DATE DUE

Fundamental Accounting Principles

The Robert N. Anthony / Willard J. Graham Series in Accounting

WILLIAM W. PYLE

KERMIT D. LARSON
The University of Texas at Austin

Fundamental Accounting Principles

1984 • TENTH EDITION

IRWIN

Homewood, Illinois 60430

© RICHARD D. IRWIN, INC., 1955, 1959, 1963, 1966, 1969,
1972, 1975, 1978, 1981, and 1984

ISBN 0-256-02970-9

Library of Congress Catalog Card No. 83–80579

Printed in the United States of America

7 8 9 0 K 1 0 9 8 7 6

Preface

Fundamental Accounting Principles is intended to provide the textual materials for the first year-long accounting course at the college and university level. This course typically has a variety of objectives. For many students, the course provides the first educational exposure to many business topics including forms of business organization, typical business practices, legal instruments such as notes, bonds, and stocks, and financial statements. Specific objectives often include: (1) developing a general understanding of financial reports and analyses that students will find useful in their personal affairs regardless of their fields of specialization, (2) introducing students to managerial decision processes and the use of accounting information by the managers of a business, (3) providing a strong foundation for subsequent courses in business and finance, and (4) initiating the coursework leading to a career in accounting. *Fundamental Accounting Principles* is designed to serve all of these objectives.

The central orientation of the book is to explain how accounting data are accumulated and how the resulting reports are prepared so that students can interpret and use accounting information intelligently and effectively. The concepts and principles that guide the preparation of accounting information are persistently emphasized so that students will be able to generalize and apply their knowledge to a variety of new situations. As new concepts and principles are gradually introduced throughout the book, they are defined, explained, and illustrated with practical applications. Thus, students need not hold abstract concepts in limbo before they see how the concepts are applied. This careful integration of conceptual principles and their application to specific business situations is a hallmark of *Fundamental Accounting Principles*.

This Tenth Edition contains substantially more important revisions than one might normally expect to observe in a book that has a successful tradition. Numerous important changes have been introduced to make the Tenth Edition an exciting, completely up-to-date product. Many of these changes have resulted from extensive input by Ninth Edition adopters. The teaching effectiveness of the book should be markedly improved in several areas. Important new topics have been covered. A substantial number of additional exercises, problems, and provocative problems have been added to the book. Yet with all of these changes, the basic objectives and philosophy of *Fundamental Accounting Principles* have not changed. The goal is to provide a rigorous and at the same time exceptionally readable teaching package. Consistent with the tradition of this book, extraordinary measures have been taken to minimize errors in the text and all supplementary materials. Students will find the book interesting to read and highly comprehensible. Instructors will find the book to be rigorous and comprehensive.

Some of the important changes in the book include the following:

1. All of the homework material in the book has been revised. The addition of several new exercises, problems, and provocative problems has increased the diversity of assignment material. This diversity is most apparent in terms of the varied levels of difficulty contained in the end-of-chapter material.

2. Some instructors prefer to minimize the time devoted to corporations during the first semester. To facilitate this preference, the revised homework material for Chapter 5 includes several assignments that are based on the single proprietorship as well as several that are based on the corporation. Thus, adopters may choose to include or exclude the corporation assignment material throughout the first half of the book.

3. Adopters of the Ninth Edition have overwhelmingly requested that the discussion of inventories in Chapter 5 and in Chapter 21 be revised to reflect a closing-entry approach. The vast majority of adopters argue that students can identify most easily with a focus on the income statement. Thus, all of the elements in the cost of goods sold calculation are transferred to Income Summary as part of the closing process. The availability of alternative procedures is, however, recognized.

4. Chapter 6 includes an expanded and updated discussion of computerized accounting information systems. The increasing importance of microcomputers in small accounting systems is emphasized.

5. Chapter 10 includes a discussion of the accelerated cost recovery

system and a more complete discussion of the difference between land and land improvements. The topic of tax allocation has been shifted to Chapter 28.

6. Editorial improvements in Chapter 11 provide clearer definitions of betterments, leases, and leaseholds. Also, reasons are provided for the fact that financial accounting depreciation records are now almost always different than tax records.

7. The present value tables in Chapter 12 and the examples involving interest throughout the book have been revised to reflect a range of interest rates that is consistent with recent real-world rates. The topic of mortgages has been moved to Chapter 12, and the difference between long-term and current liabilities is clearly defined. Also, the necessity of reclassifying the current portion of long-term obligations is explained.

8. Chapter 13 has been revised to reflect recent changes in the law and expanded to include a discussion of employee fringe benefits. The discussion of legal requirements for depositing payroll taxes and withholdings is presented more concisely.

9. The discussion of preferred stock in Chapter 15 has been expanded to include more precise illustrations of the allocation of dividends between preferred and common. In that chapter, the tax characteristics of corporations are clarified as offering potential advantages as well as disadvantages.

10. The illustrations of consolidated statements in Chapter 16 have been revised and simplified in a manner that draws more attention to the equity method and the related elimination entries. Extraneous changes in the balance sheet from one period to the next have been removed. Another important change in Chapter 16 is to insert a relatively complete discussion of temporary and long-term investments in marketable equity securities, including explanations of the cost method, lower-of-cost-or-market, and equity method. Also, the discussion of dividends has been streamlined, and the difference between legal restrictions on retained earnings and voluntary appropriations of retained earnings has been clarified.

11. Since the stock investment material has been shifted to Chapter 16, the revised Chapter 17 relates entirely to bonds. It now includes a discussion of bond investments as well as bonds payable. Also, the chapter includes a substantially expanded explanation of the straight-line method of premium or discount amortization and a tabular analysis that shows the difference between the straight-line method and the interest method.

12. Chapter 18 has been very substantially revised so that the statement of changes in financial position is presented on both a work

ing capital basis and on a cash basis. The differences between the two alternative formats are reconciled.

13. The sequence of Chapters 19 and 20 has been reversed so that the student's analysis of financial statements (Chapter 20) can incorporate the information contained in the *FASB Statement No. 33* disclosures (Chapter 19).

14. An important change in Chapter 20 has been to introduce the concept of general purpose financial statements and the objectives of financial reporting as presented in *FASB Statement of Concepts No. 1.* The philosophy is that a clear understanding of the accountant's objectives in preparing financial statements is a necessary prerequisite to a knowledgeable analysis of those statements. A provocative problem following Chapter 20 requires the student to analyze the 1982 Annual Report of Texas Instruments which is disclosed in the Appendix to the book (along with the 1982 financial statements of Equifax Inc.).

15. The sequence of Chapters 21, 22, and 23 has been changed so that responsibility and departmental accounting are now presented in Chapter 23. The content of that chapter is more closely related to subsequent chapters. This change also allows students to begin the cost and managerial accounting topics with the cost accumulation chapters. In Chapter 22, a major new illustration is introduced that clarifies not only the flow of costs but the relationship between the flow of costs in the General Ledger and the subsidiary ledgers in a job cost system.

16. An important new section on segmental reporting to outside parties has been included in Chapter 23. This section describes the basic issues involved in segmental reporting and contrasts that process with the managerial process of accounting for the departments of a business. The section on responsibility accounting has been significantly revised and expanded to include illustrations of performance reports at differing managerial levels in the firm.

17. The sequence of Chapters 24 and 25 has been reversed so that the two budgeting chapters will be adjacent to each other. An important new section of Chapter 24 contains a discussion of scatter diagrams and the process of estimating cost behavior. The concept of mixed costs is introduced in this section.

18. In Chapter 27, the discussion of rate of return on average investment has been rewritten to include situations where cash flows are received uniformly throughout the year and situations where the cash flow is received at the end of each year.

19. Chapter 28 reflects all of the changes in tax legislation that have occurred since the previous edition.

Several important changes and additions have been made in the supplementary materials for *Fundamental Accounting Principles.* These items include the following:

COMPUTERIZED PRACTICE SETS.   Two new computerized practice sets have been written to accompany the Tenth Edition. Both are designed to run on microcomputers and have been extensively class-room tested. *Lite Flight*, by Christine Sprenger and Keith Weidkamp, is a single proprietorship exercise that may be assigned after coverage of Chapter 6. *KC's Deals on Wheels*, by Christine Sprenger, Keith Weidkamp, and Clifford Burns, is a larger exercise that includes more transactions, perpetual inventories, comparative statements, notes receivable, interest, and depreciation. It may be assigned after coverage of Chapter 10.

MANUAL PRACTICE SETS.   Three manual practice sets are available for use with *Fundamental Accounting Principles.* Colorful Paint, Inc., is intended to be used at the completion of Chapter 8. An alternative practice set, Small Hardware Store, is designed as a single proprietorship and includes a variety of business papers to be used in analyzing transactions. Schwab Manufacturing Company may be assigned after coverage of Chapter 21.

WORKING PAPERS.   Separate booklets of working papers for solutions to the problems and alternate problems are available for Chapters 1–14 and Chapters 14–28. Note that Chapter 14 is included in both booklets to increase flexibility in course design.

STUDY GUIDES.   The study guides and solutions for the Tenth Edition have been revised to include more detailed outlines of each chapter. Separate booklets are available for Chapters 1–14 and Chapters 14–28.

ACHIEVEMENT TESTS.   Three alternative series of achievement tests are available in bulk to adopters. Each series includes 10 tests plus two final examinations.

MACHINE-GRADABLE TESTS and ADDITIONAL EXAMINATION MATERIALS.   The booklet of additional examination and quiz material has been thoroughly revised and expanded to include a set of machine-gradable examinations. Included in this booklet are solutions to all of the examination questions in the booklet and to the achievement tests.

COMPUTERIZED TEST BANK.   A large bank of objective test questions is available together with the Irwin Computerized Test Generator

System. Adopters may also draw upon the test bank through the use of Teletest, an in-house test preparation service for instructors who want assistance with exam preparation.

INSTRUCTOR'S LECTURE GUIDE. A completely new lecture guide to accompany the Tenth Edition of *Fundamental Accounting Principles* has been prepared by Elliott S. Levy and Laurie W. Pant of Bentley College. The lecture guide includes a topical classification of the assignment materials at the end of each chapter, a list of suggested objectives and areas for emphasis by the instructor, a detailed lecture outline for each chapter, and a list of suggested assignments.

SOLUTIONS MANUALS. Complete answers and solutions to all of the assignment material at the end of each chapter are provided in two solutions manuals. Also included are estimates of the time required by an average student to complete each problem.

TRANSPARENCIES. An expanded number of illustrative transparencies for use in teaching is available with the Tenth Edition. Transparencies of the solutions to all of the exercises and problems following each chapter are also available.

CHECK FIGURES. A list of key figures in the solutions to problems is available in quantity for distribution to students by the instructor.

Those who've made important contributions to this Tenth Edition include students, adopters, colleagues, and friends. We are particularly appreciative of the input by Alvin Black, Northeastern University; Eugene A. Braun, Northern Virginia Community College; Paul Brown, Yale University; Eric Carlsen, Kean College; Al A. Evans, Evangel College; Anna Fowler, The University of Texas at Austin; Robert Hardin, Henry Ford Community College; Jill Jones, University of West Florida; Marcella Y. Lecky, The University of Southwestern Louisiana; Elliott S. Levy, Bentley College; Janet Maly, The University of Texas at Austin; James F. McDermott, Northeastern University; Laurie W. Pant, Bentley College; L. L. Price, Ft. Steilacoom Community College; Daniel Short, The University of Texas at Austin; Sherry Stewart, Peat Marwick Mitchell; Charles E. Thompson, El Camino College; and Bill Wells, Tulsa Junior College. Patricia Kardash Lee has made an exceptional contribution through her assistance in preparing the manuscript.

William W. Pyle
Kermit D. Larson

Contents

ance. Illustration of a Bank Reconciliation. Other Internal Control Procedures. Appendix: Recording Vouchers, Pen-and-Ink System. The Unpaid Vouchers File. The Voucher System Check Register. Purchases Returns.

Promissory Notes. Calculating Interest. Recording the Receipt of a Note. Dishonored Notes Receivable. Discounting Notes Receivable. Dishonor of a Discounted Note. End-of-Period Adjustments. Reversing Entries. Bad Debts. Matching Bad Debt Losses with Sales. Allowance Method of Accounting for Bad Debts. Bad Debt Recoveries. Aging Accounts Receivable. Direct Write-Off of Bad Debts.

Matching Merchandise Costs with Revenues. Taking an Ending Inventory. Assigning Costs to Inventory Items. The Principle of Consistency. Changing Accounting Procedures. Items Included on an Inventory. Cost or Market, the Lower. Principle of Conservatism. Inventory Errors. Perpetual Inventories. Perpetual Inventory Systems. Estimated Inventories.

Cost of a Plant Asset. Nature of Depreciation. Service Life of a Plant Asset. Salvage Value. Allocating Depreciation. Depreciation for Partial Years. Apportioning Accelerated Depreciation. Depreciation on the Balance Sheet. Balance Sheet Plant Asset Values. Recovering the Costs of Plant Assets. Accelerated Depreciation for Tax Purposes. Control of Plant Assets. Plant Assets of Low Cost.

Plant Asset Disposals. Exchanging Plant Assets. Revising Depreciation Rates. Ordinary and Extraordinary Repairs. Betterments. Capital and Revenue Expenditures. Natural Resources. Intangible Assets.

PART FOUR
Accounting for Equities: Liabilities and Partners' Equities

Short-Term Notes Payable. End-of-Period Adjustments. The Concept of Present Value. Exchanging a Note for a Plant Asset. Issuing a Mortgage to Borrow Money. Liabilities from Leasing.

The Federal Social Security Act. Withholding Employees' Federal Income Taxes. City and State Income Taxes. Fair Labor Standards Act. Union Contracts.

Other Payroll Deductions. Timekeeping. The Payroll Register. Recording the Payroll. Paying the Employees. Payroll Bank Account. Employee's Individual Earnings Record. Payroll Taxes Levied on the Employer. Accruing Taxes on Wages. Employee (Fringe) Benefit Costs. Computerized Payroll Systems.

PART FIVE
Corporation Accounting

PART SIX
Financial Statements, Interpretation and Modifications

PART SEVEN
Managerial Accounting for Costs

Labor in a Job Cost System. Accounting for Overhead in a Job Cost System. Overapplied and Underapplied Overhead. Recording the Completion of a Job. Recording Cost of Goods Sold. PROCESS COST ACCOUNTING. Assembling Costs by Departments. Charging Costs to Departments. Equivalent Finished Units. Process Cost Accounting Illustrated.

Reporting on Broad Business Segments. Departmental Accounting. Departmentalizing a Business. Basis for Departmentalization. Information to Evaluate Departments. Securing Departmental Information. Allocating Expenses. Bases for Allocating Expenses. Mechanics of Allocating Expenses. Departmental Contributions to Overhead. Eliminating the Unprofitable Department. Controllable Costs and Expenses. Responsibility Accounting. Joint Costs.

PART EIGHT
Planning and Controlling Business Operations

Cost Behavior. Break-Even Point. Break-Even Graph. Sales Required for a Desired Net Income. Margin of Safety. Income from a Given Sales Level. Other Questions. Multiproduct Break-Even Point. Evaluating the Results.

The Master Budget. Benefits from Budgeting. The Budget Committee. The Budget Period. Preparing the Master Budget. Preparation of the Master Budget Illustrated.

Fixed Budgets and Performance Reports. FLEXIBLE BUDGETS. Preparing a Flexible Budget. Flexible Budget Performance Report. STANDARD COSTS. Establishing Standard Costs. Variances. Isolating Material and Labor Variances. Charging Overhead to Production. Establishing Overhead Standards. Overhead Variances. Controlling a Business through Standard Costs. Standard Costs in the Accounts.

Capital Budgeting. Accepting Additional Business. Buy or Make. Other Cost Concepts. Scrap or Rebuild Defective Units. Process or Sell. Deciding the Sales Mix.

Tax Planning. Tax Evasion and Tax Avoidance. State and Municipal Income Taxes. History and Objectives of the Federal Income Tax. Synopsis of the Federal Income Tax. Tax Effects of Business Alternatives. Tax Changes Scheduled to Take Effect in 1985. Taxes and the Distortion of Net Income. Entries for the Allocation of Taxes.

APPENDIX

Fundamental Accounting Principles

Introduction

PART ONE

1. Accounting, an Introduction to Its Concepts

Accounting, an Introduction to Its Concepts

1

After studying Chapter 1, you should be able to:

Tell the function of accounting and the nature and purpose of the information it provides.

List the main fields of accounting and tell the kinds of work carried on in each field.

List the accounting concepts and principles introduced and tell the effect of each on accounting records and statements.

Describe the purpose of a balance sheet and of an income statement and tell the kinds of information presented in each.

Recognize and be able to indicate the effects of transactions on the elements of an accounting equation.

Prepare simple financial statements.

Tell in each case the extent of the responsibility of a business owner for the debts of a business organized as a single proprietorship, a partnership, or a corporation.

Define or explain the words and phrases listed in the chapter Glossary.

Accounting is a service activity. Its function is to provide quantitative information about economic entities. The information is primarily financial in nature and is intended to be useful in making economic decisions.[1] If the entity for which the information is provided is a business, for example, the information is used by its management in answering questions such as: What are the resources of the business? What debts does it owe? Does it have earnings? Are expenses too large in relation to sales? Is too little or too much merchandise being kept? Are amounts owed by customers being collected rapidly? Will the business be able to meet its own debts as they mature? Should the plant be expanded? Should a new product be introduced? Should selling prices be increased?

In addition, grantors of credit such as banks, wholesale houses, and manufacturers use accounting information in answering such questions as: Are the customer's earning prospects good? What is its debt-paying ability? Has it paid its debts promptly in the past? Should it be granted additional credit? Likewise, governmental units use accounting information in regulating businesses and collecting taxes. Labor unions use it in negotiating working conditions and wage agreements, and investors make wide use of accounting data in investment decisions.

WHY STUDY ACCOUNTING

Information for use in answering questions like the ones listed is conveyed in accounting reports. If a person is to use these reports effectively, he or she must have some understanding of how their data were gathered and the figures were put together. He or she must appreciate the limitations of the data and the extent to which portions are based on estimates rather than precise measurements. And, he or she must understand accounting terms and concepts. Needless to say, these understandings are gained in a study of accounting.

Another reason to study accounting is to make it one's lifework. A career in accounting can be very interesting and highly rewarding.

ACCOUNTANCY AS A PROFESSION

Over the past half century, accountancy as a profession has attained a stature comparable with that of law or medicine. All states license *certified public accountants* or *CPAs* just as they license doctors and

---

[1] Accounting Principles Board, "Basic Concepts and Accounting Principles Underlying Financial Statements of Business Enterprises," *APB Statement No. 4* (New York: AICPA, October 1970), par. 9.

lawyers. The licensing helps ensure a high standard of professional service. Only individuals who have passed a rigorous examination of their accounting and related knowledge, met other education and experience requirements, and have received a license may designate themselves as certified public accountants.

The requirements for the CPA certificate or license vary with the states. In general, an applicant must be a citizen, 21 years of age, of unquestioned moral character, and a college graduate with a major concentration in accounting. Also, the applicant must pass a rigorous three-day examination in accounting theory, accounting practice, auditing, and business law. The three-day examination is uniform in all states and is given on the same days in all states. It is prepared by the American Institute of Certified Public Accountants (AICPA) which is the national professional organization of CPAs. In addition to the examination, many states require an applicant to have one or more years of work experience in the office of a CPA or the equivalent before the certificate is granted. However, some states do not require the work experience, and some states permit the applicant to substitute one or more years of experience for the college level education requirement. In 1969, the AICPA's Committee on Education and Experience Requirements for CPAs expressed the opinion that at least five years of college study are necessary to obtain the body of knowledge needed to be a CPA. For those meeting this standard, it recommended that no previous work experience be required.[2] A few states now require five years of college education. More will do so in the future. However, it will be several years before all states accept this recommendation. In the meantime, interested students can learn the requirements of any state in which they are interested by writing to its state board of accountancy.

THE WORK OF AN ACCOUNTANT

Accountants are employed in three main fields: (1) in public accounting, (2) in private accounting, or (3) in government.

Public Accounting

Public accountants are individuals who offer their professional services and those of their employees to the public for a fee, in much the same manner as a lawyer or a consulting engineer.

---

[2] *Report of the Committee on Education and Experience Requirements for CPAs* (New York: AICPA, 1969), p. 11.

AUDITING.   The principal service offered by a public accountant is auditing. Banks commonly require an *audit* of the financial statements of a company applying for a sizable loan, with the audit being performed by a CPA who is not an employee of the audited concern but an independent professional person working for a fee. Companies whose securities are offered for sale to the public generally must also have such an audit before the securities may be sold. Thereafter, additional audits must be made periodically if the securities are to continue being traded.

The purpose of an audit is to lend credibility to a company's financial statements. In making the audit, the auditor carefully examines the company's statements and the accounting records from which they were prepared. In the examination, the auditor seeks to assure that the statements fairly reflect the company's financial position and operating results and were prepared in accordance with generally accepted accounting principles from records kept in accordance with such principles. Banks, investors, and others rely on the information in a company's financial statements in making loans, granting credit, and in buying and selling securities. They depend on the auditor to verify the dependability of the information the statements contain.

MANAGEMENT ADVISORY SERVICES.   In addition to auditing, accountants commonly offer *management advisory services.* An accountant gains from an audit an intimate knowledge of the audited company's accounting procedures and its financial position. Thus, the accountant is in an excellent position to offer constructive suggestions for improving the procedures and strengthening the position. Clients expect these suggestions as a useful audit by-product. They also commonly engage CPAs to conduct additional investigations for the purpose of determining ways in which their operations may be improved. Such investigations and the suggestions growing from them are known as management advisory services.

Management advisory services include the design, installation, and improvement of a client's general accounting system and any related information system it may have for determining and controlling costs. They also include the application of machine methods to these systems, plus advice in financial planning, budgeting, forecasting, and inventory control. In fact, they include all phases of information systems and related matters.

TAX SERVICES.   In this day of increasing complexity in income and other tax laws and continued high tax rates, few important business decisions are made without consideration being given to their tax effect. A CPA, through training and experience, is well qualified to render important service in this area. The service includes not only the preparation and filing of tax returns but also advice as to how transactions may be completed so as to incur the smallest tax.

Private Accounting

Accountants employed by a single enterprise are said to be in private accounting. A small business may employ only one accountant or it may depend upon the services of a public accountant and employ none. A large business, on the other hand, may have more than a hundred employees in its accounting department. They commonly work under the supervision of a chief accounting officer, commonly called the *controller*, who is often a CPA. The title controller results from the fact that one of the chief uses of accounting data is to control the operations of a business.

The one accountant of the small business and the accounting department of a large business do a variety of work, including general accounting, cost accounting, budgeting, and internal auditing.

GENERAL ACCOUNTING. *General accounting* has to do primarily with recording transactions and preparing financial and other reports for the use of management, owners, creditors, and governmental agencies. The private accountant may design or help the public accountant design the system used in recording the transactions. He or she will also supervise the clerical or data processing staff in recording the transactions and preparing the reports.

COST ACCOUNTING. The phase of accounting that has to do with collecting, determining, and controlling costs, particularly costs of producing a given product or service, is called *cost accounting*. A knowledge of costs and controlling costs is vital to good management. Therefore, a large company may have a number of accountants engaged in this activity.

BUDGETING. Planning business activities before they occur is called *budgeting*. The objective of budgeting is to provide management with an intelligent plan for future operations. Then, after the budget plan has been put into effect, it provides summaries and reports that can be used to compare actual accomplishments with the plan. Many large companies have a number of people who devote all their time to this phase of accounting.

INTERNAL AUDITING. In addition to an annual audit by a firm of CPAs, many companies maintain a staff of internal auditors. The internal auditors constantly check the records prepared and maintained in each department or company branch. It is their responsibility to make sure that established accounting procedures and management directives are being followed throughout the company.

Governmental Accounting

Furnishing governmental services is a vast and complicated operation in which accounting is just as indispensable as in business. Elected and appointed officials must rely on data accumulated by means of accounting if they are to complete effectively their administrative duties. Accountants are responsible for the accumulation of these data. Accountants also check and audit the millions of income, payroll, and sales tax returns that accompany the tax payments upon which governmental units depend. And finally, federal and state agencies, such as the Interstate Commerce Commission, Securities and Exchange Commission, and so on, use accountants in many capacities in their regulation of business.

ACCOUNTING AND BOOKKEEPING

Many people confuse *accounting* and *bookkeeping* and look upon them as one and the same. In effect, they identify the whole with one of its parts. Actually, bookkeeping is only part of accounting, the record-making part. To keep books is to record transactions, and a bookkeeper is one who records transactions. The work is often routine and primarily clerical in nature. The work of an accountant goes far beyond this, as a rereading of the previous section will show.

ACCOUNTING STATEMENTS

Accounting statements are the end product of the accounting process, but a good place to begin the study of accounting. They are used to convey a concise picture of the profitability and financial position of a business. The two most important are the income statement and the balance sheet.

The Income Statement

A company's *income statement* (see Illustration 1–1) is perhaps more important than its balance sheet. It shows whether or not the business achieved or failed to achieve its primary objective—earning a "profit" or net income. A *net income* is earned when revenues exceed expenses, but a *net loss* is incurred if the expenses exceed the revenues. An income statement is prepared by listing the revenues earned during the period, listing the expenses incurred in earning the revenues, and subtracting the expenses from the revenues to determine if a net income or a net loss was incurred.

Illustration 1–1

COAST REALTY
Income Statement for Year Ended December 31, 19—

Revenues:		
Commissions earned	$31,450	
Property management fees	1,200	
Total revenues		$32,650
Operating expenses:		
Salaries expense	$ 7,800	
Rent expense..................	2,400	
Utilities expense	315	
Telephone expense	560	
Advertising expense	2,310	
Total operating expenses.....		13,385
Net income		$19,265

Revenues are inflows of cash or other properties received in exchange for goods or services provided to customers. Rents, dividends, and interest earned are also revenues. Coast Realty of Illustration 1–1 had revenue inflows from services that totaled $32,650.

Expenses are goods and services consumed in operating a business or other economic unit. Coast Realty consumed the services of its employees (salaries expense), the services of a telephone company, and so on.

The heading of an income statement tells the name of the business for which it is prepared and the time period covered by the statement. Both bits of information are important. However, the time covered is extremely significant, since the items on the statement must be interpreted in relation to the period of time. For example, the item "Commissions earned, $31,450" on the income statement of Illustration 1–1 has little significance until it is known that the amount represents one year's commissions and not the commissions of a week or a month.

The Balance Sheet

The purpose of a *balance sheet* is to show the financial position of a business on a specific date. It is often called a *position statement*. Financial position is shown by listing the *assets* of the business, its *liabilities* or debts, and the *equity of the owner or owners*. (An equity is a right, claim or interest.) The name of the business and the date are given in the balance sheet heading. It is understood that the item amounts shown are as of the close of business on that date.

Before a business manager, investor, or other person can make effective judgments based on balance sheet information, he or she must gain several concepts and understandings. To illustrate, assume that on August 3, Joan Ball began a new business, called World Travel Agency. During the day, she completed these transactions in the name of the business:

Aug. 3   Invested $18,000 of her personal savings in the business.
    3   Paid $15,000 of the agency's cash for a small office building and the land on which it was built (cost of the building, $10,000, and cost of the land, $5,000).
    3   Purchased on *credit* from Office Equipment Company office equipment costing $2,000. (Purchased on credit means purchased with a promise to pay at a later date.)

A balance sheet reflecting the effects of these transactions appears in Illustration 1–2. It shows that after completing the transactions, the agency has four assets, a $2,000 debt, and that its owner has an $18,000 equity in the business.

Illustration 1–2

WORLD TRAVEL AGENCY
Balance Sheet, August 3, 19—

Assets		Liabilities	
Cash	$ 3,000	Accounts payable . .	$ 2,000
Office equipment . . .	2,000	*Owner's Equity*	
Building	10,000		
Land	5,000	Joan Ball, capital . . .	18,000
		Total liabilities and	
Total assets	$20,000	owner's equity . . .	$20,000

Observe that the two sides of the balance sheet are equal. This is where it gets its name. Its two sides must always be equal because one side shows the resources of the business and the other shows who supplied the resources. For example, World Travel Agency has $20,000 of resources (assets) of which $18,000 were supplied by its owner and $2,000 by its creditors. (*Creditors* are individuals and organizations to whom the business owes debts.)

ASSETS, LIABILITIES, AND OWNER'S EQUITY

The assets of a business are, in general, the properties or economic resources owned by the business. They include cash, amounts owed to the business by its customers for goods and services sold to them on credit (called *accounts receivable*), merchandise held for sale by the business, supplies, equipment, buildings, and land. Assets may also include such intangible rights as those granted by a patent or copyright.

The liabilities of a business are its debts. They include amounts owed to creditors for goods and services bought on credit (called *accounts payable*), salaries and wages owed employees, taxes payable, notes payable, and mortgages payable.

When a business is owned by one person, the owner's interest or equity in the assets of the business is shown on a balance sheet by listing the person's name, followed by the word *capital*, and then the amount of the equity. The use of the word *capital* comes from the idea that the owner has furnished the business with resources or "capital" equal to the amount of the equity.

A liability represents a claim or right to be paid. The law recognizes this right. If a business fails to pay its creditors, the law gives the creditors the right to force the sale of the assets of the business to secure money to meet creditor claims. Furthermore, if the assets are sold, the creditors are paid first, with any remainder going to the business owner. Obviously, then, by law creditor claims take precedence over those of a business owner.

Since creditor claims take precedence over those of an owner, an owner's equity in a business is always a residual amount. Creditors recognize this. When they examine the balance sheet of a business, they are always interested in the share of its assets furnished by creditors and the share furnished by its owner or owners. The creditors recognize that if the business must be liquidated and its assets sold, the shrinkage in converting the assets into cash must exceed the equity of the owner or owners before the creditors will lose.

GENERALLY ACCEPTED ACCOUNTING PRINCIPLES

An understanding of financial statement information requires a knowledge of the generally accepted accounting principles that govern the accumulation and presentation of the data appearing on such statements. A common definition of the word *principle* is: "A broad general law or rule adopted or professed as a guide to action; a settled ground or basis of conduct or practice. . . . ." Consequently, generally accepted accounting principles may be described as broad rules adopted by the accounting profession as guides in measuring, recording, and reporting the financial affairs and activities of a business. They consist of a number of concepts, principles, and procedures that are first discussed at the points shown in the following list. They also are referred to again and again throughout this text in order to increase your understanding of the information conveyed by accounting data.

	First introduced	
	Chapter	Page
Generally accepted concepts:		
1. Business entity concept	1	16
2. Continuing-concern concept	1	17
3. Stable-dollar concept	1	18
4. Time-period concept	3	82
Generally accepted principles:		
1. Cost principle	1	16
2. Objectivity principle	1	17
3. Realization principle	1	24
4. Matching principle	3	93
5. Full-disclosure principle	8	291
6. Materiality principle	8	303
7. Consistency principle	9	323
8. Conservatism principle	9	327
Generally accepted procedures:		
These specify the ways data are processed and reported and are described and discussed throughout the text.		

SOURCE OF ACCOUNTING PRINCIPLES

Generally accepted accounting principles are not natural laws in the sense of the laws of physics and chemistry. They are man-made rules that depend for their authority upon their general acceptance by the accounting profession. They have evolved from the experience and thinking of members of the accounting profession, aided by such groups as the American Institute of Certified Public Accountants, the Financial Accounting Standards Board, the American Accounting Association, and the Securities and Exchange Commission.

The American Institute of Certified Public Accountants (AICPA) has long been influential in describing and defining generally accepted accounting principles. During the years from 1939 to 1959, it published a series of *Accounting Research Bulletins* that were recognized as expressions of generally accepted accounting principles. In 1959, it established an 18-member Accounting Principles Board (APB) composed of practicing accountants, educators, and representatives of industry, and gave the Board authority to issue opinions that were to be regarded by members of the AICPA as authoritative expressions of generally accepted accounting principles. During the years 1962 through 1973, the Board issued 31 such opinions. Added importance was given to these opinions beginning in 1964 when the AICPA ruled that its members must disclose in footnotes to published financial statements of the companies they audit any departure from generally accepted accounting principles as set forth in the *Opinions of the Accounting Principles Board.*

In 1973, after 11 years of activity, the APB was terminated. Its place was taken by a seven-member Financial Accounting Standards Board (FASB). The seven members serve full time, receive salaries, and must resign from accounting firms and other employment. They must have a knowledge of accounting, finance, and business, but are not required to be CPAs. This differs from the APB, all members of which were CPAs, who served part time, without pay, and continued their affiliations with accounting firms and other employment. The FASB issues *Statements of Financial Accounting Standards* which like the *Opinions of the Accounting Principles Board* must be considered as authoritative expressions of generally accepted accounting principles. Both the *Statements* and *Opinions* are referred to again and again throughout this text.

The American Accounting Association (AAA), an organization with strong academic ties, has also been influential in describing and defining generally accepted accounting principles. It has sponsored a number of research studies and has published many articles dealing with accounting principles. However, its influence has not been as great as the AICPA, since it has no power to impose its views on the accounting profession but must depend upon the prestige of its authors and the logic of their arguments.

The Securities and Exchange Commission (SEC) plays a prominent role in financial reporting. The SEC is an independent quasi-judicial agency of the federal government. It was established to administer the provisions of various securities and exchange acts dealing with the distribution and sale of securities. Such securities, to be sold, must be registered with the SEC. This requires the filing of audited financial statements prepared in accordance with the rules of the SEC. Furthermore, the information contained in the statements must be kept current by filing additional audited annual reports. The SEC does not appraise the registered securities. However, it attempts to safeguard investors by requiring that all materials facts affecting the worth of the securities be made public and that no important information be withheld. Its rules carry over into the annual reports of large companies and have contributed to the usefulness of these reports. In a real sense, the SEC should be viewed as the dominant authority in respect to the establishment of accounting principles. However, it has relied on the accounting profession, particularly the AICPA and the FASB, to determine and enforce accepted accounting principles. At the same time, it has pressured the accounting profession to reduce the number of acceptable accounting procedures.

UNDERSTANDING ACCOUNTING PRINCIPLES

Your authors believe that an understanding of *accounting principles* is best conveyed with examples illustrating the application of each principle. The examples must be such that a student can understand at his or her level of experience. Consequently, three *accounting concepts* and two accounting principles are introduced here. Discussions of the others are delayed until later in the text when meaningful examples of their application can be developed.

Business Entity Concept

Under the *business entity concept,* for accounting purposes, every business is conceived to be and is treated as a separate entity, separate and distinct from its owner or owners and from every other business. Businesses are so conceived and treated because, insofar as a specific business is concerned, the purpose of accounting is to record its transactions and periodically report its financial position and profitability. Consequently, the records and reports of a business should not include either the transactions or assets of another business or the personal assets and transactions of its owner or owners. To include either distorts the financial position and profitability of the business. For example, the personally owned automobile of a business owner should not be included among the assets of the owner's business. Likewise, its gas, oil, and repairs should not be treated as an expense of the business, for to do so distorts the reported financial position and profitability of the business.

Cost Principle

In addition to the *business entity concept,* an accounting principle called the *cost principle* should be borne in mind when reading financial statements. Under this principle, all goods and services purchased are recorded at cost and appear on the statements at cost. For example, if a business pays $50,000 for land to be used in carrying on its operations, the purchase should be recorded at $50,000. It makes no difference if the owner and several competent outside appraisers thought the land "worth" at least $60,000. It cost $50,000 and should appear on the balance sheet at that amount. Furthermore, if five years later, due to booming real estate prices, the land's market value has doubled, this makes no difference either. The land cost $50,000 and should continue to appear on the balance sheet at $50,000 even though its estimated market value is twice that.

In applying the *cost principle,* costs are measured on a cash or cash-equivalent basis. If the consideration given for an asset or service is cash, cost is measured at the entire cash outlay made to secure the asset or service. If the consideration is something other than cash, cost is measured at the cash-equivalent value of the consideration given or the cash-equivalent value of the thing received, whichever is more clearly evident.[3]

Why are assets and services recorded at cost and why are the balance sheet amounts for the assets not changed from time to time to reflect changing market values? The *objectivity principle* and the *continuing-concern concept* supply answers to these questions.

Objectivity Principle

The *objectivity principle* supplies the reason transactions are recorded at cost, since it requires that transaction amounts be objectively established. Whims and fancies plus, for example, something like an opinion of management that an asset is "worth more than it cost" have no place in accounting. To be fully useful, accounting information must be based on objective data. As a rule, costs are objective, since they normally are established by buyers and sellers, each striking the best possible bargain for themselves.

Continuing-Concern Concept

Balance sheet amounts for assets used in carrying on the operations of a business are not changed from time to time to reflect changing market values. A balance sheet is prepared under the assumption that the business for which it is prepared will continue in operation, and as a continuing or going concern the assets used in carrying on its operations are not for sale. In fact, they cannot be sold without disrupting the business. Therefore, since the assets are for use in the business and are not for sale, their current market values are not particularly relevant and need not be shown. Also, without a sale, their current market values usually cannot be objectively established, as is required by the *objectivity principle.*

The *continuing-concern or going-concern concept* applies in most situations. However, if a business is about to be sold or liquidated,

---

[3] APB, "Accounting for Nonmonetary Transactions," *APB Opinion No. 29* (New York: AICPA, 1973), par. 18.

the *continuing-concern concept* and the *cost and objectivity principles* do not apply in the preparation of its statements. In such cases, amounts other than costs, such as estimated market values, become more useful and informative.

The Stable-Dollar Concept

In our country, accounting transactions are measured, recorded, and reported in terms of dollars. In the measuring, recording, and reporting process, the dollar has been treated as a stable unit of measure, like a gallon, an acre, or a mile. However, unfortunately the dollar, like other currencies, is not a stable unit of measure. When the general price level (the average of all prices) changes, the value of money (its purchasing power) also changes. For example, during the past 10 years, the general price level has approximately doubled, which means that over these years the purchasing power of the dollar has declined from 100 cents to approximately 50 cents.

Nevertheless, although the instability of the dollar is recognized, accountants in their reports continue to add and subtract items acquired in different years with dollars of different sizes. In effect, they ignore changes in the size of the measuring unit. For example, assume a company purchased land some years ago for $10,000 and sold it today for $20,000. If during this period the purchasing power of the dollar declined from 100 cents to 50 cents, it can be said that the company is no better off for having purchased the land for $10,000 and sold it for $20,000 because the $20,000 will buy no more goods and services today than the $10,000 at the time of the purchase. Yet, using the dollar to measure both transactions, the accountant reports a $10,000 gain from the purchase and sale.

The instability of the dollar as a unit of measure is recognized. Therefore, the question is should the amounts shown on financial statements be adjusted for changes in the purchasing power of the dollar. Techniques have been devised to convert the historical dollars of statement amounts into dollars of current purchasing power. Such statements are called *price-level-adjusted statements*. Also, by consulting catalogs and securing current prices from manufacturers and wholesalers, it is possible to determine replacement costs for various assets owned. As a result, such costs could be used in preparing financial statements. However, financial statements showing current replacement costs and also price-level-adjusted statements require subjective judgments in their preparation. Consequently, most accountants are of the opinion that the traditional statements based on the *stable-dollar concept* are best for general publication and use. Nevertheless, they also recognize that the information conveyed by traditional statements can be made more useful if accompanied by replacement cost and/or price-level-adjusted information. This is discussed in Chapter 19.

From the discussions of the *cost principle,* the *continuing-concern concept,* and *stable-dollar concept,* it should be recognized that in most instances a balance sheet does not show the amounts at which the listed assets can be sold or replaced. Nor does it show the "worth" of the business for which it was prepared, since some of the listed assets may be salable for much more or much less than the dollar amounts at which they are shown.

BUSINESS ORGANIZATIONS

Accounting is applicable to all economic entities such as business concerns, schools, churches, fraternities, and so on. However, this text will focus on accounting for business concerns organized as single proprietorships, partnerships, and corporations.

Single Proprietorships

An unincorporated business owned by one person is called a *single proprietorship.* Small retail stores and service enterprises are commonly operated as single proprietorships. There are no legal requirements to be met in starting a single proprietorship business. Furthermore, single proprietorships are the most numerous of all business concerns.

In accounting for a single proprietorship, the *business entity concept* is applied and the business is treated as a separate entity, separate and distinct from its owner. However, insofar as the debts of the business are concerned, no such legal distinction is made. The owner of a single proprietorship business is personally responsible for its debts. As a result, if the assets of such a business are not sufficient to pay its debts, the personal assets of the proprietor may be taken to satisfy the claims of the business creditors.

Partnerships

When a business is owned by two or more people as partners, it is called a *partnership.* Like a single proprietorship, there are no special legal requirements to be met in starting a partnership business. All that is required is for two or more people to enter into an agreement to operate a business as partners. The agreement becomes a contract and may be either oral or written, but to avoid disagreements, a written contract is preferred.

For accounting purposes, a partnership business is treated as a separate entity, separate and distinct from its owners. However, just as with a single proprietorship, insofar as the debts of the business are concerned, no such legal distinction is made. A partner is personally responsible for all the debts of the partnership, both his or her own share and the shares of any partners who are unable to pay. Furthermore, the personal assets of a partner may be taken to satisfy all the debts of a partnership if other partners cannot pay.

Corporations

A business incorporated under the laws of a state or the federal government is called a *corporation*. Unlike a single proprietorship or partnership, a corporation is a separate legal entity, separate and distinct from its owners. The owners are called *stockholders* or *shareholders* because their ownership is evidenced by shares of the corporation's *capital stock* that may be sold and transferred from one shareholder to another without affecting the operation of the corporation.

Separate legal entity is the most important characteristic of a corporation. It makes a corporation responsible for its own acts and its own debts and relieves its stockholders of liability for either. It enables a corporation to buy, own, and sell property in its own name, to sue and be sued in its own name, and to enter into contracts for which it is solely responsible. In short, separate legal entity enables a corporation to conduct its business affairs as a legal person with all the rights, duties, and responsibilities of a person. However, unlike a person, it must act through agents.

A corporation is created by securing a charter from one of the 50 states or the federal government. The requirements for obtaining a charter vary; but in general, they call for filing an application with the proper governmental official and paying certain fees and taxes. If the application complies with the law and all fees and taxes have been paid, the charter is granted and the corporation comes into existence. At that point, the corporation's organizers and perhaps others buy the corporation's stock and become stockholders. Then, as stockholders they meet and elect a board of directors. The board then meets, appoints the corporation's president and other officers, and makes them responsible for managing the corporation's business affairs.

Lack of stockholder liability and the ease with which stock may be sold and transferred have enabled corporations to multiply, grow, and become the dominant form of business organization in our country. Nevertheless, because of its simplicity, it is best to begin the study of accounting with a single proprietorship.

THE BALANCE SHEET EQUATION

As previously stated, a balance sheet is so called because its two sides must always balance. The sum of the assets shown on the balance sheet must equal liabilities plus the equity of the owner or owners of the business. This equality may be expressed in equation form for a single proprietorship business as follows:

Assets = Liabilities + Owner's equity

When balance sheet equality is expressed in equation form, the resulting equation is called the *balance sheet equation.* It is also known as the *accounting equation,* since all double-entry accounting is based on it. Like any mathematical equation, its elements may be transposed and the equation expressed:

Assets − Liabilities = Owner's equity

The equation in this form illustrates the residual nature of the owner's equity. An owner's claims are secondary to the creditors' claims.

EFFECTS OF TRANSACTIONS ON THE ACCOUNTING EQUATION

A *business transaction* is an exchange of goods or services, and business transactions affect the elements of the accounting equation. However, regardless of what transactions a business completes, its accounting equation always remains in balance. Also, its assets always equal the combined claims of its creditors and its owner or owners. This may be demonstrated with the transactions of the law practice of Larry Owen, a single proprietorship business, which follow.

On July 1, Larry Owen began a new law practice by investing $5,000 of his personal cash, which he deposited in a bank account opened in the name of the business, Larry Owen, Attorney. After the investment, the one asset of the new business and the equity of Owen in the business are shown in the following equation:

Assets	=	Owner's equity
Cash, $5,000		Larry Owen, capital, $5,000

Observe that after its first transaction, the new business has one asset, cash, $5,000. Therefore, since it has no liabilities, the equity of Owen in the business is $5,000.

To continue the illustration, after the investment (transaction 2), Owen used $900 of the business cash to pay the rent for three months in advance on suitable office space and (transaction 3) $3,700 to buy office equipment. These transactions were exchanges of cash for other assets. Their effects on the accounting equation are shown in color in Illustration 1–3. Observe that the equation remains in balance after each transaction.

Illustration 1–3

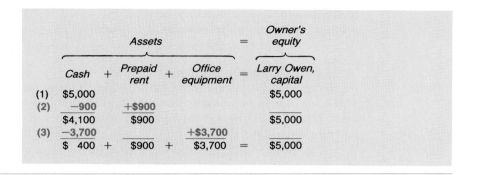

Continuing the illustration, assume that Owen needed office supplies and additional equipment in the law office. However, he felt he should conserve the cash of the law practice. Consequently, he purchased on credit from Alpha Company office equipment costing $300 and office supplies that cost $60. The effects of this transaction (4) are shown in Illustration 1–4. Note that the assets were increased by the purchase. However, Owen's equity did not change because Alpha Company acquired a claim against the assets equal to the increase in the assets. The claim or amount owed Alpha Company is called an *account payable*.

Illustration 1–4

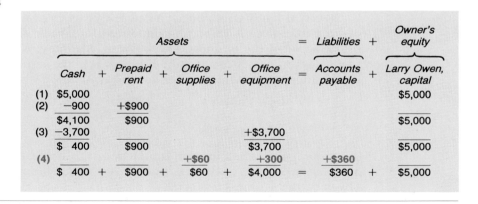

A primary objective of a business is to increase the equity of its owner or owners by earning a profit or a net income. Owen's law practice will accomplish this objective by providing legal services to its clients on a fee basis. Of course, the practice will earn a net income only if legal fees earned are greater than the expenses incurred in earning the fees. Legal fees earned and expenses incurred affect the elements of an accounting equation. To illustrate their effects, assume that on July 12, Larry Owen completed legal work for a client (transaction 5) and immediately collected $500 in cash for the services rendered. Also, the same day (transaction 6) he paid the salary of the office secretary for the first two weeks of July, a $400 expense of the business. The effects of these transactions are shown in Illustration 1–5.

Illustration 1–5

	Assets				=	Liabilities	+	Owner's equity
	Cash +	Prepaid rent +	Office supplies +	Office equipment =		Accounts payable	+	Larry Owen, capital
(1)	$5,000							$5,000
(2)	−900	+$900						
	$4,100	$900						$5,000
(3)	−3,700			+$3,700				
	$ 400	$900		$3,700				$5,000
(4)			+$60	+300		+$360		
	$ 400	$900	$60	$4,000		$360		$5,000
(5)	+500							+500
	$ 900	$900	$60	$4,000		$360		$5,500
(6)	−400							−400
	$ 500 +	$900 +	$60 +	$4,000 =		$360	+	$5,100

Observe first the effects of the legal fee. The $500 fee is a revenue, an inflow of assets from the sale of services. Note that the revenue not only increased the asset cash but also caused a $500 increase in Owen's equity. Owen's equity increased because total assets increased without an increase in liabilities.

Next observe the effects of paying the secretary's $400 salary, an expense. Note that the effects are opposite those of a revenue. Expenses are goods and services consumed in the operation of a business. In this instance, the business consumed the secretary's services. When the services were paid for, both the assets and Owen's equity in the business decreased. Owen's equity decreased because cash decreased without an increase in other assets or a decrease in liabilities.

Note this about earning a net income: A business earns a net income when its revenues exceed its expenses, and the income increases both net assets and the equity of the owner or owners. (*Net assets* are the excess of assets over liabilities.) Net assets increase because more assets flow into the business from revenues than are consumed and flow out for expenses. The equity of the owner or owners increases because net assets increase. A net loss has opposite effects.

To simplify the material and emphasize the actual effects of revenues and expenses on owner's equity, in this first chapter revenues are added directly to and expenses are deducted from the owner's capital. However, this is not done in actual practice. In actual practice, revenues and expenses are first accumulated in separate categories. They are then combined; and their combined effect, the net income or loss, is added to or deducted from owner's capital. A further discussion of this is deferred to later chapters.

REALIZATION PRINCIPLE

In transaction 5, the revenue inflow was in the form of cash. However, revenue inflows are not always in cash because of the *realization principle* (also called the *recognition principle*), which governs the recognition of revenue. This principle (1) defines a revenue as an inflow of assets (not necessarily cash) in exchange for goods or services. (2) It requires that the revenue be recognized (entered in the accounting records as revenue) at the time, but not before, it is earned. (Generally, revenue is considered to be earned at the time title to goods sold is transferred or services are rendered). (3) The principle also requires that the amount of revenue recognized be measured by the cash received plus the cash equivalent (fair value) of any other asset or assets received.

To demonstrate the recognition of a revenue inflow in a form other than cash, assume that (transaction 7) Larry Owen completed legal work for a client and billed the client $1,000 for the services rendered. Also assume that 10 days later, the client paid in full (transaction 8) for the services rendered. The effects of the two transactions are shown in Illustration 1–6.

Observe in transaction 7 that the asset flowing into the business was the right to collect $1,000 from the client, an account receivable. Compare transactions 5 and 7 and note that they differ only as to the type of asset received. Next observe that the receipt of cash (10 days after the services were rendered) is nothing more than an exchange of assets, cash for the right to collect from the client. Also note that the receipt of cash did not affect Owen's equity because the revenue was recognized in accordance with the *realization principle* and Owen's equity was increased upon completion of the services rendered.

As a final transaction assume that on July 30, Larry Owen paid Alpha Company $100 of the $360 owed for the equipment and supplies purchased in transaction 4. This transaction reduced in equal amounts both assets and liabilities, and its effects are shown in Illustration 1–7.

Illustration 1–6

	Cash +	Accounts receivable +	Prepaid rent +	Office supplies +	Office equipment =	Accounts payable +	Larry Owen, capital
(1)	$5,000						$5,000
(2)	−900		+$900				
	$4,100		$900				$5,000
(3)	−3,700				+$3,700		
	$ 400		$900		$3,700		$5,000
(4)				+$60	+300	+$360	
	$ 400		$900	$60	$4,000	$360	$5,000
(5)	+500						+500
	$ 900		$900	$60	$4,000	$360	$5,500
(6)	−400						−400
	$ 500		$900	$60	$4,000	$360	$5,100
(7)		+$1,000					+1,000
	$ 500	$1,000	$900	$60	$4,000	$360	$6,100
(8)	+1,000	− 1,000					
	$1,500 +	0 +	$900 +	$60 +	$4,000 =	$360 +	$6,100

Illustration 1–7

	Cash +	Accounts receivable +	Prepaid rent +	Office supplies +	Office equipment =	Accounts payable +	Larry Owen, capital
(1)	$5,000						$5,000
(2)	−900		+$900				
	$4,100		$900				$5,000
(3)	−3,700				+$3,700		
	$ 400		$900		$3,700		$5,000
(4)				+$60	+300	+$360	
	$ 400		$900	$60	$4,000	$360	$5,000
(5)	+500						+500
	$ 900		$900	$60	$4,000	$360	$5,500
(6)	−400						−400
	$ 500		$900	$60	$4,000	$360	$5,100
(7)		+$1,000					+1,000
	$ 500	$1,000	$900	$60	$4,000	$360	$6,100
(8)	+1,000	−1,000					
	$1,500	0	$900	$60	$4,000	$360	$6,100
(9)	−100					−100	
	$1,400 +		$900 +	$60 +	$4,000 =	$260 +	$6,100

IMPORTANT TRANSACTION EFFECTS

Look again at Illustration 1–7 and observe that every transaction affected at least two items in the equation; and in each case, after the effects were entered in the columns, the equation remained in balance. The accounting system you are beginning to study is called a *double-entry system*. It is based on the fact that every transaction affects two or more items in an accounting equation such as that in Illustration 1–7 and requires a "double entry" or, in other words, entries in two or more places. Also, the fact that the equation remained in balance after each transaction is important, for this is a proof of the accuracy with which the transactions were recorded.

BASES OF REVENUE RECOGNITION

Returning to the discussion of revenue recognition, the APB ruled that revenue is realized and in most cases should be recognized in the accounting records upon the completion of a sale or when services have been performed and are billable.[4] This is known as the *sales basis of revenue recognition.* Under it, a sale is considered to be completed when assets such as cash or the right to collect cash within a short period of time are received in exchange for goods sold or services rendered. Theoretically, revenue is earned throughout the entire performance of a service or throughout the whole process of securing goods for sale, taking a customer's order, and delivering the goods.[5] Yet, until all steps are completed and there is a right to collect the sale price, the requirements of the *objectivity principle* are not fulfilled and revenue is not recognized.

An exception to the required use of the sales basis is made for installment sales when payments are to be made over a relatively long period of time and there is considerable doubt as to the amounts that ultimately will be collected. For such sales, when collection of the full sale price is in doubt, revenue may be recognized as it is collected in cash.[6] This is known as the *cash basis of revenue recognition.*

A second exception to the required use of the sales basis applies to construction firms. Large construction jobs often take two or more years to complete. Consequently, if a construction firm has only a few jobs in process at any time and it recognizes revenue on a sales basis (upon the completion of each job), it may have a year in which no

---

[4] APB, "Omnibus Opinion—1966," *APB Opinion No. 10* (New York: AICPA, December 1966), par. 12.

[5] *APB Statement No. 4*, par. 149.

[6] *APB Opinion No. 10*, par. 12.

jobs are completed and no revenue is recognized even though the year is one of heavy activity. As a result, construction firms may and do recognize revenue on a *percentage-of-completion basis*. Under this basis, for example, if a firm has incurred 40% of the estimated cost to complete a job, it may recognize 40% of the job's contract price as revenue.

Space does not permit a full discussion of the cash basis and the percentage-of-completion basis of revenue recognition. This must be reserved for a more advanced text.

GLOSSARY

Accounting. The art of recording, classifying, reporting, and interpreting the financial data of an organization.

Accounting concept. An abstract idea that serves as a basis in the interpretation of accounting information.

Accounting equation. An expression in dollar amounts of the equivalency of the assets and equities of an enterprise, usually stated Assets = Liabilities + Owner's equity. Also called a *balance sheet equation*.

Accounting principle. A broad rule adopted by the accounting profession as a guide in measuring, recording, and reporting the financial affairs and activities of a business.

Account payable. A debt owed to a creditor for goods or services purchased on credit.

Account receivable. An amount receivable from a debtor for goods or services sold on credit.

AICPA. American Institute of Certified Public Accountants, the professional association of certified public accountants in the United States.

APB. Accounting Principles Board, a committee of the AICPA that was responsible for formulating accounting principles.

Asset. A property or economic resource owned by an individual or enterprise.

Audit. A critical exploratory review by a public accountant of the business methods and accounting records of an enterprise, made to enable the accountant to express an opinion as to whether the financial statements of the enterprise fairly reflect its financial position and operating results.

Balance sheet. A financial report showing the assets, liabilities, and owner's equity of an enterprise on a specific date. Also called a *position statement*.

Balance sheet equation. Another name for the *accounting equation*.

Bookkeeping. The record-making phase of accounting.

Budgeting. The phase of accounting dealing with planning the activities of an enterprise and comparing its actual accomplishments with the plan.

Business entity concept. The idea that a business is separate and distinct from its owner or owners and from every other business.

Business transaction. An exchange of goods, services, money, and/or the right to collect money.

Capital stock. Ownership equity in a corporation resulting from the sale of shares of the corporation's stock to its stockholders.

Continuing-concern concept. The idea that a business is a going concern that will continue to operate, using its assets to carry on its operations and, with the exception of merchandise, not offering the assets for sale.

Controller. The chief accounting officer of a large business.

Corporation. A business incorporated under the laws of a state or other jurisdiction.

Cost accounting. The phase of accounting that deals with collecting and controlling the costs of producing a given product or service.

Cost principle. The accounting rule that requires assets and services plus any resulting liabilities to be taken into the accounting records at cost.

CPA. Certified public accountant, an accountant who has met legal requirements as to age, education, experience, residence, and moral character and is licensed to practice public accounting.

Creditor. A person or enterprise to whom a debt is owed.

Debtor. A person or enterprise that owes a debt.

Equity. A right, claim, or interest in property.

Expense. Goods or services consumed in operating an enterprise.

FASB. Financial Accounting Standards Board, the seven-member board that currently has the authority to formulate and issue pronouncements of generally accepted accounting principles.

General accounting. That phase of accounting dealing primarily with recording transactions and preparing financial statements.

Going-concern concept. Another name for the *continuing-concern concept.*

Income statement. A financial statement showing revenues earned by a business, the expenses incurred in earning the revenues, and the resulting net income or net loss.

Internal auditing. A continuing examination of the records and procedures of a business by its own internal audit staff to determine if established procedures and management directives are being followed.

Liability. A debt owed.

Management advisory services. The phase of public accounting dealing with the design, installation, and improvement of a client's accounting system, plus advice on planning, budgeting, forecasting, and all other phases of accounting.

Net assets. Assets minus liabilities.

Net income. The excess of revenues over expenses.

Net loss. The excess of expenses over revenues.

Objectivity principle. The accounting rule requiring that wherever possible the amounts used in recording transactions be based on objective evidence rather than on subjective judgments.

Owner's equity.   The equity of the owner (or owners) of a business in the assets of the business.

Partnership.   An association of two or more persons to co-own and operate a business for profit.

Position statement.   Another name for the balance sheet.

Price-level-adjusted statements.   Financial statements showing item amounts adjusted for changes in the purchasing power of money.

Realization principle.   The accounting rule that defines a revenue as an inflow of assets, not necessarily cash, in exchange for goods or services and requires the revenue to be recognized at the time, but not before, it is earned.

Recognition principle.   Another name for the *realization principle.*

Revenue.   An inflow of assets, not necessarily cash, in exchange for goods and services sold.

Shareholder.   A person or enterprise owning a share or shares of stock in a corporation. Also called a *stockholder.*

Single proprietorship.   A business owned by one individual.

Stable-dollar concept.   The idea that the purchasing power of the unit of measure used in accounting, the dollar, does not change.

Stockholder.   Another name for a *shareholder.*

Tax services.   The phase of public accounting dealing with the preparation of tax returns and with advice as to how transactions may be completed in a way as to incur the smallest tax liability.

QUESTIONS FOR CLASS DISCUSSION

1. What is the nature of accounting and what is its function?
2. How does a business executive use accounting information?
3. Why do the states license certified public accountants?
4. What is the purpose of an audit? What do certified public accountants do when they make an audit?
5. A public accountant may provide management advisory services. Of what does this consist?
6. What do the tax services of a public accountant include beyond preparing tax returns?
7. Differentiate between accounting and bookkeeeping.
8. What does an income statement show?
9. As the word is used in accounting, what is a revenue? An expense?
10. Why is the period of time covered by an income statement of extreme significance?
11. What does a balance sheet show?
12. Define *(a)* asset, *(b)* liability, *(c)* equity, and *(d)* owner's equity.
13. Why is a business treated as a separate entity for accounting purposes?

14. What is required by the cost principle? Why is such a principle necessary?
15. Why are not balance sheet amounts for the assets of a business changed from time to time to reflect changes in market values?
16. A business shows office stationery on its balance sheet at its $50 cost, although the stationery can be sold for not more than $0.25 as scrap paper. What accounting principle and concept justify this?
17. In accounting, transactions are measured, recorded, and reported in terms of dollars and the dollar is assumed to be a stable unit of measure. Is the dollar a stable unit of measure?
18. What are generally accepted accounting principles?
19. Why are the *Statements* of the Financial Accounting Standards Board and the *Opinions* of the Accounting Principles Board of importance to accounting students?
20. How does separate legal entity affect the responsibility of a corporation's stockholders for the debts of the corporation? Does this responsibility or lack of responsibility for the debts of the business apply to the owner or owners of a single proprietorship or partnership business?
21. What is the balance sheet equation? What is its importance to accounting students?
22. Is it possible for a transaction to increase or decrease a single liability without affecting any other asset, liability, or owner's equity item?
23. In accounting, what does the realization principle require?

CLASS EXERCISES

Exercise 1–1

On June 30 of the current year, the balance sheet of Tennis Shop, a single proprietorship, showed the following:

Cash .... $ 2,000
Other assets 45,000
Accounts payable 17,000
Ted Lee, capital 30,000

On that date, Ted Lee sold the "Other assets" for $25,000 in preparation for ending and liquidating the business of Tennis Shop.

Required:

1. Prepare a balance sheet for the store as it would appear immediately after the sale of the assets.
2. Tell how the store's cash should be distributed in ending the business and why.

Exercise 1–2

Determine:

a. The equity of the owner in a business having $34,500 of assets and $9,300 of liabilities.
b. The liabilities of a business having $26,600 of assets and in which the owner has a $19,400 equity.

c. The assets of a business having $6,300 of liabilities and in which the owner has a $12,400 equity.

Exercise 1–3

A business had the following assets and liabilities at the beginning and at the end of a year:

	Assets	Liabilities
Beginning of year	$60,000	$15,000
End of year	75,000	20,000

Determine the net income or net loss of the business during the year under each of the following unrelated assumptions:

a. The owner of the business had made no additional investments in the business and no withdrawals of assets from the business during the year.
b. During the year, the owner made no additional investments in the business but had withdrawn $1,000 per month for personal living expenses.
c. The owner had made no withdrawals but had made a $15,000 additional investment in the business during the year.
d. The owner had withdrawn $1,000 from the business each month to pay personal living expenses and near the year-end had invested an additional $15,000 in the business.

Exercise 1–4

June Lake began the practice of dentistry and during a short period completed these transactions:

a. Invested $5,000 in cash and dental equipment having a $500 fair value in a dental practice.
b. Paid the rent on suitable office space for two months in advance, $1,000.
c. Purchased additional dental equipment for cash, $1,500.
d. Completed dental work for a patient and immediately collected $200 cash for the work.
e. Purchased additional dental equipment on credit, $800.
f. Completed $600 of dental work for a patient on credit.
g. Paid the dental assistant's wages, $300.
h. Collected $300 of the amount owed by the patient of transaction (f).
i. Paid for the equipment purchased in transaction (e).

Required:

Arrange the following asset, liability, and owner's equity titles in an equation form like Illustration 1–7: Cash; Accounts Receivable; Prepaid Rent; Dental Equipment; Accounts Payable; and June Lake, Capital. Then show by additions and subtractions the effects of the transactions on the elements of the equation. Show new totals after each transaction.

Exercise 1–5

Wayne Nash began the practice of law on October 1 of the current year; and on October 31, his records showed the following items and amounts. From the information, prepare a month-end balance sheet like Illustration 1–2 and an income statement for the month. Head the statements Wayne Nash, Attorney. (The October 31 $3,000 amount of Nash's capital is the amount of his capital after it was increased and decreased by the October revenues and expenses shown.)

Cash	$ 500	Wayne Nash, capital	$3,000
Accounts receivable	300	Legal fees earned	2,200
Prepaid rent	800	Rent expense	400
Law library	1,600	Salaries expense	500
Accounts payable	200	Telephone expense	100

PROBLEMS

Problem 1–1

Ned Able completed the following transactions:

a. Sold a personal investment in IBM stock for $9,350 and deposited $9,000 of the proceeds in a bank account opened in the name of his new business, Able TV Service.
b. Purchased for cash the repair supplies, $1,050, tools, $825, and the used truck, $2,100, of a TV repair shop that was going out of business.
c. Paid the rent on the shop space for three months in advance, $600.
d. Purchased additional tools for cash, $150.
e. Purchased additional repair supplies on credit, $250.
f. Gave the old company truck and $3,000 in cash for a new company truck.
g. Completed repair work for Walter Keller and collected $50 cash therefor.
h. Paid for the repair supplies purchased in transaction (e).
i. Completed repair work for Gary Nash on credit, $75.
j. Paid for gas and oil used in the truck, $25.
k. Gary Nash paid in full for the work of transaction (i).
l. Ned Able wrote a check on the bank account of the shop to pay a personal expense, $60.

Required:

1. Arrange the following asset, liability, and owner's equity titles in an equation like in Illustration 1–7: Cash; Accounts Receivable; Prepaid Rent; Supplies; Tools; Truck; Accounts Payable; and Ned Able, Capital.
2. Show by additions and subtractions, as in Illustration 1–7, the effects of the transactions on the elements of the equation. Show new totals after each transaction.

Problem 1–2

On October 1 of the current year, Mary Berg began the practice of law by investing $1,500 in cash and a law library having a $1,000 fair value; and during a short period, she completed the following additional transactions:

Oct. 1 Rented the furnished office of a lawyer who was retiring and paid three months' rent in advance, $900.
2 Purchased office supplies for cash, $65.
5 Purchased law books from West Publishing Company on credit, $150.
8 Completed legal work for a client and immediately collected $250 cash for the work done.
14 Completed legal work for Pine Realty on credit, $350.
15 Paid the salary of the office secretary, $350.
15 Paid $50 of the amount owed on the law books purchased on October 5.
20 Completed legal work for Guaranty Bank on credit, $400.
24 Received $200 from Pine Realty in partial payment for the legal work completed on October 14.

Oct. 31 Paid the monthly telephone bill, $20.
    31 Paid the office secretary's salary, $350.
    31 Took an inventory of unused office supplies and determined that $15 of supplies had been used and had become an expense. (Reduce the asset and owner's equity.)
    31 Recognized that one month's rent had expired and had become an expense.

Required:

1. Arrange the following asset, liability, and owner's equity titles in an equation like Illustration 1–7: Cash; Accounts Receivable; Prepaid Rent; Office Supplies; Law Library; Accounts Payable; and Mary Berg, Capital.
2. Show by additions and subtractions the effects of each transaction on the items of the equation. Show new totals after each transaction.
3. Prepare an October 31 balance sheet like Illustration 1–2 for the law practice. Head the statement Mary Berg, Attorney.
4. Analyze the increases and decreases in the last column of the equation and prepare an October income statement for the law practice.

Problem 1–3

Jack Cary began an architectural practice upon graduation from college in 1983, and the records of the practice show that it had the following assets and liabilities at the ends of 1983 and 1984:

	December 31	
	1983	*1984*
Cash	$1,200	$ 400
Accounts receivable	4,000	5,500
Prepaid rent	400	
Drafting supplies	300	200
Prepaid insurance	200	300
Office and drafting equipment	3,500	4,000
Land		25,000
Building		60,000
Accounts payable	600	500
Note payable		2,000
Mortgage payable		68,000

During the last week of 1984, Mr. Cary purchased in the name of the practice a small office building and moved the practice from rented quarters to the new building. The building and the land it occupies cost $85,000. The practice paid $17,000 in cash and assumed a mortgage liability for the balance. In order for the practice to pay the $17,000, Mr. Cary had to invest an additional $5,000 of his personal funds in the business and borrow in the name of the business $2,000 from Security Bank. To borrow the $2,000, the practice gave the bank a promissory note payable due in six months. During 1984, the practice earned a satisfactory net income that enabled Mr. Cary to withdraw $2,000 per month from the business for personal use.

Required:

1. Prepare December 31, 1983, and 1984 balance sheets for the practice like Illustration 1–2. Head the statements Jack Cary, Architect.
2. Prepare a calculation to show the amount of net income earned by the practice during 1984.

Problem 1–4   Gary Arne graduated from law school in June of the current year, passed the bar examination in his state, and on August 1 began a new law practice by investing $2,500 in cash and his college law books that had a $500 fair value. He then completed these additional transactions:

Aug. 1   Rented the furnished office of a lawyer who was retiring, paying $1,200 cash for three months' rent in advance.

     1   Purchased office supplies for cash, $35.

     1   Purchased insurance protection for one year in advance for cash by paying the premium on an insurance policy, $420.

     2   Bought the law library of the retiring lawyer for $2,500, paying $500 in cash and agreeing to pay the balance within one year.

     5   Purchased additional office supplies on credit, $50.

     8   Completed legal work for a client and immediately collected $200 cash for the work done.

   10   Completed legal work for Tops Realty on credit, $750.

   13   Purchased law books on credit, $250.

   15   Paid the salary of the legal secretary, $450.

   15   Paid for the office supplies purchased on August 5.

   18   Completed legal work for Security Bank on credit, $500.

   20   Received $750 from Tops Realty in full payment for the work completed on August 10.

   23   Completed legal work for Western Stores on credit, $450.

   28   Received $500 from Security Bank in full payment for the work completed on August 18.

   31   Paid the August telephone bill, $40.

   31   Paid the August utilities expense, $75.

   31   Paid the legal secretary's salary, $450.

   31   Recognized that one month's office rent had expired and had become an expense. (Reduce the prepaid rent and owner's equity to record the expense.)

   31   Recognized that one month's prepaid insurance had expired and had become an expense.

   31   Took an inventory of office supplies and determined that $20 of supplies had been used and had become an expense.

Required:

1. Arrange the following asset, liability, and owner's equity titles in an equation like Illustration 1–7: Cash; Accounts Receivable; Prepaid Rent; Prepaid Insurance; Office Supplies; Law Library; Accounts Payable; and Gary Arne, Capital.

2. Show the effects of the transactions on the elements of the equation by recording increases and decreases in the appropriate columns. Indicate an increase with a + and a decrease with a − before the amount. *Do not determine new balances for the items of the equation after each transaction.*

3. After recording the last transaction, determine and insert on the next line the final balance for each item of the equation and determine if the equation is in balance.

4. Prepare an August 31 balance sheet for the law practice like Illustration 1–2. Head the statement Gary Arne, Attorney.

5. Analyze the items in the last column of the equation and prepare an August income statement for the practice.

ALTERNATE PROBLEMS

Problem 1–1A
Ned Able owns and operates Able Plumbing Service, which has the following assets: cash, $915; plumbing supplies, $2,240; tools, $1,965; and truck, $4,780. The business owes Plumbing Supply Company $155 for supplies previously purchased. During a short period, the service completed these transactions:

a. Paid the rent on the shop space for two months in advance, $400.
b. Purchased tools for cash, $25.
c. Purchased plumbing supplies on credit from Plumbing Supply Company, $150.
d. Completed repair work for a customer and immediately collected $50 cash for the work done.
e. Completed repair work for Gary Hall on credit, $200.
f. Paid Plumbing Supply Company the amount owed at the beginning of the month.
g. Gary Hall paid for the work of transaction (e).
h. Gave tools carried in the accounting records at $100 plus $175 in cash for new tools priced at $275.
i. Purchased plumbing supplies on credit from Plumbing Supply Company, $200.
j. Paid the electric bill for the month, $35.
k. Ned Able withdrew $50 cash from the business to pay personal expenses.
l. Paid for the supplies purchased in transaction (c).

Required:

1. Arrange the following asset, liability, and owner's equity titles in an equation like Illustration 1–7: Cash; Accounts Receivable; Prepaid Rent; Supplies; Tools; Truck; Accounts Payable; and Ned Able, Capital.
2. Enter the beginning assets and liability under the proper titles of the equation. Determine Ned Able's beginning equity and enter it.
3. Show by additions and subtractions, as in Illustration 1–7, the effects of the transactions on the elements of the equation. Show new totals after each transaction.

Problem 1–2A
Mary Berg, a young lawyer, began her practice and completed these transactions during September of the current year:

Sept. 2 Sold a personal investment in Xerox stock for $2,845 and invested $2,500 of the proceeds in the law practice.

2 Rented the furnished office of a lawyer who was retiring and paid three months' rent in advance, $1,050.

2 Purchased the law library of the retiring lawyer for $1,750, paying $750 in cash and agreeing to pay the balance within one year.

Sept. 5 Purchased office supplies for cash, $75.

6 Purchased law books from West Publishing Company on credit, $250.

8 Completed legal work for a client and immediately collected $100 in cash for the work done.

15 Completed legal work for Security Bank on credit, $700.

15 Paid for the law books purchased on credit on September 6.

19 Completed legal work for Coast Reality on credit, $600.

25 Received $700 from Security Bank for the work completed on September 15.

30 Paid the office secretary's salary, $800.

30 Paid the monthly telephone bill, $25.

30 Recognized that one month's rent on the office had expired and become an expense. (Reduce the prepaid rent and the owner's equity.)

30 Took an inventory of unused office supplies and determined that $20 of supplies had been used and had become an expense.

Required:

1. Arrange the following asset, liability, and owner's equity titles in an equation like Illustration 1–7: Cash; Accounts Receivable; Prepaid Rent; Office Supplies; Law Library; Accounts Payable; and Mary Berg, Capital.
2. Show by additions and subtractions the effects of each transaction on the items of the equation. Show new totals after each transaction.
3. Prepare a September 30 balance sheet like Illustration 1–2 for the law practice. Head the statement Mary Berg, Attorney.
4. Analyze the increases and decreases in the last column of the equation and prepare a September income statement for the law practice.

Problem 1–3A

The records of Sue Cole's dental practice show the following assets and liabilities at the ends of 1983 and 1984:

	December 31	
	1983	*1984*
Cash	$2,000	$ 400
Accounts receivable	7,000	8,500
Dental supplies	500	600
Prepaid insurance	300	500
Prepaid rent	1,200	
Office equipment	4,000	5,000
Land		20,000
Building		65,000
Accounts payable	300	500
Mortgage payable		70,000

During the last week of December 1984, Dr. Cole purchased in the name of the practice the building in which she practices. The building and the land it occupies cost $85,000. The practice paid $15,000 in cash and assumed a mortgage liability for the balance. Dr. Cole had to invest an additional $10,000 in the practice to enable it to pay the $15,000. The practice earned a satisfactory net income during 1984, which enabled Dr. Cole to withdraw $1,750 per month from the practice for personal use.

Required:

1. Prepare balance sheets like in Illustration 1–2 for the practice as of the ends of 1983 and 1984. Head the statements Sue Cole, D.D.S.
2. Prepare a calculation to determine the amount of net income earned by the practice during 1984.

Problem 1–4A   Gary Arne graduated from law school in June of the current year and on July 1 began a new law practice by investing $2,500 in cash and his college law books that had a $400 fair value. He then completed these additional transactions:

July 1   Rented the furnished office of a lawyer who was retiring, paying $900 cash for three months' rent in advance.

1   Purchased office supplies for cash, $25.

1   Bought the law library of the retiring lawyer for $2,000, paying $500 cash and agreeing to pay the balance within one year.

2   Purchased insurance protection for one year for cash by paying the premium on an insurance policy, $360.

5   Completed legal work for a client and immediately collected $50 in cash for the work done.

7   Purchased additional office supplies on credit, $40.

10   Completed legal work for Western Realty on credit, $600.

12   Purchased law books from North Publishing Company on credit, $200.

15   Paid the salary of the office secretary, $450.

17   Paid for the office supplies purchased on July 7.

18   Completed legal work for Valley Bank on credit, $400.

20   Received payment in full for the legal work completed for Western Realty on July 10.

22   Completed additional legal work for Western Realty on credit, $350.

27   Received payment in full from Valley Bank for the legal work completed on July 18.

31   Paid the July telephone bill, $25.

31   Paid the July utilities expense, $20.

31   Paid the office secretary's salary, $450.

31   Recognized that one month's office rent had expired and had become an expense. (Reduce the prepaid rent and owner's equity to record the expense.)

31   Recognized that one month's prepaid insurance had expired.

31   Took an inventory of office supplies and determined that $15 of supplies had been used and had become an expense.

Required:

1. Arrange the following asset, liability, and owner's equity titles in an equation like Illustration 1–7: Cash, Accounts Receivable; Prepaid Rent; Prepaid Insurance; Office Supplies; Law Library; Accounts Payable; and Gary Arne, Capital.
2. Show the effects of the transactions on the elements of the equation by recording increases and decreases in the appropriate columns. Indicate

an increase with a + and a decrease with a − before the amount. *Do not determine new balances for the items of the equation after each transaction.*

3. After recording the last transaction, determine and insert on the next line the final balance for each item of the equation and determine if the equation is in balance.
4. Prepare a July 31 balance sheet for the law practice like Illustration 1–2. Head the statement Gary Arne, Attorney.
5. Analyze the items in the last column of the equation and prepare a July income statement for the practice.

PROVOCATIVE PROBLEMS

Provocative
Problem 1–1,
The Sandbar

Bob Berry has just completed the first summer's operation of a riverside concession called The Sandbar at which he sells soft drinks, candy, and sandwiches. He began the summer's operation with $4,000 in cash and a five-year lease on a boat dock and a small concession building. The lease requires a $1,200 annual rent payment, although the concession is open only from May 15 to September 15. On opening day, Bob paid the first year's rent and also purchased five boats at $450 each, paying cash. He estimated the boats would have a five-year life, after which he could sell them for $50 each.

During the summer, he purchased food, soft drinks, and candy costing $5,250, all of which was paid for by summer's end, excepting food costing $125 which was purchased during the last week's operation. He also paid electric bills, $135, and the wages of a part-time helper, $1,000; and he withdrew $200 of earnings of the concession each week for 16 weeks to pay personal expenses.

He took in $2,150 in boat rentals during the summer and sold $12,350 of food and drinks, all of which was collected in cash, excepting $150 he had not collected from Monroe Company for food, drinks, and boat rentals for an employees' party.

When he closed on September 15, he was able to return to the soft drink company several cases of drinks for which he received a $65 cash refund. However, he had to take home for consumption by his family a number of candy bars and some hamburger and buns that cost $25 and could have been sold for $50.

Prepare a September 15 balance sheet like Illustration 1–2 for the business and an income statement showing the net income earned as a result of the summer's operations. (Hint: An equation like Illustration 1–7 may be helpful in organizing the data.)

Provocative
Problem 1–2,
Rocket Delivery
Service

Bill Nash dropped out of school at the end of his first college semester but could not find a job. As a result, since he owned a Honda motorcycle having a $900 fair value, he decided to go into business for himself, and he began Rocket Delivery Service with no assets other than the motorcycle. He kept no accounting records; and now, at the year-end, has asked you to determine the net income earned by the service since it began operations the last week of January.

You find that the delivery service has an $825 year-end bank balance plus $60 of undeposited cash. Also, several customers owe the service $150 for packages delivered on credit. Likewise, the service owes $35 for gas and oil purchased with a credit card. The service still owns the motorcycle, but through hard use it has depreciated $200 since the business began operations. In addition to the motorcycle, the service has a new delivery truck that cost $6,600, has depreciated $500 since its purchase, and on which the service owes the finance company $4,000. When the truck was purchased, the service borrowed $500 from Bill Nash's father to help make the down payment on the truck. The loan was made to the delivery service, was interest free, and has not been repaid. Finally, since the service has had earnings from the beginning, Bill Nash has withdrawn $200 of its earnings each week (48 weeks) to pay personal expenses.

Determine the net income earned by the business during the period of its operations. Present figures to prove your answer. (Hint: Net income increases owner's equity.)

Processing Accounting Data

PART TWO

Recording Transactions

2

After studying Chapter 2, you should be able to:

Explain the mechanics of double-entry accounting and tell why transactions are recorded with equal debits and credits.

State the rules of debit and credit and apply the rules in recording transactions.

Tell the normal balance of any asset, liability, or owner's equity account.

Record transactions in a General Journal, post to the ledger accounts, and prepare a trial balance to test the accuracy of the recording and posting.

Define or explain the words and phrases listed in the chapter Glossary.

Transactions are the raw material of the accounting process. The process consists of identifying transactions, recording them, and summarizing their effects on periodic reports for the use of management and other decision makers.

Some years ago, almost all companies used pen and ink in recording transactions. However, today only small companies use this method, companies small enough that their bookkeeping can be done by one person working as a bookkeeper a part of his or her day. Larger, modern companies use electric bookkeeping machines and computers in recording transactions and in processing the recorded data.

Nevertheless, most students begin their study of accounting by learning a double-entry accounting system based on pen and ink. There are several reasons for this. First, pen-and-ink methods are the best methods to use in teaching beginning accounting. Second, there is little lost motion from learning a pen-and-ink system, since almost everything about it is applicable to machine and computer methods. Primarily, the bookkeeping machines and computer equipment replace pen and ink in recording and processing the accounting data, taking the drudgery out of the work. And last, for the student who will start, manage, or own a small business, one small enough to use a pen-and-ink system, the system applies as it is taught.

BUSINESS PAPERS

Business papers provide evidence of transactions completed and are the basis for accounting entries to record the transactions. For example, when goods are sold on credit, two or more copies of an invoice or sales ticket are prepared. One copy is enclosed with the goods or is delivered to the customer. The other is sent to the accounting department where it becomes the basis for an entry to record the sale. Also, when goods are sold for cash, the sales are commonly "rung up" on a cash register that prints the amount of each sale on a paper tape locked inside the register. At the end of the day, when the proper key is depressed, the register prints on the tape the total cash sales for the day. The tape is then removed and becomes the basis for an entry to record the sales. Also, when an established business purchases assets, it normally buys on credit and receives an invoice that becomes the basis for an entry to record the purchase. Likewise, when the invoice is paid, a check is issued and the check or a carbon copy becomes the basis for an entry to record the payment. Obviously, then, business papers are the starting point in the accounting process. Furthermore, verifiable business papers, particularly those originating outside the business, are also objective evidence of transactions completed and the amounts at which they should be recorded, as required by the *objectivity principle.*

ACCOUNTS

A company with an accounting system based on pen and ink or electric bookkeeping machines uses *accounts* in recording its transactions. A number of accounts are normally required, with a separate account being used for summarizing the increases and decreases in each asset, liability, and owner's equity item appearing on the balance sheet and each revenue and expense appearing on the income statement.

In its most simple form, an account looks like the letter "T," is called a *T-account,* and appears as follows:

(Place for the Name of the Item Recorded in This Account)	
(Left side)	(Right side)

Note that the "T" gives the account a left side, a right side, and a place for the name of the item, the increases and decreases of which are recorded therein.

When a T-account is used in recording increases and decreases in an item, the increases are placed on one side of the account and the decreases on the other. For example, if the increases and decreases in the cash of Larry Owen's law practice of the previous chapter are recorded in a T-account, they appear as follows:

Cash			
Investment	5,000	Prepayment of rent	900
Legal fee earned	500	Equipment purchase	3,700
Collection of account receivable	1,000	Salary payment	400
		Payment on account payable	100

The reason for putting the increases on one side and the decreases on the other is that this makes it easy to add the increases and then add the decreases. The sum of the decreases may then be subtracted from the sum of the increases to learn how much of the item recorded in the account the company has, owns, or owes. For example, the increases in the cash of the Owen law practice were:

Investment	$5,000
Legal fee earned	500
Collection of an account receivable	1,000
Sum of the increases	$6,500

And the decreases were:

```
Prepayment of office rent  ..........  $  900
Equipment purchase  ...............     3,700
Salary payment  ...................       400
Payment on account payable  .......       100
        Sum of the decreases  .......   $5,100
```

And when the sum of the decreases is subtracted from the sum of the increases,

```
Sum of the increases  .............  $6,500
Sum of the decreases  .............   5,100
    Balance of cash remaining  ...  $1,400
```

The subtraction shows the law practice has $1,400 of cash remaining.

Balance of an Account

When the increases and decreases recorded in an account are separately added and the sum of the decreases is subtracted from the sum of the increases, the procedure is called determining the *account balance*. The balance of an account is the difference between its increases and decreases. It is also the amount of the item recorded in the account that the company has, owns, or owes at the time the balance is determined.

ACCOUNTS COMMONLY USED

A business uses a number of accounts in recording its transactions. However, the specific accounts used vary from one concern to another, depending upon the assets owned, the debts owed, and the information to be secured from the accounting records. Nevertheless, although the specific accounts vary, the following accounts are common.

Asset Accounts

If useful records of a company's assets are to be kept, an individual account is needed for each kind of asset owned. Some of the more common assets for which accounts are maintained are as follows.

CASH.   Increases and decreases in cash are recorded in an account called Cash. The cash of a business consists of money or any medium of exchange that a bank will accept at face value for deposit. It includes coins, currency, checks, and postal and bank money orders. The balance of the Cash account shows both the cash on hand in the store or office and that on deposit in the bank.

NOTES RECEIVABLE.   A formal written promise to pay a definite sum of money at a fixed future date is called a *promissory note*. When amounts due from others are evidenced by promissory notes, the notes are known as notes receivable and are recorded in a Notes Receivable account.

ACCOUNTS RECEIVABLE.   Goods and services are commonly sold to customers on the basis of oral or implied promises of future payment. Such sales are known as sales on credit or sales on account; and the oral or implied promises to pay are known as accounts receivable. Accounts receivable are increased by sales on credit and are decreased by customer payments. Since it is necessary to know the amount currently owed by each customer, a separate record must be kept of each customer's purchases and payments. However, a discussion of this separate record is deferred until Chapter 6; and for the present, all increases and decreases in accounts receivable are recorded in a single account called Accounts Receivable.

PREPAID INSURANCE.   Fire, liability, and other types of insurance protection are normally paid for in advance. The amount paid is called a premium and may give protection from loss for from one to five years. As a result, a large portion of each premium is an asset for a considerable time after payment. When insurance premiums are paid, the asset *prepaid insurance* is increased by the amount paid. The increase is normally recorded in an account called Prepaid Insurance. Day by day, insurance premiums expire. Consequently, at intervals the insurance that has expired is calculated and the balance of the Prepaid Insurance account is reduced accordingly.

OFFICE SUPPLIES.   Stamps, stationery, paper, pencils, and like items are known as office supplies. They are assets when purchased, and continue to be assets until consumed. As they are consumed, the amounts consumed become expenses. Increases and decreases in the asset *office supplies* are commonly recorded in an account called Office Supplies.

STORE SUPPLIES.   Wrapping paper, cartons, bags, string, and similar items used by a store are known as store supplies. Increases and decreases in store supplies are recorded in an account of that name.

OTHER PREPAID EXPENSES.   Prepaid expenses are items that are assets at the time of purchase but become expenses as they are consumed or used. Prepaid insurance, office supplies, and store supplies are examples. Other examples are prepaid rent, prepaid taxes, and prepaid wages. Each is accounted for in a separate account.

EQUIPMENT.   Increases and decreases in such things as typewriters, desks, chairs, and office machines are commonly recorded in an account called Office Equipment. Likewise, changes in the amount of counters, showcases, cash registers, and like items used by a store are recorded in an account called Store Equipment.

BUILDINGS.   A building used by a business in carrying on its operations may be a store, garage, warehouse, or factory. However, regardless of use, an account called Buildings is commonly employed in recording the increases and decreases in the buildings owned by a business and used in carrying on its operations.

LAND.   An account called Land is commonly used in recording increases and decreases in the land owned by a business. Land and the buildings placed upon it are inseparable in physical fact. Nevertheless, it is usually desirable to account for land and its buildings in separate accounts because buildings depreciate and wear out but land does not.

Liability Accounts

Most companies do not have as many liability accounts as asset accounts; however, the following are common:

NOTES PAYABLE.   Increases and decreases in amounts owed because of promissory notes given to creditors are accounted for in an account called Notes Payable.

ACCOUNTS PAYABLE.   An account payable is an amount owed to a creditor. Accounts payable result from the purchase of merchandise, supplies, equipment, and services on credit. Since it is necessary to know the amount owed each creditor, an individual record must be kept of the purchases from and the payments to each. However, a discussion of this individual record is deferred until Chapter 6; and for the present, all increases and decreases in accounts payable are recorded in a single Accounts Payable account.

UNEARNED REVENUES.   The *realization principle* requires that revenue be earned before it is recognized as revenue. Therefore, when a company collects for its products or services before delivery, the amounts collected are unearned revenue. An unearned revenue is a liability that will be extinguished by delivering the product or service paid for in advance. Subscriptions collected in advance by a magazine publisher, rent collected in advance by a landlord, and legal fees collected in advance by a lawyer are examples. Upon receipt, the amounts collected are recorded in liability accounts such as Unearned Subscriptions, Unearned Rent, and Unearned Legal Fees. When earned by delivery, the amounts earned are transferred to the revenue accounts, Subscriptions Earned, Rent Earned, and Legal Fees Earned.

OTHER SHORT-TERM PAYABLES. Wages payable, taxes payable, and interest payable are illustrations of other short-term liabilities for which individual accounts must be kept.

MORTGAGE PAYABLE. A *mortgage payable* is a long-term debt for which the creditor has a secured prior claim against some one or more of the debtor's assets. The mortgage gives the creditor the right to force the sale of the mortgaged assets through a foreclosure if the mortgage debt is not paid when due. An account called Mortgage Payable is commonly used in recording the increases and decreases in the amount owed on a mortgage.

Owner's Equity Accounts

Several kinds of transactions affect the equity of a business owner. In a single proprietorship, these include the investment of the owner, his or her withdrawals of cash or other assets for personal use, revenues earned, and expenses incurred. In the previous chapter, all such transactions were entered in a column under the name of the owner. This simplified the material of the chapter but made it necessary to analyze the items entered in the column in order to prepare an income statement. Fortunately, such an analysis is not necessary. All that is required to avoid it is a number of accounts, a separate one for each owner's equity item appearing on the balance sheet and a separate one for each revenue and expense on the income statement. Then, as each transaction affecting owner's equity is completed, it is recorded in the proper account. Among the accounts required are the following:

CAPITAL ACCOUNT. When a person invests in a business of his or her own, the investment is recorded in an account carrying the owner's name and the word *Capital*. For example, an account called Larry Owen, Capital is used in recording the investment of Larry Owen in his law practice. In addition to the original investment, the *capital account* is used for any permanent additional increases or decreases in owner's equity.

WITHDRAWALS ACCOUNT.   Usually a person invests in a business to earn income. However, income is earned over a period of time, say, a year. Often during this period, the business owner must withdraw a portion of the earnings to pay living expenses or for other personal uses. These withdrawals reduce both assets and owner's equity. To record them, an account carrying the name of the business owner and the word *Withdrawals* is used. For example, an account called Larry Owen, Withdrawals is used to record the withdrawals of cash by Larry Owen from his law practice. The *withdrawals account* is also known as the *personal account* or *drawing account.*

An owner of a small unincorporated business often withdraws a fixed amount each week or month for personal living expenses, and often thinks of these withdrawals as a salary. However, in a legal sense they are not a salary because the owner of an unincorporated business cannot enter into a legally binding contract with himself to hire himself and pay himself a salary. Consequently, in law and custom it is recognized that such withdrawals are neither a salary nor an expense of the business but are withdrawals in anticipation of earnings.

REVENUE AND EXPENSE ACCOUNTS.   When an income statement is prepared, it is necessary to know the amount of each kind of revenue earned and each kind of expense incurred during the period covered by the statement. To accumulate this information, a number of revenue and expense accounts are needed. However, all concerns do not have the same revenues and expenses. Consequently, it is impossible to list all revenue and expense accounts to be encountered. Nevertheless, Revenue from Repairs, Commissions Earned, Legal Fees Earned, Rent Earned, and Interest Earned are common examples of revenue accounts. And Advertising Expense, Store Supplies Expense, Office Salaries Expense, Office Supplies Expense, Rent Expense, Utilities Expense, and Insurance Expense are common examples of expense accounts. It should be noted that the kind of revenue or expense recorded in each above-mentioned account is evident from its title. This is generally true of such accounts.

Real and Nominal Accounts

To add to your vocabulary, it may be said here that balance sheet accounts are commonly called *real accounts.* Presumably, this is because the items recorded in these accounts exist in objective form. Likewise, income statement accounts are called *nominal accounts* because items recorded in these accounts exist in name only.

THE LEDGER

A business may use from two dozen to several thousand accounts in recording its transactions. Each account is placed on a separate page in a bound or loose-leaf book, or on a separate card in a tray of cards. If the accounts are kept in a book, the book is called a *ledger.* If they are kept on cards in a file tray, the tray of cards is a ledger. Actually, as used in accounting, the word *ledger* means a group of accounts.

DEBIT AND CREDIT

As previously stated, a T-account has a left side and a right side. However, in accounting, the left side is called the *debit* side, abbreviated "Dr."; and the right side is called the *credit* side, abbreviated "Cr." Furthermore, when amounts are entered on the left side of an account, they are called *debits,* and the account is said to be *debited.* When amounts are entered on the right side, they are called *credits,* and the account is said to be *credited.* The difference between the total debits and the total credits recorded in an account is the *balance of the account.* The balance may be either a *debit balance* or a *credit balance.* It is a debit balance when the sum of the debits exceeds the sum of the credits and a credit balance when the sum of the credits exceeds the sum of the debits. An account is said to be *in balance* when its debits and credits are equal.

The words *to debit* and *to credit* should not be confused with *to increase* and *to decrease.* To debit means simply to enter an amount on the left side of an account. To credit means to enter an amount on the right side. Either may be an increase or a decrease. This may readily be seen by examining the way in which the investment of Larry Owen is recorded in his Cash and capital accounts that follow:

Cash		Larry Owen, Capital	
Investment 5,000			Investment 5,000

When Owen invested $5,000 in his law practice, both the business cash and Owen's equity were increased. Observe in the accounts that the increase in cash is recorded on the left or debit side of the Cash account, while the increase in owner's equity is recorded on the right or credit side. The transaction is recorded in this manner because of the mechanics of *double-entry accounting.*

MECHANICS OF DOUBLE-ENTRY ACCOUNTING

The mechanics of double-entry accounting are such that every transaction affects and is recorded in two or more accounts with equal debits and credits. Transactions are so recorded because equal debits and credits offer a means of proving the recording accuracy. The proof is, if every transaction is recorded with equal debits and credits, then the debits in the ledger must equal the credits.

The person who first devised double-entry accounting based the system on the accounting equation, $A = L + OE$. He assigned the recording of increases in assets to the debit sides of asset accounts. He then recognized that equal debits and credits were possible only if increases in liabilities and owner's equity were recorded on the opposite or credit sides of liability and owner's equity accounts. In other words, he recognized that if increases in assets were to be recorded as debits, then increases and decreases in all accounts would have to be recorded as follows:

Assets		=	Liabilities		+	Owner's equity	
Debit for increases	**Credit for** decreases		**Debit for** decreases	**Credit for** increases		**Debit for** decreases	**Credit for** increases

From the T-accounts it is possible to formulate rules for recording transactions under a double-entry system. The rules are:

1. Increases in assets are debited to asset accounts; consequently, decreases must be credited.
2. Increases in liability and owner's equity items are credited to liability and owner's equity accounts; consequently, decreases must be debited.

At this stage, beginning students will find it helpful to memorize these rules. They should also note that in a single proprietorship there are four kinds of owner's equity accounts: (1) the capital account, (2) the withdrawals account, (3) revenue accounts, and (4) expense accounts. Furthermore, for transactions affecting these accounts, students should observe these additional points:

1. The original investment of the owner of a business plus any more or less permanent changes in the investment are recorded in the capital account.
2. Withdrawals of assets for personal use, including cash to pay personal expenses, decrease owner's equity and are debited to the owner's withdrawals account.

3. Revenues increase owner's equity and are credited in each case to a revenue account that shows the kind of revenue earned.
4. Expenses decrease owner's equity and are debited in each case to an expense account that shows the kind of expense incurred.

TRANSACTIONS ILLUSTRATING THE RULES OF DEBIT AND CREDIT

The following transactions of Larry Owen's law practice illustrate the application of debit and credit rules. They also show how transactions are recorded in the accounts. The number preceding each transaction is used throughout the illustration to identify the transaction in the accounts. Note that most of the transactions are the same ones used in Chapter 1 to illustrate the effects of transactions on the accounting equation.

To record a transaction, it must be analyzed to determine what items are increased and decreased. The rules of debit and credit are then applied to determine the debit and credit effects of the increases or decreases. An analysis of each of the following transactions is given in order to demonstrate the process.

1. On July 1, Larry Owen invested $5,000 in a new law practice.

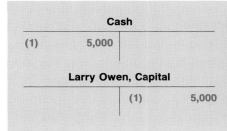

Cash	
(1) 5,000	

Larry Owen, Capital	
	(1) 5,000

Analysis of the transaction: The transaction increased the cash of the practice and at the same time it increased the equity of Owen in the business. Increases in assets are debited, and increases in owner's equity are credited. Consequently, to record the transaction, Cash should be debited and Larry Owen, Capital should be credited for $5,000.

2. Paid the office rent for three months in advance, $900.

Cash	
(1) 5,000	(2) 900

Prepaid Rent	
(2) 900	

Analysis of the transaction: The asset prepaid rent, the right to occupy the office for three months, is increased; and the asset cash is decreased. Increases in assets are debited, and decreases are credited. Therefore, to record the transaction, debit Prepaid Rent and credit Cash for $900.

3. Purchased office equipment for cash, $3,700.

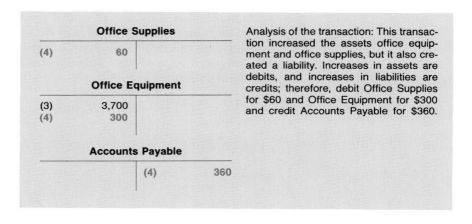

Cash

(1)	5,000	(2)	900
		(3)	3,700

Office Equipment

(3)	3,700

Analysis of the transaction: The asset office equipment is increased, and the asset cash is decreased. Debit Office Equipment and credit Cash for $3,700.

4. Purchased on credit from Alpha Company office supplies, $60, and office equipment, $300.

Office Supplies

(4)	60

Office Equipment

(3)	3,700
(4)	300

Accounts Payable

(4)	360

Analysis of the transaction: This transaction increased the assets office equipment and office supplies, but it also created a liability. Increases in assets are debits, and increases in liabilities are credits; therefore, debit Office Supplies for $60 and Office Equipment for $300 and credit Accounts Payable for $360.

5. Completed legal work for a client and immediately collected a $500 fee.

Cash

(1)	5,000	(2)	900
(5)	500	(3)	3,700

Legal Fees Earned

(5)	500

Analysis of the transaction: This revenue transaction increased both assets and owner's equity. Increases in assets are debits, and increases in owner's equity are credits. Therefore, Cash is debited; and in order to show the nature of the increase in owner's equity and at the same time accumulate information for the income statement, the revenue account Legal Fees Earned is credited.

6. Paid the secretary's salary for the first two weeks of July, $400.

	Cash		
(1)	5,000	(2)	900
(5)	500	(3)	3,700
		(6)	400

Office Salaries Expense	
(6)	400

Analysis of the transaction: The secretary's salary is an expense that decreased both assets and owner's equity. Debit Office Salaries Expense to decrease owner's equity and also to accumulate information for the income statement, and credit Cash to record the decrease in cash.

7. Signed a contract with Coast Realty to do its legal work on a fixed-fee basis for $300 per month. Received the fee for the first month and a half in advance, $450.

	Cash		
(1)	5,000	(2)	900
(5)	500	(3)	3,700
(7)	450	(6)	400

Unearned Legal Fees	
(7)	450

Analysis of the transaction: The $450 inflow increased cash, but the inflow is not a revenue until earned. Its acceptance before being earned created a liability, the obligation to do the client's legal work for the next month and a half. Consequently, debit Cash to record the increase in cash and credit Unearned Legal Fees to record the liability increase.

8. Completed legal work for a client on credit and billed the client $1,000 for the services rendered.

Accounts Receivable	
(8)	1,000

Legal Fees Earned	
(5)	500
(8)	1,000

Analysis of the transaction: Completion of this revenue transaction gave the law practice the right to collect $1,000 from the client, and thus increased assets and owner's equity. Consequently, debit Accounts Receivable for the increase in assets and credit Legal Fees Earned to increase owner's equity and at the same time accumulate information for the income statement.

9. Paid the secretary's salary for the second two weeks of the month.

Cash

(1)	1,000	(2)	900
(5)	500	(3)	3,700
(7)	450	(6)	400
		(9)	400

Office Salaries Expense

| (6) | 400 | |
| (9) | 400 | |

Analysis of the transaction: An expense that decreased assets and owner's equity. Debit Office Salaries Expense to accumulate information for the income statement and credit Cash.

10. Larry Owen withdrew $200 from the law practice to pay personal expenses.

Cash

(1)	5,000	(2)	900
(5)	500	(3)	3,700
(7)	450	(6)	400
		(9)	400
		(10)	200

Larry Owen, Withdrawals

| (10) | 200 | |

Analysis of the transaction: This transaction reduced in equal amounts both assets and owner's equity. Cash is credited to record the asset reduction; and the Larry Owen, Withdrawals account is debited for the reduction in owner's equity.

11. The client paid the $1,000 legal fee billed in transaction 8.

Cash

(1)	5,000	(2)	900
(5)	500	(3)	3,700
(7)	450	(6)	400
(11)	1,000	(9)	400
		(10)	200

Accounts Receivable

| (8) | 1,000 | (11) | 1,000 |

Analysis of the transaction: One asset was increased, and the other decreased. Debit Cash to record the increase in cash, and credit Accounts Receivable to record the decrease in the account receivable, or the decrease in the right to collect from the client.

12. Paid Alpha Company $100 of the $360 owed for the items purchased on credit in transaction 4.

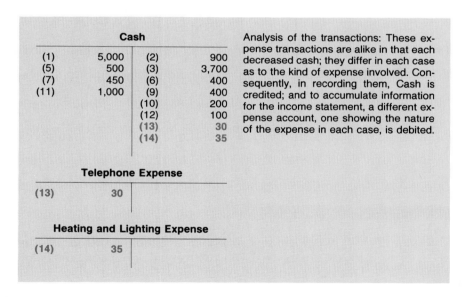

Cash

(1)	5,000	(2)	900
(5)	500	(3)	3,700
(7)	450	(6)	400
(11)	1,000	(9)	400
		(10)	200
		(12)	100

Accounts Payable

| (12) | 100 | (4) | 360 |

Analysis of the transaction: Payments to creditors decrease in like amounts both assets and liabilities. Decreases in liabilities are debited, and decreases in assets are credited. Debit Accounts Payable and credit Cash.

13. Paid the July telephone bill, $30.
14. Paid the July electric bill, $35.

Cash

(1)	5,000	(2)	900
(5)	500	(3)	3,700
(7)	450	(6)	400
(11)	1,000	(9)	400
		(10)	200
		(12)	100
		(13)	30
		(14)	35

Telephone Expense

| (13) | 30 | |

Heating and Lighting Expense

| (14) | 35 | |

Analysis of the transactions: These expense transactions are alike in that each decreased cash; they differ in each case as to the kind of expense involved. Consequently, in recording them, Cash is credited; and to accumulate information for the income statement, a different expense account, one showing the nature of the expense in each case, is debited.

THE ACCOUNTS AND THE EQUATION

In Illustration 2–1, the transactions of the Owen law practice are shown in the accounts, with the accounts brought together and classified under the elements of an accounting equation.

Illustration 2–1

		Assets			=		Liabilities		+		Owner's equity	
		Cash					Accounts Payable				Larry Owen, Capital	
(1)	5,000	(2)	900			(12)	100	(4)	360		(1)	5,000
(5)	500	(3)	3,700									
(7)	450	(6)	400				Unearned Legal Fees				Larry Owen, Withdrawals	
(11)	1,000	(9)	400					(7)	450	(10)	200	
		(10)	200									
		(12)	100								Legal Fees Earned	
		(13)	30								(5)	500
		(14)	35								(8)	1,000

Accounts Receivable

(8)	1,000	(11)	1,000

Office Salaries Expense

(6)	400	
(9)	400	

Prepaid Rent

(2)	900	

Telephone Expense

(13)	30	

Office Supplies

(4)	60	

Heating and Lighting Expense

(14)	35	

Office Equipment

(3)	3,700	
(4)	300	

PREPARING A TRIAL BALANCE

As previously stated, in a double-entry accounting system every transaction is recorded with equal debits and credits so that the equality of the debits and credits may be tested as a proof of the recording accuracy. This equality is tested at intervals by preparing a *trial balance*. A trial balance is prepared by (1) determining the balance of each account in the ledger; (2) listing the accounts having balances, with the debit balances in one column and the credit balances in another (as in Illustration 2–2); (3) adding the debit balances; (4) adding the credit balances; and then (5) comparing the sum of the debit balances with the sum of the credit balances.

Illustration 2–2

LARRY OWEN, ATTORNEY
Trial Balance, July 31, 19—

Cash	$1,185	
Prepaid rent	900	
Office supplies	60	
Office equipment	4,000	
Accounts payable		$ 260
Unearned legal fees		450
Larry Owen, capital		5,000
Larry Owen, withdrawals	200	
Legal fees earned		1,500
Office salaries expense	800	
Telephone expense	30	
Heating and lighting expense	35	
Totals	$7,210	$7,210

The illustrated trial balance was prepared from the accounts in Illustration 2–1. Note that its column totals are equal, or in other words, the trial balance is in balance. When a trial balance is in balance, debits equal credits in the ledger, and it is assumed that no errors were made in recording transactions.

THE PROOF OFFERED BY A TRIAL BALANCE

If when a trial balance is prepared it does not balance, an error or errors have been made. The error or errors may have been either in recording transactions, in determining the account balances, in copying the balances on the trial balance, or in adding the columns of the trial balance. On the other hand, if a trial balance balances, it is assumed that no errors have been made. However, a trial balance that balances is not absolute proof of accuracy. Errors may have been made that did not affect the equality of its columns. For example, an error in which a correct debit amount is debited to the wrong account or a correct credit amount is credited to the wrong account will not cause a trial balance to be out of balance. Likewise, an error in which a wrong amount is both debited and credited to the right accounts will not cause a trial balance to be out of balance. Consequently, a trial balance in balance is only presumptive proof of recording accuracy.

STANDARD ACCOUNT FORM

T-accounts like the ones shown thus far are commonly used in text-book illustrations and also in accounting classes for blackboard demonstrations. In both cases, their use eliminates details and permits the student to concentrate on ideas. However, although widely used in textbooks and in teaching, T-accounts are not used in business for recording transactions. In recording transactions, accounts like the one in Illustration 2–3 are generally used. (Note the year in the date column of the illustrated account. Throughout the remainder of this text, years will be designated 198A, 198B, 198C, and so forth. In all such situations, 198A is the earliest year, 198B is the succeeding year, and so on through the series.)

Illustration 2–3

Cash								ACCOUNT NO. *111*
DATE	EXPLANATION	POST. REF.	DEBIT		CREDIT		BALANCE	
198A July 1		G1	5 000 00				5 000 00	
1		G1			900 00		4 100 00	
3		G1			3 700 00		400 00	
12		G1	500 00				900 00	

The account of Illustration 2–3 is called a *balance column account.* It differs from a T-account in that it has columns for specific information about each debit and credit entered in the account. Also, its Debit and Credit columns are placed side by side and it has a third or Balance column. In this Balance column, the account's new balance is entered each time the account is debited or credited. As a result, the last amount in the column is the account's current balance. For example, on July 1, the illustrated account was debited for the $5,000 investment of Larry Owen, which caused it to have a $5,000 debit balance. It was then credited for $900, and its new $4,100 balance was entered. On July 3, it was credited again for $3,700, which reduced its balance to $400. Then, on July 12, it was debited for $500, and its balance was increased to $900.

When a balance column account like that of Illustration 2–3 is used, the heading of the Balance column does not tell whether the balance is a debit balance or a credit balance. However, this does not create a problem because an account is assumed to have its normal kind of balance, unless the contrary is indicated. Furthermore, an accountant is expected to know the normal balance of any account. Fortunately, this too is not difficult because the balance of an account normally results from recording in it a larger sum of increases than decreases. Consequently, if increases are recorded as debits, the account normally has a debit balance. Likewise, if increases are recorded as credits, the account normally has a credit balance. Or, increases are recorded in an account in each of the following classifications as shown, and its normal balance is:

Account classification	Increases are recorded as—	And the normal balance is—
Asset	Debits	Debit
Contra asset*	Credits	Credit
Liability	Credits	Credit
Owner's equity:		
Capital	Credits	Credit
Withdrawals	Debits	Debit
Revenue	Credits	Credit
Expense	Debits	Debit

    * Explained in the next chapter.

When an unusual transaction causes an account to have a balance opposite from its normal kind of balance, this opposite from normal kind of balance is indicated in the account by entering it in red or entering it in black and encircling the amount. Also, when a debit or credit entered in an account causes the account to have no balance, some bookkeepers place a –0– in the Balance column on the line of the entered amount. Other bookkeepers and bookkeeping machines write 0.00 in the column to indicate the account does not have a balance.

NEED FOR A JOURNAL

It is possible to record transactions by entering debits and credits directly in the accounts, as was done earlier in this chapter. However, when this is done and an error is made, the error is difficult to locate, because even with a transaction having only one debit and one credit, the debit is entered on one ledger page or card and the credit on another, and there is nothing to link the two together.

Consequently, to link together the debits and credits of each transaction and to provide in one place a complete record of each transaction, it is the universal practice in pen-and-ink systems to record all transactions in a *journal*. The debit and credit information about each transaction is then copied from the journal to the ledger accounts. These procedures are important when errors are made, since the journal record makes it possible to trace the debits and credits into the accounts and to see that they are equal and properly recorded.

The process of recording transactions in a journal is called *journalizing transactions.* Also, since transactions are first recorded in a journal and their debit and credit information is then copied from the journal to the ledger, a journal is called a *book of original entry* and a ledger a *book of final entry.*

THE GENERAL JOURNAL

The simplest and most flexible type of journal is a *General Journal.* For each transaction, it provides places for recording (1) the transaction date, (2) the names of the accounts involved, and (3) an explanation of the transaction. It also provides a place for (4) the account numbers of the accounts to which the transaction's debit and credit information is copied and (5) the transaction's debit and credit effect on the accounts named. A standard ruling for a general journal page with two of the transactions of the Owen law practice recorded therein is shown in Illustration 2–4.

Illustration 2–4

	GENERAL JOURNAL			PAGE 1	
DATE	ACCOUNT TITLES AND EXPLANATION	POST. REF.	DEBIT	CREDIT	
1984 July 5	Office Supplies		60 00		
	Office Equipment		300 00		
	Accounts Payable			360 00	
	Purchased supplies and equipment on credit.				
12	Cash		500 00		
	Legal Fees Earned			500 00	
	Collected a legal fee.				

The first entry in Illustration 2–4 records the purchase of supplies and equipment on credit, and three accounts are involved. When a transaction involves three or more accounts and is recorded with a general journal entry, a compound entry is required. A *compound journal entry* is one involving three or more accounts. The second entry records a legal fee earned.

RECORDING TRANSACTIONS IN A GENERAL JOURNAL

To record transactions in a General Journal:

1. The year is written in small figures at the top of the first column.
2. The month is written on the first line in the first column. The year and the month are not repeated except at the top of a new page or at the beginning of a new month or year.
3. The day of each transaction is written in the second column on the first line of the transaction.
4. The names of the accounts to be debited and credited and an explanation of the transaction are written in the Account Titles and Explanation column. The name of the account debited is written first, beginning at the left margin of the column. The name of the account credited is written on the following line, indented about one inch. The explanation is placed on the next line, indented about a half inch from the left margin. The explanation should be short but sufficient to explain the transaction and set it apart from every other transaction.
5. The debit amount is written in the Debit column opposite the name of the account to be debited. The credit amount is written in the Credit column opposite the account to be credited.
6. A single line is skipped between each journal entry to set the entries apart.

At the time transactions are recorded in the General Journal, nothing is entered in the *Posting Reference (Post. Ref.) column.* However, when the debits and credits are copied from the journal to the ledger, the account numbers of the ledger accounts to which the debits and credits are copied are entered in this column. The Posting Reference column is sometimes called the *Folio column.*

POSTING TRANSACTION INFORMATION

The process of copying journal entry information from the journal to the ledger is called *posting.* Normally, near the end of a day, all transactions recorded in the journal that day are posted. In the posting procedure, journal debits are copied and become ledger account debits and journal credits are copied and become ledger account credits.

The posting procedures for a journal entry are shown in Illustration 2–5, and they may be described as follows. To post a journal entry:

Illustration 2–5

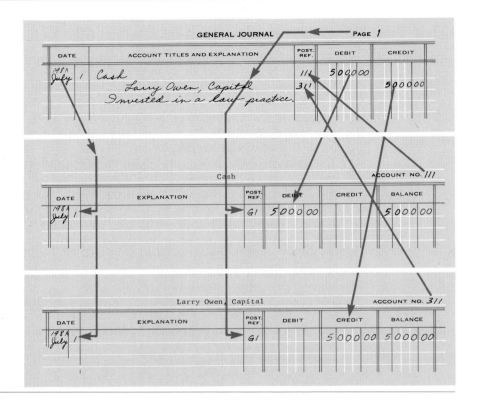

For the debit:

1. Find in the ledger the account named in the debit of the entry.
2. Enter in the account the date of the entry as shown in the journal, the *journal page number* from which the entry is being posted, and in the Debit column the debit amount. Note the letter "G" preceding the journal page number in the Posting Reference column of the account. The letter indicates that the amount was posted from the General Journal. Other journals are introduced in Chapter 6, and each is identified by a letter.
3. Determine the effect of the debit on the account balance and enter the new balance.
4. Enter in the Posting Reference column of the journal the account number of the account to which the amount was posted.

For the credit:

Repeat the foregoing steps, with the exception that the credit amount is entered in the Credit column and has a credit effect on the account balance.

Observe that the last Step (Step 4) in the posting procedure for either the debit or the credit of an entry is to insert the account number in the Posting Reference column of the journal. Inserting the account number in this column serves two purposes: (1) The account number in the journal and the journal page number in the account act as a cross-reference when it is desired to trace an amount from one record to the other. (2) Writing the account number in the journal as a last step in posting indicates that posting is completed. If posting is interrupted, the bookkeeper, by examining the journal's Posting Reference column, can easily see where posting stopped.

ACCOUNT NUMBERS

Many companies use a three-digit system in assigning numbers to their accounts. In a system commonly used by service-type concerns, accounts are assigned numbers as follows:

Asset accounts, 111 through 199.
Liability accounts, 211 through 299.
Owner's equity accounts, 311 through 399.
Revenue accounts, 411 through 499.
Operating expense accounts, 511 through 599.

Observe that asset accounts are assigned numbers with first digits of 1, liability accounts are assigned numbers with first digits of 2, and so on. In each case, the first digit of an account's number tells its balance sheet or income statement classification. The second and third digits further identify the account. However, more about this in the next chapter.

LOCATING ERRORS

When a trial balance does not balance, an error or errors are indicated. To locate the error or errors, check the journalizing, posting, and trial balance preparation steps in their reverse order. First check the addition of the columns in the trial balance to see that no error in addition was made. Then check to see that the account balances were correctly copied from the ledger. Then recalculate the account balances. If at this stage the error or errors have not been found, check the posting and then the original journalizing of the transactions.

CORRECTING ERRORS

When an error is discovered in either the journal or the ledger, it must be corrected. Such an error is never erased, for this seems to indicate an effort to conceal something. However, the method of correction will vary with the nature of the error and the stage in the accounting procedures at which it is discovered.

If an error is discovered in a journal entry before the error is posted, it may be corrected by ruling a single line through the incorrect amount or account name and writing in above the correct amount or account name. Likewise, a posted error or an error in posting in which only the amount is wrong may be corrected in the same manner. However, when a posted error involves a wrong account, it is considered best to correct the error with a correcting journal entry. For example, the following journal entry to record the purchase of office supplies was made and posted:

Oct.	14	Office Furniture and Fixtures	15.00	
		Cash		15.00
		To record the purchase of office supplies.		

Obviously, the debit of the entry is to the wrong account; consequently, the following entry is needed to correct the error:

Oct.	17	Office Supplies	15.00	
		Office Furniture and Fixtures		15.00
		To correct the entry of October 14 in which the Office Furniture and Fixtures account was debited in error for the purchase of office supplies.		

The debit of the second entry correctly records the purchase of supplies, and the credit cancels the error of the first entry. Note the full explanation of the correcting entry. Such an explanation should always be full and complete so that anyone can see exactly what has occurred.

BOOKKEEPING TECHNIQUES

Commas and Decimal Points in Dollar Amounts

When amounts are entered in a journal or a ledger, commas to indicate thousands of dollars and decimal points to separate dollars and cents are not necessary. The ruled lines accomplish this. However, when statements are prepared on unruled paper, the decimal points and commas are necessary.

Dollar Signs

Dollar signs are not used in journals or ledgers but are required on financial reports prepared on unruled paper. On such reports, a dollar sign is placed (1) before the first amount in each column of figures and (2) before the first amount appearing after a ruled line that indicates an addition or a subtraction. Examine Illustration 3–5, page 97, for examples of the use of dollar signs on a financial report.

Omission of Zeros in the Cents Columns

When an amount to be entered in a ledger or a journal is an amount of dollars and no cents, some bookkeepers will use a dash in the cents column in the place of two zeros to indicate that there are no cents. They feel that the dash is easier and more quickly made than the two zeros. This is a matter of choice in journal and ledger entries. However, on financial reports, the two zeros are preferred because they are neater in appearance.

Often in this text, where space is limited, exact dollar amounts are used in order to save space. Obviously, in such cases, neither zeros nor dashes are used to show that there are no cents involved.

GLOSSARY

Account. An accounting device used in recording and summarizing the increases and decreases in a revenue, an expense, asset, liability, or owner's equity item.

Account balance. The difference between the increases and decreases recorded in an account.

Account number. An identifying number assigned to an account.

Balance column account. An account having a column for entering the new account balance after each debit or credit is posted to the account.

Book of final entry. A ledger to which amounts are posted.

Book of original entry. A journal in which transactions are first recorded.

Business paper. A sales ticket, invoice, check, or other document arising in and evidence of the completion of a transaction.

Capital account. An account used to record the more or less permanent changes in the equity of an owner in his or her business.

Compound journal entry. A journal entry having more than one debit or more than one credit.

Credit. The right-hand side of a T-account.

Debit. The left-hand side of a T-account.

Double-entry accounting.   An accounting system in which each transaction affects and is recorded in two or more accounts with equal debits and credits.

Drawing account.   Another name for the *withdrawals account.*

Folio column.   Another name for the *Posting Reference column.*

General Journal.   A book of original entry in which any type of transaction can be recorded.

Journal.   A book of original entry in which transactions are first recorded and from which transaction amounts are posted to the ledger accounts.

Journal page number.   A posting reference number entered in the Posting Reference column of each account to which an amount is posted and which shows the page of the journal from which the amount was posted.

Ledger.   A group of accounts used by a business in recording its transactions.

Mortgage payable.   A debt, usually long term, that is secured by a special claim against one or more assets of the debtor.

Nominal accounts.   The income statement accounts.

Normal balance of an account.   The usual kind of balance, either debit or credit, that a given account has and that is a debit balance if increases are recorded in the account as debits and a credit balance if increases are recorded as credits.

Personal account.   Another name for the *withdrawals account.*

Posting.   Transcribing the debit and credit amounts from a journal to the ledger accounts.

Posting Reference (Post. Ref.) column.   A column in a journal and in each account for entering posting reference numbers. Also called a *folio column.*

Posting reference numbers.   Journal page numbers and ledger account numbers used as a cross-reference between amounts entered in a journal and posted to the ledger accounts.

Promissory note.   An unconditional written promise to pay a definite sum of money on demand or at a fixed or determinable future date.

Real accounts.   The balance sheet accounts.

T-account.   An abbreviated account form, two or more of which are used in illustrating the debits and credits required in recording a transaction.

Trial balance.   A list of accounts having balances in the ledger, the debit or credit balance of each account, the total of the debit balances, and the total of credit balances.

Withdrawals account.   The account used to record the withdrawals from a business by its owner of cash or other assets intended for personal use. Also known as *personal account* or *drawing account.*

QUESTIONS FOR CLASS DISCUSSION

1.   What is an account? What is a ledger?
2.   What determines the number of accounts a business will use?

3. What are the meanings of the following words and terms: *(a)* debit, *(b)* to debit, *(c)* credit, and *(d)* to credit?

4. Does debit always mean increase and credit always mean decrease?

5. A transaction is to be entered in the accounts. How do you determine the accounts in which amounts are to be entered? How do you determine whether a particular account is to be debited or credited?

6. Why is a double-entry accounting system so called?

7. Give the rules of debit and credit for *(a)* asset accounts and *(b)* for liability and owner's equity accounts.

8. Why are the rules of debit and credit the same for both liability and owner's equity accounts?

9. List the steps in the preparation of a trial balance.

10. Why is a trial balance prepared?

11. Why is a trial balance considered to be only presumptive proof of recording accuracy? What types of errors are not revealed by a trial balance?

12. What determines whether the normal balance of an account is a debit or a credit balance?

13. Can transaction debits and credits be recorded directly in the ledger accounts? What is gained by first recording transactions in a journal and then posting to the accounts?

14. In recording transactions in a journal, which is written first, the debit or the credit? How far is the name of the account credited indented? How far is the explanation indented?

15. What is a compound entry?

16. Are dollar signs used in journal entries? In the accounts?

17. If decimal points are not used in journal entries to separate dollars from cents, what accomplishes this purpose?

18. Define or describe each of the following:
    - *a.* Journal.
    - *b.* Ledger.
    - *c.* Book of original entry.
    - *d.* Book of final entry.
    - *e.* Folio column.
    - *f.* Posting.
    - *g.* Posting Reference column.
    - *h.* Posting reference numbers.

19. Entering in the Posting Reference column of the journal the account number to which an amount was posted is the last step in posting the amount. What is gained by making this the last step?

CLASS EXERCISES

Exercise 2–1

Prepare the following columnar form. Then (1) indicate the treatment for increases and decreases by entering the words *debited* and *credited* in the proper columns. (2) Indicate the normal balance of each kind of account by entering the word *debit* or *credit* in the last column of the form.

Kind of Account	Increases	Decreases	Normal Balance
Asset			
Liability			
Owner's capital			
Owner's withdrawals			
Revenue			
Expense			

Exercise 2–2

Place the following T-accounts on a sheet of notebook paper: Cash; Accounts Receivable; Shop Supplies; Shop Equipment; Accounts Payable; Walter Lake, Capital; Revenue from Repairs; and Rent Expense. Then record the following transactions by entering debits and credits directly in the T-accounts. Use the transaction letters to identify the amounts in the accounts.

a. Walter Lake opened a TV repair shop, called A-1 TV Service, by investing $800 in the business.
b. Paid the rent for one month on the shop space, $250.
c. Purchased shop supplies for cash, $150.
d. Purchased shop supplies, $75, and shop equipment, $200, on credit from Electronics, Inc.
e. Repaired the TV set of a customer and collected $40 cash for the service.
f. Paid Electronics, Inc., $200 of the amount owed it.
g. Repaired the TV set of Ned Brown on credit, $50.
h. Purchased additional shop equipment on credit from Electronics, Inc., $60.
i. Ned Brown paid for the repair work cf transaction (g).

Exercise 2–3

After recording the transactions of Exercise 2–2, prepare a trial balance for A–1 TV Service. Use the current date.

Exercise 2–4

A careless bookkeeper prepared the following trial balance for Handy Repair Service. It does not balance, and you have been asked to prepare a corrected trial balance. In examining the company's journal and ledger, you discover the following: (1) The debits to the Cash account total $7,625, and the credits total $5,125. (2) A $100 receipt from a customer in payment of his

HANDY REPAIR SERVICE
Trial Balance, August 31, 19—

Cash		$2,600
Accounts receivable	$3,400	
Office supplies		150
Office equipment	1,600	
Accounts payable	450	
Wages payable	100	
David Ross, capital	2,650	
Revenue from services		6,500
Rent expense	1,200	
Advertising expense		50
Totals	$9,400	$9,300

account was not posted to the Accounts Receivable account. (3) A $50 payment to a creditor was entered in the journal but was not posted to any account. (4) The first two digits in the balance of the Revenue from Services account, as shown on the trial balance prepared by the bookkeeper, were transposed in copying the account balance from the ledger to the trial balance.

Exercise 2–5   Prepare a form on notebook paper having the following three column headings: (1) Error, (2) Amount Out of Balance, and (3) Column Having Larger Total. Then for each of the following errors: (1) list the error by letter in the first column. (2) tell the amount it will cause the trial balance to be out of balance in the second column, and (3) tell in the third column which trial balance column will have the larger total as a result of the error. If an error does not affect the trial balance, write "none" in each of the last two columns.

a. A $25 debit to the Cash account was not posted.
b. A $50 debit to Store Supplies was debited to Store Equipment.
c. A $40 debit to Salaries Expense was debited to the account twice.
d. A $20 debit to Office Supplies was debited to Revenue from Sales.
e. A $45 credit to Accounts Payable was posted as a $54 credit.
f. A $10 debit to Office Supplies was posted as a $100 debit.

PROBLEMS

Problem 2–1   a. Dale Sims began a new business, called Cool Air Service, by investing these assets: cash, $1,500; office equipment, $450; tools; $800; and truck, $4,200. He then completed the following transactions:
b. Paid the rent for two months in advance on the shop space, $400.
c. Purchased repair supplies on credit, $500.
d. Traded a typewriter carried in the accounting records at $50 for additional tools.
e. Purchased for cash a new typewriter to replace the one traded, $550.
f. Paid for advertising announcing the opening of the shop, $35.
g. Completed repair work for a customer for cash, $60.
h. Completed repair work for George Thomas, $175. Accepted $100 in cash and a promise by Mr. Thomas that he would pay the balance within a short period.
i. Completed repair work for Walter Rice on credit, $85.
j. George Thomas paid the amount owed from transaction (h).
k. Paid $250 of the amount owed for the supplies purchased in transaction (c).
l. Paid the utility bills, $45.
m. Dale Sims withdrew $200 from the business to pay personal expenses.

Required:

1. Open the following T-accounts: Cash; Accounts Receivable; Repair Supplies; Prepaid Rent; Office Equipment; Tools; Truck; Accounts Payable; Dale Sims, Capital; Dale Sims, Withdrawals; Revenue from Repairs; Advertising Expense; and Utilities Expense.

2. Record the transactions by entering debits and credits directly in the T-accounts. Use the transaction letters to identify each debit and credit amount.
3. Prepare a trial balance using the current date.

Problem 2–2

Ann Evans received her CPA certificate, and during July of the current year completed these transactions:

July 1 Began a public accounting practice by transferring $2,000 from her savings account to a checking account opened in the name of the practice.
  1 Paid two months' office rent in advance, $600.
  2 Purchased office supplies, $50, and office equipment, $1,200, from Office Outfitters on credit.
  4 Paid the premiums on two insurance policies, $410.
  7 Completed accounting work for a client and immediately collected $75 therefor.
  12 Paid Office Outfitters $500 of the amount owed for the items purchased on July 2.
  13 Completed accounting work for Bond Company on credit, $300.
  15 Purchased additional office supplies on credit, $25.
  21 Completed accounting work for Kent Company on credit, $250.
  23 Received $300 from Bond Company for the work completed on July 13.
  26 Ann Evans wrote a check on the bank account of the accounting practice to pay the rent on the apartment in which she lives, $275.
  31 Paid the July utility bills of the accounting office, $30.

Required:

1. Open the following accounts: Cash; Accounts Receivable; Prepaid Rent; Prepaid Insurance; Office Supplies; Office Equipment; Accounts Payable; Ann Evans, Capital; Ann Evans, Withdrawals; Accounting Revenue; and Utilities Expense.
2. Prepare general journal entries to record the transactions, post to the accounts, and prepare a trial balance. Head the trial balance Ann Evans, CPA.

Problem 2–3

Larry Hill owns and operates Hill Real Estate Agency; and on August 1 of the current year, a trial balance of the agency's ledger carried these items:

HILL REAL ESTATE AGENCY
Trial Balance, August 1, 19—

Cash	$ 1,190	
Office supplies	145	
Office equipment	2,465	
Automobile	2,700	
Land	20,000	
Building	52,000	
Mortgage payable		$60,000
Larry Hill, capital		18,500
Totals	$78,500	$78,500

The real estate agency completed these transactions during August:

a. Purchased office supplies, $50, and office equipment, $150, on credit.
b. Sold a house and collected a $4,250 commission from the sale.
c. Paid for the items purchased on credit in transaction (a).
d. Paid for advertising that had appeared in the local paper, $175.
e. Purchased a typewriter from Office Supply Company on credit, $625.
f. Larry Hill took the old agency typewriter, carried in the accounting records at $75, home for permanent use of his high school daughter as a practice typewriter.
g. Sold a house and collected a $4,950 commission on the sale.
h. Completed property management services for Albert Pick on credit, $100.
i. Larry Hill withdrew $500 from the business to pay personal expenses.
j. Received $100 from Albert Pick for the services of transaction (h).
k. Paid the salary of the office secretary, $850.
l. Gave $5,000 in cash and the old agency car for a new agency car.
m. Paid for advertising that had appeared in the local paper, $50.
n. Paid the August Telephone bill, $35.

Required:

1. Open the following T-accounts: Cash; Accounts Receivable; Office Supplies; Office Equipment; Automobile; Land; Building; Accounts Payable; Mortgage Payable; Larry Hill, Capital; Larry Hill, Withdrawals; Commissions Earned; Management Fees Earned; Advertising Expense; Salaries Expense; and Telephone Expense.
2. Enter the August 1 trial balance amounts in the accounts, identifying each amount by writing "Bal." before it.
3. Record the transactions by entering debits and credits directly in the T-accounts. Use the transaction letters to identify the amounts in the accounts.
4. Prepare an August 31 trial balance of the accounts.

Problem 2–4

Ted Howe finished law school, and during August of the current year completed these transactions:

Aug. 1 Began a law practice by investing $2,800 in cash and a law library having a $700 fair value.
1 Paid two months' rent in advance on suitable office space, $650.
2 Purchased office equipment, $2,350, paying $350 in cash and signing a promissory note payable for the balance.
3 Purchased office supplies, $65, and office equipment, $210, from Office Outfitters on credit.
5 Completed legal work for a client and immediately collected $75 in cash therefor.
8 Paid the premium on an insurance policy, $335.
14 Completed legal work for Coast Realty on credit, $500.
15 Paid the salary of the legal secretary, $400.
18 Paid Office Outfitters $100 of the amount owed on the items purchased on August 3.

Aug. 24   Received $500 from Coast Realty for the work completed on August 14.
  28   Ted Howe withdrew $300 from the practice to pay personal expenses.
  30   Completed legal work for Security Bank on credit, $250.
  31   Paid the legal secretary's salary, $400.
  31   Paid the August utility bills, $45.
  31   Paid $15 interest expense and a $200 installment on the note payable.

Required:

1. Open the following accounts: Cash; Accounts Receivable; Prepaid Rent; Prepaid Insurance; Office Supplies; Office Equipment; Law Library; Notes Payable; Accounts Payable; Ted Howe, Capital; Ted Howe, Withdrawals; Legal Fees Earned; Salaries Expense; Utilities Expense; and Interest Expense.
2. Prepare general journal entries to record the transactions, post to the accounts, and prepare a trial balance, heading it Ted Howe, Attorney.

Problem 2–5   June Marsh graduated from college in June of the current year with a degree in architecture; and during July, she completed these transactions:

July 1   Began an architectural practice by investing cash, $1,500.
   1   Rented the furnished office and equpiment of an architect who was retiring due to illness and paid the rent for two months in advance, $800.
   1   Paid the premium on a liability insurance policy giving one year's protection, $300.
   2   Purchased drafting supplies on credit, $50.
   8   Completed a set of plans for a contractor and immediately collected $250 for the job.
  15   Completed and delivered a set of plans to Tahoe Construction Company on credit, $450.
  17   Paid for the drafting supplies purchased on July 2.
  22   Completed architectural work for Lake Realty on credit, $500.
  25   Received $450 from Tahoe Construction Company for the plans delivered on July 15.
  27   June Marsh withdrew $200 cash from the business to pay personal expenses.
  29   Purchased additional drafting supplies on credit, $45.
  31   Paid blueprinting expense incurred during the month, $75.
  31   Paid the July utility bills, $35.
  31   Recognized that one month's rent had expired and had become an expense. (Make a general journal entry to transfer the amount of the expense from the asset account to the Rent Expense account.)
  31   Recognized that one month's prepaid insurance had expired and had become an expense.
  31   Took an inventory of drafting supplies and determined that supplies costing $40 had been used and had become an expense.

Required:

1. Open the following accounts: Cash; Accounts Receivable; Prepaid Rent; Prepaid Insurance; Drafting Supplies; Accounts Payable; June Marsh, Capital; June Marsh, Withdrawals; Architectural Fees Earned; Rent Expense; Blueprinting Expense; Utilities Expense; Insurance Expense; and Drafting Supplies Expense.
2. Prepare general journal entries to record the transactions, post to the accounts, and prepare a trial balance headed June Marsh, Architect.
3. Analyze the trial balance and prepare a July 31 balance sheet like Illustration 1–2 and a July income statement for the architectural practice. (The $1,500 trial balance amount of capital for June Marsh is her July 1 beginning-of-month capital. To determine the July 31 balance sheet amount of her capital, remember that the net income increased her equity in the business and her withdrawals decreased it.)

ALTERNATE PROBLEMS

Problem 2–1A

a. Dale Sims opened a television repair shop and began business by investing cash, $5,000; repair supplies, $450; office equipment, $550; tools, $750; and truck, $2,200. He called his business Best TV Service, and during a short period completed these additional transactions:
b. Paid $25 for an advertisement announcing the opening of the shop.
c. Paid the rent for two months in advance on the shop space, $450.
d. Purchased additional office equipment for cash, $175.
e. Purchased additional tools on credit, $150.
f. Traded the old truck and $4,000 in cash for a new truck.
g. Completed repair work for cash, $50.
h. Completed repair work on credit for Walter Rice, $75.
i. Completed repair work for Barry Nash, $125. Accepted $100 in cash and Barry Nash's promise that he would pay the balance in a few days.
j. Paid $100 of the amount owed for the tools purchased on credit in transaction (e).
k. Barry Nash paid the $25 he owed.
l. Paid the utility bills, $20.
m. Dale Sims withdrew $150 from the business to pay personal expenses.

Required:

1. Open the following T-accounts: Cash; Accounts Receivable; Repair Supplies; Prepaid Rent; Office Equipment; Tools; Truck; Accounts Payable; Dale Sims, Capital; Dale Sims, Withdrawals; Revenue from Repairs; Advertising Expense; and Utilities Expense.
2. Record the transaction by entering debits and credits directly in the T-accounts. Use the transaction letters to identify each debit and credit amount.
3. Prepare a trial balance using the current data.

Problem 2–2A

Ann Evans, CPA, completed these transactions during August of the current year:

Aug. 1 Began a public accounting practice by investing $1,500 in cash and office equipment having a $1,200 fair value.

1 Purchased office supplies, $75, and office equipment, $250, from Sierra Company on credit.

1 Paid three months' rent in advance on suitable office space, $900.

5 Completed accounting work for a client and collected $60 cash therefor.

11 Paid Sierra Company $125 of the amount owed for the items purchased on August 1.

12 Paid the premium on an insurance policy, $375.

15 Completed accounting work for Nevada Company on credit, $350.

20 Ann Evans withdrew $100 from the accounting practice for personal expenses.

23 Completed accounting work for Donner Company on credit, $200.

25 Received $350 from Nevada Company for the work completed on August 15.

31 Paid the August utility bills, $35.

Required:

1. Open the following accounts: Cash; Accounts Receivable; Prepaid Rent; Prepaid Insurance; Office Supplies; Office Equipment; Accounts Payable; Ann Evans, Capital; Ann Evans, Withdrawals; Accounting Revenue; and Utilities Expense.
2. Prepare general journal entries to record the transactions, post to the accounts, and prepare a trial balance. Head the trial balance Ann Evans, CPA.

Problem 2–3A

Larry Hill began a real estate agency he called Rockhill Realty; and during a short period, he completed these transactions:

a. Began business by investing $20,000 in cash.

b. Purchased a small office building and the office equipment of Western Realty, consisting of office equipment, $4,000; land, $16,000; and building, $48,000. He paid $18,000 in cash and signed a mortgage contract to pay the balance.

c. Took his personal automobile, which had a $5,500 fair value, for permanent and exclusive use in the business.

d. Earned and collected a $5,300 commission from the sale of a house.

e. Purchased office supplies, $75, and office equipment, $250, from Office Supply Company on credit.

f. Paid the salary of the office secretary, $400.

g. Completed property management services for Neal Able on credit, $60.

h. Paid Office Supply Company for the items purchased in transaction *(e)*.

i. Received $60 from Neal Able for the services of transaction *(g)*.

j. Purchased additional office supplies on credit, $65.

k. Earned and collected a $2,700 commission from the sale of a building lot.

l. Paid the salary of the office secretary, $400.

m. Paid for newspaper advertising that had appeared, $185.

n. Paid the telephone bill, $25.

o. Larry Hill withdrew $250 from the business for personal expenses.

Required:

1. Open the following T-accounts: Cash; Accounts Receivable; Office Supplies; Office Equipment; Automobile; Land; Building; Accounts Payable; Mortgage Payable; Larry Hill, Capital; Larry Hill, Withdrawals; Commissions Earned; Management Fees Earned; Advertising Expense; Salaries Expense; and Telephone Expense.
2. Record the transactions by entering debits and credits directly in the T-accounts. Use the transaction letters to identify each debit and credit amount.
3. Prepare a trial balance, using the current date.

Problem 2–4A
Ted Howe completed these transactions during October of the current year:

Oct. 1 Began the practice of law by investing the law library acquired during his college years. The library had a $750 fair value.

2 Sold 65 shares of AT&T stock, which he had inherited from his grandfather, for $3,450 and deposited $3,000 of the proceeds in a bank account opened in the name of the practice, Ted Howe, Attorney.

3 Purchased office equipment, $2,500, paying $500 in cash and signing a promissory note payable for the balance.

4 Rented office space, paying $650, the first two months' rent in advance.

5 Paid the premium on an insurance policy taken out in the name of the law practice, $325.

6 Purchased office supplies, $60, and office equipment, $220, from Office Supply Company on credit.

9 Completed legal work for a client and immediately collected $150 therefor.

12 Completed legal work for Guaranty Bank on credit, $300.

15 Paid the legal secretary's salary, $450.

16 Paid Office Supply Company for the items purchased on October 6.

22 Received $300 from Guaranty Bank for the work completed on the 12th.

27 Ted Howe wrote a $270 check on the bank account of the law practice to pay the rent on the apartment he occupied.

30 Completed additional legal work for the Guaranty bank on credit, $200.

31 Paid $20 interest expense and a $100 installment on the note payable issued on October 3.

31 Paid the legal secretary's salary, $450.

31 Paid the October utilities, $40.

Required:

1. Open the following accounts: Cash; Accounts Receivable; Prepaid Rent; Prepaid Insurance; Office Supplies; Office Equipment; Law Library; Notes

Payable; Accounts Payable; Ted Howe, Capital; Ted Howe, Withdrawals; Legal Fees Earned; Salaries Expense; Utilities Expense; and Interest Expense.

2. Prepare general journal entries to record the transactions, post to the accounts, and prepare a trial balance.

PROVOCATIVE PROBLEMS

Provocative Problem 2–1, Bob's Lawn Service

Upon graduation from high school last summer, Bob Ross needed a job to earn a portion of his first-year college expenses. He was unable to find anything satisfactory, and he decided to go into the lawn care business. He had $300 in his savings account which he used to buy a lawn mower and other lawn care tools; but to haul the tools from job to job, he needed a truck. Consequently, he borrowed $600 from a bank, agreeing to pay 1¼% interest per month, and used the entire amount to buy a secondhand pickup.

From the beginning he had as much work as he could do, and after two months, he repaid the bank loan plus two months' interest; and on September 4, he ended the business after exactly three months' operations. Throughout the summer he had followed the practice of depositing all cash received from customers in the bank, and an examination of his checkbook record showed he had deposited $2,900. In addition, he had written checks to pay $50 for repairs to the pickup; $130 for gas, oil, and lubricants used in the truck and mower; and $25 for mower repairs. A notebook in the truck contained copies of credit card tickets that showed he owed $40 for gas and oil and that customers owed him $120 for lawn care services. He estimated that his lawn care equipment had worn out and depreciated an amount equal to one half its cost and the truck had worn out and depreciated an amount equal to one fourth its cost.

Under the assumption that Bob had withdrawn $400 from the business during the summer for spending money and to buy clothes, prepare an income statement showing the results of the summer's operations of the business and a September 4 balance sheet like Illustration 1–2. (T-accounts should prove helpful in organizing the data. Also remember that to determine Bob's ending equity in the business it is necessary to add the net income to his beginning investment and deduct his withdrawals.)

Provocative Problem 2–2, Gleaming Janitorial Service

Lee Scott lost his job and could not find another. As a result, he decided to begin a janitorial service; and on July 1, he took the last $400 of his savings and deposited it in a checking account opened in the name of the business, Gleaming Janitorial Service. The same day he signed a one-year, $2,500 promissory note payable having a 10% annual interest rate in order to borrow that amount of money from his brother. He then used the $2,500 to buy a secondhand truck needed in the business operations. He also ran a series of ads in the local paper, purchased cleaning supplies, and went to work.

He did not keep formal accounting records, but business was good from the beginning; and after six months, he tried to prepare a set of financial statements to see where the business stood. Following are the results of his efforts:

GLEAMING JANITORIAL SERVICE
Income Statement for Six Months Ended December 31, 198—

Janitorial revenue		$6,800
Operating expenses:		
Advertising expense	$ 75	
Supplies expense	300	
Gas and oil expense	250	
Salary expense	4,800	
Total operating expenses		5,425
Net income		$1,375

GLEAMING JANITORIAL SERVICE
Balance Sheet, December 31, 19—

Assets		Liabilities	
Cash	$1,775	Note payable	$2,500
Truck	2,500	*Owner's Equity*	
		Lee Scott, capital	400
		Total liabilities and	
Total assets	$4,275	owner's equity	$2,900

Since the balance sheet did not balance, and he knew it must, he has asked your help. You learn that he has deposited all receipts from his janitorial service in the bank, paid all bills by check, and owes no one other than his brother. By examining his checkbook stubs you learn that he has taken in $6,800 in cash for services rendered and paid out $75 for advertising, $250 for gas and oil used in the truck, and $300 for supplies of which one fifth are on hand unused. You also learn that the $4,800 salary expense represents six monthly withdrawals of $800 each which Lee has paid to himself. Also, customers owe the business $115 for work done on credit, and you note that although the truck has depreciated through use, this is not recognized in the statements. Likewise, Lee has not recognized that the business has used his brother's $2,500 for a half a year and therefore owes six months' interest on the note. After discussing the matter, you and Lee agree that $250 represents a fair amount of expense for six months' wear and tear on the truck.

Prepare a new income statement and a balance sheet for the business like Illustration 1–2 that reflect the foregoing information. (To determine Lee's ending equity in the business, remember that net income increased his equity and his withdrawals decreased it.)

Adjusting the Accounts and Preparing the Statements

3

After studying Chapter 3, you should be able to:

Explain why the life of a business is divided into accounting periods of equal length and why the accounts of a business must be adjusted at the end of each accounting period.

Prepare adjusting entries for prepaid expenses, accrued expenses, unearned revenues, accrued revenues, and depreciation.

Prepare entries to dispose of accrued revenue and expense items in the new accounting period.

Explain the difference between the cash and accrual bases of accounting.

Explain the importance of comparability in the financial statements of a business, period after period; and tell how the realization principle and the matching principle contribute to comparability.

Define each asset and liability classification appearing on a balance sheet, classify balance sheet items, and prepare a classified balance sheet.

Define or explain the words and phrases listed in the chapter Glossary.

The life of a business often spans many years, and its activities go on without interruption over the years. However, taxes based on annual income must be paid governmental units, and the owners and managers of a business must have periodic reports on its financial progress. Consequently, a *time-period concept* of the life of a business is required in accounting for its activities. This concept results in a division of the life of a business into time periods of equal length, called *accounting periods*. Accounting periods may be a month, three months, or a year in length, however, *annual accounting periods*, periods one year in length, are the norm.

An accounting period of any 12 consecutive months is known as a *fiscal year*. A fiscal year may coincide with the calendar year and end on December 31 or it may follow the *natural business year*. When accounting periods follow the natural business year, they end when inventories are at their lowest point and business activities are at their lowest ebb. For example, in department stores, the natural business year begins on February 1, after the Christmas and January sales, and ends the following January 31. Consequently, the annual accounting periods of department stores commonly begin on February 1 and end the following January 31.

NEED FOR ADJUSTMENTS AT THE END OF AN ACCOUNTING PERIOD

As a rule, at the end of an accounting period, after all transactions are recorded, several of the accounts in a company's ledger do not show proper end-of-period balances for preparing the statements. This is true even though all transactions were correctly recorded. The balances are incorrect for statement purposes, not through error but because of the expiration of costs brought about by the passage of time. For example, the second item on the trial balance of Owen's law practice, as prepared in Chapter 2 and reproduced again as Illustration 3–1, is "Prepaid rent, $900." This $900 represents the rent for three months paid in advance on July 1. However, by July 31, $900 is not the balance sheet amount for this asset because one month's rent, $300, has expired and become an expense and only $600 remains as an asset. Likewise, a portion of the office supplies as represented by the $60 debit balance in the Office Supplies account has been used, and the office equipment has begun to wear out and depreciate. Obviously, then, the balances of the Prepaid Rent, Office Supplies, and Office Equipment accounts as they appear on the trial balance do not reflect the proper amounts for preparing the July 31 statements. The balance of each and the balances of the Office Salaries Expense and Legal Fees Earned accounts must be *adjusted* before they will show proper amounts for the July 31 statements.

Illustration 3–1

> ### LARRY OWEN, ATTORNEY
> Trial Balance, July 31, 19—
>
> | | | |
> |---|---:|---:|
> | Cash | $1,185 | |
> | Prepaid rent | 900 | |
> | Office supplies | 60 | |
> | Office equipment | 4,000 | |
> | Accounts payable | | $ 260 |
> | Unearned legal fees | | 450 |
> | Larry Owen, capital | | 5,000 |
> | Larry Owen, withdrawals | 200 | |
> | Legal fees earned | | 1,500 |
> | Office salaries expense | 800 | |
> | Telephone expense | 30 | |
> | Heating and lighting expense | 35 | |
> | Totals | $7,210 | $7,210 |

ADJUSTING THE ACCOUNTS

Prepaid Expenses

As the name implies, a *prepaid expense* is an expense that has been paid for in advance of its use. At the time of payment, an asset is acquired that will be used or consumed, and as it is used or consumed, it becomes an expense. For example:

On July 1, the Owen law practice paid three months' rent in advance and obtained the right to occupy a rented office for the following three months. On July 1, this right was an asset valued at its $900 cost. However, day by day the agency occupied the office, and each day a portion of the prepaid rent expired and became an expense. On July 31, one month's rent, valued at one third of $900, or $300, had expired. Consequently, if the agency's July 31 accounts are to reflect proper asset and expense amounts, the following adjusting entry is required:

July	31	Rent Expense	300.00	
		Prepaid Rent		300.00
		To record the expired rent.		

Posting the adjusting entry has the following effect on the accounts:

Prepaid Rent				Rent Expense	
July 1	900	July 31	300	July 31	300

After the entry is posted, the Prepaid Rent account with a $600 balance and the Rent Expense account with a $300 balance show proper statement amounts.

To continue, early in July, the Owen law practice purchased some office supplies and placed them in the office for use. Each day the secretary used a portion. The amount used or consumed each day was an expense that daily reduced the supplies on hand. However, the daily reductions were not recognized in the accounts because day-by-day information as to amounts used and remaining was not needed. Also, bookkeeping labor could be saved if only a single amount, the total of all supplies used during the month, was recorded.

Consequently, if on July 31 the accounts are to reflect proper statement amounts, it is necessary to record the amount of office supplies used during the month. However, to do this, it is first necessary to learn the amount used. To learn the amount used, it is necessary to count or inventory the unused supplies remaining and to deduct their cost from the cost of the supplies purchased. If, for example, $35 of unused supplies remain, then $25 ($60 − $35 = $25) of supplies have been used and have become an expense. The following adjusting entry is required to record this:

July	31	Office Supplies Expense	25.00	
		Office Supplies		25.00
		To record the supplies used.		

The effect of the adjusting entry on the accounts is:

Office Supplies				Office Supplies Expense	
July 5	60	July 31	25	July 31	25

Often, unlike in the two previous examples, items that are prepaid expenses at the time of purchase are both bought and fully consumed within a single accounting period. For example, a company pays its rent in advance on the first day of each month. Each month the amount paid results in a prepaid expense that is entirely consumed before the month's end and before the end of the accounting period. In such cases, it is best to ignore the fact that an asset results from each prepayment because an adjustment can be avoided if each prepayment is originally recorded as an expense.

Other prepaid expenses that are handled in the same manner as prepaid rent and office supplies are prepaid insurance, store supplies, and factory supplies.

Depreciation

An item of equipment used in carrying on the operations of a business in effect represents a "quantity of usefulness." Also, since the equipment will eventually wear out and be discarded, the cost of its "quantity of usefulness" must be charged off as an expense over the useful life of the equipment. This is accomplished by recording *depreciation*.

Depreciation is an *expense* just like the expiration of prepaid rent. For example, if a company purchases a machine for $4,500 that it expects to use for four years, after which it expects to receive $500 for the machine as a trade-in allowance on a new machine, the company has purchased a $4,000 quantity of usefulness ($4,500 − $500 = $4,000). Furthermore, this quantity of usefulness expires or the machine depreciates at the rate of $1,000 per year [($4,500 − $500) ÷ 4 years = $1,000]. Actually, when depreciation is compared to the expiration of a prepaid expense, the primary difference is that since it is often impossible to predict exactly how long an item of equipment will be used or how much will be received for it at the end of its useful life, the amount it depreciates each accounting period is only an estimate.

Estimating and apportioning depreciation can be simple, as in the foregoing example, or it can become complex. A discussion of more complex situations is unnecessary at this point and is deferred to Chapter 10. However, to illustrate the recording of depreciation, assume that on July 31, the Owen law practice estimated its office equipment had depreciated $40 during the month. The depreciation reduced the assets and increased expenses, and the following adjusting entry is required:

July	31	Depreciation Expense, Office Equipment	40.00	
		Accumulated Depreciation, Office Equipment		40.00
		To record the July depreciation.		

The effect of the entry on the accounts is:

Office Equipment		Depreciation Expense, Office Equipment	
July 3	3,700	July 31	40
5	300		

Accumulated Depreciation, Office Equipment	
July 31	40

After the entry is posted, the Office Equipment account and its related Accumulated Depreciation, Office Equipment account together show the July 31 balance sheet amounts for this asset. The Depreciation Expense, Office Equipment account shows the amount of depreciation expense that should appear on the July income statement.

In most cases, a decrease in an asset is recorded with a credit to the account in which the asset is recorded. However, note in the illustrated accounts that this procedure is not followed in recording depreciation. Rather, depreciation is recorded in a *contra account,* the Accumulated Depreciation, Office Equipment account. (A contra account is an account the balance of which is subtracted from the balance of an associated account to show a more proper amount for the item recorded in the associated account.)

There are two good reasons for using contra accounts in recording depreciation. First, although based on objective evidence whenever possible, at its best depreciation is only an estimate. Second, the use of contra accounts better preserves the facts in the lives of items of equipment. For example, in this case, the Office Equipment account preserves a record of the equipment's cost, and the Accumulated Depreciation, Office Equipment account shows its depreciation to date.

A better understanding of the second reason for using contra accounts, along with an appreciation of why the word *accumulated* is used in the account name, can be gained when it is pointed out that depreciation is recorded at the end of each accounting period in a depreciating asset's life. As a result, at the end of the third month in the life of the law practice's office equipment, the Office Equipment and its related accumulated depreciation account will look like this:

Office Equipment		Accumulated Depreciation Office Equipment	
July 3	3,700	July 31	40
5	300	Aug. 31	40
		Sept. 30	40

And the equipment's cost and three months' *accumulated depreciation* will be shown on its September 30 balance sheet thus:

Office equipment	$4,000	
Less accumulated depreciation	120	$3,880

Accumulated depreciation accounts are sometimes found in ledgers and on statements under titles such as Allowance for Depreciation, Store Equipment or the totally unacceptable caption, Reserve for Depreciation, Office Equipment. However, more appropriate terminology is Accumulated Depreciation, Store Equipment and Accumulated Depreciation, Office Equipment. The "Accumulated" terminology is better because it is more descriptive of the depreciation procedure.

Accrued Expenses

Most expenses are recorded during an accounting period at the time they are paid. However, when a period ends there may be expenses that have been incurred but have not been paid and recorded because payment is not due. These unpaid and unrecorded expenses for which payment is not due are called *accrued expenses*. Earned but unpaid wages are a common example. To illustrate:

The Owen law practice has a secretary who is paid $40 per day or $200 per week for a week that begins on Monday and ends on Friday. The secretary's wages are due and payable every two weeks on Friday; and during July, they were paid on the 12th and 26th and recorded as follows:

Cash		Office Salaries Expense	
July 12	400	July 12	400
26	400	26	400

If the calendar for July appears as illustrated and the secretary worked on July 29, 30, and 31, then at the close of business on Wednesday, July 31, the secretary has earned three days' wages that are not paid and recorded because payment is not due. However, this $120 of earned but unpaid wages is just as much a part of the July expenses as the $800 of wages that have been paid. Furthermore, on July 31, the unpaid wages are a liability. Consequently, if the accounts are to show the correct amount of wages for July and all liabilities owed on July 31, then an adjusting entry like the following must be made:

JULY						
S	M	T	W	T	F	S
		1	2	3	4	5	6
7	8	9	10	11	12	13
14	15	16	17	18	19	20
21	22	23	24	25	26	27
28	29	30	31			

July	31	Office Salaries Expense	120.00	
		Salaries Payable		120.00
		To record the earned but unpaid wages.		

The effect of the entry on the accounts is:

Office Salaries Expense				Salaries Payable		
July 12	400				July 31	120
26	400					
31	120					

Unearned Revenues

An *unearned revenue* results when payment is received for goods or services in advance of their delivery. For instance, on July 15, Larry Owen entered into an agreement with Coast Realty to do its legal work on a fixed-fee basis for $300 per month. On that date, Owen received $450 in advance for services during the remainder of July and the month of August. The fee was recorded with this entry:

July	15	Cash	450.00	
		Unearned Legal Fees		450.00
		Received a legal fee in advance.		

Acceptance of the fee in advance increased the cash of the law practice and created a liability, the obligation to do Coast Realty's legal work for the next month and a half. However, by July 31, the law practice has discharged $150 of the liability and earned that much income, which according to the *realization principle* should appear on the July income statement. Consequently, on July 31, the following adjusting entry is required:

July	31	Unearned Legal Fees	150.00	
		Legal Fees Earned		150.00
		To record legal fees earned.		

Posting the entry has this effect on the accounts:

Unearned Legal Fees			Legal Fees Earned	
July 31	150	July 15	450	July 12	500
				19	1,000
				31	150

The effect of the entry is to transfer the $150 earned portion of the fee from the liability account to the revenue account. It reduces the liability and records as a revenue the $150 that has been earned.

Accrued Revenues

An *accrued revenue* is a revenue that has been earned but has not been collected because payment is not due. For example, assume that on July 20, Larry Owen also entered into an agreement with Guaranty Bank to do its legal work on a fixed-fee basis for $300 per month to be paid monthly. Under this assumption, by July 31, the law practice has earned one third of a month's fee, $100, which according to the *realization principle* should appear on its July income statement. Therefore, the following adjusting entry is required:

July	31	Accounts Receivable	100.00	
		Legal Fees Earned		100.00
		To record legal fees earned.		

Posting the entry has this effect on the accounts:

Accounts Receivable				Legal Fees Earned	
July 19	1,000	July 29	1,000	July 12	500
31	100			19	1,000
				31	150
				31	100

THE ADJUSTED TRIAL BALANCE

A trial balance prepared before adjustments is known as an *unadjusted trial balance,* or simply a trial balance. One prepared after adjustments is known as an *adjusted trial balance.* A July 31 adjusted trial balance for the law practice appears in Illustration 3–2.

Illustration 3–2

LARRY OWEN, ATTORNEY
Adjusted Trial Balance, July 31, 19—

Cash	$1,185	
Accounts receivable	100	
Prepaid rent	600	
Office supplies	35	
Office equipment	4,000	
Accumulated depreciation, office equipment		$ 40
Accounts payable		260
Salaries payable		120
Unearned legal fees		300
Larry Owen, capital		5,000
Larry Owen, withdrawals	200	
Legal fees earned		1,750
Office salaries expense	920	
Telephone expense	30	
Heating and lighting expense	35	
Rent expense	300	
Office supplies expense	25	
Depreciation expense, office equipment	40	
Totals	$7,470	$7,470

PREPARING STATEMENTS FROM THE ADJUSTED TRIAL BALANCE

An adjusted trial balance shows proper balance sheet and income statement amounts. Consequently, it may be used in preparing the statements. When it is so used, the revenue and expense items are arranged into an income statement, as in Illustration 3–3. Likewise, the asset, liability, and owner's equity items are arranged into a balance sheet in Illustration 3–4.

When the statements are prepared, the income statement is normally prepared first because the net income, as calculated on the income statement, is needed in completing the balance sheet's owner's equity section. Observe in Illustration 3–4 how the net income is combined with the withdrawals and the excess is added to Owen's July 1 capital. The income increased Owen's equity, and the withdrawals reduced it. Consequently, when the excess of the income over the withdrawals is added to the beginning equity, the result is the ending equity.

THE ADJUSTMENT PROCESS

The *adjustment process* described in this chapter arises from recognition that the operation of a business results in a continuous stream

Illustration 3-3

LARRY OWEN, ATTORNEY
Adjusted Trial Balance, July 31, 19—

Cash	$1,185	
Accounts receivable	100	
Prepaid rent	600	
Office supplies	35	
Office equipment	4,000	
Accumulated depreciation, office equipment		$ 40
Accounts payable		260
Salaries payable		120
Unearned legal fees		300
Larry Owen, capital		5,000
Larry Owen, withdrawals	200	
Legal fees earned		1,750
Office salaries expense	920	
Telephone expense	30	
Heating and lighting expense	35	
Rent expense	300	
Office supplies expense	25	
Depreciation expense, office equipment	40	
Totals	$7,470	$7,470

PREPARING THE INCOME STATEMENT
FROM THE ADJUSTED TRIAL BALANCE

LARRY OWEN, ATTORNEY
Income Statement for Month Ended July 31, 19—

Revenue:		
Legal fees earned		$1,750
Operating expenses:		
Office salaries expense	$920	
Telephone expense	30	
Heating and lighting expense	35	
Rent expense	300	
Office supplies expense	25	
Depreciation expense, office equipment	40	
Total operating expense		1,350
Net income		$ 400

Illustration 3–4

PREPARING THE BALANCE SHEET
FROM THE ADJUSTED TRIAL BALANCE

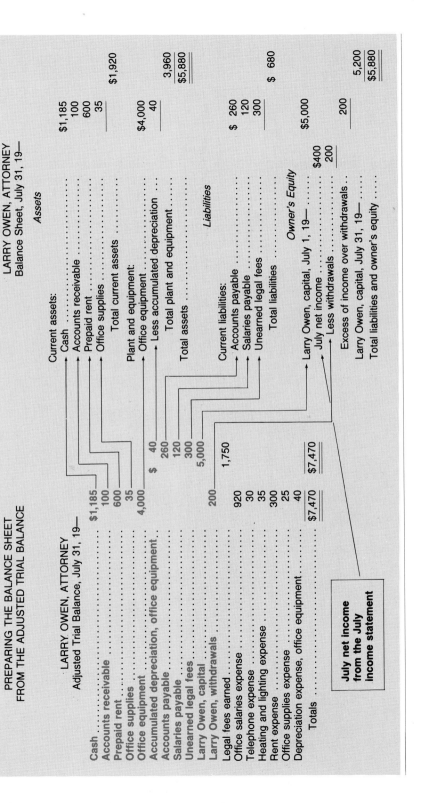

LARRY OWEN, ATTORNEY
Adjusted Trial Balance, July 31, 19—

Cash	$1,185	
Accounts receivable	100	
Prepaid rent	600	
Office supplies	35	
Office equipment	4,000	
Accumulated depreciation, office equipment		$ 40
Accounts payable		260
Unearned legal fees		120
Salaries payable		300
Larry Owen, capital		5,000
Larry Owen, withdrawals	200	
Legal fees earned		1,750
Office salaries expense	920	
Telephone expense	30	
Heating and lighting expense	35	
Rent expense	300	
Office supplies expense	25	
Depreciation expense, office equipment	40	
Totals	$7,470	$7,470

LARRY OWEN, ATTORNEY
Balance Sheet, July 31, 19—

Assets

Current assets:

Cash	$1,185	
Accounts receivable	100	
Prepaid rent	600	
Office supplies	35	
Total current assets		$1,920

Plant and equipment:

Office equipment	$4,000	
Less accumulated depreciation	40	
Total plant and equipment		3,960
Total assets		$5,880

Liabilities

Current liabilities:

Accounts payable	$ 260	
Salaries payable	120	
Unearned legal fees	300	
Total liabilities		$ 680

Owner's Equity

Larry Owen, capital, July 1, 19—		$5,000
July net income	$400	
Less withdrawals	200	
Excess of income over withdrawals		200
Larry Owen, capital, July 31, 19—		5,200
Total liabilities and owner's equity		$5,880

**July net income
from the July
income statement**

of transactions. Some of the transactions affect several accounting periods. And, the objective of the process is to allocate to each period that portion of a transaction's effects applicable to the period. For example, if a revenue is earned over several accounting periods, the adjustment process apportions and credits to each period its fair share. Likewise, if an expense benefits several periods, the adjustment process charges a fair share to each benefited period.

The adjustment process is based on two accounting principles, the *realization principle* and the *matching principle*. The *realization principle* requires that revenue be assigned to the accounting period in which it is earned, rather than to the period it is collected in cash. The *matching principle* requires that revenues and expenses be matched. As for matching revenues and expenses, it is recognized that a business incurs expenses in order to earn revenues. Consequently, it is only proper that expenses be matched with (deducted on the income statement from) the revenues they helped to produce.

The basic purpose behind the adjustment process, the *realization principle*, and the *matching principle* is to make the information on accounting statements comparable from period to period. For example, the Owen law practice paid its rent for three months in advance on July 1 and debited the $900 payment to Prepaid Rent. Then, at the end of July, it transferred $300 of this amount to its Rent Expense account and the $300 appeared on its July income statement as the July rent expense. At the end of August, it will transfer another $300 to rent expense; and at the end of September, it will transfer the third $300. As a result, the amounts shown for rent expense on its July, August, and September income statements will be comparable.

An unsatisfactory alternate procedure would be to debit the entire $900 to Rent Expense at the time of payment and permit the entire amount to appear on the July income statement as rent expense for July. However, if this were done, the July income statement would show $900 of rent expense and the August and September statements would show none. Thus, the income statements of the three months would not be comparable. In addition, the July net income would be understated $600 and the net incomes of August and September would be overstated $300 each. As a result, a person seeing only the fluctuations in net income might draw an incorrect conclusion.

ARRANGEMENT OF THE ACCOUNTS IN THE LEDGER

Normally, the accounts of a business are classified and logically arranged in its ledger. This serves two purposes: (1) it aids in locating any account and (2) it aids in preparing the statements. Obviously, statements can be prepared with the least difficulty if accounts are arranged in the ledger in the order of their statement appearance. This causes the accounts to appear on the adjusted trial balance in their statement order, which aids in rearranging the adjusted trial balance items into a balance sheet and an income statement. Consequently, the balance sheet accounts beginning with Cash and ending with the owner's equity accounts appear first in the ledger. These are followed by the revenue and expense accounts in the order of their income statement appearance.

DISPOSING OF ACCRUED ITEMS

Accrued Expenses

Several pages back, the July 29, 30, and 31 accrued wages of the secretary were recorded as follows:

July	31	Office Salaries Expense	120.00	
		Salaries Payable		120.00
		To record the earned but unpaid wages.		

When these wages are paid on Friday, August 9, the following entry is required:

Aug.	9	Salaries Payable	120.00	
		Office Salaries Expense	280.00	
		Cash		400.00
		Paid two weeks' wages.		

The first debit in the August 9 entry cancels the liability for the three days' wages accrued on July 31. The second debit records the wages of August's first seven working days as an expense of the August accounting period. The credit records the amount paid the secretary.

Accrued Revenues

On July 20, Larry Owen entered into an agreement to do the legal work of Guaranty Bank on a fixed-fee basis for $300 per month. On July 31, the following adjusting entry was made to record one third of a month's revenue earned under this contract.

July	31	Accounts Receivable	100.00	
		Legal Fees Earned		100.00
		To record legal fees earned.		

And when payment of the first month's fee is received on August 20, the following entry will be made:

Aug.	20	Cash	300.00	
		Accounts Receivable		100.00
		Legal Fees Earned		200.00
		Received legal fees earned.		

The first credit in the August 20 entry records the collection of the fee accrued at the end of July. The second credit records as revenue the fee earned during the first 20 days of August.

CASH AND ACCRUAL BASES OF ACCOUNTING

For income tax purposes, an individual or a business in which inventories of merchandise for sale are not a factor may report income on either a *cash basis* or an *accrual basis*. Under the cash basis, no adjustments are made for prepaid, unearned, and accrued items. Revenues are reported as being earned in the accounting period in which they are received in cash. Expenses are deducted from revenues in the accounting period in which cash is disbursed in their payment. As a result, under the cash basis net income is the difference between revenue receipts and expense disbursements. Under the accrual basis, on the other hand, adjustments are made for accrued and deferred (prepaid and unearned) items. Under this basis, revenues are credited to the period in which earned, expenses are matched with revenues, and no consideration is given to when cash is received and disbursed. As a result, net income is the difference between revenues earned and the expenses incurred in earning the revenues.

The cash basis of accounting is satisfactory for individuals and a few concerns in which accrued and deferred items are not important. However, it is not satisfactory for most concerns since it results in accounting reports that are not comparable from period to period. Consequently, most businesses keep their records on an accrual basis.

CLASSIFICATION OF BALANCE SHEET ITEMS

The balance sheets in the first two chapters were simple ones, and no attempt was made to classify the items. However, a balance sheet becomes more useful when its assets and liabilities are classified into significant groups, because a reader of a *classified balance sheet* can better judge the adequacy of the different kinds of assets used in the business. The reader can also better estimate the probable availability of funds to meet the various liabilities as they become due.

Accountants are not in full agreement as to the best way in which to classify balance sheet items. As a result, they are classified in several ways. A common way classifies assets into (1) current assets, (2) long-term investments, (3) plant and equipment, and (4) intangible assets. It classifies liabilities into (1) current liabilities and (2) long-term liabilities.

Of the four asset classifications listed, only two, current assets and plant and equipment, appear on the balance sheet of Valley Store, Illustration 3–5 (on the next page). The store is small and has no long-term investments and intangible assets.

Current Assets

Current assets are primarily those to which current creditors (current liabilities) may look for payment. As presently defined, current assets consist of cash and assets that are reasonably expected to be realized in cash or be sold or consumed within one year or within one *operating cycle of the business,* whichever is longer. The accounts and notes receivable of Illustration 3–5 are expected to be realized in cash. The merchandise (merchandise inventory) is expected to be sold either for cash or accounts receivable that will be realized in cash. The prepaid insurance and supplies are to be consumed.

The operating cycle of a business is the average period of time between its acquisition of merchandise or raw materials and the realization of cash from the sale of the merchandise or the sale of the products manufactured from the raw materials. In many companies, this interval is less than one year; and as a result, these companies use a one-year period in classifying current assets. However, due to an aging process or other cause, some companies have an operating cycle longer than one year. For example, distilleries must age some products for several years before the products are ready for sale. Consequently, in such companies, inventories of raw materials, manufacturing supplies, and products being processed for sale are classified as current assets, although the products made from the inventories will not be ready for sale for more than a year.

Such things as prepaid insurance, office supplies, and store supplies

Classified assets on balance sheet

Illustration 3–5

VALLEY STORE
Balance Sheet, December 31, 198A

Assets

Current assets:

Cash	$ 1,050	
Notes receivable	300	
Accounts receivable	3,961	
Merchandise inventory	20,248	
Prepaid insurance	109	
Office supplies	46	
Stores supplies	145	
Total current assets		$ 25,859

Plant and equipment:

Office equipment	$ 1,500		
Less accumulated depreciation	300	$ 1,200	
Store equipment	$ 3,200		
Less accumulated depreciation	800	2,400	
Buildings	$75,000		
Less accumulated depreciation	7,400	67,600	
Land		24,200	
Total plant and equipment			95,400
Total assets			$121,259

Liabilities

Current liabilities:

Notes payable	$ 3,000	
Accounts payable	2,715	
Wages payable	112	
Mortgage payable (current portion)	1,200	
Total current liabilities		$ 7,027

Long-term liabilities:

First mortgage payable, secured by a mortgage on land and buildings	78,800	
Total liabilities		$ 85,827

Owner's Equity

Samuel Jackson, capital, January 1, 198A		$33,721
Net income for the year	$19,711	
Less withdrawals	18,000	
Excess of income over withdrawals		1,711
Samuel Jackson, capital, December 31, 198A		35,432
Total liabilities and owner's equity		$121,259

are called *prepaid expenses*. Until consumed, they are classified as current assets. An AICPA committee said: "Prepaid expenses are not current assets in the sense that they will be converted into cash but in the sense that, if not paid in advance, they would require the use of current assets during the operating cycle."[1] This means that if the prepaid expense items were not already owned, current assets would be required for their purchase during the operating cycle.

The prepaid expenses of a business, as a total, are seldom a major item on its balance sheet. As a result, instead of listing them individually, as in Illustration 3–5, they are commonly totaled and only the total is shown under the caption "Prepaid expenses."

Long-Term Investments

The second balance sheet classification is long-term investments. Stocks, bonds, and promissory notes that will be held for more than one year or one cycle appear under this classification. Also, such things as land held for future expansion but not now being used in the business operations appear here.

Plant and Equipment

Plant assets are relatively long-lived assets of a tangible nature that are held for use in the production or sale of other assets or services. Examples are items of equipment, buildings, and land. The key words in the definition are *long-lived* and *held for use in the production or sale of other assets or services.* Land held for future expansion is not a plant asset. It is not being used to produce or sell other assets, goods, or services.

The words *Plant and equipment* are commonly used as a balance sheet caption. More complete captions are "Property, plant, and equipment" and "Land, buildings, and equipment." However, all three captions are long and unwieldy. As a result, items of plant and equipment will be called plant assets in this book.

The order in which plant assets are listed within the balance sheet classification is not uniform. However, they are often listed from the ones of least permanent nature to those of most permanent nature.

Intangible Assets

Intangible assets are assets having no physical nature. Their value is derived from the rights conferred upon their owner by possession. Goodwill, patents, and trademarks are examples.

---

[1] Committee on Accounting Procedure, "Accounting Research Bulletin No. 43," *Accounting Research and Terminology Bulletins, Final Edition* (New York: AICPA, 1961), p. 20.

Current Liabilities

Current liabilities are debts or other obligations that must be paid or liquidated within one year or one operating cycle, using presently listed current assets. Common current liabilities are notes payable, accounts payable, wages payable, taxes payable, interest payable, and unearned revenues. Also, that portion of a long-term debt due within one year or one operating cycle, for example, the $1,200 portion of the mortgage debt shown in Illustration 3–5, is a current liability. The order of their listing within the classification is not uniform. Often notes payable are listed first because notes receivable are listed first after cash in the current asset section.

Unearned revenues are classified as current liabilities because current assets will normally be required in their liquidation. For example, payments for future delivery of merchandise will be earned and the obligation for delivery will be liquidated by delivering merchandise, a current asset.

Long-Term Liabilities

The second main liability classification is long-term liabilities. Liabilities that are not due and payable for a comparatively long period, usually more than one year, are listed under this classification. Common long-term liability items are mortgages payable, bonds payable, and notes payable due more than a year after the balance sheet date.

OWNER'S EQUITY ON THE BALANCE SHEET

Single Proprietorship

The equity of the owner of a single proprietorship business may be shown on a balance sheet as follows:

Owner's Equity		
James Gibbs, capital, January 1, 198A		$23,152
Net income for the year	$10,953	
Less withdrawals	12,000	
Excess of withdrawals over income		(1,047)
James Gibbs, capital, December 31, 198A		$22,105

The withdrawals of James Gibbs exceeded his net income; and in the equity section, the excess is enclosed in parenthesis to indicate that it is a negative or subtracted amount. Negative amounts are commonly shown in this way on financial statements.

The illustrated equity section shows the increases and decreases in owner's equity resulting from earnings and withdrawals. Some accountants prefer to put these details on a supplementary schedule attached to the balance sheet and called a *statement of owner's equity*. When this is done, owner's equity is shown on the balance sheet as follows:

Owner's Equity	
James Gibbs, capital (see schedule attached)	$22,105

Partnerships

Changes in partnership equities resulting from earnings and withdrawals are commonly shown in a statement of partners' equities. Then, only the amount of each partner's equity and the total of the equalities as of the statement date are shown on the balance sheet, as follows:

Partners' Equities		
John Reed, capital	$16,534	
Robert Burns, capital	18,506	
Total equities of the partners		$35,040

Corporations

Corporations are regulated by state corporation laws. These laws require that a distinction be made between amounts invested in a corporation by its stockholders and the increase or decrease in stockholders' equity due to earnings, losses, and dividends. Consequently, stockholders' equity is commonly shown on a corporation balance sheet as follows:

Stockholders' Equity		
Common stock	$500,000	
Retained earnings	64,450	
Total stockholders' equity		$564,450

If a corporation issues only one kind of stock (others are discussed later), it is called *common stock*. The $500,000 amount shown here for this item is the amount originally invested in this corporation by its stockholders through the purchase of the corporation's stock. The $64,450 of *retained earnings* represents the increase in the stockholders' equity resulting from earnings that exceeded any losses and any *dividends* paid to the stockholders. (A dividend is a distribution of assets made by a corporation to its stockholders. A dividend of cash reduces corporation assets and the equity of its stockholders in the same way a withdrawal reduces assets and owner's equity in a single proprietorship.)

ARRANGEMENT OF BALANCE SHEET ITEMS

The balance sheet of Illustration 1–2 in the first chapter, with the liabilities and owner's equity placed to the right of the assets, is called an *account form balance sheet*. Such an arrangement emphasizes that assets equal liabilities plus owner's equity. Account form balance sheets are often reproduced on a double page with the assets on the left-hand page and the liabilities and owner's equity on the right-hand page.

The balance sheet of Illustration 3–5 is called a *report form balance sheet*. Its items are arranged vertically and better fit a single page. Both forms are commonly used, and neither is preferred.

ACCOUNT NUMBERS

A commonly used three-digit account numbering system was introduced in Chapter 2. In the system, the number assigned to an account not only identifies the account but also tells its balance sheet or income statement classification. In the system, the first digit in an account's number tells its main balance sheet or income statement classification. For example, account numbers with first digits of 1 are assigned to asset accounts. Liability accounts are assigned numbers with first digits of 2, and the accounts in each main balance sheet and income statement classification of a concern selling merchandise are assigned numbers as follows:

111 to 199 are assigned to asset accounts.
211 to 299 are assigned to liability accounts.
311 to 399 are assigned to owner's equity accounts.
411 to 499 are assigned to sales or revenue accounts.
511 to 599 are assigned to cost of goods sold accounts.
611 to 699 are assigned to operating expense accounts.
711 to 799 are assigned to other revenue and expense accounts.

In the system, the second digit further classifies an account. For example, the second digits under each of the following main classifications indicate the subclassification shown:

111 to 199.   Asset accounts

111 to 119. Current asset accounts (second digits of 1)
121 to 129. Long-term investment accounts (second digits of 2)
131 to 139. Plant asset accounts (second digits of 3)
141 to 149. Intangible asset accounts (second digits of 4)

211 to 299. Liability accounts
211 to 219. Current liability accounts (second digits of 1)
221 to 229. Long-term liability accounts (second digits of 2)

611 to 699. Operating expense accounts
611 to 629. Selling expense accounts (second digits of 1 and 2)
631 to 649. General and administrative expense accounts (second digits of 3 and 4)

The third digit of an account's number completes its identification. For example, third digits complete the identification of the following current asset accounts:

111 to 199. Asset accounts
111 to 119. Current asset accounts
111. Cash
112. Petty Cash
113. Notes Receivable
114. Accounts Receivable

The sales and cost of goods sold accounts mentioned here are discussed in Chapter 5. The division of the operating expense accounts into selling expense accounts and general and administrative expense accounts is also discussed there. In a service-type business such as the ones described in this chapter, generally all expense accounts are classified as operating expense accounts without subdividing them.

GLOSSARY

Account form balance sheet. A balance sheet with the assets on the left and the liability and owner's equity items on the right.

Accounting period. The time interval over which the transactions of a business are recorded and at the end of which its financial statements are prepared.

Accrual basis of accounting. The accounting basis in which revenues are assigned to the accounting period in which earned regardless of whether or not received in cash and expenses incurred in earning the revenues are deducted from the revenues regardless of whether or not cash has been disbursed in their payment.

Accrued expense. An expense that has been incurred during an accounting period but that has not been paid and recorded because payment is not due.

Accrued revenue. A revenue that has been earned during an accounting period but has not been received and recorded because payment is not due. *earned but not received*

Accumulated depreciation. The cumulative amount of depreciation recorded against an asset or group of assets during the entire period of time the asset or assets have been owned.

Adjusted trial balance. A trial balance showing account balances brought up to date by recording appropriate adjusting entries.

Adjusting entries. Journal entries made to assign revenues to the period in which earned and to match revenues and expenses.

Adjustment process. The end-of-period process of recording appropriate adjusting entries to assign revenues to the period in which earned and to match revenues and expenses.

Cash basis of accounting. The accounting basis in which revenues are reported as being earned in the accounting period received in cash and expenses are deducted from revenues in the accounting period in which cash is disbursed in their payment.

Classified balance sheet. A balance sheet with assets and liabilities classified into significant groups.

Common stock. The name given to a corporation's stock when it issues only one kind or class of stock.

Contra account. An account the balance of which is subtracted from the balance of an associated account to show a more proper amount for the item recorded in the associated account.

Current asset. Cash or an asset that may reasonably be expected to be realized in cash or be consumed within one year or one operating cycle of the business, whichever is longer.

Current liability. A debt or other obligation that must be paid or liquidated within one year or one operating cycle, and the payment or liquidation of which will require the use of presently classified current assets.

Depreciation. The expiration of a plant asset's "quantity of usefulness."

Depreciation expense. The expense resulting from the expiration of a plant asset's "quantity of usefulness."

Dividend. A distribution of cash or other assets made by a corporation to its stockholders.

Fiscal year. A period of any 12 consecutive months used as an accounting period.

Intangible asset. An asset having no physical existence but having value because of the rights conferred as a result of its ownership and possession.

Matching principle. The accounting rule that all expenses incurred in earning a revenue be deducted from the revenue in determining net income.

Natural business year. Any 12 consecutive months used by a business as an accounting period, at the end of which the activities of the business are at their lowest point.

Operating cycle of a business. The average period of time between the acquisition of merchandise or materials by a business and the realization of cash from the sale of the merchandise or product manufactured from the materials.

Plant and equipment.   Tangible assets having relatively long lives that are used in the production or sale of other assets or services.

Prepaid expense.   An asset that will be consumed in the operation of a business; and as it is consumed, it will become an expense.

Report form balance sheet.   A balance sheet prepared on one page, at the top of which the assets are listed, followed down the page by the liabilities and owner's equity.

Retained earnings.   Stockholders' equity in a corporation resulting from earnings in excess of losses and dividends declared.

Time-period concept.   The idea that the life of a business is divisible into time periods of equal length.

Unadjusted trial balance.   A trial balance prepared after transactions are recorded but before any adjustments are made.

Unearned revenue.   Payment received in advance for goods or services to be delivered at a later date.

QUESTIONS FOR CLASS DISCUSSION

1. Why are the balances of some of a company's accounts normally incorrect for statement purposes at the end of an accounting period even though all transactions were correctly recorded?

2. Other than to make the accounts show proper statement amounts, what is the basic purpose behind the end-of-period adjustment process?

3. A prepaid expense is an asset at the time of its purchase or prepayment. When is it best to ignore this and record the prepayment as an expense? Why?

4. What is a contra account? Give an example.

5. What contra account is used in recording depreciation? Why is such an account used?

6. What is an accrued expense? Give an example.

7. How does an unearned revenue arise? Give an example of an unearned revenue.

8. What is the balance sheet classification of an unearned revenue?

9. What is an accrued revenue? Give an example.

10. When the statements are prepared from an adjusted trial balance, why should the income statement be prepared first?

11. The adjustment process results from recognizing that some transactions affect several accounting periods. What is the objective of the process?

12. When are a concern's revenues and expenses matched?

13. Why should the income statements of a concern be comparable from period to period?

14. What is the usual order in which accounts are arranged in the ledger?

≠ 95 ╫ 102

15. Differentiate between the cash and the accrual bases of accounting?
16. What is a classified balance sheet? *╫ 103*
17. What are the characteristics of a current asset? What are the characteristics of an asset classified as plant and equipment?
18. What are current liabilities? Long-term liabilities?
19. The equity section of a corporation balance sheet shows two items, common stock and retained earnings. What does the sum of the items represent? How did each item arise?

CLASS EXERCISES

Exercise 3–1

A company has five office employees who each earn $40 per day for a five-day week that begins on Monday and ends on Friday. They were paid for the week ended December 26, and all five worked full days on Monday, Tuesday, and Wednesday, December 29, 30, and 31. January 1 of the new year was an unpaid holiday and none of the employees worked, but all worked a full day on Friday, January 2. Give in general journal form the year-end adjusting entry to record the accrued wages and the entry to pay the employees on January 2.

Exercise 3–2

Give in general journal form the year-end adjusting entry for each of the following:

a. The Prepaid Insurance account had a $985 debit balance at the end of the accounting period before adjustment for expired insurance. An examination of insurance policies showed that $540 of insurance had expired.
b. The Prepaid Insurance account had an $890 debit balance at the end of the accounting period before adjustment for expired insurance. An examination of insurance policies showed $270 of unexpired insurance.
c. The store supplies account had a $215 debit balance on January 1; store supplies costing $580 were purchased during the year; and a year-end inventory showed $235 of unconsumed store supplies on hand.
d. Four months' property taxes, estimated at $445, have accrued but are unpaid and unrecorded at the accounting period end.
e. Depreciation on store equipment for the accounting period is estimated at $2,775.

Exercise 3–3

Assume that the required adjustments of Exercise 3–2 were not made at the end of the accounting period and tell for each adjustment the effect of its omission on the income statement and balance sheet prepared at that time.

Exercise 3–4

A company paid the $1,800 premium on a three-year insurance policy on August 1, 198A.

a. How many dollars of the premium should appear on the 198A income statement as an expense?
b. How many dollars of the premium should appear on the December 31, 198A, balance sheet as an asset?

    c. Under the assumption that the Prepaid Insurance account was debited for $1,800 in recording the premium payment, give the December 31, 198A, adjusting entry to record the expired insurance.

    d. Under the assumption the bookkeeper incorrectly debited the Insurance Expense account for $1,800 in recording the premium payment, give the December 31, 198A, adjusting entry. (Hint: Did the bookkeeper's error change the answers to questions *(a)* and *(b)* of this exercise?)

Exercise 3–5
    A department store occupies most of the space in the building it owns. However, it also rents space in the building to merchants who sell compatible but not competitive merchandise.

    a. A tenant rented space in the store's building on November 1 at $400 per month, paying three months' rent in advance. The store credited Unearned Rent to record the $1,200 received. Give the store's year-end adjusting entry.

    b. Another tenant rented space at $500 per month on October 1. He paid his rent on the first day of October and again on the first day of November; but by December 31, he had not paid his December rent. Give the required year-end adjusting entry.

    c. Assume the foregoing tenant paid his rent for December and January on January 2 of the new year. Give the entry to record the receipt of the $1,000.

Exercise 3–6
    Determine the amounts indicated by the question marks in the columns below. The amounts in each column constitute a separate problem.

	(a)	*(b)*	*(c)*	*(d)*
Supplies on hand on January 1	$213	$142	$325	$?
Supplies purchased during the year	475	537	?	452
Supplies consumed during the year	?	462	622	395
Supplies remaining at the year-end	238	?	254	204

PROBLEMS

Problem 3–1
    The following information for adjustments was available on December 31, at the end of the annual accounting period. Prepare an adjusting journal entry for each unit of information.

    a. An examination of insurance policies showed the following three policies:

Policy No.	Date of purchase	Life of policy	Cost
1	November 1 of previous year	3 years	$480
2	May 1 of current year	1 year	360
3	June 1 of current year	1 year	240

Prepaid Insurance was debited for the cost of each policy at the time of its purchase.

    b. The Office Supplies account had an $85 balance at the beginning of the year, $390 of office supplies were purchased during the year, and an inventory of unused supplies on hand at the year-end totaled $115.

c. The two office employees each earn $40 per day and are paid each Friday for a workweek that begins on Monday. This year, December 31 fell on Thursday, and both employees worked Monday, Tuesday, Wednesday, and Thursday.

d. The company owns a building that it completed and occupied for the first time on May 1 of the current year. The building cost $216,000, has an estimated 30-year life, and is not expected to have any salvage value at the end of that time.

e. A company occupies most of the space in its building, but it also rents space to two tenants. One tenant agreed beginning on November 1 to rent a small amount of space at $250 per month; and on that date, he paid six months' rent in advance. The amount paid was credited to the Unearned Rent account.

f. The second tenant whose rent is also $250 per month paid his rent on the first of each month August through November, and the amounts paid were credited to Rent Earned. However, he has not paid his December rent, although he has said on several occasions that he would do so the next day.

Problem 3–2

Desert Realty operates with annual accounting periods that end each December 31. At the end of the current year, after all transactions were recorded, the trial balance that follows was taken from its ledger.

DESERT REALTY
Trial Balance, December 31, 19—

Cash	$ 4,145	
Prepaid insurance	880	
Office supplies	335	
Office equipment	3,975	
Accumulated depreciation, office equipment		$ 615
Automobile	7,645	
Accumulated depreciation, automobile		1,150
Accounts payable		75
Unearned management fees		450
Marie Sloan, capital		12,140
Marie Sloan, withdrawals	15,000	
Sales commissions earned		33,460
Office salaries expense	10,500	
Advertising expense	1,565	
Rent expense	3,600	
Telephone expense	245	
Totals	$47,890	$47,890

Required:

1. Open the accounts of the trial balance plus these additional accounts: Accounts Receivable; Salaries Payable; Management Fees Earned; Insurance Expense; Office Supplies Expense; Depreciation Expense, Office Equipment; and Depreciation Expense, Automobile. Enter the trial balance amounts in the accounts.

2. Use the following information to prepare and post adjusting entries:
   a. Insurance expired during the year, $650.
   b. An office supplies inventory showed $120 of unused office supplies on hand at the year-end.

c. Estimated depreciation of office equipment, $450; and *(d)* of automobile, $1,200.

e. Before departing on a world tour, a client entered into a contract with Desert Realty for the management of her apartment building. She paid the management fee for six months in advance, beginning on November 1, and the amount paid, $450, was credited to the Unearned Management Fees account.

f. On December 1, Desert Realty entered into a contract and began managing a small office building for a $50 monthly fee. The contract specified that payments for this service were to be made quarterly with the first payment becoming due on March 1 of next year.

g. The office employee is paid every two weeks, and on December 31 has earned $90 of wages that are unpaid and unrecorded because payment is not due.

3. Prepare an adjusted trial balance, an income statement, and a classified balance sheet.

Problem 3–3   The trial balance that follows was taken from the ledger of A–1 Moving and Storage Company at the end of its annual accounting period:

A–1 MOVING AND STORAGE
Trial Balance, December 31, 19—

Cash	$ 2,460	
Accounts receivable	680	
Prepaid insurance	2,340	
Office supplies	410	
Office equipment	3,540	
Accumulated depreciation, office equipment		$ 1,320
Trucks	43,800	
Accumulated depreciation, trucks		10,630
Buildings	156,000	
Accumulated depreciation, buildings		20,900
Land	18,000	
Accounts payable		875
Unearned storage fees		685
Mortgage payable		125,000
Ted Davis, capital		45,390
Ted Davis, withdrawals	18,400	
Revenue from moving services		78,995
Storage fees earned		2,960
Office salaries expense	10,200	
Truck drivers' wages expense	28,410	
Gas, oil, and repairs expense	2,515	
Totals	$286,755	$286,755

Required:

1. Open the accounts of the trial balance plus these additional accounts: Wages Payable; Insurance Expense; Office Supplies Expense; Depreciation Expense, Office Equipment; Depreciation Expense, Trucks; and Depreciation Expense, Buildings. Enter the trial balance amounts in the accounts.

2. Use this information to prepare and post adjusting journal entries:
    a. An examination of insurance policies showed $1,840 of insurance expired.
    b. An inventory of office supplies showed $145 of unused supplies on hand at the year-end.
    c. Estimated depreciation of office equipment, $415; *(d)* trucks, $5,450; and *(e)* buildings, $6,800.
    f. The company follows the practice of crediting the storage fees of customers who pay in advance to the Unearned Storage Fees account. Of the amount credited to this account during the year, $420 had been earned by the year-end.
    g. There were accrued storage fees earned but unrecorded in the accounts and uncollected at the year-end that totaled $110.
    h. There were $225 of accrued truck drivers' wages at the year-end.
3. After posting the adjusting entries, prepare an adjusted trial balance, an income statement, and a classified balance sheet. Payments on the mortgage principal totaling $7,200 are due within one year.

Problem 3–4

At the end of its annual accounting period, after all transactions were recorded, the trial balance that follows was taken from the ledger of Siesta Trailer Park:

SIESTA TRAILER PARK
Trial Balance, December 31, 19—

Cash	$ 2,210	
Prepaid insurance	915	
Office supplies	125	
Office equipment	1,250	
Accumulated depreciation, office equipment		$ 325
Buildings and improvements	65,000	
Accumulated depreciation, buildings and improvements		7,200
Land	90,000	
Accounts payable		215
Unearned rent		500
Mortgage payable		120,000
June Mead, capital		21,630
June Mead, withdrawals	15,000	
Rent earned		46,250
Wages expense	9,060	
Utilities expense	640	
Telephone expense	180	
Property taxes expense	1,840	
Interest expense	9,900	
Totals	$196,120	$196,120

Required:

1. Open the accounts of the trial balance plus these: Accounts Receivable; Wages Payable; Property Taxes Payable; Interest Payable; Insurance Expense; Office Supplies Expense; Depreciation Expense, Office Equipment; and Depreciation Expense, Buildings and Improvements.
2. Use the following information to prepare and post adjusting journal entries:

a. An examination of insurance policies showed $650 of insurance expired.

b. An inventory of office supplies showed $40 of unused supplies on hand.

c. Estimated depreciation on office equipment, $110; and (d) on the buildings and improvements, $3,150.

e. The company follows the practice of crediting the Unearned Rent account for rents paid in advance by tenants, and an examination revealed that one half of the $500 balance of this account had been earned by the year-end.

f. A tenant is two months in arrears with his rent payments, and this $200 of accrued revenue was unrecorded at the time the trial balance was prepared.

g. The one employee, a gardener and general handy man, works a five-day week at $35 per day. He was paid last week but has worked four days this week, December 28, 29, 30, and 31, for which he has not been paid.

h. Two months' property taxes, totaling $300, have accrued but are unpaid and unrecorded.

i. Thirty days' interest on the mortgage, $900, has accrued but is unpaid and unrecorded.

3. After posting the adjusting entries, prepare an adjusted trial balance, an income statement, and a classified balance sheet. A $4,000 payment to reduce the mortgage principal is due within one year.

Problem 3–5

The 198A and 198B balance sheets of a company showed the following asset and liability amounts at the end of each year:

	December 31	
	198A	*198B*
Prepaid insurance	$200	$500
Interest payable	100	300
Unearned property, management fees ..	400	200

The company's records showed the following amounts of cash disbursed and received for these items during 198B:

Cash disbursed to pay insurance premiums ..	$1,700
Cash disbursed to pay interest	1,400
Cash received for managing property	2,100

Required:

Present calculations to show the amounts to be reported on the 198B income statement for (a) insurance expense, (b) interest expense, and (c) property management fees earned.

ALTERNATE PROBLEMS

Problem 3–1A

The following information for adjustments was available on December 31, the end of a yearly accounting period:

a. The prepaid insurance account showed these amounts:

Prepaid Insurance

Jan.	1	Balance	165.00	
May	1		420.00	
Nov.	1		720.00	

The January balance represents the unexpired premium on a one-year policy purchased on May 1 of the previous year. The May 1 debit resulted from paying the premium on a one-year policy, and the November 1 debit represents the cost of a three-year policy.

b. The office supplies account showed these amounts:

Office Supplies

Jan.	1	Balance	115.00	
Mar.	10	Purchase	255.00	
Oct.	5	Purchase	60.00	

The December 31 year-end inventory of office supplies showed $95 of unused supplies.

c. The company owns and occupies a building that was completed and occupied for the first time on April 1 of the current year. The company had previously occupied rented quarters. The building cost $198,000, has an estimated 30-year useful life, and is not expected to have any salvage value at the end of its life.

d. The company rents portions of the space in its building to two tenants. Tenant A agreed beginning on September 1 to rent a small amount of space at $150 per month, and on that date paid six months' rent in advance. The $900 was credited to the Unearned Rent account.

e. Tenant B pays $250 rent per month on the space he occupies. During the months of June through November, he paid his rent each month on the first day of the month, and the amounts paid were credited to Rent Earned. However, he has recently experienced financial difficulties and has not yet paid his rent for December.

f. The company has two office employees who earn $40 and $50 per day, respectively. They are paid each Friday for a workweek that begins on Monday. They were paid last Friday and have worked on Monday and Tuesday, December 30 and 31 of this week.

Required:

Prepare adjusting journal entries for each of the units of information.

Problem 3–2A   A trial balance of the ledger of Sloan Realty at the end of its annual accounting period follows.

SLOAN REALTY
Trial Balance, December 31, 19—

Cash	$ 4,145	
Prepaid insurance	880	
Office supplies	335	
Office equipment	3,975	
Accumulated depreciation, office equipment		$ 615
Automobile	7,645	
Accumulated depreciation, automobile		1,150
Accounts payable		75
Unearned management fees		450
Marie Sloan, capital		12,140
Marie Sloan, withdrawals	15,000	
Sales commissions earned		33,460
Office salaries expense	10,500	
Advertising expense	1,565	
Rent expense	3,600	
Telephone expense	245	
Totals	$47,890	$47,890

Required:

1. Open the accounts of the trial balance plus these additional accounts: Accounts Receivable; Salaries Payable; Management Fees Earned; Insurance Expense; Office Supplies Expense; Depreciation Expense, Office Equipment; and Depreciation Expense, Automobile. Enter the trial balance amounts in the accounts.

2. Use the following information to prepare and post adjusting entries:
   a. An examination of insurance policies showed $615 of insurance expired at the period end.
   b. An inventory of unused office supplies showed $115 of supplies on hand.
   c. The year's depreciation on the office equipment was estimated at $500 and *(d)* on the automobile at $1,225.
   e. and *(f)* Sloan Realty has just begun to offer property management services and has signed two contracts with clients. In the first contract *(e)*, it agreed to manage a small apartment building for a $60 monthly fee payable at the end of each quarter. The contract was signed on October 15, and two and a half months' fees have accrued. In the second contract *(f)*, it agreed to manage an office building beginning on November 1. The contract called for a $150 monthly fee, and the client paid the fees for the first three months in advance at the time the contract was signed. The amount paid was credited to the Unearned Management Fees account.
   g. The office secretary is paid weekly; and on December 31, two days' wages at $40 per day have accrued.

3. Prepare an adjusted trial balance, an income statement, and a classified balance sheet.

Problem 3–3A   A trial balance of the ledger of Ted's Moving and Storage at the end of its annual accounting period carried the items that follow.

TED'S MOVING AND STORAGE
Trial Balance, December 31, 19—

Cash	$ 2,460	
Accounts receivable......................	680	
Prepaid insurance........................	2,340	
Office supplies	410	
Office equipment	3,540	
Accumulated depreciation, office equipment ..		$ 1,320
Trucks	43,800	
Accumulated depreciation, trucks		10,630
Buildings	156,000	
Accumulated depreciation, buildings.........		20,900
Land	18,000	
Accounts payable........................		875
Unearned storage fees		685
Mortgage payable........................		125,000
Ted Davis, capital.......................		45,390
Ted Davis, withdrawals	18,400	
Revenue from moving services		78,995
Storage fees earned		2,960
Office salaries expense...................	10,200	
Truck drivers' wages expense	28,410	
Gas, oil, and repairs expense	2,515	
Totals	$286,755	$286,755

Required:

1. Open the accounts of the trial balance plus these additional accounts: Wages Payable; Insurance Expense; Office Supplies Expense; Depreciation Expense, Office Equipment; Depreciation Expense, Trucks; and Depreciation Expense, Buildings. Enter the trial balance amounts in the accounts.
2. Use this information to prepare and post adjusting journal entries:
   a. An examination of insurance policies showed $2,115 of insurance expired.
   b. An office supplies inventory showed $155 of unused office supplies on hand at the period end.
   c. Estimated depreciation of office equipment, $430; *(d)* trucks, $5,875; and *(e)* buildings, $5,100.
   f. The company credits the storage fees of customers who pay in advance to the Unearned Storage Fees account. Of the $685 credited to this account during the year, $385 had been earned by the year-end.
   g. Accrued storage fees earned but unrecorded in the accounts and uncollected at the year-end totaled $140.
   h. There were $285 of earned but unpaid truck drivers' wages at the year-end.
3. After posting the adjusting journal entries, prepare an adjusted trial balance, an income statement, and a classified balance sheet. Installment payments on the mortgage totaling $9,000 are due within one year.

Problem 3–4A   An inexperienced bookkeeper prepared the first of the following income statements but forgot to adjust the accounts before its preparation. However, the oversight was discovered, and the second correct statement was prepared. Analyze the two statements and prepare the adjusting journal entries that were made between their preparation. Assume that one fourth of the additional property management fees resulted from recognizing accrued management fees and three fourths resulted from previously recorded unearned fees that were earned by the time the statements were prepared. (You will need only general journal paper for the solution of this problem. You may use the paper provided for Problems 3–4 or 3–4A or for any other unassigned problem.)

VALLEY REALTY
Income Statement for Year Ended December 31, 19—

Revenues		
Commissions earned		$39,450
Property management fees earned . .		2,110
Total revenues		$41,560
Operating expenses:		
Rent expense	$ 2,750	
Salaries expense	10,080	
Advertising expense	1,235	
Utilities expense	485	
Telephone expense	515	
Gas, oil, and repairs expense	620	
Total operating expenses		15,685
Net income		$25,875

VALLEY REALTY
Income Statement for Year Ended December 31, 19—

Revenues:		
Commissions earned		$39,450
Property management fees earned . .		2,590
Total revenues		$42,040
Operating expenses:		
Rent expense	$ 3,000	
Salaries expense	10,200	
Advertising expense	1,280	
Utilities expense	485	
Telephone expense	515	
Gas, oil, and repairs expense	635	
Office supplies expense	240	
Insurance expense	325	
Depreciation expense, office		
equipment	410	
Depreciation expense, automobile . .	915	
Taxes expense	130	
Total operating expenses		18,135
Net income		$23,905

Problem 3–5A

Lee Ross, an attorney, has always kept his accounting records on a cash basis; and at the end of 198B, he prepared the following cash basis income statement:

LEE ROSS, ATTORNEY
Income Statement for Year Ended December 31, 198B

Legal fees earned	$44,700
Expenses	16,200
Net income	$28,500

In preparing the income statement, the following amounts of accrued and deferred items were ignored at the ends of 198A and 198B:

	End of	
	198A	*198B*
Prepaid expenses	$330	$150
Accrued expenses	215	650
Accrued legal fees	360	530
Unearned legal fees	510	390

Required:

Assume that the 198A prepaid and unearned items became expenses or were earned in 198B, the ignored 198A accrued items were either received in cash or were paid in 198B, and prepare a condensed 198B accrual basis income statment for Lee Ross. Show the calculations to arrive at your income statement amounts.

PROVOCATIVE PROBLEMS

Provocative Problem 3–1, Ed's Fixit Shop

On April 1 of the current year, Ed Parr rented shop space and began a repair service he called Ed's Fixit Shop. He has not kept formal accounting records; and now, at the year-end, he wants to know how much the business has earned in its first nine months. He would also like for you to prepare an accrual basis income statement and a year-end balance sheet.

Ed has kept an accurate checkbook record of cash receipts and disbursements, which shows:

Receipts:		
Cash invested	$10,000	
Received from customers for repair services ..	26,555	$36,555
Disbursements:		
Shop rent	$ 2,000	
Shop equipment	3,200	
Truck	6,800	
Repair parts and supplies	2,850	
Insurance premium	720	
Advertising	275	
Utilities	465	
Helper's wages	5,980	
Ed Parr for personal use	12,900	35,190
Cash balance, December 31, 19—		$ 1,365

You ask a number of questions and learn that the shop rents for $200 per month on a five-year lease that calls for the payment of the first and last months' rents in advance. The shop equipment and truck were purchased and paid for on the day the business began. Ed estimates that the shop equipment will have an eight-year life, after which it will be worthless. He thinks he will drive the truck four years, after which he expects to get a $2,000 trade-in allowance on a new truck. There is a $240 invoice for shop supplies delivered yesterday that has not been recorded or paid. An inventory shows $485 of unused shop supplies on hand. The insurance premium pays for one year's protection and was taken out on the day the business began. There are $80 of accrued wages owed the helper, and customers owe the shop $315 for services received.

Mary Knott purchased Vista Trailer Park on October 1 of the current year and has operated it for three months without keeping formal accounting records. However, she has deposited all receipts in the bank and has kept an accurate checkbook record of all payments. An analysis of the receipts and payments follows.

		Receipts	Payments
Investment		$30,000	
Purchased Vista Trailer Park:			
Land	$ 35,500		
Buildings and improvements	80,000		
Office equipment	1,500		
Total	$117,000		
Less mortgage assumed	90,000		
Cash paid			$27,000
Insurance premium paid			960
Office supplies purchased			120
Wages paid			1,890
Utilities paid			265
Property taxes paid			1,540
Personal withdrawals by owner			2,600
Trailer space rentals collected		10,875	
Totals		$40,875	$34,375
Cash balance			6,500
Totals		$40,875	$40,875

Ms. Knott wants you to prepare an accrual basis income statement for the three months she has owned the trailer park and also a December 31 end of the three-month period balance sheet. A few questions on your part reveal the following:

The buildings and improvement were estimated to have 25 years of remaining useful life when purchased, and at the end of that time will have to be wrecked. It is estimated that the sale of salvaged materials will just pay the wrecking costs and the cost of clearing the site. The office equipment is in good condition. When she purchased it, Ms. Knott estimated she would use it for five years and would then trade it in on new equipment of a like nature. She thought $300 was a fair estimate of what she would receive for the old equipment when traded in at the end of the five-year period.

The $960 payment for insurance was for a policy taken out on October 1 and giving protection for two years beginning on that date. Ms. Knott estimates that one fourth of the office supplies have been used. She also says that the one employee earns $30 per day for a five-day week that ends on Friday. The employee was paid on Friday, December 27, and has worked on Monday and Tuesday, December 30 and 31, for which he has not been paid. The property tax payment represents one year's taxes paid on November 15 for a tax year beginning on October 1, the day Ms. Knott purchased the trailer park.

Included in the $10,875 trailer space rentals is $300 received from a tenant who paid his rent for four months in advance beginning on December 1. Also, two tenants have not paid their December rent. The total amount due from both is $150.

The mortgage requires the payment of 10% interest annually on the beginning principal balance and a $4,500 annual payment on the principal.

The Work Sheet and Closing the Accounts of Proprietorships, Partnerships, and Corporations

4
—

After studying Chapter 4, you should be able to:

Explain why a work sheet is prepared and be able to prepare a work sheet for a service-type business.

Explain why it is necessary to close the revenue and expense accounts at the end of each accounting period.

Prepare entries to close the temporary accounts of a service business and prepare a post-closing trial balance to test the accuracy of the end-of-period adjusting and closing procedures.

Explain the nature of the retained earnings item on corporation balance sheets.

Explain why a corporation with a deficit cannot pay a legal dividend.

Prepare entries to close the Income Summary account of a corporation and to record the declaration and payment of a dividend.

List the steps in the accounting cycle in the order in which they are completed.

Define or explain the words and phrases listed in the chapter Glossary.

As an aid in their work, accountants prepare numerous memoranda, analyses, and informal papers that serve as a basis for the formal reports given to the management or to their clients. These analyses and memoranda are called *working papers* and are invaluable tools of the accountant. The work sheet described in this chapter is such a working paper. It is prepared solely for the accountant's use. It is not given to the owner or manager of the business for which it is prepared but is retained by the accountant. Normally, it is prepared with a pencil, which makes changes and corrections easy as its preparation progresses.

WORK SHEET IN THE ACCOUNTING PROCEDURES

In the accounting procedures described in the previous chapter, at the end of an accounting period, as soon as all transactions were recorded, recall that adjusting entries were entered in the journal and posted to the accounts. Then, an adjusted trial balance was prepared and used in making an income statement and balance sheet. For a very small business, these are satisfactory procedures. However, if a company has more than a very few accounts and adjustments, errors in adjusting the accounts and in preparing the statements are less apt to be made if an additional step is inserted in the procedures. The additional step is the preparation of a *work sheet*. A work sheet is a tool of accountants upon which they (1) achieve the effect of adjusting the accounts before entering the adjustments in the accounts, (2) sort the adjusted account balances into columns according to whether the accounts are used in preparing the income statement or balance sheet, and (3) calculate and prove the mathematical accuracy of the net income. Then, after the work sheet is completed, (4) accountants use the work sheet in preparing the income statement and balance sheet and in preparing adjusting and closing entries. (Closing entries are discussed later in this chapter.)

PREPARING A WORK SHEET

The Owen law practice of previous chapters does not have sufficient accounts or adjustments to warrant the preparation of a work sheet. Nevertheless, since its accounts and adjustments are familiar, they are used here to illustrate the procedures involved.

During July, the Owen law practice completed a number of transactions. On July 31, after these transactions were recorded but *before any adjusting entries were prepared and posted,* a trial balance of its ledger appeared as in Illustration 4–1.

Illustration 4–1

```
                    LARRY OWEN, ATTORNEY
                    Trial Balance, July 31, 19—

Cash .........................    $1,185
Prepaid rent ....................     900
Office supplies..................      60
Office equipment ...............    4,000
Accounts payable ..............              $  260
Unearned legal fees.............                 450
Larry Owen, capital ............               5,000
Larry Owen, withdrawals .........     200
Legal fees earned ..............               1,500
Office salaries expense .........     800
Telephone expense ............       30
Heating and lighting expense .....    35
         Totals .................  $7,210    $7,210
```

Notice that the trial balance is an *unadjusted trial balance.* The accounts have not been adjusted for expired rent, supplies consumed, depreciation, and so forth. Nevertheless, this unadjusted trial balance is the starting point in preparing the work sheet for the law practice. The work sheet is shown in Illustration 4–2.

Note that the work sheet has five pairs of money columns and that the first pair is labeled "Trial Balance." In this first pair of columns is copied the unadjusted trial balance of the law practice. Often when a work sheet is prepared, the trial balance is prepared for the first time in its first two money columns.

The second pair of work sheet columns is labeled "Adjustments." The adjustments are entered in these columns. Note they are, with one exception, the same adjustments for which adjusting journal entries were prepared and posted in the previous chapter. The one exception is the last one, *(e),* in which the two adjustments affecting the Legal Fees Earned account are combined into one compound adjustment. They were combined because both result in credits to the same account.

Note that the adjustments on the illustrated work sheet are keyed together with letters. When a work sheet is prepared, after it is completed, the adjusting entries still have to be entered in the journal and posted to the ledger. At that time, the key letters help identify each adjustment's related debits and credits. Explanations of the adjustments on the illustrated work sheet are as follows:

Adjustment (a): To adjust for the rent expired.
Adjustment (b): To adjust for the office supplies consumed.
Adjustment (c): To adjust for depreciation of the office equipment.

Illustration 4-2

LARRY OWEN, ATTORNEY

Work Sheet for Month Ended July 31, 19—

ACCOUNT TITLES	TRIAL BALANCE		ADJUSTMENTS		ADJUSTED TRIAL BALANCE		INCOME STATEMENT		BALANCE SHEET	
	DR.	CR.	DR.	CR.	DR.	CR.	DR.	CR.	DR.	CR.
Cash	1,185 00				1,185 00				1,185 00	
Prepaid rent	900 00			(a) 300 00	600 00				600 00	
Office supplies	60 00			(b) 25 00	35 00				35 00	
Office equipment	4,000 00				4,000 00				4,000 00	
Accounts payable		260 00				260 00				260 00
Unearned legal fees		450 00	(e) 150 00			300 00				300 00
Larry Owen, capital		5,000 00				5,000 00				5,000 00
Larry Owen, withdrawals	200 00				200 00				200 00	
Legal fees earned		1,500 00		(e) 250 00		1,750 00		1,750 00		
Office salaries expense	800 00		(d) 120 00		920 00		920 00			
Telephone expense	30 00				30 00		30 00			
Heating & lighting expense	35 00				35 00		35 00			
	7,210 00	7,210 00								
Rent expense			(a) 300 00		300 00		300 00			
Office supplies expense			(b) 25 00		25 00		25 00			
Depr. expense, office equip.			(c) 40 00		40 00		40 00			
Accum. depr., office equip.				(c) 40 00		40 00				40 00
Salaries payable				(d) 120 00		120 00				120 00
Accounts receivable			(e) 100 00		100 00				100 00	
			735 00	735 00	7,470 00	7,470 00	1,350 00	1,750 00	6,120 00	5,720 00
Net income							400 00			400 00
							1,750 00	1,750 00	6,120 00	6,120 00

Adjustment (d): To adjust for the accrued secretary's salary.
Adjustment (e): To adjust for unearned and accrued revenue.

Each adjustment on the illustrated work sheet required that one or two additional account names be written in below the original trial balance. These accounts did not have balances when the trial balance was prepared. Consequently, they were not listed in the trial balance. Often, when a work sheet is prepared, the effects of the adjustments are anticipated and any additional accounts required are provided without amounts in the body of the trial balance.

When a work sheet is prepared, after the adjustments are entered in the Adjustments columns, the columns are totaled to prove the equality of the adjustments.

The third set of work sheet columns is labeled "Adjusted Trial Balance." In preparing a work sheet, each amount in the Trial Balance columns is combined with its adjustment in the Adjustments columns, if any, and is entered in the Adjusted Trial Balance columns. For example, in Illustration 4–2, the Prepaid Rent account has a $900 debit balance in the Trial Balance columns. This $900 debit is combined with the $300 credit in the Adjustments columns to give Prepaid Rent a $600 debit in the Adjusted Trial Balance columns. Rent Expense has no balance in the Trial Balance columns, but it has a $300 debit in the Adjustment columns. Therefore, no balance combined with a $300 debit gives Rent Expense a $300 debit in the Adjusted Trial Balance columns. Cash, Office Equipment, and several other accounts have trial balance amounts but no adjustments. As a result, their trial balance amounts are carried unchanged into the Adjusted Trial Balance columns. Notice that the result of combining the amounts in the Trial Balance columns with the amounts in the Adjustments columns is an adjusted trial balance in the Adjusted Trial Balance columns.

After the combined amounts are carried to the Adjusted Trial Balance columns, the Adjusted Trial Balance columns are added to prove their equality. Then, the amounts in these columns are sorted to the proper Balance Sheet or Income Statement columns according to the statement on which they will appear. This is an easy task that requires only two decisions: (1) is the item to be sorted a debit or a credit and (2) on which statement does it appear. As to the first decision, an adjusted trial balance debit amount must be sorted to either the Income Statement debit column or the Balance Sheet debit column. Likewise, a credit amount must go into either the Income Statement credit or Balance Sheet credit column. In other words, debits remain debits and credits remain credits in the sorting process. As to the second decision, it is only necessary in the sorting process to remember that revenues and expenses appear on the income statement and assets, liabilities, and owner's equity items go on the balance sheet.

After the amounts are sorted to the proper columns, the columns are totaled. At this point, the difference between the totals of the Income Statement columns is the net income or loss. The difference is the net income or loss because revenues are entered in the credit column and expenses in the debit column. If the credit column total exceeds the debit column total, the difference is a net income. If the debit column total exceeds the credit column total, the difference is a net loss. In the illustrated work sheet, the credit column total exceeds the debit column total, and the result is a $400 net income.

After the net income is determined in the Income Statement columns, it is added to the total of the Balance Sheet credit column. The reason for this is that with the exception of the balance of the capital account, the amounts appearing in the Balance Sheet columns are "end-of-period" amounts. Therefore, it is necessary to add the net income to the Balance Sheet credit column total to make the Balance Sheet columns equal. Also, adding the income to this column has the effect of adding it to the capital account.

Had there been a loss, it would have been necessary to add the loss to the debit column. This is because losses decrease owner's equity, and adding the loss to the debit column has the effect of subtracting it from the capital account.

Balancing the Balance Sheet columns by adding the net income or loss is a proof of the accuracy with which the work sheet was prepared. When the income or loss is added in the Balance Sheet columns and the addition makes these columns equal, it is assumed that no errors were made in preparing the work sheet. However, if the addition does not make the columns equal, it is proof that an error or errors were made. The error or errors may have been either mathematical or an amount may have been sorted to a wrong column.

Although balancing the Balance Sheet columns with the net income or loss is a proof of the accuracy with which a work sheet was prepared, it is not an absolute proof. These columns will balance even when errors have been made if the errors are of a certain type. For example, an expense amount carried into the Balance Sheet debit column or an asset amount carried into the debit column of the income statement section will cause both of these columns to have incorrect totals. Likewise, the net income will be incorrect. However, when such an error is made, the Balance Sheet columns will balance, but with the incorrect amount of income. Therefore, when a work sheet is prepared, care must be exercised in sorting the adjusted trial balance amounts into the correct Income Statement or Balance Sheet columns.

WORK SHEET AND THE FINANCIAL STATEMENTS

As previously stated, the work sheet is a tool of the accountant and is not for management's use or publication. However, as soon as it is completed, the accountant uses it in preparing the income statement and balance sheet that are given to management. To do this, the accountant rearranges the items in the work sheet's Income Statement columns into a formal income statement and rearranges the items in the Balance Sheet columns into a formal balance sheet.

WORK SHEET AND ADJUSTING ENTRIES

Entering the adjustments in the Adjustments columns of a work sheet does not get these adjustments into the ledger accounts. Consequently, after the work sheet and statements are completed, adjusting entries like the ones described in the previous chapter must still be entered in the General Journal and posted. The work sheet makes this easy, however, because its Adjustments columns provide the information for these entries. All that is needed is an entry for each adjustment appearing in the columns.

As for the adjusting entries for the illustrated work sheet, they are the same as the entries in the previous chapter, with the exception of the entry for adjustment *(e)*. Here a compound entry having a $150 debit to Unearned Legal Fees, a $100 debit to Accounts Receivable, and $250 credit to Legal Fees Earned is used.

CLOSING ENTRIES

After the work sheet and statements are completed, in addition to adjusting entries, it is also necessary to prepare and post *closing entries*. Closing entries clear and close the revenue and expense accounts. The accounts are cleared in the sense that their balances are transferred to another account. They are closed in the sense that they have zero balances after closing entries are posted.

WHY CLOSING ENTRIES ARE MADE

The revenue and expense accounts are cleared and closed at the end of each accounting period by transferring their balances to a summary account called *Income Summary*. Their summarized amount, which is the net income or loss, is then transferred in a single proprietorship to the owner's capital account. These transfers are necessary because—

a. Revenues actually increase the owner's equity and expenses decrease it.

b. However, throughout an accounting period these increases and decreases are accumulated in revenue and expense accounts rather than in the owner's capital account.

c. As a result, closing entries are necessary at the end of each accounting period to transfer the net effect of these increases and decreases out of the revenue and expense accounts and on to the owner's capital account.

In addition, closing entries also cause the revenue and expense account to begin each new accounting period with zero balances. This too is necessary because—

a. An income statement reports the revenues and expenses incurred during one accounting period and is prepared from information recorded in the revenue and expense accounts.

b. The revenue and expense accounts are not discarded at the end of each accounting period but are used in recording the revenues and expenses of succeeding periods.

c. Consequently, if at the end of a period the balances of these accounts are to reflect only one period's revenues and expenses, they must begin the period with zero balances.

CLOSING ENTRIES ILLUSTRATED

At the end of July, after its adjusting entries were posted but before its accounts were cleared and closed, the owner's equity accounts of Owen's law practice had the balances shown in Illustration 4–3. (An account's Balance column heading as a rule does not tell the nature of an account's balance. However, in Illustration 4–3 and in the illustrations immediately following, the nature of each account's balance is shown as an aid to the student.)

Observe in Illustration 4–3 that Owen's capital account shows only its $5,000 July 1 balance. This is not the amount of Owen's equity on July 31. Closing entries are required to make this account show the July 31 equity.

Note also the third account in Illustration 4–3, the Income Summary account. This account is used only at the end of the accounting period in summarizing and clearing the revenue and expense accounts.

Closing Revenue Accounts

Before closing entries are posted, revenue accounts have credit balances. Consequently, to clear and close a revenue account, an entry debiting the account and crediting Income Summary is required.

Illustration 4–3

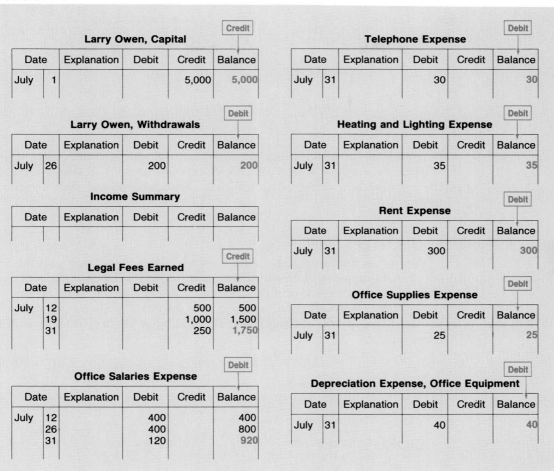

The Owen law practice has only one revenue account, and the entry to close and clear it is:

			Debit	Credit
July	31	Legal Fees Earned	1,750.00	
		Income Summary		1,750.00
		To clear and close the revenue account.		

Posting the entry has this effect on the accounts:

Legal Fees Earned				[Credit]		Income Summary				[Credit]
Date	Explanation	Debit	Credit	Balance		Date	Explanation	Debit	Credit	Balance
July 12			500	500		July 31			1,750	1,750
19			1,000	1,500						
31			250	1,750						
31		1,750		–0–						

Note that the entry clears the revenue account by transferring its balance as a credit to the Income Summary account. It also causes the revenue account to begin the new accounting period with a zero balance.

Closing Expense Accounts

Before closing entries are posted, expense accounts have debit balances. Consequently, to clear and close a concern's expense accounts, a compound entry debiting the Income Summary account and crediting each individual expense account is required. The Owen law practice has six expense accounts, and the compound entry to clear and close them is:

July	31	Income Summary	1,350.00	
		Office Salaries Expense		920.00
		Telephone Expense		30.00
		Heating and Lighting Expense		35.00
		Rent Expense		300.00
		Office Supplies Expense		25.00
		Depreciation Expense, Office Equipment ...		40.00
		To close and clear the expense accounts.		

Posting the entry has the effect shown in Illustration 4–4. Turn to Illustration 4–4 (on the next page) and observe that the entry clears the expense accounts of their balances by transferring the balances in a total as a debit to the Income Summary account. It also causes the expense accounts to begin the new period with zero balances.

Closing the Income Summary Account

After a concern's revenue and expense accounts are cleared and their balances transferred to the Income Summary account, the balance of the Income Summary account is equal to the net income or loss.

Illustration 4–4

Office Salaries Expense

Date		Explanation	Debit	Credit	Balance
July	12		400		400
	26		400		800
	31		120		920
	31			920	–0–

Telephone Expense

Date		Explanation	Debit	Credit	Balance
July	31		30		30
	31			30	–0–

Heating and Lighting Expense

Date		Explanation	Debit	Credit	Balance
July	31		35		35
	31			35	–0–

Income Summary

Date		Explanation	Debit	Credit	Balance
July	31			1,750	1,750
	31		1,350		400

Rent Expense

Date		Explanation	Debit	Credit	Balance
July	31		300		300
	31			300	–0–

$ 920
30
35
300
25
40
$1,350

Office Supplies Expense

Date		Explanation	Debit	Credit	Balance
July	31		25		25
	31			25	–0–

Depreciation Expense, Office Equipment

Date		Explanation	Debit	Credit	Balance
July	31		40		40
	31			40	–0–

When revenues exceed expenses, there is a net income and the Income Summary account has a credit balance. On the other hand, when expenses exceed revenues, there is a loss and the account has a debit balance. But, regardless of the nature of its balance, the Income Summary account is cleared and its balance, the amount of net income or loss, is transferred to the capital account.

The Owen law practice earned $400 during July. Consequently, after its revenue and expense accounts are cleared, its Income Summary account has a $400 credit balance. This balance is transferred to the Larry Owen, Capital account with an entry like this:

July	31	Income Summary	400.00	
		Larry Owen, Capital		400.00
		To clear and close the Income Summary account.		

Posting this entry has the following effect on the accounts:

Income Summary   Credit

Date		Explanation	Debit	Credit	Balance
July	31			1,750	1,750
	31		1,350		400
	31		400		–0–

Larry Owen, Capital   Credit

Date		Explanation	Debit	Credit	Balance
July	1			5,000	5,000
	31			400	5,400

Observe that the entry clears the Income Summary account, transferring its balance, the amount of the net income in this case, to the capital account.

Closing the Withdrawals Account

At the end of an accounting period, the withdrawals account shows the owner's withdrawals. The account is closed, and its debit balance is transferred to the capital account with an entry like this:

July	31	Larry Owen, Capital	200.00	
		Larry Owen, Withdrawals		200.00
		To close and clear the withdrawals account.		

Posting the entry has this effect on the accounts:

	Larry Owen, Withdrawals			Debit			Larry Owen, Capital			Credit
Date	Explanation	Debit	Credit	Balance		Date	Explanation	Debit	Credit	Balance
July 26		200		200		July 1			5,000	5,000
31			200	–0–		31			400	5,400
						31		200		5,200

After the entry closing the withdrawals account is posted, observe that the two reasons for making closing entries are accomplished: (1) All revenue and expense accounts have zero balances. (2) The net effect of the period's revenue, expense, and withdrawal transactions on the owner's equity is shown in the capital account.

Temporary Accounts

Revenue and expense accounts plus the Income Summary and withdrawals accounts are often called *temporary accounts* because in a sense the items recorded in these accounts are only temporarily recorded therein. At the end of each accounting period, through closing entries, their debit and credit effects are transferred out and on to other accounts.

SOURCES OF CLOSING ENTRY INFORMATION

Information for closing entries may be taken from the individual revenue and expense accounts. However, the work sheet provides this information in a more convenient form. Look at the work sheet on page 122. Every account having a balance in its Income Statement debit column has a debit balance in the ledger and must be credited in closing. Compare the amounts in the work sheet's Income Statement debit column with the credits in the compound closing entry on page 128. If the work sheet is used as the information source for the entry, it is not even necessary to add the entry's credits to learn the amount of the debit. The entry's debit to Income Summary is the column total.

The work sheet's Income Statement credit column is a convenient information source for the entry to close the revenue account.

THE ACCOUNTS AFTER CLOSING

At this stage, after both adjusting and closing entries have been posted, the Owen law practice accounts appear as in Illustration 4–5.

Illustration 4–5

Cash — ACCOUNT NO. 111

DATE	EXPLANATION	POST. REF.	DEBIT	CREDIT	BALANCE
198A July 1		G1	5 0 0 0 00		5 0 0 0 00
1		G1		9 0 0 00	4 1 0 0 00
3		G1		3 7 0 0 00	4 0 0 00
12		G1	5 0 0 00		9 0 0 00
12		G1		4 0 0 00	5 0 0 00
15		G1	4 5 0 00		9 5 0 00
26		G2		4 0 0 00	5 5 0 00
26		G2		2 0 0 00	3 5 0 00
29		G2	1 0 0 0 00		1 3 5 0 00
30		G2		1 0 0 00	1 2 5 0 00
31		G2		3 0 00	1 2 2 0 00
31		G2		3 5 00	1 1 8 5 00

Accounts Receivable — ACCOUNT NO. 114

DATE	EXPLANATION	POST. REF.	DEBIT	CREDIT	BALANCE
198A July 19		G2	1 0 0 0 00		1 0 0 0 00
29		G2		1 0 0 0 00	– 0 –
31		G3	1 0 0 00		1 0 0 00

Prepaid Rent — ACCOUNT NO. 115

DATE	EXPLANATION	POST. REF.	DEBIT	CREDIT	BALANCE
198A July 1		G1	9 0 0 00		9 0 0 00
31		G3		3 0 0 00	6 0 0 00

Office Supplies — ACCOUNT NO. 116

DATE	EXPLANATION	POST. REF.	DEBIT	CREDIT	BALANCE
198A July 5		G1	6 0 00		6 0 00
31		G3		2 5 00	3 5 00

Office Equipment — ACCOUNT NO. 131

DATE	EXPLANATION	POST. REF.	DEBIT	CREDIT	BALANCE
198A July 3		G1	3 7 0 0 00		3 7 0 0 00
5		G1	3 0 0 00		4 0 0 0 00

Illustration 4–5 *(continued)*

Accumulated Depreciation, Office Equipment — ACCOUNT NO. 132

DATE	EXPLANATION	POST. REF.	DEBIT	CREDIT	BALANCE
198A July 31		G3		4 0 00	4 0 00

Accounts Payable — ACCOUNT NO. 212

DATE	EXPLANATION	POST. REF.	DEBIT	CREDIT	BALANCE
198A July 5		G1		3 6 0 00	3 6 0 00
30		G2	1 0 0 00		2 6 0 00

Salaries Payable — ACCOUNT NO. 213

DATE	EXPLANATION	POST. REF.	DEBIT	CREDIT	BALANCE
198A July 31		G3		1 2 0 00	1 2 0 00

Unearned Legal Fees — ACCOUNT NO. 214

DATE	EXPLANATION	POST. REF.	DEBIT	CREDIT	BALANCE
198A July 15		G1		4 5 0 00	4 5 0 00
31		G3	1 5 0 00		3 0 0 00

Larry Owen, Capital — ACCOUNT NO. 311

DATE	EXPLANATION	POST. REF.	DEBIT	CREDIT	BALANCE
198A July 1		G1		5 0 0 0 00	5 0 0 0 00
31		G3		4 0 0 00	5 4 0 0 00
31		G3	2 0 0 00		5 2 0 0 00

Larry Owen, Withdrawals — ACCOUNT NO. 312

DATE	EXPLANATION	POST. REF.	DEBIT	CREDIT	BALANCE
198A July 26		G2	2 0 0 00		2 0 0 00
31		G3		2 0 0 00	- 0 -

Illustration 4–5 *(continued)*

Income Summary — ACCOUNT NO. 313

DATE		EXPLANATION	POST. REF.	DEBIT	CREDIT	BALANCE
198A July	31		G3		1 7 5 0 00	1 7 5 0 00
	31		G3	1 3 5 0 00		4 0 0 00
	31		G3	4 0 0 00		- 0 -

Legal Fees Earned — ACCOUNT NO. 411

DATE		EXPLANATION	POST. REF.	DEBIT	CREDIT	BALANCE
198A July	12		G1		5 0 0 00	5 0 0 00
	19		G2		1 0 0 0 00	1 5 0 0 00
	31		G3		2 5 0 00	1 7 5 0 00
	31		G3	1 7 5 0 00		- 0 -

Office Salaries Expense — ACCOUNT NO. 511

DATE		EXPLANATION	POST. REF.	DEBIT	CREDIT	BALANCE
198A July	12		G1	4 0 0 00		4 0 0 00
	26		G2	4 0 0 00		8 0 0 00
	31		G3	1 2 0 00		9 2 0 00
	31		G3		9 2 0 00	- 0 -

Telephone Expense — ACCOUNT NO. 512

DATE		EXPLANATION	POST. REF.	DEBIT	CREDIT	BALANCE
198A July	31		G2	3 0 00		3 0 00
	31		G3		3 0 00	- 0 -

Heating and Lighting Expense — ACCOUNT NO. 513

DATE		EXPLANATION	POST. REF.	DEBIT	CREDIT	BALANCE
198A July	31		G2	3 5 00		3 5 00
	31		G3		3 5 00	- 0 -

Rent Expense — ACCOUNT NO. 514

DATE		EXPLANATION	POST. REF.	DEBIT	CREDIT	BALANCE
198A July	31		G3	3 0 0 00		3 0 0 00
	31		G3		3 0 0 00	- 0 -

Illustration 4–5 *(concluded)*

	Office Supplies Expense				ACCOUNT NO. 516
DATE	EXPLANATION	POST REF	DEBIT	CREDIT	BALANCE
198A July 31		G3	2 5 00		2 5 00
31		G3		2 5 00	- 0 -

	Depreciation Expense, Office Equipment				ACCOUNT NO. 517
DATE	EXPLANATION	POST REF	DEBIT	CREDIT	BALANCE
198A July 31		G3	4 0 00		4 0 00
31		G3		4 0 00	- 0 -

Observe in the illustration that the asset, liability, and the owner's capital accounts show their end-of-period balances. Observe also that the revenue and expense accounts have zero balances and are ready for recording the new accounting period's revenues and expenses.

THE POST-CLOSING TRIAL BALANCE

It is easy to make errors in adjusting and closing the accounts. Consequently, after all adjusting and closing entries are posted, a new trial balance is prepared to retest the equality of the accounts. This new, after-closing trial balance is called a *post-closing trial balance,* and for Owen's law practice appears as in Illustration 4–6.

Illustration 4–6

LARRY OWEN, ATTORNEY
Post-Closing Trial Balance, July 31, 19—

Cash	$1,185	
Accounts receivable	100	
Prepaid rent	600	
Office supplies	35	
Office equipment	4,000	
Accumulated depreciation, office equipment		$ 40
Accounts payable		260
Salaries payable		120
Unearned legal fees		300
Larry Owen, capital		5,200
Totals	$5,920	$5,920

Compare Illustration 4–6 with the accounts having balances in Illustration 4–5. Note that only asset, liability, and the owner's capital accounts have balances in Illustration 4–5. Note also that these are the only accounts that appear on the post-closing trial balance. The revenue and expense accounts have been cleared and have zero balances at this point.

ACCOUNTING FOR PARTNERSHIPS AND CORPORATIONS

Partnership Accounting

Accounting for a partnership is like accounting for a single proprietorship except for transactions directly affecting the partners' capital and withdrawal accounts. For these transactions, there must be a capital account and a withdrawals account for each partner. Also, the Income Summary account is closed with a compound entry that allocates to each partner his or her share of the income or loss.

Corporation Accounting

A corporation's accounting also differs from that of a single proprietorship for transactions affecting the accounts that show the equity of the corporation's stockholders in the assets of the corporation. The differences result because accounting principles require a corporation to distinguish between stockholders' equity resulting from amounts invested in the corporation by its stockholders and stockholders' equity resulting from earnings. This distinction is also important because in most states a corporation cannot pay a legal dividend unless it has stockholders' equity resulting from earnings. In making the distinction, two kinds of stockholder equity accounts are kept: (1) *contributed capital accounts* and (2) *retained earnings accounts*. Amounts invested in a corporation by its stockholders are shown in a contributed capital account such as the Common Stock account. Stockholders' equity resulting from earnings is shown in a retained earnings account.

To demonstrate corporation accounting, assume that five persons secured a charter for a new corporation. Each invested $10,000 in the corporation by buying 1,000 shares of its $10 par value common stock. The corporation's entry to record their investments is:

Jan.	5	Cash	50,000.00	
		Common Stock		50,000.00
		Sold and issued 5,000 shares of $10 par value common stock.		

If during its first year the corporation earned $8,000, the entry to close its Income Summary account is:

Dec.	31	Income Summary	8,000.00	
		Retained Earnings		8,000.00
		To close the Income Summary account.		

If these were the only entries affecting the stockholders' equity during the first year, the corporation's year-end balance sheet will show the equity as follows:

Stockholders' Equity

Common stock, $10 par value, 5,000 shares authorized and outstanding	$50,000	
Retained earnings	8,000	
Total stockholders' equity		$58,000

Since a corporation is a separate legal entity, the names of its stockholders are of little or no interest to a balance sheet reader and are not shown in the equity section. However, in this case, the section does show that the corporation's stockholders have a $58,000 equity in its assets, $50,000 of which resulted from their purchase of the corporation's stock and $8,000 from earnings. As to the equity from earnings, $8,000 more assets flowed into the corporation from revenues than flowed out for expenses. This not only increased the assets but also increased the stockholders' equity in the assets by $8,000.

Many beginning students have difficulty understanding the nature of the retained earnings item in the equity section of a corporation balance sheet. They would perhaps have less difficulty if the item were labeled "Stockholders' equity resulting from earnings." However, the retained earnings caption is common. Therefore, upon seeing it, a student must recognize that it represents nothing more than stockholders' equity resulting from earnings. Furthermore, it does not represent a specific amount of cash or any other asset, since these are shown in the asset section of the balance sheet.

To continue, assume that on January 10 of the corporation's second year its board of directors met and by vote declared a $1 per share dividend payable on February 1 to the January 25 *stockholders of record* (stockholders according to the corporation's records). The entries to record the declaration and payment are as follows:

Jan.	10	Retained Earnings	5,000.00	
		Common Dividend Payable		5,000.00
		Declared a $1 per share dividend.		
Feb.	1	Common Dividend Payable	5,000.00	
		Cash		5,000.00
		Paid the dividend declared on January 10.		

Note in the two entries that the dividend declaration and payment together reduced corporation assets and stockholders' equity just as a withdrawal of cash by the owner of a single proprietorship reduces assets and the owner's equity.

A cash dividend is normally paid by mailing checks to the stockholders. Also, as in this case, three dates are normally involved in a dividend declaration and payment: (1) the *date of declaration,* (2) the *date of record,* and (3) the *date of payment.* Since stockholders may sell their stock to new investors at will, the three dates give new stockholders an opportunity to have their ownership entered in the corporation's records in time to receive the dividend. Otherwise it would go to the old stockholders.

A dividend must be formally voted by a corporation's board of directors. Furthermore, courts have generally held that the board is the final judge of when if at all a dividend should be paid. Consequently, stockholders have no right to a dividend until declared. However, as soon as a cash dividend is declared, it becomes a liability of the corporation, normally a current liability, and must be paid. Furthermore, stockholders have the right to sue and force payment of a cash dividend once it is declared.

If during its second year the corporation of this illustration suffered a $7,000 net loss, the entry to close its Income Summary account is:

Dec.	31	Retained Earnings	7,000.00	
		Income Summary		7,000.00
		To close the Income Summary account.		

Posting the entry has the effect shown on the last line of the following Retained Earnings account.

Retained Earnings

Date		Explanation	Post. Ref.	Debit	Credit	Balance
198A Dec.	31	Net income	G4		8,000.00	8,000.00
198B Jan.	10	Dividend declaration	G5	5,000.00		3,000.00
Dec.	31	Net loss	G9	7,000.00		4,000.00

After the entry was posted, due to the dividend and the net loss, the Retained Earnings account has a $4,000 debit balance. A debit balance in a Retained Earnings account indicates a negative amount of retained earnings, and a corporation with a negative amount of retained earnings is said to have a *deficit*. A deficit may be shown on a corporation's balance sheet as follows:

Stockholders' Equity

Common stock, $10 par value, 5,000 shares authorized and outstanding	$50,000
Deduct retained earnings deficit	(4,000)
Total stockholders' equity	$46,000

In most states, it is illegal for a corporation with a deficit to pay a cash dividend. Such dividends are made illegal because as a separate legal entity a corporation is responsible for its own debts. Consequently, if its creditors are to be paid, they must be paid from the corporation's assets. Therefore, making a dividend illegal when there is a deficit helps prevent a corporation in financial difficulties from paying out all of its assets in dividends and leaving nothing for payment of its creditors.

THE ACCOUNTING CYCLE

Each accounting period in the life of a business is a recurring *accounting cycle*, beginning with transactions recorded in a journal and ending with a post-closing trial balance. All steps in the cycle have now been discussed. A knowledge of accounting requires that each step be understood and its relation to the others seen. The steps in the order of their occurrence are as follows:

1. *Journalizing* . . . . Analyzing and recording transactions in a journal.

2. *Posting* . . . . Copying the debits and credits of journal entries into the ledger accounts.

3. *Preparing a trial balance* . . . Summarizing the ledger accounts and testing the recording accuracy.

4. *Preparing a work sheet* . . . . . Gaining the effects of the adjustments before entering the adjustments in the accounts. Then sorting the account balances into the Balance Sheet and Income Statement columns and finally determining and proving the income or loss.

5. *Preparing the statements* . . . Rearranging the work sheet information into a balance sheet and an income statement.

6. *Adjusting the ledger accounts* . . . . Preparing adjusting journal entries from information in the Adjustments columns of the work sheet and posting the entries in order to bring the account balances up to date.

7. *Closing the temporary accounts* . . . . Preparing and posting entries to close the temporary accounts and transfer the net income or loss to the capital account or accounts in a single proprietorship or partnership and to the Retained Earnings account in a corporation.

8. *Preparing a post-closing trial balance* . . . . Proving the accuracy of the adjusting and closing procedures.

GLOSSARY

Accounting cycle. The accounting steps that recur each accounting period in the life of a business and that begin with the recording of transactions and proceed through posting the recorded amounts, preparing a trial balance, preparing a work sheet, preparing the financial statements, preparing and posting adjusting and closing entries, and preparing a post-closing trial balance.

Closing entries. Entries made to close and clear the revenue and expense accounts and to transfer the amount of the net income or loss to a capital account or accounts or to the Retained Earnings account.

Closing procedures. The preparation and posting of closing entries and the preparation of the post-closing trial balance.

Contributed capital. Stockholders' equity in a corporation resulting among other ways from amounts invested in the corporation by its stockholders.

Date of declaration. Date on which a dividend is declared.

Date of payment. Date for the payment of a dividend.

Date of record. Date on which the stockholders who are to receive a dividend is determined.

Deficit. A negative amount of retained earnings.

Income Summary account. The account used in the closing procedures to summarize the amounts of revenues and expenses, and from which the amount of the net income or loss is transferred to the owner's capital account in a single proprietorship, the partners' capital accounts in a partnership, or the Retained Earnings account in a corporation.

Post-closing trial balance. A trial balance prepared after closing entries are posted.

Stockholders of record. A corporation's stockholders according to its records.

Temporary accounts. The revenue, expense, Income Summary, and withdrawals accounts.

Working papers. The memoranda, analyses, and other informal papers prepared by accountants and used as a basis for the more formal reports given to clients.

Work sheet. A working paper used by an accountant to bring together in an orderly manner the information used in preparing the financial statements and the adjusting and closing entries.

QUESTIONS FOR CLASS DISCUSSION

1. A work sheet is a tool accountants use to accomplish three tasks. What are these tasks?
2. Is it possible to complete the statements and adjust and close the accounts without preparing a work sheet? What is gained by preparing a work sheet?
3. At what stage in the accounting process is a work sheet prepared?
4. From where are the amounts that are entered in the Trial Balance columns of a work sheet obtained?
5. Why are the adjustments in the Adjustments columns of a work sheet keyed together with letters?
6. What is the result of combining the amounts in the Trial Balance columns with the amounts in the Adjustments columns of a work sheet?
7. Why must care be exercised in sorting the items in the Adjusted Trial Balance columns to the proper Income Statement or Balance Sheet columns?
8. In extending the items in the Adjusted Trial Balance columns of a work

sheet, what would be the effect on the net income of extending *(a)* an expense into the Balance Sheet debit column, *(b)* a liability into the Income Statement credit column, and *(c)* a revenue into the Balance Sheet debit column? Would each of these errors be automatically detected on the work sheet? Which would be automatically detected? Why?

9. Why are revenue and expense accounts called temporary accounts?

10. What two purposes are accomplished by recording closing entries?

11. What accounts are affected by closing entries? What accounts are not affected?

12. Explain the difference between adjusting and closing entries.

13. What is the purpose of the Income Summary account?

14. Why is a post-closing trial balance prepared?

15. An accounting student listed the item, "Depreciation expense, building, $1,800," on a post-closing trial balance. What did this indicate?

16. What two kinds of accounts are used in accounting for stockholders' equity in a corporation?

17. Explain how the retained earnings item found on corporation balance sheets arises.

18. What three dates are normally involved in the declaration and payment of a cash dividend?

19. Explain why the payment of a cash dividend by a corporation with a deficit is made illegal.

CLASS EXERCISES

Exercise 4–1

The balances of the following alphabetically arranged accounts appeared in the Adjusted Trial Balance columns of a work sheet. Copy the account numbers in a column on a sheet of note paper and beside each number indicate by letter the income statement or balance sheet column to which the account's balance would be sorted in completing the work sheet. Use the letter *a* to indicate the Income Statement debit column, *b* to indicate the Income Statement credit column, *c* to indicate the Balance Sheet debit column, and *d* to indicate the Balance Sheet credit column.

1. Accounts Payable.
2. Accounts Receivable.
3. Accumulated Depreciation, Repair Equipment.
4. Advertising Expense.
5. Cash.
6. Earl Gage, Capital.
7. Earl Gage, Withdrawals.
8. Prepaid Insurance.
9. Rent Expense.
10. Repair Equipment.
11. Repair Supplies.
12. Revenue from Repairs.
13. Wages Expense.

Exercise 4–2

The following item amounts are from a work sheet's Adjustments columns. From the information prepare adjusting journal entries. Use December 31 of the current year as the date.

	Adjustments	
	Debit	Credit
Prepaid insurance	....	(a) 960
Office supplies	....	(b) 180
Accumulated depreciation, office equipment....	....	(c) 115
Accumulated depreciation, delivery equipment..	....	(d) 2,210
Office salaries expense......................	(e) 40	....
Truck drivers' wages	(e) 255	....
Insurance expense, office equipment	(a) 65	....
Insurance expense, delivery equipment	(a) 895	....
Office supplies expense	(b) 180	....
Depreciation expense, office equipment	(c) 115	....
Depreciation expense, delivery equipment	(d) 2,210	....
Salaries and wages payable	....	(e) 295
Totals	3,760	3,760

Exercise 4–3

Copy the following T-accounts and their end-of-period balances on note paper. Below the copied accounts prepare journal entries to close the accounts. Post the entries to the accounts.

Ted Cook, Capital

	Dec. 31 7,500

Rent Expense

Dec. 31 1,800	

Ted Cook, Withdrawals

Dec. 31 15,600	

Wages Expense

Dec. 31 9,200	

Income Summary

Insurance Expense

Dec. 31 400	

Revenue from Services

	Dec. 31 28,000

Depreciation Expense, Equipment

Dec. 31 300	

Exercise 4–4

The following items appeared in the Income Statement columns of a December 31 work sheet prepared for Carl Dale, an attorney. Under the assumption that Mr. Dale withdrew $18,000 from the law practice during the accounting period of the work sheet, prepare entries to close his revenue, expense, Income Summary, and withdrawals accounts.

	Income Statement	
	Debit	Credit
Legal fees earned		42,000
Office salaries expense	12,000	
Rent expense	3,000	
Insurance expense	500	
Office supplies expense	200	
Depreciation expense, office equipment..	400	
	16,100	42,000
Net income	25,900	
	42,000	42,000

Exercise 4–5   Following is a list of trial balance accounts and their balances from the ledger of Fixit Shop. To save you time, the balances are in one- and two-digit numbers; however, to increase your skill in sorting adjusted trial balance amounts to the proper work sheet columns, the accounts are listed in alphabetical order.

Trial Balance Accounts and Balances

Accounts payable	$ 2	Paul Parry, withdrawals	$ 2
Accounts receivable	4	Prepaid insurance	3
Accumulated depreciation,		Revenue from services	19
shop equipment	3	Shop equipment	10
Advertising expense	1	Shop supplies	4
Cash	5	Unearned revenue	3
Notes payable	2	Utilities expense	2
Paul Parry, capital	10	Wages expense	8

Required:

1. Prepare a work sheet form on ordinary notebook paper and enter the trial balance accounts and amounts on the work sheet in their alphabetical order.
2. Complete the work sheet using the following information:
    a. Estimated depreciation on shop equipment, $2.
    b. Expired insurance, $1.
    c. Unused shop supplies on hand per inventory, $1.
    d. An examination showed that $2 of the amount listed as unearned revenue had been earned by the work sheet date.
    e. Accrued wages payable, $1.

Exercise 4–6   1. On a sheet of note paper open the following T-accounts: Cash, Accounts Receivable, Equipment, Notes Payable, Common Stock, Retained Earnings, Income Summary, Revenue from Services, and Operating Expenses.
2. Record directly in the T-accounts these transactions of a corporation:
    a. Sold and issued $10,000 of common stock for cash.
    b. Purchased $9,000 of equipment for cash.
    c. Sold and delivered $25,000 of services on credit.
    d. Collected $22,000 of accounts receivable.
    e. Paid $20,000 of operating expenses with cash.
    f. Purchased $5,000 of additional equipment, giving $3,000 in cash and a $2,000 promissory note.
    g. Closed the Revenue from Services, Operating Expenses, and Income Summary accounts.
3. Answer these questions:
    a. Does the corporation have retained earnings?
    b. Does it have any cash?
    c. If the corporation has retained earnings, why does it not also have cash?
    d. Can the corporation declare a legal cash dividend?
    e. Can it pay the dividend?
    f. In terms of assets, what does the balance of the Notes Payable account represent?

g. In terms of assets, what does the balance of the Common Stock account represent?

h. In terms of assets, what does the balance of the Retained Earnings account represent?

PROBLEMS

Problem 4–1   Joel Kane, Jerry Neal, and Larry Moss began a business on January 5, 198A, in which each man invested $30,000. During 198A, the business lost $4,500; and during 198B, it earned $33,000. On January 4, 198C, the three men agreed to pay out to themselves $18,000 of the accumulated earnings of the business; and on January 9, the $18,000 was paid out.

Required:

1. Under the assumption that the business is a partnership in which the partners share losses and gains equally, give the entries to record the investments and to close the Income Summary account at the end of 198A and again at the end of 198B. Under the further assumption that the partners shared equally in the $18,000 of earnings paid out, give the entry to record the withdrawals.
2. Under the assumption that the business is organized as a corporation and that each man invested in the corporation by buying 3,000 shares of its $10 par value common stock, give the entries to *(a)* record the investments, *(b)* close the Income Summary account at the end of 198A and again at the end of 198B, and *(c)* to record the declaration and payment of the $2 per share dividend. (Ignore corporation income taxes and assume that the three men are the corporation's board of directors.)

Problem 4–2   The following trial balance was taken from the ledger of Randy's Repair Shop at the end of its annual accounting period:

RANDY'S REPAIR SHOP
Trial Balance, December 31, 19—

Cash	$ 775	
Prepaid insurance	440	
Repair supplies	1,425	
Repair equipment	7,215	
Accumulated depreciation, repair equipment		$ 1,050
Accounts payable		260
Randy Lee, capital		5,535
Randy Lee, withdrawals	12,200	
Revenue from repairs		27,135
Wages expense	9,860	
Rent expense	1,800	
Advertising expense	265	
Totals	$33,980	$33,980

Required:

1. Enter the trial balance on a work sheet and complete the work sheet using the following information:

    a. Expired insurance, $385.

    b. An inventory of repair supplies showed $310 of unused supplies on hand.

    c. Estimated depreciation of repair equipment, $725.

    d. Wages earned by the one employee but unpaid on the trial balance date, $80.

2. Prepare an income statement and a classified balance sheet.
3. Prepare adjusting journal entries and compound closing entries.

Problem 4–3

(Covers two accounting cycles)

On June 2, Jane Ross opened a real estate office she called Hilltop Realty; and during June, she completed these transactions:

June	2	Invested $2,500 in cash and an automobile having a $7,500 fair value in the real estate agency.
	2	Rented furnished office space and paid one month's rent, $350.
	2	Purchased office supplies for cash, $115.
	13	Paid the biweekly salary of the office secretary, $400.
	15	Paid the premium on a one-year insurance policy, $720.
	27	Paid the biweekly salary of the office secretary, $400.
	27	Sold a house and collected a $5,200 commission.
	30	Paid the June telephone bill, $40.
	30	Paid for gas and oil used in the agency car during June, $85.

Required work for June:

1. Open the following accounts: Cash; Prepaid Insurance; Office Supplies; Automobile; Accumulated Depreciation, Automobile; Salaries Payable; Jane Ross, Capital; Jane Ross, Withdrawals; Income Summary; Commissions Earned; Rent Expense; Salaries Expense; Gas, Oil, and Repairs Expense; Telephone Expense; Insurance Expense; Office Supplies Expense; and Depreciation Expense, Automobile.
2. Prepare and post journal entries to record the transactions.
3. Prepare a trial balance in the Trial Balance columns of a work sheet form and complete the work sheet using the following information:

    a. One half of a month's insurance has expired.

    b. An inventory shows $85 of unused office supplies remaining.

    c. Estimated depreciation on the automobile, $100.

    d. Accrued but unpaid salary of the secretary, $40.

4. Prepare a June income statement and a June 30 classified balance sheet.
5. From the work sheet prepare and post adjusting and closing journal entries.
6. Prepare a post-closing trial balance.

During July, the real estate agency completed these transactions:

July	1	Paid the July rent on the office space, $350.
	4	Purchased additional office supplies for cash, $35.
	11	Paid the biweekly salary of the office secretary, $400.
	14	Sold a building lot and collected a $1,200 commission.
	15	Withdrew $1,500 from the business to pay personal expenses.
	25	Paid the biweekly salary of the office secretary, $400.

July 31   Paid for gas and oil used in the agency car during July, $80.
   31   Paid the July telephone bill, $35.

Required work for July:

1. Prepare and post journal entries to record the transactions.
2. Prepare a trial balance in the Trial Balance columns of a work sheet form and complete the work sheet using the following information:
   a. One month's insurance has expired.
   b. An inventory of office supplies shows $95 of unused supplies remaining.
   c. Estimated depreciation on the automobile, $100.
   d. Accrued but unpaid secretary's salary, $160.
3. Prepare a July income statement and a July 31 classified balance sheet.
4. Prepare and post adjusting and closing journal entries.
5. Prepare a post-closing trial balance.

Problem 4–4   The ledger accounts of U-Bowl Alleys showing account balances as of the end of its annual accounting period are reproduced in the booklet of working papers that accompanies this text, and a trial balance of the ledger is reproduced on a work sheet form provided there. The trial balance carries the items that follow.

U-BOWL ALLEYS
Trial Balance, December 31, 19—

Cash	$ 2,175	
Bowling supplies	1,865	
Prepaid insurance	910	
Bowling equipment	50,565	
Accumulated depreciation, bowling equipment		$10,640
Mortgage payable		12,000
Dale Hall, capital		20,285
Dale Hall, withdrawals	18,000	
Bowling revenue		56,500
Wages expense	16,655	
Advertising expense	750	
Equipment repairs expense	450	
Rent expense	4,800	
Utilities expense	2,435	
Taxes expense	220	
Interest expense	600	
Totals	$99,425	$99,425

Required:

1. If the working papers are being used, complete the work sheet provided there for the solution of this problem, using the following information. If the working papers are not being used, enter the trial balance on a work sheet form and complete the work sheet.
   a. Bowling supplies inventory, $350.
   b. Expired insurance, $780.
   c. Estimated depreciation on bowling equipment, $3,875.
   d. Wages earned but unrecorded and unpaid, $325.
   e. The lease contract on the building calls for an annual rental equal to 10% of the annual bowling revenue, with $400 payable each month

on the first day of the month. The $400 was paid each month and debited to the Rent Expense account.

f. Personal property taxes on the bowling equipment amounting to $115 have accrued but are unrecorded and unpaid.

g. The mortgage debt was incurred on September 1, and interest on the debt is at the rate of 10% annually or $100 per month. The mortgage contract calls for payments of $300 interest each three months in advance. Interest payments of $300 each were made on September 1 and December 1. The first payment on the mortage principal is not due until two years after the date on which the debt was incurred.

2. Prepare an income statement and a classified balance sheet.

3. Prepare adjusting and closing entries.

4. Post the adjusting and closing entries and prepare a post-closing trial balance. (If the working papers are not being used, omit this requirement.)

Problem 4–5   The accounts of Rocket Delivery Service showing end-of-annual accounting period balances appear in the booklet of working papers that accompanies this text, and a trial balance of the accounts is reproduced on a work sheet form there. The trial balance accounts show the amounts that follow.

ROCKET DELIVERY SERVICE
Trial Balance, December 31, 19—

Cash	$ 2,450	
Accounts receivable	355	
Prepaid insurance	1,145	
Office supplies	245	
Office equipment	2,460	
Accumulated depreciation, office equipment		$ 470
Delivery equipment	12,790	
Accumulated depreciation, delivery equipment		3,150
Accounts payable		290
Unearned delivery service revenue		450
Randy Small, capital		11,745
Randy Small, withdrawals	15,400	
Delivery service revenue		48,395
Rent expense	1,800	
Telephone expense	295	
Office salaries expense	9,060	
Truck drivers' wages expense	16,320	
Gas, oil, and repairs expense	2,180	
Totals	$64,500	$64,500

Required:

1. If the working papers are being used, complete the work sheet provided there for the solution of this problem, using the information that follows. If the working papers are not being used, enter the trial balance on a work sheet form and complete the work sheet.

   a. Expired insurance, $960.

   b. An inventory shows $100 of unused office supplies.

   c. Estimated depreciation of office equipment, $250; and *(d)* of delivery equipment, $2,350.

e. The delivery service entered into contracts with two stores during November and December to deliver packages for each on a fixed-fee basis. The contract with one store, signed on December 10, provides for a $150 monthly fee, payable on the 10th of each month after service is rendered. On December 31, two thirds of the first month's fee has been earned but is unrecorded. The other store made an advance payment on its contract, which was credited to Unearned Delivery Service Revenue. Of the $450 paid, $175 has been earned by the accounting period end.

f. Unrecorded and unpaid copies of credit card invoices show that the service owes $135 for gas and oil used in its trucks.

g. Office salaries, $50, and truck drivers' wages, $300, have accrued but are unrecorded.

2. Prepare an income statement and a classified balance sheet.
3. Prepare adjusting and closing entries.
4. Post the adjusting and closing entries to the accounts and prepare a post-closing trial balance. (Omit this requirement if the working papers are not being used.)

ALTERNATE PROBLEMS

Problem 4–1A

Fred Post, Lee Wolf, and Jerry Nash began a business on January 7, 198A, in which Fred Post invested $20,000, Lee Wolf invested $20,000, and Jerry Nash invested $40,000. During 198A, the business lost $2,000; and during 198B, it earned $32,000. On January 3, 198C, the three men agreed to pay out to themselves $16,000 of the accumulated earnings of the business; and on January 10, the $16,000 was paid out.

Required:

1. Under the assumption that the business is a partnership in which the partners share losses and gains in the ratio of their investments, give the entries to record the investments and to close the Income Summary account at the end of 198A and again at the end of 198B. Also give the January 10, 198C, entry to record the withdrawals of the partners, under the assumption that Post and Wolf each withdrew $4,000 and Nash withdrew $8,000 of the accumulated earnings.

2. Under the alternate assumption that the business is organized as a corporation and that the men invested in the corporation by buying its $10 par value common stock, with Post and Wolf each buying 2,000 shares and Nash buying 4,000 shares, give the entries *(a)* to record the investments, *(b)* to close the Income Summary account at the end of 198A and again at the end of 198B, and *(c)* to record the declaration and payment of the $2 per share dividend.

Problem 4–2A

A trial balance of the ledger of Jeff's Janitorial Service follows.

JEFF'S JANITORIAL SERVICE
Trial Balance, December 31, 19—

Cash	$ 550	
Accounts receivable	310	
Prepaid insurance	925	
Prepaid garage rent	150	
Cleaning supplies	815	
Cleaning equipment	2,750	
Accumulated depreciation, cleaning equipment ..		$ 1,410
Trucks	12,680	
Accumulated depreciation, trucks		3,790
Accounts payable		110
Unearned janitorial revenue		250
Jeff Hall, capital		9,310
Jeff Hall, withdrawals	12,600	
Janitorial revenue		26,245
Wages expense	8,650	
Garage rent expense	400	
Gas, oil, and repairs expense	1,285	
Totals	$41,115	$41,115

Required:

1. Enter the trial balance on a work sheet form and complete the work sheet using the information that follows.

   a. Expired insurance, $795.

   b. The cleaning service rents garage and equipment storage space. At the beginning of the accounting period, three months' rent was prepaid as shown by the debit balance of the Prepaid Garage Rent account. Rents for the months April through November were paid on the first day of each month and debited to the Garage Rent Expense account. The December rent was unpaid on the trial balance date.

   c. A cleaning supplies inventory shows $145 of unused cleaning supplies.

   d. Estimated depreciation on the cleaning equipment, $320, and *(e)* on the trucks, $1,845.

   f. On December 1, the janitorial service contracted and began to clean the office of Desert Insurance Agency for $125 per month. The insurance agency paid for two months' service in advance, and the amount paid was credited to the Unearned Janitorial Revenue account. The janitorial service also entered into a contract and began cleaning the office of Cactus Realty on December 15. By the month-end, a half month's revenue, $100, had been earned on this contract but is unrecorded.

   g. Wages of the one employee amounting to $115 have accrued but are unrecorded and unpaid.

2. From the work sheet prepare an income statement and a classified balance sheet.

3. Prepare adjusting and closing journal entries for the service.

Problem 4–3A   *(Covers two accounting cycles)*

On June 1 of the current year, Jane Ross began a new business she called Hilltop Realty; and during the month, she completed these transactions:

June 1 Invested $2,000 in cash and an automobile having a $5,000 fair value in the real estate agency.
 1 Rented furnished office space and paid one month's rent, $300.
 1 Paid the premium on a one-year insurance policy, $660.
 3 Purchased office supplies for cash, $100.
 12 Paid the biweekly salary of the office secretary, $350.
 18 Sold a building lot and collected a $1,250 commission.
 26 Paid the biweekly salary of the office secretary, $350.
 30 Paid for gas and oil used in the agency's car, $75.
 30 Paid the monthly telephone bill, $45.

Required work for June:

1. Open the following accounts: Cash, Prepaid Insurance; Office Supplies; Automobile; Accumulated Depreciation, Automobile; Salaries Payable; Jane Ross, Capital; Jane Ross, Withdrawals; Income Summary; Commissions Earned; Rent Expense; Salaries Expense; Gas, Oil, and Repairs Expense; Telephone Expense; Insurance Expense; Office Supplies Expense; and Depreciation Expense, Automobile.
2. Prepare and post journal entries to record the June transactions.
3. Prepare a trial balance in the Trial Balance columns of a work sheet form and complete the work sheet using the following information:
   a. One month's insurance has expired.
   b. An inventory shows $75 of unused office supplies remaining.
   c. Estimated depreciation on the automobile, $90.
   d. Accrued but unpaid salary of the secretary, $70.
4. Prepare a June income statement and a June 30 classified balance sheet.
5. Prepare and post adjusting and closing journal entries.
6. Prepare a post-closing trial balance.

During July, the following transactions were completed by the real estate agency:

July 1 Paid the July rent on the office space, $300.
 3 Sold a house and collected a $4,900 commission.
 3 Withdrew $1,000 from the business to pay personal expenses.
 10 Paid the secretary's biweekly salary, $350.
 14 Purchased additional office supplies for cash, $40.
 24 Paid the biweekly salary of the office secretary, $350.
 31 Paid the July telephone bill, $35.
 31 Paid for gas and oil used in the agency car during July, $70.

Required for July:

1. Prepare and post journal entries to record the July transactions.
2. Prepare a trial balance in the Trial Balance columns of a work sheet form and complete the work sheet using the following information:
   a. One month's insurance has expired.
   b. An inventory shows $95 of unused office supplies remaining.
   c. Estimated depreciation on the automobile, $90.
   d. Accrued but unpaid salary of the secretary, $175.

3. Prepare a July income statement and a July 31 classified balance sheet.
4. Prepare and post adjusting and closing journal entries.
5. Prepare a post-closing trial balance.

Problem 4–4A   The accounts of U-Bowl Alleys showing balances as of the end of its annual accounting period are reproduced in the booklet of working papers that accompanies this text, and a trial balance of its ledger is reproduced on a work sheet from there. The trial balance carries the items that follow.

U-BOWL ALLEYS
Trial Balance, December 31, 19—

Cash	$ 2,175	
Bowling supplies	1,865	
Prepaid insurance	910	
Bowling equipment	50,565	
Accumulated depreciation, bowling equipment		$10,640
Mortgage payable		12,000
Dale Hall, capital		20,285
Dale Hall, withdrawals	18,000	
Bowling revenue		56,500
Wages expense	16,655	
Advertising expense	750	
Equipment repairs expense	450	
Rent expense	4,800	
Utilities expense	2,435	
Taxes expense	220	
Interest expense	600	
Totals	$99,425	$99,425

Required:

1. If the working papers are being used, complete the work sheet provided there for the solution of this problem, using the following information. If the working papers are not being used, enter the trial balance on a work sheet form and complete the work sheet.
    a. Bowling supplies inventory, $280.
    b. Expired insurance, $795.
    c. Estimated depreciation on the bowling equipment, $4,150.
    d. Wages earned but unrecorded and unpaid, $275.
    e. The lease contract on the building calls for an annual rental equal to 9% of the annual bowling revenue, with $400 payable each month on the first day of the month. The $400 was paid each month and debited to the Rent Expense account.
    f. Personal property taxes on the bowling equipment amounting to $210 have accrued but are unrecorded and unpaid.
    g. The mortgage debt was incurred on May 1 of the current year, and interest on the debt is at the rate of 10% annually or $100 per month payable at the end of each quarter. Quarterly interest payments were made on July 31 and October 31. The mortgage contract also calls for annual payments of $1,000 on the anniversary date of the mortgage to reduce the amount of the debt.
2. Prepare an income statement and a classified balance sheet.
3. Prepare adjusting and closing journal entries.

4. Post the adjusting and closing entries and prepare a post-closing trial balance. (Omit this requirement if the working papers are not being used.)

Problem 4–5A   The accounts of Rocket Delivery Service showing end-of-annual accounting period balances appear in the booklet of working papers that accompanies this text, and a trial balance of the accounts is reproduced on a work sheet form there. The trial balance accounts show the amounts that follow.

ROCKET DELIVERY SERVICE
Trial Balance, December 31, 19—

Cash	$ 2,450	
Accounts receivable	355	
Prepaid insurance	1,145	
Office supplies	245	
Office equipment	2,460	
Accumulated depreciation, office equipment		$ 470
Delivery equipment	12,790	
Accumulated depreciation, delivery equipment		3,150
Accounts payable		290
Unearned delivery service revenue		450
Randy Small, capital		11,745
Randy Small, withdrawals	15,400	
Delivery service revenue		48,395
Rent expense	1,800	
Telephone expense	295	
Office salaries expense	9,060	
Truck drivers' wages expense	16,320	
Gas, oil, and repairs expense	2,180	
Totals	$64,500	$64,500

Required:

1. If the working papers are being used, complete the work sheet provided there for the solution of this problem, using the information that follows. If the working papers are not being used, enter the trial balance on a work sheet form and complete the work sheet.
   a. The delivery service entered into contracts with two stores during November and December to deliver packages on a fixed-fee basis for each store. The contract with one store, signed on December 15, provides for a $150 monthly fee, payable on the 15th of each month after service is rendered. On December 31, one half of the first month's fee has been earned but is unrecorded. The other store made an advance payment on its contract, which was credited to Unearned Delivery Service Revenue. Of the $450 paid, $300 has been earned.
   b. Expired insurance, $845.
   c. An inventory of office supplies shows $115 of unused supplies.
   d. Estimated depreciation of office equipment, $235; and (e) of delivery equipment, $2,140.
   f. The December telephone bill arrived in the mail on the last day of the month. Its $45 amount has not been paid or recorded.
   g. Office salaries, $40, and a truck drivers' wages, $160, have accrued but are unrecorded.
2. Prepare an income statement and a classified balance sheet.

3. Prepare adjusting and closing entries.
4. Post the adjusting and closing entries to the accounts and prepare a post-closing trial balance. (Omit this requirement if the working papers are not being used.)

PROVOCATIVE PROBLEMS

Provocative
Problem 4–1,
Jack Eble,
Attorney

During the first year-end closing of the accounts of Jack Eble's law practice, the office secretary and bookkeeper was in an accident and is in the hospital in a coma. Jack is certain the secretary prepared a work sheet, an income statement, and a balance sheet. However, he has only the income statement and cannot find either the work sheet or the balance sheet. He does have a trial balance of the accounts of the practice, and he wants you to prepare adjusting and closing entries from the following trial balance and income statement. He also wants you to prepare a classified balance sheet. He says that the $900 of unearned fees on the trial balance represents a retainer fee paid by Guaranty Bank. The bank retained Jack to do its legal work on October 15, agreeing to pay him $300 per month for his services. Jack says that he also has a contract with Valley Realty to do its legal work on a fixed-fee basis. The contract was signed on December 1 and provides for a $275 monthly

JACK EBLE, ATTORNEY
Trial Balance, December 31, 19—

Cash	$ 1,125	
Legal fees receivable	1,200	
Office supplies	350	
Prepaid insurance	725	
Furniture and equipment.....	6,500	
Accounts payable		$ 150
Unearned legal fees		900
Jack Eble, capital...........		7,500
Jack Eble, withdrawals	24,000	
Legal fees earned		41,900
Rent expense	3,900	
Office salaries expense	12,300	
Telephone expense	350	
Totals	$50,450	$50,450

JACK EBLE, ATTORNEY
Income Statement for Year Ended December 31, 19—

Revenue:		
Legal fees earned		$42,925
Operating expenses:		
Rent expense..............................	$ 3,600	
Office salaries expense	12,480	
Telephone expense.........................	395	
Accrued property taxes expense	130	
Office supplies expense	225	
Insurance expense	595	
Depreciation expense, furniture and equipment..	800	
Total operating expenses		18,225
Net income		$24,700

fee payable at the end of each three months. The fee for December has been earned but is unrecorded. Except for the bank and the realty firm, Jack says he has no other legal work in process.

Provocative Problem 4–2, Pay and Pack Cleaners

During his second year in college, Gary Bean, as the only heir, inherited Pay and Pack Cleaners, a cash and carry dry cleaning business, upon the death of his father. He immediately dropped out of school and took over management of the business. At the time he took over, Gary recognized he knew little about accounting. However, he reasoned that if the business cash increased, the business was doing OK. Therefore, he was pleased as he watched the balance of the concern's cash grow from $2,300 when he took over to $7,810 at the year-end. Furthermore, at the year-end he reasoned that since he had withdrawn $25,000 from the business to buy a new car and to pay personal living expenses, the business had earned $30,510 during the year. He arrived at the $30,510 by adding the $5,510 increase in cash to the $25,000 he had withdrawn from the business. Consequently, he was shocked when he received the following income statement and learned the business had earned less than the amounts withdrawn.

PAY AND PACK CLEANERS
Income Statement for Year Ended, December 31, 19—

Cleaning revenue earned		$66,980
Operating expenses:		
Salaries and wages expense	$32,460	
Cleaning supplies expense	840	
Insurance expense	1,110	
Depreciation expense, cleaning equipment	1,450	
Depreciation expense, building	4,800	
Utilities expense	2,210	
Taxes expense	660	
Total operating expenses		43,530
Net income		$23,450

After mulling the statement over for several days, Gary has asked you to explain how in a year in which the cash increased $5,510 and he had withdrawn $25,000, the business could have earned only $23,450. In examining the accounts of the business, you note that accrued salaries and wages payable at the beginning of the year were $135 but had increased to $415 at the year's end. Also, the balance of the Cleaning Supplies account had decreased $170 between the beginning and the end of the year and the balance of the Prepaid Insurance account had decreased $360. However, except for the changes in these accounts, the change in cash, and the changes in the balances of the accumulated depreciation accounts, there were no other changes in the balances of the concern's asset and liability accounts between the beginning and the end of the year. Back your explanation with a calculation accounting for the increase in cash.

Accounting for a Merchandising Concern

5

After studying Chapter 5, you should be able to:

Explain the nature of each item entering into the calculation of cost of goods sold and be able to calculate cost of goods sold and gross profit from sales.

Prepare a work sheet and the financial statements for a merchandising business using a periodic inventory system and organized as either a corporation or a single proprietorship.

Prepare adjusting and closing entries for a merchandising business organized as either a corporation or a single proprietorship.

Define or explain the words and phrases listed in the chapter Glossary.

The accounting records and reports of the Owen law practice, as described in previous chapters, are those of a service enterprise. Other service enterprises are laundries, taxicab companies, barber and beauty shops, theaters, and golf courses. Each performs a service for a commission or fee, and the net income of each is the difference between fees or commissions earned and operating expenses.

A merchandising company, on the other hand, whether a wholesaler or retailer, earns revenue by selling goods or merchandise. In such a company, a net income results when revenue from sales exceeds the cost of the goods sold plus operating expenses, as illustrated below:

XYZ Store
Condensed Income Statement

Revenue from sales	$100,000
Less cost of goods sold	60,000
Gross profit from sales	$ 40,000
Less operating expenses	25,000
Net income	$ 15,000

The store of the illustrated income statement sold for $100,000 goods that cost $60,000. It thereby earned a $40,000 gross profit from sales. From this it subtracted $25,000 of operating expenses to show a $15,000 net income.

Gross profit from sales, as shown on the illustrated income statement, is the "profit" before operating expenses are deducted. Accounting for the factors that enter into its calculation differentiates the accounting of a merchandising company from that of a service enterprise.

Gross profit from sales is determined by subtracting cost of goods sold from revenue from sales. However, before the subtraction can be made, both revenue from sales and cost of goods sold must be determined.

REVENUE FROM SALES

Revenue from sales consists of gross proceeds from merchandise sales less returns, allowances, and discounts. It may be reported on an income statement as follows:

KONA SALES, INCORPORATED
Income Statement for Year Ended December 31, 198B

Revenue from sales:		
Gross sales		$306,200
Less: Sales returns and allowances	$1,900	
Sales discounts	4,300	6,200
Net sales		$300,000

Gross Sales

The gross sales item on the partial income statement is the total cash and credit sales made by the company during the year. Cash sales were "rung up" on a cash register as each sale was completed. At the end of each day, the register total showed the amount of that day's cash sales, which was recorded with an entry like this:

Nov.	3	Cash	1,205.00	
		Sales		1,205.00
		To record the day's cash sales.		

In addition, an entry like this was used to record credit sales:

Nov.	3	Accounts Receivable	45.00	
		Sales		45.00
		Sold merchandise on credit.		

Sales Returns and Allowances

In most stores, a customer is permitted to return any unsatisfactory merchandise purchased. Or the customer is sometimes allowed to keep the unsatisfactory goods and is given an allowance or an amount off its sales price. Either way, returns and allowances result from dissatisfied customers. Consequently, it is important for management to know the amount of such returns and allowances and their relation to sales. This information is supplied by the Sales Returns and Allowances account when each return or allowance is recorded as follows:

Nov.	4	Sales Returns and Allowances	20.00	
		Accounts Receivable (or Cash)		20.00
		Customer returned unsatisfactory merchandise.		

Sales Discounts

When goods are sold on credit, the terms of payment are always made definite so there will be no misunderstanding as to the amount and time of payment. The *credit terms* normally appear on the invoice or sales ticket and are part of the sales agreement. Exact terms granted usually depend upon the custom of the trade. In some trades, it is customary for invoices to become due and payable 10 days after the end of the month *(EOM)* in which the sale occurred. Invoices in these trades carry terms, "n/10 EOM." In other trades, invoices become due and payable 30 days after the invoice date and carry terms of "n/30." This means that the net amount of the invoice is due 30 days after the invoice date.

When credit periods are long, creditors usually grant discounts, called *cash discounts,* for early payments. This reduces the amount invested in accounts receivable and tends to decrease losses from uncollectible accounts. When discounts for early payment are granted, they are made part of the credit terms and appear on the invoice as, for example, "Terms: 2/10, n/60." Terms of 2/10, n/60 mean that the *credit period* is 60 days but that the debtor may deduct 2% from the invoice amount if payment is made within 10 days after the invoice date. The 10-day period is known as the *discount period.*

Since at the time of a sale it is not known if the customer will pay within the discount period and take advantage of a cash discount, normally sales discounts are not recorded until the customer pays. For example, on November 12, Kona Sales, Incorporated, sold $100 of merchandise to a customer on credit, terms 2/10, n/60, and recorded the sale as follows:

Nov.	12	Accounts Receivable	100.00	
		Sales		100.00
		Sold merchandise, terms 2/10, n/60.		

At the time of the sale, the customer could choose either to receive credit for paying the full $100 by paying $98 any time on or before November 22, or to wait 60 days, until January 11, and pay the full $100. If the customer elected to pay by November 22 and take advantage of the cash discount, Kona Sales, Incorporated, would record the receipt of the $98 as follows:

Nov.	22	Cash	98.00	
		Sales Discounts	2.00	
		Accounts Receivable		100.00
		Received payment for the November 12 sale less the discount.		

Sales discounts are accumulated in the Sales Discounts account until the end of an accounting period. Their total is then deducted from gross sales in determining revenue from sales. This is logical. A sales discount is an "amount off" the regular price of goods that is granted for early payment. As a result, it reduces revenue from sales.

COST OF GOODS SOLD

Automobile dealers and appliance stores make a limited number of sales each day. Consequently, they can easily refer to their records at the time of each sale and record the cost of the car or appliance sold. A drugstore, on the other hand, would find this difficult. For instance, if a drugstore sells a customer a tube of toothpaste, a box of aspirin, and a magazine, it can easily record with a cash register the sale of these items at marked selling prices. However, it would be difficult to maintain records that would enable it to also "look up" and record as "cost of goods sold" the costs of the items sold. As a result, stores such as drug, grocery, and others selling a volume of low-priced items make no effort to record the cost of the goods sold at the time of each sale. Rather, they wait until the end of an accounting period, take a physical inventory, and from the inventory and their accounting records determine at that time the cost of all goods sold during the period.

The end-of-period inventories taken by drug, grocery, or like stores in order to learn the cost of the goods they have sold are called *periodic inventories*. Also, the system used by such stores in accounting for cost of goods sold is known as a *periodic inventory system*. Such a system is described and discussed in this chapter. The system used by a car or appliance dealer to record the cost of each car or appliance sold depends on a *perpetual inventory record* of cars or appliances in stock. As a result, it is known as a *perpetual inventory system of accounting for goods on hand and sold*. It is discussed in Chapter 9.

COST OF GOODS SOLD, PERIODIC INVENTORY SYSTEM

As previously said, a store using a periodic inventory system makes no effort to determine and record the cost of items sold as they are sold. Rather, it waits until the end of an accounting period and determines at one time the cost of all the goods sold during the period. And to do this, it must have information as to (1) the cost of the merchandise it had on hand at the beginning of the period, (2) the cost of the merchandise purchased during the period, and (3) the cost of the unsold goods on hand at the period end. With this information a store can, for example, determine the cost of the goods it sold during a period as follows:

Cost of goods on hand at beginning of period	$ 19,000
Cost of goods purchased during the period	232,000
Goods available for sale during the period	$251,000
Less unsold goods on hand at the period end	21,000
Cost of goods sold during the period	$230,000

The store of the calculation had $19,000 of merchandise at the beginning of the accounting period. During the period, it purchased additional merchandise costing $232,000. Consequently, it had available and could have sold $251,000 of merchandise. However, $21,000 of this merchandise was on hand unsold at the period end. Therefore, the cost of the goods it sold during the period was $230,000.

The information needed in calculating cost of goods sold is accumulated as follows.

Merchandise Inventories

The merchandise on hand at the beginning of an accounting period is called the *beginning inventory* and that on hand at the end is the *ending inventory*. Furthermore, since accounting periods follow one after another, the ending inventory of one period always becomes the beginning inventory of the next.

When a periodic inventory system is in use, the dollar amount of the ending inventory is determined by (1) counting the items on the shelves in the store and in the stockroom, (2) multiplying the count for each kind of goods by its cost, and (3) adding the costs of the different kinds.

After the dollar cost of the ending inventory is determined in this manner, it is subtracted from the cost of the goods available for sale to determine cost of goods sold. Also, by means of a journal entry, the ending inventory amount is posted to an account called Merchandise Inventory. It remains there throughout the succeeding accounting period as a record of the inventory at the end of the period ended and the beginning of the succeeding period.

It should be emphasized at this point that, other than to correct errors, entries are made in the Merchandise Inventory account only at the end of each accounting period. Furthermore, since some goods are soon sold and other goods purchased, the account does not long show the dollar amount of goods on hand. Rather, as soon as goods are sold or purchased, its balance becomes a historical record of the dollar amount of goods that were on hand at the end of the last period and the beginning of the new period.

Cost of Merchandise Purchased

Cost of merchandise purchased is determined by subtracting from purchases any discounts, returns, and allowances and then adding any freight charges on the goods purchased. However, before examining this calculation it is best to see how the amounts involved are accumulated.

Under a periodic inventory system, when merchandise is bought for resale, its cost is debited to an account called Purchases, as follows:

Nov.	5	Purchases	1,000.00	
		Accounts Payable		1,000.00
		Purchased merchandise on credit, invoice dated November 2, terms 2/10, n/30.		

The Purchases account has as its sole purpose the accumulation of the cost of all merchandise bought for resale during an accounting period. The account does not at any time show whether the merchandise is on hand or has been disposed of through sale or other means.

If a credit purchase is subject to a cash discount, payment within the discount period results in a credit to Purchases Discounts, as in the following entry:

Nov.	12	Accounts Payable	1,000.00	
		Purchases Discounts		20.00
		Cash		980.00
		Paid for the purchase of November 5 less the discount.		

When *purchases discounts* are involved, it is important that every invoice on which there is a discount be paid within the discount period, so that no discounts are lost. On the other hand, good cash management requires that no invoice be paid until the last day of its discount period. Consequently, to accomplish these objectives, every invoice must be filed in such a way that it automatically comes to the attention of the person responsible for its payment on the last day of its discount period. A simple way to do this is to provide a file with 31 folders, one for each day in a month. Then, after an invoice is recorded, it is placed in the file folder of the last day of its discount period. For example, if the last day of an invoice's discount period is November 12, it is filed in folder number 12. Then, on November 12, this invoice, together with any other invoices in the same folder, are removed and paid or refiled for payment without a discount on a later date.

Sometimes merchandise received from suppliers is not acceptable and must be returned. Or, if kept, it is kept only because the supplier grants an allowance or reduction in its price. When merchandise is returned, purchasers "get their money back"; but from a managerial point of view more is involved. Buying merchandise, receiving and inspecting it, deciding that the merchandise is unsatisfactory, and returning it is a costly procedure that should be held to a minimum. The first step in holding it to a minimum is to know the amount of returns and allowances. To make this information available, returns and allowances on purchases are commonly recorded in an account called Purchases Returns and Allowances, as follows:

Nov.	14	Accounts Payable	65.00	
		Purchases Returns and Allowances		65.00
		Returned defective merchandise.		

When an invoice is subject to a cash discount and a portion of its goods is returned before the invoice is paid, the discount applies to just the goods kept. For example, if $500 of merchandise is purchased and $100 of the goods are returned before the invoice is paid, any discount applies only to the $400 of goods kept.

Sometimes a manufacturer or wholesaler pays transportation costs on merchandise it sells. The total cost of the goods to the purchaser then is the amount paid the manufacturer or wholesaler. Other times the purchaser must pay transportation costs. When this occurs, such charges are a proper addition to the cost of the goods purchased and may be recorded with a debit to the Purchases account. However, more complete information is obtained if such costs are debited to an account called *Transportation-In,* as follows:

Nov.	24	Transportation-In	22.00	
		Cash		22.00
		Paid express charges on merchandise		
		purchased.		

When transportation charges are involved, it is important that the buyer and seller understand which party is responsible for the charges. Normally, in quoting a price, the seller makes this clear by quoting a price of, say, $400, *FOB* factory. FOB factory means free on board or loaded on board the means of transportation at the factory free of loading charges. The buyer then pays transportation costs from there. Likewise, FOB destination means the seller will pay transportation costs to the destination of the goods.

Sometimes, when terms are FOB factory, the seller will prepay the transportation costs as a service to the buyer. In such a case, if a cash discount is involved, the discount does not apply to the transportation charges.

When a classified income statement is prepared, the balances of the Purchases, Purchases Returns and Allowances, Purchases Discounts, and Transportation-In accounts are combined on it as follows to show the cost of the merchandise purchased during the period:

Purchases		$235,800
Less: Purchases returns and allowances ..	$1,200	
Purchases discounts	4,100	5,300
Net purchases		$230,500
Add transportation-in		1,500
Cost of goods purchased		$232,000

Cost of Goods Sold

The last item in the foregoing calculation is the cost of the merchandise purchased during the accounting period. It is combined with the beginning and ending inventories to arrive at cost of goods sold as follows:

Cost of goods sold:			
Merchandise inventory, January 1, 198B			$19,000
Purchases		$235,800	
Less: Purchases returns and allowances ...	$1,200		
Purchases discounts	4,100	5,300	
Net purchases		$230,500	
Add transportation-in		1,500	
Cost of goods purchased			232,000
Goods available for sale			$251,000
Merchandise inventory, December 31, 198B ..			21,000
Cost of goods sold			$230,000

Inventory Losses

Under a periodic inventory system, the cost of any merchandise lost through shrinkage, spoilage, or shoplifting is automatically included in cost of goods sold. For example, assume a store lost $500 of merchandise to shoplifters during a year. This caused its year-end inventory to be $500 less than it otherwise would have been, since these goods were not available for inclusion in the year-end count. Therefore, since the year-end inventory was $500 smaller because of the loss, the cost of the goods the store sold was $500 greater.

Many stores are troubled with shoplifting. Although under a periodic inventory system such losses are automatically included in cost of goods sold, it is often important to know their extent. Consequently, a way to estimate shoplifting losses is described in Chapter 9.

INCOME STATEMENT OF A MERCHANDISING CONCERN

A classified income statement for a merchandising concern has (1) a revenue section, (2) a cost of goods sold section, and (3) an operating expenses section. The first two sections have been discussed, but note in Illustration 5–1 how they are brought together to show gross profit from sales.

Illustration 5–1

KONA SALES, INCORPORATED
Income Statement for Year Ended December 31, 198B

Revenue from sales:			
Gross Sales			$306,200
Less: Sales returns and allowances		$ 1,900	
Sales discounts		4,300	6,200
Net sales			$300,000
Cost of goods sold:			
Merchandise inventory, January 1, 198B		$ 19,000	
Purchases	$235,800		
Less: Purchases returns and allowances	$1,200		
Purchase discounts	4,100	5,300	
Net purchases		$230,500	
Add transportation-in		1,500	
Cost of goods purchased		232,000	
Goods available for sale		$251,000	
Merchandise inventory, December 31, 198B		21,000	
Cost of goods sold			230,000
Gross profit from sales			$ 70,000
Operating expenses:			
Selling expenses:			
Sales salaries expense		$ 18,500	
Rent expense, selling space		8,100	
Advertising expense		700	
Store supplies expense		400	
Depreciation expense, store equipment		3,000	
Total selling expenses		$ 30,700	
General and administrative expenses:			
Office salaries expense		$ 25,800	
Rent expense, office space		900	
Insurance expense		600	
Office supplies expense		200	
Depreciation expense, office equipment		700	
Total general and administrative expenses		28,200	
Total operating expenses			58,900
Income from operations			$ 11,100
Less income taxes expense			1,700
Net income			$ 9,400

Observe also in Illustration 5–1 how operating expenses are classified as either "Selling expenses" or "General and administrative expenses." *Selling expenses* include expenses of storing and preparing goods for sale, promoting sales, actually making sales, and delivering goods to customers. *General and administrative expenses* include the general office, accounting, personnel, and credit and collection expenses.

Sometimes an expenditure should be divided or prorated part to selling expenses and part to general and administrative expenses. Kona Sales, Incorporated, divided the rent on its store building in this manner, as an examination of Illustration 5–1 will reveal. However, it did not prorate its insurance expense because the amount involved was so small the company felt the extra exactness did not warrant the extra work.

The last item subtracted in Illustration 5–1 is income taxes expense. This income statement was prepared for Kona Sales, Incorporated, a corporation. Of the three kinds of business organizations, corporations alone are subject to the payment of state and federal income taxes. Often on a corporation income statement, as in Illustration 5–1, the operating expenses are subtracted from gross profit from sales to arrive at income from operations, after which income taxes are deducted to arrive at net income.

WORK SHEET OF A MERCHANDISING CONCERN

A concern selling merchandise, like a service-type company, uses a work sheet in bringing together the end-of-period information needed in preparing its income statement, balance sheet, and adjusting and closing entries. Such a work sheet, that of Kona Sales, Incorporated, is shown in Illustration 5–2 on pages 168 and 169.

Illustration 5–2 differs from the work sheet in the previous chapter in several ways, the first of which is that it was prepared for a corporation. This is indicated by the word *Incorporated* in the company name. It is also indicated by the appearance on the work sheet of the Common Stock and Retained Earnings accounts. Note on lines 13 and 14 how the balances of these two accounts are carried and unchanged from the Trial Balance credit column into the Balance Sheet credit column.

Illustration 5–2 also differs in that it does not have any Adjusted Trial Balance columns. The experienced accountant commonly omits these columns from a work sheet in order to reduce the time and effort required in its preparation. He or she enters the adjustments in the Adjustments columns, combines the adjustments with the trial balance amounts, and sorts the combined amounts directly to the proper Income Statement or Balance Sheet columns in a single opera-

Illustration 5-2

KONA SALES, INCORPORATED
Work Sheet for Year Ended December 31, 198B

	ACCOUNT TITLES	TRIAL BALANCE		ADJUSTMENTS		INCOME STATEMENT		BALANCE SHEET	
		DR.	CR.	DR.	CR.	DR.	CR.	DR.	CR.
1	Cash	820000						820000	
2	Accounts receivable	1120000						1120000	
3	Merchandise inventory	1900000				1900000	2100000	2100000	
4	Prepaid insurance	90000			(a)60000			30000	
5	Store supplies	60000			(b)40000			20000	
6	Office supplies	30000			(c)20000			10000	
7	Store equipment	2910000						2910000	
8	Accumulated depreciation, store equipment		250000		(d)300000				550000
9	Office equipment	440000						440000	
10	Accumulated depreciation, office equipment		60000		(e)70000				130000
11	Accounts payable		360000						360000
12	Income taxes payable				(f)10000				10000
13	Common stock		5000000						5000000
14	Retained earnings		460000						460000
15	Sales		30620000				30620000		
16	Sales returns and allowances	190000				190000			
17	Sales discounts	430000				430000			
18	Purchases	23580000				23580000			
19	Purchases returns and allowances		120000				120000		
20	Purchases discounts		410000				410000		
21	Transportation-In	150000				150000			
22	Sales salaries expense	1850000				1850000			

Line	Account Title	Trial Balance Dr	Trial Balance Cr	Adjustments Dr	Adjustments Cr	Income Statement Dr	Income Statement Cr	Balance Sheet Dr	Balance Sheet Cr
23	Rent expense, selling space	810000				810000			
24	Advertising expense	70000				70000			
25	Store supplies expense			(b) 40000		40000			
26	Depreciation expense, store equipment			(d) 300000		300000			
27	Office salaries expense	2580000				2580000			
28	Rent expense, office space	90000				90000			
29	Insurance expense			(a) 60000		60000			
30	Office supplies expense			(c) 20000		20000			
31	Depreciation expense, office equipment			(e) 70000		70000			
32	Income taxes expense	160000		(f) 10000		170000			
33		37280000	37280000	500000	500000	32310000	33250000	7450000	6510000
34	Net income					940000			940000
35						33250000	33250000	7450000	7450000
36									
37									
38									
39									
40									
41									
42									
43									
44									
45									
46									
47									
48									

tion. In other words, the experienced accountant simply omits the adjusted trial balance in preparing a work sheet.

The remaining similarities and differences of Illustration 5–2 are best described column by column.

Account Titles Column

Several accounts that do not have trial balance amounts are listed in the Account Titles column, with each being listed in the order of its appearance on the financial statements. These accounts receive debits and credits in making the adjustments. Entering their names on the work sheet in statement order at the time the work sheet is begun makes later preparation of the statements somewhat easier. If required account names are anticipated and listed without balances, as in Illustration 5–2, but later it is discovered that a name not listed is needed, it may be entered below the trial balance totals as was done in Chapter 4.

Trial Balance Columns

The amounts in the Trial Balance columns of Illustration 5–2 are the unadjusted account balances of Kona Sales, Incorporated, as of the end of its annual accounting period. They were taken from the company's ledger after all transactions were recorded but before any end-of-period adjustments were made.

Note the $19,000 inventory amount appearing in the Trial Balance debit column on line 3. This is the amount of inventory the company had on January 1, at the beginning of the accounting period. The $19,000 was debited to the Merchandise Inventory account at the end of the previous period and remained in the account as its balance throughout the current accounting period.

Adjustments Columns

Of the adjustments appearing on the illustrated work sheet, only the adjustment for income taxes is new. A business organized as a corporation is subject to the payment of state and federal income taxes. As to the federal tax, near the beginning of each year a corporation must estimate the amount of income it expects to earn during the year. It must then pay in advance in installments an estimated tax on this income. The advance payments are debited to the Income Taxes Expense account as each installment is paid. Consequently, a corporation that expects to earn a profit normally reaches the end of the year with a debit balance in its Income Taxes Expense account. However, since the balance is an estimate and usually less than the full amount of the tax, an adjustment like that on lines 12 and 32 normally must be made to reflect the additional tax owed.

COMBINING AND SORTING THE ITEMS.   After all adjustments are entered on a work sheet like that of Illustration 5–2 and totaled, the amounts in the Trial Balance and Adjustments columns are combined and are sorted to the proper Income Statement and Balance Sheet columns. In sorting each item, two decisions are required. (1) Is the amount a debit or a credit and (2) on which statement does it appear? As to the first decision, debit amounts must be sorted to a debit column and credit amounts must go into a credit column. As to the second decision, asset, liability, and stockholders' (owners') equity items go on the balance sheet and are sorted to the Balance Sheet columns. Revenue, cost of goods sold, and expense items go on the income statement and are sorted to the Income Statement columns.

Income Statement Columns

Observe in Illustration 5–2 that revenue, cost of goods sold, and expense items maintain their debit and credit positions when sorted to the Income Statement columns. Note that sales returns and sales discounts in the debit column are in effect subtracted from sales in the credit column when the columns are totaled and the net income is determined.

Look at the beginning inventory amount on line 3. Note that the $19,000 trial balance amount is sorted to the Income Statement debit column. It is put in the Income Statement debit column because it is a debit amount and because it enters into the calculation of cost of goods sold and net income.

ENTERING THE ENDING INVENTORY ON THE WORK SHEET.   Before beginning its work sheet, the company of Illustration 5–2 determined that it had a $21,000 ending inventory. The inventory amount was determined by counting the items of unsold merchandise and multiplying the count of each kind by its cost.

In preparing a work sheet like Illustration 5–2, after all items are sorted to the proper columns, the ending inventory amount is simply inserted or "plugged" into the Income Statement credit column and the Balance Sheet debit column. Observe the $21,000 ending inventory amounts that are "plugged" into these columns on line 3 of the work sheet.

In accounting, when an amount is "plugged" into a column of figures, it is simply put in the column to accomplish an objective. In this case, the ending inventory amount is "plugged" into the Income Statement credit column so that the difference between the two Income Statement columns will equal the net income. It is put in the Balance Sheet debit column because it is the amount of an end-of-period asset that must be added to the other asset amounts in completing the work sheet. (How the ending inventory amount gets into the accounts is explained later.)

COST OF GOODS SOLD ON THE WORK SHEET

The item amounts that enter into the calculation of cost of goods sold are shown in color in the Income Statement columns of Illustration 5–2. The beginning inventory, purchases, and transportation-in amounts appear in the debit column. The amounts of the ending inventory, purchases returns and allowances, and purchases discounts appear in the credit column. Note in the following calculation that the sum of the three debit items minus the sum of the three credit items equals the $230,000 cost of goods sold shown in the income statement of Illustration 5–1.

Beginning inventory	$ 19,000		Ending inventory	$21,000
Purchases	235,800		Purchases returns	1,200
Transportation-in	1,500		Purchases discounts	4,100
Total debits	$256,300		Total credits	$26,300
Less total credits	(26,300)			
Cost of goods sold	$230,000			

Therefore, the net effect of putting the six cost of goods sold amounts in the Income Statement columns is to put the $230,000 of cost of goods sold into the columns.

COMPLETING THE WORK SHEET

After all items are sorted to the proper columns and the ending inventory amount is "plugged" in, a work sheet like Illustration 5–2 is completed by adding the columns and by determining and adding in the net income or loss, as was explained in the previous chapter.

PREPARING THE STATEMENTS

After the work sheet is completed, the items in its Income Statement columns are arranged into a formal income statement. The items in its Balance Sheet columns are then arranged into a formal balance sheet. A classified income statement prepared from information in the Income Statement columns of Illustration 5–2 is shown in Illustration 5–1. The balance sheet appears in Illustration 5–3. Observe that since none of the company's prepaid items are material in amount, they are totaled and shown as a single item on the balance sheet. The $14,000 retained earnings amount on the balance sheet is the sum of the $4,600 of retained earnings appearing on line 14 of the work sheet plus the company's $9,400 net income.

Illustration 5–3

KONA SALES, INCORPORATED
Balance Sheet, December 31, 198B

Assets

Current assets:			
Cash		$ 8,200	
Accounts receivable		11,200	
Merchandise inventory		21,000	
Prepaid expenses		600	
Total current assets			$41,000
Plant and equipment:			
Store equipment	$29,100		
Less accumulated depreciation	5,500	$23,600	
Office equipment	$ 4,400		
Less accumulated depreciation	1,300	3,100	
Total plant and equipment			26,700
Total assets			$67,700

Liabilities

Current liabilities:		
Accounts payable	$ 3,600	
Income taxes payable	100	
Total current liabilities		$ 3,700

Stockholders' Equity

Common stock, $5 par value, 10,000 shares		
authorized and oustanding	$50,000	
Retained earnings	14,000	
Total stockholders' equity		64,000
Total liabilities and stockholders' equity		$67,700

RETAINED EARNINGS STATEMENT

In addition to an income statement and a balance sheet, a third financial statement called a *retained earnings statement* is commonly prepared for a corporation. It reports the changes that have occurred in the corporation's retained earnings during the period and accounts for the difference between the retained earnings reported on balance sheets of successive accounting periods.

The retained earnings statement of Kona Sales, Incorporated, appears in Illustration 5–4. It shows that the company began the year with $8,600 of retained earnings, which is also the amount of retained earnings it reported on its previous year-end balance sheet. Its retained earnings were reduced by the declaration of $4,000 of dividends and increased by the $9,400 net income to the $14,000 reported on its current year-end balance sheet. Information as to the beginning retained earnings and the dividends declared were taken from the company's Retained Earnings account.

Illustration 5–4

KONA SALES, INCORPORATED
Retained Earnings Statement
For Year Ended December 31, 198B

Retained earnings, January 1, 198B	$ 8,600
Add 198B net income	9,400
Total	$18,000
Deduct dividends declared	4,000
Retained earnings, December 31, 198B	$14,000

RETAINED EARNINGS ACCOUNT

Illustration 5–5 shows the Retained Earnings account of Kona Sales, Incorporated. Compare the information in the account with the company's retained earnings statement. The account shows that the company began 198B with $8,600 of retained earnings. It declared and paid a $4,000 dividend in October, and it earned a $9,400 net income. The items are identified in the Explanation column of the account, but they need not be. The $9,400 net income reached the account when the closing entries, which are discussed in the next section were posted.

Illustration 5–5

Retained Earnings					Account No. 312	
Date		Explanation	Post. Ref.	Debit	Credit	Balance
198A Dec.	31	198A net income	G10		8,600	8,600
198B Oct.	15	Dividend declared	G20	4,000		4,600
Dec.	31	198B net income	G23		9,400	14,000

ADJUSTING AND CLOSING ENTRIES

After the work sheet and statements are completed, adjusting and closing entries must be prepared and posted. The entries for Kona Sales, Incorporated, are shown in Illustration 5–6. They differ from

Illustration 5–6

DATE		ACCOUNT TITLES AND EXPLANATION	POST. REF.	DEBIT	CREDIT
198B		Adjusting Entries:			
Dec.	31	Insurance Expense	653	6 0 0 00	
		Prepaid Insurance	115		6 0 0 00
	31	Store Supplies Expense	614	4 0 0 00	
		Store Supplies	116		4 0 0 00
	31	Office Supplies Expense	651	2 0 0 00	
		Office Supplies	117		2 0 0 00
	31	Depreciation Expense, Store Equipment	615	3 0 0 0 00	
		Accumulated Depr., Store Equipment	132		3 0 0 0 00
	31	Depreciation Expense, Office Equipment	655	7 0 0 00	
		Accumulated Depr., Office Equipment	134		7 0 0 00
	31	Income Taxes Expense	711	1 0 0 00	
		Income Taxes Payable	213		1 0 0 00
		Closing Entries:			
	31	Income Summary	313	32 3 1 0 0 00	
		Merchandise Inventory	113		1 9 0 0 0 00
		Sales Returns and Allowances	412		1 9 0 0 00
		Sales Discounts	413		4 3 0 0 00
		Purchases	511		23 5 8 0 0 00
		Transportation-In	514		1 5 0 0 00
		Sales Salaries Expense	611		1 8 5 0 0 00
		Rent Expense, Selling Space	612		8 1 0 0 00
		Advertising Expense	613		7 0 0 00
		Store Supplies Expense	614		4 0 0 00
		Depreciation Expense, Store Equip.	615		3 0 0 0 00
		Office Salaries Expense	651		2 5 8 0 0 00
		Rent Expense, Office Space	652		9 0 0 00
		Insurance Expense	653		6 0 0 00
		Office Supplies Expense	654		2 0 0 00
		Depreciation Expense, Office Equip.	655		7 0 0 00
		Income Taxes Expense	711		1 7 0 0 00
	31	Merchandise Inventory	113	2 1 0 0 0 00	
		Sales	411	30 6 2 0 0 00	
		Purchases Returns and Allowances	512	1 2 0 0 00	
		Purchase Discounts	513	4 1 0 0 00	
		Income Summary	313		33 2 5 0 0 00
	31	Income Summary	313	9 4 0 0 00	
		Retained Earnings	312		9 4 0 0 00

previously illustrated adjusting and closing entries in that an explanation for each entry is not given. Individual explanations may be given, but are unnecessary. The words *Adjusting entries* before the first adjusting entry and *Closing entries* before the first closing entry are sufficient to explain the entries.

As previously explained, the Adjustments columns of its work sheet provide the information needed in preparing a concern's adjusting entries. Each adjustment in the Adjustments columns requires an adjusting entry that is journalized and posted. Compare the adjusting entries in Illustration 5–6 with the adjustments on the work sheet of Illustration 5–2.

When a work sheet like Illustration 5–2 is prepared, its Income Statement columns are a source of the information needed in preparing closing entries. Look at the first closing entry of Illustration 5–6 and the items in the Income Statement debit column of Illustration 5–2. Note that Income Summary is debited for the column total and each account having an amount in the column is credited. This entry removes the $19,000 beginning inventory amount from the Merchandise Inventory account. It also clears and closes all the revenue, cost of goods sold, and expense accounts that have debit balances.

Compare the second closing entry with the items in the Income Statement credit column of Illustration 5–2. Note that each account having an amount in the column is debited and the Income Summary account is credited for the column total. This entry clears and closes the revenue and cost of goods sold accounts having credit balances. It also enters the $21,000 ending inventory amount in the Merchandise Inventory account.

CLOSING ENTRIES AND THE INVENTORIES

There is nothing essentially new about the closing entries of a merchandising company. However, their effect on the Merchandise Inventory account should be understood.

Before its closing entries are posted, the Merchandise Inventory account of Kona Sales, Incorporated, shows in its $19,000 debit balance the amount of the company's beginning-of-period inventory as follows:

	Merchandise Inventory				Account No. 113	
Date	Explanation	Post. Ref.	Debit	Credit	Balance
198A Dec. 31		G10	19,000		19,000

Then when the first closing entry is posted, its $19,000 credit to Merchandise Inventory clears the beginning inventory amount from the inventory account as follows:

Merchandise Inventory					Account No. 113
Date	Explanation	Post. Ref.	Debit	Credit	Balance
198A Dec. 31		G10	19,000		19,000
198B Dec. 31		G23		19,000	–0–

When the second closing entry is posted, its $21,000 debit to Merchandise Inventory puts the amount of the ending inventory into the inventory account, as follows:

Merchandise Inventory					Account No. 113
Date	Explanation	Post. Ref.	Debit	Credit	Balance
198A Dec. 31		G10	19,000		19,000
198B Dec. 31		G23		19,000	–0–
31		G23	21,000		21,000

The $21,000 remains throughout the succeeding year as the debit balance of the inventory account and as a historical record of the amount of inventory at the end of 198B and the beginning of 198C.

OTHER INVENTORY METHODS

There are several ways to handle the inventories in the end-of-period procedures. However, all have the same objectives. They are (1) to remove the beginning inventory amount from the inventory account and to charge (debit) it to Income Summary and (2) to enter the ending inventory amount in the inventory account and credit it to Income Summary. These objectives may be achieved with closing entries as explained in this chapter. Or, for example, adjusting entries to accomplish the same objectives may be used. Either method is satisfactory. However, most accountants prefer to use closing entries because less work is required then when adjusting entries are used.

INCOME STATEMENT FORMS

The income statement in Illustration 5–1 is called a classified income statement because its items are classified into significant groups. It is also a *multiple-step income statement* because cost of goods sold and the expenses are subtracted in steps to arrive at net income. Another income statement form, the *single-step form,* is shown in Illustration 5–7. This form is commonly used for published statements. Also, although it need not be, its information is commonly condensed as shown. Note how cost of goods sold and the expenses are added together in the illustration and are subtracted in "one step" from net sales to arrive at net income, thus the name of the form.

Illustration 5–7

KONA SALES, INCORPORATED
Income Statement for Year Ended December 31, 198B

Revenue from sales		$300,000
Expenses:		
Cost of goods sold	$230,000	
Selling expenses	30,700	
General and administrative expenses . .	28,200	
Income taxes expense	1,700	
Total expenses		290,600
Net income		$ 9,400

COMBINED INCOME AND RETAINED EARNINGS STATEMENT

Many companies combine their income and retained earnings statements into a single statement. Such a statement may be prepared in either single-step or multiple-step form. A single-step statement is shown in Illustration 5–8.

STATEMENT OF CHANGES IN FINANCIAL POSITION

In addition to the retained earnings statement, another very important financial statement commonly prepared for a corporation is the *statement of changes in financial position.* It shows where the concern secured funds and where it applied or used the funds, such as in the purchase of plant assets or the payment of dividends. A discussion of this statement is deferred until Chapter 18, after further discussion of corporation accounting.

Illustration 5–8

KONA SALES, INCORPORATED
Statement of Income and Retained Earnings
For Year Ended December 31, 198B

Revenue from sales		$300,000
Expenses:		
Cost of goods sold	$230,000	
Selling expenses	30,700	
General and administrative expenses	28,200	
Income taxes expense	1,700	
Total expenses		290,600
Net income		$ 9,400
Add retained earnings, January 1, 198B		8,600
Total		$ 18,000
Deduct dividends declared		4,000
Retained earnings, December 31, 198B		$ 14,000

DEBIT AND CREDIT MEMORANDA

Merchandise purchased that does not meet specifications, goods received that were not ordered, goods received short of the amount ordered and billed, and invoice errors are matters for adjustment between the buyer and seller. In some cases, the buyer can make the adjustment, for example, when there is an invoice error. If the buyer makes the adjustment, it must notify the seller of its action. It commonly does this by sending a *debit memorandum* or a *credit memorandum*.

A debit memorandum is a business form on which are spaces for the name and address of the concern to which it is directed and the printed words, "WE DEBIT YOUR ACCOUNT," followed by space for typing in the reason for the debit. A credit memorandum carries the words, "WE CREDIT YOUR ACCOUNT." To illustrate the use of a debit memorandum, assume a buyer discovers an invoice error that reduces the invoice total by $10. For such an error, the buyer notifies the seller with a debit memorandum reading: "WE DEBIT YOUR ACCOUNT to correct a $10 error on your November 17 invoice." A debit memorandum is sent because the correction reduces an account payable of the buyer, and to reduce an account payable requires a debit. In recording the purchase, the buyer normally marks the correction on the invoice and attaches a copy of the debit memorandum to show that the seller was notified. The buyer then debits Purchases and credits Accounts Payable for the corrected amount.

An adjustment, such as merchandise that does not meet specifications, normally requires negotiations between the buyer and the seller. In such a case, the buyer may debit Purchases for the full invoice amount and enter into negotiations with the seller for a return or a price adjustment. If the seller agrees to the return or adjustment, the seller notifies the buyer with a credit memorandum. A credit memorandum is used because the return or adjustment reduces an account receivable on the books of the seller, and to reduce an account receivable requires a credit. Upon receipt of the credit memorandum, the buyer records it by debiting Accounts Payable and crediting Purchases Returns and Allowances, if the purchase was originally recorded at the full invoice price.

From this discussion it can be seen that a debit or a credit memorandum may originate with either party to a transaction. The memorandum gets its name from the action of the originator. If the originator debits, the originator sends a debit memorandum. If the originator credits, a credit memorandum is sent.

TRADE DISCOUNTS

A *trade discount* is a deduction (often as much as 40% or more) from a *list* (or catalog) *price* that is used in determining the actual price of the goods to which it applies. Trade discounts are commonly used by manufacturers and wholesalers to avoid republication of catalogs when selling prices change. If selling prices change, catalog prices can be adjusted by merely issuing a new list of discounts to be applied to the catalog prices. Such discounts are discussed here primarily to distinguish them from the cash discounts described earlier in this chapter.

Trade discounts are not entered in the accounts by either party to a sale. For example, if a manufacturer sells on credit an item listed in its catalog at $100, less a 40% trade discount, it will record the sale as follows:

Dec.	10	Accounts Receivable	60.00	
		Sales		60.00
		Sold merchandise on credit.		

The buyer will also enter the purchase in its records at $60. Also, if a cash discount is involved, it applies only to the amount of the purchase, $60.

GLOSSARY

Cash discount. A deduction from the invoice price of goods allowed if payment is made within a specified period of time.

Credit memorandum. A memorandum sent to notify its recipient that the business sending the memorandum has in its records credited the account of the recipient.

Credit period. The agreed period of time for which credit is granted and at the end of which payment is expected.

Credit terms. The agreed terms upon which credit is granted in the sale of goods or services.

Debit memorandum. A memorandum sent to notify its recipient that the business sending the memorandum has in its records debited the account of the recipient.

Discount period. The period of time in which a cash discount may be taken.

EOM. An abbreviation meaning "end of month."

FOB. The abbreviation for "free on board," which is used to denote that goods purchased are placed on board the means of transportation at a specified geographic point free of any loading and transportation charges to that point.

General and administrative expenses. The general office, accounting, personnel, and credit and collection expenses.

Gross profit from sales. Net sales minus cost of goods sold.

List price. The catalog or other listed price from which a trade discount is deducted in arriving at the invoice price for goods.

Merchandise inventory. The unsold merchandise on hand at a given time.

Multiple-step income statement. An income statement on which cost of goods sold and the expenses are subtracted in steps to arrive at net income.

Periodic inventory system. An inventory system in which periodically, at the end of each accounting period, the cost of the unsold goods on hand is determined by counting units of each product on hand, multiplying the count for each product by its cost, and adding costs of the various products.

Perpetual inventory system. An inventory system in which an individual record is kept for each product of the units on hand at the beginning, the units purchased, the units sold, and the new balance after each purchase or sale.

Purchases discounts. Discounts taken on merchandise purchased for resale.

Retained earnings statement. A statement which reports changes in a corporation's retained earnings that occurred during an accounting period.

Sales discounts. Discounts given on sales of merchandise.

Selling expenses. The expenses of preparing and storing goods for sale, promoting sales, making sales, and if a separate delivery department is not maintained, the expenses of delivering goods to customers.

Single-step income statement. An income statement on which cost of goods sold and the expenses are added together and subtracted in one step from revenue to arrive at net income.

Trade discount. The discount that may be deducted from a catalog list price to determine the invoice price of goods.

Transportation-in. Freight, express, or other transportation costs on merchandise purchased for resale.

QUESTIONS FOR CLASS DISCUSSION

1. What is gross profit from sales?
2. May a concern earn a gross profit on its sales and still suffer a loss? How?
3. Why should a concern be interested in the amount of its sales returns and allowances?
4. Since sales returns and allowances are subtracted from sales on the income statement, why not save the effort of this subtraction by debiting all such returns and allowances directly to the Sales account?
5. What is a cash discount? If terms are 2/10, n/60, what is the length of the credit period? What is the length of the discount period?
6. How and when is cost of goods sold determined in a store using a periodic inventory system?
7. Which of the following are debited to the Purchases account of a grocery store: *(a)* the purchase of a cash register, *(b)* the purchase of a refrigerated display case, *(c)* the purchase of advertising space in a newspaper, and *(d)* the purchase of a case of tomato soup?
8. If a concern may return for full credit all unsatisfactory merchandise purchased, why should it be interested in controlling the amount of its returns?
9. When applied to transportation terms, what do the letters FOB mean? What does FOB destination mean?
10. At the end of an accounting period, which inventory, the beginning inventory or the ending, appears on the trial balance?
11. What is shown on a retained earnings statement? What is the purpose of the statement?
12. How does a single-step income statement differ from a multiple-step income statement?
13. During the year, a company purchased merchandise costing $220,000. What was the company's cost of goods sold if there were *(a)* no beginning or ending inventories? *(b)* a beginning inventory of $28,000 and no ending inventory? *(c)* a $25,000 beginning inventory and a $30,000 ending inventory? and *(d)* no beginning inventory and a $15,000 ending inventory?

14. In counting the merchandise on hand at the end of an accounting period, a clerk failed to count, and consequently omitted from the inventory, all the merchandise on one shelf. If the cost of the merchandise on the shelf was $100, what was the effect of the omission on (a) the balance sheet and (b) the income statement?

15. Suppose that the omission of the $100 from the inventory (Question 14) was not discovered. What would be the effect on the balance sheet and income statement prepared at the end of the next accounting period?

16. Distinguish between cash discounts and trade discounts. Is the amount of a trade discount on merchandise purchased credited to the Purchases Discounts account?

17. When a debit memorandum is issued, who debits, the originator of the memorandum or the company receiving it?

CLASS EXERCISES

Exercise 5–1   Campus Shop purchased merchandise having a $2,000 invoice price, terms 2/10, n/60, from a manufacturer and paid for the items within the discount period. (a) Give without dates the journal entries made by Campus Shop to record the purchase and payment and (b) give without dates the entries made by the manufacturer to record the sale and collection. (c) If Campus Shop borrowed sufficient money at 10% interest on the last day of the discount period to pay the invoice, how much did it save by borrowing to take advantage of the discount?

Exercise 5–2   The following items, with expenses condensed to conserve space, appeared in the Income Statement columns of a work sheet prepared for Pro Shop, Incorporated, as of December 31, 198B, the end of its annual accounting period. From the information prepare a multiple-step 198B income statement for the shop.

	Income statement	
	Debit	Credit
Merchandise inventory	20,000	22,000
Sales		150,000
Sales returns and allowances	500	
Sales discounts	900	
Purchases	90,000	
Purchases returns and allowances		400
Purchases discounts		1,500
Transportation-in	200	
Selling expenses	15,300	
General and administrative expenses . .	22,000	
Income taxes expense	4,300	
	153,200	173,900
Net income	20,700	
	173,900	173,900

Exercise 5–3

Part 1. Prepare entries to close the revenue, cost of goods sold, and expense accounts of Pro Shop, Incorporated, as they appear in Exercise 5–2.

Part 2. Rule a balance column Merchandise Inventory account on note paper, and under the December 31, 198A, date enter the $20,000 beginning inventory of Exercise 5–2 as its balance. Then post the portions of the closing entries that affect the account. Post first the credit that removes the beginning inventory from the account.

Exercise 5–4

Campus Shop, a single proprietorship business owned by Mary Reed, had the items that follow in the Income Statement columns of its December 31, 198B, work sheet. The expenses are condensed to conserve space. From the information given prepare a multiple-step 198B income statement for the shop.

	Income statement	
	Debit	Credit
Merchandise inventory	18,000	20,000
Sales		100,000
Sales returns and allowances	400	
Sales discounts	1,000	
Purchases	60,000	
Purchases returns and allowances		300
Purchases discounts		1,200
Transportation-in	600	
Selling expenses	14,000	
General and administrative expenses . .	6,000	
	100,000	121,500
Net income	21,500	
	121,500	121,500

Exercise 5–5

Part 1. Under the assumption that Mary Reed withdrew $15,000 from the business of Exercise 5–4 for personal living expenses during 198B, prepare entries to close the shop's revenue, cost of goods sold, expense, and withdrawals accounts.

Part 2. Rule a balance column Merchandise Inventory account on note paper and under a December 31, 198A, date enter the $18,000 beginning inventory as its balance. Then post to the account the portions of the closing entries that affect the account. Post first the credit that removes the beginning inventory from the account.

Exercise 5–6

Prepare a work sheet form having no Adjusted Trial Balance columns on note paper and copy the trial balance that follows onto the work sheet. Then complete the work sheet using the information that follows.

a. Ending store supplies inventory, $1.
b. Estimated depreciation of store equipment, $1.
c. Estimated additional income taxes expense, $1.
d. Accrued salaries payable, $2.
e. Ending merchandise inventory, $6.

BETA, INCORPORATED
Trial Balance, December 31, 19—

Cash	$ 2	
Merchandise inventory	5	
Store supplies	4	
Store equipment	11	
Accumulated depreciation, store equipment . .		$ 1
Income taxes payable		—
Salaries payable		—
Common stock, $1 par value		10
Retained earnings		2
Sales		36
Sales returns	1	
Purchases	12	
Purchases discounts		1
Transportation-in	1	
Salaries expense	7	
Rent expense	6	
Store supplies expense	—	—
Depreciation expense, store equipment	—	—
Income taxes expense	1	
Totals	$50	$50

PROBLEMS

Problem 5–1

Western Sales, Incorporated, began the year with $23,450 of retained earnings; and during the year, it declared and paid $12,000 of dividends on its outstanding common stock. At the year-end, the Income Statement columns of its work sheet carried the items that follow.

	Income statement	
	Debit	Credit
Merchandise inventory	31,315	33,110
Sales		347,885
Sales returns and allowances	2,610	
Purchases	242,450	
Purchases returns and allowances		1,095
Purchases discounts		3,535
Transportation-in	3,920	
Sales salaries expense	31,580	
Rent expense, selling space	10,500	
Advertising expense	4,310	
Store supplies expense	665	
Depreciation expense, store equipment . .	3,840	
Office salaries expense	18,815	
Rent expense, office space	1,500	
Telephone expense	645	
Office supplies expense	210	
Insurance expense	1,150	
Depreciation expense, office equipment . .	885	
Income taxes expense	5,450	
	359,845	385,625
Net income	25,780	
	385,625	385,625

Required:

1. Prepare a classified, multiple-step income statement for Western Sales, Incorporated, showing the expenses and the items that enter into cost of goods sold in detail. The company's accounting periods end on December 31.
2. Prepare a retained earnings statement for the company.
3. Also prepare a single-step statement of income and retained earnings with the items condensed as is commonly done in published financial statements.

Problem 5–2

A December 31, 198B, year-end trial balance from the ledger of The Marsh Store, a single proprietorship business, follows.

THE MARSH STORE
Trial Balance, December 31, 198B

Cash	$ 1,235	
Merchandise inventory	17,440	
Store supplies	815	
Office supplies	165	
Prepaid insurance	1,230	
Store equipment	12,125	
Accumulated depreciation, store equipment		$ 2,590
Office equipment	1,585	
Accumulated depreciation, office equipment		355
Accounts payable		2,670
Jerry Marsh, capital		32,065
Jerry Marsh, withdrawals	15,000	
Sales		95,215
Sales returns and allowances	735	
Sales discounts	975	
Purchases	57,150	
Purchases returns and allowances		370
Purchases discounts		940
Transportation-in	650	
Sales salaries expense	12,175	
Rent expense, selling space	5,400	
Advertising expense	285	
Store supplies expense	–0–	
Depreciation expense, store equipment	–0–	
Office salaries expense	6,640	
Rent expense, office space	600	
Office supplies expense	–0–	
Insurance expense	–0–	
Depreciation expense, office equipment	–0–	
Totals	$134,205	$134,205

Required:

1. Copy the trial balance on an eight-column work sheet form and complete the work sheet using the information that follows.
   a. Store supplies inventory, $165.
   b. Office supplies inventory, $60.
   c. Expired insurance, $1,010.
   d. Estimated depreciation of store equipment, $1,435.
   e. Estimated depreciation of office equipment, $190.
   f. Ending merchandise inventory, $16,990.

2. Prepare a multiple-step classified income statement showing expenses and the items entering into cost of goods sold in detail.
3. Prepare compound closing entries for the store.
4. Open a Merchandise Inventory account and enter the beginning inventory as its balance under a December 31, 198A, date. Then post those portions of the closing entries that affect the account. Post first the entry that clears the beginning inventory from the account.

Problem 5–3

(If the working papers that accompany this text are not being used, omit this problem.)

The unfinished work sheet of Novelty Shop Incorporated, is reproduced in the booklet of working papers. All adjustments have been made on the work sheet except for $500 of additional income taxes expense.

Required:

1. Enter the income tax adjustment, sort the items to the proper work sheet columns, plug in the $31,600 ending inventory, and complete the work sheet.
2. Prepare a multiple-step income statement showing the details of cost of goods sold and the expenses. Also prepare a balance sheet and a retained earnings statement. The company began 198B with $15,490 of retained earnings, and it declared and paid $12,000 of dividends during the year.
3. In addition to the foregoing statements, prepare a combined income and retained earnings statement with its items condensed as is common in published statements.
4. Prepare a balance column Merchandise Inventory account and enter the $29,810 beginning inventory under a December 31, 198A, date as its balance. Then prepare closing entries for Novelty Shop, Incorporated, and post those portions of the entries that affect the account. Post first the entry that clears the beginning inventory from the account.

Problem 5–4

Valley Sales, Incorporated, began the current year with $14,980 of retained earnings, declared and paid $10,000 of dividends, and at the year-end the trial balance that follows was taken from its ledger.

Required:

1. Copy the trial balance on an eight-column work sheet form and complete the work sheet using the information that follows.
   a. Store supplies inventory, $145; and office supplies inventory, $110.
   b. Expired insurance, $1,135.
   c. Estimated depreciation of store equipment, $2,890; and of office equipment, $820.
   d. Additional federal income tax expense, $425.
   e. Ending merchandise inventory, $25,810.
2. Prepare a multiple-step classified income statement showing expenses and the items entering into cost of goods sold in detail.
3. Prepare a retained earnings statement.
4. Prepare adjusting entries and compound closing entries.

5. In addition to the foregoing, prepare a single-step combined income and retained earnings statement with the items condensed as is commonly done in published statements.

VALLEY SALES, INCORPORATED
Trial Balance, December 31, 19—

Cash	$ 4,850	
Merchandise inventory	26,615	
Store supplies	895	
Office supplies	290	
Prepaid insurance	1,325	
Store equipment	29,350	
Accumulated depreciation, store equipment		$ 3,330
Office equipment	7,510	
Accumulated depreciation, office equipment		935
Accounts payable		1,940
Income taxes payable		–0–
Common stock, $10 par value		25,000
Retained earnings		4,980
Sales		294,845
Sales returns and allowances	710	
Purchases	197,950	
Purchases discounts		2,830
Transportation-in	2,580	
Sales salaries expense	22,575	
Rent expense, selling space	10,560	
Store supplies expense	–0–	
Depreciation expense, store equipment	–0–	
Office salaries expense	20,410	
Rent expense, office space	1,440	
Office supplies expense	–0–	
Insurance expense	–0–	
Depreciation expense, office equipment	–0–	
Income taxes expense	6,800	
Totals	$333,860	$333,860

Problem 5–5

Redrock Sales, Inc., began the current year with $15,735 of retained earnings, declared and paid $10,000 of dividends, and at the year-end the trial balance that follows was taken from its ledger.

Required:

1. Copy the trial balance on an eight-column work sheet form and complete the work sheet using the following information:
    a. Store supplies inventory, $180; and office supplies inventory, $120.
    b. Expired insurance, $1,130.
    c. Estimated depreciation of store equipment, $2,970; and of office equipment, $720.
    d. Accrued sales salaries payable, $220; and accrued office salaries payable, $120.
    e. Additional federal income taxes expense, $530.
    f. Ending merchandise inventory, $25,350.

2. Prepare a multiple-step classified income statement showing expenses and the items entering into cost of goods sold in detail.
3. Prepare a year-end classified balance sheet with the prepaid expenses combined and a retained earnings statement.
4. Prepare adjusting entries and compound closing entries.
5. In addition to the foregoing, prepare a single-step combined income and retained earnings statement with the items condensed as is commonly done in published statements.

REDROCK SALES, INC.
Trial Balance, December 31, 19—

Cash	$ 4,980	
Accounts receivable	6,235	
Merchandise inventory	24,110	
Store supplies	720	
Office supplies	315	
Prepaid insurance	1,565	
Store equipment	27,385	
Accumulated depreciation, store equipment		$ 3,210
Office equipment	5,825	
Accumulated depreciation, office equipment		845
Accounts payable		1,275
Salaries payable		–0–
Income taxes payable		–0–
Common stock		25,000
Retained earnings		5,735
Sales		318,240
Sales returns and allowances	2,830	
Purchases	221,745	
Purchases returns and allowances		910
Purchases discounts		2,990
Transportation-in	3,135	
Sales salaries expense	23,140	
Rent expense, selling space	10,450	
Store supplies expense	–0–	
Depreciation expense, store equipment	–0–	
Office salaries expense	18,820	
Rent expense, office space	950	
Office supplies expense	–0–	
Insurance expense	–0–	
Depreciation expense, office equipment	–0–	
Income taxes expense	6,000	
Totals	$358,205	$358,205

ALTERNATE PROBLEMS

Problem 5–1A   Hilltop, Incorporated, began the year with $25,580 of retained earnings, and it declared and paid $15,000 of dividends during the year. At the end of the year, the Income Statement columns of its work sheet carried the items that follow.

Required:

1. Prepare a classified, multiple-step income statement for the company, showing expenses and the cost of goods sold items in detail. The company's accounting periods end on December 31.
2. Prepare a retained earnings statement for the company.
3. Also prepare a single-step statement of income and retained earnings with the items condensed as is common on published statements.

	Income statement	
	Debit	*Credit*
Merchandise inventory	23,980	25,115
Sales		320,255
Sales returns and allowances	2,910	
Purchases	223,675	
Purchases returns and allowances		875
Purchases discounts		3,140
Transportation-in	3,270	
Sales salaries expense	27,420	
Rent expense, selling space	9,720	
Advertising expense	3,190	
Store supplies expense	515	
Depreciation expense, store equipment . .	3,240	
Office salaries expense	14,980	
Rent expense, office space	1,080	
Telephone expense	545	
Office supplies expense	215	
Insurance expense	1,020	
Depreciation expense, office equipment . .	730	
Income taxes expense	5,830	
	322,320	349,385
Net income	27,065	
	349,385	349,385

Problem 5–2A   A December 31, 198B, year-end trial balance from the ledger of The Little Store, a single proprietorship business, follows.

Required:

1. Copy the trial balance on an eight-column work sheet form and complete the work sheet using the information that follows.
   a. Ending store supplies inventory, $130.
   b. Ending office supplies inventory, $95.
   c. Expired insurance, $1,210.
   d. Estimated depreciation of store equipment, $1,550.
   e. Estimated depreciation of office equipment, $215.
   f. Ending merchandise inventory, $21,360.
2. Prepare a classified, multiple-step income statement showing the details of cost of goods sold and the expenses.
3. Prepare compound closing entries for the store.

4. Open a Merchandise Inventory account and enter the $19,950 beginning inventory as its balance under a December 31, 198A, date. Then post the portions of the closing entries that affect this account.

THE LITTLE STORE
Trial Balance, December 31, 198B

Cash	$ 1,460	
Merchandise inventory	19,950	
Store supplies	720	
Office supplies	215	
Prepaid insurance	1,445	
Store equipment	14,230	
Accumulated depreciation, store equipment		$ 5,680
Office equipment	1,710	
Accumulated depreciation, office equipment		575
Accounts payable		2,490
Jerry Marsh, capital		31,195
Jerry Marsh, withdrawals	18,000	
Sales		105,645
Sales returns and allowances	815	
Sales discounts	1,130	
Purchases	62,290	
Purchases returns and allowances		540
Purchases discounts		995
Transportation-in	375	
Sales salaries expense	11,210	
Rent expense, selling space	5,000	
Advertising expense	310	
Store supplies expense	–0–	
Depreciation expense, store equipment	–0–	
Office salaries expense	7,260	
Rent expense, office space	1,000	
Office supplies expense	–0–	
Insurance expense	–0–	
Depreciation expense, office equipment	–0–	
Totals	$147,120	$147,120

Problem 5–3A

The Good Store, a single proprietorship business, had the items that follow in the Income Statement columns of its 198B year-end work sheet.

Required:

1. Prepare a classified, multiple-step, 198B income statement for the store showing the expenses and the items entering into cost of goods sold in detail.
2. Under the assumption that Robert Good, the owner of The Good Store, withdrew $18,000 during the year to pay personal expenses, prepare compound closing entries for the store.
3. Open a balance column Merchandise Inventory account and enter the store's $24,115 beginning inventory under a December 31, 198A, date

as its balance. Then post the portions of the closing entries that affect this account.

	Income statement	
	Debit	Credit
Merchandise inventory	24,115	23,880
Sales		314,385
Sales returns and allowances	2,750	
Sales discounts	1,390	
Purchases	221,920	
Purchases returns and allowances		910
Purchases discounts		2,845
Transportation-in	2,965	
Sales salaries expense	26,650	
Rent expense, selling space	9,720	
Advertising expense	2,925	
Store supplies expense	630	
Depreciation expense, store equipment . .	3,110	
Office salaries expense	15,220	
Rent expense, office space	1,080	
Telephone expense	545	
Office supplies expense	185	
Insurance expense	1,340	
Depreciation expense, office equipment . .	675	
	315,220	342,020
Net income	26,800	
	342,020	342,020

Problem 5–4A   Grand Sales, Incorporated, began the current year with $13,075 of retained earnings, declared and paid $8,000 of dividends, and at the year-end the trial balance that follows was taken from its ledger.

Required:

1. Copy the trial balance on an eight-column work sheet form and complete the work sheet using the information that follows.
    a. Ending store supplies inventory, $215; and *(b)* ending office supplies inventory, $115.
    c. Expired insurance, $1,170.
    d. Estimated depreciation of store equipment, $3,150; and *(e)* of office equipment, $940.
    f. Additional federal income tax expense, $595.
    e. Ending merchandise inventory, $30,225.
2. Prepare a multiple-step income statement showing the expenses and cost of goods sold items in detail.
3. Prepare a retained earnings statement.
4. Prepare adjusting and compound closing entries.
5. Also prepare a single-step combined income and retained earnings statement with the items condensed as is common in published statements.

GRAND SALES, INCORPORATED
Trial Balance, December 31, 19—

Cash	$ 5,460	
Merchandise inventory	28,320	
Store supplies	1,195	
Office supplies	340	
Prepaid insurance	1,580	
Store equipment	31,395	
Accumulated depreciation, store equipment		$ 4,220
Office equipment	8,225	
Accumulated depreciation, office equipment		1,350
Accounts payable		2,160
Income taxes payable		–0–
Common stock, $10 par value		30,000
Retained earnings		5,075
Sales		312,115
Sales returns and allowances	845	
Purchases	217,980	
Purchases discounts		2,940
Transportation-in	2,630	
Sales salaries expense	21,940	
Rent expense, selling space	10,300	
Store supplies expense	–0–	
Depreciation expense, store equipment	–0–	
Office salaries expense	20,650	
Rent expense, office space	1,400	
Office supplies expense	–0–	
Insurance expense	–0–	
Depreciation expense, office equipment	–0–	
Income taxes expense	5,600	
Totals	$357,860	$357,860

Problem 5–5A

Cosmos Sales, Inc., began the current year with $26,265 of retained earnings, declared and paid $15,000 of dividends, and at the year-end the trial balance that follows was taken from its ledger.

Required:

1. Copy the trial balance on an eight-column work sheet form and complete the work sheet using the information that follows.
   a. Store supplies inventory, $315; and office supplies inventory, $165.
   b. Expired insurance, $1,470.
   c. Estimated depreciation of store equipment, $3,290; and of office equipment, $860.
   d. Accrued sales salaries payable, $310; and accrued office salaries payable, $170.
   e. Additional income taxes expense, $585.
   f. Ending merchandise inventory, $33,980.
2. Prepare a multiple-step income statement showing the expenses and cost of goods sold items in detail.
3. Prepare a year-end classified balance sheet and a retained earnings statement. Combine the prepaid expenses on the balance sheet.
4. Prepare adjusting and compound closing entries.
5. Also prepare a single-step statement of income and retained earnings with the items condensed as is common in published statements.

COSMOS SALES, INC.
Trial Balance, December 31, 19—

Cash	$ 7,275	
Accounts receivable	17,140	
Merchandise inventory	32,465	
Store supplies	1,530	
Office supplies	425	
Prepaid insurance	1,895	
Store equipment	35,650	
Accumulated depreciation, store equipment		$ 5,930
Office equipment	6,885	
Accumulated depreciation, office equipment		1,210
Accounts payable		1,525
Salaries payable		–0–
Income taxes payable		–0–
Common stock, $1 par value		50,000
Retained earnings		11,265
Sales		365,870
Sales returns and allowances	3,230	
Purchases	255,650	
Purchases returns and allowances		1,195
Purchases discounts		2,950
Transportation-in	3,235	
Sales salaries expense	25,845	
Rent expense, selling space	13,200	
Store supplies expense	–0–	
Depreciation expense, store equipment	–0–	
Office salaries expense	28,320	
Rent expense, office space	1,800	
Office supplies expense	–0–	
Insurance expense	–0–	
Depreciation expense, office equipment	–0–	
Income taxes expense	5,400	
Totals	$439,945	$439,945

PROVOCATIVE PROBLEMS

Provocative
Problem 5–1,
Western Sales

    The accountant delivered the 198B financial statements of Western Sales to the company's owner, Ed Monroe, just before closing time yesterday. Mr. Monroe took the statements home with him last night to examine but was unable to do so because of unexpected guests. This morning he inadvertently left the 198B income statement at home when he came to work. However, he has the company's 198A and 198B balance sheets which show the following in condensed form:

	December 31	
	198A	*198B*
Cash	$ 4,600	$ 6,800
Accounts receivable	6,300	5,900
Merchandise inventory	20,800	22,400
Equipment (net after depreciation)	12,400	10,800
Total assets	$44,100	$45,900

	December 31	
	198A	198B
Accounts payable (all for merchandise) ..	$ 8,100	$ 9,400
Accrued wages payable	200	400
Ed Monroe, capital	35,800	36,100
Total liabilities and owner's equity	$44,100	$45,900

He also has the company's 198B record of cash receipts and disbursements which shows:

Collection of accounts receivable $170,200

Payments for:

Accounts payable	$102,000
Wages of employees	20,400
Other operating expenses	21,600
Ed Monroe, withdrawals	24,000

Under the assumption that Western Sales makes all purchases and sales of merchandise on credit, prepare a 198B accrual basis income statement for the company based on the information given.

Provocative Problem 5–2, Colors Unlimited

Bill Nash and Harry Marsh were partners in the operation of a paint store. They disagreed, closed the store, and ended their partnership. In settlement for his partnership interest, Bill Nash received an inventory of paint having a $12,000 cost. Since there was nothing he could do with the paint, except to open a new paint store, he began such a business, called Colors Unlimited, by investing the paint and $10,000 in cash. He used $8,000 of the cash to buy store equipment, and he opened the store for business on May 1. During the succeeding eight months, he paid out $44,400 to creditors for merchandise and $16,000 in operating expenses. He also withdrew $10,000 to pay personal expenses; and at the year-end, he prepared the following balance sheet:

COLORS UNLIMITED
Balance Sheet, December 31, 19—

Cash		$ 3,000	Accounts payable (all	
Merchandise			for merchandise)	$ 2,100
inventory		14,500	Bill Nash, capital	22,800
Store equipment	$8,000			
Less depreciation ..	600	7,400	Total liabilities and	
Total assets		$24,900	owner's equity	$24,900

Based on the information given, prepare an income statement showing the results of the first eight months' operations. Support your statement with schedules showing your calculations of net income, cost of goods sold, and sales.

Accounting Systems

After studying Chapter 6, you should be able to:

Explain how columnar journals save posting labor.

Tell the kind of transaction recorded in each columnar journal described.

Explain how a controlling account and its subsidiary ledger operate and give the rule for posting to a subsidiary ledger and its controlling account.

Record transactions in and post from the columnar journals described.

Tell how the accuracy of the account balances in the Accounts Receivable and Accounts Payable Ledgers is proved and be able to make such a proof.

Describe how data is processed in a large business.

Define or explain the words and phrases listed in the chapter Glossary.

An *accounting system* consists of the business papers, records, and reports plus the procedures that are used in recording transactions and reporting their effects. Operation of an accounting system begins with the preparation of a business paper, such as an invoice or check, and includes the capture of the data entered on this paper and its flow through the recording, classifying, summarizing, and reporting steps of the system. Actually, an accounting system is a data processing system, and it is now time to introduce more efficient ways of processing data.

REDUCING WRITING AND POSTING LABOR

The General Journal used thus far is a flexible journal in which it is possible to record any transaction. However, each debit and credit entered in such a journal must be individually posted. Consequently, using a General Journal to record all the transactions of a business results in too much writing and too much labor in posting the individual debits and credits.

One way to reduce the writing and the posting labor is to divide the transactions of a business into groups of like transactions and to provide a separate *special journal* for recording the transactions in each group. For example, if the transactions of a merchandising business are examined, the majority fall into four groups. They are sales on credit, purchases on credit, cash receipts, and cash disbursements. If a special journal is provided for each group, the journals are:

1. A Sales Journal for recording credit sales.
2. A Purchases Journal for recording credit purchases.
3. A Cash Receipts Journal for recording cash receipts.
4. A Cash Disbursements Journal for recording cash payments.

In addition, a General Journal must be provided for the few miscellaneous transactions that cannot be recorded in the special journals and also for adjusting, closing, and correcting entries.

Special journals require less writing in recording transactions than does a General Journal, as the following illustrations will show. In addition, they save posting labor by providing special columns for accumulating the debits and credits of like transactions. The amounts entered in the special columns are then posted as column totals rather than as individual amounts. For example, if credit sales for, say, a month, are recorded in a Sales Journal like the one at the top of Illustration 6–1, posting labor is saved by waiting until the end of the month, totaling the sales recorded in the journal, and debiting Accounts Receivable and crediting Sales for the total.

Only seven sales are recorded in the illustrated journal. However,

Illustration 6–1

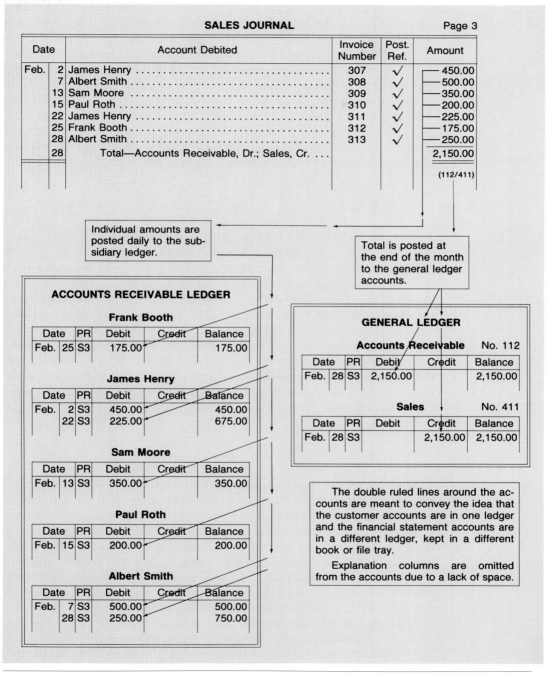

SALES JOURNAL   Page 3

Date	Account Debited	Invoice Number	Post. Ref.	Amount
Feb. 2	James Henry	307	✓	450.00
7	Albert Smith	308	✓	500.00
13	Sam Moore	309	✓	350.00
15	Paul Roth	310	✓	200.00
22	James Henry	311	✓	225.00
25	Frank Booth	312	✓	175.00
28	Albert Smith	313	✓	250.00
28	Total—Accounts Receivable, Dr.; Sales, Cr. ...			2,150.00

(112/411)

Individual amounts are posted daily to the subsidiary ledger.

Total is posted at the end of the month to the general ledger accounts.

ACCOUNTS RECEIVABLE LEDGER

Frank Booth

Date	PR	Debit	Credit	Balance
Feb. 25	S3	175.00		175.00

James Henry

Date	PR	Debit	Credit	Balance
Feb. 2	S3	450.00		450.00
22	S3	225.00		675.00

Sam Moore

Date	PR	Debit	Credit	Balance
Feb. 13	S3	350.00		350.00

Paul Roth

Date	PR	Debit	Credit	Balance
Feb. 15	S3	200.00		200.00

Albert Smith

Date	PR	Debit	Credit	Balance
Feb. 7	S3	500.00		500.00
28	S3	250.00		750.00

GENERAL LEDGER

Accounts Receivable   No. 112

Date	PR	Debit	Credit	Balance
Feb. 28	S3	2,150.00		2,150.00

Sales   No. 411

Date	PR	Debit	Credit	Balance
Feb. 28	S3		2,150.00	2,150.00

The double ruled lines around the accounts are meant to convey the idea that the customer accounts are in one ledger and the financial statement accounts are in a different ledger, kept in a different book or file tray.

Explanation columns are omitted from the accounts due to a lack of space.

if the seven sales are assumed to represent 700 sales, a better appreciation is gained of the posting labor saved by the one debit to Accounts Receivable and the one credit to Sales, rather than 700 debits and 700 credits.

The special journal of Illustration 6–1 is also called a *columnar journal* because it has columns for recording the date, the customer's name, invoice number, and the amount of each charge sale. Only charge sales can be recorded in it, and they are recorded daily with the information about each sale being placed on a separate line. Normally, the information is taken from a copy of the sales ticket or invoice prepared at the time of the sale. However, before discussing the journal further, the subject of *subsidiary ledgers* must be introduced.

SUBSIDIARY LEDGERS

The Accounts Receivable account used thus far does not readily tell how much each customer bought and paid for or how much each customer owes. As a result, a business selling on credit must maintain additional accounts receivable, one for each customer, to provide this information. These individual customer accounts are in addition to the Accounts Receivable account used thus far. They are normally kept in a book or file tray, called a *subsidiary ledger,* that is separate and distinct from the book or tray containing the financial statement accounts. Also, to distinguish the two, the book or tray containing the customer accounts is called the *Accounts Receivable Ledger,* while the one containing the financial statement accounts is known as the *General Ledger.*

POSTING THE SALES JOURNAL

When customer accounts are placed in a subsidiary ledger, a Sales Journal is posted as in Illustration 6–1. The individual sales recorded in the Sales Journal are posted each day to the proper customer accounts in the Accounts Receivable Ledger. These daily postings keep the customer accounts up to date. This is important in granting credit because the person responsible for granting credit should know in each case the amount currently owed by the credit-seeking customer. The source of this information is the customer's account. If the account is not up to date, an incorrect decision may be made.

Note the check marks in the Sales Journal's Posting Reference column. They indicate that the sales recorded in the journal were individually posted to the customer accounts in the Accounts Receivable

Ledger. Check marks rather than account numbers are used because customer accounts commonly are not numbered. Rather, as an aid in locating individual accounts, they are alphabetically arranged in the Accounts Receivable Ledger, with new accounts being added in their proper alphabetical positions as required. Consequently, numbering the accounts is impractical, since many numbers would have to be changed each time new accounts are added.

In addition to the daily postings to customer accounts, at the end of the month, the Sales Journal's Amount column is totaled and the total is debited to Accounts Receivable and credited to Sales. The credit records the month's revenue from charge sales. The debit records the resulting increase in accounts receivable.

Before going on, note again in Illustration 6–1 that the individual customer accounts in the subsidiary Accounts Receivable Ledger do not replace the Accounts Receivable account described in previous chapters but are in addition to it. The Accounts Receivable account of previous chapters must still be maintained in the General Ledger where it serves three functions: (1) It shows the total amount owed by all customers. (2) It helps keep the General Ledger a balancing ledger in which debits equal credits. (3) It offers a proof of the accuracy of the customer accounts in the subsidiary Accounts Receivable Ledger.

IDENTIFYING POSTED AMOUNTS

When several journals are posted to ledger accounts, it is necessary to indicate in the Posting Reference column before each posted amount the journal as well as the page number of the journal from which the amount was posted. The journal is indicated by using its initial. Thus, items posted from the Cash Disbursements Journal carry the initial "D" before their journal page numbers in the Posting Reference columns. Likewise, items from the Cash Receipts Journal carry the letter "R." Those from the Sales Journal carry the initial "S." Items from the Purchases Journal carry the initial "P," and from the General Journal, the letter "G."

CONTROLLING ACCOUNTS

When a company maintains an Accounts Receivable account in its General Ledger and puts its customer accounts in a subsidiary ledger, the Accounts Receivable account is said to control the subsidiary ledger and is called a *controlling account.* The extent of the control is that after all posting is completed, if no errors were made, the sum of the customer account balances in the subsidiary ledger will equal the balance of the controlling account in the General Ledger. This equality is also a proof of the total of the customer account balances.

CASH RECEIPTS JOURNAL

A Cash Receipts Journal designed to save labor through posting column totals must be a multicolumn journal. A multicolumn journal is necessary because cash receipts differ as to sources and, consequently, as to the accounts credited when cash is received from different sources. For example, if the cash receipts of a store are classified as to sources, they normally fall into three groups: (1) cash from charge customers in payment of their accounts, (2) cash from cash sales, and (3) cash from miscellaneous sources. Note in Illustration 6–2 (on the next page) how a special column is provided for the credits resulting when cash is received from each of these sources.

Cash from Charge Customers

When a Cash Receipts Journal like Illustration 6–2 is used in recording cash received from a customer in payment of the customer's account, the customer's name is entered in the journal's Account Credited column. The amount credited to the customer's account is entered in the Accounts Receivable Credit column, and the debits to Sales Discounts and Cash are entered in the journal's last two columns.

Give close attention to the Accounts Receivable credit column. Observe that (1) only credits to customer accounts are entered in this column. (2) The individual credits are posted daily to the customer accounts in the subsidiary Accounts Receivable Ledger. (3) The column total is posted at the month-end to the credit of the Accounts Receivable controlling account. This is the normal recording and posting procedure when controlling accounts and subsidiary ledgers are used. When such accounts and ledgers are used, transactions are normally entered in a journal column. The individual amounts are then posted to the subsidiary ledger accounts, and the column total is posted to the controlling account.

Cash Sales

Cash sales are commonly "rung up" each day on one or more cash registers, and their total is recorded each day with an entry having a debit to Cash and a credit to Sales. When such sales are recorded in a Cash Receipts Journal like that of Illustration 6–2, the debits to Cash are entered in the Cash debit column and a special column headed

Illustration 6–2

CASH RECEIPTS JOURNAL   Page 2

Date	Account Credited	Explanation	Post. Ref.	Other Accounts Credit	Accts. Rec. Credit	Sales Credit	Sales Dis. Debit	Cash Debit
Feb. 7	Sales	Cash sales	✓			4,450.00		4,450.00
12	James Henry	Invoice, 2/2	✓		450.00		9.00	441.00
14	Sales	Cash sales	✓			3,925.00		3,925.00
17	Albert Smith	Invoice, 2/7	✓		500.00		10.00	490.00
20	Notes Payable ..	Note to bank ...	211	1,000.00				1,000.00
21	Sales	Cash sales	✓			4,700.00		4,700.00
23	Sam Moore	Invoice, 2/13 ...	✓		350.00		7.00	343.00
25	Paul Roth	Invoice, 2/15 ...	✓		200.00		4.00	196.00
28	Sales	Cash sales	✓			4,225.00		4,225.00
28	Totals	....		1,000.00	1,500.00	17,300.00	30.00	19,770.00
				(√)	(112)	(411)	(413)	(111)

Individual amounts in the Other Accounts credit and Accounts Receivable credit columns are posted daily.

Total is not posted.

Totals posted at the end of the month.

ACCOUNTS RECEIVABLE LEDGER

Frank Booth

Date	PR	Debit	Credit	Balance
Feb. 25	S3	175.00		175.00

James Henry

Date	PR	Debit	Credit	Balance
Feb. 2	S3	450.00		450.00
12	R2		450.00	–0–
22	S3	225.00		225.00

Sam Moore

Date	PR	Debit	Credit	Balance
Feb. 13	S3	350.00		350.00
23	R2		350.00	–0–

Paul Roth

Date	PR	Debit	Credit	Balance
Feb. 15	S3	200.00		200.00
25	R2		200.00	–0–

Albert Smith

Date	PR	Debit	Credit	Balance
Feb. 7	S3	500.00		500.00
17	R2		500.00	–0–
28	S3	250.00		250.00

GENERAL LEDGER

Cash   No. 111

Date	PR	Debit	Credit	Balance
Feb. 28	R2	19,770.00		19,770.00

Accounts Receivable   No. 112

Date	PR	Debit	Credit	Balance
Feb. 28	S3	2,150.00		2,150.00
28	R2		1,500.00	650.00

Notes Payable   No. 211

Date	PR	Debit	Credit	Balance
Feb. 20	R2		1,000.00	1,000.00

Sales   No. 411

Date	PR	Debit	Credit	Balance
Feb. 28	S3		2,150.00	2,150.00
28	R2		17,300.00	19,450.00

Sales Discounts   No. 413

Date	PR	Debit	Credit	Balance
Feb. 28	R2	30.00		30.00

"Sales credit" is provided for the credits to Sales. By entering each day's cash sales in this column, the cash sales of a month may be posted at the month's end in a single amount, the column total. (Although cash sales are normally recorded daily from the cash register reading, the cash sales of Illustration 6–2 are recorded only once each week in order to shorten the illustration.)

At the time daily cash sales are recorded in the Cash Receipts Journal, some bookkeepers, as in Illustration 6–2, place a check mark in the Posting Reference column to indicate that no amount is individually posted from that line of the journal. Other bookkeepers use a double check ($\sqrt{\sqrt{}}$) to distinguish amounts not posted from amounts posted to customer accounts.

Miscellaneous Receipts of Cash

Most cash receipts are from customer collections and cash sales. However, cash is occasionally received from other sources such as, for example, the sale for cash of an unneeded asset, or a promissory note is given to a bank in order to borrow money. For miscellaneous receipts such as these, the Other Accounts credit column is provided. In an average company, the items entered in this column are few and are posted to a variety of general ledger accounts. As a result, postings are less apt to be omitted if these items are also posted daily.

The Cash Receipts Journal's Posting Reference column is used only for daily postings from the Other Accounts and Accounts Receivable columns. The account numbers appearing in the column indicate items posted to general ledger accounts. The check marks indicate either that an item like a day's cash sales was not posted or that an item was posted to the subsidiary Accounts Receivable Ledger.

Month-End Postings

The amounts in the Accounts Receivable, Sales, Sales Discounts, and Cash columns of the Cash Receipts Journal are posted as column totals at the end of the month. However, the transactions recorded in any journal must result in equal debits and credits to general ledger accounts. Consequently, debit and credit equality in a columnar journal such as the Cash Receipts Journal is proved by *crossfooting* or cross adding the column totals before they are posted. To *foot* a column of figures is to add it. To crossfoot the Cash Receipts Journal, the debit column totals are added together, the credit column totals are added together, and the two sums are compared for equality. For Illustration 6–2, the two sums appear as follows:

Debit columns		Credit columns	
Sales discounts debit	$ 30	Other accounts credit	$ 1,000
Cash debit	19,770	Accounts receivable credit ..	1,500
		Sales credit	17,300
Total	$19,800	Total	$19,800

And since the sums are equal, the debits in the journal are assumed to equal the credits.

After the debit and credit equality is proved by crossfooting, the totals of the last four columns are posted as indicated in each column heading. As for the Other Accounts column, since the individual items in this column are posted daily, the column total is not posted. Note in Illustration 6–2 the check mark below the Other Accounts column. The check mark indicates that the column total was not posted. The account numbers of the accounts to which the remaining column totals were posted are indicated in parentheses below each column.

Posting items daily from the Other Accounts column with a delayed posting of the offsetting items in the Cash column (total) causes the General Ledger to be out of balance throughout the month. However, this is of no consequence because before the trial balance is prepared, the offsetting amounts reach the General Ledger in posting the Cash column total.

POSTING RULE

Posting to a subsidiary ledger and its controlling account from two journals has been demonstrated, and a rule to cover all such postings can now be given. The rule is: *In posting to a subsidiary ledger and its controlling account, the controlling account must be debited periodically for an amount or amounts equal to the sum of the debits to the subsidiary ledger and it must be credited periodically for an amount or amounts equal to the sum of the credits to the subsidiary ledger.*

CREDITOR ACCOUNTS

As with accounts receivable, the Accounts Payable account used thus far does not show how much is owed each creditor. As a result, to secure this information, an individual account, one for each creditor, must be maintained. These creditor accounts are commonly kept in an *Accounts Payable Ledger* that is controlled by an Accounts Payable controlling account in the General Ledger. Also, the controlling account, subsidiary ledger, and columnar journal techniques demonstrated thus far with accounts receivable apply to the creditor accounts. The only difference is that a Purchases Journal and a Cash Disbursements Journal are used in recording most of the transactions affecting these accounts.

PURCHASES JOURNAL

A Purchases Journal having one money column may be used to record purchases of merchandise on credit. However, a multicolumn journal in which purchases of both merchandise and supplies can be recorded is commonly preferred. Such a journal may have the columns shown in Illustration 6–3. In the illustrated journal, the invoice date and terms together indicate the date on which payment for each purchase is due. The Accounts Payable credit column is used to record the amounts credited to each creditor's account. These amounts are posted daily to the individual creditor accounts in the Accounts Payable Ledger. The column total is posted to the Accounts Payable controlling account at the month-end. The items purchased are recorded in the debit columns and are posted in the column totals.

THE CASH DISBURSEMENTS JOURNAL AND ITS POSTING

The Cash Disbursements Journal, like the Cash Receipts Journal, has columns that make it possible to post repetitive debits and credits in column totals. The repetitive debits and credits of cash payments are debits to the Accounts Payable controlling account and credits to both Purchases Discounts and Cash. In most companies, the purchase of merchandise for cash is not common; therefore, a Purchases column is not needed and a cash purchase is recorded as on line 2 of Illustration 6–4.

Observe that the illustrated journal has a column headed "Check Number" (Ch. No.). In order to gain control over cash disbursements, all such disbursements, except petty cash disbursements, should be made by check. (Petty cash disbursements are discussed in the next chapter.) The checks should be prenumbered by the printer and should be entered in the journal in numerical order with each check's number in the column headed "Ch. No." This makes it possible to scan the numbers in the column for omitted checks. When a Cash Disbursements Journal has a column for check numbers, it is often called a *Check Register.*

A Cash Disbursements Journal or Check Register like Illustration

Illustration 6–3

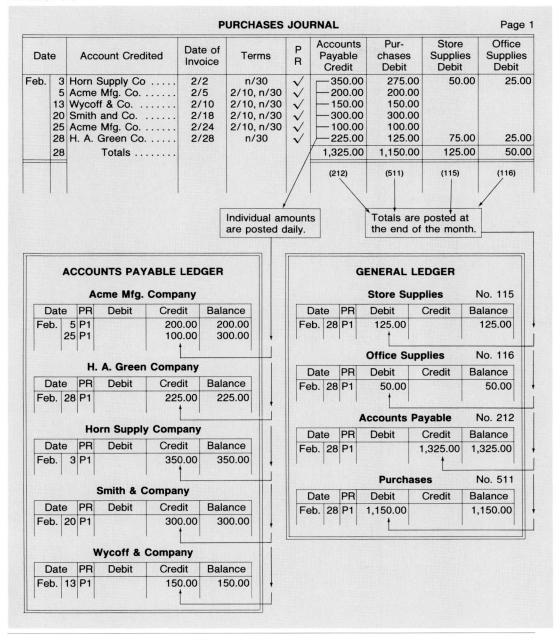

Illustration 6–4

CASH DISBURSEMENTS JOURNAL   Page 2

Date	Ch. No.	Payee	Account Debited	PR	Other Accounts Debit	Accts. Pay. Debit	Pur. Disc. Credit	Cash Credit
Feb. 3	105	L. & N. Railroad ..	Transportation-In	514	15.00			15.00
12	106	East Sales Co.	Purchases	511	25.00			25.00
15	107	Acme Mfg. Co.	Acme Mfg. Co.	✓		200.00	4.00	196.00
15	108	Jerry Hale	Salaries Expense .	611	250.00			250.00
20	109	Wycoff & Co.	Wycoff & Co.	✓		150.00	3.00	147.00
28	110	Smith & Co.	Smith & Co.	✓		300.00	6.00	294.00
28		Totals			290.00	650.00	13.00	927.00
					(✓)	(212)	(513)	(111)

Individual amounts in the Other Accounts debit column and Accounts Payable debit column are posted daily.

Totals posted at the end of the month.

ACCOUNTS PAYABLE LEDGER

Acme Mfg. Company

Date	PR	Debit	Credit	Balance
Feb. 5	P1		200.00	200.00
15	D2	200.00		–0–
25	P1		100.00	100.00

H. A. Green Company

Date	PR	Debit	Credit	Balance
Feb. 28	P1		225.00	225.00

Horn Supply Company

Date	PR	Debit	Credit	Balance
Feb. 3	P1		350.00	350.00

Smith & Company

Date	PR	Debit	Credit	Balance
Feb. 20	P1		300.00	300.00
28	D2	300.00		–0–

Wycoff & Company

Date	PR	Debit	Credit	Balance
Feb. 13	P1		150.00	150.00
20	D2	150.00		–0–

GENERAL LEDGER

Cash   No. 111

Date	PR	Debit	Credit	Balance
Feb. 28	R2	19,770.00		19,770.00
28	D2		927.00	18,843.00

Accounts Payable   No. 212

Date	PR	Debit	Credit	Balance
Feb. 28	P1		1,325.00	1,325.00
28	D2	650.00		675.00

Purchases   No. 511

Date	PR	Debit	Credit	Balance
Feb. 12	D2	25.00		25.00
28	P1	1,150.00		1,175.00

Purchases Discounts   No. 513

Date	PR	Debit	Credit	Balance
Feb. 28	D2		13.00	13.00

Transportation-In   No. 514

Date	PR	Debit	Credit	Balance
Feb. 3	D2	15.00		15.00

Salaries Expense   No. 611

Date	PR	Debit	Credit	Balance
Feb. 15	D2	250.00		250.00

6–4 is posted as follows. The individual amounts in the Other Accounts column are posted daily to the debit of the general ledger accounts named. The individual amounts in the Accounts Payable column are posted daily to the subsidiary Accounts Payable Ledger to the debit of the creditors named. At the end of the month, after the column totals are crossfooted to prove their equality, the Accounts Payable column total is posted to the debit of the Accounts Payable controlling account. The Purchases Discounts column total is credited to the Purchases Discounts account, and the Cash column total is credited to the Cash account. Since the items in the Other Accounts column are posted individually, the column total is not posted.

PROVING THE LEDGERS

Periodically, after all posting is completed, the General Ledger and the subsidiary ledgers are proved. The General Ledger is normally proved first by preparing a trial balance. If the trial balance balances, the accounts in the General Ledger, including the controlling accounts, are assumed to be correct. The subsidiary ledgers are then proved, commonly by preparing schedules of accounts receivable and accounts payable. A *schedule of accounts payable,* for example, is prepared by listing with their balances the accounts in the Accounts Payable Ledger having balances. The balances are totaled; and if the total is equal to the balance of the Accounts Payable controlling account, the accounts in the Accounts Payable Ledger are assumed to be correct. Illustration 6–5 shows a schedule of the creditor accounts having balances in the Accounts Payable Ledger of Illustration 6–4. Note that the schedule total is equal to the balance of the Accounts Payable controlling account in the General Ledger of Illustration 6–4. A *schedule of accounts receivable* is prepared in the same way as a schedule of accounts payable. Also, if its total is equal to the balance of the Accounts Receivable controlling account, the accounts in the Accounts Receivable Ledger are assumed to be correct.

Illustration 6–5

HAWAIIAN SALES COMPANY
Schedule of Accounts Payable, December 31, 19—

Acme Mfg. Company	$100
H. A. Green Company	225
Horn Supply Company	350
Total accounts payable	$675

Instead of a formal schedule to prove the accounts in a subsidiary ledger, an adding machine list may be used. For example, the balances of the accounts in the Accounts Payable Ledger may be proved by listing on an adding machine the balance of each account in the ledger, totaling the list, and comparing the total with the balance of the Accounts Payable controlling account. A similar list may be used to prove the accounts in the Accounts Receivable Ledger.

SALES TAXES

Many cities and states require retailers to collect sales taxes from their customers and periodically remit these taxes to the city or state treasurer. When a columnar Sales Journal is used, a record of taxes collected can be obtained by adding special columns in the journal as shown in Illustration 6–6.

In posting the journal, the individual amounts in the Accounts Receivable column are posted daily to customer accounts in the Accounts Receivable Ledger and the column total is posted at the end of the month to the Accounts Receivable controlling account. The individual amounts in the Sales Taxes Payable and Sales columns are not posted. However, at the end of the month the total of the Sales Taxes Payable column is credited to the Sales Taxes Payable account and the total of the Sales column is credited to Sales.

Illustration 6–6

SALES JOURNAL

Date	Account Debited	Invoice Number	P R	Accounts Receivable Debit	Sales Taxes Payable Credit	Sales Credit
Dec. 1	D. R. Horn	7-1698		103.00	3.00	100.00

A concern making cash sales upon which sales taxes are collected may add a special Sales Taxes Payable column in its Cash Receipts Journal.

SALES INVOICES AS A SALES JOURNAL

To save labor, many companies do not enter charge sales in a Sales Journal. These companies post each sales invoice total directly to the customer's account in a subsidiary Accounts Receivable Ledger. Copies of the invoices are then bound in numerical order in a binder. At the end of the month, all the invoices of that month are totaled and a general journal entry is made debiting Accounts Receivable and crediting Sales for the total. In effect, the bound invoice copies act as a Sales Journal. Such a procedure is known as direct posting of sales invoices.

SALES RETURNS

A company having only a few sales returns may record them in a General Journal with an entry like the following:

Oct.	17	Sales Returns and Allowances	412	17.50	
		Accounts Receivable—George Ball . .	112/√		17.50
		Customer returned merchandise.			

The debit of the entry is posted to the Sales Returns and Allowances account. The credit is posted to both the Accounts Receivable controlling account and to the customer's account. Note the account number and the check, 112/√, in the Posting Reference column on the credit line. This indicates that both the Accounts Receivable controlling account in the General Ledger and the George Ball account in the Accounts Receivable Ledger were credited for $17.50. Both were credited because the balance of the controlling account in the General Ledger will not equal the sum of the customer account balances in the subsidiary ledger unless both are credited.

Companies having sufficient sales returns can save posting labor by recording them in a special Sales Returns and Allowances Journal like that of Illustration 6–7. Note that this is in keeping with the gener-

Illustration 6–7

SALES RETURNS AND ALLOWANCES JOURNAL

Date		Account Credited	Explanation	Credit Memo No.	P R	Amount
Oct.	7	Robert Moore	Defective mdse	203	√	10.00
	14	James Warren	Defective mdse	204	√	12.00
	18	T. M. Jones	Not ordered	205	√	6.00
	23	Sam Smith	Defective mdse	206	√	18.00
	31	Sales Returns and Allow., Dr.; Accounts Rec., Cr.				46.00
						412/112

ally recognized idea that a company can design and use a special journal for any group of like transactions in which there are within the group sufficient transactions to warrant the journal. When a Sales Returns and Allowances Journal is used to record returns, the amounts entered in the journal are posted daily to the credit of each affected customer account. At the end of the month, the journal total is debited to Sales Returns and Allowances and credited to Accounts Receivable.

GENERAL JOURNAL ENTRIES

When columnar journals like the ones described are used, a General Journal must be provided for adjusting, closing, and correcting entries and for a few transactions that cannot be recorded in the special journals. Among these transactions, if a Sales Returns and Allowances Journal is not provided, are sales returns, purchases returns, and purchases of plant assets. Illustrative entries for the last two kinds of transactions follow:

Oct.	8	Accounts Payable—Medford Company ...	212/√	32.00	
		Purchases Returns and Allowances ..	512		32.00
		Returned defective merchandise.			
	11	Office Equipment	133	685.00	
		Accounts Payable—ABC Supply Co. .	212/√		685.00
		Purchased a typewriter.			

MACHINE METHODS

Pen-and-ink records like the ones described thus far are used by many small businesses. However, even very small businesses also use adding machines, desk calculators, and multicopy forms to save time and effort in processing accounting data. Likewise, small businesses having sufficient transactions may use electronic bookkeeping machines. Illustration 6–8 shows such a machine.

An electronic bookkeeping machine usually has a typewriter-like keyboard and the keyboard of a 10-key calculator. It also has "function" keys that direct the machine's operation, instructing it to calculate, tabulate, and/or print out stored data. A bookkeeping machine can handle accounting for sales, cash receipts, purchases, cash payments, payroll, and other transactions, as well as posting to the General Ledger.

No attempt will be made here to describe a bookkeeping machine's

Illustration 6–8

Courtesy Monroe, The Calculator Co.,
a Division of Litton Industries

operation in each of these applications. However, when used in accounting for credit sales, for example, the current page of the Sales Journal is placed in the machine. Then, for each charge sale, the operator puts the customer's account and month-end statement in the machine and depresses the proper keys to enter the information about the sale. The machine makes the entry in the Sales Journal, posts to the customer's account, updates the account balance, enters the sale on the customer's month-end statement, and updates the statement. At the same time, it accumulates the Sales Journal total for the month-end debit to Accounts Receivable and credit to Sales. Furthermore, it does all of this in one operation from one entry into the machine of the proper data. And, it is equally efficient in handling other kinds of transactions.

Bookkeeping machines like the one shown speed the processing of accounting data. They also reduce transposition errors by printing the same information on several different records in one operation. However, the speed of operation and the amount of work such a machine can do efficiently are limited. Consequently, many businesses turn to computerized data processing.

COMPUTERIZED DATA PROCESSING

Computerized data processing involves the processing of data without human intervention through the use of a machine that is far more powerful and complex than is a bookkeeping machine, a computer. A computer is capable of—

1. Inputing and storing data.
2. Performing arithmetic calculations on the data.
3. Comparing units of the data to find which are larger or smaller.
4. Sorting or rearranging data.
5. Printing reports from the data stored in the machine.

Computers vary in size and in the speed with which they process data. They range from small microcomputers similar to Illustration 6–9 to machines that with their peripheral equipment occupy a large room. Illustration 6–10 shows a large computer and its peripheral equipment. Peripheral equipment includes devices to input or output data and to store data on reels of magnetic tapes or on magnetic disks.

Illustration 6–9

Courtesy of Apple Computer, Inc.

Data may be entered into a computer by means of a computer terminal, a device that commonly has a typewriter-like keyboard, a 10-key numerical keyboard, and a TV-like screen. Data may also be entered with previously prepared punched cards, reels of magnetic tape, magnetic disks, and in other ways. For example, another means of entry uses a laser light that reads a bar code such as is found on many consumer products. Inside the computer each alphabetical letter or numerical digit of data becomes a combination of electrical or magnetic states that a computer can manipulate at very high rates of speed. Consequently, if of sufficient size, a computer can do 1 million or more additions, subtractions, multiplications, and divisions per second, all without error in a predetermined sequence according to instructions stored in the machine.

A computer can do nothing without a previously prepared set of instructions, called a *program,* that is entered and stored in the computer. However, with a properly prepared program, a computer will accept data, store and process the data, and produce the processed results, perhaps in the form of a report displayed on a TV-like screen, or typed out on an electric typewriter at the rate of approximately

Illustration 6–10

Design Model
Courtesy of International Business Machines Corporation

10 characters per second, or printed by a line printer at upwards to 2,000 lines per minute.

The Program

A computer program is a set of instructions written in a language the computer "understands." Some of the widely used languages are COBOL, BASIC, RPG, and FORTRAN. The instructions specify each operation a computer is to perform and are entered into the computer before the data to be processed. The program may contain only a few or several thousand detailed instructions. For example, the following shows the steps that must be programmed to have a computer process customers' orders for merchandise.

Instructions to Be Programmed for Processing Customers' Orders

1. For the first item on the customer's order, compare the quantity ordered with the quantity on hand as shown by inventory data stored in the computer.
   a. If the quantity ordered is not on hand:
      (1) Prepare a back order notifying the customer that the goods are not available but will be shipped as soon as a new supply is received.
      (2) Go to the next item on the customer's order.

b. If the quantity on hand is greater than the amount ordered:
  (1) Deduct the amount ordered from the amount on hand.
  (2) Prepare instructions to ship the goods.
  (3) Compare the amount of the item remaining after filling the customer's order with the reorder point for the item.
   (a) If the amount remaining is greater than the reorder point:
    1. Go to the next item on the customer's order.
   (b) If the amount remaining is less than the reorder point:
    1. Compute the amount to be purchased and prepare documents for the purchase.
    2. Go to the next item on the customer's order.

In addition to these instructions, a program for processing customer orders would have instructions for preparing invoices, recording sales, and updating customer accounts.

Designing the Program

Computers have the ability to compare two numbers and decide which is larger. This ability makes it possible for the computer to process data one way or another, depending on the result of the comparison. Note that this ability to compare numbers is essential if the computer is to follow instructions such as those for processing customer orders.

If a computer is to process data correctly, a person (the programmer) must first design a program for the computer to follow. In designing the program, the programmer determines in advance the alternative sets of calculations or processing steps to be made. Then, the programmer must devise the appropriate comparisons that will identify the circumstances under which each particular set of processing steps should be performed. Finally, the programmer must write specific instructions telling the computer how to process the data. A computer can follow through the program's maze of decisions and alternate instructions rapidly and accurately. However, if it encounters an exception not anticipated in the program, it is helpless and can only process the exception incorrectly or stop.

The ability to store a program and data and then to race through the maze of decisions and alternate instructions is what distinguishes a computer from an electronic bookkeeping machine. Some electronic bookkeeping machines can do an addition, a multiplication, or a division at the speed of a computer. Yet with all this speed, their operating rates are relatively slow, since they must depend on a person to push their function keys to tell them what to do.

Modes of Operation

Computers operate in one of two modes: either batch processing or online processing. In the batch mode, the program and data to be processed are inputed to the computer, processed, and then removed from the computer before another batch is begun. Then, the program for a new job and a new set of data are entered and the new job is processed. Batch processing may result in customers' orders being processed daily, the payroll being run each week, financial statements being prepared monthly, and the processing of other jobs on a periodic basis. Because transactions are processed in groups or batches, this mode of operation may require less computer capacity, is usually less expensive than online operation and is used when an immediate processing or an immediate computer response is not required.

In online processing, the program is kept in the computer along with any required data. As new data are entered, they are instantly processed by the computer. For example, in some department stores, the cash registers are connected directly into the store's computer. In addition to cash sales, the registers are used as follows in recording charge sales. After the customer selects merchandise for purchase, the salesperson uses the customer's plastic credit card to print the customer's name on a blank sales ticket. The sales ticket is then placed in the Forms Printer of the cash register and the sale is recorded. The register prints all pertinent information on the sales ticket and totals it. In order to finalize the sale, controls within the register require that the salesperson depress the proper register keys to record the customer's account number. This, in effect, posts the sale to the customer's account. The salesperson does not actually post to the account. Rather, the data entered with the cash register's keys causes the store's computer to update the customer's account. The computer will also produce the customer's month-end statement, ready for mailing.

Another example of online operation is found in supermarkets, where each item of merchandise is imprinted with a machine-readable price tag similar to Illustration 6–11. At one of the store's checkout stands, each item of merchandise selected by a customer is passed over an optical scanner in the countertop or an optical scanner in a wand is passed over each item's price tag. This actuates the cash register and eliminates the need for handkeying information into the register. It also transmits the sales information to a computer that updates the store's inventory records and prepares orders to a central warehouse to restock any item in low supply. At closing time, the computer prints out detailed summaries of the day's sales and item inventories. It thus provides management with up-to-the-minute information that could not otherwise be obtained.

Other examples of online operations are found in banks, airlines, and factories. However, all have the same results: they reduce human labor, create more accurate records, and provide management with both better and more up-to-date reports. Furthermore, when there are sufficient transactions, they do the work at less cost per transaction.

Time Sharing

Computer service companies provide computer service to many concerns on a time-sharing basis, using computers that are capable of working on many jobs simultaneously. In providing such service, the computer service company installs an input-output device on the premises of a subscriber to its service. The input-output device is connected to the service company's computer through wires leased from the phone company. The subscriber uses the input-output device to input data into the service company's computer. It is held in storage there until processing time is available, usually within a few seconds. The computer then processes the data and transmits the results to the subscriber. For this service the subscriber pays a monthly fee plus a charge for the computer time used.

Through *time sharing*, a growing number of concerns are using computers, even very small businesses. For example, a dentist or a physician practicing alone is a small business. Yet a significant number of such dentists and physicians have their accounts receivable and customer billing done by computer service companies.

Microcomputers

Another important factor leading to the expanded use of computers is the development of microcomputers (one of which is shown in Illustration 6–9). These very small computers have become less expensive in recent years and are now affordable by very small businesses and individuals. As more and more people become proficient in using these machines, manual accounting systems will be replaced by computerized systems.

RECORDING ACTUAL TRANSACTIONS

Transactions may be recorded in a pen-and-ink journal or with a bookkeeping machine or on a computer terminal, depending on the accounting system of the business completing the transactions. Nevertheless, in the remainder of this text, general journal entries will be used to illustrate the recording of most transactions. The general journal entries are intended to show the items increased and decreased by the transactions. The student should recognize that the entries actually would be made in a General Journal, or a columnar special journal, or with a bookkeeping machine or a computer terminal, depending on the accounting system of the business completing the transactions.

GLOSSARY

Accounting system. The business papers, records, reports, and procedures used by a business in recording transactions and reporting their effects.

Accounts Payable Ledger. A subsidiary ledger having an account for each creditor.

Accounts Receivable Ledger. A subsidiary ledger having an account for each customer.

Batch processing. A mode of computer operation in which a program and data are entered in the computer, processed, and removed from the computer before the next program and data are entered.

Check Register. A book of original entry for recording payments by check.

Columnar journal. A book of original entry having columns for entering specific data about each transaction of a group of like transactions.

Computer. A complex electronic machine that has the capacity to store a program of instructions and data, process the data rapidly according to the instructions, and prepare reports showing the results of the processing operation.

Controlling account. A general ledger account that controls the accounts in a subsidiary ledger.

Crossfoot. To add the column totals of a journal or a report.

Foot. To add a column of figures.

General Ledger. A ledger containing the financial statement accounts of a business.

Online processing. A mode of computer operation in which the program and required data are maintained in the computer so that as new data are entered, they are processed instantly.

Program. A set of computer instructions for processing data.

Schedule of accounts payable. A list of creditor account balances with the total.

Schedule of accounts receivable. A list of customer account balances with the total.

Special journal. A columnar book of original entry for recording one kind of transaction.

Subsidiary ledger. A group of accounts other than general ledger accounts which show the details underlying the balance of a controlling account in the General Ledger.

Time sharing. A process by which several users of a computer, each having an input-output device, can input data into a single computer and, as processing time becomes available, having their data processed and transmitted back to their output device.

QUESTIONS FOR CLASS DISCUSSION

1. How does a columnar journal save posting labor?
2. Why should sales to and receipts of cash from charge customers be recorded and posted daily?
3. What functions are served by the Accounts Receivable controlling account?
4. Both credits to customer accounts and credits to miscellaneous accounts are individually posted from a Cash Receipts Journal like that of Illustration 6–2. Why not put both kinds of credits in the same column and thus save journal space?
5. How is a multicolumn journal crossfooted? Why is such a journal crossfooted?
6. How is the equality of a controlling account and its subsidiary ledger accounts maintained?
7. Describe how copies of a company's sales invoices may be used as a Sales Journal.
8. When a general journal entry is used to record a returned charge sale, the credit of the entry must be posted twice. Does this cause the trial balance to be out of balance? Why or why not?
9. How does one tell from which journal a particular amount in a ledger account was posted?
10. How is a schedule of accounts payable prepared? How is it used to prove the balances of the creditor accounts in the Accounts Payable Ledger? What may be substituted for a formal schedule?
11. After all posting is completed, the balance of the Accounts Receivable controlling account does not agree with the sum of the balances in the Accounts Receivable Ledger. If the trial balance is in balance, where is the error apt to be?

CLASS EXERCISES

Exercise 6–1   A concern that uses a Sales Journal, a Purchases Journal, a Cash Receipts Journal, a Cash Disbursements Journal, and a General Journal like the ones described in this chapter completed the following transactions. List the transactions by letter and opposite each letter give the name of the journal in which the transaction should be recorded.

 a. Purchased merchandise on credit.
 b. Purchased office supplies on credit.
 c. Purchased office equipment on credit.
 d. Returned merchandise purchased on credit.
 e. Sold merchandise for cash.
 f. Sold merchandise on credit.
 g. Gave a customer credit for merchandise purchased on credit and returned.
 h. A customer paid for merchandise previously purchased on credit.
 i. A customer returned merchandise sold for cash; a check was issued.
 j. Paid a creditor.
 k. Recorded adjusting and closing entries.

Exercise 6–2   At the end of November, the Sales Journal of Best Company showed the following sales on credit:

SALES JOURNAL

Date		Account Debited	Invoice Number	P R	Amount
Nov.	2	Jerry Marsh	345		300.00
	9	Dale Evans	346		250.00
	16	Ted Bates	347		200.00
	27	Jerry Marsh	348		100.00
	30	Total			850.00

The company had also recorded the return of merchandise with the following entry:

Nov.	18	Sales Returns and Allowances	50.00	
		Accounts Receivable—Ted Bates		50.00
		Customer returned merchandise.		

Required:

1. On a sheet of notebook paper open a subsidiary Accounts Receivable Ledger having a T-account for each customer listed in the Sales Journal. Post to the customer accounts the entries of the Sales Journal and also the portion of the general journal entry that affects a customer's account.
2. Open a General Ledger having T-accounts for Accounts Receivable, Sales,

and Sales Returns and Allowances. Post the Sales Journal's total and the portions of the general journal entry that affect these accounts.

3. Prove the subsidiary ledger accounts with a schedule of accounts receivable.

Exercise 6–3

New Company, a company that posts its sales invoices directly and then binds the invoices to make them into a Sales Journal, had the following sales during October:

Oct. 3	John Fox	$ 800
6	Gary Ball	1,100
11	Jerry Dale	1,600
18	Gary Ball	2,200
21	Jerry Dale	700
27	Walter Scott	1,500
	Total	$7,900

Required:

1. On a sheet of notebook paper open a subsidiary Accounts Receivable Ledger having a T-account for each customer with an invoice bound in the Sales Journal. Post the invoices to the subsidiary ledger.
2. Give the general journal entry to record the end-of-month total of the Sales Journal.
3. Open an Accounts Receivable controlling account and a Sales account and post the general journal entry.
4. Prove the subsidiary Accounts Receivable Ledger with a schedule of accounts receivable.

Exercise 6–4

A company that records credit sales in a Sales Journal and records sales returns in its General Journal made the following errors. List each error by letter, and opposite each letter tell when the error will be discovered:

a. Correctly recorded a $75 sale in the Sales Journal but posted it to the customer's account as a $750 sale.
b. Made an addition error in totaling the Amount column of the Sales Journal.
c. Posted a sales return recorded in the General Journal to the Sales Returns and Allowances account and to the Accounts Receivable account but did not post to the customer's account.
d. Posted a sales return to the Accounts Receivable account and to the customer's account but did not post to the Sales Returns and Allowances account.
e. Made an addition error in determining the balance of a customer's account.

Exercise 6–5

Following are the condensed journals of a merchandising concern. The journal column headings are incomplete in that they do not indicate whether the columns are debit or credit columns.

Required:

1. Prepare T-accounts on a sheet of ordinary notebook paper for the following general ledger and subsidiary ledger accounts. Separate the accounts of each ledger group as follows:

General Ledger Accounts
- Cash
- Accounts Receivable
- Prepaid Insurance
- Store Equipment
- Notes Payable
- Accounts Payable
- Sales
- Sales Returns
- Sales Discounts
- Purchases
- Purchases Returns
- Purchases Discounts

Accounts Receivable Ledger Accounts
- Customer A
- Customer B
- Customer C

Accounts Payable Ledger Accounts
- Company One
- Company Two
- Company Three

2. Without referring to any of the illustrations showing complete column headings for the journals, post the following journals to the proper T-accounts.

SALES JOURNAL

Account	Amount
Customer A	1,000
Customer B	1,500
Customer C	2,000
Total	4,500

PURCHASES JOURNAL

Account	Amount
Company One	1,200
Company Two	1,400
Company Three	1,600
Total	4,200

GENERAL JOURNAL

....	...	Sales Returns	200.00	
		Accounts Receivable—Customer C		200.00
	...	Accounts Payable—Company Three	300.00	
		Purchases Returns		300.00

CASH RECEIPTS JOURNAL

Account	Other Accounts	Accounts Receivable	Sales	Sales Discounts	Cash
Customer A	.....	1,000	.....	20	980
Cash Sales	.....	.....	1,450	.....	1,450
Notes Payable.................	2,000	.....	.....	.....	2,000
Cash Sales	.....	.....	1,650	.....	1,650
Customer C	.....	1,500	.....	30	1,470
Store Equipment	150	.....	.....	.....	150
	2,150	2,500	3,100	50	7,700

CASH DISBURSEMENTS JOURNAL

Accounts	Other Accounts	Accounts Payable	Purchases Discounts	Cash
Prepaid Insurance	100	. . . . .	. . . . .	100
Company Two	. . . . .	1,400	28	1,372
Company Three	. . . . .	1,300	26	1,274
Store Equipment	500	. . . . .	. . . . .	500
	600	2,700	54	3,246

PROBLEMS

Problem 6–1

(If the working papers that accompany this text are not being used, omit this problem.)

It is June 21 and you have just taken over the accounting work of Sierra Company, a concern operating with annual accounting periods that end each May 31. The company's previous accountant journalized its transactions through June 19 and posted all items that required posting as individual amounts, as an examination of the journals and ledgers in the booklet of working papers will show.

The company completed these transactions beginning on June 21:

June 21 Purchased on credit from Lee Supply Company merchandise, $545; store supplies, $80; and office supplies, $55. Invoice dated June 21, terms n/10 EOM.

22 Received an $85 credit memorandum from Pace Company for merchandise received on June 18 and returned for credit.

23 Received a $20 credit memorandum from Lee Supply Company for office supplies received on June 21 and returned for credit.

24 Sold merchandise on credit to Alan Hall, Invoice No. 716, $615. (Terms of all credit sales are 2/10, n/60.)

25 Issued a credit memorandum to John Long for defective merchandise sold on June 18 and returned for credit, $65.

25 Purchased store equipment on credit from Lee Supply Company invoice dated June 24, terms n/10 EOM, $735.

26 Issued Check No. 723 to Pace Company in payment of its June 16 invoice less the return and the discount.

26 Received payment for Alan Hall for the June 16 sale less the discount.

27 Issued Check No. 724 to Clark Company in payment of its June 17 invoice less the discount.

27 Sold merchandise on credit to Roy Ness, Invoice No. 717, $825.

27 Sold a local church group a roll of wrapping paper (store supplies) for cash at cost, $30.

28 Received payment from John Long for the June 18 sale less the return and the discount.

29 Received merchandise and an invoice dated June 26, terms 2/10, n/60, from Clark Company, $945.

June 29 Douglas Murphy, the owner of Sierra Company, used Check No. 725 to withdraw $1,000 cash from the business for personal use.

30 Issued Check No. 726 to Gary Beal, the company's only sales employee, in payment of his salary for the last half of June, $320.

30 Issued Check No. 727 to Nevada Power Company in payment of the June electric bill, $185.

30 Cash sales for the last half of the month, $9,995. (Cash sales are usually recorded daily but are recorded only twice in this problem in order to reduce the repetitive transactions.)

Required:

1. Record the transactions in the journals provided.
2. Post to the customer and creditor accounts and also post any amounts that should be posted as individual amounts to the general ledger accounts. (Normally, these amounts are posted daily, but they are posted only once by you in this problem because they are few in number.)
3. Foot and crossfoot the journals and make the month-end postings.
4. Prepare a June 30 trial balance and prove the subsidiary ledgers by preparing schedules of accounts receivable and payable.

Problem 6–2

Bedrock Company completed these transactions during February of the current year:

Feb. 2 Sold merchandise on credit to Dale Dent, Invoice No. 711, $800. (Terms of all credit sales are 2/10, n/60.)

3 Received merchandise and an invoice dated January 30, terms 2/10, n/60, from Able Company, $1,750.

4 Sold merchandise on credit to Gary Glen, Invoice No. 712, $1,250.

5 Purchased on credit from Best Company merchandise, $1,855; store supplies, $75; and office supplies, $35. Invoice dated February 4, terms n/10 EOM.

7 Borrowed $5,000 by giving First National Bank a promissory note payable.

9 Purchased office equipment on credit from More Company, invoice dated February 6, terms n/10 EMO, $625.

9 Sent Able Company Check No. 414 in payment of its January 30 invoice less the discount.

11 Sold merchandise on credit to Carl Cole, Invoice No. 713, $1,650.

12 Received payment from Dale Dent of the February 2 sale less the discount.

14 Received payment from Gary Glen of the February 4 sale less the discount.

14 Received merchandise and an invoice dated February 11, terms 2/10, n/60, from Old Company, $1,985.

14 Issued Check No. 415, payable to Payroll, in payment of sales salaries for the first half of the month, $855. Cashed the check and paid the employees.

14 Cash sales for the first half of the month, $18,460. (Normally, cash sales are recorded daily; however, they are recorded only twice in this problem to reduce the number of repetitive entries.)

Feb. 14 *Post to the customer and creditor accounts and also post any amounts that should be posted as individual amounts to the general ledger accounts. (Normally, such items are posted daily; but you are asked to post them on only two occasions in this problem because they are few in number.)*

16 Purchased on credit from Best Company merchandise, $410; store supplies, $45; and office supplies, $30. Invoice dated February 12, terms n/10, EOM.

17 Received a credit memorandum from Old Company for unsatisfactory merchandise received on February 14 and returned for credit, $85.

18 Received a credit memorandum from More Company for office equipment received on February 9 and returned for credit, $130.

21 Received payment from Carl Cole for the sale of February 11 less the discount.

21 Issued Check No. 416 to Old Company in payment of its invoice of February 11 less the return and the discount.

24 Sold merchandise on credit to Carl Cole, Invoice No. 714, $835.

26 Sold merchandise on credit to Gary Glen, Invoice No. 715, $775.

28 Issued Check No. 417, payable to Payroll, in payment of sales salaries for the last half of the month, $855. Cashed the check and paid the employees.

28 Cash sales for the last half of the month, $20,215.

28 *Post to the customer and creditor accounts and post any amounts that should be posted as individual amounts to general ledger accounts.*

28 *Foot and crossfoot the journals and make the month-end postings.*

Required:

1. Open the following general ledger accounts: Cash, Accounts Receivable, Store Supplies, Office Supplies, Office Equipment, Notes Payable, Accounts Payable, Sales, Sales Discounts, Purchases, Purchases Returns and Allowances, Purchases Discounts, and Sales Salaries Expense.

2. Open the following accounts receivable ledger accounts: Carl Cole, Dale Dent, and Gary Glen.

3. Open the following accounts payable ledger accounts: Able Company, Best Company, More Company, and Old Company.

4. Enter the transactions in a Sales Journal, a Purchases Journal, a Cash Receipts Journal, a Cash Disbursements Journal, and a General Journal similar to the ones illustrated in this chapter. Post when instructed to do so.

5. Prepare a trail balance and prove the subsidiary ledgers by preparing schedules of accounts receivable and payable.

Problem 6–3

Block Company completed these transactions during February of the current year:

Feb. 2 Received merchandise and an invoice dated January 31, terms 2/10, n/60, from Dale Company, $2,800.

3 Sold merchandise on credit to Ted Barr, Invoice No. 815, $850. (Terms of all credit sales are 2/10, n/60.)

Feb. 4 Sold merchandise on credit to Ray Deal, Invoice No. 816, $1,250.

6 Purchased store equipment on credit from Store Sales Company, invoice dated February 2, terms n/10 EOM, $775.

7 Cash sales for the week ended February 7, $8,455.

7 *Post to the customer and creditor accounts and also post any amounts that should be posted as individual items to the general ledger accounts. (Normally, such items are posted daily; but to simplify the problem, you are asked to post them only once each week.)*

9 Sold unneeded store equipment at cost for cash, $85.

9 Issued Check No. 612 to *The Daily News* for advertising, $115.

10 Sold merchandise on credit to Fred Cole, Invoice No. 817, $750.

10 Purchased on credit from West Company merchandise, $1,530; store supplies, $95; and office supplies, $55. Invoice dated February 9, terms n/10 EOM.

10 Issued Check No. 613 to Dale Company in payment of its January 31 invoice less the discount.

13 Received payment from Ted Barr for the sale of February 3 less the discount.

14 Received payment from Ray Deal for the sale of February 4 less the discount.

14 Cash sales for the week ended February 14, $9,130.

14 *Post to the customer and creditor accounts and also post any amounts that should be posted as individual items to the general ledger accounts.*

16 Sold merchandise on credit to Fred Cole, Invoice No. 818, $1,180.

16 Issued Check No. 614, payable to Payroll, in payment of the sales salaries for the first half of the month, $975. Cashed the check and paid the employees.

17 Issued a credit memorandum to Fred Cole for defective merchandise sold on February 16 and returned for credit, $130.

18 Received a credit memorandum from Store Sales Company for store equipment received on February 6 and returned for credit, $65.

18 Sold merchandise on credit to Ted Barr, Invoice No. 819, $865.

19 Received merchandise and an invoice dated February 16, terms 2/10, n/60, from Hill Company, $3,470.

20 Received payment from Fred Cole for the sale of February 10 less the discount.

21 Cash sales for the week ended February 21, $9,550.

21 *Post to the customer and creditor accounts and any amounts that should be posted to the general ledger accounts.*

23 Purchased on credit from West Company merchandise, $1,840; store supplies, $65; and office supplies, $45. Invoice dated February 20, terms n/10 EOM.

23 Received merchandise and an invoice dated February 17, terms 2/10, n/60, from Dale Company, $2,150.

23 Received a credit memorandum from Hill Company for defective merchandise received on February 19 and returned for credit, $120.

25 Sold merchandise on credit to Ray Deal, Invoice No. 820, $935.

26 Received payment from Fred Cole for the February 16 sale less the return and the discount.

Feb. 26   Issued Check No. 615 to Hill Company in payment of its February 16 invoice less the return and the discount.

27   Issued Check No. 616 to Dale Company in payment of its February 17 invoice less the discount.

28   Issued Check No. 617, payable to Payroll, in payment of the sales salaries for the last half of the month, $950. Cashed the check and paid the employees.

28   Cash sales for the week ended February 28, $9,310.

28   *Post to the customer and creditor accounts and any amounts that should be posted to the general ledger accounts as individual items.*

28   *Foot and crossfoot the journals and make the month-end postings.*

Required:

1.   Open the following general ledger accounts: Cash, Accounts Receivable, Store Supplies, Office Supplies, Store Equipment, Accounts Payable, Sales, Sales Returns and Allowances, Sales Discounts, Purchases, Purchases Returns and Allowances, Purchases Discounts, Sales Salaries Expense, and Advertising Expense.

2.   Open the following accounts receivable ledger accounts: Ted Barr, Fred Cole, and Ray Deal.

3.   Open the following accounts payable ledger accounts: Dale Company, Hill Company, Store Sales Company, and West Company.

4.   Prepare a Sales Journal, a Purchases Journal, a Cash Receipts Journal, a Cash Disbursements Journal, and a General Journal similar to the ones illustrated in this chapter. Enter the transactions in the journals and post when instructed to do so.

5.   Prepare a trial balance of the General Ledger and prove the subsidiary ledgers by preparing schedules of accounts receivable and payable.

Problem 6–4   Lakeside Sales completed these transactions during February of the current year:

Feb. 1   Purchased merchandise on credit from Hardy Company, invoice dated January 29, terms 2/10, n/60, $1,950.

2   Issued Check No. 812 to *The Gazette* for advertising expense, $125.

2   Sold merchandise on credit to Ben Blue, Invoice 711, $765. (The terms of all credit sales are 2/10, n/60.)

3   Sold merchandise on credit to John Moss, Invoice No. 712, $850.

5   Purchased on credit from Old Company merchandise, $135; store supplies, $70; and office supplies, $45. Invoice dated February 4, terms n/10 EOM.

8   Received a $25 credit memorandum from Old Company for unsatisfactory store supplies received on February 5 and returned for credit.

8   Issued Check No. 813 to Hardy Company in payment of its January 29 invoice, less the discount.

9   Issued a $65 credit memorandum to Ben Blue for defective merchandise sold on February 2 and returned for credit.

10   Sold merchandise on credit to Fred Gage, Invoice No. 713, $650.

11   Purchased store equipment on credit from Best Company, invoice dated February 8, terms n/10 EOM, $515.

Feb. 12   Received payment from Ben Blue for the February 2 sale, less the return and the discount.

13   Received payment from John Moss for the February 3 sale, less the discount.

14   Sold merchandise on credit to Ben Blue, Invoice No. 714, $950.

15   Issued Check No. 814, payable to payroll, in payment of the sales salaries for the first half of the month, $1,210. Cashed the check and paid the employees.

15   Cash sales for the first half of the month, $12,445. (Cash sales are usually recorded daily from the cash register readings. However, they are recorded only twice in this problem to reduce the repetitive transactions.)

15   *Post the items that are posted as individual amounts from the journals. (Normally, such items are posted daily; but since they are few in number in this problem, you are asked to post them on only two occasions.)*

18   Purchased merchandise on credit from Flint Company, invoice dated February 15, terms 2/10, n/60, $1,460.

19   Borrowed $5,000 from Security Bank by giving a note payable.

20   Received payment from Fred Gage for the February 10 sale, less the discount.

21   Purchased on credit from Best Company merchandise, $315; store supplies, $60; and office supplies, $40. Invoice dated February 19, terms n/10 EOM.

22   Purchased merchandise on credit from Hardy Company, invoice dated February 19, terms 2/10, n/60, $1,155.

23   Received a $60 credit memorandum from Flint Company for defective merchandise received on February 18 and returned.

24   Received payment from Ben Blue for the February 14 sale, less the discount.

25   Issued Check No. 815 to Flint Company in payment of its February 15 invoice, less the return and the discount.

27   Sold merchandise on credit to John Moss, Invoice No. 715, $895.

28   Sold merchandise on credit to Fred Gage, Invoice No. 716, $685.

28   Issued Check No. 816, payable to Payroll, in payment of the sales salaries for the last half of the month, $1,195.

28   Cash sales for the last half of the month were $14,880.

28   *Post the remaining items from the journals that are posted as individual amounts.*

28   *Foot and crossfoot the journals and make the month-end postings.*

Required:

1.   Open the following general ledger accounts: Cash, Accounts Receivable, Store Supplies, Office Supplies, Store Equipment, Notes Payable, Accounts Payable, Sales, Sales Returns and Allowances, Sales Discounts, Purchases, Purchases Returns and Allowances, Purchases Discounts, Advertising Expense, and Sales Salaries Expense.

2.   Open these subsidiary accounts receivable ledger accounts: Ben Blue, Fred Gage, and John Moss.

3. Open these subsidiary accounts payable ledger accounts: Best Company, Flint Company, Hardy Company, and Old Company.
4. Prepare a General Journal, a Sales Journal, a Purchases Journal, a Cash Receipts Journal, and a Cash Disbursements Journal like the ones illustrated in this chapter.
5. Enter the transactions in the journals and post when instructed to do so.
6. Prepare a trial balance and prove the subsidiary ledgers with schedules of accounts receivable and payable.

ALTERNATE PROBLEMS

Problem 6–1A

(If the working papers that accompany this text are not being used, omit this problem.)

It is June 21 and you have just been hired as accountant of Hillside Sales, a concern that operates with annual accounting periods that end each May 31. The company's previous accountant journalized its transactions through June 19 and posted all items that required posting as individual amounts, as an examination of the journals and ledgers in the booklet of working papers will reveal.

Hillside Sales completed these transactions beginning on June 21:

June 21 Sold merchandise on credit to Roy Ness, Invoice No. 716, $715. (The terms of all credit sales are 2/10, n/60.)

23 Purchased on credit from Lee Supply Company merchandise, $495; store supplies, $75; and office supplies, $35. Invoice dated June 23, terms n/10 EOM.

24 Issued a credit memorandum to John Long for defective merchandise sold on June 18 and returned for credit, $165.

25 Received a credit memorandum from Pace Company for merchandise received on June 18 and returned for credit, $35.

25 Received a credit memorandum from Lee Supply Company for store supplies received on June 23 and returned for credit, $45.

26 Issued Check No. 723 to Pace Company in payment of its June 16 invoice less the return and the discount.

26 Received payment from Alan Hall for the sale of June 16 less the discount.

27 Issued Check No. 724 to Clark Company in payment of its June 17 invoice less the discount.

27 Sold merchandise on credit to Ted Reed, Invoice No. 717, $1,165.

27 Sold the merchant next door a roll of wrapping paper (store supplies) at cost for cash, $25.

28 Received payment from John Long for the June 18 sale less the return and the discount.

28 Purchased store equipment from Lee Supply Company on credit, invoice dated June 28, terms n/10 EOM, $840.

29 Received merchandise and an invoice dated June 27, terms 2/10, n/60, from Acme Company, $875.

June 30 Douglas Murphy, the owner of Hillside Sales, used Check No. 725 to withdraw $750 cash from the business for personal use.

30 Issued Check No. 726 to Gary Beal, the company's only sales employee, in payment of his salary for the last half of the month plus some overtime, $365.

30 Issued Check No. 727 to Eastern Utility to pay the June electric bill, $165.

30 Cash sales for the last half of the month were $9,325. (Cash sales are usually recorded daily, but you are asked to record them only once in this problem in order to reduce repetitive transactions.)

Required:

1. Record the transaction in the journals provided.
2. Post to the customer and creditor accounts and also post any amounts that should be posted as individual amounts to general ledger accounts. (Normally, these amounts are posted daily, but they are posted only once in this problem in order to simplify it.)
3. Foot and crossfoot the journals and make the month-end postings.
4. Prepare a June 30 trial balance and prove the subsidiary ledgers with schedules of accounts receivable and accounts payable.

Problem 6–2A

Camel Company completed these transactions during April of the current year:

Apr. 2 Received merchandise and an invoice dated March 30, terms 2/10, n/60, from Old Company, $1,965.

3 Sold merchandise on credit to Gary Glen, Invoice No. 632, $1,350. (Terms of all credit sales are 2/10, n/60.)

5 Purchased office equipment on credit from Best Company, invoice dated April 4, terms n/10 EOM, $795.

6 Purchased on credit from Able Company merchandise, $840; store supplies, $65; and office supplies, $40. Invoice dated April 3, terms n/10 EOM.

7 Received a credit memorandum from Old Company for unsatisfactory merchandise received on April 2 and returned for credit, $115.

7 Received a credit memorandum from Best Company for office equipment received on April 5 and returned for credit, $75.

9 Issued Check No. 510 to Old Company in payment of its March 30 invoice less the return and the discount.

11 Sold merchandise on credit to Dale Dent, Invoice No. 633, $1,450.

13 Received payment from Gary Glen for the April 3 sale less the discount.

14 Borrowed $2,500 from Valley Bank by giving a promissory note payable.

15 Issued Check No. 511, payable to Payroll, in payment of the sales salaries for the first half of the month, $925. Cashed the check and paid the employees.

15 Cash sales for the first half of the month were $20,215. (Normally, cash sales are recorded daily. They are recorded only twice in this problem to reduce the number of repetitive entries.)

Apr. 15 *Post to the customer and creditor accounts and also post any amounts that should be posted as individual items to the general ledger accounts. (Normally, such items are posted daily, but you are asked to post them only on two occasions in this problem because they are few in number.)*

17 Sold merchandise on credit to Carl Cole, Invoice No. 634, $1,150.

18 Sold merchandise on credit to Dale Dent, Invoice No. 635, $950.

19 Received merchandise and an invoice dated April 16 from More Company, terms 2/10, n/60, $1,550.

20 Purchased on credit from Able Company merchandise, $515; store supplies, $55; and office supplies, $35. Invoice dated April 17, terms n/10 EOM.

21 Received payment from Dale Dent for the sale of April 11 less the discount.

23 Sold merchandise on credit to Gary Glen, Invoice No. 636, $1,725.

25 Sold merchandise on credit to Carl Cole, Invoice No. 637, $1,415.

26 Issued Check No. 512 to More Company in payment of its April 16 invoice less the discount.

27 Received payment from Carl Cole for the April 17 sale less the discount.

28 Received payment from Dale Dent for the April 18 sale less the discount.

30 Issued Check No. 513, payable to Payroll, in payment of the sales salaries for the last half of the month, $925. Cashed the check and paid the employees.

30 Cash sales for the last half of the month, $19,610.

30 *Post to the customer and creditor accounts and post any amounts that should be posted as individual items to the general ledger accounts.*

30 *Foot and crossfoot the journals and make the month-end postings.*

Required:

1. Open the following general ledger accounts: Cash, Accounts Receivable, Store Supplies, Office Supplies, Office Equipment, Notes Payable, Accounts Payable, Sales, Sales Discounts, Purchases, Purchases Returns and Allowances, Purchases Discounts, and Sales Salaries Expense.

2. Open the following accounts receivable ledger accounts: Carl Cole, Dale Dent, and Gary Glen.

3. Open the following accounts payable ledger accounts: Able Company, Best Company, More Company, and Old Company.

4. Enter the transactions in a Sales Journal, a Purchases Journal, a Cash Receipts Journal, a Cash Disbursements Journal, and a General Journal like the ones illustrated in this chapter. Post when instructed to do so.

5. Prepare a trial balance and prove the subsidiary ledgers by preparing schedules of accounts receivable and payable.

Problem 6–3A

Clark Company completed these transactions during February of the current year:

Feb. 2 Sold merchandise on credit to Fred Cole, Invoice No. 911, $900. (Terms of all credit sales are 2/10, n/60.)

2 Received merchandise and an invoice dated January 30, terms 2/10, n/60, from Dale Company, $1,795.

3 Purchased store equipment from Store Sales Company, invoice dated February 3, terms n/10 EOM, $885.

4 Sold merchandise on credit to Ray Deal, Invoice No. 912, $1,400.

5 Purchased on credit from Hill Company merchandise, $1,635; store supplies, $85; and office supplies, $55. Invoice dated February 4, terms n/10 EOM.

6 Received a credit memorandum from Dale Company for defective merchandise received on February 2 and returned for credit, $45.

7 Received a credit memorandum from Store Sales Company for office equipment received on February 3 and returned for credit, $60.

7 Cash sales for the week ended February 7, $9,310.

7 *Post to the customer and creditor accounts and post any amounts that should be posted as individual items to the general ledger accounts. (Normally, such items are posted daily; but to simplify the problem, you are asked to post them weekly.)*

9 Issued Check No. 815 to Dale Company in payment of its January 30 invoice less the return and the discount.

9 Sold unneeded store equipment at cost for cash, $55.

11 Sold merchandise on credit to Ted Barr, Invoice No. 913, $1,540.

12 Received payment from Fred Cole for the February 2 sale less the discount.

14 Received payment from Ray Deal for the February 4 sale less the discount.

14 Received merchandise and an invoice dated February 11, terms 2/10, n/60, from West Company, $1,650.

14 Issued Check No. 816, payable to Payroll, in payment of the sales salaries for the first half of the month, $935. Cashed the check and paid the employees.

14 Cash sales for the week ended February 14, $8,985.

14 *Post to the customer and creditor accounts and also any amounts to be posted as individual amounts to the general ledger accounts.*

16 Issued a $90 credit memorandum to Ted Barr for defective merchandise sold on February 11 and returned for credit.

17 Received merchandise and an invoice dated February 14, terms 2/10, n/60 from West Company, $1,850.

18 Purchased on credit from Hill Company merchandise, $415; store supplies, $40; and office supplies, $30. Invoice dated February 16, terms n/10 EOM.

18 Sold merchandise on credit to Fred Cole, Invoice No. 914, $1,100.

21 Received payment from Ted Barr for the February 11 sale less the return and the discount.

21 Issued Check No. 817 to West Company in payment of its February 11 invoice less the discount.

21 Cash sales for the week ended February 21, $9,860.

Feb. 21   *Post to the customer and creditor accounts and also post any amounts to be posted as individual items to the general ledger accounts.*

     24   Issued Check No. 818 to West Company in payment of its February 14 invoice less the discount.

     26   Sold merchandise on credit to Ted Barr, Invoice No. 915, $1,125.

     27   Sold merchandise on credit to Ray Deal, Invoice No. 916, $985.

     28   Issued Check No. 819 to *The Gazette* for advertising, $135.

     28   Issued Check No. 820, payable to Payroll, for sales salaries, $955.

     28   Received payment from Fred Cole for the February 18 sale less the discount.

     28   Cash sales for the week ended February 28, $9,440.

     28   *Post to the customer and creditor accounts and also post any amounts to be posted as individual items to the general ledger accounts.*

     28   *Foot and crossfoot the journals and make the month-end postings.*

Required:

1. Open the following general ledger accounts: Cash, Accounts Receivable, Store Supplies, Office Supplies, Store Equipment, Accounts Payable, Sales, Sales Returns and Allowances, Sales Discounts, Purchases, Purchases Returns and Allowances, Purchases Discounts, Sales Salaries Expense, and Advertising Expense.

2. Open these accounts receivable ledger accounts: Ted Barr, Fred Cole, and Ray Deal.

3. Open these accounts payable ledger accounts: Dale Company, Hill Company, Store Sales Company, and West Company.

4. Prepare a Sales Journal, a Purchases Journal, a Cash Receipts Journal, a Cash Disbursements Journal, and a General Journal similar to the ones illustrated in this chapter. Enter the transactions in the journals and post when instructed to do so.

5. Prepare a trial balance of the General Ledger and prove the subsidiary ledgers by preparing schedules of accounts receivable and payable.

Sigma Company—A Minipractice Set

(If the working papers that accompany this text are not being used, omit this minipractice set.)

Assume it is Monday, February 2, the first business day of the month, and you have just been hired as accountant by Sigma Company, a company that operates with monthly accounting periods. All of the company's accounting work has been completed through the end of January, its ledgers show January 31 balances, and you are ready to begin work by recording the following transactions:

Feb. 2   Issued Check No. 510 to Desert Realty in payment of the February rent, $950. (Use two lines to record the transaction. Charge 90% of the rent to Rent Expense, Selling Space and the balance to Rent Expense, Office Space.)

      3   Purchased on credit from Fine Supply Company merchandise, $2,245; store supplies, $85; and office supplies, $50. Invoice dated February 2, terms n/10 EOM.

      3   Sold merchandise on credit to Stern Brothers, Invoice No. 815, $1,500. (The terms of all credit sales are 2/10, n/60.)

Feb. 4 Received a $130 credit memorandum from Good Company for merchandise received on January 29 and returned for credit.

5 Issued a $110 credit memorandum to Bush Company for defective merchandise sold on January 30 and returned for credit.

6 Issued Check No. 511 to Good Company to pay for the $1,630 of merchandise received on January 29, less the return and a 2% discount.

7 Sold store supplies to the merchant next door at cost for cash, $25.

9 Received payment from Bush Company for the sale of January 30 less the return and the discount.

10 Purchased office equipment on credit from Fine Supply Company, invoice dated February 9, terms n/10 EOM, $745.

11 Received merchandise and an invoice dated February 9, terms 2/10, n/60, from Reliable Company, $2,750.

13 Received payment from Stern Brothers for the February 3 sale less the discount.

14 Issued Check No. 512, payable to Payroll, in payment of sales salaries, $485, and office salaries, $425. Cashed the check and paid the employees.

14 Cash sales for the first half of the month, $6,575. (Such sales are normally recorded daily. They are recorded only twice in this problem in order to reduce the number of repetitive transactions.)

14 *Post to the customer and creditor accounts and post any amounts that are posted to the general ledger accounts as individual amounts. (Such items are normally posted daily; but you are asked to post them only at the end of each two weeks because they are few in number.)*

16 Received a $95 credit memorandum from Fine Supply Company for defective office equipment received on February 10 and returned for credit.

16 Sold merchandise on credit to Owl Electric Company, Invoice No. 816, $2,250.

17 Received merchandise and an invoice dated February 14, terms 2/10, n/60, from Quick Company, $3,250.

19 Issued Check No. 513 to Reliable Company in payment of its February 9 invoice less the discount.

20 Sold merchandise on credit to Bush Company, Invoice No. 817, $1,435.

21 Sold merchandise on credit to Morgan and Son, Invoice No. 818, $1,215.

23 Purchased on credit from Fine Supply Company merchandise, $2,970; store supplies, $70; and office supplies, $25. Invoice dated February 21, terms n/10 EOM.

24 Issued Check No. 514 to Quick Company in payment of its February 14 invoice less the discount.

25 Received merchandise and an invoice dated February 22, terms 2/10, n/60, from Reliable Company, $3,190.

26 Received payment from Owl Electric Company for the February 16 sale less the discount.

Feb. 27   Dale Nash, the owner of Sigma Company, used Check No. 515 to withdraw $1,000 from the business for personal use.

   28   Issued Check No. 516, payable to Payroll, in payment of sales salaries, $485, and office salaries, $425. Cashed the check and paid the employees.

   28   Issued Check No. 517 to Public Utility in payment of the February electric bill, $195.

   28   Cash sales for the last half of the month were $6,160.

   28   *Post to the customer and creditor accounts and any amounts that are posted as individual amounts to the general ledger accounts.*

   28   *Foot and crossfoot the journals and make the month-end postings.*

Required:

1.   Enter the transactions in the journals and post when instructed to do so.
2.   Prepare a trial balance in the Trial Balance columns of the work sheet form provided and complete the work sheet using the following information:
   a.   Ending merchandise inventory, $21,220.
   b.   Expired insurance, $115.
   c.   Ending store supplies inventory, $195; and office supplies inventory, $95.
   d.   Estimated depreciation of store equipment, $135; and of office equipment, $40.
3.   Prepare a multiple-step classified February income statement and a February 28 classified balance sheet.
4.   Prepare and post adjusting and closing entries.
5.   Prepare a post-closing trial balance and prove the subsidiary ledgers with schedules of accounts payable and accounts receivable.

Accounting for Assets

PART THREE

Accounting for Cash

7

After studying Chapter 7, you should be able to:

Explain why internal control procedures are needed in a large concern and state the broad principles of internal control.

Describe internal control procedures to protect cash received from cash sales, cash received through the mail, and cash disbursements.

Tell how a petty cash fund operates and be able to make entries in a Petty Cash Record and the entries required to reimburse a petty cash fund.

Explain why the bank balance and the book balance of cash are reconciled and be able to prepare such a reconciliation.

Tell how recording invoices at net amounts helps to gain control over cash discounts taken and be able to account for invoices recorded at net amounts.

Define or explain the words and phrases listed in the chapter Glossary.

Cash has universal usefulness, small bulk for high value, and no convenient identification marks by which ownership may be established. Consequently, in accounting for cash, the procedures for protecting it from fraud and theft are very important. They are called *internal control procedures*. Internal control procedures apply to all assets owned by a business and to all phases of its operations.

INTERNAL CONTROL

In a small business, the owner-manager commonly controls the entire operation through personal supervision and direct participation in the activities of the business. For example, he or she commonly buys all the assets, goods, and services bought by the business. Such a manager also hires and closely supervises all employees, negotiates all contracts, and signs all checks. As a result, in signing checks, for example, he or she knows from personal contact and observation that the assets, goods, and services for which the checks are in payment were received by the business. However, as a business grows, it becomes increasingly difficult to maintain this personal contact. Therefore, at some point it becomes necessary for the manager to delegate responsibilities and rely on internal control procedures rather than personal contact in controlling the operations of the business. In a properly designed system, the procedures encourage adherence to prescribed managerial policies. They also promote operational efficiencies; protect the business assets from waste, fraud, and theft; and ensure accurate and reliable accounting data.

Internal control procedures vary from company to company, depending on such factors as the nature of the business and its size. However, discussions of some of the broad principles of internal control follow.[1]

1. Responsibilities Should Be Clearly Established

Good internal control necessitates that responsibilities be clearly established, and for a given task, one person be made responsible. When responsibility is shared and something goes wrong, it is difficult to determine who was at fault. For example, when two salesclerks share the same cash drawer and there is a shortage, it is normally impossible to tell which clerk is at fault. Each will tend to blame the other. Neither can prove that he or she is not responsible. In such a

---

[1] For a discussion that continues to offer an unusually balanced analysis of the principles of internal control, see AICPA, *Internal Control* (New York, 1949).

situation, each clerk should be assigned a separate cash drawer or one of the clerks should be given responsibility for making all change.

2. Adequate Records Should Be Maintained

Good records provide a means of control by placing responsibility for the care and protection of assets. Poor records invite laxity and often theft. When a company has poor accounting control over its assets, dishonest employees soon become aware of this and are quick to take advantage.

3. Assets Should Be Insured and Employees Bonded

Assets should be covered by adequate casualty insurance, and employees who handle cash and negotiable assets should be bonded. Bonding provides a means for recovery if a loss occurs. It also tends to prevent losses, since a bonded employee is less apt to take assets if the employee knows a bonding company must be dealt with when the shortage is revealed.

4. Record Keeping and Custody Should Be Separated

A fundamental principle of internal control requires that the person who has access to or is responsible for an asset should not maintain the accounting record for that asset. When this principle is observed, the custodian of an asset, knowing that a record of the asset is being kept by another person, is not apt to either misappropriate the asset or waste it; and the record keeper, who does not have access to the asset, has no reason to falsify the record. Furthermore, if the asset is to be misappropriated and the theft concealed in the records, collusion is necessary.

5. Responsibility for Related Transactions Should Be Divided

Responsibility for a divisible transaction or a series of related transactions should be divided between individuals or departments in such a manner that the work of one acts as a check on that of another. This does not mean there should be duplication of work. Each employee or department should perform an unduplicated portion. For example, responsibility for placing orders, receiving the merchandise, and paying the vendors should not be given to one individual or department. To do so is to invite laxity in checking the quality and quantity of goods received, and carelessness in verifying the validity and accuracy of invoices. It also invites the purchase of goods for an employee's personal use and the payment of fictitious invoices.

6. Mechanical Devices Should Be Used Whenever Practicable

Cash registers, check protectors, time clocks, and mechanical counters are examples of control devices that should be used whenever practicable. A cash register with a locked-in tape makes a record of each cash sale. A check protector by perforating the amount of a check into its face makes it very difficult to change the amount. A time clock registers the exact time an employee arrived on the job and when the employee departed.

INTERNAL CONTROL FOR CASH

A good system of internal control for cash should provide adequate procedures for protecting both cash receipts and cash disbursements. In the procedures, three basic principles should always be observed. First, there should be a separation of duties so that the people responsible for handling cash and for its custody are not the same people who keep the cash records. Second, all cash receipts should be deposited in the bank, intact, each day. Third, all payments should be made by check. The one exception to the last principle is that small disbursements may be made in cash from a petty cash fund. Petty cash funds are discussed later in this chapter.

The reason for the first principle is that a division of duties necessitates collusion between two or more people if cash is to be embezzled and the theft concealed in the accounting records. The second, requiring that all receipts be deposited intact each day, prevents an employee from making personal use of the money for a few days before depositing it. And, requiring that all receipts be deposited intact and all payments be made by check provides in the records of the bank a separate and external record of all cash transactions that may be used to prove the company's own records.

The exact procedures used to achieve control over cash vary from company to company. They depend upon such things as company size, number of employees, cash sources, and so on. Consequently, the following procedures are only illustrative of some that are in use.

Cash from Cash Sales

Cash sales should be rung up on a cash register at the time of each sale. To help ensure that correct amounts are rung up, each register should be so placed that customers can see the amounts rung up. Also, the clerks should be required to ring up each sale before wrapping the merchandise. Finally, each cash register should have a locked-in tape on which the amount of each sale and total sales are printed by the register.

Good cash control, as previously stated, requires a separation of custody for cash from record keeping for cash. For cash sales, this separation begins with the cash register. The salesclerk who has access to the cash in the register should not have access to its locked-in tape. At the end of each day, the salesclerk is usually required to count the cash in the register and to turn the cash and its count over to an employee in the cashier's office. The employee in the cashier's office, like the salesclerk, has access to the cash and should not have access to the register tape or other accounting records. A third employee, commonly from the accounting department, removes the tape from the register. He or she compares its total with the cash turned over to the cashier's office and uses the tape's information as a basis for the entry recording cash sales. This employee who has access to the register tape does not have access to the cash and therefore cannot take any. Likewise, since the salesclerk and the employee from the cashier's office do not have access to the cash register tape, they cannot take cash without the shortage being revealed.

Cash Received through the Mail

Control of cash coming in through the mail begins with a mail clerk who opens the mail and makes a list in triplicate of the money received. The list should give each sender's name, the purpose for which the money was sent, and the amount. One copy of the list is sent to the cashier with the money. The second copy goes to the bookkeeper. The third copy is kept by the mail clerk. The cashier deposits the money in the bank, and the bookkeeper records the amounts received in the accounting records. Then, if the bank balance is reconciled (discussed later) by a fourth person, errors or fraud by the mail clerk, the cashier, or bookkeeper will be detected. They will be detected because the cash deposited and the records of three people must agree. Furthermore, fraud is impossible, unless there is collusion. The mail clerk must report all receipts or customers will question their account balances. The cashier must deposit all receipts because the bank balance must agree with the bookkeeper's cash balance. The bookkeeper and the person reconciling the bank balance do not have access to cash and, therefore, have no opportunity to withhold any.

Cash Disbursements

It is important to gain control over cash from sales and cash received through the mail. However, most large embezzlements have not involved cash receipts but have been accomplished through the payment of fictitious invoices. Consequently, procedures for controlling cash disbursements are equally as important and sometimes more important than those for cash receipts.

To gain control over cash disbursements, all disbursements should be made by check, excepting those from petty cash. If authority to sign checks is delegated to some person other than the business owner, that person should not have access to the accounting records. This helps prevent a fraudulent disbursement being made and concealed in the accounting records.

In a small business, the owner-manager usually signs checks and normally knows from personal contact that the items for which the checks pay were received by the business. However, this is impossible in a large business. In a large business, internal control procedures must be substituted for personal contract. The procedures tell the person who signs checks that the obligations for which the checks pay are proper obligations, properly incurred, and should be paid. Often these procedures take the form of a *voucher system*.

THE VOUCHER SYSTEM AND CONTROL

A voucher system helps gain control over cash disbursements as follows: (1) It permits only designated departments and individuals to incur obligations that will result in cash disbursements. (2) It establishes procedures for incurring such obligations and for their verification, approval, and recording. (3) It permits checks to be issued only in payment of properly verified, approved, and recorded obligations. Finally (4), it requires that every obligation be recorded at the time it is incurred and every purchase be treated as an independent transaction, complete in itself. It requires this even though a number of purchases may be made from the same company during a month or other billing period.

When a voucher system is in use, control over cash disbursements begins with the incurrence of obligations that will result in cash disbursements. Only specified departments and individuals are authorized to incur such obligations, and the kind each may incur is limited. For example, in a large store, only the purchasing department may incur obligations by purchasing merchandise. However, to gain control, the purchasing-receiving-and-paying procedures are divided among several departments. They are the departments requesting that merchandise be purchased, the purchasing department, the receiving department, and the accounting department. To coordinate and control the responsibilities of these departments, business papers are used. A list of the papers follows, and an explanation of each will show how a large concern may gain control over cash disbursements resulting from the purchase of merchandise.

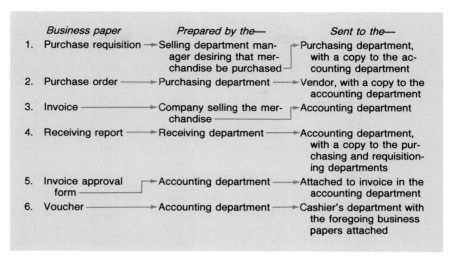

	Business paper	Prepared by the—	Sent to the—
1.	Purchase requisition →	Selling department manager desiring that merchandise be purchased	Purchasing department, with a copy to the accounting department
2.	Purchase order →	Purchasing department →	Vendor, with a copy to the accounting department
3.	Invoice →	Company selling the merchandise →	Accounting department
4.	Receiving report →	Receiving department →	Accounting department, with a copy to the purchasing and requisitioning departments
5.	Invoice approval form →	Accounting department →	Attached to invoice in the accounting department
6.	Voucher →	Accounting department →	Cashier's department with the foregoing business papers attached

Purchase Requisition

The department managers in a large store cannot be permitted to place orders directly with supply sources. If each manager were permitted to deal directly with wholesalers and manufacturers, the amount of merchandise purchased and the resulting liabilities could not be controlled. Therefore, to gain control over purchases and resulting liabilities, department managers are commonly required to place all orders through the purchasing department. In such cases, the function of the several department managers in the purchasing procedure is to inform the purchasing department of their needs. Each manager performs this function by preparing in triplicate and signing a business paper called a *purchase requisition*. On the requisition, the manager lists the merchandise needs of his or her department. The original and a duplicate copy of the purchase requisition are sent to the purchasing department. The third copy is retained by the requisitioning department as a check on the purchasing department.

Purchase Order

A *purchase order* is a business form used by the purchasing department in placing an order with a manufacturer or wholesaler. It authorizes the supplier to ship the merchandise ordered and takes the place of a typewritten letter placing the order. On receipt of a purchase requisition from a selling department, the purchasing department prepares four or more copies of the purchase order. The copies are distributed as follows:

Copy 1, the original copy, is sent to the supplier as a request to purchase and as authority to ship the merchandise listed.

Copy 2, with a copy of the purchase requisition attached, is sent to the accounting department where it will ultimately be used in approving the invoice of the purchase for payment.

Copy 3 is sent to the department issuing the requisition to acknowledge the requisition and tell the action taken.

Copy 4 is retained on file by the purchasing department.

Invoice

An *invoice* is an itemized statement of goods bought and sold. It is prepared by the seller or *vendor*, and to the seller it is a sales invoice. However, when the same invoice is received by the buyer or *vendee*, it becomes a purchase invoice to the buyer. Upon receipt of a purchase order, the manufacturer or wholesaler receiving the order ships the ordered merchandise to the buyer and mails a copy of the invoice covering the shipment. The goods are delivered to the buyer's receiving department. The invoice is sent directly to the buyer's accounting department.

Receiving Report

Most large companies maintain a special department assigned the duty of receiving all merchandise or other assets purchased. As each shipment is received, counted, and checked, the receiving department prepares four or more copies of a *receiving report*. On this report are listed the quantity, description, and condition of the items received. The original copy is sent to the accounting department. The second copy is sent to the department that requisitioned the merchandise. The third copy is sent to the purchasing department. The fourth copy is retained on file in the receiving department. The copies sent to the purchasing and requisitioning departments act as notification of the arrival of the goods.

Invoice Approval Form

When the receiving report arrives in the accounting department, it has in its possession copies of the—

1. Requisition listing the items that were to be ordered.
2. Purchase order that lists the merchandise actually ordered.

3. Invoice showing quantity, description, unit price, and total of the goods shipped by the seller.
4. Receiving report that lists quantity and condition of the items received.

With the information of these papers, the accounting department is in position to approve the invoice for entry on the books and ultimate payment. In approving the invoice, the accounting department checks and compares the information on all the papers. To facilitate the checking procedure and to ensure that no step is omitted, an *invoice approval form* is commonly used. This may be a separate business paper that is attached to the invoice, or the information shown in Illustration 7–1 may be stamped directly on the invoice with a rubber stamp.

As each step in the checking procedure is completed, the clerk making the check initials the invoice approval form. Initials in each space on the form indicate the following:

Illustration 7–1

INVOICE APPROVAL FORM

Purchase order number _____

Requisition check _____

Purchase order check _____

Receiving report check _____

Invoice check:

Price approval _____

Calculations _____

Terms _____

Approved for payment:

_____

1. Requisition check . . . . The items on the invoice agree with the requisition and were requisitioned.
2. Purchase order check . . . . . . The items on the invoice agree with the purchase order and were ordered.
3. Receiving report check . . . . . The items on the invoice agree with the receiving report and were received.

4. Invoice check:

Price approval . . . . The invoice prices are the agreed prices.

Calculations . . . . The invoice has no mathematical errors.

Terms . . . . The terms are the agreed terms.

The Voucher

When a voucher system is in use, after the invoice is checked and approved, a *voucher* is prepared. A voucher is a business paper on which a transaction is summarized, its correctness certified, and its recording and payment approved. Vouchers vary somewhat from company to company. However, in general, they are so designed that the invoice, bill, or other documents from which they are prepared are attached to and folded inside the voucher. This makes for ease in filing. The inside of a voucher is shown in Illustration 7–2, and the outside in Illustration 7–3. The preparation of a voucher is a simple task requiring only that a clerk enter the required information in the

Illustration 7–2: Inside of a voucher

Voucher No. ___767___

VALLEY SUPPLY COMPANY
Eugene, Oregon

Date ___Oct. 1, 19--___

Pay to ___A. B. Seay Wholesale Company___

City ___Salem___   State ___Oregon___

For the following: (attach all invoices and supporting papers)

Date of Invoice	Terms	Invoice Number and Other Details	Amount
Sept. 30, 19--	2/10, n/60	Invoice No. C-11756	800.00
		Less Discount	16.00
		Net Amount Payable	784.00

Payment Approved

___P. C. Neal___
Auditor

proper blank spaces on a voucher form. The information is taken from the invoice and its supporting documents. After the voucher is completed, the invoice and its supporting documents are attached to and folded inside the voucher. The voucher is then sent to the desk of the chief clerk or auditor who makes an additional check, approves the accounting distribution (the accounts to be debited), and approves the voucher for recording.

After being approved and recorded, a voucher is filed until its due date, when it is sent to the office of the company cashier or other disbursing officer for payment. Here the person responsible for issuing checks depends upon the approved voucher and its signed supporting documents to verify that the obligation is a proper obligation, properly incurred, and should be paid. For example, the purchase requisition and purchase order attached to the voucher confirm that the purchase was authorized. The receiving report shows that the items were received, and the invoice approval form verifies that the invoice was checked for errors. As a result, there is little chance for fraud, unless all the documents were stolen and the signatures forged, or there was collusion.

Illustration 7–3:   Outside of a voucher

ACCOUNTING DISTRIBUTION

Voucher No. _767_

Account Debited	Amount
Purchases	800.00
Transportation-In	
Store Supplies	
Office Supplies	
Sales Salaries	

Due Date____ October 6, 19-- _____

Pay to ___ A.B. Seay Wholesale Co. _____
City ____ Salem _____
State ____ Oregon _____

Total Vouch. Pay.Cr.	800.00

Summary of Charges:
Total Charges _____ 800.00 ____
Discount _____ 16.00 ____
Net Payment _____ 784.00 ____

Record of Payment:
Paid _____
Check No. _____

THE VOUCHER SYSTEM AND EXPENSES

Under a voucher system, to gain control over disbursements, every obligation that will result in a cash disbursement must be approved for payment and recorded as a liability at the time it is incurred. This includes all expenses. As a result, for example, when the monthly telephone bill is received, it is verified and any long-distance calls are approved. A voucher is then prepared, and the telephone bill is attached to and folded inside the voucher. The voucher is then recorded, and a check is issued in its payment, or the voucher is filed for payment at a later date.

Requiring that an expense be approved for payment and recorded as an expense and a liability at the time it is incurred helps ensure that every expense payment is approved when information for its approval is available. Often invoices, bills, and statements for such things as equipment repairs are received weeks after the work is done. If no record of the repairs exists, it is difficult at that time to determine whether the invoice or bill is a correct statement of the amount owed. Also, if no records exist, it is possible for a dishonest employee to arrange with an outsider for more than one payment of an obligation, for payment of excessive amounts, and for payment of goods and services not received, all with kickbacks to the dishonest employee.

RECORDING VOUCHERS

Normally a company large enough to use a voucher system will use bookkeeping machines or punched cards, magnetic tape, and a computer in recording its transactions. Consequently, for this reason and also because the primary purpose of this discussion is to describe the control techniques of a voucher system, a pen-and-ink system of recording vouchers is not described here. However, such a system is described in the Appendix at the end of this chapter.

THE PETTY CASH FUND

A basic principle in controlling cash disbursements is that all such disbursements be made by check. However, an exception to this rule is made for petty cash disbursements. Every business must make many small payments for items such as postage, express charges, telegrams, and small items of supplies. If each such payment is made by check, many checks for immaterial amounts are written. This is both time consuming and expensive. Therefore, to avoid writing checks for small amounts, a petty cash fund is established, and such payments are made from this fund.

When a petty cash fund is established, an estimate is made of the total small payments likely to be disbursed during a short period, usually not more than a month. A check is drawn and debited to the Petty Cash account for an amount slightly in excess of this estimate. The check is cashed, and the money is turned over to a member of the office staff who is designated *petty cashier* and who is responsible for the petty cash and for making payments therefrom.

The petty cashier usually keeps the petty cash in a locked box in the office safe. As each disbursement is made, a *petty cash receipt,* Illustration 7–4, is signed by the person receiving payment. The receipt is entered in the *Petty Cash Record* (Illustration 7–6) and then placed with the remaining money in the petty cashbox. Under this system, the petty cashbox should always contain paid petty cash receipts and money equal to the amount of the fund.

Illustration 7–4

RECEIVED OF PETTY CASH

No. -1- $ 1.65

DATE Nov. 3 19 --

FOR Telegram

CHARGE TO Miscellaneous General Expenses
ACCOUNT

APPROVED BY *CaB.*

RECEIVED BY *Bob Tone*

TOPS—FORM 3008

Courtesy Tops Business Forms

Each disbursement reduces the money and increases the sum of the receipts in the petty cashbox. When the money is nearly exhausted, the fund is reimbursed. To reimburse the fund, the petty cashier presents the receipts for petty cash payments to the company cashier who retains the receipts and gives the petty cashier a check for their sum. When this check is cashed and the proceeds returned to the petty cashbox, the money in the box is restored to its original amount and the fund is ready to begin anew the cycle of its operations.

PETTY CASH FUND ILLUSTRATED

To avoid writing numerous checks for small amounts, a company established a petty cash fund on November 1, designating one of its office clerks, Ned Fox, petty cashier. A check for $35 was drawn, cashed, and the proceeds turned over to the clerk. The entry to record the check is shown in Illustration 7–5. The effect of the entry was to transfer $35 from the regular Cash account to the Petty Cash account.

Illustration 7–5

CASH DISBURSEMENTS JOURNAL

Date	Ch. No.	Payee	Account Debited	P R	Other Accts. Debit	Cash Credit
Nov. 1	58	Ned Fox, Petty Cashier	Petty Cash............		35.00	35.00

The Petty Cash account is debited when the fund is established. It is not debited or credited again unless the size of the fund is changed. If the fund is exhausted and reimbursements occur too often, the fund should be increased. This results in an additional debit to the Petty Cash account and a credit to the regular Cash account for the amount of the increase. If the fund is too large, part of its cash should be returned to general cash.

During the first month of the illustrated fund's operation, the following petty cash payments were made:

Nov. 3	Telegram	$ 1.65
7	Purchased paper clips	0.50
12	Express on purchases	3.75
18	Postage on sale	3.80
19	Food for employee working overtime.....	3.60
20	Purchased postage stamps	10.00
21	Express on purchases	2.80
27	Repair of typewriter	7.50
	Total	$33.60

As each amount was disbursed, a petty cash receipt was signed by the person receiving payment. Each receipt was then recorded in the Petty Cash Record and placed in the petty cashbox. The Petty Cash Record with the paid receipts entered is shown in Illustration 7–6.

The Petty Cash Record is a supplementary record and not a book of original entry. A book of original entry is a journal or register from which postings are made. A supplementary record is one in which information is summarized but not posted. Rather, the summarized information is used as a basis for an entry in a regular journal or register, which is posted.

Illustration 7–6

PETTY CASH RECORD

Date	Explanation	Re-ceipt No.	Receipts	Payments	Postage	Trans-porta-tion-In	Misc. General Expense	Miscellaneous Payments Account	Amount
Nov. 1	Established fund (Ch. No. 58)		35.00						
3	Telegram	1		1.65			1.65		
7	Purchased paper clips	2		0.50				Office supplies	0.50
12	Express on purchases	3		3.75		3.75			
18	Postage on sale	4		3.80				Delivery expense	3.80
19	Overtime meals	5		3.60			3.60		
20	Purchased postage stamps	6		10.00	10.00				
21	Express on purchases	7		2.80		2.80			
27	Repair of typewriter	8		7.50			7.50		
27	Totals		35.00	33.60	10.00	6.55	12.75		4.30
	Balance			1.40					
	Totals		35.00	35.00					
Nov. 27	Balance		1.40						
27	Replenished fund (Ch. No. 106)		33.60						

To continue the illustration, on November 27, after the last of the listed payments was made, only $1.40 in money remained in the fund. The petty cashier recognized that this would probably not cover another payment, so he gave his $33.60 of paid petty cash receipts to the company cashier in exchange for a $33.60 check to replenish the fund. On receiving the check, he ruled and balanced his Petty Cash Record (see Illustration 7–6) and entered the amount of the replenishing check. He then cashed the check and was ready to begin anew payments from the fund.

The reimbursing check was recorded in the Cash Disbursements Journal with the second entry of Illustration 7–7. Information for this entry was secured from a summarization of the entries in the Petty Cash Record. Its debits are to accounts affected by payments from the fund. Note that such an entry is necessary to get debits into the accounts for amounts paid from a petty cash fund. Consequently, petty cash must be reimbursed at the end of each accounting period, as well as at any time the money in the fund is low. If the fund is not reimbursed at the end of each accounting period, the asset petty cash is overstated and the expenses and assets of the petty cash payments are understated on the financial statements.

Illustration 7–7

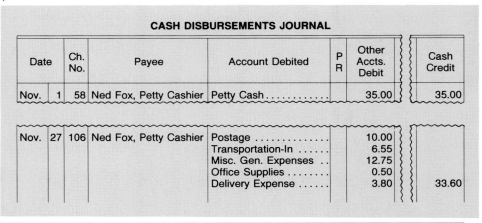

CASH DISBURSEMENTS JOURNAL

Date	Ch. No.	Payee	Account Debited	P R	Other Accts. Debit	Cash Credit
Nov. 1	58	Ned Fox, Petty Cashier	Petty Cash............		35.00	35.00
Nov. 27	106	Ned Fox, Petty Cashier	Postage		10.00	
			Transportation-In		6.55	
			Misc. Gen. Expenses ..		12.75	
			Office Supplies		0.50	
			Delivery Expense		3.80	33.60

Many companies use a Petty Cash Record like the one described here. Other companies are of the opinion that such a record is unnecessary. In the latter, when the petty cash fund is reimbursed, the petty cashier sorts the paid petty cash receipts into groups according to the expense or other accounts to be debited in recording payments from the fund. Each group is then totaled, and a summary of the totals is used in making the reimbursing entry.

Occasionally, at the time of a petty cash expenditure, a petty cashier will forget to secure a receipt, and by the time the fund is reimbursed will have forgotten the expenditure. This causes the fund to be short. If at reimbursement time the petty cash fund is short and no errors or omitted entries can be found, the shortage is entered in the Petty Cash Record as a payment in the Miscellaneous Payments column. It is then recorded as an expense in the reimbursing entry with a debit to the Cash Over and Short account discussed in the next section.

CASH OVER AND SHORT

Regardless of care exercised in making change, customers are sometimes given too much change or are shortchanged. As a result, at the end of a day the actual cash from a cash register is commonly not equal to the cash sales "rung up" on the register. When this occurs and, for example, actual cash as counted is $557 but the register shows cash sales of $556, the entry in general journal form to record sales and the overage is:

Nov.	23	Cash	557.00	
		Cash Over and Short		1.00
		Sales		556.00
		Day's cash sales and overage.		

If, on the other hand, cash is short, the entry in general journal form to record sales and the shortage is:

Nov.	24	Cash	621.00	
		Cash Over and Short	4.00	
		Sales		625.00
		Day's cash sales and shortage.		

Over a period of time, cash overages should about equal cash shortages. However, customers are more prone to report instances in which they are given too little change. Therefore, amounts of cash short are apt to be greater than amounts of cash over. Consequently, the *Cash Over and Short account* normally reaches the end of the accounting period with a debit balance. When it does so, the balance represents an expense. The expense may appear on the income statement as a separate item in the general and administrative expense section. Or if the amount is small, it may be combined with other miscellaneous expenses and appear as part of the item, miscellaneous expenses. When Cash Over and Short reaches the end of the period with a credit balance, the balance represents revenue and normally appears on the income statement as part of the item, miscellaneous revenues.

RECONCILING THE BANK BALANCE

Once each month banks furnish each commercial depositor a bank statement that shows (1) the balance of the depositor's account at the beginning of the month; (2) checks and any other amounts deducted from the account; (3) deposits and any other amounts added to the account; and (4) the account balance at the end of the month, according to the records of the bank. A bank statement is shown in Illustration 7–8.

Banks commonly mail a depositor's bank statement. Included in the envelope with the statement are the depositor's *canceled checks* and any debit or credit memoranda that have affected the account. The checks returned are the ones the bank has paid during the month.

Illustration 7–8

MERCHANT'S NATIONAL BANK
Eugene, Oregon

STATEMENT OF ACCOUNT

| BALANCE BROUGHT FORWARD | | STATEMENT OF BALANCE | | CHECKS RETURNED |
Date	Balance	Date	Balance	
9/30/——	1,578.00	10/31/——	2,050.00	8

Valley Company
10th and Pine Sts.
Eugene, Oregon

CHECKS IN DETAIL				DEPOSITS		DATE		BALANCE	
DM	3 00					10	1	1575	00
	55 00					10	2	1520	00
	120 00		200 00			10	5	1200	00
				240	00	10	6	1440	00
	25 00		75 00	150	00	10	10	1490	00
				180	00	10	18	1670	00
	10 00		50 00			10	23	1610	00
			135 00	100	00	10	25	1575	00
		DM	20 00			10	28	1555	00
				CM 495	00	10	30	2050	00

If no error is reported within ten days this account will be considered correct.

They are called canceled checks because they are canceled by stamping or punching to show that they have been paid. During any month, in addition to the checks the depositor has drawn, the bank may deduct from the depositor's account amounts for service charges, items deposited that are uncollectible, and for errors. The bank notifies the depositor of each such deduction with a debit memorandum. A copy of the memorandum is always included with the monthly statement. The bank may also add amounts to the depositor's account for errors and for amounts collected for the depositor. A credit memorandum is used to notify of any additions.

If all receipts are deposited intact and all payments, other than petty cash payments, are made by check, the bank statement becomes a device for proving the depositor's cash records. The proof normally begins with the preparation of a *reconciliation of the bank balance.*

Need for Reconciling the Bank Balance

Normally, when the bank statement arrives, the balance of cash as shown by the statement does not agree with the balance shown by the depositor's accounting records. Consequently, in order to prove the accuracy of both the depositor's records and those of the bank, it is necessary to *reconcile* and account for any differences between the two balances.

Numerous things may cause the bank statement balance to differ from the depositor's book balance of cash. Some are the following:

1. *Outstanding checks.* These are checks that have been drawn by the depositor and deducted on the depositor's records but have not reached the bank for payment and deduction.
2. *Unrecorded deposits.* Companies often make deposits at the end of each business day, after the bank has closed. These deposits are made in the bank's night depository and are not recorded by the bank until the next business day. Consequently, if a deposit is placed in the night depository the last day of the month, it does not appear on the bank statement for that month.
3. *Charges for service and uncollectible items.* A bank often deducts amounts from a depositor's account for services rendered and for items deposited that it is unable to collect. Insufficient funds checks are the most common of the latter. The bank notifies the depositor of each such deduction with a debit memorandum. If the item is material in amount, the memorandum is mailed to the depositor on the day of the deduction. Furthermore, in a well-managed company, each such deduction is recorded on the day the memorandum is received. However, occasionally there are unrecorded amounts near the end of the month.

4. *Collections.* Banks often act as collecting agents for their depositors, collecting for a small fee promissory notes and other items. When an item such as a promissory note is collected, the bank usually adds the proceeds to the depositor's account. It then sends a credit memorandum as notification of the transaction. As soon as the memorandum is received, it should be recorded. Occasionally, there are unrecorded amounts near the end of the month.

5. *Errors.* Regardless of care and systems of internal control for automatic error detection, both the bank and the depositor make errors that affect the bank balance. Occasionally, these errors are not discovered until the balance is reconciled.

Steps in Reconciling the Bank Balance

The steps in reconciling the bank balance are the following:

1. Compare the deposits listed on the bank statement with deposits shown in the accounting records. Note any discrepancies and discover which is correct. List any errors or unrecorded items.

2. When canceled checks are returned by the bank, they are in a stack in the order of their listing on the bank statement. While the checks are in this order, compare each with its bank statement listing. Note any discrepancies or errors.

3. Rearrange the returned checks in numerical order, the order in which they were written. Secure the previous month's reconciliation and determine if any checks outstanding at the end of the previous month are still outstanding. If there are any, list them. Also, see that any deposits that were unrecorded by the bank at the end of the previous month have been recorded.

4. Insert among the canceled checks any bank memoranda according to their dates. Compare each check with its entry in the accounting records. Note for correction any discrepancies, and list any unpaid checks or unrecorded memoranda.

5. Prepare a reconciliation of the bank statement balance with the book balance of cash. Such a reconciliation is shown in Illustration 7–9.

6. Determine if any debits or credits appearing on the bank statement are unrecorded in the books of account. Make journal entries to record them.

ILLUSTRATION OF A BANK RECONCILIATION

To illustrate a bank reconciliation, assume that Valley Company found the following when it attempted to reconcile its bank balance of October 31. The bank balance as shown by the bank statement was $2,050, and the cash balance according to the accounting records was $1,373. Check No. 124 for $150 and Check No. 126 for $200 were outstanding and unpaid by the bank. A $145 deposit, placed in the bank's night depository after banking hours on October 31, was unrecorded by the bank at the time the bank statement was mailed. Among the returned checks was a credit memorandum showing the bank had collected a note receivable for the company on October 30, crediting the proceeds, $500 less a $5 collection fee, to the company account. Also returned with the bank statement was a $3 debit memorandum for checks printed by the bank and a NSF (not sufficient funds) check for $20. This check had been received from a customer, Frank Jones, on October 25, and had been included in that day's deposit. The collection of the note, the return of the NSF check, and the check printing charge were unrecorded on the company books. The statement reconciling these amounts is shown in Illustration 7–9.

Illustration 7–9

VALLEY COMPANY
Bank Reconciliation as of October 31, 19—

Book balance of cash		$1,373	Bank statement balance		$2,050
Add:			Add:		
Proceeds of note less			Deposit of 10/31		145
collection fee		495			$2,195
		$1,868			
Deduct:			Deduct:		
NSF check of Frank Jones ..	$20		Outstanding checks:		
Check printing charge	3	23	No. 124	$150	
			No. 126	200	350
Reconciled balance		$1,845	Reconciled balance		$1,845

A bank reconciliation helps locate any errors made by either the bank or the depositor. It discloses any items that have been entered on the company books but have not come to the bank's attention. Also, it discloses items that should be recorded on the company books but are unrecorded on the date of the reconciliation. For example, in the reconciliation illustrated, the reconciled cash balance, $1,845, is the true cash balance. However, at the time the reconciliation is completed, Valley Company's accounting records show a $1,373 book balance. Consequently, entries must be made to adjust the book balance, increasing it to the true cash balance. This requires three entries. The first in general journal form is:

Nov.	2	Cash	495.00	
		Collection Expense	5.00	
		Notes Receivable		500.00
		To record the proceeds and collection charge of a note collected by the bank.		

This entry is self-explanatory. The bank collected a note receivable, deducted a collection fee, and deposited the difference to the Valley Company account. The entry increases the amount of cash on the books, records the collection expense, and reduces notes receivable.

The second entry is:

Nov.	2	Accounts Receivable—Frank Jones	20.00	
		Cash		20.00
		To charge back the NSF check received from Frank Jones.		

This entry records the NSF check returned as uncollectible. The check was received from Jones in payment of his account and was deposited as cash. The bank, unable to collect the check, deducted $20 from the Valley Company account. This made it necessary for the company to reverse the entry made when the check was received. After recording the returned check, the company will endeavor to collect the $20 from Jones. If after all legal means of collection have been exhausted and the company is still unable to collect, the amount will be written off as a bad debt. (Bad debts are discussed in the next chapter.)

The third entry debits the check printing charge to Miscellaneous General Expenses and in general journal form is:

Nov.	2	Miscellaneous General Expenses	3.00	
		Cash		3.00
		Check printing charge.		

OTHER INTERNAL CONTROL PROCEDURES

Internal control procedures apply to every phase of a company's operations from purchases through sales, cash receipts, cash disbursements, and the control of plant assets. Many of these procedures are discussed in later chapters. However, the way in which a company can gain control over purchases discounts is discussed here where there is time and space for problems illustrating the technique.

Recall that thus far the following entries in general journal form have been used in recording the receipt and payment of an invoice for merchandise purchased.

Oct.	2	Purchases	1,000.00	
		Accounts Payable		1,000.00
		Purchased merchandise, terms 2/10, n/60.		
	12	Accounts Payable	1,000.00	
		Purchases Discounts		20.00
		Cash		980.00
		Paid the invoice of October 2.		

The invoice of these entries was recorded at its *gross*, $1,000, amount. This is the way in which invoices are recorded in many companies. However, well-managed companies follow the practice of taking all offered cash discounts. In many of these companies, invoices are recorded at their *net*, after discount amounts. To illustrate, a company that records invoices at net amounts purchased merchandise having a $1,000 invoice price, terms 2/10, n/60. On receipt of the goods, it deducted the offered $20 discount from the gross invoice amount and recorded the purchase with this entry:

Oct.	2	Purchases	980.00	
		Accounts Payable		980.00
		Purchased merchandise on credit.		

If the invoice for this purchase is paid within the discount period (all invoices should be so paid), the cash disbursements entry to record the payment has a debit to Accounts Payable and a credit to Cash for $980. However, if payment is not made within the discount period and the discount is *lost*, an entry like the following must be made in the General Journal either before or when the invoice is paid:

Dec.	1	Discounts Lost.............................	20.00	
		Accounts Payable		20.00
		To record the discount lost.		

A check for the full $1,000 invoice amount is then drawn, recorded, and mailed to the creditor.

Advantage of the Net Method

When invoices are recorded at gross amounts, the amount of discounts taken is deducted from the balance of the Purchases account on the income statement to arrive at the cost of merchandise purchased. However, when invoices are recorded at gross amounts, if through oversight or carelessness discounts are lost, the amount of discounts lost does not appear in any account or on the income statement and may not come to the attention of management. On the other hand, when purchases are recorded at net amounts, the amount of discounts taken does not appear on the income statement. However, the amount of discounts lost is called to management's attention through the appearance on the income statement of the expense account, Discounts Lost, as in the condensed income statement of Illustration 7–10.

Illustration 7–10

XYZ COMPANY
Income Statement for Year Ended December 31, 19—

Sales	$100,000
Cost of goods sold	60,000
Gross profit from sales	$ 40,000
Operating expenses	28,000
Income from operations	$ 12,000
Other revenues and expenses:	
Discounts lost	(150)
Net income	$ 11,850

Of the two methods, recording invoices at their net amounts probably supplies management with the more valuable information, the amount of discounts lost through oversight, carelessness, or other cause. It also gives management better control over the work of the people responsible for taking cash discounts. If discounts are lost, someone must explain why. As a result, few discounts are lost through carelessness.

APPENDIX

RECORDING VOUCHERS, PEN-AND-INK SYSTEM

When a voucher system is in use, an account called Vouchers Payable replaces the Accounts Payable account described in previous chapters. And, for every transaction that will result in a cash disbursement, a voucher is prepared and credited to this account. For example, when merchandise is purchased, the voucher covering the transaction is recorded with a debit to Purchases and a credit to Vouchers Payable. Likewise, when a plant asset is purchased or an expense is incurred, the voucher of the transaction is recorded with a debit to the proper plant asset or expense account and a credit to Vouchers Payable.

In a pen-and-ink system, vouchers are recorded in a *Voucher Register* similar to Illustration 7A–1. Such a register has a Vouchers Payable credit column and a number of debit columns. The exact debit columns vary from company to company, but merchandising concerns always provide a Purchases debit column. Also, as long as space is available, special debit columns are provided for transactions that occur frequently. In addition, an Other Accounts debit column is provided for transactions that do not occur often.

In recording vouchers in a register like that of Illustration 7A–1, all information about each voucher, other than information about its payment, is entered as soon as the voucher is approved for recording. The information as to payment date and the number of the paying check is entered later as each voucher is paid.

In posting a Voucher Register like that in Illustration 7A–1, the columns are first totaled and crossfooted to prove their equality. The Vouchers Payable column total is then credited to the Vouchers Payable account. The totals of the Purchases, Transportation-In, Sales Salaries Expense, Advertising Expense, Delivery Expense, and Office Salaries Expense are debited to these accounts. None of the individual amounts in these columns are posted. However, the individual amounts in the Other Accounts column are posted as individual amounts and the column total is not posted.

THE UNPAID VOUCHERS FILE

When a voucher system is in use, some vouchers are paid as soon as they are recorded. Others must be filed until payment is due. As an aid in taking cash discounts, vouchers for which payment is not due are generally filed in an unpaid vouchers file under the dates on which they are to be paid.

The file of unpaid vouchers takes the place of a subsidiary Accounts Payable Ledger. Actually, the file is a subsidiary ledger of amounts owed creditors. Likewise, the Vouchers Payable account is in effect a controlling account controlling the unpaid vouchers file. Consequently, after posting is completed at the end of a month, the balance of the Vouchers Payable account should equal the sum of the unpaid vouchers in the unpaid vouchers file. This is verified each month by preparing a schedule or an adding machine list of the unpaid vouchers

Illustration 7A–1

Page 32				When and How Paid		Vouch-ers Payable Credit	Pur-chases Debit	Transpor-tation-In Debit		VOUCHER
Date 19—		Voucher No.	Payee	Date	Check No.				
Oct.	1	767	A. B. Seay Co.	10/6	733	800.00	800.00		1
	1	768	Daily Sentinel	10/9	744	53.00			2
	2	769	Seaboard Supply Co.	10/12	747	235.00	155.00	10.00	3
	6	770	George Smith	10/6	734	85.00			4
	6	771	Frank Jones	10/6	735	95.00			5
	6	772	George Roth	10/6	736	95.00			6
	30	998	First National Bank	10/30	972	505.00			33
									34
	30	999	Pacific Telephone Co.	10/30	973	18.00			35
	31	1000	Tarbell Wholesale Co.			235.00	235.00		36
	31	1001	Office Equipment Co.	10/31	974	195.00			37
	31		Totals			5,079.00	2,435.00	156.00	38
						(213)	(511)	(514)	39
									40
									41

in the file and comparing its total with the balance of the Vouchers Payable account. In addition, the unpaid vouchers in the file are compared with the unpaid vouchers shown in the Voucher Register's record of payments column. The number of each paying check and the payment date are entered in the Voucher Register's payments column as each voucher is paid. Consequently, the vouchers in the register without check numbers and payment dates should be the same as those in the unpaid vouchers file.

THE VOUCHER SYSTEM CHECK REGISTER

In a pen-and-ink voucher system, checks drawn in payment of vouchers are recorded in a simplified Check Register. It is simplified because under a voucher system no obligation is paid until a voucher covering the payment is prepared and recorded. Likewise, no check is drawn except in payment of a specific voucher. Consequently, all checks drawn result in debits to Vouchers Payable and credits to Cash, unless a discount must be recorded. Then, there are credits to both Purchases Discounts and to Cash. Such a register is shown in Illustration

REGISTER   Page 32

	Sales Salaries Expense Debit	Adver- tising Expense Debit	Delivery Expense Debit	Office Salaries Expense Debit	Other Accounts Debit		
					Account Name	Post. Ref.	Amount Debit
1							
2		53.00					
3					Store Supplies	117	70.00
4				85.00			
5	95.00						
6	95.00						
33					Notes Payable	211	500.00
34					Interest Expense	721	5.00
35					Telephone Expense	655	18.00
36							
37					Office Equipment	134	195.00
38	740.00	115.00	358.00	340.00			935.00
39	(611)	(612)	(615)	(651)			(✓)
40							
41							

7A–2. Note that it has columns for debits to Vouchers Payable and credits to Purchases Discounts and to Cash. In posting, all amounts entered in these columns are posted in the column totals.

PURCHASES RETURNS

Occasionally, an item must be returned after the voucher recording its purchase has been prepared and entered in the Voucher Register. In such cases, the return may be recorded with a general journal entry similar to the following:

Nov.	5	Vouchers Payable	15.00	
		Purchases Returns and Allowances		15.00
		Returned defective merchandise.		

In addition to the entry, the amount of the return is deducted on the voucher and the credit memorandum and other documents verify-

Illustration 7A–2

CHECK REGISTER

Date 19—		Payee	Voucher No.	Check No.	Vouchers Payable Debit	Purchases Discounts Credit	Cash Credit
Oct.	1	C. B. & Y. RR. Co.	765	728	14.00		14.00
	3	Frank Mills	766	729	73.00		73.00
	3	Ajax Wholesale Co.	753	730	250.00	5.00	245.00
	4	Normal Supply Co.	747	731	100.00	2.00	98.00
	5	Office Supply Co.	763	732	43.00		43.00
	6	A. B. Seay Co.	767	733	800.00	16.00	784.00
	6	George Smith	770	734	85.00		85.00
	6	Frank Jones	771	735	95.00		95.00
	30	First National Bank	998	972	505.00		505.00
	30	Pacific Telephone Co.	999	973	18.00		18.00
	31	Office Equipment Co.	1001	974	195.00		195.00
	31	Totals			6,468,00	28.00	6,440.00
					(213)	(512)	(111)

ing the return are attached to the voucher. Then, when the voucher is paid, a check is drawn for its corrected amount.

GLOSSARY

Bank reconciliation. An analysis explaining the difference between an enterprise's book balance of cash and its bank statement balance.

Canceled checks. Checks paid by the bank and canceled by punching or stamping.

Cash Over and Short account. An account in which are recorded cash overages and cash shortages arising from making change.

Discounts lost. Cash discounts offered but not taken.

Gross method of recording invoices. Recording invoices at the full amount of the sale price without deducting offered cash discounts.

Internal controls system. The methods and procedures adopted by a business to control its operations and protect its assets from waste, fraud, and theft.

Invoice. A document listing items sold, together with prices, the customer's name, and the terms of sale.

Invoice approval form. A document used in checking an invoice and approving it for recording and payment.

Net method of recording invoices. Recording invoices at the full amount of the sale price less offered cash discounts.

Outstanding checks. Checks that have been written, recorded, and sent or given to payees but have not been received by the bank, paid, and returned.

Purchase order. A business form used in placing an order for the purchase of goods from a vendor.

Purchase requisition. A business form used within a business to ask the purchasing department of the business to buy needed items.

Receiving report. A form used within a business to notify the proper persons of the receipt of goods ordered and of the quantities and condition of the goods.

Reconcile. To account for the difference between two amounts.

Vendee. The purchaser of something.

Vendor. The individual or enterprise selling something.

Voucher. A business paper used in summarizing a transaction and approving it for recording and payment.

Voucher Register. A book of original entry in which approved vouchers are recorded.

Voucher system. An accounting system used to control the incurrence and payment of obligations requiring the disbursement of cash.

QUESTIONS FOR CLASS DISCUSSION

1. Internal control procedures are important in every business, but at what stage in the development of a business do they become critical?
2. Name some of the broad principles of internal control.
3. Why should the person who keeps the record of an asset be a different person from the one responsible for custody of the asset?
4. Why should responsibility for a sequence of related transactions be divided among different departments or individuals?
5. In a small business, it is sometimes impossible to separate the functions of record keeping and asset custody, and it is sometimes impossible to divide responsibilities for related transactions. What should be substituted for these control procedures?
6. What is meant by the phrase *all receipts should be deposited intact?* Why should all receipts be deposited intact on the day of receipt?
7. Why should a company's bookkeeper not be given responsibility for receiving cash for the company nor the responsibility for signing checks or making cash disbursements in any other way?
8. In purchasing merchandise in a large store, why are the department managers not permitted to deal directly with the sources of supply?
9. What are the duties of the selling department managers in the purchasing procedures of a large store?
10. Tell *(a)* who prepares, *(b)* who receives, and *(c)* the purpose of each of the following business papers:

a. Purchase requisition.   d. Receiving report.

b. Purchase order.   e. Invoice approval form.

c. Invoice.   f. Voucher.

11. Do all companies need a voucher system? At what approximate point in a company's growth would you recommend the installation of such a system?

12. When a disbursing officer issues a check in a large business, he or she usually cannot know from personal contact that the assets, goods, or services for which the check pays were received by the business or that the purchase was properly authorized. However, if the company has an internal control system, the officer can depend on the system. Exactly what documents does the officer depend on to tell that the purchase was authorized and properly made and the goods were actually received?

13. Why are some cash payments made from a petty cash fund? Why are not all payments made by check?

14. What is a petty cash receipt? When a petty cash receipt is prepared, who signs it?

15. Explain how a petty cash fund operates.   #252

16. Why must a petty cash fund be reimbursed at the end of each accounting period?

17. What are two results of reimbursing the petty cash fund?

18. What is a bank statement? What kind of information appears on a bank statement? #258

19. What is the meaning of the phrase *to reconcile?* Book balance + actual Cash in bank

20. Why are the bank statement balance of cash and the depositor's book balance of cash reconciled?

21. What valuable information becomes readily available to management when invoices are recorded at net amounts? Is this information readily available when invoices are recorded at gross amounts?

CLASS EXERCISES

Exercise 7–1

A company established a $25 petty cash fund on September 5. Two weeks later, on September 19, there were $1.75 in cash in the fund and receipts for these expenditures: postage, $6.50; transportation-in, $7.25; miscellaneous general expenses, $5; and office supplies, $4.50. *(a)* Give in general journal form the entry to establish the fund and *(b)* the entry to reimburse it on September 19. *(c)* Assume that since the fund was exhausted so quickly, it was not only reimbursed on September 19 but also increased in size to $50. Give the entry to reimburse and increase the fund to $50.

Exercise 7–2

A company established a $50 petty cash fund on October 3. On November 30, there were $23 in cash in the fund and receipts for these expenditures: transportation-in, $9.75; miscellaneous general expenses, $8.50; and office supplies, $7.75. The petty cashier could not account for the $1 shortage in the fund. Give in general journal form *(a)* the entry to establish the fund and *(b)* the November 30 entry to reimburse the fund and reduce it to $25.

Exercise 7–3   Southside Shop deposits all receipts intact on the day received and makes all payments by check; and on November 30, after all posting was completed, its Cash account showed a $1,510 debit balance; but its November 30 bank statement showed only $1,299 on deposit in the bank on that day. Prepare a bank reconciliation for the shop, using the following information:

a. Outstanding checks, $200.
b. Included with the November canceled checks returned by the bank was a $4 debit memorandum for bank services.
c. Check No. 512, returned with the canceled checks, was correctly drawn for $24 in payment of the telephone bill and was paid by the bank on November 7, but it had been recorded with a debit to Telephone Expense and a credit to Cash as though it were for $42.
d. The November 30 cash receipts, $425, were placed in the bank's night depository after banking hours on that date and were unrecorded by the bank at the time the November bank statement was mailed.

Exercise 7–4   Give in general journal form any entries that Southside Shop should make as a result of having prepared the bank reconciliation of the previous exercise.

Exercise 7–5   Sage Company incurred $7,000 of operating expenses in October, a month in which its sales were $25,000. The company began October with a $13,000 merchandise inventory and ended the month with a $14,000 inventory. During the month, it purchased merchandise having a $16,000 invoice price, all of which was subject to a 2% discount for prompt payment. The company took advantage of the discounts on $11,000 of the purchases; but through an error in filing, it did not earn and could not take the discount on a $5,000 invoice paid on October 30.

Required:

1. Prepare an October income statement for the company under the assumption that it records invoices at gross amounts.
2. Prepare a second income statement for the company under the assumption that it records invoices at net amounts.

PROBLEMS

Problem 7–1   Lee Best, owner of a small business, established a petty cash fund on the advice of his accountant. During the fund's first month, the following petty cash transactions were completed.

Nov. 3 Drew Check No. 633, payable to Ted Moss, petty cashier. Cashed the check and delivered the $50 proceeds and the Petty Cash Record to the newly appointed petty cashier.
      5 Purchased postage stamps with $15 from petty cash.

Nov. 8 Paid Parcel Delivery Service $4.25 COD delivery charges on merchandise purchased for resale.

10 Paid $8 for minor repairs to an office typewriter.

13 Paid the laundry truck driver $3.50 upon the delivery of a package of shirts Mr. Best had left at the laundry and had asked that they be delivered to the office.

17 Paid Parcel Delivery Service $3.75 COD delivery charges on merchandise purchased for resale.

18 Gave Mrs. Best, wife of the business owner, $5 for cab fare and other personal expenses.

23 Paid Quick Delivery Service $2.50 to deliver merchandise sold to a customer.

27 Purchased office supplies with petty cash, $2.25.

30 Drew Check No. 710 to reimburse the fund for expenditures and a $1.25 shortage the petty cashier could not explain.

Required:

Record the transactions in a Petty Cash Record and, where required, in a Cash Disbursements Journal similar to the ones illustrated in this chapter. Balance and rule the Petty Cash Record before entering the replenishing check. Skip a line between entries in the Cash Disbursements Journal to set the entries apart.

Problem 7–2   A business established a petty cash fund, appointed Jane Hill, an office secretary, petty cashier, and then completed these transaction:

Dec. 1 Drew Check No. 889 for $30 to establish the fund, cashed the check, and delivered the proceeds and the Petty Cash Record to the new petty cashier.

3 Paid $5.25 COD delivery charges on merchandise purchased for resale.

5 Purchased postage stamps with $15 from petty cash.

6 Paid $6 for minor repairs to an office desk.

8 Purchased paper clips with petty cash, $2.50.

8 Drew Check No. 915 to replenish the petty cash fund; and because the fund was exhausted so rapidly, made the check large enough to increase the size of the fund to $50.

10 Paid $5 to have the office windows washed.

17 Paid $3.75 COD delivery charges on merchandise purchased for resale.

20 Paid Rocket Delivery Service $2.50 to deliver merchandise sold to a customer.

23 Purchased postage stamps with $15 of petty cash.

24 Paid $4.75 COD delivery charges on merchandise purchased for resale.

27 Paid Rocket Delivery Service $3.25 to deliver merchandise sold to a customer.

31 In reimbursing the fund at the end of the accounting period, the

petty cashier found she had only $15 in cash in the fund and she could not account for the shortage. Drew Check No. 998 to reimburse the fund for expenditures and the shortage.

Required:

Record the transactions in a Petty Cash Record and, where required, in a Cash Disbursements Journal similar to the ones illustrated in this chapter. Balance and rule the Petty Cash Record at the time of each reimbursement. Skip a line between entries in the Cash Disbursements Journal to set the entries apart.

Problem 7–3   The following information was available to reconcile Brill Company's book balance of cash with its bank statement balance as of December 31:

a.   The December 31 cash balance according to the accounting records was $2,780, and the bank statement balance for that date was $2,653.
b.   Two checks, No. 722 for $103 and No. 726 for $93, were outstanding on November 30 when the book and bank statement balances were last reconciled. Check No. 726 was returned with the December canceled checks, but Check No. 722 was not.
c.   Check No. 803 for $79 and Check No. 805 for $73, both written and entered in the accounting records in December, were not among the canceled checks returned.
d.   When the December checks were compared with entries in the accounting records, it was found that Check No. 751 had been correctly drawn for $183 in payment for store supplies but was entered in the accounting records in error as though it were drawn for $138.
e.   Two debit memoranda and a credit memorandum were included with the returned checks and were unrecorded at the time of the reconciliation. The credit memorandum indicated that the bank had collected a $500 note receivable for the company, deducted a $4 collection fee, and credited the balance to the company's account. One of the debit memoranda was for $32 and had attached to it a NSF check in that amount that had been received from a customer, Dale Hill, in payment of his account. The second debit memorandum was for a special printing of checks and was for $12.
f.   The December 31 cash receipts, $789, had been placed in the bank's night depository after banking hours on that date and did not appear on the bank statement.

Required:

Prepare a December 31 bank reconciliation for the company and the entries in general journal form required to adjust the company's book balance of cash to the reconciled balance.

Problem 7–4   Olive Company reconciled its book and bank statement balances of cash on October 31 with two checks outstanding, No. 713 for $275 and No. 716 for $142. The following information was available for the November 30 reconciliation:

Olive Company 17th and High Streets		Statement of account with FIRST NATIONAL BANK		
Date	Checks and Other Debits		Deposits	Balance
Nov. 1	Balance brought forward			1,912.00
2	275.00			1,637.00
3	218.00		312.00	1,731.00
5	302.00			1,429.00
9	737.00			692.00
12	75.00	132.00		485.00
14			551.00	1,036.00
18	284.00			752.00
21			512.00	1,264.00
28	343.00		472.00	1,393.00
29	43.00 NSF			1,350.00
30	3.00 SC		995.00 CM	2,342.00

Code: CM Credit Memorandum   NSF Not sufficient funds check
        DM Debit Memorandum   SC Service charge

CASH RECEIPTS DEPOSITED

Date			Cash Debit
Nov. 3			312.00
14			551.00
21			512.00
28			472.00
30			247.00
30			2,094.00

CASH DISBURSEMENTS

Check Number			Cash Credit
718			218.00
719			320.00
720			75.00
721			737.00
722			132.00
723			136.00
724			284.00
725			343.00
726			53.00
			2,298.00

From the General Ledger:

CASH

Date	Explanation	PR	Debit	Credit	Balance
Oct. 31	Balance	✓			1,495.00
Nov. 30	Total receipts	R-8	2,094.00		3,589.00
30	Total disbursements	D-9		2,298.00	1,291.00

Check No. 719 was correctly drawn for $302 in payment for office equipment; however, the bookkeeper misread the amount and entered in the accounting records with a debit to Office Equipment and a credit to Cash as though it were for $320.

The NSF check was received from a customer, Ted Lee, in payment of his account. Its return is unrecorded. The credit memorandum resulted from a $1,000 note collected for Olive Company by the bank. The bank had deducted a $5 collection fee. The collection is not recorded.

Required:

1. Prepare a November 30 bank reconciliation for the company.
2. Prepare in general journal form the entries needed to adjust the book balance of cash to the reconciled balance.

Problem 7–5   The August 31 credit balance in the Sales account of Apex Sales showed it had sold $48,500 of merchandise during the month. The company began August with a $54,600 merchandise inventory and ended the month with a $45,100 inventory. It had incurred $16,600 of operating expenses during the month, and it had also recorded the following transactions:

Aug. 1 Received merchandise purchased at a $5,000 invoice price, invoice dated July 28, terms 2/10, n/30.

5 Received a $500 credit memorandum (invoice price) for merchandise received on August 1 and returned for credit.

11 Received merchandise purchased at an $8,000 invoice price, invoice dated August 9, terms 2/10, n/30.

15 Received merchandise purchased at a $7,500 invoice price, invoice dated August 12, terms 2/10, n/30.

19 Paid for the merchandise received on August 11, less the discount.

22 Paid for the merchandise received on August 15, less the discount.

27 The invoice received on August 1 had been refiled in error, after the credit memorandum was attached, for payment on this the last day of its credit period, causing the discount to be lost. Paid the invoice.

Required:

1. Assume the company records invoices at gross amounts and *(a)* prepare general journal entries to record the transactions. *(b)* Prepare an August income statement for the concern.
2. Assume the company records invoices at net amounts and *(a)* prepare general journal entries to record the transactions. *(b)* Prepare a second income statement for the company under this assumption.

Problem 7–6   *(This problem is based on information in the Appendix to this chapter.)* Lee Company completed these transactions involving vouchers payable:

Oct. 2 Recorded Voucher No. 751 payable to Tipton Company for merchandise having $950 invoice price, invoice dated September 28, terms FOB factory, 2/10, n/30. The vendor had prepaid the freight, $45, adding the amount to the invoice and bringing its total to $995.

4 Recorded Voucher No. 752 payable to *The Times* for advertising expense, $110. Issued Check No. 748 in payment of the voucher.

5 Received a credit memorandum for merchandise having a $150 invoice price. The merchandise had been received from Tipton Company on October 2 and returned for credit.

9 Recorded Voucher No. 753 payable to Lake Realty for one month's rent on the space occupied by the store, $500. Issued Check No. 749 in payment of the voucher.

Oct. 11 Recorded Voucher No. 754 payable to Beta Supply Company for store supplies, $65, terms n/10 EOM.

14 Recorded Voucher No. 755 payable to Phoenix Company for merchandise having a $1,250 invoice price, invoice dated October 11, terms FOB factory, 2/10, n/60. The vendor had prepaid the freight charges, $50, adding the amount to the invoice and bringing its total to $1,300.

15 Recorded Voucher No. 756 payable to Payroll for sales salaries, $500, and office salaries $375. Issued Check No. 750 in payment of the voucher. Cashed the check and paid the employees.

18 Recorded Voucher No. 757 payable to West Company for merchandise having a $750 invoice price, invoice dated October 15, terms 2/10, n/60, FOB factory. The vendor had prepaid the freight charges, $35, adding the amount to the invoice and bringing its total to $785.

21 Issued Check No. 751 in payment of Voucher No. 755.

26 Recorded Voucher No. 758 payable to Phoenix Company for merchandise having a $1,500 invoice price, invoice dated October 22, terms FOB factory, 2/10, n/60. The vendor had prepaid the freight charges, $70, adding the amount to the invoice and bringing its total to $1,570.

28 Discovered that Voucher No. 751 had been filed in error for payment on the last day of its credit period rather than on the last day of its discount period, causing the discount to be lost. Issued Check No. 752 in payment of the voucher.

31 Recorded Voucher No. 759 payable to Payroll for sales salaries, $500, and office salaries $375. Issued Check No. 753 in payment of the voucher. Cashed the check and paid the employees.

Required:

1. Assume that Lee Company records vouchers at gross amounts, and prepare a Voucher Register, a Check Register, and a General Journal and record the transactions.
2. Prepare a Vouchers Payable account and post those entry portions that affect the account.
3. Prove the balance of the Vouchers Payable account by preparing a schedule of vouchers payable.

ALTERNATE PROBLEMS

Problem 7–1A

George Sears established a petty cash fund for his business and appointed Ned Barr, an office clerk, petty cashier. During the fund's first month, these transactions were completed:

Apr. 3 Drew Check No. 410 for $50 payable to Ned Barr, petty cashier. Cashed the check and delivered the proceeds and the Petty Cash Record to the new petty cashier.

5 Paid United Delivery Service $4.50 COD delivery charges on merchandise purchased for resale.

Apr. 7 Gave Mrs. Sears, wife of the business owner, $5 from petty cash for lunch money.

10 Purchased postage stamps with $7.50 of petty cash.

14 Paid United Delivery Service $4.75 COD delivery charges on merchandise purchased for resale.

17 Paid the Bright Laundry's delivery truck driver $3.50 upon the delivery of some laundry Mr. Sears had left at the laundry and asked that it be delivered to the office.

21 Paid $7.50 for minor repairs to an office typewriter.

23 Purchased office supplies with petty cash, $5.25.

25 Paid United Delivery Service $5.25 COD delivery charges on merchandise purchased for resale.

28 Paid $5 from petty cash to have the office windows washed.

30 Drew Check No. 485 to reimburse the fund for expenditures and a $0.75 shortage.

Required:

Record the transactions in a Petty Cash Record and, where required, in a Cash Disbursements Journal similar to the ones in this chapter. Skip a line between entries in the Cash Disbursements Journal to set the entries apart.

Problem 7–2A   A company completed these petty cash transactions during December of the current year:

Dec. 2 Drew Check No. 672 for $25 to establish a petty cash fund. Appointed Jane Drew, an office employee, petty cashier. Cashed the check and turned the proceeds and the Petty Cash Record over to her.

4 Purchased postage stamps with $7.50 from petty cash.

5 Paid $5 from petty cash to have the office windows washed.

8 Purchased office supplies with $2.50 from petty cash.

9 Paid $3.25 COD delivery charges on merchandise purchased for resale.

10 Paid $5 for minor repairs to an office chair.

10 Drew Check No. 691 to reimburse the petty cash fund; and because it was exhausted so quickly, made the check large enough to increase the size of the fund to $50.

12 Gave Mrs. Carl Dent, wife of the owner of the business, $10 from petty cash for cab fare and lunch money.

15 Paid $4.75 COD delivery charges on merchandise purchased for resale.

17 Carl Dent, the owner of the business, signed a petty cash receipt and took $1 from petty cash for coffee money.

18 Purchased postage stamps with $15 from petty cash.

27 Paid $6.25 COD delivery charges on merchandise purchased for resale.

28 Paid $8.25 from petty cash for repairs to an office typewriter.

31 In reimbursing the petty cash fund at the end of the accounting period, Jane Drew had only $3 in cash in the fund. She could not account for the shortage. Consequently, she prepared a petty cash

receipt for the amount of the shortage, had Mr. Dent approve it, and recorded it in her Petty Cash Record. She then exchanged her paid petty cash receipts for a $47 check, No. 745, to reimburse the fund.

Required:

Enter the transactions in a Petty Cash Record and, where required, in a Cash Disbursements Journal similar to the ones illustrated in this chapter. Skip a line between entries in the Cash Disbursements Journal to set the entries apart.

Problem 7–3A　　　The following information was available to reconcile Vale Company's November 30 book balance of cash with its bank statement balance of that date:

a. After all posting was completed on November 30, the company's Cash account had a $1,989 debit balance, but its bank statement showed a $2,615 balance.
b. Checks No. 721 for $102 and No. 726 for $197 were outstanding on the October 31 bank reconciliation. Check No. 726 was returned with the November canceled checks, but Check No. 721 was not.
c. In comparing the canceled checks returned with the bank statement with the entries in the accounting records, it was found that Check No. 801 for the purchase of office equipment was correctly drawn for $258 but was entered in the accounting records as though it were for $285. It was also found that Check No. 835 for $125 and Check No. 837 for $50, both drawn in November, were not among the canceled checks returned with the statement.
d. A credit memorandum enclosed with the bank statement indicated that the bank had collected a $1,000 noninterest-bearing note for the concern, deducted a $5 collection fee, and had credited the remainder to the concern's account.
e. A debit memorandum with a $126 NSF check received from a customer, David Green, attached was among the canceled checks returned.
f. Also among the canceled checks was a $5 debit memorandum for bank services. None of the memoranda had been recorded.
g. The November 30 cash receipts, $542, were placed in the bank's night depository after banking hours on that date and their amount did not appear on the bank statement.

Required:

1. Prepare a bank reconciliation for the company.
2. Prepare entries in general journal form to adjust the company's book balance of cash to the reconciled balance.

Problem 7–4A　　　Mesa Company reconciled its bank balance on November 30 with two checks, No. 808 for $262 and No. 813 for $93 outstanding. The following information is available for the December 31 reconciliation:

Mesa Company 1475 North Main Street		Statement of account with VALLEY NATIONAL BANK	
Date	Checks and Other Debits	Deposits	Balance
Dec. 1	Balance brought forward		1,834.00
2	262.00		1,572.00
3	225.00	223.00	1,570.00
5	306.00		1,264.00
6	846.00		418.00
12		945.00	1,363.00
15	51.00 117.00		1,195.00
22		649.00	1,844.00
28	321.00	748.00	2,271.00
30	240.00 NSF		2,031.00
31	3.00 SC	495.00 CM	2,523.00

Code: CM Credit Memorandum   NSF Not sufficient funds check
          DM Debit Memorandum   SC Service charge

CASH RECEIPTS DEPOSITED

Date		Cash Debit
Dec. 3		223.00
12		945.00
22		649.00
28		748.00
31		319.00
31		2,884.00

CASH DISBURSEMENTS

Check Number		Cash Credit
814		306.00
815		225.00
816		846.00
817		51.00
818		117.00
819		312.00
820		129.00
821		163.00
		2,149.00

From the General Ledger:

CASH

Date	Explanation	PR	Debit	Credit	Balance
Nov. 30	Balance	✓			1,479.00
Dec. 31		R-9	2,884.00		4,363.00
31		D-9		2,149.00	2,214.00

Check No. 819 was correctly drawn for $321 in payment for store equipment purchased; however, the bookkeeper misread the amount and entered it in the accounting records with a debit to Store Equipment and a credit to Cash as though it were for $312. The bank paid and deducted the correct amount.

The NSF check was received from a customer, Jerry Mays, in payment of his account. Its return was unrecorded. The credit memorandum resulted from a $500 note which the bank had collected for the company, deducted a $5 collection fee, and deposited the balance in the company's account. The collection was not recorded.

Required:

1. Prepare a bank reconciliation for Mesa Company.
2. Prepare in general journal form the entries needed to bring the company's book balance of cash into agreement with the reconciled balance.

Problem 7–5A

The October 31 credit balance in the Sales account of Kappa Sales showed it had sold $52,400 of merchandise during the month. The company began October with a $45,800 merchandise inventory and ended the month with a $36,200 inventory. It had incurred $17,500 of operating expenses during the month, and it had also recorded the following transactions:

Oct. 3 Received merchandise purchased at a $6,000 invoice price, invoice dated September 30, terms 2/10, n/30.

7 Received a $1,000 credit memorandum (invoice price) for merchandise received on October 3 and returned for credit.

10 Received merchandise purchased at a $9,000 invoice price, invoice dated October 8, terms 2/10, n/30.

14 Received merchandise purchased at an $8,500 invoice price, invoice dated October 12, terms 2/10, n/30.

18 Paid for the merchandise received on October 10, less the discount.

22 Paid for the merchandise received on October 14, less the discount.

30 Discovered that the invoice received on October 3 had been refiled in error, after the credit memorandum was attached, for payment on this the last day of its credit period, causing the discount to be lost. Paid the invoice.

Required:

1. Assume that the company records invoices at gross amounts and *(a)* prepare general journal entries to record the transactions. *(b)* Prepare an October income statement for the concern.
2. Assume that the company records invoices at net amounts and *(a)* prepare general journal entries to record the transactions. *(b)* Prepare a second income statement for the company under this assumption.

Problem 7–6A

(This problem is based on information in the Appendix to this chapter.) Nye Company completed these transactions involving vouchers payable:

Nov. 1 Recorded Voucher No. 911 payable to Dale Company for merchandise having a $750 invoice price, invoice dated October 28, terms FOB destination, 2/10, n/30.

5 Recorded Voucher No. 912 payable to Hill Company for merchandise having a $1,150 invoice price, invoice dated November 3, terms FOB factory, 2/10, n/60. The vendor had prepaid the freight charges, $50, adding the amount to the invoice and bringing its total to $1,200.

6 Received a credit memorandum for merchandise having a $250 invoice price. The merchandise was received on November 1, Voucher No. 911, and returned for credit.

13 Issued Check No. 910 in payment of Voucher No. 912.

Nov. 15 Recorded Voucher No. 913 payable to Payroll for sales salaries, $400, and office salaries, $300. Issued Check No. 911 in payment of the voucher. Cashed the check and paid the employees.

18 Recorded Voucher No. 914 payable to Office Outfitters for the purchase of office equipment having a $300 invoice price, terms n/10 EOM.

22 Recorded Voucher No. 915 payable to *The News* for advertising expense, $125. Issued Check No. 912 in payment of the voucher.

25 Recorded Voucher No. 916 payable to Bell Company for merchandise having an $850 invoice price, invoice dated November 22, terms FOB factory, 2/10, n/60. The vendor had prepaid the freight charges, $30, adding the amount to the invoice and bringing its total to $880.

27 Discovered that Voucher No. 911 had been filed in error for payment on the last day of its credit period rather than on the last day of its discount period, causing the discount to be lost. Issued Check No. 913 in payment of the voucher, less the return.

30 Recorded Voucher No. 917 payable to Payroll for sales salaries, $400, and office salaries, $300. Issued Check No. 914 in payment of the voucher. Cashed the check and paid the employees.

Required:

Assume that Nye Company records vouchers at gross amounts. *(a)* Prepare a Voucher Register, a Check Register, and a General Journal and record the transactions. *(b)* Prepare a Vouchers Payable account and post those portions of the journal and register entries that affect the account. *(c)* Prove the balance of the Vouchers Payable account by preparing a schedule of unpaid vouchers.

PROVOCATIVE PROBLEMS

Provocative Problem 7–1, Zest Manufacturing Company

Zest Manufacturing Company began business a dozen years ago in a very small way, but has since grown rapidly. Last year its sales were in excess of $8,000,000. However, its purchasing procedures have not kept pace with its growth. When a plant supervisor or department head needs raw materials, plant assets, or supplies, he or she tells the purchasing department manager by phone or in person. The purchasing department manager prepares a purchase order in duplicate, sends one copy to the company selling the goods, and keeps the other copy in the files. When the invoice arrives, it is sent directly to the purchasing department. When the goods arrive, receiving department personnel count and inspect the items and prepare one copy of a receiving report which is sent to the purchasing department. The purchasing department manager attaches the receiving report and the retained copy of the purchase order to the invoice; and if all is in order, stamps the invoice "approved for payment" and signs his name. The invoice and its supporting documents are then sent to the accounting department to be recorded and filed until due. On its due date, the invoice and its supporting documents are sent to the office of the company treasurer where a check in payment is prepared and mailed. The number of the paying check is entered on the invoice, and the invoice is sent to the accounting department for an entry to record its payment.

Do the procedures of Zest Manufacturing Company make it fairly easy for someone in the company to institute the payment of fictitious invoices by the company? If so, who is the person and what would the person have to do to receive payment of a fictitious invoice. What changes should be made in the company's purchasing procedures, and why should each change be made?

Provocative
Problem 7–2,
Poor Internal
Control

The bookkeeper at Lee's Home Store will retire next week after more than 40 years with the store, having been hired by the father of the store's present owner. He has always been a very dependable employee, and as a result has been given more and more responsibilities over the years. Actually, for the past 15 years, he has "run" the store's office, keeping books, verifying invoices, and issuing checks in their payment, which in the absence of the store's owner, Ted Lee, he could sign. In addition, at the end of each day, the store's salesclerks turn over their daily cash receipts to the old bookkeeper, who after counting the money and comparing the amounts with the cash register tapes, which he is responsible for removing from the cash registers, makes the journal entry to record cash sales and then deposits the money in the bank. He also reconciles the bank balance each month with his book balance of cash.

Mr. Lee, the store's owner, realizes he cannot expect a new bookkeeper to accomplish as much in a day as the old bookkeeper; and since the store is not large enough to warrant more than one office employee, he recognizes he must take over some of the old bookkeeper's duties when he retires. Mr. Lee already places all orders for merchandise and supplies and closely supervises all employees and does not want to add more to his duties than necessary.

Name the internal control principle violated here and tell which of the old bookkeeper's tasks should be taken over by Mr. Lee in order to improve the store's internal control over cash.

Notes and Accounts Receivable

8

After studying Chapter 8, you should be able to:

Calculate interest on promissory notes and the discount on notes receivable discounted.

Prepare entries to record the receipt of a promissory note and its payment or dishonor.

Prepare entries to record the discounting of a note receivable and its payment by the maker or its dishonor.

Prepare reversing entries and explain the advantage of making such entries.

Prepare entries accounting for bad debts both by the allowance method and the direct write-off method.

Explain the full-disclosure principle and the materiality principle.

Define or explain the words and phrases listed in the chapter Glossary.

Companies selling merchandise on the installment plan commonly take promissory notes from their customers. Likewise, when the credit period is long, as in the sale of farm machinery, promissory notes are often required. Also, creditors frequently ask for promissory notes from customers who are granted additional time in which to pay their past-due accounts. In these situations, creditors prefer notes to accounts receivable because the notes may be readily turned into cash before becoming due by discounting (selling) them to a bank. Likewise, notes are preferred because if a lawsuit is needed to collect, a note represents written acknowledgment by the debtor of both the debt and its amount. Also, notes are preferred because they generally earn interest.

PROMISSORY NOTES

A promissory note is an unconditional promise in writing to pay on demand or at a fixed or determinable future date a definite sum of money. In the note shown in Illustration 8–1, Hugo Brown promises to pay Frank Black or his order a definite sum of money at a fixed future date. Hugo Brown is the *maker* of the note. Frank Black is the *payee.* To Hugo Brown, the illustrated note is a *note payable,* a liability. To Frank Black, the same note is a *note receivable,* an asset.

The illustrated Hugo Brown note bears interest at 12%. Interest is a charge for the use of money. To a borrower, interest is an expense. To a lender, it is a revenue. A note may be interest bearing or it may be noninterest bearing. If a note bears interest, the rate or the amount of interest must be stated on the note.

Illustration 8–1

$ 1,000.00   Eugene, Oregon   March 9, 19--

_____Thirty days_____ after date_____ I _____ promise to pay to

the order of_____ Frank Black _____

One thousand and no/100--- dollars

for value received with interest at____ 12% _____

payable at__ First National Bank of Eugene, Oregon _____

_____ Hugo Brown _____

CALCULATING INTEREST

Unless otherwise stated, the rate of interest on a note is the rate charged for the use of the principal for one year. The formula for calculating interest is:

$$\text{Principal of the note} \times \text{Annual rate of interest} \times \text{Time of the note expressed in years} = \text{Interest}$$

For example, interest on a $1,000, 12%, one-year note is calculated:

$$\$1,000 \times \frac{12}{100} \times 1 = \$120$$

Most note transactions involve a period less than a full year, and this period is usually expressed in days. When the time of a note is expressed in days, the actual number of days elapsing, not including the day of the note's date but including the day on which it falls due, are counted. For example, a 90-day note, dated July 10, is due on October 8. This October 8 due date, called the *maturity date*, is calculated as follows:

Number of days in July	31
Minus the date of the note	10
Gives the number of days the note runs in July	21
Add the number of days in August	31
Add the number of days in September	30
Total through September 30	82
Days in October needed to equal the time of the note, 90 days, also the maturity date of the note—October	8
Total time the note runs in days	90

Occasionally, the time of a note is expressed in months. In such cases, the note matures and is payable in the month of its maturity on the same day of the month as its date. For example, a note dated July 10 and payable three months after date is payable on October 10.

In calculating interest, it was once almost the universal practice to treat a year as having just 360 days. This simplified most interest calculations. However, the practice is no longer so common. Nevertheless, to simplify the calculation of interest in assigned problems and to be consistent in the illustrations and problems, the practice is continued in this text. It makes the interest calculation on a 90-day, 12%, $1,000 note as follows:

$$\text{Principal} \times \text{Rate} \times \frac{\text{Exact days}}{360} = \text{Interest}$$

or

$$\$1{,}000 \times \frac{12}{100} \times \frac{90}{360} = \text{Interest}$$

or

$$\cancel{\$1{,}000}^{\,10} \times \frac{\cancel{12}^{\,3}}{\cancel{100}} \times \frac{\cancel{90}}{\cancel{360}_{\,4}} = \$30$$

RECORDING THE RECEIPT OF A NOTE

Notes receivable are recorded in a single Notes Receivable account. Each note may be identified in the account by writing the name of the maker in the Explanation column on the line of the entry recording its receipt or payment. Only one account is needed because the individual notes are on hand. Consequently, the maker, rate of interest, due date, and other information may be learned by examining each note.

A note received at the time of a sale is recorded as follows:

Dec.	5	Notes Receivable	650.00	
		Sales		650.00
		Sold merchandise, terms six-month, 14% note.		

When a note is taken in granting a time extension on a past-due account receivable, the creditor usually attempts to collect part of the past-due account in cash. This reduces the debt and requires the acceptance of a note for a smaller amount. For example, Monroe Company agrees to accept $232 in cash and a $500, 60-day, 14% note from Joseph Cook in settlement of his $732 past-due account. When Monroe receives the cash and note, the following entry in general journal form is made:

Oct.	5	Cash	232.00	
		Notes Receivable	500.00	
		Accounts Receivable—Joseph Cook		732.00
		Received cash and a note in settlement of an account.		

Observe that this entry changes the form of $500 of the debt from an account receivable to a note receivable.

When Cook pays the note, this entry in general journal form is made:

Dec.	4	Cash	511.67	
		Notes Receivable		500.00
		Interest Earned		11.67
		Collected the Joseph Cook note.		

In the December 4 entry, the interest on $500 for 60 days at 14% is $11.666+. It is the general business practice to round up to the nearest full cent when a calculation results in a half cent or more. Likewise, a fraction less than a half cent is rounded down.

DISHONORED NOTES RECEIVABLE

Occasionally, the maker of a note either cannot or will not pay the note at maturity. When a note's maker refuses to pay at maturity, the note is said to be *dishonored.* Dishonor does not relieve the maker of the obligation to pay. Furthermore, every legal means should be made to collect. However, collection may require lengthy legal proceedings.

The balance of the Notes Receivable account should show only the amount of notes that have not matured. Consequently, when a note is dishonored, its amount should be removed from the Notes Receivable account and charged back to the account of its maker. To illustrate, Monroe Company holds an $800, 14%, 60-day note of George Jones. At maturity, Jones dishonors the note. To remove the dishonored note from its Notes Receivable account, the company makes the following entry:

Oct.	14	Accounts Receivable—George Jones	818.67	
		Interest Earned		18.67
		Notes Receivable		800.00
		To charge the account of George Jones for his dishonored note.		

Charging a dishonored note back to the account of its maker serves two purposes. It removes the amount of the note from the Notes Receivable account, leaving in the account only notes that have not matured. It also records the dishonored note in the maker's account. The second purpose is important. If in the future the maker of the dishonored note again applies for credit, his or her account will show all past dealings, including the dishonored note.

Observe in the entry that the Interest Earned account is credited for interest earned even though it was not collected. The reason for this is that Jones owes both the principal and the interest. Consequently, his account should reflect the full amount owed on the date of the entry.

DISCOUNTING NOTES RECEIVABLE

As previously stated, a note receivable is preferred to an account receivable because the note can be turned into cash before maturity by discounting (selling) it to a bank. In *discounting a note receivable,* the owner endorses and delivers the note to the bank in exchange for cash. The bank holds the note to maturity and then collects its maturity value from the maker. To illustrate, assume that on May 28, Symplex Company received a $1,200, 60-day, 12% note dated May 27 from John Owen. It held the note until June 2 and then discounted it at its bank at 14%. Since the maturity date of this note is July 26, the bank must wait 54 days after discounting the note to collect from Owen. These 54 days are called the *discount period* and are calculated as follows:

Time of the note in days		60
Less time held by Symplex Company:		
Number of days in May	31	
Less the date of the note	27	
Days held in May	4	
Days held in June	2	
Total days held		6
Discount period in days		54

At the end of the discount period, the bank expects to collect the *maturity value* of this note from Owen. Therefore, as is customary, it bases its discount on the maturity value of the note, which is calculated as follows:

Principal of the note	$1,200
Interest on $1,200 for 60 days at 12% ..	24
Maturity value	$1,224

In this case, the bank's discount rate, or the rate of interest it charges for lending money, is 14%. Consequently, in discounting the note, it will deduct 54 days' interest at 14% from the note's maturity value and will give Symplex Company the remainder. The remainder is called the *proceeds of the note.* The amount of interest deducted is known as *bank discount.* The bank discount and the proceeds are calculated as follows:

Maturity value of the note	$1,224.00
Less interest on $1,224 for 54 days at 14% ..	25.70
Proceeds...................................	$1,198.30

Observe in this case that the proceeds, $1,198.30, are $1.70 less than the $1,200 principal amount of the note. Consequently, Symplex will make this entry in recording the discount transaction:

June	2	Cash	1,198.30	
		Interest Expense	1.70	
		Notes Receivable		1,200.00
		Discounted the John Owen note for 54 days at 14%.		

In recording the transaction, Symplex in effect offsets the $24 of interest it would have earned by holding the note to maturity against the $25.70 discount charged by the bank and records only the difference, the $1.70 excess of expense.

In the situation just described, the principal of the discounted note exceeded the proceeds. However, in many cases, the proceeds exceed the principal. When this happens, the difference is credited to Interest Earned. For example, suppose that instead of discounting the John Owen note on June 2, Symplex held the note and discounted it on June 26. If the note is discounted on June 26 at 14%, the discount period is 30 days, the discount is $14.28, and the proceeds of the note are $1,209.72, calculated as follows:

Maturity value of the note	$1,224.00
Less interest on $1,224 at 14% for 30 days ..	14.28
Proceeds...................................	$1,209.72

And since the proceeds exceed the principal, the transaction is recorded as follows:

June	26	Cash	1,209.72	
		Interest Earned		9.72
		Notes Receivable		1,200.00
		Discounted the John Owen note for 30 days at 14%.		

Contingent Liability

A person or company discounting a note is ordinarily required to endorse the note because an endorsement, unless it is qualified, makes the endorser contingently liable for payment of the note.[1] The *contingent liability* depends upon the note's dishonor by its maker. If the maker pays, the endorser has no liability. However, if the maker defaults, the endorser's contingent liability becomes an actual liability and the endorser must pay the note for the maker.

A contingent liability, since it can become an actual liability, may affect the credit standing of the person or concern contingently liable. Consequently, a discounted note should be shown as such in the Notes Receivable account. Also, if a balance sheet is prepared before the discounted note's maturity date, the contingent liability should be indicated on the balance sheet. For example, if in addition to the John Owen note, Symplex Company holds $500 of other notes receivable, the record of the discounted John Owen note may appear in its Notes Receivable account as follows:

Notes Receivable					
Date	Explanation	Post. Ref.	Debit	Credit	Balance
May 28	John Owen note	G6	1,200.00		1,200.00
June 7	Earl Hill note	G6	500.00		1,700.00
26	Discounted the J. Owen note	G7		1,200.00	500.00

The contingent liability resulting from discounted notes receivable is commonly shown on a balance sheet by means of a footnote. If Symplex Company follows this practice, it will show the $500 of notes it has not discounted and the contingent liability resulting from discounting the John Owen note on its June 30 balance sheet as follows:

---

[1] A qualified endorsement is one in which the endorser states in writing that he or she will not be liable for payment.

```
Current assets:
  Cash ............................................. $ 5,315
  Notes receivable (Footnote 2) ....................     500
  Accounts receivable .............................  21,475
```

Footnote 2: Symplex Company is contingently liable for $1,200 of notes receivable discounted.

Full-Disclosure Principle

The balance sheet disclosure of contingent liabilities is required under the *full-disclosure principle.* Under this principle, it is held that financial statements and their accompanying footnotes should disclose fully and completely all relevant data of a material nature relating to the financial position of the company for which they are prepared. This does not necessarily mean that the information should be detailed, for details can at times obscure. It simply means that all information necessary to an appreciation of the company's position be reported in a readily understandable manner and that nothing of a significant nature be withheld. For example, any of the following would be considered relevant and should be disclosed.

CONTINGENT LIABILITIES. In addition to discounted notes, a company that is contingently liable due to possible additional tax assessments, pending lawsuits, or product guarantees should disclose this on its statements.

LONG-TERM COMMITMENTS UNDER A CONTRACT. If the company has signed a long-term lease requiring a material annual payment, this should be disclosed even though the liability does not appear in the accounts. Also, if the company has pledged certain of its assets as security for a loan, this should be revealed.

ACCOUNTING METHODS USED. Whenever there are several acceptable accounting methods that may be followed, a company should report in each case the method used, especially when a choice of methods can materially affect reported net income. For example, a company should report by means of footnotes accompanying its statements the inventory method or methods used, depreciation methods, method of recognizing revenue under long-term construction contracts, and the like.[2]

---

[2] APB, "Disclosure of Accounting Policies," *APB Opinion No. 22* (New York: AICPA, April 1972), pars. 12, 13.

DISHONOR OF A DISCOUNTED NOTE

A bank always tries to collect a discounted note directly from the maker. If it is able to do so, the one who discounted it will not hear from the bank and will need to do nothing more in regard to the note. However, according to law, if a discounted note is dishonored, the bank must before the end of the next business day notify each endorser of the note if it is to hold the endorsers liable on the note. To notify the endorsers, the bank will normally protest the dishonored note. To protest a note, the bank prepares and mails before the end of the next business day a *notice of protest* to each endorser. A notice of protest is a statement, usually attested by a notary public, that says the note was duly presented to the maker for payment and payment was refused. The cost of protesting a note is called a *protest fee,* and the bank will look to the one who discounted the note for payment of both the note's maturity value and the protest fee.

For example, suppose that instead of paying the $1,200 note previously illustrated, John Owen dishonored it. In such a situation, the bank would notify Symplex Company immediately of the dishonor by mailing a notice of protest and a letter asking payment of the note's maturity value plus the protest fee. If the protest fee is, say, $5, Symplex must pay the bank $1,229. In recording the payment, Symplex will charge the $1,229 to the account of John Owen, as follows:

July	27	Accounts Receivable—John Owen	1,229.00	
		Cash		1,229.00
		To charge the account of Owen for the maturity value of his dishonored note plus the protest fee.		

Of course, upon receipt of the $1,229, the bank will deliver to Symplex the dishonored note. Symplex Company will then make every legal effort to collect from Owen, not only the maturity value of the note and protest fee but also interest on both from the date of dishonor until the date of final settlement. However, it may not be able to collect, and after exhausting every legal means to do so, it may have to write the account off as a bad debt. Normally, in such cases, no additional interest is taken onto the books before the write-off.

Although dishonored notes commonly have to be written off as bad debts, some are also eventually paid by their makers. For example, if 30 days after dishonor, John Owen pays the maturity value of his dishonored note, the protest fee, and interest at 12% on both for 30 days beyond maturity, he will pay the following:

```
Maturity value .......................  $1,224.00
Protest fee ........................       5.00
Interest on $1,229 at 12% for 30 days ..  12.29
        Total ........................  $1,241.29
```

And Symplex will record receipt of his money as follows:

Aug.	25	Cash	1,241.29	
		Interest Earned		12.29
		Accounts Receivable—John Owen		1,229.00
		Dishonored note and protest fee collected with interest.		

END-OF-PERIOD ADJUSTMENTS

If any notes receivable are outstanding at the accounting period end, their accrued interest should be calculated and recorded. For example, on December 16, a company accepted a $3,000, 60-day, 12% note from a customer in granting an extension on a past-due account. If the company's accounting period ends on December 31, by then $15 interest has accrued on this note and should be recorded with this adjusting entry:

Dec.	31	Interest Receivable	15.00	
		Interest Earned		15.00
		To record accrued interest on a note receivable.		

The adjusting entry causes the interest earned to appear on the income statement of the period in which it was earned. It also causes the interest receivable to appear on the balance sheet as a current asset.

Collecting Interest Previously Accrued

When the note is collected, the transaction may be recorded as follows:

Feb.	14	Cash	3,060.00	
		Interest Earned		45.00
		Interest Receivable.....................		15.00
		Notes Receivable		3,000.00
		Received payment of a note and its interest.		

The entry's credit to Interest Receivable records collection of the interest accrued at the end of the previous period.

REVERSING ENTRIES

To correctly record a transaction like that of the February 14 entry just shown, a bookkeeper must remember the accrued interest recorded at the end of the previous year and divide the amount of interest received between the Interest Earned and Interest Receivable accounts. Many bookkeepers find this difficult, and they avoid "the need to remember" by preparing and posting entries to reverse any end-of-period adjustments of accrued items. These *reversing entries* are made after the adjusting and closing entries are posted and are normally dated the first day of the new accounting period.

To demonstrate reversing entries, assume that a company accepted a $3,000, 12%, 60-day note dated December 19, 12 days before the end of its annual accounting period. Sixty days' interest on this note is $60; and by December 31, $12 of the $60 has been earned. Consequently, the company's bookkeeper should make the following adjusting and closing entries to record the accrued interest on the note and to close the Interest Earned account.

Dec.	31	Interest Receivable	12.00	
		Interest Earned		12.00
		To record the accrued interest.		
	31	Interest Earned	12.00	
		Income Summary		12.00
		To close the Interest Earned account.		

In addition to the adjusting and closing entries, if the bookkeeper chooses to make reversing entries, he or she will make the following entry to reverse the accrued interest adjusting entry:

Jan.	1	Interest Earned	12.00	
		Interest Receivable		12.00
		To reverse the accrued interest adjusting entry.		

Observe that the reversing entry is debit for credit and credit for debit the reverse of the adjusting entry it reverses. After the adjusting, closing, and reversing entries are posted, the Interest Receivable and Interest Earned accounts appear as follows:

Interest Receivable

Date		Explanation	Dr.	Cr.	Bal.
Dec.	31	Adjusting	12		12
Jan.	1	Reversing		12	–0–

Interest Earned

Date		Explanation	Dr.	Cr.	Bal.
Dec.	31	Adjusting		12	12
	31	Closing	12		–0–
Jan.	1	Reversing	12		(12)

Notice that the reversing entry cancels the $12 of interest appearing in the Interest Receivable account. It also causes the accrued interest to appear in the Interest Earned account as a $12 debit. (Remember that an encircled balance means a balance opposite from normal.) Consequently, due to the reversing entry, when the note and interest are paid on February 17, the bookkeeper can record the transaction with this entry:

Feb.	17	Cash	3,060.00	
		Interest Earned		60.00
		Notes Receivable		3,000.00
		Received payment of a note and interest.		

The entry's $60 credit to Interest Earned includes both the $12 of interest earned during the previous period and the $48 of interest earned during the current period. However, when the entry is posted, because of the previously posted reversing entry, the balance of the Interest Earned account shows only the $48 of interest applicable to the current period, as follows:

Interest earned

Date		Explanation	Dr.	Cr.	Bal.
Dec.	31	Adjusting		12	12
	31	Closing	12		–0–
Jan.	1	Reversing	12		⑫
Feb.	17	Payment		60	48

Reversing entries are applicable to all accrued items, such as accrued interest earned, accrued interest expense, accrued taxes, and accrued salaries and wages. Nevertheless, they are not required, but are a matter of convenience that enable a bookkeeper to forget an accrued item once its adjusting entry has been reversed.

BAD DEBTS

When goods and services are sold on credit, there are almost always a few customers who do not pay. The accounts of such customers are called *bad debts* and are a loss and an expense of selling on credit.

It might be asked: Why do merchants sell on credit if bad debts result? The answer is, of course, that they sell on credit in order to increase sales and profits. They are willing to take a reasonable loss from bad debts in order to increase sales and profits. Therefore, bad debt losses are an expense of selling on credit, an expense incurred in order to increase sales. Consequently, if the requirements of the *matching principle* are met, bad debt losses must be matched against the sales they helped produce.

MATCHING BAD DEBT LOSSES WITH SALES

Credit sales that result in bad debt losses are made in one accounting period, but final recognition that the customers will not pay commonly does not occur until a later period. Final recognition waits until every means of collecting has been exhausted, which may take a year or more. Therefore, if bad debt losses are matched with the sales they helped to produce, they must be matched on an estimated basis. The *allowance method of accounting for bad debts* does just that.

ALLOWANCE METHOD OF ACCOUNTING FOR BAD DEBTS

Under the allowance method of accounting for bad debts, an estimate is made at the end of each accounting period of the total bad debts that are expected to result from the period's sales. An allowance is then provided for the loss. This has two advantages: (1) the estimated loss is charged to the period in which the revenue is recognized; and (2) the accounts receivable appear on the balance sheet at their estimated realizable value, a more informative balance sheet amount.

Estimating Bad Debts

In making the year-end estimate of bad debts that are expected to result from the year's sales, companies commonly assume that "history will repeat." For example, over the past several years, Alpha Company has experienced bad debt losses equal to one half of 1% of its charge sales. During the past year, its charge sales were $300,000. Consequently, if history repeats, Alpha Company can expect $1,500 of bad debt losses to result from the year's sales ($300,000 × 0.005 = $1,500).

Recording the Estimated Bad Debts Loss

Under the allowance method of accounting for bad debts, the estimated bad debts loss is recorded at the end of each accounting period with a work sheet adjustment and an adjusting entry. For example, Alpha Company will record its $1,500 estimated bad debts loss with a work sheet adjustment and an adjusting entry like the following:

Dec.	31	Bad Debts Expense	1,500.00	
		Allowance for Doubtful Accounts		1,500.00
		To record the estimated bad debts.		

The debit on this entry causes the estimated bad debts loss to appear on the income statement of the year in which the sales were made. As a result, the estimated $1,500 expense of selling on credit is matched with the $300,000 of revenue it helped to produce.

Bad debt losses normally appear on the income statement as an administrative expense rather than as a selling expense because granting credit is usually not a responsibility of the sales department. Therefore, since the sales department is not responsible for granting credit, it should not be held responsible for bad debt losses. The sales department is usually not given responsibility for granting credit because it is feared the sales department would at times be swayed in its judgment of a credit risk by its desire to make a sale.

Bad Debts in the Accounts

If at the time its bad debts adjusting entry is posted, Alpha Company has $20,000 of accounts receivable, its Accounts Receivable and Allowance for Doubtful Accounts accounts will show these balances:

Accounts Receivable		Allowance for Doubtful Accounts	
Dec. 31 20,000			Dec. 31 1,500

The bad debts adjusting entry reduces the accounts receivable to their estimated realizable value. However, note that the credit of the entry is to the contra account, Allowance for Doubtful Accounts. It is necessary to credit the contra account because at the time of the adjusting entry it is not known for certain which customers will fail to pay. (The total loss from bad debts can be estimated from past experience. However, the exact customers who will not pay cannot be known until every means of collecting from each has been exhausted.) Consequently, since the bad accounts are not identifiable at the time of the adjusting entry, they cannot be removed from the subsidiary Accounts Receivable Ledger. As a result, the Allowance for Doubtful Accounts account must be credited instead of the controlling account. The allowance account must be credited because to credit the controlling account without removing the bad accounts from the subsidiary ledger would cause the controlling account balance to differ from the sum of the balances in the subsidiary ledger.

Allowance for Doubtful Accounts on the Balance Sheet

When the balance sheet is prepared, the *allowance for doubtful accounts* is subtracted thereon from the accounts receivable to show the amount that is expected to be realized from the accounts, as follows:

Current assets:		
Cash		$11,300
Accounts receivable	$20,000	
Less allowance for doubtful accounts.....	(1,500)	18,500
Merchandise inventory		67,200
Prepaid expenses		1,100
Total current assets		$98,100

Writing off a Bad Debt

When an allowance for doubtful accounts is provided, accounts deemed uncollectible are written off against this allowance. For example, after spending a year trying to collect, Alpha Company finally concluded the $100 account of George Vale was uncollectible and made the following entry to write it off:

Jan.	23	Allowance for Doubtful Accounts	100.00	
		Accounts Receivable—George Vale		100.00
		To write off an uncollectible account.		

Posting the credit of the entry to the Accounts Receivable account removes the amount of the bad debt from the controlling account. Posting it to the George Vale account removes the amount of the bad debt from the subsidiary ledger. Posting the entry has this effect on the general ledger accounts:

Accounts Receivable				Allowance for Doubtful Accounts			
Dec. 31	20,000	Jan. 23	100	Jan. 23	100	Dec. 31	1,500

Two points should be observed in the entry and accounts. First, although bad debts are an expense of selling on credit, the allowance account rather than an expense account is debited in the write-off. The allowance account is debited because the expense was recorded at the end of the period in which the sale occurred. At that time, the loss was foreseen, and the expense was recorded in the estimated bad debts adjusting entry.

Second, although the write-off removed the amount of the account receivable from the ledgers, it did not affect the estimated realizable amount of Alpha Company's accounts receivable, as the following tabulation shows:

	Before write-off	After write-off
Accounts receivable	$20,000	$19,900
Less allowance for doubtful accounts	1,500	1,400
Estimated realizable accounts receivable	$18,500	$18,500

Bad Debts Written Off Seldom Equal the Allowance Provided

The uncollectible accounts from a given year's sales seldom, if ever, exactly equal the allowance provided for their loss. If accounts written off are less than the allowance provided, the allowance account reaches the end of the year with a credit balance. On the other hand, if accounts written off exceed the allowance provided, the allowance account reaches the period end with a debit balance, which is then eliminated with the new bad debts adjusting entry. In either case, no harm is done if the allowance provided is approximately equal to the bad debts written off and is neither continually excessive nor insufficient.

Often when the addition to the allowance for doubtful accounts is based on a percentage of sales, the passage of several accounting periods is required before it becomes apparent the percentage is either too large or too small. In such cases, when it becomes apparent the percentage is incorrect, a change in the percentage should be made.

BAD DEBT RECOVERIES

Frequently, errors in judgment are made and accounts written off as uncollectible are later sometimes collected in full or in part. If an account is written off as uncollectible and later the customer pays part or all of the amount previously written off, the payment should be shown in the customer's account for future credit action. It should be shown because when a customer fails to pay and his or her account is written off, the customer's credit standing is impaired. Later when the customer pays, the payment helps restore the credit standing. When an account previously written off as a bad debt is collected, two entries are made. The first reinstates the customer's account and has the effect of reversing the original write-off. The second entry records the collection of the reinstated account.

For example, assume that George Vale, whose account was previously written off, pays in full on August 15. The entries in general journal form to record the bad debt recovery are:

Aug.	15	Accounts Receivable—George Vale	100.00	
		Allowance for Doubtful Accounts		100.00
		To reinstate the account of George Vale written off on January 23.		
	15	Cash	100.00	
		Accounts Receivable—George Vale		100.00
		In full of account.		

In this case, George Vale paid the entire amount previously written off. Sometimes after an account is written off the customer will pay a portion of the amount owed. The question then arises, should the entire balance of the account be returned to accounts receivable or just the amount paid? The answer is a matter of judgment. If it is thought the customer will pay in full, the entire amount owed should be returned. However, only the amount paid should be returned if it is thought that no more will be collected.

AGING ACCOUNTS RECEIVABLE

In estimating bad debt losses, many companies *age their accounts receivable*. This consists of preparing a schedule of accounts receivable with their balances entered in columns according to age, as in Illustration 8–2. After such a schedule is prepared, executives of the sales and credit departments examine each account listed and by judgment decide which are probably uncollectible. Normally, most of the accounts on the schedule are current and not past due. These are examined for possible losses but receive less scrutiny than past-due accounts. The older accounts are more apt to prove uncollectible. These receive the greatest attention. After decisions are made as to which accounts are probably uncollectible, the allowance account is adjusted to provide for them.

Illustration 8–2

Schedule of Accounts Receivable by Age					
Customer's Name	Not Due	1 to 30 Days Past Due	31 to 60 Days Past Due	61 to 90 Days Past Due	Over 90 Days Past Due
Charles Abbot	45.00				
Frank Allen	53.00				
George Arden			14.00		
Paul Baum					27.00

To illustrate this adjustment, assume that a company ages its accounts receivable and estimates that accounts totaling $1,950 are probably uncollectible. Assume further that the company has a $250 credit balance in its allowance account. Under these assumptions, the company will make the following adjusting entry to increase the balance of the allowance account to the amount needed to provide for the estimated uncollectible accounts:

Dec.	31	Bad Debts Expense	1,700.00	
		Allowance for Doubtful Accounts		1,700.00
		To increase the allowance for doubtful accounts to $1,950.		

The $1,700 credit of the entry increases the balance of the allowance account to the $1,950 needed to provide for the estimated bad debts. If it had been assumed that the allowance account had a $150 debit balance before adjustment, rather than the assumed $250 credit balance, it would have been necessary to increase the entry amounts to $2,100 ($150 + $1,950) in order to bring the account balance up to the required amount.

Aging accounts receivable and increasing the allowance for doubtful accounts to an amount sufficient to provide for the accounts deemed uncollectible normally provides a better balance sheet figure than does the percent of sales method, a figure closer to realizable value. However, the aging method may not as closely match revenues and expenses as the percent of sales method.

DIRECT WRITE-OFF OF BAD DEBTS

The allowance method of accounting for bad debts better fulfills the requirements of the *matching principle.* Consequently, it is the method that should be used in most cases. However, under certain circumstances another method, called the *direct write-off method,* may be used. Under this method, when it is decided that an account is uncollectible, it is written off directly to Bad Debts Expense with an entry like this:

Nov.	23	Bad Debts Expense	52.50	
		Accounts Receivable—Dale Hall		52.50
		To write off the uncollectible account.		

The debit of the entry charges the bad debt loss directly to the current year's Bad Debts Expense account. The credit removes the balance of the account from the subsidiary ledger and controlling account.

If an account previously written off directly to Bad Debts Expense is later collected in full, the following entries are used to record the recovery:

Mar.	11	Accounts Receivable—Dale Hall	52.50	
		Bad Debts Expense		52.50
		To reinstate the account of Dale Hall previously written off.		
	11	Cash	52.50	
		Accounts Receivable—Dale Hall		52.50
		In full of account.		

Sometimes a bad debt previously written off directly to the Bad Debts Expense account is recovered in the year following the write-off. If at that time the Bad Debts Expense account has no balance from other write-offs and no write-offs are expected, the credit of the entry recording the recovery can be to a revenue account called Bad Debt Recoveries.

Direct Write-off Mismatches Revenues and Expenses

The direct write-off method commonly mismatches revenues and expenses. The mismatch results because the revenue from a bad debt sale appears on the income statement of one year while the expense of the loss is deducted on the income statement of the following or a later year. Nevertheless, it may still be used in situations where its use does not materially affect reported net income. For example, it may be used in a concern where bad debt losses are immaterial in relation to total sales and net income. In such a concern, the use of direct write-off comes under the accounting *principle of materiality.*

The Principle of Materiality

Under the *principle of materiality,* it is held that a strict adherence to any accounting principle, in this case the *matching principle,* is not required when adherence is relatively difficult or expensive and the lack of adherence does not materially affect reported net income. Or in other words, failure to adhere is permissible when the failure does not produce an error or misstatement sufficiently large as to influence a financial statement reader's judgment of a given situation.

GLOSSARY

Aging accounts receivable. Preparing a schedule listing accounts receivable by the number of days each account has been unpaid.

Allowance for doubtful accounts. The estimated amount of accounts receivable that will prove uncollectible.

Allowance method of accounting for bad debts. The accounting procedure whereby an estimate is made at the end of each accounting period of the portion of the period's credit sales that will prove uncollectible, and an entry is made to charge this estimated amount to an expense account and to an allowance account against which actual uncollectible accounts can be written off.

Bad debt. An uncollectible account receivable.

Bank discount. The amount of interest a bank deducts in lending money.

Contingent liability. A potential liability that may become an actual liability if certain events occur.

Direct write-off method of accounting for bad debts. The accounting procedure whereby uncollectible accounts are written off directly to an expense account.

Discount period of a note. The number of days for which a note is discounted.

Discounting a note receivable. Selling a note receivable to a bank or other concern.

Dishonoring a note. Refusing to pay a promissory note on its due date.

Full-disclosure principle. The accounting rule requiring that financial statements and their accompanying notes disclose all information of a material nature relating to the financial position and operating results of the company for which the statements are prepared.

Maker of a note. One who signs a note and promises to pay it at maturity.

Materiality principle. The accounting rule that a strict adherence to any accounting principle is not required when adherence is relatively difficult or expensive and lack of adherence will not materially affect reported net income.

Maturity date of a note. The date on which a note and any interest are due and payable.

Maturity value of a note. Principal of the note plus any interest due on the note's maturity date.

Notes receivable discounted. The amount of notes receivable that have been discounted or sold.

Notice of protest. A document that gives notice that a promissory note was presented for payment on its due date and payment was refused.

Payee of a note. The one to whom a promissory note is made payable.

Proceeds of a discounted note. The maturity value of a note minus any interest deducted because of its being discounted before maturity.

Protest fee. The fee charged for preparing and issuing a notice of protest.

Reversing entry. An entry that reverses the adjusting entry for an accrued item.

QUESTIONS FOR CLASS DISCUSSION

1. Why does a business prefer a note receivable to an account receivable?
2. Define:
   a. Promissory note.
   b. Payee of a note.
   c. Maturity date.
   d. Dishonored note.
   e. Notice of protest.
   f. Discount period of a note.
   g. Maker of a note.
   h. Principal of a note.
   i. Maturity value.
   j. Contingent liability.
3. What are the due dates of the following notes: *(a)* a 90-day note dated June 10, *(b)* a 60-day note dated May 13, and *(c)* a 90-day note dated November 12?
4. Distinguish between bank discount and cash discount.
5. What does the full-disclosure principle require in a company's accounting statements?

6. In meeting the requirements of the matching principle, why must bad debt losses be matched on an estimated basis?

7. In estimating bad debt losses, it is commonly assumed that "history will repeat." How is this assumption used in estimating bad debt losses?

8. A company had $484,000 of charge sales in a year. How many dollars of bad debt losses may the company expect to experience from these sales if its past bad debt losses have averaged one fourth of 1% of charge sales?

9. What is a contra account? Why are estimated bad debt losses credited to a contra account rather than to the Accounts Receivable controlling account?

10. Classify the following accounts: *(a)* Accounts Receivable, *(b)* Allowance for Doubtful Accounts, and *(c)* Bad Debts Expense.

11. Explain why writing off a bad debt against the allowance account does not reduce the estimated realizable amount of a company's accounts receivable.

12. Why does the direct write-off method of accounting for bad debts commonly fail in matching revenues and expenses?

13. What is the essence of the accounting principle of materiality?

CLASS EXERCISES

Exercise 8–1

Prepare general journal entries to record these transactions:

Mar. 3 Accepted a $600, 60-day, 12% note dated this day from Earl Kane in granting a time extension on his past-due account.

May 2 Earl Kane dishonored his note when presented for payment.

Dec. 31 After exhausting all legal means of collecting, wrote off the account of Earl Kane against the allowance for doubtful accounts.

Exercise 8–2

Prepare general journal entries to record these transactions:

June 7 Sold merchandise to Jerry Hill, $1,200, terms 2/10, n/60.

Aug. 12 Received $200 in cash and a $1,000, 60-day, 12% note dated August 10 in granting a time extension on the amount due from Jerry Hill.

16 Discounted the Jerry Hill note at the bank at 14%.

Oct. 14 Since notice protesting the Jerry Hill note had not been received, assumed that it had been paid.

Exercise 8–3

Prepare general journal entries to record these transactions:

Aug. 15 Accepted a $1,500, 60-day, 12% note dated August 13 from Dale Ball in granting a time extension on his past-due account.

25 Discounted the Dale Ball note at the bank at 14%.

Oct. 13 Received notice protesting the Dale Ball note. Paid the bank the maturity value of the note plus a $4 protest fee and canceled the discount liability.

Nov. 11 Received payment from Dale Ball of the maturity value of his dishonored note, the protest fee, and interest at 12% on both for 30 days beyond maturity.

Exercise 8–4

On July 6, Tri-City Sales sold Robert Todd merchandise having a $1,500 catalog list price, less a 20% trade discount, 2/10, n/60. Todd was unable to pay and was granted a time extension on receipt of his 60-day, 12% note for the amount of the debt, dated September 10. Tri-City Sales held the note until October 16, when it discounted the note at its bank at 15%. The note was not protested. Answer these questions:

a. How many dollars of trade discount were granted on the sale?
b. How many dollars of cash discount could Todd have earned?
c. What was the maturity date of the note?
d. How many days were in the discount period?
e. How much bank discount was deducted by the bank?
f. What were the proceeds of the discounted note?

Exercise 8–5

Northland Sales accepted a $4,500, 12%, 60-day note dated December 11, 20 days before the end of its annual accounting period, in granting a time extension on the past-due account of Lee Best.

Required:

1. Give in general journal form the entries made by Northland Sales (a) to record receipt of the note on December 11, (b) to record the accrued interest on the note on December 31, (c) to close the Income Summary account, (d) to reverse the accrued interest adjusting entry, and (e) to record payment of the note and interest on February 9.
2. Open balance column accounts for Interest Receivable and Interest Earned and post the portions of the foregoing entries that affect these accounts.

Exercise 8–6

On December 31, at the end of its annual accounting period, a company estimated it would lose as bad debts an amount equal to one fourth of 1% of its $648,000 of charge sales made during the year, and it made an addition to its allowance for doubtful accounts equal to that amount. On the following May 10, it decided the $110 account of Albert Lee was uncollectible and wrote it off as a bad debt. Two months later, on July 10, Mr. Lee unexpectedly paid the amount previously written off. Give the required entries in general journal form to record these transactions.

Exercise 8–7

At the end of each year, a company ages its accounts receivable and increases its allowance for doubtful accounts by an amount sufficient to provide for the estimated uncollectible accounts. At the end of last year, it estimated it would not be able to collect $3,400 of its total accounts receivable. (a) Give the entry to increase the allowance account under the assumption it had a $150 credit balance before the adjustment. (b) Give the entry under the assumption the allowance account had a $225 debit balance before the adjustment.

PROBLEMS

Problem 8–1

Prepare general journal entries to record these transactions:

Jan. 3   Accepted a $1,275, 60-day, 12% note dated this day in granting a time extension on the past-due account of Ted Lee.

Mar. 4   Ted Lee paid the maturity value of his $1,275 note.

    7   Accepted a $900, 60-day, 12% note dated this day in granting a time extension on the past-due account of Frank Jones.

May 6   Frank Jones dishonored his note when presented for payment.

    10   Accepted a $1,200, 90-day, 12% note dated May 8 in granting a time extension on the past-due account of Joel Kane.

    14   Discounted the Joel Kane note at the bank at 14%.

Aug. 10   Since notice protesting the Joel Kane note had not been received, assumed that it had been paid.

    12   Accepted a $1,500, 60-day, 12% note dated August 11 in granting a time extension on the past-due account of Fred Lang.

Sept. 4   Discounted the Fred Lang note at the bank at 15%.

Oct. 11   Received notice protesting the Fred Lang note. Paid the bank the maturity value of the note plus a $5 protest fee.

    12   Received an $1,800, 60-day, 12% note dated this day from Earl Larr in granting a time extension on his past-due account.

Nov. 11   Discounted the Earl Larr note at the bank at 15%.

Dec. 12   Received notice protesting the Earl Larr note. Paid the bank the maturity value of the note plus a $4 protest fee.

    23   Received payment from Earl Larr of the maturity value of his dishonored note, the protest fee, and interest on both for 12 days beyond maturity at 12%.

Dec. 31   Wrote off the accounts of Frank Jones and Fred Lang against the allowance for doubtful accounts.

Problem 8–2

Prepare general journal entries to record these transactions:

Dec. 16   Accepted a $1,400, 60-day, 12% note dated this day in granting a time extension on the past-due account of Carl Dent.

    31   Made an adjusting entry to record the accrued interest on the Carl Dent note.

    31   Made an adjusting entry to increase the allowance for doubtful accounts by an amount equal to one third of 1% of the year's $829,500 of credit sales.

    31   Closed the Interest Earned and Bad Debts Expense accounts.

    31   Reversed the accrued interest adjusting entry, dating the reversing entry January 1.

Feb. 14   Received payment from Carl Dent of the maturity value of his note.

    15   Accepted a $1,350, 90-day, 12% note dated this day in granting a time extension on the past-due account of Ted Bush.

    25   Discounted the Ted Bush note at the bank at 14%.

May 17   Received notice protesting the Ted Bush note. Paid the bank the maturity value of the note plus a $5 protest fee.

    18   Accepted $250 in cash and an $1,800, 60-day, 12% note dated May

16 in granting a time extension on the past-due account of Fred Hall.

June   3   Discounted the Fred Hall note at the bank at 15%.

July   16   Received notice protesting the Fred Hall note. Paid the bank the maturity value of the note plus a $4 protest fee.

Aug.   20   Received payment from Fred Hall of the maturity value of his dishonored note, the protest fee, and interest on both for 36 days beyond maturity at 12%.

Dec.   28   Decided the account of Ted Bush was uncollectible and wrote it off as a bad debt.

Problem 8–3   Prepare general journal entries to record these transactions:

Dec.   16   Accepted an $1,800, 60-day, 12% note dated this day in granting Dale Parr a time extension on his past-due account.

       31   Made an adjusting entry to record the accrued interest on the Dale Parr note.

       31   Closed the Interest Earned account.

       31   Reversed the accrued interest adjusting entry, dating the entry January 1.

Jan.   15   Discounted the Dale Parr note at the bank at 14%.

Feb.   15   Received notice protesting the Dale Parr note. Paid the bank the maturity value of the note plus a $5 protest fee.

Mar.   3   Accepted a $1,200, 12%, 60-day note dated this day in granting a time extension on the past-due account of Walter Allen.

       27   Discounted the Walter Allen note at the bank at 15%.

May   5   Since notice protesting the Walter Allen note had not been received, assumed that it had been paid.

June   8   Accepted a $1,400, 60-day, 12% note dated this day in granting a time extension on the past-due account of David Green.

Aug.   7   Received payment of the maturity value of the David Green note.

       10   Accepted a $1,600, 60-day, 12% note dated this day in granting Alfred Moss a time extension on his past-due account.

Sept. 15   Discounted the Alfred Moss note at the bank at 15%.

Oct.   10   Received notice protesting the Alfred Moss note. Paid the bank the maturity value of the note plus a $4 protest fee.

Nov.   9   Received payment from Alfred Moss of the maturity value of his dishonored note, the protest fee, and interest on both for 30 days beyond maturity at 12%.

Dec.   27   Wrote off the Dale Parr account against the allowance for doubtful accounts.

Problem 8–4   Prepare general journal entries to record these transactions:

Dec.   11   Accepted a $2,400, 60-day, 12% note dated this day in granting a time extension on the past-due account of Walter Jacks.

       31   Made an adjusting entry to record the accrued interest on the Walter Jacks note.

       31   Closed the Interest Earned account.

       31   Reversed the accrued interest adjusting entry, dating the entry January 1.

Feb.	9	Received payment of the maturity value of the Walter Jacks note.
	11	Accepted a $900, 60-day, 12% note dated this day in granting a time extension on the past-due account of Harold Dane.
	15	Accepted a $1,200, 90-day, 12% note dated this day in granting a time extension on the past-due account of David Kane.
	21	Discounted the David Kane note at the bank at 15%.
Apr.	12	Harold Dane dishonored his note when presented for payment.
May	19	Since notice protesting the David Kane note had not been received, assumed that it had been paid at maturity.
	24	Accepted a $750, 60-day, 12% note dated this day in granting a time extension on the past-due account of Earl Voss.
June	29	Discounted the Earl Voss note at the bank at 15%.
July	24	Received notice protesting the Earl Voss note. Paid the bank the maturity value of the note plus a $5 protest fee.
Aug.	5	Accepted a $1,200, 60-day, 12% note dated this day in granting a time extension on the past-due account of Lee Marsh.
	29	Discounted the Lee Marsh note at the bank at 15%.
Oct.	5	Received a notice protesting the Lee Marsh note. Paid the bank the maturity value of the note plus a $6 protest fee.
Dec.	3	Received payment from Lee Marsh of the maturity value of his dishonored note, the protest fee, and interest on both for 60 days beyond maturity at 12%.
	28	Wrote off the accounts of Harold Dane and Earl Voss against the allowance for doubtful accounts.

Problem 8–5   A company completed these transactions:

Dec.	11	Accepted a $2,700, 60-day, 12% note dated this day and $325 in cash in granting a time extension on the past-due account of Gary Carr.
	31	Aged the accounts receivable and estimated that $2,235 of the accounts would prove uncollectible. Examined the Allowance for Doubtful Accounts account and determined that it had a $145 debit balance. Made an adjusting entry to provide for the estimated bad debts.
	31	Made an adjusting entry to record the accrued interest on the Gary Carr note.
	31	Closed the Bad Debts Expense and Interest Earned accounts.
Feb.	9	Received payment of the maturity value of the Gary Carr note.
	11	Learned of the bankruptcy of Earl Hall and made a claim on his receiver in bankruptcy for the $545 owed by Mr. Hall for merchandise purchased on credit.
Mar.	5	Learned that Joel Kane had gone out of business, leaving no assets to attach. Wrote off his $315 account as a bad debt.
Apr.	24	Accepted $365 in cash and a $1,000, 60-day, 12% note dated this day in granting a time extension on the past-due account of Jerry West.
May	24	Discounted the Jerry West note at the bank at 14%.
June	24	Received notice protesting the Jerry West note. Paid the bank the maturity value of the note plus a $5 protest fee.

July   2   Joel Kane paid $150 of the amount written off on March 5. In a
letter accompanying the payment, he stated that his finances had
improved and he expected to pay the balance owed within a short
time.

Aug. 12   Received $110 from the receiver in bankruptcy of Earl Hall. A letter
accompanying the payment said that no more would be paid. Recorded the receipt of the $110 and wrote off the balance owed as
a bad debt.

Oct.   5   Decided that the Jerry West account was uncollectible and wrote
it off as a bad debt.

Dec. 22   Made a compound entry to write off the accounts of Harold Bane,
$395, and Fred Small, $215.

    31   Aged the accounts receivable and determined that $2,400 of the
accounts would probably prove uncollectible. Made an adjusting
entry to provide for them.

    31   Closed the Bad Debts Expense account and the Interest Earned
account.

Required:

1.   Open Interest Receivable, Allowance for Doubtful Accounts, Interest
Earned, and Bad Debts Expense accounts. Enter the $145 debit balance
in the Allowance for Doubtful Accounts account.
2.   Prepare general journal entries to record the transactions and post the
portions of the entries that affect the accounts opened.

ALTERNATE PROBLEMS

Problem 8–1A   Prepare general journal entries to record these transactions:

Jan.   5   Accepted a $1,600, 60-day, 12% note dated this day in granting a
time extension on the past-due account of Harold Green.

Mar.   6   Harold Green dishonored his note when presented for payment.

    12   Accepted a $1,500, 90-day, 12% note dated this day in granting a
time extension on the past-due account of Allen Cole.

    18   Discounted the Allen Cole note at the bank at 14%.

June 16   Since notice protesting the Allen Cole note had not been received,
assumed that it had been paid.

    18   Accepted $335 in cash and an $800, 60-day, 12% note dated this
day in granting a time extension on the past-due account of Walter
Evans.

July 12   Discounted the Walter Evans note at the bank at 15%.

Aug. 19   Received notice protesting the Walter Evans note. Paid the bank
the maturity value of the note plus a $5 protest fee.

Aug. 28   Accepted a $1,500, 60-day, 12% note dated this day in granting a
time extension on the past-due account of Larry Dent.

Oct.   3   Discounted the Larry Dent note at the bank at 14%.

    28   Received notice protesting the Larry Dent note. Paid the bank the
maturity value of the note plus a $6 protest fee.

Nov. 26 Received payment from Larry Dent of the maturity value of his dishonored note, the protest fee, and interest on both for 30 days beyond maturity at 12%.

Dec. 27 Decided the accounts of Harold Green and Walter Evans were uncollectible and wrote them off against the allowance for doubtful accounts.

Problem 8–2A Prepare general journal entries to record these transactions:

Dec. 16 Accepted $250 in cash and a $1,600, 60-day, 12% note dated this day in granting a time extension on the past-due account of Dale Dodd.

31 Made an adjusting entry to record the accrued interest on the Dale Dodd note.

31 Made an adjusting entry to increase the allowance for doubtful accounts by an amount equal to one third of 1% of the year's $936,000 of credit sales.

31 Closed the Interest Earned and Bad Debts Expense accounts.

31 Reversed the accrued interest adjusting entry, dating the reversing entry January 1.

Jan. 15 Discounted the Dale Dodd note at the bank at 14%.

Feb. 15 Received notice protesting the Dale Dodd note. Paid the bank the maturity value of the note plus a $4 protest fee.

Mar. 16 Received payment from Dale Dodd of the maturity value of his dishonored note, the protest fee, and interest on both for 30 days beyond maturity at 12%.

20 Accepted a $2,400, 90-day, 12% note dated this day in granting a time extension on the past-due account of Edward Brill.

26 Discounted the Edward Brill note at the bank at 15%.

June 19 Received notice protesting the Edward Brill note. Paid the bank the maturity value of the note plus a $5 protest fee.

Aug. 26 Accepted a $900, 60-day, 12% note dated this day in granting a time extension on the past-due account of Fred Gage.

Oct. 25 Fred Gage dishonored his note when presented for payment.

Dec. 18 Decided the Edward Brill and Fred Gage accounts were uncollectible and wrote them off against the allowance for doubtful accounts.

Problem 8–3A Prepare general journal entries to record these transactions:

Dec. 16 Accepted a $2,000, 60-day, 12% note dated this day in granting a time extension on the past-due account of Larry Taylor.

31 Made an adjusting entry to record the accrued interest on the Larry Taylor note.

31 Closed the Interest Earned account.

31 Reversed the accrued interest adjusting entry, dating the reversing entry January 1.

Jan. 15 Discounted the Larry Taylor note at the bank at 14%.

Feb. 15 Since notice protesting the Larry Taylor note had not been received, assumed that it had been paid.

Mar. 1 Accepted a $1,400, 90-day, 12% note dated this day in granting a time extension on the past-due account of John Rust.

7 Discounted the John Rust note at the bank at 15%.

May 31 Received notice protesting the John Rust note. Paid the bank the maturity value of the note plus a $6 protest fee.

June 29 Received payment from John Rust of the maturity value of his dishonored note, the protest fee, and interest on both for 30 days beyond maturity at 12%.

July 2 Accepted a $750, 60-day, 12% note dated July 1 in granting a time extension on the past-due account of Gary Jones.

Aug. 30 Gary Jones dishonored his note when presented for payment.

31 Accepted $425 in cash and a $900, 60-day, 12% note dated this day in granting a time extension on the past-due account of Ted Nash.

Oct. 6 Discounted the Ted Nash note at the bank at 15%.

31 Received notice protesting the Ted Nash note. Paid the bank the maturity value of the note plus a $6 protest fee.

Dec. 27 Decided the Gary Jones and Ted Nash accounts were uncollectible and wrote them off against the allowance for doubtful accounts.

Problem 8–4A   Prepare general journal entries to record these transactions:

Jan. 5 Accepted $450 in cash and a $1,350, 60-day, 12% note dated this day in granting a time extension on the past-due account of Earl Ross.

Mar. 6 Earl Ross dishonored his note when presented for payment.

12 Accepted a $1,600, 60-day, 12% note dated this day in granting a time extension on the past-due account of Carl Lane.

Apr. 5 Discounted the Carl Lane note at the bank at 15%.

May 14 Since notice protesting the Carl Lane note had not been received, assumed that it had been paid.

18 Accepted a $2,400, 90-day, 12% note dated this day in granting a time extension on the past-due account of Dale Hall.

28 Discounted the Dale Hall note at the bank at 15%.

Aug. 17 Received notice protesting the Dale Hall note. Paid the bank the maturity value of the note plus a $6 protest fee.

Sept. 9 Received payment from Dale Hall of the maturity value of his dishonored note, the protest fee, and interest on both for 24 days beyond maturity at 12%.

10 Accepted a $900, 60-day, 12% note dated this day in granting a time extension on the past-due account of Joel Kane.

30 Discounted the Joel Kane note at the bank at 14%.

Nov. 10 Received notice protesting the Joel Kane note. Paid the bank the maturity value of the note plus a $5 protest fee.

21 Accepted a $1,500, 60-day, 12% note dated this day in granting a time extension on the past-due account of Larry Parr.

Dec. 28 Decided the accounts of Earl Ross and Joel Kane were uncollectible and wrote them off against the allowance for doubtful accounts.

31 Made an adjusting entry to record the accrued interest on the Larry Parr note.

Dec. 31 Made an adjusting entry to increase the allowance for doubtful accounts by an amount equal to one fourth of 1% of the year's $968,000 of charge sales.

31 Closed the Interest Earned and Bad Debts Expense accounts.

31 Reversed the accrued interest adjusting entry, dating the reversing entry January 1.

Jan. 20 Received payment from Larry Parr of the maturity value of his note.

Problem 8–5A A company completed these transactions:

Dec. 1 Accepted $215 in cash and a $750, 60-day, 12% note dated this day in granting a time extension on the past-due account of Lee Moss.

31 Made an adjusting entry to record the accrued interest on the Lee Moss note.

31 Examined the Allowance for Doubtful Accounts account and determined that it had a $115 credit balance. Made an adjusting entry to provide an addition to the allowance equal to one fourth of 1% of the year's $964,000 of charge sales.

31 Closed the Interest Earned and Bad Debts Expense accounts.

Jan. 30 Received payment of the maturity value of the Lee Moss note.

Feb. 3 Learned of the bankruptcy of George Hall and made a claim on his receiver in bankruptcy for the $380 owed by Mr. Hall for merchandise purchased on credit.

Mar. 12 After making every effort to collect, decided the $470 account of Carl Voss was uncollectible and wrote it off as a bad debt.

June 15 Received a letter from Carl Voss enclosing a $150 payment on the account written off on March 12. He stated in his letter that his finances had improved and that he expected to pay the balance owed within a short time.

Nov. 3 Received $95 from George Hall's receiver in bankruptcy. A letter accompanying the payment stated that no more would be paid. Made an entry to record the cash received and to write off the balance of Hall's account.

Dec. 22 Made a compound entry to write off the accounts of Earl Parks, $860; Fred Davis, $690; and Walter Sears, $765.

31 Provided an addition to the allowance for doubtful accounts equal to one fourth of 1% of the year's $996,000 of charge sales.

31 Closed the Interest Earned and Bad Debts Expense accounts.

Required:

1. Open these accounts: Interest Receivable, Allowance for Doubtful Accounts, Interest Earned, and Bad Debts Expense. Enter the $115 credit balance in the Allowance for Doubtful Accounts account. Prepare general journal entries to record the transactions and post the entry portions affecting the accounts opened.

2. Prepare an alternate bad debts adjusting entry for the second December 31 of the problem under the assumption that rather than providing an addition to the allowance account equal to one fourth of 1% of charge

sales, the company aged its accounts receivable, estimated that $2,300 of accounts were probably uncollectible, and increased its allowance to provide for them.

PROVOCATIVE PROBLEMS

Provocative Problem 8–1, an Embezzlement

When his auditor arrived early in January to begin the annual audit, Robert Cole, the owner of Specialty Sales, asked that careful attention be given the accounts receivable. Two things caused this request: (1) During the previous week, Mr. Cole had met Ted Beck, a former customer, on the street, and had asked him about his account which had recently been written off as uncollectible. Mr. Beck had indignantly replied that he had paid his $255 account in full, and he later produced a canceled check endorsed by Specialty Sales to prove it. (2) The income statement prepared for the quarter ended the previous December 31 showed an unusually large volume of sales returns. The bookkeeper who had prepared the statement was a new employee, having begun work on October 1, after being hired on the basis of out-of-town letters of reference. In addition to doing all the record keeping, the bookkeeper also acts as cashier, receiving and depositing the cash from both cash sales and that received through the mail.

In the course of his investigation, the auditor prepared from the company's records the following analysis of the accounts receivable for the period October 1 through December 31:

	Aker	Beck	Cash	Dent	Eads	Fish	Glen
Balance, October 1	$ 210	$ 125	$ 345	$ 250	$ 130	$ 545	$ 410
Sales	695	130	530		660	420	575
Total	$ 905	$ 255	$ 875	$ 250	$ 790	$ 965	$ 985
Collections	(510)		(395)		(410)	(490)	(615)
Returns	(85)	(45)	(40)		(80)	(60)	(25)
Bad debts written off		(210)		(250)			
Balance, December 31	$ 310	–0–	$ 440	–0–	$ 300	$ 415	$ 345

The auditor communicated with all charge customers and learned that although their account balances as of December 31 agreed with the amounts shown in the company's records, the individual transactions did not. They reported credit purchases totaling $3,435 during the three-month period and $85 of returns for which credit had been granted. Correspondence with Mr. Dent, the customer whose $250 account had been written off, revealed that he had become bankrupt and his creditor claims had been settled by his receiver in bankruptcy at $0.22 on the dollar. The checks had been mailed by his receiver on October 30, and all had been paid and returned by the bank, properly endorsed by the recipients.

Under the assumption the bookkeeper has embezzled cash from the company, determine the total amount he has taken and attempted to conceal with false accounts receivable entries. Account for the deficiency by listing the concealment methods used and the amount he attempted to conceal with each method. Also outline an internal control system that will help protect the company's cash from future embezzlement. Assume the company will hire a new bookkeeper, but that it is small and can have only one office employee who must do all the bookkeeping.

Walter Barr has operated Elegant Shop for five years. Three years ago he liberalized the shop's credit policy in an effort to increase credit sales. Credit sales have increased, but Walt is concerned with the effects of the more liberalized credit policy. Bad debts written off (the store uses the direct write-off method) have increased materially in the last three years, and now Walt wonders if the increase justifies the substantial bad debt losses that he is certain have resulted from the more liberal credit policy.

An examination of the shop's credit sales records, bad debt losses, and accounts receivable for the five years' operations reveal:

	1st year	2d year	3d year	4th year	5th year
Credit sales	$100,000	$110,000	$150,000	$180,000	$200,000
Cost of goods sold	60,000	66,200	89,900	108,300	120,100
Gross profit from credit sales	$ 40,000	$ 43,800	$ 60,100	$ 71,700	$ 79,900
Expenses other than bad debts	30,000	32,900	45,200	53,800	60,000
Income before bad debts	$ 10,000	$ 10,900	$ 14,900	$ 17,900	$ 19,900
Bad debts written off	100	440	750	2,340	2,400
Income from credit sales	$ 9,900	$ 10,460	$ 14,150	$ 15,560	$ 17,500
Bad debts by year of sales	$ 400	$ 330	$ 1,950	$ 2,160	$ 2,800

The last line in the tabulation results from reclassifying bad debt losses by the years in which the sales that resulted in the losses were made. Consequently, the $2,800 of fifth-year losses includes $1,610 of estimated bad debts that are still in the accounts receivable.

Prepare a schedule showing in columns by years income from credit sales before bad debt losses, bad debts incurred, and the resulting net income from credit sales. Then below the income figures show for each year bad debts written off as a percentage of sales followed on the next line by bad debts incurred as a percentage of sales. Also prepare a report answering Mr. Barr's concern about the new credit policy and recommending any changes you consider desirable in his accounting for bad debts.

Inventories and Cost of Goods Sold

9

After studying Chapter 9, you should be able to:

Calculate the cost of an inventory based on *(a)* specific invoice prices, *(b)* weighted-average cost, *(c)* FIFO, and *(d)* LIFO.

Explain the income tax effect of the use of LIFO.

Tell what is required by the accounting principle of consistency and why the application of this principle is important.

Tell what is required of a concern when it changes its accounting procedures.

Tell what is required by the accounting principle of conservatism.

Explain the effect of an inventory error on the income statements of the current and succeeding years.

Tell how a perpetual inventory system operates.

Estimate an inventory by the retail method and by the gross profit method.

Define or explain the words and phrases listed in the chapter Glossary.

A merchandising business earns revenue by selling merchandise. For such a business, the phrase *merchandise inventory* is used to describe the aggregate of the items of tangible personal property it holds for sale. As a rule, the items are sold within a year or one cycle. Consequently, the inventory is a current asset, usually the largest current asset on a merchandising company's balance sheet.

MATCHING MERCHANDISE COSTS WITH REVENUES

An AICPA committee said: "A major objective of accounting for inventories is the proper determination of income through the process of matching appropriate costs against revenues."[1] The matching process referred to is one with which the student is already familiar. For inventories, it consists of determining how much of the cost of the goods that were for sale during a period should be deducted from the period's revenue and how much should be carried forward as inventory to be matched against a future period's revenue.

In separating cost of goods available for sale into its components of cost of goods sold and cost of goods not sold, the key problem is that of assigning a cost to the goods not sold or to the ending inventory. However, it should be borne in mind that the procedures for assigning a cost to the ending inventory are also the means of determining cost of goods sold. For whatever portion of the cost of goods for sale is assigned to the ending inventory, the remainder goes into cost of goods sold.

TAKING AN ENDING INVENTORY

As previously stated, when a periodic inventory system is in use, the dollar amount of the ending inventory is determined by counting the items of unsold merchandise remaining in the store, multiplying the count for each kind by its cost, and adding the costs for all the kinds. In making the count, items are less apt to be counted twice or omitted from the count if prenumbered *inventory tickets* like the one in Illustration 9–1 are used. Before beginning the inventory, a sufficient number of the tickets, at least one for each kind of product on hand, is issued to each department in the store. Next, a clerk counts the quantity of each product and from the count and the price tag attached to the merchandise fills in the information on the inventory

---

[1] Committee on Accounting Procedures, "Accounting Research Bulletin No. 43," *Accounting Research and Terminology Bulletins, Final Edition* (New York: AICPA, 1961), p. 28.

ticket and attaches it to the counted items. After the count is completed, each department is examined for uncounted items. At this stage, inventory tickets are attached to all counted items. Consequently, any products without tickets attached are uncounted. After all items are counted and tickets attached, the tickets are removed and sent to the accounting department for completion of the inventory. To ensure that no ticket is lost or left attached to merchandise, all the prenumbered tickets issued are accounted for when the tickets arrive in the accounting department.

Illustration 9–1

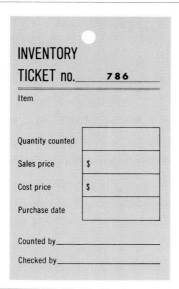

In the accounting department, the information on the tickets is copied on inventory summary sheets. The sheets are then completed by multiplying the number of units of each product by its cost. This gives the dollar amount of each product in the inventory, and the total for all the products is the dollar total of the inventory.

ASSIGNING COSTS TO INVENTORY ITEMS

In completing an inventory, it is necessary to assign costs to the inventory items. This offers no problem when costs remain fixed. However, when identical items were purchased during a period at different costs, a problem arises as to which costs apply to the ending inventory and which apply to the goods sold. There are four commonly used ways of assigning costs to goods in the ending inventory and to goods sold. They are (1) specific invoice prices; (2) weighted-average cost; (3) first-in, first-out; and (4) last-in, first-out. Each is a *generally accepted accounting procedure.*

To illustrate the four, assume that a company has on hand at the end of an accounting period 12 units of Product X. Also, assume that the company began the year and purchased Product X during the year as follows:

Jan.	1	Beginning inventory	10 units @ $100 =	$1,000
Mar.	13	Purchased	15 units @ $108 =	1,620
Aug.	17	Purchased	20 units @ $120 =	2,400
Nov.	10	Purchased	10 units @ $125 =	1,250
		Total	55 units	$6,270

Specific Invoice Prices

When it is possible to identify each item in an inventory with a specific purchase and its invoice, *specific invoice prices* may be used to assign costs. For example, assume that 6 of the 12 unsold units of Product X were from the November purchase and 6 were from the August purchase. Under this assumption, costs are assigned to the inventory and goods sold by means of specific invoice prices as follows:

Total cost of 55 units available for sale	$6,270
Less ending inventory priced by means of specific invoices:	
6 units from the November purchase at $125 each $750	
6 units from the August purchase at $120 each 720	
12 units in ending inventory	1,470
Cost of goods sold	$4,800

Weighted Average

Under this method, prices for the units in the beginning inventory and in each purchase are weighted by the number of units in the beginning inventory and in each purchase and are averaged to find the *weighted-average cost* per unit as follows:

```
10 units @ $100 =  $1,000
15 units @ $108 =   1,620
20 units @ $120 =   2,400
10 units @ $125 =   1,250
55                 $6,270

$6,270 ÷ 55 = $114, weighted-average cost per unit
```

After the weighted-average cost per unit is determined, this average is used to assign costs to the inventory and the units sold as follows:

```
Total cost of 55 units available for sale ...............  $6,270
Less ending inventory priced on a weighted-average
    cost basis: 12 units at $114 each...................   1,368
Cost of goods sold ....................................   $4,902
```

First-in, First-out

In a merchandising business, clerks are instructed to sell the oldest merchandise first. Consequently, when this instruction is followed, merchandise tends to flow out on a first-in, first-out basis. When first-in, first-out is applied in pricing an inventory, it is assumed that costs follow this pattern. As a result, the costs of the last items received are assigned to the ending inventory and the remaining costs are assigned to goods sold. When first-in, first-out, or *FIFO* as it is often called from its first letters, is used, costs are assigned to the inventory and goods sold as follows:

```
Total cost of 55 units available for sale ................      $6,270
Less ending inventory priced on a basis of FIFO:
    10 units from the November purchase at $125 each ..... $1,250
     2 units from the August purchase at $120 each ........   240
    12 units in the ending inventory ......................     1,490
Cost of goods sold ......................................      $4,780
```

Last-in, First-out

Under this method of inventory pricing, commonly called *LIFO,* the costs of the last goods received are matched with revenue from sales. The theoretical justification for this is that a going concern must at all times keep a certain amount of goods in stock. Consequently, when goods are sold, replacements are purchased. Thus, it is a sale that causes the replacement of goods. If costs and revenues are then matched, replacement costs should be matched with the sales that induced the acquisitions.

Under LIFO, costs are assigned to the 12 remaining units of Product X and to the goods sold as follows:

Total cost of 55 units available for sale		$6,270
Less ending inventory priced on a basis of LIFO:		
10 units in the beginning inventory at $100 each	$1,000	
2 units from the first purchase at $108 each	216	
12 units in the ending inventory		1,216
Cost of goods sold		$5,054

Notice that this method of matching costs and revenue results in the final inventory being priced at the cost of the oldest 12 units.

Tax Effect of LIFO

During periods of rising prices, LIFO offers a tax advantage to its users. This advantage arises because when compared with other methods the application of LIFO results in assigning greatest amounts of costs to goods sold. This in turn results in the smallest reported net incomes and income taxes.

The use of LIFO is not limited to companies in which goods are actually sold on a last-in, first-out basis. A company may choose LIFO even though it actually sells goods on a first-in, first-out basis, or on an indiscriminate basis.

Comparison of Methods

In a stable market where prices remain unchanged, the inventory pricing method is of little importance. For when prices are unchanged over a period of time, all methods give the same cost figures. However, in a changing market where prices are rising or falling, each method may give a different result. This may be seen by comparing the costs of the units in the ending inventory and the units of Product X sold as calculated by the several methods discussed. These costs are as follows:

	Ending inventory	Cost of units sold
Based on specific invoice prices	$1,470	$4,800
Based on weighted average	1,368	4,902
Based on FIFO	1,490	4,780
Based on LIFO	1,216	5,054

Each of the four pricing methods is recognized as a generally accepted accounting procedure, and arguments can be advanced for the use of each. Specific invoice prices exactly match costs and revenues. However, this method is of practical use only for relatively high-priced items of which only a few units are kept in stock and sold. Weighted-average costs tend to smooth out price fluctuations. FIFO causes the last costs incurred to be assigned to the ending inventory. It thus provides an inventory valuation for the balance sheet that most closely approximates current replacement cost. LIFO causes last costs incurred to be assigned to cost of goods sold. Therefore, it results in a better matching of current costs with revenues. However, the method used commonly affects the amounts of reported ending inventory, cost of goods sold, and net income. Consequently, the *full-disclosure principle* requires that a company show in its statements by means of footnotes or other manner the pricing method used.[2]

THE PRINCIPLE OF CONSISTENCY

Look again at the table of costs for Product X. Note that a company can change its reported net income for an accounting period simply by changing its inventory pricing method. However, the change would violate the accounting *principle of consistency.* Furthermore, it would make a comparison of the company's inventory and income with previous periods more or less meaningless.

As with inventory pricing, more than one generally accepted method or procedure has been derived in accounting practice to account for an item or an activity. In each case, one method may be considered better for one enterprise, while another may be considered more satisfactory for a concern operating under different circumstances. Nevertheless, the *principle of consistency* requires a persistent application by a company of any selected accounting method or

---

[2] APB, "Disclosure of Accounting Policies," *APB Opinion No. 22* (New York: AICPA, April 1972), pars. 12, 13.

procedure, period after period. As a result, a reader of a company's financial statements may assume that in keeping its records and in preparing its statements the company used the same procedures employed in previous years. Only on the basis of this assumption can meaningful comparisons be made of the data in a company's statements year after year.

CHANGING ACCOUNTING PROCEDURES

In achieving comparability, the *principle of consistency* does not require that a method or procedure once chosen can never be changed. Rather, if a company decides that a different acceptable method or procedure from the one in use will better serve its needs, a change may be made. However, when such a change is made, the *full-disclosure principle* requires that the nature of the change, justification for the change, and the effect of the change on net income be disclosed in notes accompanying the statements.[3]

ITEMS INCLUDED ON AN INVENTORY

A company's inventory should include all goods owned by the business and held for sale, regardless of where the goods may be located at the time of the inventory. In the application of this rule, there are generally no problems with respect to most items. For most items, all that is required is to see that they are counted, that nothing is omitted, and that nothing is counted more than once. However, goods in transit, goods sold but not delivered, goods on consignment, and obsolete and damaged goods do require special attention.

When goods are in transit on the inventory date, the purchase should be recorded and the goods should appear on the purchaser's inventory if ownership has passed to the purchaser. Generally, if the buyer is responsible for paying the transportation charges, ownership passes as soon as the goods are loaded aboard the means of transportation. Likewise, if the seller is to pay the transportation charges, ownership passes when the goods arrive at their destination.

Goods on consignment are goods shipped by their owner (known as the *consignor*) to another person or firm (called the *consignee*) who is to sell the goods for the owner. Consigned goods belong to the consignor and should appear on the consignor's inventory.

Damaged goods and goods that have deteriorated or become obso-

---

[3] APB, "Accounting Changes," *APB Opinion No. 20* (New York: AICPA, July 1971), par. 17.

lete should not be placed on the inventory if they are not salable. If such goods are salable but at a reduced price, they should be placed on the inventory at a conservative estimate of their realizable value (sale price less the cost of making the sale). This causes the accounting period in which the goods were damaged, deteriorated, or became obsolete to suffer the resultant loss.

Elements of Inventory Cost

As applied to inventories, cost means the sum of the applicable expenditures and charges directly or indirectly incurred in bringing an article to its existing condition and location.[4] Therefore, the cost of an inventory item includes the invoice price, less the discount, plus any additional incidental costs necessary to put the goods into place and condition for sale. The additional incidental costs include import duties, transportation, storage, insurance, and any other applicable costs, such as those incurred during an aging process.

If incurred, any of the foregoing enter into the cost of an inventory. However, in pricing an inventory, most concerns do not take into consideration the incidental costs of acquiring merchandise. They price the inventory on the basis of invoice prices only, and treat all incidental costs as expenses of the period in which incurred.

Although not correct in theory, treating incidental costs as expenses of the period in which incurred is commonly permissible and often best. In theory, a share of each incidental cost should be assigned to every unit purchased. This causes a portion of each to be carried forward in the inventory to be matched against the revenue of the period in which the inventory is sold. However, the expense of computing costs on such a precise basis usually outweighs any benefit from the extra accuracy. Consequently, when possible, most companies take advantage of the *principle of materiality* and treat such costs as expenses of the period in which incurred.

COST OR MARKET, THE LOWER

Over the years, the traditional rule for pricing inventory items has been *the lower of cost or market*. "Cost" is the price that was paid for an item when it was purchased. "Market" is the price that would have to be paid to purchase or replace the item on the inventory date. The use of this rule gained its wide acceptance because it placed an inventory on the balance sheet at a conservative figure, the lower

---

[4] *Accounting Research and Terminology Bulletins, Final Edition,* p. 28.

of what the inventory cost or its replacement cost on the balance sheet date.

The argument advanced to support the use of lower of cost or market was that if the replacement cost of an inventory item had declined, then its selling price would probably have to be reduced. Since this might result in a loss, the loss should be anticipated and taken in the year of the price decline. It was a good argument. However, selling prices do not always exactly and quickly follow cost prices. As a result, the application of the rule often resulted in misstating net income in the year of a price decline and again in the succeeding year. For example, suppose that a firm purchased merchandise costing $1,000; marked it up to a $1,500 selling price; and sold one half of the goods. The gross profit on the goods sold would be calculated as follows:

```
Sales ................... $750
Cost of goods sold ......   500
Gross profit on sales .....  $250
```

However, if the $500 replacement cost of the unsold goods declined to $450 by the inventory date, an income statement based upon the traditional application of cost or market would show the following:

```
Sales ......................        $750
Cost of goods sold:
    Purchases ................ $1,000
        Less ending inventory .....   450   550
Gross profit on sales..........     $200
```

The $450 would be a conservative balance sheet figure for the unsold goods. However, if these goods were sold at their full price early in the following year, the $450 inventory figure would have the erroneous effect of deferring $50 of income to the second year's income statement as follows:

```
Sales ................... $750
Cost of goods sold:
    Beginning inventory .....   450
Gross profit on sales...... $300
```

Merchants are prone to be slow in marking down goods; they normally try to sell merchandise at its full price if possible. Consequently, the illustrated situation is not uncommon. For this reason, the lower-of-cost-or-market rule has been modified as follows for situations in which replacement costs are below actual costs.[5]

1. Goods should be placed on an inventory at cost, even though replacement cost is lower, if there has not been and there is not expected to be a decline in selling price.
2. Goods should at times be placed on an inventory at a price below cost but above replacement cost. For example, suppose the cost of an item that is normally bought for $20 and sold for $30 declines from $20 to $16, and its selling price declines from $30 to $27. The normal profit margin on this item is one third of its selling price. If this normal margin is applied to $27, the item should be placed on the inventory at two thirds of $27, or at $18. This is below cost but above replacement cost.
3. At times, goods should be placed on an inventory at a price below replacement cost. For example, assume that the goods described in the preceding paragraph can only be sold for $18.50 and that the disposal costs are estimated at $3. In this case, the goods should be placed on the inventory at $15.50, a price below their replacement cost of $16.

PRINCIPLE OF CONSERVATISM

Decisions based on estimates and opinions as to future events affect financial statements. Financial statements are also affected by the selection of accounting procedures. The *principle of conservatism* holds that accountants should be conservative in their estimates and opinions and in the selection of procedures, choosing those that neither unduly understate nor overstate the situation.

Something called balance sheet conservatism was once considered the "first" principle of accounting. Its objective was to place every item on the balance sheet at a conservative figure. This in itself was commendable. However, it was often carried too far and resulted not only in the misstatement of asset values but also in unconservative income statements. For example, when prices are falling, the blind application of the lower of cost or market to inventories may result in a conservative balance sheet figure for inventories. It may also result in an improper deferring of net income and in inaccurate income statements. Consequently, accountants recognize that balance sheet conservatism does not outweigh other factors. They favor practices that result in a fair statement of net income period after period.

---

[5] Ibid., pp. 30, 31.

INVENTORY ERRORS

An error in determining the end-of period inventory will cause misstatements in cost of goods sold, gross profit, net income, current assets, and owner's equity. Also, the ending inventory of one period is the beginning inventory of the next. Therefore, the error will carry forward and cause misstatements in the succeeding period's cost of goods sold, gross profit, and net income. Furthermore, since the amount involved in an inventory is often large, the misstatements can be material without being readily apparent.

To illustrate the effects of an inventory error, assume that in each of the years 198A, 198B, and 198C, a company had $100,000 in sales. If the company maintained a $20,000 inventory throughout the period and made $60,000 in purchases in each of the years, its cost of goods sold each year was $60,000 and its annual gross profits were $40,000. However, assume the company incorrectly calculated its December 31, 198A, inventory at $18,000 rather than $20,000. The error would have the effects shown in Illustration 9–2.

Illustration 9–2

	198A		198B		198C	
Sales		$100,000		$100,000		$100,000
Cost of goods sold:						
Beginning inventory	$20,000		$18,000*		$20,000	
Purchases	60,000		60,000		60,000	
Goods for sale	$80,000		$78,000		$80,000	
Ending inventory	18,000*		20,000		20,000	
Cost of goods sold		62,000		58,000		60,000
Gross profit		$ 38,000		$ 42,000		$ 40,000
* Should have been $20,000.						

Observe in Illustration 9–2 that the $2,000 understatement of the December 31, 198A, inventory caused a $2,000 overstatement in 198A cost of goods sold and a $2,000 understatement in gross profit and net income. Also, since the ending inventory of 198A became the beginning inventory of 198B, the error caused an understatement in the 198B cost of goods sold and a $2,000 overstatement in gross profit and net income. However, by 198C the error had no effect.

In Illustration 9–2, the December 31, 198A, inventory is understated. Had it been overstated, it would have caused opposite results—the 198A net income would have been overstated and the 198B income understated.

It has been argued that an inventory mistake is not too serious, since the error it causes in reported net income the first year is exactly offset by an opposite error in the second. However, such reasoning is unsound. It fails to consider that management, creditors, and owners base many important decisions on fluctuations in reported net income. Consequently, such mistakes should be avoided.

PERPETUAL INVENTORIES

Companies selling a limited number of products of relatively high value often keep perpetual or book inventories. Also, concerns that use computers in processing their accounting data commonly keep such records. Furthermore, the essential information provided is the same whether accumulated by computer or with pen and ink.

A perpetual or book inventory based on pen and ink makes use of a subsidiary record card for each product in stock. On these individual cards, the number of units received is recorded as units are received and the number of units sold is recorded as units are sold. Then, after each receipt or sale, the balance remaining is recorded. (An inventory record card for Product Z is shown in Illustration 9–3.) At any time,

Illustration 9–3

Item	Product Z			Location in stock room	Bin 8					
Maximum	25			Minimum	5					

Date	Received			Sold			Balance		
	Units	Cost	Total	Units	Cost	Total	Units	Cost	Balance
1/1							10	10.00	100.00
1/5				5	10.00	50.00	5	10.00	50.00
1/8	20	10.50	210.00				5	10.00	
							20	10.50	260.00
1/10				3	10.00	30.00	2	10.00	
							20	10.50	230.00

each perpetual inventory card tells the balance on hand of any one product; and the total of all cards is the amount of the inventory.

The January 10 sale on the card of Illustration 9–3 indicates that the inventory of this card is kept on a first-in, first-out basis, since the sale is recorded as being from the oldest units in stock. Perpetual inventories may also be kept on a last-in, first-out basis. When this is done, each sale is recorded as being from the last units received, until these are exhausted, then sales are from the next to last, and so on.

When a company keeps perpetual inventory records, it normally also makes a once-a-year physical count of each kind of goods in stock in order to check the accuracy of its book inventory records.

Perpetual inventories not only tell the amount of inventory on hand at any time but they also aid in controlling the total amount invested in inventory. Each perpetual inventory card may have on it the maximum and minimum amounts of that item that should be kept in stock. By keeping the amount of each item within these limits, an oversupply or an undersupply of inventory is avoided.

PERPETUAL INVENTORY SYSTEMS

Under a *perpetual inventory system,* cost of goods sold during a period, as well as the ending inventory, may be determined from the accounting records. Under such a system, an account called Merchandise is used in the place of the Purchases and Merchandise Inventory accounts. It is a controlling account that controls the numerous perpetual inventory cards described in previous paragraphs.

When merchandise is purchased by a concern using a perpetual inventory system, the acquisition is recorded as follows:

Jan.	8	Merchandise	210.00	
		Accounts Payable—Blue Company		210.00
		Purchased merchandise on credit.		

In addition to the entry debiting the purchase to the Merchandise account, entries are also made on the proper perpetual inventory cards in the Received columns to show the kinds of merchandise bought. (See Illustration 9–3.)

When a sale is made, since the inventory cards show the cost of each item sold, it is possible to record both the sale and the cost of the goods sold. For example, if goods that according to the inventory cards cost $30 are sold for $50, cost of goods sold and the sale may be recorded as follows:

Jan.	10	Accounts Receivable—George Black	50.00	
		Cost of Goods Sold	30.00	
		Sales		50.00
		Merchandise		30.00
		Sold merchandise on credit.		

In addition to the credit in this entry to the Merchandise account for the cost of the goods sold, the costs of the items sold are also deducted in the Sold columns of the proper inventory cards.

Note the debit to the Cost of Goods Sold account in the entry just given. If this account is debited at the time of each sale for the cost of the goods sold, the debit balance of the account will show at the end of the accounting period the cost of all goods sold during the period.

Note also the debit and the credit to the Merchandise account as they appear in the two entries just given. If this account is debited for the cost of merchandise purchased and credited for the cost of merchandise sold, at the end of an accounting period its debit balance will show the cost of the unsold goods on hand, the ending inventory.

ESTIMATED INVENTORIES

Retail Method

Good management requires that income statements be prepared more often than once each year, and inventory information is necessary in their preparation. However, taking a physical inventory in a retail store is both time consuming and expensive. Consequently, many retailers use the so-called *retail inventory method* to estimate inventories for monthly or quarterly statements. These monthly or quarterly statements are called *interim statements*, since they are prepared in between the regular year-end statements.

ESTIMATING AN ENDING INVENTORY BY THE RETAIL METHOD. When the retail method is used to estimate an inventory, a store's records must show the amount of inventory it had at the beginning of the period both *at cost* and *at retail*. At cost for an inventory means just that, while "at retail" means the dollar amount of the inventory at the marked selling prices of the inventory items.

In addition to the beginning inventory, the records must also show the amount of goods purchased during the period both at cost and at retail plus the net sales at retail. The last item is easy; it is the balance of the Sales account less returns and discounts. Then, with this information the interim inventory is estimated at follows: (Step 1) The amount of goods that were for sale during the period both at cost and at retail is first computed. Next (Step 2), "at cost" is divided by "at retail" to obtain a cost ratio. Then (Step 3), sales (at retail) are deducted from goods for sale (at retail) to arrive at the ending inventory (at retail). And finally (Step 4), the ending inventory at retail is multiplied by the cost ratio to reduce it to a cost basis. These calculations are shown in Illustration 9–4.

Illustration 9–4

		At cost	At retail
(Step 1)	Goods available for sale:		
	Beginning inventory	$20,500	$ 34,500
	Net purchases	39,500	65,500
	Goods available for sale	$60,000	$100,000
(Step 2)	Cost ratio: $60,000 ÷ $100,000 = 60%		
(Step 3)	Deduct sales at retail		70,000
	Ending inventory at retail		$ 30,000
(Step 4)	Ending inventory at cost ($30,000 × 60%)	$18,000	

This is the essence of Illustration 9–4: (1) The store had $100,000 of goods (at marked selling prices) for sale during the period. (2) These goods cost 60% of the $100,000 total amount at which they were marked for sale. (3) The store's records (its Sales account) showed that $70,000 of these goods were sold, leaving $30,000 of merchandise unsold and presumably in the ending inventory. Therefore, (4) since cost in this store is 60% of retail, the estimated cost of this ending inventory is $18,000.

An ending inventory calculated as in Illustration 9–4 is an estimate arrived at by deducting sales (goods sold) from goods for sale. Inventories estimated in this manner are satisfactory for interim statements, but for year-end statements, or at least once each year, a store should take a physical inventory.

USING THE RETAIL METHOD TO REDUCE A PHYSICAL INVENTORY TO COST.   Items for sale in a store normally have price tickets attached that show selling prices. Consequently, when a store takes a physical inventory, it commonly takes the inventory at the marked selling prices of the inventoried items. It then reduces the dollar total of this inventory to a cost basis by applying its cost ratio. It does this because the selling prices are readily available and the application of the cost ratio eliminates the need to look up the invoice price of each inventoried item.

For example, assume that the store of Illustration 9–4, in addition to estimating its inventory by the retail method, also takes a physical inventory at the marked selling prices of the inventoried goods. Assume further that the total of this physical inventory is $29,600. Under these assumptions, the store may arrive at a cost basis for this inventory, without having to look up the cost of each inventoried item, simply by applying its cost ratio to the $29,600 inventory total as follows:

$$\$29,600 \times 60\% = \$17,760$$

The $17,760 cost figure for this store's ending physical inventory is a satisfactory figure for year-end statement purposes. It is also acceptable to the Internal Revenue Service for tax purposes.

INVENTORY SHORTAGE. An inventory determined as in Illustration 9–4 is an estimate of the amount of goods that should be on hand. However, since it is arrived at by deducting sales from goods for sale, it does not reveal any actual shortages due to breakage, loss, or theft. Nevertheless, the amount of such shortages may be determined by first estimating an inventory as in Illustration 9–4 and then taking a physical inventory at marked selling prices.

For example, by means of the Illustration 9–4 calculations, it was estimated the store of this discussion had a $30,000 ending inventory at retail. However, in the previous section, it was assumed that this same store took a physical inventory and had only $29,600 of merchandise on hand. Therefore, if this store should have had $30,000 of goods in its ending inventory as determined in Illustration 9–4, but had only $29,600 when it took a physical inventory, it must have had a $400 inventory shortage at retail or a $240 shortage at cost ($400 $\times$ 60% = $240).

MARKUPS AND MARKDOWNS. The calculation of a cost ratio is often not as simple as that shown in Illustration 9–4. It is not simple because many stores not only have a *normal markup* (often called a *markon*) that they apply to items purchased for sale but also make *additional markups* and *markdowns*. A normal markup or markon is the normal amount or percentage that is applied to the cost of an item to arrive at its selling price. For example, if a store's normal markup is 50% on cost and it applies this markup to an item that cost $10, it will mark the item for sale at $15. Normal markups appear in the calculation of a store's cost ratio as the difference between net purchases at cost and at retail.

Additional markups are markups made in addition to normal markups. Stores commonly give goods of outstanding style or quality such additional markups because they can get a higher than normal price for such goods. They also commonly mark down for a clearance sale any slow-moving merchandise.

When a store using the retail inventory method makes additional markups and markdowns, it must keep a record of them. It then uses the information in calculating its cost ratio and in estimating an interim inventory as in Illustration 9–5.

Observe in Illustration 9–5 that the store's $80,000 of goods for sale at retail were reduced $54,000 by sales and $2,000 by markdowns, a total of $56,000. (To understand the markdowns, visualize this effect of a markdown. The store had an item for sale during the period at

Illustration 9–5

	At cost	At retail
Goods available for sale:		
Beginning inventory	$18,000	$27,800
Net purchases	34,000	50,700
Additional markups		1,500
Goods available for sale	$52,000	$80,000
Cost ratio: $52,000 ÷ $80,000 = 65%		
Sales at retail...................................		$54,000
Markdowns.......................................		2,000
Total sales and markdowns		$56,000
Ending inventory at retail ($80,000 less $56,000).....		$24,000
Ending inventory at cost ($24,000 × 65%).........	$15,600	

$25. The item did not sell; and to move it, the manager marked its price down from $25 to $20. By this act, the amount of goods for sale in the store at retail was reduced by $5. Likewise, by a number of such markdowns during the year, goods for sale at retail in the store of Illustration 9–5 were reduced $2,000). Now back to the calculations of Illustration 9–5. The store's $80,000 of goods for sale were reduced $54,000 by sales and $2,000 by markdowns, leaving an estimated $24,000 ending inventory at retail. Therefore, since "cost" is 65% of "retail," the ending inventory at "cost" is $15,600.

Observe in Illustration 9–5 that markups enter into the calculation of the cost ratio but markdowns do not. It has long been customary in using the retail inventory method to add additional markups but to ignore markdowns in computing the percentage relation between goods for sale at cost and at retail. The justification for this was and is that a more conservative figure for the ending inventory results, a figure that approaches "cost or market, the lower." A further discussion of this phase of the retail inventory method is reserved for a more advanced text.

Gross Profit Method

Often retail price information about beginning inventory, purchases, and markups is not kept. In such cases, the retail inventory method cannot be used. However, if a company knows its normal gross profit margin or rate; has information at cost in regard to its beginning inventory, net purchases, and transportation-in; and knows the amount of its sales and sales returns, the company can estimate its ending inventory by the *gross profit method.*

For example, on March 27, the inventory of a company was totally destroyed by a fire. The company's average gross profit rate during the past five years has been 30% of net sales. And on the date of the fire, the company's accounts showed the following balances:

Sales	$31,500
Sales returns	1,500
Inventory, January 1, 19—.....	12,000
Net purchases	20,000
Transportation-in	500

With this information, the gross profit method may be used to estimate the company's inventory loss for insurance purposes. The first step in applying the method is to recognize that whatever portion of each dollar of net sales was gross profit, the remaining portion was cost of goods sold. Consequently, if the company's gross profit rate averaged 30%, then 30% of each dollar of net sales was gross profit and 70% was cost of goods sold. The 70% is used in estimating the inventory and inventory loss as in Illustration 9–6.

Illustration 9–6

Goods available for sale:		
Inventory, January 1, 19—.........................		$12,000
Net purchases	$20,000	
Add transportation-in...............................	500	20,500
Goods available for sale		$32,500
Less estimated cost of goods sold:		
Sales	$31,500	
Less sales returns	(1,500)	
Net sales...	$30,000	
Estimated cost of goods sold (70% × $30,000)		(21,000)
Estimated March 27 inventory and inventory loss..........		$11,500

To understand Illustration 9–6, recall that in a normal situation an ending inventory is subtracted from goods for sale to determine cost of goods sold. Then observe in Illustration 9–6 that the opposite subtraction is made. Estimated cost of goods sold is subtracted from goods for sale to arrive at the estimated ending inventory.

In addition to its use in insurance cases, as in this illustration, the gross profit method is also commonly used by accountants in checking on the probable accuracy of a physical inventory taken and priced in the normal way.

GLOSSARY

Conservatism principle. The rule that accountants should be conservative in their estimates and opinions and in their selection of procedures.

Consignee. One to whom something is consigned or shipped.

Consignor. One who consigns or ships something to another person or enterprise.

Consistency principle. The accounting rule requiring a persistent application of a selected accounting method or procedure, period after period.

FIFO inventory pricing. The pricing of an inventory under the assumption that the first items received were the first items sold.

Gross profit inventory method. A procedure for estimating an ending inventory in which an estimated cost of goods sold based on past gross profit rates is subtracted from the cost of goods available for sale to arrive at an estimated ending inventory.

Interim statements. Financial statements prepared in between the regular annual statements.

Inventory cost ratio. The ratio of goods available for sale at cost to goods available for sale at retail prices.

LIFO inventory pricing. The pricing of an inventory under the assumption that the last items received were the first items sold.

Lower-of-cost-or-market pricing of an inventory. The pricing of inventory at the lower of what each item actually cost or what it would cost to replace each item on the inventory date.

Markdown. A reduction in the marked selling price of an item.

Markon. The normal percentage of its cost that is added to the cost of an item to arrive at its selling price.

Markup. An addition to the normal markon given to an item.

Normal markup. A phrase meaning the same as markon.

Periodic inventory system. An inventory system in which inventories and cost of goods sold are based on periodic physical inventories.

Perpetual inventory system. An inventory system in which inventories and cost of goods sold are based on book inventory records.

Retail inventory method. A method for estimating an ending inventory based on the ratio of the cost of goods for sale at cost and cost of goods for sale at marked selling prices.

Specific invoice inventory pricing. The pricing of an inventory where each inventory item can be associated with a specific invoice and be priced accordingly.

Weighted-average cost inventory pricing. An inventory pricing system in which the units in the beginning inventory of a product and in each purchase of the product are weighted by the number of units in the beginning inventory and in each purchase to determine a weighted-average cost per unit of the product, and after which this weighted-average cost is used to price the ending inventory of the product.

QUESTIONS FOR CLASS DISCUSSION

1. It has been said that cost of goods sold and ending inventory are opposite sides of the same coin. What is meant by this?

2. Give the meanings of the following when applied to inventory; *(a)* first-in, first-out; *(b)* FIFO; *(c)* last-in, first-out; *(d)* LIFO; *(e)* cost; *(f)* market; *(g)* cost or market, the lower; *(h)* perpetual inventory; *(i)* physical inventory; and *(j)* book inventory.

3. If prices are rising, will the LIFO or the FIFO method of inventory valuation result in the higher gross profit?

4. May a company change its inventory pricing method at will?

5. What is required by the accounting principle of consistency?

6. If a company changes one of its accounting procedures, what is required of it under the full-disclosure principle?

7. Of what does the cost of an inventory item consist?

8. Why are incidental costs commonly ignored in pricing an inventory? Under what accounting principle is this permitted?

9. What is meant when it is said that inventory errors "correct themselves"?

10. If inventory errors "correct themselves," why be concerned when such errors are made?

11. What is required of an accountant under the principle of conservatism?

12. Give the meanings of the following when applied in the retail method of estimating an inventory: *(a)* at cost, *(b)* at retail, *(c)* cost ratio, *(d)* normal markup, *(e)* markon, *(f)* additional markup, and *(g)* markdown.

CLASS EXERCISES

Exercise 9–1

A company began a year and purchased Product Z as follows:

Jan. 1	Beginning inventory ..	10 units @	$9.20	= $	92
Feb. 5	Purchased	40 units @	$10.00	=	400
June 8	Purchased	20 units @	$10.60	=	212
Aug. 3	Purchased	30 units @	$11.20	=	336
Dec. 9	Purchased	20 units @	$11.00	=	220
	Total	120 units			$1,260

Required:

Under the assumption the ending inventory consisted of 30 units, 10 from each of the last three purchases, determine the share of the $1,260 cost of the units for sale that should be assigned to the ending inventory and to goods sold under each of the following assumptions: *(a)* costs are assigned on the basis of specific invoice prices, *(b)* costs are assigned on a weighted-average cost basis, *(c)* costs are assigned on the basis of FIFO, and *(d)* costs are assigned on the basis of LIFO.

Exercise 9–2   A small shop had $80,000 of sales during each of three consecutive years, and it purchased merchandise costing $50,000 during each of the years. It also maintained a $10,000 inventory from the beginning to the end of the three-year period. However, it made an error that caused its December 31, end-of-year-one, inventory to appear on its statements at $11,000, rather than the correct $10,000.

Required:

1. State the actual amount of the shop's gross profit in each of the years.
2. Prepare a comparative income statement like the one illustrated in this chapter to show the effect of this error on the shop's cost of goods sold and gross profit for each of Year 1, Year 2, and Year 3.

Exercise 9–3   During an accounting period, a store sold $78,000 of merchandise at marked retail prices. At the period end, the following information was available from its records:

	At cost	At retail
Beginning inventory.....	$15,000	$21,000
Net purchases	55,000	74,000
Additional markups		5,000
Markdowns		2,000

Use the retail method to estimate the store's ending inventory at cost.

Exercise 9–4   Assume that in addition to estimating its ending inventory by the retail method, the store of Exercise 9–3 also took a physical inventory at the marked selling prices of the inventory items. Assume further that the total of this physical inventory at marked selling prices was $19,500. Then *(a)* determine the amount of this inventory at cost and *(b)* determine the store's inventory shrinkage from breakage, theft, or other cause at retail and at cost.

Exercise 9–5   On January 1, a store had a $17,000 inventory at cost. During the first quarter of the year, it purchased $65,000 of merchandise, returned $500, and paid freight charges on merchandise purchased totaling $3,500. During the past several years, the store's gross profit on sales has averaged 35%. Under the assumption the company had $100,000 of sales during the first quarter of the year, use the gross profit method to estimate its end of the first quarter inventory.

PROBLEMS

PROBLEM 9–1   A company began a year with 300 units of Product A in its inventory that cost $50 each, and it made successive purchases of the product as follows:

Mar.   1   400 units @ $60 each.
June 10   500 units @ $70 each.
Aug. 29   400 units @ $80 each.
Nov. 15   400 units @ $60 each.

Required:

1. Prepare a calculation showing the number and total cost of the units that were for sale during the year.
2. Assume the company had 500 of the units in its December 31 year-end inventory and prepare calculations showing the portions of the total costs of the units for sale during the year that should be assigned to the ending inventory and to cost of goods sold *(a)* first on a FIFO basis, *(b)* then on a LIFO basis, and finally *(c)* on a weighted-average cost basis.

Problem 9–2

Last year, Beta Company sold 8,500 units of its product at $10 per unit. It incurred operating expenses of $2 per unit in selling the units, and it began the year and made successive purchases of the product as follows:

January 1, beginning inventory .. 1,000 units costing $5.60 per unit

Purchases:

January 29	1,000 units costing $6.00 per unit
March 15	3,000 units costing $6.20 per unit
July 12	4,000 units costing $6.50 per unit
November 3	1,000 units costing $7.00 per unit

Required:

Prepare a comparative income statement for the company showing in adjacent columns the net incomes earned from the sale of the product under the assumptions the company priced its ending inventory on the basis of: *(a)* FIFO, *(b)* LIFO, and *(c)* weighted-average cost.

Problem 9–3

The perpetual inventory record card for Article X showed the following beginning balance and transactions during January of this year:

Jan.	1	Balance 12 units costing $6 each.
	4	Received 20 units costing $7 each.
	9	Sold 10 units.
	15	Sold 15 units.
	19	Received 20 units costing $8 each.
	24	Sold 5 units.
	29	Sold 16 units.

Required:

1. Under the assumption the company keeps its records on a FIFO basis, enter the beginning balance and the transactions on a perpetual inventory record card like the one illustrated in this chapter.
2. Under the assumption the company keeps its inventory records on a LIFO basis, enter the beginning inventory and the transactions on a second inventory record card.
3. Assume the 16 units sold on January 29 were sold on credit to Lee Hall at $12.50 each and prepare a general journal entry to record the sale and cost of goods sold on a LIFO basis.

Problem 9–4

Pro Shop takes a year-end physical inventory at marked selling prices and uses the retail method to reduce the inventory total to a cost basis for statement purposes. It also uses the retail method to estimate the amount of inventory it should have at the end of a year, and by comparison determines any inventory shortage due to shoplifting or other cause. At the end of last year, its physical inventory at marked selling prices totaled $20,950, and the following information was available from its records:

	At cost	At retail
January 1 inventory.....	$12,210	$ 18,100
Purchases.............	83,385	119,900
Purchases returns......	1,415	1,950
Additional markups.....		2,450
Markdowns............		1,530
Sales.................		117,340
Sales returns..........		1,870

Required:

1. Use the retail method to estimate the shop's year-end inventory at cost.
2. Use the retail method to reduce the shop's year-end physical inventory to a cost basis.
3. Prepare a schedule showing the inventory shortage at cost and at retail.

Problem 9–5

The records of The Man's Store provided the following information for the year ended December 31:

	At cost	At retail
January 1 beginning inventory.....	$ 23,830	$ 31,350
Purchases......................	162,116	229,590
Purchases returns...............	2,210	3,160
Additional markups.............		4,700
Markdowns.....................		1,170
Sales.........................		228,240
Sales returns...................		2,880

Required:

1. Prepare an estimate of the store's year-end inventory by the retail method.
2. Under the assumption the store took a year-end physical inventory at marked selling prices that totaled $35,100, prepare a schedule showing the store's loss from theft or other cause at cost and at retail.

Problem 9–6

On Monday morning, May 7, the manager of The Good Shop unlocked the store to learn that thieves had broken in over the weekend and stolen the store's entire inventory. The following information for the period, January 1 to May 7 was available to establish the amount of loss:

January 1 merchandise inventory at cost..	$ 32,500
Purchases	92,310
Purchases returns.....................	415
Transportation-in	560
Sales................................	139,875
Sales returns	1,375

Required:

Under the assumption the store had earned an average 32% gross profit on sales during the past five years, prepare a statement showing the estimated loss.

Problem 9–7 Village Shop wants an estimate of its March 31, end-of-first quarter inventory. During the last five years, its gross profit rate has averaged 34%; and the following information for the year's first quarter is available from its records:

January 1, beginning inventory ..	$ 38,750
Purchases	91,400
Purchases returns	850
Transportation-in	1,130
Sales	144,640
Sales returns	2,140

Required:

Use the gross profit method to prepare an estimate of the shop's March 31 inventory.

ALTERNATE PROBLEMS

Problem 9–1A A company began a year with 20 units of a product that cost $60 each, and it made successive purchases of the product as follows:

Jan. 15   60 units @ $75 each.
May 10   50 units @ $80 each.
Aug. 17   30 units @ $90 each.
Nov. 30   40 units @ $85 each.

Required:

1. Prepare a calculation showing the number and total cost of the units for sale during the year.
2. Under the assumption the company had 50 of the units in its December 31 end-of-year inventory, prepare calculations showing the portions of the total cost of the units for sale during the year that should be assigned to the ending inventory and to the units sold *(a)* first on a FIFO basis, *(b)* then on a LIFO basis, and *(c)* finally on a weighted-average cost basis.

Problem 9–2A Moss Company incurred $50,000 of operating expenses last year in selling 850 units of its Product Z at $200 per unit. It began the year and purchased the product as follows:

January 1 inventory ..... 100 units @ $121 each

Purchases:
  January 28 .... 300 units @ $120 each
  April 29 .... 200 units @ $125 each
  July 27 .... 300 units @ $129 each
  December 2 .... 100 units @ $132 each

Required:

Prepare a comparative income statement for the company showing in adjacent columns the net incomes earned from the sale of the product under the assumptions the company priced its ending inventory on the basis of: *(a)* FIFO, *(b)* LIFO, and *(c)* weighted-average cost.

Problem 9–3A The inventory record for Item ABC showed these transactions:

Jan. 1 Balance 5 units costing $5 each.
    2 Received 10 units costing $5.40 each.
    6 Sold 3 units.
   10 Sold 8 units.
   14 Received 8 units costing $6 each.
   18 Sold 3 units.
   28 Sold 4 units.

Required:

1. Assume the perpetual inventory record card for Item ABC is kept on a FIFO basis and enter the beginning balance and transactions on the card.
2. Assume the perpetual inventory record for Item ABC is kept on a LIFO basis and enter the beginning balance and transactions on a second card.
3. Assume the four units sold on January 28 were sold on credit at $8 each to Ted Lee and give the entry to record the sale and the cost of goods sold on a LIFO basis.

Problem 9–4A

The Smart Shop takes a year-end physical inventory at marked selling prices and by the retail inventory method reduces the total to a cost basis for statement purposes. It also estimates its year-end inventory by the retail method and by a comparison determines the amount of any inventory shortage. At the end of last year, the following information from the store's records and from its physical inventory was available:

	At cost	At retail
January 1 beginning inventory	$ 18,500	$ 28,450
Purchases	143,880	217,180
Purchases returns	1,180	1,820
Additional markups		4,190
Markdowns		2,110
Sales		220,120
Sales returns		1,830
December 31 physical inventory		27,200

Required:

1. Prepare an estimate of the store's year-end inventory at cost.
2. Use the store's cost ratio to reduce the amount of its year-end physical inventory to a cost basis.
3. Prepare a schedule showing the inventory shortage at cost and at retail.

Problem 9–5A

The records of The Small Store provided the following information for the year ended December 31:

	At cost	At retail
Year's sales		$221,560
Sales returns		2,345
January 1 inventory	$ 21,540	32,950
Purchases	146,490	219,735
Purchases returns	980	1,470
Additional markups		5,785
Markdowns		1,285

Required:

1. Use the retail method to prepare an estimate of the store's year-end inventory at cost.

2. Under the assumption that the store took a year-end physical inventory at the marked selling prices of the inventory items that totaled $35,800, prepare a calculation to show the store's loss from theft or other cause at cost and at retail.

Problem 9–6A

The Top Store suffered a disastrous fire during the night of May 12, and everything except its accounting records, which were in a fireproof vault, was destroyed. As an insurance adjuster, you have been called on to determine the store's inventory loss. The following information is available from its accounting records for the period January 1 through May 12:

Merchandise inventory, January 1, at cost .. $23,400
Purchases 63,520
Purchases returns 1,260
Transportation-in 660
Sales 94,730
Sales returns 2,230

The accounting records also show that the store's gross profit rate has averaged 34% over the past four years.

Required:

Use the gross profit method to prepare an estimate of the store's inventory loss.

Problem 9–7A

Little Company's gross profit rate has averaged 32% during the past five years, and the following information covering the period January 1 through June 30 of the current year was taken from its records:

January 1 inventory at cost ..... $ 42,850
Purchases 123,900
Purchases returns 1,200
Transportation-in 2,680
Sales 189,900
Sales returns 3,400

Required:

Use the gross profit method to prepare an estimate of the company's June 30 inventory.

PROVOCATIVE PROBLEMS

Provocative Problems 9–1, Boot Center

Boot Center suffered extensive smoke and water damage and a small amount of fire damage on October 3. The store carried adequate insurance, and the insurance company's claims adjuster appeared the same day to inspect the damage. After completing his survey, the adjuster agreed with Al Berg, the store's owner, that the inventory could be sold to a company specializing in fire sales for about one fourth of its cost. The adjuster offered Mr. Berg $25,000 in full settlement for the damage to the inventory. He suggested that the offer be accepted and said he had authority to deliver at once a check for that amount. He also pointed out that a prompt settlement would provide funds to replace the inventory in time for the store to participate in the Christmas shopping season.

Mr. Berg felt the loss might exceed $25,000, but he recognized that a time-consuming count and inspection of each item in the inventory would be required to establish the loss more precisely; and he was reluctant to take the time for the inventory, since he was anxious to get back into business before the Christmas rush, the season making the largest contribution to his annual net income. Yet he was also unwilling to take a substantial loss on the insurance settlement; so he asked for and received a one-day period in which to consider the insurance company offer, and he immediately went to his records for the following information:

	At cost	At retail
a. January 1 inventory	$ 35,550	$ 55,600
Purchases, January 1 through October 3	233,250	364,100
Net sales, January 1 through October 3		361,700

b. On March 1, the remaining inventory of winter footwear was marked down from $16,000 to $12,000, and placed on sale in the annual end-of-winter-season sale. Three fourths of the shoes were sold. The markdown on the remainder was canceled, and the shoes were returned to their regular retail prices. (A markdown cancellation is subtracted from a markdown, and a markup cancellation is subtracted from a markup.)

c. In May, a special line of imported Italian shoes proved popular, and 84 pairs were marked up from their normal $49 retail price to $54 per pair. Sixty pairs were sold at the higher price; and on July 5, the markup on the remaining 24 pairs was canceled and they were returned to their regular $49 per pair price.

d. Between January 1 and October 3, markdowns totaling $1,800 were taken on several odd lots of shoes.

Recommend whether or not you think Mr. Berg should accept the insurance company's offer. Back your recommendation with figures.

Provocative Problem 9–2, Discount Furniture Store

Night before last, June 5, Discount Furniture Store suffered a disastrous fire that destroyed its entire inventory. Ted Bates, the store's owner, has filed a $99,200 inventory loss claim with the store's insurance company. When asked by the insurance adjusters on what he based his claim, he replied that during the day before the fire he had marked every item in the store down 20% in preparation for the annual summer clearance sale, and during the marking down process he had taken an inventory of the merchandise in the store. Furthermore, he said, "It's a big loss, but I am giving you fellows (the insurance company) the benefit of the 20% markdown in filing this claim."

When it was explained to Mr. Bates that he had to back his loss claim with more than his word as to the amount of the loss, he produced the following information from his pre-sale inventory and accounting records, which fortunately were in a fireproof vault and were not destroyed in the fire.

a. The store had earned a 34% average gross profit on sales during the last five years.

b. The store's books were closed on the previous December 31.

c. After posting was completed, the accounts showed the following June 5 balances:

```
Merchandise inventory, January 1 balance..  $ 86,500
Purchases ..............................      235,800
Purchases returns ......................       2,450
Transportation-in ......................       2,880
Sales ..................................     369,420
Sales returns ..........................       4,420
```

d. Mr. Bates's pre-fire inventory totaled $124,000 at pre-markdown prices.

Required:

1. Prepare a calculation showing the estimated amount of Discount Furniture Store's inventory loss.
2. Present figures to show how Mr. Bates arrived at the amount of his loss claim.
3. Present figures based on the amount of the pre-markdown inventory amount, $124,000, to substantiate the inventory estimate arrived at in Part 1 above.

Plant and Equipment

10

After studying Chapter 10, you should be able to:

Tell what is included in the cost of a plant asset.

Allocate the cost of lump-sum purchases to the separate assets being purchased.

Describe the causes of depreciation and the reasons for depreciation accounting.

Calculate depreciation by the *(a)* straight-line, *(b)* units-of-production, *(c)* declining-balance, and *(d)* sum-of-the-years'-digits methods.

Explain how the original cost of a plant asset is recovered through the sale of the asset's product or service.

Explain how the accelerated cost recovery system defers income taxes.

Define or explain the words and phrases listed in the chapter Glossary.

Tangible assets that are used in the production or sale of other assets or services and that have a useful life longer than one accounting period are called *plant and equipment* or *plant assets*. The phrase *fixed assets* was used for many years. However, it is rapidly disappearing from published balance sheets. The more descriptive "plant and equipment" or perhaps "property, plant, and equipment" is now used more often.

Use in the production or sale of other assets or services is the characteristic that distinguishes a plant asset from an item of merchandise or an investment. An office or factory machine held for sale by a dealer is merchandise to the dealer. Likewise, land purchased and held for future expansion but presently unused is classified as a long-term investment. Only when the asset is put to use in the production or sale of other assets or services should it be classified as plant and equipment. However, standby equipment for use in case of a breakdown or for use during peak periods of production is a plant asset. Also, when equipment is removed from service and held for sale, it ceases to be a plant asset.

A productive or service life longer than one accounting period distinguishes an item of plant and equipment from an item of supplies. An item of supplies may be consumed in a single accounting period. If consumed, its cost is charged to the period of consumption. The productive life of a plant asset, on the other hand, is longer than one period. It contributes to production for several periods. Therefore, as a result of the *matching principle,* its cost must be allocated to these periods in a systematic and rational manner.[1]

COST OF A PLANT ASSET

Cost is the basis for recording the acquisition of a plant asset. The cost of a plant asset includes all normal and reasonable expenditures necessary to get the asset in place and ready to use. For example, the cost of a factory machine includes its invoice price, less any discount for cash, plus freight, unpacking, and assembling costs. Cost also includes any special concrete base or foundation, electrical or power connections, and adjustments needed to place the machine in operation. In short, the cost of a plant asset includes all normal, necessary, and reasonable costs incurred in getting the asset in place and ready to produce.

---

[1] APB, "Basic Concepts and Accounting Principles Underlying Financial Statements of Business Enterprises," *APB Statement No. 4* (New York: AICPA, October 1970), par. 159.

A cost must be normal and reasonable as well as necessary if it is to be properly included in the cost of a plant asset. For example, if a machine is damaged by being dropped in unpacking, repairs should not be added to its cost. They should be charged to an expense account. Likewise, a fine paid for moving a heavy machine on city streets without proper permits is not part of the cost of the machine. However, if secured, the cost of the permits would be.

After being purchased but before being put to use, a plant asset must sometimes be repaired or remodeled before it meets the needs of the purchaser. In such a case, the repairing or remodeling expenditures are part of its cost and should be charged to the asset account. Furthermore, depreciation charges should not begin until the asset is put in use.

When a plant asset is constructed by a business for its own use, cost includes material and labor costs plus a reasonable amount of overhead or indirect expenses such as heat, lights, power, and depreciation on the machinery used in constructing the asset. Cost also includes architectural and design fees, building permits, and insurance during construction. Needless to say, insurance on the same asset after it has been placed in production is an expense.

When land is purchased for a building site, its cost includes the amount paid for the land plus any real estate commissions. It also includes escrow and legal fees, fees for examining and insuring the title, and any accrued property taxes paid by the purchaser, as well as expenditures for surveying, clearing, grading, draining, and landscaping. All are part of the cost of the land. Furthermore, any assessments incurred at the time of purchase or later for such things as the installation of streets, sewers, and sidewalks should be debited to the Land account since they add a more or less permanent value to the land.

Land purchased as a building site sometimes has an old building that must be removed. In such cases, the entire purchase price, including the amount paid for the to-be-removed building, should be charged to the Land account. Also, the cost of removing the old building, less any amounts recovered through the sale of salvaged materials, should be charged to this account.

Since land has an unlimited life, it is not subject to depreciation. However, *land improvements* such as parking lot surfaces, fences, and lighting systems have limited useful lives. Such costs improve the value or usefulness of land but must be charged to separate Land Improvement accounts and subjected to depreciation. Finally, a separate Building account must be charged for the cost of purchasing or constructing a building to be used as a plant asset.

Often land, land improvements, and buildings are purchased together for one lump sum. When this occurs, the purchase price must be apportioned among the assets on some fair basis, since some of the assets depreciate and some do not. A fair basis may be tax-assessed values or appraised values. For example, assume that land independently appraised at $30,000, land improvements appraised at $10,000, and a building appraised at $60,000 are purchased together for $90,000. The cost may be apportioned on the basis of appraised values as follows:

	Appraised value	Percent of total	Apportioned cost
Land	$ 30,000	30	$27,000
Land improvements	10,000	10	9,000
Building	60,000	60	54,000
Totals	$100,000	100	$90,000

NATURE OF DEPRECIATION

When a plant asset is purchased, in effect a quantity of usefulness that will contribute to production throughout the service life of the asset is acquired. However, since the life of any plant asset (other than land) is limited, this quantity of usefulness will in effect be consumed by the end of the asset's service life. Consequently, depreciation, as the term is used in accounting, is nothing more than the expiration of a plant asset's quantity of usefulness, and the recording of depreciation is a process of allocating and charging the cost of this usefulness to the accounting periods that benefit from the asset's use.

For example, when a company purchases an automobile to be used in the business, it in effect purchases a quantity of usefulness, a quantity of transportation. The cost of this quantity of usefulness is the cost of the car less whatever will be received for it when sold or traded in at the end of its service life. Recording depreciation on the car is a process of allocating the cost of this usefulness to the accounting periods that benefit from the car's use. Note that it is not the recording of physical deterioration nor the recording of the decline in the car's market value. Depreciation is a process of allocating cost.

The foregoing is in line with the pronouncements of the AICPA's Committee on Accounting Procedure which described depreciation as follows:

> The cost of a productive facility is one of the costs of the services it renders during its useful economic life. Generally accepted accounting principles require that this cost be spread over the expected useful life of the facility in such a way as to allocate it as equitably as possible to the periods during which services are obtained from the use of the facility.

This procedure is known as depreciation accounting, a system of accounting which aims to distribute the cost or other basic value of tangible capital assets, less salvage (if any), over the estimated useful life of the unit . . . in a systematic and rational manner. It is a process of allocation, not of valuation.[2]

SERVICE LIFE OF A PLANT ASSET

The *service life* of a plant asset is the period of time it will be used in producing or selling other assets or services. This may not be the same as the asset's potential life. For example, typewriters have a potential six- or eight-year life. However, if a company finds that it is economically wise to trade its old typewriters on new ones every three years, in this company typewriters have a three-year service life. Furthermore, in this business, the cost of new typewriters less their trade-in value should be charged to depreciation expense over this three-year period.

Predicting a plant asset's service life is sometimes difficult because several factors are often involved. Wear and tear from use determine the useful life of some assets. However, two additional factors, *inadequacy* and *obsolescence*, often need be considered. When a business acquires plant assets, it should acquire assets of a size and capacity to take care of its foreseeable needs. However, a business often grows more rapidly than anticipated. In such cases, the capacity of the plant assets may become too small for the productive demands of the business long before they wear out. When this happens, inadequacy is said to have taken place. Inadequacy cannot easily be predicted. Obsolescence, like inadequacy, is also difficult to foresee because the exact occurrence of new inventions and improvements normally cannot be predicted. Yet, new inventions and improvements often cause an asset to become obsolete and make it wise to discard the obsolete asset long before it wears out.

A company that has previously used a particular type of asset may estimate the service life of a new asset of like kind from past experience. A company without previous experience with a particular asset must depend upon the experience of others or upon engineering studies and judgment. The Internal Revenue Service publishes information giving estimated service lives for hundreds of new assets. Many business executives refer to this information in estimating the life of a new asset.

---

[2] Committee on Accounting Procedure, "Accounting Research Bulletin No. 43," *Accounting Research and Terminology Bulletins, Final Edition* (New York: AICPA, 1961), p. 76. Copyright (1961) by the American Institute of CPAs.

SALVAGE VALUE

The total amount of depreciation that should be taken over an asset's service life is the asset's cost minus its *salvage value*. The salvage value of a plant asset is the portion of its cost that is recovered at the end of its service life. Some assets such as typewriters, trucks, and automobiles are traded in on similar new assets at the end of their service lives. The salvage values of such assets are their trade-in values. Other assets may have no trade-in value and little or no salvage value. For example, at the end of its service life, some machinery can be sold only as scrap metal.

When the disposal of a plant asset involves certain costs, as in the wrecking of a building, the salvage value is the net amount realized from the sale of the asset. The net amount realized is the amount received for the asset less its disposal cost. In the case of a machine, the cost to remove the machine often will equal the amount that can be realized from its sale. In such a case, the machine has no salvage value.

ALLOCATING DEPRECIATION

Many methods of allocating a plant asset's total depreciation to the several accounting periods in its service life have been suggested and are used. Four of the more common are the *straight-line method,* the *units-of-production method,* the *declining-balance method,* and the *sum-of-the-years'-digits method.* Each is acceptable and falls within the realm of *generally accepted accounting principles.*

Straight-Line Method

When the straight-line method is used, the cost of the asset minus its estimated salvage value is divided by the estimated number of accounting periods in the asset's service life. The result is the amount of depreciation to be taken each period. For example, if a machine costs $550, has an estimated service life of five years, and an estimated $50 salvage value, its depreciation per year by the straight-line method is $100 and is calculated as follows:

$$\frac{\text{Cost } - \text{ Salvage}}{\text{Service life in years}} = \frac{\$550 - \$50}{5} = \$100$$

Note that the straight-line method allocates an equal share of an asset's total depreciation to each accounting period in its life.

Units-of-Production Method

The purpose of recording depreciation is to charge each accounting period in which an asset is used with a fair share of its cost. The straight-line method charges an equal share to each period; and when plant assets are used about the same amount in each accounting period, this method rather fairly allocates total depreciation. However, in some lines of business, the use of certain plant assets varies greatly from accounting period to accounting period. For example, a contractor may use a particular piece of construction equipment for a month and then not use it again for many months. For such an asset, since use and contribution to revenue may not be uniform from period to period, it is argued that the *units-of-production method* better meets the requirements of the *matching principle* than does the straight-line method.

When the units-of-production method is used in allocating depreciation, the cost of an asset minus its estimated salvage value is divided by the estimated units it will produce during its entire service life. This calculation gives depreciation per unit of production. Then, the amount the asset is depreciated in any one accounting period is determined by multiplying the units produced in that period by the depreciation per unit. Units of production may be expressed as units of product or in any other unit of measure such as hours of use or miles driven. For example, a truck costing $6,000 is estimated to have a $2,000 salvage value. If it is also estimated that during the truck's service life it will be driven 50,000 miles, the depreciation per mile, or the depreciation per unit of production is $0.08 and is calculated as follows:

$$\frac{\text{Cost} - \text{Salvage value}}{\text{Estimated units of production}} = \text{Depreciation per unit of production}$$

or

$$\frac{\$6,000 - \$2,000}{50,000 \text{ miles}} = \$0.08 \text{ per mile}$$

If these estimates are used and the truck is driven 20,000 miles during its first year, depreciation for the first year is $1,600. This is 20,000 miles at $0.08 per mile. If the truck is driven 15,000 miles in the second year, depreciation for the second year is 15,000 times $0.08, or $1,200.

Declining-Balance Method *omit*

Some depreciation methods result in larger depreciation charges during the early years of an asset's life and smaller charges in the later years. These methods are called *accelerated depreciation*. The declining-balance method is one of these. Under this method, depreciation of up to twice the straight-line rate, without considering salvage value, may be applied each year to the declining book value of a new plant asset. If this method is followed and twice the straight-line rate is used, depreciation on an asset is determined as follows: (1) calculate a straight-line depreciation rate for the asset; (2) double this rate; and (3) at the end of each year in the asset's life, apply this doubled rate to the asset's remaining *book value*. (The book value of a plant asset is its cost less accumulated depreciation; it is the net amount shown for the asset on the books.)

If this method is used to charge depreciation on a $10,000 new asset that has an estimated five-year life and no salvage value, these steps are followed: (Step 1) A straight-line depreciation rate is calculated by dividing 100% by five (years) to determine the straight-line annual depreciation rate of 20%; (Step 2) this rate is doubled; and (Step 3) annual depreciation charges are calculated as in the following table:

Year	Annual depreciation calculation	Annual depreciation expense	Remaining book value
1st year	40% of $10,000	$4,000.00	$6,000.00
2d year	40% of 6,000	2,400.00	3,600.00
3d year	40% of 3,600	1,440.00	2,160.00
4th year	40% of 2,160	864.00	1,296.00
5th year	40% of 1,296	518.40	777.60

Under the declining-balance method, the book value of a plant asset never reaches zero. Consequently, when the asset is sold, exchanged, or scrapped, any remaining book value is used in determining the gain or loss on the disposal. However, if an asset has a salvage value, the asset may not be depreciated beyond its salvage value. For example, if instead of no salvage value, the foregoing $10,000 asset has an estimated $1,000 salvage value, depreciation for its fifth year is limited to $296. This is the amount required to reduce the asset's book value to its salvage value.

Sum-of-the-Years'-Digits Method

Another frequently used method of accelerated depreciation is called *sum-of-the-years' digits*. Under the sum-of-the-years'-digits method, the years in an asset's service life are added. Their sum becomes the denominator of a series of fractions used in allocating total depreciation to the periods in the asset's service life. The numerators of the fractions are the years in the asset's life in their reverse order. For example, assume a machine is purchased that costs $7,000, has an estimated five-year life, and has an estimated $1,000 salvage value. The sum-of-the-years' digits in the asset's life are:

$$1 + 2 + 3 + 4 + 5 = 15$$

and annual depreciation charges are calculated as follows:

Year	Annual depreciation calculation	Annual depreciation expense
1st year	$5/15$ of $6,000	$2,000
2d year	$4/15$ of 6,000	1,600
3d year	$3/15$ of 6,000	1,200
4th year	$2/15$ of 6,000	800
5th year	$1/15$ of 6,000	400
Total depreciation		$6,000

When a plant asset has a long life, the sum-of-the-years' digits in its life may be calculated by using the formula: $SYD = n[(n + 1)/2]$. For example, sum-of-the-years' digits for a five-year life is: $5\left(\dfrac{5 + 1}{2}\right) = 15$.

Accelerated depreciation methods are advocated by many accountants who claim that their use results in a more equitable "use charge" for long-lived plant assets than other methods. These accountants point out, for example, that as assets grow older, repairs and maintenance increase. Therefore, when smaller amounts of depreciation are added to increasing repair costs, a more equitable total expense charge to match against revenue results. Also, they point out that as an asset grows older, in some instances its ability to produce revenue is reduced. For example, rentals from an apartment building may be higher in the earlier years of its life but then decline as the building becomes less attractive. In such cases, many accountants argue that the requirements of the *matching principle* are better met with heavier depreciation charges in the earlier years and lighter charges in the later years of the asset's life.

DEPRECIATION FOR PARTIAL YEARS

Plant assets may be purchased or disposed of any time during the year. When an asset is purchased (or disposed of) at some time other than the beginning (or end) of an accounting period, depreciation must be recorded for part of a year. Otherwise, the year of purchase or the year of disposal is not charged with its share of the asset's depreciation. For example, assume a machine costing $4,600 and having an estimated five-year service life and a $600 salvage value is purchased on October 8 and the annual accounting period ends on December 31. Three months' depreciation on the machine must be recorded on the latter date. Three months are three twelfths of a year. Consequently, if straight-line depreciation is used, the three months' depreciation is calculated as follows:

$$\frac{\$4,600 - \$600}{5} \times \frac{3}{12} = \$200$$

Note that depreciation was calculated for a full three months, even though the asset was purchased on October 8. Depreciation is an estimate; therefore, calculation to the nearest full month is usually sufficiently accurate. This means that depreciation is usually calculated for a full month on assets purchased before the 15th of the month. Likewise, depreciation for the month of purchase is normally disregarded if the asset is purchased after the middle of the month.

The entry to record depreciation for three months on the machine purchased on October 8 is:

Dec.	31	Depreciation Expense, Machinery	200.00	
		Accumulated Depreciation, Machinery		200.00
		To record depreciation for three months.		

On December 31, 198B, and at the end of each of the following three years, a journal entry to record a full year's depreciation on this machine is required. The entry is:

Dec.	31	Depreciation Expense, Machinery	800.00	
		Accumulated Depreciation, Machinery		800.00
		To record depreciation for one year.		

After the December 31, 198E, depreciation entry is recorded, the accounts showing the history of this machine appear as follows:

Machinery		Accumulated Depreciation, Machinery	
Oct. 8, '8A 4,600			Dec. 31, '8A 200
			Dec. 31, '8B 800
			Dec. 31, '8C 800
			Dec. 31, '8D 800
			Dec. 31, '8E 800

If this machine is disposed of during 198F, two entries must be made to record the disposal. The first records 198F depreciation to the date of disposal, and the second records the actual disposal. For example, assume that the machine is sold for $800 on June 24, 198F. To record the disposal, depreciation for six months (depreciation to the nearest full month) must first be recorded. The entry for this is:

June	24	Depreciation Expense, Machinery	400.00	
		Accumulated Depreciation, Machinery		400.00
		To record depreciation for one-half year.		

After making the entry to record depreciation to the date of sale, a second entry to record the actual sale is made. This entry is:

June	24	Cash	800.00	
		Accumulated Depreciation, Machinery	3,800.00	
		Machinery		4,600.00
		To record the sale of a machine at book value.		

In this instance, the machine was sold for its book value. Plant assets are commonly sold for either more or less than book value, and cases illustrating this are described in the next chapter.

APPORTIONING ACCELERATED DEPRECIATION

When accelerated depreciation is used and accounting periods do not coincide with the years in an asset's life, depreciation must be apportioned between periods if it is to be properly charged. For example, the machine for which sum-of-the-years'-digits depreciation is calculated on page 355 is to be depreciated $2,000 during its first year, $1,600 during its second year, and so on for its five-year life. If this machine is placed in use on April 1 and the annual accounting periods of its owner end on December 31, the machine will be in use for three fourths of a year during the first accounting period in its life. Consequently, this period should be charged with $1,500 depreciation ($2,000 × ¾ = $1,500). Likewise, the second accounting period should be charged with $1,700 depreciation [(¼ × $2,000) + (¾ × $1,600) = $1,700]. Similar calculations should be used for the remaining periods in the asset's life.

DEPRECIATION ON THE BALANCE SHEET

In presenting information about the plant assets of a business, the *full-disclosure principle* requires that both the cost of such assets and their accumulated depreciation be shown by major classes in the statements or in related footnotes. Also, a general description of the depreciation method or methods used must be given in a balance sheet footnote or other manner.[3] To comply, the plant assets of a business may be shown on its balance sheet or in a schedule accompanying the balance sheet as follows:

	Cost	Accumulated depreciation	Book value	
Plant assets:				
Store equipment	$ 12,400	$1,500	$10,900	
Office equipment	3,600	450	3,150	
Building	72,300	7,800	64,500	
Land	15,000		15,000	
Totals	$103,300	$9,750		$93,550

When plant assets are thus shown and the depreciation methods described, a much better understanding can be gained by a balance sheet reader than if only information as to undepreciated cost is given. For example, $50,000 of assets with $40,000 of accumulated depreciation are quite different from $10,000 of new assets. Yet, the net undepreciated cost is the same in both cases. Likewise, the picture is different if the $40,000 of accumulated depreciation resulted from accelerated depreciation rather than straight-line depreciation.

---

[3] Accounting Principles Board, "Omnibus Opinion—1967," *APB Opinion No. 12* (New York: AICPA, December 1967), par. 5.

BALANCE SHEET PLANT ASSET VALUES

From the discussion thus far, students should recognize that the recording of depreciation is not primarily a valuing process. Rather, it is a process of allocating the costs of plant assets to the several accounting periods that benefit from their use. Because the recording of depreciation is a cost allocation process rather than a valuing process, plant assets are reported in balance sheets at their remaining (undepreciated) costs, not at market values.

The fact that balance sheets show undepreciated costs rather than market values seems to disturb many beginning accounting students. It should not. Normally, a company has no intention of selling its plant assets. Consequently, the market values of these assets may be of little significance to financial statement readers. Students should recognize that a balance sheet is prepared under the assumption the company is a going concern. This means the company is expected to continue in business long enough to recover the original costs of its plant assets through the sale of its products.

The assumption that a company will continue in business long enough to recover its plant asset costs through the sale of its products is known in accounting as the *continuing- or going-concern concept.* It provides the justification for carrying plant assets on the balance sheet at cost less accumulated depreciation; in other words, at the share of their cost applicable to future periods. It is also the justification for carrying at cost such things as stationery imprinted with the company name, though salable only as scrap paper. In all such instances, the intention is to use the assets in carrying on the business operations. They are not for sale, so it is pointless to place them on the balance sheet at market or realizable values, whether these values are greater or less than book values.

Uninformed financial statement readers sometimes mistakenly think that the accumulated depreciation shown on a balance sheet represents funds accumulated to buy new assets when present assets must be replaced. However, an informed reader recognizes that accumulated depreciation represents the portion of an asset's cost that has been charged off to depreciation expense during its life. Accumulated depreciation accounts are contra accounts having credit balances that cannot be used to buy anything. Furthermore, an informed reader knows that if a business has cash with which to buy assets, it is shown on the balance sheet as a current asset "Cash."

RECOVERING THE COSTS OF PLANT ASSETS

A company that earns a profit or breaks even (neither earns a profit nor suffers a loss) eventually recovers the original cost of its plant assets through the sale of its products. This is best explained with a condensed income statement like that of Illustration 10–1 which shows that Even Steven Company broke even during the year of the illustrated income statement. However, in breaking even it also recovered $5,000 of the cost of its plant assets through the sale of its products. It recovered the $5,000 because $100,000 flowed into the company from sales and only $95,000 flowed out to pay for goods sold, rent, and salaries. No funds flowed out for depreciation expense. As a result, the company recovered this $5,000 portion of the cost of its plant assets through the sale of its products. Furthermore, if the company remains in business for the life of its plant assets, either breaking even or earning a profit, it will recover their entire cost in this manner.

Illustration 10–1

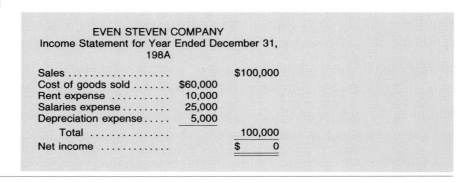

EVEN STEVEN COMPANY
Income Statement for Year Ended December 31, 198A

Sales		$100,000
Cost of goods sold	$60,000	
Rent expense	10,000	
Salaries expense	25,000	
Depreciation expense	5,000	
Total		100,000
Net income		$ 0

At this point students commonly ask, "Where is the recovered $5,000?" The answer is that the company may have the $5,000 in the bank. However, the funds may also have been spent to increase merchandise inventory, to buy additional equipment, to pay off a debt, or they may have been withdrawn by the business owner. In short, the funds may still be in the bank or they may have been used for any purpose for which a business uses funds.

ACCELERATED DEPRECIATION FOR TAX PURPOSES

The use of accelerated depreciation in preparing financial statements does not require that such methods also be used for tax purposes. However, the tax laws of the United States, as codified in the *Internal Revenue Code,* allow the use of accelerated methods in various circumstances. For certain assets purchased prior to 1981, the law allowed declining-balance or sum-of-the-years'-digits methods. However, for assets purchased after 1980, a new system of accelerated depreciation was adopted for tax purposes. The Economic Recovery Tax Act of 1981 arbitrarily classified depreciable property into classes with 3-year, 5-year, 10-year, or 15-year lives. These periods are usually much shorter than the actual economic lives of the assets. For example, the three-year class includes: (1) automobiles; (2) light trucks; (3) tangible and personal property used in research and development activities; and (4) tangible personal property normally recognized by the Internal Revenue Service as having a useful life of four years or less. Normally, assets such as the above would be expected to have useful lives longer than three years.

When calculating depreciation for tax purposes, salvage values on assets purchased after 1980 are ignored. A straight-line method may be used. However, many taxpayers choose the *accelerated cost recovery system (ACRS)*, which is a unique, accelerated depreciation method prescribed in the tax law for assets purchased after 1980. The depreciation rates under the ACRS method are specified in the law. For example, the depreciation rates for property in the 3-year, 5-year, and 10-year classes are shown in Illustration 10–2.

Illustration 10–2

ACCELERATED COST RECOVERY SYSTEM
Annual Depreciation as a Percent of Original Cost

	For property in the		
	Three-year class	*Five-year class*	*Ten-year class*
1st year	25	15	8
2d year	38	22	14
3d year	37	21	12
4th year		21	10
5th year		21	10
6th year			10
7th year			9
8th year			9
9th year			9
10th year			9

Note that the first year's rate is intended to approximate depreciation for one-half year. The 1981 law requires taxpayers to use this half-year convention in depreciating personal property regardless of when the asset was purchased during the year.

Even the straight-line methods prescribed in the law for assets purchased after 1980 can have an accelerated effect. To illustrate, for assets in the 3-year class, the taxpayer may choose to use straight line over 3, 5, or 12 years, subject to the one-half year convention for the first year.

For example, a company buys a light truck that is expected to last about five years. The following table shows how depreciation for tax purposes can be accelerated by using the three-year, straight-line option, or even more so by using the ACRS rates:

DEPRECIATION RATES EACH YEAR

| | Straight line | | |
Year	Five-year (useful life)	Three-year option	ACRS
1	10%	16.7%	25%
2	20	33.3	38
3	20	33.3	37
4	20	16.7	0
5	20	0	0
6	10	0	0

Students should understand that ACRS depreciation generally is not acceptable for use in preparing financial statements. ACRS is not acceptable because it allocates depreciation over a shorter period of time than the estimated useful life of the asset. However, using ACRS depreciation for tax purposes may have an important tax advantage.

The tax advantage of accelerated depreciation is that it *defers the payment of income taxes* from the early years of a plant asset's life until its later years. Taxes are deferred because accelerated depreciation causes larger amounts of depreciation to be charged to the early years. This results in smaller amounts of income and income taxes in these years. However, the taxes are only deferred; they are not avoided. The larger depreciation charges in earlier years are offset by smaller (or even zero) depreciation charges in later years. Thus, larger amounts of income and income taxes are reported and paid in the later years. Nevertheless, through accelerated depreciation a company gains the "interest-free" use of the deferred tax dollars until the later years of a plant asset's life.

Special problems in measuring net income may occur when a company uses one depreciation method for financial accounting purposes and another for tax purposes. These problems are discussed in Chapter 28.

CONTROL OF PLANT ASSETS

Good internal control for plant assets requires specific identification of each plant asset and formal records. It also requires periodic inventories in which each plant asset carried in the records is identified and its continued existence and use are verified. For identification purposes, each plant asset is commonly assigned a serial number at the time it is acquired. The serial number is stamped, etched, or affixed to the asset with a small decal not easily removed or altered. The exact kind of records kept depends upon the size of the business and the number of its plant assets. They range from handwritten records to punched cards and computer tapes. However, regardless of their nature, all provide the same basic information contained in the handwritten records which follow.

In keeping plant asset records, businesses normally divide their plant assets into functional groups and provide in their General Ledger separate asset and accumulated depreciation accounts for each group. For example, a store will normally provide an Office Equipment account and an Accumulated Depreciation, Office Equipment account. It will also provide a Store Equipment account and an Accumulated Depreciation, Store Equipment account. In short, the store will normally provide in its General Ledger a separate plant asset account and a separate accumulated depreciation account for each functional group of plant assets it owns. Furthermore, each plant asset account and its related accumulated depreciation account is normally a controlling account controlling detailed subsidiary records. For example, the Office Equipment account and the Accumulated Depreciation, Office Equipment account control a subsidiary *Office Equipment Ledger* having a separate record for each individual item of office equipment. Likewise, the Store Equipment account and its related Accumulated Depreciation, Store Equipment account become controlling accounts over a subsidiary *Store Equipment Ledger.* In a handwritten system, these subsidiary records are kept on plant asset record cards.

To illustrate handwritten plant asset records, assume that a company's office equipment consists of just one desk and a chair. The general ledger record of these assets is maintained in the Office Equipment controlling account and the Accumulated Depreciation, Office Equipment controlling account. Since in this case there are only two assets, only two subsidiary record cards are needed. The general ledger and subsidiary ledger record of these assets appear as in Illustration 10–3.

Observe at the top of the cards the plant asset numbers assigned to these two items of office equipment. In each case, the assigned number consists of the number of the Office Equipment account, 132, followed by the asset's number. As previously stated, these numbers are stenciled on or otherwise attached to the items of office equipment as a means of identification and to increase control over the items. The remaining information on the record cards is more or less self-evident. Note how the balance of the general ledger account, Office Equipment, is equal to the sum of the balances in the asset record section of the two subsidiary ledger cards. The general ledger account controls this section of the subsidiary ledger. Observe also how the Accumulated Depreciation, Office Equipment account controls the depreciation record section of the cards. The disposition section at the bottom of the card is used to record the final disposal of the asset. When the asset is discarded, sold, or exchanged, a notation telling of the final disposition is entered here. The card is then removed from the subsidiary ledger and filed for future reference.

Illustration 10–3

Plant Asset
No. *132-1*

SUBSIDIARY PLANT ASSET AND DEPRECIATION RECORD

Item _Office chair_   General Ledger
Description _Office chair_   Account _Office Equipment_

                                     Purchased
Mfg. Serial No._____   from _Office Equipment Co._
Where Located _Office_
Person Responsible for the Asset _Office Manager_
Estimated Life _12 years_ Estimated Salvage Value _$4.00_
Depreciation per Year _$6.00_ per Month _$0.50_

Date	Explanation	P R	Asset Record			Depreciation Record		
			Dr.	Cr.	Bal.	Dr.	Cr.	Bal.
July 2, 198A		G1	76.00		76.00			
Dec. 31, 198A		G23					3.00	3.00
Dec. 31, 198B		G42					6.00	9.00
Dec. 31, 198C		G65					6.00	15.00

Final Disposition of the Asset _____

Illustration 10–3 *(concluded)*

Plant Asset
No. *132-2*

SUBSIDIARY PLANT ASSET AND DEPRECIATION RECORD

General Ledger
Item *Desk*   Account *Office Equipment*
Description *Office desk*

Purchased
Mfg. Serial No. _____ from *Office Equipment Co.*
Where Located *Office*
Person Responsible for the Asset *Office Manager*
Estimated Life *12 years* Estimated Salvage Value *$25.00*
Depreciation per Year *$36.00* per Month *$3.00*

Date	Explanation	P R	Asset Record			Depreciation Record		
			Dr.	Cr.	Bal.	Dr.	Cr.	Bal.
July 2, 198A		G1	457.00		457.00			
Dec. 31, 198A		G23					18.00	18.00
Dec. 31, 198B		G42					36.00	54.00
Dec. 31, 198C		G65					36.00	90.00

Final Disposition of the Asset _____

Office Equipment   ACCOUNT NO. 132

DATE	EXPLANATION	FO-LIO	DEBIT	CREDIT	BALANCE
198A July 2	Desk and chair	G1	5 3 3 00		5 3 3 00

Accumulated Depreciation, Office Equipment   ACCOUNT NO. 132A

DATE	EXPLANATION	FO-LIO	DEBIT	CREDIT	BALANCE
198A Dec. 31		G23		2 1 00	2 1 00
198B Dec. 31		G42		4 2 00	6 3 00
198C Dec. 31		G65		4 2 00	1 0 5 00

PLANT ASSETS OF LOW COST

Individual plant asset records are expensive to keep. Consequently, many companies establish a minimum, say, $50 or $100, and do not keep such records for assets costing less than the minimum. Rather, they charge the cost of such assets directly to an expense account at the time of purchase. Furthermore, if about the same amount is expended for such assets each year, this is acceptable under the *materiality principle.*

GLOSSARY

[handwritten: 1986 Tax Laws   27½ Years   1987 = 19 years]

Accelerated cost recovery system (ACRS).   A unique, accelerated depreciation method prescribed in the tax law for assets placed in service after 1980. *[handwritten: #357]*

Accelerated depreciation.   Any depreciation method resulting in greater amounts of depreciation expense in the early years of a plant asset's life and lesser amounts in later years.

Book value.   The carrying amount for an item in the accounting records. When applied to a plant asset, it is the cost of the asset minus its accumulated depreciation.

Declining-balance depreciation.   A depreciation method in which up to twice the straight-line rate of depreciation, without considering salvage value, is applied to the remaining book value of a plant asset to arrive at the asset's annual depreciation charge.

Fixed asset.   A plant asset.

Inadequacy.   The situation where a plant asset does not produce enough product to meet current needs.

Internal Revenue Code.   The codification of the numerous tax laws passed by Congress.

Land improvements.   Assets that improve or increase the value or usefulness of land but have a limited useful life and are subject to depreciation.

Obsolescence.   The situation where because of new inventions and improvements, an old plant asset can no longer produce its product on a competitive basis.

Office Equipment Ledger.   A subsidiary ledger having a record card for each item of office equipment owned.

Salvage value.   The share of a plant asset's cost recovered at the end of its service life through a sale or as a trade-in allowance on a new asset.

Service life.   The period of time a plant asset is used in the production and sale of other assets or services.

Store Equipment Ledger.   A subsidiary ledger having a record card for each item of store equipment owned.

Straight-line depreciation.   A depreciation method that allocates an equal share of the total estimated amount a plant asset will be depreciated during its service life to each accounting period in that life. *[handwritten: #352]*

Sum-of-the-years'-digits depreciation. A depreciation method that allocates depreciation to each year in a plant asset's life on a fractional basis. The denominator of the fractions used is the sum-of-the-years' digits in the estimated service life of the asset, and the numerators are the years' digits in reverse order.

Units-of-production depreciation. A depreciation method that allocates depreciation on a plant asset based on the relation of the units of product produced by the asset during a given period to the total units the asset is expected to produce during its entire life.

QUESTIONS FOR CLASS DISCUSSION

1. What are the characteristics of assets classified as plant and equipment? *#348*

2. What is the balance sheet classification of land held for future expansion? Why is such land not classified as a plant asset?

3. What is the difference between land and land improvements?

4. What in general is included in the cost of a plant asset? *#348*

5. A company asked for bids from several machine shops for the construction of a special machine. The lowest bid was $12,500. The company decided to build the machine itself and did so at a total cash outlay of $10,000. It then recorded the machine's construction with a debit to Machinery for $12,500, a credit to Cash for $10,000, and a credit to Gain on the Construction of Machinery for $2,500. Was this a proper entry? Discuss.

6. As used in accounting, what is the meaning of the term *depreciation?*

7. Is it possible to keep a plant asset in such an excellent state of repair that recording depreciation is unnecessary? *Yes. after normal length of use.*

8. A company has just purchased a machine that has a potential life of 15 years. However, the company's management believes that the development of a more efficient machine will make it necessary to replace the machine in eight years. What period of useful life should be used in calculating depreciation on this machine?

9. A building estimated to have a useful life of 30 years was completed at a cost of $85,000. It was estimated that at the end of the building's life it would be wrecked at a cost of $1,000 and that materials salvaged from the wrecking operation would be sold for $2,000. How much straight-line depreciation should be charged on the building each year?

10. Define the following terms as used in accounting for plant assets:

    a. Trade-in value.   *c.* Book value.   *e.* Inadequacy.
    b. Market value.   *d.* Salvage value.   *f.* Obsolescence.

11. When straight-line depreciation is used, an equal share of the total amount a plant asset is to be depreciated during its life is assigned to each accounting period in that life. Describe a situation in which this may not be a fair basis of allocation. Name a more fair basis for the situation described.

12. What is the sum-of-the-years' digits in the life of a plant asset that will be used for 12 years?

13. Does the recording of depreciation cause a plant asset to appear on the balance sheet at market value? What is accomplished by recording depreciation? *350*

14. What is the essence of the going-concern concept of a business?

15. Explain how a business that breaks even recovers the cost of its plant assets through the sale of its products? Where are the funds thus recovered? *Deprociation of Assets*

16. Does the balance of the Accumulated Depreciation, Machinery account represent funds accumulated to replace the machinery as it wears out? Tell in your own words what the balance of such an account represents.

CLASS EXERCISES

Exercise 10–1

A machine was purchased for $2,000, terms 2/10, n/60, FOB shipping point. The manufacturer prepaid the freight charges, $110, adding the amount to the invoice and bringing its total to $2,110. The machine required a special concrete base and power connections costing $285, and $270 was paid a millwright to assemble the machine and get it into operation. In moving the machine onto its concrete base, it was dropped and damaged. The damages cost $70 to repair; and after being repaired, $30 of raw materials were consumed in adjusting the machine so it would produce a satisfactory product. The adjustments were normal for this type of machine and were not the result of its having been damaged. The product produced while the adjustments were being made was not salable. Prepare a calculation to show the cost of this machine for accounting purposes.

Exercise 10–2

A company paid $145,000 for real estate plus $3,000 in closing costs. The real estate included land appraised at $45,000; land improvements appraised at $18,000; and a building appraised at $117,000. The company's plan is to use the building as a factory. Prepare a calculation showing the allocation of cost to the assets purchased and present the journal entry to record the purchase.

Exercise 10–3

Three machines were purchased for $8,400 at an auction sale of a bankrupt company's machinery. The purchaser paid $400 to transport the machines to its factory. Machine 1 was twice as big and weighed twice as much as Machine 2. Machines 2 and 3 were approximately equal in size and weight. The machines had the following appraised values and installation costs:

	Machine 1	Machine 2	Machine 3
Appraised values	$5,000	$4,000	$3,000
Installation costs	300	200	150

Determine the cost of each machine for accounting purposes.

Exercise 10–4

A machine was installed in a factory at a $15,800 cost. Its useful life was estimated at five years or 50,000 units of product with an $800 trade-in value. During its second year, the machine produced 12,000 units of product. Determine the machine's second-year depreciation with depreciation calculated in each of the following ways: *(a)* straight-line basis, *(b)* units-of-production basis, *(c)* declining-balance basis at twice the straight-line rate, and *(d)* sum-of-the-years'-digits basis.

Exercise 10–5   A company purchased a machine for $12,000 on September 30, 198A. Depreciation was recorded on December 31, 198A, 198B, and 198C, assuming the straight-line method, a four-year life, and no salvage value. The machine was sold for its book value on August 31, 198D. *(a)* Give the entry to record the partial year's depreciation on August 31, 198D. *(b)* Give the entry to record the sale.

Exercise 10–6   A machine that cost $30,000 was purchased on July 3, 198A. The machine is expected to last five years and have a $5,000 salvage value. Declining-balance depreciation is to be used at twice the straight-line rate. Assuming the annual accounting period ends on December 31, present the journal entries to record depreciation on *(a)* December 31, 198A, and *(b)* December 31, 198B.

Exercise 10–7   In January 1984, a machine was purchased for $600,000. It will be used in research and development activities for six years and then sold at an estimated salvage value of $50,000. The machine is in the three-year class for tax purposes. Prepare a schedule showing each year's depreciation for tax purposes assuming *(a)* five-year straight-line, *(b)* three-year straight-line, and *(c)* ACRS depreciation rates.

PROBLEMS

Problem 10–1   In early 1984, Bear Company paid $230,000 for real estate that included a tract of land on which two buildings were located. The plan was to demolish Building A and build a new store in its place. Building B was to be used as a company office and was appraised to have a value of $65,000, with a useful life of 15 years and a $5,000 salvage value. A lighted parking lot near Building B had improvements valued at $26,000 that were expected to last another 10 years and have no salvage value. In its existing condition, the tract of land was estimated to have a value of $169,000.

Bear Company incurred the following additional costs:

Cost to demolish Building A . . . . $ 25,000
Cost to landscape new building site   8,000
Cost to build new building (Building C), having a useful life of 30 years
    and a $30,000 salvage value   300,000
Cost of new land improvements near Building C, which have a 15-year
    useful life and no salvage value   35,000

Required:

1. Prepare a form having the following column headings: Land, Building B, Building C, Land Improvements B, and Land Improvements C. Allocate the costs incurred by Bear Company to the appropriate columns and total each column.

2. Prepare a single journal entry dated March 30 to record all of the costs incurred, assuming they were all paid in cash.
3. Prepare December 31 adjusting entries to record depreciation for the nine months of 1984 during which the assets were in use. Use sum-of-the-years'-digits depreciation for the newly constructed Building C and Land Improvements C and straight-line depreciation for Building B and Land Improvements B.

Problem 10–2

On January 3, 198A, Fox Company paid $20,000 for equipment that had a five-year estimated life and $4,000 salvage value. During its life, the equipment would produce 18,000 units of product. During the succeeding five years, production from the equipment was: 198A, 2,700; 198B, 1,800; 198C, 4,500; 198D, 5,400; and 198E, 3,600.

Required:

1. Prepare a five-column table that shows depreciation to be taken each year on the machine. In Column 1, list the year. In Column 2, show depreciation under the straight-line method. In Column 3, show depreciation under the units-of-production method. In Column 4, show depreciation under sum-of-the-years'-digits method. In Column 5, show depreciation under the declining-balance method at twice the straight-line rate.
2. Now suppose the equipment was purchased on April 1, 198A, instead of on January 3. Production in 198A remained 2,700 units. Calculate the depreciation to be taken in 198A and in 198B under each of the four methods listed in Requirement 1.

Problem 10–3

Nelson Corporation recently negotiated a lump-sum purchase of several assets from a truck dealer who was planning to change locations. The purchase was completed on October 1, 1984, at a total cash price of $260,000, and included a warehouse with land and certain land improvements and a new light truck. The estimated market value of each asset is: warehouse, $178,750; land, $55,000; land improvements, $27,500; and truck, $13,750.

Required:

1. Prepare a schedule to allocate the lump-sum purchase price to the separate assets that were purchased. Also present the general journal entry to record the purchase.
2. Calculate the 1985 depreciation expense on the warehouse using the sum-of-the-years'-digits method and assuming a 15-year life and a $9,000 salvage value.
3. Calculate the 1984 depreciation expense on the land improvements assuming a 10-year life and declining-balance depreciation at twice the straight-line rate.
4. The truck is in the three-year class for tax purposes but is expected to last six years and have a salvage value of $1,000. Prepare a schedule showing each year's depreciation on the truck for tax purposes, assuming five-year straight-line, three-year straight-line, and ACRS depreciation.

Problem 10–4   On March 16, 198A, a company made a lump-sum purchase of two machines from another company that was going out of business. The machines cost $48,600 and were placed in use on April 4, 198A. This additional information about the machines is available:

Machine number	Appraised value	Salvage value	Estimated life	Installation cost	Depreciation method
1......	$24,000	$1,200	4 years	$ 600	Sum-of-the-years' digits
2......	30,000	2,000	4 years	1,000	Declining balance at twice the straight-line rate

Depreciation was taken on the machines at the end of 198A, 198B, and 198C and during the first week in January 198D, the company decided to sell and replace them. Consequently, on January 12, 198D, it sold Machine 1 for $4,350, and on January 14 it sold Machine 2 for $4,375.

Required:

1. Prepare a form with the following columnar headings:

Machine Number	198A Depreciation	198B Depreciation	198C Depreciation	198D Depreciation	198E Depreciation

Enter the machine numbers in the first column and the amounts of depreciation in the remaining columns.

2. Prepare general journal entries to record the purchase of the machines, their installation, the depreciation for each year they were in use, and their sale. Assume cash was paid and received in all transactions and the installation charges were paid for on the day the machines were put in use.

Problem 10–5   Monroe Company completed the following plant asset transactions:

198A
Jan. 7 Purchased on credit from Quicko, Inc., a Quicko calculator, $550. The serial number of the machine was X2X345. Its service life was estimated at eight years with a $70 trade-in value. It was assigned plant asset number 132–1.

   9 Purchased on credit from Office Outfitters an Accurate typewriter for $380. The machine's serial number was MMM-0156, and it was assigned plant asset number 132-2. Its service life was estimated at four years with a $44 trade-in value.

Dec. 31 Recorded the straight-line depreciation on the office equipment for 198A.

198B
June 3 Sold the Accurate typewriter for $261 cash.

   4 Purchased on credit for $415 from Speedy Typewriter Company a Speedy typewriter. The machine's serial number was MO7781, and it was assigned plant asset number 132–3. Its service life was estimated at four years with a $55 trade-in value.

Dec. 31   Recorded the straight-line depreciation on the office equipment for 198B.

Required:

1. Open an Office Equipment account and an Accumulated Depreciation, Office Equipment account plus subsidiary plant asset record cards as needed.
2. Prepare general journal entries to record the transactions. Post to the general ledger accounts and subsidiary record cards.
3. Prove the December 31, 198B, balances of the Office Equipment and Accumulated Depreciation, Office Equipment accounts by preparing a schedule showing the cost and accumulated depreciation of each plant asset owned by the company on that date.

ALTERNATE PROBLEMS

Problem 10–1A

In mid-1984, Smoothie Company paid $420,000 for real estate that included a tract of land on which two buildings were located. Smoothie planned to tear down Building One and build a new factory in its place. Building Two was to be used as a warehouse and was appraised to have a value of $138,000, with a useful life of 12 years and a $6,000 salvage value. A lighted parking lot near Building Two had improvements valued at $69,000 that were expected to last another six years and have no salvage value. In its existing condition, the tract of land was estimated to have a value of $253,000.

Smoothie Company incurred the following additional costs:

Cost to demolish Building One	$ 29,000
Cost to landscape new building site	14,000
Cost to build new building (Building Three), having a useful life of 25 years and a $50,000 salvage value	450,000
Cost of new land improvements near Building Three, which have a 10-year useful life and no salvage value	40,000

Required:

1. Prepare a form having the following column headings: Land, Building Two, Building Three, Old Land Improvements, and New Land Improvements. Allocate the costs incurred by Smoothie Company to the appropriate columns and total each column.
2. Prepare a single journal entry dated July 30 to record all of the costs incurred, assuming they were all paid in cash.
3. Prepare December 31 adjusting entries to record depreciation for the five months of 1984 during which the assets were in use. Use declining-balance depreciation at twice the straight-line rate for the newly constructed Building Three and the New Land Improvements and straight-line depreciation for Building Two and the Old Land Improvements.

Problem 10–2A

On January 6, 198A, Stellor Company paid $80,000 for equipment that had a five-year estimated life and $8,000 salvage value. During its life, the equipment would produce 24,000 units of product. During the succeeding five years, production from the equipment was: 198A, 1,200; 198B, 3,600; 198C, 8,400; 198D, 6,000; and 198E, 4,800.

Required:

1. Prepare a five-column table that shows depreciation to be taken each year on the machine. In Column 1, list the year. In Column 2, show depreciation under the straight-line method. In Column 3, show depreciation under the units-of-production method. In Column 4, show depreciation under sum-of-the-years'-digits method. In Column 5, show depreciation under the declining-balance method at twice the straight-line rate.
2. Now suppose the equipment was purchased on August 1, 198A, instead of on January 6. Production in 198A remained 1,200 units. Calculate the depreciation to be taken in 198A and 198B under each of the four methods listed in Requirement 1.

Problem 10–3A
On April 1, 1985, Otter Company made a lump-sum purchase of several assets for a total cash price of $240,000. The purchase included land, certain land improvements, a building, and a new light truck. The estimated market value of each asset is: land, $71,400; land improvements, $56,100; building, $117,300; and truck, $10,200.

Required:

1. Prepare a schedule to allocate the lump-sum purchase price to the separate assets that were purchased. Also present the general journal entry to record the purchase.
2. Calculate the 1986 depreciation expense on the building using the sum-of-the-years'-digits method and assuming a 12-year life and a $9,000 salvage value.
3. Calculate the 1985 depreciation expense on the land improvements assuming an eight-year life and declining-balance depreciation at twice the straight-line rate.
4. The truck is in the three-year class for tax purposes but is expected to last six years and have a salvage value of $1,000. Prepare a schedule showing each year's depreciation on the truck for tax purposes, assuming five-year straight-line, three-year straight-line, and ACRS depreciation.

Problem 10–4A
On August 3, 198A, a company made a lump-sum purchase of two machines at a bankruptcy sale. The machines cost $27,300 and were placed in use on August 30, 198A. This additional information about the machines is available:

Machine number	Appraised value	Salvage value	Estimated life	Installation cost	Depreciation method
1......	$15,000	$ 500	4 years	$ 800	Sum-of-the-years'-digits
2......	20,000	1,500	4 years	1,200	Declining balance

The machines were depreciated at the end of 198A, 198B, and 198C. Machine 2's depreciation was calculated at twice the straight-line rate. During the first week in January 198D, the company decided to replace the machines, and on January 10 it sold them in separate sales for cash, Machine 1 for $3,300, and Machine 2 for $3,500.

Required:

1. Prepare a form with the following headings:

Machine Number	198A Depreciation	198B Depreciation	198C Depreciation	198D Depreciation	198E Depreciation

Fill in the machine numbers in the first column and the amounts of depreciation in the remaining columns.

2. Prepare general journal entries to record the purchase of the machines, their installation, the depreciation for each year they were in use, and their sale. Assume cash was paid and received in all transactions and the installation charges were paid for on the day the machines were put in use.

Problem 10–5A   Bargain Mart completed these transactions involving plant assets:

198A

Jan. 3   Purchased on credit from Store Equipment Company an Econ Scale priced at $265. The serial number of the scale was B-23452, its service life was estimated at 10 years with a trade-in value of $25, and it was assigned plant asset No. 132–1.

Apr. 7   Purchased on credit from Store Equipment Company a Regal cash register priced at $323. The serial number of the register was 3–32564, its service life was estimated at eight years with a trade-in value of $35, and it was assigned plant asset No. 132–2.

Dec. 31   Recorded the straight-line depreciation on the store equipment for 198A.

198B

Oct. 28   Sold the Regal cash register to Ted Beal for $266 cash.

     28   Purchased a new Accurate cash register on credit from Beta Equipment Company for $360. The serial number of the register was XXX-12345, its service life was estimated at 10 years with a trade-in value of $48, and it was assigned plant asset No. 132–3.

Dec. 31   Recorded the straight-line depreciation on the store equipment for 198B.

Required:

1. Open general ledger accounts for Store Equipment and for Accumulated Depreciation, Store Equipment. Prepare a subsidiary plant asset record card for each item of equipment purchased.

2. Prepare general journal entries to record the transactions and post to the proper general ledger and subsidiary ledger accounts.

3. Prove the December 31, 198B, balances of the Store Equipment and Accumulated Depreciation, Store Equipment accounts by preparing a list showing the cost and accumulated depreciation on each item of store equipment owned by Bargain Mart on that date.

PROVOCATIVE PROBLEMS

Buildex Company was organized early in January of the current year; and in making your audit of the company's records at the end of the year, you discover that the company's bookkeeper has debited an account called Land, Buildings, and Equipment for what he thought was the cost of the company's new factory. The account has a $824,400 debit balance made up of the following items:

Cost of land and an old building on the land purchased as the site of the company's new factory (appraised value of the land, $80,000, and of the old building, $10,000)	$ 84,600
Attorney's fees resulting from land purchase	500
Escrow fees resulting from land purchase	300
Cost of removing old building from plant site	1,800
Surveying and grading plant site	2,800
Cost of retaining wall and the placing of tile to drain the site	1,200
Cost of new building	381,900
Architect's fee for planning building	23,100
Cost of paving parking lot	8,600
Lights for parking lot	400
Landscaping	2,700
Machinery (including the $800 cost of a machine dropped and made useless while being unloaded from a freight car)	312,500
Fine and permit to haul heavy machinery on city streets. The company was cited for hauling machinery without a permit. It then secured the permit. (Fine, $200; cost of permit, $50)	250
Cost of hauling machinery on city streets	2,950
Cost of replacing damaged machine	800
Total	$824,400

In auditing the company's other accounts, it was discovered that the bookkeeper had credited the $300 proceeds from the sale of materials salvaged from the old building removed from the plant site to an account called Miscellaneous Revenues.

An examination of the payroll records showed that an account called Superintendence had been debited for the plant superintendent's $15,000 salary for the 10-month period, March 1 through December 31. From March 1 through August 31 the superintendent had supervised construction of the factory building. During September, October, and November, he had supervised installation of the factory machinery. The factory began manufacturing operations on December 1.

Required:

1. Prepare a form having the following four column headings: Land, Land Improvements, Buildings, and Machinery. List the items and sort their amounts to the proper columns. Show a negative amount in parentheses. Total the columns.
2. Under the assumption that the company's accounts had not been closed, prepare an entry to remove the foregoing item amounts from the accounts in which they were incorrectly entered and record them in the proper accounts.

3. The company closes its books annually on December 31. Prepare the entry to record the partial year's depreciation on the plant assets using the straight-line method. Assume the building and land improvements are estimated to have 30-year lives and no salvage values and that the machinery is estimated to have a 12-year life and a salvage value equal to 10% of its cost.

Provocative Problem 10–2, a Comparison of Companies

Delta Company and Swamp Company are almost identical. Each began operations on January 9 of this year with $36,000 of equipment having an eight-year life and a $4,000 salvage value. Each purchased merchandise during the year as follows:

Jan. 9	120 units @ $200 per unit =	$ 24,000
Mar. 11	150 units @ $240 per unit =	36,000
July 7	225 units @ $250 per unit =	56,250
Oct. 20	125 units @ $270 per unit =	33,750
		$150,000

And now, on December 31 at the end of the first year, each has 130 units of merchandise in its ending inventory. However, Delta Company will use straight-line depreciation in arriving at its net income for the year, while Swamp Company will use declining-balance depreciation at twice the straight-line rate. Also, Delta Company will use FIFO in costing its ending inventory and Swamp Company will use LIFO. The December 31 trial balances of the two concerns carried these amounts:

	Delta Company		Swamp Company	
Cash	$ 3,500		$ 3,500	
Accounts receivable	8,000		8,000	
Equipment	36,000		36,000	
Accounts payable		$ 18,000		$ 18,000
David Delta, capital		44,000		
Samuel Swamp, capital				44,000
Sales		170,000		170,000
Purchases	150,000		150,000	
Salaries expense	15,000		15,000	
Rent expense	12,000		12,000	
Other expenses	7,500		7,500	
Totals	$232,000	$232,000	$232,000	$232,000

Required:

Prepare an income statement for each company and a schedule accounting for the difference in their reported net incomes. Write a short answer to this question: Which, if either, of the companies is the more profitable and why?

Plant and Equipment; Intangible Assets

11

After studying Chapter 11, you should be able to:

Prepare entries to record the purchase and sale or discarding of a plant asset.

Prepare entries to record the exchange of plant assets under accounting rules and under income tax rules and tell which rules should be applied in any given exchange.

Make the calculations and prepare the entries to account for revisions in depreciation rates.

Make the calculations and prepare the entries to account for plant asset repairs and betterments.

Prepare entries to account for wasting assets and for intangible assets.

Define or explain the words and phrases listed in the chapter Glossary.

Some of the problems met in accounting for property, plant, and equipment were discussed in the previous chapter. Additional problems involving plant assets and some of the accounting problems encountered with intangible assets are examined in this chapter.

PLANT ASSET DISPOSALS

Sooner or later a plant asset wears out, becomes obsolete, or becomes inadequate. When this occurs, the asset is discarded, sold, or traded in on a new asset. The entry to record the disposal depends on which action is taken.

Discarding a Plant Asset

When an asset's accumulated depreciation is equal to its cost, the asset is said to be fully depreciated; and if a fully depreciated asset is discarded, the entry to record the disposal is:

Jan.	7	Accumulated Depreciation, Machinery	1,500.00	
		Machinery		1,500.00
		Discarded a fully depreciated machine.		

Although often discarded, sometimes a fully depreciated asset is kept in use. In such situations, the asset's cost and accumulated depreciation should not be removed from the accounts; they should remain on the books until the asset is sold, traded, or discarded. Otherwise, the accounts do not show its continued existence. However, no additional depreciation should be recorded, since the reason for recording depreciation is to charge an asset's cost to depreciation expense. In no case should the expense exceed the asset's cost.

Sometimes an asset is discarded before being fully depreciated. For example, suppose an error was made in estimating the service life of a $1,000 machine and it becomes worthless and is discarded after having only $800 of depreciation recorded against it. In such a situation, there is a loss and the entry to record the disposal is:

Jan.	10	Loss on Disposal of Machinery	200.00	
		Accumulated Depreciation, Machinery	800.00	
		Machinery		1,000.00
		Discarded a worthless machine.		

Discarding a Damaged Plant Asset

Occasionally, before the end of its service life, a plant asset is wrecked in an accident or destroyed by fire. For example, a machine that cost $900 and that had been depreciated $400 was totally destroyed in a fire. If the loss was partially covered by insurance and the insurance company paid $350 to settle the loss claim, the entry to record the machine's destruction is:

Jan.	12	Cash	350.00	
		Loss from Fire	150.00	
		Accumulated Depreciation, Machinery	400.00	
		Machinery		900.00
		To record the destruction of machinery and the receipt of insurance compensation.		

If the machine were uninsured, the entry to record its destruction would not have a debit to Cash and the loss from fire would be $500.

Selling a Plant Asset

When a plant asset is sold, if the selling price exceeds the asset's book value, there is a gain. If the price is less than book value, there is a loss. For example, assume that a machine that cost $5,000 and had been depreciated $4,000 is sold for a price in excess of its book value, say, for $1,200. In this case, there is a gain, and the entry to record the sale is:

Jan.	4	Cash	1,200.00	
		Accumulated Depreciation, Machinery	4,000.00	
		Machinery		5,000.00
		Gain on the Sale of Plant Assets		200.00
		Sold a machine at a price in excess of book value.		

However, if the machine is sold for $750, there is a $250 loss, and the entry to record the sale is:

Jan.	4	Cash	750.00	
		Loss on the Sale of Plant Assets	250.00	
		Accumulated Depreciation, Machinery	4,000.00	
		Machinery		5,000.00
		Sold a machine at a price below book value.		

EXCHANGING PLANT ASSETS

Some plant assets are sold at the end of their useful lives. Others, such as machinery, automobiles, and office equipment, are commonly exchanged for new, up-to-date assets of like purpose. In such exchanges, a trade-in allowance is normally received on the old asset, with the balance being paid in cash. The APB ruled that in recording the exchanges, a material book loss should be recognized in the accounts but a book gain should not.[1] A book loss is experienced when the trade-in allowance is less than the book value of the traded asset. A book gain results from a trade-in allowance that exceeds the book value of the traded asset.

Recognizing a Material Book Loss

To illustrate recognition of a material book loss on an exchange of plant assets, assume that a machine that cost $18,000 and had been depreciated $15,000 was traded in on a new machine having a $21,000 cash price. A $1,000 trade-in allowance was received, and the $20,000 balance was paid in cash. Under these assumptions, the book value of the old machine is $3,000, calculated as follows:

Cost of old machine	$18,000
Less accumulated depreciation.....	15,000
Book value	$ 3,000

And since the $1,000 trade-in allowance resulted in a $2,000 loss on the exchange, the transaction should be recorded as follows:

Jan.	5	Machinery	21,000.00	
		Loss on Exchange of Machinery	2,000.00	
		Accumulated Depreciation, Machinery	15,000.00	
		Machinery		18,000.00
		Cash		20,000.00
		Exchanged old machine and cash for a new machine of like purpose.		

---

[1] APB, "Accounting for Nonmonetary Transactions," *APB Opinion No. 29* (New York: AICPA, May 1973), par. 22. Copyright (1973) by the American Institute of CPAs.

The $21,000 debit to Machinery puts the new machine in the accounts at its cash price. The debit to Loss on Exchange of Machinery records the loss. The old machine is removed from the accounts with the $15,000 debit to accumulated depreciation and the $18,000 credit to Machinery.

Nonrecognition of a Book Gain

When there is a book gain on an exchange of plant assets, the APB ruled that the new asset should be taken into the accounts at an amount equal to the book value of the traded-in asset plus the cash given. This results in the nonrecognition of the gain. For example, assume that in acquiring the $21,000 machine of the previous section a $4,500 trade-in allowance, rather than a $1,000 trade-in allowance, was received, and the $16,500 balance was paid in cash. A $4,500 trade-in allowance would result in a $1,500 gain on the exchange. However, in recording the exchange, the book gain should not be recognized in the accounts. Rather, it should be absorbed into the cost of the new machine by taking the new machine into the accounts at an amount equal to the sum of the book value of the old machine plus the cash given. This is $19,500 and is calculated as follows:

Book value of old machine	$ 3,000
Cash given in the exchange	16,500
Cost basis for the new machine	$19,500

And the transaction should be recorded as follows:

Jan.	5	Machinery	19,500.00	
		Accumulated Depreciation, Machinery	15,000.00	
		Machinery		18,000.00
		Cash		16,500.00
		Exchanged old machine and cash for a new machine of like purpose.		

Observe that the $19,500 recorded amount for the new machine is equal to its cash price less the $1,500 book gain on the exchange ($21,000 − $1,500 = $19,500). In other words, the $1,500 book gain was absorbed into the amount at which the new machine was recorded. The $19,500 is called the *cost basis* of the new machine and is the amount used in recording depreciation on the machine or any gain or loss on its sale.

The APB based its ruling that gains on plant asset exchanges should not be recognized on the opinion that ". . . revenue should not be recognized merely because one productive asset is substituted for a similar productive asset but rather should be considered to flow from the production and sale of the goods or services to which the substituted productive asset is committed."[2] In other words, the APB's opinion was that any gain from a plant asset exchange should be taken in the form of increased net income resulting from smaller depreciation charges on the asset acquired. In this case, depreciation calculated on the recorded $19,500 cost basis of the new machine is less than if calculated on the machine's $21,000 cash price.

Tax Rules and Plant Asset Exchanges

Because depreciation methods for financial statement purposes are often different from those used for tax purposes, companies usually must keep two sets of depreciation records on each asset. Even where the depreciation methods and estimated lives are the same for tax and accounting purposes, two sets of records may be necessary. This is caused by the fact that *income tax rules* and accounting principles do not agree on the treatment of losses on plant asset exchanges. In the case of a gain, the tax rules and accounting principles agree.

According to the Internal Revenue Service, when an old asset is traded in on a new asset of like purpose, either a gain or a loss on the exchange must be absorbed into the cost of the new machine. This cost basis then becomes for tax purposes the amount that must be used in calculating depreciation on the new asset or any gain or loss on its sale or exchange. Consequently, for tax purposes, the cost basis of an asset acquired in an exchange is the sum of the book value of the old asset plus the cash given, and it makes no difference whether there is a gain or a loss on the exchange.

Since accounting principles and tax rules differ in their treatment of a loss on a plant asset exchange, two sets of depreciation records must be kept for the new asset even if the depreciation method and estimated life are the same for tax and accounting purposes. One set must be kept for determining net income for accounting purposes, and the other for determining the depreciation deduction for tax purposes. Keeping two sets of records is obviously more costly than keeping one. Yet, when an exchange results in a material loss, the loss should be recorded and the two sets of records kept. On the other hand, when an exchange results in an immaterial loss, it is permissible under the *principle of materiality* to avoid the two sets of records by putting the new asset on the books at its cost basis for tax purposes.

---

[2] Ibid., par. 16.

For example, an old typewriter that cost $500 was traded in at $50 on a new $600 typewriter, with the $550 difference being paid in cash. Depreciation on the old typewriter in the amount of $420 had been taken both for tax and accounting purposes. In this case, the old typewriter's book value is $80; and with the trade-in of $50, there was a $30 book loss on the exchange. However, the $30 loss is an immaterial amount; and the following method, called the income tax method, may be used in recording the exchange:

Jan.	7	Office Equipment	630.00	
		Accumulated Depreciation, Office Equipment ...	420.00	
		Office Equipment		500.00
		Cash		550.00
		Traded an old typewriter and cash for a new typewriter.		

The $630 at which the new typewriter is taken into the accounts by the income tax method is its cost basis for tax purposes and is calculated as follows:

Book value of old typewriter ($500 less $420)	$ 80
Cash paid ($600 less the $50 trade-in allowance)	550
Income tax basis of the new typewriter	$630

Not recording the loss on this exchange and taking the new typewriter into the accounts at its cost basis for income tax purposes violates the ruling of the APB that a loss on a plant asset exchange should be recorded. However, when there is an immaterial loss on an exchange, as in this case, the violation is permissible under the *principle of materiality*. Under this principle, an adherence to any accounting principle, including rulings of the APB and the FASB, is not required when the cost to adhere is proportionally great and the lack of adherence does not materially affect reported periodic net income. In this case, failing to record the $30 loss on the exchange would not materially affect the average company's statements.

REVISING DEPRECIATION RATES

An occasional error in estimating the useful life of a plant asset is to be expected. Furthermore, when such an error is discovered, it is corrected by spreading the remaining amount the asset is to be depreciated over its remaining useful life.[3] For example, seven years ago a machine was purchased at a cost of $10,500. At that time, the machine was estimated to have a 10-year life with a $500 salvage value. Therefore, it was depreciated at the rate of $1,000 per year [($10,500 − $500) ÷ 10 = $1,000]; and it began its eighth year with a $3,500 book value calculated as follows:

Cost	$10,500
Less seven years' accumulated depreciation ..	7,000
Book value	$ 3,500

Assume that at the beginning of its eighth year the estimated number of years remaining in this machine's useful life is changed from three to five years with no change in salvage value. Under this assumption, depreciation for each of the machine's remaining years should be calculated as follows:

$$\frac{\text{Book value} - \text{Salvage value}}{\text{Remaining useful life}} = \frac{\$3,500 - \$500}{5 \text{ years}} = \$600 \text{ per year}$$

And $600 of depreciation should be recorded on the machine at the end of the eighth and each succeeding year in its life.

If depreciation is charged at the rate of $1,000 per year for the first seven years of this machine's life and $600 per year for the next five, depreciation expense is overstated during the first seven years and understated during the next five. However, if a business has many plant assets, the lives of some will be underestimated and the lives of others will be overestimated at the time of purchase. Consequently, such errors will tend to cancel each other out with little or no effect on the income statement.

ORDINARY AND EXTRAORDINARY REPAIRS

Repairs made to keep an asset in its normal good state of repair are classified as *ordinary repairs*. A building must be repainted and its roof repaired. A machine must be cleaned, oiled, adjusted, and have any worn small parts replaced. Such repairs and maintenance

---

[3] APB, "Accounting Changes," *APB Opinion No. 20* (New York: AICPA, July 1971), par. 31.

are necessary, and their costs should appear on the current income statement as an expense.

Extraordinary repairs are major repairs made not to keep an asset in its normal good state of repair but to extend its service life beyond that originally estimated. As a rule, the cost of such repairs should be debited to the repaired asset's accumulated depreciation account under the assumption they make good past depreciation, add to the asset's useful life, and benefit future periods. For example, a machine was purchased for $8,000 and depreciated under the assumption it would last eight years and have no salvage value. As a result, at the end of the machine's sixth year its book value is $2,000, calculated as follows:

Cost of machine	$8,000
Less six years' accumulated depreciation ..	6,000
Book value	$2,000

If at the beginning of the machine's seventh year a major overhaul extends its estimated useful life three years beyond the eight originally estimated, the $2,100 cost should be recorded as follows:

Jan.	12	Accumulated Depreciation, Machinery	2,100.00	
		Cash (or Accounts Payable)		2,100.00
		To record extraordinary repairs.		

In addition, depreciation for each of the five years remaining in the machine's life should be calculated as follows:

Book value before extraordinary repairs	$2,000
Extraordinary repairs	2,100
Total	$4,100
Annual depreciation expense for remaining years ($4,100 ÷ 5 years)	$ 820

And, if the machine remains in use for five years after the major overhaul, the five annual $820 depreciation charges will exactly write off its new book value, including the cost of the extraordinary repairs.

BETTERMENTS

A *betterment* involves modifying an existing plant asset to make it more efficient, usually by replacing part of the asset with an improved or superior part. The result of a betterment is a more efficient or more productive asset, but not necessarily one having a longer life. For example, if the manual controls on a machine are replaced with automatic controls, the cost of labor may be reduced. When a betterment is made, its cost should be debited to the improved asset's account, say, the Machinery account, and depreciated over the remaining service life of the asset. Also, the cost and applicable depreciation of the replaced asset portion should be removed from the accounts.

CAPITAL AND REVENUE EXPENDITURES

A *revenue expenditure* is one that should appear on the current income statement as an expense that is deducted from the period's revenues. Expenditures for ordinary repairs, rent, and salaries are examples. Expenditures for betterments and for extraordinary repairs, on the other hand, are examples of what are called *capital expenditures* or *balance sheet expenditures*. They should appear on the balance sheet as asset increases.

Obviously, care must be exercised to distinguish between capital and revenue expenditures when transactions are recorded. For if errors are made, such errors often affect a number of accounting periods. For instance, an expenditure for a betterment initially recorded in error as an expense overstates expenses in the year of the error and understates net income. Also, since the cost of a betterment should be depreciated over the remaining useful life of the bettered asset, depreciation expense of future periods is understated and net income is overstated.

NATURAL RESOURCES

Natural resources such as standing timber, mineral deposits, and oil reserves are known as wasting assets. In their natural state they represent inventories that will be converted into a product by cutting, mining, or pumping. However, until cut, mined, or pumped they are noncurrent assets and commonly appear on a balance sheet under such captions as "Timberlands," "Mineral deposits," or "Oil reserves."

Natural resources are accounted for at cost, and appear on the balance sheet at cost less accumulated *depletion*. The amount such assets are depleted each year by cutting, mining, or pumping is commonly calculated on a "units-of-production" basis. For example, if a mineral deposit having an estimated 500,000 tons of available ore is purchased for $500,000, the depletion charge per ton of ore mined is $1. Furthermore, if 85,000 tons are mined during the first year, the depletion charge for the year is $85,000 and is recorded as follows:

Dec.	31	Depletion of Mineral Deposit	85,000.00	
		Accumulated Depletion, Mineral Deposit ...		85,000.00
		To record depletion of the mineral deposit.		

On the balance sheet prepared at the end of the first year, the mineral deposit should appear at its $500,000 cost less $85,000 accumulated depletion. If the 85,000 tons of ore are sold by the end of the first year, the entire $85,000 depletion charge reaches the income statement as the depletion cost of the ore mined and sold. However, if a portion remains unsold at the year-end, the depletion cost of the unsold ore is carried forward on the balance sheet as part of the cost of the unsold ore inventory, a current asset.

Often, machinery must be installed or a building constructed in order to exploit a natural resource. The costs of such assets should be depreciated over the life of the natural resource with annual depreciation charges that are in proportion to the annual depletion charges. For example, if a machine is installed in a mine and one eighth of the mine's ore is removed during a year, one eighth of the amount the machine is to be depreciated should be recorded as a cost of the ore mined.

INTANGIBLE ASSETS

Intangible assets have no physical existence; rather, they represent certain legal rights and economic relationships that are beneficial to the owner. Patents, copyrights, leaseholds, goodwill, trademarks, and organization costs are examples. Notes and accounts receivable are also intangible in nature. However, these appear on the balance sheet as current assets rather than under the intangible assets classification.

Intangible assets are accounted for at cost and should appear on the balance sheet in the intangible asset section at cost or at that portion of cost not previously written off. Normally, the intangible asset section follows on the balance sheet immediately after the plant and equipment section. Intangibles should be systematically amortized or written off to expense accounts over their estimated useful lives, which in no case should exceed 40 years. Amortization is a process similar to the recording of depreciation. However, amortization of intangibles is limited to the straight-line method unless it can be demonstrated that another method is more appropriate.

Patents

Patents are granted by the federal government to encourage the invention of new machines and mechanical devices. A patent gives its owner the exclusive right to manufacture and sell a patented machine or device for a period of 17 years. When patent rights are purchased, all costs of acquiring the rights may be debited to an account called Patents. Also, the costs of a successful lawsuit in defense of a patent may be debited to this account.

A patent gives its owner exclusive rights to the patented device for 17 years. However, its cost should be *amortized* or written off over a shorter period if its useful or economic life is estimated to be less than 17 years. For example, if a patent costing $25,000 has an estimated useful life of only 10 years, the following adjusting entry is made at the end of each year in the patent's life to write off one tenth of its cost:

Dec.	31	Amortization of Patents	2,500.00	
		Patents		2,500.00
		To write off one tenth of patent costs.		

The entry's debit causes $2,500 of patent costs to appear on the annual income statement as one of the costs of the patented product manufactured. The credit directly reduces the balance of the Patents account. Normally, patents are written off directly to the Patents account as in this entry.

Copyrights

A *copyright* is granted by the federal government and in most cases gives its owner the exclusive right to publish and sell a musical, literary, or artistic work during the life of the composer, author, or artist and for 50 years thereafter. Many copyrights have value for a much shorter time, and their costs should be amortized over the shorter period. Often, the only cost of a copyright is the fee paid the Copyright Office. If this fee is not material, it may be charged directly to an expense account. Otherwise, the copyright costs should be capitalized and the periodic amortization of a copyright should be charged to Amortization Expense, Copyrights.

Leaseholds

Property is rented under a contract called a *lease*. The person or company owning the property and granting the lease is called the *lessor*. The person or company securing the right to possess and use the property is called the *lessee*. The rights granted the lessee under the lease are called a *leasehold*.

Some leases require no advance payment from the lessee but do require monthly rent payments. In such cases, a Leasehold account is not needed, and the monthly payments are debited to a Rent Expense account. Sometimes a long-term lease is so drawn that the last year's rent must be paid in advance at the time the lease is signed. When this occurs, the last year's advance payment is debited to the Leasehold account. It remains there until the last year of the lease, at which time it is transferred to Rent Expense.

Often, a long-term lease, one running 20 or 25 years, becomes very valuable after a few years because its required rent payments are much less than current rentals for identical property. In such cases, the increase in value of the lease should not be entered on the books since no extra cost was incurred in acquiring it. However, if the property is subleased and a cash payment is made for the rights under the old lease, the new tenant should debit the payment to a Leasehold account and write it off as additional rent expense over the remaining life of the lease.

Leasehold Improvements

Long-term leases often require the lessee to pay for any alterations or improvements to the leased property, such as new partitions and store fronts. Normally, the costs of *leasehold improvements* are debited to an account called Leasehold Improvements. Also, since the improvements become part of the property and revert to the lessor at the end of the lease, their cost should be amortized over the life of the lease or the life of the improvements, whichever is shorter. The amortization entry commonly debits Rent Expense and credits Leasehold Improvements.

Goodwill

The term *goodwill* has a special meaning in accounting. In accounting, *a business is said to have goodwill when its rate of expected future earnings is greater than the rate of earnings normally realized in its industry.* Above-average earnings and the existence of goodwill may be demonstrated as follows with Companies A and B, both of which are in the same industry:

	Company A	Company B
Net assets (other than goodwill)	$100,000	$100,000
Normal rate of return in this industry	10%	10%
Normal return on net assets	$ 10,000	$ 10,000
Expected net income	10,000	15,000
Expected earnings above average	$ 0	$ 5,000

Company B is expected to have an above-average earnings rate compared to its industry and is said to have goodwill. This goodwill may be the result of excellent customer relations, the location of the business, monopolistic privileges, superior management, or a combination of factors. Furthermore, a prospective investor would normally be willing to pay more for Company B than for Company A if the investor agreed the extra earnings rate should be expected. Thus, goodwill is an asset having value, and it can be sold.

Accountants are in agreement that goodwill should not be recorded unless it is bought or sold. This normally occurs only when a business is purchased and sold in its entirety. When this occurs, the goodwill of the business may be valued in several ways. Examples of three follow:

1. The buyer and seller may place an arbitrary value on the goodwill of a business being sold. For instance, a seller may be willing to sell a business having an above-average earnings rate for $115,000 and a buyer may be willing to pay that amount. If they both agree that the net assets of the business other than its goodwill have a $100,000 value, they are arbitrarily valuing the goodwill at $15,000.

2. Goodwill may be valued at some multiple of that portion of expected earnings which is above average. For example, if a company is expected to have $5,000 each year in above-average earnings, its goodwill may be valued at, say, four times that portion of its earnings which are above average, or at $20,000. In this case, it may also be said that the goodwill is valued at four years' above-average earnings. However, regardless of how it is said, this too is placing an arbitrary value on the goodwill.

3. The portion of a company's earnings that is above average may be capitalized in order to place a value on its goodwill. For example, if a business is expected to continue to have $5,000 each year in earnings that are above average and the normal rate of return on invested capital in its industry is 10%, the excess earnings may be capitalized at 10% and a $50,000 value may be placed on its goodwill ($5,000 ÷ 10% = $50,000). Note that this values the goodwill at the amount that must be invested at the normal rate of

return in order to earn the extra $5,000 each year ($50,000 × 10% = $5,000). It is a satisfactory method if the extra earnings are expected to continue indefinitely. However, this may not happen. Consequently, extra earnings are often capitalized at a rate higher than the normal rate of the industry, say, in this case, at twice the normal rate or at 20%. If the extra earnings are capitalized at 20%, the goodwill is valued at $25,000 ($5,000 ÷ 20% = $25,000).

There are other ways to value goodwill. Nevertheless, in the final analysis, goodwill is always valued at the price a seller is willing to accept and a buyer is willing to pay.

Trademarks and Trade Names

Proof of prior use of a trademark or trade name is sufficient under common law to prove ownership and right of use. However, both may be registered at the Patent Office at a nominal cost for the same purpose. The cost of maintaining or enhancing the value of a trademark or trade name, perhaps through advertising, should be charged to an expense account in the period or periods incurred. However, if a trademark or trade name is purchased, its cost should be amortized as explained in the next section.

Amortization of Intangibles

Some intangibles, such as patents, copyrights, and leaseholds, have determinable lives based on a law, contract, or the nature of the asset. The costs of such assets should be amortized over the shorter of their legal existence or the period expected to be benefited by their use. Other intangibles, such as goodwill, trademarks, and trade names, have indeterminable lives. However, the APB ruled that the value of any intangible will eventually disappear. As a result, a reasonable estimate of the period of usefulness of such assets should be made. Their costs should then be amortized over the periods estimated to be benefited by their use, which in no case should exceed 40 years.[4]

GLOSSARY

Amortize. To periodically write off as an expense a share of the cost of an asset, usually an intangible asset.

---

[4] APB, "Intangible Assets," *APB Opinion No. 17* (New York: AICPA, August 1970), par. 29.

Betterment. A modification of an existing plant asset to make it more efficient, usually by replacing part of the asset with an improved or superior part.

Capital expenditure. An expenditure that increases net assets.

Copyright. An exclusive right granted by the federal government to publish and sell a musical, literary, or artistic work for a period of years.

Depletion. The amount that a wasting asset, e.g., timber, mineral deposits, oil reserves, is depleted through cutting, mining, or pumping.

Extraordinary repairs. Major repairs that extend the service life of a plant asset beyond the number of years originally estimated.

Goodwill. That portion of the value of a business due to its expected ability to earn a rate of return greater than the average in its industry.

Income tax rules. Rules governing how income for tax purposes and income taxes are to be calculated.

Intangible asset. An asset having no physical existence but having value due to the rights resulting from its ownership and possession.

Lease. A contract that grants the right to possess and use property.

Leasehold. The rights granted to a lessee under the terms of a lease contract.

Leasehold improvements. Improvements to leased property made by the lessee.

Lessee. An individual granted possession of property under the terms of a lease contract.

Lessor. The individual or enterprise that has granted possession and use of property under the terms of a lease contract.

Ordinary repairs. Repairs made to keep a plant asset in its normal good operating condition.

Patent. An exclusive right granted by the federal government to manufacture and sell a given machine or mechanical device for a period of years.

Revenue expenditure. An expenditure that should be deducted from current revenue on the income statement.

QUESTIONS FOR CLASS DISCUSSION

1. When should a loss on the exchange of a plant asset be recorded? When is it permissible to absorb a loss into the cost basis of the new plant asset? Should a gain on a plant asset exchange be recorded as such?

2. When plant assets of like purpose are exchanged, what determines the cost basis of the newly acquired asset for federal income tax purposes?

3. When the loss on an exchange of plant assets is immaterial in amount, what advantage may result from taking the newly acquired asset into the records at the amount of its cost basis for tax purposes?

4. When an old plant asset is traded in at a book loss on a new asset of like purpose, the loss is not recognized for tax purposes. In the end, this normally does not work a financial hardship on the taxpayer. Why?

5. What is the essence of the accounting principle of materiality?

6. If, at the end of four years, it is discovered that a machine that was expected to have a five-year life will actually have an eight-year life, how is the error corrected?

7. Distinguish between ordinary repairs and replacements and extraordinary repairs and replacements.

8. How should ordinary repairs to a machine be recorded? How should extraordinary repairs be recorded?

9. What is a betterment? How should a betterment to a machine be recorded?

10. Distinguish between revenue expenditures and capital expenditures.

11. What are the characteristics of an intangible asset?

12. In general, how are intangible assets accounted for?

13. Define (a) lease, (b) lessor, (c) leasehold, and (d) leasehold improvement.

14. In accounting, when is a business said to have goodwill?

CLASS EXERCISES

Exercise 11-1

A company traded in its old truck on a new truck, receiving a $3,700 trade-in allowance and paying the remaining $12,300 in cash. The old truck had cost $11,000, and straight-line depreciation of $6,000 had been recorded under the assumption it would last five years and have a $1,000 salvage value. Answer the following questions: (a) What was the book value of the old truck? (b) What is the loss on the exchange? (c) Assuming the loss is deemed to be material, what amount should be debited to the New Truck account? (d) Assuming the loss is not material and the income tax method is used to record the exchange, what amount should be debited to the New Truck account?

Exercise 11-2

A machine that cost $4,000 and that had been depreciated $2,500 was disposed of on January 4. Give without explanations the entries to record the disposal under each of the following unrelated assumptions:

a. The machine was sold for $1,750 cash.
b. The machine was sold for $600 cash.
c. The machine was traded in on a new machine of like purpose having a $4,500 cash price. A $1,750 trade-in allowance was received, and the balance was paid in cash.
d. A $600 trade-in allowance was received for the machine on a new machine of like purpose having a $4,500 cash price. The balance was paid in cash, and the loss was considered material.
e. Transaction (d) was recorded by the income tax method because the loss was considered immaterial.

Exercise 11-3

A machine that cost $12,000 was depreciated on a straight-line basis for six years under the assumption it would have an eight-year life and a $2,000 trade-in value. At that point it was recognized that the machine had four years of remaining useful life, after which it would have an estimated $1,500 trade-in value. *(a)* Determine the machine's book value at the end of its sixth year. *(b)* Determine the amount of depreciation to be charged against the machine during each of the remaining years in its life.

Exercise 11–4 A company owns a building that appeared on its balance sheet at the end of last year at its original $246,000 cost less $205,000 accumulated depreciation. The building has been depreciated on a straight-line basis under the assumption it would have a 30-year life and no salvage value. During the first week in January of the current year, major structural repairs were completed on the building at a $64,000 cost. The repairs did not improve the building's usefulness but they did extend its expected life for 10 years beyond the 30 years originally estimated. *(a)* Determine the building's age on last year's balance sheet date. *(b)* Give the entry to record the cost of the repairs. *(c)* Determine the book value of the building after its repairs were recorded. *(d)* Give the entry to record the current year's depreciation.

Exercise 11–5 On January 1, 198A, a company paid $90,000 for an ore body containing 900,000 tons of ore, and it installed machinery costing $150,000, having an estimated 12-year life and no salvage value, and capable of removing the entire ore body in 10 years. The company began mining operations on April 1, and it mined 60,000 tons of ore during the remaining nine months of the year. Give the entries to record the December 31, 198A, depletion of the ore body and the depreciation of the mining machinery.

Exercise 11–6 On January 7, 198A, Able Company purchased the copyright to a trade manual for $30,000. The copyright legally protects its owner for 30 more years. However, management believes the trade manual can be successfully published and sold for only six more years. Prepare journal entries to record *(a)* the purchase of the copyright and *(b)* annual amortization of the copyright on December 31, 198A.

PROBLEMS

Problem 11–1 A company completed these transactions involving the purchase and operation of delivery trucks.

198A
July 7 Paid cash for a new truck, $5,700 plus $285 state and city sales taxes. The truck was estimated to have a four-year life and a $1,500 salvage value.
     10 Paid $315 for special racks and shelves installed in the truck. The racks and shelves did not increase the truck's estimated trade-in value.
Dec. 31 Recorded straight-line depreciation on the truck.

198B
June 26 Paid $410 to install an air-conditioning unit in the truck. The unit increased the truck's estimated trade-in value $50.
Dec. 31 Recorded straight-line depreciation on the truck.

198C

May 29   Paid $55 for repairs to the truck's rear bumper damaged when the driver backed into a loading dock.

Dec. 31   Recorded straight-line depreciation on the truck.

198D

Aug. 26   Traded the old truck and $4,885 in cash for a new truck. The new truck was estimated to have a three-year life and a $1,600 trade-in value, and the invoice for the exchange showed these items:

Price of the truck	$ 6,200
Trade-in allowance granted	$(1,500)
Balance	$ 4,700
State and city sales taxes	185
Balance paid in cash	$ 4,885

The loss on the exchange was considered to be material.

29   Paid $615 for special shelves and racks installed in the truck.

Dec. 31   Recorded straight-line depreciation on the new truck.

Required:

Prepare general journal entries to record the transactions.

Problem 11–2

A company completed the following transactions involving machinery:

Machine No. 133–51 was purchased on April 1, 198A, at an installed cost of $5,400. Its useful life was estimated at four years with a $600 trade-in value. Straight-line depreciation was recorded on the machine at the end of 198A and 198B, and on July 2, 198C, it was traded in on Machine No. 133–85. A $3,000 trade-in allowance was received, and the balance was paid in cash.

Machine No. 133–85 was purchased on July 2, 198C, at an installed cost of $7,000, less the trade-in allowance received on Machine 133–51. The new machine's life was estimated at five years with $700 trade-in value. Sum-of-the-years'-digits depreciation was recorded on each December 31 of its life, and on January 4, 198H, it was sold for $1,000.

Machine No. 133–72 was purchased on January 5, 198C, at an installed cost of $5,000. Its useful life was estimated at five years, after which it would have a $500 trade-in value. Declining-balance depreciation at twice the straight-line rate was recorded on the machine at the end of 198C, 198D, and 198E; and on January 1, 198F, it was traded on Machine No. 133–99. A $900 trade-in allowance was received, the balance was paid in cash, the loss was considered immaterial, and the income tax method was used to record the transaction.

Machine No. 133–99 was purchased on January 1, 198F, at a $5,900 installed cost, less the trade-in allowance received on Machine No. 133–72. It was estimated the new machine would produce 100,000 units of product during its useful life, after which it would have a $600 trade-in value. Units-of-production depreciation was recorded on the machine for 198F, a period in which it produced 10,000 units of product. Between January 1 and October 12, 198G, the machine produced 15,000 more units, and on the latter date it was sold for $4,000.

Required:

Prepare general journal entries to record *(a)* the purchase of each machine, *(b)* the depreciation recorded on the first December 31 of each machine's life, and *(c)* the disposal of each machine. Treat the entries for the first two machines as one series of transactions and those of the next two machines as an unrelated second series. Only one entry is needed to record the exchange of one machine for another.

Problem 11–3

Part 1.   On January 7, 1975, a company purchased and placed in operation a machine estimated to have a 10-year life and no salvage value. The machine cost $15,000 and was depreciated on a straight-line basis. On January 3, 1979, a $600 device that increased its output by one fourth was added to the machine. The device did not change the machine's estimated life nor its zero salvage value. During the first week of January 1982, the machine was completely overhauled at a $4,500 cost (paid for on January 9). The overhaul added three additional years to the machine's estimated life but did not change its zero salvage value. On June 27, 1983, the machine was destroyed in a fire and the insurance company settled the loss claim for $5,000.

Required:

Prepare general journal entries to record *(a)* the purchase of the machine, *(b)* the 1975 depreciation, *(c)* the addition of the new device, *(d)* the 1979 depreciation, *(e)* the machine's overhaul, *(f)* the 1982 depreciation, and *(g)* the insurance settlement.

Part 2.   A company purchased Machine A at a $12,400 installed cost on January 5, 1977, and depreciated it on a straight-line basis at the end of 1977, 1978, 1979, and 1980 under the assumption it would have a 10-year life and a $2,400 salvage value. After more experience and before recording 1981 depreciation, the company revised its estimate of the machine's remaining years downward from six years to four and revised the estimate of its salvage value downward to $2,000. On April 2, 1983, after recording 1981, 1982, and part of a year's depreciation for 1983, the company traded in Machine A on Machine B, receiving a $5,000 trade-in allowance. Machine B cost $16,300, less the trade-in allowance, and the balance was paid in cash. Machine B was depreciated on a straight-line basis on December 31, 1983, under the assumption it would have a six-year life and a $2,300 salvage value.

Required:

Prepare entries to record *(a)* the purchase of Machine A, *(b)* its 1977 depreciation, *(c)* its 1981 depreciation, *(d)* the exchange of the machines, and *(e)* the 1983 depreciation on Machine B.

Problem 11–4

Part 1.   Ten years ago Safety Products Company leased space in a building for a period of 20 years. The lease contract calls for $18,000 annual rental payments on each January 1 throughout the life of the lease, and also provides that the lessee must pay for all additions and improvements to the leased property. Recent construction nearby has made the location more valuable, and on December 20 Safety Products Company subleased the space to Tekcon,

Inc., for the remaining 10 years of the lease, beginning on the next January 1. Tekcon, Inc., paid $40,000 for the privilege of subleasing the property and in addition agreed to assume and pay the building owner the $18,000 annual rental charges. During the first 10 days after taking possession of the leased space, Tekcon, Inc., remodeled the shop front of the leased space at a cost of $56,000. The remodeled shop front is estimated to have a life equal to the remaining life of the building, 20 years, and was paid for on January 12.

Required:

Prepare entries in general journal form to record: *(a)* Tekcon, Inc.'s payment to sublease the shop space, *(b)* its payment of the annual rental charge to the building owner, and *(c)* payment for the new shop front. Also, prepare the adjusting entries required at the end of the first year of the sublease to amortize *(d)* a proper share of the $40,000 cost of the sublease and *(e)* a proper share of the shop front cost.

Part 2. On March 12 of the current year, Deepdrill Company paid $680,000 for mineral land estimated to contain 4,000,000 tons of recoverable ore. It installed machinery costing $120,000, having a 12-year life and no salvage value, and capable of exhausting the mine in 10 years. The machinery was paid for on July 5, three days after mining operations began. During the first six months' operations the company mined 165,000 tons of ore.

Required:

Prepare entries to record *(a)* the purchase of the mineral land, *(b)* the installation of the machinery, *(c)* the first six months' depletion under the assumption that the land will be valueless after the ore is mined, and *(d)* the first six months' depreciation on the machinery.

Problem 11–5   Fast Company's balance sheet on December 31, 198A, is as follows:

Cash	$ 18,000
Merchandise inventory	26,000
Buildings	80,000
Accumulated depreciation	(21,000)
Land	45,000
Total assets	$148,000
Accounts payable	$ 12,000
Long-term note payable	31,000
Common stock	75,000
Retained earnings	30,000
Total liabilities and owners' equity	$148,000

In Fast Company's industry, earnings average 12% of common stockholders' equity. Fast Company, however, is expected to earn $21,000 annually. The owners of Fast Company believe that the balance sheet amounts are reasonable estimates of fair market values except for goodwill. In discussing a plan to sell the company, they argue that goodwill should be recognized by capitalizing the amount of earnings above average at a rate of 15%. On the other hand, the prospective purchaser argues that goodwill should be valued at 5 times the earnings above average.

Required:

1. Calculate the amount of goodwill claimed by Fast Company's owners.
2. Calculate the amount of goodwill according to the purchaser.
3. Suppose the purchaser finally agrees to pay the full price requested by Fast Company's owners. If the expected earnings level is obtained and the goodwill is amortized over the longest permissible time period, what will be the net income for the first year after the company is purchased.
4. If the purchaser pays the full price requested by Fast Company's owners, what percentage of the purchaser's investment will be earned as net income the first year?

ALTERNATE PROBLEMS

Problem 11–1A   Prepare general journals to record these transactions involving the purchase and operation of a secondhand truck:

198A

Jan. 8   Purchased for $3,850 cash a secondhand delivery truck having an estimated three years of remaining useful life and an $800 trade-in value.

       9   Paid Service Garage for the following:

Minor repairs to the truck's motor	$ 32
New tires for the truck	218
Gas and oil	9
Total	$259

Dec. 31   Recorded straight-line depreciation on the truck.

198B

Jan. 4   Paid $550 to install a hydraulic loader on the truck. The loader increased the truck's trade-in value to $850.

June 27   Paid Service Garage for the following:

Minor repairs to the truck's motor	$22
New battery for the truck	38
Gas and oil	8
Total	$68

Nov. 3   Paid $55 for repairs to the hydraulic loader damaged when the driver backed into a loading dock.

Dec. 31   Recorded straight-line depreciation on the truck.

198C

Jan. 11   Paid Service Garage $350 to overhaul the truck's motor, replacing its bearings and rings and extending the truck's life one year beyond the original three years planned. However, it was also estimated that the extra year's operation would reduce the truck's trade-in value to $650.

Dec. 31   Recorded straight-line depreciation on the truck.

198D

July 7 Traded the old truck on a new one having a $5,600 cash price. Received a $1,200 trade-in allowance and paid the balance in cash. (Assume that the loss is not material.)

Problem 11–2A

A company completed the following transactions involving machinery:

Machine No. 133–5 was purchased on May 2, 1976, at an installed cost of $3,000. Its useful life was estimated at five years with no trade-in value. Straight-line depreciation was recorded on the machine at the end of 1976 and 1977; and on January 5, 1978, it was traded in on Machine No. 133–23. An $1,800 trade-in allowance was received, the loss was considered immaterial, and the income tax method was used to record the exchange.

Machine No. 133–23 was purchased on January 5, 1978, at an installed cost of $4,600, less the trade-in allowance received for Machine No. 133–5. Its life was estimated at five years with a $600 trade-in value. Sum-of-the-years'-digits depreciation was recorded on the machine on each December 31 of its life, and it was sold on October 7, 1982, for $800.

Machine No. 133–25 was purchased on January 9, 1978, at an installed cost of $6,400. Its useful life was estimated at four years, after which it would have a $400 salvage value. Declining-balance depreciation at twice the straight-line rate was recorded on the machine on each December 31 of its life, and it was traded in on Machine No. 133–30 on January 4, 1982. A $900 trade-in allowance was received.

Machine No. 133–30 was purchased on January 4, 1982, at an installed cost of $7,000 less the trade-in allowance received on Machine No. 133–25. It was estimated the new machine would produce 12,000 units of product during its life, after which it would have a $500 trade-in value. It produced 2,500 units of product in 1982 and 500 additional units in 1983 before its sale for $4,000 on June 3, 1983.

Required:

Prepare general journal entries to record (a) the purchase of each machine, (b) the depreciation recorded on the first December 31 of each machine's life, and (c) the disposal of each machine. (Treat the entries for the first two machines as one series of transactions and those of the next two machines as an unrelated second series. Only one entry is needed to record the exchange of one machine for another.)

Problem 11–3A

Prepare general journal entries to record the following transactions. Use straight-line depreciation.

1978

Jan. 10 Purchased and placed in operation Machine No. 133–8 at an $18,000 installed cost. The machine's useful life was estimated at six years with no salvage value.

Dec. 31 Recorded depreciation on the machine.

1979

Mar. 14 After a little over 14 months of satisfactory use, Machine No. 133–8 was cleaned, inspected, oiled, and adjusted by a factory representative at a cost of $215.

Dec. 31 Recorded depreciation on Machine No. 133–8.

1980

June 28 Added a new device to Machine No. 133–8 at a $700 cost. The device did not change the machine's expected life nor change its zero salvage value, but it did increase its output by one fourth.

Dec. 31 Recorded depreciation on the machine.

1981

Dec. 31 Recorded depreciation on the machine.

1982

Jan. 9 Repaired and completely overhauled Machine No. 133–8 at a $4,000 cost, consisting of $400 for ordinary repairs and $3,600 for extraordinary repairs. The extraordinary repairs were expected to extend the machine's expected useful life for two years beyond the six years originally expected but were not expected to change its zero salvage value.

Dec. 31 Recorded depreciation on the machine.

1983

July 9 Machine No. 133–8 was destroyed in a fire. The insurance company settled the loss claim for $5,000.

Problem 11–4A

Part 1. Thirteen years ago Haynes Company leased a building for a 25-year period. The lease contract requires a $20,000 annual rental payment on each January 1 throughout the life of the lease, and it requires the lessee to pay for all improvements to the leased property. Due to traffic pattern changes, the lease has become more valuable; and on December 19, Haynes subleased the property for the remaining 12 years of the lease, beginning on January 1, to Hot Tubs. Hot Tubs paid Haynes Company $50,000 for its rights under the lease, and it also agreed to pay the annual rental charges directly to the building owner. In addition, during the first two weeks of January, it remodeled the front of the leased building at a $32,000 total cost, paying the contractor on January 14. The remodeled store front was estimated to have a life equal to the remaining life of the building, 24 years.

Required:

Prepare general journal entries to record Hot Tubs' payments for the sublease, the annual rental charge, and the new store front. Also, prepare the end-of-year adjusting entries to amortize portions of the sublease cost and the cost of the building improvements.

Part 2. On March 2, 198A, Constructor Company paid $300,000 for land containing an estimated 1,000,000 cubic yards of gravel suitable for preparing concrete. The gravel was to be removed by stripping, and the company estimated that it would cost $90,000 to return the land to a condition that would meet governmental safety and ecological standards, after which the land could be sold for its rehabilitation cost. The company installed machinery costing $210,000 (paid for on June 27), having a 10-year life and no salvage value, and capable of exhausting the site in 8 years. During the first six months of operations, ending December 31, the company removed 60,000 yards of gravel.

Required:

Prepare general journal entries to record *(a)* the purchase of the land, *(b)* the installation of the machinery, *(c)* the first six months' depreciation, and *(d)* the first six months' depletion.

Problem 11–5A

The owners of Granger Company are negotiating with a potential buyer for the sale of the company. The balance sheet of Granger Company discloses the following:

Total assets	$360,000
Liabilities	140,000
Common stockholders' equity	$220,000

Granger Company is expected to earn an annual net income of $35,000, even though the industry's average earnings is only 11% of common stockholders' equity.

The owners and the potential buyer agree that the balance sheet fairly values the assets and liabilities of the company, except for unrecorded goodwill. The owners believe goodwill should be measured by capitalizing earnings above average at a rate of 16%. The potential buyer believes goodwill should be measured by multiplying earnings above average times 5.

Required:

1. Calculate the amount of goodwill implied by the owners' belief.
2. Calculate the amount of goodwill implied by the potential buyer's belief.
3. Suppose the buyer agrees to pay the price asked by the owners. If the expected earnings level is obtained and the goodwill is amortized over the longest permissible period, what will be the net income for the first year after the company is purchased?
4. If the buyer pays the full price asked by the owners, what percentage of the buyer's investment will be earned as net income in the first year?

PROVOCATIVE PROBLEMS

Provocative
Problem 11–1,
Err Company

In helping to verify the records of Err Company, you find the following entries:

1984				
Oct.	20	Cash	8,500.00	
		Loss from Fire	3,500.00	
		Accumulated Depreciation, Machinery	9,000.00	
		Machinery		21,000.00
		Received payment of fire loss claim.		
Nov.	15	Cash	24,000.00	
		Factory Land		24,000.00
		Sold unneeded factory land.		

An investigation revealed that the first entry resulted from recording an $8,500 check from an insurance company in full settlement of a loss claim resulting from the destruction of a machine in a small plant fire on September 29, 1984. The machine had originally cost $18,000, was put in operation on January 5, 1980, and had been depreciated on a straight-line basis at the end of each of the first four years in its life under the assumption it would have an eight-year life and no salvage value. During the first week of January 1984, the machine had been overhauled at a $3,000 cost. The overhaul did not increase the machine's capacity nor change its zero salvage value. However, it was expected that the overhaul would lengthen the machine's service life two years beyond the eight originally expected.

The second entry resulted from recording a check received from selling a portion of a tract of land. The tract was adjacent to the company's plant and had been purchased the year before. It cost $32,000, and $3,000 was paid for clearing and grading it. Both amounts had been debited to the Factory Land account. The land was to be used for storing raw materials; but after the grading was completed, it was obvious the company did not need the entire tract, and it was pleased when it received an offer from a purchaser who was willing to pay $18,000 for the east half or $24,000 for the west half. The company decided to sell the west half, and it recorded receipt of the purchaser's check with the entry previously given.

Were any errors made in recording the transactions described here? If so, describe the errors and in each case give an entry or entries that will correct the account balances under the assumption the 1984 revenue and expense accounts have not been closed.

Provocative Problem 11–2, Ray Burchette

Ray Burchette wishes to buy an established business and is considering Companies A and B, both of which have been in business for exactly five years, during which time Company A has reported an average annual net income of $11,835 and Company B has reported an average of $14,250. However, the incomes are not comparable, since the companies have not used the same accounting procedures. Current balance sheets of the companies show these items:

	Company A	Company B
Cash	$ 6,700	$ 8,200
Accounts receivable	51,600	58,500
Allowance for doubtful accounts	(3,200)	–0–
Merchandise inventory	71,300	86,100
Store equipment	28,800	25,600
Accumulated depreciation, store equipment	(24,000)	(16,000)
Total assets	$131,200	$162,400
Current liabilities	$ 62,400	$ 68,900
Owners' equity	68,800	93,500
Total liabilities and owners' equity	$131,200	$162,400

Company A has used the allowance method in accounting for bad debts and has added to its allowance each year an amount equal to 1% of sales. However, this seems excessive since an examination shows only $1,500 of its accounts that are probably uncollectible. Company B, on the other hand, has used the direct write-off method but has been slow to write off bad debts, and an examination of its accounts shows $3,000 of accounts that are probably uncollectible.

During the past five years, Company A has priced its inventories on a LIFO basis with the result that its current inventory appears on its balance sheet at an amount that is $12,000 below replacement cost. Company B has used FIFO, and its ending inventory appears at approximately its replacement cost.

Both companies have assumed eight-year lives and no salvage value in depreciating equipment; however, Company A has used sum-of-the-years'-digits depreciation, while Company B has used straight line. Mr. Burchette is of the opinion that straight-line depreciation has resulted in Company B's equipment appearing on its balance sheet at approximately its fair market value and that it would have had the same result for Company A.

Mr. Burchette is willing to pay what he considers fair market value for the assets of either business, not including cash, but including goodwill measured at four times average annual earnings in excess of 15% on the fair market value of the net tangible assets. He defines net tangible assets as all assets other than goodwill, including accounts receivable, minus liabilities. He will also assume the liabilities of the purchased business, paying its owner the difference between total assets purchased and the liabilities assumed.

Required:

Prepare the following schedules: *(a)* a schedule showing the net tangible assets of each company at their fair market values according to Mr. Burchette, *(b)* a schedule showing the revised net incomes of the companies based on FIFO inventories and straight-line depreciation, *(c)* a schedule showing the calculation of each company's goodwill, and *(d)* a schedule showing the amount Mr. Burchette would pay for each business.

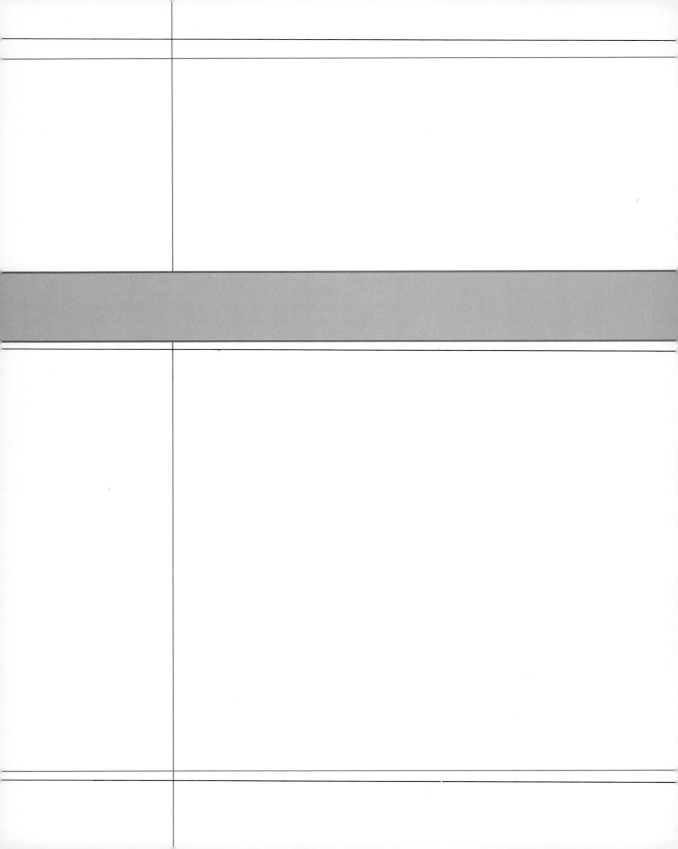

Accounting for Equities: Liabilities and Partners' Equities

PART FOUR

Current and Long-Term Liabilities

12

After studying Chapter 12, you should be able to:

Prepare entries to record transactions involving short-term notes payable.

Explain the concept of present value.

Calculate the present value of a sum of money to be received a number of periods in the future.

Calculate the present value of a sum of money to be received periodically for a number of periods in the future.

Account for a plant asset purchased with a long-term note payable.

Account for a plant asset acquired through leasing.

Define and explain the words and phrases listed in the chapter Glossary.

A liability is a legal obligation requiring the future payment of an asset, the future performance of a service, or the creation of another liability. In accounting for liabilities, the *cost principle* applies and each liability is accounted for at the cost of the asset or service received in exchange for the liability.

A business normally has several kinds of liabilities which are classified as either current or long-term liabilities. Current liabilities are debts or other obligations the liquidation of which is expected to require the use of existing current assets or the creation of other current liabilities.[1] Current liabilities are due within one year of the balance sheet date or the operating cycle of the business, whichever is longer. Accounts payable, short-term notes payable, wages payable, payroll and other taxes payable, and unearned revenues are common examples of current liabilities. *Long-term liabilities* are obligations that will not require the use of existing current assets in their liquidation because they are not to be paid or liquidated within one year or one operating cycle, whichever is longer.

Accounts payable, wages payable, and unearned revenues were discussed in previous chapters. Liabilities resulting from payrolls are discussed in Chapter 13. Consequently, this chapter is devoted to notes payable, liabilities from leasing, and mortgages payable. A discussion of the long-term liability, bonds payable, is deferred to Chapter 17.

SHORT-TERM NOTES PAYABLE

Short-term notes payable often arise in gaining an extension of time in which to pay an account payable. They frequently arise in borrowing from a bank.

Note Given to Secure a Time Extension on an Account

A note payable may be given to secure an extension of time in which to pay an account payable. For example, Brock Company cannot pay its past-due, $600 account with Ajax Company, and Ajax Company has agreed to accept Brock Company's 60-day, 12%, $600 note in granting an extension on the due date of the debt. Brock Company will record the issuance of the note as follows:

---

[1] APB, "Basic Concepts and Accounting Principles Underlying Financial Statements of Business Enterprises," *APB Statement No. 4* (New York: AICPA, October 1970), par. 198.

Aug.	23	Accounts Payable—Ajax Company	600.00	
		Notes Payable		600.00
		Gave a 60-day, 12% note to extend the due date on the amount owed.		

Observe that the note does not pay or retire the debt. It merely changes it from an account payable to a note payable. Ajax Company should prefer the note to the account because in case of default and a lawsuit the note improves its legal position, since the note is written evidence of the debt and its amount.

When the note becomes due, Brock Company will give Ajax Company a check for $612 and record the payment of the note and its interest with an entry like this:

Oct.	22	Notes Payable	600.00	
		Interest Expense	12.00	
		Cash		612.00
		Paid our note with interest.		

Borrowing from a Bank

In lending money, banks distinguish between *loans* and *discounts*. In case of a loan, the bank collects interest when the loan is repaid. In a discount, it deducts interest at the time the loan is made. To illustrate loans and discounts, assume that H. A. Green wishes to borrow approximately $2,000 for 60 days at the prevailing 15% rate of interest.

A LOAN. In a loan transaction, the bank will lend Green $2,000 in exchange for a signed promissory note. The note will read: "Sixty days after date I promise to pay $2,000 with interest at 15%." Green will record the transaction as follows:

Sept.	10	Cash	2,000.00	
		Notes Payable		2,000.00
		Gave the bank a 60-day, 15% note.		

When the note and interest are paid, Green makes this entry:

Nov.	9	Notes Payable	2,000.00	
		Interest Expense	50.00	
		Cash		2,050.00
		Paid the 60-day, 15% note.		

Observe that in a loan transaction the interest is paid at the time the loan is repaid.

A DISCOUNT.   If it is the practice of Green's bank to deduct interest at the time a loan is made, the bank will discount Green's $2,000 note. If it discounts the note at 15% for 60 days, it will deduct from the face amount of the note 60 days' interest at 15%, which is $50, and will give Green the difference, $1,950. The $50 of deducted interest is called the *bank discount,* and the $1,950 are the *proceeds* of the discounted note. Green will record the transaction as follows:

Sept.	10	Cash	1,950.00	
		Interest Expense	50.00	
		Notes Payable		2,000.00
		Discounted a $2,000 note payable at 15%.		

When the note matures, Green is required to pay the bank just the face amount of the note, $2,000, and Green will record the transaction like this:

Nov.	9	Notes Payable	2,000.00	
		Cash		2,000.00
		Paid the discounted note payable.		

Since interest is deducted in a discount transaction at the time the loan is made, the note used in such a transaction must state that only the principal amount is to be repaid at maturity. Such a note may read: "Sixty days after date I promise to pay $2,000 with no interest," and is commonly called a noninterest-bearing note. However, banks are not in business to lend money interest free. Interest is paid in a discount transaction. But since it is deducted at the time the loan is made, the note must state that no additional interest is to be collected at maturity. Nevertheless, interest is collected in a discount transaction and at a rate slightly higher than in a loan transaction at the same stated interest rate. For example, in this instance, Green paid $50 for the use of $1,950 for 60 days, which was at an effective interest rate just a little in excess of 15% on the $1,950 received.

END-OF-PERIOD ADJUSTMENTS

Accrued Interest Expense

Interest accrues daily on all interest-bearing notes. Consequently, if any notes payable are outstanding at the end of an accounting period, the accrued interest should be recorded. For example, a company gave its bank a $4,000, 60-day, 13.5% note on December 16 to borrow that amount of money. If the company's accounting period ends on December 31, by then 15 days' or $22.50 interest has accrued on this note. It may be recorded with this adjusting entry:

Dec.	31	Interest Expense	22.50	
		Interest Payable		22.50
		To record accrued interest on a note payable.		

The adjusting entry causes the $22.50 accrued interest to appear on the income statement as an expense of the period benefiting from 15 days' use of the money. It also causes the interest payable to appear on the balance sheet as a current liability.

When the note matures in the next accounting period, its payment may be recorded as follows:

Feb.	14	Notes Payable	4,000.00	
		Interest Payable	22.50	
		Interest Expense	67.50	
		Cash		4,090.00
		Paid a $4,000 note and its interest.		

Interest on this note for 60 days is $90. In the illustrated entry, the $90 is divided between the interest accrued at the end of the previous period, $22.50, and interest applicable to the current period, $67.50. Some accountants avoid the necessity of making this division by reversing the accrued interest adjusting entry as a last step in their end-of-period work.

Discount on Notes Payable

When a note payable is discounted at a bank, interest based on the principal of the note is deducted and the interest is normally recorded as interest expense. Furthermore, since most such notes run for 30, 60, or 90 days, the interest is usually an expense of the period in which it is deducted. However, when the time of a note extends beyond a single accounting period, an adjusting entry is required. For example, on December 11, 198A, a company discounted at 15% its own $6,000, 60-day, noninterest-bearing note payable. It recorded the transaction as follows:

198A				
Dec.	11	Cash	5,850.00	
		Interest Expense	150.00	
		Notes Payable		6,000.00
		Discounted our noninterest-bearing, 60-day note at 15%.		

If this company operates with accounting periods that end each December 31, 20 days' interest on this note, or $50 of the $150 of discount, is an expense of the 198A accounting period, and 40 days' interest or $100 is an expense of 198B. Consequently, if revenues and expenses are matched, the company must make the following December 31, 198A, adjusting entry:

198A				
Dec.	31	Discount on Notes Payable	100.00	
		Interest Expense		100.00
		To set up as a contra liability the interest applicable to 198B.		

The adjusting entry removes from the Interest Expense account the $100 of interest that is applicable to 198B. It leaves in the account the $50 that is an expense of 198A. The $50 then appears on the 198A income statement as an expense, and the $100 appears on the December 31, 198A, balance sheet. If this is the only note the company has outstanding, the $100 is deducted on the balance sheet as follows:

Current liabilities:		
Notes payable	$6,000	
Less discount on notes payable.....	100	$5,900

When the adjusted discount on notes payable is subtracted as a contra liability, the net liability on the balance sheet shows the amount received in discounting the note plus the accrued interest on the note to the balance sheet date. In this example, $5,850 was received in discounting the note, and accrued interest on the note is $50. Together they total $5,900, which is the net liability to the bank on December 31.

The $100 interest set out as discount on notes payable in the previous paragraphs becomes an expense early in 198B. Consequently, sooner or later it must be taken from the Discount on Notes Payable account and returned to the Interest Expense account. Accountants commonly make this return with a *reversing entry*. The entry is made as the last step in the end-of-period work and is dated the first day of the new accounting period. Such a reversing entry appears as follows:

198B				
Jan.	1	Interest Expense	100.00	
		Discount on Notes Payable		100.00
		To reverse the adjusting entry that set out		
		discount on notes payable.		

Observe that the reversing entry is debit for credit and credit for debit the reverse of the adjusting entry it reverses. That is where it gets its name. Also, observe that it returns the $100 interest to the expense account so that it will appear on the 198B income statement as an expense without further ado.

THE CONCEPT OF PRESENT VALUE

The concept of present value enters into many financing and investing decisions and any resulting liabilities. Consequently, an understanding of it is important. The concept is based on the idea that the right to receive, say, $1 a year from today is worth somewhat less than $1 today. Or stated another way, $1 to be received a year hence has a *present value* of somewhat less than $1. How much less depends on how much can be earned on invested funds. If, say, a 10% annual return can be earned, the expectation of receiving $1 a year hence has a present value of $0.9091. This can be verified as follows: $0.9091 invested today to earn 10% annually will earn $0.0909 in one year, and when the $0.0909 earned is added to the $0.9091 invested—

Investment	$0.9091
Earnings	0.09091
Total	$1.00001

the investment plus the earnings equal $1.00001, which rounds to the $1 expected.

Likewise, the present value of $1 to be received two years hence is $0.8265 if a 10% compound annual return is expected. This also can be verified as follows: $0.8265 invested to earn 10% compounded annually will earn $0.08265 the first year it is invested, and when the $0.08265 earned is added to the $0.8265 invested—

Investment	$0.8265
First year earnings	0.08265
End-of-year-one amount.....	$0.90915

the investment plus the first year's earnings total $0.90915. And during the second year, this $0.90915 will earn $0.090915, which when added to the end-of-first-year amount—

End-of-year-one amount	$0.90915
Second year earnings	0.090915
End-of-year-two amount	$1.000065

equals $1.000065, which rounds to the $1 expected at the end of the second year.

Present Value Tables

The present value of $1 to be received any number of years in the future can be calculated by using the formula, $1/(1 + i)^n$. The i is the interest rate, and n is the number of years to the expected receipt. However, the formula need not be used, since tables showing present values computed with the formula at various interest rates are readily available. Table 12–1, with its amounts rounded to four decimal places, is such a table. (Four decimal places would not be sufficiently accurate for some uses but will suffice here.)

Observe in Table 12–1 that the first amount in the 10% column is the 0.9091 used in the previous section to introduce the concept of present value. The 0.9091 in the 10% column means that the expectation of receiving $1 a year hence when discounted for one period, in this case one year, at 10%, has a present value of $0.9091. Then, note that the second amount in the 10% column is the 0.8265 previously used, which means that the expectation of receiving $1 two years hence, discounted at 10%, has a present value of $0.8265.

Table 12–1

Present Value of $1 at Compound Interest

Periods hence	4½%	5%	6%	7%	8%	9%	10%	12%	14%	16%
1	0.9569	0.9524	0.9434	0.9346	0.9259	0.9174	0.9091	0.8929	0.8772	0.8621
2	0.9157	0.9070	0.8900	0.8734	0.8573	0.8417	0.8265	0.7972	0.7695	0.7432
3	0.8763	0.8638	0.8396	0.8163	0.7938	0.7722	0.7513	0.7118	0.6750	0.6407
4	0.8386	0.8227	0.7921	0.7629	0.7350	0.7084	0.6830	0.6355	0.5921	0.5523
5	0.8025	0.7835	0.7473	0.7130	0.6806	0.6499	0.6209	0.5674	0.5194	0.4761
6	0.7679	0.7462	0.7050	0.6663	0.6302	0.5963	0.5645	0.5066	0.4556	0.4104
7	0.7348	0.7107	0.6651	0.6228	0.5835	0.5470	0.5132	0.4524	0.3996	0.3538
8	0.7032	0.6768	0.6274	0.5820	0.5403	0.5019	0.4665	0.4039	0.3506	0.3050
9	0.6729	0.6446	0.5919	0.5439	0.5003	0.4604	0.4241	0.3606	0.3075	0.2630
10	0.6439	0.6139	0.5584	0.5084	0.4632	0.4224	0.3855	0.3220	0.2697	0.2267
11	0.6162	0.5847	0.5268	0.4751	0.4289	0.3875	0.3505	0.2875	0.2366	0.1954
12	0.5897	0.5568	0.4970	0.4440	0.3971	0.3555	0.3186	0.2567	0.2076	0.1685
13	0.5643	0.5303	0.4688	0.4150	0.3677	0.3262	0.2897	0.2292	0.1821	0.1452
14	0.5400	0.5051	0.4423	0.3878	0.3405	0.2993	0.2633	0.2046	0.1597	0.1252
15	0.5167	0.4810	0.4173	0.3625	0.3152	0.2745	0.2394	0.1827	0.1401	0.1079
16	0.4945	0.4581	0.3937	0.3387	0.2919	0.2519	0.2176	0.1631	0.1229	0.0930
17	0.4732	0.4363	0.3714	0.3166	0.2703	0.2311	0.1978	0.1456	0.1078	0.0802
18	0.4528	0.4155	0.3503	0.2959	0.2503	0.2120	0.1799	0.1300	0.0946	0.0691
19	0.4333	0.3957	0.3305	0.2765	0.2317	0.1945	0.1635	0.1161	0.0830	0.0596
20	0.4146	0.3769	0.3118	0.2584	0.2146	0.1784	0.1486	0.1037	0.0728	0.0514

Using a Present Value Table

To demonstrate the use of the *present value table,* Table 12–1, assume that a company has an opportunity to invest $55,000 in a project, the risks of which it feels justify a 12% compound return. The investment will return $20,000 at the end of the first year, $25,000 at the end of the second year, $30,000 at the end of the third year, and nothing thereafter. Will the project return the original investment plus the 12% demanded? The calculations of Illustration 12–1, which use the first three amounts in the 12% column of the Table 12–1, indicate that it will. In Illustration 12–1, the expected returns in the second column are multiplied by the present value amounts in the third column to determine the present values in the last column. Since the total of the present values exceeds the required investment by $4,142, the project will return the $55,000 investment, plus a 12% return thereon, and $4,142 extra.

In Illustration 12–1, the present value of each year's return was separately calculated, after which the present values were added to determine their total. Separately calculating the present value of each of several returns from an investment is necessary when the returns

Illustration 12–1

Years hence	Expected returns	Present value of $1 at 12%	Present value of expected returns
1	$20,000	0.8929	$17,858
2	$25,000	0.7972	19,930
3	$30,000	0.7118	21,354
Total present value of the returns			$59,142
Less investment required			55,000
Excess over 12% demanded			$ 4,142

are unequal, as in this example. However, in cases where the periodic returns are equal, there are shorter ways of calculating the sum of their present values. For instance, suppose a $17,500 investment will return $5,000 at the end of each year in its five-year life and an investor wants to know the present value of these returns, discounted at 12%. In this case, the periodic returns are equal, and a short way to determine their total present value at 12% is to add the present values of $1 at 12% for periods one through five (from Table 12–1), as follows—

0.8929
0.7972
0.7118
0.6355
0.5674
3.6048

and then to multiply $5,000 by the total. The $18,024 result ($5,000 × 3.6048 = $18,024) is the same as would be obtained by calculating the present value of each year's return and adding the present values. However, although the result is the same either way, the method demonstrated here requires four fewer multiplications.

Present Value of $1 Received Periodically for a Number of Periods

Table 12–2 is based on the idea demonstrated in the previous paragraph. To summarize, the present value of a series of equal returns to be received at periodic intervals is nothing more than the sum of the present values of the individual returns. Note the amount on the table's fifth line in the 12% column. It is the same 3.6048 amount arrived at in the previous section by adding the first five present values of $1 at 12%. All the amounts shown in Table 12–2 could be arrived

Table 12–2

Present Value of $1 Received Periodically for a Number of Periods

Periods hence	4½%	5%	6%	7%	8%	9%	10%	12%	14%	16%
1	0.9569	0.9524	0.9434	0.9346	0.9259	0.9174	0.9091	0.8929	0.8772	0.8621
2	1.8727	1.8594	1.8334	1.8080	1.7833	1.7591	1.7355	1.6901	1.6467	1.6052
3	2.7490	2.7232	2.6730	2.6243	2.5771	2.5313	2.4869	2.4018	2.3216	2.2459
4	3.5875	3.5460	3.4651	3.3872	3.3121	3.2397	3.1699	3.0374	2.9137	2.7982
5	4.3900	4.3295	4.2124	4.1002	3.9927	3.8897	3.7908	3.6048	3.4331	3.2743
6	5.1579	5.0757	4.9173	4.7665	4.6229	4.4859	4.3553	4.1114	3.8887	3.6847
7	5.8927	5.7864	5.5824	5.3893	5.2064	5.0330	4.8684	4.5638	4.2883	4.0386
8	6.5959	6.4632	6.2098	5.9713	5.7466	5.5348	5.3349	4.9676	4.6389	4.3436
9	7.2688	7.1078	6.8017	6.5152	6.2469	5.9953	5.7590	5.3283	4.9464	4.6065
10	7.9127	7.7217	7.3601	7.0236	6.7101	6.4177	6.1446	5.6502	5.2161	4.8332
11	8.5289	8.3064	7.8869	7.4987	7.1390	6.8052	6.4951	5.9377	5.4527	5.0286
12	9.1186	8.8633	8.3838	7.9427	7.5361	7.1607	6.8137	6.1944	5.6603	5.1971
13	9.6829	9.3936	8.8527	8.3577	7.9038	7.4869	7.1034	6.4236	5.8424	5.3423
14	10.2228	9.8986	9.2950	8.7455	8.2442	7.7862	7.3667	6.6282	6.0021	5.4675
15	10.7395	10.3797	9.7123	9.1079	8.5595	8.0607	7.6061	6.8109	6.1422	5.5755
16	11.2340	10.8378	10.1059	9.4467	8.8514	8.3126	7.8237	6.9740	6.2651	5.6685
17	11.7072	11.2741	10.4773	9.7632	9.1216	8.5436	8.0216	7.1196	6.3729	5.7487
18	12.1600	11.6896	10.8276	10.0591	9.3719	8.7556	8.2014	7.2497	6.4674	5.8179
19	12.5933	12.0853	11.1581	10.3356	9.6036	8.9501	8.3649	7.3658	6.5504	5.8775
20	13.0079	12.4622	11.4699	10.5940	9.8182	9.1286	8.5136	7.4694	6.6231	5.9288

at by adding amounts found in Table 12–1. However, there would be some slight variations due to rounding.

When available, Table 12–2 is used to determine the present value of a series of equal amounts to be received at periodic intervals. For example, what is the present value of a series of ten $1,000 amounts, with one $1,000 amount to be received at the end of each of 10 successive years, discounted at 8%? To determine the answer, go down the 8% column to the amount opposite 10 periods (years in this case). It is 6.7101, and $6.7101 is the present value of $1 to be received annually at the end of each of 10 years, discounted at 8%. Therefore, the present value of the ten $1,000 amounts is 1,000 times $6.7101, or $6710.10.

Discount Periods Less than a Year in Length

In the examples thus far, the discount periods have been measured in intervals one year in length. Often discount periods are based on intervals shorter than a year. For instance, although interest rates on corporation bonds are usually quoted on an annual basis, the interest on such bonds is normally paid semiannually. As a result, the present value of the interest to be received on such bonds must be based on interest periods six months in length.

To illustrate a calculation based on six-month interest periods, assume an investor wants to know the present value of the interest that will be received over a period of five years on some corporation bonds. The bonds have a $10,000 par value, and interest is paid on them every six months at a 14% annual rate. Although the interest rate is stated as an annual rate of 14%, it is actually a rate of 7% per six-month interest period. Consequently, the investor will receive $10,000 times 7% or $700 in interest on these bonds at the end of each six-month interest period. In five years, there are 10 such periods. Therefore, if these 10 receipts of $700 each are to be discounted at the interest rate of the bonds, to determine their present value, go down the 7% column of Table 12–2 to the amount opposite 10 periods. It is 7.0236, and the present value of the ten $700 semiannual receipts is 7.0236 times $700, or $4,916.52.

EXCHANGING A NOTE FOR A PLANT ASSET

When a relatively high-cost plant asset is purchased, particularly if the credit period is long, a note is sometimes given in exchange for the purchased asset. If the amount of the note is approximately equal to the cash price for the asset and the interest on the note is at approximately the prevailing rate, the transaction is recorded as follows:

Feb	12	Store Equipment	4,500.00	
		Notes Payable		4,500.00
		Exchanged a $4,500, three-year, 16% note payable for a refrigerated display case.		

A note given in exchange for a plant asset has two elements, which may or may not be stipulated in the note. They are (1) a dollar amount equivalent to the bargained cash price of the asset and (2) an interest factor to compensate the supplier for the use of the funds that otherwise would have been received in a cash sale. Consequently, when a note is exchanged for a plant asset and the face amount of the note approximately equals the cash price of the asset and the note's interest rate is at or near the prevailing rate, the asset may be recorded at the face amount of the note as in the previous illustration.

In addition to paying interest, a long-term note commonly requires the borrower to make periodic payments to reduce the debt. For example, if the note in the previous illustration requires semiannual interest payments plus semiannual $750 payments to reduce the debt, the following entry is used to record the first semiannual payment:

Aug.	12	Notes Payable	750.00	
		Interest Expense [(16% × $4,500) ÷ 2]	360.00	
		Cash		1,100.00

Sometimes no interest rate is stated on a note, or the interest rate is unreasonable, or the face amount of the note materially differs from the cash price for the asset. In such cases, the asset should be recorded at its cash price or at the present value of the note, whichever is more clearly determinable.[2] In such a situation, to record the asset at the face amount of the note would cause the asset, the liability, and interest expense to be misstated. Furthermore, the misstatements could be material in case of a long-term note.

To illustrate a situation in which a note having no interest rate stated is exchanged for a plant asset, assume that on January 2, 198A, a noninterest-bearing, five-year, $10,000 note payable is exchanged for a factory machine, the cash price of which is not readily determinable. If the prevailing rate for interest on the day of the exchange is 14%, the present value of the note on that day is $5,194 [based on the fifth amount in the 14% column of Table 12–1 ($10,000 × 0.5194 = $5,194)], and the exchange should be recorded as follows:

198A				
Jan.	2	Factory Machinery	5,194.00	
		Discount on Notes Payable	4,806.00	
		Long-Term Notes Payable		10,000.00
		Exchanged a five-year, noninterest-bearing note for a machine.		

The $5,194 debit amount in the entry is the present value of the note on the day of the exchange. It is also the cost of the machine and is the amount to be used in calculating depreciation and any future loss or gain on the machine's sale or exchange. The entry's notes payable and discount amounts together measure the liability resulting

---

[2] APB, "Interest on Receivables and Payables," *APB Opinion No. 21* (New York: AICPA, August 1971), pars. 8 and 12.

from the transaction. They should appear on a balance sheet prepared immediately after the exchange as follows:

Long-term liabilities:
Long-term notes payable $10,000
Less unamortized discount based on the 14% interest
rate prevailing on the date of issue 4,806 $5,194

The $4,806 discount is a contra liability and also the interest element of the transaction. Column 3 of Illustration 12–2 shows the portions of the $4,806 that should be amortized and charged to Interest Expense at the end of each of the five years in the life of the note.

The first year's amortization entry is:

198A			
Dec.	31	Interest Expense	727.00	
		Discount on Notes Payable		727.00
		To amortize a portion of the discount on our long-term note.		

The $727 amortized is interest at 14% on the note's $5,194 value on the day it was exchanged for the machine. [The $727 is rounded to the nearest full dollar, as are all the Column 3 amounts ($5,194 × 14% = $727.16).]

Posting the amortization entry causes the note to appear on the December 31, 198A, balance sheet as follows:

Long-term liabilities:
Long-term notes payable $10,000
Less unamortized discount based on the 14% interest
rate prevailing on the date of issue 4,079 $5,921

Illustration 12–2

Year	Beginning-of-year carrying amount	Discount to be amortized each year	Unamortized discount at the end of year	End-of-year carrying amount
198A	$5,194	$ 727	$4,079	$ 5,921
198B	5,921	829	3,250	6,750
198C	6,750	945	2,305	7,695
198D	7,695	1,077	1,228	8,772
198E	8,772	1,228	–0–	10,000

Compare the net amount at which the note is carried on the December 31, 198A, balance sheet with the net amount shown for the note on the balance sheet prepared on its date of issue. Observe that the *carrying amount* increased $727 between the two dates. The $727 is the amount of discount amortized and charged to Interest Expense at the end of 198A.

At the end of 198B and each succeeding year, the remaining amounts of discount shown in Column 3 of Illustration 12–2 should be amortized and charged to Interest Expense. This will cause the carrying amount of the note to increase each year by the amount of discount amortized that year and to reach $10,000, the note's maturity value, at the end of the fifth year. Payment of the note may then be recorded as follows:

198F					
Jan.	2	Long-Term Notes Payable	10,000.00	
		Cash		10,000.00
		Paid our long-term noninterest-bearing note.		

Now return to Illustration 12–2. Each end-of-year carrying amount in the last column is determined by subtracting the end-of-year unamortized discount from the $10,000 face amount of the note. For example, $10,000 − $4,079 = $5,921. Each beginning-of-year carrying amount is the same as the previous year's end-of-year amount. The amount of discount to be amortized each year is determined by multiplying the beginning-of-year carrying amount by the 14% interest rate prevailing at the time of the exchange. For example, $5,921 × 14% = $829 (rounded). Each end-of-year amount of unamortized discount is the discount remaining after subtracting the discount amortized that year. For example, $4,806 − $727 = $4,079.

In the balance sheet at the end of each year, the carrying amount of a note payable must be divided into two parts. The portion to be paid during the next year must be shown as a current liability, with the remaining portion shown as a long-term liability.

ISSUING A MORTGAGE TO BORROW MONEY

When a business seeks to borrow money by signing a long-term note payable, the lender may also be given a mortgage on some of the plant assets of the business. The mortgage actually involves two legal documents. The first is the long-term note payable, sometimes called a mortgage note, which is secured by a second legal document called a *mortgage* or a *mortgage contract*. In the note payable (the mortgage note), the borrower promises to repay the money borrowed and to pay interest. The mortgage or mortgage contract commonly requires the borrower (the mortgagor) to keep the property in a good state of repair and to carry adequate insurance. In addition, it grants the mortgage holder the right to foreclose in case the mortgagor fails to perform any of the duties required by the mortgage note and the mortgage contract. In a foreclosure, a court takes possession of the mortgaged property for the mortgage holder and may order its sale. If the property is sold, the proceeds go first to pay court costs and then the claims of the mortgage holder. Any money remaining is paid to the former owner of the property.

Whether or not a long-term note payable is a mortgage note or is unsecured, accounting for the note is the same. However, the existence of mortgages on some or all of a business's plant assets should be disclosed in a footnote to the financial statements.

LIABILITIES FROM LEASING

The leasing of plant assets, rather than purchasing them, has increased tremendously in recent years, primarily because leasing does not require a large cash outflow at the time the assets are acquired. Leasing has been called off balance sheet financing because assets leased under certain conditions do not appear on the balance sheet of the lessee. However, some leases have essentially the same economic consequences as if the lessee secured a loan and purchased the leased asset. Such leases are called *capital leases* or *financing leases*. The FASB ruled that a lease meeting any one of the following criteria is a capital lease.[3]

1. Ownership of the leased asset is transferred to the lessee at the end of the lease period.
2. The lease gives the lessee the option of purchasing the leased asset at less than fair value at some point during or at the end of the lease period.
3. The period of the lease is 75% or more of the estimated service life of the leased asset.
4. The present value of the minimum lease payments is 90% or more of the fair value of the leased asset.

---

[3] FASB, "Accounting for Leases," *FASB Statement No. 13* (Stamford, Conn., 1976), par. 7. Copyright © by the Financial Accounting Standards Board, High Ridge Park, Stamford, Conn. 06905, U.S.A. Quoted (or excerpted) with permission. Copies of the complete document are available from the FASB.

A lease that does not meet any one of the four criteria is classified as an *operating lease*.

To illustrate accounting for leases, assume that Alpha Company plans to produce a product requiring the use of a new machine costing approximately $35,000 and having an estimated 10-year life and no salvage value. Alpha Company does not have $35,000 in available cash and is planning to lease the machine as of December 31, 198A. It will lease the machine under one of the following contracts, each of which requires Alpha Company to pay maintenance, taxes, and insurance on the machine: (1) Lease the machine for five years, annual payments of $7,500 payable at the end of each of the five years, the machine to be returned to the lessor at the end of the lease period. (2) Lease the machine for five years, annual payments of $10,000 payable at the end of each of the five years, the machine to become the property of Alpha Company at the end of the lease period.

If the interest rate available to Alpha Company is 16%, the first lease contract does not meet any of the four criteria of the FASB. Therefore, it is an operating lease. If Alpha Company chooses this contract, it should make no entry to record the lease contract. However, each annual rental payment should be recorded as follows:

198B					
Dec.	31	Machinery Rentals Expense	7,500.00	
		Cash		7,500.00
		Paid the annual rent on a leased machine.		

Alpha Company should also charge to expense all payments for taxes, insurance, and any repairs to the machine. But since the leased machine was not recorded as an asset, depreciation expense is not recorded. Alpha should also append a footnote to its income statement giving a general description of the leasing arrangements.

The second lease contract meets the first and fourth criteria of the FASB and is a capital lease. It is in effect a purchase transaction with the lessor company financing the purchase of the machine for Alpha Company. To charge each of the $10,000 lease payments to an expense account would overstate expenses during the first five years of the machine's life and understate expenses during the last five. It would also understate the company's assets and liabilities. Consequently, the FASB ruled that such a lease should be treated as a purchase transaction and be recorded on the lease date at the present value of the lease payments.

If Alpha Company chooses the second lease contract and the interest rate available to Alpha on such contracts is 16% annually, it should (based on the fifth amount in the 16% column of Table 12–2) multiply $10,000 by 3.2743 to arrive at a $32,743 present value for the five lease payments. It should then make this entry:

198A				
Dec.	31	Machinery	32,743.00	
		Discount on Lease Financing	17,257.00	
		Long-Term Lease Liability		50,000.00
		Purchased a machine through a long-term lease contract.		

The $32,743 is the cost of the machine. As with any plant asset, it should be charged off to depreciation expense over the machine's expected service life. Note, however, that the expected service life of a leased asset may be limited to the term of the lease. If the lessee does not have the right to ownership at the end of the lease, and the lease period is less than the asset's expected life, the lease period becomes the useful life of the asset.

The $17,257 discount is the interest factor in the transaction. The long-term lease liability less the amount of the discount measures the net liability resulting from the purchase. The two items should appear on a balance sheet prepared immediately after the transaction as follows:

Long-term liabilities:		
Long-term lease liability[4]	$50,000	
Less unamortized discount based on the 16%		
interest rate available on the date		
of the contract	17,257	$32,743

If Alpha Company plans to depreciate the machine on a straight-line basis over its 10-year life, it should make the following entries at the end of the first year in the life of the lease:

---

[4] To simplify the illustration, the fact that the first installment on the lease should probably be classified as a current liability is ignored here and should be ignored in the problems at the end of the chapter.

198B				
Dec.	31	Depreciation Expense, Machinery .... Accumulated Depreciation, Machinery ..... To record depreciation on the machine.	3,274.30	3,274.30
	31	Long-Term Lease Liability .... Cash .... Made the annual payment on the lease.	10,000.00	10,000.00
	31	Interest Expense .... Discount on Lease Financing .... Amortized a portion of the discount on the lease financing.	5,239.00	5,239.00

The first two entries need no comment. The $5,239 amortized in the third entry is interest at 16% for one year on the $32,743 beginning-of-year carrying amount of the lease liability ($32,743 × 16% = $5,239). The $5,239 is rounded to the nearest full dollar, as are all amounts in Column 5 of Illustration 12–3.

Posting the entries recording the $10,000 payment and the amortization of the discount causes the lease liability to appear on the December 31, 198B, balance sheet as follows:

Long-term liabilities:
Long-term lease liability $40,000
Less unamortized discount based on the 16% interest
rate prevailing on the date of the contract 12,018 $27,982

Illustration 12–3

Year	Beginning-of-year lease liability	Beginning-of-year unamortized discount	Beginning-of-year carrying amount	Discount to be amortized	Unamortized discount at the end of year	End-of-year lease liability	End-of-year carrying amount
198B	$50,000	$17,257	$32,743	$5,239	$12,018	$40,000	$27,982
198C	40,000	12,018	27,982	4,477	7,541	30,000	22,459
198D	30,000	7,541	22,459	3,593	3,948	20,000	16,052
198E	20,000	3,948	16,052	2,568	1,380	10,000	8,620
198F	10,000	1,380	8,620	1,380*	–0–	–0–	–0–

* Adjusted for rounding.

At the end of 198C and each succeeding year thereafter, the remaining amounts in Column 5 of Illustration 12–3 should be amortized. This, together with $10,000 annual payments, will reduce the carrying amount of the lease liability to zero by the end of the fifth year.

Return again to Illustration 12–3, Column 5. Each year's amount of discount to be amortized is determined by multiplying the beginning-of-year carrying amount of the lease liability by 16%. For example, the 198C amount to be amortized is $4,477 ($27,982 × 16% = $4,477 rounded). Likewise, each end-of-year carrying amount is determined by subtracting the end-of-year unamortized discount from the remaining end-of-year lease liability. For example, the December 31, 198C, carrying amount is $30,000 − $7,541 = $22,459.

GLOSSARY

Bank discount.   Interest charged and deducted by a bank in discounting a note.

Capital lease.   A lease having essentially the same economic consequences as if the lessee had secured a loan and purchased the leased asset.

Carrying amount of a note.   The face amount of a note minus the unamortized discount on the note.

Carrying amount of a lease.   The remaining lease liability minus the unamortized discount on the lease financing.

Financing lease.   Another name for a capital lease.

Long-term liabilities.   Debts or obligations that will not require the use of existing current assets in their liquidation because they are not to be paid or liquidated within one year or one operating cycle, whichever is longer.

Mortgage.   A lien or prior claim to an asset or assets given by a borrower to a lender as security for a loan.

Mortgage contract.   A document setting forth the terms under which a mortgage loan is made.

Operating lease.   A lease not meeting any of the criteria of the FASB that would make it a capital lease.

Present value.   The estimated worth today of an amount of money to be received at a future date.

Present value table.   A table showing the present value of one amount to be received at various future dates when discounted at various interest rates.

QUESTIONS FOR CLASS DISCUSSION

1.   Define *(a)* a current liability and *(b)* a long-term liability.
2.   The legal position of a company may be improved by its acceptance of

a promissory note in exchange for granting a time extension on the due date of a customer's debt. Why?

3. What distinction do banks make between loans and discounts?

4. Which is to the advantage of a bank *(a)* making a loan to a customer in exchange for the customer's $1,000, 60-day, 9% note or *(b)* making a loan to the customer by discounting the customer's $1,000 noninterest-bearing note for 60 days at 9%? Why?

5. Distinguish between bank discount and cash discount.

6. What determines the present value of $1,000 to be received at some future date?

7. If a $5,000, noninterest-bearing, five-year note is exchanged for a machine, what two elements of the transaction are represented in the $5,000 face amount of the note?

8. If the Machinery account is debited for $5,000 and Notes Payable is credited for $5,000 in recording the machine of Question 7, what effects will this have on the financial statements?

9. What is the advantage of leasing a plant asset instead of purchasing it?

10. Distinguish between a capital lease and an operating lease. Which causes an asset and a liability to appear on the balance sheet?

11. At what amount is a machine acquired through a capital lease recorded?

12. What two legal documents are involved when money is borrowed by mortgaging property? What does each document require of the mortgagor?

CLASS EXERCISES

Exercise 12–1

On December 16, 198A, a company borrowed $60,000 by giving a 60-day, 10% note payable to a bank. The company does not make reversing entries. Prepare general journal entries to record *(a)* the issuance of the note, *(b)* the required year-end adjusting entry, and *(c)* the entry to pay the note.

Exercise 12–2

On December 16, 198A, a company discounted its own $60,000, 60-day note payable at the bank. The discount rate was 10%. Prepare general journal entries to record *(a)* the issuance of the note, *(b)* the required year-end adjusting entry, *(c)* the reversing entry on January 1, 198B, and *(d)* the entry to pay the note.

Exercise 12–3

Present calculations to show the following: *(a)* The present value of $15,000 to be received five years hence, discounted at 12%. *(b)* The total present value of three payments consisting of $8,000 to be received one year hence, $12,000 to be received two years hence, and $16,000 to be received three years hence, all discounted at 10%. *(c)* The present value of five payments of $4,000 each, with a payment to be received at the end of each of the next five years, discounted at 14%.

Exercise 12–4

Equipment was purchased on January 1 of the current year, with the terms of purchase including $2,000 cash plus a $7,000, noninterest-bearing, four-year note. The available interest rate on this date was 8%. *(a)* Prepare the entry to record the purchase of the machine. *(b)* Show how the liability will appear on a balance sheet prepared on the day of the purchase. *(c)* Prepare the entry to amortize a portion of the discount on the note at the end of its first year.

Exercise 12–5   On January 1, 198A, a day when the available interest rate was 12%, a company had an opportunity to either buy a machine for $21,000 cash or lease it for six years under a contract calling for a $5,000 annual lease payment at the end of each of the next six years, with the machine becoming the property of the lessee company at the end of that period. The company decided to lease the machine. Prepare entries to record *(a)* the leasing of the machine, *(b)* the amortization of the discount of the lease financing at the end of the first year, and *(c)* the first annual payment under the lease.

PROBLEMS

Problem 12–1   Prepare general journal entries to record these transactions:

Mar. 5   Purchased merchandise on credit from Monroe Company, invoice dated March 3, terms 2/10, n/60, $4,000.

May 2   Borrowed money at Guaranty Bank by discounting our own $6,000 note payable for 60 days at 14%.

8   Gave Monroe Company $1,000 cash and a $3,000, 60-day, 14% note to secure an extension on our past-due account.

July 1   Paid the note discounted at Guaranty Bank on May 2.

7   Paid the note given Monroe Company on May 8.

Nov. 1   Borrowed money at Guaranty Bank by discounting our own $8,000 note payable for 90 days at 15%.

Dec. 1   Borrowed money at Security Bank by giving a $4,000, 60-day, 15% note payable.

31   Made an adjusting entry to remove from the Interest Expense account the interest applicable to next year on the note discounted at Guaranty Bank on November 1.

31   Made an adjusting entry to record the accrued interest on the note given Security Bank on December 1.

31   Made a reversing entry dated January 1 to return to the Interest Expense account the interest on the note discounted at Guaranty Bank.

Jan. 30   Paid the note discounted at Guaranty Bank on November 1.

30   Paid the note given Security Bank on December 1.

Problem 12–2   On January 2, 198A, a company gave its own $70,000, noninterest-bearing, four-year note payable in exchange for a machine the cash price of which was not readily determinable. The market rate for interest on such notes on the day of the exchange was 10% annually.

Required:

1. Prepare a form with the following columnar headings and calculate and fill in the required amounts for the four years the note is outstanding. (Round all amounts to the nearest full dollar.)

Year	Beginning-of-Year Carrying Amount	Discount to Be Amortized Each Year	Unamortized Discount at End of Year	End-of-Year Carrying Amount

2. Prepare general journal entries to record *(a)* the acquisition of the machine, *(b)* the discount amortized at the end of each year, and *(c)* the payment of the note on January 2, 198E.
3. Show how the note should appear on the December 31, 198C, balance sheet.

Problem 12–3

Lee Jordan has worked with a yacht designer and shipyard in planning the construction of a 100-foot, gaff-rigged schooner that Jordan expects to acquire and place in charter service. The yacht will be completed and ready for service four years hence. If Jordan pays for the yacht upon completion (Payment Plan A), it will cost $450,000. However, two alternative payment plans are available. Plan B would require an immediate payment of $325,000. Plan C would require four annual payments of $95,000, the first of which would be made one year hence. In evaluating the three alternatives, Jordan decides to assume an interest rate of 10%.

Required:

Calculate the present value of each payment plan and indicate which plan Jordan should follow.

Problem 12–4

Cranston Company leased a machine on January 1, 198A, under a contract calling for annual payments of $20,000 on December 31 at the end of each of four years, with the machine becoming the property of the lessee company after the fourth $20,000 payment. The machine was estimated to have an eight-year life and no salvage value, and the interest rate available to Cranston for equipment loans on the day the lease was signed was 10%. The machine was delivered on January 3, 198A, and was immediately placed in operation. At the beginning of the eighth year in the machine's life, it was overhauled at a $1,275 total cost. The overhaul was paid for on January 10, and it did not increase the machine's efficiency but it did add an additional year to its expected service life. On March 30, during the ninth year in the machine's life, it was traded in on a new machine of like purpose having a $60,000 cash price. A $5,000 trade-in allowance was received, and the balance was paid in cash.

Required:

1. Prepare a schedule with the columnar headings of Illustration 12–3. Enter the years 198A through 198D in the first column and complete the schedule by filling in the proper amounts. (Round all amounts to the nearest full dollar.)

2. Prepare the entry to record the leasing of the machine.
3. Using straight-line depreciation, prepare the required entries as of the end of the second year in the life of the lease. Also show how the machine and the lease liability should appear on the December 31, 198B, balance sheet.
4. Prepare the entries to record the machine's overhaul and the depreciation on the machine at the end of its eighth year.
5. Prepare the March 30, 198I, entries to record the exchange of the machines.

Problem 12–5

The Airflo Charter Company needs two new airplanes, each of which has an estimated service life of nine years. The planes could be purchased for $120,000 each, but Airflo does not have the cash available to pay for them. Instead, Airflo agrees to lease Plane 1 for six years, after which the plane remains the property of the lessor. In addition, Aiflo agrees to lease Plane 2 for eight years, after which the plane remains the property of the lessor. According to the lease contracts, Airflo must pay $25,000 annually for each plane ($50,000 for two planes), with the payments to be made at the end of each lease year. Both leases were signed on December 31, 198A, at which time the prevailing interest rate available to Airflo for equipment loans was 12%.

Required:

1. Prepare any required entries to record the lease of *(a)* Plane 1 and *(b)* Plane 2.
2. Prepare the required entries as of the end of the first year in *(a)* the life of Plane 1 and *(b)* the life of Plane 2. (Round all amounts to the nearest full dollar and use straight-line depreciation.)
3. Plane 1 was returned to the lessor on December 31, 198G, the end of the sixth year. Prepare the required entries as of the end of the sixth year in *(a)* the life of Plane 1 and *(b)* the life of Plane 2.
4. Show how Plane 2 and the lease liability for the plane should appear on the balance sheet as of the end of the sixth year in the life of the lease (after the year-end lease payment).

ALTERNATE PROBLEMS

Problem 12–1A

Prepare general journal entries to record these transactions:

Apr. 1 Gave $1,500 cash and a $6,000, 14%, 120-day note to purchase store equipment.
May 14 Borrowed money at the bank by discounting our own $3,000 note payable for 60 days at 14%.
July 13 Paid the note discounted at the bank on May 14.
    30 Paid the $6,000 note of the April 1 transaction.
Aug. 31 Purchased merchandise on credit from Acme Company, invoice dated August 29, terms 2/10, n/60, $2,400.
Nov. 1 Gave Acme Company a $2,400, 15%, 90-day note dated this day to secure a time extension on our past-due account.

Dec. 1 Borrowed money at Security Bank by discounting our own $4,000 note payable for 90 days at 15%.

31 Made an adjusting entry to record the accrued interest on the note given Acme Company on November 1.

31 Made an adjusting entry to remove from the Interest Expense account the interest applicable to next year on the note discounted at Security Bank on December 1.

31 Made a reversing entry dated January 1 to return to the Interest Expense account the interest on the note discounted at Security Bank on December 1.

Jan. 30 Paid the note given Acme Company on November 1.

Mar. 1 Paid the note discounted at Security Bank on December 1.

Problem 12–2A
A company exchanged a $40,000, noninterest-bearing, four-year note payable on January 1, 198A, for a machine the cash price of which was not readily determinable. The market rate for interest on such notes on the day of the exchange was 12% annually.

Required:

1. Prepare a form with the following columnar headings and calculate and fill in the required amounts for the four years the note is outstanding. (Round all dollar amounts to the nearest whole dollar.)

Year	Beginning-of-Year Carrying Amount	Discount to Be Amortized Each Year	Unamortized Discount at End of Year	End-of-Year Carrying Amount

2. Prepare general journal entries to record *(a)* the acquisition of the machine, *(b)* the discount amortized at the end of each year, and *(c)* the payment of the note on January 1, 198E.

3. Show how the note should appear on the December 31, 198B, balance sheet.

Problem 12–3A
Franklin Company plans to order and purchase some special drilling equipment that will be constructed and ready for service five years hence. If Franklin pays for the equipment upon completion (Payment Plan A), it will cost $200,000. However, two alternative payment plans are available. Plan B would require an immediate payment of $110,000. Plan C would require five annual payments of $30,000, the first of which would be made one year hence. In evaluating the three alternatives, Jordan decides to assume an interest rate of 12%.

Required:

Calculate the present value of each payment plan and indicate which plan Franklin should follow.

Problem 12–4A
A company needed a new machine in its operations. The machine could be purchased for $38,000 cash or it could be leased for four years under a contract calling for annual payments of $13,000 at the end of each of the

four years in the life of the lease, with the machine becoming the property of the lessee after the last lease payment. The machine's service life was estimated at six years with no salvage value. The company decided to lease the machine; and on December 31, 198A, a day when the prevailing interest rate was 16%, it signed the lease contract. The machine was delivered two days later and was placed in operation on January 5, 198B. On April 1, during the sixth year in the life of the machine, it was traded in on a new machine of like purpose having a $40,000 cash price. A $7,500 trade-in allowance was received, and the balance was paid in cash.

Required:

1. Prepare a schedule with the columnar headings of Illustration 12–3. Enter the years 198B through 198E in the first column and complete the schedule by filling in the proper amounts. (Round all amounts to the nearest full dollar.)
2. Prepare the entry to record the leasing of the machine.
3. Using straight-line depreciation, prepare the required entries as of the end of the first year in the life of the machine and the lease. Show how the machine and the lease liability should appear on the December 31, 198B, balance sheet.
4. Prepare the required entries as of the end of the third year in the life of the lease and the machine. Show how the machine and the lease liability should appear on the December 31, 198D, balance sheet.
5. Prepare the April 1, 198G, entries to record the depreciation for 198G on the old machine and to record the exchange of the old and new machines.

Problem 12–5A   On December 31, 198A, a day when the available interest rate for equipment loans was 14%, a company leased two machines. Machine 1 was leased for six years under a contract calling for a $30,000 lease payment at the end of each year in the life of the lease, with the machine becoming the property of the lessee company after the sixth lease payment. Machine 2 was leased for four years under a contract calling for a $30,000 annual lease payment at the end of each year in the life of the lease and the machine to be returned to the lessor at the end of the fourth year. Each machine could have been purchased for $130,000 cash, and each machine was estimated to have no salvage value at the end of an estimated 10-year life.

Required:

1. Prepare any required entries to record the lease of (a) Machine 1 and (b) Machine 2.
2. Prepare the required entries as of the end of the first year in (a) the life of Machine 1 and (b) the life of Machine 2. (Round all amounts to the nearest full dollar and use straight-line depreciation.)
3. Machine 2 was returned to the lessor on December 31, 198E, the end of the fourth year. Prepare the required entries as of the end of the fourth year in (a) the life of Machine 1 and (b) the life of Machine 2.
4. Show how Machine 1 and the lease liability for the machine should appear on the balance sheet prepared at the end of the fourth year in the life of the lease.

PROVOCATIVE PROBLEM

Provocative
Problem 12–1,
Gilpin Company

Gilpin Company is considering a plan to purchase some equipment from Smith Company and has asked you to assist in analyzing the situation. The equipment may be purchased for $110,000 and then will be leased by Gilpin under a 10-year lease contract to a customer for $20,000 payable at the end of each year. After the lease expires, Gilpin expects to sell the equipment for $30,000.

Required:

1. Suppose Gilpin has $110,000 cash available to buy the equipment and requires a 14% rate of return on its investments. Should Gilpin buy the equipment and lease it to the customer?
2. As an alternative to paying cash, Gilpin can invest the $110,000 in other operations for five years and earn 14% annually on its investment. If this is done, the equipment may be purchased by signing a $200,000, five-year, noninterest-bearing note payable to Smith Company. Should Gilpin pay $110,000 now or sign the $200,000 note?
3. Now suppose Gilpin does not have the option of signing a $200,000, five-year, noninterest-bearing note. Instead, the company may either pay $110,000 cash or lease the equipment from Smith Company for eight years, after which the equipment would become the property of Gilpin. The lease contract would require $25,000 payments at the end of each year. If Gilpin leases the equipment, it will invest the $110,000 available cash in other operations and earn 14% on the investment. Should Gilpin pay cash or lease the equipment from Smith?

Payroll Accounting

13

After studying Chapter 13, you should be able to:

List the taxes that are withheld from employees' wages and the payroll taxes that are levied on employers.

Calculate an employee's gross pay and the various deductions from the pay.

Prepare a Payroll Register and make the entries to record its information and to pay the employees.

Explain the operation of a payroll bank account.

Calculate and prepare the entries to record the payroll taxes levied on an employer and to record employee fringe benefit costs.

Define or explain the words and phrases listed in the chapter Glossary.

Wages or salaries generally amount to one of the largest expenses incurred by a business. Accounting for these items involves much more than simply recording liabilities and cash payments to employees. Payroll acounting also includes (1) amounts withheld from employees' wages, (2) payroll taxes levied on the employer, and (3) employee (fringe) benefits paid by the employer. Certain federal and state laws directly affect several aspects of payroll accounting. Thus, the discussion of this chapter begins with an overview of the more pertinent of these laws.

THE FEDERAL SOCIAL SECURITY ACT

The federal Social Security Act provides for a number of programs, two of which materially affect payroll accounting. These are (1) a federal old-age and survivors' benefits program with medical care for the aged and (2) a joint federal-state unemployment insurance program.

Federal Old Age and Survivors' Benefits Program

The Social Security Act provides that a qualified worker in a covered industry who reaches the age of 62 and retires shall receive monthly retirement benefits for the remainder of his or her life, and certain medical benefits after reaching 65. It further provides benefits for the family of a worker covered by the act who dies either before or after reaching retirement age and benefits for covered workers who become disabled. The benefits in each case are based upon the earnings of the worker during the years of his or her employment in covered industries.

No attempt will be made here to list or discuss the requirements to be met by a worker or the worker's family to qualify for benefits. In general, any person who works for an employer covered by the act for a sufficient length of time qualifies himself or herself and family. All companies and individuals who employ one or more persons and are not specifically exempted are covered by the law.

Social Security (FICA) Taxes

Funds for the payment of old-age, survivors', and medical benefits under the Social Security Act come from payroll taxes. These taxes are imposed under a law called the Federal Insurance Contributions Act and are called *FICA taxes.* They are also commonly called social security taxes. These FICA taxes are imposed in equal amounts on covered employers and their employees. At this writing, the act imposes a 1983 tax on both employers and their employees amounting to 6.7% of the first $35,700 paid to each employee. It also provides for rate increases as follows:

	Tax on employees	Tax on employers
1985	7.05	7.05
1986 through 1989	7.15	7.15
1990 and after	7.65	7.65

The maximum amount of wages subject to FICA taxes is very apt to change; and if history is any indication, Congress will change the rates listed above (probably increasing them) before they become effective. Consequently, since changes are almost certain, you are asked to use an assumed FICA tax rate of 7% on the first $35,700 of wages paid each employee each year in solving the problems at the end of this chapter. The assumed 7% rate is used because it simplifies calculations and because a specific rate may not be correct for the remaining years this text will be used.

The Federal Insurance Contributions Act in addition to setting rates requires that an employer—

1. Withhold from the wages of each employee each payday an amount of FICA tax calculated at the current rate. FICA taxes are withheld from each paycheck during the year until the tax-exempt point is reached.
2. Pay a payroll tax equal to the sum of the FICA taxes withheld from the wages of all employees.
3. Periodically deposit to the credit of the Internal Revenue Service in a bank authorized to receive such deposits (called a *federal depository bank*) both the amounts withheld from the employees' wages and the employer's tax.
4. Within one month after the end of each calendar quarter, file a tax information return known as Employer's Quarterly Federal Tax Return, Form 941. (See Illustration 13–1.)
5. Furnish each employee before January 31 following each year a Wage and Tax Statement, Form W–2, which tells the employee the amounts of his or her wages that were subject to FICA and federal income taxes and the amounts of such taxes withheld. (A W–2 Form is shown in Illustration 13–2.)
6. Send copies of the W–2 Forms to the Social Security Administration, which posts to each employee's social security account the amount of the employee's wages subject to FICA tax and the FICA tax withheld. These posted amounts become the basis for determin-

Illustration 13–1

| Form **941** (Rev. January 1983) Department of the Treasury Internal Revenue Service | **Employer's Quarterly Federal Tax Return** ▶ For Paperwork Reduction Act Notice, see page 2. | | OMB No. 1545–0029 Expires 12–31–85 |

			T
			FF
Your name, address, employer identification number, and calendar quarter of return. (If not correct, please change.) ▶	┌ Name (as distinguished from trade name) Trade name, if any **Graphic Planners, Inc.** Address and ZIP code **907 Falcon Trail** **Austin, Texas 78746**	Date quarter ended **Sept. 30, 1982** Employer identification number **74–1633163**	FD
			FP
			I
			T
			If address is different from prior return, check here ▶ ☐

Record of Federal Tax Liability
(Complete if line 13 is $500 or more)

If you made eighth-monthly deposits using the 95% rule, check here . . . . ▶ ☐

If you are a first-time 3-banking-day depositor, check here . . . . ▶ ☐

See the instructions under rule 4 on page 4 for details.

Date wages paid		Tax liability
Day		
First month of quarter	1st through 3rd . . . **A**	
	4th through 7th . . . **B**	
	8th through 11th . . . **C**	
	12th through 15th . . **D**	
	16th through 19th . . **E**	
	20th through 22nd . . **F**	
	23rd through 25th . . **G**	
	26th through last . . . **H**	
I	Total . . . . . . ▶	2,920.40
Second month of quarter	1st through 3rd . . . **I**	
	4th through 7th . . . **J**	
	8th through 11th . . . **K**	
	12th through 15th . . **L**	
	16th through 19th . . **M**	
	20th through 22nd . . **N**	
	23rd through 25th . . **O**	
	26th through last . . **P**	
II	Total . . . . . . ▶	2,550.60
Third month of quarter	1st through 3rd . . . **Q**	
	4th through 7th . . . **R**	
	8th through 11th . . . **S**	
	12th through 15th . . **T**	
	16th through 19th . . **U**	
	20th through 22nd . . **V**	
	23rd through 25th . . **W**	
	26th through last . . **X**	
III	Total . . . . . ▶	2,644.75
IV	Total for quarter (add lines I, II, and III)	8,115.75

If you are not liable for returns in the future, write "FINAL" . . . . ▶

Date final wages paid . . . . ▶

1	Number of employees (except household) employed in the pay period that includes March 12th (complete first quarter only) . . . . . ▶		
2	Total wages and tips subject to withholding, plus other employee compensation . . . . . ▶	34,370	50
3	Total income tax withheld from wages, tips, pensions, annuities, sick pay, gambling, etc. . ▶	3,510	10
4	Adjustment of withheld income tax for preceding quarters of calendar year . . . . . . ▶		
5	Adjusted total of income tax withheld	3,510	10
6	Taxable FICA wages paid: $____34,370__50___ × 13.4% (.134) equals tax	4,605	65
7 a	Taxable tips reported: $_____ × 6.7% (.067) equals tax		
b	Tips deemed to be wages (see instructions): $_____ × 6.7% (.067) equals tax		
8	Total FICA taxes (add lines 6, 7a, and 7b) . . .	4,605	65
9	Adjustment of FICA taxes (see instructions) . ▶		
10	Adjusted total of FICA taxes	4,605	65
11	Total taxes (add lines 5 and 10) . . . . . ▶	8,115	75
12	Advance earned income credit (EIC) payments, if any		
13	Net taxes (subtract line 12 from line 11). This must equal line IV	8,115	75

14	Total deposits for quarter, including any overpayment applied from a prior quarter, from your records . ▶	8,115 75
15	Undeposited taxes due (subtract line 14 from line 13). Enter here and pay to Internal Revenue Service . ▶	– 0 –
16	If line 14 is more than line 13, enter overpayment here ▶ $_____ and check if to be: ☐ Applied to next return, or ☐ Refunded.

Under penalties of perjury, I declare that I have examined this return, including accompanying schedules and statements, and to the best of my knowledge and belief it is true, correct, and complete.

Signature ▶ *Walter W. West*   Title ▶ President   Date ▶ Oct. 26, 1982

Please file this form with your Internal Revenue Service Center (see instructions on "Where to File").   Form **941** (Rev. 1–83)

Illustration 13–2

1 Control number	22222		OMB No. 1545–0008	

2 Employer's name, address, and ZIP code	3 Employer's identification number 74–1633163	4 Employer's State number 56–5678

Graphic Planners, Inc.
907 Falcon Trail
Austin, Texas 78746

5 Stat. employee ☒ | De-ceased | Pension plan | Legal rep. | 942 emp. | Sub-total | Cor-rection | Void

6 | 7 Advance EIC payment

8 Employee's social security number 302-02-0222	9 Federal income tax withheld 2,487.20	10 Wages, tips, other compensation 24,560.60	11 FICA tax withheld 1,645.56

12 Employee's name, address, and ZIP code

Charles Robert Lusk
1310 East 5th Street
Austin, Texas 78711

13 FICA wages 24,560.60 | 14 FICA tips

16 Employer's use

Form **W-2 Wage and Tax Statement** 1982   Copy B To be filed with employee's FEDERAL tax return. This information is being furnished to the Internal Revenue Service.   Department of the Treasury Internal Revenue Service

ing the employee's retirement and survivors' benefits. In addition to the posting, the Social Security Administration transmits to the Internal Revenue Service the amount of each employee's wages subject to federal income tax and the amount of such tax withheld.

7. Keep a record for four years for each employee that shows among other things wages subject to FICA taxes and the taxes withheld. (The law does not specify the exact form of the record. However, most employers keep individual employee earnings records similar to the one shown later in this chapter.)

Observe that in addition to reporting its employees' and employer's FICA taxes on Form 941 (Illustration 13–1), an employer also reports the amount of its employees' wages that were subject to federal income taxes and the amount of such taxes that were withheld. (The withholding of employees' federal income taxes is discussed later in this chapter.) Employees' wages subject to federal income tax is shown on line 2 of Illustration 13–1, and the amount of tax withheld is reported on lines 3, 4, and 5. The combined amount of the employees' and employer's FICA taxes is reported on line 6 where it says, "Taxable FICA wages paid . . . $34,370.50 multiplied by 13.4% = Tax, $4,605.65." The 13.4% is the sum of the (1982) 6.7% tax withheld from the employees' wages plus the 6.7% tax levied on the employer.

The frequency with which an employer must deposit to the credit of the Internal Revenue Service the FICA and employees' withheld income taxes depends on the amounts involved. If the sum of the FICA taxes plus the employees' income taxes is less than $500 for a quarter, the taxes may be paid when the employer files an Employer's Quarterly Tax Return, Form 941. This return is due on April 30, July

31, October 31, and January 31 following the end of each calendar quarter. A check for the taxes, if less than $500, may be attached to the return, or the taxes may be deposited in a federal depository bank at the time the return is filed. The check or the deposit is recorded in the same manner as a check paying any other liability.

If the taxes exceed $500 at the end of any month but are less than $3,000, payment must be made within 15 days after the end of the month. Companies with large payrolls may have to make tax payments as often as eight times each month. Note in Illustration 13–1 that each month is divided into eight periods. When the taxes exceed $3,000 at the end of any period, they must be paid within three banking days after the end of that period.

In the example shown in Illustration 13–1, the employer's tax liability exceeded $500 but was less than $3,000 at the end of each month during the quarter. It is assumed in the illustration that the employer paid the amounts due within 15 days after the end of each month.

Joint Federal-State Unemployment Insurance Program

The federal government participates with the states in a joint federal-state unemployment insurance program. Within this joint program each state has established and now administers its own unemployment insurance program under which it provides unemployment benefits to its insured workers. The federal government approves the state programs and pays a portion of their administrative expenses.

The federal money for administering the state programs is raised by a tax imposed under a law called the Federal Unemployment Tax Act. This act levies a *payroll tax* on employers of one or more people. Note that the tax is imposed on employers only. Employees pay nothing. Also the money from this tax is used for administrative purposes and not to pay benefits. In periods of high unemployment, however, these funds may also be loaned to states that have temporary fund deficits.

Historically, in 1935 when the Federal Unemployment Tax Act was first passed, only one state had an unemployment insurance program. At that time, Congress passed certain sections of the Social Security Act and the Federal Unemployment Tax Act with two purposes in view. The first was to induce the individual states to create satisfactory unemployment insurance programs of their own. The second was to provide funds to be distributed to the states for use in administering the state programs. These acts were successful in accomplishing their first purpose. All states immediately created unemployment benefit programs. Today, the acts remain in effect for their second purpose, to provide funds to be distributed to the states, and also to retain a measure of federal control over the state programs.

THE FEDERAL UNEMPLOYMENT TAX ACT. At this writing the Federal Unemployment Tax Act requires employers of one or more employees to:

1. Pay an excise tax (FUTA tax) equal to 3.5% of the first $7,000 in wages paid each employee, less a maximum credit of 2.7% for contributions to a state program. Since all states have unemployment tax programs, the net federal tax is normally 0.8%. The current law also calls for rate changes beginning in 1985 to 6.2% less a maximum state credit of 5.4%. Thus, when states make the necessary increases in their tax, the net federal rate will remain at 0.8%.

2. On or before January 31 following the end of each year, file a tax return, called an "Employer's Annual Federal Unemployment Tax Return, Form 940," reporting the amount of the tax. (Ten additional days are allowed for filing if all required tax deposits are made on a timely basis, and the full amount of the tax is paid on or before January 31.)

3. Keep records to substantiate the information on the tax return. (In general, the records required by other payroll laws and the regular accounting records satisfy this requirement.)

An employer's federal unemployment tax for the first three quarters of a year must be deposited in a federal depository bank by the last day of the month following each quarter (i.e., on April 30, July 31, and October 31). However, no deposit is required if the tax for a quarter plus the undeposited tax for previous quarters is $100 or less. The tax for the last quarter of a year plus the undeposited tax for previous quarters must be deposited or paid on or before January 31 following the end of the tax year. If the Employer's Annual Federal Unemployment Tax Return is filed on or before that date, a check for the last quarter's tax and any undeposited tax for previous quarters may be attached to the form.

STATE UNEMPLOYMENT INSURANCE PROGRAMS. While the various state unemployment insurance programs differ in some respects, all have three common objectives. They are:

1. To pay unemployment benefits for limited periods to unemployed individuals. (To be eligible for benefits, an unemployed individual must have worked for a tax-paying employer covered by the law. In general, the state laws cover employers of from one to four or more employees who are not specifically exempted.)

2. To encourage the stabilization of employment by covered employers. (In all states this is accomplished by a so-called *merit-rating plan*. Under a merit-rating plan, an employer who provides steady

employment for employees gains a merit rating that substantially reduces its state unemployment tax rate.)

3. To establish and operate employment facilities that assist unemployed individuals in finding suitable employment and assist employers in finding employees.

All states support their unemployment insurance programs by placing a payroll tax on employers. A few states place an additional tax on employees. The basic rate in most states at the time of this writing is 2.7% of the first $7,000 paid each employee. However, an employer can gain a merit rating that will reduce this basic rate to as little as 0.5% in some states and to zero in others. An employer gains a merit rating by not laying employees off during slack seasons, thereby avoiding their drawing of unemployment benefits. And, to most employers such a rating offers an important tax savings. For example, an employer with just 10 employees who each earn $7,000 or more per year can save $1,540 of state unemployment taxes each year by gaining a merit rating that reduces its state unemployment tax rate from 2.7% to 0.5%. Given the current federal law (as explained previously), the basic rate in most states will probably increase beginning in 1985 from 2.7% to 5.4%. However, merit ratings will continue to provide significant reductions.

The states vary as to required unemployment tax reports. Nevertheless, in general, all require a tax return and payment of the required tax within one month after the end of each calendar quarter. Also, since the benefits paid an eligible unemployed individual are based upon earnings, the tax return must usually name each employee and summarize the employee's wages.

In addition to reports and payment of taxes, all states require employers to maintain certain payroll records. These vary but in general require a payroll record for each pay period showing the pay period dates, hours worked, and taxable earnings of each employee. An individual earnings record for each employee is also commonly required. The earnings record generally must show about the same information that is required by social security laws. In addition, information is also commonly required as to (1) the date an employee was hired, rehired, or reinstated after a layoff; (2) the date the employee quit, was discharged, or laid off; and (3) the reason for termination.

WITHHOLDING EMPLOYEES' FEDERAL INCOME TAXES

With few exceptions, an employer of one or more persons is required to calculate, withhold, and remit to the Internal Revenue Service the federal income taxes of its employees. The amount of tax to be withheld from each employee's wages is determined by the amount of the wages earned and the number of the employee's income tax exemptions, which for payroll purposes are called *withholding allowances*. At this writing, each exemption or withholding allowance exempts $1,000 of the employee's yearly earnings from income tax. An employee is allowed one exemption for himself or herself, additional exemptions if the employee or the employee's spouse is blind or over 65, and an exemption for each dependent. Every covered employee is required to furnish his or her employer an employee's withholding allowance certificate, called a Form W–4, on which the employee indicates the number of exemptions claimed.

Most employers use a *wage bracket withholding table* similar to the one shown in Illustration 13–3 to determine the federal income taxes to be withheld from employees' *gross pay*. The illustrated table is for married employees and is applicable when a pay period is one week. Different tables are provided for single employees and for biweekly, semimonthly, and monthly pay periods. Somewhat similar tables are also available for determining FICA tax withholdings.

Determining the federal income tax to be withheld from an employee's gross wages is quite easy when a withholding table is used. First, the employee's wage bracket is located in the first two columns. Then, the amount to be withheld is found on the line of the wage bracket in the column showing the exemption allowances to which the em-

Illustration 13–3

MARRIED Persons — **WEEKLY** Payroll Period
(For Wages Paid After June 1982 and Before July 1983)

And the wages are—		And the number of withholding allowances claimed is—										
At least	But less than	0	1	2	3	4	5	6	7	8	9	10 or more
		The amount of income tax to be withheld shall be—										
$310	$320	$42.70	$39.10	$35.40	$31.80	$28.10	$24.80	$21.70	$18.70	$15.60	$12.50	$9.40
320	330	44.60	41.00	37.30	33.70	30.00	26.40	23.30	20.30	17.20	14.10	11.00
330	340	46.50	42.90	39.20	35.60	31.90	28.30	24.90	21.90	18.80	15.70	12.60
340	350	48.40	44.80	41.10	37.50	33.80	30.20	26.50	23.50	20.40	17.30	14.20
350	360	50.30	46.70	43.00	39.40	35.70	32.10	28.40	25.10	22.00	18.90	15.80
360	370	52.70	48.60	44.90	41.30	37.60	34.00	30.30	26.70	23.60	20.50	17.40
370	380	55.10	50.50	46.80	43.20	39.50	35.90	32.20	28.60	25.20	22.10	19.00
380	390	57.50	52.80	48.70	45.10	41.40	37.80	34.10	30.50	26.80	23.70	20.60
390	400	59.90	55.20	50.60	47.00	43.30	39.70	36.00	32.40	28.70	25.30	22.20
400	410	62.30	57.60	53.00	48.90	45.20	41.60	37.90	34.30	30.60	26.90	23.80
410	420	64.70	60.00	55.40	50.80	47.10	43.50	39.80	36.20	32.50	28.80	25.40
420	430	67.10	62.40	57.80	53.20	49.00	45.40	41.70	38.10	34.40	30.70	27.10
430	440	69.50	64.80	60.20	55.60	51.00	47.30	43.60	40.00	36.30	32.60	29.00
440	450	71.90	67.20	62.60	58.00	53.40	49.20	45.50	41.90	38.20	34.50	30.90
450	460	74.30	69.60	65.00	60.40	55.80	51.20	47.40	43.80	40.10	36.40	32.80
460	470	77.00	72.00	67.40	62.80	58.20	53.60	49.30	45.70	42.00	38.30	34.70
470	480	79.70	74.50	69.80	65.20	60.60	56.00	51.40	47.60	43.90	40.20	36.60
480	490	82.40	77.20	72.20	67.60	63.00	58.40	53.80	49.50	45.80	42.10	38.50
490	500	85.10	79.90	74.70	70.00	65.40	60.80	56.20	51.60	47.70	44.00	40.40
500	510	87.80	82.60	77.40	72.40	67.80	63.20	58.60	54.00	49.60	45.90	42.30
510	520	90.50	85.30	80.10	74.90	70.20	65.60	61.00	56.40	51.70	47.80	44.20
520	530	93.20	88.00	82.80	77.60	72.60	68.00	63.40	58.80	54.10	49.70	46.10
530	540	95.90	90.70	85.50	80.30	75.10	70.40	65.80	61.20	56.50	51.90	48.00
540	550	98.60	93.40	88.20	83.00	77.80	72.80	68.20	63.60	58.90	54.30	49.90
550	560	101.30	96.10	90.90	85.70	80.50	75.30	70.60	66.00	61.30	56.70	52.10

ployee is entitled. The column heading numbers refer to the number of exemption allowances claimed by an employee.

In addition to determining and withholding income tax from each employee's wages every payday, employers are required to—

1. Periodically deposit the withheld taxes to the credit of the Internal Revenue Service.
2. Within one month after the end of each calendar quarter, file a report showing the income taxes withheld. This report is the Employer's Quarterly Federal Tax Return, Form 941, discussed previously and shown in Illustration 13–1. It is the same report required for FICA taxes.
3. On or before January 31 following each year, give each employee a Wage and Tax Statement, Form W–2, which tells the employee (1) his or her total wages for the preceding year, (2) wages subject to FICA taxes, (3) income taxes withheld, and (4) FICA taxes withheld. A copy of this statement must also be given to each terminated employee within 30 days after his or her last wage payment.
4. On or before January 31 following the end of each year, send the Social Security Administration copies of all W–2 forms given employees. The Social Security Administration transmits the information as to employees' earnings and withheld taxes to the Internal Revenue Service.

CITY AND STATE INCOME TAXES

In addition to deducting employees' federal income taxes, employers in many cities and in many states must also deduct employees' city and state income taxes. When levied, the city and state taxes are handled much the same as federal income taxes.

FAIR LABOR STANDARDS ACT

The Fair Labor Standards Act, often called the Wages and Hours Law, sets minimum hourly wages and maximum hours of work per week for employees, with certain exceptions, of employers engaged either directly or indirectly in interstate commerce. The law at this writing sets a $3.35 per hour minimum wage for employees in most occupations and a 40-hour workweek. It also provides that if an employee covered by the act works more than 40 hours in one week, he or she must be paid for the hours in excess of 40 at his or her regular pay rate plus an overtime premium of at least one half the regular rate. This gives an employee an overtime rate of at least one and one half times his or her regular hourly rate. The act also requires employers to maintain records for each covered employee similar to the employee's individual earnings record of Illustration 13–8.

UNION CONTRACTS

Employers commonly operate under contracts with their employees' union that provide even better terms than the Wages and Hours Law. For example, union contracts often provide for time and one half for work in excess of eight hours in any one day, time and one half for work on Saturdays, and double time for Sundays and holidays. When an employer is under such a union contract, since the contract terms are better than those of the Wages and Hours Law, the contract terms take precedence over the law.

In addition to specifying working hours and wage rates, union contracts often provide for the collection of employees' union dues by the employer. Such a requirement commonly provides that the employer deduct dues from the wages of each employee and remit the amounts deducted to the union. The employer is usually required to remit once each month and to report the name and amount deducted from each employee's pay.

OTHER PAYROLL DEDUCTIONS

In addition to the payroll deductions discussed thus far, employees may individually authorize additional deductions, such as deductions for the purchase of U.S. savings bonds; to pay health, hospital, or life insurance premiums; to repay loans from the employer or the employees' credit union; and to pay for merchandise purchased from the employer and for donations to charitable organizations.

TIMEKEEPING

Compiling a record of the time worked by each employee is called *timekeeping.* In an individual company, the method of compiling such a record depends upon the nature of the business and the number of its employees. In a very small business, timekeeping may consist of no more than pencil notations of each employee's working time made in a memorandum book by the manager or owner. On the other hand, in larger companies, a time clock or several time clocks are often used to record on *clock cards* each employee's time of arrival and departure. When time clocks are used, they are usually placed near entrances to the office, store, or factory. At the beginning of each payroll period a clock card for each employee similar to Illustration 13–4 is placed in a rack for use by the employee. Upon arriving at work, an employee takes his or her card from the rack and places it in a slot in the time clock. This actuates the clock to stamp the date and arrival time on the card. The employee then returns the card to the rack and proceeds to the employee's place of work. Upon leaving the plant, store, or office for lunch or at the end of the day, the procedure is repeated. The employee takes the card from the rack, places it in the clock, and the time of departure is automatically stamped. As a result, at the end of each pay period, the card shows the hours the employee was at work.

Illustration 13–4

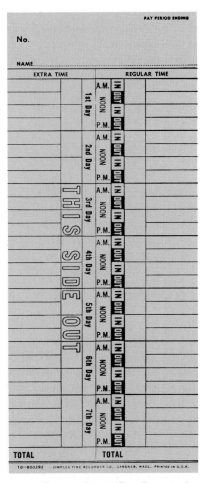

Courtesy Simplex Time Recorder Co.

THE PAYROLL REGISTER

Each pay period the total hours worked as compiled on clock cards or otherwise is summarized in a Payroll Register. A typical example of such a register is shown in Illustration 13–5. The illustrated register is for a weekly pay period and shows the payroll data for each employee on a separate line. The column headings and the data recorded in the columns are, for the most part, self-explanatory.

The columns under the heading "Daily Time" show the hours worked each day by each employee. The total of each employee's hours is entered in the column headed "Total Hours." If hours worked include overtime hours, these are entered in the column headed "O.T. Hours."

The column headed "Reg. Pay Rate" is for the hourly pay rate of each employee. Total hours worked multiplied by the regular pay rate equals regular pay. Overtime hours multiplied by the overtime premium rate equals overtime premium pay. And, regular pay plus overtime premium pay is the gross pay of each employee.

Under the heading "Deductions," the amounts withheld from each employee's gross pay for FICA taxes are shown in the column marked "FICA Taxes." These amounts are determined by multiplying the gross pay of each employee by the FICA tax rate in effect. In this and the remaining illustrations of this chapter, it is assumed that the rate is 7% on the first $35,700 paid each employee.

As previously stated, the income tax withheld from each employee depends upon his or her gross pay and exemptions. This amount is commonly determined by the use of a wage bracket withholding table; and when determined, it is entered in the column headed "Federal Income Taxes."

The column headed "Hosp. Ins." shows the amounts withheld to pay for hospital insurance for the employees and their families. The total withheld from all employees is a current liability of the employer until paid to the insurance company. Likewise, the total withheld for employees' union dues is a current liability until paid to the union. The column marked "Union Dues" in the illustrated Payroll Register is for this deduction.

Additional columns may be added to the Payroll Register for any other deductions that occur sufficiently often to warrant special columns. For example, a company that regularly deducts amounts from its employees' pay for U.S. savings bonds may add a special column for this deduction.

An employee's gross pay less total deductions is the employee's *net pay* and is entered in the column headed "Net Pay." The total of this column is the amount to be paid the employees. The numbers of the checks used in paying the employees are entered in the column headed "Check No."

Illustration 13–5

		Daily Time									Earnings			
Employees	Clock Card No.	M	T	W	T	F	S	S	Total Hours	O.T. Hours	Reg. Pay Rate	Regular Pay	O.T. Premium Pay	Gross Pay
Robert Austin	114	8	8	8	8	8			40		5.00	200.00		200.00
Judy Cross	102	8	8	8	8	8			40		7.50	300.00		300.00
John Cruz	108	0	8	8	8	8	8		40		7.00	280.00		280.00
Kay Keife	109	8	8	8	8	8	8		48	8	7.00	336.00	28.00	364.00
Lee Miller	112	8	8	8	8	0			32		7.00	224.00		224.00
Dale Sears	103	8	8	8	8	8	4		44	4	7.50	330.00	15.00	345.00
Totals												1,670.00	43.00	1,713.00

Payroll
Week ended

The two columns under the heading "Distribution" are for sorting the various salaries into kinds of salary expense. Here each employee's gross salary is entered in the proper column according to the type of work performed. The column totals then indicate the amounts to be debited to the salary expense accounts.

RECORDING THE PAYROLL

Generally, a Payroll Register such as the one shown is a supplementary memorandum record. As such, its information is not posted directly to the accounts but is first recorded with a general journal entry, which is then posted. The entry to record the payroll shown in Illustration 13–5 is:

June	26	Sales Salaries Expense	1,168.00	
		Office Salaries Expense	545.00	
		FICA Taxes Payable		119.91
		Employees' Income Taxes Payable		183.10
		Employees' Hospital Insurance Payable		160.00
		Employees' Union Dues Payable		20.00
		Accrued Payroll Payable		1,229.99
		To record the June 26 payroll.		

Register
June 26, 19--

	Deductions				Payment		Distribution	
FICA Taxes	Federal Income Taxes	Hosp. Ins.	Union Dues	Total Deduc- tions	Net Pay	Check No.	Sales Salaries	Office Salaries
14.00	15.30	20.00		49.30	150.70	893		200.00
21.00	41.30	28.00	5.00	95.30	204.70	894	300.00	
19.60	28.10	28.00	5.00	80.70	199.30	895	280.00	
25.48	48.60	28.00	5.00	107.08	256.92	896	364.00	
15.68	12.30	28.00	5.00	60.98	163.02	897	224.00	
24.15	37.50	28.00		89.65	255.35	898		345.00
119.91	183.10	160.00	20.00	483.01	1,229.99		1,168.00	545.00

The debits of the entry were taken from the Payroll Register's distribution column totals. They charge the employees' gross earnings to the proper salary expense accounts. The credits to FICA Taxes Payable, Employees' Income Taxes Payable, Employees' Hospital Insurance Payable, and Employees' Union Dues Payable record these amounts as current liabilities. The credit to Accrued Payroll Payable records as a liability the net amount to be paid the employees.

PAYING THE EMPLOYEES

Almost every business pays its employees with checks. In a company having few employees, these checks are often drawn on the regular bank account and entered in a Cash Disbursements Journal (or Check Register) like the one described in Chapter 6. Each check is debited to the Accrued Payroll Payable account. Therefore, posting labor can be saved by adding an Accrued Payroll Payable column in the journal. If such a column is added, entries to pay the employees of the Illustration 13–5 payroll will appear as in Illustration 13–6.

Although not required by law, most employers furnish each employee an earnings statement each payday. The objective of the statement is to inform the employee and give the employee a record of hours worked, gross pay, deductions, and net pay that may be retained. The statement usually takes the form of a detachable paycheck portion

Illustration 13–6

CASH DISBURSEMENTS JOURNAL

Date		Check No.	Payee	Account Debited	P R	Other Accounts Debit	Accts. Pay. Debit	Accr. Payroll Pay Debit	Pur. Dis. Credit	Cash Credit
June	26	893	Robert Austin	Accrued Payroll				150.70		150.70
	26	894	Judy Cross	"				204.70		204.70
	26	895	John Cruz	"				199.30		199.30
	26	896	Kay Keife	"				256.92		256.92
	26	897	Lee Miller	"				163.02		163.02
	26	898	Dale Sears	"				255.35		255.35

that is removed before the check is cashed. A paycheck with a detachable earnings statement is reproduced in Illustration 13–7.

PAYROLL BANK ACCOUNT

A business with many employees normally makes use of a special *payroll bank account* in paying its employees. When such an account

Illustration 13–7

Robert Austin	40		5.00	200.00		200.00	14.00	15.30		20.00	49.30	$150.70
Employee	Total Hours	O.T. Hours	Reg. Pay Rate	Reg- ular Pay	O.T. Prem. Pay	Gross Pay	F.I.C.A. Taxes	In- come Taxes	Union Dues	Hosp. Ins.	Total Deduc- tions	Net Pay

STATEMENT OF EARNINGS AND DEDUCTIONS FOR EMPLOYEE'S RECORDS—DETACH BEFORE CASHING CHECK

VALLEY SALES COMPANY

2590 Chula Vista Street • Eugene, Oregon

No. 893

PAY TO THE
ORDER OF___Robert Austin_____ DATE June 26, 19-- $ 150.70

--One-hundred-fifty dollars and seventy cents- - - - - - - - - - - - - - -

VALLEY SALES COMPANY

James R. Morris

Merchants National Bank
Eugene, Oregon

is used, one check for the total of the payroll is drawn on the regular bank account and deposited in the special payroll bank account. Then, individual payroll checks are drawn on this special account. Because only one check for the payroll total is drawn on the regular bank account each payday, use of a special payroll bank account simplifies reconciliation of the regular bank account. It may be reconciled without considering the payroll checks outstanding, and there may be many of these.

A company using a special payroll bank account completes the following steps in paying its employees:

1. First, it records the information shown on its Payroll Register in the usual manner with a general journal entry similar to the one previously illustrated. This entry causes the sum of the employees' net pay to be credited to the liability account Accrued Payroll Payable.
2. Next, a single check payable to Payroll Bank Account for the total of the payroll is drawn and entered in the Check Register. This results in a debit to Accrued Payroll Payable and a credit to Cash.
3. The check is then endorsed and deposited in the payroll bank account. This transfers an amount of money equal to the payroll total from the regular bank account to the special payroll bank account.
4. Last, individual payroll checks are drawn on the special payroll bank account and delivered to the employees. These pay the employees and, as soon as all employees cash their checks, exhaust the funds in the special account.

A special Payroll Check Register may be used in connection with a payroll bank account. However, most companies do not use such a register but prefer to enter the payroll check numbers in their Payroll Register, making it act as a Check Register.

EMPLOYEE'S INDIVIDUAL EARNINGS RECORD

An *Employee's Individual Earnings Record,* Illustration 13–8, provides for each employee in one record a full year's summary of the employee's working time, gross earnings, deductions, and net pay. In addition, it accumulates information that—

1. Serves as a basis for the employer's state and federal payroll tax returns.
2. Indicates when an employee's earnings have reached the tax-exempt points for FICA and state and federal unemployment taxes.
3. Supplies data for the Wage and Tax Statement, Form W–2, which must be given to the employee at the end of the year.

Illustration 13–8

EMPLOYEE'S INDIVIDUAL EARNINGS RECORD

Employee's Name __Robert Austin__ S.S. Acct. No. __307-03-2195__ Employee No. __114__

Home Address __111 South Greenwood__ Notify in Case of Emergency __Margaret Austin__ Phone No. __964-9834__

Employed __June 7, 1980__ Date of Termination _____ Reason _____

Date of Birth __June 6, 1962__ Date Becomes 65 __June 6, 2027__ Male (x) Female ( ) Married ( ) Single (x) Number of Exemptions __1__ Pay Rate __$5.00__

Occupation __Clerk__ Place __Office__

Date		Time Lost		Time Wk.		Reg. Pay	O.T. Prem. Pay	Gross Pay	F.I.C.A. Taxes	Federal Income Taxes	Hosp. Ins.	Union Dues	Total Deductions	Net Pay	Check No.	Cumulative Pay
Per. Ends	Paid	Hrs.	Reason	Total	O.T. Hours											
1/5	1/5			40		200.00		200.00	14.00	15.30	20.00		49.30	150.70	173	200.00
1/12	1/12			40		200.00		200.00	14.00	15.30	20.00		49.30	150.70	201	400.00
1/19	1/19			40		200.00		200.00	14.00	15.30	20.00		49.30	150.70	243	600.00
1/26	1/26	4	Sick	36		180.00		180.00	12.60	14.10	20.00		46.70	130.70	295	780.00
2/2	2/2			40		200.00		200.00	14.00	15.30	20.00		49.30	150.70	339	980.00
2/9	2/9			40		200.00		200.00	14.00	15.30	20.00		49.30	150.70	354	1,180.00
2/16	2/16			40		200.00		200.00	14.00	15.30	20.00		49.30	150.70	397	1,380.00
2/23	2/23			40		200.00		200.00	14.00	15.30	20.00		49.30	150.70	446	1,580.00
6/26	6/26			40		200.00		200.00	14.00	15.30	20.00		49.30	150.70	893	5,180.00

The payroll information on an Employee's Individual Earnings Record is taken from the Payroll Register. The information as to earnings, deductions, and net pay is first recorded on a single line in the Payroll Register. It is posted each pay period from there to the earnings record. Note the last column of the record. It shows an employee's cumulative earnings and is used to determine when the earnings reach the maximum amounts taxed and are no longer subject to the various payroll taxes.

PAYROLL TAXES LEVIED ON THE EMPLOYER

As previously explained, FICA taxes are levied in equal amounts on both covered employers and their employees. However, only employers are required to pay federal and, usually, state unemployment taxes. Each time a payroll is recorded, a general journal entry is also made to record the employer's FICA and state and federal unemployment taxes. For example, the entry to record the employer's payroll taxes on the payroll of Illustration 13–5 is:

June	26	Payroll Taxes Expense	128.66	
		FICA Taxes Payable		119.91
		State Unemployment Taxes Payable		6.75
		Federal Unemployment Taxes Payable		2.00
		To record the employer's payroll taxes.		

The $128.66 debit of the entry records as an expense the sum of the employer's payroll taxes. The $119.91 credit to FICA Taxes Payable is equal to and matches the FICA taxes deducted from the employees' pay and is credited to the same FICA Taxes Payable account. The $6.75 credit to State Unemployment Taxes Payable results from the assumptions that the employer's state unemployment tax rate is 2.7% on the first $7,000 paid each employee and that the employees have cumulative earnings prior to this pay period and earnings subject to the various taxes as shown in Illustration 13–9. Observe in the illustration that four employees have earned more than $7,000 and their pay is assumed, as in most states, to be exempt from state unemployment tax. One employee has previously earned $6,950 and only the first $50 of his pay is subject to tax. The wages of the remaining em-

Illustration 13–9

			Earnings Subject to—	
Employees' Cumulative Earnings through the Last Pay Period and Earnings Subject to the Various Taxes				
Employees	Earnings through Last Pay Period	Earnings This Pay Period	FICA Taxes	State and Federal Unemployment Taxes
Robert Austin	$5,180.00	$ 200.00	$ 200.00	$200.00
Judy Cross	7,910.00	300.00	300.00	
John Cruz	7,280.00	280.00	280.00	
Kay Keife	7,945.00	364.00	364.00	
Lee Miller	6,950.00	224.00	224.00	50.00
Dale Sears	7,995.00	345.00	345.00	
Totals		$1,713.00	$1,713.00	$250.00

ployee are taxable in full. Consequently, the $6.75 credit to State Unemployment Taxes Payable in the entry recording the employer's payroll taxes resulted from multiplying the wages subject to tax ($250) by the assumed 2.7% rate.

As the law is presently amended, an employer's federal unemployment tax is also based on the first $7,000 in wages paid each employee. Therefore the $2 federal unemployment tax liability in the illustrated journal entry resulted from multiplying $250 by the 0.8% rate.

ACCRUING TAXES ON WAGES

Payroll taxes are levied on wages actually paid; consequently, there is no legal liability for taxes on accrued wages. Nevertheless, if the requirements of the *matching principle* are to be met, both accrued wages and the accrued taxes on the wages should be recorded at the end of an accounting period. However, since there is no legal liability and the amounts of such taxes vary little from one accounting period to the next, most employers apply the *materiality principle* and do not accrue payroll taxes.

EMPLOYEE (FRINGE) BENEFIT COSTS

In addition to the wages earned by employees and the related payroll taxes paid by the employer, many companies provide their employees a variety of benefits. Since the costs of these benefits are paid by the employer, and the benefits are in addition to the amount of wages earned, they are often called fringe benefits. For example, an employer may pay for part (or all) of the employees' health insurance, life insurance, and disability insurance. Another frequent employee benefit involves employer contributions to a retirement income plan.

The entries for employee benefit costs are similar to those used for payroll taxes. For example, assume the employer with the previously described $1,713 payroll has agreed to match the employees' contributions for hospital insurance and also to contribute 10% of employees' salaries to a retirement program. The entry to record these employee benefits is:

Jan.	7	Employees' Benefits Expense	331.30	
		Employees' Hospital Insurance Payable		160.00
		Employees' Retirement Program Payable ..		171.30

Payroll taxes and employee benefits costs are often a major category of expense incurred by a company. They may amount to well over 25% of the salaries earned by employees.

COMPUTERIZED PAYROLL SYSTEMS

Manually prepared records like the ones described in this chapter are found in many small companies, and very satisfactorily meet their needs. However, companies having many employees commonly use computers to process their payroll. The computer programs are designed to take advantage of the fact that each pay period the same calculations are performed and that much of the same information must be entered for each employee in the Payroll Register, on the employee's earnings record, and on the employees' paycheck. The computers simultaneously store or print the information in all three places.

GLOSSARY

Clock card. A card used by an employee to record his or her time of arrival and departure to and from work.

Employees' Individual Earnings Record. A record of an employee's hours worked, gross pay, deductions, net pay, and certain personal information about the employee.

Federal depository bank. A bank authorized to receive as deposits amounts of money payable to the federal government.

Federal unemployment tax. A tax levied by the federal government and used to pay a portion of the costs of the joint federal-state unemployment programs.

FICA taxes. Federal Insurance Contributions Act taxes, otherwise known as social security taxes.

Gross pay. The amount an employee earns before any deductions.

Merit rating. A rating granted to an employer by a state, which is based on whether or not the employer's employees have experienced periods of unemployment. A good rating reduces the employer's unemployment tax rate.

Net pay. Gross pay minus deductions.

Payroll bank account. A special bank account into which at the end of each pay period the total amount of an employer's payroll is deposited and on which the employees' payroll checks are drawn.

Payroll tax. A tax levied on the amount of a payroll or on the amount of an employee's gross pay.

State unemployment tax. A tax levied by a state, the proceeds from which are used to pay benefits to unemployed workers.

Timekeeping.   Making a record of the time each employee is at his or her place of work.

Wage bracket withholding table.   A table showing the amounts to be withheld from employees' wages at various levels of earnings.

Withholding allowance.   An amount of an employee's annual earnings not subject to income tax.

QUESTIONS FOR CLASS DISCUSSION

#436

1. What are FICA taxes? Who pays these taxes, and for what purposes are the funds from FICA taxes used?

2. Company A has one employee from whose pay it withholds each week $8.75 of federal income tax and $13.02 of FICA tax. Company B has 30 employees from whose pay it withholds each month a total of $800 of employee FICA taxes and $900 of federal income taxes. When must each of these companies remit these amounts to the Internal Revenue Service?

3. What benefits are paid to unemployed workers from funds raised by the Federal Unemployment Insurance Act? Why was this act passed?

Employer

4. Who pays federal unemployment insurance taxes? What is the net tax rate? *. 8 of 13 0*

5. What are the objectives of state unemployment insurance laws? Who pays state unemployment insurance taxes?

6. What is a state unemployment merit rating? Why are such merit ratings granted?

7. What determines the amount that must be deducted from an employee's wages for federal income taxes?

8. What is a wage bracket withholding table? Use the wage bracket withholding table in Illustration 13–3 to find the income tax to be withheld from the wages of a married employee with three exemptions who earned $445 in a week.

9. What does the Fair Labor Standards Act require of a covered employer?

10. How is a clock card used in recording the time an employee is on the job?

11. How is a special payroll bank account used in paying the wages of employees?

12. At the end of an accounting period, a firm's special payroll bank account has a $562.35 balance because the payroll checks of two employees have not cleared the bank. Should this $562.35 appear on the firm's balance sheet? If so, where?

13. What information is accumulated on an employee's individual earnings record? Why must this information be accumulated? For what purposes is the information used?

#4

14. What payroll taxes are levied on the employer? What taxes are deducted from the wages of an employee? *F.I.C.A.:- Unemployment tax*

15. What are employee fringe benefits? Name some examples.

CLASS EXERCISES

Exercise 13–1   Henry Smith, an employee of a company subject to the Fair Labor Standards Act, worked 46 hours during the week ended January 7. His pay rate is $8 per hour, and his wages are subject to no deductions other than FICA and federal income taxes. He claims three income tax exemptions. Calculate his regular pay, overtime premium pay, gross pay, FICA tax deduction at an assumed 7% rate, income tax deduction (use the wage bracket withholding table of Illustration 13–3), total deductions, and net pay.

Exercise 13–2   On January 4, at the end of its first weekly pay period in the year, the column totals of a company's Payroll Register showed that its sales employees had earned $1,900 and its office employees had earned $1,000. The employees were to have FICA taxes withheld at an assumed 7% rate plus $410 of federal income taxes, $70 of union dues, and $320 of hospital insurance premiums. Calculate the amount of FICA taxes to be withheld and give the general journal entry to record the Payroll Register.

Exercise 13–3   The following information as to earnings and deductions for the pay period ended May 20 was taken from a company's payroll records:

Employees' Names	Gross Pay	Earnings to End of Previous Week	Federal Income Taxes	Health Insurance Deductions
June Abbot ...	$ 300	$ 3,240	$ 38.00	$ 26.50
John Cotton ...	450	5,880	56.50	38.50
Fred Green ...	450	8,110	56.50	38.50
Sally Nash	1,500	36,610	210.00	38.50
	$2,700		$361.00	$142.00

Required:

1. Calculate the employees' FICA tax withholdings at an assumed 7.0% rate on the first $35,700 paid each employee. Also calculate total FICA taxes withheld, total deductions, and net pay.
2. Prepare a general journal entry to record the payroll. Assume all employees work in the office.

Exercise 13–4   Use the information provided in Exercise 13–3 to complete the following requirements:

1. Prepare a general journal entry to record the employer's payroll taxes resulting from the payroll. Assume a state unemployment tax rate of 1% and a net federal unemployment tax of 0.8% on the first $7,000 paid each employee.
2. Prepare a general journal entry to record the following employee benefits incurred by the company: *(a)* health insurance costs equal to the amounts contributed by each employee and *(b)* contributions equal to 10% of gross pay for each employee's retirement income program.

Exercise 13–5   Alto Company's employees earn a gross pay of $10 per hour and work 40 hours each week. The FICA tax rate is 7%, the federal unemployment tax rate is 0.8%, and the state unemployment tax rate is 2.7%. In addition, Alto Company contributes 10% of gross pay to a retirement program for employees and pays medical insurance premiums of $22 per week per employee. What is Alto Company's total cost of employing a person for one hour? (Assume that individual wages are less than the $7,000 unemployment tax limit.)

PROBLEMS

Problem 13–1   On January 3, at the end of the first weekly pay period of the year, a company's Payroll Register showed that its employees had earned $4,500 of sales salaries and $1,100 of office salaries. The employees were to have FICA taxes withheld from their wages at an assumed 7% rate plus $790 of federal income taxes, $224 of hospital insurance, and $75 of union dues.

Required:

1. Calculate the total of the FICA Taxes Payable column in the Payroll Register, and prepare a general journal entry to record the register information.
2. Prepare a general journal entry to record the employer's payroll taxes resulting from the payroll. Assume the company has a merit rating that reduces its state unemployment tax rate to 1.8% of the first $7,000 paid each employee.
3. Under the assumption the company uses a payroll bank account and special payroll checks in paying its employees, give the check resister entry (Check No. 777) to transfer funds equal to the payroll from the regular bank account to the payroll bank account.
4. Answer this question: After the check register entry is made and posted, are additional debit and credit entries required to record the payroll checks and pay the employees?

Problem 13–2   The payroll records of Fix-all Company provided the following information for the weekly pay period ended December 21.

Employees	Clock Card No.	Daily Time							Pay Rate	Federal Income Taxes	Hospi-tal Insur-ance	Union Dues	Earnings to End of Previous Week
		M	T	W	T	F	S	S					
Darla Algoe	11	8	8	8	8	7	4	0	$15.00	$ 96.60	$ 25.00	$ 9.50	$31,000
John Fox	12	8	8	8	8	8	2	0	16.00	90.10	25.00	9.50	35,500
Dale Kohler	13	8	8	8	8	7	0	0	15.00	75.00	25.00	9.50	6,400
Jerry Mozena	14	8	8	8	8	8	1	0	12.00	61.90	20.00	9.50	24,000
Kay Gilpin	15	8	8	8	8	8	4	0	18.00	109.50	25.00		36,000
										$433.10	$120.00	$38.00	

Required:

1. Enter the relevant information in the proper columns of a Payroll Register and complete the register using a FICA tax rate of 7% on the first $35,700

paid each employee. Assume the company is subject to the Fair Labor Standards Act. Charge the wages of Kay Gilpin to Office Salaries Expense and the wages of the remaining employees to Technicians' Wages Expense.

2. Prepare a general journal entry to record the payroll register information.
3. Make the check register entry (Check No. 157) to transfer funds equal to the payroll from the regular bank account to the payroll bank account under the assumption the company uses special payroll checks and a payroll bank account in paying its employees. Assume the first payroll check is numbered 491 and enter the payroll check numbers in the Payroll Register.
4. Prepare a general journal entry to record the employer's payroll taxes resulting from the payroll. Assume the company has a merit rating that reduces its state unemployment tax rate to 2.3% of the first $7,000 paid each employee.

Problem 13–3   A company subject to the Fair Labor Standards Act accumulated the following payroll information for the weekly pay period ended December 19:

| Employees | Clock Card No. | Daily Time | | | | | | | Pay Rate | Income Tax Exemptions | Medical Insurance | Union Dues | Earnings to End of Previous Week |
		M	T	W	T	F	S	S					
Mike Linder	40	8	6	8	8	8	4	0	$ 8.50	1	$27.00	$9.00	$17,000
Mark Mangum	41	8	8	8	7	8	4	0	8.00	2	27.00	9.00	6,100
Tim Snook	42	8	8	8	8	8	0	0	9.00	4	27.00	9.00	18,150
Kathy White	43	8	8	8	9	9	0	0	12.00	3	27.00		22,600

Required:

1. Enter the relevant information in the proper columns of a Payroll Register and complete the register using a 7% FICA tax rate on the wages of each employee, since the wages of none had reached the $35,700 tax exempt point. Use the wage bracket withholding table of Illustration 13–3 to determine the federal income tax to be withheld from the wages of each employee. Assume all employees are married and the first one is a salesperson, the second two work in the shop, and the last one works in the office.
2. Prepare a general journal entry to record the payroll register information.
3. Make the check register entry to transfer funds equal to the payroll from the regular bank account to the payroll bank account (Check No. 370) under the assumption the company uses special payroll checks and a payroll bank account in paying its employees. Assume the first payroll check is numbered 715 and enter the payroll check numbers in the Payroll Register.
4. Prepare a general journal entry to record the employer's payroll taxes resulting from the payroll. Assume the company has a merit rating that reduces its state unemployment tax rate to 1.9% of the first $7,000 paid each employee.
5. Prepare a general journal entry to accrue employee fringe benefit costs for the week. Assume the company matches the employees' payments for medical insurance and contributes an amount equal to 10% of each employee's gross pay to a retirement program.

Problem 13–4   A company has four employees to each of whom it pays $850 per month on the last day of each month. On June 1, the following accounts and balances appeared in its ledger:

a. FICA Taxes Payable, $476. (The balance of this account represents the liability for both the employer and employees' FICA taxes for the May 31 payroll only.)
b. Employees' Federal Income Taxes Payable, $404 (liability for May only).
c. Federal Unemployment Taxes Payable, $136 (liability for first five months of the year).
d. State Unemployment Taxes Payable, $170 (liability for April and May).
e. Employees' Hospital Insurance Payable, $600 (liability for April and May).

During June and July, the company completed the following payroll related transactions:

June 12   Issued Check No. 755 payable to Security Bank, a federal depository bank authorized to receive FICA and employee income tax payments from employers. The check was for $880 and was in payment of the May FICA and employee income taxes.
     30   Prepared a general journal entry to record the June Payroll Register which had the following column totals:

FICA Taxes	Federal Income Taxes	Hospital Insurance Deductions	Total Deductions	Net Pay	Office Salaries	Shop Wages
$238	$404	$300	$942	$2,458	$850	$2,550

June 30   Issued Check No. 828 payable to Payroll Bank Account in payment of the June payroll. Endorsed the check, deposited it in the payroll bank account, and issued payroll checks to the employees.
     30   Prepared and posted a general journal entry to record the employer's payroll taxes resulting from the June payroll. The company has a merit rating that reduces its state unemployment tax rate to 2.5% of the first $7,000 paid each employee.
July 14   Issued Check No. 883 payable to Security Bank. The check was in payment of the June FICA and employee income taxes.
     14   Issued Check No. 884 payable to Apex Insurance Company. The check was for $900 and was in payment of the April, May, and June employees' hospital insurance.
     14   Issued Check No. 885 to the State Tax Commission for the April, May, and June state unemployment taxes. Mailed the check along with the second quarter tax return to the State Tax Commission.
     31   Issued Check No. 915 payable to Security Bank in payment of the employer's federal unemployment taxes for the first two quarters of the year.
     31   Mailed to the Internal Revenue Service the Employer's Quarterly Tax Return reporting the FICA taxes and the employees' federal income tax deductions for the second quarter of the year.

Required:

Prepare the necessary general journal and check register entries to record the transactions.

ALTERNATE PROBLEMS

Problem 13–1A   On January 5, at the end of the first weekly pay period of the year, the column totals of a company's Payroll Register indicated its sales employees had earned $2,650, its office employees had earned $1,250, and its delivery employee $300. The employees were to have FICA taxes withheld from their wages at an assumed 7% rate plus $420 federal income taxes, $190 hospital insurance deductions, and $45 of union dues.

Required:

1. Calculate the total of the FICA Taxes Payable column in the Payroll Register, and prepare a general journal entry to record the register information.
2. Prepare a general journal entry to record the employer's payroll taxes resulting from the payroll. Assume the company has a merit rating that reduces its state unemployment tax rate to 2.4% of the first $7,000 paid each employee.
3. Under the assumption the company uses special payroll checks and a payroll bank account in paying its employees, give the check register entry (Check No. 611) to transfer funds equal to the payroll from the regular bank account to the payroll bank account.
4. Answer this question: after the check register entry is made and posted, are additional debit and credit entries required to record the payroll checks and pay the employees?

Problem 13–2A   The following information was taken from the payroll records of Compu-Serve Company for the weekly pay period ending December 24.

Employees	Clock Card No.	M	T	W	T	F	S	S	Pay Rate	Federal Income Taxes	Hospital Insurance	Union Dues	Earnings to End of Previous Week
Julie Albers	14	8	8	8	8	8	0	0	$15.00	$ 84.00	$18.00		$35,500
Roy First	15	8	8	8	7	8	6	0	14.00	80.64	24.00	$10.00	32,130
Kim Mayo	16	8	8	8	8	8	0	0	13.00	52.00	18.00	10.00	30,050
John Porter	17	8	8	8	8	8	3	0	14.00	93.45	18.00	10.00	16,100
Dick Tieman	18	8	8	7	8	8	2	0	12.00	54.12	18.00	10.00	4,310
										$364.21	$96.00	$40.00	

Required:

1. Enter the relevant information in the proper columns of a Payroll Register and complete the register using a 7% FICA tax rate on the first $35,700 paid each employee. Assume the company has a union contract that requires time and a half for work on Saturdays. Charge the wages of Julie

Albers to Office Salaries Expense and the wages of the remaining employees to Technicians' Wages Expense.

2. Prepare a general journal entry to record the payroll register information.

3. Assume the company uses special payroll checks drawn on a payroll bank account in paying its employees, and make the check register entry (Check No. 160) to transfer funds equal to the payroll from the regular bank account to the payroll bank account. Also assume the first payroll check is No. 790 and enter the payroll check numbers in the Payroll Register.

4. Prepare a general journal entry to record the employer's payroll taxes resulting from the payroll. Assume the concern has a merit rating that reduces its state unemployment tax rate to 1.2% of the first $7,000 paid each employee.

Problem 13–3A   The following information for the weekly pay period ended December 9 was taken from the records of a company subject to the Fair Labor Standards Act:

| Employees | Clock Card No. | Daily Time | | | | | | | Pay Rate | Income Tax Exemptions | Medical Insurance | Union Dues | Earnings to End of Previous Week |
		M	T	W	T	F	S	S					
Bob Bebe	18	8	8	8	6	8	4	0	$8.00	2	$26.50		$15,760
Frank Grey	19	8	8	8	6	8	6	0	7.00	3	20.00		6,300
Sue Hitch........	20	8	8	8	6	8	8	0	8.50	4	20.00	$10.00	17,700
Molly Kimbal	21	8	8	8	6	8	8	0	7.50	1	26.50	10.00	6,900

Required:

1. Enter the relevant information in the proper columns of a Payroll Register and complete the register. Use a 7% FICA tax rate to calculate the FICA tax of each employee. Use the wage bracket withholding table of Illustration 13–3 to determine the federal income taxes to be withheld from the wages of the employees. Assume that all employees are married and that the first employee works in the office, the second is a salesperson, and the last two work in the shop.

2. Prepare a general journal entry to record the payroll register information.

3. Make the check register entry (Check No. 399) to transfer funds equal to the payroll from the regular bank account to the payroll bank account. Assume the first payroll check is numbered 812 and enter the payroll check numbers in the Payroll Register.

4. Prepare a general journal entry to record the employer's payroll taxes resulting from the payroll. Assume the company has a merit rating that reduces its state unemployment tax rate to 1.5% of the first $7,000 paid each employee.

5. Prepare a general journal entry to accrue employee fringe benefit costs for the week. Assume the company matches the employees' payments for medical insurance and contributes an amount equal to 10% of each employee's gross pay to a retirement program.

Problem 13–4A   Smothers Company has four employees to each of whom it pays $900 per month on the last day of each month. On June 1, the following accounts and balances appeared in its ledger:

FICA taxes payable (liability for the employer's and employees'
  taxes resulting from the May 31 payroll) $504.00
Employees' federal income taxes payable (liability for the May 31
  payroll deductions) 424.00
Federal unemployment taxes payable (liability for first five months
  of the year) 144.00
State unemployment taxes payable (liability for April and May) 108.00
Employees' hospital insurance payable (liability for April and
  May) 168.00

During June and July, the company completed the following payroll related transactions:

June 14   Issued Check No. 816 payable to Guaranty Bank, a federal depository bank authorized to accept FICA and employee income tax payments from employers. The check was for $928 and was in payment of the May FICA and employee income taxes.

30   Prepared and posted a general journal entry to record the June Payroll Register. The register had the following column totals:

Gross pay $3,600
Employees' FICA taxes payable 252
Employees' federal income taxes payable 424
Employees' hospital insurance payable 84
Total deductions 760
Net pay 2,840
Sales salaries 2,700
Office salaries 900

30   Issued Check No. 863 payable to Payroll Bank Account in payment of the June payroll. Endorsed the check, deposited it in the payroll bank account, and issued payroll checks to the employees.

30   Prepared and posted a general journal entry to record the employer's payroll taxes resulting from the June 30 payroll. Due to a merit rating the company's state unemployment tax rate was 1.5% of the first $7,000 paid each employee, and no employee had earned that amount.

July 15   Issued Check No. 911 payable to Guaranty Bank. The check was in payment of the June FICA and employee income taxes.

15   Issued Check No. 912 to the State Tax Commission for the April, May, and June state unemployment taxes. Mailed the check along with the second quarter tax return to the State Tax Commission.

20   Issued Check No. 933 payable to Security Insurance Company. The check was for $252 and was in payment of the April, May, and June employees' hospital insurance.

31   Issued Check No. 989 payable to Guaranty Bank in payment of the federal unemployment tax for the first two quarters.

31   Mailed the Internal Revenue Service the Employer's Quarterly Tax Return, Form 941, reporting the FICA taxes and the employees' federal income tax deductions for the second quarter.

Required:

Prepare the necessary general journal and check register entries to record the transactions.

PROVOCATIVE PROBLEMS

Provocative Problem 13–1, Centex Snoshove Company

Centex Snoshove Company has 200 regular employees, all earning in excess of $7,000 per year. The company's plant and office are located in a state in which the maximum unemployment tax rate is 2.7% of the first $7,000 paid each employee. However, the company has an excellent past unemployment record and a merit rating that reduces its state unemployment tax rate to 0.5% of the first $7,000 paid each employee.

The company has recently received an order for snow shovels from a large chain of department stores. The order should be very profitable and will probably be repeated each year. In filling the order, Centex can stamp out the parts for the shovels with present machines and employees. However, it will have to add 40 persons to its work force for 40 hours per week for 10 weeks to assemble the shovels and pack them for shipment.

The company can hire these workers and add them to its own payroll or it can secure the services of 40 people through Handy Labor, Inc., a company in the business of supplying temporary help. If the temporary help is secured through Handy Labor, Inc., Centex will pay Handy Labor, Inc., $8.50 per hour for each hour worked by each person supplied. The people will be employees of Handy Labor, Inc., and it will pay their wages and all taxes on the wages. On the other hand, if Centex employs the workers and places them on its payroll, it will pay them $7 per hour and will also pay the following payroll taxes on their wages: FICA tax, 7% (assumed rate); federal unemployment tax, 0.8% on the first $7,000 paid each employee; state unemployment tax, 2.7% on the first $7,000 paid each employee. (The state unemployment tax rate will be 2.7% because if the company hires the temporary people and terminates them each year after 10 weeks, it will lose its merit rating.)

Should Centex place the temporary help on its own payroll or should it secure their services through Handy Labor, Inc.? Justify your answer.

Provocative Problem 13–2, Technical Service Company

Technical Service Company employs a highly skilled technician at an annual salary of $42,000. The company pays federal unemployment taxes of 0.8% and state unemployment taxes of 2.0% on the first $7,000 of the technician's wages. FICA taxes are 7% of the first $35,700. The company also pays $110 per month for the employee's medical insurance. Effective July 1, the company agreed to contribute 10% of the technician's gross pay to a retirement program.

What was the total monthly cost of employing the technician in January, May, August, and December? Assuming the employee works 170 hours each month, what is the cost per hour in January? If the annual gross salary is increased by $3,000, what will be the increase in the total annual costs of employing the technician?

Partnership Accounting

14

After studying Chapter 14, you should be able to:

List the characteristics of a partnership and explain the importance of mutual agency and unlimited liability by a person about to become a partner.

Allocate partnership earnings to partners *(a)* on a stated fractional basis, *(b)* in the partners' capital ratio, and *(c)* through the use of salary and interest allowances.

Prepare entries for *(a)* the sale of a partnership interest, *(b)* the admission of a new partner by investment, and *(c)* the retirement of a partner by the withdrawal of partnership assets.

Prepare entries required in the liquidation of a partnership.

Define or explain the words and phrases listed in the chapter Glossary.

A majority of the states have adopted the Uniform Partnership Act to govern the formation and operation of partnerships. This act defines a *partnership* as "an association of two or more persons to carry on as co-owners a business for profit." A partnership has been further defined as "an association of two or more competent persons under a contract to combine some or all their property, labor, and skills in the operation of a business." Both of these definitions tell something of a partnership's legal nature. However, a better understanding of a partnership as a form of business organization may be gained by examining some of its characteristics.

CHARACTERISTICS OF A PARTNERSHIP

A Voluntary Association

A partnership is a voluntary association into which a person cannot be forced against his or her will. This is because a partner is responsible for the business acts of his or her partners when the acts are within the scope of the partnership. Also, a partner is personally liable for all of the debts of his or her partnership. Consequently, partnership law recognizes it is only fair that a person be permitted to select the people he or she wishes to join in a partnership. Normally, a person will select only financially responsible people in whose judgment he or she has respect.

Based on a Contract

One advantage of a partnership as a form of business organization is the ease with which it may be begun. All that is required is that two or more legally competent people agree to be partners. Their agreement becomes a *contract*. It should be in writing, with all anticipated points of future disagreement covered. However, it is binding if only orally expressed.

Limited Life

The life of a partnership is always limited. Death, *bankruptcy,* or anything that takes away the ability of one of the partners to contract automatically ends a partnership. In addition, since a partnership is based on a contract, if the contract is for a definite period, the partnership ends when that period expires. If the contract does not specify a time period, the partnership ends when the business for which it was created is completed. Or, if no time is stated and the business cannot be completed but goes on indefinitely, the partnership may be terminated at will by any one of the partners.

Mutual Agency

Normally, there is *mutual agency* in a partnership. This means that under normal circumstances, every partner is an agent of the partnership and can enter into and bind it to any contract within the apparent scope of its business. For example, a partner in a merchandising business can bind the partnership to contracts to buy merchandise, lease a store building, borrow money, or hire employees. These are all within the scope of a merchandising firm. On the other hand, a partner in a law firm, acting alone, cannot bind his or her partners to a contract to buy merchandise for resale or rent a store building. These are not within the normal scope of a law firm's business.

Partners among themselves may agree to limit the right of any one or more of the partners to negotiate certain contracts for the partnership. Such an agreement is binding on the partners and on outsiders who know of the agreement. However, it is not binding on outsiders who are unaware of its existence. Outsiders who are unaware of anything to the contrary have a right to assume that each partner has the normal agency rights of a partner.

Mutual agency offers an important reason for care in the selection of partners. Good partners benefit all; but a poor partner can do great damage. Mutual agency plus unlimited liability are the reasons most partnerships have only a few members.

Unlimited Liability

When a partnership business is unable to pay its debts, the creditors may satisfy their claims from the personal assets of the partners. Furthermore, if the property of a partner is insufficient to meet his or her share, the creditors may turn to the assets of the remaining partners who are able to pay. Thus, a partner may be called on to pay all the debts of his or her partnership and is said to have *unlimited liability* for its debts.

Unlimited liability may be illustrated as follows. Ned Albert and Carol Bates each invested $5,000 in a store to be operated as a partnership, under an agreement to share losses and gains equally. Albert has no property other than his $5,000 investment. Bates owns her own home, a farm, and has sizable savings in addition to her investment. The partners rented store space and bought merchandise and fixtures costing $30,000. They paid $10,000 in cash and promised to pay the balance at a later date. However, the night before the store opened the building in which it was located burned and the merchandise and fixtures were totally destroyed. There was no insurance, all the partnership assets were lost, and Albert has no other assets. Consequently, the partnership creditors may collect the full $20,000 of their claims from Bates. However, Bates may look to Albert for payment of half at a later date, if Albert ever becomes able to pay.

ADVANTAGES AND DISADVANTAGES OF A PARTNERSHIP

Limited life, mutual agency, and unlimited liability are disadvantages of a partnership. Yet, a partnership has advantages over both the single proprietorship and corporation forms of organization. A partnership has the advantage of being able to bring together more money and skills than a single proprietorship. It is much easier to organize than a corporation. It does not have the corporation's governmental supervision nor its extra burden of taxation. And, partners may act freely and without the necessity of stockholders' and directors' meetings, as is required in a corporation.

PARTNERSHIP ACCOUNTING

Partnership accounting is exactly like that of a single proprietorship except for transactions that directly affect the partners' equities. Because ownership rights in a partnership are divided between two or more partners, there must be (1) a capital account for each partner, (2) a withdrawals account for each partner, and (3) an accurate measurement and division of earnings.

Each partner's capital account is credited, and asset accounts showing the nature of the assets invested are debited in recording the investment of each partner. A partner's withdrawals are debited to his or her withdrawals account. And, in the end-of-period closing procedure, the capital account is credited for a partner's share of the net income. Obviously, these procedures are not new; only the added accounts are new, and they need no further consideration here. However, the matter of dividing earnings among partners requires additional discussion.

NATURE OF PARTNERSHIP EARNINGS

Law and custom recognize that partners cannot enter into an employer-employee contractual relationship with themselves. Hence, partners cannot legally hire themselves and pay themselves a salary. Furthermore, law and custom recognize that a partner works for partnership profits and not a salary. Also, law and custom recognize that a partner invests in a partnership for earnings and not for interest. However, it should be recognized that partnership earnings do include a return for services, even though the return is contained within the earnings and is not a salary in a legal sense. Likewise, partnership earnings include a return on invested capital, although the return is not interest in the legal sense of the term. Furthermore, if partnership earnings are to be fairly shared, it is often necessary to recognize this. For example, if one partner contributes five times as much capital as another, it is only fair that this be taken into consideration in the method of sharing. Likewise, if the services of one partner are much more valuable than those of another, some provision should be made for the unequal service contributions.

DIVISION OF EARNINGS

The law provides that in the absence of a contrary agreement, all partnership earnings are shared equally by the partners. However, partners may agree to any method of sharing. If they agree to a method of sharing earnings but say nothing of losses, losses are shared in the same way as earnings.

Several methods of sharing partnership earnings may be employed. All attempt in one way or another to recognize differences in service contributions or in investments, when such differences exist. Three frequently used methods to share earnings are: (1) on a stated fractional basis, (2) based on the ratio of capital investments, or (3) based on salary and interest allowances and the remainder in a fixed ratio.

EARNINGS ALLOCATED ON A STATED FRACTIONAL BASIS

The easiest way to divide partnership earnings is to give each partner a stated fraction of the total. A division on a fractional basis may provide for an equal sharing if service and capital contributions are equal. An equal sharing may also be provided when the greater capital contribution of one partner is offset by a greater service contribution of another. Or, if the service and capital contributions are unequal, a fixed ratio may easily provide for an unequal sharing. All that is necessary in any case is for the partners to agree as to the fractional share to be given each.

For example, the partnership agreement of Morse and North may provide that each partner is to receive half the earnings. Or the agreement may provide for two thirds to Morse and one third to North. Or it may provide for three fourths to Morse and one fourth to North. Any fractional basis may be agreed upon as long as the partners feel earnings are fairly shared. For example, assume the agreement of Morse and North provides for a two-thirds and one-third sharing, and earnings for a year are $30,000. After all revenue and expense accounts are closed, if earnings are $30,000, the partnership Income Summary account has a $30,000 credit balance. It is closed, and the earnings are allocated to the partners with the following entry:

Dec.	31	Income Summary	30,000.00	
		A. P. Morse, Capital		20,000.00
		R. G. North, Capital		10,000.00
		To close the Income Summary account and allocate the earnings.		

DIVISION OF EARNINGS BASED ON THE RATIO OF CAPITAL INVESTMENTS

If the business of a partnership is of a nature that earnings are closely related to money invested, a division of earnings based on the ratio of partners' investments offers a fair sharing method. To illustrate this method, assume that Chase, Davis, and Fall have agreed to share earnings in the ratio of their investments. If these are Chase, $50,000, Davis, $30,000, and Fall, $40,000, and if the earnings for the year are $48,000, the respective shares of the partners are calculated as follows:

Step 1:   Chase, capital .... $ 50,000
           Davis, capital 30,000
           Fall, capital 40,000
              Total invested..... $120,000

Step 2:   Share of earnings to Chase $\frac{\$50,000}{\$120,000} \times \$48,000 = \$20,000$

           Share of earnings to Davis $\frac{\$30,000}{\$120,000} \times \$48,000 = \$12,000$

           Share of earnings to Fall $\frac{\$40,000}{\$120,000} \times \$48,000 = \$16,000$

The entry to allocate the earnings to the partners is then:

Dec.	31	Income Summary	48,000.00	
		T. S. Chase, Capital		20,000.00
		S. A. Davis, Capital.....................		12,000.00
		R. R. Fall, Capital		16,000.00
		To close the Income Summary account and allocate the earnings.		

SALARIES AND INTEREST AS AIDS IN SHARING

Sometimes partners' capital contributions are unequal. Also, the service contributions of the partners may not be equal. Even in partnerships in which all partners work full time, the services of one partner may be more valuable than the services of another. When these situations occur and, for example, the capital contributions are unequal, the partners may allocate a portion of their net income to themselves in the form of interest, so as to compensate for the unequal investments. Or, when service contributions are unequal, they may use salary allowances as a means of compensating for unequal service contributions. Or, when investment and service contributions are both unequal, they may use a combination of interest and salary allowances in an effort to share earnings fairly.

For example, Hill and Dale began a partnership business of a kind in which Hill has had experience and could command a $36,000 annual salary working for another firm of like nature. Dale is new to the business and could expect to earn not more than $24,000 working elsewhere. Furthermore, Hill invested $30,000 in the business and Dale invested $10,000. Consequently, the partners agreed that in order to compensate for the unequal service and capital contributions, they will share losses and gains as follows:

1. A share of the profits equal to interest at 10% is to be allowed on the partners' initial investments.
2. Annual salary allowances of $36,000 per year to Hill and $24,000 per year to Dale are to be allowed.
3. The remaining balance of income or loss is to be shared equally.

Under this agreement, a first year $69,000 net income would be shared as in Illustration 14–1.

After the shares in the net income are determined, the following entry is used to close the Income Summary account. Observe in the

Illustration 14–1

	Share to Hill	Share to Dale	Income allocated
Total net income			$69,000
Allocated as interest:			
Hill (10% on $30,000)	$ 3,000		
Dale (10% on $10,000)		$ 1,000	
Total allocated as interest			4,000
Balance of income after interest allowances			$65,000
Allocated as salary allowances:			
Hill	36,000		
Dale		24,000	
Total allocated as salary allowances			60,000
Balance of income after interest and salary allowances			$ 5,000
Balance allocated equally:			
Hill	2,500		
Dale		2,500	
Total allocated equally			5,000
Balance of income			–0–
Shares of the partners	$41,500	$27,500	

entry that the credit amounts may be taken from the first two column totals of the computation of Illustration 14–1.

Dec.	31	Income Summary	69,000.00	
		Hill, Capital		41,500.00
		Dale, Capital		27,500.00
		To close the Income Summary account and allocate the earnings.		

In a legal sense, partners do not work for salaries, nor do they invest in a partnership to earn interest. They invest and work for earnings. Consequently, when a partnership agreement provides for salaries and interest, the partners should understand that the salaries and interest are not really salaries and interest. They are only a means of sharing losses and gains.

In the illustration just completed, the $69,000 net income exceeded the salary and interest allowances of the partners. However, the partners would use the same method to share a net income smaller than their salary and interest allowances, or to share a loss. For example,

Illustration 14–2

	Share to Hill	Share to Dale	Income allocated
Total net income			$ 45,000
Allocated as interest:			
Hill (10% on $30,000)	$ 3,000		
Dale (10% on $10,000)		$ 1,000	
Total allocated as interest			4,000
Balance of income after interest allowances			$ 41,000
Allocated as salary allowances:			
Hill	36,000		
Dale		24,000	
Total allocated as salary allowances			60,000
Balance of income after interest and salary allowances (a negative amount)			$(19,000)
Balance allocated equally:			
Hill	(9,500)		
Dale		(9,500)	
Total allocated equally			(19,000)
Balance of income			–0–
Shares of the partners	$29,500	$15,500	

assume that Hill and Dale earned only $45,000 in a year. A $45,000 net income would be shared by the partners as in Illustration 14–2.

A net loss would be shared by Hill and Dale in the same manner as the foregoing $45,000 net income. The only difference being that the loss-and-gain-sharing procedure would begin with a negative amount of income, in other words, a net loss. The amount allocated equally would then be a larger negative amount.

PARTNERSHIP FINANCIAL STATEMENTS

In most respects, partnership financial statements are like those of a single proprietorship. However, one common difference is that the income allocation is often shown on the income statement following the reported net income. For example, an income statement prepared for Hill and Dale might show the allocation of the $45,000 net income of Illustration 14–2 as in Illustration 14–3.

Illustration 14–3

HILL AND DALE
Income Statement for Year Ended December 31, 19—

Sales		$332,400
~~		
~~		
Net income		$ 45,000
Allocation of net income to the partners:		
To Hill:		
Interest at 10% on investment	$ 3,000	
Salary allowance	36,000	
Total	$ 39,000	
Less one half the remaining deficit	(9,500)	
Share of the net income		$ 29,500
To Dale:		
Interest at 10% on investment	$ 1,000	
Salary allowance	24,000	
Total	$ 25,000	
Less one half the remaining deficit	(9,500)	
Share of the net income		15,500
Net income allocated		$ 45,000

ADDITION OR WITHDRAWAL OF A PARTNER

A partnership is based on a contract between specific individuals. Consequently, an existing partnership is ended when a partner withdraws or a new partner is added. A partner may sell his or her partnership interest and withdraw from a partnership. Also, a partner may withdraw his or her equity, taking partnership cash or other assets. Likewise, a new partner may join an existing partnership by purchasing an interest from one or more of its partners or by investing cash or other assets in the business.

Sale of a Partnership Interest

Assume that Abbott, Burns, and Camp are partners in a partnership that has no liabilities and the following assets and equities:

Assets		*Equities*	
Cash	$ 3,000	Abbott, capital	$ 5,000
Other assets	12,000	Burns, capital	5,000
		Camp, capital	5,000
Total assets	$15,000	Total equities	$15,000

Camp's equity in this partnership is $5,000. If Camp sells this equity to Davis for $7,000, Camp is selling a $5,000 interest in the partnership assets. The entry on the partnership books to transfer the equity is:

Feb.	4	Camp, Capital	5,000.00	
		Davis, Capital		5,000.00
		To transfer Camp's equity in the partner-		
		ship assets to Davis.		

After this entry is posted, the assets and equities of the new partnership are:

Assets		Equities	
Cash	$ 3,000	Abbott, capital	$ 5,000
Other assets	12,000	Burns, capital	5,000
		Davis, capital	5,000
Total assets	$15,000	Total equities	$15,000

Two points should be noted in regard to this transaction. First, the $7,000 Davis paid Camp is not recorded in the partnership books. Camp sold and transferred a $5,000 equity in the partnership assets to Davis. The entry that records the transfer is a debit to Camp, Capital and a credit to Davis, Capital for $5,000. Furthermore, the entry is the same whether Davis pays Camp $7,000, or $70,000. The amount is paid directly to Camp. It is a side transaction between Camp and Davis and does not affect partnership assets.

The second point to be noted is that Abbott and Burns must agree to the sale and transfer if Davis is to become a partner. Abbott and Burns cannot prevent Camp from selling the interest to Davis. On the other hand, Camp cannot force Abbott and Burns to accept Davis as a partner. If Abbott and Burns agree to accept Davis, a new partnership is formed and a new contract with a new loss-and-gain-sharing ratio must be drawn. If Camp sells to Davis and either Abbott or Burns refuses to accept Davis as a partner, under the Uniform Partnership Act Davis gets Camp's share of partnership gains and losses and Camp's share of partnership assets if the firm is liquidated. However, Davis gets no voice in the management of the firm until admitted as a partner.

Investing in an Existing Partnership

Instead of purchasing the equity of an existing partner, an individual may gain an equity by investing assets in the business, with the invested assets becoming the property of the partnership. For example, assume that the partnership of Evans and Gage has assets and equities as follows:

Assets		Equities	
Cash	$ 3,000	Evans, capital	$20,000
Other assets	37,000	Gage, capital	20,000
Total assets	$40,000	Total equities	$40,000

Also, assume that Evans and Gage have agreed to accept Hart as a partner with a one-half interest in the business upon his investment of $40,000. The entry to record Hart's investment is:

Mar.	2	Cash	40,000.00	
		Hart, Capital		40,000.00
		To record the investment of Hart.		

After the entry is posted, the assets and equities of the new partnership appear as follows:

Assets		Equities	
Cash	$43,000	Evans, capital	$20,000
Other assets	37,000	Gage, capital	20,000
		Hart, capital	40,000
Total assets	$80,000	Total equities	$80,000

In this case, Hart has a 50% equity in the assets of the business. However, he does not necessarily have a right to one half of its net income. The sharing of losses and gains is a separate matter on which the partners must agree. Furthermore, the agreed method may bear no relation to their capital ratio.

A Bonus to the Old Partners

Sometimes, when the equity of a partnership is worth more than the amounts of equity recorded in the accounting records, its partners may require an incoming partner to give a bonus for the privilege of joining the firm. For example, Judd and Kirk operate a partnership business, sharing its earnings equally. The partnership's accounting records show that Judd has a $38,000 equity in the business, and Kirk has a $32,000 equity. They have agreed to allow Lee a one-third equity and a one-third share of the partnership's earnings upon the investment of $50,000. Lee's equity is determined with a calculation like this:

Equities of the existing partners ($38,000 + $32,000) ..	$ 70,000
Investment of the new partner	50,000
Total equities in the new partnership	$120,000
Equity of Lee (⅓ of total)	$ 40,000

And the entry to record Lee's investment is:

May	15	Cash	50,000.00	
		Lee, Capital		40,000.00
		Judd, Capital		5,000.00
		Kirk, Capital		5,000.00
		To record the investment of Lee.		

The $10,000 difference between the $50,000 invested by Lee and the $40,000 credited to his capital account is a bonus that is shared by Judd and Kirk in their loss-and-gain-sharing ratio. Such a bonus is always shared by the old partners in their loss-and-gain-sharing ratio. This is fair because the bonus compensates the old partners for increases in the worth of the partnership that have not yet been recorded as income.

RECORDING GOODWILL. Instead of allowing bonuses to the old partners, goodwill may be recorded in the admission of a new partner, with the amount of the goodwill being used to increase the equities of the old partners. This can be justified only if the old partnership has a sustained earnings rate in excess of the average for its industry. However, in practice, goodwill is seldom recognized upon the admission of a new partner. Instead, the bonus method is used.

Bonus to the New Partner

Sometimes the members of an existing partnership may be very anxious to bring a new partner into their firm. The business may need additional cash or the new partner may have exceptional abilities or business contacts that will increase profits. In such a situation, the old partners may be willing to give the new partner a larger equity in the business than the amount of his or her investment. For example, Moss and Owen are partners with capital account balances of $30,000 and $18,000, respectively, and sharing losses and gains in a 2 to 1 ratio. The partners are anxious to have Pitt join their partnership and will allow him a one-fourth equity in the firm if he will invest $12,000. If Pitt accepts, his equity in the new firm is calculated as follows:

Equities of the existing partners ($30,000 + $18,000) ..	$48,000
Investment of the new partner	12,000
Total equities in the new partnership	$60,000
Equity of Pitt (¼ of total)	$15,000

And the entry to record Pitt's investment is:

June	1	Cash	12,000.00	
		Moss, Capital	2,000.00	
		Owen, Capital	1,000.00	
		Pitt, Capital		15,000.00
		To record the investment of Pitt.		

Note that Pitt's bonus is contributed by the old partners in their loss-and-gain-sharing ratio. Also remember that Pitt's one-fourth equity does not necessarily entitle him to one fourth of the earnings of the business, since the sharing of losses and gains is a separate matter for agreement by the partners.

Withdrawal of a Partner

The best practice in regard to a partner's withdrawal from a partnership is for the partners to provide in advance in their partnership contract the procedures to be followed. Such procedures commonly provide for an audit of the accounting records and a revaluation of the partnership assets. The revaluation is very desirable since it places the assets on the books at current values. It also causes the retiring partner's capital account to reflect the current value of the partner's equity. Often in such cases the agreement also provides that the retiring partner is to withdraw assets equal to the book amount of the revalued equity.

For example, assume that Blue is retiring from the partnership of Smith, Blue, and Short. The partners have always shared losses and gains in the ratio of Smith, one half; Blue, one fourth; and Short, one fourth. Their partnership agreement provides for an audit and asset revaluation upon the retirement of a partner. Just prior to the audit and revaluation, their balance sheet shows the following assets and equities:

Assets			Equities		
Cash		$11,000	Smith, capital		$22,000
Merchandise inventory .		16,000	Blue, capital		10,000
Equipment	$20,000		Short, capital		10,000
Less accum. depr. ..	5,000	15,000			
Total assets		$42,000	Total equities		$42,000

The audit and appraisal indicate the merchandise inventory is over-valued by $4,000. Also, due to market changes, the partnership equipment should be valued at $25,000 with accumulated depreciation of $8,000. The entries to record these revaluations are:

Oct.	31	Smith, Capital	2,000.00	
		Blue, Capital	1,000.00	
		Short, Capital.............................	1,000.00	
		Merchandise inventory		4,000.00
		To revalue the inventory.		
	31	Equipment	5,000.00	
		Accumulated Depreciation, Equipment		3,000.00
		Smith, Capital		1,000.00
		Blue, Capital		500.00
		Short, Capital		500.00
		To revalue the equipment.		

Note in the illustrated entries that losses and gains are shared in the partners' loss-and-gain-sharing ratio. Losses and gains from asset revaluations are always so shared. The fairness of this is easy to see when it is remembered that if the partnership did not terminate, such losses and gains would sooner or later be reflected on the income statement.

After the entries revaluing the partnership assets are recorded, a balance sheet will show these revalued assets and equities for Smith, Blue, and Short:

Assets			Equities		
Cash		$11,000	Smith, capital		$21,000
Merchandise inventory .		12,000	Blue, capital		9,500
Equipment	$25,000		Short, capital		9,500
Less accum. depr. ..	8,000	17,000			
Total assets		$40,000	Total equities		$40,000

After the revaluation, if Blue withdraws, taking assets equal to his revalued equity, the entry to record the withdrawal is:

Oct.	31	Blue, Capital	9,500.00	
		Cash		9,500.00
		To record the withdrawal of Blue.		

In withdrawing, Blue does not have to take cash in settlement of his equity. He may take any combination of assets to which the partners agree, or he may take the new partnership's promissory note. Also, the withdrawal of Blue generally creates a new partnership. Consequently, a new partnership contract and a new loss-and-gain-sharing agreement may be required.

Partner Withdraws Taking Assets of Less Value than His Book Equity

Sometimes when a partner retires, the remaining partners may not wish to have the assets revalued and the new values recorded. In such cases, the partners may agree, for example, that the assets are overvalued. And, due to the overvalued assets, the retiring partner should in settlement of his equity take assets of less value than the book value of his equity. Sometimes, too, when assets are not overvalued, the retiring partner may be so anxious to retire that he is willing to take less than the current value of his equity just to get out of the partnership.

When a partner retires taking assets of less value than his equity, he is in effect leaving a portion of his book equity in the business. In such cases, the remaining partners share the unwithdrawn equity portion in their loss-and-gain-sharing ratio. For example, assume that Black, Brown, and Green are partners sharing gains and losses in a 2:2:1 ratio. Their assets and equities are:

Assets		Equities	
Cash	$ 5,000	Black, capital	$ 6,000
Merchandise	9,000	Brown, capital	6,000
Store equipment	4,000	Green, capital	6,000
Total assets	$18,000	Total equities	$18,000

Brown is so anxious to withdraw from the partnership that he is willing to retire if permitted to take $4,500 in cash in settlement for his equity. Black and Green agree to the $4,500 withdrawal, and Brown retires. The entry to record the retirement is:

Mar.	4	Brown, Capital	6,000.00	
		Cash		4,500.00
		Black, Capital		1,000.00
		Green, Capital		500.00
		To record the withdrawal of Brown.		

In retiring, Brown did not withdraw $1,500 of his book equity. This is divided between Black and Green in their loss-and-gain-sharing ratio. The loss-and-gain-sharing ratio of the original partnership was Black, 2; Brown, 2; and Green, 1. Therefore in the original partnership, Black and Green shared in a 2 to 1 ratio. Consequently, the unwithdrawn book equity of Brown is shared by Black and Green in this ratio.

Partner Withdraws Taking Assets of Greater Value than His Book Equity

There are two common reasons for a partner receiving upon retirement assets of greater value than his book equity. First, certain of the partnership assets may be undervalued. Or, the partners continuing the business may be so anxious for the retiring partner to withdraw that they are willing to give him assets of greater value than his book equity.

When assets are undervalued and the partners do not wish to change the recorded values, the partners may agree to permit a retiring member to withdraw assets of greater value than his book equity. In such cases, the retiring partner is, in effect, withdrawing his own book equity and a portion of his partners' equities. For example, assume that Jones, Thomas, and Finch are partners sharing gains and losses in a $3:2:1$ ratio. Their assets and equities are:

Assets		Equities	
Cash	$ 5,000	Jones, capital	$ 9,000
Merchandise	10,000	Thomas, capital	6,000
Equipment	3,000	Finch, capital	3,000
Total assets	$18,000	Total equities	$18,000

Finch wishes to withdraw from the partnership. Jones and Thomas plan to continue the business. The partners agree that certain of their assets are undervalued, but they do not wish to increase the recorded values. They further agree that if current values were recorded, the asset total would be increased $6,000 and the equity of Finch would be increased $1,000. Therefore, the partners agree that $4,000 is the proper value for Finch's equity and that he may withdraw that amount in cash. The entry to record the withdrawal is:

May	7	Finch, Capital..............................	3,000.00	
		Jones, Capital	600.00	
		Thomas, Capital	400.00	
		Cash		4,000.00
		To record the withdrawal of Finch.		

DEATH OF A PARTNER

A partner's death automatically dissolves and ends a partnership, and the deceased partner's estate is entitled to receive the amount of his or her equity. The partnership contract should contain provisions for settlement in case a partner dies. Included should be provisions for *(a)* an immediate closing of the books to determine earnings since the end of the previous accounting period and *(b)* a method for determining and recording current values for the assets. After earnings are shared and the current value of the deceased partner's equity is determined, the remaining partners and the deceased partner's estate must agree to a disposition of the equity. They may agree to its sale to the remaining partners or to an outsider, or they may agree to the withdrawal of assets in settlement. Entries for both of these procedures have already been discussed.

LIQUIDATIONS

When a partnership is liquidated, its business is ended. The assets are converted into cash, and the creditors are paid. The remaining cash is then distributed to the partners, and the partnership is dissolved. Although many combinations of circumstances occur in liquidations, only three are discussed here.

All Assets Realized before a Distribution; Assets Are Sold at a Profit

A partnership liquidation under this assumption may be illustrated with the following example. Ottis, Skinner, and Parr have operated a partnership for a number of years, sharing losses and gains in a 3:2:1 ratio. Due to several unsatisfactory conditions, the partners decide to liquidate as of December 31. On that date, the books are closed, the income from operations is transferred to the partners' capital accounts, and the following balance sheet is prepared:

Assets		Liabilities and Owners' Equity	
Cash	$10,000	Accounts payable	$ 5,000
Merchandise inventory	15,000	Ottis, capital	15,000
Other assets	25,000	Skinner, capital	15,000
		Parr, capital	15,000
		Total liabilities and	
Total assets	$50,000	owners' equity	$50,000

In a liquidation, either a gain or a loss normally results from the sale of each group of assets. These losses and gains are called "losses and gains from realization." They are shared by the partners in their loss-and-gain-sharing ratio. If Ottis, Skinner, and Parr sell their inventory for $12,000 and their other assets for $34,000, the sales and the net gain allocation are recorded as follows:

Jan.	12	Cash	12,000.00	
		Loss or Gain from Realization	3,000.00	
		Merchandise inventory		15,000.00
		Sold the inventory at a loss.		
	15	Cash	34,000.00	
		Other Assets		25,000.00
		Loss or Gain from Realization		9,000.00
		Sold the other assets at a profit.		
	15	Loss or Gain from Realization	6,000.00	
		Ottis, Capital		3,000.00
		Skinner, Capital		2,000.00
		Parr, Capital		1,000.00
		To allocate the net gain from realization to the partners in their 3:2:1 loss-and-gain-sharing ratio.		

Careful attention should be given to the last journal entry. In a partnership termination, when assets are sold at a loss or gain, the loss or gain is allocated to the partners in their loss-and-gain-sharing ratio. In solving liquidation problems, students sometimes attempt to allocate the assets to the partners in their loss-and-gain-sharing ratio. Obviously this is not correct. It is not assets but losses and gains that are shared in the loss-and-gain-sharing ratio.

After the merchandise and other assets of Ottis, Skinner, and Parr are sold and the net gain is allocated, a new balance sheet shows the following:

Assets		Liabilities and Owners' Equity	
Cash	$56,000	Accounts payable	$ 5,000
		Ottis, capital	18,000
		Skinner, capital	17,000
		Parr, capital	16,000
		Total liabilities and	
Total assets	$56,000	owners' equity	$56,000

Observe that the one asset, cash, $56,000, exactly equals the sum of the liabilities and the equities of the partners.

After partnership assets are realized and the gain or loss shared, entries are made to distribute the realized cash to the proper parties. Since creditors have first claim, they are paid first. After the creditors are paid, the remaining cash is divided among the partners. Each partner has the right to cash equal to his equity or, in other words, cash equal to the balance of his capital account. The entries to distribute the cash of Ottis, Skinner, and Parr are:

Jan.	15	Accounts payable	5,000.00	
		Cash		5,000.00
		To pay the claims of the creditors.		
	15	Ottis, Capital	18,000.00	
		Skinner, Capital	17,000.00	
		Parr, Capital	16,000.00	
		Cash		51,000.00
		To distribute the remaining cash to the partners according to their capital account balances.		

Notice that after losses and gains are shared and the creditors are paid, each partner receives liquidation cash equal to the balance remaining in his capital account. The partners receive these amounts because a partner's capital account balance shows his equity in the one partnership asset, cash.

All Assets Realized before a Distribution; Assets Sold at a Loss; Each Partner's Capital Account Is Sufficient to Absorb His Share of the Loss

In a partnership liquidation, the assets are sometimes sold at a net loss. For example, if contrary to the previous assumptions the inventory of Ottis, Skinner, and Parr is sold for $9,000 and the other assets for $13,000, the entries to record the sales and loss allocation are:

Jan.	12	Cash	9,000.00	
		Loss or Gain from Realization	6,000.00	
		Merchandise Inventory...................		15,000.00
		Sold the inventory at a loss.		
	15	Cash	13,000.00	
		Loss or Gain from Realization	12,000.00	
		Other Assets		25,000.00
		Sold the other assets at a loss.		
	15	Ottis, Capital	9,000.00	
		Skinner, Capital	6,000.00	
		Parr, Capital	3,000.00	
		Loss or Gain from Realization		18,000.00
		To allocate the loss from realization to the partners in their loss-and-gain-sharing ratio.		

After the entries are posted, a balance sheet shows that the partnership cash exactly equals the liabilities and the equities of the partners, as follows:

Assets		Liabilities and Owners' Equity	
Cash	$32,000	Accounts payable	$ 5,000
		Ottis, capital	6,000
		Skinner, capital	9,000
		Parr, capital	12,000
		Total liabilities and	
Total assets	$32,000	owners' equity	$32,000

The following entries are required to distribute the cash to the proper parties:

Jan.	15	Accounts Payable	5,000.00	
		Cash		5,000.00
		To pay the partnership creditors.		
	15	Ottis, Capital	6,000.00	
		Skinner, Capital	9,000.00	
		Parr, Capital	12,000.00	
		Cash		27,000.00
		To distribute the remaining cash to the partners according to the balances of their capital accounts.		

Notice again that after losses are shared and creditors are paid, each partner receives cash equal to his capital account balance.

All Assets Realized before a Distribution; Assets Sold at a Loss; a Partner's Capital Account Is Not Sufficient to Cover His Share of the Loss

Sometimes, a partner's share of realization losses is greater than the balance of his capital account. In such cases, the partner must, if he can, cover the deficit by paying cash into the partnership. For example, assume contrary to the previous illustrations that Ottis, Skinner, and Parr sell their merchandise for $3,000 and the other assets for $4,000. The entries to record the sales and the loss allocation are:

Jan.	12	Cash	3,000.00	
		Loss or Gain from Realization	12,000.00	
		Merchandise Inventory		15,000.00
		Sold the inventory at a loss.		
	15	Cash	4,000.00	
		Loss or Gain from Realization	21,000.00	
		Other Assets		25,000.00
		Sold the other assets at a loss.		
	15	Ottis, Capital	16,500.00	
		Skinner, Capital	11,000.00	
		Parr, Capital	5,500.00	
		Loss or Gain from Realization		33,000.00
		To record the allocation of the loss from realization to the partners in their loss-and-gain-sharing ratio.		

After the entry allocating the realization loss is posted, the capital account of Ottis has a $1,500 debit balance and appears as follows:

Ottis, Capital

Date		Explanation	Debit	Credit	Balance
Dec.	31	Balance			15,000.00
Jan.	15	Share of loss from realization	16,500.00		(1,500.00)

The partnership agreement provides that Ottis is allocated one half the losses or gains. Consequently, since his capital account balance is not large enough to absorb his loss share in this case, he must, if he can, pay $1,500 into the partnership to cover the *deficit*. If he is able to pay, the following entry is made:

Jan.	15	Cash	1,500.00	
		Ottis, Capital		1,500.00
		To record the additional investment of Ottis to cover his share of realization losses.		

After the $1,500 is received, the partnership has $18,500 in cash. The following entries are then made to distribute the cash to the proper parties:

Jan.	15	Accounts Payable	5,000.00	
		Cash		5,000.00
		To pay the partnership creditors.		
	15	Skinner, Capital	4,000.00	
		Parr, Capital	9,500.00	
		Cash		13,500.00
		To distribute the remaining cash to the partners according to the balances of their capital accounts.		

When a partner's share of partnership losses exceeds his capital account balance, he may be unable to make up the deficit. In such cases, since each partner has unlimited liability, the deficit must be borne by the remaining partner or partners. For example, assume that Ottis is unable to pay in the $1,500 necessary to cover the deficit in his capital account. If Ottis is unable to pay, his deficit must be shared by Skinner and Parr in their loss-and-gain-sharing ratio. The partners share losses and gains in the ratio of Ottis, 3; Skinner, 2; and Parr, 1. Therefore, Skinner and Parr share in a 2 to 1 ratio. Consequently, the $1,500 by which Ottis's share of the losses exceeded his capital account balance is apportioned between them in this ratio. Normally, the defaulting partner's deficit is transferred to the capital accounts of the remaining partners. This is accomplished for Ottis, Skinner, and Parr with the following entry:

Jan.	15	Skinner, Capital	1,000.00	
		Parr, Capital	500.00	
		Ottis, Capital		1,500.00
		To transfer the deficit of Ottis to the capital accounts of Skinner and Parr.		

After the deficit is transferred, the capital accounts of the partners appear as in Illustration 14–4.

Illustration 14–4

Ottis, Capital

Date		Explanation	Debit	Credit	Balance
Dec.	31	Balance			15,000.00
Jan.	15	Share of loss from realization	16,500.00		(1,500.00)
	15	Deficit to Skinner and Parr		1,500,00	–0–

Skinner, Capital

Date		Explanation	Debit	Credit	Balance
Dec.	31	Balance			15,000.00
Jan.	15	Share of loss from realization	11,000.00		4,000.00
	15	Share of Ottis's deficit	1,000.00		3,000.00

Parr, Capital

Date		Explanation	Debit	Credit	Balance
Dec.	31	Balance			15,000.00
Jan.	15	Share of loss from realization	5,500.00		9,500.00
	15	Share of Ottis's deficit	500.00		9,000.00

After the deficit is transferred, the $17,000 of liquidation cash is distributed with the following entries:

Jan.	15	Accounts Payable	5,000.00	
		Cash		5,000.00
		To pay the partnership creditors.		
	15	Skinner, Capital	3,000.00	
		Parr, Capital	9,000.00	
		Cash		12,000.00
		To distribute the remaining cash to the partners according to their capital account balances.		

It should be understood that the inability of Ottis to meet his loss share at this time does not relieve him of liability. If he becomes able to pay at some future time, Skinner and Parr may collect from him the full $1,500. Skinner may collect $1,000, and Parr, $500.

GLOSSARY

Deficit. A negative amount of an item.

Liquidation. The winding up of a business by converting its assets to cash and distributing the cash to the proper parties.

Mutual agency. The legal situation in a partnership whereby each partner is an agent of the partnership and is able to bind the partnership to contracts within the normal scope of the partnership business.

Partnership. An association of two or more persons to carry on a business as co-owners for profit.

Partnership contract. The document setting forth the agreed terms under which the members of a partnership will conduct the partnership business.

Unlimited liability.   The legal situation in a partnership that makes each partner responsible for paying all the debts of the partnership if his or her partners are unable to pay a share.

QUESTIONS FOR CLASS DISCUSSION

1. Hill and Dale are partners. Hill dies, and his son claims the right to take his father's place in the partnership. Does he have this right? Why?
2. If Ted Hall cannot legally enter into a contract, can he become a partner?
3. If a partnership contract does not state the period of time the partnership is to exist, when does the partnership end?
4. What is the meaning of the term *mutual agency* as applied to a partnership?
5. Jack and Jill are partners in the operation of a store. Jack without consulting Jill enters into a contract for the purchase of merchandise for resale

by the store. Jill contends that she did not authorize the order and refuses to take delivery. The vendor sues the partners for the contract price of the merchandise. Will the firm have to pay? Why?

6. Would your answer to Question 5 differ if Jack and Jill were partners in a public accounting firm?

7. May partners limit the right of a member of their firm to bind their partnership to contracts? Is such an agreement binding *(a)* on the partners and *(b)* on outsiders?

8. What is the meaning of the term *unlimited liability* when it is applied to members of a partnership?

9. Kennedy, Porter, and Foulke have been partners for three years. The partnership is dissolving, Kennedy is leaving the firm, and Porter and Foulke plan to carry on the business. In the final settlement, Kennedy places a $45,000 salary claim against the partnership. His contention is that since he devoted all of his time for three years to the affairs of the partnership, he has a claim for a salary of $15,000 for each year. Is his claim valid? Why?

10. The partnership agreement of Martin and Tritt provides for a two-thirds, one-third sharing of income but says nothing of losses. The operations for a year result in a loss. Martin claims the loss should be shared equally since the partnership agreement said nothing of sharing losses. Do you agree?

11. A, B, and C are partners with capital account balances of $6,000 each. D gives A $7,500 for his one-third interest in the partnership. The bookkeeper debits A, Capital and credits D, Capital for $6,000. D objects. He wants his capital account to show a $7,500 balance, the amount he paid for his interest. Explain why D's capital account is credited for $6,000.

12. After all partnership assets are converted to cash and all creditor claims have been paid, the remaining cash should equal the sum of the balances of the partners' capital accounts. Why?

13. J, K, and L are partners. In a liquidation, J's share of partnership losses exceeds his capital account balance. He is unable to meet the deficit from his personal assets, and the excess losses are shared by his partners. Does this relieve J of liability?

CLASS EXERCISES

Exercise 14–1   Linda Stewart and Steve Schwab began operating a partnership in January 198A. Linda invested $30,000, and Steve invested $20,000. On several occasions during the first year, they discussed alternative methods of allocating profits and losses but had not reached an agreement at year-end.

Required:

1. If the first year's net income was $90,000, how should it be allocated to the partners?

2. If the partners had agreed to share earnings in their investment ratio, how should the $90,000 be allocated?

3. If Linda worked 10 hours per week in the business and Steve worked 40 hours, and they agreed that earnings should be shared on the basis of the number of hours worked, how should the $90,000 be allocated?
4. Suppose the partners had agreed to share earnings by granting 12% interest on their investments, salary allowances of $15,000 to Linda and $30,000 to Steve, and the balance equally. How should the $90,000 be allocated?

Exercise 14–2

Linda Stewart and Steve Schwab, the partners of Exercise 14–1, have agreed to share earnings and losses by granting 12% interest on their investments, salary allowances of $15,000 to Linda and $30,000 to Steve, and the balance equally. Calculate the allocation to the partners of *(a)* a $40,000 net income and *(b)* a $20,000 net loss.

Exercise 14–3

The partners in A-1 Partnership have agreed that partner Smith may sell his $50,000 equity in the partnership to Jones, for which Jones will pay Smith $38,000. Present the partnership's journal entry to record the sale on August 30.

Exercise 14–4

The M&M Partnership has total partners' equity of $80,000, which is made up of McGowen, Capital, $60,000, and Messerly, Capital, $20,000. The partners share gains and losses in a ratio of 70% to McGowen and 30% to Messerly. On February 1, Fletcher is admitted to the partnership and given a 20% interest in equity and in gains and losses. Prepare the journal entry to record the entry of Fletcher under each of the following unrelated assumptions. Fletcher invests cash of *(a)* $20,000; *(b)* $30,000; and *(c)* $12,000.

Exercise 14–5

Felix, Garfield, and Nermal have been partners sharing losses and gains in a 2:3:1 ratio. On June 30, the date Nermal retires from the partnership, the equities of the partners are Felix, $35,000; Garfield, $30,000; and Nermal, $10,000.

Required:

Present general journal entries to record Nermal's retirement under each of the following unrelated assumptions:

a. Nermal is paid $10,000 in partnership cash for his equity.
b. Nermal is paid $15,000 in partnership cash for his equity.
c. Nermal is paid $8,000 in partnership cash for his equity.

Exercise 14–6

The Fit, Start, and Stop partnership was begun with investments by the partners as follows: Fit, $25,000; Start, $15,000; and Stop, $20,000. The first year of operations did not go well, and the partners finally decided to liquidate the partnership, sharing all losses equally. On December 31, after all assets were converted to cash and all creditors were paid, only $6,000 in partnership cash remained.

Required:

1. Calculate the capital account balances of the partners after the liquidation of assets and payment of creditors.

2. Assume that any partner with a deficit pays cash to the partnership to cover the deficit. Then, present the general journal entries on December 31 to record the cash receipt from the deficient partner and the final disbursement of cash to the partners.
3. Now make the contrary assumption that any partner with a deficit is not able to reimburse the partnership. Present journal entries *(a)* to transfer the deficit of any deficient partners to the other partners and *(b)* to record the final disbursement of cash to the partners.

PROBLEMS

Problem 14–1   Doug Coleman, John Martin, and Betty Smith formed the CMS Partnership by making capital contributions of $40,000, $60,000, and $80,000, respectively. They anticipate annual net incomes of $90,000 and are considering the following alternative plans of sharing gains and losses: *(a)* equally; *(b)* in the ratio of their initial investments; or *(c)* interest allowances of 10% on initial investments, salary allowances of $20,000 to Coleman, $10,000 to Martin, and $24,000 to Smith, with any remaining balance shared equally.

Required:

1. Prepare a schedule with the following column headings:

Income Sharing Plan	Calculations	Coleman	Martin	Smith

Use the schedule to show how a net income of $90,000 would be distributed under each of the alternative plans being considered.
2. Prepare the section of the partner's first year income statement showing the allocation of income to the partners assuming they agree to use alternative *(c)* and the net income actually earned is $45,000.
3. Prepare the December 31 journal entry to close the Income Summary account assuming they agree to use alternative *(c)* and the net income is $45,000.

Problem 14–2   Spoede and Brown have made lengthy plans for their new partnership that will require capital contributions of $200,000, 40% to be contributed by Spoede and 60% by Brown. Spoede will work full time managing the business, and Brown will work one-half time. They expect it will generate incomes as follows: Year 1, $25,000 net loss; and Year 2, $70,000 net income.
The partners are considering the following plans for sharing gains and losses:

a. In the ratio of their beginning investments, which they will maintain without change.
b. In the ratio of the time they devote to the business.
c. Salary allowances of $30,000 to Spoede and $12,000 to Brown, and the balance in the ratio of their investments.

d. Salary allowances as in *(c)* above, a 12% interest allowance on their investments, and the balance equally.

e. In the partnership agreement, the partners say nothing about sharing losses and gains.

Required:

1. Prepare a schedule with the following column headings for each of the first two years:

Income Sharing Plan	Year _____		
	Calculations	Spoede	Brown

2. Complete each schedule by showing how the partnership income would be allocated to the partners under each of the four plans being considered. Round your answers to the nearest whole dollar.

Problem 14–3

Part 1. Jackson, Grimes, and Holten are partners with capital balances as follows: Jackson, $60,000; Grimes, $35,000; and Holten, $25,000. The partners share losses and gains in a 3:1:2 ratio. Prepare general journal entries to record the June 30 withdrawal of Holten from the partnership under each of the following unrelated assumptions:

a. Holten sells his interest to Smith for $32,000 after Jackson and Grimes approve the entry of Smith as a partner.

b. Holten gives his interest to a son-in-law, Ray Phillips. Jackson and Grimes accept Phillips as a partner.

c. Holten is paid $25,000 in partnership cash for his equity.

d. Holten is paid $37,000 in partnership cash for his equity.

e. Holten is paid $5,000 in partnership cash plus delivery equipment recorded on the partnership books at $22,000 less accumulated depreciation of $12,000.

Part 2. Assume that Holten does not retire from the partnership described in *Part 1.* Instead, Dawes is to be admitted to the partnership on June 30 and is to have a 25% equity. Prepare general journal entries to record the entry of Dawes into the partnership under each of the following unrelated assumptions:

a. Dawes invests $40,000.

b. Dawes invests $30,000.

c. Dawes invests $50,000.

Problem 14–4

Mann, Olson, and Peters plan to liquidate their partnership. They have always shared losses and gains in a 5:3:2 ratio, and on the day of the liquidation their balance sheet appeared as follows:

MANN, OLSON, AND PETERS
Balance Sheet, March 31, 19—

Assets		Liabilities and Owners' Equity	
Cash	$ 3,500	Accounts payable	$13,500
Other assets	45,000	Kay Mann, capital	10,000
		Paul Olson, capital	20,000
		Jan Peters, capital	5,000
		Total liabilities and	
Total assets	$48,500	owners' equity	$48,500

Required:

Prepare general journal entries to record the sale of the other assets and the distribution of the cash to the proper parties under each of the following unrelated assumptions:

a. The other assets are sold for $50,500.

b. The other assets are sold for $30,000.

c. The other assets are sold for $22,000, and the partner with the deficit can and does pay in the amount of his deficit.

d. The other assets are sold for $20,000, and the partners have no assets other than those invested in the business.

Problem 14–5   Until April 7 of the current year, Dirks, Thomas, and Zoller were partners sharing losses and gains in their capital ratio. On that date, Dirks suffered a heart attack and died. Thomas and Zoller immediately ended the business operations and prepared the following adjusted trial balance:

DIRKS, THOMAS, AND ZOLLER
Adjusted Trial Balance, April 7, 19—

Cash..................................	$ 4,500	
Accounts receivable	10,500	
Allowance for doubtful accounts..........		$ 500
Supplies inventory	23,000	
Equipment	13,500	
Accumulated depreciation, equipment		3,500
Land..................................	4,500	
Building	50,000	
Accumulated depreciation, building		9,500
Accounts payable		3,000
Mortgage payable		10,000
Ted Dirks, capital......................		30,000
Sally Thomas, capital		30,000
Bob Zoller, capital		15,000
Ted Dirks, withdrawals	1,000	
Sally Thomas, withdrawals...............	1,000	
Bob Zoller, withdrawals	1,000	
Revenues		39,000
Expenses	31,500	
Totals	$140,500	$140,500

Required:

1. Prepare April 7 entries to close the revenue, expense, income summary, and withdrawals accounts of the partnership.

2. Assume the estate of Dirks agreed to accept the land and building and assume the mortgage thereon in settlement of its claim against the partnership assets, and that Thomas and Zoller planned to continue the business and rent the building from the estate. Give the April 20 entry to transfer the land, building, and mortgage and to settle with the estate.

3. Assume that in the place of the foregoing the estate of Dirks demanded a cash settlement and the business had to be sold to a competitor who gave $68,000 for the noncash assets and assumed the mortgage but not the accounts payable. Give the April 20 entry to transfer the noncash assets and mortgage to the competitor, and give the entries to allocate the loss to the partners and to distribute the partnership cash to the proper parties.

ALTERNATE PROBLEMS

Problem 14–1A   Kay Linn, Ed Cramer, and Dale Swan formed the LCS Partnership by making capital contributions of $70,000, $80,000, and $50,000, respectively. They anticipate annual net incomes of $120,000 and are considering the following alternative plans of sharing gains and losses: *(a)* equally; *(b)* in the ratio of their initial investments; *(c)* interest allowances of 12% on initial investments, salary allowances of $30,000 to Linn, $10,000 to Cramer, and $20,000 to Swan, with any remaining balance shared equally.

Required:

1. Prepare a schedule with the following column headings:

Income Sharing Plan	Calculations	Linn	Cramer	Swan

Use the schedule to show how a net income of $120,000 would be distributed under each of the alternative plans being considered.

2. Prepare the section of the partner's first year income statement showing the allocation of income to the partners assuming they agree to use alternative *(c)* and the net income actually earned is $30,000.

3. Prepare the December 31 journal entry to close the Income Summary account assuming they agree to use alternative *(c)* and the net income is $30,000.

Problem 14–2A   Winslow and Friar are planning a new partnership that will require capital contributions of $200,000, 30% to be contributed by Winslow and 70% by Friar. Winslow will work full time managing the business, and Friar will work two-thirds time. They expect it will generate incomes as follows: Year 1, $10,000 net loss; and Year 2, $80,000 net income.

The partners are considering the following plans for sharing gains and losses:

a. In the ratio of their beginning investments, which they will maintain without change.
b. In the ratio of the time they devote to the business.
c. Salary allowances of $36,000 to Winslow and $24,000 to Friar, and the balance in the ratio of their investments.
d. Salary allowances as in *(c)* above, an 11% interest allowance on their investments, and the balance equally.
e. In the partnership agreement, the partners say nothing about sharing losses and gains.

Required:

1. Prepare a schedule with the following column headings for each of the first two years:

Income Sharing Plan	Year _____		
	Calculations	Winslow	Friar

2. Complete each schedule by showing how the partnership income would be allocated to the partners under each of the four plans being considered.

Problem 14–3A

Part 1. Grange, Slade, and Trainer are partners with capital balances as follows: Grange, $75,000; Slade, $25,000; and Trainer, $50,000. The partners share losses and gains in a 2:4:2 ratio. Prepare general journal entries to record the November 30 withdrawal of Trainer from the partnership under each of the following unrelated assumptions:

a. Trainer sells his interest to Catz for $21,000 after Grange and Slade approve the entry of Catz as a partner.
b. Trainer gives his interest to a son-in-law, S. Butters. Grange and Slade accept Butters as a partner.
c. Trainer is paid $50,000 in partnership cash for his equity.
d. Trainer is paid $35,000 in partnership cash for his equity.
e. Trainer is paid $30,000 in partnership cash plus delivery equipment recorded on the partnership books at $40,000 less accumulated depreciation of $12,000.

Part 2. Assume that Trainer does not retire from the partnership described in *Part 1*. Instead, Atwell is to be admitted to the partnership on November 30 and is to have a 20% equity. Prepare general journal entries to record the entry of Atwell under each of the following unrelated assumptions:

a. Atwell invests $37,500.
b. Atwell invests $25,000.
c. Atwell invests $60,000.

Problem 14–4A

Eaton, James, and Coxon, who have always shared losses and gains in a 2:2:1 ratio, plan to liquidate their partnership. Just prior to the liquidation their balance sheet appeared as follows:

EATON, JAMES, AND COXON
Balance Sheet, May 6, 19—

Assets		Liabilities and Owners' Equity	
Cash	$ 2,500	Accounts payable	$10,500
Other assets	44,000	X. M. Eaton, capital	8,000
		T. D. James, capital	20,000
		A. T. Coxon, capital	8,000
		Total liabilities and	
Total assets	$46,500	owners' equity	$46,500

Required:

Under the assumption the other assets are sold and the cash is distributed to the proper parties on May 12, give the entries for the sales, the loss or gain allocations, and the distributions if—

a. The other assets are sold for $50,000.
b. The other assets are sold for $31,500.
c. The other assets are sold for $21,500, and the partner with a deficit can and does pay in the amount of his deficit.
d. The other assets are sold for $20,250, and the partners have no assets other than those invested in the business.

Problem 14–5A

Dame, Pharr, and Wrey are partners. Dame devotes full time to partnership affairs; Pharr and Wrey devote very little time; and as a result, they share gains and losses in a $3:1:1$ ratio. Of late, the business has not been too profitable, and the partners have decided to liquidate. Just prior to the first realization sale, a partnership balance sheet appeared as follows:

DAME, PHARR, AND WREY
Balance Sheet, July 4, 19—

Assets			Liabilities and Owners' Equity	
Cash		$ 2,500	Accounts payable	$ 7,000
Accounts receivable		9,500	Dame, capital	6,000
Merchandise			Pharr, capital	12,000
inventory		16,000	Wrey, capital	12,000
Equipment	$12,000			
Less accum. depr.	3,000	9,000		
			Total liabilities and	
Total assets		$37,000	owners' equity	$37,000

The assets were sold, the creditors were paid, and the remaining cash was distributed to the partners on the following dates:

July 5   The accounts receivable were sold for $6,500.
    11   The merchandise inventory was sold for $11,000.
    14   The equipment was sold for $5,000.
    16   The creditors were paid.
    16   The remaining cash was distributed to the partners.

Required:

1. Prepare general journal entries to record the asset sales, the allocation of the realization loss, and the payment of the creditors.

2. Under the assumption that the partner with a deficit can and does pay in the amount of his deficit on July 16, give the entry to record the receipt of his cash and the distribution of partnership cash to the remaining partners.

3. Under the assumption that the partner with a deficit cannot pay, give the entry to allocate his deficit to his partners. Then give the entry to distribute the partnership cash to the remaining partners.

PROVOCATIVE PROBLEMS

Provocative
Problem 14–1,
Tracy and
Bachman

Tracy and Bachman are partners who share annual losses equally. If the partnership earns a net income, the first $50,000 is allocated 20% to Tracy and 80% to Bachman so as to reflect the time devoted to the business by each partner. Gains in excess of $50,000 are shared equally.

Required:

1. Prepare a schedule showing how the 198A net income of $60,000 should be allocated to the partners.
2. Immediately after the closing entries were posted on December 31, 198A, the partners discovered unrecorded accounts payable amounting to $75,000. Bachman suggests that the $75,000 should be allocated equally among the partners as a loss. Tracy disagrees and argues that an entry should be made to record the accounts payable and correct the capital accounts to reflect a $15,000 net loss for 198A.
   a. Give the January 1, 198B, journal entry to record the accounts payable and allocate the loss to the partners according to Bachman's suggestion.
   b. Now give the January 1, 198B, journal entry to record the accounts payable and correct the capital accounts according to Tracy's argument. Show how you calculated the amounts in the entry.
3. Which partner do you think is right? Why?

Provocative
Problem 14–2,
Fast Feet

Ned Fry and Roy Lee operate Fast Feet, a sporting goods store, as a partnership enterprise. Fry has a $42,000 equity in the business, and Lee has a $25,500 equity. They share losses and gains by allowing annual salary allowances of $15,000 per year to Fry and $12,000 to Lee, with any remaining balance being shared 60% to Fry and 40% to Lee.

Joe Fry, Ned Fry's son, has been working in the store on a salary basis. He was an outstanding high school and college athlete and has maintained his contacts with coaches and athletes since graduating from college, and thus attracts a great deal of business to the store. Actually, one third of the past three years' sales can be traced directly to Joe's association with the store, and it is reasonable to assume he was instrumental in attracting even more.

Joe is paid $1,000 per month, but feels this is not sufficient to induce him to remain with the firm as an employee. However, he likes his work and would like to remain in the sporting goods business. What he really wants is to become a partner in the business.

His father is anxious for him to remain in the business and proposes the following:

a. That Joe be admitted to the partnership with a 20% equity in the partnership assets.

b. That he, Ned Fry, transfer from his capital account to that of Joe's one half the 20% interest; that Joe contribute to the firm's assets a noninterest-bearing note for the other half; and that he, Ned Fry, will guarantee payment of the note.

c. That losses and gains be shared by continuing the $15,000 and $12,000 salary allowances of the original partners and that Joe be given a $12,000 annual salary allowance, after which any remaining loss or gain would be shared 40% to Ned Fry, 40% to Roy Lee, and 20% to Joe Fry.

Prepare a report to Mr. Lee on the advisability of accepting Mr. Fry's proposal. Under the assumption that net incomes for the past three years have been $37,000, $41,000, and $43,000, respectively, prepare schedules showing *(a)* how net income was allocated during the past three years and *(b)* how it would have been allocated had the proposed new agreement been in effect. Also, *(c)* prepare a schedule showing the partners' capital interests as they would be immediately after the admission of Joe.

Provocative Problem 14–3, a partner retires

The balance sheet of the Serve-all Partnership on December 31, 198A, is as follows:

Assets		Liabilities and Owners' Equity	
Cash	$12,000	Gifford, capital	$ 6,000
Other assets	15,000	Hobson, capital	9,000
Land	9,000	Lemke, capital	21,000
		Total liabilities and	
Total assets	$36,000	owners' equity	$36,000

The loss-and-gain-sharing percentages are: Gifford, 25%; Hobson, 25%; and Lemke, 50%. Gifford wishes to withdraw from the partnership, and the partners finally agree that the land owned by the partnership should be transferred to Gifford in full payment for his equity. In reaching this decision, they recognize that the land has appreciated since it was purchased and is now worth $16,000. If Gifford retires on January 1, 198B, what journal entries should be made on that date?

Corporation Accounting

PART FIVE

Organization and Operation of Corporations

15

After studying Chapter 15, you should be able to:

State the advantages and disadvantages of the corporate form of business organization and explain how a corporation is organized and managed.

Describe the differences in accounting for the owners' equity in a partnership and the stockholders' equity in a corporation.

Record the issuance of par value stock at par or at a premium in exchange for cash or other assets.

Record the issuance of no-par stock with or without a stated value.

Record transactions involving stock subscriptions and explain the effects of subscribed stock on corporation assets and stockholders' equity.

Explain the concept of minimum legal capital and explain why corporation laws governing minimum legal capital were written.

State the differences between common and preferred stocks and explain why preferred stock is issued.

Describe the meaning and significance of par, book, market, and redemption values of corporate stock.

Define or explain the words and phrases listed in the chapter Glossary.

The three common types of business organizations are single proprietorships, partnerships, and corporations. Of the three, corporations are fewer in number. In dollar volume, however, they transact more business than do the other two combined. In terms of their economic impact, corporations are clearly the most important form of business organization. Almost every student will at some time either work for or own an interest in a corporation. For these reasons, an understanding of corporations and corporation accounting is important to all students of business.

ADVANTAGES OF THE CORPORATE FORM

[handwritten note: double Taxation factor 1. income + dividends 2. dividends]

Corporations have become the dominant type of business in our country because of the advantages offered by this form of business organization. Among the advantages are the following:

Separate Legal Entity

A corporation is a separate legal entity, separate and distinct from its stockholders who are its owners. Because it is a separate legal entity, a corporation, through its agents, may conduct its affairs with the same rights, duties, and responsibilities as a person.

Lack of Stockholders' Liability

As a separate legal entity a corporation is responsible for its own acts and its own debts, and its shareholders have no liability for either. From the viewpoint of an investor, this is perhaps the most important advantage of the corporate form.

Ease of Transferring Ownership Rights

Ownership rights in a corporation are represented by shares of stock that generally can be transferred and disposed of any time the owner wishes. Furthermore, the transfer has no effect on the corporation and its operations.

Continuity of Life

A corporation's life may continue for the time stated in its charter, which may be of any length permitted by the laws of the state of its incorporation. Furthermore, at the expiration of the stated time, the charter may normally be renewed and the period extended. Thus, a perpetual life is possible for a successful corporation.

No Mutual Agency

Mutual agency does not exist in a corporation. A corporation stockholder, acting as a stockholder, has no power to bind the corporation to contracts. Stockholders' participation in the affairs of the corporation is limited to the right to vote in the stockholders' meetings. Consequently, stockholders need not exercise the care of partners in selecting people with whom they associate themselves in the ownership of a corporation.

Ease of Capital Assembly

Lack of stockholders' liability, lack of mutual agency, and the ease with which an ownership interest may be transferred make it possible for a corporation to assemble large amounts of capital from the combined investments of many stockholders. Actually, a corporation's capital-raising ability is as a rule limited only by the profitableness with which it can employ the funds. This is very different from a partnership. In a partnership, capital-raising ability is always limited by the number of partners and their individual wealth. The number of partners is in turn usually limited because of mutual agency and unlimited liability.

DISADVANTAGES OF THE CORPORATE FORM

Governmental Regulation

Corporations are created by fulfilling the requirements of a state's corporation laws, and the laws subject a corporation to considerable state regulation and control. Single proprietorships and partnerships escape this regulation and also many governmental reports required of corporations.

Taxation

Corporations as business units are subject to the same taxes as single proprietorships and partnerships. In addition, corporations are subject to several taxes not levied on either of the other two. The most burdensome of these are state and federal income taxes that together may take 50% of a corporation's pretax income. However, for the stockholders of a corporation, the burden does not end there. The income of a corporation is taxed twice, first as corporation income and again as personal income when distributed to the stockholders as dividends. This differs from single proprietorships and partnerships, which as business units are not subject to income taxes. Their income is normally taxed only as the personal income of their owners.

While the tax characteristics of a corporation are generally viewed as a disadvantage, in some instances they may work to the advantage of stockholders. If the stockholders have very large personal incomes and pay taxes at rates that exceed the corporate rate, the corporation may choose to avoid paying dividends. By not paying dividends, the income of the corporation is, at least temporarily, taxed only once at the lower corporate rate.

ORGANIZING A CORPORATION

A corporation is created by securing a charter from one of the states. The requirements that must be met to secure a charter vary with the states. In general, however, a charter application must be signed by three or more subscribers to the prospective corporation's stock (who are called the incorporators). It must then be filed with the proper state official. If the application complies with the law and all fees are paid, the charter is issued and the corporation comes into existence. The subscribers then purchase the corporation's stock and become stockholders. After this, they meet and elect a board of directors who are made responsible for directing the corporation's affairs.

ORGANIZATION COSTS

The *costs* of organizing a corporation, such as legal fees, promoters' fees, and amounts paid the state to secure a charter, are called organization costs and are debited on incurrence to an asset account called Organization Costs. Theoretically, the sum of these costs represents an intangible asset from which the corporation will benefit throughout its life. However, this is an indeterminable period. Therefore, a corporation should make a reasonable estimate of the benefit period, which in no case should exceed 40 years, and write off its organization costs over the estimated period.[1] Although not necessarily related to the benefit period, income tax rules permit a corporation to write off organization costs as a tax-deductible expense over a period of not less than five years. Consequently, many corporations adopt five years as the period over which to write off such costs. There is no theoretical justification for this, but it is generally accepted in practice. Organization costs are usually immaterial in amount; and under the *principle of materiality,* the write-off eliminates an unnecessary balance sheet item.

---

[1] APB, "Intangible Assets," *APB Opinion No. 17* (New York: AICPA, August 1970), par. 29.

MANAGEMENT OF A CORPORATION

Although ultimate control of a corporation rests with its stockholders, this control is exercised indirectly through the election of the board of directors. The individual stockholder's right to participate in management begins and ends with a vote in the stockholders' meeting, where each stockholder has one vote for each share of stock owned.

Normally a corporation's stockholders meet once each year to elect directors and transact such other business as is provided in the corporation's bylaws. Theoretically, stockholders owning or controlling the votes of 50% plus one share of a corporation's stock can elect the board and control the corporation. Actually, because many stockholders do not attend the annual meeting, a much smaller percentage is frequently sufficient for control. Commonly, stockholders who do not attend the annual meeting delegate to an agent their voting rights. This is done by signing a legal document called a *proxy*, which gives the agent the right to vote the stock.

A corporation's board of directors is responsible and has final authority for the direction of corporation affairs. However, it may act only as a collective body. An individual director, as a director, has no power to transact corporation business. And, as a rule, although it has final authority, a board will limit itself to establishing policy. It will then delegate the day-by-day direction of corporation business to the corporation's administrative officers whom it selects and elects.

A corporation's administrative officers are commonly headed by a president who is directly responsible to the board for supervising the corporation's business. To aid the president, many corporations have one or more vice presidents who are vested with specific managerial powers and duties. In addition, the corporation secretary keeps the minutes of the meetings of the stockholders and directors. In a small corporation, the secretary may also be responsible for keeping a record of the stockholders and the changing amounts of their stock interest.

STOCK CERTIFICATES AND THE TRANSFER OF STOCK

When a person invests in a corporation by buying its stock, the person receives a stock certificate as evidence of the shares purchased. Usually, in a small corporation, only one certificate is issued for each block of stock purchased. The one certificate may be for any number of shares. For example, the certificate of Illustration 15–1 is for 50 shares. Large corporations commonly use preprinted 100-share denomination certificates in addition to blank certificates that may be made out for any number of shares.

Illustration 15–1

An owner of stock may transfer at will either part or all of the shares represented by a stock certificate. To do so, the owner completes and signs the transfer endorsement on the reverse side of the certificate and sends the certificate to the corporation secretary in a small corporation or to the corporation's transfer agent in a large one. The old certificate is canceled and retained, and a new certificate is issued to the new stockholder.

Transfer Agent and Registrar

A large corporation whose stock is sold on a major stock exchange must have a registrar and a transfer agent who are assigned the responsibilities of transferring the corporation's stock. Also, the registrar is assigned the duty of keeping stockholder records and preparing official lists of stockholders for stockholders' meetings and for payment of dividends. Usually, registrars and transfer agents are large banks or trust companies.

When the owner of stock in a corporation having a registrar and a transfer agent wishes to transfer the stock to a new owner, he or she completes the transfer endorsement on the back of the stock certificate and, usually through a stockbroker, sends the certificate to the transfer agent. The transfer agent cancels the old certificate and issues one or more new certificates which the agent sends to the registrar. The registrar enters the transfer in the stockholder records and sends the new certificate or certificates to the proper owners.

CORPORATION ACCOUNTING

Corporation accounting was initially discussed in Chapter 4. In that discussion, entries were shown to record several basic transactions. An issue of common stock for cash was recorded. A net income (credit balance) was closed from Income Summary to Retained Earnings. The declaration and later payment of cash dividends were recorded. And, a net loss was closed from Income Summary to Retained Earnings. *At this point, students should review the discussion in Chapter 4 on pages 136 through 139 which explains these entries.* After completing that review, keep in mind that the stockholders' equity accounts of a corporation are divided into (1) contributed capital accounts and (2) retained earnings accounts. Also, remember that when a corporation's board of directors declares a cash dividend on the *date of declaration,* a legal liability of the corporation is incurred. The board of directors declares that on a specific future date, the *date of record,* the stockholders according to the corporation's records will be designated as those to receive the dividend. Finally, on the *date of payment,* the liability for the declared cash dividend is paid by the corporation.

The financial statements of a corporation were first illustrated in Chapter 5. The income statement was shown in Illustration 5–1 on page 166; the balance sheet was shown in Illustration 5–3 on page 173; and the retained earnings statement was shown in Illustration 5–4 on page 174. Reviewing these illustrations, students should note that income taxes were deducted on the income statement as an expense. Recall that a business that is organized as a corporation must pay income taxes, while a proprietorship or partnership does not pay income taxes. Also, cash dividends to stockholders are not an expense of the corporation; they are not deducted on the income statement. Instead, dividends are a distribution *of* net income, and are subtracted on the retained earnings statement. Finally, notice that the stockholders' equity in Illustration 5–3 is divided into common stock and retained earnings.

STOCKHOLDERS' EQUITY ACCOUNTS COMPARED TO PARTNERSHIP ACCOUNTS

To demonstrate the use of separate accounts for contributed capital and retained earnings as found in corporation accounting and to contrast their use with the accounts used in partnership accounting, assume the following. On January 5, 198A, a partnership involving two equal partners and a corporation having five stockholders were formed. Assume further that $25,000 was invested in each. In the partnership, J. Olm invested $10,000 and A. Baker invested $15,000; in the corporation, each of the five stockholders bought 500 shares of its $10 par value common stock at $10 per share. Without dates and explanations, general journal entries to record the invesments are:

	PARTNERSHIP			CORPORATION	
Cash	10,000		Cash	25,000	
J. Olm, Capital		10,000	Common Stock		25,000
Cash	15,000				
A. Baker, Capital		15,000			

After the entries were posted, the owners' equity accounts of the two companies appeared as follows:

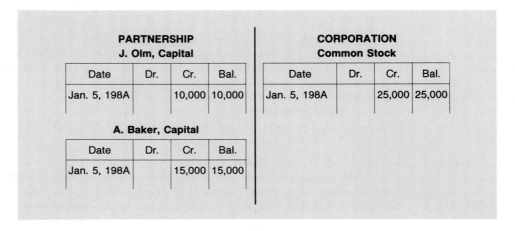

PARTNERSHIP
J. Olm, Capital

Date	Dr.	Cr.	Bal.
Jan. 5, 198A		10,000	10,000

A. Baker, Capital

Date	Dr.	Cr.	Bal.
Jan. 5, 198A		15,000	15,000

CORPORATION
Common Stock

Date	Dr.	Cr.	Bal.
Jan. 5, 198A		25,000	25,000

To continue the illustration, assume that during 198A, each company earned a net income of $8,000 and also distributed $5,000 to its owners.

The partners share income equally, and the cash distribution was also divided equally. The corporation declared the dividends on December 20, 198A, and both companies made the cash payments to owners on December 25, 198A. The entries to record the distribution of cash to partners and the declaration and payments of dividends to stockholders are as follows:

PARTNERSHIP			CORPORATION		
J. Olm, Withdrawals	2,500		Retained Earnings	5,000	
A. Baker, Withdrawals	2,500		Dividends Payable		5,000
Cash		5,000			
			Dividends Payable	5,000	
			Cash		5,000

At the end of the year, the entries to close the Income Summary account are as follows:

PARTNERSHIP			CORPORATION		
Income Summary	8,000		Income Summary	8,000	
J. Olm, Capital		4,000	Retained Earnings		8,000
A. Baker, Capital		4,000			

Finally, the entry to close the withdrawals accounts is:

PARTNERSHIP			CORPORATION
J. Olm, Capital	2,500		
A. Baker, Capital	2,500		
J. Olm, Withdrawals		2,500	
A. Baker, Withdrawals		2,500	

After posting the above entries, the owners' equity accounts of the two companies are as follows:

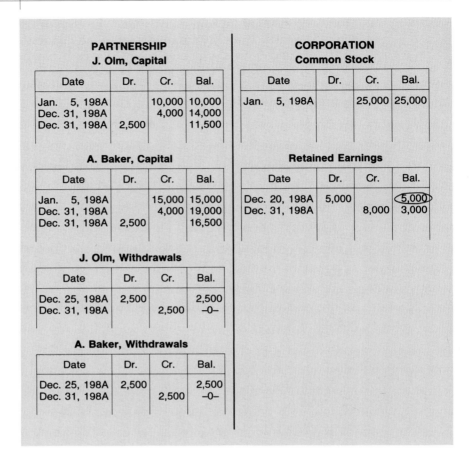

PARTNERSHIP
J. Olm, Capital

Date	Dr.	Cr.	Bal.
Jan. 5, 198A		10,000	10,000
Dec. 31, 198A		4,000	14,000
Dec. 31, 198A	2,500		11,500

A. Baker, Capital

Date	Dr.	Cr.	Bal.
Jan. 5, 198A		15,000	15,000
Dec. 31, 198A		4,000	19,000
Dec. 31, 198A	2,500		16,500

J. Olm, Withdrawals

Date	Dr.	Cr.	Bal.
Dec. 25, 198A	2,500		2,500
Dec. 31, 198A		2,500	–0–

A. Baker, Withdrawals

Date	Dr.	Cr.	Bal.
Dec. 25, 198A	2,500		2,500
Dec. 31, 198A		2,500	–0–

CORPORATION
Common Stock

Date	Dr.	Cr.	Bal.
Jan. 5, 198A		25,000	25,000

Retained Earnings

Date	Dr.	Cr.	Bal.
Dec. 20, 198A	5,000		5,000
Dec. 31, 198A		8,000	3,000

Observe that in the partnership, after all entries have been posted, the $28,000 equity of the owners appears in the capital accounts of the partners:

J. Olm, capital	$11,500
A. Baker, capital	16,500
Total owners' equity	$28,000

By comparison, the stockholders' equity of the corporation is divided between the contributed capital account and the Retained Earnings account, as follows:

Common stock	$25,000
Retained earnings	3,000
Total stockholders' equity	$28,000

AUTHORIZATION AND ISSUANCE OF STOCK

When a corporation is organized, it is authorized in its charter to issue a certain amount of stock. The stock may be of one kind, *common stock,* or both common and preferred stock may be authorized. (Preferred stock is discussed later in this chapter.) However, regardless of whether one or two kinds of stock are authorized, the corporation may issue no more of each than the amount authorized by its charter.

Often a corporation will secure an authorization to issue more stock than it plans to sell at the time of its organization. This provides the means for future expansion through the sale of the additional stock, without the need of applying to the state for the right to issue more. When a balance sheet is prepared, both the amount of stock authorized and the amount issued are commonly shown in the equity section as on page 516.

Sale of Stock for Cash

When stock is sold for cash and immediately issued, an entry in general journal form like the following may be used to record the sale and issuance:

June	5	Cash	300,000.00	
		Common Stock		300,000.00
		Sold at par and issued 30,000 shares of $10 par value common stock.		

Exchanging Stock for Noncash Assets

A corporation may accept assets other than cash in exchange for its stock. When it does so, the transaction may be recorded like this:

Apr.	3	Machinery..................................	10,000.00	
		Buildings..................................	25,000.00	
		Land	5,000.00	
		Common Stock		40,000.00
		Exchanged 4,000 shares of $10 par value common stock for machinery, buildings, and land.		

A corporation may also give shares of its stock to its promoters in exchange for their services in organizing the corporation. In such a case, the corporation receives the intangible asset of being organized in exchange for its stock. The transaction is recorded as follows:

Apr.	5	Organization Costs	5,000.00	
		Common Stock		5,000.00
		Gave the promoters 500 shares of $10 par value common stock in exchange for their services in organizing the corporation.		

PAR VALUE AND MINIMUM LEGAL CAPITAL

Many stocks have a *par value*. The par value of a stock is an arbitrary value the issuing corporation chose for the stock at the time it sought authorization of the stock. A corporation may choose to issue stock having a par value of any amount, but par values of $100, $25, $10, $5, and $1 are common.

When a corporation issues par value stock, the par value is printed on each certificate and is used in accounting for the stock. Also, in many states when a corporation issues par value stock, it establishes for itself a *minimum legal capital* equal to the par value of the issued stock. For example, if a corporation issues 1,000 shares of $100 par value stock, it establishes for itself a minimum legal capital of $100,000.

Laws establishing minimum legal capital normally require stockholders in a corporation to invest assets equal in value to minimum legal capital or be liable to the corporation's creditors for the deficiency. In other words, these laws require stockholders to give a corporation par value for its stock or be liable for the difference. Minimum legal capital requirements also make illegal any payments to stockholders for dividends or their equivalent when these payments reduce stockholders' equity below minimum legal capital.

Corporation laws governing minimum legal capital were written in an effort to protect corporation creditors. The authors of these laws reasoned as follows: A corporation's creditors may look only to the assets of the corporation for satisfaction of their claims. Consequently, when a corporation is organized, its stockholders should provide it with a fund of assets equal to its minimum legal capital. Thereafter, this fund of assets should remain with the corporation and should not be returned to the stockholders in any form until all creditor claims are paid.

Par value helps establish minimum legal capital and is used in accounting for par value stock. However, it does not establish a stock's worth nor the price at which a corporation may issue the stock. If purchasers are willing to pay more than par, a corporation may sell and issue its stock at a price above par. If purchasers will not pay par, it may be possible in some states for a corporation to issue its stock at a price below par.

STOCK PREMIUMS AND DISCOUNTS

Premiums

When a corporation sells and issues stock at a price above the stock's par value, the stock is said to be issued at a *premium*. For example, if a corporation sells and issues its $10 par value common stock at $12 per share, the stock is sold at a $2 per share premium. Although a premium is an amount in excess of par paid by purchasers of newly issued stock, it is not considered a profit to the issuing corporation. Rather a premium is part of the investment of stockholders who pay more than par for their stock.

In accounting for stock sold at a premium, the premium is recorded separately from the par value of the stock to which it applies. For example, if a corporation sells and issues 10,000 shares of its $10 par value common stock for cash at $12 per share, the sale is recorded as follows:

Dec.	1	Cash	120,000.00	
		Premium on Common Stock		20,000.00
		Common Stock		100,000.00
		Sold and issued 10,000 shares of $10 par value common stock at $12 per share.		

When stock is issued in exchange for assets other than cash and the fair value of the assets exceeds the par value of the stock, a premium is recorded. If fair value for the assets cannot be determined within reasonable limits, a price established by recent sales of the stock may be used in recording the exchange. This too may require that a premium be recorded.

When the equity section of a balance sheet is prepared, stock premium is added to the par value of the stock to which it applies, as follows:

Stockholders' Equity

Common stock, $10 par value, 25,000 shares authorized, 20,000 shares issued	$200,000	
Add premium on common stock	30,000	
Total contributed capital		$230,000
Retained earnings		82,400
Total stockholders' equity		$312,400

Discounts

Stock issued at a price below par is said to be issued at a *discount.* Many states prohibit the issuance of stock at a discount because the discount allows stockholders to invest less than the minimum legal capital. In those states in which stock may be issued at a discount, purchasers of the stock usually become contingently liable to the issuing corporation's creditors for the amount of the discount. Consequently, stock is seldom issued at a discount, and a discussion of stock discounts is of little practical importance. However, if stock were issued at less than par, the discount would be debited to a discount account and subtracted on the balance sheet from the par value of the stock to which it applies.

NO-PAR STOCK

At one time, all stocks were required to have a par value. Today, all jurisdictions permit the issuance of *no-par stocks* or stocks without a par value. The primary advantage claimed for no-par stock is that since it does not have a par value, it may be issued at any price without having a *discount liability* attached. Also, printing a par value, say, $100, on a stock certificate may cause a person lacking in knowledge to believe a share of the stock to be worth $100 when it actually may be worthless. Therefore, eliminating the par value helps force such a person to examine the factors that give a stock value, which are earnings, dividends, and future prospects.

In some states, the entire proceeds from the sale of no-par stock becomes minimum legal capital and must be credited to a no-par stock account. In these states, if a corporation issues 1,000 shares of no-par stock at $42 per share, the transaction is recorded like this:

Oct.	20	Cash	42,000.00	
		No-Par Common Stock		42,000.00
		Sold and issued 1,000 shares of no-par common stock at $42 per share.		

In other states, a corporation may place a *stated value* on its no-par stock. The stated value then becomes minimum legal capital and is credited to the no-par stock account. If the stock is issued at an amount in excess of stated value, the excess is credited to a contributed capital account called, for instance, Contributed Capital in Excess of Stated Value of No-Par Stock. In these states, if a corporation issues at $42 per share 1,000 shares of no-par common stock on which it has placed a $25 per share stated value, the transaction is recorded as follows:

Oct.	20	Cash	42,000.00	
		No-Par Common Stock		25,000.00
		Contributed Capital in Excess of Stated Value, No-Par Common Stock		17,000.00
		Sold at $42 per share 1,000 shares of no-par stock having a $25 per share stated value.		

In still other states, a corporation may place a stated value on its no-par stock and record the transaction as in the preceding entry, but the entire proceeds from the sale of the stock are included in minimum legal capital.

SALE OF STOCK THROUGH SUBSCRIPTIONS

Often stock is sold for cash and immediately issued. Often, too, especially in organizing a new corporation, stock is sold by means of *subscriptions*. In the latter instance, a person wishing to become a stockholder signs a subscription blank or a subscription list, agreeing to buy a certain number of the shares at a specified price. When the subscription is accepted by the corporation, it becomes a contract; and the corporation acquires an asset, the right to receive payment from the subscriber. At the same time, the subscriber gains an equity in the corporation equal to the amount the subscriber agrees to pay. Payment may be in one amount or in installments.

To illustrate the sale of stock through subscriptions, assume that on June 6, Northgate Corporation accepted subscriptions to 5,000 shares of its $10 par value common stock at $12 per share. The subscription contracts called for a 10% down payment to accompany the subscriptions and the balance in two equal installments due in 30 and 60 days.

The subscriptions are recorded with the following entry:

June	6	Subscriptions Receivable, Common Stock	60,000.00	
		Premium on Common Stock		10,000.00
		Common Stock Subscribed		50,000.00
		Accepted subscriptions to 5,000 shares of $10 par value common stock at $12 per share.		

Notice that the subscriptions receivable account is debited at the time the subscriptions are accepted for the sum of the stock's par value and premium. This is the amount the subscribers agree to pay. Notice, too, that the stock subscribed account is credited for par value and that the premium is credited to a premium account at the time the subscriptions are accepted. The subscriptions receivable and stock subscribed accounts are of temporary nature. The subscriptions receivable will be turned into cash when the subscribers pay for their stock. Likewise, when payment is completed, the subscribed stock will be issued and will become outstanding stock. Normally, subscribed stock is not issued until completely paid for.

Receipt of the down payments and the two installment payments may be recorded with these entries:

June	6	Cash	6,000.00	
		Subscriptions Receivable, Common Stock . .		6,000.00
		Collected 10% down payments on the common stock subscribed.		
July	6	Cash	27,000.00	
		Subscriptions Receivable, Common Stock . .		27,000.00
		Collected the first installment payments on the common stock subscribed.		
Aug.	5	Cash	27,000.00	
		Subscriptions Receivable, Common Stock . .		27,000.00
		Collected the second installment payments on the common stock subscribed.		

In this case, the down payments accompanied the subscriptions. Consequently, the entry to record the receipt of the subscriptions and the entry to record the down payments may be combined.

When stock is sold through subscriptions, the stock is usually not issued until the subscriptions are paid in full. However, as soon as the subscriptions are paid, the stock is issued. The entry to record the issuance of the Northgate common stock appears as follows:

Aug.	5	Common Stock Subscribed	50,000.00	
		Common Stock		50,000.00
		Issued 5,000 shares of common stock sold through subscriptions.		

Most subscriptions are collected in full, although not always. Sometimes a subscriber fails to pay. If this happens, the subscription contract must be canceled. In such a case, if the subscriber has made a partial payment on the contract, the amount paid may be returned. Or, a smaller amount of stock than that subscribed, an amount equal to the partial payment, may be issued. Or, in some states, the subscriber's partial payment may be kept by the corporation to compensate for any damages suffered.

Subscriptions Receivable and Stock Subscribed on the Balance Sheet

Subscriptions receivable are normally to be collected within a relatively short time. Consequently, they appear on the balance sheet as a current asset. If a corporation prepares a balance sheet after accepting subscriptions to its stock but before the stock is issued, it should show both its issued stock and its subscribed stock on the balance sheet as follows:

Common stock, $10 par value, 25,000 shares authorized, 20,000 shares issued	$200,000
Unissued common stock subscribed, 5,000 shares	50,000
Total common stock issued and subscribed	$250,000
Add premium on common stock	40,000
Amount contributed and subscribed by the common stockholders	$290,000

RIGHTS OF COMMON STOCKHOLDERS

When investors buy a corporation's common stock, they acquire all the specific rights granted by the corporation's charter to its common stockholders. They also acquire the general rights granted stockholders by the laws of the state in which the company is incorporated.

The laws vary, but common stockholders generally have the following rights:

1. The right to vote in the stockholders' meetings.
2. The right to sell or otherwise dispose of their stock.
3. The right of first opportunity to purchase any additional shares of common stock issued by the corporation. (This is called the common stockholders' *preemptive right*. It gives common stockholders the opportunity to maintain their proportionate interest in the corporation. For example, a stockholder who owns one fourth of a corporation's common stock has the first opportunity to buy one fourth of any new common stock issued. This enables the stockholder to maintain a one-fourth interest.)
4. The right to share pro rata with other common stockholders in any dividends distributed to common stockholders.
5. The right to share in any assets remaining after creditors are paid if the corporation is liquidated.

PREFERRED STOCK

A corporation may issue more than one kind or class of stock. If two classes are issued, one is generally known as common stock and the other as *preferred stock*. Preferred stock generally has a par value and, like common stock, may be sold at a price that is greater than par (or perhaps less than par). Separate contributed capital accounts are used to record the issuance of preferred stock. For example, if 50 shares of $100 par, preferred stock are issued for $6,000 cash, the entry to record the issue is:

June	1	Cash	6,000.00	
		Preferred Stock		5,000.00
		Premium on Preferred Stock		1,000.00

Preferred stock is so called because of the preferences granted to its owners. These commonly include a preference as to payment of *dividends,* and may include a preference in the distribution of assets if the corporation is liquidated.

A preference as to dividends does not give an absolute right to dividends. Rather, if dividends are declared, it gives the preferred stockholders the right to receive their preferred dividend before the common stockholders are paid a dividend. In other words, if dividends are declared, a dividend must be paid the preferred stockholders before a dividend may be paid to the common stockholders. However, if the directors are of the opinion that no dividends should be paid, then neither the preferred nor the common stockholders receive a dividend.

Dividends to common stockholders are limited only by the earning power of the corporation and the judgment of its board of directors. Dividends to preferred stock, however, are generally limited to a fixed maximum amount. When preferred stock is so limited, it is called *nonparticipating preferred stock*. For example, a corporation has outstanding 1,000 shares of $100 par, 9%, nonparticipating, preferred stock and 4,000 shares of $50 par, common stock. If the corporation's board of directors declares cash dividends of $42,000 in a year, this amount would be allocated as follows:

	To preferred	To common
First, to preferred [9% × (1,000 × $100)]	$9,000	
Remainder to common		$33,000

While most preferred stock is nonparticipating, some preferred stock may be paid additional dividends in excess of the stated percentage or amount that is preferred. Such preferred stock is called *participating preferred stock*. Participating preferred stock may be fully participating or partially participating.

To illustrate fully participating preferred stock, assume that the 1,000 shares of $100 par, 9% preferred stock in the previous example are fully participating. Now the allocation of $42,000 cash dividends in a year would be as follows:

	To preferred	To common
First, to preferred [9% × (1,000 × $100)]....	$ 9,000	
Next, to common [9% × (4,000 × $50)]		$18,000
Remainder maintains equal percentage to preferred and common:		
($42,000 − $9,000 − $18,000 = $15,000)		
$15,000 × ($100,000 ÷ $300,000)	5,000	
$15,000 × ($200,000 ÷ $300,000)		10,000
Totals	$14,000	$28,000

Observe that the first step satisfies the preferred stock's right to 9% before any dividends are paid to common. Next, the common shares receive 9%. Finally, any additional dividends are allocated on the basis of the relative par value amounts outstanding. As a consequence, both preferred and common shares are paid the same percentage (14% in this case). This is confirmed by the following calculation:

	Par value	Total dividend	Percent of par
Preferred (1,000 × $100) ..	$100,000	$14,000	14
Common (4,000 × $50) ...	200,000	28,000	14
Totals	$300,000	$42,000	14

No matter how much larger the dividend declaration might be, fully participating preferred stock has the right to participate with common on an equal percentage basis.

As mentioned before, participating preferred stock may be fully participating or partially participating. With partially participating preferred stock, the right to receive additional dividends beyond the basic preferred percentage is limited to a stated amount or percentage. Continuing with the previous example, the 1,000 shares of 9%, preferred stock might be participating up to an additional 3%. If so, the preferred shares would have received no more than 12% × $100,000, or $12,000. Of the $42,000 dividends declared, the remaining $30,000 would be paid entirely to common.

In addition to being participating or nonparticipating, preferred stock is either *cumulative* or *noncumulative*. If stock is cumulative, any undeclared dividends accumulate each year until paid. If preferred stock is noncumulative, the right to receive dividends is forfeited in any year that dividends are not declared.

The accumulation of dividends on cumulative preferred stocks does not guarantee payment. Dividends cannot be guaranteed because earnings from which they are paid cannot be guaranteed. However, when a corporation issues cumulative preferred stock, it does agree to pay its cumulative preferred stockholders both their current dividends and any unpaid back dividends called *dividends in arrears*, before it pays a dividend to its common stockholders.

In addition to the preferences it receives, preferred stock carries with it all the rights of common stock, unless such rights are specifically denied in the corporation charter. Commonly, preferred stock is denied the right to vote in the stockholders' meetings.

Preferred Dividends in Arrears on the Balance Sheet Date

A liability for a dividend does not come into existence until the dividend is declared by the board of directors; and unlike interest, dividends do not accrue. Consequently, if on the dividend date a corporation's board of directors fails to declare a dividend on its cumulative preferred stock, the dividend in arrears is not a liability and does not appear on the balance sheet as such. However, if there are preferred dividends in arrears, the *full-disclosure principle* requires that this information appear on the balance sheet, and normally such information is given in a balance sheet footnote. When a balance sheet does not carry such a footnote, a balance sheet reader has the right to assume that there are no dividends in arrears.

WHY PREFERRED STOCK IS ISSUED

Two common reasons why preferred stock is issued can best be shown by means of an example. Suppose that three persons with a total of $100,000 to invest wish to organize a corporation requiring $200,000 capital. If they sell and issue $200,000 of common stock, they will have to share control with other stockholders. However, if they sell and issue $100,000 of common stock to themselves and sell to outsiders $100,000 of 8%, cumulative preferred stock having no voting rights, they can retain control of the corporation for themselves.

Also, suppose the three promoters expect their new corporation to earn an annual after-tax return of $24,000. If they sell and issue $200,000 of common stock, this will mean a 12% return. However, if they sell and issue $100,000 of each kind of stock, retaining the common for themselves, they can increase their own return to 16%, as follows:

Net after-tax income	$24,000
Less preferred dividends at 8%	(8,000)
Balance to common stockholders (equal to 16% on their $100,000 investment)	$16,000

In this case, the common stockholders earn 16% because the dividends on the preferred stock are less than the amount that is earned on the preferred stockholders' investment.

STOCK VALUES

In addition to a par value, stocks may have a redemption value, a market value, and a book value.

Redemption Value

Redemption values apply to preferred stocks. Corporations that issue preferred stock often reserve the right to redeem or retire the stock by paying a specified amount to the preferred stockholders. The amount a corporation agrees to pay to redeem a share of its preferred stock is set at the time the stock is issued and is called the redemption value of the stock. Normally, the redemption value includes the par value of the stock plus a premium. To this amount must be added any dividends in arrears.

Market Value

The market value of a share of stock is the price at which a share can be bought or sold. Market values are influenced by earnings, dividends, future prospects, and general market conditions.

Book Value

The *book value of a share of stock* measures the equity of the owner of one share of the stock in the net assets of the issuing corporation. If a corporation has issued only common stock, its book value per share is determined by dividing total stockholders' equity by the number of shares outstanding. For example, if total stockholders' equity is $285,000 and there are 10,000 shares outstanding, the book value per share is $28.50 ($285,000 ÷ 10,000 = $28.50).

To compute book values when both common and preferred stock are outstanding, the preferred stock is assigned a portion of the total stockholders' equity equal to its redemption value (or par value if there is no redemption value) plus any cumulative dividends in arrears. The remaining stockholders' equity is then assigned to the common shares outstanding. After this, the book value of each class is determined by dividing its share of stockholders' equity by the number of shares of that class outstanding. For instance, assume a corporation has the stockholders' equity shown in Illustration 15–2. If the preferred stock is redeemable at $103 per share and two years' of cumulative preferred dividends are in arrears, the book values of the corporation's shares are calculated as follows:

Total stockholders' equity		$ 447,000	
Less equity applicable to preferred shares:			
Redemption value	$103,000		
Cumulative dividends in arrears	14,000	(117,000)	
Equity applicable to common shares			$330,000
Book value of preferred shares ($117,000 ÷ 1,000)			$117
Book value of common shares ($330,000 ÷ 10,000)			33

Illustration 15–2

Stockholders' Equity

Preferred stock, $100 par value, 7% cumulative and nonparticipating, 2,000 shares authorized, 1,000 shares issued and outstanding	$100,000	
Premium on preferred stock	5,000	
Total capital contributed by preferred stockholders		$105,000
Common stock, $25 par value, 12,000 shares authorized, 10,000 shares issued and outstanding	$250,000	
Premium on common stock	10,000	
Total capital contributed by common stockholders		260,000
Total contributed capital		$365,000
Retained earnings		82,000
Total stockholders' equity		$447,000

Corporations in their annual reports to their shareholders often highlight the increase that has occurred in the book value of the corporation's shares during a year. Book value may also be of significance in a contract. For example, a stockholder may enter into a contract to sell shares at their book value at some future date. However, book value should not be confused with *liquidation value* because if a corporation is liquidated, its assets will probably sell at prices quite different from the amounts at which they are carried on the books. Also, book value generally has little bearing upon the market value of stock. Dividends, earning capacity, and future prospects are usually of much more importance. For instance a common stock having a $11 book value may sell for $25 per share if its earnings, dividends, and prospects are good. However, it may sell for $5 per share if these factors are unfavorable.

GLOSSARY

Book value of a share of stock. The equity represented by one share of stock in the issuing corporation's net assets.

Common stock. Stock of a corporation that has only one class of stock; if there is more than one class, the class that has no preferences relative to the corporation's other classes of stock.

Common stock subscribed. Unissued common stock for which the issuing corporation has a subscription contract to issue.

Cumulative preferred stock. Preferred stock on which undeclared dividends accumulate annually until paid.

Discount on stock. The difference between the par value of stock and the amount below par value contributed by stockholders.

Dividend.   A distribution made by a corporation to its stockholders of cash, other assets, or additional shares of the corporation's own stock.

Dividends in arrears.   Unpaid prior period dividends on preferred stock which must be paid before dividends are paid to common stockholders.

Minimum legal capital.   An amount, as defined by state law, that stockholders must invest in a corporation or be contingently liable to its creditors.

Noncumulative preferred stock.   A preferred stock for which the right to receive dividends is forfeited in any year in which dividends are not declared.

No-par stock.   A class of stock having no par value.

Organization costs.   Costs of bringing a corporation into existence, such as legal fees, promoters' fees, and amounts paid the state to secure a charter.

Participating preferred stock.   Preferred stock that has the right to share in dividends above the fixed amount or percentage which is preferred.

Par value.   An arbitrary value placed on a share of stock at the time the corporation seeks authorization of the stock.

Preemptive right.   The right of a common stockholder to have the first opportunity to purchase additional shares of common stock issued by the corporation.

Preferred stock.   Stock the owners of which are granted certain preferences over common stockholders, such as a preference to payment of dividends or in the distribution of assets in a liquidation.

Premium on stock.   The amount of capital contributed by stockholders above the stock's par value.

Proxy.   A legal document that gives an agent of a stockholder the right to vote the stockholder's shares.

Redemption value of stock.   The amount a corporation must pay for the return of a share of preferred stock previously issued by the corporation.

Stated value of no-par stock.   An amount, established by a corporation's board of directors, that is credited to the no-par stock account at the time the stock is issued.

Stock subscription.   A contractual commitment to purchase unissued shares of stock and become a stockholder.

QUESTIONS FOR CLASS DISCUSSION

1. What are the advantages and disadvantages of the corporate form of business organization?
2. What is a proxy?
3. What are organization costs? List several.
4. What are the duties and responsibilities of a corporation's registrar and transfer agent?
5. Why is a corporation the stock of which is sold on a stock exchange required to have a registrar and transfer agent? Why is such a corporation required to have both a registrar and a transfer agent?

6. List the general rights of common stockholders. *#519*

7. What is the preemptive right of common stockholders?

8. Laws place no limit on the amounts partners may withdraw from a partnership. On the other hand, laws regulating corporations place definite limits on the amounts corporation owners may withdraw from a corporation in dividends. Why is there a difference? *514*

9. What is a stock premium? What is a stock discount? *516*

10. Does a corporation earn a profit by selling its stock at a premium? Does it incur a loss by selling its stock at a discount? *NO! Operating only.*

11. Why do corporation laws make purchasers of stock at a discount contingently liable for the discount? To whom are such purchasers contingently liable?

12. What is the main advantage of no-par stock?

13. What are the balance sheet classifications of the accounts: *(a)* Subscriptions Receivable, Common Stock and *(b)* Common Stock Subscribed?

14. What are the meanings of the following when applied to preferred stock: *(a)* preferred, *(b)* participating, *(c)* nonparticipating, *(d)* cumulative, and *(e)* noncumulative?

15. What are the meanings of the following terms when applied to stock: *(a)* par value, *(b)* book value, *(c)* market value, and *(d)* redemption value? *generally same as Par Value*

#514   2-525   #524   #524

CLASS EXERCISES

Exercise 15–1

Prepare general journal entries on August 15 to record the following issuances of stock by various corporations:

1. Ten shares of $50 par, common stock are issued for $700 cash.
2. Fifty shares of no-par common stock are issued to promoters in exchange for their efforts in organizing the corporation. The promoters' efforts are estimated to be worth $3,000, and the stock has no stated value.
3. Assume the same facts as in 2 above, except that the stock has a $20 stated value.

Exercise 15–2

Kay Smith and Ed Townes begin a new business on January 18 by investing $25,000 each in the company. Assume that on December 25, it is decided that $4,000 of the company's cash will be distributed equally between the owners. Checks for $2,000 are prepared and given to the owners on December 30. On December 31, the company reports a $7,000 net income. Prepare journal entries to record the investments by the owners, the distribution of cash to the owners, and the closing of the Income Summary account assuming: *(a)* the business is a partnership and *(b)* the business is a corporation that issued 250 shares of $100 par value, common stock to each owner.

Exercise 15–3

On February 22, Donay Company accepted subscriptions to 100,000 shares of its $1 par value common stock at $1.10 per share. The subscription contracts called for one fifth of the subscription price to accompany each contract as a down payment and the balance to be paid on March 15. Give the entries to record *(a)* the subscription, *(b)* the down payments, *(c)* receipt of the remaining amounts due on the subscriptions, and *(d)* issuance of the stock.

Exercise 15–4

When first organized, a corporation issued 1,000 shares of $100 par, 8% cumulative, nonparticipating preferred stock, and 6,000 shares of $50 par value common stock. During the first three years of operation, the following amounts of dividends were declared and paid: first year, $–0–; second year, $14,000; and third year, $40,000. Calculate the total dividends paid each year to each class of stockholders.

Exercise 15–5

Assume that the preferred stock in the previous exercise was cumulative and fully participating. What would be the total dividends paid each year to each class of stockholders?

Exercise 15–6

XYZ Corporation has outstanding 20,000 shares of $10 par common stock and 6,000 shares of $50 par, 9% noncumulative and fully participating preferred stock. For each class of shareholders, calculate the percent on par to be paid and the dividend per share to be paid if total dividends declared this year are $70,000.

Exercise 15–7

The stockholders' equity section from a corporation's balance sheet appeared as follows:

Stockholders' Equity

Preferred stock, 10% cumulative and nonparticipating, $15 par value, $17 redemption value, 8,000 shares issued and outstanding . .	$120,000
Common stock, $6 par value, 40,000 shares issued and outstanding . .	240,000
Retaining earnings	72,000
Total stockholders' equity	$432,000

Required:

1. Determine the book value per share of the preferred stock and of the common stock under the assumption there are no dividends in arrears on the preferred stock.
2. Determine the book value per share for each kind of stock under the assumption that two years' dividends are in arrears on the preferred stock.

PROBLEMS

Problem 15–1

Bevo Corporation is authorized to issue 4,000 shares of $100 par value, 9% cumulative and nonparticipating, preferred stock and 60,000 shares of $15 par value common stock. It then completed these transactions:

May 23 Accepted subscriptions to 30,000 shares of common stock at $18 per share. Down payments equal to 20% of the subscription price accompanied each subscription.

    30 Gave the corporation's promoters 800 shares of common stock for their services in getting the corporation organized. The board valued the services at $14,000.

June 7 Accepted subscriptions to 2,000 shares of preferred stock at $120 per share. The subscriptions were accompanied by 50% down payments.

23 Collected the balance due on the May 23 common stock subscriptions and issued the stock.

29 Accepted subscriptions to 1,000 shares of preferred stock at $110 per share. The subscriptions were accompanied by 50% down payments.

July 6 Collected the balance due on the June 7 preferred stock subscriptions and issued the stock.

Required:

1. Prepare general journal entries to record the transactions.
2. Prepare the stockholders' equity section of the corporation's balance sheet as of the close of business on July 6.

Problem 15–2   Uzi Company received a charter granting the right to issue 200,000 shares of $1 par value common stock and 10,000 shares of 8%, cumulative and nonparticipating, $50 par value preferred stock. It then completed these transactions:

198A
Feb. 19 Issued 45,000 shares of common stock at par for cash.

22 Gave the corporation's promoters 30,000 shares of common stock for their services in getting the corporation organized. The directors valued the services at $50,000.

Mar. 30 Exchanged 100,000 shares of common stock for the following assets at fair market values: land, $25,000; buildings, $100,000; and machinery, $125,000.

Dec. 31 Closed the Income Summary account. A $25,000 loss was incurred.

198B
Jan. 12 Issued 1,000 shares of preferred stock at par.

Dec. 15 Accepted subscriptions to 10,000 shares of common stock at $1.80 per share. Down payments of 25% accompanied the subscription contracts.

31 Closed the Income Summary account. A $69,000 net income was earned.

198C
Jan. 5 The board of directors declared an 8% dividend to preferred shares and $0.10 per share to outstanding common shares, payable on January 25 to the January 12 stockholders of record.

31 Paid the previously declared dividends.

Required:

1. Prepare general journal entries to record the transactions.
2. Prepare a stockholders' equity section as of the close of business on January 31, 198C.

Problem 15–3   Greenbriar Company has outstanding 10,000 shares of $10 par value, 7%, preferred stock and 20,000 shares of $10 par value common stock. During a seven-year period, the company paid out the following amounts in dividends: 198A, nothing; 198B, $24,000; 198C, nothing; 198D, $31,000; 198E, $18,000; 198F, $30,000; and 198G, $36,000.

Required:

1. Prepare three schedules with columnar headings as follows:

Year	Amount Distributed in Dividends	Total to Preferred	Balance Due Preferred	Total to Common	Dividend per Share Preferred	Dividend per Share Common

2. Complete a schedule under each of the following assumptions, showing for each year the total dollars paid the preferred stockholders, the balance due the preferred stockholders, and so on. There were no dividends in arrears for the years prior to 198A.
   a. The preferred stock is noncumulative and nonparticipating.
   b. The preferred stock is cumulative and nonparticipating.
   c. The preferred stock is cumulative and fully participating.

Problem 15–4   *Part 1.* Dugger Company's balance sheet includes the following information:

Stockholders' Equity

Eight percent cumulative and nonparticipating, $50 par value, preferred stock, authorized and issued 1,000 shares	$ 50,000
Common stock, $10 par value, 25,000 shares authorized and issued	250,000
Retained earnings	60,000
Total stockholders' equity	$360,000

Required:

Assume that the preferred stock has a redemption value of $55 plus any dividends in arrears. Calculate the book values per share of the preferred and common stocks under each of the following assumptions:

a. There are no dividends in arrears on the preferred stock.
b. One year's dividends are in arrears on the preferred stock.
c. Three years' dividends are in arrears on the preferred stock.

Part 2. Taft Corporation has had outstanding since its organization 12,000 shares of $20 par value, 8%, preferred stock and 32,000 shares of $5 par value common stock. No dividends have been paid this year, and two prior years' dividends are in arrears on the preferred stock. However, the company has recently prospered and the board of directors wants to know how much cash will be required for dividends if a $1.50 per share dividend is paid on the common stock.

Required:

Prepare a schedule showing the amounts of cash required for dividends to each class of stockholders under each of the following assumptions:

a. The preferred stock is noncumulative and nonparticipating.
b. The preferred stock is cumulative and nonparticipating.
c. The preferred stock is cumulative and fully participating.
d. The preferred stock is cumulative and participating to 10%.

Problem 15–5   Kite Corporation's common stock is selling on a stock exchange today at $7.25 per share, and a just-published balance sheet shows the stockholders' equity in the corporation as follows:

Stockholders' Equity

Preferred stock, 7% cumulative and nonparticipating, $10 par value, 10,000 shares authorized and outstanding	$100,000
Common stock, $5 par value, 50,000 shares authorized and outstanding	250,000
Retained earnings	84,000
Total shareholders' equity	$434,000

Required:

Answer these questions: (1) What is the market value of the corporation's common stock? (2) What are the par values of its *(a)* preferred stock and *(b)* common stock? (3) If there are no dividends in arrears, what are the book values of the *(a)* preferred stock and *(b)* common stock? (4) If two years' dividends are in arrears on the preferred stock, what are the book values of the *(a)* preferred stock and *(b)* common stock? (Assume the preferred stock carries the right to the return of par value plus dividends in arrears in a liquidation.)

ALTERNATE PROBLEMS

Problem 15–1A   The charter of Burkey Corporation grants it the right to issue 5,000 shares of $100 par value, 8% cumulative and nonparticipating, preferred stock and 80,000 shares of $20 par value common stock. It then completed these transactions:

Oct. 10 Exchanged 25,000 shares of common stock for the following assets at fair values: land, $40,000; buildings, $180,000; and machinery, $305,000.

13 Accepted subscriptions to 8,000 shares of common stock at $21.50 per share. The subscription contracts were accompanied by 10% down payments.

14 Accepted subscriptions and $52,500 in down payments on 2,000 shares of preferred stock at $105 per share.

20 Gave the corporation's attorneys $5,000 in cash and 200 shares of common stock for their services in securing the corporation charter. The services were valued by the board of directors at $9,200.

Nov. 8 Collected the balance due on the October 13 common stock subscriptions and issued the stock.

11 Collected the balance due on the preferred stock subscriptions and issued the stock.

30 Accepted subscriptions accompanied by 10% down payments to 10,000 shares of common stock at $23 per share.

Required:

1. Prepare general journal entries to record the transactions.
2. Prepare the stockholders' equity section of the corporation's balance sheet as of the close of business on November 30.

Problem 15–2A   Guthrie Corporation received a charter granting it the right to issue 100,000 shares of $5 par value common stock and 20,000 shares of 8%, cumulative and nonparticipating, $50 par value preferred stock. It then completed these transactions:

198A
Mar. 2 Issued 16,000 shares of common stock at par for cash.
     30 Issued 2,000 shares of common stock to the corporation's attorneys for their services in getting the corporation organized. The directors placed a $10,000 value on the services.
Apr. 7 Exchanged 60,000 shares of common stock for the following assets at their fair market values: land, $50,000; buildings, $200,000; and machinery, $125,000.
Dec. 31 Closed the Income Summary account. There was a $15,000 loss.

198B
Jan. 15 Issued 1,500 shares of preferred stock at $60 per share.
Dec. 1 Accepted subscriptions to 12,000 shares of common stock at $7. Down payments of 20% accompanied the subscription contracts.
     31 Closed the Income Summary account. There was an $86,000 net income.

198C
Jan. 3 The board of directors declared an 8% dividend to preferred shares and $0.15 per share to outstanding common shares, payable on February 5 to the January 15 stockholders of record.
Feb. 28 Paid the dividend previously declared.

Required:

1. Prepare general journal entries to record the transactions.
2. Prepare the stockholders' equity section of the corporation's balance sheet as of the close of business on February 28, 198C.

Problem 15–3A   Gateway Company has outstanding 10,000 shares of $10 par value, 9% preferred stock and 30,000 shares of $10 par value common stock. During a seven-year period, it paid out the following amounts in dividends: 198A, $5,000; 198B, nothing; 198C, $7,000; 198D, $24,000; 198E, $24,000; 198F, $30,000; and 198G, $54,000. There were no dividends in arrears for the years before 198A.

Required:

1. Prepare three schedules with columnar headings as follows:

Year	Amount Distributed in Dividends	Total to Preferred	Balance Due Preferred	Total to Common	Dividend per Share Preferred	Dividend per Share Common

2. Complete a schedule under each of the following assumptions, showing for each year the total dollars paid the preferred stockholders, the balance due the preferred stockholders, and so forth.

   a. The preferred stock is noncumulative and nonparticipating.

   b. The preferred stock is cumulative and nonparticipating.

   c. The preferred stock is cumulative and participating to 10% of its par value.

Problem 15–4A

Part 1. Following are the stockholders' equity sections from the balance sheets of three corporations. From the information given calculate the book value per share of the preferred and of the common stock of each corporation.

1. Stockholders' equity:

    Eight percent cumulative and nonparticipating, $10 par value, $12 redemption value, preferred stock, authorized and issued 8,000 shares .... $ 80,000

    Common stock, $5 par value, authorized and issued 60,000 shares 300,000

    Retained earnings 106,000

       Total stockholders' equity $486,000

2. Stockholders' equity:

    Cumulative and nonparticipating, $50 par value, 6% preferred stock, 10,000 shares issued and outstanding $500,000*

    Common stock, $1 par value, 200,000 shares issued and outstanding 200,000

    Retained earnings 80,000

       Total stockholders' equity $780,000

  * The preferred stock is not redeemable and has no assigned redemption value. One year's dividends are in arrears.

3. Stockholders' equity:

    Preferred stock, $50 par value, 7% cumulative and nonparticipating, 5,000 shares issued and outstanding $250,000*

    Common stock, $1 par value, 500,000 shares issued and outstanding 500,000

    Total contributed capital $750,000

    Deficit .... (70,000)

       Total stockholders' equity $680,000

  * Redemption value of preferred stock is $55 plus two years' dividends which are in arrears.

Part 2. A corporation's common stock is selling on the stock exchange today at $13.75 per share, and a just-published balance sheet shows the stockholders' equity in the company as follows:

Stockholders' Equity

Preferred stock, $100 par value, 8% cumulative and nonparticipating, issued and outstanding 4,000 shares	$400,000*
Common stock, $10 par value, issued and outstanding 30,000 shares	300,000
Total contributed capital	$700,000
Retained earnings	110,000
Total stockholders' equity	$810,000

* The preferred stock is not redeemable.

Required:

Answer these questions: (1) What is the market value of the corporation's common stock? (2) What are the par values of its *(a)* preferred stock and *(b)* common stock? (3) If there are no dividends in arrears, what are the book values per share of the *(a)* preferred stock and *(b)* common stock? (4) If two years' dividends are in arrears on the preferred stock, what are the book values per share of the *(a)* preferred stock and the *(b)* common stock?

Problem 15–5A

The stockholders' equity sections from three corporation balance sheets follow:

1. Stockholders' equity:

Cumulative and nonparticipating, $100 par value, 6% preferred stock, authorized and issued 1,000 shares	$ 100,000
Common stock, $25 par value, 10,000 shares authorized and issued	250,000
Retained earnings	64,000
Total stockholders' equity	$ 414,000

2. Stockholders' equity:

Preferred stock, $100 par value, 7% cumulative and nonparticipating, 500 shares authorized and issued	$ 50,000*
Common stock, $100 par value, 500 shares authorized and issued	50,000
Retained earnings	6,000
Total stockholders' equity	$ 106,000

* The current year's dividend is unpaid on the preferred stock.

3. Stockholders' equity:

Cumulative and nonparticipating, $10 par value, 7% preferred stock, 100,000 shares authorized and issued	$1,000,000*
Common stock, $25 par value, 100,000 shares authorized and issued	2,500,000
Total contributed capital	$3,500,000
Deficit	(540,000)
Total stockholders' equity	$2,960,000

* Three years' dividends are in arrears on the preferred stock.

Required:

Prepare a schedule showing the book values per share of the preferred and common stock of each corporation under the assumption that the preferred stock carries the right to the return of par value plus dividends in arrears in a liquidation.

PROVOCATIVE PROBLEMS

Karen Dabney has decided to invest $10,000 in one of two securities: Wisetec Corporation common stock or the preferred stock issued by Hypercon Company. The companies manufacture and sell competing products, and both have been in business about the same length of time—four years in the case of Wisetec Corporation and five years for Hypercon Company. Also, the two companies have about the same amounts of stockholders' equity, as the following equity sections from their latest balance sheets show:

WISETEC CORPORATION

Common stock, $5 par value, 200,000 shares authorized, 80,000 shares issued	$400,000
Retained earnings	200,000
Total stockholders' equity	$600,000

HYPERCON COMPANY

Preferred stock, $100 par value, 7% cumulative and nonparticipating, 2,000 shares authorized and issued	$200,000*
Common stock, $10 par value, 40,000 shares authorized and issued	400,000
Retained earnings	15,000
Total stockholders' equity	$615,000

* The current and two prior years' dividends are in arrears on the preferred stock.

Wisetec Corporation did not pay a dividend on its common stock during its first year's operations; however, since then, for the past three years, it has paid a $0.25 per share annual dividend on the stock. The stock is currently selling for $7.80 per share. The preferred stock of Hypercon Company, on the other hand, is selling for $91 per share. Ms. Dabney favors this stock as an investment. She feels the stock is a real bargain since it is not only selling below its par value but also $30 below book value, and as she says, "Since it is a preferred stock, the dividends are guaranteed." Too, she feels the common stock of Wisetec Corporation, selling at 4% above book value and 56% above par value while paying only a $0.25 per share dividend, is overpriced.

a. Is the preferred stock of Hypercon Company selling at a price $30 below its book value, and is the common stock of Wisetec Corporation selling at a price 4% above book value and 56% above par value?
b. From an analysis of the stockholders' equity sections, express your opinion of the two stocks as investments and describe some of the factors Ms. Dabney should consider in choosing between the two securities.

James Awn and William Allen have operated a stereophonic supply firm, Stereophonic Supply, for a number of years as partners sharing losses and gains in a 3 to 2 ratio. They have entered into an agreement with Francis Lawton to reorganize their firm into a corporation and have just received a charter granting their corporation, Stereo Suppliers, Inc., the right to issue 20,000 shares of $5 par value common stock. On the date of the reorganization,

April 9 of the current year, a trial balance of the partnership ledger appears as follows:

STEREOPHONIC SUPPLY
Trial Balance
April 9, 19—

Cash	$ 5,100	
Accounts receivable	9,300	
Allowance for doubtful accounts		$ 350
Merchandise inventory	42,250	
Store equipment	9,800	
Accumulated depreciation, store equipment . .		2,100
Buildings	50,000	
Accumulated depreciation, buildings		10,000
Land	12,500	
Accounts payable		5,550
Mortgage payable		35,000
James Awn, capital		45,250
William Allen, capital		30,700
Totals	$128,950	$128,950

The agreement between the partners and Lawton carries these provisions:

1.   The partnership assets are to be revalued as follows:
   a.   The $300 account receivable of Disco Shop is known to be uncollectible and is to be written off as a bad debt, after which *(b)* the allowance for doubtful accounts is to be increased to 5% of the remaining accounts receivable.
   c.   The merchandise inventory is to be written down to $38,000 to allow for damaged and shopworn goods.
   d.   Insufficient depreciation has been taken on the store equipment; consequently, its book value is to be decreased to $6,500 by increasing the balance of the accumulated depreciation account.
   e.   The building is to be written up to its replacement cost, $65,000, and the balance of the accumulated depreciation account is to be increased to show the building to be one-fifth depreciated.
2.   After the partnership assets are revalued, the assets and liabilities are to be transferred to the corporation in exchange for its stock, with each partner accepting stock at par value for his equity in the partnership.
3.   Francis Lawton is to buy any remaining stock for cash at par value.

After reaching the agreement outlined, the three men hired you as accountant for the new corporation. Your first task is to determine the amount of stock each person should receive, and to prepare entries on the corporation's books to record the issuance of stock in exchange for the partnership assets and liabilities and the issuance of stock to Lawton for cash. In addition, prepare a balance sheet for the corporation as it should appear after the firm is reorganized and all its stock is issued.

Provocative
Problem 15–3,
Fling
Corporation

The management of Fling Corporation is considering the expansion of its business operations to a new and exciting line of business in which newly invested assets can be expected to earn 16% per year. At the present time, Fling Corporation has only 10,000 shares of $50 par, common stock outstanding, no other contributed capital accounts, and retained earnings of $100,000. Existing operations consistently earn approximately $60,000 each year. To finance the new expansion, management is considering three alternatives: *(a)* Issuing 2,500 shares of $100 par, 9% cumulative, nonparticipating, nonvoting, preferred stock. Investment advisors of the company have concluded that these shares could be issued at par. *(b)* Issuing 2,000 shares of $100 par, 9% cumulative, fully participating, nonvoting, preferred stock. The investment advisors conclude that these shares could be sold for $125 per share. *(c)* Issuing 4,000 shares of common stock at $62.50 per share.

In evaluating these three alternatives, Fling Corporation management has asked you to calculate the dividends that would be distributed to each class of stockholder based on the assumption that each year the board of directors will declare dividends equal to the total net income earned by the corporation.

Required:

1. Prepare calculations showing the distribution of dividends to preferred and common stockholders under each of three alternative financing plans. Also calculate dividends per share of preferred and dividends per share of common.
2. Assume that you own 1,000 of the common shares outstanding prior to the expansion and that you will not acquire or purchase any of the newly issued shares. Based on your analysis in Requirement 1, which of the three financing plans would you prefer? Alternatively, would you prefer that the proposed expansion in operations be rejected?

Additional Corporation Transactions and Stock Investments

16

After studying Chapter 16, you should be able to:

Record stock dividends and compare them with stock splits.

Record purchases and sales of treasury stock and describe their effects on stockholders' equity.

Describe restrictions and appropriations of retained earnings and the disclosure of such items in the financial statements.

State the criteria for classifying stock investments as current assets or as long-term investments.

Describe the circumstances under which the cost method of accounting for stock investments is used and the circumstances under which the equity method is used.

Record and maintain the accounts for stock investments according to the cost method and the equity method.

Prepare consolidated financial statements that include such matters as excess of investment cost over book value and minority interests.

Define or explain the words and phrases listed in the chapter Glossary.

When a corporation earns a net income, more assets flow into the business from revenues than flow out for expenses. As a result, a net income increases both assets and stockholders' equity. The increase in stockholders' equity appears on the corporation's balance sheet as retained earnings. Once retained earnings were commonly called *earned surplus*. However, since the word *surplus* is subject to misinterpretation, the AICPA's Committee on Terminology recommended that its use be discontinued. Consequently, the term *surplus* has all but disappeared from published balance sheets.

RETAINED EARNINGS AND DIVIDENDS

In most states, a corporation must have retained earnings in order to pay a cash dividend. However, the payment of a cash dividend reduces in equal amounts both cash and stockholders' equity. Consequently, in order to pay a cash dividend, a corporation must have not only a credit balance in its Retained Earnings account but also cash with which to pay the dividend. If cash or assets that will shortly become cash are not available, a board of directors may think it wise to forgo the declaration of a dividend, even though retained earnings exist. Often, the directors of a corporation with a large retained earnings balance will not declare a dividend because all current assets will be needed in the operation of the business.

In considering the wisdom of a dividend, a board of directors must recognize that earnings are a source of assets. Perhaps some assets from earnings should be paid out in dividends and some should be retained for emergencies and to pay dividends in years when earnings are not sufficient to pay normal dividends. Also, if a corporation is to expand, management may wish to finance the expansion by using assets acquired through earnings rather than by borrowing or selling equity.

Entries for the declaration and distribution of a cash dividend were presented on page 138 and need not be repeated here.

DISTRIBUTIONS FROM CONTRIBUTED CAPITAL

Generally, contributed capital may not be returned to stockholders as dividends. However, in some states, dividends may be debited or charged to certain contributed capital accounts. Seldom may dividends be deducted from the par or stated value of the outstanding stock. However, the exact contributed capital accounts to which a corporation may charge dividends depend upon the laws of the state of its incorporation. For this reason, it is usually wise for a board of directors to secure competent legal advice before voting to charge dividends to any contributed capital account.

STOCK DIVIDENDS

A *stock dividend* is a distribution by a corporation of shares of its own stock to its stockholders without any consideration being received in return from its stockholders. Usually, the distribution is prompted by a desire to give the stockholders some evidence of their interest in retained earnings without distributing cash or other assets that the board of directors wants to retain in the business. A clear distinction should be made between a cash dividend and a stock dividend. A cash dividend reduces both assets and stockholders' equity. A stock dividend differs in that shares of the corporation's own stock rather than cash are distributed. Such a dividend has no effect on assets, total capital, or the amount of a stockholder's equity.

A stock dividend has no effect on corporation assets, total capital, and the amount of a stockholder's equity because it involves nothing more than a transfer of retained earnings to contributed capital. To illustrate this, assume that Northwest Corporation has the following stockholders' equity:

Stockholders' Equity		
Common stock, $10 par value, authorized 15,000 shares, issued and outstanding 10,000 shares	$100,000	
Premium on common stock	8,000	
Total contributed capital	$108,000	
Retained earnings	35,000	
Total stockholders' equity		$143,000

Assume further that on December 28, the directors of Northwest Corporation declared a 10% or 1,000-share stock dividend distributable on January 20 to the stockholders of record on January 15.

If the market value of Northwest Corporation's stock on December 28 is $15 per share, the following entries would record the dividend declaration and distribution:

Dec.	28	Retained Earnings	15,000.00	
		Common Stock Dividend Distributable		10,000.00
		Premium on Common Stock		5,000.00
		To record the declaration of a 1,000-share common stock dividend.		
Jan.	20	Common Stock Dividend Distributable	10,000.00	
		Common Stock		10,000.00
		To record the distribution of a 1,000-share common stock dividend.		

Note that the entries shift $15,000 of the stockholders' equity from retained earnings to contributed capital, or as it is said, $15,000 of retained earnings are *capitalized*. Note also that the amount of retained earnings capitalized is equal to the market value of the 1,000 shares issued ($15 × 1,000 shares = $15,000).

As previously pointed out, a stock dividend does not distribute assets to the stockholders; it does not affect in any way the corporation assets. Likewise, it has no effect on total capital and on the equities of the individual stockholders. To illustrate these last points, assume that Johnson owned 100 shares of Northwest Corporation's stock prior to the stock dividend. The corporation's total contributed and retained capital before the dividend and the book value of Johnson's 100 shares were as follows:

Common stock (10,000 shares)	$100,000
Premium on common stock	8,000
Retained earnings	35,000
Total contributed and retained capital	$143,000

$143,000 ÷ 10,000 shares outstanding = $14.30 per share book value.
$14.30 × 100 = $1,430 for the book value of Johnson's 100 shares.

A 10% stock dividend gives a stockholder one new share for each 10 shares previously held. Consequently, Johnson received 10 new shares. After the dividend, the contributed capital and retained earnings of the corporation and the book value of Johnson's holdings are as follows:

Common stock (11,000 shares)	$110,000
Premium on common stock	13,000
Retained earnings	20,000
Total contributed and retained capital	$143,000

$143,000 ÷ 11,000 shares outstanding = $13 per share book value.
$13 × 110 = $1,430 for the book value of Johnson's 110 shares.

Before the stock dividend, Johnson owned 100/10,000 or 1/100 of the Northwest Corporation stock and his holdings had a $1,430 book value. After the dividend, he owned 110/11,000 or 1/100 of the corporation and his holdings still had a $1,430 book value. In other words, there was no effect on his equity other than that it was repackaged from 100 units into 110. Likewise, the only effect on corporation capital was a permanent transfer to contributed capital of $15,000 from retained earnings. Consequently, insofar as both the corporation and Johnson are concerned, there was no shift in equities or corporation assets.

Why Stock Dividends Are Distributed

If a stock dividend has no effect on corporation assets and stockholders' equities other than to repackage the equities into more units, why are such dividends declared and distributed? One of the reasons for the declaration of stock dividends is directly related to the market price of a corporation's common stock. For example, if a profitable corporation grows by retaining earnings, the price of its common stock also tends to grow. Eventually, the price of a share may become high enough to prevent some investors from considering a purchase of the stock. Thus, the corporation may declare stock dividends to keep the price of its shares from growing too high. For this reason, some corporations declare small stock dividends each year.

Stockholders may benefit from a stock dividend in another way. Often, corporations declaring stock dividends continue to pay the same cash dividend per share after a stock dividend as before, with the result that stockholders receive more cash each time dividends are declared.

Amount of Retained Earnings Capitalized

Some stockholders may incorrectly believe that earnings are distributed in a stock dividend. Consequently, it was decided that the amount of retained earnings capitalized in a small stock dividend and made unavailable for future dividends should equal the market value of the shares to be distributed.[1] A *small stock dividend* was defined as one of 25% or less of the previously outstanding shares.

A small stock dividend is likely to have only a small impact on the price of the stock. On the other hand, a large stock dividend normally has a pronounced impact, and for this reason is not apt to be perceived as a distribution of earnings. Therefore, in recording a large stock dividend (over 25%), it is necessary to capitalize retained earnings only to the extent required by law. As a result, in most states, a corporation may record a large stock dividend by debiting Retained Earnings and crediting the stock account for the par value of the shares issued.[2]

---

[1] Committee on Accounting Procedure, "Accounting Research Bulletin No. 43," *Accounting Research and Terminology Bulletins, Final Edition* (New York: AICPA, 1961), chap. 7, sec. B, pars. 10, 13.

[2] Ibid., chap. 7, sec. B, par. 11.

Stock Dividends on the Balance Sheet

Since a stock dividend is "payable" in stock rather than in assets, it is not a liability of its issuing corporation. Therefore, if a balance sheet is prepared between the declaration and distribution dates of a stock dividend, the amount of the dividend distributable should appear on the balance sheet in the stockholders' equity section as follows:

Common stock, $10 par value, 50,000 shares authorized, 20,000 shares issued	$200,000
Common stock subscribed, 5,000 shares	50,000
Common stock dividend distributable, 1,900 shares	19,000
Total common stock issued and to be issued	$269,000
Capital contributed by common stockholders in excess of the par value of their shares	46,000
Total capital contributed and subscribed by common stockholders	$315,000

In addition to the stock dividend distributable, note in the equity section the item "Capital contributed by common stockholders in excess of the par value of their shares." This item resulted from common stock premiums and is probably carried in the ledger in the Premium on Common Stock account. However, as in this case, items are commonly shown on the balance sheet under more descriptive captions than the name of the account in which they are recorded.

STOCK SPLITS

Sometimes, when a corporation's stock is selling at a high price, the corporation will call it in and issue two, three, or more new shares in the place of each previously outstanding share. For example, a corporation having outstanding $100 par value stock selling for $375 a share may call in the old shares and issue to the stockholders four shares of $25 par, or 10 shares of $10 par, or any number of shares of no-par stock in exchange for each $100 share formerly held. This is known as a *stock split* or a *stock split-up,* and its usual purpose is to reduce the market price of the stock and, consequently, to facilitate trading in the stock.

A stock split has no effect on total stockholders' equity, the equities of the individual stockholders, or on the balances of any of the contributed capital or retained earnings accounts. Consequently, all that is required in recording a stock split is a memorandum entry in the stock account reciting the facts of the split. For example, such a memorandum might read, "Called in the outstanding $100 par value common stock and issued 10 shares of $10 par value common stock for each old share previously outstanding." Also, there would be a change in the description of the stock on the balance sheet.

TREASURY STOCK

Corporations often reacquire shares of their own stock. Sometimes a corporation will purchase its own stock on the open market to be given to employees as a bonus or to be used in acquiring other corporations. Occasionally, shares are bought in order to maintain a favorable market for the stock. Regardless of the reason, if a corporation reacquires shares of its own stock, such stock is known as *treasury stock*. Treasury stock is a corporation's own stock that has been issued and then reacquired either by purchase or gift. Notice that the stock must be the corporation's own stock. The acquisition of stock of another corporation does not create treasury stock. Furthermore, treasury stock must have been issued and then reacquired. This distinguishes treasury stock from unissued stock. The distinction is important because stock once issued at par or above and then reacquired as treasury stock may be legally reissued at a discount without discount liability. Although treasury stock differs from unissued stock in that it may be sold at a discount without discount liability, in other respects it has the same status as unissued stock. Neither of the two is an asset. Both are subtracted from authorized stock to determine outstanding stock when such things as book values are calculated. Neither receives cash dividends nor has a vote in the stockholders' meetings.

PURCHASE OF TREASURY STOCK[3]

When a corporation purchases its own stock, it reduces in equal amounts both its assets and its stockholders' equity. To illustrate this, assume that on May 1 of the current year, the condensed balance sheet of Curry Corporation appears as in Illustration 16–1.

If on May 1, Curry Corporation purchases 1,000 shares of its outstanding stock at $11.50 per share, the transaction is recorded as follows:

---

[3] There are several ways of accounting for treasury stock transactions. This text discusses the so-called cost basis, which seems to be the most widely used. Other methods are left for a more advanced course.

May	1	Treasury Stock, Common	11,500.00	
		Cash		11,500.00
		Purchased 1,000 shares of treasury stock at $11.50 per share.		

The debit of the entry records a reduction in the equity of the stockholders. The credit records a reduction in assets. Both are equal to the cost of the treasury stock. After the entry is posted, a new balance sheet will show the reductions as in Illustration 16–2.

Notice in the second balance sheet that the cost of the treasury stock appears in the stockholders' equity section as a deduction from common stock and retained earnings. In comparing the two balance sheets, notice that the treasury stock purchase reduces both assets

Illustration 16–1

CURRY CORPORATION
Balance Sheet, May 1, 19—

Assets		*Capital*	
Cash	$ 30,000	Common stock, $10 par value, authorized and issued 10,000 shares	$100,000
Other assets	95,000	Retained earnings	25,000
Total assets	$125,000	Total capital	$125,000

Illustration 16–2

CURRY CORPORATION
Balance Sheet, May 1, 19—

Assets		*Capital*	
Cash	$ 18,500	Common stock, $10 par value, authorized and issued 10,000 shares of which 1,000 are in the treasury	$100,000
Other assets	95,000	Retained earnings of which $11,500 is restricted by the purchase of treasury stock	25,000
		Total	$125,000
		Less cost of treasury stock	11,500
Total assets	$113,500	Total capital	$113,500

and stockholders' equity by the $11,500 cost of the stock. Also, observe that the dollar amount of issued stock remains at $100,000 and is unchanged from the first balance sheet. The amount of *issued stock* is not changed by the purchase of treasury stock. However, the purchase does reduce *outstanding stock*. In Curry Corporation, the purchase reduced the outstanding stock from 10,000 to 9,000 shares.

There is a distinction between issued stock and outstanding stock. Issued stock may or may not be outstanding. Outstanding stock has been issued and remains currently outstanding. Only outstanding stock is effective stock, receives cash dividends, and is given a vote in the meetings of stockholders.

Restricting Retained Earnings by the Purchase of Treasury Stock

The purchase of treasury stock by a corporation has the same effect on its assets and stockholders' equity as the payment of a cash dividend. Both transfer corporation assets to stockholders and thereby reduce assets and stockholders' equity. Consequently, in most states, a corporation may purchase treasury stock or it may pay cash dividends, but the sum of both cannot exceed the amount of its retained earnings available for dividends.

Unlike the payment of a cash dividend, the purchase of treasury stock does not reduce the balance of the Retained Earnings account. However, the purchase does place a restriction on the amount of retained earnings available for dividends. Note how the restriction is shown in Illustration 16–2. It is also commonly shown by means of a balance sheet footnote.

The restriction of retained earnings because of treasury stock purchases is a matter of state law. Other types of legal restrictions on retained earnings may be imposed by law or by contract.

REISSUING TREASURY STOCK

When treasury stock is reissued, it may be reissued at cost, above cost, or below cost. If reissued at cost, the entry to record the transaction is the reverse of the entry used to record the purchase.

Although treasury stock may be sold at cost, it is commonly sold at a price either above or below cost. When sold above cost, the amount received in excess of cost is credited to a contributed capital account called Contributed Capital, Treasury Stock Transactions. For example, if Curry Corporation sells for $12 per share 500 of the treasury shares purchased at $11.50 per share, the entry to record the transaction appears as follows:

June	3	Cash	6,000.00	
		Contributed Capital, Treasury Stock		
		Transactions		250.00
		Treasury Stock		5,750.00
		Sold at $12 per share 500 treasury shares		
		that cost $11.50 per share.		

When treasury stock is reissued at a price below cost, the entry to record the sale depends upon whether or not there is contributed capital from previous treasury stock transactions. If there is no such contributed capital, the "loss" is debited to Retained Earnings. However, if there is such contributed capital, the "loss" is debited to the account of this contributed capital to the extent of its balance. Any remainder is then debited to Retained Earnings. For example, if Curry Corporation sells its remaining 500 shares of treasury stock at $10 per share, the entry to record the sale is:

July	10	Cash	5,000.00	
		Contributed Capital, Treasury Stock		
		Transactions	250.00	
		Retained Earnings	500.00	
		Treasury Stock		5,750.00
		Sold at $10 per share 500 treasury shares		
		that cost $11.50 per share.		

RETIREMENT OF STOCK

A corporation may purchase shares of its own stock with the intent of retiring the stock rather than holding it as treasury stock. Such shares are permanently canceled upon receipt. The purchase and retirement of stock is permissible if the interests of creditors and other stockholders are not jeopardized.

When stock is purchased for retirement, all capital items related to the shares being retired are removed from the accounts. If there is a "gain" on the transaction, it should be credited to contributed capital. On the other hand, a loss should be debited to Retained Earnings.

For example, assume a corporation originally issued its $10 par value common stock at $12 per share, with the premium being credited to Premium on Common Stock. If the corporation later purchased for retirement 1,000 shares of this stock at the price for which it was issued, the entry to record the retirement is:

Apr.	12	Common Stock	10,000.00	
		Premium on Common Stock	2,000.00	
		Cash		12,000.00
		Purchased and retired 1,000 shares of common stock at $12 per share.		

If on the other hand the corporation paid $11 per share instead of $12, the entry for the retirement is:

Apr.	12	Common Stock	10,000.00	
		Premium on Common Stock	2,000.00	
		Cash		11,000.00
		Contributed Capital from the Retirement of Common Stock		1,000.00
		Purchased and retired 1,000 shares of common stock at $11 per share.		

Or, if the corporation paid $15 per share, the entry for the purchase and retirement is:

Apr.	12	Common Stock	10,000.00	
		Premium on Common Stock	2,000.00	
		Retained Earnings	3,000.00	
		Cash		15,000.00
		Purchased and retired 1,000 shares of common stock at $15 per share.		

APPROPRIATIONS OF RETAINED EARNINGS

A corporation may *appropriate retained earnings* for some special purpose or purposes and show the amounts appropriated as separate items in the equity section of its balance sheet. In contrast to retained earnings *restrictions* which are binding by law or by contract, appropriations of retained earnings are voluntarily made by the board of directors. Such appropriations may be recorded by transferring portions of retained earnings from the Retained Earnings account to accounts such as Retained Earnings Appropriated for Contingencies or Retained Earnings Appropriated for Plant Expansion.

The appropriations do not reduce total retained earnings. Rather, their purpose is to inform balance sheet readers that portions of retained earnings are not available for the declaration of cash dividends.

When the contingency or other reason for an appropriation has passed, the appropriation account is eliminated by returning its balance to the Retained Earnings account.

Appropriations of retained earnings were once common, but such appropriations are seldom seen on balance sheets today. Today, the same information is conveyed with less chance of misunderstanding by means of footnotes accompanying the financial statements.

STOCKS AS INVESTMENTS

The stock transactions illustrated thus far have been transactions in which a corporation sold and issued its own stock. Such transactions represent only a small portion of the daily transactions in stocks. Most stock sales involve transactions between investors which are arranged through brokers who charge a commission for their services.

Brokers acting as agents for their customers buy and sell stocks and bonds on exchanges such as the New York Stock Exchange. Some securities are not listed or traded on an organized stock exchange, and brokers act for their customers to buy and sell such securities in the "over-the-counter" market. Each security in this market is handled by one or more brokers who receive from other brokers offers to buy or sell the security at specific "bid" or "ask" prices. Stock prices are quoted on the basis of dollars and ⅛ dollars per share. For example, a stock quoted at 46⅛ means $46.125 per share, and a stock quoted at 25½ means $25.50 per share.

CLASSIFYING INVESTMENTS

Equity securities generally include common and preferred stocks. Many equity securities are actively traded, so that "sales prices or bid and ask prices are currently available on a national securities exchange or in the over-the-counter market." Such securities are called *marketable equity securities.*[4] If, in addition to being marketable, a stock investment is held as "an investment of cash available for current operations," it is classified as a current asset.[5]

Investments that are not intended as a ready source of cash in case of need are classified as *long-term investments*. They include funds

---

[4] FASB, "Accounting for Certain Marketable Securities," *Statement of Financial Accounting Standards No. 12* (Stamford, Conn., 1975), par. 7.

[5] Committee on Accounting Procedure, "Accounting Research Bulletin No. 43," *Accounting Research and Terminology Bulletins, Final Edition* (New York: AICPA, 1961), chap. 3, sec. A, par. 4.

earmarked for a special purpose, such as bond sinking funds, as well as land or other assets owned but not employed in the regular operations of the business. They also include investments in stocks that are not marketable or that, although marketable, are not intended to serve as a ready source of cash. Long-term investments appear on the balance sheet in a classification of their own titled "Long-term investments."

ACCOUNTING FOR INVESTMENTS IN STOCK

Most investments in a corporation's stock represent a small percentage of the total amount of stock outstanding. As a consequence, the investor does not exercise a significant influence over the financial or operating policies of the corporation. However, in some cases, an investor will buy a large portion of the outstanding stock of a corporation in order to influence or control its operations. For example, corporations frequently buy a large share of another corporation's stock in order to influence its activities as well as to receive part of its income.

The method of accounting for stock investments on the books of the investor depends upon whether the investor has the ability to significantly influence the operating and financial policies of the corporation. If the investor can exercise a significant influence, the accounting method used is called the equity method. If the investor does not have a significant influence, the accounting method used is called the cost method. In general, ownership of 20% or more of the voting stock of a corporation is presumptive evidence of the ability to significantly influence its operations.[6] Thus, common stock investments of 20% or more of the voting stock usually are accounted for according to the equity method while investments of less than 20% usually are accounted for according to the cost method. There may be instances, however, where the accountant concludes that the 20% test of significant influence should be overruled by other, more persuasive, evidence.[7]

The Cost Method of Accounting for Stock Investments

When stock is purchased as either a short- or long-term investment, the purchase is recorded at total cost, which includes any commission paid to the broker. For example, 1,000 (10%) of Dot Corporation's 10,000 outstanding common shares were purchased as an investment

---

[6] APB, "The Equity Method of Accounting for Investments in Common Stock," *APB Opinion No. 18* (New York: AICPA, 1971), par. 17.

[7] FASB, "Criteria for Applying the Equity Method of Accounting for Investments in Common Stock," *FASB Interpretation No. 35* (Stamford, Conn., 1981), pars. 3–4.

at 23¼ plus a $300 broker's commission. The entry to record the transaction is:

Sept.	10	Investment in Dot Corporation Stock	23,550.00	
		Cash		23,550.00
		Purchased 1,000 shares of stock for $23,250 plus a $300 broker's commission.		

Observe that nothing is said about a premium or a discount on the Dot Corporation stock. Premiums and discounts are normally recorded only by the corporation that issues the stock. An investor records the entire cost as a debit to the investment account, even though the cost may be above or below par value.

When the cost method is used to account for either a short- or long-term investment and a dividend is received on the stock, an entry similar to the following is made:

Oct.	5	Cash	1,000.00	
		Dividends Earned		1,000.00
		Received a $1 per share dividend on the stock		

Dividends on stocks do not accrue; consequently, an end-of-period entry to record accrued dividends is never made. However, if a balance sheet is prepared after a dividend is declared but before it is paid, an entry debiting Dividends Receivable and crediting Dividends Earned would be appropriate.

A dividend in shares of stock is not income, and a debit and credit entry recording it should not be made. However, a memorandum entry or a notation as to the additional shares should be made in the investment account. Also, receipt of a stock dividend does affect the per share cost of the old shares. For example, if a 20-share dividend is received on 100 shares originally purchased for $1,500 or at $15 per share, the cost of all 120 shares is $1,500 and the cost per share is $12.50 ($1,500 ÷ 120 shares = $12.50 per share).

Under the cost method, when an investment in stock is sold and the proceeds net of any sales commission differ from cost, a gain or loss must be recorded. For example, consider the 1,000 shares of Dot Corporation common stock that were purchased at a cost of $23,550. If these shares are sold at 25¾ less a sales commission of $315, there is a $1,885 gain, and the transaction is recorded:

Jan.	7	Cash	25,435.00	
		Investment in Dot Corporation Stock		23,550.00
		Gain on Sale of Investments		1,885.00
		Sold 1,000 shares of stock for $25,750 less		
		a $315 commission.		

If the net amount received for these shares had been less than their $23,550 cost, there would have been a loss on the transaction.

Lower of Cost or Market

For balance sheet presentation, an investment in stock that is not marketable is accounted for at cost. However, investments in marketable equity securities are divided into two portfolios: (1) those to be shown as current assets and (2) those to be shown as long-term investments. Then the total current market value of each portfolio is calculated and compared to the total cost of each portfolio. Each portfolio is reported at the lower of cost or market.[8]

In the case of the current asset portfolio, a decline in total market value below the previous balance sheet valuation (or cost) is reported in the income statement as a loss. Subsequent recoveries of market value are reported in the income statement as gains, but market value increases above original cost are not recorded.[9]

In the case of long-term investment portfolios of marketable equity securities, market value declines are reported in the income statement *only* if they appear to be permanent. Usually, they are not assumed to be permanent, in which case the market value decline is disclosed as a separate item in the stockholders' equity section of the balance sheet.[10]

The Equity Method of Accounting for Common Stock Investments

If a common stock investor has a significant influence over or even controls the investee, the equity method of accounting for the investment must be used. When the stock is acquired, the purchase is recorded at cost just as it is under the cost method. For example, on January 1, 198A, James, Inc., purchased 3,000 shares (30%) of RMS,

---

[8] FASB, "Accounting for Certain Marketable Securities," par. 8.
[9] Ibid., par. 11.
[10] Ibid., pars. 11, 21.

Inc., common stock for a total cost of $70,650. The entry to record the purchase on the books of James, Inc., is as follows:

Jan.	1	Investment in RMS, Inc.	70,650.00	
		Cash		70,650.00
		Purchased 3,000 shares of common stock.		

Under the equity method, it is recognized that the earnings of the investee corporation not only increase the net assets of the investee corporation but also increase the investor's equity in the assets. Consequently, when the investee closes its books and reports the amount of its earnings, the investor takes up its share of those earnings in its investment account. For example, RMS, Inc., reported net income of $20,000. James, Inc.'s entry to record its share of these earnings is:

Dec.	31	Investment in RMS, Inc.	6,000.00	
		Earnings from Investment in RMS, Inc.		6,000.00
		To record 30% equity in investee's earnings of $20,000.		

The debit records the increase in James, Inc.'s equity in RMS, Inc. The credit causes 30% of RMS, Inc.'s net income to appear on James, Inc.'s income statement as earnings from the investment, and James, Inc., closes the earnings to its Income Summary account and on to its Retained Earnings account just as it would close earnings from any investment.

If, instead of a net income, the investee corporation incurs a loss, the investor debits the loss to an account called Loss from Investment and credits and reduces its Investment in Stock account. It then transfers the loss to its Income Summary account and on to its Retained Earnings account.

Dividends paid by an investee corporation decrease the investee's assets and retained earnings, and also decrease the investor's equity in the investee. Since, under the equity method, the investor records its equity in the full amount of earnings reported by an investee, the receipt of dividends does not constitute income; instead, dividend receipts from the investee represent a decrease in the equity. For example, RMS, Inc., declared and paid $10,000 in dividends on its common stock. The entry to record James, Inc.'s share of these dividends, which it received on January 9, 198B, is:

Jan.	9	Cash	3,000.00	
		Investment in RMS, Inc.		3,000.00
		To record receipt of 30% of the $10,000 dividend paid by RMS, Inc.		

Notice that the carrying value of a common stock investment, accounted for by the equity method, changes in reflection of the investor's equity in the undistributed earnings of the investee. For example, after the above transactions have been recorded on the books of James, Inc., the investment account would appear as follows:

Investment in RMS, Inc.

Date		Explanation	Debit	Credit	Balance
198A					
Jan.	1	Investment	70,650.00		70,650.00
Dec.	31	Share of earnings	6,000.00		76,650.00
198B					
Jan.	9	Share of dividend		3,000.00	73,650.00

When common stock, accounted for by the equity method, is sold, the gain or loss on the sale is determined by comparing the proceeds from the sale with the carrying value of the stock on the date of sale. For example, on January 10, 198B, James, Inc., sold its RMS, Inc., stock for $80,000. The entry to record the sale is as follows:

Jan.	10	Cash	80,000.00	
		Investment in RMS, Inc.		73,650.00
		Gain on Sale of Investments		6,350.00
		Sold 3,000 shares of stock for $80,000.		

PARENT AND SUBSIDIARY CORPORATIONS

Corporations commonly own stock in and may even control other corporations. For example, if Corporation A owns more than 50% of the voting stock of Corporation B, Corporation A can elect Corporation B's board of directors and thus control its activities and resources. In such a situation, the controlling corporation, Corporation A, is known as the *parent company* and Corporation B is called a *subsidiary*.

When a corporation owns all the outstanding stock of a subsidiary, it can take over the subsidiary's assets, cancel its stock, and fuse the subsidiary into the parent company. However, instead of operating the business as a single corporation, there are often financial, legal, and tax advantages if a large business is operated as a parent company that controls one or more subsidiaries. Actually, most large companies are parent corporations owning one or more subsidiaries.

When a business is operated as a parent company with subsidiaries, separate accounting records are kept for each corporation. Also, from a legal viewpoint, the parent and each subsidiary are separate entities with all the rights, duties, and responsibilities of a separate corporation. However, investors in the parent company depend on the parent to present a set of *consolidated statements* that show the results of all operations under the parent's control, including those of any subsidiaries. In these statements, the assets and liabilities of all affiliated companies are combined on a single balance sheet and their revenues and expenses are combined on a single income statement, as though the business were in fact a single company.

CONSOLIDATED BALANCE SHEETS

When parent and subsidiary balance sheets are consolidated, duplications in items are eliminated so that the combined figures do not show more assets and equities than actually exist. For example, a parent's investment in a subsidiary is evidenced by shares of stock that are carried as an asset in the parent company's records. However, these shares actually represent an equity in the subsidiary's assets. Consequently, if the parent's investment in a subsidiary and the subsidiary's assets were both shown on the consolidated balance sheet, the same resources would be counted twice. To prevent this, the parent's investment and the subsidiary's capital accounts are offset and eliminated in preparing a consolidated balance sheet.

Likewise, a single enterprise cannot owe a debt to itself. This would be analogous to a student borrowing $20 for a date from funds saved for next semester's expenses and then preparing a balance sheet showing the $20 as both a receivable from himself and a payable to himself. To prevent such double counting, intercompany debts and receivables are also eliminated in preparing a consolidated balance sheet.

Balance Sheets Consolidated at Time of Acquisition

When a parent's and a subsidiary's assets are combined in the preparation of a consolidated balance sheet, a work sheet is normally used to effect the consolidation. Illustration 16–3 shows such a work sheet.

Illustration 16–3

PARENT COMPANY AND SUBSIDIARY COMPANY
Work Sheet for a Consolidated Balance Sheet, January 1, 198A

	Parent Company	Subsidiary Company	Eliminations		Consolidated Amounts
			Debit	Credit	
Assets					
Cash......................	5,000	15,000			20,000
Notes receivable	10,000			(a) 10,000	
Investment in Subsidiary					
Company	115,000			(b) 115,000	
Other assets	190,000	117,000			307,000
	320,000	132,000			327,000
Liabilities and Equities					
Accounts payable	15,000	7,000			22,000
Notes payable		10,000	(a) 10,000		
Common stock	250,000	100,000	(b) 100,000		250,000
Retained earnings	55,000	15,000	(b) 15,000		55,000
	320,000	132,000	125,000	125,000	327,000

It was prepared to consolidate the accounts of Parent Company and its subsidiary, called Subsidiary Company, on January 1, 198A, the day Parent Company acquired Subsidiary Company through the cash purchase of all its outstanding $10 par value common stock. The stock had a book value of $115,000, or $11.50 per share, which in this first illustration is the amount Parent Company is assumed to have paid for it. Explanation of the work sheet's two eliminating entries follow.

ENTRY *(a).* On the day it acquired Subsidiary Company, Parent Company lent Subsidiary Company $10,000 for use in the subsidiary's operations. It took the subsidiary's note as evidence of the transaction. This intercompany debt was in reality a transfer of funds within the organization. Consequently, since it did not increase the total assets and total liabilities of the affiliated companies, it is eliminated by means of entry *(a).* To understand this entry, recall that the subsidiary's promissory note is represented by a $10,000 debit in Parent Company's Notes Receivable account. Then, observe that the first credit in the Eliminations column exactly offsets and eliminates this item. Next, recall that the subsidiary's note appears as a credit in its Notes Payable account. Then, observe that the $10,000 debit in the Eliminations column completes the elimination of this intercompany debt.

ENTRY *(b)*.   When a parent company buys a subsidiary's stock, the investment appears on the parent's balance sheet as an asset, "Investment in Subsidiary." The investment represents an equity in the subsidiary's net assets. Consequently, to show both the subsidiary's (net) assets and the parent company's investment in the subsidiary on a consolidated balance sheet would be to double count those resources. As a result, on the work sheet the amount of the parent's investment (an equity in the subsidiary's assets) is offset against the subsidiary's stockholder equity accounts, which also represent an equity in the assets, and both are eliminated.

After the intercompany items are eliminated on a work sheet like Illustration 16–3, the assets of the parent and the subsidiary and the remaining equities in these assets are combined and carried into the work sheet's last column. The combined amounts are then used to prepare a consolidated balance sheet showing all the assets and equities of the parent and its subsidiary.

Parent Company Does Not Buy All of Subsidiary's Stock and Does Not Pay Book Value

In the situation just described, Parent Company purchased all of its subsidiary's stock, paying book value for it. Often, a parent company purchases less than 100% of a subsidiary's stock, and commonly pays a price either above or below book value. To illustrate such a situation, assume Parent Company purchased for cash only 80% of its subsidiary's stock rather than 100%, and that it paid $13 per share, a price $1.50 above the stock's book value.

These new assumptions result in a more complicated work sheet entry to eliminate the parent's investment and the subsidiary's stockholders' equity accounts. The entry is complicated by (1) the minority interest in the subsidiary and (2) the excess over book value paid by the parent company for the subsidiary's stock.

MINORITY INTEREST.   When a parent buys a controlling interest in a subsidiary, the parent company is the subsidiary's majority stockholder. However, when the parent owns less than 100% of the subsidiary's stock, the subsidiary has other stockholders who own a *minority interest* in its assets and share its earnings. Consequently, when there is a minority interest, the minority interest must be set out as on the last line of Illustration 16–4 in making the work sheet entry to eliminate the stockholders' equity accounts of the subsidiary. In this case, the minority stockholders have a 20% interest in the subsidiary. Consequently, 20% of the subsidiary's common stock and retained earnings accounts [($100,000 + $15,000) × 20% = $23,000] is set out on the work sheet as the minority interest.

Illustration 16–4

			Eliminations		Consolidated
	Parent Company	Subsidiary Company	Debit	Credit	Amounts
Assets					
Cash.....................	16,000	15,000			31,000
Notes receivable	10,000			(a) 10,000	
Investment in Subsidiary					
Company	104,000			(b) 104,000	
Other assets	190,000	117,000			307,000
Excess of cost					
over book value			(b) 12,000		12,000
	320,000	132,000			350,000
Liabilities and Equities					
Accounts payable	15,000	7,000			22,000
Notes payable		10,000	(a) 10,000		
Common stock	250,000	100,000	(b) 100,000		250,000
Retained earnings	55,000	15,000	(b) 15,000		55,000
Minority interest				(b) 23,000	23,000
	320,000	132,000	137,000	137,000	350,000

PARENT COMPANY AND SUBSIDIARY COMPANY
Work Sheet for a Consolidated Balance Sheet, January 1, 198A

EXCESS OF INVESTMENT COST OVER BOOK VALUE.   Parent Company paid $13 per share for its 8,000 shares of Subsidiary Company's stock. Consequently, the cost of these shares exceeded their book value by $12,000, calculated as follows:

Cost of stock (8,000 shares at $13 per share) ..	$104,000
Book value (8,000 shares at $11.50 per share)..	92,000
Excess of cost over book value	$ 12,000

Now observe how this excess of cost over book value is set out on the work sheet in eliminating the parent's investment in the subsidiary. Then, it is carried into the Consolidated Amounts column as an asset.

After the work sheet of Illustration 16–4 was completed, the consolidated amounts in the last column were used to prepare the consolidated balance sheet of Illustration 16–5. Note the treatment of the minority interest in the balance sheet. The minority stockholders have a $23,000 equity in the consolidated assets of the affiliated companies. Many have

Illustration 16–5

PARENT COMPANY AND SUBSIDIARY
Consolidated Balance Sheet, January 1, 198A

Assets

Cash	$ 31,000	
Other assets	307,000	
Goodwill from consolidation	12,000	
Total assets		$350,000

Liabilities and Stockholders' Equity

Liabilities:		
Accounts payable		$ 22,000
Minority interest		23,000
Stockholders' equity:		
Common stock	$250,000	
Retained earnings	55,000	
Total stockholders' equity		305,000
Total liabilities and stockholders' equity		$350,000

argued that this item should be disclosed in the stockholders' equity section. Others believe it should be shown in the long-term liabilities section. However, a more common alternative is to disclose the minority interest as a separate item between the liabilities and stockholders' equity sections, as is shown in Illustration 16–5.

Next, observe that the $12,000 excess over book value paid by the parent company for the subsidiary's stock appears on the consolidated balance sheet as the asset described as "Goodwill from consolidation." When a parent company purchases an interest in a subsidiary, it may pay more than book value for its equity because (1) certain of the subsidiary's assets are carried on the subsidiary's books at less than fair value. It also may pay more because (2) certain of the subsidiary's liabilities are carried at book values which are greater than fair values, or (3) the subsidiary's earnings prospects are good enough to justify paying more than the net fair (market) value of its assets and liabilities. In this illustration, it is assumed that the book values of Subsidiary Company's assets and liabilities are their fair values. However, Subsidiary Company's expected earnings justified paying $104,000 for an 80% equity in the subsidiary's net assets (assets less liabilities).

The APB ruled that where a company pays more than book value because the subsidiary's assets are undervalued or its liabilities are overvalued, the cost in excess of book value should be allocated to those assets and liabilities so that they are restated at fair values. After the subsidiary's assets and liabilities have been restated to reflect fair values, any remaining cost in excess of book value should be reported on the consolidated balance sheet as "Goodwill from consolidation."[11]

Occasionally, a parent company pays less than book value for its interest in a subsidiary. In such a case, since a "bargain" purchase is very unlikely, the logical reason for a price below book value is that certain of the subsidiary's assets are carried on its books at amounts in excess of fair value. In such a situation, the APB ruled that the amounts at which the overvalued assets are placed on the consolidated balance sheet should be reduced accordingly.[12]

EARNINGS AND DIVIDENDS OF A SUBSIDIARY

As previously discussed, a parent accounts for its investment in a subsidiary according to the equity method. As a consequence, the parent's recorded net income and Retained Earnings account include the parent's equity in the net income earned by the subsidiary since the date of acquisition. Also, the balance of the parent's Investment in Subsidiary account increases (or decreases) each year by an amount equal to the parent's equity in the subsidiary's earnings (or loss) less the parent's share of any dividends paid by the subsidiary.

For example, assume that Subsidiary Company of this illustration earned $12,500 during its first year as a subsidiary and at year-end paid out $7,500 in dividends. Parent Company recorded its 80% equity in these earnings and dividends as follows:

Dec.	31	Investment in Subsidiary Company	10,000.00	
		Earnings from Investment in Subsidiary		10,000.00
		To record 80% of the net income reported by Subsidiary Company.		
Dec.	31	Cash	6,000.00	
		Investment in Subsidiary Company		6,000.00
		To record the receipt of 80% of the $7,500 dividend paid by Subsidiary Company.		

CONSOLIDATED BALANCE SHEETS AT A DATE AFTER ACQUISITION

Illustration 16–6 shows the December 31, 198B, work sheet to consolidate the balance sheets of Parent Company and Subsidiary Com-

---

[11] APB, "Business Combinations," *APB Opinion No. 16* (New York: AICPA, 1970), par. 87.

[12] Ibid., par. 91.

Illustration 16–6

	Parent Company	Subsidiary Company	Eliminations Debit	Eliminations Credit	Consolidated Amounts

PARENT COMPANY AND SUBSIDIARY COMPANY
Work Sheet for a Consolidated Balance Sheet, December 31, 198A

	Parent Company	Subsidiary Company	Eliminations — Debit	Eliminations — Credit	Consolidated Amounts
Assets					
Cash......................	22,000	20,000			42,000
Notes receivable	10,000			*(a)* 10,000	
Investment in Subsidiary Company	108,000			*(b)* 108,000	
Other assets	190,000	117,000			307,000
Excess of cost over book value			*(b)* 12,000		12,000
	330,000	137,000			361,000
Liabilities and Equities					
Accounts payable	15,000	7,000			22,000
Notes payable		10,000	*(a)* 10,000		
Common stock...........	250,000	100,000	*(b)* 100,000		250,000
Retained earnings	65,000	20,000	*(b)* 20,000		65,000
Minority interest				*(b)* 24,000	24,000
	330,000	137,000	142,000	142,000	361,000

pany. To simplify the illustration, it is assumed that Parent Company had no transactions during the year other than to record its equity in Subsidiary Company's earnings and dividends. Also, the other assets and liabilities of Subsidiary Company did not change, and the subsidiary has not paid the note given Parent Company.

Compare Illustration 16–6 with 16–4 and note the changes in Parent Company's balance sheet (the first column). Parent Company's Cash increased from $16,000 to $22,000 as a result of the dividends received from the subsidiáry. The Investment in Subsidiary Company account increased from $104,000 to $108,000 as a result of the equity method entries during the year. Finally, Parent Company's Retained Earnings increased by $10,000, which was the parent's equity in the subsidiary's earnings.

In the second column of Illustration 16–6, note only two changes: (1) Subsidiary Company's Cash balance increased by $5,000, which is the difference between its $12,500 net income and $7,500 payment of dividends. (2) Retained Earnings also increased from $15,000 to $20,000, which is the amount eliminated on the work sheet.

Two additional items in Illustration 16–6 require explanation. First, the minority interest set out on the year-end work sheet is greater than on the beginning-of-year work sheet (Illustration 16–4). The minority stockholders have a 20% equity in Subsidiary Company, and the $24,000 shown on the year-end work sheet is 20% of the year-end balances of the Subsidiary's Common Stock and Retained Earnings accounts. This $24,000 is $1,000 greater than the beginning-of-year minority interest because the subsidiary's retained earnings increased $5,000 during the year and the minority stockholder's share of this increase is 20% or $1,000. Second, the $12,000 amount set out as the excess cost of Parent Company's investment over its book value is, in this illustration, the same on the end-of-year work sheet as on the work sheet at the beginning. The APB ruled that such excess cost or "goodwill" should be amortized by systematic charges to income over the accounting periods estimated to be benefited.[13] An explanation of the amortization entries is left to a more advanced text.

OTHER CONSOLIDATED STATEMENTS

Consolidated income statements and consolidated retained earnings statements are also prepared for affiliated companies. However, a discussion of the procedures to prepare these statements is deferred to an advanced accounting course. Knowledge of the procedures is not necessary for a general understanding of such statements. At this point, the reader need only recognize that all duplications in items and all profit arising from intercompany transactions are eliminated in their preparation. Also, the amounts of net income and retained earnings that are reported in consolidated statements are equal to the amounts recorded by the parent under the equity method.

THE CORPORATION BALANCE SHEET

A number of balance sheet sections have been illustrated in this and previous chapters. To bring together as much of the information from all these sections as space allows, the balance sheet of Betco Corporation is shown in Illustration 16–7.

Betco Corporation's balance sheet is a consolidated balance sheet, as indicated in the title and by the items "Goodwill from consolidation" and "Minority interest." In preparing the balance sheet, Betco Corporation's investment in its subsidiary was eliminated. Consequently, the Toledo Corporation stock shown on the consolidated balance sheet represents an investment in an unconsolidated (outside) company that is not a subsidiary of either Betco or Betco's subsidiary.

---

[13] APB, "Intangible Assets," *APB Opinion No. 17* (New York: AICPA, 1970), pars. 27–31.

Illustration 16–7

BETCO CORPORATION
Consolidated Balance Sheet, December 31, 198A

Assets

Current assets:

Cash		$ 15,000
Marketable securities		5,000
Accounts receivable	$50,000	
Less allowance for doubtful accounts	1,000	49,000
Merchandise inventory		115,000
Subscriptions receivable, common stock		15,000
Prepaid expenses		1,000
Total current assets			$200,000

Long-term investments:

Bond sinking fund		$ 15,000
Toledo Corporation common stock		5,000
Total long-term investments		20,000

Plant assets:

Land		$ 50,000
Buildings	$285,000	
Less accumulated depreciation	30,000	255,000
Store equipment	$ 85,000	
Less accumulated depreciation	20,000	65,000
Total plant assets		370,000

Intangible assets:

Goodwill from consolidation		10,000
Total assets		$600,000

Liabilities

Current liabilities:

Notes payable	$ 10,000	
Accounts payable	14,000	
State and federal income taxes payable	16,000	
Total current liabilities		$ 40,000

Long-term liabilities:

First 8% real estate mortgage bonds, due in 199E	$100,000	
Less unamortized discount based on the 8¼% market rate for bond interest prevailing on the date of issue	2,000	98,000
Total liabilities		$138,000
Minority interest		15,000

Stockholders' Equity

Contributed capital:

Common stock, $10 par value, authorized 50,000 shares, issued 30,000 shares of which 1,000 are in the treasury	$300,000	
Unissued common stock subscribed, 2,500 shares	25,000	
Capital contributed by the stockholders in excess of the par value of their shares	33,000	
Total contributed capital	$358,000	
Retained earnings (Note 1)	105,000	
Total contributed and retained capital	$463,000	
Less cost of treasury stock	16,000	
Total stockholders' equity		447,000
Total liabilities and stockholders' equity		$600,000

Note 1: Retained earnings in the amount of $31,000 is restricted under an agreement with the corporation's bondholders and because of the purchase of treasury stock, leaving $74,000 of retained earnings not so restricted.

GLOSSARY

Appropriated retained earnings. Retained earnings voluntarily earmarked for a special use as a means of informing stockholders that assets from earnings equal to the appropriations are unavailable for dividends.

Cost method of accounting for stock investments. The investment is recorded at total cost and maintained at that amount; subsequent investee earnings and dividends do not affect the investment account.

Earned surplus. A synonym for retained earnings, no longer in use.

Equity method of accounting for stock investments. The investment is recorded at total cost, investor's equity in subsequent earnings of the investee increases the investment account, and subsequent dividends of the investee reduce the investment account.

Long-term investments. Investments, not intended as a ready source of cash in case of need, such as bond sinking funds, land, and marketable securities that are not held as a temporary investment of cash.

Marketable equity securities. Common and preferred stocks that are actively traded so that sales prices or bid and ask prices are currently available on a national securities exchange or in the over-the-counter market.

Minority interest. Stockholders' equity in a subsidiary not owned by the parent corporation.

Parent company. A corporation that owns a controlling interest (more than 50% of the voting stock is required) in another corporation.

Restricted retained earnings. Retained earnings that are unavailable for dividends as a result of law or binding contract.

Small stock dividend. A stock dividend 25% or less of a corporation's previously outstanding shares.

Stock dividend. A distribution by a corporation of shares of its own common stock to its common stockholders without any consideration being received in return therefor.

Stock split. The act of a corporation of calling in its stock and issuing more than one new share in exchange for each share previously outstanding.

Subsidiary. A corporation that is controlled by another (parent) corporation because the parent owns more than 50% of the subsidiary's voting stock.

Treasury stock. Issued stock that has been reacquired by the issuing corporation.

QUESTIONS FOR CLASS DISCUSSION

1. What are the effects in terms of assets and stockholders' equity of the declaration and distribution of (a) a cash dividend and (b) a stock dividend?
2. What is the difference between a stock dividend and a stock split?
3. Courts have held that a dividend in the stock of the distributing corporation is not taxable income to its recipients. Why?

4. If a balance sheet is prepared between the date of declaration and the date of distribution of a dividend, how should the dividend be shown if it is to be distributed in *(a)* cash and *(b)* stock?

5. What is treasury stock? How is it like unissued stock? How does it differ from unissued stock? What is the legal significance of this difference?

6. General Plastics Corporation bought 1,000 shares of Capital Steel Corporation stock and turned it over to its treasurer for safekeeping. Is this treasury stock? Why or why not?

7. What is the effect of a treasury stock purchase in terms of assets and stockholders' equity?

8. Distinguish between issued stock and outstanding stock.

9. Why do state laws place limitations on the purchase of treasury stock?

10. What is meant by "marketable securities?"

11. Under what conditions should a stock investment be classified as a current asset?

12. In accounting for common stock investments, when should the cost method be used? When should the equity method be used?

13. When a parent corporation uses the equity method to account for its investment in a subsidiary, what recognition is given by the parent corporation to the income or loss reported by the subsidiary? What recognition is given to dividends declared by the subsidiary?

14. What are consolidated financial statements?

15. What account balances must be eliminated in preparing a consolidated balance sheet? Why are they eliminated?

16. Why would a parent corporation pay more than book value for the stock of a subsidiary?

17. When a parent pays more than book value for the stock of a subsidiary, how should this additional cost be allocated in the consolidated balance sheet?

18. What is meant by "minority interest?" Where is this item disclosed on a consolidated balance sheet?

CLASS EXERCISES

Exercise 16–1   Stockholders' equity in a corporation appeared as follows on March 9:

Common stock, $10 par value, 100,000	
shares authorized, 60,000 shares issued	$600,000
Premium on common stock	48,000
Total contributed capital	$648,000
Retained earnings	90,000
Total stockholders' equity	$738,000

On that date, when the stock was selling at $14 per share, the corporation's directors voted a 5% stock dividend distributable on April 1 to the March 15 stockholders of record. The stock was selling at $13.25 per share at the close of business on April 1.

Required:

1. Give the entries to record the declaration and distribution of the dividend.
2. Under the assumption that Gary White owned 100 of the shares on March 9 and received his dividend shares on April 1, prepare a schedule showing the number of shares he held on March 9 and April 1, with their total book values and total market values.

Exercise 16–2   On January 31, the stockholders' equity section of a corporation's balance sheet appeared as follows:

Stockholders' Equity

Common stock, $25 par value, 20,000 shares authorized and issued ..	$500,000
Retained earnings	75,000
Total stockholders' equity	$575,000

On January 31, the corporation purchased 1,000 shares of treasury stock at $35 per share. Give the entry to record the purchase and prepare a stockholders' equity section as it would appear immediately after the purchase.

Exercise 16–3   On February 15, the corporation of Exercise 16–2 sold at $37 per share 500 of the treasury shares purchased on January 31; and on March 1, it sold the remaining treasury shares at $32 per share. Give the entries to record the sales.

Exercise 16–4   Give entries in general journal form to record the following events on the books of A Company:

198A

Jan. 10   Purchased 10,000 shares of B Company common stock for $125,000 plus broker's fee of $3,500. B Company has 100,000 shares of common stock outstanding, and A Company does not have a significant influence on B Company policies.

Apr. 15   B Company declared and paid a cash dividend of $0.50 per share.

Dec. 31   B Company announced that net income for the year amounted to $140,000.

198B

Apr. 14   B Company declared and paid a cash dividend of $0.40 per share.

July 9   B Company declared and issued a stock dividend of one additional share for each 10 shares already outstanding.

Dec. 26   A Company sold 5,500 shares of B Company for $70,000.

31   B Company announced that net income for the year amounted to $75,000.

Exercise 16–5   Give entries in general journal form to record the following events on the books of Jag Company:

198A

Jan. 5   Purchased 10,000 shares of Kay Company for $125,000 plus broker's fee of $3,500. Kay Company has 40,000 shares of common stock outstanding and has acknowledged the fact that its policies will be significantly influenced by Jag.

Apr. 20   Kay Company declared and paid a cash dividend of $0.50 per share.
Dec. 31   Kay Company announced that net income for the year amounted to $56,000.

198B
Apr. 22   Kay Company declared and paid a cash dividend of $0.40 per share.
July   9   Kay Company declared and issued a stock dividend of one additional share for each 10 shares already outstanding.
Dec. 31   Kay Company announced that net income for the year amounted to $30,000.
      31   Jag Company sold 5,500 shares of Kay Company for $70,000.

Exercise 16–6

On June 30, Company Y had the following stockholders' equity:

Common stock, $10 par value, 10,000 shares issued and outstanding . . $100,000
Retained earnings   25,000
      Total stockholders' equity $125,000

On the date of the equity section, Company X purchased 8,000 of Company Y's outstanding shares, paying $15 per share, and a work sheet to consolidate the balance sheets of the two companies was prepared. Give the entry made on this work sheet to eliminate Company X's investment and Company Y's stockholders' equity account balances.

Exercise 16–7

During the year following its acquisition by Company X (see Exercise 16–6), Company Y earned $5,000, paid out $3,000 in dividends, and retained the balance for use in its operations. Give the entry under these assumptions to eliminate Company X's investment and Company Y's stockholders' equity account balances as of the end of the year.

PROBLEMS

Problem 16–1

At the beginning of the current year, Austin Corporation's stockholders' equity consisted of the following:

Common stock, $25 par value, 30,000
      shares authorized, 24,000 shares issued . . $600,000
Premium on common stock   90,000
Retained earnings 230,000
      Total stockholders' equity $920,000

During the year, the company completed these transactions:

June   6   Purchased 1,000 shares of treasury stock at $40 per share.
      23   The directors voted a $0.50 per share cash dividend payable on July 25 to the July 20 stockholders of record.
July 25   Paid the dividend declared on June 23.
Aug. 10   Sold 500 of the treasury shares at $45 per share.
Oct. 20   Sold 500 of the treasury shares at $38 per share.
Dec. 15   The directors voted a $0.50 per share cash dividend payable on January 20 to the January 15 stockholders of record, and they voted

a 2% stock dividend distributable on January 30 to the January 20 stockholders of record. The market value of the stock was $40 per share.

31 Closed the Income Summary account and carried the company's $60,000 net income to Retained Earnings.

Required:

1. Prepare general journal entries to record the transactions.
2. Prepare a retained earnings statement for the year and the stockholders' equity section of the company's year-end balance sheet.

Problem 16–2   Last October 31, Breaker Corporation had a $211,800 credit balance in its Retained Earnings account. On that date, the corporation had 100,000 authorized shares of $10 par, common stock of which 60,000 shares had been issued at $12 and were outstanding. It then completed the following transactions:

Oct. 28 The board of directors declared a 20 cents per share dividend on the common stock, payable on December 3 to the November 25 stockholders of record.

Dec. 3 Paid the dividend declared on October 28.

5 The board declared a 5% stock dividend, distributable on December 30 to the December 22 stockholders of record. The stock was selling at $18 per share, and the directors voted to use this amount in recording the dividend.

30 Distributed the foregoing stock dividend.

31 The corporation earned $94,500 during the year.

Jan. 6 The board of directors voted to split the corporation's stock 2 for 1 by calling in the old stock and issuing two $5 par value shares for each old $10 share held. The stockholders voted approval of the split and authorization of 200,000 new $5 par value shares to replace the $10 shares; all legal requirements were met; and the split was completed on February 1.

Required:

1. Prepare general journal entries to record the foregoing transactions and to close the Income Summary account at the year-end. (No entry is required for the stock split; however, a memorandum reciting the facts would be entered in the Common Stock account.)
2. Under the assumption Mike Linder owned 500 of the $10 par value shares on October 27 and neither bought nor sold any shares during the period of the transactions, prepare a schedule showing in one column the book value per share of the corporation's stock and in the second column the book value of Linder's shares at the close of business on each of October 27, October 28, December 3, December 30, December 31, and February 1.
3. Prepare three stockholders' equity sections for the corporation, the first showing the stockholders' equity on October 27, the second on December 31, and the third on February 1.

Problem 16–3   The equity sections from the 198A and 198B balance sheets of Towers Corporation appeared as follows:

Stockholders' Equity
(As of December 31, 198A)

Common stock, $5 par value, 250,000 shares authorized, 50,000 shares issued	$250,000
Premium on common stock	100,000
Total contributed capital	$350,000
Retained earnings	420,000
Total contributed capital and retained earnings	$770,000

Stockholders' Equity
(As of December 31, 198B)

Common stock, $5 par value, 250,000 shares authorized, 54,800 shares issued of which 2,000 are in the treasury ..	$274,000
Premium on common stock	133,600
Total contributed capital	$407,600
Retained earnings	385,000
Total	$792,600
Less: Cost of treasury stock	21,000
Total contributed capital and retained earnings	$771,600

On February 15, May 17, August 14, and again on November 15, 198B, the board of directors declared $0.30 per share dividends on the outstanding stock. The treasury stock was purchased on July 23. On August 14, while the stock was selling for $12 per share, the corporation declared a 10% stock dividend on the outstanding shares. The new shares were issued on September 15.

Required:

Under the assumption that there were no transactions affecting retained earnings other than the ones given, determine the 198B net income of Towers Corporation. Present calculations to prove your net income figure.

Problem 16–4   Fan Corporation was organized on January 1, 198A, for the purpose of investing in the shares of other companies. Fan Corporation immediately issued 1,000 shares of $100 par, common stock for which it received $100,000 cash. On January 2, 198A, Fan Corporation purchased 5,000 shares (20%) of Breeze Company's outstanding stock at a cost of $100,000. The following transactions and events subsequently occurred:

198A
May 17   Breeze Company declared and paid a cash dividend of $1 per share.
Dec. 31   Breeze Company announced that its net income for the year was $40,000.

198B
June 1   Breeze Company declared and issued a stock dividend of one share for each two shares already outstanding.
Oct. 7   Breeze Company declared and paid a cash dividend of $0.75 per share.

Dec. 31 Breeze Company announced that its net income for the year was $48,000.

198C

Jan. 3 Fan Corporation sold all of its investment in Breeze Company for $112,000 cash.

Part 1. Because Fan Corporation owns 20% of Breeze Company's outstanding stock, Fan Corporation is presumed to have a significant influence over Breeze Company.

Required:

1. Give the entries on the books of Fan Corporation to record the above events regarding its investment in Breeze Company.
2. Calculate the cost per share of Fan Corporation's investment, as reflected in the investment account on January 1, 198C.
3. Calculate Fan Corporation's retained earnings balance on January 5, 198C, after a closing of the books.

Part 2. Although Fan Corporation owns 20% of Breeze Company's outstanding stock, a thorough investigation of the surrounding circumstances indicates that Fan Corporation does not have a significant influence over Breeze Company, and the cost method is the appropriate method of accounting for the investment.

Required:

1. Give the entries on the books of Fan Corporation to record the above events regarding its investment in Breeze Company.
2. Calculate the cost per share of Fan Corporation's investment, as reflected in the investment account on January 1, 198C.
3. Calculate Fan Corporation's retained earnings balance on January 5, 198C, after a closing of the books.

Problem 16–5

Batts Corporation purchased 60% of Hogg Company's stock at $25 per share on January 1, 198A. On that date, Batts Corporation had retained earnings of $96,100. Hogg Company had retained earnings of $25,000, and had outstanding 7,500 shares of $10 par, common stock, originally issued at par.

Part 1

Required:

1. Give the elimination entry to be used on a work sheet for a consolidated balance sheet, January 1, 198A.
2. Determine the amount of consolidated retained earnings that should be shown on a consolidated balance sheet, January 1, 198A.

Part 2. During the year ended December 31, 198A, Batts Corporation paid cash dividends of $10,000 and earned net income of $20,000 excluding earnings from its investment in Hogg Company. Hogg Company earned net income of $15,000 and paid dividends of $7,000. Except for Batts Corporation's

Retained Earnings account and the Investment in Hogg Company account, the balance sheet accounts for the two companies on December 31, 198A, are as follows:

	Batts Corporation	Hogg Company
Cash	$ 42,000	$ 15,000
Notes receivable	10,000	
Merchandise	104,300	29,000
Building (net)	126,500	52,000
Land	40,000	35,000
Investment in Monroe Company	?	
Total assets	$?	$131,000
Accounts payable	$ 35,000	$ 13,000
Notes payable		10,000
Common stock	290,000	75,000
Retained earnings	?	33,000
Total liabilities and stockholders' equity ...	$?	$131,000

Batts Corporation loaned $10,000 to Hogg Company during 198A, for which Hogg Company signed a note. On December 31, 198A, that note had not been repaid.

Required:

1. Calculate the December 31, 198A, balances in Batts Corporation's Investment in Hogg Company account and Retained Earnings account.
2. Complete a work sheet to consolidate the balance sheets of the two companies.

Problem 16–6   The following items appeared in the first two columns of a work sheet prepared to consolidate the balance sheets of Company A and Company B on the day Company A gained control of Company B by purchasing 17,000 shares of its $5 par value common stock at $6.50 per share:

	Company A	Company B
Assets		
Cash	$ 7,500	$ 11,000
Note receivable, Company B	10,000	
Accounts receivable, net	28,000	24,000
Inventories	42,000	35,000
Investment in Company B	110,500	
Equipment, net	80,000	70,000
Buildings, net	85,000	
Land	20,000	
Total assets	$383,000	$140,000
Liabilities and Stockholders' Equity		
Accounts payable	$ 21,000	$ 10,000
Note payable, Company A		10,000
Common stock	250,000	100,000
Retained earnings	112,000	20,000
Total liabilities and stockholders' equity ...	$383,000	$140,000

At the time Company A acquired control of Company B, it took Company B's note in exchange for $10,000 in cash and it sold and delivered $2,000 of equipment at cost to Company B on open account (account receivable). Both transactions are reflected in the foregoing accounts.

Required:

1. Prepare a work sheet to consolidate the balance sheets of the two companies and prepare a consolidated balance sheet.
2. Under the assumption that Company B earned $10,000 during the first year after it was acquired by Company A, paid out $6,000 in dividends, and retained the balance of the earnings in its operations, give the entry to eliminate Company A's investment in the subsidiary and Company B's stockholders' equity accounts at the year's end.

ALTERNATE PROBLEMS

Problem 16–1A   The stockholders' equity in Foster Corporation consisted of the following at the beginning of the current year:

```
Common stock, $5 par value, 100,000 shares authorized,
    75,000 shares issued and outstanding .................  $375,000
Premium on common stock ...........................    37,500
Retained earnings .....................................    70,000
          Total stockholders' equity .......................  $445,000
```

During the year, the company completed these transactions affecting its stockholders' equity:

Feb. 12   Purchased 6,000 shares of treasury stock at $7.50 per share.
June 30   The directors voted a 10 cents per share cash dividend payable on July 20 to the July 15 stockholders of record.
July 20   Paid the previously declared cash dividend.
Aug. 18   Sold 4,000 of the treasury shares at $8 per share.
Nov. 12   Sold the remaining treasury shares at $7.25 per share.
Dec. 21   The directors voted a 5% stock dividend distributable on January 20 to the January 15 stockholders of record. The stock was selling at $7.50 per share.
      31   Closed the Income Summary account and carried the company's $40,000 net income to Retained Earnings.

Required:

1. Prepare general journal entries to record the transactions.
2. Prepare a retained earnings statement for the year and the stockholders' equity section of the company's year-end balance sheet.

Problem 16–2A   On September 30, the stockholders' equity of Extra Company appeared as follows:

Stockholders' Equity

Common stock, $25 par value, 10,000 shares authorized, 8,000 shares issued	$200,000
Premium on common stock	40,000
Total contributed capital	$240,000
Retained earnings	141,600
Total stockholders' equity ....*....	$381,600

On October 2, the board of directors declared a 40 cents per share cash dividend payable on October 31 to the October 20 stockholders of record. On November 28, the board declared a 10% stock dividend distributable on December 30 to the December 20 stockholders of record. The stock was selling for $50 per share on the day of the declaration, and the board voted to use this price in recording the dividend. The corporation earned $35,200, after taxes, during the year of the foregoing transactions; and on January 8 of the following year, the board voted to split the corporation's stock 2½ for 1 by calling in the old stock and issuing 25 shares of $10 par value common stock for each 10 shares of the old $25 par value stock held. The stockholders voted approval of the split and authorization of 25,000 shares of new $10 par value stock to replace the old stock; all legal requirements were met; and the split was completed on February 15.

Required:

1. Prepare general journal entries to record the transactions and to close the Income Summary account. (No entry is needed for the split; however, a memorandum reciting the facts would be entered in the Common Stock account.)
2. Under the assumption that Larry Chambers owned 200 of the $25 par value shares on September 30 and neither bought nor sold any shares during the foregoing period, prepare a schedule showing the book value per share of the corporation's stock in one column and the book value of Chambers' total shares in a second column at the close of business on the following dates: September 30, October 2, October 31, December 30, December 31, and February 15.
3. Prepare the stockholders' equity section of the corporation's balance sheet as of the close of business on December 31, and prepare another equity section as of the close of business on February 15.

Problem 16–3A   On December 31, 198A, Baker Corporation had 20,000 shares of $10 par, common stock outstanding and a retained earnings balance of $345,000. During 198B, the board of directors declared cash dividends of $0.25 per outstanding share on each of the following dates: January 30, April 16, July 25, and October 26. During February 198B, the board declared a 5 for 1 stock split, calling in the existing shares and issuing five $2 par shares for each of the old $10 par shares.

On June 1, Baker Corporation acquired 4,000 of its outstanding shares, paying $10 per share. And on October 2, the company declared a 5% stock dividend on the outstanding shares to be distributed October 12. At the time of the declaration, the stock was selling for $8 per share.

On December 31, 198B, Baker Corporation's retained earnings balance was $290,000, including $40,000 that was restricted as a consequence of the purchase of treasury stock.

Required:

Under the assumption that there were no transactions affecting retained earnings other than the ones given, determine the 198B net income of Baker Corporation. Present calculations to prove your net income figure.

Problem 16-4A   Big Company was organized as an investment company on January 1, 198A, and immediately issued 1,500 shares of $80 par, common stock in exchange for $140,000 cash. On January 4, 198A, Big Company acquired 10,000 shares (20%) of Bang Company's outstanding stock for $140,000. The following transactions and events subsequently occurred.

198A
Apr. 25   Bang Company declared and paid cash dividends of $75,000.
Dec. 31   Bang Company announced that its net income for the year was $90,000.

198B
Apr. 28   Bang Company declared and issued a stock dividend of one share for each five shares already outstanding.
Nov. 12   Bang Company declared and paid cash dividends of $60,000.
Dec. 31   Bang Company announced that its net income for the year was $115,000.

198C
Jan.   4   Big Company sold all of its Bang Company stock for $145,000.

Part 1.   Since Big Company owns 20% of Bang Company's outstanding stock, Big Company is presumed to have a significant influence over Bang Company, and the equity method is the appropriate method of accounting for the investment.

Required:

1.   Give the entries on the books of Big Company to record the above events regarding its investment in Bang Company.
2.   Calculate the cost per share of Big Company's investment, as reflected in the investment account on January 1, 198C.
3.   Calculate Big Company's retained earnings balance on January 5, 198C, after a closing of the books.

Part 2.   Although Big Company owns 20% of Bang Company's outstanding stock, a thorough investigation of the surrounding circumstances indicates that Big Company does not have a significant influence over Bang Company, and the cost method is the appropriate method of accounting for the investment.

Required:

1.   Give the entries on the books of Big Company to record the above events regarding its investment in Bang Company.

2. Calculate the cost per share of Big Company's investment, as reflected in the investment account on January 1, 198C.
3. Calculate Big Company's retained earnings balance on January 6, 198C, after a closing of the books.

Problem 16–6A   The following assets and equities appeared on the balance sheets of Company X and Company Y on the day Company X gained control of Company Y by purchasing 3,600 shares of its $25 par value common stock at $35 per share.

	Company X	Company Y
Assets		
Cash	$ 8,000	$ 12,000
Note receivable, Company Y	5,000	
Accounts receivable, net	37,000	22,000
Inventories	35,000	32,000
Investment in Company Y	126,000	
Equipment, net	75,000	70,000
Buildings, net	100,000	
Land	25,000	
Total assets	$411,000	$136,000
Liabilities and Stockholders' Equity		
Note payable, Company X		$ 5,000
Accounts payable	$ 24,000	11,000
Common stock	300,000	100,000
Premium on common stock	30,000	5,000
Retained earnings	57,000	15,000
Total liabilities and stockholders' equity ...	$411,000	$136,000

At the time Company X gained control of Company Y, it took Company Y's note in exchange for equipment that cost Company X $5,000 and it also sold and delivered $2,000 of inventory at cost to Company Y on open account (account receivable). Both transactions are reflected in the foregoing accounts.

Required:

1. Prepare a work sheet to consolidate the balance sheets of the two companies and prepare a consolidated balance sheet.
2. Under the assumption Company Y earned $9,600 during the year after it was acquired by Company X, paid out $5,600 in dividends, and retained the balance in its operations, give the entry to eliminate Company X's investment in the subsidiary and Company Y's stockholders' equity accounts at the year's end.

PROVOCATIVE PROBLEMS

Provocative Problem 16–1, Expo Company   Sally King purchased 500 shares of Expo Company stock at $15 per share on January 1, 198A, when the corporation had the following stockholders' equity:

```
Common stock, $10 par value, 250,000 shares authorized,
   150,000 shares issued and outstanding ................  $1,500,000
Contributed capital in excess of par value ................     250,000
Retained earnings  ........................................     400,000
         Total stockholders' equity ........................  $2,150,000
```

Since purchasing the 500 shares, Ms. King has neither purchased nor sold any additional shares of the company's stock; and on December 31 of each year, she has received dividends on the shares held as follows: 198A, $330; 198B, $425; and 198C, $550.

On June 30, 198A, at a time when its stock was selling for $17.50 per share, Expo Company declared a 10% stock dividend that was distributed one month later. On August 15, 198B, the corporation doubled the number of its authorized shares and split its stock 2 for 1; and on January 1, 198C, it purchased 10,000 shares of treasury stock at $9 per share. The shares were still in its treasury at year-end.

Required:

Under the assumption that Expo Company's stock had a book value of $13.50 per share on December 31, 198A, a book value of $7.20 per share on December 31, 198B, and a book value of $7.70 on December 31, 198C, do the following:

1. Prepare statements showing the nature of the stockholders' equity in the corporation at the end of 198A, 198B, and 198C.
2. Prepare a schedule showing the amount of the corporation's net income for each of 198A, 198B, and 198C, under the assumption that the changes in the company's retained earnings during the three-year period resulted solely from earnings and dividends.

Provocative Problem 16–2, Condo Corporation

On November 3, stockholders' equity in Condo Corporation consisted of the following:

```
Common stock, $10 par value, 150,000 shares authorized,
   100,000 shares issued and outstanding ..................  $1,000,000
Capital contributed by the common stockholders in excess of
   the par value of their shares ...........................     150,000
Retained earnings .........................................     650,000
         Total stockholders' equity ........................  $1,800,000
```

On November 3, when the stock was selling at $20 per share, the corporation's directors voted a 20% stock dividend, distributable on December 1 to the November 25 stockholders of record. The directors also voted an $0.85 per share annual cash dividend, payable on December 20 to the December 15 stockholders of record. The amount of the latter dividend was a disappointment to some stockholders, since the company had for a number of years paid a $1 per share annual cash dividend.

Jack Clifford owned 1,000 shares of Condo Corporation stock on November 25, which he had purchased a number of years ago, and as a result he received his dividend shares. He continued to hold all of his shares until after he received the December 20 cash dividend. However, he did note that his stock had a $20 per share market value on November 3, a market value it held until the close of business on November 25, when the market value declined to $17.50 per share.

Give the entries to record the declaration and payment of the dividends involved here, and answer these questions:

a. What was the book value of Clifford's total shares on November 3, and what was the book value on December 1, after he received his dividend shares?

b. What fraction of the corporation did Clifford own on November 3, and what fraction did he own on December 1?

c. What was the market value of Clifford's total shares on November 3, and what was the market value at the close of business on November 25?

d. What did Clifford gain from the stock dividend?

Provocative
Problem 16–3,
Indiana
Company

At the recent stockholders' meeting of Indiana Company, one of the stockholders made the following statements: "I have owned shares of Indiana Company for several years, but am now questioning whether management is telling the truth in the annual financial statements. At the end of 198A, you announced that Indiana Company had just acquired a 30% interest in the outstanding stock of Southern Airlines. You also stated that the 80,000 shares had cost Indiana Company $8,000,000. In the financial statements for 198B, you told us that the investments of Indiana Company were proving to be very profitable, and reported that earnings from all investments had amounted to more than $2.3 million. In the financial statements for 198C, you explained that Indiana Company had sold the Southern Airlines shares during the first week of the year, receiving $9,100,000 cash proceeds from the sale. Nevertheless, the income statement for 198C reports only a $200,000 gain on the sale (before taxes). I realize that Southern Airlines did not pay any dividends during 198B, but it was very profitable. As I recall, it reported net income of $3,000,000 for 198B. Personally, I do not think you should have sold the shares. But, much more importantly, you reported to us that our company gained only $200,000 from the sale. How can that be true if the shares were purchased for $8,000,000 and were sold for $9,100,000?"

Explain to this stockholder why the $200,000 gain is correctly reported.

Bonds Payable and Investments

17

After studying Chapter 17 you should be able to:

Explain the difference between a share of stock and a bond.

State the advantages and disadvantages of securing capital by issuing bonds.

Explain how bond interest rates are established.

Use present value tables to calculate the premium or discount on a bond issue.

Prepare entries to account for bonds issued between interest dates at par.

Prepare entries to account for bonds sold on their date of issue at par, at a discount, and at a premium.

Explain the purpose and operation of a bond sinking fund and prepare entries to account for the operation of such a fund.

Describe the procedures used to account for investments in bonds.

Define or explain the words and phrases listed in the chapter Glossary.

The phrase *stocks and bonds* commonly appears on the financial pages of newspapers and is often heard in conversations. However, there are important differences between stocks and bonds. A share of stock represents an equity or ownership right in a corporation. For example, if a person owns 1,000 of the 10,000 shares of common stock a corporation has outstanding, the person has an equity in the corporation measured at one tenth of the corporation's total stockholders' equity and has an equity in one tenth of the corporation's earnings. If on the other hand a person owns a $1,000, 8%, 20-year bond issued by a corporation, the *bond* represents a debt or a liability of the corporation.[1] Its owner has two rights: (1) the right to receive 8% or $80 interest each year the bond is outstanding and (2) the right to be paid $1,000 when the bond matures 20 years after its date of issue.

This chapter begins with a discussion of bonds from the perspective of the corporation that issues the bonds. Later in the chapter, investments in bonds are also considered.

WHY BONDS ARE ISSUED

A corporation in need of long-term funds may secure the funds by issuing additional shares of stock or by selling bonds. Each has its advantages and disadvantages. Stockholders are owners, and issuing additional stock spreads ownership, control of management, and earnings over more shares. Bondholders, on the other hand, are creditors and do not share in either management or earnings. However, bond interest must be paid whether there are any earnings or not. Otherwise, the bondholders may foreclose and take the assets pledged for their security.

Nevertheless, issuing bonds, rather than additional stock, will commonly result in increased earnings for the owners (the common stockholders) of the issuing corporation. For example, assume a corporation with 200,000 shares of common stock outstanding needs $1,000,000 to expand its operations. The corporation's management estimates that after the expansion, the company can earn $600,000 annually before bond interest, if any, and corporation income taxes. Two plans for securing the needed funds are proposed. Plan No. 1 calls for issuing 100,000 additional shares of the corporation's common stock at $10 per share. This will increase the total outstanding shares to 300,000. Plan No. 2 calls for the sale at par of $1,000,000 of 8% bonds. Illustration 17–1 shows how the plans will affect the corporation's earnings.

---

[1] The federal government and other governmental units, such as cities, states, and school districts, also issue bonds. However, the discussions in this chapter are limited to the bonds of corporations.

Illustration 17–1

	Plan 1	Plan 2
Earnings before bond interest and income taxes	$ 600,000	$ 600,000
Deduct bond interest expense		(80,000)
Income before corporation income taxes	$ 600,000	$ 520,000
Deduct income taxes (assumed 50% rate)	(300,000)	(260,000)
Net income	$ 300,000	$ 260,000
Plan 1 income per share (300,000 shares)	$1.00	
Plan 2 income per share (200,000 shares)		$1.30

Corporations are subject to state and federal income taxes, which together may take as much as 50% of the corporation's before-tax income. However, bond interest expense is a deductible expense in arriving at income subject to taxes. Consequently, when the combined state and federal tax rate is 50%, as in Illustration 17–1, the tax reduction from issuing bonds equals one half the annual interest on the bonds. In other words, the tax savings in effect pays one half the interest cost of the bond.

BORROWING BY ISSUING BONDS

When a large corporation wishes to borrow several millions of dollars, it will often borrow by issuing bonds. Bonds are issued because few banks or insurance companies are able or willing to make a loan of such size. Also, bonds enable the corporation to divide the loan among many lenders.

Borrowing by issuing bonds is in many ways similar to borrowing by giving a mortgage. Actually, the real difference is that a number of bonds, often in denominations of $1,000, are issued in the place of a single promissory note. For all practical purposes, each bond is a promissory note, promising to pay a definite sum of money to its holder, or owner of record, at a fixed future date. Like promissory notes, bonds bear interest; and like a mortgage note, they are often secured by a mortgage. However, since bonds may be owned and transferred during their lives by a number of people, they differ from promissory notes in that they do not name the lender.

When a company issues bonds secured by a mortgage, it normally sells the bonds to an investment firm, known as the *underwriter*. The underwriter in turn resells the bonds to the public. In addition to the underwriter, the company issuing bonds selects a trustee to represent the bondholders. In most cases, the trustee is a large bank or trust company to which the company issuing the bonds executes and delivers the mortgage contract that acts as security for the bonds. It is the duty of the trustee to see that the company fulfills all of the pledged responsibilities of the mortgage contract, or as it is often called, the *deed of trust*. It is also the duty of the trustee to foreclose if any pledges are not fulfilled.

CHARACTERISTICS OF BONDS

Over the years, corporation lawyers and financiers have created a wide variety of bonds, each with different combinations of characteristics. For example, bonds may be *serial bonds* or *sinking fund bonds*. When serial or term bonds are issued, portions of the issue become due and are paid in installments over a period of years. Sinking fund bonds differ in that they are paid at maturity in one lump sum from a sinking fund created for that purpose. Sinking funds are discussed later in this chapter.

Bonds may also be either *registered bonds* or *coupon bonds*. Ownership of registered bonds is registered or recorded with the issuing corporation. This offers some protection from loss or theft. Interest payments on such bonds are usually made by checks mailed to the registered owners. Coupon bonds obtain their name from the interest coupons attached to each bond. A coupon is provided for each interest payment during the life of the bond. The coupons are detached as they become due and are deposited with a bank for collection. Often, ownership of a coupon bond is not registered. Such unregistered bonds are payable to the bearer and are called bearer paper. Ownership of unregistered bonds is transferred by delivery. Sometimes bonds are registered as to principal with interest payments by coupons.

Bonds also may be secured or unsecured. Unsecured bonds are called *debentures* and depend upon the general credit standing of the issuing corporation for security. Only financially strong companies are able to sell unsecured bonds or bonds that are not secured by a mortgage.

ISSUING BONDS

When a corporation issues bonds, the bonds are printed and the deed of trust is drawn and deposited with the trustee of the bondholders. At that point a memorandum describing the bond issue is commonly entered in the Bonds Payable account. Such a memorandum might read, "Authorized to issue $8,000,000 of 9%, 20-year bonds dated January 1, 19—, and with interest payable semiannually on each July

1 and January 1." As in this case, bond interest is usually payable semiannually.

After the deed of trust is deposited with the trustee of the bondholders, all or a portion of the bonds may be sold. If all are sold at their *par value,* also called their *face amount,* an entry like the following is made to record the sale:

Jan.	1	Cash	8,000,000.00	
		Bonds Payable.....................		8,000,000.00
		Sold 9%, 20-year bonds at par on their interest date.		

When the semiannual interest is paid on these bonds, the transaction is recorded as follows:

July	1	Bond Interest Expense	360,000.00	
		Cash		360,000.00
		Paid the semiannual interest on the bonds.		

And when the bonds are paid at maturity, an entry like the following is made:

Jan.	1	Bonds Payable	8,000,000.00	
		Cash		8,000,000.00
		Paid bonds at maturity.		

BONDS SOLD BETWEEN INTEREST DATES

Sometimes bonds are sold on their date of issue, which is also their interest date, as in the previous illustration. More often they are sold after their date of issue and between interest dates. In such cases, it is customary to charge and collect from the purchasers the interest that has accrued on the bonds since the previous interest payment and to return this accrued interest to the purchasers on the next interest date. For example, assume that on March 1, a corporation sold at par $100,000 of 9% bonds on which interest is payable semiannually on each January 1 and July 1. (Small dollar amounts are used to conserve space.) The entry to record the sale between interest dates is:

Mar.	1	Cash	101,500.00	
		Bond Interest Expense.................		1,500.00
		Bonds Payable........................		100,000.00
		Sold $100,000 of 9%, 20-year bonds on which two months' interest has accrued.		

At the end of four months, on the July 1 semiannual interest date, the purchasers of these bonds are paid a full six months' interest. This payment includes four months' interest earned by the bondholders after March 1 and the two months' accrued interest collected from them at the time the bonds were sold. The entry to record the payment is:

July	1	Bond Interest Expense	4,500.00	
		Cash		4,500.00
		Paid the semiannual interest on the bonds.		

After both of these entries are posted, the Bond Interest Expense account has a $3,000 debit balance and appears as follows:

Bond Interest Expense			
July 1 (Payment)	4,500.00	Mar. 1 (Accrued interest)	1,500.00

The $3,000 debit balance represents the interest on the $100,000 of bonds at 9% for the four months from March 1 to July 1.

It may seem strange to charge bond purchasers for accrued interest when bonds are sold between interest dates, and to return this accrued interest in the next interest payment. However, this is the custom. All bond transactions are "plus accrued interest," and there is a good reason for the practice. For instance, if a corporation sells portions of a bond issue on different dates during an interest period without collecting the accrued interest, it must keep records of the purchasers and the dates on which they bought bonds. Otherwise, it cannot pay the correct amount of interest to each. However, if it charges each buyer for accrued interest at the time of the purchase, it need not keep records of the purchasers and their purchase dates. It can pay a full period's interest to all purchasers for the period in which they bought their bonds; each receives the interest earned and gets back the accrued interest paid at the time of the purchase.

BOND INTEREST RATES

At this point students who are not sure of their understanding of the concept of present value should turn back to Chapter 12 and review this concept before going further into this chapter.

A corporation issuing bonds specifies in the deed of trust and on each bond the interest rate it will pay. This rate is called the *contract rate*. It is usually stated on an annual basis, although bond interest is normally paid semiannually. Also, it is applied to the par value of the bonds to determine the dollars of interest the corporation will pay. For example, if a corporation issues a $1,000, 8% bond on which interest is paid semiannually, $80 will be paid each year in two semiannual installments of $40 each.

Although the contract rate establishes the interest a corporation will pay, it is not necessarily the interest the corporation will incur in issuing bonds. The interest it will incur depends upon what lenders consider their risks are in lending to the corporation and upon the current *market rate for bond interest.* The market rate for bond interest is the rate borrowers are willing to pay and lenders are willing to take for the use of money at the level of risk involved. It fluctuates from day to day as the supply and demand for loanable funds fluctuate. It goes up when the demand for bond money increases and the supply decreases, and it goes down when the supply increases and the demand decreases.

Also, note that on any single day, the market rate for bond interest is not the same for all corporations. The rate for a specific corporation's bonds depends on the level of risk investors attach to those bonds. As the perceived level of risk increases, the rate increases.

A corporation issuing bonds usually offers a contract rate of interest equal to what it estimates the market will demand on the day the bonds are to be issued. If its estimate is correct, and the contract rate and market rate coincide on the day the bonds are issued, the bonds will sell at par, their face amount. However, when bonds are sold, their contract rate seldom coincides with the market rate. As a result, bonds usually sell either at a premium or at a discount.

BONDS SOLD AT A DISCOUNT

When a corporation offers to sell bonds carrying a contract rate below the prevailing market rate, the bonds will sell at a *discount*. Given the level of risk, investors can get the market rate of interest elsewhere for the use of their money, so they will buy the bonds only at a price that will yield the prevailing market rate on the investment. What price will they pay and how is it determined? The price they will pay is the *present value* of the expected returns from the investment. It is determined by discounting the returns at the current market rate for bond interest.

To illustrate how bond prices are determined, assume that on a day when the market rate for bond interest is 9%, a corporation offers to sell and issue bonds having a $100,000 par value, a 10-year life, and on which interest is to be paid semiannually at an 8% annual rate.[2] In exchange for current dollars, the buyers of these bonds will gain two monetary rights:

1. The right to receive $100,000 at the end of the bond issue's 10-year life.
2. The right to receive $4,000 in interest at the end of each 6-month interest period throughout the 10-year life of the bonds.

Since both are rights to receive money in the future, to determine their present value, the amounts to be received are discounted at the market rate of interest. If the market rate is 9% annually, it is 4½% semiannually; and in 10 years, there are 20 semiannual periods. Consequently, using the last number in the 4½% column of Table 12–1, page 415, to discount the first amount and the last number in the 4½% column of Table 12–2, page 417, to discount the series of $4,000 amounts, the present value of the rights and the price informed buyers will offer for the bonds is:

Present value of $100,000 to be received 20 periods hence, discounted at 4½% per period ($100,000 × 0.4146) $41,460
Present value of $4,000 to be received periodically for 20 periods, discounted at 4½% ($4,000 × 13.008) 52,032
Present value of the bonds $93,492

If the corporation accepts the $93,492 offered for its bonds and sells them on their date of issue, the sale will be recorded with an entry like this:

Jan.	1	Cash	93,492.00	
		Discount on Bonds Payable	6,508.00	
		Bonds Payable		100,000.00
		Sold 8%, 10-year bonds at a discount on their date of issue.		

---

[2] The spread between the contract rate and the market rate of interest on a new bond issue is seldom more than a fraction of a percent. However, a spread of a full percent is used here to simplify the illustrations.

If the corporation prepares a balance sheet on the day the bonds are sold, it may show the bonds in the long-term liability section as follows:

Long-term liabilities:
First-mortgage, 8% bonds payable, due January 1,
199A $100,000
Less unamortized discount based on the 9%
market rate for bond interest prevailing on the
date of issue 6,508 $93,492

On a balance sheet, any unamortized discount on a bond issue is deducted from the par value of the bonds to show the amount at which the bonds are carried on the books, called the *carrying amount.*

Amortizing the Discount

The corporation of this discussion received $93,492 for its bonds, but in 10 years it must pay the bondholders $100,000. The difference, the $6,508 discount, is a cost of using the $93,492 that is incurred because the contract rate of interest on the bonds was below the prevailing market rate. It is a cost that must be paid when the bonds mature. However, each semiannual interest period in the life of the bond issue benefits from the use of the $93,492. Consequently, it is only fair that each should bear a fair share of this cost.

STRAIGHT-LINE METHOD.   The procedure for dividing a discount and charging a share to each period in the life of the applicable bond issue is called *amortizing* a discount. A simple method of amortizing a discount is the *straight-line method,* a method in which an equal portion of the discount is amortized each interest period. If this method is used to amortize the $6,508 discount of this discussion, the $6,508 is divided by 20, the number of interest periods in the life of the bond issue, and $325 ($6,508 ÷ 20 = $325.40, or $325) of the discount is amortized at the end of each interest period with an entry like this:

July	1	Bond Interest Expense	4,325.00	
		Discount on Bonds Payable		325.00
		Cash		4,000.00
		To record payment of six months' interest and amortization of one twentieth of the discount.		

Illustration 17–2

Period	Beginning-of-period carrying amount	Interest expense to be recorded	Interest to be paid the bondholders	Discount to be amortized	Unamortized discount at end of period	End-of-period carrying amount
1	$93,492	$4,325	$4,000	$325	$6,183	$ 93,817
2	93,817	4,325	4,000	325	5,858	94,142
3	94,142	4,325	4,000	325	5,533	94,467
4	94,467	4,325	4,000	325	5,208	94,792
5	94,792	4,325	4,000	325	4,883	95,117
6	95,117	4,325	4,000	325	4,558	95,442
7	95,442	4,325	4,000	325	4,233	95,767
8	95,767	4,325	4,000	325	3,908	96,092
9	96,092	4,325	4,000	325	3,583	96,417
10	96,417	4,325	4,000	325	3,258	96,742
11	96,742	4,325	4,000	325	2,933	97,067
12	97,067	4,325	4,000	325	2,608	97,392
13	97,392	4,325	4,000	325	2,283	97,717
14	97,717	4,325	4,000	325	1,958	98,042
15	98,042	4,325	4,000	325	1,633	98,367
16	98,367	4,325	4,000	325	1,308	98,692
17	98,692	4,325	4,000	325	983	99,017
18	99,017	4,325	4,000	325	658	99,342
19	99,342	4,325	4,000	325	333	99,667
20	99,667	4,333*	4,000	333*	–0–	100,000

* Adjusted to compensate for accumulated rounding of amounts.

Illustration 17–2, with amounts rounded to full dollars, shows the interest expense to be recorded, the discount to be amortized, and so forth, when the straight-line method of amortizing a discount is applied to the bonds in this discussion. In examining Illustration 17–2, note these points:

1. The bonds were sold at a $6,508 discount, which when subtracted from their face amount gives a beginning-of-Period-1 carrying amount of $93,492.
2. The semiannual $4,325 interest expense amounts equal $4,000 paid to bondholders plus $325 amortization of discount.
3. Interest to be paid bondholders each period is determined by multiplying the par value of the bonds by the contract rate of interest ($100,000 × 4% = $4,000).
4. The discount to be amortized each period is $6,508 ÷ 20 = $325.40, or $325.
5. The unamortized discount at the end of each period is determined by subtracting the discount amortized that period from the unamortized discount at the beginning of the period.
6. The end-of-period carrying amount for the bonds is determined

by subtracting the end-of-period amount of unamortized discount from the face amount of the bonds. For example, at the end of Period 1: $100,000 − $6,183 = $93,817.

Straight-line amortization once was commonly used. However, the APB ruled that it may now be used only in situations where the results do not materially differ from those obtained through use of the so-called interest method.[3]

INTEREST METHOD. When the interest method is used, the interest expense to be recorded each period is determined by applying a constant rate of interest to the beginning-of-period carrying amount of the bonds. The constant rate applied is the market rate for the bonds at the time the bonds were issued. The discount amortized each period is then determined by subtracting the interest to be paid the bondholders from the interest expense to be recorded. Illustration 17–3 shows the interest expense to be recorded, the discount to be amortized,

Illustration 17–3

Period	Beginning-of-period carrying amount	Interest expense to be recorded	Interest to be paid the bondholders	Discount to be amortized	Unamortized discount at end of period	End-of-period carrying amount
1	$93,492	$4,207	$4,000	$207	$6,301	$ 93,699
2	93,699	4,216	4,000	216	6,085	93,915
3	93,915	4,226	4,000	226	5,859	94,141
4	94,141	4,236	4,000	236	5,623	94,377
5	94,377	4,247	4,000	247	5,376	94,624
6	94,624	4,258	4,000	258	5,118	94,882
7	94,882	4,270	4,000	270	4,848	95,152
8	95,152	4,282	4,000	282	4,566	95,434
9	95,434	4,295	4,000	295	4,271	95,729
10	95,729	4,308	4,000	308	3,963	96,037
11	96,037	4,322	4,000	322	3,641	96,359
12	96,359	4,336	4,000	336	3,305	96,695
13	96,695	4,351	4,000	351	2,954	97,046
14	97,046	4,367	4,000	367	2,587	97,413
15	97,413	4,384	4,000	384	2,203	97,797
16	97,797	4,401	4,000	401	1,802	98,198
17	98,198	4,419	4,000	419	1,383	98,617
18	98,617	4,438	4,000	438	945	99,055
19	99,055	4,457	4,000	457	488	99,512
20	99,512	4,488*	4,000	488	–0–	100,000

* Adjusted to compensate for accumulated rounding of amounts.

---

[3] APB, "Interest on Receivables and Payables," *APB Opinion No. 21* (New York: AICPA, August 1971), par. 15.

and so forth, when the interest method is applied to the bonds in this discussion.

Compare Illustration 17–3 with 17–2 and note these unique aspects of the interest method as shown in Illustration 17–3.

1. The interest expense amounts result from multiplying each beginning-of-period carrying amount by the 4½% semiannual market rate that prevailed when the bonds were issued. For example, $93,492 × 4½% = $4,207 and $93,699 × 4½% = $4,216.
2. The discount to be amortized each period is determined by subtracting the amount of interest to be paid the bondholders from the amount of interest expense.

When the interest method is used in amortizing a discount, the periodic amortizing entries are like the entries used with the straight-line method; only the dollar amounts are different. For example, the entry to pay the bondholders and amortize a portion of the discount at the end of the first semiannual interest period of the bond issue in Illustration 17–3 is:

July	1	Bond Interest Expense	4,207.00	
		Discount on Bonds Payable		207.00
		Cash		4,000.00
		To record payment to the bondholders and amortization of a portion of the discount.		

Similar entries, differing only in the amount of interest expense recorded and discount amortized, are made at the end of each semiannual interest period in the life of the bond issue.

Consider the differences between the interest method of amortizing a discount and the straight-line method (previously discussed). The following table shows these financial statement differences:

	Interest-method amortization			Straight-line amortization		
Period	Beginning-of-period carrying amount	Interest expense to be recorded	Interest expense as a percent of carrying amount	Beginning-of-period carrying amount	Interest expense to be recorded	Interest expense as a percent of carrying amount
1	$93,492	$4,207	4.5	$93,492	$4,325	4.63
11	96,037	4,322	4.5	96,742	4,325	4.47
19	99,055	4,457	4.5	99,342	4,325	4.35

The table shows the beginning-of-period carrying amount of the bond liability and the interest expense for each of three six-month periods during the life of the bonds. The first three columns of the table show that in each and every six-month period, the interest method provides an interest expense amount that is 4.5% of the beginning-of-period carrying amount. The last three columns show the amounts that would result from using the straight-line method. Observe that when the straight-line method is used, the percentage changes each period. Recall that the bonds were issued at a price that reflected a discounting of cash flows at 4.5% per six-month period. The interest method is most consistent with this fact; and it is the preferred method.

Because the above example involves a bond discount, the straight-line method results in a declining percentage. When a premium is amortized, the straight-line method results in an increasing percentage. In either case, however, the straight-line method can be used only where the results do not differ materially from those obtained through use of the interest method.

BONDS SOLD AT A PREMIUM

When a corporation offers to sell bonds carrying a contract rate of interest above the prevailing market rate for the risks involved, the bonds will sell at a *premium*. Buyers will bid up the price of the bonds, going as high, but no higher, than a price that will return the current market rate of interest on the investment. What price will they pay? They will pay the present value of the expected returns from the investment, determined by discounting these returns at the market rate of interest for the bonds. For example, assume that on a given day a corporation offers to sell bonds having a $100,000 par value and a 10-year life with interest to be paid semiannually at an 11% annual rate. On that day, the market rate of interest for the corporation's bonds is 10%. Buyers of these bonds will discount the expectation of receiving $100,000 in 10 years and the expectation of receiving $5,500 semiannually for 20 periods at the current 10% market rate as follows:

Present value of $100,000 to be received 20 periods hence, discounted at 5% per period ($100,000 × 0.3769)	$ 37,690
Present value of $5,500 to be received periodically for 20 periods, discounted at 5% ($5,500 × 12.4622)	68,542
Present value of the bonds	$106,232

Investors will offer the corporation a total of $106,232 for its bonds. If the corporation accepts and sells the bonds on their date of issue, say, May 1, 198A, it will record the sale as follows:

198A				
May	1	Cash	106,232.00	
		Premium on Bonds Payable		6,232.00
		Bonds Payable		100,000.00
		Sold bonds at a premium on their date of issue.		

It may then show the bonds on a balance sheet prepared on the day of the sale as follows:

Long-term liabilities:
First-mortgage, 11% bonds payable, due May 1, 199A $100,000
Add unamortized premium based on the 10%
market rate for bond interest prevailing on the
date of issue 6,232 $106,232

On a balance sheet, any unamortized premium on bonds payable is added to the par value of the bonds to show the carrying amount of the bonds, as illustrated.

Amortizing the Premium

Although the corporation discussed here received $106,232 for its bonds, it will have to repay only $100,000 to the bondholders at maturity. The difference, the $6,232 premium, represents a reduction in the cost of using the $106,232. It should be amortized over the life of the bond issue in such a manner as to lower the recorded bond interest expense. If the $6,232 premium is amortized by the interest method, Illustration 17–4 shows the amounts of interest expense to be recorded each period, the premium to be amortized, and so forth.

Observe in Illustration 17–4 that the premium to be amortized each period is determined by subtracting the interest to be recorded from the interest to be paid the bondholders.

Based on Illustration 17–4, the entry to record the first semiannual interest payment and premium amortization is:

	198A				
	Nov.	1	Bond Interest Expense	5,313.00	
			Premium on Bonds Payable	187.00	
			Cash		5,500.00
			To record payment of the bondholders and amortization of a portion of the premium.		

Note how the amortization of the premium results in a reduction in the amount of interest expense recorded. Similar entries having decreasing amounts of interest expense and increasing amounts of premium amortized are made at the ends of the remaining periods in the life of the bond issue.

ACCRUED BOND INTEREST EXPENSE

Often when bonds are sold, the bond interest periods do not coincide with the issuing company's accounting periods. In such cases, it is necessary at the end of each accounting period to make an adjustment

Illustration 17–4

Period	Beginning-of-period carrying amount	Interest expense to be recorded	Interest to be paid the bondholders	Premium to be amortized	Unamortized premium at end of period	End-of-period carrying amount
1	$106,232	$5,313	$5,500	$187	$6,045	$106,045
2	106,045	5,302	5,500	198	5,847	105,847
3	105,847	5,292	5,500	208	5,639	105,639
4	105,639	5,282	5,500	218	5,421	105,421
5	105,421	5,271	5,500	229	5,192	105,192
6	105,192	5,260	5,500	241	4,951	104,951
7	104,951	5,248	5,500	252	4,699	104,699
8	104,699	5,235	5,500	265	4,434	104,434
9	104,434	5,222	5,500	278	4,156	104,156
10	104,156	5,208	5,500	292	3,864	103,864
11	103,864	5,193	5,500	307	3,557	103,557
12	103,557	5,178	5,500	322	3,235	103,235
13	103,235	5,162	5,500	338	2,897	102,897
14	102,897	5,145	5,500	355	2,542	102,542
15	102,542	5,127	5,500	373	2,169	102,169
16	102,169	5,108	5,500	392	1,777	101,777
17	101,777	5,089	5,500	411	1,366	101,366
18	101,366	5,068	5,500	432	934	100,934
19	100,934	5,047	5,500	453	481	100,481
20	100,481	5,019*	5,500	481	–0–	100,000

* Adjusted to compensate for accumulated rounding of amounts.

for accrued interest. For example, it was assumed that the bonds of Illustration 17–4 were issued on May 1, 198A, and interest was paid on these bonds on November 1 of that year. If the accounting periods of the corporation end each December 31, on December 31, 198A, two months' interest has accrued on these bonds, and the following adjusting entry is required:

198A				
Dec.	31	Bond Interest Expense	1,767.33	
		Premium on Bonds Payable	66.00	
		Bond Interest Payable		1,833.33
		To record two months' accrued interest and amortize one third of the premium applicable to the interest period.		

Two months are one third of a semiannual interest period. Consequently, the amounts in the entry are one third of the amounts applicable to the second interest period in the life of the bond issue. Similar entries will be made on each December 31 throughout the life of the issue. However, the amounts will differ, since in each case they will apply to a different interest period.

When the interest is paid on these bonds on May 1, 198B, an entry like this is required:

198B				
May	1	Bond Interest Expense	3,534.67	
		Bond Interest Payable	1,833.33	
		Premium on Bonds Payable	132.00	
		Cash		5,500.00
		Paid the interest on the bonds, a portion of which was previously accrued, and amortized four months' premium.		

SALE OF BONDS BY INVESTORS

A purchaser of a bond may not hold it to maturity but may sell it after a period of months or years to another investor at a price determined by the market rate for bond interest on the day of the sale. The market rate for bond interest on the day of the sale determines the price because the new investor could get this current rate elsewhere. Therefore, the investor will discount the right to receive the bond's face amount at maturity and the right to receive its interest for the remaining periods of its life at the current market rate to determine the price to pay for the bond. As a result, since bond interest rates may vary greatly over a period of months or years, a bond that originally sold at a premium may later sell at a discount, and vice versa.

REDEMPTION OF BONDS

Bonds are commonly issued with the provision that they may be redeemed at the issuing corporation's option, usually upon the payment of a redemption premium. Such bonds are known as *callable bonds*. Corporations commonly insert redemption clauses in deeds of trust because if interest rates decline, it may be advantageous to call and redeem outstanding bonds and issue in their place new bonds paying a lower interest rate.

Not all bonds have a provision giving their issuing company the right to call. However, even though the right is not provided, a company may secure the same effect by purchasing its bonds on the open market and retiring them. Often such action is wise when a company has funds available and its bonds are selling at a price below their carrying amount. For example, assume that a company has outstanding on their interest date $1,000,000 of bonds on which there is $12,000 unamortized premium. The bonds are selling at 98½ (98½% of par value), and the company decides to buy and retire one tenth of the issue. The entry to record the purchase and retirement is:

Apr.	1	Bonds Payable	100,000.00	
		Premium on Bonds Payable	1,200.00	
		Gain on the Retirement of Bonds		2,700.00
		Cash		98,500.00
		To record the retirement of bonds.		

The retirement resulted in a $2,700 gain in this instance because the bonds were purchased at a price $2,700 below their carrying amount.

In the last paragraph, the statement was made that the bonds were selling at 98½. Bond quotations are commonly made in this manner. For example, a bond may be quoted for sale at 101¼. This means the bond is for sale at 101¼% of its par value, plus accrued interest, of course, if applicable.

BOND SINKING FUND

Bonds appeal to some investors because bonds usually provide greater security than stocks. A corporation may further increase the security of its bonds by "securing" them with a mortgage on certain of its assets. Often it will give additional security by agreeing in its deed of trust to create a *bond sinking fund*. This is a fund of assets accumulated during the life of the bonds to pay the bondholders at maturity.

When a corporation agrees to create a bond sinking fund, it normally agrees to create the fund by making periodic cash deposits with a sinking fund trustee. It is the duty of the trustee to safeguard the cash, to invest it in securities of reasonably low risk, and to add the interest or dividends earned to the sinking fund. Generally, when the bonds become due, it is also the duty of the sinking fund trustee to sell the sinking fund securities and to use the proceeds to pay the bondholders.

When a sinking fund is created, the amount that must be deposited periodically in order to provide enough money to retire a bond issue at maturity will depend upon the net rate of compound interest that can be earned on the invested funds. The rate is a compound rate because earnings are continually reinvested by the sinking fund trustee to earn an additional return. It is a net rate because the fee for the trustee's services commonly is deducted from the earnings.

To illustrate the operation of a sinking fund, assume a corporation issues $1,000,000 par value, 10-year bonds and agrees to deposit with a sinking fund trustee at the end of each year in the bond issue's life sufficient cash to create a fund large enough to retire the bonds at maturity. If the trustee is able to invest the funds in such a manner as to earn a 7% net return, $72,378 must be deposited each year and the fund will grow to maturity (in rounded dollars) as shown in Illustration 17–5.

Illustration 17–5

End of year	Amount deposited	Interest earned on fund balance	Balance in fund after deposit and interest
1	$72,378	$ –0–	$ 72,378
2	72,378	5,066	149,822
3	72,378	10,488	232,688
4	72,378	16,288	321,354
5	72,378	22,495	416,227
6	72,378	29,136	517,741
7	72,378	36,242	626,361
8	72,378	43,845	742,584
9	72,378	51,981	866,943
10	72,378	60,679*	1,000,000

* Adjusted for rounding.

When a sinking fund is created by periodic deposits, the entry to record the amount deposited each year appears as follows:

Dec.	31	Bond Sinking Fund	72,378.00	
		Cash		72,378.00
		To record the annual sinking fund deposit.		

Each year the sinking fund trustee invests the amount deposited, and each year it collects and reports the earnings on the investments. The earnings report results in an entry to record the sinking fund income. For example, if $72,378 is deposited at the end of the first year in the sinking fund, the accumulation of which is shown in Illustration 17–5, and 7% is earned, the entry to record the sinking fund earnings of the second year is:

Dec.	31	Bond Sinking Fund	5,066.00	
		Sinking Fund Earnings		5,066.00
		To record the sinking fund earnings.		

Sinking fund earnings appear on the income statement as financial revenue in a section titled "Other revenues and expenses." A sinking fund is the property of the company creating the fund and should appear on its balance sheet in the long-term investments section.

When bonds mature, it is usually the duty of the sinking fund trustee to convert the fund's investments into cash and pay the bondholders. Normally the sinking fund securities, when sold, produce either a little more or a little less cash than is needed to pay the bondholders. If more cash than needed is produced, the extra cash is returned to the corporation; and if less cash is produced than needed, the corporation must make up the deficiency. For example, if the securities in the sinking fund of a $1,000,000 bond issue produce $1,001,325 when converted to cash, the trustee will use $1,000,000 to pay the bondholders and will return the extra $1,325 to the corporation. The corporation will then record the payment of its bonds and the return of the extra cash with an entry like the following:

Jan.	3	Cash	1,325.00	
		Bonds Payable	1,000,000.00	
		Bond Sinking Fund		1,001,325.00
		To record payment of our bonds and the return of extra cash from the sinking fund.		

RESTRICTION ON DIVIDENDS DUE TO OUTSTANDING BONDS

To protect a corporation's financial position and the interests of its bondholders, a deed of trust may restrict the dividends the corporation may pay while its bonds are outstanding. Commonly, the restriction provides that the corporation may pay dividends in any year only to the extent that the year's earnings exceed sinking fund requirements.

CONVERTIBLE BONDS

To make an issue more attractive, bond owners may be given the right to exchange their bonds for a fixed number of shares of the issuing company's common stock. Such bonds are known as *convertible bonds.* They offer investors initial investment security, and if the issuing company prospers and the market value of its stock goes up, an opportunity to share in the prosperity by converting their bonds to stock. Conversion is always at the bondholders' option and is not exercised except when doing so is to their advantage.

When bonds are converted into stock, the bondholders' claims as creditors are transformed into ownership equity. The generally accepted rule for measuring the contribution for the issued shares is that the carrying amount of the converted bonds becomes the book value of the capital contributed for the new shares. For example, assume the following: (1) A company has outstanding $1,000,000 of bonds upon which there is $8,000 unamortized discount. (2) The bonds are convertible at the rate of a $1,000 bond for 90 shares of the company's $10 par value common stock. And (3) $100,000 in bonds have been presented on their interest date for conversion. The entry to record the conversion is:

May	1	Bonds Payable	100,000.00	
		Discount on Bonds Payable		800.00
		Common Stock		90,000.00
		Premium on Common Stock		9,200.00
		To record the conversion of bonds.		

Note in this entry that the bonds' $99,200 carrying amount sets the accounting value for the capital contributed. Usually, when bonds have a conversion privilege, it is not exercised until the stock's market value and normal dividend payments are sufficiently high to make the conversion profitable to the bondholders.

INVESTMENTS IN BONDS

The discussion of bonds has thus far focused on the issuing corporation. Attention is now shifted to the purchasers of bonds. When bonds are purchased as an investment, they are recorded at cost, including any brokerage fees. If interest has accrued at the date of purchase, it is also paid for by the purchaser and is recorded with a debit to Bond Interest Receivable. The entry to record a bond purchase is as follows:

May	1	Investment in X Corporation Bonds	46,400.00	
		Bond Interest Receivable	1,500.00	
		Cash		47,900.00
		Purchased 50 $1,000, 9%, 10-year bonds dated December 31, 198A, at a price of 92 plus a $400 brokerage fee and accrued interest.		

Note that the $46,400 cost of the bonds was 92% × $50,000 par value plus the $400 brokerage fee, which leaves a discount of $3,600. Most companies do not record the discount (or premium) in a separate account. The investment account is simply debited for the net cost. The accrued interest on May 1 was 4/12 × 9% × $50,000, or $1,500.

Assuming interest is paid semiannually on June 30 and December 31, the entry to record the receipt of interest on June 30 would be as follows:

June	30	Cash	2,250.00	
		Bond Interest Receivable		1,500.00
		Bond Interest Earned		750.00

This entry correctly reflects the fact that the purchaser owned the bonds for two months during which time interest amounted to 2/12 × 9% × $50,000, or $750. However, recall that the bonds were purchased at a discount and observe that the June 30 entry does not include any amortization of the discount. This is acceptable only if the bonds are held as a short-term, temporary investment. Under these conditions, the bond investment is shown as a current asset at cost. The market value of the bonds on the date of the balance sheet should also be reported parenthetically, as follows:

Current assets:
    Investment in X Corp. Bonds (market value is $xx,xxx) $46,400

When the bonds are sold, the gain or loss on the sale is calculated as the difference between the sale proceeds and cost.

What if the bonds are held as a long-term investment? In this case, one should expect the market value of the bonds to move generally toward par value as the maturity date approaches. Therefore, any discount (or premium) should be amortized so that each interest period includes some amortization in the calculation of interest earned. The procedures for amortizing discount or premium on bond investments parallel those that were discussed and applied previously to bonds payable. The only difference is that the amount of discount (premium) to be amortized is debited (credited) directly to the investment account. As a consequence, on the maturity date, the investment account balance will equal the par value on the bonds.

GLOSSARY

Bond. A type of long-term note payable issued by a corporation or a political subdivision.

Bond discount. The difference between the par value of a bond and the price at which it is issued when issued at a price below par.

Bond premium. The difference between the par value of a bond and the price at which it is issued when issued at a price above par.

Bond sinking fund. A fund of assets accumulated to pay a bond issue at maturity.

Callable bond. A bond that may be called in and redeemed at the option of the corporation or political subdivision that issued it.

Carrying amount of a bond issue. The par value of a bond issue less any unamortized discount or plus any unamortized premium.

Contract rate of bond interest The rate of interest that is applied to the par value of bonds to determine the annual cash payment to the bondholders.

Convertible bond. A bond that may be converted into shares of its issuing corporation's stock at the option of the bondholder.

Coupon bond. A bond having coupons that are detached by the bondholder to collect interest on the bond.

Debenture bond. An unsecured bond.

Deed of trust. The contract between a corporation and its bondholders governing the duties of the corporation in relation to the bonds.

Face amount of a bond. The bond's par value.

Market rate of bond interest. The interest rate that a corporation is willing to pay and investors are willing to take for the use of their money to buy that corporation's bonds.

Par value of a bond. The face amount of the bond, which is the amount the borrower agrees to repay at maturity and the amount on which interest payments are based.

Registered bond. A bond the ownership of which is recorded with the issuing corporation or political subdivision.

Serial bonds. An issue of bonds that will be repaid in installments over a period of years.

Sinking fund. A fund of assets accumulated for some purpose.

Sinking fund bonds. Bonds which require that a separate fund of assets be accumulated during the life of the bonds for the purpose of repaying the bondholders at maturity.

QUESTIONS FOR CLASS DISCUSSION

1. What is the primary difference between a share of stock and a bond?
2. What is a deed of trust? What are some of the provisions commonly contained in a deed of trust?
3. Define or describe *(a)* registered bonds, *(b)* coupon bonds, *(c)* serial bonds, *(d)* sinking fund bonds, *(e)* callable bonds, *(f)* convertible bonds, and *(g)* debenture bonds.
4. Why does a corporation issuing bonds between interest dates charge and collect accrued interest from the purchasers of the bonds?
5. As it relates to a bond issue, what is the meaning of "contract rate of interest"? What is the meaning of "market rate for bond interest"?
6. What determines bond interest rates?
7. When the straight-line method is used to amortize bond discount, how is the interest expense to be reported each period calculated?
8. When the interest method is used to amortize bond discount or premium, how is the interest expense to be reported each period calculated?
9. If a $1,000 bond is sold at 98¼, at what price is it sold? If a $1,000 bond is sold at 101½, at what price is it sold?
10. If the quoted price for a bond is 97¾, does this include accrued interest?
11. What purpose is served by creating a bond sinking fund?
12. How are bond sinking funds classified for balance sheet purposes?
13. Convertible bonds are often popular with investors. Why?
14. What is the difference between the accounting procedures for bonds held as a short-term investment and for bonds held as a long-term investment?

CLASS EXERCISES

Exercise 17–1

On May 1 of the current year, a corporation sold at par plus accrued interest $2,000,000 of its 9.6% bonds. The bonds were dated January 1 of the current year, with interest payable on each July 1 and January 1. *(a)* Give the entry to record the sale. *(b)* Give the entry to record the first interest payment. *(c)* Set up a T-account for Bond Interest Expense and post the portions of the entries that affect the account. Answer these questions: *(d)* How many months' interest were accrued on these bonds when they were sold? *(e)* How many months' interest were paid on July 1? *(f)* What is the balance of the Bond Interest Expense account after the entry recording the first interest payment is posted? *(g)* How many months' interest does this balance represent? *(h)* How many months' interest did the bondholders earn during the first interest period?

Exercise 17–2   On April 1 of the current year, a corporation sold $1,000,000 of its 9.4%, 10-year bonds. The bonds were dated April 1 of the current year, with interest payable on each October 1 and April 1. Give the entries to record the sale at 98¼ and the first semiannual interest payment under the assumption that the straight-line method is used to amortize the discount.

Exercise 17–3   On January 1 of the current year, a corporation sold $500,000 of its 9.9%, 10-year bonds at a price that reflected a 12% market rate for bond interest. Interest is payable each June 30 and December 31. Calculate the sales price of the bonds and prepare a general journal entry to record the sale of the bonds. (Use the present value tables, Tables 12–1 and 12–2, pages 415 and 417.)

Exercise 17–4   The corporation of Exercise 17–3 uses the interest method of amortizing bond discount or premium. Under the assumption the corporation of Exercise 17–3 sold its bonds for $439,882, prepare a schedule with the columnar headings of Illustration 17–3 and present the amounts in the schedule for the first two interest periods. Also, prepare general journal entries to record the first and second payments of interest to bondholders. (Round all amounts to the nearest whole dollar.)

Exercise 17–5   A corporation sold $200,000 of its own 10%, nine-year bonds on November 1, 198A, at a price that reflected a 9% market rate of bond interest. The bonds pay interest each May 1 and November 1. *(a)* Calculate the price at which the bonds sold and *(b)* prepare a general journal entry to record the sale. (Use the present value tables, Tables 12–1 and 12–2, pages 415 and 417.)

Exercise 17–6   Assume the bonds of Exercise 17–5 sold for $212,160 and that the corporation uses the interest method to amortize bond discount or premium. Prepare general journal entries to accrue interest on December 31, 198A, and to record the first payment of interest on May 1, 198B.

Exercise 17–7   A corporation sold $1,000,000 of its 9.5%, 10-year bonds at 97¼ on their date of issue, January 1, 19—. Five years later, on January 1, after the bond interest for the period had been paid and 40% of the total discount on the issue had been amortized, the corporation purchased $100,000 par value of the bonds on the open market at 99¾ and retired them. Give the entry to record the retirement.

Exercise 17–8   On January 1, 198A, a corporation sold $600,000 of eight-year sinking fund bonds. The corporation expects to earn 9% on assets deposited with the sinking fund trustee and is required to deposit $54,400 with the trustee at the end of each year in the life of the bonds. *(a)* Prepare a general journal entry to record the first deposit of $54,400 with the trustee on January 1, 198B. *(b)* Prepare a general journal entry on December 31, 198B, to record the $4,825 earnings for 198B reported to the corporation by the trustee. *(c)* After the final payment to the trustee, the sinking fund had an accumulated balance of $601,500. Prepare the general journal entry to record the payment to the bondholders on January 1, 199A.

Exercise 17–9   On November 2, 198B, Best Company purchased 20 $1,000 par value, 14%, 10-year Zero Corporation bonds dated December 31, 198A. The bonds pay interest semiannually on June 30 and December 31. Best Company bought the bonds at 94 plus a $500 brokerage fee and accrued interest; it intends to hold the bonds as a temporary investment. Prepare journal entries for Best Company to record the purchase and to record the receipt of interest on December 31, 198A.

PROBLEMS

Problem 17–1   A corporation sold $500,000 of its own 8.6%, 10-year bonds on their date of issue, January 1, 198A. Interest was payable on the bonds on each June 30 and December 31, and they were sold at a price to yield the buyers a 9% annual return. The corporation uses the straight-line method of amortizing discount or premium.

Required:

1. Prepare a calculation to show the price at which the bonds were sold. (Use the present value tables, Tables 12–1 and 12–2, pages 415 and 417.)
2. Prepare a form with the columnar headings of Illustration 17–2 and fill in the amounts for the first two interest periods of the bond issue. Round all amounts to the nearest whole dollar.
3. Prepare entries in general journal form to record the sale of the bonds and the first two payments of interest.

Problem 17–2   On January 1, 198A, a corporation sold $800,000 of its own 9.5%, 10-year bonds. The bonds were dated January 1, 198A, with interest payable on each June 30 and December 31, and were sold to yield the buyers a 9% annual return. The corporation uses the interest method of amortizing premium or discount.

Required:

1. Prepare a calculation to show the price at which the bonds were sold. (Use the present value tables, Tables 12–1 and 12–2, pages 415 and 417.)
2. Prepare a form with the columnar headings of Illustration 17–4 and fill in the amounts for the first two interest periods of the bond issue. Round all amounts to the nearest whole dollar.

3. Prepare entries in general journal form to record the sale of the bonds and the first two payments of interest.

Problem 17–3 Prepare general journal entries to record the following transactions of Fry Corporation. Use the present value tables, Tables 12–1 and 12–2, pages 415 and 417, as necessary, to calculate the amounts in your entries and round all amounts to the nearest whole dollar.

198A

Jan. 1 Sold $1,000,000 of its own 8.1%, 10-year bonds dated January 1, 198A, with interest payable on each June 30 and December 31. The bonds sold for a price that reflected a 9% market rate of bond interest.

June 30 Paid the semiannual interest on the bonds and amortized a portion of the discount calculated by the straight-line method.

Dec. 31 Paid the semiannual interest on the bonds and amortized a portion of the discount calculated by the straight-line method.

31 Deposited $63,000 with the sinking fund trustee to establish the sinking fund to repay the bonds.

198B

Dec. 30 Received the report of the sinking fund trustee that the sinking fund had earned $6,200.

199A

Jan. 1 Received a report from the sinking fund trustee which noted that the bondholders had been paid $1,000,000 on that day. Included was a $1,900 check for the extra cash accumulated in the sinking fund.

Problem 17–4 Prepare general journal entries to record the following bond transactions of a corporation. Round all dollar amounts to the nearest whole dollar.

198A

Oct. 1 Sold $4,000,000 par value of its own 10.9%, 10-year bonds at a price to yield the buyers a 10% annual return. The bonds were dated October 1, 198A, with interest payable on each April 1 and October 1.

Dec. 31 Made an adjusting entry to record the accrued interest on the bonds and to amortize the premium applicable to 198A. The interest method was used in calculating the premium amortized.

198B

Apr. 1 Paid the semiannual interest on the bonds and amortized the remainder of the premium applicable to the first interest period.

Oct. 1 Paid the semiannual interest on the bonds and amortized the premium applicable to the second interest period of the issue.

198D

Oct. 1 After recording the entry paying the semiannual interest on the bonds on this date and amortizing a portion of the premium, the carrying amount of the bonds on the corporation's books was $4,178,300, and it purchased one tenth of the bonds at 97½ and retired them.

Problem 17–5   On December 31, 198A, Zilker Corporation sold $3,000,000 of 10-year, 10.6% bonds payable at a price that reflected a 12% market rate of bond interest. The bonds pay interest on June 30 and December 31. Use the present value tables, Tables 12–1 and 12–2, pages 415 and 417, as necessary, in calculating the amounts in your answers and round all amounts to the nearest whole dollar.

Required:

1. Present a general journal entry to record the sale of the bonds.
2. Present general journal entries to record the first and second payments of interest on June 30, 198B, and on December 31, 198B, assuming straight-line amortization of premium or discount.
3. Present general journal entries to record the first and second payments of interest on June 30, 198B, and on December 31, 198B, assuming the use of the interest method to amortize premium or discount.
4. Prepare a schedule like the one on page 588 that has columns for the beginning-of-period carrying amount, interest expense to be reported, and interest expense as a percentage of carrying amount, assuming use of the (1) interest method, and (2) straight-line method. In completing the schedule, present the amounts for Period 1 and Period 2.

ALTERNATE PROBLEMS

Problem 17–1A   A corporation sold $700,000 of its own 8.5%, eight-year bonds on their date of issue, January 1, 198A. Interest was payable on the bonds on each June 30 and December 31, and they were sold at a price to yield the buyers a 9% annual return. The corporation uses the straight-line method of amortizing premium or discount.

Required:

1. Prepare a calculation to show the price at which the bonds were sold. (Use the present value tables, Tables 12–1 and 12–2, pages 415 and 417.) Round amounts to the nearest whole dollar.
2. Prepare a form with the columnar headings of Illustration 17–2 and fill in the amounts for the first two interest periods of the bond issue.
3. Prepare general journal entries to record the sale of the bonds and the first two payments of interest.

Problem 17–2A   On January 1, 198A, a corporation sold $600,000 of its own 11%, nine-year bonds. The bonds were dated January 1, 198A, with interest payable on each June 30 and December 31, and were sold to yield the buyers a 12% annual return. The corporation uses the interest method of amortizing premium or discount.

Required:

1. Prepare a calculation to show the price at which the bonds were sold. (Use the present value tables, Tables 12–1 and 12–2, pages 415 and 417.)
2. Prepare a form with the columnar headings of Illustration 17–3 and fill

in the amounts for the first two interest periods of the bond issue. Round all amounts to the nearest whole dollar.

3. Prepare entries in general journal form to record the sale of the bonds and the first two payments of interest.

Problem 17–3A   Prepare general journal entries to record the following transactions of Shedd Corporation. Use the present value tables, Tables 12–1 and 12–2, pages 415 and 417, as necessary, to calculate the amounts in your entries and round all amounts to the nearest whole dollar.

198A

Dec. 31   Sold $5,000,000 of its own 9.6%, eight-year bonds dated December 31, 198A, with interest payable on each June 30 and December 31. The bonds sold for a price that reflected a 9% market rate of bond interest.

198B

June 30   Paid the semiannual interest on bonds and amortized a portion of the premium calculated by the straight-line method.

Dec. 31   Paid the semiannual interest on the bonds and amortized a portion of the premium calculated by the straight-line method.

31   Deposited $453,500 with the sinking fund trustee to establish the sinking fund to repay the bonds.

198C

Dec. 30   Received the report of the sinking fund trustee that the sinking fund had earned $41,200.

199A

Dec. 31   Received a report from the sinking fund trustee which noted that the bondholders had been paid $5,000,000 on that day. Included was a $9,300 check for the extra cash accumulated in the sinking fund.

Problem 17–4A   Prepare general journal entries to record the following bond transactions of Kardash Corporation. Round all dollar amounts to the nearest whole dollar.

198A

Aug. 1   Sold $800,000 par value of its own 11%, 10-year bonds at a price to yield the buyers a 12% annual return. The bonds were dated August 1, 198A, with interest payable on each February 1 and August 1.

Dec. 31   Made an adjusting entry to record the accrued interest on the bonds and to amortize the discount applicable to 198A. The interest method was used in calculating the discount amortized.

198B

Feb. 1   Paid the semiannual interest on the bonds and amortized the remainder of the discount applicable to the first interest period.

Aug. 1   Paid the semiannual interest on the bonds and amortized the discount applicable to the second interest period of the issue.

198D

Aug. 1   After recording the entry paying the semiannual interest on the bonds on this date and amortizing a portion of the discount, the carrying amount of the bonds on the corporation's books was $763,047, and it purchased one tenth of the bonds at 98 and retired them.

Problem 17–5A
On December 31, 198A, Manning Corporation sold $2,000,000 of eight-year, 10.2% bonds payable at a price that reflected a 12% market rate of bond interest. The bonds pay interest on June 30 and December 31. Use the present value tables, Tables 12–1 and 12–2, pages 415 and 417, as necessary, in calculating the amounts in your answers and round all amounts to the nearest whole dollar.

Required:

1. Present a general journal entry to record the sale of the bonds.
2. Present general journal entries to record the first and second payments of interest on June 30, 198B, and on December 31, 198B, assuming straight-line amortization of premium or discount.
3. Present general journal entries to record the first and second payments of interest on June 30, 198B, and on December 31, 198B, assuming the use of the interest method to amortize premium or discount.
4. Prepare a schedule like the one on page 588 that has columns for the beginning-of-period carrying amount, interest expense to be reported, and interest expense as a percentage of carrying amount, assuming use of the (1) interest method and (2) straight-line method. In completing the schedule, present the amounts for Period 1 and Period 2.

Provocative Problems

Provocative Problem 17–1, Fisher Corporation
Ownership equity in Fisher Corporation is represented by 200,000 shares of outstanding common stock on which the corporation has earned an unsatisfactory average of $0.45 per share during each of the last three years. And, as a result of the unsatisfactory earnings, management of the corporation is planning an expansion that will require the investment of an additional $1,000,000 in the business. The $1,000,000 is to be acquired either by selling an additional 100,000 shares of the company's common stock at $10 per share or selling at par $1,000,000 of 8%, 20-year bonds. Management estimates that the expansion will double the company's before-tax earnings the first year after it is completed and will increase before-tax earnings an additional 25% over that level in the years that follow.

The company's management wants to finance the expansion in the manner that will serve the best interests of present stockholders and they have asked you to determine this for them. In your report express an opinion as to the relative merits and disadvantages of each of the proposed ways of securing the funds needed for the expansion. Attach to your report a schedule showing expected earnings per share of the common stockholders under each method of financing. In preparing your schedule, assume the company presently pays out in state and federal income taxes 50% of its before-tax earnings and that it will continue to pay out the same share after the expansion.

Financial Statements, Interpretation and Modifications

PART SIX

Statement of Changes in Financial Position

18

After studying Chapter 18, you should be able to:

List the items included in working capital and explain why an adequate amount of working capital is important in the operation of a business.

List a number of sources and uses of working capital.

Explain why the net income reported on an income statement is not the amount of working capital generated by operations.

Describe the adjustments that must be made to the reported net income figure in order to determine the amount of working capital generated by operations.

Prepare a statement of changes in financial position on a working capital basis.

Prepare an analysis of changes in working capital items.

Prepare a statement of changes in financial position on a cash basis.

Define or explain the words and phrases listed in the chapter Glossary.

When financial statements are prepared for a business, the income statement shows the income earned or the loss incurred during the accounting period. The retained earnings statement summarizes the changes in retained earnings, and the balance sheet shows the end-of-period financial position. However, for a better understanding of the financing and investing activities of the business, more information is needed. This information is supplied by a *statement of changes in financial position*. Such a statement summarizes the changes that occurred in the financial position of the business by showing where it acquired resources during the period and where it applied or used resources. Often, the statement is designed to emphasize the change in the *working capital* of the business. Other companies design the statement to explain the changes in cash, or to explain the changes in cash plus temporary investments.

WORKING CAPITAL

The working capital of a business is the excess of its current assets over its current liabilities. The more important of a company's current assets are usually its cash, accounts receivable, and merchandise. The merchandise is normally acquired through the use of short-term credit, primarily accounts payable. It is sold and turned into accounts receivable, which are collected and turned into cash. The cash is then used to pay bills so that short-term credit can be used again to buy more merchandise. As a result, it can be said that a company's current assets and current liabilities circulate. Furthermore, in the circulation it is important for the current assets to exceed the current liabilities by an adequate amount.

An adequate excess of current assets over current liabilities or, in other words, an adequate amount of working capital, enables a business to meet current debts, carry sufficient inventory, take advantage of cash discounts, and offer favorable credit terms to customers. A company that is deficient in working capital and unable to do these things is in a poor competitive position. Its survival may even be threatened, unless its working capital position can be improved. Inadequacy of working capital has ended the business lives of many companies even though total assets far exceeded total liabilities.

Funds

Many people use the word *funds* to mean cash. Others point out that temporary investments are available to be sold and used as cash if the needs of a business require such sales. Hence, they use the word *funds* to mean cash plus temporary investments. Still others use the word *funds* to mean working capital. They argue that working capital circulates, and the portion not needed to pay existing current debts will become cash within the current operating cycle.

None of these definitions of funds is clearly superior to the others. All of them share the general idea that funds involve relatively liquid resources that are or soon will be available to pay dividends, buy plant assets, pay long-term debt, or satisfy other resource needs of the business.

A statement of changes in financial position describes the sources and uses of funds during an accounting period. However, since the term *funds* is used in more than one way, confusion is avoided if more precise descriptions are used. If the statement is designed to explain working capital changes, the phrases "sources of working capital" and "uses of working capital" should be used. Similarly, if the statement is designed to explain cash changes, the phrases "sources of cash" and "uses of cash" should be used.

The following discussion is organized so as to explain first the preparation of the statement of changes in financial position on a working capital basis. Later, the necessary alterations to prepare the statement on a cash basis are considered.

SOURCES AND USES OF WORKING CAPITAL

Transactions that increase working capital are called *sources of working capital*, and transactions that decrease working capital are called *uses of working capital*. If the working capital of a business increased during an accounting period, more working capital was generated by its transactions than was used. On the other hand, if working capital decreased, more working capital was used than was generated.

Sources of Working Capital

Some of the more common sources of working capital are as follows:

CURRENT OPERATIONS. Funds in the form of cash and accounts receivable flow into a business from sales, and most expenses and goods sold result in outflows of funds. Consequently, working capital is increased by normal operations if the inflow of funds from sales exceeds the outflows for goods sold and expenses. However, the net income figure appearing on an income statement generally does not represent the amount of working capital generated by operations because some expenses listed on the income statement do not cause working capital outflows in the period of the statement.

For example, Rexel Sales Company of Illustration 18–1 experienced

Illustration 18–1

REXEL SALES COMPANY
Income Statement for Year Ended December 31, 19—

Sales		$50,000
Cost of goods sold		30,000
Gross profit from sales		$20,000
Operating expenses:		
Sales salaries expense	$8,000	
Rent expense	1,200	
Depreciation expense, equipment	1,000	10,200
Net income		$ 9,800

a $50,000 funds inflow from sales during the year. It also experienced outflows of $30,000 for goods sold, $8,000 for salaries, and $1,200 for rent. However, there was no outflow of working capital for depreciation expense. Consequently, during the period, the company gained working capital from operations equal to the sum of its reported net income plus the recorded depreciation, or it gained $9,800 plus $1,000 or $10,800 of working capital from operations.

Business executives sometimes speak of depreciation as a source of funds, but it is not. Look again at Illustration 18–1. Sales are the source of working capital on this statement. No funds flowed into this company from recording depreciation. In this case, as with every business, the revenues are the source of working capital from operations. However, since depreciation, unlike most expenses, does not cause a funds outflow in the current period, it must be added to the net income to determine working capital from operations.

LONG-TERM LIABILITIES. Transactions that increase long-term liabilities increase working capital or are so treated. Therefore, they are sources of working capital regardless of whether long-term notes, mortgages, or bonds are involved. On the other hand, short-term credit, whether obtained from banks or other creditors, is not a source of working capital because short-term credit does not increase working capital. For example, if $10,000 is borrowed for, say, six months, both current assets and current liabilities are increased. However, since both are increased the same amount, total working capital is unchanged.

SALE OF NONCURRENT ASSETS. When a plant asset, long-term investment, or other noncurrent asset is sold for cash or receivables, working capital is increased by the amount of the sale. Therefore, such sales are sources of working capital.

SALE OF CAPITAL STOCK. The issuance of stock for cash or current receivables increases current assets; and as a result, such sales are sources of funds. Likewise, an additional investment of current assets by a single proprietor or partner is also a source of working capital.

Uses of Working Capital

Common uses of working capital are the following:

PURCHASE OF NONCURRENT ASSETS. When noncurrent assets such as plant and equipment or long-term investments are purchased, working capital is reduced. Consequently, such purchases are uses of working capital.

PAYMENT OF NONCURRENT LIABILITIES. Payment of a long-term debt such as a mortgage reduces working capital and is a use of working capital. Likewise, a contribution to a debt retirement fund, bond sinking fund, or other special noncurrent fund is also a use of working capital.

CAPITAL REDUCTIONS. The withdrawals of cash or other current assets by a proprietor, the purchase of treasury stock, or the purchase of stock for retirement reduce working capital and are uses of working capital.

DECLARATION OF A DIVIDEND. The declaration of a dividend that is to be paid in cash or other current assets reduces working capital and is a use of working capital. Note that it is the declaration, not the payment, that uses working capital. The declaration creates a current liability, dividends payable, and therefore reduces working capital as soon as it is voted by the board of directors. The final payment of a dividend previously declared does not affect working capital because it reduces current assets and current liabilities in equal amounts.

STATEMENT OF CHANGES IN FINANCIAL POSITION, WORKING CAPITAL BASIS

As previously stated, a statement of changes in financial position summarizes and discloses the financing and investing activities of the business for which it was prepared. The statement covers a period of time and may be designed to account for the change in the company's working capital during the period.

Illustration 18–2 shows the 198B statement of changes in financial position for Delta Company. The illustration also includes a companion statement called an analysis of changes in working capital items. These

Illustration 18-2

DELTA COMPANY
Statement of Changes in Financial Position
For Year Ended December 31, 198B

Sources of working capital:
Current operations:
  Net income $12,200
  Add expenses not requiring outlays of working
    capital in the current period:
    Depreciation of buildings and equipment   4,500
    Working capital provided by operations $16,700
Other sources:
  Sales of common stock 12,500
    Total sources of working capital $29,200

Uses of working capital:
Purchase of office equipment .... $ 500
Purchase of store equipment....................... 6,000
Addition to building 15,000
Reduction of mortgage debt 2,500
Declaration of dividends 3,100
    Total uses of working capital 27,100
Net increase in working capital .... $ 2,100

DELTA COMPANY
Analysis of Changes in Working Capital Items
For Year Ended December 31, 198B

	Dec. 31, 198B	Dec. 31, 198A	Working capital Increases	Working capital Decreases
Current assets:				
Cash	$ 7,500	$ 4,800	$ 2,700	
Accounts receivable, net	8,000	9,500		$ 1,500
Merchandise inventory	31,500	32,000		500
Prepaid expenses	1,000	1,200		200
Total current assets	$48,000	$47,500		
Current liabilities:				
Notes payable	$ 2,500	$ 1,500		1,000
Accounts payable	16,700	19,600	2,900	
Dividends payable	1,000	700		300
Total current liabilities	$20,200	$21,800		
Working capital	$27,800	$25,700		
			$ 5,600	$ 3,500
Net increase in working capital ...				2,100
			$ 5,600	$ 5,600

two statements are normally presented together to enhance the usefulness of the statement of changes in financial position.[1]

Observe in Illustration 18–2 that the changes in working capital that took place during 198B can be described two different ways. At the bottom of the illustration, the analysis of changes in working capital items simply lists the beginning and ending balances in the current asset and current liability items. Next, it shows whether the change in each item involved an increase or decrease in working capital. The difference between the total increases and total decreases obviously amounts to the net increase or decrease. The analysis of changes in working capital items provides a clear description of the changes in working capital components. But, it gives no indication of what caused those changes.

At the top of Illustration 18–2, the statement of changes in financial position takes an entirely different approach to describing the change in working capital. It shows the types of financing and investing activities that caused the changes in working capital.

The ability of an enterprise to generate funds in its operations is an important factor in evaluating its ability to pay dividends, to finance new investment opportunities, and to grow. Consequently, the amount of working capital generated by operations is commonly summarized first on a statement of changes in financial position. Normally, the summary begins with the amount of the net income reported on the income statement. To this are added any expenses deducted on the income statement that did not decrease working capital, such as depreciation, depletion, and bond discount amortization. (Bond premium amortization is deducted from the income figure on the statement.) The resulting amount is then described as, for example, "Working capital provided by operations." (If the summary begins with a net loss, rather than a net income, and the net loss exceeds the expenses that did not decrease working capital, the resulting amount may be described as "Working capital used in operations.")

Working capital is also secured from sources other than operations. These are shown next on the statement of changes in financial position. The uses of working capital are then listed, after which the net increase or decrease in working capital is shown.

PREPARING A STATEMENT OF CHANGES IN FINANCIAL POSITION

If a statement of changes in financial position is prepared on a working capital basis, the primary focus is on the *noncurrent accounts*. (The

---

[1] APB, "Reporting Changes in Financial Position," *APB Opinion No. 19* (New York: AICPA, 1971), par. 12.

noncurrent accounts are the accounts other than the current asset and current liability accounts.) The noncurrent accounts are examined because (1) only a few transactions affected these accounts and (2) almost every one either increased or decreased working capital.

Normally, in making an audit of a company's noncurrent accounts, the auditor makes a list of the transactions that affected these accounts during the period under review. This list is then used along with the company's balance sheets as of the beginning and end of the period to prepare the statement of changes in financial position. The compara-

Illustration 18–3

DELTA COMPANY
Comparative Balance Sheet
December 31, 198B, and December 31, 198A

	198B	198A
Assets		
Current assets:		
Cash	$ 7,500	$ 4,800
Accounts receivable, net	8,000	9,500
Merchandise inventory	31,500	32,000
Prepaid expenses	1,000	1,200
Total current assets	$ 48,000	$ 47,500
Plant and equipment:		
Office equipment	$ 3,500	$ 3,000
Accumulated depreciation, office equipment	(900)	(600)
Store equipment	26,200	21,000
Accumulated depreciation, store equipment	(5,200)	(4,200)
Buildings	95,000	80,000
Accumulated depreciation, buildings	(10,600)	(8,200)
Land	25,000	25,000
Total plant and equipment	$133,000	$116,000
Total assets	$181,000	$163,500
Liabilities		
Current liabilities:		
Notes payable	$ 2,500	$ 1,500
Accounts payable	16,700	19,600
Dividends payable	1,000	700
Total current liabilities	$ 20,200	$ 21,800
Long-term liabilities:		
Mortgage payable	$ 17,500	$ 20,000
Total liabilities	$ 37,700	$ 41,800
Stockholders' Equity		
Common stock, $10 par value	$115,000	$100,000
Premium on common stock	8,500	5,000
Retained earnings	19,800	16,700
Total stockholders' equity	$143,300	$121,700
Total liabilities and stockholders' equity	$181,000	$163,500

tive balance sheet of Illustration 18–3 and the following list of transactions that affected the noncurrent accounts of Delta Company were used in preparing the Illustration 18–2 statement of changes in financial position.

a. Purchased office equipment costing $500 during the year.
b. Purchased store equipment that cost $6,000.
c. Discarded and junked fully depreciated store equipment that cost $800 when new.
d. Added a new addition to the building that cost $15,000.
e. Earned a $12,200 net income during the year.
f. Delta Company deducted on its 198B income statement $300 of depreciation on office equipment, (g) $1,800 on its store equipment, and (h) $2,400 on its building.
i. Made a $2,500 payment on the mortgage.
j. Declared a 5% stock dividend at a time when the company's stock was selling for $12 per share.
k. Sold and issued 1,000 shares of common stock at $12.50 per share.
l. Declared cash dividends totaling $3,100 during the year.

Steps in Preparing a Statement of Changes in Financial Position

Three steps are involved in preparing a statement of changes in financial position. They are the following:

1. Prepare an analysis of changes in working capital items.
2. Prepare a working paper to account for the changes in the company's noncurrent accounts and in the process set out on the working paper the period's sources and uses of working capital.
3. Use the working paper to prepare the formal statement of changes in financial position.

ANALYSIS OF CHANGES IN WORKING CAPITAL ITEMS

Information for preparing the analysis of changes in working capital items is taken from balance sheets as of the beginning and end of the period under review. For Delta Company, the analysis of changes in working capital items was presented at the bottom of Illustration 18–2. Observe how the beginning and ending account balances were taken directly from the balance sheets presented in Illustration 18–3. The current asset and current liability items in the analysis and the preparation of the analysis need little discussion. However, students sometimes have difficulty understanding how, for example, an increase in a current liability results in a decrease in working capital. They should not, for when a current liability increases, a larger amount is subtracted from current assets in determining working capital.

PREPARING THE WORKING PAPER, WORKING CAPITAL BASIS

Delta Company's sources and uses of working capital resulted from simple transactions, and a statement of changes in financial position could be prepared for the company without a working paper. However, the working paper helps to organize the information needed for the statement and also offers a proof of the accuracy of the work.

The working paper for Delta Company's statement of changes in financial position is shown in Illustration 18–4. Such a working paper is prepared as follows:

1. First, the amount of working capital at the beginning of the period under review is entered on the first line in the first money column and the amount of working capital at the end is entered in the last column.
2. Next, the noncurrent balance sheet amounts are entered on the working paper. The amounts or account balances as of the beginning of the period are entered in the first money column and those of the end in the last. Observe that debit items are listed first and are followed by credit items. This is a convenience that places the accumulated depreciation items with the liability and capital amounts.
3. After the noncurrent account balances are entered, the working capital amount and debit items in each column are added. Next, the credit items are added to be certain that debits equal credits.
4. After the items are added to see that debits equal credits, the phrase "Sources of working capital:" is written on the line following the total of the credit items. Sufficient lines are then skipped to allow for listing all possible sources and then the phrase "Uses of working capital:" is written.
5. Next, analyzing entries are entered in the second and third money columns. These entries do two things: (1) they account for or explain the amount of change in each noncurrent account and (2) they set out the sources and uses of working capital. (The analyzing entries on the illustrated working paper are discussed later in this chapter.)
6. After the last analyzing entry is entered, the working paper is completed by adding the Analyzing Entries columns to determine their equality. The information as to sources and uses of working capital is then used to prepare the formal statement of changes in financial position.

In passing, it should be observed that the working paper is prepared solely for the purpose of bringing together information as to sources and uses of working capital. Its analyzing entries are never entered in the accounts.

Illustration 18–4

DELTA COMPANY
Working Paper for Statement of Changes in Financial Position
(Working Capital Basis)
For Year Ended December 31, 198B

	Account Balances 12/31/8A	Analyzing Entries Debit	Analyzing Entries Credit	Account Balances 12/31/8B
Debits				
Working capital	25,700			27,800
Office equipment	3,000	*(a)* 500		3,500
Store equipment.........................	21,000	*(b)* 6,000	*(c)* 800	26,200
Buildings	80,000	*(d)* 15,000		95,000
Land	25,000			25,000
Totals	154,700			177,500
Credits				
Accumulated depreciation, office equipment ..	600		*(f)* 300	900
Accumulated depreciation, store equipment ..	4,200	*(c)* 800	*(g)* 1,800	5,200
Accumulated depreciaiton, buildings	8,200		*(h)* 2,400	10,600
Mortgage payable........................	20,000	*(i)* 2,500		17,500
Common stock	100,000		*(j)* 5,000	115,000
			(k) 10,000	
Premium on common stock	5,000		*(j)* 1,000	8,500
			(k) 2,500	
Retained earnings	16,700	*(j)* 6,000	*(e)* 12,200	19,800
		(l) 3,100		
Totals	154,700			177,500
Sources of working capital:				
Current operations:				
Net income		*(e)* 12,200		
Depreciation of office equipment		*(f)* 300		
Depreciation of store equipment		*(g)* 1,800		
Depreciation of buildings		*(h)* 2,400		
Other sources:				
Sale of stock		*(k)* 12,500		
Uses of working capital:				
Purchase of office equipment			*(a)* 500	
Purchase of store equipment			*(b)* 6,000	
Addition to building			*(d)* 15,000	
Reduction of mortgage			*(i)* 2,500	
Declaration of dividends			*(l)* 3,100	
Totals		63,100	63,100	

Analyzing Entries

As previously stated, in addition to setting out sources and uses of working capital, the analyzing entries on the working paper also account for or explain the amount of change in each noncurrent account. The change in each noncurrent account is explained with one or more analyzing entries because every transaction that caused an increase or decrease in working capital also increased or decreased a noncurrent account. Consequently, when all increases and decreases in noncurrent accounts are explained by means of analyzing entries, all sources and uses of working capital are set out on the working paper.

The analyzing entries on the working paper of Illustration 18–4 account for the changes in Delta Company's noncurrent accounts and set out its sources and uses of working capital. Explanations of the entries follow:

a. During the year, Delta Company purchased new office equipment that cost $500. This required the use of working capital and also caused a $500 increase in the balance of its Office Equipment account. Consequently, analyzing entry (a) has a $500 debit to Office Equipment and a like credit to "Uses of working capital: Purchase of office equipment." The debit accounts for the change in the Office Equipment account, and the credit sets out the use of working capital.

b. Delta Company purchased $6,000 of new store equipment during the period. This required the use of $6,000 of working capital, and the use is set out with analyzing entry (b). However, the $6,000 debit of the entry does not fully account for the change in the balance of the Store Equipment account. Analyzing entry (c) is also needed.

c. During the period under review, Delta Company discarded and junked fully depreciated store equipment. The equipment originally had cost $800, and the entry made to record the disposal decreased the company's Store Equipment and related accumulated depreciation accounts by $800. However, the disposal had no effect on the company's working capital. Nevertheless, analyzing entry (c) must be made to account for the changes in the accounts. Otherwise all changes in the company's noncurrent accounts will not be explained. Unless all changes are explained, the person preparing the working paper cannot be certain that all sources and uses of working capital have been set out on the working paper.

d. Delta Company used $15,000 to increase the size of its building. The cost of the addition was debited to the Buildings account, and analyzing entry (d) sets out this use of working capital.

e. Delta Company reported a $12,200 net income for 198B, and the income was a source of working capital. In the end-of-year closing procedures, the amount of this net income was transferred from the company's Income Summary account to its Retained Earnings account. It helped change the balance of the latter account from $16,700 at the beginning of the year to $19,800 at the year-end. Observe the analyzing entry that sets out this source of working capital. The entry's debit sets out the net income as a source of working capital, and the credit helps explain the change in the Retained Earnings account.

f. *(g)*, and *(h)*. On its 198B income statement, Delta Company deducted $300 of depreciation expense on its office equipment, $1,800 on its store equipment, and $2,400 on its building. As previously explained, although depreciation is a rightful deduction from revenues in arriving at net income, any depreciation so deducted must be added to net income in determining working capital from operations. The debits of entries *(f)*, *(g)*, and *(h)* show the depreciation taken by the company as part of the working capital generated by operations. The credits of the entries either account for or help account for the changes in the accumulated depreciation accounts.

i. On June 10, Delta Company made a $2,500 payment on the mortgage on its plant and equipment. The payment required the use of working capital, and it reduced the balance of the Mortgage Payable account by $2,500. Entry *(i)* sets out this use of working capital and accounts for the change in the Mortgage Payable account.

j. At the September board meeting, the directors of the company declared a 5% or 500-share stock dividend on a day the company's stock was selling at $12 per share. The declaration and later distribution of this dividend had no effect on the company's working capital. However, it did decrease Retained Earnings by $6,000 and increase the Common Stock account by $5,000 and increase the Premium on Common Stock account by $1,000. Entry *(j)* accounts for the changes in the accounts resulting from the dividend.

k. In October, the company sold and issued 1,000 shares of its common stock for cash at $12.50 per share. The sale was a source of working capital that increased the balance of the company's Common Stock account by $10,000 and the balance of its Premium on Common Stock account by $2,500. Entry *(k)* sets out this source of working capital and completes the explanation of the changes in the stock and premium accounts.

l. At the end of each of the first three quarters in the year, the company declared a $700 quarterly cash dividend. Then, on December 22, it declared a $1,000 dividend, payable on the following January 15. The fourth dividend brought the total cash dividends declared during the year to $3,100. Each declaration required the use of working capital, and each reduced the balance of the Retained Earnings account. On the working paper, the four dividends are combined and one analyzing entry is made for the $3,100 use of working capital. The entry's debit helps account for the change in the balance of the Retained Earnings account, and its credit sets out the use of working capital.

After the last analyzing entry is entered on the working paper, an examination is made to be certain that all changes in the noncurrent accounts listed on the paper have been explained with analyzing entries. To make this examination, the debits and credits in the Analyzing Entries columns opposite each beginning account balance are added to or subtracted from the beginning balance. The result must equal the ending balance. For example, the $3,000 beginning debit balance of office equipment plus the $500 debit of analyzing entry (a) equals the $3,500 ending amount of office equipment. Likewise, the $21,000 beginning balance of store equipment plus the $6,000 debit and minus the $800 credit equals the $26,200 ending balance for this asset, and so on down the working paper until all changes are accounted for. Then, if in every case the debits and credits opposite each beginning balance explain the change in the balance, all sources and uses of working capital have been set out on the working paper and the working paper is completed by adding the amounts in its Analyzing Entries columns.

Preparing the Statement of Changes in Financial Position from the Working Paper

After the working paper is completed, the sources and uses of working capital set out on the bottom of the paper are used to prepare the formal statement of changes in financial position. This is a simple task that requires little more than a relisting of the sources and uses of working capital on the formal statement. A comparison of the items appearing on the statement of Illustration 18–2 with the items at the bottom of the working paper of Illustration 18–4 will show this.

A Net Loss on the Working Paper

When a business incurs a net loss, the amount of the loss is debited to its Retained Earnings account in the end-of-period closing procedures. Then, when the working paper for the statement of changes in financial position is prepared, the words *Net loss* are substituted for *Net income* in its sources of working capital section. The amount of the loss is then debited to Retained Earnings and credited to "Net loss" on the working paper. After this, the loss is placed on the formal statement of changes in financial position as the first monetary item and the expenses not requiring outlays of working capital are deducted therefrom. If the net loss is less than these expenses, the resulting amount is working capital provided by operations. If the net loss exceeds these expenses, the result is working capital used in operations.

BROAD CONCEPT OF FINANCING AND INVESTING ACTIVITIES

The APB held that a statement of changes in financial position should be based on a broad concept of the financing and investing activities of a business. Also, it should disclose all important aspects of such activities even though elements of working capital are not directly affected.[2] For example, the acquisition of a building in exchange for a mortgage or the conversion of bonds to stock are transactions that do not directly affect elements of working capital. However, the Board has held that such transactions should be disclosed on the statement of changes in financial position even though working capital is not directly involved. For example, if a building is acquired by issuing a mortgage, the issuance of the mortgage should be disclosed on the statement as a source of working capital, "Mortgage issued to acquire building." Likewise the acquisition of the building should appear as a use of working capital, "Building acquired by issuing a mortgage."

STATEMENT OF CHANGES IN FINANCIAL POSITION, CASH BASIS

The primary purpose of a statement of changes in financial position is to show where a company acquired resources and where it applied or used resources. As previously mentioned, such statements may be designed to account for the change in working capital, or they may be designed to account for the change in cash. The terminology used in the statement should clearly indicate which basis is being emphasized. For example, when the cash basis is used, terminology such as "Cash provided by operations" should be used rather than "Working capital provided by operations."

The procedures for preparing a statement of changes in financial position on a cash basis are similar to the ones used when the statement is prepared on a working capital basis. The only differences relate to the working capital accounts.

When the cash basis is used, the noncash working capital items must be included among the potential sources and uses of cash. Thus, increases in current assets (other than Cash) represent uses of cash. Decreases in current assets (other than Cash) represent sources of cash. Conversely, increases in current liabilities represent increases in cash and decreases in current liabilities represent uses of cash.

---

[2] Ibid., par. 8.

Consider, for example, the noncash working capital accounts of Delta Company:

DELTA COMPANY
Analysis of Changes in Noncash Working Capital Items
For Year Ended December 31, 198B

	Dec. 31, 198B	Dec. 31, 198A	Effect on cash	
			Increases	Decreases
Current assets:				
Accounts receivable, net	$ 8,000	$ 9,500	$1,500	
Merchandise inventory	31,500	32,000	500	
Prepaid expenses	1,000	1,200	200	
Total current assets, excluding cash	$40,500	$42,700		
Current liabilities:				
Notes payable	$ 2,500	$ 1,500	1,000	
Accounts payable	16,700	19,600		$2,900
Dividends payable	1,000	700	300	
Total current liabilities	$20,200	$21,800		
Working capital, excluding cash	$20,300	$20,900		

Observe that the changes in five of the working capital items had the effect of increasing cash. Only one change, accounts payable, had the effect of decreasing cash. How should the changes in these noncash working capital items be shown on the statement?

Separating Material Items from the Net Change in Working Capital

One possibility would be to show each working capital change as a source or use of cash. However, many of these individual changes are small in amount. Even if a change appears material, it probably resulted from a large number of small transactions. Therefore, to avoid excessive detail, the changes in noncash working capital items may be lumped together and shown as a single source or use of cash. If, however, the amount of any particular item is thought to be material, it should be extracted and listed separately.

In evaluating the working capital items for Delta Company, the $1,500 change in Accounts Receivable and the $2,900 change in Accounts Payable may at first appear to be material. However, they probably resulted from many small transactions and should not be shown separately.

To illustrate how items may be extracted and listed separately, assume that the $1,000 increase in Notes Payable resulted from a single bank loan. Also, the $300 increase in Dividends Payable should be extracted, combined with the dividend declaration of $3,100, and shown as a $2,800 payment of dividends. Recall that dividend declarations use working capital and dividend payments do not. On a cash basis, it must be recognized that dividend declarations do not use cash and dividend payments do.

The necessary adjustments to Delta Company's working capital are as follows:

	Dec. 31, 198B	Dec. 31, 198A	Increase (decrease)
Total current assets, excluding cash............	$40,500	$42,700	
Total current liabilities	$20,200	$21,800	
Less:			
Notes payable	(2,500)	(1,500)	
Dividends payable.......................	(1,000)	(700)	
Total current liabilities, excluding notes payable and dividends payable	$16,700	$19,600	
Working capital, excluding cash, notes payable and dividends payable	$23,800	$23,100	$700

The net effect of the remaining working capital items is a $700 use of cash, that is, $23,800 − $23,100 = $700. In addition, the Notes Payable increase should be shown as a $1,000 source of cash and the payments of dividends should be shown as a $2,800 use of cash.

With this additional information, the statement of changes in financial position can be prepared. To highlight the differences between preparing the statement on a working capital basis and on a cash basis, the statement originally presented on a working capital basis in Illustration 18–2 is reproduced and modified to reflect a cash basis in Illustration 18–5. Each modification is shown in color.

Disclosure of Increases (or Decreases) in Working Capital Items

In Illustration 18–5, observe that the "increases in working capital" is shown as an adjustment to net income in the calculation of cash provided by operations. Some companies may show this item among "Uses of cash" or, if positive, among "Other sources" of cash. However, most working capital item changes represent differences between revenue and expense items on an accrual basis and revenue and expense items on a cash basis. Therefore, on a statement of changes in financial position (cash basis), the change in working capital should be shown as an addition to or subtraction from net income when calculating cash provided by operations.

For example, suppose that Delta Company's Sales revenue for 198B was $50,000. This amount would have appeared on the 198B income

Illustration 18–5

DELTA COMPANY
Statement of Changes in Financial Position
For Year Ended December 31, 198B

Sources of cash:		
Current operations:		
Net income	$12,200	
Add expenses not requiring outlays of cash in the current period:		
Depreciation of buildings and equipment	4,500	
Subtract increases in working capital (excluding cash, notes payable, and dividends payable)	(700)	
Cash provided by operations	$16,000	
Other sources:		
Sales of common stock	12,500	
Increase in notes payable	1,000	
Total sources of cash		$29,500
Uses of cash:		
Purchase of office equipment	$ 500	
Purchase of store equipment	6,000	
Addition to building	15,000	
Reduction of mortgage debt	2,500	
Payment of dividends	2,800	
Total uses of cash		26,800
Net increase in cash		$ 2,700

statement that resulted in a net income of $12,200. Recall that Accounts Receivable (net) decreased from $9,500 at the end of 198A to $8,000 at the end of 198B. This means that the cash generated from sales to customers was $50,000 + $1,500 = $51,500. In a similar manner, the expenses on the income statement could be converted to a cash basis by adjusting them for changes in merchandise inventory, prepaid expenses, and accounts payable. Whether the changes in these working capital items are listed separately or shown as a single item, they are most appropriately included in the calculation of cash provided by operations.

PREPARING THE WORKING PAPER

Illustration 18–6 shows Delta Company's working paper for a statement of changes in financial position on a cash basis. Compare Illustration 18–4 and Illustration 18–5 and observe the differences. Instead of aggregating all of the working capital items on a single line (as is done in Illustration 18–4), each current asset and current liability is listed separately in Illustration 18–6.

Illustration 18–6

DELTA COMPANY
Working Paper for Statement of Changes in Financial Position
(Cash Basis)
For Year Ended December 31, 198B

	Account Balances 12/31/8A	Analyzing Entries Debit	Analyzing Entries Credit	Account Balances 12/31/8B
Debits				
Cash	4,800			7,500
Accounts receivable, net	9,500		(m) 1,500	8,000
Merchandise inventory	32,000		(n) 500	31,500
Prepaid expenses	1,200		(o) 200	1,000
Office equipment	3,000	(a) 500		3,500
Store equipment	21,000	(b) 6,000	(c) 800	26,200
Buildings	80,000	(d) 15,000		95,000
Land	25,000			25,000
Totals	176,500			197,700
Credits				
Notes payable	1,500		(p) 1,000	2,500
Accounts payable	19,600	(q) 2,900		16,700
Dividends payable	700		(r) 300	1,000
Accumulated depreciation, office equipment ..	600		(f) 300	900
Accumulated depreciation, store equipment ..	4,200	(c) 800	(g) 1,800	5,200
Accumulated depreciation, buildings	8,200		(h) 2,400	10,600
Mortgage payable	20,000	(i) 2,500		17,500
Common stock	100,000		(j) 5,000	115,000
			(k) 10,000	
Premium on common stock	5,000		(j) 1,000	8,500
			(k) 2,500	
Retained earnings	16,700	(j) 6,000	(e) 12,200	19,800
		(l) 3,100		
Totals	176,500			197,700
Sources of cash:				
Current operations:				
Net income		(e) 12,200		
Depreciation of office equipment		(f) 300		
Depreciation of store equipment		(g) 1,800		
Depreciation of buildings		(h) 2,400		
Increases (decreases) in working capital (excluding cash, notes payable, and dividends payable)		(m) 1,500	(q) 2,900	
		(n) 500		
		(o) 200		
Other sources:				
Sale of stock		(k) 12,500		
Increase in notes payable		(p) 1,000		
Uses of cash:				
Purchase of office equipment			(a) 500	
Purchase of store equipment			(b) 6,000	
Addition to building			(d) 15,000	
Reduction of mortgage			(i) 2,500	
Payment of dividends		(r) 300	(l) 3,100	
Totals		69,500	69,500	

The analyzing entries in Illustration 18–4 are repeated in Illustration 18–6 and have been assigned the same identifying letters *(a)* through *(l)*. Illustration 18–6 also contains additional analyzing entries *(m)* through *(r)* to explain the change in each working capital item except cash. Note that the analyzing entries for accounts receivable *(m)*, merchandise inventory *(n)*, prepaid expenses *(o)*, and accounts payable *(q)* result in a single item "Increase (decrease) in working capital. . . ." This item is listed in the "Sources of cash, Current operations" category.

The completed working paper in Illustration 18–6 contains all of the necessary information to prepare the statement of changes in financial position as shown in Illustration 18–5.

USING A CASH PLUS TEMPORARY INVESTMENTS BASIS

If a statement of changes in financial position is designed to explain the change in cash plus temporary investments, only minor modifications to the statement and working paper are necessary. The cash and temporary investment balances are added and treated as a single item. All other working capital items are listed separately on the working paper and analyzed in exactly the same manner as if a cash basis is used.

GLOSSARY

Funds. Relatively liquid resources that are or soon will be available to meet the needs of the business; defined as cash, or cash plus investments, or working capital.

Net working capital. A synonym for working capital.

Source of working capital. A transaction that increases working capital.

Statement of changes in financial position. A statement that reports the financing and investing activities of a business during a period, generally indicating their effects on working capital, or cash, or cash plus temporary investments.

Use of working capital. A transaction that decreased working capital.

Working capital. The excess of a company's current assets over its current liabilities.

QUESTIONS FOR CLASS DISCUSSION

1. What are three different meanings of the word *funds?*
2. List several sources of working capital and several uses of working capital.
3. Explain why such expenses as depreciation, amortization of patents, and amortization of bond discount are added to the net income in order to determine working capital provided by operations.

4. Some people speak of depreciation as a source of funds. Is depreciation a source of funds?

5. On May 14, a company borrowed $30,000 by giving its bank a 60-day, interest-bearing note. Was this transaction a source of working capital?

6. A company began an accounting period with a $90,000 merchandise inventory and ended it with a $50,000 inventory. Was the decrease in inventory a source of working capital?

7. What is shown on a statement of changes in financial position?

8. Why are the noncurrent accounts examined to discover changes in working capital?

9. When a working paper for the preparation of a statement of changes in financial position is prepared, all changes in noncurrent balance sheet accounts are accounted for on the working paper. Why?

10. Under what conditions are the changes in working capital items shown on a statement of changes in financial position?

11. A company discarded and wrote off fully depreciated store equipment. What account balances appearing on the statement of changes in financial position working paper were affected by the write-off? What analyzing entry was made on the working paper to account for the write-off? If the write-off did not affect working capital, why was the analyzing entry made on the working paper?

12. Explain why a decrease in a current liability represents an increase in working capital.

13. Under what conditions should (a) declarations of dividends and (b) payments of dividends appear on the statement of changes in financial position?

CLASS EXERCISES

Exercise 18–1   Given the following condensed income statement, calculate the working capital provided by operations:

WESTWOOD CORPORATION
Income Statement for Year Ended December 31, 198A

Sales		$900,000
Cost of goods sold		520,000
Gross profit from sales		$380,000
Operating expenses:		
Salaries and wages (including $1,000 accrued)	$125,000	
Depreciation expense	15,000	
Rent expense	36,000	
Amortization of patents	3,000	
Bad debts expense (allowance method)	4,000	183,000
Operating income		$197,000
Bond interest expense (including $6,000 accrued and $1,500 of bond discount amortized)		13,500
Net income		$183,500

Exercise 18–2   From the following list of transactions completed by Columbia Shipping during 198B, prepare a statement of changes in financial position designed to explain the change in working capital.

a. Columbia Shipping earned $250,000 net income during 198B.
b. Issued a five-year note payable in the amount of $300,000 and paid $80,000 in cash for a new computerized reservations system.
c. Declared cash dividends totaling $25,000 during the year.
d. Depreciation totaled $140,000 on all depreciable assets.
e. Purchased on-line computer terminals costing $75,000.
f. Purchased miscellaneous equipment totaling $84,000.
g. Made mortgage payments of $136,000.
h. Sold and issued 10,000 shares of common stock at $11.30 per share.

Exercise 18–3   Use the information provided in Exercise 18–2 plus the following information on Columbia Shipping's current asset and current liability accounts to prepare a statement of changes in financial position designed to explain the change in cash.

	Dec. 31, 198B	Dec. 31, 198A
Cash	$ 59,000	$24,000
Accounts receivable, net	116,000	75,000
Prepaid expenses	12,000	7,000
Accounts payable	35,000	51,000
Dividends payable	–0–	6,000

Exercise 18–4   The 198B and 198A trial balances of Kit Corporation follow. From the information, prepare an analysis of changes in working capital items for 198B.

	198B		198A	
Cash	$ 10,000		$ 15,000	
Notes receivable	5,000		3,000	
Accounts receivable, net	25,000		30,000	
Merchandise inventory	55,000		50,000	
Prepaid expenses	2,000		1,000	
Equipment	109,000		250,000	
Accumulated depreciation, equipment		$ 25,000		$ 20,000
Notes payable		10,000		8,000
Accounts payable		18,000		20,000
Taxes payable		4,000		5,000
Wages payable		2,000		1,000
Mortgage payable (due 199C)		25,000		25,000
Common stock		100,000		100,000
Retained earnings		22,000		170,000
Totals	$206,000	$206,000	$349,000	$349,000

Exercise 18–5   Carpet Company's 198B and 198A balance sheets carried the following items:

	December 31	
	198B	*198A*
Debits		
Cash	$10,500	$ 4,000
Accounts receivable, net	8,000	9,000
Merchandise inventory	21,000	18,000
Equipment	18,000	15,000
Totals.......................	$57,500	$46,000
Credits		
Accumulated depreciation, equipment ..	$ 4,000	$ 3,000
Accounts payable	7,000	5,000
Taxes payable	1,000	2,000
Dividends payable	1,500	–0–
Common stock, $10 par value	27,000	25,000
Premium on common stock...........	6,000	5,000
Retained earnings	11,000	6,000
Totals.......................	$57,500	$46,000

Required:

   Prepare a statement of changes in financial position working paper that is designed to explain the changes in working capital, and prepare the formal statement. Also prepare an analysis of changes in working capital items. Use the following information from the company's 198B income statement and accounts:

a. The company earned $10,000 during 198B.
b. Its equipment depreciated $1,500 in 198B.
c. Equipment costing $3,500 was purchased.
d. Fully depreciated equipment that cost $500 was discarded and its cost and accumulated depreciation were removed from the accounts.
e. Two hundred shares of stock were sold and issued at $15 per share.
f. The company declared $5,000 of cash dividends during the year and paid $3,500.

Exercise 18–6   Use the information provided in Exercise 18–5 to prepare a working paper for a statement of changes in financial position that is designed to explain the change in cash.

PROBLEMS

Problem 18–1   Zandu Company's 198B and 198A balance sheets carried these items:

	December 31	
	198B	*198A*
Debits		
Cash	$ 8,400	$ 4,300
Accounts receivable, net	8,000	10,000
Merchandise inventory	31,500	32,000
Prepaid expenses	1,000	1,200
Equipment	30,100	24,000
Totals.......................	$79,000	$71,500

	December 31	
	198B	*198A*
Credits		
Accumulated depreciation, equipment ..	$ 6,100	$ 4,800
Accounts payable	14,300	17,900
Notes payable (short-term)	2,500	1,500
Mortgage payable	6,000	10,000
Common stock, $10 par value	30,000	25,000
Premium on common stock...........	2,500	
Retained earnings	17,600	12,300
Totals.......................	$79,000	$71,500

Required:

Prepare a statement of changes in financial position working paper and a formal statement that are designed to explain the change in working capital. Also prepare an analysis of changes in working capital items. Use the following additional information from the company's 198B income statement and accounting records:

a. Net income for the year, $8,300.
b. The equipment depreciated $2,100 during the year.
c. Fully depreciated equipment that cost $800 was discarded, and its cost and accumulated depreciation were removed from the accounts.
d. Equipment costing $6,900 was purchased.
e. The mortgage was reduced by a $4,000 payment.
f. Five hundred shares of common stock were issued at $15 per share.
g. Cash dividends totaling $3,000 were declared and paid.

Problem 18–2   Iris Company's 198B and 198A balance sheets carried these items:

	December 31	
	198B	*198A*
Debits		
Cash	$ 12,700	$ 11,800
Accounts receivable, net	34,900	33,400
Merchandise inventory	85,900	86,700
Other current assets	2,000	1,800
Office equipment	5,400	6,100
Store equipment	31,700	27,800
Totals	$172,600	$167,600
Credits		
Accumulated depreciation, office equipment ..	$ 2,500	$ 2,400
Accumulated depreciation, store equipment ..	7,400	6,500
Accounts payable........................	19,500	23,700
Notes payable (short-term)	4,500	–0–
Federal income taxes payable	3,500	2,300
Dividends payable	–0–	2,500
Common stock, $5 par value	105,000	100,000
Premium on common stock	8,500	5,500
Retained earnings	21,700	24,700
Totals	$172,600	$167,600

An examination of the company's statements and accounts showed:

a. A $15,000 net income was earned in 198B.
b. Depreciation charged on office equipment, $600; and on store equipment, $1,500.
c. Office equipment that had cost $700 and had been depreciated $500 was sold for its book value.
d. Store equipment costing $4,500 was purchased.
e. Fully depreciated store equipment that cost $600 was discarded, and its cost and accumulated depreciation were removed from the accounts.
f. Cash dividends totaling $10,000 were declared during the year.
g. A 1,000-share stock dividend was declared and distributed during the year at a time the company's stock was selling at $8 per share.

Required:

Prepare a statement of changes in financial position working paper and a formal statement of changes in financial position for the company. The statement should be designed to explain the change in working capital. Also prepare an analysis of changes in working capital items.

Problem 18–3

Refer to the information provided in problem 18–2. In that problem, the increase in Notes Payable resulted from Iris Company's borrowing of $4,500 from the bank in late December 198B.

Required:

1. Prepare a schedule showing the 198B change in Iris Company's working capital, excluding cash, notes payable, and dividends payable.
2. Prepare a working paper for a statement of changes in financial position that is designed to explain the change in cash. Also prepare the formal statement. The short-term bank loan should be disclosed separately on the statement.

Problem 18–4

Doris May, as a single proprietor, operates May's Craft Store. The store's balance sheets at the end of 198B and 198A carried this information:

	December 31	
	198B	*198A*
Debits		
Cash	$ 9,700	$ 6,400
Accounts receivable, net	16,800	17,200
Merchandise inventory	36,400	33,700
Other current assets	500	800
Store equipment	13,100	8,400
Totals	$76,500	$66,500
Credits		
Accumulated depreciation, store equipment	$ 1,800	$ 3,200
Accounts payable	14,200	16,800
Doris May, capital	60,500	46,500
Totals	$76,500	$66,500

The 198B statement showing changes in the proprietor's Capital account carried the following information:

Doris May, capital, January 1, 198B		$46,500
Add additional investment		5,000
Total investment		$51,500
Net income per income statement	$15,000	
Less withdrawals	6,000	
Excess of income over withdrawals ...		9,000
Doris May, capital, December 31, 198B		$60,500

The store equipment accounts showed: (1) $1,200 depreciation expense on store equipment recorded in 198B; (2) store equipment costing $4,800 was purchased; (3) equipment carried on the books on the day of its exchange at its $2,800 cost, less $2,400 accumulated depreciation, was traded on new equipment having a $2,900 cash price, and a $400 trade-in allowance was received; and (4) fully depreciated equipment that cost $200 was junked and its cost and accumulated depreciation were removed from the accounts.

Required:

Prepare a statement of changes in financial position working paper and a formal statement of changes in financial position. Both should be designed to explain the change in working capital. Also prepare an analysis of changes in working capital items.

Problem 18–5

The debit and credit amounts from B-G Corporation's 198B and 198A balance sheets and its noncurrent accounts follow:

	December 31	
	198B	*198A*
Debits		
Cash.....................................	$ 19,900	$ 22,900
Accounts receivable, net	30,400	32,100
Merchandise inventory	55,100	56,400
Prepaid expenses	1,900	1,700
Store equipment	40,400	32,800
Land.....................................	30,000	30,000
Building	181,000	112,500
Totals	$358,700	$288,400
Credits		
Accumulated depreciation, store equipment ..	$ 16,200	$ 13,700
Accumulated depreciation, building	23,600	20,200
Accounts payable	25,700	24,600
Wages payable	2,100	1,800
Income taxes payable....................	4,100	4,200
Mortgage interest payable	1,000	
Cash dividends payable	5,000	7,500
Mortgage payable	50,000	
Common stock, $10 par value	150,000	150,000
Premium on common stock	18,000	15,000
Stock dividend distributable	7,500	
Retained earnings	55,500	51,400
Totals	$358,700	$288,400

Store Equipment

Date		Explanation	Debit	Credit	Balance
198B					
Jan.	1	Balance			32,800
Apr.	4	Purchased new equipment	8,700		41,500
	7	Discarded equipment		1,100	40,400

Accumulated Depreciation, Store Equipment

Date		Explanation	Debit	Credit	Balance
198B					
Jan.	1	Balance			13,700
Apr.	7	Discarded equipment	1,100		12,600
Dec.	31	Year's depreciation		3,600	16,200

Land

Date		Explanation	Debit	Credit	Balance
198B					
Jan.	1	Balance			30,000

Building

Date		Explanation	Debit	Credit	Balance
198B					
Jan.	1	Balance			112,500
Mar.	17	Building addition	68,500		181,000

Accumulated Depreciation, Building

Date		Explanation	Debit	Credit	Balance
198B					
Jan.	1	Balance			20,200
Dec.	31	Year's depreciation		3,400	23,600

Mortgage Payable

Date		Explanation	Debit	Credit	Balance
198B					
Mar.	15	Issuance of mortgage		50,000	50,000

Common Stock

Date		Explanation	Debit	Credit	Balance
198B Jan.	1	Balance			150,000

Premium on Common Stock

Date		Explanation	Debit	Credit	Balance
198B Jan.	1	Balance			15,000
Dec.	23	Stock dividend		3,000	18,000

Stock Dividend Distributable

Date		Explanation	Debit	Credit	Balance
198B Dec.	23	Stock dividend		7,500	7,500

Retained Earnings

Date		Explanation	Debit	Credit	Balance
198B Jan.	1	Balance			51,400
Dec.	23	Stock dividend	10,500		40,900
	23	Cash dividend	5,000		35,900
	31	Net income		19,600	55,500

Required:

Prepare a statement of changes in financial position working paper and a formal statement of changes in financial position. They should be designed to explain the change in B-G Corporation's working capital. Also prepare an analysis of changes in working capital items.

Problem 18–6   Refer to the information about B-G Corporation presented in Problem 18–5.

Required:

1. Prepare a schedule showing the 198B change in B-G Corporation's working capital, excluding cash and cash dividends payable.
2. Prepare a working paper for a statement of changes in financial position on a cash basis. Also prepare the formal statement.

ALTERNATE PROBLEMS

Problem 18–1A The December 31, 198B, and 198A balance sheets of Anchor, Inc., carried the following items:

	December 31	
	198B	*198A*
Assets		
Cash	$ 10,500	$ 7,200
Accounts receivable, net	12,750	14,250
Merchandise inventory	47,250	48,000
Prepaid expenses	1,500	1,800
Equipment..........................	45,150	36,000
Accumulated depreciation, equipment ...	(9,150)	(7,200)
Total assets	$108,000	$100,050
Liabilities and Stockholders' Equity		
Notes payable	$ 3,750	$ 2,250
Accounts payable	21,450	26,850
Mortgage payable	9,000	15,000
Common stock, $7.50 par value	45,000	37,500
Premium on common stock	3,750	
Retained earnings	25,050	18,450
Total liabilities and stockholders' equity .	$108,000	$100,050

The company's 198B income statement and accounts revealed the following:

a. Net income for the year, $11,100.
b. The equipment depreciated $3,150 during the year.
c. Fully depreciated equipment that cost $1,200 was discarded, and its cost and accumulated depreciation were removed from the accounts.
d. Equipment costing $10,350 was purchased.
e. The mortgage was reduced by a $6,000 payment.
f. One thousand shares of common stock were issued at $11.25 per share.
g. Cash dividends totaling $4,500 were declared and paid.

Required:

Prepare a statement of changes in financial position working paper and a statement of changes in financial position. Design the working paper and statement to explain the change in working capital. Also prepare an analysis of changes in working capital items.

Problem 18–2A The 198B and 198A balance sheets of Whisper Corporation carried these items:

	December 31	
	198B	198A
Debits		
Cash	$ 16,200	$ 12,600
Accounts receivable, net	29,100	32,900
Merchandise inventory	85,200	86,400
Prepaid expenses.......................	1,500	1,800
Office equipment	5,000	5,600
Store equipment	29,800	28,300
Totals	$166,800	$167,600
Credits		
Accumulated depreciation, office equipment..	$ 2,600	$ 2,400
Accumulated depreciation, store equipment ..	7,500	6,500
Accounts payable.......................	18,400	21,100
Notes payable (short-term)................	10,000	5,000
Dividends payable	4,000	2,400
Common stock, $10 par value.............	110,000	100,000
Premium on common stock	6,500	5,500
Retained earnings	7,800	24,700
Totals	$166,800	$167,600

Required:

Use the following additional information and prepare a statement of changes in financial position working paper and a statement of changes in financial position. They should be designed to explain the change in working capital. Also prepare an analysis of changes in working capital items.

a. The company suffered a $1,900 net loss during 198B.
b. Depreciation expense charged on office equipment during the year, $500; and on store equipment, $1,700.
c. Office equipment carried at its $600 cost less $300 accumulated depreciation was sold at its book value.
d. Store equipment costing $2,200 was purchased.
e. Fully depreciated store equipment that cost $700 was discarded, and its cost and accumulated depreciation were removed from the accounts.
f. Cash dividends totaling $4,000 were declared during the year.
g. A 1,000-share stock dividend was declared and distributed. On the declaration date the company's shares were selling at $11 each.

Problem 18–3A   Refer to the information provided in Problem 18–2A. In that problem the increase in Notes Payable resulted from Whisper Corporation's borrowing of $5,000 from the bank in late December 198B.

Required:

1. Prepare a schedule showing the 198B change in Whisper Corporation's working capital, excluding cash, notes payable, and dividends payable.
2. Prepare a working paper for a statement of changes in financial position that is designed to explain the change in cash. Also prepare the formal statement. The short-term bank loan should be disclosed separately on the statement.

Problem 18–4A   The 198B and 198A balance sheets of Windfoil Company carried the following debit and credit amounts:

	December 31	
	198B	*198A*
Debits		
Cash	$ 16,100	$ 22,300
Accounts receivable, net	16,200	15,600
Merchandise inventory	50,200	51,400
Prepaid expenses	1,300	1,100
Store equipment	26,000	24,300
Office equipment	4,400	4,200
Land	20,000	
Building	100,000	
Totals	$234,200	$118,900
Credits		
Accumulated depreciation, store equipment ..	$ 5,200	$ 3,600
Accumulated depreciation, office equipment..	1,400	1,300
Accumulated depreciation, building	1,200	
Accounts payable	17,300	18,700
Taxes payable	4,400	4,100
Mortgage payable	80,000	
Common stock, $10 par value	100,000	80,000
Premium on common stock	4,000	
Retained earnings	20,700	11,200
Totals	$234,200	$118,900

An examination of the company's 198B income statement and accounting records showed:

a. A $15,500 net income for the year.
b. Depreciation on store equipment, $2,400; on office equipment, $400; and on the building, $1,200.
c. Store equipment that cost $2,500 was purchased during the year.
d. Fully depreciated store equipment that cost $800 was discarded and its cost and accumulated depreciation were removed from the accounts.
e. Office equipment that cost $500 and had been depreciated $300 was traded in on new office equipment priced at $700. A $200 trade-in allowance was received.
f. During the year, the company purchased the land and building it occupied and had previously rented, paying $40,000 in cash and giving a 20-year mortgage for the balance.
g. Two thousand shares of common stock were issued at $12 per share.
h. Cash dividends totaling $6,000 were declared during the year.

Required:

Prepare a statement of changes in financial position working paper and a formal statement of changes in financial position. Both should be designed to explain the changes in working capital. Also prepare an analysis of changes in working capital items.

Problem 18–5A   The Farwood Company's December 31, 198B, and 198A balance sheet accounts reveal the following:

	December 31	
	198B	*198A*
Debits		
Cash....................................	$ 29,900	$ 26,100
Accounts receivable, net	57,200	46,500
Merchandise inventory	71,400	88,800
Prepaid expenses	6,500	9,100
Store equipment	37,700	35,200
Land.....................................	50,000	50,000
Building	160,000	126,000
Totals	$412,700	$381,700
Credits		
Accumulated depreciation, store equipment ..	$ 13,200	$ 15,500
Accumulated depreciation, building	54,000	42,000
Accounts payable	41,600	46,700
Wages payable	4,400	6,600
Income taxes payable.....................	12,800	9,500
Mortgage interest payable	1,200	–0–
Cash dividends payable	7,000	4,000
Mortgage payable	15,000	–0–
Common stock, $10 par value	80,000	80,000
Premium on common stock................	20,000	16,000
Stock dividend distributable................	8,000	–0–
Retained earnings	155,500	161,400
Totals	$412,700	$381,700

An investigation of the 198B changes in the noncurrent accounts provides the following information:

Store Equipment:
Beginning balance	$ 35,200
Purchase of new equipment	8,500
Discarded equipment	(6,000)
Ending balance	$ 37,700

Accumulated Depreciation, Store Equipment:
Beginning balance	$ 15,500
Discarded equipment	(6,000)
Depreciation for 198B....................	3,700
Ending balance	$ 13,200

Land:
Beginning balance	$ 50,000

Building:
Beginning balance	$126,000
Building addition........................	34,000
Ending balance	$160,000

Accumulated Depreciation, Building:
Beginning balance .... $ 42,000
Depreciation for 198B 12,000
Ending balance .... $ 54,000

Mortgage Payable:
Beginning balance .... $ –0–
Loan to finance building 15,000
Ending balance .... $ 15,000

Common Stock:
Beginning and ending balance .... $ 80,000

Premium on Common Stock:
Beginning balance .... $ 16,000
Stock dividend 4,000
Ending balance .... $ 20,000

Stock Dividend Distributable:
Beginning balance .... $ –0–
Stock dividend 8,000
Ending balance .... $ 8,000

Retained Earnings:
Beginning balance $161,400
Stock dividend .... (12,000)
Cash dividend .... (28,000)
Net income 34,100
Ending balance $155,500

Required:

Prepare a statement of changes in financial position working paper and a formal statement of changes in financial position. They should be designed to explain the change in Farwood Company's working capital. Also prepare an analysis of changes in working capital items.

Problem 18–6A   Refer to the information about Farwood Company presented in Problem 18–5A.

Required:

1. Prepare a schedule showing the 198B change in Farwood Company's working capital, excluding cash and cash dividends payable.
2. Prepare a working paper for a statement of changes in financial position on a cash basis. Also prepare the formal statement.

PROVOCATIVE PROBLEMS

Provocative Problem 18–1, Lonestar Products   At the end of 198B, the accountant of Lonestar Products prepared the following analysis of changes in working capital accounts, statement of changes in financial position, and income statement for the store's owner, Mike Linder:

Analysis of Changes in Working Capital Items
For Year Ended December 31, 198B

	Dec. 31, 198B	Dec. 31, 198A	Working Capital Increases	Working Capital Decreases
Current assets:				
Cash	$ 3,000	$15,000		$12,500
Accounts receivable	38,000	32,000	$ 6,000	
Merchandise inventory	35,000	25,000	10,000	
Prepaid expenses	1,000	500	500	
Total current assets	$77,000	$73,000		
Current liabilities:				
Notes payable	$ 5,000	$ –0–		5,000
Accounts payable	21,000	25,000	4,000	
Salaries and wages payable ..	1,000	2,000	1,000	
Total current liabilities ...	$27,000	$27,000		
Working capital	$50,000	$46,000		
			$21,500	$17,500
Increase in working capital				4,000
			$21,500	$21,500

Statement of Changes in Financial Position
For Year Ended December 31, 198B

Sources of working capital:
  Current operations:
    Net income $30,000
    Add depreciation of plant assets 12,000
      Total sources of working capital .. $42,000

Working capital was used for:
  Purchases of new plant assets $20,000
  Reduction of mortgage............... 6,000
  Personal withdrawals of proprietor 12,000
    Total uses of working capital   38,000
Increase in working capital .... $ 4,000

Comparative Income Statements
For Years Ended December 31, 198B, and 198A

	198B		198A	
Sales		$300,000		$250,000
Cost of goods sold:				
Inventory, January 1	$ 25,000		$ 30,000	
Purchases	190,000		150,000	
Goods for sale	$215,000		$180,000	
Inventory, December 31	35,000		25,000˙	
Cost of goods sold		180,000		155,000
Gross profit from sales		$120,000		$ 95,000
Operating expenses:				
Salaries and wages	$ 76,000		$ 69,000	
Depreciation of plant assets ...	12,000		9,500	
Insurance and supplies	2,000		1,500	
Total operating expenses ..		90,000		80,000
Net income		$ 30,000		$ 15,000

When Mr. Linder saw the income statement, he was amazed to learn that net income had doubled in 198B, and he could not understand how this could happen in a year in which cash had declined to the point that he had found it necessary in late December to secure a $5,000 short-term bank loan in order to meet current expenses. His accountant pointed to the statement of changes in financial position by way of explanation, but this statement only confused Mr. Linder further. He could not understand how depreciation could be a source of working capital, while a bank loan was not, and he could not understand how working capital could increase $4,000 at a time when cash decreased $12,500.

Explain the points Mr. Linder finds confusing. Attach to your explanation a statement of changes in financial position that explains the change in cash and a schedule that reconciles the change in working capital with the change in cash.

Provocative Problem 18–2, Waltrick Auto Parts

Terry Kowalczyk and Jack Deitrick own Waltrick Auto Parts. During 198B, they remodeled and replaced $30,000 of the store's fully depreciated equipment with new equipment costing $37,500. By the year-end, they were having trouble meeting the store's current expenses and had to secure a $9,000 short-term bank loan. To meet cash needs, Jack had to make an additional investment of $7,500 in the business. At the year-end, Terry, who manages the business, asked the Waltrick accountant to prepare a report that summarizes the financing and investing activities of the business. As a result, the accountant prepared the following statement:

WALTRICK AUTO PARTS
Statement of Changes in Financial Position
For Year Ended December 31, 198B

Sources of working capital:		
Income from operations	$26,550	
Depreciation on store equipment	7,500	
Additional investment by Deitrick	7,500	
New mortgage to purchase equipment	18,750	$60,300
Uses of working capital:		
Purchase of new equipment (financed in part by		
mortgage)	$37,500	
Personal withdrawals of partners	18,000	55,500
Net increase in working capital		$ 4,800

On reading the report, Jack was confused by the $4,800 increase in working capital in a year he knew his store's bank balance had decreased by $12,000. Also, he could not understand how depreciation was a source of working capital but the $9,000 bank loan was not. What should Terry say by way of explaining these points to Jack? Also, can you reconcile the difference between the $4,800 increase in working capital and the $12,000 decrease in cash? Finally, present a statement of changes in financial position that explains the change in cash.

The following post-closing trial balances were used by the accountant in preparing the store's statement of changes in financial position:

WALTRICK AUTO PARTS
198B and 198A Post-Closing Trial Balances

	Dec. 31, 198B		Dec. 31, 198A	
Cash	$ 3,750		$ 15,750	
Accounts receivable	26,400		21,450	
Allowance for doubtful accounts		$ 750		$ 450
Merchandise inventory	44,400		26,100	
Prepaid expenses	1,200		750	
Store equipment	67,500		60,000	
Accumulated depr., store equipment ..		16,500		39,000
Notes payable		9,000		
Accounts payable		15,000		17,250
Accrued payables		900		1,050
Mortgage payable (due 198F–8H)		18,750		
Terry Kowalczyk, capital		50,350		40,500
Jack Deitrick, capital		32,000		25,800
Totals	$143,250	$143,250	$124,050	$124,050

Accounting for Price-Level Changes

19

After studying Chapter 19, you should be able to:

Describe the effects of inflation on historical financial statements.

Explain how price-level changes are measured.

Tell how to construct both general and specific price-level indexes.

Describe the use of price indexes in constant dollar accounting.

Restate unit-of-money financial statements for general price-level changes.

Explain how purchasing power gains and losses arise and how they are computed and integrated into constant dollar financial statements.

State the differences between general price-level-adjusted costs and current values such as exit prices and current costs.

Explain what current costs measure and the use of recoverable amounts in current cost accounting.

Describe the reporting requirements of *FASB Statement No. 33*.

Define or explain the words and phrases listed in the chapter Glossary.

Perhaps all accountants agree that conventional financial statements provide useful information for making economic decisions. However, many accountants also agree that conventional financial statements fail to adequately account for the impact of price-level changes. Usually, this means a failure to adequately account for the impact of inflation. Indeed, this failure of conventional financial statements may sometimes even make the statements misleading. That is, the statements may imply certain facts that are inconsistent with the real state of affairs. As a result, decision makers may be inclined to make decisions that are inconsistent with their objectives.

In what ways do conventional financial statements fail to account for inflation? The general problem is that transactions are recorded in terms of the historical number of dollars received or paid. These amounts are not adjusted even though subsequent price changes may dramatically change the purchasing power of the dollars received or paid. For example, Old Company purchased 10 acres of land for $25,000. At the end of each accounting period thereafter, Old Company presented a balance sheet showing "Land, $25,000." Six years later, after inflation of 97%, New Company purchased 10 acres of land that was adjacent and nearly identical to Old Company's land. New Company paid $49,250 for the land. In comparing the conventional balance sheets of the two companies, which own identical pieces of property, the following balances are observed:

	Balance Sheets	
	Old Company	*New Company*
Land	$25,000	$49,250

Without knowing the details that underlie these balances, a statement reader is likely to conclude that New Company either has more land than does Old Company or that New Company's land is more valuable. But, both companies own 10 acres, which are identical in value. The entire difference between the prices paid by the two companies is explained by the 97% inflation between the two purchase dates. That is, $25,000 × 1.97 = $49,250.

The failure of conventional financial statements to adequately account for inflation also shows up in the income statement. For example, assume that in the previous example, machinery was purchased instead of land. Also, assume that the machinery of Old Company and New Company is identical except for age; it is being depreciated on a straight-line basis over a 10-year period, with no salvage value. As a result, the annual income statements of the two companies show the following:

Income Statements	Old Company	New Company
Depreciation expense, machinery	$2,500	$4,925

Although assets of equal value are being depreciated, the income statements show that New Company's depreciation expense is 97% higher than is Old Company's. And, if all other revenue and expense items are the same, Old Company will appear more profitable than New Company. This is inconsistent with the fact that both companies own the same machines that are subject to the same depreciation factors. Furthermore, although Old Company will appear more profitable, it must pay more income taxes due to the apparent extra profits. Old Company also may not recover the full replacement cost of its machinery through the sale of its product.

Some of the procedures used in conventional accounting tend to reduce the impact of price-level changes on the income statement. LIFO inventory pricing and accelerated depreciation are examples. However, these are only partial solutions, since they do not offset the impact on both the income statement and the balance sheet.

Because of these deficiencies in conventional accounting practices, accountants have devoted increasing attention to alternatives that make comprehensive adjustments for the effects of price-level changes. This chapter discusses the two that have received the greatest attention. The first alternative involves adjusting conventional financial statements for changes in the general level of prices. This is called *constant dollar accounting,* or *general price-level adjusted accounting.* Later, consideration is given to another alternative, *current cost accounting.* This makes adjustments for changes in the specific prices of the specific assets owned by the company.

UNDERSTANDING PRICE-LEVEL CHANGES

In one way or another, all readers of this book have experienced the effects of inflation, which is a general increase in the prices paid for goods and services. Of course, the prices of specific items do not all change at the same rate. Even when most prices are rising, the prices of some goods or services may be falling. For example, consider the following prices of four different items:

Item	Price/unit in 1983	Price/unit in 1984	Percent change
A	$1.00	$1.30	+30
B	2.00	2.20	+10
C	1.50	1.80	+20
D	3.00	2.70	−10
Totals	$7.50	$8.00	

What can be said to describe these price changes? One possibility is to state the percentage change in the price per unit of each item (see above). This information is very useful for some purposes. But, it does not show the average effect or impact of the price changes that occurred. A better indication of the average effect would be to determine the average increase in the per unit prices of the four items. Thus: $8.00/$7.50 − 1.00 = 6.7% average increase in per unit prices.[1] However, even this average probably fails to show the impact of the price changes on most individuals or businesses. It is a good indicator only if the typical buyer purchased an equal number of units of each item. But what if these items are typically purchased in the following ratio? For each unit of A purchased, 2 units of B, 5 units of C, and 1 unit of D are purchased. With a different number of each item being purchased, the impact of changing prices must take into account the typical quantity of each item purchased. Hence, the average change in the price of the A, B, C, D "market basket" would be calculated as follows:

Item	Units purchased	1983 prices		Units purchased	1984 prices	
A	1 unit	× $1.00 =	$ 1.00	1 unit	× $1.30 =	$ 1.30
B	2 units	× $2.00 =	4.00	2 units	× $2.20 =	4.40
C	5 units	× $1.50 =	7.50	5 units	× $1.80 =	9.00
D	1 unit	× $3.00 =	3.00	1 unit	× $2.70 =	2.70
Totals			$15.50			$17.40

Weighted-average price change = $17.40/$15.50 − 1.00 = 12%

It may now be said that the annual rate of inflation in the prices of these four items was 12%. Of course, not every individual and business will purchase these four items in exactly the same proportion of 1 unit of A, 2 units of B, 5 units of C, and 1 unit of D. As a consequence,

---

[1] Throughout this chapter amounts are rounded to the nearest $\frac{1}{10}$ percent or to the nearest full dollar.

the stated 12% inflation rate is only an approximation of the impact of price changes on each buyer. But if these proportions represent the typical buying pattern, the stated 12% inflation rate fairly reflects the inflationary impact on the average buyer.

CONSTRUCTION OF A PRICE INDEX

When the cost of purchasing a given market basket is determined for each of several periods, the results can be expressed as a *price index*. In constructing a price index, one year is arbitrarily selected as the "base" year. The cost of purchasing the market basket in that year is then assigned a value of 100. For example, suppose the cost of purchasing the A, B, C, D market basket in each year is:

```
1978 ......  $ 9.00
1979 ......   11.00
1980 ......   10.25
1981 ......   12.00
1982 ......   13.00
1983 ......   15.50
1984 ......   17.40
```

If 1981 is selected as the base year, then the $12 cost for 1981 is assigned a value of 100. The index number for each of the other years is then calculated and expressed as a percent of the base year's cost. For example, the index number for 1980 is 85, or ($10.25/$12.00 × 100 = 85). The index numbers for the remaining years are calculated in the same way. The entire price index for the years 1978 through 1984 is presented in Illustration 19–1.

Having constructed a price index for the A, B, C, D market basket, it is possible to make comparative statements about the cost of purchasing these items in various years. For example, it may be said that

Illustration 19–1

Year	Calculations of price level	Price index
1978	($9.00/$12.00) × 100 =	75
1979	($11.00/$12.00) × 100 =	92
1980	($10.25/$12.00) × 100 =	85
1981	($12.00/$12.00) × 100 =	100
1982	($13.00/$12.00) × 100 =	108
1983	($15.50/$12.00) × 100 =	129
1984	($17.40/$12.00) × 100 =	145

the price level in 1984 was 45% (145/100) higher than it was in 1981; the price level in 1984 was 34% (145/108) higher than it was in 1982; and 12% (145/129) higher than it was in 1983. Stated another way, it may be said that $1 in 1984 would purchase the same amount of A, B, C, D as would $0.69 in 1981 (100/145 = 0.69). Also, $1 in 1984 would purchase the same amount of A, B, C, D as would $0.52 in 1978 (75/145 = 0.52).

USING PRICE INDEX NUMBERS

In accounting, the most important use of a price index is to restate dollar amounts of cost that were paid in earlier years into the current price level. In other words, a specific dollar amount of cost in a previous year can be restated in terms of the comparable number of dollars that would be incurred if the cost were paid with dollars of the current amount of purchasing power. For example, suppose that $1,000 were paid in 1980 to purchase items A, B, C, D. Stated in terms of 1984 prices, that 1980 cost is $1,000 × (145/85) = $1,706. As another example, if $1,500 were paid for A, B, C, D in 1981, that 1981 cost, restated in terms of 1984 prices, is $1,500 × (145/100) = $2,175.

Note that the 1981 cost of $1,500 correctly states the number of monetary units (dollars) expended for items A, B, C, D in 1981. Also, the 1980 cost of $1,000 correctly states the units of money expended in 1980. And, these two costs can be added together to determine the cost for the two years, stated in terms of the historical number of monetary units (units of money) expended. However, in a very important way, the 1980 monetary units do not mean the same thing as do the 1981 monetary units. A dollar (one monetary unit) in 1980 represented a different amount of purchasing power than did a dollar in 1981. Both of these dollars represent different amounts of purchasing power than a dollar in 1984. If one intends to communicate the amount of purchasing power expended or incurred, the historical number of

Illustration 19–2

Year cost was incurred	Monetary units expended	Adjustment to 1981 dollars	Historical cost stated in 1981 dollars	Adjustment to 1984 dollars	Historical cost stated in 1984 dollars
1980	$1,000	1,000 × (100/85)	$1,176	1,176 × (145/100)	$1,706*
1981	1,500	—	1,500	1,500 × (145/100)	2,175
Total cost	$2,500		$2,676		$3,881

* Raised $1 to correct for rounding. An alternative calculation is $1,000 × (145/85) = $1,706.

monetary units must be adjusted so that they are stated in terms of dollars with the same amount of purchasing power. For example, the total amount of cost incurred during 1980 and 1981 could be stated in terms of the purchasing power of 1981 dollars, or stated in terms of the purchasing power of 1984 dollars. These calculations are presented in Illustration 19–2.

SPECIFIC VERSUS GENERAL PRICE-LEVEL INDEXES

Price changes and price-level indexes can be calculated for narrow groups of commodities or services, such as housing construction material costs; or for broader groups of items, such as all construction costs; or for very broad groups of items, such as all items produced in the economy. A *specific price-level index,* as for housing construction materials, indicates the changing purchasing power of a dollar spent for items in that specific category, that is, to pay for housing construction materials. A *general price-level index,* as for all items produced in the economy, indicates the changing purchasing power of a dollar, in general. Two general price-level indexes are the Consumer Price Index for All Urban Consumers (prepared by the Bureau of Labor Statistics) and the Gross National Product (GNP) Implicit Price Deflator (prepared by the U.S. Department of Commerce).

USING PRICE INDEXES IN ACCOUNTING

There are at least two important accounting systems that use price indexes to develop comprehensive financial statements. Both are major alternatives to the conventional accounting system in general use in the United States. One alternative, called current cost accounting, uses specific price-level indexes (along with appraisals and other means) to develop statements that report assets and expenses in terms of the current costs to acquire those assets or services. Additional consideration is given to this alternative later in this chapter.

The other alternative is called constant dollar accounting. It uses general price-level indexes to restate the conventional, unit-of-money financial statements into dollar amounts that represent current, general purchasing power. In the past, most proposals for making constant dollar financial statements suggested using the GNP Implicit Price Deflator because it is the broadest index of general price-level changes.[2]

---

[2] See, for example, APB "Financial Statements Restated for General Price Level Changes," *APB Statement No. 3* (New York: AICPA, 1969), par. 30; and also FASB, "Financial Reporting in Units of General Purchasing Power," *Proposed Statement of Financial Accounting Standards, Exposure Draft* (Stamford, Conn., 1974), par. 35.

However, the FASB's *Statement No. 33* requires use of the Consumers' Price Index for All Urban Consumers (CPI).[3] The following sections of this chapter explain how a general price index, such as the CPI, is used to prepare constant dollar financial statements.

CONSTANT DOLLAR ACCOUNTING

Conventional financial statements disclose revenues, expenses, assets, liabilities, and owners' equity in terms of the historical monetary units exchanged when the transactions occurred. As such, they are sometimes referred to as *unit-of-money* or *nominal dollar financial statements*. This is intended to emphasize the difference between conventional statements and constant dollar statements. In the latter, the dollar amounts shown are adjusted for changes in the general purchasing power of the dollar.

Students should understand clearly that the same principles for determining depreciation expense, cost of goods sold, accruals of revenue, and so forth, apply to both unit-of-money statements and constant dollar statements. The same generally accepted accounting principles apply to both. The only difference between the two is that constant dollar statements reflect adjustments for general price-level changes; unit-of-money statements do not. As a matter of fact, constant dollar financial statements are prepared by adjusting the amounts appearing on the unit-of-money financial statements.

CONSTANT DOLLAR ACCOUNTING FOR ASSETS

The effect of general price-level changes on investments in assets depends on the nature of the assets involved. Some assets, called *monetary assets*, represent money or claims to receive a fixed amount of money. The number of dollars owned or to be received does not change, regardless of changes that may occur in the purchasing power of the dollar. Examples of monetary assets are cash, accounts receivable, notes receivable, and investments in bonds.

Because the amount of money owned or to be received from a monetary asset does not change with price-level changes, the constant dollar balance sheet amount of a monetary asset is not adjusted for general price-level changes. For example, if $200 in cash was owned at the end of 1983 and was held throughout 1984, during which time

---

[3] FASB, "Financial Reporting and Changing Prices," *Statement of Financial Accounting Standards No. 33* (Stamford, Conn., 1979), par. 39. Copyright © by the Financial Accounting Standards Board, High Ridge Park, Stamford, Conn. 06905, U.S.A. Quoted (or excerpted) with permission. Copies of the complete document are available from the FASB.

the general price-level index increased from 150 to 168,[4] the cash reported on both the December 31, 1983, and 1984, constant dollar balance sheets is $200. However, although no balance sheet adjustment is made, it is important to note that an investment in monetary assets held during a period of inflation results in a loss of purchasing power. The $200 would buy less at the end of 1984 than it would have at the end of 1983. This reduction in purchasing power constitutes a loss. The amount of the loss is calculated as follows:

Monetary asset balance on December 31, 1983	$ 200
Adjustment to reflect an equal amount of purchasing power on December 31, 1984: $200 × 168/150	$ 224
Amount of monetary asset balance on December 31, 1984	(200)
General purchasing power loss	$ 24

Nonmonetary assets are defined as all assets other than monetary assets. The prices at which nonmonetary assets may be bought and sold tend to increase or decrease over time as the general price level increases or decreases. Consequently, as the general price level changes, investments in nonmonetary assets tend to retain the amounts of purchasing power originally invested. As a result, the reported amounts of nonmonetary assets on constant dollar balance sheets are adjusted to reflect changes in the price level that have occurred since the nonmonetary assets were acquired.

For example, assume $200 was invested in land (a nonmonetary asset) at the end of 1983, and the investment was held throughout 1984. During this time, the general price index increased from 150 to 168. The constant dollar balance sheets would disclose the following amounts:

Asset	December 31, 1983, constant dollar balance sheet	Adjustment to December 31, 1984, price level	December 31, 1984, constant dollar balance sheet
Land	$200	$200 × (168/150)	$224

The $224 shown as the investment in land at the end of 1984 has the same amount of general purchasing power as did $200 at the end of 1983. Thus, no change in general purchasing power was recognized from holding the land.

---

[4] Observe that these index numbers, and those used in the remaining sections of the chapter, are different from those that were calculated on page 651. Since the earlier calculations were based on only four items (A, B, C, D), that index would not be appropriate to illustrate a general price index, which must reflect the prices of many, many items.

CONSTANT DOLLAR ACCOUNTING FOR LIABILITIES AND STOCKHOLDERS' EQUITY

The effect of general price-level changes on liabilities depends on the nature of the liability. Most liabilities are monetary items, but stockholders' equity and a few liabilities are nonmonetary items.[5] *Monetary liabilities* represent fixed amounts that are owed. The number of dollars to be paid does not change regardless of changes in the general price level.

Since monetary liabilities are unchanged in amounts owed even when price levels change, monetary liabilities are not adjusted for price-level changes. However, a company with monetary liabilities outstanding during a period of general price-level change will experience a general purchasing power gain or loss. Assume, for example, that a note payable for $300 was outstanding on December 31, 1983, and remained outstanding throughout 1984. During that time, the general price index increased from 150 to 168. On the constant dollar balance sheets for December 31, 1983, and 1984, the note payable would be reported at $300. The general purchasing power gain or loss is calculated as follows:

Monetary liability balance on December 31, 1983	$ 300
Adjustment to reflect an equal amount of purchasing power on December 31, 1984: $300 × (168/150)	$ 336
Amount of monetary liability balance on December 31, 1984	(300)
General purchasing power gain	$ 36

The $336 at the end of 1984 has the same amount of general purchasing power as $300 had at the end of 1983. Since the company can pay the note with $300, the $36 difference is a gain in general purchasing power realized by the firm. Alternatively, if the general price index had decreased during 1984, the monetary liability would have resulted in a general purchasing power loss.

Nonmonetary liabilities are obligations that are not fixed in amount. They therefore tend to change with changes in the general price level. For example, product warranties may require that a manufacturer pay for repairs and replacements for a specified period of time after the product is sold. The amount of money required to make the repairs or replacements tends to change with changes in the general price

---

[5] Depending on its nature, preferred stock may be treated as a monetary item. If so, it is an exception to the general rule that stockholders' equity items are nonmonetary items.

level. Consequently, there is no purchasing power gain or loss associated with such warranties. Further, the balance sheet amount of such a nonmonetary liability must be adjusted to reflect changes in the general price index that occur after the liability comes into existence. Stockholders' equity items, with the possible exception of preferred stock, are also nonmonetary items. Hence, they also must be adjusted for changes in the general price index.

Illustration 19–3 summarizes the impact of general price-level changes on monetary items and nonmonetary items. The illustration indicates what adjustments must be made in preparing a constant dollar balance sheet and what purchasing power gains and losses must be recognized on a constant dollar income statement.

Illustration 19–3

Financial statement item	When the general price level rises (inflation)		When the general price level falls (deflation)	
	Balance sheet adjustment required	Income statement gain or loss	Balance sheet adjustment required	Income statement gain or loss
Monetary assets	No	Loss	No	Gain
Nonmonetary assets	Yes	None	Yes	None
Monetary liabilities	No	Gain	No	Loss
Nonmonetary equities and liabilities*	Yes	None	Yes	None

* However, a nonmonetary liability may require an additional adjustment to assure that the balance sheet shows the current estimated amount to satisfy the liability.

PREPARING COMPREHENSIVE, CONSTANT DOLLAR FINANCIAL STATEMENTS

The previous discussion of price indexes and of constant dollar accounting for assets, liabilities, and stockholders' equity provides a basis for understanding the procedures used in preparing comprehensive constant dollar financial statements. In the following discussion, examples of these procedures are based on the unit-of-money (nominal dollar) financial statements for Delivery Service Company (Illustration 19–4).

Delivery Service Company was organized on January 1, 1983. Of the original $30,000 invested in the company, $25,000 was used to buy delivery trucks. The trucks are being depreciated over five years on a straight-line basis. They have a $5,000 salvage value. Since the company was organized, the general price index has changed as follows:

	Price
Date	index
December 1982	130
June 1983 (also average for 1983) ..	140
December 1983	150
Average for 1984	160
December 1984	168

Illustration 19–4

DELIVERY SERVICE COMPANY
Balance Sheets
December 31, 1983, and 1984

	1983	1984
Cash	$ 8,000	$30,000
Land (acquired December 31, 1983)	12,000	12,000
Delivery equipment (acquired January 1, 1983) ..	25,000	25,000
Accumulated depreciation	(4,000)	(8,000)
Total assets	$41,000	$59,000
Note payable (issued July 1, 1983)	$ 5,000	$ 5,000
Capital stock (issued January 1, 1983)	30,000	30,000
Retained earnings	6,000	24,000
Total liabilities and stockholders' equity	$41,000	$59,000

DELIVERY SERVICE COMPANY
Income Statement
For Year Ended December 31, 1984

Delivery revenues	$100,000
Depreciation expense	(4,000)
Other expenses	(78,000)
Net income	$ 18,000

Delivery Service Company's cash balance increased from $8,000 to $30,000 during 1984 and is explained as follows:

Beginning cash balance	$ 8,000
Revenues, earned uniformly throughout the year ..	100,000
Expenses, paid uniformly throughout the year	(78,000)
Ending cash balance	$ 30,000

Restatement of the Balance Sheet

In preparing a constant dollar balance sheet, the account balances are first classified as being monetary items or nonmonetary items. Since monetary items do not change regardless of changes in the price level, each monetary item is placed on the constant dollar balance sheet without adjustment. Each nonmonetary item, on the other hand, must be adjusted for the price-level changes occurring since the original transactions that gave rise to the item.

The restatement of Delivery Service Company's balance sheet is presented in Illustration 19–5. Observe that the monetary items "Cash" and "Note payable" are transferred without adjustment from the unit-of-money column to the price-level-adjusted column. All of the remaining items are nonmonetary and are adjusted. The land was purchased on December 31, 1983, when the price level was 150.[6] Thus, the historical cost of the land is restated from December 1983 dollars to December 1984 dollars (price index 168) as follows: $12,000 \times (168/150) =$ $13,440. The delivery equipment was purchased on January 1, 1983, at the same time the capital stock was issued. Therefore, "Delivery equipment," "Accumulated depreciation," and "Capital stock" are restated from January 1983 prices (index number 130) to December 1984 prices by applying the restatement factor of 168/130.

The retained earnings balance of $24,000 cannot be adjusted in a single step because this balance resulted from more than one transaction. However, the correct, adjusted amount of retained earnings can

Illustration 19–5

DELIVERY SERVICE COMPANY
Restatement of Balance Sheet
December 31, 1984

	Unit-of-money balances	Restatement factor from price index	Price-level-adjusted amounts
Cash	$30,000	—	$ 30,000
Land	12,000	168/150	13,440
Delivery equipment	25,000	168/130	32,308
Less accumulated depreciation	(8,000)	168/130	(10,338)
Total assets	$59,000		$ 65,410
Note payable	$ 5,000	—	$ 5,000
Capital stock	30,000	168/130	38,769
Retained earnings	24,000	(See discussion)	21,641
Total liabilities and stockholders' equity	$59,000		$ 65,410

[6] Normally, price index numbers are determined for a period of time, such as one quarter or one month, and are not determined for a specific point in time, such as December 31. For example, the CPI for All Urban Consumers is prepared for each month. Thus, the index number for December is used to approximate the price level on December 31.

be determined simply by "plugging" the necessary amount to make the balance sheet balance, as follows:

Total assets, adjusted		$ 65,410
Less: Note payable	$ 5,000	
Capital stock	38,769	(43,769)
Necessary retained earnings ..		$ 21,641

The process of confirming this restated retained earnings amount is explained later in the chapter.

Students should recognize that Delivery Service Company is a simplified illustration. Only two of its balance sheet amounts (cash and retained earnings) resulted from more than one transaction. In a more complex case, most account balances would reflect several past transactions that took place at different points in time. In such a situation, the adjustment procedures are more detailed. For example, suppose that the $12,000 balance in the Land account resulted from three different purchases of land, as follows:

January 1, 1983, purchased land for	$ 3,000
July 1, 1983, purchased land for	4,000
December 31, 1983, purchased land for ..	5,000
Total	$12,000

Under this assumption, the following adjustments would be required to prepare the constant dollar balance sheet as of December 31, 1984:

	Unit-of-money balances	Restatement factor from price index	Restated to December 31, 1984, general, price level
Land purchased on:			
January 1, 1983......	$ 3,000	168/130	$ 3,877
July 1, 1983	4,000	168/140	4,800
December 31, 1983 ..	5,000	168/150	5,600
Total	$12,000		$14,277

Restatement of the Income Statement

To prepare a constant dollar income statement, every individual revenue and expense transaction must be restated from the price index level on the date of the transaction to the price index level at the end of the year. The restated amounts are then listed on the constant dollar income statement along with the purchasing power gain or loss that resulted from holding or owing monetary items.

The calculations to restate the 1984 income statement of Delivery Service Company from units of money to the price-level-adjusted amounts are presented in Illustration 19–6.

Illustration 19–6

	Unit-of-money amounts	Restatement factor from price index	Price-level-adjusted amounts
DELIVERY SERVICE COMPANY Restatement of Income Statement For Year Ended December 31, 1984			
Delivery service revenues	$100,000	168/160	$105,000
Depreciation expense	(4,000)	168/130	(5,169)
Other expenses	(78,000)	168/160	(81,900)
	$ 18,000		$ 17,931
Purchasing power loss (from Illustration 19–7)			(1,460)
Net income	$ 18,000		$ 16,471

As previously mentioned, Delivery Service Company's revenues were received and its other expenses were incurred in many transactions that occurred throughout the year. To be completely precise, each of these individual transactions would have to be separately restated. However, these revenues and expenses occurred in a nearly uniform pattern throughout the year. Restating the total revenue and the total other expenses from the average price level during the year (160) to the end-of-year price level (168) is therefore an acceptable approximation procedure.

The unit-of-money amount of depreciation expense on delivery trucks ($4,000) was determined by taking 20% of the $25,000 − $5,000 cost to be depreciated. Since this cost was incurred on January 1, 1983, the restatement of depreciation expense must be based on the price index for that date (130) and on the index number for the end of 1984 (168).

Purchasing Power Gain or Loss

As was explained, the purchasing power gain or loss experienced by Delivery Service Company (shown in Illustration 19–6) stems from the amount of monetary assets held and monetary liabilities owed by the company during the year. During 1984, cash was the only monetary asset held by the company; the only monetary liability was a $5,000 note payable. The purchasing power gain or loss for these items is calculated in Illustration 19–7.

Illustration 19–7

DELIVERY SERVICE COMPANY
Calculation of Purchasing Power Gain or Loss
For Year Ended December 31, 1984

	Unit-of-money amounts	Restatement factor from price index	Restated to December 31, 1984	Gain or loss
Cash:				
Beginning balance	$ 8,000	168/150	$ 8,960	
Delivery revenue receipts	100,000	168/160	105,000	
Payments for expenses	(78,000)	168/160	(81,900)	
Ending balance, adjusted			$ 32,060	
Ending balance, actual	$ 30,000		(30,000)	
Purchasing power loss				$2,060
Note payable: beginning balance	$ 5,000	168/150	$ 5,600	
Ending balance, actual	$ 5,000		(5,000)	
Purchasing power gain				(600)
Net purchasing power loss				$1,460

Note in Illustration 19–7 that the purchasing power loss from holding cash must take into account the changes in the cash balance that occurred during the year. First, the beginning cash balance of $8,000 is restated as an equivalent amount of general purchasing power at the end of the year. Since the December 1984 price index was 168 and the December 1983 price index was 150, the balance is restated as follows: $8,000 × 168/150 = $8,960. Next, each cash change is adjusted from the price level at the time the change occurred to the price level at the end of the year. In the example, cash receipts from revenues occurred uniformly throughout the year. Therefore, the average price index number for the year (160) is used to approximate the price level in effect when the revenues were received. The $100,000 cash received from revenues during the year is restated to the equivalent general purchasing power at the year's end, as follows: $100,000 × 168/160 = $105,000. Cash payments for expenses were also made uniformly throughout the year, so they are restated using the same index numbers. In other words, the $78,000 of cash expenses are restated as follows: $78,000 × 168/160 = $81,900. With the initial cash balance and the cash changes restated into end-of-year purchasing power, the adjusted end-of-year purchasing power for cash is $32,060. Since the actual ending cash balance is only $30,000, the $2,060 difference represents a loss of general purchasing power.

The $5,000 note payable was issued on July 1, 1983, when the price index was 140. Nevertheless, the purchasing power gain associated with this monetary liability is calculated by adjusting the $5,000 from the beginning-of-1984 price level, when the index number was 150. Since the calculation is being made for the purpose of preparing a 1984 constant dollar income statement, only the purchasing power gain arising from inflation during 1984 should be included. The gain associated with the price index change from 140 to 150 occurred during 1983, and would have been included in the constant dollar income statement for 1983.

Adjusting the Retained Earnings Balance

The December 31, 1984, adjusted retained earnings balance was previously determined by "plugging" the amount necessary to make liabilities plus stockholders' equity equal to total assets (page 660). Alternatively, if a constant dollar balance sheet for December 31, 1983, was available, the adjusted retained earnings balance on that date could be restated to the December 31, 1984, price level. Then the constant dollar net income for 1984 could be added to determine constant dollar retained earnings at December 31, 1984. For example, had constant dollar financial statements been prepared for 1983, the $6,000 retained earnings balance in units of money (see Illustration 19–4) would have been adjusted to a December 31, 1983, general price-level-adjusted amount of $4,616.[7] With this additional information, the adjusted retained earnings balance for December 31, 1984, is calculated as follows:

	Restated to December 31, 1983, general price level	Factor from price index	Restated to December 31, 1984, general price level
Retained earnings, December 31, 1983	$4,616	168/150	$ 5,170
Constant dollar net income for 1984 (see Illustration 19–6)			16,471
Dividends declared during 1984			–0–
Retained earnings, December 31, 1984 ...			$21,641

[7] Notice that the $4,616 price-level-adjusted retained earnings on December 31, 1983, is smaller than the $6,000 units-of-money amount. This decrease was caused by the same factors that caused the adjusted net income for 1984 to be less than the unit-of-money net income (see Illustration 19–6).

CONSTANT DOLLAR ACCOUNTING AND CURRENT VALUES

Early in this chapter, the fact that prices do not all change at the same rate was discussed. Indeed, when the general price level is rising, some specific prices may be falling. If this were not so, if prices all changed at the same rate, then constant dollar accounting would report current values on the financial statements. For example, suppose that a company purchased land for $50,000 on January 1, 1983, when the general price index was 130. Then the price level increased until December 1984, when the price index was 168. A constant dollar balance sheet for this company on December 31, 1984, would report the land at $50,000 × 168/130 = $64,615. If all prices increased at the same rate during that period, the price of the land would have increased from $50,000 to $64,615, and the company's constant dollar balance sheet would coincidentally disclose the land at its current value.

However, since all prices do not change at the same rate, the current value of the land may differ substantially from the constant dollar amount of $64,615. For example, assume that the company obtained an appraisal of the land and determined that its current value on December 31, 1984, was $80,000. The difference between the original purchase price of $50,000 and the current value of $80,000 can be explained as follows:

Unrealized holding gain	$80,000 − $64,615 = $15,385
Adjustment for general price-level increase	$64,615 − $50,000 = 14,615
	$30,000

In that case, the constant dollar balance sheet would report land at $64,615, which is $15,385 ($80,000 − $64,615) less than its current value. This illustrates a very important fact concerning constant dollar accounting; it is not a form of current value accounting. Rather, constant dollar accounting restates original transaction prices into equivalent amounts of current, *general* purchasing power. Only if current, *specific* purchasing power were the basis of valuation would the balance sheet display current values.

CURRENT VALUE ACCOUNTING

Constant dollar accounting often has been proposed as a way of improving accounting information. Proponents argue that conventional, unit-of-money financial statements have questionable relevance to decision makers. Conventional statements may even be misleading in a world of persistent, long-run inflation. Since constant dollar accounting adjusts for general price-level changes, its proponents believe that constant dollar financial statements provide a more meaningful portrayal of a company's past operations and financial position. And, they argue, constant dollar accounting is sufficiently objective to allow its practical application without damaging the credibility of financial statements.

Other accountants argue that even constant dollar accounting fails to communicate to statement readers the economic values of most relevance. They would design financial statements so that each item in the statements is measured in terms of current value.

Some arguments for *current value accounting* conclude that the current liquidation price or "exit value" of an item is the most appropriate basis of valuation for financial statements. However, other arguments, which appear to be more widely supported, conclude that the price to replace an item, its *current cost,* is the best basis of financial statement valuation.

CURRENT COST ACCOUNTING

Current Costs on the Income Statement

In the current cost approach to accounting, the reported amount of each expense should be the number of dollars that would be required, at the time the expense is incurred, to acquire the resources consumed. For example, assume that the annual sales of a company included an item that was sold in May for $1,500 and the item had been acquired on January 1 for $500. Also, suppose that in May, at the time of the sale, the cost to replace this item was $700. Then the annual current cost income statement would show sales of $1,500 less cost of goods sold of $700. To state this idea more generally, when an asset is acquired and then held for a time before it expires, the historical cost of the asset likely will differ from its current cost at the time it expires. *Current cost accounting* requires that the reported amount of expense be measured at the time the asset expires.

The result of measuring expenses in terms of current costs is that revenue is matched with the current (at the time of the sale) cost of the resources that were used to earn the revenue. Thus, operating profit is not positive unless revenues are sufficient to replace all of the resources that were consumed in the process of producing those revenues. The operating profit figure is therefore thought to be an important (and improved) basis for evaluating the effectiveness of operating activities.

Current Costs on the Balance Sheet

On the balance sheet, current cost accounting requires that assets be reported at the amounts that would have to be paid to purchase them as of the balance sheet date. Similarly, liabilities should be reported at the amounts that would have to be paid to satisfy the liabilities as of the balance sheet date. Note that this valuation basis is similar to constant dollar accounting in that a distinction exists between monetary and nonmonetary assets and liabilities. Monetary assets and liabilities are fixed in amount regardless of price-level changes. Therefore, monetary assets need not be adjusted in amount. But all of the nonmonetary items must be evaluated at each balance sheet date to determine the best approximation of current cost.

A little reflection on the variety of assets reported on balance sheets will confirm the presence of many difficulties in obtaining reliable estimates of current costs. In some cases, specific price indexes may provide the most reliable source of current cost information. In other cases, where an asset is not new and has been partially depreciated, its current cost may be estimated by determining the cost to acquire a new asset of like nature. Depreciation on the old asset is then based on the current cost of the new asset. Clearly, the accountant's professional judgment is an important factor in developing current cost data.

FASB REQUIREMENTS FOR CONSTANT DOLLAR AND CURRENT COST INFORMATION

In October 1979, the FASB issued *Statement No. 33,* which contains reporting requirements for both constant dollar and current cost information. These requirements became effective for financial statements issued after December 24, 1979, but with a one-year delay of the current cost requirements if a reporting company had difficulty implementing the requirements more quickly.[8] The requirements apply only to large companies with assets of more than $1 billion or inventories plus property, plant, and equipment (before deducting depreciation) of more than $125 million.[9]

Statement No. 33 does not affect the conventional financial statements; only supplemental information is required. The supplemental information to be presented includes:[10]

a. Income from continuing operations[11] adjusted for general price-level changes.

---

[8] *FASB Statement No. 33,* pars. 67–69.

[9] Ibid., par. 23.

[10] Ibid., pars. 29–37.

[11] Income from continuing operations excludes the effects of accounting changes, extraordinary items, and income or loss from operations that are being discontinued. Detailed discussions of these items are left to a more advanced accounting course.

b. The general purchasing power gain or loss.

c. Income from continuing operations on a current cost basis.

d. Current cost of inventory at the end of the year.

e. Current cost of property, plant, and equipment at the end of the year.

f. The increase or decrease in the current cost of inventory, property, plant, and equipment, net of general price-level changes.

g. A five-year summary of selected financial data.

Examples of the required disclosures are presented in Illustrations 19–8 and 19–9. Compare the requirements listed above as items *(a)* through *(f)* with the information shown in Illustration 19–8. Each of the required items is disclosed.

Observe in Illustration 19–8 that the only restated income statement items are "Cost of goods sold" and "Depreciation and amortization expense." These are the only income statement items (plus depletion expense, if any) that must be restated to meet the minimum FASB requirements. Net sales, other operating expense, interest expense,

---

Illustration 19–8

Statement of Income from Continuing Operations
Adjusted for Changing Prices
For the Year Ended December 31, 198E
($000)

	As reported in the primary statements	Adjusted for general inflation	Adjusted for changes in specific prices (current costs)
Net sales and other operating revenues	$253,000	$253,000	$253,000
Cost of goods sold	197,000	204,384	205,408
Depreciation and amortization expense	10,000	14,130	19,500
Other operating expenses	20,835	20,835	20,835
Interest expense	7,165	7,165	7,165
Provision for income taxes	9,000	9,000	9,000
	$244,000	$255,514	$261,908
Income (loss) from continuing operations	$ 9,000	$ (2,514)	$ (8,908)
Gain from decline in purchasing power of net amounts owed		$ 7,729	$ 7,729
Increase in specific prices (current cost) of inventories and property, plant, and equipment held during the year*			$ 24,608
Effect of increase in general price level			18,959
Excess of increase in specific prices over increase in the general price level			$ 5,649

* At December 31, 198E, current cost of inventory was $65,700 and current cost of property, plant, and equipment, net of accumulated depreciation was $85,100.

Adapted from *FASB Statement No. 33,* Appendix A, Schedule B, p. 33.

Illustration 19–9

Five-Year Comparison of Selected Supplementary Financial Data Adjusted for Effects of Changing Prices ($000 of average 198E dollars)					
	Years ended December 31				
	198A	*198B*	*198C*	*198D*	*198E*
Net sales and other operating revenues	$265,000	$235,000	$240,000	$237,063	$253,000
Historical cost information adjusted for general inflation					
Income (loss) from continuing operations	(2,249)	(3,086)	(2,795)	(2,761)	(2,514)
Income (loss) from continuing operations per common share ..	(1.56)	(2.13)	(1.93)	(1.91)	(1.68)
Net assets at year-end	47,812	51,150	54,110	55,518	57,733
Current cost information					
Income (loss) from continuing operations	(3,650)	(4,039)	(5,100)	(4,125)	(8,908)
Income (loss) from continuing operations per common share ..	(2.52)	(2.79)	(3.53)	(2.75)	(5.94)
Excess of increase in specific prices over increase in the general price level	1,892	1,659	140	2,292	5,649
Net assets at year-end	68,850	73,100	77,170	79,996	81,466
Gain from decline in purchasing power of net amounts owed ...	7,950	6,080	6,420	7,027	7,729
Cash dividends declared per common share	2.59	2.43	2.26	2.16	2.00
Market price per common share at year-end	32	31	43	39	35
Average consumer price index ...	170.5	181.5	195.4	205.0	220.9

Adapted from *FASB Statement No. 33*, Appendix A, Schedule B, p. 34.

and provision for income taxes do not have to be restated. These latter items may well have been affected by inflation. And the FASB would *permit* companies to adjust such items. But the Board does not require it.

Note that the general purchasing power gain or loss is called "gain from decline in purchasing power of net amounts owed." The FASB decided not to include this item in the calculation of income (loss) from continuing operations; instead, it is shown separately.

The five-year summary of financial data is shown in Illustration 19–9. Observe that the constant cost and current cost information is shown for the years 198A through 198E.

Using Recoverable Amounts That Are Lower than Current Cost

In general, *current cost* is the cost that would be required to currently acquire (or replace) an asset or service. Current cost accounting involves reporting assets and expenses in terms of their current costs. However, the FASB recognized an important exception to this general description of current cost accounting. That exception involves the use of recoverable amounts.

In the case of an asset about to be sold, the recoverable amount is its net realizable value. In other words, the recoverable amount is the asset's expected sales price less related costs to sell. If an asset is to be used rather than sold, the recoverable amount is the present value of future cash flows expected from using the asset. A recoverable amount is reported instead of current cost whenever the recoverable amount appears to be materially and permanently lower than current cost. Both the asset and the expense associated with using it (or selling it) should be measured in terms of the recoverable amount.[12]

The reason for using recoverable amounts emphasizes the value of an asset to its owner. The idea is that an asset should not be reported at an amount that is larger than its value to its owner. If the recoverable amount of an asset is less than its current cost, a business is not likely to replace it. A business would not be willing to pay more for an asset than it could expect to recover from using or selling the asset. Hence, the value of the asset to the business can be no higher than the recoverable amount. When value to the business is less than current cost, it is believed that current cost is not relevant to an analysis of the business. Following this line of reasoning, *Statement No. 33* calls for reporting current cost or recoverable amount, if lower.

Using Recoverable Amounts Lower than Historical Cost in Constant Dollars

In constant dollar accounting, assets and their associated expenses are generally reported in terms of historical cost, adjusted for general price-level changes. However, the FASB requirements for constant dollar accounting involve the same "recoverable amount" exception as is applied in the case of current cost accounting. In other words, recoverable amounts must be substituted for historical costs in constant dollars if the recoverable amounts are lower. The Board argues that using recoverable amounts in such cases avoids overstating the "worth" of assets.[13]

To see an actual example of the disclosures required by the FASB,

---

[12] *FASB Statement No. 33*, pars. 62–63.

[13] Ibid., pars. 62, 195.

turn to the Appendix at the end of this book which contains the 1982 annual report of Texas Instruments. The supplementary financial information in that report (pages 1001 through 1004) contains the *Statement No. 33* disclosures.

THE MOMENTUM TOWARD MORE COMPREHENSIVE PRICE-LEVEL ACCOUNTING

The question of whether procedures of accounting for price-level changes should be implemented has been debated and discussed for many years. Granted, inflation (and taxes) has caused the expanded use of certain procedures such as LIFO. But the first significant requirements to report inflation-adjusted information were not imposed until 1976. At that time, the Securities and Exchange Commission (SEC) began to require certain large companies to report supplemental information on a replacement cost basis. They were required to estimate the

> . . . current replacement cost of inventories and productive capacity at the end of each fiscal year for which a balance sheet is required and the approximate amount of cost of sales and depreciation based on replacement cost for the two most recent full fiscal years.[14]

The SEC's replacement cost disclosure requirements generated many complaints and public statements of opposition by corporate managements. Thus, when *FASB Statement No. 33* was issued in 1979, the SEC withdrew its 1976 requirements and supported those specified by the FASB.

The SEC's action was limited to large companies, and the required information was obviously much less than a complete set of financial statements prepared on a replacement cost basis. Nevertheless, the SEC action represented a major break with the U.S. tradition of relying totally on unit-of-money financial statements.

The FASB requirements constituted another major step toward improved accounting for price-level changes. While still limited to large companies and still substantially less than complete financial statements, they involve both constant dollar and current cost information, with important inclusions of income statement information. Whether or not current cost accounting and/or constant dollar accounting will eventually be required in most financial statements remains to be seen. No doubt, conventional, unit-of-money financial statements will continue to represent the primary basis of U.S. accounting in the near future. But a basic shift to one or the other inflation accounting alternative is a distinct possibility. Both constant dollar accounting and current

---

[14] Securities and Exchange Commission, *Accounting Series Release No. 190* (Washington, D.C., 1976).

cost accounting are being used in some countries. The strength of the calls for expanded usage of them in the United States will probably depend on how much future inflation as well as specific price changes undermine the perceived relevance of existing reporting methods.

GLOSSARY

Constant dollar accounting. An accounting system that adjusts unit-of-money financial statements for changes in the general purchasing power of the dollar. Also called *general price-level adjusted accounting*.

Current cost. On the income statement, the numbers of dollars that would be required, at the time the expense is incurred, to acquire the resources consumed. On the balance sheet, the amounts that would have to be paid to replace the assets or satisfy the liabilities as of the balance sheet date.

Current cost accounting. An accounting system that uses specific price-level indexes (and other means) to develop financial statements that report items such as assets and expenses in terms of the current costs to acquire or replace those assets or services.

Current value accounting. An accounting system that provides financial statements in which current values are reported; different versions of current value are possible, for example, current replacement costs or current exit values.

General price-level-adjusted (GPLA) accounting. Synonym for *constant dollar accounting*.

General price-level index. A measure of the changing purchasing power of a dollar in general; measures the price changes for a broad market basket that includes a large variety of goods and services, for example, the Gross National Product Implicit Price Deflator or the Consumers Price Index for All Urban Consumers.

General purchasing power gain or loss. The gain or loss that results from holding monetary assets and/or owing monetary liabilities during a period in which the general price-level changes.

Monetary assets. Money or claims to receive a fixed amount of money with the number of dollars to be received not changing regardless of changes in the general price level.

Monetary liabilities. Fixed amounts that are owed, with the number of dollars to be paid not changing regardless of changes in the general price level.

Price index. A measure of the changes in prices of a particular market basket of goods and/or services.

Specific price-level index. An indicator of the changing purchasing power of a dollar spent for items in a specific category; includes a much more narrow range of goods and services than does a general price index.

Unit-of-money financial statments. Conventional financial statements that disclose revenues, expenses, assets, liabilities, and owners' equity in terms of the historical monetary units exchanged at the time the transactions occurred.

QUESTIONS FOR CLASS DISCUSSION

1. Some people argue that conventional financial statements fail to adequately account for inflation. What is the general problem with conventional financial statements that generates this argument?

2. Are there any procedures used in conventional accounting that offset the effects of inflation on financial statements? Give some examples.

3. What is the fundamental difference in the price-level adjustments made under current cost accounting and under constant dollar accounting?

4. Explain the difference between an "average change in per unit prices" and a "weighted-average change in per unit prices."

5. What is the significance of the "base" year in constructing a price index? How is the base year chosen?

6. For accounting purposes, what is the most important use of a price index?

7. What is the difference between a specific price-level index and a general price-level index?

8. What is meant by "unit-of-money" financial statements?

9. Define *monetary assets*.

10. Explain the meaning of *nonmonetary assets*.

11. Define *monetary liabilities* and *nonmonetary liabilities*. Give examples of both.

12. If the monetary assets held by a firm exceed its monetary liabilities throughout a period in which prices are rising, which should be recorded on a constant dollar income statement—a purchasing power gain or loss? What if monetary liabilities exceed monetary assets during a period in which prices are falling?

13. If accountants preferred to display current values in the financial statements, would they use constant dollar accounting or current cost accounting? Are there any other alternatives?

14. Describe the meaning of *operating profit* under a current cost accounting system.

15. "The distinction between monetary assets and nonmonetary assets is just as important for current cost accounting as it is for general price-level-adjusted accounting." Is this statement true? Why?

16. *FASB Statement No. 33* requires several specific disclosures of constant dollar items and current cost items. List the general disclosure requirements of *FASB Statement No. 33*.

CLASS EXERCISES

Exercise 19–1   Market basket No. 1 consists of 3 units of W, 4 units of X, and 2 units of Z. Market basket No. 2 consists of 2 units of X, 3 units of Y, and 4 units of Z. The per unit prices of each item during 198A and during 198B are as follows:

Item	198A price per unit	198B price per unit
W	$1.00	$0.60
X	3.00	3.10
Y	5.00	4.80
Z	1.00	1.80

Required:

Compute the annual rate of inflation for market basket No. 1 and for market basket No. 2.

Exercise 19–2

The following total prices of a specified market basket were calculated for each of the years 198A through 198E:

Year	Total price
198A	$12,000
198B	15,000
198C	19,000
198D	21,000
198E	29,000

Required:

1. Using 198C as the base year, prepare a price index for the five-year period.
2. Convert the index from a 198C base year to a 198E base year.

Exercise 19–3

A company's plant and equipment consisted of equipment purchased during 198A for $150,000, land purchased during 198C for $40,000, and a building purchased during 198E for $260,000. The general price index during these and later years was as follows:

198A	100
198B	110
198C	120
198D	130
198E	140
198F	150
198G	160

Required:

1. Assuming the above price index adequately represents end-of-year price levels, calculate the amount of each cost that would be shown on a constant dollar balance sheet for *(a)* December 31, 198F, and *(b)* December 31, 198G. Ignore any accumulated depreciation.
2. Would the constant dollar income statement for 198G disclose any purchasing power gain ·or loss as a consequence of holding the above assets? If so, how much?

Exercise 19–4

Determine whether the following items are monetary or nonmonetary items.

1. Trade accounts receivable.
2. Petty cash.
3. Notes receivable.

4. Goodwill.
5. Income taxes payable.
6. Retained earnings deficit.
7. Merchandise.
8. Product warranties liability.
9. Common stock subscribed.
10. Prepaid rent.
11. Furniture and fixtures.
12. Common stock.
13. Prepaid fire and casualty insurance.
14. Accounts payable.

Exercise 19–5   Calculate the general purchasing power gain or loss in 198B given the following information:

Time period	Price index
December 198A	100
Average during 198B	120
December 198B	150

a.   The Cash balance on December 31, 198A, was $500. During 198B, cash sales occurred uniformly throughout the year and amounted to $1,500. Payments of expenses also occurred evenly throughout the year and amounted to $600.

b.   Accounts payable amounted to $200 on December 31, 198A. Additional accounts payable amounting to $800 were recorded evenly throughout 198B. The only payment of accounts during the year was $100 in late December.

c.   A note payable of $250 was issued during 198A and was repaid on December 30, 198B.

PROBLEMS

Problem 19–1   The costs of purchasing a common "market basket" in each of several years are as follows:

Year	Cost of market basket
198A	$30,000
198B	31,800
198C	34,000
198D	33,800
198E	40,000
198F	42,000
198G	41,200
198H	45,000

Required:

1. Construct a price index using 198E as the base year.
2. Using the index constructed in Requirement 1, what was the percent increase in prices from 198F to 198H?

3. Using the index constructed in Requirement 1, how many dollars in 198H does it take to have the same purchasing power as $1 in 198B?

4. Using the index constructed in Requirement 1, if $14,000 were invested in land during 198A and $17,000 were invested in land during 198E, what would be reported as the total land investment on a constant dollar balance sheet prepared in 198G? What would your answer be if the investments were in U.S. long-term bonds rather than in land?

Problem 19–2

Fister Corporation purchased machinery for $720,000 on January 2, 198B. The equipment was expected to last six years and have no salvage value; straight-line depreciation was to be used. The equipment was sold on December 31, 198D, for $510,000. End-of-year general price index numbers during this period of time were as follows:

```
198A .....  110.0
198B .....  137.5
198C .....  165.0
198D .....  192.5
```

Required:

1. What should be presented for the equipment and accumulated depreciation on a constant dollar balance sheet dated December 31, 198B?

2. How much depreciation expense should be shown on the constant dollar income statement for 198C?

3. How much depreciation expense should be shown on the constant dollar income statement for 198D?

4. How much gain on the sale of equipment would be reported on the conventional, unit-of-money income statement for 198D?

5. After adjusting the equipment's cost and accumulated depreciation to the end-of-198D price level, how much gain in (loss of) general purchasing power was realized by the sale of the equipment?

Problem 19–3

The Algona Bus Line's only monetary item during 198D was cash, the balance of which changed during the year as follows:

Beginning balance	$ 10,500
Revenues received evenly throughout the year	60,000
Payments of expenses (spread evenly throughout the year)	(42,000)
Dividends declared and paid in mid-March 198D	(3,000)
Dividends declared and paid in mid-September 198D ..	(3,000)
Ending balance	$ 22,500

The unit-of-money income statement for 198D appeared as follows:

Sales		$ 60,000
Cash expense	$42,000	
Depreciation expense, equipment ..	7,000	
Amortization expense, patents	4,000	
Total expenses		(53,000)
Net income		$ 7,000

The depreciation expense refers to equipment purchased in December 198A, and the amortization expense refers to patents acquired in December

198B. General price index numbers covering the periods of time mentioned above are as follows:

December 198A 180.0
December 198B 200.0
December 198C 225.0
March 198D 236.7
September 198D 254.7
December 198D 270.0
Average for 198D..... 240.0

Required:

1. Calculate the general purchasing power gain or loss experienced by Algona Bus Line in 198D.
2. Prepare a schedule that restates the income statement for 198D from units of money to constant dollar amounts.

Problem 19–4   The directors of Luong Company have expressed an interest in constant dollar financial statements and the concepts of purchasing power gains and losses. The price index in December 198A was 120; and in December 198B, it was 140. The average price index during 198B was 128.

The unit-of-money financial statements for Luong Company are presented below. The increase in notes payable during 198B occurred on July 15, at which time the reported price index was 125. The funds derived from the increase in notes payable were used to increase the cash balance. Luong Company purchased the equipment several years ago when the price index was 105.

LUONG COMPANY
Balance Sheets
December 31, 198A, and 198B

	198A	*198B*
Cash	$120,000	$210,000
Accounts receivable	100,000	100,000
Equipment (net of depreciation)	80,000	75,000
Total assets.........................	$300,000	$385,000
Notes payable	$100,000	$140,000
Capital stock	100,000	100,000
Retained earnings	100,000	145,000
Total liabilities and stockholders' equity ..	$300,000	$385,000

LUONG COMPANY
Income Statement
For Year Ended December 31, 198B

Revenues............................		$200,000
Depreciation expense	$ 5,000	
Other expenses	150,000	155,000
Net income		$ 45,000

Required:

1. Calculate the purchasing power gain or loss incurred by Luong Company during 198B. You should assume that revenues were received in cash evenly throughout the year and that expenses other than depreciation were paid in cash evenly throughout the year.

2. Prepare a schedule to restate the income statement for 198B from units of money to constant dollars.

Problem 19–5

Luong Company, for which data were presented in Problem 19–4, was organized at a time when the price index was 105. All of the $100,000 capital stock was issued at that time.

Required:

1. Based on the above information and the data provided in Problem 19–4, prepare a constant dollar balance sheet for Luong Company as of December 31, 198B. (The retained earnings balance may be determined simply by "plugging" in the amount that is necessary to make the balance sheet balance.)
2. On Luong Company's constant dollar balance sheet on December 31, 198A, retained earnings was reported as $97,144. Assuming that constant dollar net income for 198B was $23,332, present a calculation that confirms the retained earnings balance as it is reported on the constant dollar balance sheet for December 31, 198B.

Problem 19–6

The 198B income statement of ABC Company and its comparative balance sheets for December 31, 198A, and December 31, 198B, are as follows:

ABC COMPANY
Income Statement
For Year Ended December 31, 198B

Sales revenue		$50,000
Cost of goods sold:		
Beginning inventory	$ 7,000	
Purchases	26,000	
Total available merchandise	$33,000	
Ending inventory	8,000	25,000
Gross profit		$25,000
Depreciation expense	$ 2,000	
Other expenses	13,000	15,000
Net income		$10,000

ABC COMPANY
Balance Sheets
December 31, 198A, and 198B

	198A	*198B*
Cash	$ 5,000	$ 4,500
Accounts receivable	15,000	20,000
Notes receivable	5,000	5,000
Inventory	7,000	8,000
Building	40,000	40,000
Accumulated depreciation	(2,000)	(4,000)
Land	25,000	25,000
Total assets	$95,000	$98,500
Accounts payable	$25,000	$20,000
Notes payable	10,000	10,000
Common stock	50,000	50,000
Retained earnings	10,000	18,500
Total liabilities and stockholders' equity . .	$95,000	$98,500

Selected index numbers from a general price-level index are:

	General price index
January 198A	110
June 198A (Also average for 198A)	120
December 198A	130
June 198B (Also average for 198B)	140
December 198B	150

Additional information regarding ABC Company is as follows:

a. All sales are on credit and recorded to Accounts Receivable. Cash collections of Accounts Receivable occurred evenly throughout the year.

b. All merchandise purchases were credited to Accounts Payable and cash payments of Accounts Payable occurred evenly throughout the year. The beginning inventory was acquired when the price index was 120.

c. Other expenses ($13,000) were paid in cash evenly throughout the year.

d. Dividends of $1,500 were paid to stockholders in late December 198B.

e. The Building and Land accounts reflect assets that were acquired in January 198A. The outstanding stock was issued on January 1, 198A.

f. The changes during the year in Cash, Accounts Payable, and Accounts Receivable, are as follows:

Cash

Beginning balance	5,000	Payments of accounts	31,000
Receipts from customers	45,000	Other expenses	13,000
		Dividend payments	1,500

Accounts Payable

Cash payments	31,000	Beginning balance	25,000
		Merchandise purchases	26,000

Accounts Receivable

Beginning balance	15,000	Cash receipts	45,000
Credit sales	50,000		

Required:

1. Calculate the purchasing power gain or loss to be reported on the constant dollar income statement for 198B.

2. Prepare the constant dollar income statement for 198B.

3. Prepare a constant dollar balance sheet as of December 31, 198B. (Retained earnings may be determined by "plugging" in the amount necessary to make the balance sheet balance.)

4. Based on the additional information that the constant dollar balance sheet on December 31, 198A, disclosed a retained earnings balance of $12,946, calculate the constant dollar retained earnings balance on December 31, 198B, so as to confirm the "plugged" amount used in answering Requirement 3.

ALTERNATE PROBLEMS

Problem 19–1A   The costs of purchasing a common "market basket" in each of several years are as follows:

Year	Cost of market basket
198A	$41,000
198B	44,000
198C	43,500
198D	48,000
198E	50,000
198F	54,000
198G	57,000
198H	56,000

Required:

1. Construct a price index using 198D as the base year.
2. Using the index constructed in Requirement 1, what was the percent increase in prices from 198E to 198H?
3. Using the index constructed in Requirement 1, how many dollars in 198H does it take to have the same purchasing power as $1 in 198B?
4. Using the index constructed in Requirement 1, if $18,000 were invested in land during 198A and $24,000 were invested in land during 198E, what would be reported as the total land investment on a constant dollar balance sheet prepared in 198G? What would your answer be if the investments were in corporate bonds which pay a fixed rate of interest rather than in land?

Problem 19–2A   Castor Company purchased machinery for $420,000 on January 2, 198B. The machinery was expected to last five years and have no salvage value; straight-line depreciation was to be used. The machinery was sold on December 30, 198E, for $175,000. End-of-year general price index numbers during this period of time were the following:

198A	128.0
198B	153.6
198C	192.0
198D	179.2
198E	211.2

Required:

1. What should be presented for the machinery and accumulated depreciation on a constant dollar balance sheet dated December 31, 198C?
2. How much depreciation expense should be shown on the constant dollar income statement for 198D?
3. How much depreciation expense should be shown on the constant dollar income statement for 198E?
4. How much gain on the sale of machinery would be reported on the conventional, unit-of-money income statement for 198E?

5. After adjusting the machinery's cost and accumulated depreciation to the end-of-198E price level, how much gain in (loss of) general purchasing power was realized by the sale of the machinery?

Problem 19–3A

The conventional, unit-of-money income statement of P. K. Lee Company for 198F appears as follows:

Sales		$90,000
Cash expenses	$40,000	
Depreciation expense, machinery.....	15,000	
Amortization expense, patent	10,000	
Total expenses...............		65,000
Net income		$25,000

Cash was the only monetary item held by the company during 198F, and the changes that occurred in the Cash account during the year were as follows:

Beginning balance	$ 14,000
Revenues received uniformly during the year......	90,000
Payment of dividend on April 3, 198F	(18,000)
Payment of expenses evenly throughout the year ..	(40,000)
Purchase of land on December 28, 198F	(30,000)
Ending balance...............................	$ 16,000

The only depreciable asset belonging to P. K. Lee Company is a machine that was purchased early in January 198B. The patent owned by the company was purchased in late December 198C. General price index numbers covering the periods of time mentioned above are as follows:

December 198A	80.0
December 198B	95.0
December 198C	105.0
December 198D	110.0
December 198E	108.0
April 198F	110.0
December 198F	120.0
Average for 198F.....	112.0

Required:

1. Calculate the general purchasing power gain or loss experienced by P. K. Lee Company in 198F.
2. Prepare a schedule that restates the income statement for 198F from units of money to constant dollar amounts.

Problem 19–4A

The unit-of-money income statement for 198B and December 31, 198A, and 198B, balance sheets of Service Company are given below:

SERVICE COMPANY
Income Statement
For Year Ended December 31, 198B

Commissions revenue ..		$120,000
Depreciation expense ..	$15,000	
Other expenses	80,000	95,000
Net income		$ 25,000

SERVICE COMPANY
Balance Sheets
December 31, 198A, and 198B

	198A	198B
Cash	$ 70,000	$100,000
Accounts receivable	30,000	55,000
Equipment (net of depreciation)	90,000	75,000
Total assets	$190,000	$230,000
Notes payable	$ 50,000	$ 65,000
Capital stock	130,000	130,000
Retained earnings	10,000	35,000
Total liabilities and stockholders' equity ..	$190,000	$240,000

Selected numbers from a general price-level index are as follows:

	Price index
December 198A	80
Average during 198B	90
September 198B	95
December 198B	105

The increase in notes payable during 198B occurred on September 10, and the funds derived from the increase in notes payable were used to increase the cash balance. Service Company purchased the equipment at a time when the general price index was 62.

Required:

1. Calculate the purchasing power gain or loss incurred by Service Company during 198B. You should assume that all commissions were earned evenly throughout the year and were debited to Accounts Receivable. Cash receipts from receivables ($95,000) were also distributed evenly throughout the year, and expenses other than depreciation were paid in cash evenly throughout the year.
2. Prepare a schedule to restate the income statement for 198B from units of money to constant dollars.

Problem 19–5A Assume the same facts as were presented in Problem 19–4A. In addition, Service Company was organized some time ago when the price index was 59. All of the capital stock ($130,000) was issued at that time.

Required:

1. Based on the above information and the data provided in Problem 19–4A, prepare a constant dollar balance sheet for Service Company on December 31, 198B. (The retained earnings balance may be determined simply by "plugging" in the amount that is necessary to make the balance sheet balance.)
2. On Service Company's constant dollar balance sheet on December 31, 198A, retained earnings was reported as a deficit of $10,142.48. Assuming that Service Company reported a constant dollar net loss for 198B of $1,028, present a calculation that confirms the retained earnings balance as it is reported on the constant dollar balance sheet for December 31, 198B.

PROVOCATIVE PROBLEMS

Provocative
Problem 19–1,
Adler Company

Adler Company purchased a plot of land in 198A when the general price index was 94. The land cost $200,000 and was zoned for heavy industrial use. In 198D, the general price index is 118. However, a specific price index for heavy industrial property in the general area of the land in question has risen from 80 in 198A to 140 in 198D.

Adler Company has no intention of building a plant on the property. It is being held only as an investment and will eventually be sold. Some of the employees of Adler Company have been arguing over the matter of how the land should be presented in the balance sheet at the close of 198D and also over the amount of real economic benefit the company will have obtained from the investment if the land were to be sold immediately. Prepare an analysis which recognizes the alternative balance sheet valuation possibilities and which will help resolve the dispute.

Provocative
Problem 19–2,
Steamboat
Company

Steamboat Company has often been willing to consider new, innovative ways of reporting to its stockholders. For example, it has presented supplemental constant dollar financial statements in its annual reports. The constant dollar balance sheets of Steamboat Company for December 31, 198A, and 198B, were as follows:

STEAMBOAT COMPANY
Constant Dollar Balance Sheets

	As presented on December 31, 198B	As presented on December 31, 198A
Assets		
Cash	$ 12,000	$ 5,000
Accounts receivable	20,000	10,000
Notes receivable	5,000	—
Inventory	6,455	3,240
Equipment	49,636	42,955
Accumulated depreciation	(14,182)	(6,136)
Land	39,123	24,545
Total assets	$118,032	$79,604
Liabilities and Stockholders' Equity		
Accounts payable	$ 17,000	$ 3,500
Notes payable	9,000	2,500
Common stock	70,909	61,364
Retained earnings	21,123	12,240
Total liabilities and stockholders' equity	$118,032	$79,604

A new member of Steamboat Company's board of directors has expressed interest in the relationship between constant dollar statements and unit-of-money statements. The board member understands that constant dollar statements are derived from unit-of-money statements, but wonders if the process can be reversed. Specifically, you are asked to show how the constant dollar balance sheets for December 31, 198A, and 198B could be restated back into unit-of-money statements.

Additional information:

1. The outstanding stock was issued in January 198A, and the company's equipment was purchased at that time. The equipment has no salvage value and is being depreciated over seven years.
2. The note receivable was acquired on June 30, 198B.
3. Notes payable consists of two notes, one for $2,500 which was issued on January 1, 198A, and the other for $6,500 which was issued on January 1, 198B.
4. The land account includes two parcels, one of which was acquired for $20,000 on January 1, 198A. The remaining parcel was acquired in June 198B.
5. Selected numbers from a general price-level index are:

   January 198A 110
   June 198A (also average for 198A) . . 125
   December 198A 135
   June 198B (also average for 198B) . . 145
   December 198B 156

6. The inventory at the end of each year was acquired evenly throughout that year.

Analyzing Financial Statements

20

After studying Chapter 20, you should be able to:

List the three broad objectives of financial reporting by business enterprises.

Describe comparative financial statements, how they are prepared, and the limitations associated with interpreting them.

Prepare common-size comparative statements and interpret them.

Explain the importance of working capital in the analysis of financial statements and list the typical ratios used to analyze working capital.

Calculate the common ratios used in analyzing the balance sheet and income statement and state what each ratio is intended to measure.

State the limitations associated with using financial statement ratios and the sources from which standards for comparison may be obtained.

Define or explain the words and phrases listed in the chapter Glossary.

A large variety of persons are interested in receiving and analyzing financial information about business firms. They range from managers, employees, directors, customers, suppliers, owners, lenders, and potential investors to brokers, regulatory authorities, lawyers, economists, labor unions, financial advisors, and the financial press. Some of these groups, such as managers and some regulatory agencies, have the ability to require a company to prepare specialized financial reports designed to meet their specific interests. Many other groups must rely on the *general-purpose financial statements* that are periodically published by the companies. General-purpose financial statements usually include the income statement, balance sheet, statement of retained earnings, and statement of changes in financial position. These statements are typically accompanied by a variety of additional financial information such as that contained in the footnotes to the financial statements. See, for example, the financial statements and related footnotes of Texas Instruments shown in the Appendix beginning on page 987. Financial information about companies may also be obtained from a variety of news announcements issued from time to time by management.

The process of preparing and issuing financial information about a company is called *financial reporting*. While this is broader than general-purpose financial statements, the objectives of those statements are essentially the same as are the objectives of financial reporting.

OBJECTIVES OF FINANCIAL REPORTING

The great variety of persons who use financial information about a business undoubtedly differ widely in their reasons for analyzing that information. Nevertheless, the FASB suggests that such users are "generally interested in [the business'] ability to generate favorable cash flows because their decisions relate to amounts, timing, and uncertainties of expected cash flows."[1] Based on this general assumption about the interests of financial information users, the FASB has prescribed three broad objectives of financial reporting. Those objectives are as follows:

1. —Financial reporting should provide information that is useful to present and potential investors and creditors and other users in making rational investment, credit, and similar decisions. The information should be comprehensible to those who have a reasonable understanding of busi-

---

[1] FASB, "Objectives of Financial Reporting by Business Enterprises," *Statement of Financial Accounting Concepts No. 1* (Stamford, Conn., 1978), par. 25. Copyright © by the Financial Accounting Standards Board, High Ridge Park, Stamford, Conn. 06905, U.S.A. Quoted (or excerpted) with permission. Copies of the complete document are available from the FASB.

ness and economic activities and are willing to study the information with reasonable diligence.

2. —Financial reporting should provide information to help present and potential investors and creditors and other users in assessing the amounts, timing, and uncertainty of prospective cash receipts from dividends or interest and the proceeds from the sale, redemption, or maturity of securities or loans. Since investors' and creditors' cash flows are related to enterprise cash flows, financial reporting should provide information to help investors, creditors, and others assess the amounts, timing, and uncertainty of prospective net cash inflows to the related enterprise.

3. —Financial reporting should provide information about the economic resources of an enterprise, the claims to those resources (obligations of the enterprise to transfer resources to other entities and owners' equity), and the effects of transactions, events, and circumstances that change its resources and claims to those resources.[2]

These three objectives of financial reporting were published by the FASB as the first step in a long-run project of developing a new conceptual framework for financial accounting.[3] Such a conceptual framework is intended to assist accountants in resolving questions about how accounting problems should be solved. In addition, however, the objectives provide important background information for the person who is beginning to learn how to analyze financial statements.

Although the user of financial information may have other reasons for analyzing financial statements, he or she should understand that the authoritative body for establishing accounting principles (the FASB) intends for financial reporting (and financial statements) to be focused on these basic objectives. The primary idea is that financial reporting should help the information user predict the amounts, timing, and uncertainty of future net cash inflows to the business. The methods of analysis and techniques explained in this chapter should contribute to this process.

When the financial statements of a business are analyzed, individual statement items are in themselves generally not too significant. However, relationships between items and groups of items plus changes that have occurred are significant. As a result, financial statement analysis requires that relationships between items and groups of items and changes in items and groups be described.

---

[2] Ibid., p. viii.

[3] Other major sections of the FASB's conceptual framework project published to date include "Qualitative Characteristics of Accounting Information," *Statement of Financial Accounting Concepts No. 2* (May 1980); "Elements of Financial Statements of Business Enterprises," *Statement of Financial Accounting Concepts No. 3* (December 1980); and "Objectives of Financial Reporting by Nonbusiness Organizations," *Statement of Financial Accounting Concepts No. 4* (December 1980).

COMPARATIVE STATEMENTS

Changes in statement items can usually best be seen when item amounts for two or more successive accounting periods are placed side by side in columns on a single statement. Such a statement is called a *comparative statement*. Each of the financial statements, or portions thereof, may be presented in the form of a comparative statement.

In its most simple form, a comparative balance sheet consists of the item amounts from two or more of a company's successive balance sheets arranged side by side so that changes in amounts may be seen. However, such a statement can be improved by also showing in both dollar amounts and in percentages the changes that have occurred. When this is done, as in Illustration 20–1, large dollar and large percentage changes become more readily apparent.

A comparative income statement is prepared in the same manner as a comparative balance sheet. Income statement amounts for two or more successive periods are placed side by side, with dollar and percentage changes in additional columns. Such a statement is shown in Illustration 20–2.

Analyzing and Interpreting Comparative Statements

In analyzing and interpreting comparative data, it is necessary for the analyst to select for study any items showing significant dollar or percentage changes. The analyst then tries to determine the reasons for each change and if possible whether they are favorable or unfavorable. For example, in Illustration 20–1, the first item, "Cash," shows a large decrease. At first glance this appears unfavorable. However, when the decrease in "Cash" is considered with the decrease in "Investments" and the increases in "Store equipment," "Buildings," and "Land," plus the increase in "Mortgage payable," it becomes apparent the company has materially increased its plant assets between the two balance sheet dates. Further study reveals the company has apparently constructed a new building on land it has held as an investment until needed in this expansion. Also, it seems the company paid for its new plant assets by reducing cash, selling its Apex Company common stock, and issuing a $50,000 mortgage.

As an aid in controlling operations, a comparative income statement is usually more valuable than a comparative balance sheet. For example, in Illustration 20–2, "Gross sales" increased 14.1% and "Net sales" increased 13.9%. At the same time, "Sales returns" increased 32.4%, or at a rate more than twice that of gross sales. Returned sales represent wasted sales effort and indicate dissatisfied customers. Consequently, such an increase in returns should be investigated, and the reason

Illustration 20–1

ANCHOR SUPPLY COMPANY
Comparative Balance Sheet
December 31, 198B, and December 31, 198A

	Years Ended December 31		Amount of Increase or (Decrease) during 198B	Percent of Increase or (Decrease) during 198B
	198B	198A		
Assets				
Current assets:				
Cash	$ 18,000	$ 90,500	$ (72,500)	(80.1)
Accounts receivable, net	68,000	64,000	4,000	6.3
Merchandise inventory	90,000	84,000	6,000	7.1
Prepaid expenses	5,800	6,000	(200)	(3.3)
Total current assets	$181,800	$244,500	$ (62,700)	(25.6)
Long-term investments:				
Real estate	–0–	$ 30,000	$ (30,000)	(100.0)
Apex Company common stock	–0–	50,000	(50,000)	(100.0)
Total long-term investments	–0–	$ 80,000	$ (80,000)	(100.0)
Plant and equipment:				
Office equipment, net	$ 3,500	$ 3,700	$ (200)	(5.4)
Store equipment, net	17,900	6,800	11,100	163.2
Buildings, net	176,800	28,000	148,800	531.4
Land	50,000	20,000	30,000	150.0
Total plant and equipment	$248,200	$ 58,500	$189,700	324.3
Total assets	$430,000	$383,000	$ 47,000	12.3
Liabilities				
Current liabilities:				
Notes payable	$ 5,000	–0–	$ 5,000	
Accounts payable	43,600	$ 55,000	(11,400)	(20.7)
Taxes payable	4,800	5,000	(200)	(4.0)
Wages payable	800	1,200	(400)	(33.3)
Total current liabilities	$ 54,200	$ 61,200	$ (7,000)	(11.4)
Long-term liabilities:				
Mortgage payable	$ 60,000	$ 10,000	$ 50,000	500.0
Total liabilities	$114,200	$ 71,200	$ 43,000	60.4
Capital				
Common stock, $10 par value	$250,000	$250,000	–0–	–0–
Retained earnings	65,800	61,800	$ 4,000	6.5
Total capital	$315,800	$311,800	$ 4,000	1.3
Total liabilities and capital	$430,000	$383,000	$ 47,000	12.3

Illustration 20–2

ANCHOR SUPPLY COMPANY
Comparative Income Statement
Years Ended December 31, 198B, and 198A

	Years Ended December 31		Amount of Increase or (Decrease) during 198B	Percent of Increase or (Decrease) during 198B
	198B	198A		
Gross sales............................	$973,500	$853,000	$120,500	14.1
Sales returns and allowances	13,500	10,200	3,300	32.4
Net sales...............................	$960,000	$842,800	$117,200	13.9
Cost of goods sold	715,000	622,500	92,500	14.9
Gross profit from sales	$245,000	$220,300	$ 24,700	11.2
Operating expenses:				
Selling expenses:				
Advertising expense	$ 7,500	$ 5,000	$ 2,500	50.0
Sales salaries expense	113,500	98,000	15,500	15.8
Store supplies expense	3,200	2,800	400	14.3
Depreciation expense, store equipment .	2,400	1,700	700	41.2
Delivery expense	14,800	14,000	800	5.7
Total selling expenses	$141,400	$121,500	$ 19,900	16.4
General and administrative expenses:				
Office salaries expense	$ 41,000	$ 40,050	$ 950	2.4
Office supplies expense	1,300	1,250	50	4.0
Insurance expense	1,600	1,200	400	33.3
Depreciation expense, office equipment .	300	300	–0–	–0–
Depreciation expense, buildings	2,850	1,500	1,350	90.0
Bad debts expense	2,250	2,200	50	2.3
Total general and admin. expenses .	$ 49,300	$ 46,500	$ 2,800	6.0
Total operating expenses	$190,700	$168,000	$ 22,700	13.5
Operating income	$ 54,300	$ 52,300	$ 2,000	3.8
Less interest expense..................	2,300	1,000	1,300	130.0
Income before taxes	$ 52,000	$ 51,300	$ 700	1.4
Income taxes	19,000	18,700	300	1.6
Net income	$ 33,000	$ 32,600	$ 400	1.2

for the increase determined if at all possible. Also, in addition to the large increase in the "Sales returns," it is significant that the rate of increase in "Cost of goods sold" is greater than that of "Net sales." This is an unfavorable trend and should be remedied if at all possible.

In attempting to account for Anchor Supply Company's increase in sales, the increases in advertising and in plant assets merit attention. It is reasonable to expect an increase in advertising to increase sales. It is also reasonable to expect an increase in plant assets to result in a sales increase.

Calculating Percentage Increases and Decreases

When percentage increases and decreases are calculated for comparative statements, the increase or decrease in an item is divided by the amount shown for the item in the base year. No problems arise in these calculations when positive amounts are shown in the base year. However, when no amount is shown or a negative amount is shown in the base year, a percentage increase or decrease cannot be calculated. For example, in Illustration 20–1, there were no notes payable at the end of 198A and a percentage change for this item cannot be calculated.

In this text, percentages and ratios are typically rounded to one or two decimal places. However, there is no uniform agreement on this matter. In general, percentages should be carried out to the point of assuring that meaningful information is conveyed. However, they should not be carried so far that the significance of relationships tend to become "lost" in the length of the numbers.

Trend Percentages

Trend percentages or index numbers emphasize changes that have occurred from period to period and are useful in comparing data covering a number of years. Trend percentages are calculated as follows:

1. A base year is selected, and each item amount on the base year statement is assigned a weight of 100%.
2. Then, each item from the statements for the years after the base year is expressed as a percentage of its base year amount. To determine these percentages, the item amounts in the years after the base year are divided by the amount of the item in the base year.

For example, if 198A is made the base year for the following data, the trend percentages for "Sales" are calculated by dividing by $210,000 the amount shown for "Sales" in each year after the first. The trend percentages for "Cost of goods sold" are found by dividing by $145,000 the amount shown for "Cost of goods sold" in each year after the first. And, the trend percentages for "Gross profit" are found by dividing the amounts shown for "Gross profit" by $65,000.

	198A	198B	198C	198D	198E	198F
Sales..................	$210,000	$204,000	$292,000	$284,000	$310,000	$324,000
Cost of goods sold.....	145,000	139,000	204,000	198,000	218,000	229,000
Gross profit	$ 65,000	$ 65,000	$ 88,000	$ 86,000	$ 92,000	$ 95,000

When these divisions are made, the trends for these three items appear as follows:

	1981A	198B	198C	198D	198E	198F
Sales................	100%	97%	139%	135%	148%	154%
Cost of goods sold.....	100	96	141	137	150	158
Gross profit	100	100	135	132	142	146

It is interesting to note in the illustrated trends that while after the second year the sales trend is upward, the cost of goods sold trend is upward at a slightly more rapid rate. This indicates a contracting gross profit rate and should receive attention.

It should be pointed out in a discussion of trends that the trend for a single balance sheet or income statement item is seldom very informative. However, a comparison of trends for related items often tells the analyst a great deal. For example, a downward sales trend with an upward trend for merchandise inventory, accounts receivable, and loss on bad debts would generally indicate an unfavorable situation. On the other hand, an upward sales trend with a downward trend or a slower upward trend for accounts receivable, merchandise inventory, and selling expenses would indicate an increase in operating efficiency.

Common-Size Comparative Statements

The comparative statements illustrated thus far do not show proportional changes in items except in a general way. Changes in proportions are often shown and emphasized by *common-size comparative statements.*

A common-size statement is so called because its items are shown in common-size figures, figures that are fractions of 100%. For example, on a common-size balance sheet (1) the asset total is assigned a value of 100%. (2) The total of the liabilities and owner's equity is also assigned a value of 100%. Then (3), each asset, liability, and owners' equity item is shown as a percentage of total assets (or total equities). When a company's successive balance sheets are shown in this manner (see Illustration 20–3), proportional changes are emphasized.

A common-size income statement is prepared by assigning net sales a 100% value and then expressing each statement item as a percent of net sales. Such a statement is an informative and useful tool. If the 100% sales amount on the statement is assumed to represent one sales dollar, then the remaining items show how each sales dollar was distributed to costs, expenses, and profit. For example, on the compara-

Illustration 20–3

ANCHOR SUPPLY COMPANY
Common-Size Comparative Balance Sheet
December 31, 198B, and December 31, 198A

	Years Ended December 31		Common-Size Percentages	
	198B	198A	198B	198A
Assets				
Current assets:				
Cash	$ 18,000	$ 90,500	4.19	23.63
Accounts receivable, net	68,000	64,000	15.81	16.71
Merchandise inventory	90,000	84,000	20.93	21.93
Prepaid expenses	5,800	6,000	1.35	1.57
Total current assets	$181,800	$244,500	42.28	63.84
Long-term investments:				
Real estate	–0–	$ 30,000		7.83
Apex Company common stock	–0–	50,000		13.05
Total long-term investments	–0–	$ 80,000		20.88
Plant and equipment:				
Office equipment, net	$ 3,500	$ 3,700	0.81	0.97
Store equipment, net	17,900	6,800	4.16	1.78
Buildings, net	176,800	28,000	41.12	7.31
Land	50,000	20,000	11.63	5.22
Total plant and equipment	$248,200	$ 58,500	57.72	15.28
Total assets	$430,000	$383,000	100.00	100.00
Liabilities				
Current liabilities:				
Notes payable	$ 5,000	–0–	1.16	
Accounts payable	43,600	$ 55,000	10.14	14.36
Taxes payable	4,800	5,000	1.12	1.31
Wages payable	800	1,200	0.19	0.31
Total current liabilities	$ 54,200	$ 61,200	12.61	15.98
Long-term liabilities:				
Mortgage payable	$ 60,000	$ 10,000	13.95	2.61
Total liabilities	$114,200	$ 71,200	26.56	18.59
Capital				
Common stock, $10 par value	$250,000	$250,000	58.14	65.27
Retained earnings	65,800	61,800	15.30	16.14
Total capital	$315,800	$311,800	73.44	81.44
Total liabilities and capital	$430,000	$383,000	100.00	100.00

Illustration 20–4

ANCHOR SUPPLY COMPANY
Common-Size Comparative Income Statement
Year Ended December 31, 198B, and 198A

	Years Ended December 31		Common-Size Percentages	
	198B	198A	198B	198A
Gross sales	$973,500	$853,000	101.41	101.21
Sales returns and allowances	13,500	10,200	1.41	1.21
Net sales	$960,000	$842,800	100.00	100.00
Cost of goods sold	715,000	622,500	74.48	73.86
Gross profit from sales	$245,000	$220,300	25.52	26.14
Operating expenses:				
Selling expenses:				
Advertising expense	$ 7,500	$ 5,000	0.78	0.59
Sales salaries expense	113,500	98,000	11.82	11.63
Store supplies expense	3,200	2,800	0.33	0.33
Depreciation expense, store equipment	2,400	1,700	0.25	0.20
Delivery expense	14,800	14,000	1.54	1.66
Total selling expenses	$141,400	$121,500	14.72	14.41
General and administrative expenses:				
Office salaries expense	$ 41,000	$ 40,050	4.27	4.75
Office supplies expense	1,300	1,250	0.14	0.15
Insurance expense	1,600	1,200	0.17	0.14
Depreciation expense, office equipment	300	300	0.03	0.04
Depreciation expense, buildings	2,850	1,500	0.30	0.18
Bad debts expense	2,250	2,200	0.23	0.26
Total general and administrative expenses ...	$ 49,300	$ 46,500	5.14	5.52
Total operating expenses	$190,700	$168,000	19.86	19.93
Operating income	$ 54,300	$ 52,300	5.66	6.21
Less interest expense	2,300	1,000	0.24	0.12
Income before taxes	$ 52,000	$ 51,300	5.42	6.09
Income taxes	19,000	18,700	1.98	2.22
Net income	$ 33,000	$ 32,600	3.44	3.87

tive income statement shown in Illustration 20–4, the 198A cost of goods sold consumed 73.86 cents of each sales dollar. In 198B, cost of goods sold consumed 74.48 cents of each sales dollar. While this increase is small, if in 198B the proportion of cost of goods sold had remained at the 198A level, almost $6,000 of additional gross profit would have been earned.

Common-size percentages point out efficiencies and inefficiencies that are otherwise difficult to see. For this reason, they are a valuable management tool. To illustrate, sales salaries of Anchor Supply Company took a higher percentage of each sales dollar in 198B than in

198A. On the other hand, office salaries took a smaller percentage. Furthermore, although the loss from bad debts is greater in 198B than in 198A, loss from bad debts took a smaller proportion of each sales dollar in 198B than in 198A.

ANALYSIS OF WORKING CAPITAL

When balance sheets are analyzed, working capital always receives close attention because an adequate amount of working capital enables a company to meet current debts, carry sufficient inventories, and take advantage of cash discounts. However, the amount of working capital a company has is not a measure of these abilities. This may be demonstrated as follows with Companies A and B:

	Company A	Company B
Current assets	$100,000	$20,000
Current liabilities	90,000	10,000
Working capital	$ 10,000	$10,000

Companies A and B have the same amounts of working capital. However, Company A's current liabilities are nine times its working capital, while Company B's current liabilities and working capital are equal. As a result, if liabilities are to be paid on time, Company A must experience much less shrinkage and delay in converting its current assets to cash than Company B. Thus, the amount of a company's working capital is not a measure of its working capital position. However, the relation of its current assets to its current liabilities is such a measure.

Current Ratio

The relation of a company's current assets to its current liabilities is known as its *current ratio*. A current ratio is calculated by dividing current assets by current liabilities. The current ratio of the foregoing Company B is calculated as follows:

$$\frac{\text{Current assets, \$20,000}}{\text{Current liabilities, \$10,000}} = 2$$

After the division is made, the relation can be described by saying that Company B's current assets are two times its current liabilities, or simply Company B's current ratio is 2 to 1.

The current ratio is the relation of current assets and current liabilities expressed mathematically. A high current ratio indicates a large proportion of current assets to current liabilities. The higher the ratio, the better is a company's current position, and normally the more capable it is of meetings its current obligations.

For years, bankers and other credit grantors measured a credit-seeking company's debt-paying ability by whether or not it had a 2 to 1 current ratio. Today, most credit grantors realize that the 2 to 1 rule of thumb is not an adequate test of debt-paying ability. They realize that whether or not a company's current ratio is good or bad depends upon at least three factors:

1. The nature of the company's business.
2. The composition of its current assets.
3. The turnover of certain of its current assets.

The nature of a company's business has much to do with whether or not its current ratio is adequate. A public utility that has no inventories other than supplies and grants little or no credit can operate on a current ratio of less than 1 to 1. On the other hand, because a misjudgment of style can make an inventory of goods for sale almost worthless, a company in which style is the important sales factor may find a current ratio of much more than 2 to 1 to be inadequate. Consequently, when the adequacy of working capital is studied, consideration must be given to the type of business under review.

Also, in an analysis of a company's working capital, the composition of its current assets should be considered. Normally, a company with a high proportion of cash to accounts receivable and merchandise is in a better position to meet quickly its current obligations than is a company with most of its current assets tied up in accounts receivable and merchandise. The company with cash can pay its current debts at once. The company with accounts receivable and merchandise must often turn these items into cash before it can pay.

Acid-Test Ratio

An easily calculated check on current asset composition is the *acid-test ratio,* also called the *quick ratio* because it is the ratio of "quick assets" to current liabilities. "Quick assets" are cash, notes receivable, accounts receivable, and temporary investments in marketable securities. They are the current assets that can quickly be turned into cash. An acid-test ratio of 1 to 1 is normally considered satisfactory. However, this is a rule of thumb and should be applied with care. The acid-test ratio of Anchor Supply Company as of the end of 198B is calculated as follows:

Quick assets:		Current liabilities:	
Cash	$18,000	Notes payable	$ 5,000
Accounts receivable	68,000	Accounts payable	43,600
		Taxes payable	4,800
		Wages payable	800
Total	$86,000	Total	$54,200

Acid-test ratio is $86,000 ÷ $54,200 = 1.59 or is 1.6 to 1

Certain current asset turnovers affect working capital requirements. For example, assume Companies A and B sell the same amounts of merchandise on credit each month. However, Company A grants 30-day terms to its customers, while Company B grants 60 days. Both collect their accounts at the end of the credit periods granted. But as a result of the difference in terms, Company A turns over or collects its accounts twice as rapidly as does Company B. Also, as a result of the more rapid turnover, Company A requires only one half the investment in accounts receivable that is required of Company B and can operate with a smaller current ratio.

Accounts receivable turnover is calculated by dividing net sales for a year by the year-end accounts receivable. Anchor Supply Company's turnovers for 198B and 198A are calculated as follows:

		198B	*198A*
a.	Net sales for year	$960,000	$842,800
b.	Year-end accounts receivable	68,000	64,000
	Times accounts receivable were turned over *(a ÷ b)*	14.1	13.2

The turnover of 14.1 times in 198B in comparison to 13.2 in 198A indicates the company's accounts receivable were collected more rapidly in 198B.

The year-end amount of accounts receivable is commonly used in calculating accounts receivable turnover. However, if year-end accounts receivable are not representative, an average of the year's accounts receivable by months should be used. Also, credit sales should be used rather than the sum of cash and credit sales; and accounts receivable before subtracting the allowance for doubtful accounts should be used. However, information as to credit sales is seldom available in a published balance sheet. Likewise, many published balance sheets report accounts receivable at their net amount. Consequently, total sales and net accounts receivable must often be used.

Days' Sales Uncollected

Accounts receivable turnover is one indication of the speed with which a company collects its accounts. *Days' sales uncollected* is another indication of the same thing. To illustrate the calculation of days' sales uncollected, assume a company had charge sales during a year of $250,000, and that it has $25,000 of accounts receivable at the year-end. In other words, one tenth of its charge sales, or the charge sales made during one tenth of a year, or the charge sales of 36.5 days ($\frac{1}{10} \times 365$ days in a year $= 36.5$ days) are uncollected. This calculation of days' sales uncollected in equation form appears as follows:

$$\frac{\text{Accounts receivable, \$25,000}}{\text{Charge sales, \$250,000}} \times 365 = 36.5 \text{ days' sales uncollected}$$

Days' sales uncollected takes on more meaning when credit terms are known. According to a rule of thumb, a company's days' sales uncollected should not exceed one and one-third times the days in its credit period when it does not offer discounts and one and one-third times the days in its discount period when it does. If the company, whose days' sales uncollected is calculated in the illustration just given, offers 30-day terms, then 36.5 days is within the rule-of-thumb amount. However, if its terms are 2/10, n/30, its days' sales uncollected seem excessive.

Turnover of Merchandise Inventory

A company's *merchandise turnover* is the number of times its average inventory is sold during an accounting period. A high turnover is considered an indication of good merchandising. Also, from a working capital point of view, a company with a high turnover requires a smaller investment in inventory than one producing the same sales with a low turnover. Merchandise turnover is calculated by dividing cost of goods sold by average inventory. Cost of goods sold is the amount of merchandise at cost that was sold during an accounting period. Average inventory is the average amount of merchandise at cost on hand during the period. The 198B merchandise turnover of Anchor Supply Company is calculated as follows:

$$\frac{\text{Cost of goods sold, \$715,000}}{\text{Average merchandise inventory, \$87,000}} = \text{Merchandise turnover of 8.2 times}$$

The cost of goods sold is taken from the company's 198B income statement. The average inventory is found by dividing by two the sum of the $84,000, January 1, 198B, inventory and the $90,000, December 31, 198B, inventory. In a company in which beginning and ending inventories are not representative of the inventory normally on hand, a more accurate turnover may be secured by using the average of all the 12 month-end inventories.

STANDARDS OF COMPARISON

When financial statements are analyzed by computing ratios and turnovers, the analyst must determine whether the ratios and turnovers obtained are good, bad, or just average. Furthermore, in making the decision, the analyst must have some basis for comparison. The following are available:

1. A trained analyst may compare the ratios and turnovers of the company under review with mental standards acquired from past experiences.
2. An analyst may calculate for purposes of comparison the ratios and turnovers of a selected group of competitive companies in the same industry as the one whose statements are under review.
3. Published ratios and turnovers such as those published by Dun & Bradstreet may be used for comparison.
4. Some local and national trade associations gather data from their members and publish standard or average ratios for their trade or industry. These offer the analyst a very good basis of comparison when available.
5. Rule-of-thumb standards may be used as a basis for comparison.

Of these five standards, the ratios and turnovers of a selected group of competitive companies normally offer the best basis for comparison. Rule-of-thumb standards should be applied with care if erroneous conclusions are to be avoided.

OTHER BALANCE SHEET AND INCOME STATEMENT RELATIONS

Several balance sheet and income statement relationships in addition to those dealing with working capital are important to the analyst. Some of the more important are discussed below.

Capital Contributions of Owners and Creditors

The share of a company's assets contributed by its owners and the share contributed by creditors are always of interest to the analyst.

The owners' and creditors' contributions of Anchor Supply Company are calculated as follows:

		198B	198A
a.	Total liabilities	$114,200	$ 71,200
b.	Total owners' equity	315,800	311,800
c.	Total liabilities and owners' equity	$430,000	$383,000
	Creditors' equity (a ÷ c)............	26.6%	18.6%
	Owners' equity (b ÷ c).............	73.4%	81.4%

Creditors like to see a high proportion of owners' equity because owners' equity acts as a cushion that absorbs losses. The greater the equity of the owners in relation to liabilities, the greater the losses that can be absorbed by the owners before the creditors begin to lose.

From the creditors' standpoint, a high percentage of owners' equity is desirable. However, if an enterprise can earn a return on borrowed capital that is in excess of the capital's cost, then a reasonable amount of creditors' equity is desirable from the owners' viewpoint.

Pledged Plant Assets to Long-Term Liabilities

Companies commonly borrow by issuing a note or bonds secured by a mortgage on certain of their plant assets. The ratio of pledged plant assets to long-term debt is often calculated to measure the security granted to mortgage or bondholders by the pledged assets. This ratio is calculated by dividing the pledged assets' book value by the liabilities for which the assets are pledged. It is calculated for Anchor Supply Company as of the end of 198B and 198A as follows:

		198B	198A
	Buildings, net	$176,800	$28,000
	Land	50,000	20,000
a.	Book value of pledged plant assets	$226,800	$48,000
b.	Mortgage payable	$ 60,000	$10,000
	Ratio of pledged assets to secured liabilities (a ÷ b)	3.8 to 1	4.8 to 1

The usual rule-of-thumb minimum for this ratio is 2 to 1. However, the ratio needs careful interpretation because it is based on the *book value* of the pledged assets. Book values often bear little or no relation to the amount that would be received for the assets in a foreclosure or a liquidation. As a result, estimated liquidation values or foreclosure values are normally a better measure of the protection offered bond or mortgage holders by pledged assets. Also, the long-term earning ability of the company whose assets are pledged is usually more important to long-term creditors than the pledged assets' book value.

Times Fixed Interest Charges Earned

The number of times fixed interest charges were earned is often calculated to measure the security of the return offered to bondholders or a mortgage holder. The amount of income before the deduction of fixed interest charges and income taxes is available to pay the fixed interest charges. Consequently, the calculation is made by dividing income before fixed interest charges and income taxes by fixed interest charges. The result is the number of times fixed interest charges were earned. Often, fixed interest charges are considered secure if the company consistently earns its fixed interest charges two or more times each year.

Rate of Return on Total Assets Employed

The return earned on total assets employed is a measure of management's performance. Assets are used to earn a profit, and management is responsible for the way in which they are used. Consequently, the return on assets employed is a measure of management's performance.

The return figure used in this calculation should be after-tax income plus interest expense. Interest expense is included because it is a return paid creditors for assets they have supplied. Likewise, if the amount of assets has fluctuated during the year, an average of the beginning- and end-of-year assets employed should be used.

The rates of return earned on the average total assets employed by Anchor Supply Company during 198B and 198A are calculated as follows:

		198B	198A
	Net income after taxes	$ 33,000	$ 32,600
	Add interest expense	2,300	1,000
a.	Net income plus interest plus expense	$ 35,300	$ 33,600
b.	Average total assets employed	$406,500	$380,000
	Rate of return on total assets employed *(a ÷ b)*	8.7%	8.8%

In the case of Anchor Supply Company, the change in the rates is not too significant. It is also impossible to tell whether the returns are good or bad without some basis of comparison. The best comparison would be the returns earned by similar-size companies engaged in the same kind of business. A comparison could also be made with the returns earned by this company in previous years. Neither of these is available in this case.

Rate of Return on Common Stockholders' Equity

A primary reason for the operation of a corporation is to earn a net income for its common stockholders. The rate of return on the common stockholders' equity is a measure of the success achieved in this area. Usually an average of the beginning- and end-of-year equities is used in calculating the return. For Anchor Supply Company, the 198B and 198A calculations are as follows:

		198B	198A
a.	Net income after taxes	$ 33,000	$ 32,600
b.	Average stockholders' equity	313,800	309,000
	Rate of return on stockholders' equity (a ÷ b)	10.5%	10.6%

Compare Anchor Supply Company's returns on stockholders' equity with its returns on total assets employed and note that the return on the stockholders' equity is greater in both years. The greater returns resulted from using borrowed money.

When there is preferred stock outstanding, the preferred dividend requirements must be subtracted from net income to arrive at the common stockholders' share of income to be used in this calculation.

Earnings per Common Share

Earnings per common share data are among the most commonly quoted figures on the financial pages of daily newspapers. Such data are used by investors in evaluating the past performance of a business, in projecting its future earnings, and in weighing investment opportunities. Because of the significance attached to earnings per share data by investors and others, the APB concluded that earnings per common share or net loss per common share data should be shown on the face of a published income statement.[4]

---

[4] APB, "Earnings per Share," *APB Opinion No. 15* (New York: AICPA, 1969), par. 12.

For corporations having only common stock outstanding, the amount of earnings per share is determined by dividing net income by the number of common shares outstanding. For example, Anchor Supply Company of previous illustrations earned $33,000 in 198B and it had 25,000 common shares outstanding. Consequently, the amount of its earnings per common share is calculated:

$$\frac{\text{Net income, }\$33,000}{25,000\text{ common shares}} = \$1.32\text{ per share}$$

Where there are also nonconvertible preferred shares outstanding, the year's preferred dividend requirement must be deducted from net income before dividing by the number of outstanding common shares. Also, if the number of common shares changed during the year, a weighted-average number of shares (weighted by the length of time each number of shares was outstanding) is used in the calculation.

Many corporations, like Anchor Supply Company, have simple capital structures consisting only of common stock and, perhaps, preferred stock that is not convertible into common stock. Other corporations have more complex capital structures that include preferred stocks and bonds that are convertible into common stock at the option of the owners. In the latter corporations, if conversion should occur, earnings per share would undoubtedly change due solely to the conversion. Recognizing this, the APB provided specific requirements in *Opinion No. 15* for calculating and reporting earnings per share for corporations with complex capital structures. However, these requirements are so lengthy and involved that a discussion must be left to an advanced course.

Price-Earnings Ratio

Price-earnings ratios are commonly used in comparing investment opportunities. A price-earnings ratio is calculated by dividing market price per share by earnings per share. For example, if Anchor Supply Company's common stock sold at $12 per share at the end of 198B, the stock's end-of-year price-earnings ratio is calculated as:

$$\frac{\text{Market price per share, }\$12}{\text{Earnings per share, }\$1.32} = 9.09$$

After the calculation is made, it may be said that the stock had a 9.1 price-earnings ratio at the end of 198B, or it may be said that approximately $9.10 was required at that time to buy $1 of the company's 198B earnings.

In comparing price-earnings ratios, it must be remembered that such ratios vary from industry to industry. For example, in the steel industry, a price-earnings ratio of 8 to 10 is normal, while in a growth industry, such as microcomputers, a price-earnings ratio of 20 to 25 might be expected.

GLOSSARY

Accounts receivable turnover.   An indication of how long it takes a company to collect its accounts, calculated by dividing net sales or credit sales by ending or average accounts receivable.

Acid-test ratio.   The relation of quick assets, such as cash, notes receivable, accounts receivable, and temporary investments in marketable securities, to current liabilities, calculated as quick assets divided by current liabilities.

Common-size comparative statements.   Comparative financial statements in which each amount is expressed as a percentage of a base amount. In the balance sheet, total assets is usually selected as the base amount and is expressed as 100%. In the income statement, net sales is usually selected as the base amount.

Comparative statement.   A financial statement with data for two or more successive accounting periods placed in columns side by side in order to better illustrate changes in the data.

Current ratio.   The relation of a company's current assets to its current liabilities, that is, current assets divided by current liabilities.

Financial reporting.   The process of preparing and issuing financial information about a company.

General-purpose financial statements.   Financial statements (usually including the income statement, balance sheet, statement of retained earnings, and statement of changes in financial position) published by a company for use by persons who do not have the ability to obtain specialized financial reports designed to meet their interests.

Merchandise turnover.   The number of times a company's average inventory is sold during an accounting period, calculated by dividing cost of goods sold by average merchandise inventory.

Price-earnings ratio.   Market price per share of common stock divided by earnings per share.

Quick ratio.   A synonym for acid-test ratio.

Rate of return on common stockholders' equity.   Net income after taxes and dividends on preferred stock divided by average common stockholders' equity.

Rate of return on total assets employed.   Net income after taxes, plus interest expense, expressed as a percentage of total assets employed during the period.

Times fixed interest charges earned.   An indicator of a company's ability to satisfy fixed interest charges, calculated as net income before fixed interest charges and income taxes divided by fixed interest charges.

QUESTIONS FOR CLASS DISCUSSION

1. What are the three broad objectives of financial reporting prescribed by the FASB?

2. Comparative balance sheets often have columns showing increases and decreases in both dollar amounts and percentages. Why is this so?

3. When trends are calculated and compared, what item trends should be compared with the trend of sales?

4. What is meant by *common-size* financial statements?

5. What items are assigned a value of 100% *(a)* on a common-size balance sheet and *(b)* on a common-size income statement?

6. Why is working capital given special attention in the process of analyzing balance sheets?

7. For the following transactions indicate which increase working capital, which decrease working capital, and which have no effect on working capital:
   a. Collected accounts receivable.
   b. Borrowed money by giving a 90-day interest-bearing note.
   c. Declared a cash dividend.
   d. Paid a cash dividend previously declared.
   e. Sold plant assets at their book value.
   f. Sold merchandise at a profit.

8. List several factors that have an effect on working capital requirements.

9. A company has a 2 to 1 current ratio. List several reasons why this ratio may not be adequate.

10. State the significance of each of the following ratios and turnovers and tell how each is calculated:
    a. Current ratio.
    b. Acid-test ratio.
    c. Turnover of accounts receivable.
    d. Turnover of merchandise inventory.
    e. Rate of return on common stockholders' equity
    f. Ratio of pledged plant assets to long-term liabilities.

11. How are days' sales uncollected calculated? What is the significance of the number of days' sales uncollected?

12. Why do creditors like to see a high proportion of total assets being financed by owners' equity?

13. What is the ratio of pledged plant assets to long-term liabilities supposed to measure? Why must this ratio be interpreted with care?

14. What does the rate of return on assets employed tell about management?

15. How are earnings per share calculated in a corporation having outstanding only common stock and preferred stock that is not convertible into common stock?

16. How is a price-earnings ratio calculated?

CLASS EXERCISES

Exercise 20–1   Calculate trend percentages for the following items and tell whether the situation shown by the trends is favorable or unfavorable:

	198E	198D	198C	198B	198A
Sales.................	$364,000	$347,200	$333,200	$316,400	$280,000
Cost of goods sold......	252,000	235,200	226,800	201,600	168,000
Accounts receivable.....	43,400	39,200	37,800	35,000	28,000

Exercise 20–2   Where possible, calculate percentages of increase and decrease for the following unrelated items. The parentheses indicate deficit items.

	198B	198A
Equipment, net	$112,500	$75,000
Notes receivable	–0–	7,000
Notes payable	14,000	–0–
Retained earnings	(1,500)	15,000
Cash	9,000	(2,000)

Exercise 20–3   Express the following income statement information in common-size percentages and tell whether the situation shown is favorable or unfavorable.

STANDISH COMPANY
Comparative Income Statement
For Years Ended December 31, 198B, and 198A

	198B	198A
Sales	$150,000	$110,000
Cost of goods sold	100,500	70,400
Gross profit from sales	$ 49,500	$ 39,600
Operating expenses	37,500	26,400
Net income	$ 12,000	$ 13,200

Exercise 20–4   The end-year statements of Marathon Company follow:

MARATHON COMPANY
Balance Sheet, December 31, 198A

Assets		Liabilities and Stockholders' Equity	
Cash	$ 18,000	Accounts payable	$ 25,000
Accounts receivable, net	22,000	Mortgage payable, secured by	
Merchandise inventory	30,000	a lien on the plant assets ...	90,000
Prepaid expenses	5,000	Common stock $10 par value .	60,000
Plant assets, net	150,000	Retained earnings	50,000
		Total liabilities and	
Total assets	$225,000	stockholders' equity	$225,000

MARATHON COMPANY
Income Statement for Year Ended December 31, 198A

Sales		$420,000
Cost of goods sold:		
Merchandise inventory, January 1, 198A	$ 42,600	
Purchases	284,000	
Goods available for sale	$326,600	
Merchandise inventory, December 31, 198A ..	36,600	
Cost of goods sold		290,000
Gross profit on sales		$130,000
Operating expenses		105,000
Operating income		$ 25,000
Mortgage interest expense		3,000
Income before taxes		$ 22,000
Income taxes		4,000
Net income		$ 18,000

Required:

Calculate the following: *(a)* current ratio, *(b)* acid-test ratio, *(c)* days' sales uncollected, *(d)* merchandise turnover, *(e)* capital contribution of owners expressed as a percent, *(f)* ratio of pledged plant assets to long-term debt, *(g)* times fixed interest charges earned, *(h)* return on stockholders' equity, and *(i)* earnings per share. (Assume all sales were on credit and the stockholders' equity was $98,000 on January 1.)

Exercise 20–5
    Common-size and trend percentages for a company's sales, cost of goods sold, and expenses follow:

Common-Size Percentages				**Trend Percentages**			
	198C	*198B*	*198A*		*198C*	*198B*	*198A*
Sales..............	100.0	100.0	100.0	Sales	92.0	97.0	100.0
Cost of goods sold ..	55.4	58.8	60.0	Cost of goods sold ..	85.0	95.0	100.0
Expenses	29.3	29.9	30.0	Expenses	90.0	96.7	100.0

Required:

Present statistics to prove whether the company's net income increased, decreased, or remained unchanged during the three-year period represented above.

PROBLEMS

Problem 20–1
    The year-end statements of Faster Company follow:

FASTER COMPANY
Income Statement for Year Ended December 31, 198A

Sales		$663,000
Cost of goods sold:		
Merchandise inventory, January 1, 198A	$ 49,140	
Purchases	416,520	
Goods available for sale	$465,660	
Merchandise inventory, December 31, 198A	44,460	
Cost of goods sold		421,200
Gross profit from sales		$241,800
Operating expenses		206,310
Operating income		$ 35,490
Mortgage interest expense		5,460
Income before taxes		$ 30,030
Income taxes		6,630
Net income		$ 23,400

FASTER COMPANY
Balance Sheet, December 31, 198A

Assets		Liabilities and Stockholders' Equity	
Cash	$ 11,180	Accounts payable	$ 30,940
Temporary investments	13,000	Accrued wages payable	1,430
Notes receivable	3,900	Income taxes payable	6,630
Accounts receivable, net	33,150	Mortgage payable, secured by	
Merchandise inventory	44,460	a lien on the plant assets ...	88,400
Prepaid expenses	1,560	Common stock, $5 par value ..	130,000
Plant assets, net	221,000	Retained earnings	70,850
		Total liabilities and	
Total assets	$328,250	stockholders' equity	$328,250

Required:

Calculate the following: *(a)* current ratio, *(b)* acid-test ratio, *(c)* days' sales uncollected, *(d)* merchandise turnover, *(e)* ratio of pledged plant assets to long-term debt, *(f)* times fixed interest charges earned, *(g)* return on total assets employed, *(h)* return on stockholders' equity, and *(i)* earnings per share. Assume all sales were on credit, the assets totaled $321,750 on January 1, and the stockholders' equity at the beginning of the year was $189,150.

Problem 20–2   The condensed statements of Ames Corporation follow:

AMES CORPORATION
Comparative Income Statements
For Years Ended December 31, 198C, 198B, and 198A
($000)

	198C	198B	198A
Sales	$15,000	$13,500	$12,000
Cost of goods sold	10,725	9,720	8,532
Gross profit from sales	$ 4,275	$ 3,780	$ 3,468
Selling expenses	$ 2,250	$ 2,038	$ 1,824
Administrative expenses	1,410	1,283	1,176
Total expenses	$ 3,660	$ 3,321	$ 3,000
Income before taxes	$ 615	$ 459	$ 468
State and federal income taxes ..	294	224	228
Net income	$ 321	$ 235	$ 240

AMES CORPORATION
Comparative Balance Sheets
December 31, 198C, 198B, and 198A
($000)

	198C	198B	198A
Assets			
Current assets	$1,044	$ 922	$1,125
Long-term investments	–0–	8	75
Plant and equipment	3,996	4,014	3,600
Total assets	$5,040	$4,944	$4,800
Liabilities and Capital			
Current liabilities	$ 435	$ 420	$ 375
Common stock	3,150	3,150	3,000
Other contributed capital	92	92	75
Retained earnings	1,363	1,282	1,350
Total liabilities and capital	$5,040	$4,944	$4,800

Required:

1. Calculate each year's current ratio.
2. Express the income statement data in common-size percentages.
3. Express the balance sheet data in trend percentages.
4. Comment on any significant relationships revealed by the ratios and percentages.

Problem 20–3

Following are data from the statements of two companies selling similar products:

Data from the Current Year-End Balance Sheets

	Sled Company	Zip Company
Cash	$ 11,900	$ 20,000
Notes receivable	7,700	3,200
Accounts receivable	42,000	64,000
Merchandise inventory	58,800	87,680
Prepaid expenses	1,680	3,520
Plant and equipment, net	232,120	274,400
Total assets	$354,200	$452,800
Current liabilities	$ 56,000	$ 80,000
Mortgage payable	70,000	86,000
Common stock, $10 par value	140,000	160,000
Retained earnings	88,200	132,800
Total liabilities and capital	$354,200	$452,800

Data from the Current Year's Income Statements

Sales	$672,000	$880,000
Cost of goods sold	528,080	699,840
Interest expense	4,200	5,600
Net income	23,373	28,896

Beginning-of-Year Data

Merchandise inventory	$ 53,200	$ 85,120
Total assets	345,800	443,200
Stockholders' equity	217,000	285,120

Required:

1. Calculate current ratios, acid-test ratios, merchandise turnovers, and days' sales uncollected for the two companies. Then state which company you think is the better short-term credit risk and why.
2. Calculate earnings per share, rate of return on total assets employed, and rate of return on stockholders' equity. Then, under the assumption that each company's stock can be purchased at book value, state which company's stock you think is the better investment and why.

Problem 20–4

The condensed comparative statements of Hondo Crutch Company follow:

HONDO CRUTCH COMPANY
Comparative Income Statements
For Years Ended December 31, 198G–198A
($000)

	198G	*198F*	*198E*	*198D*	*198C*	*198B*	*198A*
Sales	$872	$840	$760	$680	$572	$500	$400
Cost of goods sold	604	585	515	430	360	310	250
Gross profit from sales	$268	$255	$245	$250	$212	$190	$150
Operating expenses	238	220	197	138	118	110	100
Income before taxes	$ 30	$ 35	$ 48	$112	$ 94	$ 80	$ 50

HONDO CRUTCH COMPANY
Comparative Balance Sheets
December 31, 198G–198A
($000)

	198G	*198F*	*198E*	*198D*	*198C*	*198B*	*198A*
Assets							
Cash	$ 4	$ 10	$ 12	$ 15	$ 17	$ 14	$ 20
Accounts receivable, net	92	90	88	62	54	52	40
Merchandise inventory	226	218	204	165	141	118	100
Other current assets	2	4	2	6	4	4	2
Long-term investments	–0–	–0–	–0–	38	38	38	38
Plant and equipment, net	440	450	446	202	204	198	200
Total assets	$764	$772	$752	$488	$458	$424	$400
Liabilities and Capital							
Current liabilities	$159	$156	$140	$ 90	$ 82	$ 64	$ 50
Long-term liabilities	178	180	182	34	36	38	40
Common stock	250	250	250	200	200	200	200
Premium on common stock ..	60	60	60	50	50	50	50
Retained earnings	117	126	120	114	90	72	60
Total liabilities and capital....	$764	$772	$752	$488	$458	$424	$400

Required:

1. Calculate trend percentages for the items of the statements.
2. Analyze and comment on any situations shown in the statements.

Problem 20–5

Tack Company began the month of July with $270,000 of current assets, a 3 to 1 current ratio, and a 1.8 to 1 acid-test ratio. During the month, it completed the following transactions:

Aug. 1 Bought $30,000 of merchandise on account. (The company uses a perpetual inventory system.)

6 Sold for $40,000 merchandise that cost $22,000.
9 Collected a $7,000 account receivable.
10 Paid a $18,000 account payable.
16 Wrote off a $4,000 bad debt against the allowance for doubtful accounts.
17 Declared a $1 per share cash dividend on the 15,000 shares of outstanding common stock.
22 Paid the dividend declared on July 18.
29 Borrowed $20,000 by giving the bank a 60-day, 12% note.
30 Borrowed $60,000 by placing a 10-year mortgage on the plant.
31 Used the $60,000 proceeds of the mortgage to buy additional machinery.

Required:

Prepare a schedule showing the company's current ratio, acid-test ratio, and working capital after each of the foregoing transactions. Round to two decimal places.

ALTERNATE PROBLEMS

Problem 20–1A The year-end statements of Seat Cover Company follow:

SEAT COVER COMPANY
Balance Sheet, December 31, 198A

Assets		Liabilities and Stockholders' Equity	
Cash	$ 17,000	Accounts payable	$ 42,300
Temporary investments	11,000	Accrued wages payable	1,600
Notes receivable	3,500	Income taxes payable	6,700
Accounts receivable, net	31,400	Mortgage payable, secured by	
Merchandise inventory	110,700	a lien on the plant assets ...	75,000
Prepaid expenses	2,400	Common stock, $10 par value .	100,000
Plant assets, net	189,000	Retained earnings	139,400
		Total liabilities and	
Total assets	$365,000	stockholders' equity	$365,000

SEAT COVER COMPANY
Income Statement for Year Ended December 31, 198A

Sales		$520,000
Cost of goods sold:		
Merchandise inventory, January 1, 198A	$ 36,700	
Purchases	306,500	
Goods available for sale	$343,200	
Merchandise inventory, December 31, 198A	37,300	
Cost of goods sold		305,900
Gross profit from sales		$214,100
Operating expenses		142,600
Operating income		$ 71,500
Mortgage interest expense		6,000
Income before taxes		$ 65,500
Income taxes		13,900
Net income		$ 51,600

Required:

Calculate the following: *(a)* current ratio, *(b)* acid-test ratio, *(c)* days' sales uncollected, *(d)* merchandise turnover, *(e)* ratio of pledged plant assets to long-term debt, *(f)* times fixed interest charges earned, *(g)* return on total assets employed, *(h)* return on stockholders' equity, and *(i)* earnings per share. Assume all sales were on credit, assets employed at the beginning of the year totaled $335,000, and stockholders' equity at the beginning of the year was $210,600.

Problem 20–2A   The condensed statements of Heeling Company follow:

HEELING COMPANY
Comparative Income Statements
For Years Ended December 31, 198C, 198B, and 198A
($000)

	198C	*198B*	*198A*
Sales............................	$9,000	$8,000	$7,000
Cost of goods sold...............	5,000	4,400	4,000
Gross margin on sales	$4,000	$3,600	$3,000
Selling expenses	$ 920	$ 880	$ 800
Administrative expenses	650	610	600
Total expenses	$1,570	$1,490	$1,400
Income before taxes	$2,430	$2,110	$1,600
State and federal income taxes.....	780	700	600
Net income	$1,650	$1,410	$1,000

HEELING COMPANY
Comparative Balance Sheets
December 31, 198C, 198B, and 198A
($000)

	198C	*198B*	*198A*
Assets			
Current assets	$ 510	$ 540	$ 650
Plant and equipment	2,500	2,410	2,100
Total assets.....................	$3,010	$2,950	$2,750
Liabilities and Capital			
Current liabilities	$ 200	$ 220	$ 180
Common stock, $10 par value	1,200	1,200	1,200
Other contributed capital...........	300	300	300
Retained earnings	1,310	1,230	1,070
Total liabilities and capital	$3,010	$2,950	$2,750

Required:

1. Calculate each year's current ratio.
2. Express the income statement data in common-size percentages.
3. Express the balance sheet data in trend percentages.
4. Comment on any significant relationships revealed by the ratios and percentages.

Problem 20–3A   Following are the condensed 198B and 198A statements of Andersen Tools:

ANDERSEN TOOLS
Comparative Income Statements
For Years Ended December 31, 198B, and 198A

	198B	198A
Sales (all on credit)	$585,000	$530,000
Cost of goods sold:		
Merchandise inventory, January 1	$ 49,000	$ 42,000
Purchases	297,400	289,100
Goods for sale	$346,400	$331,100
Merchandise inventory, December 31	47,000	45,000
Cost of goods sold	$299,400	$286,100
Gross profit from sales	$285,600	$243,900
Operating expenses	201,500	184,700
Income before taxes	$ 84,100	$ 59,200

ANDERSEN TOOLS
Comparative Balance Sheets
December 31, 198B, and 198A

	198B	198A
Assets		
Cash	$ 17,500	$ 16,000
Accounts receivable.....................	42,900	49,200
Merchandise inventory	61,100	54,300
Plant assets, net........................	136,800	109,900
Total assets............................	$258,300	$229,400
Liabilities and Stockholders' Equity		
Accounts payable	$ 30,100	$ 31,400
Notes payable (short term)................	20,000	17,000
Mortgage payable (due in 1990)	35,000	35,000
Common stock	100,000	100,000
Retained earnings	73,200	46,000
Total liabilities and stockholders' equity	$258,300	$229,400

Required:

1. Calculate common-size percentages for sales, cost of goods sold, gross profit from sales, operating expenses, and income before taxes; and calculate the current ratio, acid-test ratio, merchandise turnover, and days' sales uncollected for each of the two years.
2. Comment on the situation shown by your calculations.

Problem 20–4A   The condensed comparative statements of Rocky's Racecar Manufacturing Company follow:

ROCKY'S RACECAR MANUFACTURING COMPANY
Comparative Income Statements
For Years Ended December 31, 198E–198A
($000)

	198E	198D	198C	198B	198A
Sales	$780	$620	$560	$510	$450
Cost of goods sold	733	565	497	427	352
Gross profit from sales	$ 47	$ 55	$ 63	$ 83	$ 98
Operating expenses	16	15	14	12	10
Income before taxes	$ 31	$ 40	$ 49	$ 71	$ 88

ROCKY'S RACECAR MANUFACTURING COMPANY
Comparative Balance Sheets
December 31, 198E–198A
($000)

	198E	198D	198C	198B	198A
Assets					
Cash........................	$ 6	$ 6	$ 10	$ 20	$ 19
Accounts receivable, net	21	16	13	21	21
Merchandise inventory	269	250	230	169	167
Other current assets	3	2	2	7	1
Long-term investments	0	0	0	42	40
Plant assets, net	236	243	250	299	321
Total assets	$535	$517	$505	$559	$569
Liabilities and Capital					
Current liabilities	$ 88	$ 80	$ 77	$ 98	$100
Long-term liabilities	80	76	70	103	130
Common stock................	200	200	200	200	200
Premium on common stock.....	36	36	36	36	36
Retained earnings	131	125	122	122	103
Total liabilities and capital	$535	$517	$505	$559	$569

Required:

1. Calculate trend percentages for the items of the statements.
2. Assuming flexibility in the use of plant assets, analyze the situation and suggest reasons for the poor financial position and possibilities for recovery.

Problem 20–5A

Haines Company had $162,000 of current assets, a 2.7 to 1 current ratio, and a 1.25 to 1 quick ratio. It then completed the following transactions:

a. Collected a $6,000 account receivable.
b. Wrote off a $4,000 bad debt against the allowance for doubtful accounts.
c. Borrowed $25,000 by giving its bank a 60-day, 6% note.
d. Bought $18,000 of merchandise on credit. The company uses a perpetual inventory system.
e. Declared a $0.75 per share cash dividend on its 16,000 shares of outstanding common stock.
f. Paid the dividend declared in (e) above.
g. Declared a 1,000-share stock dividend. The stock was selling at $15 per share on the day of the declaration.
h. Distributed the dividend stock of (g) above.
i. Sold for $20,000 merchandise that cost $12,000.

Required:

Prepare a schedule showing the company's current ratio, its acid-test ratio, and the amount of its working capital after each of the foregoing transactions. Round to two decimal places.

PROVOCATIVE PROBLEMS

Provocative
Problem 20–1,
Leeward Sales
Company

You are the controller of Leeward Sales Company. In preparation for the next meeting of the company's board of directors, you have calculated the following ratios, turnovers, and percentages to enable you to answer questions:

	198C	198B	198A
Current ratio	2.10 to 1	2.01 to 1	1.90 to 1
Acid-test ratio	1.16 to 1	1.24 to 1	1.30 to 1
Merchandise turnover	10.1 times	10.6 times	11.0 times
Accounts receivable turnover	8.0 times	8.6 times	8.9 times
Return on stockholders' equity	6.30%	6.86%	7.10%
Return on total assets	6.65%	6.70%	7.01%
Sales to plant assets	5.11 to 1	4.93 to 1	4.70 to 1
Sales trend	125.00	116.00	100.00
Selling expenses to net sales	15.06%	15.95%	16.35%

Required:

Using the statistics given, answer each of the following questions and explain how you arrived at your answer.

1. Is it becoming easier for the company to meet its current debts on time and to take advantage of cash discounts?
2. Is the company collecting its accounts receivable more rapidly?
3. Is the company's investment in accounts receivable decreasing?
4. Are dollars invested in inventory increasing?
5. Is the company's investment in plant assets increasing?
6. Is the stockholders' investment becoming more profitable?
7. Is the company using debt leverage to the advantage of its stockholders?
8. Did the dollar amount of selling expenses decrease during the three-year period?

Provocative
Problem 20–2, a
Comparison of
Companies

Echo and Factor are competing companies with similar backgrounds. The stock of both companies is traded locally, and each stock can be purchased at its book value. J. T. Smith has an opportunity to invest in either company but is undecided as to which is the better managed company and which is the better investment. Prepare a report to J. T. Smith stating which company you think is the better managed and which company's stock you think may be the better investment. Back your report with any ratios, turnovers, and other analyses you think pertinent.

December 31, 198A, Balance Sheets

	Echo Company	Factor Company
Cash	$ 49,400	$ 47,600
Accounts receivable, net	121,600	133,450
Merchandise inventory	161,500	174,250
Prepaid expenses	3,800	5,100
Plant and equipment, net	608,000	595,000
Total assets	$ 944,300	$ 955,400

	Echo Company	Factor Company
Current liabilities	$ 142,500	$ 166,600
Mortgage payable	201,400	187,000
Common stock, $10 par value	380,000	340,000
Retained earnings	220,400	261,800
Total liabilities and capital	$ 944,300	$ 955,400

Income Statements for the Year Ended December 31, 198A

	Echo Company	Factor Company
Sales	$2,318,000	$2,371,500
Cost of goods sold	1,634,950	1,688,100
Gross profit on sales	$ 683,050	$ 683,400
Operating expenses..............	532,000	571,200
Operating income...............	$ 151,050	$ 112,200
Interest expense................	19,950	18,700
Income before taxes	$ 131,100	$ 93,500
Income taxes	50,540	33,830
Net income	$ 80,560	$ 59,670

January 1, 198A, Data

	Echo Company	Factor Company
Merchandise inventory	$ 127,300	$ 148,750
Total assets	912,000	935,000
Stockholders' equity	589,000	612,000

Provocative
Problem 20–3,
Texas
Instruments

Use the financial statements and related footnotes of Texas Instruments shown in the Appendix beginning on page 987 to complete the following requirements:

Required:

1. Calculate the following ratios and turnovers for 1982 and 1981: *(a)* current ratio, *(b)* acid-test ratio, *(c)* days' sales uncollected, *(d)* merchandise turnover (assume the December 31, 1980, balance of Inventories was $442,-700,000), *(e)* rate of return on total assets employed (assume total assets on December 31, 1980, amounted to $2,413,700,000), and *(f)* rate of return on stockholders' equity (assume total stockholders' equity on December 31, 1980, was $1,164,500,000.)
2. Express the income statements for 1982 and 1981 in common-size percentages.
3. Review the financial statements and related footnotes of Texas Instruments and write a brief summary of the results of 1982 compared to 1981.

Managerial Accounting for Costs

PART SEVEN

Manufacturing Accounting

21

After studying Chapter 21, you should be able to:

Describe the basic differences in the financial statements of manufacturing companies and merchandising companies.

Describe the procedures inherent in a general accounting system for a manufacturing company.

List the different accounts that appear on a manufacturing company's books and state what the accounts represent.

Explain the purpose of a manufacturing statement, how one is composed, and how the statement is integrated with the primary financial statements.

Prepare financial statements for a manufacturing company from a work sheet.

Prepare the adjusting and closing entries for a manufacturing company.

Explain the procedures for assigning costs to the different manufacturing inventories.

Define or explain the words and phrases listed in the chapter Glossary.

In previous chapters, consideration has been given to the accounting problems of service-type and merchandising companies. In this chapter, some problems of manufacturing enterprises are examined.

Manufacturing and merchandising companies are alike in that both depend upon the sale of one or more commodities or products for revenue. However, they differ in one important way. A merchandising company buys the goods it sells in the same condition in which they are sold. On the other hand, a manufacturing company buys raw materials that it manufactures into the finished products it sells. For example, a shoe store buys shoes and sells them in the same form in which they are purchased; but a manufacturer of shoes buys leather, cloth, glue, nails, and dye and turns these items into salable shoes.

BASIC DIFFERENCE IN ACCOUNTING

The basic difference in accounting for manufacturing and merchandising companies grows from the idea in the preceding paragraph. That is the idea that a merchandising company buys the goods it sells in their finished ready-for-sale state. A manufacturer must create what it sells from raw materials. As a result, the merchandising company can easily determine the cost of the goods it has bought for sale by examining the debit balance of its Purchases account. In contrast, the manufacturer must combine the balances of a number of material, labor, and overhead accounts to determine the cost of the goods it has manufactured for sale.

To emphasize this difference, the cost of goods sold section from a merchandising company's income statement is condensed and presented below alongside the cost of goods sold section of a manufacturing company.

Merchandising Company		Manufacturing Company	
Cost of goods sold:		Cost of goods sold:	
Beginning merchandise inventory	$14,200	Beginning finished goods inventory	$ 11,200
Cost of goods purchased	34,150	Cost of goods manufactured (see Manufacturing Statement)	170,500
Goods available for sale	$48,350	Goods available for sale	$181,700
Ending merchandise inventory	12,100	Ending finished goods inventory	10,300
Cost of goods sold	$36,250	Cost of goods sold	$171,400

Notice in the cost of goods sold section from the manufacturing company's income statement that the inventories of goods for sale are called *finished goods inventories* rather than merchandise inventories. Notice too that the "Cost of goods purchased" element of the merchandising company becomes "Cost of goods manufactured (see Manufacturing Statement)" on the manufacturer's income statement. These differences exist because the merchandising company buys its goods ready for sale, while the manufacturer creates its salable products from raw materials.

The words *see Manufacturing Statement* refer the income statement reader to a separate schedule called a manufacturing statement (see page 729) which shows the costs of manufacturing the products produced by a manufacturing company. The records and techniques used in accounting for these costs are the distinguishing characteristics of manufacturing accounting.

SYSTEMS OF ACCOUNTING IN MANUFACTURING COMPANIES

The accounting system used by a manufacturing company may be either a so-called general accounting system like the one described in this chapter or a cost accounting system. A general accounting system uses periodic physical inventories of raw materials, goods in process, and finished goods; and it has as its goal the determination of the total cost of all goods manufactured during each accounting period. Cost accounting systems differ in that they use perpetual inventories and have as their goal the determination of the unit cost of manufacturing a product or performing a service. Such systems are discussed in Chapter 22.

ELEMENTS OF MANUFACTURING COSTS

A manufacturer takes *raw materials* and by applying *direct labor* and *factory overhead* converts these materials into finished products. Raw materials, direct labor, and factory overhead are the "elements of manufacturing costs."

Raw Materials

Raw materials are the commodities that enter into and become a part of a finished product. Such items as leather, dye, cloth, nails, and glue are raw materials used by shoe manufacturers. Raw materials are often called *direct materials*. Since direct materials physically become part of the finished product, the cost of direct materials is easily traced to units of product or batches of production, and the direct materials cost of production can be directly charged to units of product or batches of production without the use of arbitrary or highly judgmental cost allocation procedures.

Direct materials are distinguished from *indirect materials* or factory supplies which are such items as grease and oil for machinery, cleaning fluids, and so on. Indirect materials are not easily traced to specific units or batches of production and are accounted for as factory overhead.

The materials of a manufacturer are called raw materials, even though they may not necessarily be in their natural raw state. For example, leather is manufactured from hides, nails from steel, and cloth from cotton. Nevertheless, leather, nails, and cloth are the raw materials of a shoe manufacturer even though they are the finished products of previous manufacturers.

Direct Labor

Direct labor is often described as the labor of those people who work, either with machines or hand tools, specifically on the materials converted into finished products. The cost of direct labor can therefore be easily associated with and charged to the units or batches of production to which the labor was applied. In manufacturing, direct labor is distinguished from *indirect labor*. Indirect labor is the labor of superintendents, foremen, millwrights, engineers, janitors, and others who do not work specifically on the manufactured products but do aid in production. The labor provided by these workers often makes production possible but is not applied specifically to the finished product. Indirect labor is accounted for as a factory overhead cost.

In a general accounting system, an account called *Direct Labor* is debited each payday for the wages of those workers who work directly on the product. Likewise, each payday, the wages of indirect workers are debited to one or more indirect labor accounts. Also, at the end of each period, the amounts of accrued direct and indirect labor are recorded in the direct and indirect labor accounts by means of adjusting entries. From this it can be seen that a manufacturing company's payroll accounting is similar to that of a merchandising company. When a cost accounting system is not involved, no new techniques are required and only the new direct and indirect labor accounts distinguish the payroll accounting of a manufacturer from that of a merchant.

Factory Overhead

Factory overhead, often called *manufacturing overhead* or *factory burden,* includes all manufacturing costs other than direct materials and direct labor costs. Factory overhead may include:

Indirect labor.	Heat, lights, and power.
Factory supplies.	Depreciation of plant and equipment.
Repairs to buildings and equipment.	Amortization of patents.
Insurance on plant and equipment.	Small tools written off.
Taxes on plant and equipment.	Workmen's compensation insurance.
Taxes on raw materials and work in process.	Payroll taxes on the wages of the factory workers.

Factory overhead does not include selling and administrative expenses. Selling and administrative expenses are not factory overhead because they are not incurred in the manufacturing process. These costs could be calling selling and administrative overhead, but not factory overhead.

All factory overhead costs are accumulated in overhead cost accounts that vary in number and description from company to company. The exact accounts used in each case depend upon the nature of the company and the information desired. For example, one account called Expired Insurance on Plant Equipment may be maintained, or separate expired insurance accounts for buildings and the different kinds of equipment may be used. Regardless of the accounts used, overhead costs are recorded in the same ways as are selling and administrative expenses. Some, such as indirect labor and light and power, are recorded in registers or journals as they are paid and are then posted to the accounts. Other costs, such as depreciation and expired insurance, are recorded in the accounts through adjusting entries.

ACCOUNTS UNIQUE TO A MANUFACTURING COMPANY

Because of the nature of its operations, a manufacturing company's ledger normally contains more accounts than that of a merchandising company. However, some of the same accounts are found in the ledgers of both, for example, Cash, Accounts Receivable, Sales, and many selling and administrative expenses. Nevertheless, many accounts are unique to a manufacturing company. For instance, accounts such as Machinery and Equipment, Accumulated Depreciation of Machinery and Equipment, Factory Supplies, Factory Supplies Used, Raw Materials Inventory, Raw Material Purchases, Goods in Process Inventory, Finished Goods Inventory, and Manufacturing Summary are normally found only in the ledgers of manufacturing companies. Some of these accounts merit special attention.

Raw Material Purchases Account

When a general accounting system is in use, the cost of all raw materials purchased is debited to an account called Raw Material Purchases. Often a special column is provided in the Voucher Register or other special journal for the debits of the individual purchases. Thus, it is possible to periodically post these debits in one amount, the column total.

Raw Materials Inventory Account

When a general accounting system is in use, the raw materials on hand at the end of each accounting period are determined by a physical inventory count; and through a closing entry, the cost of this inventory is debited to Raw Materials Inventory. That account becomes a record of the materials on hand at the end of one period and the beginning of the next.

Goods in Process Inventory Account

Most manufacturing companies have on hand at all times partially processed products called *goods in process* or *work in process*. These are products in the process of being manufactured, products that have received a portion or all of their materials and have had some labor and overhead applied but that are not completed.

When a general manufacturing accounting system is used, the amount of goods in process at the end of each accounting period is determined by a physical inventory count; and through a closing entry, the cost of this inventory is debited to Goods in Process Inventory. This account then becomes a record of the goods in process at the end of one period and the beginning of the next.

Finished Goods Inventory Account

The *finished goods* of a manufacturer are the equivalent of a store's merchandise; they are products in their completed state ready for sale. Actually, the only difference is that a manufacturing company creates its finished goods from raw materials, while a store buys its merchandise in a finished, ready-for-sale state.

In a general accounting system, the amount of finished goods on hand at the end of each period is determined by a physical inventory; and through a closing entry, the cost of this inventory is debited to Finished Goods Inventory. That account provides a record of the finished goods at the end of one period and the beginning of the next.

The three inventories—raw materials, goods in process, and finished goods—are classified as current assets for balance sheet purposes. Factory supplies is also a current asset.

INCOME STATEMENT OF A MANUFACTURING COMPANY

The income statement of a manufacturing company is similar to that of a merchandising company. To see this, compare the income statement of Kona Sales Incorporated, Illustration 5–1 on page 166, with that of Excel Manufacturing Company, Illustration 21–1. Notice that the revenue, selling, and general and administrative expense sections are very similar. However, when the cost of goods sold sections are compared, a difference is apparent. Here the item "Cost of goods

Illustration 21–1

THE EXCEL MANUFACTURING COMPANY
Income Statement for Year Ended December 31, 198A

Revenue:			
Sales			$310,000
Cost of goods sold:			
Finished goods inventory, January 1, 198A		$ 11,200	
Cost of goods manufactured (see Manufacturing Statement)		170,500	
Goods available for sale		$181,700	
Finished goods inventory, December 31, 198A		10,300	
Cost of goods sold			171,400
Gross profit			$138,600
Operating expenses:			
Selling expenses:			
Sales salaries expense	$18,000		
Advertising expense	5,500		
Delivery wages expense	12,000		
Shipping supplies expense	250		
Delivery equipment insurance expense	300		
Depreciation expense, delivery equipment	2,100		
Total selling expenses		$ 38,150	
General and administrative expenses:			
Office salaries expense	$15,700		
Miscellaneous general expense	200		
Bad debts expense	1,550		
Office supplies expense	100		
Depreciation expense, office equipment	200		
Total general and administrative expenses		17,750	
Total operating expenses			55,900
Operating income			$ 82,700
Financial expense:			
Mortgage interest expense			4,000
Income before state and federal income taxes			$ 78,700
Less state and federal income taxes			32,600
Net income			$ 46,100
Net income per common share (20,000 shares outstanding)			$ 2.31

manufactured" replaces the "Purchases" element, and finished goods inventories take the place of merchandise inventories.

Observe the cost of goods sold section of Excel Manufacturing Company's income statement. Only the *total* cost of goods manufactured is shown. It would be possible to expand this section to show the detailed costs of the materials, direct labor, and factory overhead entering into the cost of goods manufactured. However, this would make the income statement long and unwieldy. Consequently, the common practice is to show only the total cost of goods manufactured on the income statement and to attach a supporting schedule showing the details. This supporting schedule is called a *schedule of the cost of goods manufactured* or a *manufacturing statement.*

MANUFACTURING STATEMENT

The cost elements of manufacturing are raw materials, direct labor, and factory overhead; and a manufacturing statement is normally constructed in such a manner as to emphasize these elements. Notice in Illustration 21–2 that the first section of the statement shows the cost of raw materials used. Also observe the manner of presentation is the same as that used on the income statement of a merchandising company to show cost of goods purchased and sold.

The second section shows the cost of direct labor used in production, and the third section shows factory overhead costs. If overhead accounts are not too numerous, the balance of each is often listed in this third section, as in Illustration 21–2. However, if overhead accounts are numerous, only the total of all may be shown. In such cases, the total is supported by a separate schedule showing each cost.

In the fourth section, the calculation of costs of goods manufactured is completed. Here the cost of the beginning goods in process inventory is added to the sum of the manufacturing costs to show the total cost of all goods in process during the period. From this total, the cost of the goods still in process at the end of the period is subtracted to show cost of the goods manufactured.

The manufacturing statement is prepared from the Manufacturing Statement columns of a work sheet. The items that appear on the statement are summarized in these columns, and all that is required in constructing the statement is a rearrangement of the items into the proper statement order. Illustration 21–3 shows the manufacturing work sheet.

WORK SHEET FOR A MANUFACTURING COMPANY

In examining Illustration 21–3, note first that there are no Adjusted Trial Balance columns. The experienced accountant commonly omits

Illustration 21-2

EXCEL MANUFACTURING COMPANY
Manufacturing Statement for Year Ended December 31, 198A

1	Raw materials:		
	Raw materials inventory, January 1, 198A............	$ 8,000	
	Raw materials purchased $85,000		
	Freight on raw materials purchased 1,500		
	Delivered cost of raw materials purchased	86,500	
	Raw materials available for use.....................	$94,500	
	Raw materials inventory, December 31, 198A	9,000	
	Raw materials used		$ 85,500
2	Direct labor		60,000
3	Factory overhead costs:		
	Indirect labor	$ 9,000	
	Supervision	6,000	
	Power	2,600	
	Repairs and maintenance	2,500	
	Factory taxes.....................................	1,900	
	Factory supplies used	500	
	Factory insurance expired.........................	1,200	
	Small tools written off	200	
	Depreciation of machinery and equipment	3,500	
	Depreciation of building...........................	1,800	
	Amortization of patents	800	
4	Total factory overhead costs		30,000
	Total manufacturing costs...................		$175,500
	Add goods in process inventory, January 1, 198A.....		2,500
	Total goods in process during the year		$178,000
	Deduct goods in process inventory,		
	December 31, 198A		7,500
	Cost of goods manufactured		$170,500

such columns to save time and effort. How a work sheet without Adjusted Trial Balance columns is prepared and how this saves time and effort were explained in Chapter 5.

To understand the work sheet of Illustration 21–3, recall that a work sheet is a tool with which the accountant—

1. Achieves the effect of adjusting the accounts before entering the adjustments in a journal and posting them to the accounts.
2. Sorts the adjusted account balances into columns according to the financial statement upon which they appear.
3. Calculates and confirms the mathematical accuracy of the net income.

With the foregoing in mind, a primary difference between the work sheet of a manufacturing company and that of a merchandising company is an additional set of columns. Insofar as the adjustments are concerned, they are made in the same way on both kinds of work

Illustration 21-3

THE EXCEL MANUFACTURING COMPANY
Manufacturing Work Sheet for Year Ended December 31, 198A

Account Titles	Trial Balance Dr.	Trial Balance Cr.	Adjustments Dr.	Adjustments Cr.	Mfg. Statement Dr.	Mfg. Statement Cr.	Income Statement Dr.	Income Statement Cr.	Balance Sheet Dr.	Balance Sheet Cr.
Cash	11,000								11,000	
Accounts receivable	32,000								32,000	
Allowance for doubtful accounts		300		(a) 1,550						1,850
Raw materials inventory	8,000				8,000	9,000			9,000	
Goods in process inventory	2,500				2,500	7,500			7,500	
Finished goods inventory	11,200						11,200	10,300	10,300	
Office supplies	150			(b) 100					50	
Shipping supplies	300			(c) 250					50	
Factory supplies	750			(d) 500					250	
Prepaid insurance	1,800			(e) 1,500					300	
Small tools	1,300			(f) 200					1,100	
Delivery equipment	9,000								9,000	
Accumulated depreciation of delivery equipment		1,900		(g) 2,100						4,000
Office equipment	1,700								1,700	
Accumulated depreciation of office equipment		200		(h) 200						400
Machinery and equipment	72,000								72,000	
Accumulated depr. of machinery and equipment		3,000		(i) 3,500						6,500
Factory building	90,000								90,000	
Accumulated depreciation of factory building		1,500		(j) 1,800						3,300
Land	9,500								9,500	
Patents	12,000			(k) 800					11,200	
Accounts payable		14,000								14,000
Mortgage payable		50,000								50,000
Common stock, $5 par value		100,000								100,000
Retained earnings		3,660								3,660
Sales		310,000						310,000		
Raw material purchases	85,000				85,000					
Freight on raw materials	1,500				1,500					
Direct labor	59,600		(l) 400		60,000					
Indirect labor	8,940		(l) 60		9,000					

	Trial Balance Dr.	Trial Balance Cr.	Adjustments Dr.	Adjustments Cr.	Mfg. Dr.	Mfg. Cr.	Income Statement Dr.	Income Statement Cr.	Balance Sheet Dr.	Balance Sheet Cr.
Supervision	6,000				6,000					
Power expense	2,600				2,600					
Repairs and maintenance	2,500				2,500					
Factory taxes	1,900				1,900					
Sales salaries expense	18,000						18,000			
Advertising expense	5,500						5,500			
Delivery wages expense	11,920		(l) 80				12,000			
Office salaries expense	15,700						15,700			
Miscellaneous general expense	200						200			
Mortgage interest expense	2,000		(m) 2,000				4,000			
	484,560	484,560								
Bad debts expense			(a) 1,550				1,550			
Office supplies expense			(b) 100				100			
Shipping supplies expense			(c) 250				250			
Factory supplies used			(d) 500		500					
Factory insurance expired			(e) 1,200		1,200					
Delivery equipment insurance expense			(e) 300				300			
Small tools written off			(f) 200		200					
Depreciation expense, delivery equipment			(g) 2,100				2,100			
Depreciation expense, office equipment			(h) 200				200			
Depreciation of machinery and equipment			(i) 3,500		3,500					
Depreciation of building			(j) 1,800		1,800					
Amortization of patents			(k) 800		800					
Accrued wages payable				(l) 540						540
Mortgage interest payable				(m) 2,000						2,000
State and federal income taxes expense			(n) 32,600				32,600			
State and federal income taxes payable				(n) 32,600		16,500				32,600
			47,640	47,640		170,500				
Cost of goods manufactured to Income Statement columns						170,500				
					187,000	187,000	274,200	320,300	264,950	218,850
Net income							46,100			46,100
							320,300	320,300	264,950	264,950

sheets. Also, the mathematical accuracy of the net income is confirmed in the same way. However, since an additional accounting statement, the manufacturing statement, is prepared for a manufacturing company, the work sheet of such a company has an additional set of columns, the Manufacturing Statement columns, into which are sorted the items appearing on the manufacturing statement.

PREPARING A MANUFACTURING COMPANY'S WORK SHEET

A manufacturing company's work sheet is prepared in the same manner as that of a merchandising company. First, a trial balance of the ledger is entered in the Trial Balance columns. Next, information for the adjustments is assembled, and the adjustments are entered in the Adjustments columns. The adjustments information for the work sheet shown in Illustration 21–3 is as follows:

a. Estimated bad debt losses ½% of sales, or $1,550.
b. Office supplies used, $100.
c. Shipping supplies used, $250.
d. Factory supplies used, $500.
e. Expired insurance on factory, $1,200; and expired insurance on the delivery equipment, $300.
f. The small tools inventory shows $1,100 of usable small tools on hand. As is frequently done, small hand tools are in this case accounted for in the same manner as are supplies.
g. Depreciation of delivery equipment, $2,100.
h. Depreciation of office equipment, $200.
i. Depreciation of factory machinery and equipment, $3,500.
j. Depreciation of factory building, $1,800.
k. Yearly amortization of ¼₇ of the cost of patents, $800.
l. Accrued wages: direct labor, $400; indirect labor, $60; delivery wages, $80. All other employees paid monthly on the last day of each month.
m. One-half year's interest accrued on the mortgage, $2,000.
n. State and federal income taxes expense, $32,600.

After the adjustments are completed, the amounts in the Trial Balance columns are combined with the amounts in the Adjustments columns and are sorted to the proper Manufacturing Statement, Income Statement, or Balance Sheet columns, according to the statement on which they appear.

In the sorting process, just two decisions are required for each item: First, does the item have a debit balance or a credit balance; and second, on which statement does it appear? The first decision is necessary because a debit item must be sorted to a debit column and a credit item to a credit column. As for the second, a work sheet is a tool for sorting items according to their statement appearance. Asset, liability, and owners' equity items appear on the balance sheet and are sorted to the Balance Sheet columns. The finished goods inventory plus the revenue, selling, general and administrative, and financial expense items should appear on the income statement and are sorted to the Income Statement columns. And finally, the raw material, goods in process, direct labor, and factory overhead items appear on the manufacturing statement and are sorted to the Manufacturing Statement columns.

After the trial balance items with their adjustments are sorted to the proper statement columns, the ending inventory amounts are entered on the work sheet. The raw materials and goods in process inventories appear on the manufacturing statement. Therefore, the ending raw materials and goods in process inventory amounts are entered in the Manufacturing Statement credit and Balance Sheet debit columns. They must be entered in the Manufacturing Statement credit column in order to make the difference between the two columns equal cost of goods manufactured. Likewise, since these inventory amounts represent end-of-period assets, they must be entered in the Balance Sheet debit column with the other assets.

The ending finished goods inventory is the equivalent of an ending merchandise inventory and receives the same work sheet treatment. It is entered in the Income Statement credit column and the Balance Sheet debit column. It is entered in the Income Statement credit column so that the net income may be determined; and since it is a current asset, it must also be entered in the Balance Sheet debit column.

After the ending inventories are entered on the work sheet, the Manufacturing Statement columns are added and their difference determined. This difference is the cost of the goods manufactured; and after it is determined, it is entered in the Manufacturing Statement credit column to make the two columns equal. Also, it is entered in the Income Statement debit column, the same column in which the balance of the Purchases account of a merchant is entered. After this, the work sheet is completed in the usual manner.

PREPARING STATEMENTS

After completion, the manufacturing work sheet is used in preparing the statements and in making adjusting and closing entries. The manufacturing statement is prepared from the information in the work sheet's Manufacturing Statement columns, the income statement from the information in the Income Statement columns, and the balance sheet from information in the Balance Sheet columns. After this, the adjusting and closing entries are entered in the journal and posted.

ADJUSTING ENTRIES

The adjusting entries of a manufacturing company are prepared in the same way as those of a merchandising company. An adjusting entry is entered in the General Journal for each adjustment appearing in the work sheet Adjustments columns. No new techniques are required.

CLOSING ENTRIES

The account balances that enter into the calculation of cost of goods manufactured reflect the manufacturing costs for a particular accounting period and must be closed at the end of each period. Normally they are closed to a Manufacturing Summary account, which is in turn closed to the Income Summary account.

The entries to close the manufacturing accounts of Excel Manufacturing Company are as follows:

Dec.	31	Manufacturing Summary	187,000.00	
		Raw Materials Inventory		8,000.00
		Goods in Process Inventory		2,500.00
		Raw Material Purchases		85,000.00
		Freight on Raw Materials		1,500.00
		Direct Labor		60,000.00
		Indirect Labor		9,000.00
		Supervision		6,000.00
		Power Expense		2,600.00
		Repairs and Maintenance		2,500.00
		Factory Taxes		1,900.00
		Factory Supplies Used		500.00
		Factory Insurance Expired		1,200.00
		Small Tools Written Off		200.00
		Depreciation of Machinery and Equipment		3,500.00
		Depreciation of Building		1,800.00
		Amortization of Patents		800.00
		To close those manufacturing accounts having debit balances.		
	31	Raw Materials Inventory	9,000.00	
		Goods in Process Inventory	7,500.00	
		Manufacturing Summary		16,500.00
		To set up the ending raw materials and goods in process inventories and to remove their balances from the Manufacturing Summary account.		

The entries are taken from the information in the Manufacturing Statement columns of the Illustration 21–3 work sheet. Compare the first entry with the information shown in the Manufacturing Statement debit column. Note how the debit to the Manufacturing Summary account is taken from the column total, and how each account having a balance in the column is credited to close it. Also observe that the second entry has the effect of subtracting the ending raw materials and goods in process inventories from the manufacturing costs shown in the work sheet's debit column.

The effect of the two entries is to cause the Manufacturing Summary account to have a debit balance equal to the $170,500 cost of goods manufactured. This $170,500 balance is closed to the Income Summary account along with the other cost and expense accounts having balances in the Income Statement debit column. Observe the following entry which is used to close the accounts having balances in the Income Statement debit column of the Illustration 21–3 work sheet and especially note its last credit.

Dec.	31	Income Summary	274,200.00	
		Finished Goods Inventory		11,200.00
		Sales Salaries Expense		18,000.00
		Advertising Expense		5,500.00
		Delivery Wages Expense		12,000.00
		Office Salaries Expense		15,700.00
		Miscellaneous General Expense		200.00
		Mortgage Interest Expense		4,000.00
		Bad Debts Expense		1,550.00
		Office Supplies Expense		100.00
		Shipping Supplies Expense		250.00
		Delivery Equipment Insurance Expense		300.00
		Depreciation Expense, Delivery Equipment		2,100.00
		Depreciation Expense, Office Equipment		200.00
		State and Federal Income Taxes Expense		32,600.00
		Manufacturing Summary		170,500.00
		To close the income statement accounts having debit balances.		

After the foregoing entry, the remainder of the income statement accounts of Illustration 21–3 are closed as follows:

Dec.	31	Finished Goods Inventory	10,300.00	
		Sales	310,000.00	
		Income Summary		320,300.00
		To close the Sales account and to bring the ending finished goods inventory on the books.		
	31	Income Summary	46,100.00	
		Retained Earnings		46,100.00
		To close the Income Summary account.		

INVENTORY VALUATION PROBLEMS OF A MANUFACTURER

In a manufacturing company using a general accounting system, at the end of each period, an accounting value must be placed on the inventories of raw materials, goods in process, and finished goods. No particular problems are encountered in valuing raw materials because the items are in the same form in which they were purchased and a cost or market price may be applied. However, placing a valuation on goods in process and finished goods is generally not as easy. These goods consist of raw materials to which certain amounts of labor and overhead have been added. They are not in the same form in which they were purchased. Consequently, a price paid a previous producer cannot be used to measure their inventory value. Instead, their inventory value must be built up by adding together estimates of the raw materials, direct labor, and overhead costs applicable to each item.

Estimating raw material costs applicable to a goods in process or finished goods item is usually not too difficult. Likewise, a responsible plant official normally can estimate an item's percentage of completion and then make a reasonably accurate estimate of the direct labor applicable to an item. However, estimating factory overhead costs presents more of a problem, which is often solved by assuming that factory overhead costs are closely related to direct labor costs. This is often a fair assumption. Frequently there is a close relation between direct labor costs and such indirect costs as supervision, power, repairs, and so forth. Furthermore, when this relation is used to apply overhead costs, it is assumed that the relation of overhead costs to the direct labor costs in each goods in process and finished goods item is the same as the relation between total factory overhead costs and total direct labor costs for the accounting period.

For example, an examination of the manufacturing statement in Illustration 21–2 shows that Excel Manufacturing Company's total direct labor costs were $60,000 and its overhead costs were $30,000. Or, in other words, during the year the company incurred in the production of all its products $2 of direct labor for each $1 of factory overhead costs; overhead costs were 50% of direct labor cost.

Overhead costs, $30,000 ÷ Direct labor, $60,000 = 50%

Consequently, in estimating the overhead applicable to a goods in process or finished goods item, Excel Manufacturing Company may assume that this 50% overhead rate is applicable. Since total overhead costs were 50% of total labor costs, it would appear reasonable to assume that this relationship applies to each goods in process and finished goods item.

If Excel Manufacturing Company makes this assumption and its goods in process inventory consists of 1,000 units of Item X with each unit containing $3.75 of raw material and having $2.50 of applicable direct labor, then the goods in process inventory is valued as shown in Illustration 21–4.

Illustration 21–4

Product	Estimated Raw Material Cost	Estimated Direct Labor Applicable	Overhead (50% of Direct Labor)	Estimated Total Unit Cost	No. of Units	Estimated Inventory Cost
Item X	$3.75	$2.50	$1.25	$7.50	1,000	$7,500.00

Excel Manufacturing Company may use the same procedure in placing an accounting value on the items of its finished goods inventory.

GLOSSARY

Direct labor. The labor of those people who work specifically on the conversion of raw materials into finished products; in other words, labor that can be easily associated with units of product.

Direct materials. A synonym for raw materials.

Factory overhead. All manufacturing costs other than for direct materials and direct labor.

Finished goods. Products in their completed state, ready for sale; equivalent to a store's merchandise.

Indirect labor. The labor of superintendents, foremen, millwrights, engineers, janitors, and others that contribute to production but do not work specifically on the manufactured products, and whose labor therefore cannot be easily associated with specific units of product.

Indirect materials. Commodities that are used in production but that do not enter into and become a part of the finished product, for example, grease and oil for machinery, or cleaning fluid.

Manufacturing overhead. A synonym for factory overhead. Also called manufacturing burden.

Manufacturing statement. A financial report showing the costs incurred to manufacture a product or products during a period. Also called schedule of the cost of goods manufactured.

Raw materials. Commodities that enter into and become a part of a finished product; therefore, commodities that are easily associated with specific units of product.

Work in process. Products in the process of being manufactured that have received a portion or all of their materials and have had some labor and overhead applied but that are not completed. Also called goods in process.

QUESTIONS FOR CLASS DISCUSSION

1. Manufacturing costs consist of three elements. What are they?

2. Explain how the income statement of a manufacturing company differs from the income statement of a merchandising company.

3. What are (a) direct labor, (b) indirect labor, (c) direct material, (d) indirect material, and (e) factory overhead costs?

4. Factory overhead costs include a variety of items. List several examples of factory overhead costs.

5. Name several accounts that are often found in the ledgers of both manufacturing and merchandising companies. Name several accounts that are found only in the ledgers of manufacturing companies.

6. What three new inventory accounts appear in the ledger of a manufacturing company?

7. How are the raw material inventories handled on the work sheet of a manufacturing company? How are the goods in process inventories handled? How are the finished goods inventories handled?

8. Which inventories of a manufacturing company receive the same work sheet treatment as the merchandise inventories of a merchandising company?

9. Which inventories of a manufacturing company appear on its manufacturing statement? Which appear on the income statement?

10. What accounts are summarized in the Manufacturing Summary account? What accounts are summarized in the Income Summary account?

11. What are the three manufacturing cost elements emphasized on the manufacturing statement?

12. What account balances are carried into the Manufacturing Statement columns of the manufacturing work sheet? What account balances are carried into the Income Statement columns? What account balances are carried into the Balance Sheet columns?

13. Why is the cost of goods manufactured entered in the Manufacturing Statement credit column of a work sheet and again in the Income Statement debit columns?

14. May prices paid a previous manufacturer for items of raw materials be used to determine the balance sheet value of the items in the raw material inventory? Why? May such prices also be used to determine the balance sheet values of the goods in process and finished goods inventories? Why?

15. Standard Company used an overhead rate of 75% of direct labor cost to apply overhead to the items of its goods in process inventory. If the

manufacturing statement of the company showed total overhead costs of $98,400, how much direct labor did it show?

CLASS EXERCISES

Exercise 21–1

After Bluenose Corporation posted its adjusting entries on December 31, 198A, the general ledger included the following account balances. (Some accounts in the general ledger have not been listed.)

Sales	$360,000
Raw materials inventory, January 1, 198A	20,000
Goods in process inventory, January 1, 198A	23,000
Finished goods inventory, January 1, 198A	29,000
Raw material purchases	58,000
Direct labor	69,000
Factory supplies used	7,000
Indirect labor	17,000
Machinery repairs	3,000
Rent expense, factory building	25,000
Selling expenses, controlling	43,000
Administrative expenses, controlling	51,000

On December 31, 198A, the inventories of Bluenose Company were determined to be:

Raw materials inventory	$18,000
Goods in process inventory	16,000
Finished goods inventory.....................	27,000

Given the above information, prepare a manufacturing statement for Bluenose Corporation.

Exercise 21–2

Use the information provided in Exercise 21–1 and prepare an income statement for Bluenose Corporation.

Exercise 21–3

Refer to the information provided in Exercise 21–1 and prepare closing entries for Bluenose Corporation.

Exercise 21–4

A company that uses the relation between overhead and direct labor costs to apply overhead to its goods in process and finished goods inventories incurred the following costs during a year: materials, $95,000; direct labor, $80,000; and factory overhead costs, $160,000. (a) Determine the company's overhead rate. (b) Under the assumption the company's $12,500 goods in process inventory had $3,000 of direct labor costs, determine the inventory's material costs. (c) Under the assumption the company's $17,000 finished goods inventory had $5,000 of material costs, determine the inventory's labor cost and overhead costs.

Exercise 21–5

The December 31 trial balance of Bohn's Deck Company follows:

BOHN'S DECK COMPANY
Trial Balance, December 31, 198A

Cash	$ 450	
Accounts receivable	510	
Allowance for doubtful accounts		$ 160
Raw materials inventory	190	
Goods in process inventory	410	
Finished goods inventory	250	
Factory supplies	330	
Prepaid factory insurance	350	
Factory machinery	2,160	
Accumulated depreciation, factory machinery ..		400
Common stock		1,500
Retained earnings		600
Sales....................................		8,100
Raw material purchases	1,700	
Freight on raw materials	100	
Direct labor	1,100	
Indirect labor	340	
Power	580	
Machinery repairs	150	
Rent expense, factory	600	
Selling expenses, controlling	870	
Administrative expenses, controlling	670	
	$10,760	$10,760

Additional information to be used in preparing a work sheet for 198A financial statements is as follows:

a. Ending inventories:
    Raw materials, $320.
    Goods in process, $530.
    Finished goods, $180.
    Factory supplies, $70.
b. Allowance for doubtful accounts should be increased by $220.
c. Expired factory insurance for the year is $250.
d. Depreciation of factory machinery amounted to $280.
e. Accrued payroll on December 31:
    Direct labor, $440.
    Indirect labor, $160.
    Office salaries, $110. (Debit Administrative Expenses, controlling account.)

Required:
Prepare a work sheet for the year ended December 31, 198A.

PROBLEMS

Problem 21–1   A work sheet prepared by Steel Net Company at the end of last year had the following items in its Manufacturing Statement columns:

	Manufacturing Statement	
	Debit	Credit
Raw materials inventory	30,750	33,750
Goods in process inventory	36,750	?
Raw material purchases	135,750	
Direct labor	225,000	
Indirect labor	89,000	
Heat, lights, and power	42,250	
Machinery repairs	13,000	
Rent expense, factory	30,000	
Property taxes, machinery	8,000	
Expired factory insurance	6,500	
Factory supplies used	15,250	
Depreciation expense, machinery	38,250	
Amortization of patents	5,250	
	675,750	?
Cost of goods manufactured		?
	675,750	675,750

Steel Net Company's work sheet does not show the amount of the ending goods in process inventory and cost of goods manufactured. However, the company makes a single product; and on December 31, at the end of last year, there were 3,000 units of goods in process with each unit containing an estimated $2.625 of materials and having had an estimated $3.75 of direct labor applied.

Required:

1. Calculate the relation between direct labor and factor overhead costs and use this relation to place an accounting value on the ending goods in process inventory.
2. After placing a value on the ending goods in process inventory, prepare a manufacturing statement for the company.
3. Prepare entries to close the manufacturing accounts and to summarize their balances in the Manufacturing Summary account.
4. Prepare an entry to close the Manufacturing Summary account.

Problem 21–2   The following items appeared in the Manufacturing Statement and Income Statement columns of a work sheet prepared for Ditto, Inc., on December 31, 198A:

	Manufacturing Statement		Income Statement	
	Debit	Credit	Debit	Credit
Raw materials inventory	18,900	18,150	....	...,....
Goods in process inventory	22,200	19,350	....	....
Finished goods inventory	....	....	24,150	28,200
Sales.....................................	....	....	....	542,250
Raw material purchases	88,500	.......:	....	....
Discounts on raw material purchases........	....	1,200	....	....
Direct labor	135,000	....	....	....
Indirect labor	20,700	....	....	....
Factory supervision	18,000	....	....	....
Heat, lights, and power	27,600	....	....	....
Machinery repairs	6,750	....	....	....
Rent expense, factory	10,800	....	....	....
Property taxes, machinery.................	2,550	....	....	....
Selling expenses, controlling	....	....	46,200	....
Administrative expenses, controlling	....	....	43,350	....
Expired factory insurance	3,600	....	....	....
Factory supplies used	9,150	....	....	....
Depreciation expense, factory machinery	15,750	....	....	....
Small tools written off	600	....	....	....
Amortization of patents	3,750	....	....	....
State and federal income taxes expense.....	....	....	44,250	....
	383,850	38,700	....	....
Cost of goods manufactured	....	345,150	345,150	....
	383,850	383,850	503,100	570,450
Net income			67,350	....
			570,450	570,450

Required:

1. From the information given prepare an income statement and a manufacturing statement for the company.
2. Prepare compound closing entries for the company.

Problem 21–3

Manudot Company began this year with the following inventories: raw materials, $18,400; goods in process, $20,600; and finished goods, $25,000. The company uses the relation between its overhead and direct labor costs to apply overhead to its inventories of goods in process and finished goods; and at the end of this year its inventories were assigned these costs:

	Raw materials	Goods in process	Finished goods
Material costs	$17,200	$5,600	$ 9,000
Direct labor costs	–0–	7,200	11,200
Overhead costs	–0–	?	14,000
Totals	$17,200	?	$34,200

And this additional information was available from the company's records:

Total factory overhead costs incurred during the year..... $165,000
Cost of all goods manufactured during the year.......... 396,800

Required:

On the basis of the information given plus any data you can derive from it, prepare a manufacturing statement for Manudot Company.

Problem 21–4   The December 31, 198A, trial balance of Nagle Manufacturing Company's ledger carried the following items:

NAGLE MANUFACTURING COMPANY
Trial Balance, December 31, 198A

Cash	$ 32,300	
Accounts receivable	36,200	
Allowance for doubtful accounts		$ 200
Raw materials inventory	37,100	
Goods in process inventory	34,400	
Finished goods inventory	48,700	
Prepaid factory insurance	4,100	
Factory supplies	13,100	
Machinery	227,500	
Accumulated depreciation, machinery		78,400
Accounts payable		25,300
Common stock		100,000
Retained earnings		94,900
Sales		692,500
Raw materials purchased	185,100	
Direct labor	159,500	
Indirect labor	36,600	
Heat, lights, and power	13,600	
Machinery repairs	9,400	
Selling expenses, controlling	81,200	
Administrative expenses, controlling	72,500	
Totals	$991,300	$991,300

The following adjustments and inventory information was available at year-end:

a. Allowance for doubtful accounts to be increased to $1,700. (Debit Administrative Expenses, controlling account.)
b. An examination of policies showed $3,100 of factory insurance expired.
c. An inventory of factory supplies showed $9,700 of factory supplies used.
d. Estimated depreciation of factory machinery, $31,300.
e. Accrued direct labor, $500; and accrued indirect labor, $300.
f. Accrued state and federal income taxes payable amount to $37,500.
g. Year-end inventories:
   (1) Raw materials, $36,700.
   (2) Goods in process consisted of 3,200 units of product with each unit containing an estimated $3.65 of materials and having had an estimated $4 of direct labor applied.
   (3) Finished goods inventory consisted of 3,000 units of product with each unit containing an estimated $7.50 of materials and having had an estimated $6 of direct labor applied.

Required:

1. Enter the trial balance on a work sheet form and make the adjustments from the information given. Then sort the items to the proper Manufacturing Statement, Income Statement, and Balance Sheet columns.
2. After the Direct Labor and factory overhead accounts have been adjusted and carried into the Manufacturing Statement columns, determine the relation between direct labor and overhead costs and use this relation to determine the overhead applicable to each unit of goods in process and finished goods. Next, calculate the balance sheet values for these inventories, enter the inventory amounts on the work sheet, and complete the work sheet.
3. From the work sheet prepare a manufacturing statement and an income statement.
4. Prepare compound closing entries.

Problem 21–5 A trial balance of Clipper Company's ledger on December 31, 198A, the end of an annual accounting period, appeared as follows:

CLIPPER COMPANY
Trial Balance, December 31, 198A

Cash	$ 14,800	
Raw materials inventory	13,700	
Goods in process inventory	12,500	
Finished goods inventory	15,100	
Prepaid factory insurance	3,600	
Factory supplies	6,800	
Factory machinery	168,200	
Accumulated depreciation, factory machinery		$ 31,300
Small tools	4,100	
Patents	6,700	
Common stock		100,000
Retained earnings		16,700
Sales		370,000
Raw material purchases	62,000	
Discounts on raw material purchases		1,200
Direct labor	98,400	
Indirect labor	12,100	
Factory supervision	11,700	
Heat, lights, and power	17,900	
Machinery repairs	4,200	
Rent expense, factory	6,000	
Property taxes, machinery	1,700	
Selling expenses, controlling	31,400	
Administrative expenses, controlling	28,300	
Totals	$519,200	$519,200

Additional information:

a. Expired factory insurance, $2,400.
b. Factory supplies used, $5,900.
c. Depreciation of factory machinery, $10,200.
d. Small tools written off, $500.
e. Amortization of patents, $1,400.
f. Accrued wages payable:

(1) Direct labor, $1,600.
(2) Indirect labor, $700.
(3) Factory supervision, $300.

g. Ending inventories:
(1) Raw materials, $13,200.
(2) Goods in process consisted of 2,500 units of product with each unit containing an estimated $1.10 of raw materials and having had an estimated $2 of direct labor applied.
(3) Finished goods consisted of 2,000 units of product with each unit containing an estimated $2.60 of raw materials and having had an estimated $3.60 of direct labor applied.

h. Estimated state and federal income taxes payable, $30,000.

Required:

1. Enter the trial balance on a work sheet form. Make the adjustments from the information given. Sort the items to the proper Manufacturing Statement, Income Statement, and Balance Sheet columns.

2. After the Direct Labor account and the factory overhead cost accounts have been adjusted and carried into the Manufacturing Statement columns, determine the relation between overhead costs and direct labor cost and use the relation to determine the amount of overhead applicable to each unit of goods in process and finished goods. After overhead applicable to each unit of goods in process and finished goods is determined, calculate the inventory values of the goods in process and finished goods inventories. Enter these inventory amounts on the work sheet and complete the work sheet.

3. From the work sheet prepare a manufacturing statement and an income statement.

4. Prepare closing entries.

ALTERNATE PROBLEMS

Problem 21–1A   Following are the items from the Manufacturing Statement columns of Trainer Manufacturing Company's work sheet prepared at the end of last year. The illustrated columns show the items as they appeared after all adjustments were completed but before the ending work in process inventory was calculated and entered and before the cost of goods manufactured was calculated.

Trainer Manufacturing Company makes a single product called Wrenchit. On December 31, at the end of last year, the goods in process inventory consisted of 5,000 units of Wrenchit with each unit containing an estimated $2.40 of raw materials and having had an estimated $6 of direct labor applied:

	Manufacturing Statement	
	Debit	Credit
Raw materials inventory	63,600	57,900
Goods in process inventory..........................	53,400	?
Raw materials purchased	244,200	
Direct labor......................................	300,000	
Indirect labor	50,700	
Factory supervision	36,000	
Heat, lights, and power	25,800	
Machinery repairs	18,900	
Rent expense, factory	21,600	
Property taxes, machinery	5,700	
Factory insurance expired	9,900	
Factory supplies used	22,200	
Depreciation expense, factory machinery	50,700	
Small tools written off	1,500	
	904,200	?
Cost of goods manufactured.........................		?
	904,200	904,200

Required:

1. Calculate the relation between direct labor and factory overhead costs and use this relation to determine the value of the ending goods in process inventory.
2. After placing a value on the ending goods in process inventory, determine the cost of goods manufactured.
3. Prepare a manufacturing statement for Trainer Manufacturing Company.
4. Prepare entries to close the manufacturing accounts and to summarize their balances in the Manufacturing Summary account.
5. Prepare an entry to close the Manufacturing Summary account.

Problem 21–2A   The following alphabetically arranged items were taken from the Manufacturing Statement and Income Statement columns of Awesome Manufacturing Company's year-end work sheet:

Advertising	$ 3,600	Goods in process, December 31	$ 22,500
Depreciation, machinery	6,300	Finished goods, January 1	31,500
Depreciation, office equipment	1,500	Finished goods, December 31	25,200
Depreciation, selling equipment........	1,800	Miscellaneous factory expenses	1,500
Direct labor	116,400	Office salaries	12,600
Factory supplies used	3,300	Raw material purchases	154,500
Federal income taxes expense	24,300	Rent expense, factory building	14,400
Freight on raw materials	4,500	Rent expense, office space	4,200
Heat and power, factory	6,000	Rent expense, selling space	4,800
Indirect labor	10,500	Repairs to machinery.................	55,400
Inventories:		Sales...............................	540,300
Raw materials, January 1	29,400	Sales discounts	10,200
Raw materials, December 31	30,300	Sales salaries	52,500
Goods in process, January 31	24,600	Superintendence, factory	21,600

Required:

Prepare an income statement and a manufacturing statement for the company.

Problem 21–3A

Graphic Products Company incurred a total of $868,800 of material, labor, and factory overhead costs in manufacturing its product last year, and of this amount, $374,400 represented factory overhead costs. The company began last year with the following inventories: raw materials, $33,600; goods in process, $58,000; and finished goods, $70,000. It applies overhead to its goods in process and finished goods inventories on the basis of the relation of overhead to direct labor costs; and at the end of last year, it assigned the following costs to its inventories:

	Raw materials	Goods in process	Finished goods
Material costs	$36,800	$18,800	$23,000
Direct labor costs	–0–	19,200	23,200
Overhead costs	–0–	?	34,800
Totals	$36,800	$?	$81,000

Required:

On the basis of the information given plus any information you can derive from it, prepare a manufacturing statement for Graphic Products Company.

Problem 21–4A

The December 31, 198A, trial balance of Sapp Manufacturing Company's ledger carried the following items:

SAPP MANUFACTURING COMPANY
Trial Balance, December 31, 198A

Cash	$ 25,500	
Accounts receivable	31,600	
Allowance for doubtful accounts		$ 300
Raw materials inventory	39,600	
Goods in process inventory	21,200	
Finished goods inventory	41,400	
Prepaid factory insurance	6,400	
Factory supplies	9,700	
Machinery	185,000	
Accumulated depreciation, machinery ...		57,700
Accounts payable		34,600
Common stock		50,000
Retained earnings		56,900
Sales		671,500
Raw materials purchased	145,900	
Direct labor	163,800	
Indirect labor	22,500	
Heat, lights, and power	19,300	
Machinery repairs	6,100	
Selling expenses, controlling	72,900	
Administrative expenses, controlling	80,100	
Totals	$871,000	$871,000

The following adjustments and inventory information was available at year-end:

a. Allowance for doubtful accounts to be increased to $1,500. (Debit Administrative Expenses, controlling account.)
b. An examination of policies showed $4,200 of factory insurance expired.
c. An inventory of factory supplies showed $6,200 of factory supplies used.
d. Estimated depreciation of factory machinery, $26,500.
e. Accrued direct labor, $1,200; and accrued indirect labor, $400.

   f. Accrued state and federal income taxes payable amount to $32,800.

   g. Year-end inventories:

     (1) Raw materials, $30,600.

     (2) Goods in process consisted of 2,900 units of product with each unit containing an estimated $4.10 of materials and having had an estimated $3.75 of direct labor applied.

     (3) Finished goods inventory consisted of 3,600 units of product with each unit containing an estimated $6.90 of materials and having had an estimated $5.50 of direct labor applied.

Required:

1. Enter the trial balance on a work sheet form and make the adjustments from the information given. Then sort the items to the proper Manufacturing Statement, Income Statement, and Balance Sheet columns.
2. After the Direct Labor and factory overhead accounts have been adjusted and carried into the Manufacturing Statement columns, determine the relation between direct labor and overhead costs and use this relation to determine the overhead applicable to each unit of goods in process and finished goods. Next, calculate the balance sheet values for these inventories (rounded to the nearest whole dollar). Enter the inventory amounts on the work sheet and complete the work sheet.
3. From the work sheet prepare a manufacturing statement and an income statement.
4. Prepare compound closing entries.

Problem 21–5A   Betcha Manufacturing Company prepared the following trial balance at the end of its annual accounting period:

BETCHA MANUFACTURING COMPANY
Trial Balance, December 31, 198A

Cash	$ 17,500	
Raw materials inventory	13,300	
Goods in process inventory	15,300	
Finished goods inventory	16,600	
Prepaid factory insurance	4,200	
Factory supplies	6,400	
Factory machinery	175,500	
Accumulated depreciation, factory machinery		$ 28,800
Small tools	3,700	
Patents	4,500	
Common stock		100,000
Retained earnings		34,400
Sales		359,700
Raw material purchases	61,800	
Discounts on raw material purchases		1,000
Direct labor	89,100	
Indirect labor	13,300	
Factory supervision	11,800	
Heat, lights, and power	17,900	
Machinery repairs	4,400	
Rent expense, factory	7,200	
Property taxes, machinery	800	
Selling expenses, controlling	31,400	
Administrative expenses, controlling	29,200	
Totals	$523,900	$523,900

Additional information:

a. Expired factory insurance, $2,200.
b. Factory supplies used, $6,300.
c. Depreciation of factory machinery, $9,900.
d. Small tools written off, $700.
e. Amortization of patents, $1,300.
f. Accrued wages payable:
  (1) Direct labor, $900.
  (2) Indirect labor, $500.
  (3) Factory supervision, $200.
g. Ending inventories:
  (1) Raw materials, $12,800.
  (2) Goods in process consisted of 4,000 units of product with each unit containing an estimated $1.40 of materials and having had an estimated $1 of direct labor applied.
  (3) Finished goods consisted of 3,000 units of product with each unit containing an estimated $1.96 of raw materials and having an estimated $2.40 of direct labor applied.
h. Estimated state and federal income taxes expense, $29,000.

Required:

1. Enter the trial balance on a work sheet form. Make the adjustments from the information given. Sort the items to the proper Manufacturing Statement, Income Statement, and Balance Sheet columns.
2. After the Direct Labor account and factory overhead cost accounts have been adjusted and carried into the Manufacturing Statement columns, determine the relation between direct labor and overhead costs and use this relation to determine the overhead applicable to each unit of goods in process and finished goods. After the amounts of overhead applicable to the units of goods in process and finished goods are determined, calculate the balance sheet values of these inventories, enter these inventory amounts on the work sheet, and complete the work sheet.
3. From the work sheet prepare a manufacturing statement and an income statement.
4. Prepare compound closing entries.

PROVOCATIVE PROBLEMS

Provocative
Problem 21–1,
Modular Power
Company

Modular Power Company has been in operation for three years, manufacturing and selling a single product. Sales have increased materially each year but profits have increased only slightly. The company president, Tom Pickle, has asked you to analyze the situation and tell him why. Mr. Pickle is primarily a production man and knows little about accounting. The company bookkeeper knows a debit from a credit, is an excellent clerk, but has little accounting training.

The company's condensed income statements for the past three years show:

	198A	198B	198C
Sales	$375,000	$525,000	$600,000
Cost of goods sold:			
Finished goods inventory, January 1	–0–	$ 22,500	$ 67,500
Cost of goods manufactured	247,500	384,000	420,750
Goods for sale	$247,500	$406,500	$488,250
Finished goods inventory, December 31	22,500	67,500	90,000
Cost of goods sold	$225,000	$339,000	$398,250
Gross profit from sales	$150,000	$186,000	$201,750
Selling and administrative expenses	112,500	147,000	162,000
Net income	$ 37,500	$ 39,000	$ 39,750

Further investigation yields the following additional information:

a. The company sold 5,000 units of its product during the first year in business, 7,000 during the second year, and 8,000 during the third. All sales were priced at $75 per unit, and no discounts were granted.

b. There were 500 units in the finished goods inventory at the end of the first year, 1,500 at the end of the second, and 2,000 at the end of the third.

c. The units in the finished goods inventory were valued each year at 60% of their selling price, or at $45 per unit.

Required:

Prepare a report for Mr. Pickle that shows *(a)* the number of units of product manufactured each year, *(b)* the cost each year to manufacture a unit of product, and *(c)* the selling and administrative expenses per unit of product sold each year. Also, *(d)* prepare an income statement showing the correct net income each year, using a FIFO basis for pricing the finished goods inventory. And finally, *(e)* express an opinion as to why net income has not kept pace with the rising sales volume.

Provocative
Problem 21–2,
Custom Boats

Several years ago Will Patterson took over the operation of his family's boat shop. The shop previously specialized in manufacturing power boats, but recently it has turned more and more to building sailboats to the specifications of its customers. The seasonality of this business means that shop activity is rather slow during October, November, and December.

Will has tried to increase business during the slow months. However, most prospective customers who come into the shop during these months are shoppers; and when Will quotes a price for a new boat, they commonly decide the price is too high and walk out. Will thinks the trouble arises from his application of a rule established by his father when he ran the shop. The rule is that in pricing a job to a customer, "always set the price so as to make a 10% profit over and above all costs, and be sure that all costs are included."

Will says that in pricing a job, the material and labor costs are easy to figure but that overhead is another thing. His overhead consists of depreciation of building and machinery, heat, lights, power, taxes, and so on, which in total run to $3,000 per month whether he builds any boats or not. Furthermore, when he follows his father's rule, he has to charge more for a boat built during the slow months because the overhead is spread over fewer jobs. He readily admits that this seems to drive away business during the months he needs business most, but he finds it difficult to break his father's rule, for as he says, "Dad did all right in this business for many years."

Required:

Explain with assumed figures to illustrate your point why Will charges more for a boat made in December than for one built in May, a very busy month. Suggest how Will might solve this pricing problem and still follow his father's rule.

Provocative Problem 21–3, Lonestar Manufacturing Company

Lonestar Manufacturing Company had outstanding 15,000 shares of $12 par value common stock on January 1, 198A. The stock was issued at par. The assets and liabilities of the company on that date were as follows:

Cash	$40,000
Accounts receivable	20,000
Raw materials inventory	25,000
Goods in process inventory	30,000
Finished goods inventory	35,000
Plant and equipment, net	85,000
Accounts payable	20,000

During 198A, the company paid no dividends, although it earned a 198A net income (ignore income taxes) of $18,750. At the year-end, the amounts of the company's accounts receivable, accounts payable, and common stock outstanding were the same as of the beginning of the year. However, its cash decreased $3,750, its raw materials inventory increased by 40%, its goods in process inventory increased by 25%, and its finished goods inventory increased by one half during the year. The net amount of its plant and equipment decreased $12,500 due to depreciation, chargeable four fifths to factory overhead costs and one fifth to general and administrative expenses. The year's direct labor costs were $50,000, and factory overhead costs excluding depreciation were 60% of that amount. Cost of finished goods sold was $125,000, and all sales were made at prices 50% above cost. Selling expenses were 10%, and general and administrative expenses excluding depreciation were 12% of sales.

Required:

Based on the information given and on amounts you can derive therefrom, prepare a manufacturing work sheet for the company.

Cost Accounting, Job Order, and Process

<u>22</u>

After studying Chapter 22, you should be able to:

State the conditions under which job order cost accounting should be used and those under which process cost accounting should be used.

Describe how costs for individual jobs are accumulated on job cost sheets and how control accounts are charged with the total costs of all jobs.

Allocate overhead to jobs and distribute any over- or underapplied overhead.

Describe how costs are accumulated by departments under process costing.

Explain what an equivalent finished unit is and how equivalent finished units are used in calculating unit costs.

Prepare a process cost summary.

Define or explain the words and phrases listed in the chapter Glossary.

When a company uses a general manufacturing accounting system such as that described in the previous chapter, physical counts of inventories are required at the end of each accounting period in order to determine cost of goods manufactured. Furthermore, cost of goods manufactured as determined under such a system is the cost of all goods that were manufactured during the period; usually, no effort is made to determine unit costs. In contrast to a general manufacturing accounting system, a *cost accounting system* is based on perpetual inventories and emphasizes unit costs and the control of costs.

There are two common types of cost accounting systems: (1) job order cost systems and (2) process cost systems. However, of the two there are an infinite number of variations and combinations. A job order system is described first.

JOB ORDER COST ACCOUNTING

In job order cost accounting a *job* is a turbine, machine, or other product manufactured especially for and to the specifications of a customer. A job may also be a single construction project of a contractor. A *job lot* is a quantity of identical items, such as 500 typewriters, manufactured in one lot as a job or single order; and a *job order cost system* is one in which costs are assembled in terms of jobs or job lots of product.

As previously stated, a job cost system differs from a general accounting system in that its primary objective is the determination of the cost of producing each job or job lot. A job cost system also differs in that all inventory accounts used in such a system are perpetual inventory accounts that control subsidiary ledgers. For example, in a job cost system, the purchase and use of all materials are recorded in a perpetual inventory account called Materials. The Materials account controls a subsidiary ledger having a separate ledger card (Illustration 22–1) for each different kind of material used. Likewise, in a job cost system, the Goods in Process and Finished Goods accounts are also perpetual inventory accounts controlling subsidiary ledgers.

In addition to perpetual inventory controlling accounts, job cost accounting is also distinguished by the flow of manufacturing costs through the accounts. Costs flow from the Materials, Factory Payroll, and Overhead Costs accounts into and through the Goods in Process and Finished Goods accounts and on to the Cost of Goods Sold account. This flow is diagrammed in Illustration 22–2 on the next page. An examination of the diagram will show that costs flow through the accounts in the same way materials, labor, and overhead are placed in production in the factory, are combined to become finished goods, and finally are sold.

Illustration 22–1

MATERIALS LEDGER CARD

Item _Whatsit clip_   Stock No. _C-347_   Location in Storeroom _Bin 137_

Maximum _400_   Minimum _150_   Number to Reorder _200_

	Received				Issued				Balance		
Date	Receiving Report No.	Units	Unit Price	Total Price	Requi- sition No.	Units	Unit Price	Total Price	Units	Unit Price	Total Price
3/1									180	1.00	180.00
3/5					4345	.20	1.00	20.00	160	1.00	160.00
3/11					4416	10	1.00	10.00	150	1.00	150.00
3/12	C-114	200	1.00	200.00					350	1.00	350.00
3/25					4713	21	1.00	21.00	329	1.00	329.00

Illustration 22–2 also shows the relationships between the controlling accounts and the subsidiary ledgers in a job cost system. In order to better understand the role played by each component of the system, students should refer back to Illustration 22–2 as they study the discussion of each component.

JOB COST SHEETS

The heart of a job cost system is a subsidiary ledger of *job cost sheets* called a *Job Cost Ledger*. The costs sheets are used to accumulate costs by jobs. A separate cost sheet is used for each job.

Observe in Illustration 22–3 that a job cost sheet is designed to accumulate costs. Although this accumulation is discussed in more detail later, it may be summarized as follows. When a job is begun, information regarding the customer, job number, and job description is recorded on a blank cost sheet and the cost sheet is placed in the Job Cost Ledger. Identifying each job with a job number simplifies the process of charging materials, labor, and overhead to the job. As materials are required for the job, they are transferred from the materials storeroom and are used to complete the job. At the same time their cost is charged to the job in the Materials column of the job's cost sheet. Labor used directly on the job is likewise charged to the job in the Labor column; and when the job is finished, the amount

Illustration 22–2: Cost Flows and Subsidiary Ledgers for a Job Cost System

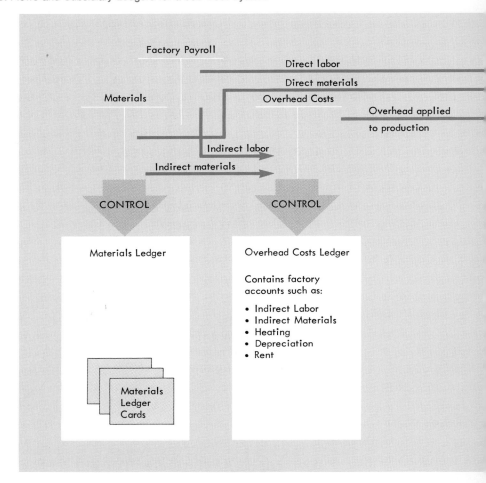

of overhead applicable is entered in the Overhead Costs Applied column. After this, the cost totals are summarized and the job's total cost is determined.

THE GOODS IN PROCESS ACCOUNT

The job cost sheets in the Job Cost Ledger are controlled by the Goods in Process account, which is kept in the General Ledger. And, the Goods in Process account and its subsidiary ledger of cost sheets

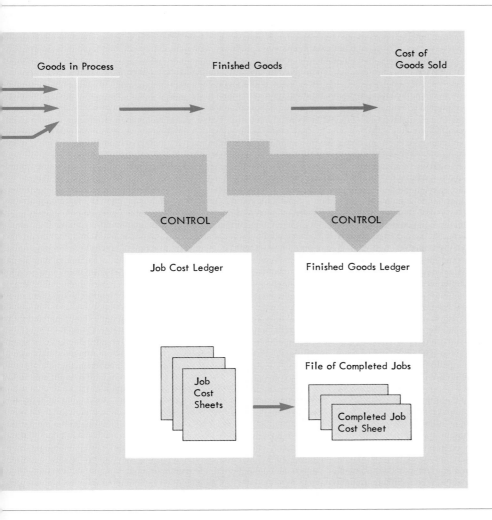

operate in the usual manner of controlling accounts and subsidiary ledgers. The material, labor, and overhead costs debited to each individual job on its cost sheet must be debited to the Goods in Process account either as individual amounts or in totals. Likewise all credits to jobs on their cost sheets must be credited individually or in totals to the Goods in Process account.

In addition to being a controlling account, the Goods in Process account is a perpetual inventory account. At the beginning of a cost period, the cost of any unfinished jobs in process appears in the Goods in Process account as a debit balance. Throughout the cost period,

Illustration 22–3

JOB COST SHEET

Customer's Name _Cone Lumber Company_   Job No. _7452_

Address _Eugene, Oregon_

Job Description _10 H.P. electric motor to customer's specifications_

Date Promised _4/1_   Date Started _3/23_   Date Completed _3/29_

Date	Materials		Labor		Overhead Costs Applied		
	Requisition No.	Amount	Time Ticket No.	Amount	Date	Rate	Amount
19-- Mar. 23	4698	53.00	C-3422	12.00	3/29	150 percent of the direct labor	$123.00
24			C-3478 C-3479	16.00 6.00			
25	4713	21.00	C-4002	16.00			
26			C-4015	10.00			
27			C-4032	12.00			
28			C-4044	10.00			
	Total	74.00	Total	82.00			

Summary of Costs

Materials _____ $ 74.00

Labor _____ 82.00

Overhead _____ 123.00

Total Cost of the job _____ 279.00

Remarks: Completed and shipped 3/29

materials, labor, and overhead are placed in production, and periodically their costs are debited to the account (note the last three debits in the Goods in Process account that follows). Also, throughout the period the cost of each job completed (the sum of the job's material, labor, and overhead costs) is credited to the account as each job is finished. As a result, the account functions as a perpetual inventory account. After all entries are posted, the debit balance shows the cost of the unfinished jobs still in process. This current balance is obtained and maintained without having to take a physical count of inventory, except as an occasional means of confirming the account balance. For example, the following Goods in Process account shows a $12,785 March 31 ending inventory of unfinished jobs in process.

Goods in Process

Date		Explanation	Debit	Credit	Balance
Mar.	1	Balance, beginning inventory			2,850
	10	Job 7449 completed		7,920	(5,070)
	18	Job 7448 completed		9,655	(14,725)
	24	Job 7450 completed		8,316	(23,041)
	29	Job 7452 completed		279	(23,320)
	29	Job 7451 completed		6,295	(29,615)
	31	Materials used	17,150		(12,465)
	31	Labor applied	10,100		(2,365)
	31	Overhead applied	15,150		12,785

ACCOUNTING FOR MATERIALS UNDER A JOB COST SYSTEM

Under a job cost system, all materials purchased are placed in a materials storeroom under the care of a storeroom keeper, and are issued to the factory only in exchange for properly prepared material *requisitions* (Illustration 22–4). The storeroom provides physical control over materials. The requisitions enhance the control and also provide a means of charging material costs to jobs or, in the case of indirect materials, to factory overhead costs. The use of requisitions is described in the next paragraphs.

When a material is needed in the factory, a material requisition is prepared and signed by a superintendent or other responsible person. The requisition identifies the material and shows the job number or overhead account to which it is to be charged and is given to the storeroom keeper in exchange for the material. The storeroom keeper collects the requisitions and then forwards them, in batches, to the accounting department.

Issuing units of material to the factory obviously reduces the amount of that particular material in the storeroom. Consequently, when a material requisition reaches the accounting department, it is first recorded in the Issued column of the materials ledger card of the material issued. This reduces the number of units of that material shown to be on hand. Note the last entry in Illustration 22–1, which records the requisition of Illustration 22–4.

Illustration 22–4

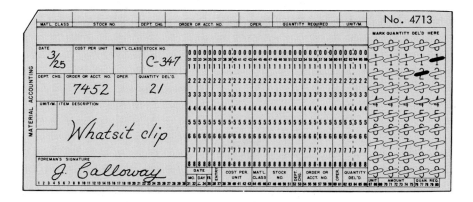

Materials issued to the factory may be used on jobs or for some overhead task, such as machinery repairs. Consequently, after being entered in the Issued columns of the proper materials ledger cards, a batch of requisitions is sorted by jobs and overhead accounts and charged to the proper jobs and overhead accounts. Materials used on jobs are charged to the jobs in the Materials columns of the job cost sheets. (Note the last entry in the Materials column on the cost sheet of Illustration 22–3 where the requisition of Illustration 22–4 is recorded.) Materials used for overhead tasks are charged to the proper overhead accounts in the Overhead Costs Ledger. A company using a job cost system commonly has an Overhead Costs controlling account in its General Ledger that controls a subsidiary Overhead Costs Ledger having an account for each overhead cost, such as Heating and Lighting or Machinery Repairs. Consequently, a requisition for light bulbs, for example, is charged to the Heating and Lighting account in the subsidiary Overhead Costs Ledger.

Material ledger cards, job cost sheets, and overhead cost accounts are all subsidiary ledger accounts controlled by accounts in the General Ledger. Consequently, in addition to the entries just described, entries must also be made in the controlling accounts. To make these entries, the requisitions charged to jobs and the requisitions charged to overhead accounts are accumulated until the end of a month or other cost period when they are separately totaled. If, for example, the requisitions charged to jobs during the month total $17,150 and those charged to overhead accounts total $320, an entry like the following is made:

Mar.	31	Goods in Process	17,150.00	
		Overhead Costs	320.00	
		Materials		17,470.00
		To record the materials used during March.		

The debit to Goods in Process in the illustrated entry is equal to the sum of the requisitions charged to jobs as detailed on the job cost sheets during March. The debit to Overhead Costs is equal to the sum of the requisitions charged to overhead accounts, and the credit to Materials is equal to the sum of all requisitions entered in the Issued columns of the material ledger cards during the month.

ACCOUNTING FOR LABOR IN A JOB COST SYSTEM

Time clocks, clock cards, and a Payroll Register similar to those described in an earlier chapter are commonly used in factories to record the hours and cost of the direct and indirect labor provided by employees. Without the complications of payroll taxes, income taxes, and other deductions, the entry to pay the employees is as follows:

Mar.	7	Factory Payroll	2,900.00	
		Cash		2,900.00
		To record the factory payroll and pay the employees.		

This entry is repeated at the end of each pay period. Thus, at the end of a month or other cost period, the Factory Payroll account has a series of debits (see Illustration 22–6) like the debit of this entry. The sum of these debits is the total amount paid to employees for the direct and indirect labor during the month.

The clock cards just mentioned are a record of hours worked each day by each employee, but they do not show how the employees spent their time or the specific jobs and overhead tasks on which they worked. Consequently, if the hours worked by each employee are to be charged to specific jobs and overhead accounts, another record called a *labor time ticket* must be prepared. Labor time tickets like the one shown in Illustration 22–5 describe how each employee's time was spent while at work.

Illustration 22–5: A Labor Time Ticket

The time ticket of Illustration 22–5 is a "pen-and-ink" ticket and is suitable for use in a plant in which only a small number of such tickets are prepared and recorded each day. In a plant in which many tickets are prepared, a time ticket that can be made into a punched card similar to Illustration 22–4 would be more suitable.

Labor time tickets serve as a basis for charging jobs and overhead accounts for an employee's wages. Throughout each day a labor time ticket is prepared each time an employee moves from one job or over-

Illustration 22–6

Factory Payroll

Date		Explanation	Debit	Credit	Balance
Mar.	7	Weekly payroll payment	2,900		2,900
	14	Weekly payroll payment	2,950		5,850
	21	Weekly payroll payment	3,105		8,955
	28	Weekly payroll payment	3,040		11,995
	31	Labor cost summary		12,600	(605)

head task to another. The tickets may be prepared by the worker, the worker's supervisor, or a clerk called a timekeeper. If the employee works on only one job all day, only one ticket is prepared. If more than one job is worked on, a separate ticket is made for each. At the end of the day all the tickets prepared that day are sent to the accounting department.

In the accounting department, the direct labor time tickets are charged to jobs on the job cost sheets (see the first entry in the Labor column of Illustration 22–3 where the ticket of Illustration 22–5 is recorded), and the indirect labor tickets are charged to overhead accounts in the Overhead Costs Ledger. The tickets are then accumulated until the end of the cost period when they are separately totaled. If, for example, the direct labor tickets total $10,100 and the indirect labor tickets total $2,500, the following entry is made:

Mar.	31	Goods in Process	10,100.00	
		Overhead Costs	2,500.00	
		Factory Payroll		12,600.00
		To record the March time tickets.		

The first debit in the illustrated entry is the sum of all direct labor time tickets charged to jobs on the job cost sheets, and the second debit is the sum of all tickets charged to overhead accounts. The credit is the total of the month's labor time tickets, both direct and indirect. Notice in Illustration 22–6 that after this credit is posted, the Factory Payroll account has a $605 credit balance. This $605 is the accrued factory payroll payable at the month's end, and it is also the dollar amount of time tickets prepared and recorded during the last three days of March.

ACCOUNTING FOR OVERHEAD IN A JOB COST SYSTEM

In a job cost system, if the cost of each job is to be determined at the time it is finished, it is necessary to associate with each job the cost of its materials, labor, and overhead. Requisitions and time tickets make possible a direct association of material and labor costs with jobs. However, overhead costs are incurred for the benefit of all jobs and cannot be related directly to any one job. Consequently, to associate overhead with jobs it is necessary to relate overhead to another variable, such as direct labor costs, and to apply overhead to jobs by means of a *predetermined overhead application rate.*

A predetermined overhead application rate based on direct labor cost is established before a cost period begins by (1) estimating the total overhead that will be incurred during the period; (2) estimating the cost of the direct labor that will be incurred during the period; then (3), calculating the ratio, expressed as a percentage, of the estimated overhead to the estimated direct labor cost. For example, if a cost accountant estimates that a factory will incur $180,000 of overhead during the next year and that $120,000 of direct labor will be applied to production during the year, these estimates are used to establish an overhead application rate of 150%, calculated as follows:

$$\frac{\text{Next year's estimated overhead costs, \$180,000}}{\text{Next year's estimated direct labor costs, \$120,000}} = 150\%$$

After a predetermined overhead application rate is established, it is used throughout the year to apply overhead to jobs as they are finished. Overhead is assigned to each job, and its cost is calculated as follows: (1) As each job is completed, the cost of its materials is determined by adding the amounts in the Materials column of its cost sheet. Then (2), the cost of its labor is determined by adding the amounts in the Labor column. Next (3), the applicable overhead cost is calculated by multiplying the job's total labor cost by the predetermined overhead application rate and is entered in the Overhead Costs Applied column. Finally (4), the job's material, labor, and overhead costs are entered in the summary section of the cost sheet and totaled to determine the total cost of the job.

The predetermined overhead application rate is also used to assign overhead to any jobs still in process at the cost period end. Then, the total overhead assigned to all jobs during the period is recorded in the accounts with an entry like this:

Mar.	31	Goods in Process	15,150.00	
		Overhead Costs		15,150.00
		To record the overhead applied to jobs during March.		

The illustrated entry assumes that the overhead applied to all jobs during March totaled $15,150. After it is posted, the Overhead Costs account appears as in Illustration 22–7.

In the Overhead Costs account of Illustration 22–7, the actual overhead costs incurred during March are represented by four debits. The first two need no explanation; the third represents the many payments for such things as water, telephone, and so on; the fourth represents such things as depreciation, expired insurance, taxes, and so forth.

When overhead is applied to jobs on the basis of a predetermined overhead rate based upon direct labor costs, it is assumed that the

Illustration 22–7

Overhead Costs

Date		Explanation	P R	Debit	Credit	Balance
Mar.	31	Indirect materials	G24	320		320
	31	Indirect labor	G24	2,500		2,820
	31	Miscellaneous payments	D89	3,306		6,126
	31	Accrued and prepaid items	G24	9,056		15,182
	31	Applied			15,150	32

overhead applicable to a particular job bears the same relation to the job's direct labor cost as the total estimated overhead of the factory bears to the total estimated direct labor costs. This assumption may not be proper in every case. However, when the ratio of overhead to direct labor cost is approximately the same for all jobs, an overhead rate based upon direct labor cost offers an easily calculated and fair basis for assigning overhead to jobs. In those cases in which the ratio of overhead to direct labor cost does not remain the same for all jobs, some other relationship must be used. Often overhead rates based upon the ratio of overhead to direct labor hours or overhead to machine-hours are used. However, a discussion of these alternative bases is reserved for a course in cost accounting.

OVERAPPLIED AND UNDERAPPLIED OVERHEAD

When overhead is applied to jobs by means of an overhead application rate based on estimates, the Overhead Costs account seldom, if ever, has a zero balance. At times actual overhead incurred exceeds overhead applied, and at other times overhead applied exceeds actual overhead incurred. When the account has a debit balance (overhead incurred in excess of overhead applied), the balance is known as *underapplied overhead* (see Illustration 22–7); and when it has a credit balance (overhead applied in excess of overhead incurred), the balance is called *overapplied overhead*. Usually the balance is small and fluctuates from debit to credit throughout a year. However, any remaining balance in the account at the end of each year must be disposed of before a new accounting period begins.

If the year-end balance of the Overhead Costs account is material in amount, it is reasonable that it be disposed of by apportioning it among the goods still in process, the finished goods inventory, and cost of goods sold. This has the effect of restating the inventories and goods sold at "actual" cost. For example, assume that at the end of an accounting period, (1) a company's Overhead Costs account has a $1,000 debit balance (underapplied overhead) and (2) the company had charged the following amounts of overhead to jobs during the period: jobs still in process, $10,000; jobs finished but unsold, $20,000; and jobs finished and sold, $70,000. In such a situation, the following entry apportions the underapplied overhead fairly among the jobs worked on during the period:

Dec.	31	Goods in Process	100.00	
		Finished Goods	200.00	
		Cost of Goods Sold	700.00	
		Overhead Costs		1,000.00
		To clear the Overhead Costs account and charge the underapplied overhead to the work of the accounting period.		

When the amount of over- or underapplied overhead is immaterial, all of it is closed to Cost of Goods Sold under the assumption that the major share of these costs would be charged to this account anyway and any extra exactness gained from prorating would not be worth the extra record keeping involved.

RECORDING THE COMPLETION OF A JOB

When a job is completed, its cost is transferred from the Goods in Process account to the Finished Goods account. For example, the following entry transfers the cost of the job the cost sheet of which appears on page 758.

Mar.	29	Finished Goods	279.00	
		Goods in Process		279.00
		To transfer the cost of Job No. 7452 to Finished Goods.		

At the same time this entry is made, the completed job's cost sheet is removed from the Job Cost Ledger, marked "completed," and filed. This is in effect the equivalent of posting a credit to the Job Cost Ledger equal to the credit to the Goods in Process controlling account.

RECORDING COST OF GOODS SOLD

When a cost system is in use, the cost to manufacture a job or job lot of product is known as soon as the goods are finished. Consequently, when goods are sold, since their cost is known, the cost can be recorded at the time of sale. For example, if goods costing $279 are sold for $450, the cost of the goods sold may be recorded at the time of sale as follows:

Mar.	29	Accounts Receivable—Cone Lumber Co.	450.00	
		Cost of Goods Sold	279.00	
		Sales		450.00
		Finished Goods		279 00
		Sold for $450 goods costing $279.		

When cost of goods sold is recorded at the time of each sale, the balance of the Cost of Goods Sold account shows at the end of an accounting period the cost of goods sold during the period.

PROCESS COST ACCOUNTING

A *process* is a step in manufacturing a product, and a *process cost system* is one in which costs are assembled in terms of processes or manufacturing steps.

Process cost systems are found in companies producing cement, flour, or other products the production of which is characterized by a large volume of standardized units manufactured on a more or less continuous basis. In such companies, responsibility for completing each step in the production of a product is assigned to a department. Costs are then assembled by departments, and the efficiency of each department is measured by comparing planned and actual processing costs incurred in processing the units of product that flow through the department.

ASSEMBLING COSTS BY DEPARTMENTS

When costs are assembled by departments in a process cost system, a separate goods in process account is used for the costs of each department. For example, assume a company makes a product from metal that is cut to size in a cutting department, then sent to a bending department to be bent into shape, and then on to a painting department to be painted. Such a company would collect costs in three goods

Illustration 22–8

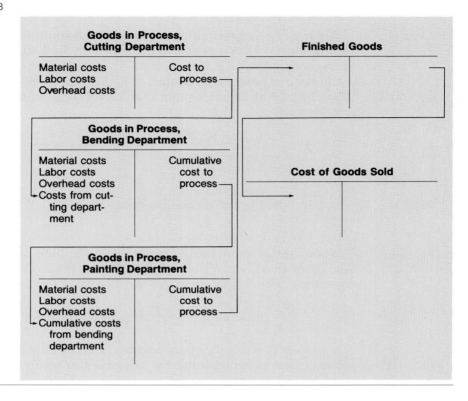

in process accounts, one for each department, and costs would flow through the accounts as in Illustration 22–8.

Observe in Illustration 22–8 that each department's material, labor, and overhead costs are charged to the department's goods in process account. (It is assumed there were additional materials charged directly to the bending department.) Observe too how costs are transferred from department to department, just as the product is physically transferred in the manufacturing procedure. The cost to cut the product in the cutting department is transferred to the bending department; and the sum of the costs in the first two departments is transferred to the third department; and finally, the sum of the processing costs in all three departments, which is the total cost to make the product, is transferred to finished goods.

CHARGING COSTS TO DEPARTMENTS

Since there are no jobs in a process cost system, accounting for material and labor costs in such a system is much simplified. Material requisitions may be used. However, a consumption report kept by the storeroom keeper and showing the materials issued to each department during a cost period is often substituted. Likewise, labor time tickets may be used; but since most employees spend all their working time in the same department, an end-of-period summary of the payroll records is usually all that is required in charging labor to the departments. And since there are no jobs, there is no need to distinguish between direct and indirect materials and direct and indirect labor. All that is required is that material and labor costs, both direct and indirect, be charged to the proper departments.

The lack of jobs also simplifies accounting for overhead in a process cost system. Since there are no jobs to charge with overhead on completion, predetermined overhead application rates are not required and actual overhead incurred may be charged directly to the goods in process accounts of the departments.

EQUIVALENT FINISHED UNITS

A basic objective of a process cost system is the determination of unit processing costs for material, labor, and overhead in each processing department. This requires that (1) material, labor, and overhead costs be accumulated for each department for a cost period of, say, a month; (2) a record be kept of the number of units processed in each department during the period; and then (3) that costs be divided by units processed to determine unit costs. However, it should be observed that when a department begins and ends a cost period with partially processed units of product, the units completed in the department are not an accurate measure of the department's total production. When the production of the period includes completing units that were partially finished at the beginning of the period and also includes working on units that remain partially finished at the end of the period, the following question arises: How many units did the department produce during the period? In other words, how many units would have been produced if all activity in the department had been concentrated on units that were started this period and finished this period? The answer is the number of *equivalent finished units* produced by the department during the period. Thus, when a department's beginning and ending inventories include partially finished units, the department's production for the period must be measured in terms of *equivalent finished units* and unit costs become *equivalent finished unit costs.*

The idea of an equivalent finished unit is based on the assumption that it takes the same amount of labor, for instance, to one-half finish each of two units of product as it takes to fully complete one, or it takes the same amount of labor to one-third finish each of three units as to complete one. Also, since a department may add materials to production at a different rate than it adds labor and overhead, separate measures of production are often required for materials, for labor, and for overhead. For example, a department may have added enough materials to produce 1,000 equivalent finished units, and during the same period, the department may have added enough labor and overhead to produce 900 equivalent finished units. The concept of equivalent finished units and the related calculations are discussed further in the Delta Processing Company illustration that follows.

PROCESS COST ACCOUNTING ILLUSTRATED

The process cost system of Delta Processing Company, a company manufacturing a patented home remedy called Noxall, is used to illustrate process cost accounting.

The procedure for manufacturing Noxall is as follows: Material A is finely ground in Delta Processing Company's grinding department. Then, it is transferred to the mixing department where Material B is added, and the two materials are thoroughly mixed. The mixing process results in the finished product, Noxall, which is transferred on completion to finished goods. All the Material A placed in process in the grinding department is placed in process at the beginning of the grinding process, but the Material B added in the mixing department is added evenly throughout its process. In other words, a product one-third mixed in the latter department has received one third of its Material B and a product three-fourths mixed has received three fourths. Labor and overhead are applied evenly throughout each department's process.

At the end of the April cost period, after entries recording materials, labor, and overhead were posted, the company's two goods in process accounts appeared as follows:

Goods in Process, Grinding Department

Date		Explanation	Debit	Credit	Balance
Apr.	1	Beginning inventory			4,250
	30	Materials	9,900		14,150
	30	Labor	5,700		19,850
	30	Overhead	4,275		24,125

Goods in Process, Mixing Department

Date		Explanation	Debit	Credit	Balance
Apr.	1	Beginning inventory			3,785
	30	Materials	2,040		5,825
	30	Labor	3,570		9,395
	30	Overhead	1,020		10,415

The production reports prepared by the company's two department managers give the following information about inventories and goods started and finished in each department during the month:

	Grinding department	Mixing department
Units in the beginning inventories of goods in process	30,000	16,000
April 1 stage of completion of the beginning inventories of goods in process	⅓	¼
Units started in process and finished during period	70,000	85,000
Total units finished and transferred to next department or to finished goods	100,000	101,000
Units in the ending inventories of goods in process	20,000	15,000
Stage of completion of ending inventories of goods in process	¼	⅓

Process Cost Summary

After receiving the production reports, the company's cost accountant prepared a process cost summary, Illustration 22–9, for the grinding department. A process cost summary is a report unique to a processing company. A separate report is prepared for each processing department and shows (1) the costs charged to the department, (2) the department's equivalent unit processing costs, and (3) the assignment of costs to the department's goods in process inventories and its goods started and finished.

COSTS CHARGED TO THE DEPARTMENT.   Observe in Illustration 22–9 that a process cost summary has three sections. In the first, headed Costs Charged to the Department, are summarized the costs charged to the department. Information for this section comes from the department's Goods in Process account. Compare the first section of Illustration 22–9 with the Goods in Process account of the grinding department shown on page 770.

Illustration 22–9

DELTA PROCESSING COMPANY
Process Cost Summary, Grinding Department
For Month Ended April 30, 198A

1

COSTS CHARGED TO THE DEPARTMENT:

Material requisitioned	$ 9,900
Labor charged	5,700
Overhead costs incurred	4,275
Total processing costs..	$19,875
Goods in process at the beginning of the month	4,250
Total costs to be accounted for	$24,125

2

EQUIVALENT UNIT PROCESSING COSTS:

	Units involved	Fraction of a unit added	Equivalent units added
Material:			
Beginning inventory............................	30,000	–0–	–0–
Units started and finished	70,000	One	70,000
Ending inventory	20,000	One	20,000
			90,000

Equivalent unit processing cost for material: $9,900 ÷ 90,000 = $0.11

	Units involved	Fraction of a unit added	Equivalent units added
Labor and overhead:			
Beginning inventory............................	30,000	⅔	20,000
Units started and finished	70,000	One	70,000
Ending inventory	20,000	¼	5,000
			95,000

Equivalent unit processing cost for labor: $5,700 ÷ 95,000 = $0.06
Equivalent unit processing cost for overhead: $4,275 ÷ 95,000 = $0.045

3

ASSIGNMENT OF COSTS TO THE WORK OF THE DEPARTMENT:

Goods in process, one-third processed at the beginning of April:

Costs charged to the beginning inventory of goods in process during previous month	$4,250	
Material added (all added during March)	–0–	
Labor applied (20,000 × $0.06)	1,200	
Overhead applied (20,000 × $0.045)..................................	900	
Cost to process...		$ 6,350

Goods started and finished in the department during April:

Material added (70,000 × $0.11)	$7,700	
Labor applied (70,000 × $0.06)	4,200	
Overhead applied (70,000 × $0.045).................................	3,150	
Cost to process...		15,050
Total cost of the goods processed in the department and transferred to the mixing department (100,000 units at $0.214 each)*		$21,400

Goods in process, one-fourth processed at the end of April:

Material added (20,000 × $0.11)	$2,200	
Labor applied (5,000 × $0.06)	300	
Overhead applied (5,000 × $0.045)	225	
Cost to one-fourth process		2,725
Total costs accounted for		$24,125

* Note that the $0.214 is an average unit cost based on all 100,000 units finished. Other alternatives such as FIFO and LIFO are deferred to a more advanced course.

EQUIVALENT UNIT PROCESSING COSTS.   The second section of a process cost summary shows the calculation of equivalent unit costs. The information for this section as to units involved and fractional units applicable to the inventories comes from the production report prepared by the department manager. Information as to material, labor, and overhead costs comes from the first section of the summary.

Notice in the second section of Illustration 22–9 that there are two separate equivalent unit calculations. Two calculations are required because material, labor, and overhead are not added in the same proportions and at the same stages in the processing procedure of this department. As previously stated, all material is added at the beginning of this department's process, and labor and overhead are added evenly throughout the process. Consequently, the number of equivalent units of material added is not the same as the number of equivalent units of labor and overhead added.

Observe in the calculation of equivalent finished units for materials that the beginning-of-month inventory is assigned no additional material. In the grinding department, all material placed in process is placed there at the beginning of the process. The 30,000 beginning inventory units were begun during March and were one-third completed at the beginning of April. Consequently, these units received all their material during March when their processing was first begun.

Note also how the $9,900 cost of the material charged to the department in April is divided by 90,000 equivalent units of material to arrive at an $0.11 per equivalent unit cost for material consumed in this department.

Now move on to the calculation of equivalent finished units for labor and overhead and note that the beginning inventory units were each assigned two thirds of a unit of labor and overhead. If these units were one-third completed on April 1, then two thirds of the work done on these units was done in April. Beginning students often have difficulty with this. Students commonly assign only an additional one-third unit of labor and overhead when two thirds is required.

Before going further, observe that the essence of the equivalent unit calculation for labor and overhead is that to do two thirds of the work on 30,000 units, all the work on 70,000 units, and one fourth the work on 20,000 units is the equivalent of completing all the work on 95,000 units. Consequently, the $5,700 of labor cost and $4,275 of overhead cost charged to the department are each divided by 95,000 to determine equivalent unit costs for labor and overhead.

ASSIGNMENT OF COSTS TO THE WORK OF THE DEPARTMENT.   When a department begins and ends a cost period with partially processed units of product, it is necessary to apportion the department's costs between the units that were in process in the department at the beginning of the period, the units started and finished during the period, and the ending inventory units. This division is necessary to determine the cost of the units completed in the department during the period; and the division and assignment of costs are shown in the third section of the process cost summary.

Notice in the third section of Illustration 22–9 how costs are assigned to the beginning inventory. The first amount assigned is the $4,250 beginning inventory costs. This amount represents the material, labor, and overhead costs used to one-third complete the inventory during March, the previous cost period. Normally, the second charge to a beginning inventory is for additional material assigned to it. However, in the grinding department no additional material costs are assigned the beginning inventory because these units received all of their material when their processing was first begun during the previous month. The second charge to the beginning inventory is for labor. The $1,200 portion of applicable labor costs is calculated by multiplying the number of equivalent finished units of labor used to complete the beginning inventory by the cost of an equivalent finished unit of labor (20,000 equivalent finished units at $0.06 each). The third charge to the beginning inventory is for overhead. The applicable $900 portion is determined by multiplying the equivalent finished units of overhead used to complete the beginning inventory by the cost of an equivalent finished unit of overhead (20,000 $\times$ $0.45).

After costs are assigned to the beginning inventory, the procedures used in their assignment are repeated for the units started and finished. Then, the cost of the units completed and transferred to finished goods, in this case the cost of the 30,000 beginning inventory units plus the cost of the 70,000 units started and finished, is determined by adding the costs assigned to the two groups. In this situation, the total is $21,400 or $0.214 per unit ($21,400 $\div$ 100,000 units = $0.214 per unit).

Before proceeding further, notice in the second section of the grinding department's process cost summary that the equivalent finished unit cost for materials is $0.11, for labor is $0.06, and for overhead is $0.045, a total of $0.215. Notice, however, in the third section of the summary that the unit cost of the 100,000 units finished and transferred is $0.214, which is less than $0.215. It is less because costs were less in the department during the previous month and the 30,000 beginning units were one-third processed at these lower costs.

Transferring Costs from One Department to the Next

The grinding department's process cost summary is completed by assigning costs to the ending inventory; and after the summary was completed, the accountant prepared the following entry to transfer from the grinding department to the mixing department the cost of the 100,000 units processed in the department and transferred during April. Information for the entry as to the cost of the units transferred was taken from the third section of Illustration 22–9.

Apr.	30	Goods in Process, Mixing Department	21,400.00	
		Goods in Process, Grinding Department . . .		21,400.00
		To transfer the cost of the 100,000 units of product transferred to the mixing department.		

Posting this entry had the effect on the accounts shown in Illustration 22–10. Observe that the effect is one of transferring and advancing costs from one department to the next just as the product is physically transferred and advanced in the manufacturing procedure.

Process Cost Summary—Mixing Department

After posting the entry transferring to the mixing department the grinding department costs of the units transferred, the cost accountant prepared a process cost summary for the mixing department. Information required in its preparation was taken from the mixing department's goods in process account and production report. This summary appeared as in Illustration 22–11.

Two points in Illustration 22–11 require special attention. The first

Illustration 22–10

Goods in Process, Grinding Department

Date		Explanation	Debit	Credit	Balance
Apr.	1	Beginning inventory			4,250
	30	Materials	9,900		14,150
	30	Labor	5,700		19,850
	30	Overhead	4,275		24,125
	30	Units to mixing department		21,400	2,725

Goods in Process, Mixing Department

Date		Explanation	Debit	Credit	Balance
Apr.	1	Beginning inventory			3,785
	30	Materials	2,040		5,825
	30	Labor	3,570		9,395
	30	Overhead	1,020		10,415
	30	Units from grinding department	21,400		31,815

Illustration 22–11

DELTA PROCESSING COMPANY
Process Cost Summary, Mixing Department
For Month Ended April 30, 198A

COSTS CHARGED TO THE DEPARTMENT:

Materials requisitioned	$ 2,040
Labor charged	3,570
Overhead costs incurred	1,020
Total processing costs	$ 6,630
Goods in process at the beginning of the month	3,785
Cost transferred from the grinding department (100,000 units at $0.214 each)	21,400
Total costs to be accounted for	$31,815

EQUIVALENT UNIT PROCESSING COSTS:

	Units involved	Fraction of a unit added	Equivalent units added
Materials, labor, and overhead:			
Beginning inventory	16,000	¾	12,000
Units started and finished	85,000	One	85,000
Ending inventory	15,000	⅓	5,000
Total equivalent units			102,000

Equivalent unit processing cost for materials: $2,040 ÷ 102,000 = $0.02
Equivalent unit processing cost for labor: $3,570 ÷ 102,000 = $0.035
Equivalent unit processing cost for overhead: $1,020 ÷ 102,000 = $0.01

ASSIGNMENT OF COSTS TO THE WORK OF THE DEPARTMENT:

Goods in process, one fourth completed at the beginning of April:

Costs charged to the beginning inventory of goods in process during previous month	$ 3,785	
Materials added (12,000 × $0.02)	240	
Labor applied (12,000 × $0.035)	420	
Overhead applied (12,000 × $0.01)	120	
Cost to process		$ 4,565

Goods started and finished in the department during April:

Costs in the grinding department (85,000 × $0.214)	$18,190	
Materials added (85,000 × $0.02)	1,700	
Labor applied (85,000 × $0.035)	2,975	
Overhead applied (85,000 × $0.01)	850	
Cost to process		23,715
Total accumulated cost of goods transferred to finished goods (101,000 units at $0.28)		$28,280

Goods in process, one third processed at the end of April:

Costs in the grinding department (15,000 × $0.214)	$ 3,210	
Materials added (5,000 × $0.02)	100	
Labor applied (5,000 × $0.035)	175	
Overhead applied (5,000 × $0.01)	50	
Cost to one-third process		3,535
Total costs accounted for		$31,815

is the calculation of equivalent finished units. Since the materials, labor, and overhead added in the mixing department are all added evenly throughout the process of this department, only a single equivalent unit calculation is required. This differs from the grinding department, the previous department, where two equivalent unit calculations were required. Two were required because material was not placed in process at the same stage in the processing procedure as were labor and overhead.

The second point needing special attention in the mixing department cost summary is the method of handling the grinding department costs transferred to this department. During April, 100,000 units of product, with accumulated grinding department costs of $21,400, were transferred to the mixing department. Of these 100,000 units, 85,000 were started in process in the department, finished, and transferred to finished goods. The remaining 15,000 were still in process in the department at the end of the cost period.

Notice in the first section of Illustration 22–11 how the $21,400 of grinding department costs transferred to the mixing department are added to the other costs charged to the department. Compare the information in this first section with the mixing department's Goods in Process account as it is shown on page 771 and again in Illustration 22–10.

Notice again in the third section of the mixing department's process cost summary how the $21,400 of grinding department costs are apportioned between the 85,000 units started and finished and the 15,000 units still in process in the department. The 16,000 beginning goods in process units received none of this $21,400 charge because they were transferred from the grinding department during the previous month. Their grinding department costs are included in the $3,785 beginning inventory costs.

The third section of the mixing department's process cost summary shows that 101,000 units of product (16,000 beginning inventory units plus 85,000 started and finished) with accumulated costs of $28,280 were completed in the department during April and transferred to finished goods. The cost accountant used the entry below to transfer the accumulated cost of these 101,000 units from the mixing department's goods in process account to the Finished Goods account. Posting the entry had the effect shown in Illustration 22–12.

Apr.	30	Finished Goods	28,280.00	
		Goods in Process, Mixing Department		28,280.00
		To transfer the accumulated grinding department and mixing department costs of the 101,000 units transferred to Finished Goods.		

Illustration 22–12

Goods in Process, Mixing Department

Date		Explanation	Debit	Credit	Balance
Apr.	1	Beginning inventory			3,785
	30	Materials	2,040		5,825
	30	Labor	3,570		9,395
	30	Overhead	1,020		10,415
	30	Units from grinding department	21,400		31,815
	30	Units to finished goods		28,280	3,535

Finished Goods

Date		Explanation	Debit	Credit	Balance
Apr.	30	Units from mixing department	28,280		28,280

GLOSSARY

Cost accounting system. An accounting system based on perpetual inventory records that is designed to emphasize the determination of unit costs and the control of costs.

Equivalent finished units. A measure of production with respect to materials or labor, expressed as the number of units that could have been manufactured from start to finish during a period given the amount of materials or labor used during the period.

Job. A special production order to meet a customer's specifications.

Job Cost Ledger. A subsidiary ledger to the Goods in Process account in which are kept the job cost sheets of unfinished jobs.

Job cost sheet. A record of the costs incurred on a single job.

Job lot. A quantity of identical items manufactured in one lot or single order.

Job order cost system. A cost accounting system in which costs are assembled in terms of jobs or job lots.

Labor time ticket. A record of how an employee's time at work was used; the record serves as the basis for charging jobs and overhead accounts for the employee's wages.

Overapplied overhead. The amount by which overhead applied on the basis of a predetermined overhead application rate exceeds overhead actually incurred.

Predetermined overhead application rate. A rate that is used to charge overhead cost to production; calculated by relating estimated overhead cost for a period to another variable such as estimated direct labor cost.

Process cost system. A cost accounting system in which costs are assembled in terms of steps in manufacturing a product.

Requisition. A document that identifies the materials needed for a specific job and the account to which the materials cost should be charged, and that is given to a storeroom keeper in exchange for the materials.

Underapplied overhead. The amount by which actual overhead incurred exceeds the overhead applied to production, based on a predetermined application rate and evidenced by a debit balance in the overhead account at the end of the period.

QUESTIONS FOR CLASS DISCUSSION

1. What are the two primary types of cost accounting systems? Indicate which of the two would best fit the needs of a manufacturer who *(a)* produces special-purpose machines designed to fit the particular needs of each customer, *(b)* produces electric generators in lots of 10, and *(c)* manufactures copper tubing.

2. Define the following terms in the context of cost accounting:

   a. Job order cost system.
   b. Process cost system.
   c. Job.
   d. Job lot.
   e. Job cost sheet.
   f. Labor time ticket.
   g. Materials requisition.
   h. Process cost summary.

3. The Materials account and the Goods in Process account each serve as a control account for a subsidiary ledger. What subsidiary ledgers do these accounts control?

4. How is the inventory of goods in process determined in a general accounting system like that described in Chapter 21? How may this inventory be determined in a job cost system?

5. What is the purpose of a job cost sheet? What is the name of the ledger containing the job cost sheets of the unfinished jobs in process? What account controls this ledger?

6. What business papers provide the information that is used to make the job cost sheet entries for *(a)* materials and *(b)* labor?

7. Refer to the job cost sheet of Illustration 22–3. How was the amount of overhead costs charged to this job determined?

8. How is a predetermined overhead application rate established? Why is such a predetermined rate used to charge overhead to jobs?

9. Why does a company using a job cost system normally have either overapplied or underapplied overhead at the end of each accounting period?

10. At the end of a cost period, the Overhead Costs controlling account has a debit balance. Does this represent overapplied or underapplied overhead?

11. What are the basic differences in the products and in the manufacturing procedures of a company to which a job cost system is applicable as opposed to a company to which a process cost system is applicable?

12. What is an equivalent finished unit of labor? Of materials?

13. What is the assumption on which the idea of an equivalent finished unit of, for instance, labor is based?

14. What is the production of a department measured in equivalent finished units if it began an accounting period with 8,000 units of product that were one-fourth completed at the beginning of the period, started and finished 50,000 units during the period, and ended the period with 6,000 units that were one-third processed at the period end?

15. The process cost summary of a department commonly has three sections. What is shown in each section?

CLASS EXERCISES

Exercise 22–1

Part 1. During December 198A, Cowan Company's cost accountant established the company's 198B overhead application rate based on direct labor cost. In setting the rate, the cost accountant estimated the company would incur $200,000 of overhead costs during 198B and it would apply $160,000 of direct labor to the products that would be manufactured during 198B. Determine the rate.

Part 2. During February 198B, the company of Part 1 began and completed Job No. 715. Determine the job's cost under the assumption that on its completion the job's cost sheet showed the following materials and labor charged to it:

		JOB COST SHEET					
Customer's Name		Richfield, Inc.				Job No. 715	
Job Description		400 Watt Power Supply					

Date	Materials		Labor		Overhead Costs Applied		
	Requisition Number	Amount	Time Ticket Number	Amount	Date	Rate	Amount
Feb. 2	1524	85.00	2116	50.00			
3	1527	75.00	2117	60.00			
4	1531	390.00	2122	70.00			

Exercise 22–2

In December 198A, a cost accountant for Mandle Company established the following overhead application rate for applying overhead to the jobs that would be completed during 198B:

$$\frac{\text{Estimated overhead costs, \$342,000}}{\text{Estimated direct labor costs, \$380,000}} = 90\%$$

At the end of 198B, the company's accounting records showed that $350,000 of overhead costs had actually been incurred during 198B and $400,000 of direct labor, distributed as follows, had been applied to jobs during the year.

Direct labor on jobs completed and sold	$340,000
Direct labor on jobs completed and in the finished goods inventory	40,000
Direct labor on jobs still in process	20,000
	$400,000

Required:

1. Set up an Overhead Costs T-account and enter on the proper sides the amounts of overhead costs incurred and applied. State whether overhead was overapplied or underapplied during the year.
2. Give the entry to close the Overhead Costs account and allocate its balance between jobs sold, jobs finished but unsold, and jobs in process.

Exercise 22-3

Hayes Company uses a job cost system in which overhead is charged to jobs on the basis of direct labor cost. At the end of a year, the company's Goods in Process account showed the following:

Goods in Process			
Materials	170,000	To finished goods	411,000
Labor	120,000		
Overhead	150,000		

Required:

1. Determine the overhead application rate used by the company under the assumption that the labor and overhead costs actually incurred were the same as the amounts estimated.
2. Determine the cost of the labor and the cost of the overhead charged to the one job in process at year-end under the assumption it had $11,000 of materials charged to it.

Exercise 22-4

During a cost period, a department finished and transferred 56,000 units of product to finished goods, of which 16,000 were in process in the department at the beginning of the cost period and 40,000 were begun and completed during the period. The 16,000 beginning inventory units were three fourths completed when the period began. In addition to the 56,000 units completed, 12,000 more units were in process in the department, one half completed when the period ended.

Required:

Calculate the equivalent units of product completed in the department during the cost period.

Exercise 22-5

Assume the department of Exercise 22-4 had $40,000 of labor charged to it during the cost period of the exercise and that labor is applied in the process of the department evenly throughout the process.

Required:

Calculate the cost of an equivalent unit of labor in the department and the portion of the department's $40,000 labor cost that should be assigned to each of its inventories and to the units started and finished.

Exercise 22-6

A department completed and transferred to finished goods 48,000 units of product during a cost period. Of these units, 12,000 were in process and were one third completed at the beginning of the period and 36,000 units were begun and completed during the period. In addition to the 48,000 units completed, 10,000 more units were in process in the department, three fifths processed at the period end.

Required:

Calculate the equivalent units of material added to the product processed in the department during the period under each of the following unrelated assumptions: *(a)* All material added to the product of the department is added when the department's process is first begun. *(b)* The material added to the product of the department is added evenly throughout the department's process. *(c)* One half the material added in the department is added when the department's process is first begun and the other half is added when the process is three fourths completed.

PROBLEMS

Problem 22–1

A cost accountant for Davis Company estimated before a year began that the company would incur during the year the direct labor cost of 20 persons working 2,000 hours each at an average rate of $6 per hour. The accountant also estimated that the following overhead costs would be incurred during the year:

Indirect labor	$ 31,500
Superintendence	24,000
Rent of factory building	14,400
Heat, lights, and power	9,600
Insurance expense	6,800
Depreciation of machinery	48,400
Machinery repairs	6,000
Supplies expense	3,000
Miscellaneous factory expenses	2,700
Total	$146,400

At the end of the year for which the estimates were made, the cost records showed the company had actually incurred $145,600 of overhead costs and had completed and sold five jobs that had direct labor costs as follows: Job No. 603, $50,800; Job No. 604, $46,400; Job No. 605, $43,400; Job No. 606, $45,600; and Job No. 607, $49,800. In addition, Job No. 608 was in process at the period end and had had $5,000 of direct labor and its share of overhead costs charged.

Required:

Under the assumption the company used a predetermined overhead application rate based on the foregoing overhead and direct labor estimates, determine: *(a)* the predetermined application rate used, *(b)* the total overhead applied to jobs during the year, and *(c)* the over- or underapplied overhead at the year-end. *(d)* Under the further assumption that the company considered the amount of its over- or underapplied overhead to be immaterial, give the entry to close the Overhead Costs account.

Problem 22–2

A company completed the following transactions and activities, among others, during a cost period:

a. Purchased materials on account, $16,000.
b. Paid factory wages, $12,400.
c. Paid miscellaneous factory overhead costs, $800.
d. Material requisitions were used during the cost period to charge materials to jobs. The requisitions were then accumulated until the end of the cost period at which time they were totaled and recorded with a general journal entry. (Instructions for this entry are given in Item *j.*) An abstract of the requisitions showed the following materials charged to jobs. (Charge the materials to the jobs by making entries directly in the job T-accounts in the subsidiary Job Cost Ledger.)

Job No. 1.....	$ 2,600
Job No. 2.....	1,300
Job No. 3.....	2,800
Job No. 4.....	3,000
Job No. 5.....	600
Total ...	$10,300

e. Labor time tickets were used to charge jobs with direct labor. The tickets were then accumulated until the end of the cost period at which time they were totaled and recorded with a general journal entry. (Instructions for the entry are given in Item *k.*) An abstract of the tickets showed the following labor charged to jobs. (Charge the labor to the jobs by making entries directly in the job T-accounts in the Job Cost Ledger.)

Job No. 1.....	$ 2,400
Job No. 2.....	1,400
Job No. 3.....	2,600
Job No. 4.....	2,800
Job No. 5.....	400
Total ...	$ 9,600

f. Job Nos. 1, 3, and 4 were completed and transferred to finished goods. A predetermined overhead application rate, 150% of direct labor cost, was used to apply overhead to each job upon its completion. (Enter the overhead in the job T-accounts; mark the jobs "completed"; and make a general journal entry to transfer their costs to the Finished Goods account.)
g. Job Nos. 1 and 3 were sold on account for a total of $24,000.
h. At the end of the cost period charged overhead to the jobs in process at the rate of 150% of direct labor cost. (Enter the overhead in the job T-accounts.)
i. At the end of the cost period made a general journal entry to record: depreciation, factory building, $2,300; depreciation, machinery, $4,100; expired factory insurance, $600; and accrued factory taxes payable, $1,200.
j. Separated the material requisitions into direct material requisitions and indirect material requisitions, totaled each kind, and made a general journal entry to record them. The requisition totals were:

Direct materials	$10,300
Indirect materials.....	2,000
Total	$12,300

k. Separated the labor time tickets into direct labor time tickets and indirect labor time tickets, totaled each kind, and made a general journal entry to record them. The time ticket totals were:

Direct labor	$ 9,600
Indirect labor	3,100
Total	$12,700

l. Determined the total overhead assigned to all jobs and made a general journal entry to record it.

Required:

1. Open the following general ledger T-accounts: Materials, Goods in Process, Finished Goods, Factory Payroll, Overhead Costs, and Cost of Goods Sold.
2. Open an additional T-account for each of the five jobs. Assume that each job's T-account is a job cost sheet in a subsidiary Job Cost Ledger.
3. Prepare general journal entries to record the applicable information of Items *a, b, c, f, g, i, j, k,* and *l.* Post the entry portions that affect the general ledger accounts opened.
4. Enter the applicable information of Items *d, e, f,* and *h* directly in the T-accounts that represent job cost sheets.
5. Present statistics to prove the balances of the Goods in Process and Finished Goods accounts.
6. List the general ledger accounts and tell what is represented by the balance of each.

Problem 22–3

If the working papers that accompany this text are not being used, omit this problem.

The Bancroft Company manufactures to the special order of its customers a machine called an astroviewer. On January 1, the company had a $2,230 materials inventory but no inventories of goods in process and finished goods. However, on that date it began Job No. 1, an astroviewer for Nearsight Company, and Job No. 2, for Farsight Company; and during the January cost period, it completed the following activities and transactions:

a. Recorded invoices for the purchase of materials on credit. The invoices and receiving reports carried this information:

Receiving Report No. 1, Material A, 200 units at $11 each.
Receiving Report No. 2, Material B, 300 units at $5 each.
(Record the invoices with a single general journal entry and post to the general ledger T-accounts, using the transaction number to identify the amounts in the accounts. Enter the receiving report information on the proper materials ledger cards.)

b. Materials were requisitioned as follows:

Requisition No. 1, for Job No. 1, 100 units of Material A.
Requisition No. 2, for Job No. 1, 120 units of Material B.
Requisition No. 3, for Job No. 2, 80 units of Material A.
Requisition No. 4, for Job No. 2, 100 units of Material B.
Requisition No. 5, for 10 units of machinery lubricant.
(Enter the the requisition amounts for direct materials on the materials ledger cards and on the job cost sheets. Enter the indirect material amount on the proper materials ledger card and debit it to the Indirect Materials account in the subsidiary Overhead Costs Ledger. Assume the requisitions are accumulated until the end of the month and will

be recorded with a general journal entry. Instructions for this entry follow in the problem.)

c. Received the following labor time tickets from the timekeeping department:

Time tickets Nos. 1 through 60 for direct labor on Job No. 1, $1,000.
Time tickets Nos. 61 through 100 for direct labor on Job No. 2, $800.
Time tickets Nos. 101 through 120 for machinery repairs, $375.
(Charge the direct labor time tickets to the proper jobs and charge the indirect labor time tickets to the Indirect Labor account in the subsidiary Overhead Costs Ledger. Assume the time tickets are accumulated until the end of the month for recording with a general journal entry.)

d. Made the following cash disbursements during the month:
Paid the month's factory payroll, $2,110.
Paid for miscellaneous overhead items totaling $1,000.
(Record the payments with general journal entries and post the general ledger accounts. Enter the charge for miscellaneous overhead items in the subsidiary Overhead Costs Ledger.)

e. Finished Job No. 1 and transferred it to the finished goods warehouse.
(The company charges overhead to each job by means of a predetermined overhead application rate based on direct labor costs. The rate is 80%. (1) Enter the overhead charge on the cost sheet of Job No. 1. (2) Complete the cost summary section of the cost sheet. (3) Mark "Finished" on the cost sheet. (4) Prepare and post a general journal entry to record the job's completion and transfer to finished goods.)

f. Prepared and posted a general journal entry to record both the cost of goods sold and the sale of Job No. 1 to Nearsight Company, sale price $5,000.

g. At the end of the cost period, charged overhead to Job No. 2 based on the amount of direct labor applied to the job thus far. (Enter the applicable amount of overhead on the job's cost sheet.)

h. Totaled the requisitions for direct materials, totaled the requisitions for indirect materials, and made and posted a general journal entry to record them.

i. Totaled the direct labor time tickets, totaled the indirect labor time tickets, and made and posted a general journal entry to record them.

j. Determined the amount of overhead applied to jobs and made and posted a general journal entry to record it.

Required:

1. Record the transactions as instructed in the narrative.
2. Complete the statements in the book of working papers by filling in the blanks.

Problem 22–4

In the grinding department of a manufacturing company, labor is added to the department's product evenly throughout its processing. During a cost period, 75,000 units of product were finished in this department and transferred to finished goods. Of these 75,000 units, 22,500 were in process at the beginning of the period and 52,500 were begun and completed during the period. The 22,500 beginning goods in process units were one fifth completed when the period began. In addition to the foregoing units, 13,500 additional units were in process and were one-third completed at the period end.

Required:

Under the assumption that $62,100 of labor was charged to the grinding department during the period, determine (a) the equivalent units of labor applied to the department's product, (b) the cost of an equivalent unit of labor, and (c) the portion of the $62,100 that should be charged to the beginning inventory, the units started and finished, and the ending inventory.

Problem 22–5

The product of So Hi Manufacturing Company is produced on a continuous basis in a single processing department in which material, labor, and overhead are added to the product evenly throughout the manufacturing process.

At the end of the May 198A cost period, after the material, labor, and overhead costs were charged to the Goods in Process account of the single processing department, the account appeared as follows:

Goods in Process

May 1	Balance	6,810	
31	Materials	26,625	
31	Labor	54,315	
31	Overhead	75,615	
		163,365	

During the cost period, the company finished and transferred to finished goods 108,000 units of the product, of which 13,500 were in process at the beginning of the period and 94,500 were begun and finished during the period. The 13,500 units that were in process were one third processed when the period began. In addition to the foregoing units, 12,000 additional units were in process and were one fourth completed at the end of the cost period.

Required:

1. Prepare a process cost summary for the department.
2. Draft the general journal entry to transfer to Finished Goods the cost of the product finished in the department during the month.

Problem 22–6

Central Processing Company manufactures a simple product on a continuous basis in one department. All materials are added in the manufacturing process of this product when the process is first begun. Labor and overhead are added evenly throughout the process.

During the current April cost period, the company completed and transferred to finished goods 86,000 units of the product. These consisted of 10,000 units that were in process at the beginning of the period and 76,000 units begun and finished during the period. The 10,000 beginning goods in process units were complete as to materials and four fifths complete as to labor and overhead when the period began. In addition to the foregoing units, 12,000 additional units were in process at the end of the period, complete as to materials and one half complete as to labor and overhead.

Since the company has only one processing department, it has only one

Goods in Process account. At the end of the period, after entries recording material, labor, and overhead had been posted, the account appeared as follows:

Goods in Process

Apr. 1	Balance	15,999	
30	Materials	81,180	
30	Labor	29,232	
30	Overhead	44,604	
		171,015	

Required:

Prepare a process cost summary and the entry to transfer to Finished Goods the cost of the product completed in the department during April.

ALTERNATE PROBLEMS

Problem 22–1A   Late in 198A, the cost accountant for Caspari Company established the 198B overhead application rate by estimating that the company would assign 10 persons to direct labor tasks during 198B and that each person would work 2,000 hours at $7.50 per hour during the year. At the same time the accountant estimated that the company would incur the following amounts of overhead costs during 198B:

Indirect labor	$ 50,000
Factory building rent	30,000
Depreciation expense, machinery	37,500
Machinery repairs expense	7,500
Heat, lights, and power	15,000
Factory supplies expense	2,500
Total	$142,500

At the end of 198B, the accounting records showed the company had actually incurred $146,400 of overhead costs during the year while completing four jobs and beginning the fifth. The completed jobs were assigned overhead on completion, and the in-process job was assigned overhead at year-end. The jobs had the following direct labor costs:

Job No. 1 (sold and delivered)	$ 32,000
Job No. 2 (sold and delivered)	32,500
Job No. 3 (sold and delivered)	35,500
Job No. 4 (in finished goods inventory)	35,000
Job No. 5 (in process, unfinished)	17,500
Total	$152,500

Required:

1. Determine the overhead application rate established by the cost accountant under the assumption it was based on direct labor cost.
2. Determine the total overhead applied to jobs during the year and the amount of over- or underapplied overhead at year-end.
3. Give the entry to dispose of the over- or underapplied overhead by prorat-

ing it between goods in process, finished goods inventory, and cost of goods sold.

Problem 22–2A   During its first cost period, a company completed the following activities and transactions:

a. Purchased materials on account, $22,000.
b. Paid factory wages, $18,800.
c. Paid miscellaneous factory overhead costs, $3,000.
d. Material requisitions were used during the cost period to charge materials to jobs. The requisitions were accumulated until the end of the cost period and then were totaled and recorded with a general journal entry. (Instructions for the entry are given in Item *j*.) An abstract of the requisitions showed the following materials charged to jobs. (Charge the materials to the jobs by making entries directly in the job T-accounts in the subsidiary Job Cost Ledger.)

Job No. 1	$ 4,000
Job No. 2	2,100
Job No. 3	3,900
Job No. 4	4,300
Job No. 5	800
Total	$15,100

e. Labor time tickets were used to charge jobs with direct labor. The tickets were accumulated until the end of the cost period and then were totaled and recorded with a general journal entry. (Instructions for the entry are given in Item *k*.) An abstract of the tickets showed the following labor charged to jobs. (Charge the labor to the jobs by making entries directly in the job T-accounts in the Job Cost Ledger.)

Job No. 1	$ 3,800
Job No. 2	2,200
Job No. 3	4,000
Job No. 4	3,600
Job No. 5	400
Total	$14,000

f. Job Nos. 1, 3, and 4 were completed and transferred to finished goods. A predetermined overhead application rate, 200% of direct labor cost, was used to apply overhead to each job upon its completion. (Enter the overhead in the job T-accounts; mark the jobs "completed"; and make a general journal entry to transfer their costs to the Finished Goods account.)
g. Job Nos. 1 and 4 were sold on account for a total of $40,000.
h. At the end of the cost period, charged overhead to the jobs in process, using the 200% of direct labor cost application rate. (Enter the overhead in the job T-accounts.)
i. Made a general journal entry at the end of the cost period to record depreciation on the factory building, $6,000; machinery depreciation, $6,700; expired factory insurance, $1,200; and accrued factory taxes payable, $2,000.
j. Separated the material requisitions into direct material requisitions and indirect material requisitions, totaled each kind, and made a general journal entry to record them. The requisition totals were:

Direct materials $15,100
Indirect materials   4,000
Total $19,100

k. Separated the labor time tickets into direct labor time tickets and indirect labor time tickets, totaled each kind, and made a general journal entry to record them. The time ticket totals were:

Direct labor $14,000
Indirect labor   5,000
Total $19,000

l. Determined the total overhead assigned to all jobs and made a general journal entry to record it.

Required:

1. Open the following general ledger T-accounts: Materials, Goods in Process, Finished Goods, Factory Payroll, Overhead Costs, and Cost of Goods Sold.
2. Open an additional T-account for each of the five jobs. Assume that each job's T-account is a job cost sheet in a subsidiary Job Cost Ledger.
3. Prepare general journal entries to record the applicable information of Items *a, b, c, f, g, i, j, k,* and *l.* Post the entry portions that affect the general ledger accounts opened.
4. Enter the applicable information of Items *d, e, f,* and *h* directly in the T-accounts that represent job cost sheets.
5. Present statistics to prove the balances of the Goods in Process and Finished Goods accounts.
6. List the general ledger accounts and tell what is represented by the balance of each.

Problem 22–4A   The PKL Gadget Company is a one-department operation in which labor and overhead are added to the department's product evenly throughout the production process. In July, 21,000 units of product were transferred from the shop to finished goods inventory. Included in these 21,000 units were 8,000 units from the June 30 work in process inventory, at which time those units were one fourth finished. In addition to the beginning inventory, 27,000 units were placed in process during July. On July 31, the units which remained in process were one half complete. Total overhead costs incurred during July were $187,200.

Required:

Determine *(a)* the equivalent units of production in July to be used in applying overhead costs to the product of the shop, *(b)* the overhead cost of an equivalent unit of production, and *(c)* the portion of July overhead cost that should be charged to completing the units in beginning inventory, to units started and finished during July, and to the ending inventory.

Problem 22–5A   Two operations, forming and finishing, are used in the manufacturing procedure of Northeastern Manufacturing Company. The procedure is begun in the forming department and completed in the finishing department.

At the beginning of the May cost period there were 2,500 units of product in the forming department that were three fifths processed. These units were completed during the period and transferred to the finishing department. Also, the processing of 15,500 additional units was begun in the forming department during the period. Of these 15,500 units, 11,500 were finished and transferred to the molding department. The remaining 4,000 units were in the department in a one-half processed state at the end of the period.

It is assumed that the material, labor, and overhead applied in the forming department are applied evenly throughout the process of the department.

At the end of the cost period, after entries recording materials, labor, and overhead were posted, the company's Goods in Process, Forming Department account appeared as follows:

Goods in Process, Forming Department

May 1	Balance	11,604	
31	Materials	37,120	
31	Labor	48,836	
31	Overhead	24,360	
		121,920	

Required:

1. Prepare a process cost summary for the forming department.
2. Prepare the journal entry to transfer to the finishing department the cost of the goods completed in the forming department and transferred.

Problem 22–6A   The product of Springfield Company is manufactured in one continuous process in which all materials are entered into production at the beginning of the process. Labor and overhead are applied evenly throughout the process.

Springfield Company's Goods in Process account reflects the following charges during the month of October:

Beginning balance	$ 9,600
Materials added to production	42,294
Labored charged to production	33,948
Overhead charged to production	50,922

During October, the company completed the manufacture of 12,000 units of product. These included 2,100 units that had entered production the previous month, and on October 1 were complete as to materials and two-thirds complete as to labor and overhead. At the end of October, 3,400 units remained in process, completed as to materials and one-half complete as to labor and overhead.

Required:

Prepare a process cost summary and the entry to transfer to Finished Goods the cost of the product completed during October.

PROVOCATIVE PROBLEMS

Provocative Problem 22–1, Lopez Company   The Lopez Company uses a job order cost system in accounting for manufacturing costs, and following are a number of its general ledger accounts with the January 1 balances and some January postings shown. The postings are incomplete. Commonly only the debit or credit of a journal entry appears in the accounts, with the offsetting debits and credits being omitted. Also, the amounts shown represent total postings for the month and no date appears. However, this additional information is available: *(a)* The company charges jobs with overhead on the basis of direct labor cost, using a 150% overhead application rate. *(b)* The $42,500 debit in the Overhead Costs account represents the sum of all overhead costs for January other than indirect materials and indirect labor. *(c)* The accrued factory payroll on January 31 was $7,500.

Materials			
Jan. 1 Bal.	27,500	30,000	
	37,500		

Factory Payroll			
47,500	Jan. 1 Bal.	5,000	

Goods in Process			
Jan. 1 Bal.	15,000	120,000	
Materials	25,000		
Labor	40,000		

Cost of Goods Sold			

Finished Goods			
Jan. 1 Bal.	30,000	125,000	

Factory Overhead Costs			
42,500			

Required:

Copy the accounts on a sheet of paper, supply the missing debits and credits, and tie together the debits and credits of an entry with key letters. Answer these questions: *(a)* What was the January 31 balance of the Finished Goods account? *(b)* How many dollars of factory labor cost (direct plus indirect) were incurred during January? *(c)* What was the cost of the goods sold during January? *(d)* How much overhead was actually incurred during the month? *(e)* How much overhead was charged to jobs during the month? *(f)* Was overhead overapplied or underapplied during the month?

Provocative
Problem 22–2,
Santorini
Company

The production facility of the Santorini Company was nearly destroyed on April 7, 198B, as a consequence of an explosion and fire in the plant. Assets lost in the blaze included all of the inventories. In addition, many of the accounting records were destroyed. In preparation for settlement with the insurance company, you are requested to estimate the amounts of raw materials, goods in process, and finished goods destroyed. Through your investigation, you determined that the company used a job order cost system, and you also obtained the following additional information:

a. The company's December 31, 198A, balance sheet showed the following inventory amounts: materials, $15,000; goods in process, $21,000; and finished goods, $24,000. The balance sheet also showed a $3,000 liability for accrued factory wages payable.
b. The overhead application rate used by the company was 70% of direct labor cost.
c. Goods costing $81,000 were sold and delivered to customers between January 1 and April 7, 198B.

    d. Materials purchased between January 1 and April 7 amounted to $31,000, and $27,000 of direct and indirect materials were issued to the factory during the same period.

    e. Factory wages totaling $35,000 were paid between January 1 and April 7, and there were $1,000 of accrued factory wages payable on the latter date.

    f. The debits to the Overhead Costs account during the period before the fire totaled $21,000 of which $3,000 was for indirect materials and $5,000 was for indirect labor.

    g. The cost of goods finished and transferred to finished goods inventory during the January 1 to April 7 period amounted to $76,000.

    h. It was decided that the April 7 balance of the Overhead Costs account should be apportioned between goods in process, finished goods, and cost of goods sold. Between January 1 and April 7, the company had charged the following amounts of overhead to jobs: to jobs sold, $12,740; to jobs finished but unsold, $3,920; and to jobs still in process on April 7, $2,940.

    Determine the April 7 inventories of materials, goods in process, and finished goods. (T-accounts may be helpful in organizing the data.)

Provocative Problem 22–3, Webb Company

    The processing department of Webb Company began January 198A with 10,000 units in the goods in process inventory, each of which was 40 percent complete. During January, an additional 120,000 units were entered into the production process.

    A total of 105,000 units were completed and transferred to finished goods. If January's equivalent units of production amounted to 106,000 units, how many units remained in process at the end of the month and what was their average stage of completion?

Accounting for the Segments and Departments of a Business; Responsibility Accounting

23

After studying Chapter 23, you should be able to:

Describe the segmental information disclosed in the financial reports of large companies having operations in several lines of business.

List the four basic issues faced by accountants in developing segmental information.

State the reasons for departmentalization of businesses.

Describe the types of expenses that should be allocated among departments, the bases for allocating such expenses, and the procedures involved in the allocation process.

Explain the differences between reports designed to measure the profitability of a department and reports that are used to evaluate the performance of a department manager.

Describe the problems associated with allocation of joint costs between departments.

Define or explain the words and phrases listed in the chapter Glossary.

In previous chapters, attention was focused on understanding financial statements and related accounting information for a *whole* business. This chapter shifts the attention to accounting for the "parts" or subunits of a business. This is normally called *segmental reporting* or *departmental accounting.* Information on the subunits of a business may be useful to (1) outsiders generally interested in an overall evaluation of the business and (2) internal managers responsible for planning and controlling the operations of the business.

The term *segmental reporting* is used most often in reference to published information for the use of outsiders; this information generally relates to a company's operations in different industries or geographical areas. Usually, the term *departmental accounting* relates to information on the subunits of a business that is prepared for the use of internal managers.

REPORTING ON BROAD BUSINESS SEGMENTS

When a company is large and has operations in more than one type of business, outsiders may gain a better understanding of the overall business by examining information on each segment. For example, Illustration 23–1 shows segmental information provided in the annual report of The Southland Corporation.

Segmental Information to Be Disclosed

In Illustration 23–1, observe that the activities of the business are grouped into four major segments: the Stores Group, the Dairies Group, the Special Operations Group, and Gasoline Supply. Some additional activities do not fit into any of these major groups and are lumped into a category called Corporate. Note that five different items of information are presented for each segment. They are:

1. Revenues.
2. Operating profits (before interest and taxes).
3. Identifiable assets.
4. Capital expenditures.
5. Depreciation and amortization expense.

Large firms that operate in more than one industry are required to disclose these items of information on each industrial segment of the business. In addition, they may be required to report (1) a geographical distribution of sales and (2) sales to major customers. Additional examples of reported segmental information are shown in the Appendix beginning on page 987. Note that segmental information is included

Illustration 23–1

16. Segment Information:

The Stores Group includes all convenience and grocery stores in the United States and Canada, as well as those activities (such as distribution and food preparation) which derive the majority of their revenues and operating profits from support of these stores. The Dairies Group includes milk and ice cream processing and distribution. The Special Operations Group includes the ice, chemical, Tidel and Chief Auto Parts divisions. Gasoline Supply includes gasoline storage facilities and gasoline wholesaling operations. Corporate items reflect income, expenses and assets not allocable to segments.

Intersegment sales are accounted for on a cost-plus-markup basis. Expenses directly identifiable with a segment and certain allocated income and expenses are used to determine operating profit by segment.

Amounts for 1981 and 1980 have been restated to reflect the retroactive application of SFAS No. 52. The effect was not material.

Segment information is as follows (000's omitted):

	1982	1981	1980
Revenues:			
Stores Group	$5,721,099	$5,144,087	$4,307,876
Dairies Group	584,422	568,560	534,699
Special Operations Group	165,154	140,904	122,645
Gasoline Supply	1,259,493	103,754	—
Corporate	9,031	7,725	8,864
	7,739,199	5,965,030	4,974,084
Intersegment revenues:			
Dairies Group	(229,833)	(198,329)	(175,251)
Special Operations Group	(13,745)	(14,069)	(16,228)
Gasoline Supply	(713,238)	(18,472)	—
Consolidated revenues	$6,782,383	$5,734,160	$4,782,605
Operating profits:			
Stores Group	$ 224,916	$ 219,887	$ 174,399
Dairies Group	12,457	13,333	15,325
Special Operations Group	(3,137)	(9,503)	(3,053)
Gasoline Supply	23,009	2,994	—
Consolidated operating profits	257,245	226,711	186,671
Interest expense	(48,735)	(47,587)	(46,337)
Corporate expense — net	(19,769)	(14,363)	(9,191)
Consolidated earnings before income taxes	$ 188,741	$ 164,761	$ 131,143
Identifiable assets (including capital leases) at December 31:			
Stores Group	$1,253,280	$1,216,037	$1,180,889
Dairies Group	114,799	120,313	116,051
Special Operations Group	97,122	96,463	95,617
Gasoline Supply	140,006	107,045	—
Corporate	237,377	132,313	103,685
Total identifiable assets	$1,842,584	$1,672,171	$1,496,242
Capital expenditures (excluding capital leases):			
Stores Group	$ 184,677	$ 150,301	$ 92,112
Dairies Group	15,966	14,213	9,656
Special Operations Group	11,164	11,462	10,712
Gasoline Supply	15,681	14,700	—
Corporate	109,800	33,215	2,030
	$ 337,288	$ 223,891	$ 114,510
Depreciation and amortization expense:			
Stores Group	$ 99,200	$ 85,009	$ 74,870
Dairies Group	8,648	7,930	7,474
Special Operations Group	5,327	4,538	4,488
Gasoline Supply	3,571	203	—
Corporate	4,955	3,151	3,015
	$ 121,701	$ 100,831	$ 89,847

in the reports of both Texas Instruments (pages 988 through 1,004) and Equifax Inc. (pages 1,005 and 1,019).

Four Basic Issues in Segmental Reporting

Companies face four basic problems in developing segmental information. Detailed guidelines for dealing with these problems are provided by the FASB. While the study of these guidelines is too detailed for inclusion at this introductory level, students should be aware of each basic issue.

1. IDENTIFYING SIGNIFICANT SEGMENTS. The operations of a business may not be neatly organized in terms of segments that are important to financial statement readers. For purposes of segmental reporting, the business must be divided into enough segments to show the basic industries in which the business operates. On the other hand, it should not be divided into so many segments that the information becomes confusing.

2. TRANSFER PRICING BETWEEN SEGMENTS. Sometimes one or more segments of a business make sales of products or services to the other segments. These sales are eliminated when the overall statements for the business are prepared. However, sales between segments should not be eliminated when evaluating the performance of each segment. Sales between segments result in revenues to the selling segment and costs to the purchasing segment. The problem is to determine a fair price at which to report such sales, so that the profitability of both the selling segment and the purchasing segment are fairly measured.

3. MEASURING SEGMENTAL PROFITABILITY. Even if each segment operates as a highly independent unit, some expenses of the business will benefit more than one segment. Some of these common expenses can be allocated to the segments on a reasonable basis. Others may defy meaningful allocation. The accountant must first decide which expenses are to be allocated and which are to be left unallocated when measuring the profitability of each segment. For those expenses to be allocated, the accountant must then determine the most reasonable basis for allocation.

4. IDENTIFYING SEGMENTAL ASSETS. Many assets are easily identified with specific segments because they are used solely by one segment or another. Other assets are shared by more than one segment. The accountant must determine reasonable bases for allocating shared assets to the segments that benefit from the assets.

DEPARTMENTAL ACCOUNTING

The previous discussion of segmental reporting related primarily to large businesses that have operations in more than one industry. However, students should not presume that accounting for the subunits of a business is limited to large companies with diverse operations. Businesses are divided into subunits or departments whenever they become too large to be effectively managed as a single unit.

Accounting for the departments of a business is characterized by two primary goals. One goal is to provide information that management can use in evaluating the profitability or cost effectiveness of each department. The second goal is to assign costs and expenses to the particular managers who are responsible for controlling those costs and expenses. In this way, the performance of managers can be evaluated in terms of their responsibilities. Thus, departmental accounting is closely related to what is called *responsibility accounting*.

DEPARTMENTALIZING A BUSINESS

Most businesses are large and complex enough to require that they be divided into subunits or departments. When a business is departmentalized, a manager is usually placed in charge of each department. If the business grows even larger, each department may be further divided into smaller segments. Thus, a particular manager can be assigned responsibilities over the activities of a unit that is not too large for the manager to effectively oversee and control. Also, departments can be organized so that the specialized skills of each manager can be used most effectively.

BASIS FOR DEPARTMENTALIZATION

In a departmentalized business, there are two basic kinds of departments, *productive departments* and *service departments*. In a factory, the productive departments are those engaged directly in manufacturing operations. In a store, they are the departments making sales. Departmental divisions in a factory are commonly based on manufacturing processes employed or products or components manufactured. The divisions in a store are usually based on kinds of goods sold, with each selling or productive department being assigned the sale of one or more kinds of merchandise. In either type of business, the service departments, such as the general office, advertising, purchasing, payroll, and personnel departments, assist or perform services for the productive departments.

INFORMATION TO EVALUATE DEPARTMENTS

When a business is divided into departments, management must be able to find out how well each department is performing. Thus, it is necessary for the accounting system to supply information by departments as to resources expended and outputs achieved. This requires that revenue and expense information be measured and accumulated by departments. However, before going further it should be observed that such information is generally not made public, since it might be of considerable benefit to competitors. Rather, it is for the use of management in controlling operations, appraising performances, allocating resources, and in taking remedial actions. For example, if one of several departments is particularly profitable, perhaps it should be expanded. Or, if a department is showing poor results, information as to its revenues, costs, and expenses may point to a proper remedial action.

The information used to evaluate a department depends on whether the department is a *cost center* or a *profit center.* A cost center is a unit of the business that incurs costs (or expenses) but does not directly generate revenues. The productive departments of a factory and such service departments as the general office, advertising, and purchasing departments are cost centers. A profit center differs from a cost center in that it not only incurs costs but also generates revenues. The selling departments of a store are profit centers. In judging efficiencies in the two kinds of centers, managers of cost centers are judged on their ability to control costs and keep costs within a satisfactory range. Managers of profit centers, on the other hand, are judged on their ability to generate earnings, which are the excess of revenues over costs.

SECURING DEPARTMENTAL INFORMATION

Modern cash registers enable a merchandising company to accumulate information as to sales and sales returns by departments. Often, the registers transfer the information directly into the store's computer. This kind of system is capable of much more than accumulating sales information by departments. The cash registers will print all pertinent information on the sales ticket given to the customer, total the ticket, and initiate entries to record credit sales in the customer's account. Also, if the required information as to type of goods sold is keyed into the registers by means of code numbers, the computer can print out detailed daily departmental summaries of goods sold and item inventories of unsold goods.

Cash registers also enable a small store to determine daily totals for sales and sales returns by departments. However, since the registers often are not connected to a computer, the totals must be accumulated by some other method. Two methods are commonly used. A small store may provide separate Sales and Sales Returns accounts in its ledger for each of its departments or it may use analysis sheets. Either method may also be used to accumulate information as to purchases and purchases returns by departments.

If a store chooses to provide separate Sales, Sales Returns, Purchases, and Purchases Returns accounts in its ledger for each of its departments, it may also provide columns in its journals to record transactions by departments. Illustration 23–2 shows such a journal for recording sales by departments. The amounts to be debited to the customers' accounts are entered in the Accounts Receivable Debit column and are posted to these accounts each day. The column's total is debited to the Accounts Receivable controlling account at the end of the month. The departmental sales are entered in the last three columns and are posted as column totals at the end of the month.

Illustration 23–2

SALES JOURNAL

Date		Account Debited	Invoice Number	P R	Accounts Receivable Debit	Departmental Sales		
						Dept. 1 Credit	Dept. 2 Credit	Dept. 3 Credit
Oct.	1	Walter Marshfield	737		145.00	90.00	55.00	. . . . .
	1	Thomas Higgins	738		85.00	. . . . .	40.00	45.00

Separate departmental accounts are practical only for a store having a limited number of departments. In a store having more than a few departments, a more practical procedure is to use departmental sales analysis sheets.

When a store uses departmental sales analysis sheets, it provides only one undepartmentalized general ledger account for sales, another account for sales returns, another for purchases, and another for purchases returns; and it records its transactions and posts to these accounts as though it were not departmentalized. In addition to this, each day it also summarizes its transactions by departments and enters the summarized amounts on analysis sheets. For example, a company using analysis sheets, in addition to recording sales in its usual manner, will total each day's sales by departments and enter the daily totals on a sales analysis sheet like Illustration 23–3. As a result, at the end of a month or other period, the column totals of the analysis sheet show

Illustration 23–3

Departmental Sales Analysis Sheet

Date		Men's Wear Dept.	Boys' Wear Dept.	Shoe Dept.	Leather Goods Dept.	Women's Wear Dept.
May	1	$357.15	$175.06	$115.00	$ 75.25	$427.18
	2	298.55	136.27	145.80	110.20	387.27

sales by departments, and the grand total of all the columns should equal the balance of the Sales account.

When a store uses departmental analysis sheets, it uses one analysis sheet to accumulate sales figures, another for sales returns, another for purchases, and still another for purchases returns. At the end of the period, the several analysis sheets show the store's sales, sales returns, purchases, and purchases returns by departments. If the store then takes inventories by departments, it can calculate gross profits by departments.

Accumulating information and arriving at a gross profit figure for each selling department in a departmentalized business is not too difficult, as the discussion thus far reveals. However, to go beyond this and arrive at useful departmental net income figures is not so easy. As a result, many companies make no effort to calculate more than gross profits by departments.

ALLOCATING EXPENSES

If a business attempts to measure not only departmental gross profit but also departmental net income, special problems are confronted. They involve dividing the expenses of the business among the selling departments of the business. Some expenses, called *direct expenses,* are easily traced to specific departments. The direct expenses of a department are easily traced to the department because they are incurred for the sole benefit of that department. For example, the salary of an employee who works in only one department is a direct expense of that department.

The expenses of a business include both direct expenses and *indirect expenses.* Indirect expenses are incurred for the joint benefit of more than one department. For example, where two or more departments share a single building, the expenses of renting, heating, and lighting the building jointly benefit all of the departments in the building. Although such indirect expenses cannot be easily traced to a specific department, they must be allocated among the departments that benefited from the expenses. Each indirect expense should be allocated on a basis that fairly approximates the relative benefit received by each department. However, measuring the benefit each department receives from an indirect expense is often difficult. Even after a reasonable allocation basis is chosen, considerable doubt often exists regarding the proper share to be charged to each department.

To illustrate the allocation of an indirect expense, assume that a jewelry store purchases janitorial services from an outside firm. The jewelry store then allocates the cost among its three departments according to the floor space occupied. The cost of janitorial services for a short period is $280, and the amounts of floor space occupied are:

```
Jewelry department ............ 250 sq. ft.
Watch repair department ........ 125
China and silver department ..... 500
        Total ................. 875 sq. ft.
```

The calculations to allocate janitorial expense to the departments are:

$$\text{Jewelry department:} \quad \frac{250}{875} \times \$280 = \$80$$

$$\text{Watch repair department:} \quad \frac{125}{875} \times \$280 = \$40$$

$$\text{China and silver department:} \quad \frac{500}{875} \times \$280 = \$160$$

Students should note that the concepts of *direct* costs or expenses and *indirect* costs or expenses can be usefully applied in a variety of situations in addition to departmental accounting. In general, direct costs are easily traced to or associated with a "cost object." In this chapter, the cost object of significance is the department. However, other cost objects may also be of interest. For example, recall that the discussion of Chapters 21 and 22 dealt with manufacturing companies. In that context, the cost object was a unit or batch of product. Direct costs were recognized to be those that can be easily identified with a unit of product. Other costs that are essential to the manufacturing process but that cannot be easily traced to specific units of product were called indirect costs.

BASES FOR ALLOCATING EXPENSES

In the following paragraphs, bases for allocating some common indirect expenses are discussed. In the discussions, no hard-and-fast rules are given because several factors are often involved in an expense allocation and the relative importance of the factors varies from situation to situation. As previously stated, indirect expenses are, by definition, subject to doubt as to how they should be allocated between departments. Judgment rather than hard-and-fast rules is required, and different accountants may not agree on the proper basis for allocating an indirect expense.

Wages and Salaries

An employee's wages may be either a direct or an indirect expense. If an employee's time is spent all in one department, the employee's wages are a direct expense of the benefited department; but if an employee works in more than one department, the wages become an indirect expense to be allocated between or among the benefited departments. Normally, working time spent in each department is a fair basis for allocating wages.

A supervisory employee may supervise more than one department; and in such cases, the time spent in each department is usually a fair basis for allocating his or her salary. However, since a supervisory employee is frequently on the move from department to department, the time spent in each is often difficult to measure. Consequently, some companies allocate the salary of such an employee to his or her departments on the basis of the number of employees in each department, while others make the allocation on the basis of the supervised departments' sales. When a supervisor's salary is allocated on the basis of employees, it is assumed that he or she is supervising people and the time spent in each department is related to the number of employees in each. When the salary is allocated on the basis of sales, it is assumed that the time devoted to each department is related to the department's production.

Rent or Depreciation and Related Expenses of Buildings

Rent expense is normally allocated to benefited departments on the basis of the amount and value of the floor space occupied by each. Furthermore, since all customers who enter a store must pass the departments by the entrance and only a fraction of these people go beyond the first floor, ground floor space is more valuable for retail purposes than is basement or upper floor space, and space near the entrance is more valuable than is space in an out-of-the-way corner.

Yet, since there is no exact measure of floor space values, all such values and the allocations of rent based on such values must depend on judgment. Fair allocations depend on the use of good judgment, statistics as to customer traffic patterns, and the opinions of experts who are familiar with current rental values. When a building is owned instead of being rented, expenses such as depreciation, taxes, and insurance on the building are allocated like rent expense.

Advertising

When a store advertises a department's products, if the advertising is effective, people come into the store to buy the products. However, at the same time they also often buy other unadvertised products. Consequently, advertising benefits all departments, even those the products of which are not advertised. Thus, many stores treat advertising as an indirect expense and allocate it on the basis of sales. When advertising costs are allocated on a sales basis, a department producing $\frac{1}{10}$ of the total sales is charged with $\frac{1}{10}$ of the advertising cost; a department producing $\frac{1}{8}$ of the sales is charged with $\frac{1}{8}$.

Although in many stores advertising costs are allocated to departments on the basis of sales, in others each advertisement is analyzed and the cost of the column inches of newspaper space or minutes of TV or radio time devoted to the products of a department is charged to the department.

Depreciation of Equipment

Depreciation on equipment used solely in one department is a direct expense of that department; and if detailed plant asset records are kept, the depreciation applicable to each department may be determined by examining the records. Where adequate records are not maintained, depreciation must be treated as an indirect expense and allocated to the departments on the basis of the value of the equipment in each. Where items of equipment are used by more than one department, the relative number of hours used is usually a fair basis of allocating depreciation costs by each department.

Heating and Lighting Expense

Heating and lighting expense is usually allocated on the basis of floor space occupied under the assumption that the amount of heat and the number of lights, their wattage, and the extent of their use are uniform throughout the store. Should there be a material variation in lighting, however, further analysis and a separate allocation may be advisable.

Service Departments

In order to manufacture products and make sales, the productive departments must have the services supplied by departments such as the general office, personnel, payroll, advertising, and purchasing departments. Such departments are called *service departments*. Since service departments do not produce revenues, they are evaluated as cost centers rather than as profit centers. Although each service department should be separately evaluated, the costs it incurs must also be allocated among the departments it services. Thus, the costs of service departments are, in effect, indirect expenses of the selling departments; and the allocation of service department costs to selling departments is required if net incomes of the selling departments are to be calculated. The following list shows commonly used bases for these allocations:

Departments	Commonly Used Expense Allocation Bases
General office department	Number of employees in each department or sales.
Personnel department	Number of employees in each department.
Payroll department	Number of employees in each department.
Advertising department	Sales or amounts of advertising charged directly to each department.
Purchasing department	Dollar amounts of purchases or number of purchase invoices processed.
Cleaning and maintenance department	Square feet of floor space occupied.

MECHANICS OF ALLOCATING EXPENSES

It would be difficult or impossible to analyze each indirect expense incurred and allocate and charge portions to several departmental expense accounts at the time of incurrence or payment. Consequently, expense amounts paid or incurred, both direct and indirect, are commonly accumulated in undepartmentalized expense accounts until the end of a period, when a *departmental expense allocation sheet* (see Illustration 23–4) is used to allocate and charge each expense to the benefited departments.

To prepare an expense allocation sheet, the names of the to-be-allocated expenses are entered in the sheet's first column along with the names of the service departments. Next, the bases of allocation are entered in the second column, and the expense amounts are entered in the third. Then, each expense is allocated according to the basis shown, and the allocated portions are entered in the departmental columns. After this, the departmental columns are totaled and the

Illustration 23–4

BETA HARDWARE STORE
Departmental Expense Allocation Sheet
Year Ended December 31, 19—

Undepartmentalized Expense Accounts and Service Departments	Bases of Allocation	Expense Account Balance	Allocation of Expenses to Departments				
			General Office Dept.	Purchasing Dept.	Hardware Dept.	Housewares Dept.	Appliances Dept.
Salaries expense	Direct, payroll records	51,900	13,300	8,200	15,600	7,000	7,800
Rent expense	Amount and value of space	12,000	500	500	6,000	1,400	3,600
Heating and lighting	Floor space	2,000	100	100	1,000	200	600
Advertising expense	Sales	1,000	.....	.....	500	300	200
Depreciation, equipment	Direct, depreciation records	1,500	500	300	400	100	200
Supplies expense	Direct, requisitions	900	200	100	300	200	100
Insurance expense	Value of assets insured	2,500	400	200	900	600	400
Total expenses by departments		71,800	15,000	9,400	24,700	9,800	12,900
Allocation of service department expenses:							
General office department	Sales		15,000		7,500	4,500	3,000
Purchasing department	Purchase requisitions			9,400	3,900	3,400	2,100
Total expenses applicable to selling departments		71,800			36,100	17,700	18,000

Illustration 23–5

	Hardware department	Housewares department	Appliances department	Combined
BETA HARDWARE STORE				
Departmental Income Statement				
Year Ended December 31, 19—				
Sales	$119,500	$71,700	$47,800	$239,000
Cost of goods sold	73,800	43,800	30,200	147,800
Gross profit on sales	$ 45,700	$27,900	$17,600	$ 91,200
Gross profit percentages	38.2%	38.9%	36.8%	38.2%
Operating expenses:				
Salaries expense	$ 15,600	$ 7,000	$ 7,800	$ 30,400
Rent expense	6,000	1,400	3,600	11,000
Heating and lighting expense	1,000	200	600	1,800
Advertising expense	500	300	200	1,000
Depreciation expense, equipment	400	100	200	700
Supplies expense	300	200	100	600
Insurance expense	900	600	400	1,900
Share of general office department expenses	7,500	4,500	3,000	15,000
Share of purchasing department expenses	3,900	3,400	2,100	9,400
Total operating expenses	$ 36,100	$17,700	$18,000	$ 71,800
Net income (loss)	$ 9,600	$10,200	$ (400)	$ 19,400

service department column totals are allocated in turn to the selling departments. Upon completion, the amounts in the departmental columns are available for preparing income statements showing net income by departments, as in Illustration 23–5.

DEPARTMENTAL CONTRIBUTIONS TO OVERHEAD

Some people argue that departmental net incomes do not provide a fair basis for evaluating departmental performance. This is because the assumptions and somewhat arbitrary decisions involved in allocating the indirect expenses impact on the net income figures. The criticism of departmental net incomes is most likely heard in companies where indirect expenses represent a large portion of total expenses. Those who criticize departmental net income numbers usually suggest the substitution of what are known as *departmental contributions to overhead*. A department's contribution to overhead is the amount its revenues exceed its direct costs and expenses. Illustration 23–6 shows the departmental contributions to overhead for Beta Company.

Compare the performance of the appliance department as it is

Illustration 23–6

BETA HARDWARE STORE
Income Statement Showing Departmental Contributions to Overhead
Year Ended December 31, 19—

	Hardware department	Housewares department	Appliances department	Combined
Sales	$119,500	$71,700	$47,800	$239,000
Cost of goods sold	73,800	43,800	30,200	147,800
Gross profit on sales	$ 45,700	$27,900	$17,600	$ 91,200
Direct expenses:				
Salaries expense	$ 15,600	$ 7,000	$ 7,800	$ 30,400
Depreciation expense, equipment	400	100	200	700
Supplies expense	300	200	100	600
Total direct expenses	$ 16,300	$ 7,300	$ 8,100	$ 31,700
Departmental contributions to overhead	$ 29,400	$20,600	$ 9,500	$ 59,500
Contribution percentages	24.6%	28.7%	19.9%	24.9%
Indirect expenses:				
Rent expense				$ 11,000
Heating and lighting expense				1,800
Advertising expense				1,000
Insurance expense				1,900
General office department expense				15,000
Purchasing department expense				9,400
Total indirect expenses				$ 40,100
Net income				$ 19,400

shown in Illustrations 23–5 and 23–6. Illustration 23–5 shows an absolute loss of $400 resulting from the department's operations. On the other hand, Illustration 23–6 shows a positive contribution to overhead of $9,500, which is 19.9% of sales. While this contribution is not as good as for the other departments, it appears much better than the $400 loss. Which is the better basis of evaluation? To resolve the matter, one must critically review the bases used for allocating the indirect expenses to departments. In the final analysis, answering the question is a matter of judgment.

ELIMINATING THE UNPROFITABLE DEPARTMENT

When a department's net income shows a loss or when its contribution to overhead appears very poor, management may consider the extreme action of eliminating the department. However, in considering this extreme action, neither the net income figure nor the contribution to overhead provides the best information on which to base a decision. Instead, consideration should be given to the department's *escapable expenses* and *inescapable expenses.* Escapable expenses are those that would be avoided if the department were eliminated; inescapable expenses are those that would continue even though the department were eliminated. For example, the management of Beta Company is considering whether to eliminate its appliances department. An evaluation of the inescapable expenses and escapable expenses of the appliances department reveals the following:

	Escapable expenses	Inescapable expenses
Salaries expense	$ 7,800	
Rent expense		$3,600
Heating and lighting expense		600
Advertising expense	200	
Depreciation expense, equipment		200
Supplies expense	100	
Insurance expense (merchandise and equipment)	300	100
Share of office department expenses	2,200	800
Share of purchasing department expenses	1,000	1,100
Totals	$11,600	$6,400

If the appliances department is discontinued, its $6,400 of inescapable expenses will have to be borne by the remaining departments; thus, until the appliances department's annual loss exceeds $6,400, Beta Company is better off continuing the unprofitable department. In addition, another factor must be weighed when considering the elimination of an unprofitable department. Often, the existence of a department, even though unprofitable, contributes to the sales and profits of the other departments. In such a case, a department might be continued even when its losses exceed its inescapable expenses.

CONTROLLABLE COSTS AND EXPENSES

Net income figures and contributions to overhead are used in judging departmental efficiencies, but is either a good index of how well a department manager has performed? The answer is that neither may be a good index. Since many expenses entering into the calculation of a department's net income or into its contribution to overhead may be beyond the control of the department's manager, neither net income nor contribution to overhead is the best means of judging how well the manager has performed. Instead, the performance of a manager should be evaluated in terms of *controllable costs and expenses.*

What is the distinguishing characteristic of controllable costs and expenses? The critical factor is that the manager must have the power to determine or at least strongly influence the amounts to be expended. Controllable costs and expenses are not the same thing as direct costs and expenses. Direct costs and expenses are easily traced and therefore chargeable to a specific department, but the amounts expended may or may not be under the control of the department's manager. For example, a department manager often has little or no control over the amount of equipment assigned to the department and the resulting depreciation expense. Also, the manager has no control over his or her own salary. On the other hand, a department manager commonly has some control over the employees and the amount of work they do. Also, the manager normally has some control over supplies used in the department.

When controllable costs and expenses are used in judging a manager's efficiency, statistics are prepared showing the department's output and its controllable costs and expenses. The statistics of the current period are then compared with prior periods and with planned levels, and the manager's performance is judged.

The concepts of *controllable costs* and *uncontrollable costs* must be defined with reference to a particular manager and within a definite time period. Without these two reference points, all costs are controllable; that is, all costs are controllable at some level of management if the time period is long enough. For example, a cost such as property insurance may not be controllable at the level of a department manager, but it is subject to control by the executive who is responsible for obtaining insurance coverage for the company. Likewise, the executive responsible for obtaining insurance coverage may not have any control over insurance expense resulting from insurance contracts presently in force. But when a contract expires, the executive is free to renegotiate and thus has control over the long run. Thus, it is recognized that all costs are subject to the control of some manager at some point in time. Revenues are likewise subject to the control of some manager.

RESPONSIBILITY ACCOUNTING

The concept of controllable costs and expenses provides the basis for a system of responsibility accounting. In responsibility accounting, each manager is held responsible for the costs and expenses that fall under the manager's control. Prior to each period of activity, plans are developed that specify the expected costs or expenses under the control of each manager. Those plans are called *responsibility accounting budgets*. To secure the cooperation of each manager and to be sure that the budgets represent reasonable goals, each manager should be closely involved in the preparation of his or her budget.

The accounting system is then designed to accumulate costs and expenses so that timely reports can be made to each manager of the costs for which the manager is responsible. These reports (called *perfor-mance reports*) compare actual costs and expenses to the budgeted amounts. Managers use these reports to focus their attention on the specific areas in which actual costs exceed budgeted amounts. With this information in hand, they proceed to take corrective action.

Performance reports are also used to evaluate the effectiveness of each manager. The reports allow managers to be evaluated in terms of their ability to control costs and keep them within budgeted amounts. Importantly, managers are not held responsible for costs over which they have no control. Further consideration is given to perfor-mance reports in Chapter 26.

A responsibility accounting system must reflect the fact that control over costs and expenses applies to several levels of management. For example, consider the partial organization chart shown in Illustration 23–7. In Illustration 23–7, the lines connecting the various managerial

Illustration 23–7

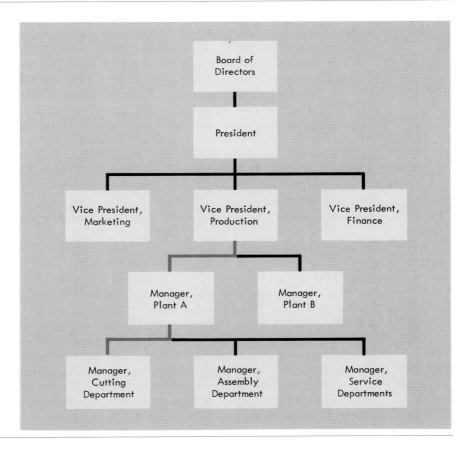

positions represent lines of authority. Thus, while each department manager is responsible for the controllable costs and expenses incurred in his or her department, those same costs are subject to the general control of the plant manager. More generally, those costs are also subject to the control of the vice president of production, and of the president, and finally of the board of directors.

At the lowest levels of management, responsibilities and costs over which control is exercised are limited. Consequently, performance reports for this management level cover only those costs over which the department managers exercise control. Moving up the management hierarchy, responsibilities and control broaden, and reports to higher level managers are broader and cover a wider range of costs. However, reports to higher level managers normally do not contain the details reported to their subordinates. Rather, the details reported to lower level managers are normally summarized on the reports to their superiors. The details are summarized for two reasons: (1) lower level managers are primarily responsible and (2) too many details can be confusing. If reports to higher level managers contain too much detail, they may draw attention away from the broad, more important issues confronting the company.

Illustration 23–8 shows summarized performance reports for three of the management levels depicted in Illustration 23–7. Observe in Illustration 23–8 how the costs under the control of the cutting department manager are totaled and included among the controllable costs of the plant manager. Similarly, the costs under the control of the plant manager are totaled and included among the controllable costs of the vice president of production. In this manner, a responsibility accounting system provides information that is relevant to the control responsibilities of each management level.

In conclusion, it should be said that the ability to produce vast amounts of raw data mechanically and electronically has far outstripped our ability to use the data. What is needed is the ability to select the data that is meaningful for planning and control. This is recognized in responsibility accounting, and every effort is made to get the right information to the right person at the right time, and the right person is the person who can control the cost or revenue.

JOINT COSTS

Joint costs are encountered in some manufacturing companies and are introduced here because they have much in common with indirect expenses. A *joint cost* is a cost incurred to secure two or more essentially different products. For example, a meat-packing company incurs a joint cost when it buys a pig from which it will get bacon, hams, shoul-

Illustration 23–8

Performance Reports

Vice President, Production

For the month of July

Controllable costs	Budgeted amount	Actual amount	Over (under) budget
Salaries, plant managers	$ 80,000	$ 80,000	$ –0–
Quality control costs	21,000	22,400	1,400
Office costs	29,500	28,800	(700)
Plant A	276,700	279,500	2,800
Plant B	390,000	380,600	(9,400)
Totals	$797,200	$791,300	$(5,900)

Manager, Plant A

For the month of July

Controllable costs	Budgeted amount	Actual amount	Over (under) budget
Salaries, department managers	$ 75,000	$ 78,000	$ 3,000
Depreciation	10,600	10,600	–0–
Insurance	6,800	6,300	(500)
Cutting department	79,600	79,900	300
Assembly department	61,500	60,200	(1,300)
Service Department 1	24,300	24,700	400
Service Department 2	18,900	19,800	900
Totals	$276,700	$279,500	$ 2,800

Manager, Cutting Department

For the month of July

Controllable costs	Budgeted amount	Actual amount	Over (under) budget
Raw materials	$ 26,500	$ 25,900	$ (600)
Direct labor	32,000	33,500	1,500
Indirect labor	7,200	7,000	(200)
Supplies	4,000	3,900	(100)
Other controllable costs	9,900	9,600	(300)
Totals	$ 79,600	$ 79,900	$ 300

ders, liver, heart, hide, pig feet, and a variety of other products. Likewise, a sawmill incurs joint costs when it buys a log and saws it into portions of Clears, Select Structurals, No. 1 Common, No. 2 Common, and other grades of lumber. In both cases, as with all joint costs, the problem is one of allocating the costs to the several joint products.

A joint cost may be, but is not commonly, allocated on some physical basis, such as the ratio of pounds, square feet, or gallons of each joint product to total pounds, square feet, or gallons of all joint products flowing from the cost. The reason this method is not commonly used is that the resulting cost allocations may be completely out of keeping with the market values of the joint products, and thus may cause certain of the products to sell at a profit while other products always show a loss. For example, a sawmill bought for $30,000 a number of logs that when sawed produced a million board feet of lumber in the grades and amounts shown in Illustration 23–9.

Observe in Illustration 23–9 that the logs produced 200,000 board feet of No. 3 Common lumber and that this is two tenths of the total lumber produced from the logs. If the No. 3 lumber is assigned two tenths of the $30,000 cost of the logs, it will be assigned $6,000 of the cost ($30,000 × $\frac{2}{10}$ = $6,000); and since this lumber can be sold for only $4,000, the assignment will cause this grade to show a loss. As a result, as in this situation, to avoid always showing a loss on one or more of the products flowing from a joint cost, such costs are commonly allocated to the joint products *in the ratio of the market values of the joint products at the point of separation.*

The ratios of the market values of the joint products flowing from the $30,000 of log cost are shown in the last column of Illustration 23–9. If these ratios are used to allocate the $30,000 cost, the cost will be apportioned between the grades as follows:

```
Structural:      $30,000  ×  12/50  =  $ 7,200
No. 1 Common:    $30,000  ×  18/50  =    10,800
No. 2 Common:    $30,000  ×  16/50  =     9,600
No. 3 Common:    $30,000  ×   4/50  =     2,400
                                       $30,000
```

Observe that if the No. 3 Common is allocated a share of the $30,000 joint cost based on market values by grades, it is allocated $2,400 of the $30,000. Furthermore, when the $2,400 is subtracted from the

Illustration 23–9

Grade of Lumber	Production in Board Feet	Market Price per 1,000 Board Feet	Market Value of Production of Each Grade	Ratio of Market Value of Each Grade to Total
Structural	100,000	$120	$12,000	12/50
No. 1 Common	300,000	60	18,000	18/50
No. 2 Common	400,000	40	16,000	16/50
No. 3 Common	200,000	20	4,000	4/50
	1,000,000		$50,000	

grade's $4,000 market value, $1,600 remains to cover other after-separation costs and provide a profit.

GLOSSARY

Controllable costs or expenses.   Costs for which the manager has the power to determine or strongly influence amounts to be expended.

Cost center.   A unit of a business that incurs costs or expenses but does not directly generate revenues.

Departmental accounting.   Accounting for the "parts" or subunits of a business, especially relating to the development of subunit information for the use of internal managers.

Departmental contribution to overhead.   The amount by which a department's revenues exceed its direct costs and expenses.

Direct costs or expenses.   Costs that are easily traced to or associated with a cost object, for example, costs incurred by a department for the sole benefit of the department.

Escapable expenses.   Costs that would end with an unprofitable department's elimination.

Indirect costs or expenses.   Costs that are not easily traced to a cost object, for example, costs incurred for the joint benefit of more than one department.

Inescapable expenses.   Expenses that would continue even though the department were eliminated.

Joint cost.   A single cost incurred to secure two or more essentially different products.

Productive departments.   Subunits of a business, the operations of which involve manufacturing or selling the goods or services of a business.

Profit center.   A unit of a business that incurs costs and generates revenues.

Responsibility accounting.   An accounting system designed to accumulate controllable costs in timely reports to be given to each manager determined responsible for the costs, and also to be used in judging the performance of each manager.

Responsibility accounting budget.   A plan that specifies the expected costs and expenses falling under the control of a manager.

Segmental reporting.   Providing information about the subunits of a business, especially published information about a company's operations in different industries or geographical areas.

Service departments.   Departments that do not manufacture or produce revenue but which supply other departments with essential services.

Uncontrollable cost.   A cost the amount of which a specific manager cannot control within a given period of time.

QUESTIONS FOR CLASS DISCUSSION

1. What is the difference, if any, between segmental reporting and departmental accounting?
2. What are five items of segmental information about operations in different industries that may be required disclosures in the annual report of a company?
3. What are four basic issues confronted by the accountant in developing information on broad industrial segments?
4. Why is a business divided into departments?
5. What are two primary goals of departmental accounting?
6. Differentiate between productive departments and service departments.
7. Name several examples of service departments.
8. Are service departments analyzed as cost centers or as profit centers? Why?
9. How is a departmental sales analysis sheet used in determining sales by departments?
10. Differentiate between direct and indirect expenses.
11. Suggest a basis for allocating each of the following expenses to departments: *(a)* salary of a supervisory employee, *(b)* rent, *(c)* heat, *(d)* electricity used in lighting, *(e)* janitorial services, *(f)* advertising, *(g)* expired insurance, and *(h)* taxes.
12. How is a departmental expense allocation sheet used in allocating expenses to departments?
13. How reliable are the amounts shown as net incomes for the various departments of a store when expenses are allocated to the departments?
14. How is a department's contribution to overhead measured?
15. As the terms are used in departmental accounting, what are *(a)* escapable expenses and *(b)* inescapable expenses?
16. What are controllable costs and expenses?
17. Why should a manager be closely involved in preparing his or her responsibility accounting budget?
18. In responsibility accounting, who is the right person to be given timely reports and statistics on a given cost?
19. What is a joint cost? How are joint costs normally allocated?

CLASS EXERCISES

Exercise 23-1   Answer the following questions about the segmental information contained in the 1982 annual report of Texas Instruments shown on pages 988 through 1,004.

1. What are the industrial segments into which Texas Instruments' operations are divided?

2. What was the 1982 net sales of the Digital Products segment *(a)* to outside parties and *(b)* to other segments of Texas Instruments?
3. Which segment earned the largest profit in 1982?
4. In which segment did Texas Instruments have the largest investment of identifiable assets at the end of 1982?

Exercise 23–2

A company rents for $100,000 per year all the space in a building, which is assigned to its departments as follows:

Department A: 2,000 square feet of first-floor space
Department B: 1,000 square feet of first-floor space
Department C: 600 square feet of second-floor space
Department D: 900 square feet of second-floor space
Department E: 1,500 square feet of second-floor space

The company allocates 60% of the total rent to the first floor and 40% to the second floor, and then allocates the rent of each floor to the departments on that floor on the basis of the space occupied. Determine the rent to be allocated to each department.

Exercise 23–3

A company rents for $36,000 per year all the space in a small building, and it occupies the space as follows:

Department A: 2,500 square feet of first-floor space
Department B: 1,500 square feet of first-floor space
Department C: 4,000 square feet of second-floor space

Determine the rent expense to be allocated to each department under the assumption that first-floor space rents for twice as much as second-floor space in the city in which this company is located.

Exercise 23–4

David Malone works part-time in the men's shoe department and in the men's clothing department of Western Department Store. His work consists of waiting on customers who enter either department and also in straightening and rearranging merchandise in either department as needed after it has been shown to customers. The store allocates his $16,000 in annual wages to the two departments in which he works. Last year the division was based on a sample of the time Malone spent working in the two departments. To obtain the sample, observations were made on several days throughout the year of the manner in which Malone spent his time while at work. Following are the results of the observations:

Observed manner in which employee spent his time	Elapsed time in minutes
Selling in men's shoe department	1,850
Straightening and rearranging merchandise in men's shoe department	350
Selling in men's clothing department	1,425
Straightening and rearranging merchandise in men's clothing department	375
Doing nothing while waiting for a customer to enter one of the selling departments	250

Required:

Prepare a calculation to show the shares of the employee's wages that should be allocated to the departments.

Exercise 23–5

Manor Company has two service departments, the office department and the purchasing department, and two sales departments, tools and paint. During 198A, the departments had the following direct expenses: general office department, $3,800; purchasing department, $2,800; tools department, $10,000; and paint department, $7,000. The departments occupy the following amounts of floor space: office, 600; purchasing, 400; tools, 1,200; and paint, 800. The tools department had three times as many dollars of sales during the year as did the paint department, and during the year the purchasing department processed twice as many purchase orders for the tools department as it did for the paint department.

Required:

Prepare an expense allocation sheet for Manor Company on which the direct expenses are entered by departments, the year's $24,000 of rent expense is allocated to the departments on the basis of floor space occupied, office department expenses are allocated to the sales departments on the basis of sales, and purchasing department expenses are allocated on the basis of purchase orders processed.

Exercise 23–6

Ken Cubbage is the manager of the automobile service department of a large department store. A 198A income statement for the department included the following:

Revenues:		
Sales of services	$290,000	
Sales of parts	220,000	$510,000
Costs and expenses:		
Cost of parts sold	$109,000	
Wages (hourly)	180,000	
Salary of manager	30,000	
Payroll taxes	21,000	
Supplies	47,000	
Depreciation of building	18,000	
Utilities	32,000	
Interest on long-term debt	14,000	
Income taxes allocated to department	20,000	
Total costs and expenses		471,000
Department net income		$ 39,000

Which of the income statement items do you think should be excluded from a report to be used in evaluating Mr. Cubbage's performance? State your reasons. If the exclusion of some items is questionable, list those items and explain why the exclusion is questionable.

Exercise 23-7   Kimble Development Company has just completed a subdivision containing 25 building lots, of which 20 lots are for sale at $15,000 each and 5 are for sale at $30,000 each. The land for the subdivision cost $110,000, and the company spent $130,000 on street and utilities improvements. Assume that the land and improvement costs are to be assigned to the lots as joint costs and determine the share of the costs to assign to a lot in each price class.

PROBLEMS

Problem 23-1   Overby Company occupies all the space in a two-story building, and it has an account in its ledger called Building Occupancy to which it charged the following during the past year:

Depreciation, building	$16,000
Interest, building mortgage	13,200
Taxes, building and land	4,900
Heating expenses	2,200
Lighting expense	2,900
Cleaning and maintenance......	11,200
Total	$50,400

The building has 6,000 square feet of floor space on each of its two floors, a total of 12,000 square feet; and the bookkeeper divided the $50,400 by 12,000 and charged the selling departments on each floor with $4.20 of occupancy cost for each square foot of floor space occupied.

Bob Dunn, the manager of a second-floor department occupying 2,000 square feet of floor space, saw the $4.20 per square foot, or $8,400 of occupancy cost, charged to his department and complained. He cited a recent real estate board study that showed average rental charges for like space, including heat but not including lights, cleaning, and maintenance, as follows:

Ground-floor space ..... $4.50 per sq. ft.
Second-floor space..... $3.00 per sq. ft.

Required:

Prepare a computation showing how much building occupancy cost you think should have been charged to Bob Dunn's department last year.

Problem 23-2   Ranger Company began its operations one year ago with two selling departments and one office department. The year's operating results are:

RANGER COMPANY
Departmental Income Statement for Year Ended December 31, 198A

	Dept. A	Dept. B	Combined
Revenue from sales	$80,000	$50,000	$130,000
Cost of goods sold	52,000	30,000	82,000
Gross profit from sales	$28,000	$20,000	$ 48,000
Direct expenses:			
Sales salaries	$10,500	$ 6,000	$ 16,500
Advertising	900	675	1,575
Store supplies used	400	200	600
Depreciation of equipment	1,075	575	1,650
Total direct expenses	$12,875	$ 7,450	$ 20,325
Allocated expenses:			
Rent expense	$ 4,800	$ 2,400	$ 7,200
Heating and lighting expense	1,200	600	1,800
Share of office department expenses	4,800	3,000	7,800
Total allocated expenses	$10,800	$ 6,000	$ 16,800
Total expenses	$23,675	$13,450	$ 37,125
Net income	$ 4,325	$ 6,550	$ 10,875

The company plans to open a third selling department which it estimates will produce $30,000 in sales with a 35% gross profit margin and will require the following direct expenses: sales salaries, $4,500; advertising, $450; store supplies, $175; and depreciation of equipment, $350.

A year ago, when operations began, it was necessary to rent store space in excess of requirements. This extra space was assigned to and used by Departments A and B during the year; but when the new department, Department C, is opened, it will take one fourth of the space presently assigned to Department A and one sixth of the space assigned to Department B.

The company allocates its general office department expenses to its selling departments on the basis of sales, and it expects the new department to cause a $525 increase in general office department expenses.

The company expects Department C to bring new customers into the store who in addition to buying goods in the new department will also buy sufficient merchandise in the two old departments to increase their sales by 5% each. And, although the old departments' sales are expected to increase, their gross profit percentages are not expected to change. Likewise, their direct expenses, other than supplies, are not expected to change. The supplies used will increase in proportion to sales.

Required:

Prepare a departmental income statement showing the company's expected operations with three selling departments.

Problem 23–3   Algona Company is considering the elimination of its unprofitable Department B. The company's income statement for last year appears as follows:

ALGONA COMPANY
Income Statement for Year Ended December 31, 19—

	Dept. A	Dept. B	Combined
Sales	$108,000	$51,600	$159,600
Cost of goods sold	59,800	37,500	97,300
Gross margin on sales	$ 48,200	$14,100	$ 62,300
Operating expenses:			
Direct expenses:			
Advertising	$ 1,350	$ 990	$ 2,340
Store supplies used	1,260	810	2,070
Depreciation of store equipment	1,090	660	1,750
Total direct expenses	$ 3,700	$ 2,460	$ 6,160
Allocated expenses:			
Sales salaries	$ 22,750	$13,650	$ 36,400
Rent expense	3,800	1,800	5,600
Bad debts expense	410	340	750
Office salaries	6,825	4,095	10,920
Insurance expense	400	200	600
Miscellaneous office expenses	550	300	850
Total allocated expenses	$ 34,735	$20,385	$ 55,120
Total expenses	$ 38,435	$22,845	$ 61,280
Net income (loss)	$ 9,765	$ (8,745)	$ 1,020

If Department B is eliminated:

a. The company has one office worker who earns $210 per week or $10,920 per year and four salesclerks each of whom earns $175 per week or $9,100 per year. At present the salaries of two and one-half salesclerks are charged to Department A and one and one-half salesclerks to Department B. The sales salaries and office salaries presently assigned to Department B can be avoided if the department is eliminated. However, management is considering another plan, as follows. It is the opinion of management that two salesclerks may be dismissed if Department B is eliminated, leaving only two full-time clerks in Department A and making up the difference by assigning the office worker to part-time sales work in the department. It is felt that although the office worker has not devoted half of his time to the office work of Department B, if he devotes the same amount of time to selling in Department A during rush hours as he has to the office work of Department B, it will be sufficient to carry the load.

b. The lease on the store building is long term and cannot be changed; therefore, the space presently occupied by Department B will have to be used by and charged to Department A. Likewise, Department A will have to make whatever use of Department B's equipment it can, since the equipment has little or no sales value.

c. The elimination of Department B will eliminate the Department B advertising expense, losses from bad debts, and store supplies used. It will also eliminate 80% of the insurance expense allocated to the department (the portion on merchandise) and 25% of the miscellaneous office expenses presently allocated to Department B.

Required:

1. List in separate columns the amounts of Department B's escapable and inescapable expenses.
2. Under the assumption that Department A's sales and gross profit will not be affected by the elimination of Department B, prepare an income statement showing what the company can expect to earn from the operation of Department A after Department B is eliminated. Assume that the plan of assigning part of the office worker's time to the sales force is used.

Problem 23-4

Jack and Susan Roberts own a farm that produces potatoes. Last year after preparing the following income statement, Jack remarked to Susan that they should have fed the No. 3 potatoes to the pigs and thus avoided the loss from the sale of this grade.

JACK AND SUSAN ROBERTS

Income from the Production and Sale of Potatoes

For Year Ended December 31, 198A

	Results by Grades			Combined
	No. 1	No. 2	No. 3	
Sales by grades:				
No. 1, 300,000 lbs. @ $0.045 per lb......	$13,500			
No. 2, 500,000 lbs. @ $0.04 per lb.......		$20,000		
No. 3, 200,000 lbs. @ $0.03 per lb.......			$6,000	
Combined				$39,500
Costs:				
Land preparation, seed, planting, and cultivating @ $0.01422 per lb......	$ 4,266	$ 7,110	$2,844	$14,220
Harvesting, sorting, and grading @ $0.01185 per lb.....................	3,555	5,925	2,370	11,850
Marketing @ $0.00415 per lb...........	1,245	2,075	830	4,150
Total costs	$ 9,066	$15,110	$6,044	$30,220
Net income (or loss)	$ 4,434	$ 4,890	$ (44)	$ 9,280

On the foregoing statement, Jack and Susan divided their costs among the grades on a per pound basis. They did this because with the exception of marketing costs, their records did not show costs per grade. As to marketing costs, the records did show that $4,020 of the $4,150 was the cost of placing the No. 1 and No. 2 potatoes in bags and hauling them to the warehouse of the produce buyer. Bagging and hauling costs were the same for both grades. The remaining $130 of marketing costs was the cost of loading the No. 3 potatoes into trucks of a potato starch factory that bought these potatoes in bulk and picked them up at the farm.

Required:

Prepare an income statement that will show better the results of producing and marketing the potatoes.

Problem 23–5   Mineola Company has three selling departments, X, Y, and Z, and two service departments, general office and purchasing. At the end of 198A, its bookkeeper brought together the following information for use in preparing the year-end statements:

	Dept. X	Dept. Y	Dept. Z
Sales	$95,400	$51,200	$73,400
Purchases	67,900	35,300	41,800
January 1 (beginning) inventory	12,300	8,500	10,200
December 31 (ending) inventory.....	14,500	9,400	7,300

Mineola Company treats salaries, supplies used, and depreciation as direct departmental expenses. The payroll, requisition, and plant asset records showed the following amounts of these expenses by departments:

	Salaries expense	Supplies used	Depreciation of equipment
General office	$ 9,345	$ 235	$ 625
Purchasing department	6,160	195	375
Department X	10,360	385	850
Department Y	5,510	215	450
Department Z	8,140	295	500
	$39,515	$1,325	$2,800

The company incurred the following amounts of indirect expenses:

Rent expense	$6,600
Advertising expense	5,500
Expired insurance..............	750
Heating and lighting expense.....	1,750
Janitorial expense	2,100

Mineola Company allocates the foregoing expenses to its departments as follows:

a. Rent expense on the basis of the amount and value of floor space occupied. The general office and purchasing departments occupy space in the rear of the store that is not as valuable as space in the front; consequently, $600 of the total rent is allocated to these two departments in proportion to the space occupied by each. The remainder of the rent is divided between the selling departments in proportion to the space occupied. The five departments occupy these amounts of space: general office, 600 square feet; purchasing department, 400 square feet; Department X, 3,000 square feet; Department Y, 1,500 square feet; and Department Z, 1,500 square feet.

b. Advertising expense on the basis of sales.

c. Expired insurance on the basis of equipment book values. The book values of the equipment in the departments are: general office, $3,500; purchasing department, $2,000; Department X, $9,000; Department Y, $5,000; and Department Z, $5,500.

d. Heating and lighting and janitorial expenses on the basis of floor space occupied.

Mineola Company allocates its general office department expenses to its selling departments on the basis of sales, and it allocates purchasing department expenses on the basis of purchases.

Required:

1. Prepare a departmental expense allocation sheet for the company.
2. Prepare a departmental income statement showing sales, cost of goods sold, expenses, and net incomes by departments and for the entire store.
3. Prepare a second departmental income statement showing departmental contributions to overhead and overall net income.

Problem 23–6

Tekcon Company's Denver plant is managed by Joyce Goodwin, who is responsible for all costs of the Denver operation other than her own salary. The plant is divided into two production departments and an office department. The gadgets and the doodads departments manufacture different products and have separate managers; the office department is managed by the plant manager. Tekcon Company prepares a monthly budget for each of the production departments (gadgets and doodads) and then accumulates costs in a manner that assigns all of the Denver plant costs to the departments.

The department budgets and cost accumulations for the month of June were as follows:

	Budget		Actual costs		
	Gadgets dept.	Doodads dept.	Gadgets dept.	Doodads dept.	Combined
Raw materials	$195,000	$140,000	$209,000	$143,500	$352,500
Wages	110,000	100,000	116,600	103,200	219,800
Salary—department manager	25,000	22,000	25,000	23,000	48,000
Supplies used	10,000	9,000	8,600	9,900	18,500
Depreciation of equipment	6,000	5,000	6,000	5,800	11,800
Heating and lighting	20,000	10,000	25,000	12,500	37,500
Rent on building	24,000	12,000	24,000	12,000	36,000
Share of office department costs	41,000	41,000	38,800	38,800	77,600
	$431,000	$339,000	$453,000	$348,700	$801,700

Office department costs consisted of the following:

	Budget	Actual
Salary—plant manager	$42,000	$42,000
Other salaries	28,000	26,500
Other costs	12,000	9,100

Each department manager is responsible for the purchase and maintenance of equipment in the department. Heating and lighting cost and building rent are allocated to the production departments on the basis of relative space used by those departments.

Required:

Prepare responsibility accounting performance reports on the managers of each production department and on the plant manager.

ALTERNATE PROBLEMS

Problem 23–1A   Atlantic Super Store has in its ledger an account called Building Occupancy Costs to which it charged the following last year:

Building rent	$54,000
Lighting expense	2,000
Cleaning and maintenance.....	10,000
Total	$66,000

The store occupies all the space in a building having selling space on three levels—basement level, street level, and second-floor level. Each level has 5,000 square feet of selling space, a total of 15,000 square feet; and the bookkeeper divided the $66,000 of building occupancy cost by 15,000 and charged each selling department with $4.40 of building occupancy cost for each square foot of space occupied.

When Joe Phelps, the manager of a basement-level department having 1,500 square feet of floor space, saw the $4.40 per square foot of building occupancy cost charged to his department, he complained. In this complaint, he cited a recent local real estate study that showed average charges for like space, including heat but not including lights and janitorial service, as follows:

Basement-level space	$2 per sq. ft.
Street-level space	$6 per sq. ft.
Second-floor-level space	$4 per sq. ft.

Required:

Prepare a computation showing the amount of building occupancy cost you think should be charged to Joe Phelps' department.

Problem 23–2A   The Colorado Company began business last year with two selling departments and a general office department. It had the following results for the year:

COLORADO COMPANY
Departmental Income Statement for Year Ended December 31, 198A

	Dept. 1	Dept. 2	Combined
Sales	$120,000	$60,000	$180,000
Cost of goods sold	84,000	36,000	120,000
Gross profit from sales	$ 36,000	$24,000	$ 60,000
Direct expenses:			
Sales salaries	$ 12,500	$ 7,200	$ 19,700
Advertising expense	1,125	750	1,875
Store supplies used	600	300	900
Depreciation of equipment	1,025	550	1,575
Total direct expenses	$ 15,250	$ 8,800	$ 24,050
Allocated expenses:			
Rent expense	$ 5,400	$ 3,600	$ 9,000
Heating and lighting expense	1,080	720	1,800
Share of general office expenses	7,000	3,500	10,500
Total allocated expenses	$ 13,480	$ 7,820	$ 21,300
Total expenses	$ 28,730	$16,620	$ 45,350
Net income	$ 7,270	$ 7,380	$ 14,650

The company plans to add a third selling department which it estimates will produce $40,000 in sales with a 35% gross profit margin. The new department will require the following estimated direct expenses: sales salaries, $4,500; advertising expense, $450; store supplies, $250; and depreciation on equipment, $525.

When the company began its operations, it was necessary to rent a store room having selling space in excess of requirements. This extra space was assigned to and used by Departments 1 and 2 during the year; but when Department 3 is opened, it will take over one third the space presently assigned to Department 1 and one sixth the space assigned to Department 2. The space reductions are not expected to affect the operations or sales of the old departments.

The company allocates its general office department expenses to its selling departments on the basis of sales. It expects the new department to cause a $950 increase in general office department expenses.

The company expects the addition of Department 3 to bring new customers to the store who in addition to buying Department 3 merchandise will also do sufficient buying in the old departments to increase their sales by 5% each. It is not expected that the increase in sales in the old departments will affect their gross profit percentages nor any of their direct expenses other than supplies. It is expected the supplies used will increase in proportion to sales.

Required:

Prepare a departmental income statement showing the company's expected operating results with three departments.

Problem 23–4A Joan Holtz's business produced and sold a half million pounds of apples last year, and she prepared the following statement to show the results:

JOAN HOLTZ
Income from the Sale of Apples, Year Ended December 31, 198A

	Results by Grades			Combined
	No. 1	No. 2	No. 3	
Sales by grades:				
No. 1, 200,000 lbs. @ $0.11 per lb.	$22,000			
No. 2, 200,000 lbs. @ $0.07 per lb.		$14,000		
No. 3, 100,000 lbs. @ $0.04 per lb.			$ 4,000	
Combined sales				$40,000
Costs:				
Tree pruning and orchard care @				
$0.021 per lb.	$ 4,200	$ 4,200	$ 2,100	$10,500
Fruit picking, grading, and sorting				
@ $0.0252 per lb.	5,040	5,040	2,520	12,600
Marketing @ $0.0084 per lb.	1,680	1,680	840	4,200
Total costs	$10,920	$10,920	$ 5,460	$27,300
Net income (or loss)	$11,080	$ 3,080	$(1,460)	$12,700

Upon completing the statement, Ms. Holtz thought a wise course of future action might be to leave the No. 3 apples on the trees to fall off and be plowed under when the ground is cultivated between the trees, and thus avoid the loss from their sale. However, before doing so she consulted you.

When you examined the statement, you recognized that Ms. Holtz had divided all her costs by 500,000 and allocated them on a per pound basis. You asked her about the marketing costs and learned that $3,960 of the $4,200 was incurred in placing the No. 1 and No. 2 fruit in boxes and delivering them to the warehouse of the fruit buyer. The cost for this was the same for both grades. You also learned that the remaining $240 was for loading the No. 3 fruit on the trucks of a cider manufacturer who bought this grade of fruit in bulk at the orchard for use in making apple cider.

Required:

Prepare an income statement that will reflect better the results of producing and marketing the apples.

Problem 23–5A

Triple Company carries on its operations with two service departments, the general office department and the purchasing department, and with three selling departments, A, B, and C. At the end of its annual accounting period the company's accountant prepared the following adjusted trial balance:

TRIPLE COMPANY
Adjusted Trial Balance, December 31, 198A

Cash	$ 7,875	
Merchandise inventory, Department A	9,300	
Merchandise inventory, Department B	18,200	
Merchandise inventory, Department C	14,500	
Supplies	620	
Equipment	36,940	
Accumulated depreciation, equipment		$ 10,135
Mary Triple, capital		72,925
Mary Triple, withdrawals	9,000	
Sales, Department A		52,400
Sales, Department B		104,200
Sales, Department C		68,400
Purchases, Department A	34,400	
Purchases, Department B	79,300	
Purchases, Department C	41,700	
Salaries expense	36,855	
Rent expense	7,500	
Advertising expense	5,625	
Expired insurance	500	
Heating and lighting expense	1,200	
Depreciation of equipment	1,820	
Supplies used	1,125	
Janitorial services	1,600	
Totals	$308,060	$308,060

Required:

1. Prepare a departmental expense allocation sheet for Triple Company, using the following information:

a. Triple Company treats salaries, supplies used, and depreciation of equipment as direct departmental expenses. The payroll, requisition, and plant asset records show the following amounts of these expenses by departments:

	Salaries expense	Supplies used	Depreciation of equipment
General office	$10,295	$ 145	$ 250
Purchasing department	7,040	130	220
Department A	4,660	275	425
Department B	8,320	315	615
Department C	6,540	260	310
	$36,855	$1,125	$1,820

b. The company treats the remainder of its expenses as indirect and allocates them as follows:

(1) Rent expense on the basis of the amount and value of floor space occupied. The general office occupies 600 square feet, and the purchasing department occupies 400 square feet on a balcony at the rear of the store. This space is not as valuable as space on the main floor; therefore, the store allocates $500 of its rent to these two departments on the basis of space occupied and allocates the remainder to the selling departments on the basis of the main-floor space they occupy. The selling departments occupy main-floor space as follows: Department A, 2,000 square feet; Department B, 3,500 square feet; and Department C, 1,500 square feet.

(2) Advertising expense on the basis of sales.

(3) Insurance expense on the basis of the book values of the equipment in the departments, which are: general office, $2,500; purchasing, $2,000; Department A, $6,500; Department B, $9,500; and Department C, $4,500.

(4) Heating and lighting and janitorial services on the basis of floor space occupied.

c. The company allocates general office department expenses to the selling departments on the basis of sales, and it allocates purchasing department expenses on the basis of purchases.

2. Prepare a departmental income statement for the company showing sales, cost of goods sold, expenses, and net incomes by departments and for the entire store. The year-end inventories were Department A, $11,600; Department B, $23,400; and Department C, $13,400.

3. Prepare a second income statement for the company showing departmental contributions to overhead and overall net income.

Problem 23–6A   Modular Power, Inc.'s Toledo plant is managed by Tim Andersen, who is responsible for all costs of the Toledo operation other than his own salary. The plant is divided into two production departments and an office department. The metals and the fibers departments manufacture different products and have separate managers; the office department is managed by the plant manager. Modular Power prepares a monthly budget for each of the production departments (metals and fibers) and then accumulates costs in a manner that assigns all of the Toledo plant costs to the departments.

The department budgets and cost accumulations for the month of May were as follows:

	Budget		Actual costs		
	Metals dept.	Fibers dept.	Metals dept.	Fibers dept.	Combined
Raw materials	$230,000	$280,000	$223,500	$287,600	$ 511,100
Wages	168,000	198,000	173,900	192,900	366,800
Salary–department manager	26,000	28,000	27,500	28,000	55,500
Supplies used	7,500	8,000	9,600	9,200	18,800
Depreciation of equipment	14,000	10,000	14,000	11,000	25,000
Heating and lighting	16,000	24,000	19,440	29,160	48,600
Rent on building	10,000	15,000	10,000	15,000	25,000
Share of office department costs.....	65,000	65,000	69,500	69,500	139,000
	$536,500	$628,000	$547,440	$642,360	$1,189,800

Office department costs consisted of the following:

	Budget	Actual
Salary–plant manager	$54,000	$54,000
Other salaries	60,000	62,000
Other costs	16,000	23,000

Each department manager is responsible for the purchase and maintenance of equipment in the department. Heating and lighting cost and building rent are allocated to the production departments on the basis of relative space used by those departments.

Required:

Prepare responsibility accounting performance reports on the managers of each production department and on the plant manager.

PROVOCATIVE PROBLEMS

Provocative
Problem 23–1, a
Real Estate Deal

Bob Cramer, Jan Sullins, and Tim Lane entered into a partnership for the purpose of developing and selling a plot of land currently owned by Cramer. Sullins invested $52,000 cash in the partnership, Cramer invested his land at its $60,000 fair market value, and Lane invested $8,000; and they agreed to share losses and gains equally. Lane was to provide the necessary real estate expertise to make the project a success. The partnership installed streets and water mains costing $60,000 and divided the land into 14 building lots. They priced Lots 1, 2, 3, and 4 for sale at $12,000 each; Lots 5, 6, 7, 8, 9, 10, 11, and 12 at $14,000 each; and Lots 13 and 14 at $16,000 each. The partners agreed that Lane could take Lot 13 at cost for his personal use. The remaining lots were sold, and the partnership dissolved. Determine the amount of partnership cash each partner should receive in the dissolution.

The Electro-Drive Company bookkeeper prepared the following income statement for March of the current year:

ELECTRO-DRIVE COMPANY
Income Statement for March 198A

	Motor department	Compressor department	Combined
Sales	$40,000	$60,000	$100,000
Cost of goods sold	28,600	42,900	71,500
Gross profit on sales	$11,400	$17,100	$ 28,500
Warehousing expenses	$ 2,950	$ 2,950	$ 5,900
Selling expenses	5,600	6,100	11,700
General and administrative expenses	1,525	1,525	3,050
Total expenses	$10,075	$10,575	$ 20,650
Net income	$ 1,325	$ 6,525	$ 7,850

The company is a wholesaler of motors and compressors and is organized on a departmental basis. However, the company manager does not feel that the bookkeeper's statement reflects the profit situation in the company's two selling departments and he has asked you to redraft it with any supporting schedules or comments you think desirable. Your investigation reveals the following:

1. The company sold 500 motors and 400 compressors during March. The bookkeeper apportioned cost of goods sold between the two departments on an arbitrary basis. A compressor actually costs the company twice as much as a motor.
2. A motor and a compressor are of approximately the same weight and bulk. However, because there are two styles of motors and three styles of compressors, the company must carry a 50% greater inventory of compressors, than motors.
3. The company occupies its building on the following bases:

	Area of space	Value of space
Warehouse	80%	60%
Motor sales office	5	10
Compressor sales office	5	10
General office	10	20

4. Warehousing expenses for March consisted of the following:

Wages expense	$3,000
Depreciation of building	2,000
Heating and lighting expenses	500
Depreciation of warehouse equipment.....	400
Total	$5,900

The bookkeeper had charged all of the building's depreciation plus all of the heating and lighting expenses to warehousing expenses.
5. Selling expenses for March consisted of the following:

	Motor department	Compressor department
Sales salaries	$4,000	$4,500
Advertising	1,500	1,500
Depreciation of office equipment	100	100
Totals	$5,600	$6,100

Sales salaries and depreciation were charged to the two departments on the basis of actual amounts incurred. Advertising was apportioned by the bookkeeper. The company has an established advertising budget based on dollars of sales which it followed rather closely in March.

6.   General and administrative expenses for March consisted of the following:

Salaries and wages	$2,800
Depreciation of office equipment	200
Miscellaneous office expenses	50
Total	$3,050

Provocative Problem 23–3, Camera Corporation

Camera Corporation wholesales high-quality cameras that are designed for specialized industrial usage. Operations of the company during the past year resulted in the following:

	Standard	Deluxe
Units sold	900	300
Selling price per unit	$300	$400
Cost per unit	160	210
Sales commission per unit	45	60
Indirect selling and administrative expenses	75	100

Indirect selling and administrative expenses totaled $97,500 and were allocated between the sales of Standard and Deluxe units on the basis of their relative sales volumes. The Standard model produced $270,000 of revenue, and the Deluxe model produced $120,000; thus, the Standard model was assigned 27/39 of the $97,500 of indirect expenses and the Deluxe model was assigned 12/39. After allocating the total indirect expenses to the two models, the indirect expenses per unit were determined by dividing the total by the number of units sold. Hence, the Standard model's cost per unit was $75 and the Deluxe model's cost per unit was $100.

Management of Camera Corporation is attempting to decide between three courses of action and asks you to evaluate which of the three courses is most desirable. The three alternatives are: (1) through advertising push the sales of the Standard model, (2) through advertising push the sales of the Deluxe model, or (3) do no additional advertising, in which case sales of each model will continue at present levels. The demand for cameras is fairly stable, and an increase in the number of units of one model sold will cause an equally large decrease in unit sales of the other model. However, through the expenditure of $3,000 for advertising, the company can shift the sale of 150 units of the Standard model to the Deluxe model, or vice versa, depending upon which model receives the advertising attention. Should the company advertise; and if so, which model? Back your position with income statements.

Planning and Controlling Business Operations

PART EIGHT

Cost-Volume-Profit Analysis

24

After studying Chapter 24, you should be able to:

Describe the different types of cost behavior experienced by a typical company.

State the assumptions that underlie cost-volume-profit analysis and explain how these assumptions restrict the usefulness of the information obtained from the analysis.

Prepare and interpret a scatter diagram of past costs and sales volume.

Calculate a break-even point for a single product company and graphically plot its costs and revenues.

Describe some extensions that may be added to the basic cost-volume-profit analysis of break-even point.

Calculate a composite sales unit for a multiproduct company and a break-even point for such a company.

Define or explain the words and phrases listed in the chapter Glossary.

Cost-volume-profit analysis is a means of predicting the effect of changes in costs and sales levels on the income of a business. In its simplest form, it involves the determination of the sales level at which a company neither earns a profit nor incurs a loss, or in other words, the point at which it breaks even. For this reason, cost-volume-profit analysis is often called break-even analysis. However, the technique can be expanded to answer additional questions, such as: What sales volume is necessary to earn a desired net income? What net income will be earned if unit selling prices are reduced in order to increase sales volume? What net income will be earned if a new machine that will reduce unit labor costs is installed? What net income will be earned if we change the sales mix? When the technique is expanded to answer such additional questions, the descriptive phrase *cost-volume-profit analysis* is more appropriate than *break-even analysis*.

COST BEHAVIOR

Conventional cost-volume-profit analyses require that costs be classified as either fixed or variable. Some costs are definitely fixed in nature. Others are strictly variable. But, when costs are examined, some are observed to be neither completely fixed nor completely variable.

Fixed Costs

A *fixed cost* remains unchanged in total amount over a wide range of production levels. For example, if the factory building is rented for, say, $1,000 per month, this cost remains the same whether the factory operates on a one-shift, two-shift, or an around-the-clock basis. Likewise, the cost is the same whether one hundred units of product are produced in a month, one thousand units are produced, or any other number up to the full production capacity of the plant. Note, however, that while the total amount of a fixed cost remains constant as the level of production changes, fixed costs per unit of product decrease as volume increases. For example, if rent is $1,000 per month and two units of product are produced in a month, the rent cost per unit is $500; but if production is increased to 10 units per month, rent cost per unit decreases to $100. Likewise it decreases to $2 per unit if production is increased to 500 units per month.

When production volume is plotted on a graph, units of product are shown on the horizontal axis and dollars of cost are shown on the vertical axis. Fixed costs are then expressed as a horizontal line, since the total amount of fixed costs remains constant at all levels of production. This is shown in the Illustration 24–1 graph where the

Illustration 24–1

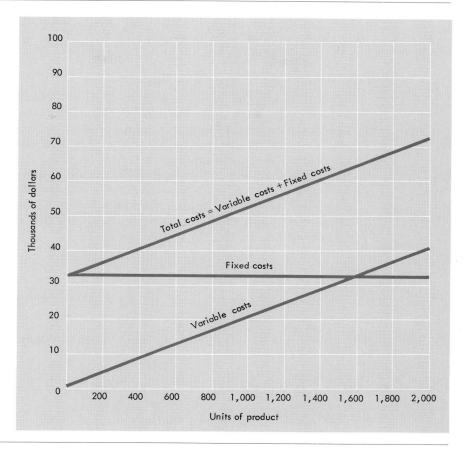

fixed costs remain at $32,000 at all production levels up to 2,000 units of product.

Variable Costs

A *variable cost* changes in total amount as production volume changes. For example, the cost of the material that enters into a product is a variable cost. If material costing $20 is required in the production of one unit of product, total material costs are $20 if one unit of product is manufactured, $40 if two units are manufactured, $60 if three units are manufactured, and so on up for any number of units. In other words, the variable cost per unit of production remains constant while the total amount of variable cost changes in direct proportion to changes in the level of production. Variable costs appear on a graph as a straight line with a positive slope; the line rises as the production volume increases, as in Illustration 24–1.

Semivariable Costs and Stair-Step Costs

All costs are not necessarily either fixed or variable. For example, some costs go up in steps. Consider the salaries of production supervisors. Supervisory salaries may be more or less fixed for any production volume from zero to the maximum that can be completed on a one-shift basis. Then, if an additional shift must be added to increase production, a whole new group of supervisors must be hired and supervisory salaries go up by a lump-sum amount. Total supervisor costs then remain fixed at this level until a third shift is added when they increase by another lump sum. Costs such as these are called *stair-step costs* and are shown graphically in Illustration 24–2.

Illustration 24–2

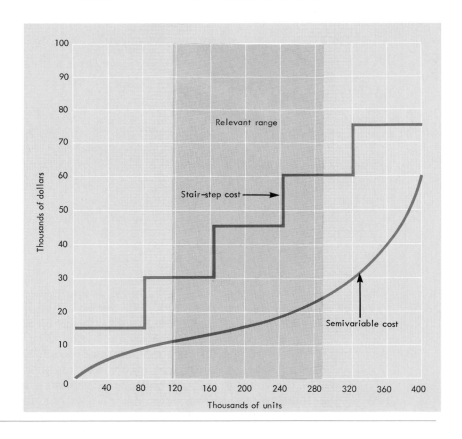

In addition to stair-step costs, some costs may be semivariable or curvilinear in nature. *Semivariable costs* go up with volume increases, but when plotted on a graph, they must be plotted as a curved line (see Illustration 24–2). These costs change with production-level changes, but not proportionately.

For example, at low levels of production, the addition of more laborers may allow each laborer to specialize so that the whole crew becomes more efficient. Each new laborer increases the total cost, but the increased production more than compensates for the increased cost so that the cost per unit is reduced. Eventually, however, the addition of more laborers in a given plant may cause inefficiencies; laborers may begin to waste time bumping into each other. Thus, the addition of a new laborer may add some production, but the cost per unit increases.

Cost Assumptions

Conventional *cost-volume-profit analysis* is based on relationships that can be expressed as straight lines. Costs are assumed to be either fixed or variable. With the costs expressed as straight lines, the lines are then analyzed in order to answer a variety of questions. The reliability of the answers secured through application of the technique rests on three basic assumptions. If a cost-volume-profit analysis is to be reliable:

1. The per unit selling price must be constant. (The selling price per unit must remain the same regardless of production level.)
2. The costs classified as "variable" must, in fact, behave as variable costs; that is, the actual (variable) cost per unit of production must remain constant.
3. The costs classified as "fixed" must, in fact, remain constant over wide changes in the level of production.

When these assumptions are met, costs and revenues may be correctly represented by straight lines. However, the actual behavior of costs and revenues often is not completely consistent with these assumptions, and if the assumptions are violated by significant amounts, the results of cost-volume-profit analysis will not be reliable. Yet, there are at least two reasons why these assumptions tend to provide reliable analyses.

AGGREGATING COSTS MAY SUPPORT ASSUMPTIONS. While individual variable costs may not act in a truly variable manner, the process of adding such costs together may offset such violations of the assumption. In other words, the assumption of variable behavior may be satisfied in respect to total variable costs even though it is violated in respect to individual variable costs. Similarly, the assumption that fixed costs remain constant may be satisfied for total fixed costs even though individual fixed costs may violate the assumption.

RELEVANT RANGE OF OPERATIONS.   Another reason why the assumptions that revenues, variable costs, and fixed costs can be reasonably represented as straight lines is that the assumptions are only intended to apply over the *relevant range of operations.* The relevant range of operations, as plotted in Illustration 24–2, is the normal operating range for the business. It excludes the extremely high and low levels that are not apt to be encountered. Thus, a specific fixed cost is expected to be truly fixed only within the relevant range. It may be that beyond the limits of the relevant range, the fixed cost would not remain constant.

The previous discussion defined variable costs and fixed costs in terms of levels of production activity. However, in cost-volume-profit analysis, the level of activity is usually measured in terms of sales volume, whether stated as sales dollars or number of units sold. Thus, an additional assumption is frequently made that the level of production is the same as the level of sales, or if they are not the same, that the difference will not be enough to materially damage the reliability of the analysis.

It must also be recognized that cost-volume-profit analysis yields approximate answers to questions concerning the interrelations of costs, volume, and profits. So long as management understands that the answers provided are approximations, cost-volume-profit analysis can be a useful managerial tool.

Estimating Cost Behavior

The process of estimating the behavior of a company's costs requires judgment and, to the extent past data is available, a careful examination of past experience. Initially, the individual costs should be reviewed and classified as fixed or variable based on the accountant's understanding of how each cost is likely to behave. Some costs may be classified quite easily. For example, raw materials costs of a manufacturer or cost of goods sold of a merchandiser are undoubtedly variable costs. Similarly, a constant monthly rent expense or the monthly salaries of administrative personnel are clearly fixed costs.

MIXED COSTS.   Although some costs are easily classified as variable or fixed, the behavior of other costs may be less obvious. For example, compensation to sales personnel might include a constant monthly salary plus a commission based on sales. A cost of this type is called a *mixed cost* (see Illustration 24–3). Instead of classifying a mixed cost

Illustration 24–3:   Mixed Cost

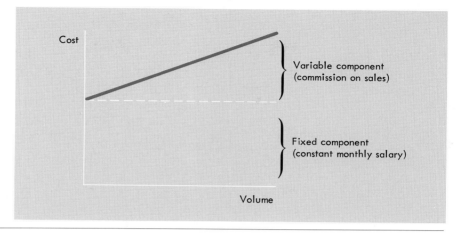

as variable or fixed, it should be divided into its separate fixed and variable components so that each can be classified correctly.

SCATTER DIAGRAMS.   Classifying costs as fixed or variable should be based, to the extent possible, on an analysis of past experience. One helpful technique of analyzing past experience is to display past data on a *scatter diagram,* such as is shown in Illustration 24–4. In preparing a scatter diagram, volume in dollars or units is measured on the horizontal axis and cost is measured on the vertical axis. The cost and volume of each period are entered as a single point on the diagram.

Illustration 24–4 shows a scatter diagram of a company's total costs and sales for each of 12 months. Each point shows the total costs incurred and the sales volume during a given month. For example, in one month, sales amounted to $30,000 and total costs were $26,000. These results were entered on the diagram as the point labeled "A."

ESTIMATED LINE OF COST BEHAVIOR.   In Illustration 24–4, observe the *estimated line of cost behavior.* This line attempts to reflect the average relationship between total costs and sales volume. Several alternative methods can be used to derive this line.

A crude means of deriving this line is called the *high-low method.* To use this method, all that is required is to identify the two points in the diagram that represent the highest total cost and the lowest total cost. A line is then drawn between these two points. The most obvious deficiency in this approach is that it totally ignores all of the available cost and sales volume points except the highest and lowest.

Illustration 24–4

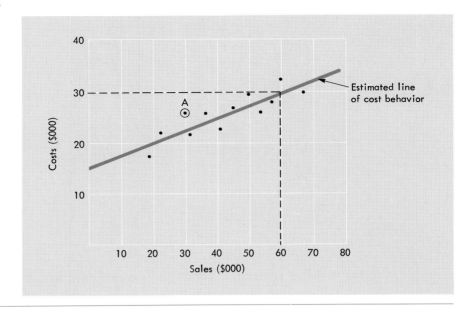

Another, somewhat better approach is to visually inspect the scatter of points and draw a line through the scatter that appears to provide an average reflection of the relationship between costs and volume. For quick and rough analyses, this approach is often satisfactory.

More sophisticated methods of approximating cost behavior are also available. Among these, perhaps the most often used is the statistical method of *least-squares regression*. This method requires fairly extensive calculations but results in an approximation that can be described as a line that best fits the actual cost and sales volume experience of the company. The calculations for least-squares regressions are typically covered in statistics courses and are applied to accounting data in more advanced cost accounting courses.

Return to Illustration 24–4 and observe that the sales volume each month ranged from approximately $20,000 to $67,000. If the estimated line of cost behavior is extended too far beyond this range, it is likely to be an unreliable basis for predicting actual costs. Note, however, that the line has been extended downward to the point at which it intersects the horizontal axis ($15,000). This should be interpreted as follows: Assuming sales volume in the range of past operations ($20,000 to $67,000), the company's total costs apparently include fixed costs of approximately $15,000.

Variable costs per sales dollar are represented in Illustration 24–4 by the slope of the estimated line of cost behavior. The slope may be calculated by comparing any two points on the line. To estimate variable cost per sales dollar, the change in total cost between the two points is divided by the change in sales volume between the two points.

For example, in Illustration 24–4, two points could be selected and the variable cost per sales dollar calculated as follows:

	Sales	Cost
First point	$60,000	$30,000
Second point.....	–0–	15,000
Changes	$60,000	$15,000

$$\frac{\text{Change in cost}}{\text{Change in sales}} = \frac{\$15,000}{\$60,000} = \$0.25 \text{ of cost per sales dollar}$$

An analysis of past experience may allow the accountant to estimate total fixed costs and variable costs per unit of volume without making a detailed classification of each individual cost. However, the accountant will have greater confidence in the analysis if individual costs are classified and the results are tested against observations of past experience. In testing the classifications, scatter diagrams may be prepared for individual costs, total variable costs, total fixed costs, and total costs.

BREAK-EVEN POINT

A company's *break-even point* is the sales level at which it neither earns a profit nor incurs a loss. It may be expressed either in units of product or in dollars of sales. To illustrate, assume that Alpha Company sells a single product for $100 per unit and incurs $70 of variable costs per unit sold. If the fixed costs involved in selling the product are $24,000, the company breaks even on the product as soon as it sells 800 units or as soon as sales volume reaches $80,000. This break-even point may be determined as follows:

1. Each unit sold at $100 recovers its $70 variable costs and contributes $30 toward the fixed costs.
2. The fixed costs are $24,000; consequently, 800 units ($24,000 ÷ $30 = 800) must be sold to pay the fixed costs.
3. And 800 units at $100 each produce an $80,000 sales volume.

The $30 amount by which the sales price exceeds variable costs per unit is this product's *contribution margin per unit.* In other words, the contribution margin per unit is the amount that the sale of one unit contributes toward recovery of the fixed costs and then toward a profit.

Also, the contribution margin of a product expressed as a percentage of its sales price is its *contribution rate.* For instance, the contribution rate of the $100 product of this illustration is 30% ($30 ÷ $100 = 30%).

With contribution margin and contribution rate defined, it is possible to set up the following formulas for calculating a break-even point in units and in dollars:

$$\text{Break-even point in units} = \frac{\text{Fixed costs}}{\text{Contribution margin per unit}}$$

$$\text{Break-even point in dollars} = \frac{\text{Fixed costs}}{\text{Contribution rate}}$$

Application of the second formula to figures for the product of this illustration gives this result:

$$\text{Break-even point in dollars} = \frac{\$24,000}{30\%} = \frac{\$24,000}{0.30} = \$80,000$$

Although the solution in the present example comes out evenly, a contribution rate should be carried out several decimal places to avoid minor rounding errors when calculating the break-even point in dollars. In solving the exercises and problems at the end of this chapter, for example, calculations of contribution rate should be carried to six decimal places unless the requirements state otherwise. Calculated either way, Alpha Company's break-even point may be verified with an income statement, as in Illustration 24–5. Observe in the illustration that revenue from sales exactly equals the sum of the fixed and variable costs at the break-even point. Recognizing this will prove helpful in understanding the material that follows in this chapter.

Illustration 24–5

ALPHA COMPANY		
Income Statement at the Break-Even Point		
Sales (800 units @ $100 each)		$80,000
Costs:		
Fixed costs...........................	$24,000	
Variable costs (800 units @ $70 each).....	56,000	80,000
Net income...............................		$ –0–

BREAK-EVEN GRAPH

A cost-volume-profit analysis may be shown graphically as in Illustration 24–6. When presented in this form, the graph is commonly called a break-even graph or break-even chart. On such a graph, the horizontal axis shows units sold and the vertical axis shows both dollars of sales and dollars of costs; costs and revenues are plotted as straight lines. The illustrated graph shows the break-even point of Alpha Company. A break-even graph is prepared as follows:

1. The line representing fixed costs is plotted at the fixed cost level. Note that it is a horizontal line, since the fixed costs are the same at all sales levels. Actually, the fixed costs line is not essential to the analysis; however, it contributes important information and is commonly plotted on a break-even chart.

Illustration 24–6

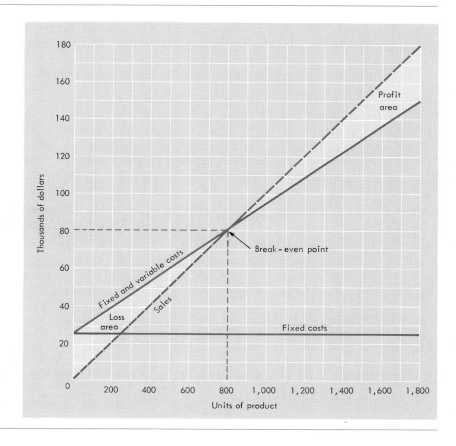

2. Next, the sales line is projected from the point of zero units and zero dollars of sales to the point of maximum sales shown on the graph. In choosing the maximum number of units to be shown, a better graph results if the number chosen is such that it will cause the break-even point to appear near the center of the graph.

3. Next, the variable cost plus fixed cost line is plotted. Note that it begins at the fixed cost level and, as a result, shows total costs at all production levels. At the zero sales level, there are no variable costs, only fixed costs. However, at any level above zero sales, all the fixed costs are present and so are the variable costs for that level. Also observe that the variable cost plus fixed cost line intersects the sales line at the break-even point. It intersects at this point because at the break-even point the revenue from sales exactly equals the sum of the fixed and variable costs, or in other words, the total costs.

In reading a break-even chart, the vertical distance between the sales line and the total cost line represents a loss to the left of the break-even point and a profit to the right of it. The amount of profit or loss at any given sales level can be determined from the graph by measuring the vertical distance between the sales line and the total cost line at the given level.

SALES REQUIRED FOR A DESIRED NET INCOME

A slight extension of the concept behind the break-even calculation will produce a formula that may be used in determining the sales level necessary to produce a desired net income. The formula is:

$$\text{Sales at desired income level} = \frac{\text{Fixed costs} + \text{Net income} + \text{Income taxes}}{\text{Contribution rate}}$$

To illustrate the formula's use, assume that Alpha Company of the previous discussion, the company having $24,000 of fixed costs and a 30% contribution rate, has set a $20,000 after-tax income goal for itself. Assume further that in order to have a $20,000 net income, the company must earn $28,500 and pay $8,500 in income taxes. Under these assumptions, $175,000 of sales are necessary to produce a $20,000 net income. This is calculated as follows:

$$\text{Sales at desired income level} = \frac{\text{Fixed costs} + \text{Net income} + \text{Income taxes}}{\text{Contribution rate}}$$

$$\text{Sales at desired income level} = \frac{\$24,000 + \$20,000 + \$8,500}{30\%}$$

$$\text{Sales at desired income level} = \frac{\$52,500}{30\%} = \$175,000$$

In the formula just given, the contribution rate was used as the divisor and the resulting answer was in dollars of sales. The contribution margin can also be used as the divisor; when it is, the resulting answer is in units of product.

MARGIN OF SAFETY

The difference between a company's current sales and sales at its break-even point, when sales are above the break-even point, is known as its margin of safety. The *margin of safety* is the amount sales may decrease before the company will incur a loss. It may be expressed in units of product, dollars, or as a percentage of sales. For example, if current sales are $100,000 and the break-even point is $80,000, the margin of safety is $20,000, or 20% of sales, calculated as follows:

$$\frac{\text{Sales} - \text{Break-even sales}}{\text{Sales}} = \text{Margin of safety}$$

or

$$\frac{\$100,000 - \$80,000}{\$100,000} = \text{20\% margin of safety}$$

INCOME FROM A GIVEN SALES LEVEL

Cost-volume-profit analysis goes beyond break-even analysis and can be used to answer other questions. For example, what income will result from a given sales level? To understand the analysis used in answering this question, recall the factors that enter into the calculation of income. When expressed in equation form, they are:

$$\text{Sales} - (\text{Fixed costs} + \text{Variable costs}) = \text{Income}$$

or

$$\text{Income} = \text{Sales} - (\text{Fixed costs} + \text{Variable costs})$$

This equation may be used to calculate the income that will result at a given sales level. For example, assume that Alpha Company of the previous illustrations wishes to know what income will result if its sales level can be increased to $200,000. That would be 2,000 units of its product at $100 per unit. To determine the answer, recall that the variable costs per unit of this product are $70 and note that the $70 is 0.7 of the product's selling price. Consequently, variable costs for 2,000 units of the product are 0.7 of the selling price of these units, or (0.7 × $200,000) = $140,000. Alpha Company's fixed costs are $24,000. Therefore, if these known factors are substituted in the equation for determining income, the equation will read:

$$\text{Income} = \$200,000 - [\$24,000 + (0.7 \times \$200,000)]$$
$$\text{Income} = \$200,000 - \$164,000$$
$$\text{Income} = \$36,000$$

The $36,000 is "before-tax" income; and as a result, if Alpha Company wishes to learn its after-tax income from the sale of 2,000 units of its product, it will have to apply the appropriate tax rates to the $36,000.

OTHER QUESTIONS

A company may wish to know what would happen to its break-even point if it reduced the selling price of its product in order to increase sales. Or it might wish to know what would happen if it installed a new machine that would increase its fixed costs but which would reduce variable costs. These are two of several possible questions involving changes in selling prices and costs. At first glance such changes seem to violate the basic assumptions on which cost-volume-profit analysis is based. But this is not true. A constant selling price, truly variable costs, and truly fixed costs are assumed to hold for any analysis involving the assumed price and costs. However, changes may be made, and if made, the new price and new costs are assumed to remain constant for the analyses involving that price and those costs. The fact that changes can be made in these factors is helpful for planning purposes because the effect of changes can be predicted before the changes are actually made.

To illustrate the effect of changes, assume that Alpha Company is considering the installation of a new machine that will increase the fixed costs of producing and selling its product from $24,000 to $30,000. However, the machine will reduce the variable costs from $70 per unit of product to $60. The selling price of the product will remain unchanged at $100, and the company wishes to know what its break-even point will be if the machine is installed. Examination of the costs shows that the installation will not only increase the company's fixed costs but it will also change the contribution margin and contribution rate of the company's product. The new contribution margin will be $40, that is, ($100 − $60) = $40, and the new contribution rate will be 40%, that is, ($40 ÷ $100) = 0.4 or 40%. Consequently, if the machine is installed, the company's new break-even point will be:

$$\text{Break-even point in dollars} = \frac{\$30,000}{0.4} = \$75,000$$

In addition to their use in determining Alpha Company's break-even point, the new fixed costs and the new contribution rate may be used to determine the sales level needed to earn a desired net income. They may also be used to determine the expected income at a given sales level, or to answer other questions the company will want to answer before installing the new machine.

MULTIPRODUCT BREAK-EVEN POINT

The break-even point for a company selling a number of products can be determined by using a hypothetical unit made up of units of each of the company's products in their expected *sales mix*. Such a hypothetical unit is really a composite unit and is treated in all analyses as though it were a single product. To illustrate the use of such a hypothetical unit, assume that Beta Company sells three products, A, B, and C, and it wishes to calculate its break-even point. Unit selling prices for the three products are Product A, $5; Product B, $8; and Product C, $4. The sales mix or ratio in which the products are expected to be sold is 4:2:1, and the company's fixed costs are $48,000. Under these assumptions a composite unit selling price for the three products can be calculated as follows:

4 units of Product A @ $5 per unit =	$20
2 units of Product B @ $8 per unit =	16
1 unit of Product C @ $4 per unit =	4
Selling price of a composite unit	$40

Also, if the variable costs of selling the three products are Product A, $3.25; Product B, $4.50; and Product C, $2, the variable costs of a composite unit of the products are:

4 units of Product A @ $3.25 per unit =	$13
2 units of Product B @ $4.50 per unit =	9
1 unit of Product C @ $2.00 per unit =	2
Variable costs of a composite unit	$24

With the variable costs and selling price of a composite unit of the company's products calculated, the contribution margin for a composite unit may be determined by subtracting the variable costs of a composite unit from the selling price of such a unit, as follows:

$40 − $24 = $16 contribution margin per composite unit

The $16 contribution margin may then be used to determine the company's break-even point in composite units. The break-even point is:

$$\text{Break-even point in composite units} = \frac{\text{Fixed costs}}{\text{Composite contribution margin per unit}}$$

$$\text{Break-even point in composite units} = \frac{\$48,000}{\$16}$$

$$\text{Break-even point} = 3,000 \text{ composite units}$$

The company breaks even when it sells 3,000 composite units of its products. However, to determine the number of units of each product it must sell to break even, the number of units of each product in the composite unit must be multiplied by the number of composite units needed to break even, as follows:

Product A:	4	× 3,000	=	12,000 units
Product B:	2	× 3,000	=	6,000 units
Product C:	1	× 3,000	=	3,000 units

The accuracy of all these computations can be verified by preparing an income statement showing the company's revenues and costs at the break-even point. Such a statement is shown in Illustration 24–7.

A composite unit made up of units of each of a company's products in their expected sales mix may be used in answering a variety of cost-volume-profit questions. In making all such analyses, it is assumed that the product mix remains constant at all sales levels just as the other factors entering into an analysis are assumed to be constant.

Illustration 24–7

BETA COMPANY
Income Statement at the Break-Even Point

Sales:			
Product A (12,000 units @ $5)			$ 60,000
Product B (6,000 units @ $8)			48,000
Product C (3,000 units @ $4)			12,000
Total revenues			$120,000
Costs:			
Fixed costs		$48,000	
Variable costs:			
Product A (12,000 units @ $3.25)	$39,000		
Product B (6,000 units @ $4.50)	27,000		
Product C (3,000 units @ $2.00)	6,000		
Total variable costs		72,000	
Total costs			120,000
Net income			–0–

Nevertheless, this does not prevent changes in the assumed sales mix in order to learn what would happen if the mix were changed. However, problems involving changes in the sales mix require a recomputation of the composite unit selling price and composite unit variable costs for each change in the mix.

EVALUATING THE RESULTS

Cost-volume-profit analyses have their greatest use in predicting what will happen when changes are made in selling prices, product mix, and the various cost factors. However, in evaluating the results of such analyses, several points should be kept in mind. First, the analyses are used to predict future results. Therefore, the data used in the formulas and on the graphs are assumed or forecasted data. Consequently, the results of the analyses are no more reliable than the data used. Second, cost-volume-profit analyses as presented here are based on the assumptions that in any one analysis selling price will remain constant, fixed costs are truly fixed, and variable costs are truly variable. These assumptions do not always reflect reality. Therefore, at best the answers obtained through cost-volume-profit analyses are approximations. However, if this is recognized, cost-volume-profit analyses can be useful to management in making decisions.

The cost-volume-profit analyses presented in this chapter are based on the assumption that revenues and costs may be expressed as straight lines; and as pointed out, such an assumption does not always hold. Therefore, it should be noted that cost-volume-profit analyses based on curvilinear relationships are also possible. However, the use of curvilinear relationships requires rather sophisticated mathematics, and a discussion is deferred to a more advanced text.

GLOSSARY

Break-even point. The sales level at which a company neither earns a profit nor incurs a loss.

Contribution margin per unit. The dollar amount that the sale of one unit contributes toward recovery of fixed costs and then toward a profit.

Contribution rate. The contribution margin per unit expressed as a percentage of sales price.

Cost-volume-profit analysis. A method of predicting the effects of changes in costs and sales level on the income of a business.

Estimated line of cost behavior. A line that attempts to reflect the average relationship between cost and volume.

Fixed cost.   A cost that remains unchanged in total amount over a wide range of production levels.

High-low method.   A crude technique for deriving an estimated line of cost behavior that connects the highest and lowest costs shown on a scatter diagram with a straight line.

Least-squares regression.   A sophisticated method of deriving an estimated line of cost behavior; the resulting estimate can be described as a line that best fits the actual cost and volume data of a company.

Margin of safety.   The amount by which a company's current sales exceed the sales necessary to break even.

Mixed cost.   A cost that includes two components, one of which is fixed and one of which is variable.

Relevant range of operations.   The normal operating range for the business, which excludes extremely high and low levels of production that are not apt to be encountered.

Sales mix.   The ratio in which a company's different products are sold.

Scatter diagram.   A graph used to display the relationship between costs and volume in which the cost and volume for each period is shown as a point on the diagram.

Semivariable cost.   A cost that changes with production volume but not in the same proportion.

Stair-step cost.   A cost that remains constant over a range of production, then increases by a lump sum if production is expanded beyond this range, then remains constant over another range of production increases, and so forth.

Variable cost.   A cost that changes in total amount proportionately with production-level changes.

QUESTIONS FOR CLASS DISCUSSION

1.   Why is cost-volume-profit analysis used?

2.   What is a fixed cost? Name two fixed costs.

3.   When there are fixed costs in manufacturing a product and the number of units manufactured is increased, do fixed costs per unit increase or decrease? Why?

4.   What is a variable cost? Name two variable costs.

5.   What is a semivariable cost?

6.   The reliability of cost-volume-profit analysis rests upon three basic assumptions. What are they?

7.   What two factors tend to make it possible to classify costs as either fixed or variable?

8.   What is a mixed cost? How should a mixed cost be classified for the purpose of cost-volume-profit analysis?

9. How are scatter diagrams used in the process of estimating the behavior of a company's costs?
10. What is the primary weakness of the high-low method of deriving an estimated line of cost behavior?
11. What is the break-even point in the sale of a product?
12. A company sells a product for $90 per unit. The variable costs of producing and selling the product are $54 per unit. What is the product's contribution margin per unit? What is its contribution rate?
13. If a straight line is begun at the fixed cost level on a break-even graph and the line rises at the variable cost rate, what does the line show?
14. When a break-even graph is prepared, why are the fixed costs plotted as a horizontal line?
15. What is a company's margin of safety?
16. What is meant by the sales mix of a company?
17. If a company produces and sells more than one product, the reliability of cost-volume-profit analysis depends on an additional assumption in regard to sales mix. What is that assumption?

CLASS EXERCISES

Exercise 24–1

The past experience of a company discloses the following information about a particular cost and sales volume:

Period	Sales	Cost X
1.....	$16,000	$ 8,200
2.....	22,000	10,500
3.....	15,000	8,300
4.....	23,000	10,000
5.....	19,000	9,100
6.....	12,000	7,300

Required:

Prepare a scatter diagram of the cost and volume data, estimate the line of cost behavior, and decide whether the cost is a variable, fixed, or mixed cost.

Exercise 24–2

Otter Company manufactures a single product that it sells for $106 per unit. The variable costs of manufacturing the product are $82 per unit, and the annual fixed costs incurred in manufacturing it are $119,160. Calculate the company's *(a)* contribution margin, *(b)* contribution rate, *(c)* break-even point for the product in units, and *(d)* break-even point in dollars of sales. The calculation of contribution rate should be carried to six decimal places.

Exercise 24–3

Prepare an income statement for Otter Company's operations (Exercise 24–2) showing sales, fixed costs, and variable costs at the break-even point. Also, if Otter Company's fixed costs increased by $9,480, calculate how many additional sales (in dollars) would be necessary to break even.

Exercise 24–4

Assume that Otter Company of Exercise 24–2 wishes to earn a $36,000 annual after-tax income from the sale of its product, and that it must pay 50% of its income in state and federal income taxes. Calculate (a) the number of units of its product it must sell to earn a $36,000 after-tax income from the sale of the product and (b) the number of dollars of sales that are needed to earn a $36,000 after-tax income.

Exercise 24–5

The sales manager of Otter Company (Exercise 24–2) thinks that within two years annual sales of the company's product will reach 6,400 units while the sale price will go up to $125. Variable costs are expected to increase only $10 per unit, and fixed costs are not expected to change. Calculate the company's (a) before-tax income from the sale of these units and (b) calculate its after-tax income from the sale of the units.

Exercise 24–6

Dual Company markets Products X and Y which it sells in the ratio of five units of Product X at $8 per unit to each two units of Product Y at $30 per unit. The variable costs of marketing Product X are $3.40 per unit, and the variable costs for Product Y are $9.50 per unit. The annual fixed costs for marketing both products are $135,040. Calculate (a) the selling price of a composite unit of these products, (b) the variable costs per composite unit, (c) the break-even point in composite units, and (d) the number of units of each product that will be sold at the break-even point.

PROBLEMS

Problem 24–1

Ketch Company has collected the following monthly total cost and sales volume data related to its recent operations:

Period	Costs	Sales
1	$35,000	$44,000
2	37,500	36,000
3	30,000	24,000
4	27,500	32,000
5	25,000	20,000
6	40,000	48,000
7	45,000	60,000
8	37,500	40,000
9	36,000	56,000
10	42,500	68,000
11	42,500	56,000
12	42,500	60,000

Required:

1. Design a diagram with sales volume marked off in $8,000 intervals on the horizontal axis and cost marked off in $5,000 intervals on the vertical axis. Record the cost and sales data of Ketch Company as a scatter of points on the diagram.
2. Based on your visual inspection of the scatter diagram, draw an estimated line of cost behavior that appears to show the average relationship between cost and sales.

3. Based on the estimated line of cost behavior, estimate the amount of Ketch Company's fixed costs.
4. Use the estimated line of cost behavior to approximate cost when sales volume is $20,000 and when sales volume is $60,000. Calculate an estimate of variable cost per sales dollar.

Problem 24–2

Abilene Company manufactures a number of products, one of which, Product A, is produced and sold quite independently from the others and sells for $600 per unit. The fixed costs of manufacturing Product A are $85,500, and the variable costs are $410 per unit. In solving Requirements 1 (b) and 4 (below), the calculation of a contribution rate should be carried to six decimal places.

Required:

1. Calculate the company's break-even point in the sale of Product A (a) in units and (b) in dollars of sales.
2. Prepare a break-even graph for Product A. Use 1,000 as the maximum number of units on your graph and 675 as the maximum number of dollars (in thousands).
3. Prepare an income statement showing sales, fixed costs, and variable costs for Product A at the break-even point.
4. Determine the sales volume in dollars that the company must achieve to earn a $28,500 after-tax (40% rate) income from the sale of Product A.
5. Determine the after-tax income the company will earn from a $465,000 sales level for Product A.

Problem 24–3

Waterloo Company incurred a $5,000 loss last year in selling 5,000 units of its Product A, as the following income statement shows:

WATERLOO COMPANY
Last Year's Income Statement for Product A

Sales		$125,000
Costs:		
Fixed	$ 30,000	
Variable	100,000	130,000
Net loss from sale of Product A		$ (5,000)

The production manager has pointed out that the variable costs of Product A can be reduced 25% by installing a machine that performs operations presently done by hand. However, the new machine will increase fixed costs by $8,000 annually.

Required:

1. Calculate last year's dollar break-even point for Product A.
2. Calculate the dollar break-even point for Product A under the assumption the new machine is installed.
3. Prepare a break-even chart under the assumption the new machine is installed. Use 6,000 as the maximum number of units on your chart.
4. Prepare an income statement showing expected annual results with the new machine installed. Assume no change in the selling price of Product A, no change in the number of units sold, and a 50% income tax rate.

5. Calculate the sales level required to earn a $42,000 per year after-tax income with the new machine installed and no change in the selling price of Product A. Prepare an income statement showing the results at this sales level.

Problem 24–4   Last year Bedford Company earned an unsatisfactory 2.5% after-tax return on sales from the sale of 50,000 packages of its Product 801 at $2.50 each. The company buys Product 801 in bulk and packages it for resale. Following are last year's costs for the product:

Cost of bulk Product 801 (sufficient for 50,000 packages) $62,500
Packaging materials and other variable packaging costs $12,500
Fixed costs $43,750
Income tax rate 50%

It has been suggested that if the selling price of the product is reduced 10% and a slight change is made in its packaging, the number of units sold can be doubled. The packaging change will increase packaging costs 10% per unit, but doubling the sales volume will allow the company to take advantage of a quantity discount of 5% on the product's bulk purchase price. The packaging and volume changes will not affect fixed costs.

Required:

1. Calculate the dollar break-even points for Product 801 at the $2.50 per unit sales price and at $2.25 per unit.
2. Prepare a break-even chart for the sale of the product at each price. Use 100,000 units as the upper limit of your charts.
3. Prepare a condensed comparative income statement showing the anticipated results of selling the product at $2.50 per unit and the estimated results of selling it at $2.25 per unit.

Problem 24–5   Renko Company sells two products, S and T, which are produced and sold independently. Last year, the company sold 8,000 units of each of these products at $120 per unit, earning $105,000 from the sale of each as the following condensed income statement shows:

	Product S	Product T
Sales	$960,000	$960,000
Costs:		
Fixed costs	$150,000	$600,000
Variable costs	600,000	150,000
Total costs	$750,000	$750,000
Income before taxes	$210,000	$210,000
Income taxes (50% rate)	105,000	105,000
Net income	$105,000	$105,000

Required:

1. Calculate the break-even point for each product in units.
2. Prepare a break-even graph for each product. Use 10,000 as the maximum number of units on each graph.

3. Prepare a condensed income statement showing in separate columns the net income the company will earn from the sale of each product under the assumption that without a change in selling prices, the number of units of each product sold declines to 5,926 units.
4. Prepare a second condensed income statement showing in separate columns the net income the company will earn if the number of units of each product increases 25%.

Problem 24-6   Mulberry Company manufactures and sells three products, A, B, and C. Product A sells for $16 per unit, Product B sells for $8 per unit, and Product C sells for $7 per unit. Their sales mix is in the ratio of 4:5:8, and the variable costs of manufacturing and selling the products have been: Product A, $12; Product B, $6; and Product C, $5. The fixed costs of manufacturing the three products are $134,400. A special material labeled 650 has been used in manufacturing both Products A and B; however, a new material called 710 has just become available, and if it is substituted for material 650, it will reduce the variable cost of manufacturing Product A by $0.75 and Product B by $0.20. However, fixed costs will go up to $138,000 because of special equipment needed to process material 710.

Required:

1. Determine the company's break-even point in dollars and the number of units of each product sold at the break-even point under the assumption that material 650 is used in manufacturing Products A and B. Show all pertinent calculations.
2. Determine the company's break-even point in dollars and the number of units of each product sold at the break-even point under the assumption that the new material 710 is used in manufacturing Products A and B. Show all pertinent calculations.

ALTERNATE PROBLEMS

Problem 24-1A   Cradle Company has collected the following monthly total cost and sales volume data related to its recent operations:

Period	Costs	Sales
1	$38,000	$52,000
2	41,000	43,000
3	33,000	28,000
4	30,000	38,000
5	27,000	24,000
6	44,000	57,000
7	49,000	72,000
8	41,000	48,000
9	39,000	67,000
10	46,000	81,000
11	46,000	67,000
12	46,000	72,000

Required:

1. Design a diagram with sales volume marked off in $8,000 intervals on the horizontal axis and cost marked off in $5,000 intervals on the vertical axis. Record the cost and sales data of Cradle Company as a scatter of points on the diagram.
2. Based on your visual inspection of the scatter diagram, draw an estimated line of cost behavior that appears to show the average relationship between cost and sales.
3. Based on the estimated line of cost behavior, estimate the amount of Cradle Company's fixed costs.
4. Use the estimated line of cost behavior to approximate cost when sales volume is $32,000 and when sales volume is $80,000. Calculate an estimate of variable cost per sales dollar.

Problem 24–2A   Among the products sold by Nelson Company is Product B, which is produced and sold independently from the other products of the company, and which sells for $320 per unit. The fixed costs of manufacturing and selling Product B are $39,000, and the variable costs are $260 per unit.

Required:

1. Calculate the company's break-even point in the sale of Product B *(a)* in units and *(b)* in dollars of sales.
2. Prepare a break-even graph for Product B, using 1,000 as the maximum number of units on the graph.
3. Prepare an income statement showing sales, fixed costs, and variable costs for Product B at the break-even point.
4. Determine the sales volume in dollars required to achieve a $3,000 after-tax (50% rate) income from the sale of Product B.
5. Determine the after-tax income the company will earn from a $313,600 sales level for Product B.

Problem 24–3A   Dodgen Company lost $1,000 last year in selling 2,000 units of its Product X, as the following income statement shows:

DODGEN COMPANY
Last Year's Sales of Product X

Sales		$100,000
Costs:		
Fixed	$26,000	
Variable	75,000	101,000
Net loss from sales of Product X		$ (1,000)

The company management is convinced that if a new machine is installed, enough piece-rate labor and spoiled materials can be saved to reduce the variable costs of manufacturing Product X by 20%. However, the new machine will increase fixed costs $2,400 annually.

Required:

1. Calculate last year's dollar break-even point for Product X.
2. Calculate the dollar break-even point under the assumption the new machine is installed.
3. Prepare a break-even chart under the assumption the new machine is installed. Use 3,000 as the maximum number of units on your chart.
4. Prepare an income statement showing expected annual results with the new machine installed, no change in Product X's price, and sales at last year's level. Assume a 50% income tax rate.
5. Calculate the sales level required to earn a $10,000 per year after-tax income with the new machine installed and no change in the selling price of Product X. Prepare an income statement showing the results at this sales level.

Problem 24–4A

Last year Wayne Company sold 20,000 units of its product at $20 per unit. To manufacture and sell the product required $100,000 of fixed manufacturing costs and $20,000 of fixed selling and administrative expenses. Last year's variable costs and expenses per unit were:

Material	$8.00
Direct labor (paid on a piece-rate basis)	3.00
Variable manufacturing overhead costs	0.60
Variable selling and administrative expenses.....	0.40

A new material has just come on the market that will cut the material cost of producing the product in half if substituted for the material presently being used. The substitution will have no effect on the product's quality; but it will give the company a choice in pricing the product. (1) The company can maintain the present per unit price, sell the same number of units, and make an extra $4 per unit profit as a result of the substitution. Or (2) it can reduce the product's price $4 per unit to an amount equal to the material savings and, because of the reduction, increase the number of units sold by 60%. If the latter choice is made, the fixed manufacturing overhead and fixed selling and administrative expenses will not change and the remaining variable costs and expenses will vary with volume.

Required:

1. Calculate the break-even point in dollars for each alternative.
2. Prepare a break-even chart for each. The company's production capacity is 40,000 units, and this should be used as the upper limit of your charts.
3. Prepare a comparative income statement showing sales, total fixed costs, and total variable costs and expenses, operating income, income taxes (50% rate), and net income for each alternative.

Problem 24–5A

Double Company has two essentially unrelated divisions, each of which produces a single product. The two products, A and B, are produced and sold independently. Coincidentally, each product sold last year at a price of $150 and 5,000 units of each product were sold.

Last year's income statements for the two products are as follows:

	Product A	Product B
Sales	$750,000	$750,000
Costs:		
Fixed costs	$500,000	$150,000
Variable costs	150,000	500,000
Total costs	$650,000	$650,000
Income before taxes	$100,000	$100,000
Income taxes (40% rate)	40,000	40,000
Net income	$ 60,000	$ 60,000

Required:

1. Calculate the break-even point for each product in units.
2. Prepare a break-even graph for each product. Use 10,000 as the maximum number of units on each graph.
3. Prepare a condensed income statement showing in separate columns the net income the company will earn from the sale of each product under the assumption that without a change in selling prices, the number of units of each product sold declines to 4,167 units.
4. Prepare a second condensed income statement showing in separate columns the net income the company will earn if the number of units of each product increases 100%.

Problem 24–6A

Tacky Company manufactures and sells three products, X, Y, and Z, which sell for $24 per unit, $20 per unit, and $16 per unit, respectively. Their sales mix is in the ratio of 2:5:8, and the variable costs of manufacturing and selling the products have been: Product X, $16; Product Y, $14; and Product Z, $10. Fixed manufacturing, selling, and administrative costs amount to $488,800.

The management of Tacky Company is considering the purchase of a new machine that will be used in the manufacture of Products Y and Z. If the machine is purchased, fixed manufacturing costs will increase by $99,200. However, variable costs of Product Y will decrease by $2 per unit and variable costs of Product Z will decrease by $1 per unit.

Required:

1. Determine the company's break-even point in dollars and the number of units of each product sold at the break-even point assuming the new machine is not purchased. Show all necessary calculations.
2. Determine the company's break-even point in dollars and the number of units of each product sold at the break-even point assuming that the new machine is purchased. Show all pertinent calculations.

PROVOCATIVE PROBLEMS

Provocative Problem 24–1, Nitro Corporation

Nitro Corporation produces a high-quality fertilizer at its Iowa plant. The plant produced at near capacity last year with the results shown in the following condensed income statement:

Sales (300,000 lbs.)	$600,000
Cost of goods manufactured and sold (fixed, $100,000;	
variable, $240,000)	340,000
Gross margin	$260,000
Selling and administrative expenses (fixed, $80,000;	
variable, $60,000)	140,000
Income before taxes	$120,000

Big Spender Company has offered Nitro a two-year contract whereby Big Spender will buy 200,000 pounds of the additive annually at $1.60 per pound for export sales. Delivery on the contract would require a plant addition that would double fixed manufacturing costs. The contract would not affect present selling and administrative expenses. Variable manufacturing costs per unit would be the same in the new plant as they have been in the old plant.

Required:

Management is not certain it should enter into the contract and has asked for your opinion, including the following:

1. An estimated income statement for the first year following the plant addition, assuming no change in domestic sales.
2. A comparison of break-even sales levels before the plant addition and after the contract with Big Spender expires. Assume after-contract sales and expense levels, other than fixed manufacturing costs, will be at the same levels as last year.
3. A statement showing net income after the contract expiration but at sales and expense levels of last year, other than fixed manufacturing costs.

Provocative
Problem 24–2,
Faces Company

Faces Company manufactures and sells Frowns, Scowls, and Grimaces. Last year's sales mix for the three products was in the ratio of $6:1:3$, with combined sales totaling 12,000 units. Frowns sell for $120 each and have a 20% contribution rate. Scowls sell for $100 each and have a 25% contribution rate, and Grimaces sell for $90 each and have a 40% contribution rate. The fixed costs of manufacturing and selling the products amount to $161,214. The company estimates that combined sales of the three products will continue at the 12,000 unit level next year. However, the sale manager is of the opinion that if the company's advertising and sales efforts are slanted further toward Scowls and Grimaces during the coming year, with no increases in the amounts of money expended, the sales mix of the three products can be changed to the ratio of $3:3:4$.

Required:

Should the company change its sales mix through advertising and sales efforts? What effect will the change have on the composite contribution rate of the three products? What effect will it have on the company's break-even point? Back your answers with figures. Calculations of contribution rate should be carried to seven decimal places.

Provocative
Problem 24–3,
Bentley
Company

Bentley Company operated at near capacity during 198A, and a 20% annual increase in the demand for its product is expected in 198B. As a result the company's management is trying to decide how to meet this demand. Two alternatives are being considered. The first calls for changes that will increase variable costs to 55% of the selling price of the company's product but will not change fixed costs. The second calls for a capital investment that will increase fixed costs 15% but will not affect variable costs.

Bentley Company's income statement for 198A provided the following summarized information:

Sales		$450,000
Costs:		
Variable costs	$216,000	
Fixed costs	160,000	376,000
Income before taxes		$ 74,000

Required:

Which alternative do you recommend? Back your recommendation with income statement information and any other data you consider relevant.

The Master Budget: A Formal Plan for the Business

After studying Chapter 25, you should be able to:

Explain the importance of budgeting.

Describe the specific benefits derived from budgeting.

List the sequence of steps required to prepare a master budget.

Prepare each budget in a master budget and explain the importance of each budget to the overall budgeting process.

Integrate the individual budgets into planned financial statements.

Define or explain the words and phrases listed in the chapter Glossary.

The process of managing a business consists of two basic elements: planning and control. If a business is to accomplish the variety of objectives expected of it, management must first carefully plan the activities and events the business should enter into and accomplish during future weeks, months, and years. Then, as the activities take place, they must be monitored and controlled so that actual events conform as closely as possible to the plan.

The management functions of planning and control are perhaps equally important to the long-run success of a business. Nevertheless, most business failures appear to result from inadequate planning. Countless pitfalls can be avoided if management carefully anticipates the future conditions within which the business will operate and prepares a detailed plan of the activities the business should pursue. Furthermore, the plans for future business activities should be formally organized and preserved. This process of planning future business actions and expressing those plans in a formal manner is called *budgeting*. Correspondingly, a *budget* is a formal statement of future plans. Since the economic or financial aspects of the business are primary matters of consideration, budgets are usually expressed in monetary terms.

THE MASTER BUDGET

When the plan to be formalized is a comprehensive or overall plan for the business, the resulting budget is called a *master budget*. As an overall plan, the master budget should include specific plans for expected sales, the units of product to be produced, the materials or merchandise to be purchased, the expense payments to be made, the long-term assets to be purchased, and the amount of cash to be borrowed, if any. The planned activities of each subunit of the business should be separately organized and presented within the master budget. Thus, the master budget for a business consists of several sub-budgets, all of which articulate or join with each other to form the overall, coordinated plan for the business. As finally presented, the master budget typically includes sales, expense, production, equipment, and cash budgets. Also, the expected financial results of the planned activities may be expressed in terms of a planned income statement for the budget period and a planned balance sheet for the end of the budget period.

BENEFITS FROM BUDGETING

All business managements engage in planning; some planning is absolutely necessary if business activities are to continue. However, a typical characteristic of poor management is sloppy or incomplete planning. But, if management plans carefully and formalizes its plans completely enough, that is, if management engages in a thorough budgeting process, it may expect to obtain the following benefits.

Study, Research, and a Focus on the Future

When a business plans with sufficient care and detail to prepare a budget, the planning process usually involves thorough study and research. Not only should this result in the best conceivable plans but it should also instill in executives the habit of doing a reasonable amount of research and study before decisions are made. In short, budgeting tends to promote good decision-making processes. In addition, the items of interest to a budgetary investigation lie in the future. Thus, the attention of management is focused on future events and the associated opportunities available to the business. The pressures of daily operating problems naturally tend to take precedence over planning, thereby leaving the business without carefully thought-out objectives. Budgeting counteracts this tendency by formalizing the planning process; it makes planning an explicit responsibility of management.

The Basis for Evaluating Performance

The control function of management requires that performance be evaluated in light of some norms or objectives. On the basis of this evaluation, appropriate corrective actions can be implemented. In evaluating performance, there are two alternative norms or objectives against which actual performance can be compared: (1) past performance or (2) expected (budgeted) performance. Although past performance is sometimes used as the basis of comparison, budgeted performance is generally superior for determining whether actual performance is acceptable or in need of corrective action. Past performance fails to take into account all of the environmental changes that may impact on the performance level. For example, in the evaluation of sales performance, past sales occurred under economic conditions that may have been dramatically different from those that apply to the current sales effort. Economy-wide fluctuations, competitive shifts within the industry, new product line developments, increased or decreased advertising commitments, and so forth, all tend to invalidate comparisons between past performance and present performance. On the other hand, budgeted (anticipated) performance levels are developed after a research and study process that attempts to take such environmental factors into account. Thus, budgeting provides the benefit of a superior basis for evaluating performance and a more effective control mechanism.

Coordination

Coordination requires that a business be operated as a whole rather than as a group of separate departments. When a budget plan is prepared, each department's objectives are determined in advance, and these objectives are coordinated. For example, the production department is budgeted to produce approximately the number of units the selling department can sell. The purchasing department is budgeted to buy raw materials on the basis of budgeted production; and the hiring activities of the personnel department are budgeted to take into account budgeted production levels. Obviously, the departments and activities of a business must be closely coordinated if the business operations are to be efficient and profitable. Budgeting provides this coordination.

Communication

In a very small business, adequate communication of business plans might be accomplished by direct contact between the employees. Frequent conversations could perhaps serve as the means of communicating management's plans for the business. However, oral conversations often leave ambiguities and potential confusion if not backed up by documents that clearly state the content of the plans. Further, businesses need not be very large before informal conversations become obviously inadequate. When a budget is prepared, the budget becomes a means of informing the organization not only of plans that have been approved by management but also of budgeted actions management wishes the organization to take during the budget period.

A Source of Motivation

As previously mentioned, budgets provide the standards against which actual performance is evaluated. Because of this, the budget and the manner in which it is used can significantly affect the attitudes of those who are to be evaluated. If management is not careful, the budgeting process may have a negative impact on the attitudes of employees. Budgeted levels of performance must be realistic. Also, the personnel who will be evaluated in terms of a budget should be consulted and involved in preparing the budget. Finally, the subsequent evaluations of performance must not be given critically without offering the affected employees an opportunity to explain the reasons for performance failures. These three factors are important: (1) If the affected employees are consulted when the budget is prepared, (2) if obtainable objectives are budgeted, and (3) if the subsequent evaluations of performance are made fairly with opportunities provided to explain performance deficiencies, budgeting can be a strongly positive, motivating force in the organization. Budgeted performance levels can provide goals that individuals will attempt to attain or even exceed as they fulfill their responsibilities to the organization.

THE BUDGET COMMITTEE

The task of preparing a budget should not be made the responsibility of any one department; and the budget definitely should not be handed down from above as the "final word." Rather, budget figures and budget estimates should be developed from "the bottom up." For example, the sales department should have a hand in preparing sales estimates. Similarly, the production department should have initial responsibility for preparing its own expense budget. Otherwise, production and salespeople may say the budget figures are meaningless because they were prepared by front office personnel who know little if anything of sales and production problems.

Although budget figures should be developed from "the bottom up," the preparation of a budget needs central guidance. This is commonly supplied by a budget committee of department heads or other high-level executives who are responsible for seeing that budget figures are realistic and coordinated. If a department submits budget figures that do not reflect proper performance, the figures should be returned to the department with the budget committee's comments. The originating department then either adjusts the figures or defends them. It should not change the figures just to please the committee, since it is important that all parties agree that the figures are reasonable and attainable.

THE BUDGET PERIOD

Budget periods normally coincide with accounting periods. This means that in most companies the budget period is one year in length. However, in addition to their annual budgets, many companies prepare long-range budgets that set forth major objectives for periods of 3 to 5 or 10 years in advance. These long-range budgets are particularly important in planning for major expenditures of capital to buy plant and equipment. Additionally, the financing of major capital projects, for example, by issuing bonds, by issuing stock, by retaining earnings, and so forth, can be anticipated and planned as a part of preparing long-range budgets.

Long-range budgets of 2, 3, 5, and 10 years should reflect the planned accomplishment of long-range objectives. Within this context, the annual master budget for a business reflects the objectives that have been adopted for the next year. The annual budget, however, is commonly broken down into quarterly or monthly budgets. Short-term budgets of a quarter or a month are useful yardsticks that allow management to evaluate actual performance and take corrective actions promptly. After the quarterly or monthly results are known, the actual performance is compared to the budgeted amounts in a report similar to that disclosed in Illustration 25–1.

Many businesses follow the practice of "continuous" budgeting and are said to prepare *rolling budgets*. As each monthly or quarterly budget period goes by, these firms revise their entire set of budgets, adding new monthly or quarterly sales, production, expense, equipment, and cash budgets to replace the ones that have elapsed. Thus,

Illustration 25–1

CONSOLIDATED STORES, INC.
Income Statement with Variations from Budget for Month Ended April 30, 19—

	Actual	Budget	Variations
Sales	$63,500	$60,000	$+3,500
Less: Sales returns and allowances	1,800	1,700	+100
Sales discounts	1,200	1,150	+50
Net sales	$60,500	$57,150	$+3,350
Cost of goods sold:			
Merchandise inventory, April 1, 19—	$42,000	$44,000	$−2,000
Purchases, net	39,100	38,000	+1,100
Freight-in	1,250	1,200	+50
Goods for sale	$82,350	$83,200	$ −850
Merchandise inventory, April 30, 19—	41,000	44,100	−3,100
Cost of goods sold	$41,350	$39,100	$+2,250
Gross profit	$19,150	$18,050	$+1,100
Operating expenses:			
Selling expenses:			
Sales salaries	$ 6,250	$ 6,000	$ +250
Advertising expense	900	800	+100
Store supplies used	550	500	+50
Depreciation of store equipment	1,600	1,600	
Total selling expenses	$ 9,300	$ 8,900	$ +400
General and administrative expenses:			
Office salaries	$ 2,000	$ 2,000	
Office supplies used	165	150	$ +15
Rent	1,100	1,100	
Expired insurance	200	200	
Depreciation of office equipment	100	100	
Total general and administrative expenses	$ 3,565	$ 3,550	$ +15
Total operating expenses	$12,865	$12,450	$ +415
Income from operations	$ 6,285	$ 5,600	$ +685

at any point in time, monthly or quarterly budgets are available for a full year in advance.

PREPARING THE MASTER BUDGET

As indicated in the previous discussion, the master budget consists of a number of budgets that collectively express the planned activities of the business. The number and arrangement of the budgets included in the master budget depend on the size and complexity of the business. However, a master budget typically includes:

1. Operating budgets.
   a. Sales budget.
   b. For merchandising companies: Merchandise purchases budget.
   c. For manufacturing companies:
      (1) Production budget (stating the number of units to be produced).
      (2) Manufacturing budget.
   d. Selling expense budget.
   e. General and administrative expense budget.
2. Capital expenditures budget, which includes the budgeted expenditures for new plant and equipment.
3. Financial budgets.
   a. Budgeted statement of cash receipts and disbursements, called the cash budget.
   b. Budgeted income statement.
   c. Budgeted balance sheet.

In addition to these budgets, numerous supporting calculations or schedules may be required.

Some of the budgets listed above cannot be prepared until other budgets on the list are first completed. For example, the merchandise purchases budget cannot be prepared until the sales budget is available, since the number of units to be purchased depends upon how many units are to be sold. As a consequence, preparation of the budgets within the master budget must follow a definite sequence, as follows:

First: The sales budget must be prepared first because the operating and financial budgets depend upon information provided by the sales budget.

Second: The remaining operating budgets are prepared next. For manufacturing companies, the production budget must be prepared prior to the manufacturing budget, since the number of units to be manufactured obviously affects the amounts of materials, direct labor, and overhead to be budgeted.

Other than this, the budgets for manufacturing costs or merchandise costs, general and administrative expenses, and selling expenses may be prepared in any sequence.

Third: If capital expenditures are anticipated during the budget period, the capital expenditures budget is prepared next. This budget usually depends upon long-range sales forecasts more than it does upon the sales budget for the next year.

Fourth: Based upon the information provided in the above budgets, the budgeted statement of cash receipts and disbursements is prepared. If this budget discloses an imbalance between disbursements and planned receipts, the previous plans may have to be revised.

Fifth: The budgeted income statement is prepared next. If the plans contained in the master budget result in unsatisfactory profits, the entire master budget may be revised to incorporate any corrective measures available to the firm.

Sixth: The budgeted balance sheet for the end of the budget period is prepared last. An analysis of this statement may also lead to revisions in the previous budgets. For example, the budgeted balance sheet may disclose too much debt resulting from an overly ambitious capital expenditures budget, and revised plans may be necessary.

PREPARATION OF THE MASTER BUDGET ILLUSTRATED

The following sections explain the procedures involved in preparing the budgets that comprise the master budget. Northern Company, a wholesaler of a single product, provides an illustrative basis for the discussion. The September 30, 198A, balance sheet for Northern Company is presented in Illustration 25–2. The master budget for Northern

Illustration 25–2

NORTHERN COMPANY
Balance Sheet, September 30, 198A

Cash	$ 20,000	Accounts payable	$ 58,200
Accounts receivable	42,000	Loan from bank	10,000
Inventory (9,000 units @ $6)	54,000	Accrued income taxes payable	
Equipment*	200,000	(due October 15, 198A)	20,000
Less accumulated depreciation	(36,000)	Common stock	150,000
		Retained earnings	41,800
Total	$280,000	Total	$280,000

* The equipment is being depreciated on a straight-line basis over 10 years. Estimated salvage value is $20,000.

Company is prepared on a monthly basis, with a budgeted balance sheet prepared for the end of each quarter. Also, a budgeted income statement is prepared for each quarter. In the following sections, Northern Company budgets are prepared for October, November, and December 198A.

Sales Budget

The *sales budget* provides an estimate of goods to be sold and revenue to be derived from sales. It is the starting point in the budgeting procedure, since the plans of all departments are related to sales and expected revenue. The sales budget commonly grows from a reconciliation of forecasted business conditions, plant capacity, proposed selling expenses such as advertising, and estimates of sales. As to sales estimates, since people normally feel a greater responsibility for reaching goals they have had a hand in setting, the sales personnel of a company are often asked to submit, through the sales manager, estimates of sales for each territory and department. The final sales budget is then based on these estimates as reconciled for the forecasted business conditions, selling expenses, and so forth.

During September 198A, Northern Company sold 7,000 units of product at a price of $10 per unit. After obtaining the estimates of sales personnel and considering the economic conditions affecting the market for Northern Company's product, the sales budget (Illustration 25–3) is established for October, November, and December 198A. Since the purchasing department must base December 198A purchases on estimated sales for January 198B, the sales budget is expanded to include January 198B.

Observe in Illustration 25–3 that the sales budget is more detailed than simple projections of total sales; both unit sales and unit prices are forecasted. Some budgeting procedures are less detailed, expressing the budget only in terms of total sales volume. Also, many sales budgets

Illustration 25–3

NORTHERN COMPANY
Monthly Sales Budget
October 198A–January 198B

	Budgeted unit sales		Budgeted unit price		Budgeted total sales
September 198A (actual)	7,000	×	$10	=	$ 70,000
October 198A	10,000	×	10	=	100,000
November 198A	8,000	×	10	=	80,000
December 198A	14,000	×	10	=	140,000
January 198B	9,000	×	10	=	90,000

are far more detailed than the one illustrated. The more detailed sales budgets may show units and unit prices for each of many different products, classified by salesperson and by territory or by department.

Merchandise Purchases Budget

A variety of sophisticated techniques have been developed to assist management in making inventory purchase decisions. All of these techniques recognize that the number of units to be added to inventory depends upon the budgeted sales volume. Whether a company manufactures or purchases the product it sells, budgeted future sales volume is the primary factor to be considered in most inventory management decisions.

The amount of merchandise or materials to be purchased each month is determined as follows:

Budgeted sales for the month	XXX
Add the budgeted end-of-month inventory	XXX
Required amount of available merchandise	XXX
Deduct the beginning-of-month inventory	(XXX)
Inventory to be purchased	XXX

The calculation may be made in either dollars or in units. If the calculation is in units and only one product is involved, the number of dollars of inventory to be purchased may be determined by multiplying units to be purchased by the cost per unit.

After considering the cost of maintaining an investment in inventory and the potential cost associated with a temporary inventory shortage, Northern Company has decided that the number of units in its inventory at the end of each month should equal 90% of the next month's sales. In other words, the inventory at the end of October should equal 90% of the budgeted November sales, the November ending inventory should equal 90% of the expected December sales, and so on. Also, the company's suppliers have indicated that the September 198A per unit cost of $6 can be expected to remain unchanged through January 198B. Based on these factors the company prepared the merchandise purchases budget of Illustration 25–4.

The calculations of Northern Company's merchandise purchases budget differ slightly from the basic calculation previously given in that the first lines are devoted to determining the desired end-of-month inventory. Also, budgeted sales are added to the desired end-of-month inventory instead of vice versa, and on the last lines the number of dollars of inventory to be purchased is determined by multiplying units to be purchased by the cost per unit.

Illustration 25–4

	October	November	December
NORTHERN COMPANY Merchandise Purchases Budget October, November, and December 198A			
Next month's budgeted sales (in units)	8,000	14,000	9,000
Ratio of inventory to future sales	×90%	×90%	×90%
Desired end-of-month inventory	7,200	12,600	8,100
Budgeted sales for the month (in units)	10,000	8,000	14,000
Required units of available merchandise	17,200	20,600	22,100
Deduct beginning-of-month inventory	(9,000)	(7,200)	(12,600)
Number of units to be purchased	8,200	13,400	9,500
Budgeted cost per unit	×$6	×$6	×$6
Budgeted cost of merchandise purchases	$49,200	$80,400	$57,000

It was previously mentioned that some budgeting procedures are designed to provide only the total dollars of budgeted sales. Likewise, the merchandise purchases budget may not state the number of units to be purchased, and may be expressed only in terms of the total cost of merchandise to be purchased. In such situations, it is assumed that there is a constant relationship between sales and cost of goods sold. For example, Northern Company expects that cost of goods sold will equal 60% of sales. (Note that the budgeted sales price is $10 and the budgeted unit cost is $6.) Thus, its cost of purchases can be budgeted in dollars on the basis of budgeted sales without requiring information on the number of units involved.

Production Budgets and Manufacturing Budgets

Since Northern Company does not manufacture the product it sells, its budget for acquiring goods to be sold is a merchandise purchases budget (Illustration 25–4). If Northern Company had been a manufacturing company, a production budget rather than a merchandise purchases budget would be required. In a *production budget,* the number of units to be produced each month is shown. For Northern Company such a budget would be very similar to a merchandise purchases budget. It would differ in that the number of units to be purchased each month (see Illustration 25–4) would be described as the number of units to be manufactured each month. Also, it would not show costs, since a production budget is always expressed entirely in terms of units of product and does not include budgeted production costs. Such costs are shown in the manufacturing budget, which is based on the production volume shown in the production budget.

A *manufacturing budget* shows the budgeted costs for raw materials, direct labor, and manufacturing overhead. In many manufacturing companies, the manufacturing budget is actually prepared in the form of three subbudgets: a raw materials purchases budget, a direct labor budget, and a manufacturing overhead budget. These budgets show the total budgeted cost of goods to be manufactured during the budget period.

Selling Expense Budget

The responsibility for preparing a budget of selling expenses typically falls on the vice president of marketing or the equivalent sales manager. Although budgeted selling expenses should affect the expected amount of sales, the typical procedure is to prepare a sales budget first and then to budget selling expenses. Estimates of selling expenses are based on the tentative sales budget and upon the experience of previous periods adjusted for known changes. After the entire master budget is prepared on a tentative basis, it may be decided that the projected sales volume is inadequate. If so, subsequent adjustments in the sales budget would generally require that corresponding adjustments be made in the selling expense budget.

Northern Company's selling expenses consist of commissions paid to sales personnel and a $24,000 per year salary, paid on a monthly basis to the sales manager. Sales commissions amount to 10% of total sales and are paid during the month the sales are made. The selling expense budget for Northern Company is presented in Illustration 25–5.

General and Administrative Expenses

General and administrative expenses usually are the responsibility of the office manager, who should therefore be charged with the task

Illustration 25–5

NORTHERN COMPANY
Selling Expense Budget
October, November, and December 198A

	October	November	December	Total
Budgeted sales	$100,000	$80,000	$140,000	$320,000
Sales commission percentage	×10%	×10%	×10%	×10%
Sales commissions	$ 10,000	$ 8,000	$ 14,000	$ 32,000
Salary for sales manager ($24,000/12 = $2,000 per month)	2,000	2,000	2,000	6,000
Total selling expenses	$ 12,000	$10,000	$ 16,000	$ 38,000

Illustration 25–6

NORTHERN COMPANY
General and Administrative Expense Budget
October, November, and December 198A

	October	November	December	Total
Administrative salaries				
($54,000/12 = $4,500)	$4,500	$4,500	$4,500	$13,500
Depreciation of equipment				
($18,000/12 = $1,500)	1,500	1,500	1,500	4,500
	$6,000	$6,000	$6,000	$18,000

of preparing the budget for these items. The amounts of some general and administrative expenses may depend upon budgeted sales volume. However, most of these expenses depend more upon other factors such as management policies, inflationary influences, and so forth, than they do upon monthly fluctuations in sales volume. Although interest expense and income tax expense are frequently classified as general and administrative expenses, they generally cannot be budgeted at this point in the budgeting sequence. Interest expense must await preparation of the cash budget, which determines the need for loans, if any. Income tax expense must await preparation of the budgeted income statement, at which time taxable income and income tax expense can be estimated.

General and administrative expenses for Northern Company include administrative salaries amounting to $54,000 per year and depreciation of $18,000 per year on equipment (see Illustration 25–2). The salaries are paid each month as they are earned. Illustration 25–6 shows the budget for these expenses.

Capital Expenditures Budget

The capital expenditures or plant and equipment budget lists equipment to be scrapped and additional equipment to be purchased if the proposed production program is carried out. The purchase of additional equipment requires funds; and anticipating equipment additions in advance normally makes it easier to provide the funds. Also, at times, estimated production may exceed plant capacity. Budgeting makes it possible to anticipate this and either revise the production schedule or increase plant capacity. Planning plant and equipment purchases is called capital budgeting, and this is discussed in more detail in Chapter 27.

Northern Company does not anticipate any sales or retirements of equipment through December 198A. However, management plans to acquire additional equipment for $25,000 cash near the end of December 198A.

Cash Budget

After tentative sales, merchandise purchases, expenses, and capital expenditures budgets have been developed, the *cash budget* is prepared. This budget is especially important; a company should have at all times enough cash to meet needs, but it should not hold too much cash. Too much cash is undesirable because it often cannot be profitably invested. A cash budget requires management to forecast cash receipts and disbursements, and usually results in better cash management. Also, it enables management to arrange well in advance for loans to cover any anticipated cash shortages.

In preparing the cash budget, anticipated receipts are added to the beginning cash balance and anticipated expenditures are deducted. If the resulting cash balance is inadequate, the required additional cash is provided in the budget through planned increases in loans.

Much of the information that is needed to prepare the cash budget can be obtained directly from the previously prepared operating and capital expenditures budgets. However, further investigation and additional calculations may be necessary to determine the amounts to be included.

Illustration 25–7 shows the cash budget for Northern Company. October's beginning cash balance was obtained from the September 30, 198A, balance sheet (Illustration 25–2).

Budgeted sales of Northern Company are shown in Illustration 25–3. An investigation of previous sales records indicates that 40% of Northern Company's sales are for cash. The remaining 60% are credit sales, and customers can be expected to pay for these sales in the month after the sales are made. Thus, the budgeted cash receipts from customers are calculated as follows:

	September	October	November	December
Sales	$70,000	$100,000	$80,000	$140,000
Credit sales percentage	×60%	×60%	×60%	×60%
Accounts receivable, end of month	$42,000	$ 60,000	$48,000	$ 84,000
Cash sales percentage		×40%	×40%	×40%
Cash sales		$ 40,000	$32,000	$ 56,000
Collections of accounts receivable		42,000	60,000	48,000
Total cash receipts		$ 82,000	$92,000	$104,000

Illustration 25–7

NORTHERN COMPANY
Cash Budget
October, November, and December 198A

	October	November	December
Beginning cash balance	$ 20,000	$ 20,000	$ 22,272
Cash receipts from customers	82,000	92,000	104,000
Totals	$102,000	$112,000	$126,272
Cash disbursements:			
Payments for merchandise	$ 58,200	$ 49,200	$ 80,400
Sales commissions (Illustration 25–5)	10,000	8,000	14,000
Salaries: Sales (Illustration 25–5)	2,000	2,000	2,000
Administrative (Illustration 25–6)	4,500	4,500	4,500
Accrued income taxes payable	20,000		
Dividends ($150,000 × 0.02 = $3,000)		3,000	
Interest on loan from bank:			
$10,000 × 0.01 = $100	100		
$22,800 × 0.01 = $228		228	
Purchase of equipment			25,000
Total cash disbursements	$ 94,800	$ 66,928	$125,900
Balance	$ 7,200	$ 45,072	$ 372
Additional loan from bank	12,800		19,628
Repayment of loan from bank		(22,800)	
Ending cash balance	$ 20,000	$ 22,272	$ 20,000
Loan balance, end of month	$ 22,800	$ -0-	$ 19,628

Observe in the calculation that the October cash receipts consist of $40,000 from cash sales ($100,000 × 40%) plus the collection of $42,000 of accounts receivable as calculated in the previous column. Also, note that each month's total cash receipts are listed on the second line of Illustration 25–7.

Northern Company's purchases of merchandise are entirely on account, and full payments are made regularly in the month following purchase. Thus, in Illustration 25–7, the cash disbursements for purchases are obtained from the September 30, 198A, balance sheet (Illustration 25–2), and from the merchandise purchases budget (Illustration 25–4), as follows:

September 30, accounts payable equal October payments	$58,200
October purchases equal November payments	49,200
November purchases equal December payments	80,400

Sales commissions and all salaries are paid monthly, and the budgeted cash disbursements for these items are obtained from the selling expense budget (Illustration 25–5) and the general and administrative expense budget (Illustration 25–6).

As indicated in the September 30, 198A, balance sheet (Illustration 25–2), accrued income taxes are paid in October. Estimated income tax expense for the quarter ending December 31 is 40% of net income and is due in January 198B.

Northern Company pays 2% quarterly cash dividends, and the November payment of $3,000 is the planned disbursement for this item. Also, Northern Company has an agreement with the bank whereby additional loans are granted at the end of each month if they are necessary to maintain a minimum cash balance of $20,000 at the end of the month. Interest is paid at the end of each month at the rate of 1% per month; and if the cash balance at the end of a month exceeds $20,000, the excess is used to repay the loans to the bank. Illustration 25–7 indicates that the $10,000 loan from the bank at the end of September was not sufficient to provide a $20,000 cash balance at the end of October, and as a result, the loan was increased by $12,800 at the end of October. The entire loan was repaid at the end of November, and $19,628 was again borrowed at the end of December.

Budgeted Income Statement

One of the final steps in preparing a master budget is to summarize the effects of the various budgetary plans on the income statement. The necessary information to prepare a budgeted income statement is drawn primarily from the previously prepared budgets or from the investigations that were made in the process of preparing those budgets.

For many companies, the volume of information that must be summarized in the budgeted income statement and the budgeted balance sheet is so large that a work sheet must be used to accumulate all of the budgeted transactions and to classify them in terms of their impact on the income statement and/or on the balance sheet. However, the transactions and account balances of Northern Company are few in number, and the budgeted income statement (and balance sheet) can be prepared simply by inspecting the previously discussed budgets and recalling the information that was provided in the related discussions. Northern Company's budgeted income statement is shown in Illustration 25–8.

Budgeted Balance Sheet

If a work sheet is used to prepare the budgeted income statement and balance sheet, the first two columns of the work sheet are used

Illustration 25–8

NORTHERN COMPANY
Budgeted Income Statement for Three Months Ended December 31, 198A

Sales (Illustration 25–3, 32,000 units @ $10)		$320,000
Cost of goods sold (32,000 units @ $6)		192,000
Gross profit		$128,000
Operating expenses:		
Sales commissions (Illustration 25–5)	$32,000	
Sales salaries (Illustration 25–5)	6,000	
Administrative salaries (Illustration 25–6)	13,500	
Depreciation on equipment (Illustration 25–6)	4,500	
Interest expense (Illustration 25–7)	328	(56,328)
Net income before income taxes		$ 71,672
Income tax expense ($71,672 × 40%)		(28,669)
Net income		$ 43,003

to list the estimated post-closing trial balance of the period prior to the budget period. Next, the budgeted transactions and adjustments are entered in the second pair of work sheet columns in the same manner as end-of-period adjustments are entered on an ordinary work sheet. For example, if the budget calls for sales on account of $250,000, the name of the Sales account is entered on the work sheet in the

Illustration 25–9

NORTHERN COMPANY
Budgeted Balance Sheet, December 31, 198A

Assets

Cash (Illustration 25–7)		$ 20,000
Accounts receivable (page 876)		84,000
Inventory (Illustration 25–4, 8,100 units @ $6)		48,600
Equipment (Illustrations 25–2 and 25–7)	$225,000	
Less accumulated depreciation (Illustrations		
25–2 and 25–6)	40,500	184,500
Total assets		$337,100

Liabilities and Stockholders' Equity

Liabilities:		
Accounts payable (Illustration 25–4)	$ 57,000	
Accrued income taxes payable (Illustration 25–8)	28,669	
Bank loan payable (Illustration 25–7)	19,628	$105,297
Stockholders' equity:		
Common stock (Illustration 25–2)	$150,000	
Retained earnings (see discussion)	81,803	231,803
Total liabilities and stockholders' equity		$337,100

Account Titles column below the names of the post-closing trial balance accounts; and then Sales is credited and Accounts Receivable is debited for $250,000 in the second pair of money columns. After all budgeted transactions and adjustments are entered on the work sheet, the estimated post-closing trial balance amounts in the first pair of money columns are combined with the budget amounts in the second pair of columns and are sorted to the proper Income Statement and Balance Sheet columns of the work sheet. Finally, the information in these columns is used to prepare the budgeted income statement and budgeted balance sheet.

As previously mentioned, the transactions and account balances of Northern Company are few in number, and its budgeted balance sheet, shown in Illustration 25–9 (on the previous page), can be prepared simply by inspecting the previously prepared budgets and recalling the related discussions of those budgets.

Observe that the retained earnings balance in Illustration 25–9 is $81,803. This amount was determined as follows:

Retained earnings, September 30, 198A (Illustration 25–2)	$41,800
Net income for three months ended December 31, 198A (Illustration 25–8)	43,003
Total	$84,803
Dividends declared in November, 198A (Illustration 25–7)	(3,000)
Retained earnings, December 31, 198A	$81,803

GLOSSARY

Budget. A formal statement of future plans, usually expressed in monetary terms.

Budgeting. The process of planning future business actions and expressing those plans in a formal manner.

Capital expenditures budget. A listing of the plant and equipment to be purchased if the proposed production program is carried out. Also called the plant and equipment budget.

Cash budget. A forecast of cash receipts and disbursements.

Manufacturing budget. A statement of the estimated costs for raw materials, direct labor, and manufacturing overhead associated with producing the number of units estimated in the production budget.

Master budget. A comprehensive or overall plan for the business that typically includes budgets for sales, expenses, production, equipment, cash, and also a planned income statement and balance sheet.

Merchandise purchases budget. An estimate of the units (or cost) of merchandise to be purchased by a merchandising company.

Production budget. An estimate of the number of units to be produced during a budget period.

Rolling budgets. A sequence of revised budgets that are prepared in the practice of continuous budgeting.

Sales budget. An estimate of goods to be sold and revenue to be derived from sales; serves as the usual starting point in the budgeting procedure.

QUESTIONS FOR CLASS DISCUSSION

1. What is a budget? What is a master budget?
2. What are the benefits from budgeting?
3. How does the process of budgeting tend to promote good decision making?
4. What are the two alternative norms or objectives against which actual performance is sometimes compared and evaluated? Which of the two is generally superior?
5. Why should each department be asked to prepare or at least to participate in the preparation of its own budget estimates?
6. What are the duties of the budget committee?
7. What is the normal length of a master budget period? How far in advance are long-range budgets generally prepared?
8. What is meant by the terms *continuous* budgeting and *rolling* budgets?
9. What are the three primary types of budgets that make up the master budget?
10. In comparing merchandising companies and manufacturing companies, what differences show up in the operating budgets?
11. What is the sequence that is followed in preparing the set of budgets that collectively make up the master budget?
12. What is a sales budget? A selling expense budget? A capital expenditures budget?
13. What is the difference between a production budget and a manufacturing budget?
14. What is a cash budget? Why must it be prepared after the operating budgets and the capital expenditures budget?

CLASS EXERCISES

Exercise 25–1   The sales budget of Alpha Store's camera department calls for $9,500 sales during March. The department expects to begin March with a $4,600 inventory and end the month with a $5,200 inventory. Its cost of goods sold averages 65% of sales.

Required:

Prepare a merchandise purchases budget for the camera department showing the amount of goods to be purchased during March.

Exercise 25–2   Tacket Company manufactures a product called Altex. The company's management estimates there will be 6,600 units of Altex in the March 31 finished goods inventory, that 14,700 units will be sold during the year's second quarter, that 17,500 units will be sold during the third quarter, and that 19,200 units will be sold during the fourth quarter. Management also believes the company should begin each quarter with units in the finished goods inventory equal to 30% of the next quarter's budgeted sales.

Required:

Prepare a production budget showing the units of Altex to be manufactured during the year's second quarter and third quarter.

Exercise 25–3   A company has budgeted the following cash receipts and cash disbursements from operations during the second quarter of 198A:

	Receipts	Disbursements
April	$225,000	$190,000
May	110,000	230,850
June	195,000	145,000

According to a credit agreement with the bank, the company promises to maintain a minimum, end-of-month cash balance of $25,000. In return, the bank has agreed to provide the company the right to receive loans up to $150,000 with interest of 12% per year, paid monthly on the last day of the month. If the loan must be increased during the last 10 days of a month to provide enough cash to pay bills, interest will not begin to be charged until the end of the month.

The company is expected to have a cash balance of $25,000 and a loan balance of $15,000 on March 31, 198A.

Required:

Prepare a monthly cash budget for the second quarter of 198A.

Exercise 25–4   Using the following information, prepare a cash budget showing expected cash receipts and disbursements for the month of June and the balance expected on June 30, 198A.

a. Beginning cash balance on June 1: $42,000.
b. Budgeted sales for June: $280,000; 40% are collected in the month of sale, 50% in the next month, 5% in the following month, and 5% are uncollectible.
c. Sales for May: $320,000.
d. Sales for April: $240,000.
e. Budgeted merchandise purchases for June: $180,000; 50% are paid in month of purchase; 50% are paid in the month following purchase.
f. Merchandise purchased in May: $120,000.
g. Budgeted cash disbursements for salaries in June: $80,000.

h. Depreciation expense in June: $4,000.
i. Other cash expenses budgeted for June: $20,000.
j. Budgeted taxes payable in June: $45,000.
k. Budgeted interest payable on bank loan in June: $3,000.

Exercise 25–5

Based on the information provided in Exercise 25–4 and the additional information that follows, prepare a budgeted income statement for the month of June and a budgeted balance sheet for June 30, 198A.

a. Cost of goods sold is 50% of sales.
b. The inventory at the end of May was $54,000.
c. Salaries payable on May 31 was $14,000 and is expected to be $8,000 on June 30.
d. The Equipment account shows a balance of $410,000. On May 31, Accumulated Depreciation had a balance of $105,000.
e. The $3,000 cash payment of interest represents the 1% monthly expense on a bank loan of $300,000.
f. Income taxes payable on May 31 amounted to $45,000, and the income tax rate applicable to the company is 40%.
g. The 5% of sales that prove to be uncollectible are debited to Bad Debts Expense and credited to Allowance for Doubtful Accounts during the month of sale. However, specific accounts that prove to be uncollectible are not written off until the second month after the sale, at which time all accounts not yet collected are so written off.
h. The only balance sheet accounts other than those implied by the previous discussion are Common Stock, which shows a balance of $100,000, and Retained Earnings, which showed a balance of $70,000 on May 31.

PROBLEMS

Problem 25–1

Tool Manufacturing Company manufactures a steel product called a Gripper. Each Gripper requires 10 pounds of steel and is produced in a single operation by a stamping process. The company's management estimates there will be 1,400 units of the product and 7 tons of steel on hand on March 31 of the current year, and that 11,000 units of the product will be sold during the year's second quarter. Management also believes that due to the possibility of a strike in the steel industry, the company should begin the third quarter with a 20-ton steel inventory and 2,000 finished Grippers. Steel can be purchased for approximately $480 per ton ($0.24 per pound).

Required:

Prepare a second-quarter production budget and a second-quarter steel purchases budget for the company.

Problem 25–2

During the latter part of February, the owner of New Springs Store approached the bank for a $16,000 loan to be made on April 1 and repaid 60 days thereafter with interest at 15%. The owner planned to increase the store's inventory by $16,000 during March and needed the loan to pay for the merchandise during April. The bank's loan officer was interested in New Springs Store's ability to repay the loan and asked the owner to forecast the store's May 31 cash position.

On March 1, New Springs Store was expected to have a $6,000 cash balance, $34,000 of accounts receivable, and $21,000 of accounts payable. Its budgeted sales, purchases, and cash expenditures for the following three months are as follows:

	March	April	May
Sales.....................	$30,000	$33,000	$29,000
Merchandise purchases	34,600	18,000	17,000
Payroll	3,000	3,000	3,000
Rent	1,000	1,000	1,000
Other cash expenses	1,600	1,800	1,900
Repayment of bank loan.....			16,400

The budgeted March purchases include the inventory increase. All sales are on account; and past experience indicates 80% is collected in the month following the sale, 15% in the next month, 4% in the next, and the remainder is not collected. Application of this experience to the March 1 accounts receivable balance indicates $27,200 of the $34,000 will be collected during March, $5,100 during April, and $1,360 during May. All merchandise is paid for in the month following its purchase.

Required:

Prepare cash budgets for March, April, and May 198A for New Springs Store under the assumption the bank loan will be paid on May 31.

Problem 25–3   Shafer Company has a cash balance of $36,000 on June 1, 198A. The product sold by the company sells for $30 per unit. Actual and projected sales are:

April, actual	$240,000
May, actual	180,000
June, estimated	300,000
July, estimated	240,000
August, estimated.....	216,000

Experience has shown that 50% of the billings are collected in the month of sale, 30% in the second month, 15% in the third month, and 5% will prove to be uncollectible.

All purchases are payable within 15 days. Thus, approximately 50% of the purchases in a month are due and payable in the next month. The unit purchase cost is $22. Shafer Company's management had established a policy of maintaining an end-of-month inventory of 100 units plus 50% of the next month's unit sales, and the June 1 inventory is consistent with this policy.

Selling and general administrative expenses (excluding depreciation) for the year amount to $540,000 and are distributed evenly throughout the year.

Required:

Prepare a monthly cash budget for June and July, with supporting schedules showing cash receipts from collections of receivables and cash payments for merchandise purchases.

Problem 25–4

James Company buys merchandise at $5.80 per unit and sells it at $10 per unit. Sales personnel are paid a commission of 10% of sales. The September 198A income statement of James Company is as follows:

JAMES COMPANY
Income Statement for September 198A

Sales	$100,000
Cost of goods sold	58,000
Gross profit	$ 42,000
Expenses:	
Sales commissions	$ 10,000
Advertising	6,000
Store rent	2,000
Administrative salaries	4,000
Depreciation expense	1,000
Other expenses	3,000
Total	$ 26,000
Net income	$ 16,000

The management of James Company expects the September results to be repeated during October, November, and December. However, certain changes are being considered. Management believes that if selling price is reduced to $9 and advertising expenses are increased by 50%, unit sales will increase at a rate of 10% each month during the last quarter of 198A. If these changes are made, merchandise will still be purchased at $5.80 per unit. Sales personnel will continue to earn a commission of 10%, and the remaining expenses will remain constant.

Required:

Prepare a budgeted income statement that shows in three columns the planned results of operations for October, November, and December 198A, assuming the changes are implemented. Based on the budgeted income statements, decide whether management should make the changes.

Problem 25–5

During March 198A, the management of Flyer Corporation prepared a budgeted balance sheet for March 31, 198A, which is presented below.

FLYER CORPORATION
Budgeted Balance Sheet for March 31, 198A

Cash	$ 12,500	Accounts payable	$ 20,000
Accounts receivable	37,500	Loan from bank	12,500
Inventory	62,500	Taxes payable (due	
Equipment	150,000	June 15, 198A)	30,000
Accumulated		Common stock	125,000
depreciation	(15,000)	Retained earnings	60,000
Total	$247,500	Total	$247,500

In the process of preparing a master budget for April, May, and June 198A, the following information has been obtained:

a. The product sold by Flyer Corporation is purchased for $10 per unit and resold for $15 per unit. Although the inventory level on March 31 (6,250 units) is smaller than desired, management has established a new inventory policy whereby the end-of-month inventory should be 80% of the next month's expected sales (in units). Budgeted unit sales are: April, 25,000; May, 22,500; June, 30,000; and July, 30,000.

b. Total sales each month are 50% for cash and 50% on account. Of the credit sales, 80% are collected in the first month after the sale and 20% in the second month after the sale. Similarly, 80% of the Accounts Receivable balance on March 31 should be collected during April and 20% should be collected in May.

c. Merchandise purchased by the company is paid for as follows: 70% in the month after purchase and 30% in the second month after purchase. Similarly, 70% of the Accounts Payable balance on March 31 will be paid during April and 30% will be paid during May.

d. Sales commissions amounting to 10% of sales are paid each month. Additionally, the salary of the sales managers is $30,000 per year.

e. Repair expenses amount to $1,250 per month and are paid in cash. General administrative salaries amount to $270,000 per year.

f. The equipment shown in the March 31, 198A, balance sheet was purchased one year ago. It is being depreciated over 10 years according to the straight-line method. Regarding new purchases of equipment, management has decided to take a full month's depreciation (rounded to the nearest dollar) during the month the equipment is purchased, and to use straight-line depreciation over 10 years, assuming no salvage value. The company plans to purchase additional equipment worth $27,000 in April, $15,000 in May, and $36,000 in June.

g. The company plans to acquire some land in June at a cost of $250,000. The land will not require a cash outlay until the last day of June. Thus, if a bank loan is necessary, the first payment of interest will be due at the end of July.

h. Flyer Corporation has an arrangement with the bank whereby additional loans are available as they are needed at a rate of 12% per year, paid monthly. If part or all of a loan is repaid during a month, the payment will be made on the last day of the month, along with any interest that is due. Flyer Corporation has agreed to maintain an end-of-month cash balance of at least $12,500.

i. The income tax rate applicable to the company is 40%. However, tax on the income for the second quarter of 198A will not be paid until July.

Required:

Prepare a master budget for the second quarter of 198A, with the operating budgets, capital expenditures budget, and the cash budget prepared on a monthly basis. The budgeted income statement should show operations for the second quarter, and the budgeted balance sheet should be prepared as of June 30, 198A. The operating budgets included in the master budget should include a sales budget (showing both budgeted unit sales and dollar sales), a merchandise purchases budget, a selling expense budget, and a general and administrative expense budget. Round all amounts to the nearest dollar.

ALTERNATE PROBLEMS

Problem 25–1A

Thompson Corporation sells three products that it purchases in their finished ready-for-sale state. The company's April 1 inventories are Product X, 7,800 units; Product Y, 7,500 units; and Product Z, 12,600 units. The company's management is disturbed because each product's April 1 inventory is excessive in relation to immediately expected sales. Consequently, management has set as a goal a month-end inventory for each product that is equal to one half the following month's expected sales. Expected sales in units for April, May, June, and July are as follows:

	Expected sales in units			
	April	May	June	July
Product X.....	10,000	9,200	10,000	7,600
Product Y.....	5,600	5,600	6,800	7,200
Product Z.....	12,000	10,800	10,400	11,600

Required:

Prepare purchases budgets in units for the three products for each of April, May, and June 198A.

Problem 25–2A

Beach Company expects to have a $5,800 cash balance on December 31, 198A. It also expects to have a $35,200 balance of accounts receivable and $20,900 of accounts payable. Its budgeted sales, purchases, and cash expenditures for the first three months of 198B are:

	January	February	March
Sales	$24,000	$18,000	$27,000
Purchases	14,000	17,300	18,000
Payroll	2,400	2,400	2,800
Rent...........................	1,000	1,000	1,000
Other cash expenses	1,200	1,600	1,400
Purchase of store equipment	—	5,000	—
Payment of quarterly dividend.....	—	—	4,000

All sales are on account; and past experience indicates that 85% will be collected in the month following the sale, 10% in the next month, and 4% in the third month. Notwithstanding these expectations for future sales, an analysis of the December 31 accounts receivable balance indicates that $28,000 of the $35,200 balance will be collected in January, $5,200 in February, and $1,600 in March.

Purchases of merchandise on account are paid in the month following each purchase; likewise, the store equipment will be paid for in the month following its purchase.

Required:

Prepare cash budgets for the months of January, February, and March 198B.

Problem 25–3A

The actual and projected monthly sales of Wimp Company are as follows:

September 198A, actual $240,000
October 198A, actual 160,000
November 198A, estimated 190,000
December 198A, estimated 230,000
January 198B, estimated 210,000

Experience has shown that 40% of the sales are collected in the month of sale, 40% are collected in the first month after the sale, 18% in the second month after the sale, and 2% prove to be uncollectible.

Merchandise purchased by the Wimp Company is paid for 10 days after the date of purchase. Thus, approximately one third of the purchases in a month are due and paid for in the next month. Wimp Company pays $25 per unit of merchandise and subsequently sells the merchandise for $50 per unit. Wimp Company always plans to maintain an end-of-month inventory of 250 units plus 60% of the next month's unit sales, and the October 31, 198A, inventory is consistent with this policy.

In addition to cost of goods sold, Wimp Company incurs other operating expenses (excluding depreciation) of $582,000 per year, and they are distributed evenly throughout the year. On October 31, 198A, the company has a cash balance of $40,000.

Required:

Prepare a monthly cash budget for November and December, with supporting schedules showing cash receipts from collections of receivables and cash payments for merchandise purchases. Round all amounts to the nearest dollar.

Problem 25–4A   Crutchfield Company buys merchandise at $14 per unit and sells it at $25 per unit. Sales personnel are paid a commission of 10% of sales. The June 198A income statement of Crutchfield Company is as follows:

CRUTCHFIELD COMPANY
Income Statement for June 198A

Sales	$225,000
Cost of goods sold	126,000
Gross profit	$ 99,000
Expenses:	
Sales commissions	$ 22,500
Advertising	16,000
Store rent	5,000
Administrative salaries	6,000
Depreciation expense	3,000
Other expenses	7,500
Total	$ 60,000
Net income	$ 39,000

The management of Crutchfield Company expects the June results to be repeated during July, August, and September. However, certain changes are being considered. Management believes that if selling price is reduced to $22 and advertising expenses are increased by 40%, unit sales will increase at a rate of 10% each month during the third quarter of 198A. If these changes are made, merchandise will still be purchased at $14 per unit. Sales personnel will continue to earn a commission of 10%, and the remaining expenses will remain constant.

Required:

Prepare a budgeted income statement that shows in three columns the planned results of operations for July, August, and September 198A, assuming the changes are implemented. Based on the budgeted income statements, decide whether management should make the changes.

Problem 25–5A

Shortly before the end of 198A, Dot Company's management prepared a budgeted balance sheet for December 31, 198A, as follows:

DOT COMPANY
Balance Sheet for December 31, 198A

Cash	$ 5,000	Accounts payable		$ 8,000
Accounts receivable	15,000	Loan from bank		5,000
Inventory	25,000	Taxes payable (due March		
Equipment	60,000	15, 198B)		12,000
Accumulated depreciation	(6,000)	Common stock		50,000
		Retained earnings		24,000
Total	$99,000	Total		$99,000

In the process of preparing a master budget for January, February, and March 198B, the following information has been obtained:

a. The product sold by Dot Company is purchased for $10 per unit and resold for $15 per unit. Although the inventory level on December 31, 198A (2,500 units), is smaller than desired, management has established a new inventory policy for 198B whereby the end-of-month inventory should be 80% of the next month's expected sales (in units). Budgeted unit sales are: January, 10,000; February, 9,000; March, 12,000; April, 12,000.

b. Total sales each month are 50% for cash and 50% on account. Of the credit sales, 80% are collected in the first month after the sale and 20% in the second month after the sale. Similarly, 80% of the Accounts Receivable balance on December 31, 198A, should be collected during January and 20% should be collected in February.

c. Merchandise purchased by the company is paid for as follows: 70% in the month after purchase and 30% in the second month after purchase. Similarly, 70% of the Accounts Payable balance on December 31, 198A, will be paid during January and 30% will be paid during February.

d. Sales commissions amounting to 10% of sales are paid each month. Additionally, the salary of the sales manager is $12,000 per year.

e. Repair expenses amount to $500 per month and are paid in cash. General administrative salaries amount to $108,000 per year.

f. The equipment shown in the December 31, 198A, balance sheet was purchased one year ago. It is being depreciated over 10 years according to the straight-line method. Regarding new purchases of equipment, management has decided to take a full month's depreciation (rounded to the nearest dollar) during the month the equipment is purchased, and to use straight-line depreciation over 10 years, assuming no salvage value. The company plans to purchase additional equipment worth $10,000 in January, $5,000 in February, and $15,000 in March.

g. The company plans to acquire some land in March at a cost of $100,000. The land will not require a cash outlay until the last day of March. Thus, if a bank loan is necessary, the first payment of interest will be due at the end of April.

h. Dot Company has an arrangement with the bank whereby additional loans are available as they are needed at a rate of 10% per year, paid monthly. If part or all of a loan is repaid during a month, the payment will be made on the last day of the month, along with any interest that is due. Dot Company has agreed to maintain an end-of-month cash balance of at least $5,000.

i. The income tax rate applicable to the company is 40%. However, tax on the income for the first quarter of 198B will not be paid until April.

Required:

Prepare a master budget for the first quarter of 198B, with the operating budgets, capital expenditures budget, and the cash budget prepared on a monthly basis. The budgeted income statement should show operations for the first quarter, and the budgeted balance sheet should be prepared as of March 31, 198B. The operating budgets included in the master budget should include a sales budget (showing both budgeted unit sales and dollar sales), a merchandise purchases budget, a selling expense budget, and a general and administrative expense budget. Round all amounts to the nearest dollar.

PROVOCATIVE PROBLEMS

Provocative
Problem 25–1,
Contek
Company

Contek Company produces a Product X that requires six pounds of soluform per unit of X. The owner of Contek Company is in the process of negotiating with the bank for the approval to make loans as they are needed by the company. One of the important items in their discussion has been the question of how much cash will be needed to pay for purchases of soluform. Contek Company purchases soluform on account, and the resulting payables are paid in cash as follows: 60% during the month after purchase and 40% during the second month after purchase. The company plans to manufacture enough units of X to maintain an end-of-month inventory of finished units equal to 70% of the next month's sales, and enough soluform is purchased each month to maintain an end-of-month inventory equal to 50% of the next month's production requirements. Budgeted sales (in units) are as follows: February, 4,000; March, 6,000; April, 7,000; and May, 8,000. On January 31, 198A, the following data are available: finished units of Product X on hand, 2,800; pounds of soluform on hand, 16,200; Accounts Payable, $140,000 due in February plus $60,000 due in March.

In recent months, the price of soluform has varied substantially, and the owner estimates that during the next few months the price could range from $10 to $15 per pound. You are asked to assist the owner by estimating the cash payments to be made in February, in March, and in April. In preparing your answer, you should prepare separate estimates based on a $10 price and a $15 price.

The Lonestar Corporation has budgeted the following monthly sales volumes: April, 20,000 units; May, 12,000 units; June, 18,000 units; and July, 30,000 units. The company policy is to maintain an end-of-month finished goods inventory equal to 4,000 units plus 25% of the next month's budgeted sales in units. Consistent with this policy, the April 1 inventory was 9,000 units.

An analysis of Lonestar Corporation's manufacturing costs show the following:

Material cost per unit $6.10
Direct labor cost per unit $4.50
Fixed manufacturing overhead costs .... $18,000 per month
Variable manufacturing overhead costs ..... $2.20 per unit manufactured

Required:

Prepare production budgets and manufacturing budgets for the months of April, May, and June.

Flexible Budgets; Standard Costs

After studying Chapter 26, you should be able to:

State the deficiencies of fixed budgets.

Prepare flexible budgets and state their advantages.

State what standard costs represent, how they are determined, and how they are used in the evaluation process.

Calculate material, labor, and overhead variances, and state what each variance indicates about the performance of a company.

Explain the relevance of standard cost accounting to the management philosophy known as *management by exception.*

Define or explain the words and phrases listed in the chapter Glossary.

The development of a master plan for a business was discussed in Chapter 25; consideration was also given to the importance of controlling subsequent operations. This function of control was recognized as one of the two basic functions of management. In order to control business operations, management must obtain information or feedback regarding how closely actual operations conform to the plans. To the extent possible, the comparison of actual performance with planned performance should direct management's attention toward the reasons why actual performance differs from planned performance. Flexible budgets and standard costs are important techniques that are used to help management determine why actual performance differs from the plan.

FIXED BUDGETS AND PERFORMANCE REPORTS

In preparing a master budget as discussed in Chapter 25, the initial step is to determine the expected sales volume for the budget period. All of the subsequent budget procedures are based on this specific estimate of sales volume. The amount of each budgeted cost is based on the assumption that a specific or fixed amount of sales will take place. When a budget is based on a single estimate of sales or production volume, the budget is called a *fixed* or *static budget*. In budgeting the total amount of each cost, a fixed budget gives no consideration to the possibility that the actual sales or production volume may be different from the fixed or budgeted amount.

If a company uses only fixed budgets, the comparison of actual performance with the budgeted performance is presented in a performance report such as that shown in Illustration 26–1.

The budgeted sales volume of Tampa Manufacturing Company is 10,000 units (see Illustration 26–1). Also, to simplify the discussion, production volume is assumed to equal sales volume; and no beginning or ending inventory is maintained by the company. In evaluating Tampa Manufacturing Company's operations, management should be interested in answering such questions as: Why is the actual income from operations $13,400 higher than the budgeted amount? Are the prices being paid for each expense item too high? Is the manufacturing department using too much raw material? Is it using too much direct labor? The performance report shown in Illustration 26–1 provides little help in answering questions such as these. Since the actual sales volume was 2,000 units higher than the budgeted amount, it may be assumed that this increase caused total dollar sales and many of the expenses to be higher. But other factors may have influenced the amount of income, and the fixed budget performance report fails to provide management much information beyond the fact that the sales volume was higher than budgeted.

Illustration 26–1

> **TAMPA MANUFACTURING COMPANY**
> Fixed Budget Performance Report
> For Month Ended November 30, 198A
>
> | | Fixed budget | Actual performance | Variances |
> |---|---|---|---|
> | Sales: In units .... | 10,000 | 12,000 | |
> | In dollars .... | $100,000 | $125,000 | $25,000 F |
> | Cost of goods sold: | | | |
> | Raw materials .... | $ 10,000 | $ 13,000 | $ 3,000 U |
> | Direct labor .... | 15,000 | 20,000 | 5,000 U |
> | Overhead: | | | |
> | Factory supplies .... | 2,000 | 2,100 | 100 U |
> | Utilities .... | 3,000 | 4,000 | 1,000 U |
> | Depreciation of machinery .... | 8,000 | 8,000 | — |
> | Supervisory salaries .... | 11,000 | 11,000 | — |
> | Selling expenses: | | | |
> | Sales commissions .... | 9,000 | 10,800 | 1,800 U |
> | Shipping expenses .... | 4,000 | 4,300 | 300 U |
> | General and administrative expenses: | | | |
> | Office supplies .... | 5,000 | 5,200 | 200 U |
> | Insurance expense .... | 1,000 | 1,200 | 200 U |
> | Depreciation of office equipment .... | 7,000 | 7,000 | — |
> | Administrative salaries .... | 13,000 | 13,000 | — |
> | Total expenses .... | $ 88,000 | $ 99,600 | $11,600 U |
> | Income from operations .... | $ 12,000 | $ 25,400 | $13,400 F |
>
> F = Favorable variance; that is, compared to the budget, the actual cost or revenue
>   contributes to a higher income.
> U = Unfavorable variance; that is, compared to the budget, the actual cost or revenue
>   contributes to a lower income.

FLEXIBLE BUDGETS

To help answer questions such as those mentioned above, many companies prepare *flexible* or *variable budgets.* In contrast to fixed budgets, which are based on one fixed amount of budgeted sales or production, flexible budgets recognize that different levels of activity should produce different amounts of cost.

PREPARING A FLEXIBLE BUDGET

To prepare a flexible budget, each type of cost is examined to determine whether it should be classified as a variable cost or as a fixed cost. Recall from Chapter 24 that the total amount of a variable cost changes in direct proportion to a change in the level of activity. Thus, variable cost per unit of activity remains constant. On the other hand,

Illustration 26–2

TAMPA MANUFACTURING COMPANY
Flexible Budget
For Month Ended November 30, 198A

	Fixed budget	Variable cost per unit	Total fixed cost	Flexible budget for unit sales of 12,000	Flexible budget for unit sales of 14,000
Sales: In units	10,000			12,000	14,000
In dollars	$100,000	$10.00		$120,000	$140,000
Variable costs:					
Raw materials	$ 10,000	$ 1.00		$ 12,000	$ 14,000
Direct labor	15,000	1.50		18,000	21,000
Factory supplies	2,000	0.20		2,400	2,800
Utilities	3,000	0.30		3,600	4,200
Sales commissions	9,000	0.90		10,800	12,600
Shipping expenses	4,000	0.40		4,800	5,600
Office supplies	5,000	0.50		6,000	7,000
Total variable costs	$ 48,000	$ 4.80		$ 57,600	$ 67,200
Contribution margin	$ 52,000	$ 5.20		$ 62,400	$ 72,800
Fixed costs:					
Depreciation of machinery ..	$ 8,000		$ 8,000	$ 8,000	$ 8,000
Supervisory salaries	11,000		11,000	11,000	11,000
Insurance expense	1,000		1,000	1,000	1,000
Depreciation of office equipment	7,000		7,000	7,000	7,000
Administrative salaries	13,000		13,000	13,000	13,000
Total fixed costs	$ 40,000		$40,000	$ 40,000	$ 40,000
Income from operations	$ 12,000			$ 22,400	$ 32,800

the total amount of a fixed cost remains unchanged regardless of changes in the level of activity (within the relevant or normal operating range of activity).[1]

After each cost item is classified as variable or fixed, each variable cost is expressed as a constant amount of cost per unit of sales (or per sales dollar). Fixed costs are, of course, budgeted in terms of the total amount of each fixed cost that is expected regardless of the sales volume that may occur within the relevant range.

Illustration 26–2 shows how the fixed budget of Tampa Manufacturing Company is reformulated as a flexible budget. Compare the first column of Illustration 26–2 with the first column of Illustration 26–1. Notice that seven of the expenses have been reclassified as variable

---

[1] In Chapter 24, it was recognized that some costs are neither strictly variable nor strictly fixed. However, in the present discussion, it is assumed that all costs can be reasonably classified as being either variable or fixed.

costs; the remaining five expenses have been reclassified as fixed costs. This classification results from an investigation of each expense incurred by Tampa Manufacturing Company, and the classification should not be misunderstood. It does not mean that these particular expenses are always variable costs in every company. For example, Office Supplies Expense may frequently be a fixed cost, depending upon the nature of the company's operations. Nevertheless, Tampa Manufacturing Company's accountant investigated this item and concluded that the Office Supplies cost behaves as a variable cost.

Observe in Illustration 26–2 that the variable costs of Tampa Manufacturing Company are listed together, totaled, and subtracted from sales. As explained in Chapter 24, the difference between sales and variable costs is identified as the contribution margin. The budgeted amounts of fixed costs are then listed and totaled.

In Illustration 26–2, columns 2 and 3 show the flexible budget amounts that may be applied to any volume of sales that occurs. The last two columns merely illustrate what form the flexible budget takes when the budget amounts are applied to particular sales volumes.

Recall from Illustration 26–1 that Tampa Manufacturing Company's actual sales volume for November 198A was 12,000 units. This was 2,000 units more than the 10,000 units originally forecasted in the master budget. The effect of this sales increase on the income from operations can be determined by comparing the budget for 10,000 units with the budget for 12,000 units (see Illustration 26–2). At a sales volume of 12,000 units, the budgeted income from operations is $22,400, whereas the budget for sales of 10,000 units shows income from operations of $12,000. Thus, if sales volume is 12,000 rather than 10,000 units, management should expect income from opertions to be higher by $10,400 ($22,400 − $12,000). In other words, the difference between the $25,400 actual income from operations (see Illustration 26–1) and the $12,000 income from operations shown on the master budget can be analyzed, as follows:

Actual income from operations (12,000 units)	$25,400
Income from operations on master budget (10,000 units)	12,000
Difference to be explained	$13,400
Income from operations:	
On the flexible budget for 12,000 units $22,400	
On the budget for 10,000 units 12,000	
Additional income caused by increase in sales volume	(10,400)
Unexplained difference	$ 3,000

This $3,000 unexplained difference is the amount by which the actual income from operations exceeds budgeted income from operations as shown on the flexible budget for a sales volume of 12,000 units. As management seeks to determine what steps should be taken to control Tampa Manufacturing Company's operations, the next step is to determine what caused this $3,000 unexplained difference. Information to help answer this question is provided by a flexible budget performance report.

FLEXIBLE BUDGET PERFORMANCE REPORT

A *flexible budget performance report* is designed to analyze the difference between actual performance and budgeted performance, where the budgeted amounts are based on the actual sales volume or level of activity. The report should direct management's attention toward those particular costs or revenues where actual performance has differed substantially from the budgeted amount.

The flexible budget performance report for Tampa Manufacturing Company is presented in Illustration 26–3.

Observe in Illustration 26–3 the $5,000 favorable variance in total dollar sales. Since the actual number of units sold amounted to 12,000 and the budget was also based on unit sales of 12,000, the $5,000 variance must have resulted entirely from a difference between the average price per unit and the budgeted price per unit. Further analysis of the $5,000 variance is as follows:

Average price per unit, actual	$125,000/12,000	=	$10.42
Budgeted price per unit	$120,000/12,000	=	10.00
Favorable variance in price per unit	$5,000/12,000	=	$ 0.42

The variances in Illustration 26–3 direct management's attention toward the areas in which corrective action may be necessary to control Tampa Manufacturing Company's operations. In addition, students should recognize that each of the cost variances can be analyzed in a manner similar to the above discussion of sales. Each of the expenses can be thought of as involving the use of a given number of units of the expense item, and paying a specific price per unit. Following this approach, each of the cost variances shown in Illustration 26–3 might result in part from a difference between the actual price per unit and the budgeted price per unit (a price variance); and they may also result in part from a difference between the actual number of units used and the budgeted number of units to be used (a quantity variance). This line of reasoning, called variance analysis, is discussed more completely in the following section on standard costs.

Illustration 26–3

TAMPA MANUFACTURING COMPANY
Flexible Budget Performance Report
For Month Ended November 30, 198A

	Flexible budget	Actual performance	Variances
Sales (12,000 units)	$120,000	$125,000	$5,000 F
Variable costs:			
Raw materials	$ 12,000	$ 13,000	$1,000 U
Direct labor	18,000	20,000	2,000 U
Factory supplies	2,400	2,100	300 F
Utilities	3,600	4,000	400 U
Sales commissions	10,800	10,800	
Shipping expenses	4,800	4,300	500 F
Office supplies	6,000	5,200	800 F
Total variable costs	$ 57,600	$ 59,400	$1,800 U
Contribution margin	$ 62,400	$ 65,600	$3,200 F
Fixed costs:			
Depreciation of machinery	$ 8,000	$ 8,000	
Supervisory salaries	11,000	11,000	
Insurance expense	1,000	1,200	$ 200 U
Depreciation of office equipment	7,000	7,000	
Administrative salaries	13,000	13,000	
Total fixed costs	$ 40,000	$ 40,200	$ 200 U
Income from operations	$ 22,400	$ 25,400	$3,000 F

F = Favorable variance; that is, compared to the budget, the actual cost or revenue
   contributes to a higher income.
U = Unfavorable variance; that is, compared to the budget, the actual cost or revenue
   contributes to a lower income.

STANDARD COSTS

In Chapter 22, it was said that there are two basic types of manufacturing cost systems, job order and process, but a large number of variations of the two. A *standard cost system,* one based on *standard* or *budgeted costs,* is such a variation.

The costs of a job or a process as discussed in Chapter 22 were historical costs, historical in the sense that they had been incurred and were "history" by the time they were recorded. Such costs are useful; but to judge whether or not they are reasonable or what they should be, management needs a basis of comparison. Standard costs offer such a basis.

Standard costs are the costs that should be incurred under normal conditions in producing a given product or part or in performing a particular service. They are established by means of engineering and accounting studies made before the product is manufactured or the service performed. Once established, standard costs are used to judge the reasonableness of the actual costs incurred when the product or service is produced. Standard costs are also used to place responsibilities when actual costs vary from standard.

Accountants speak of *standard material cost, standard labor cost,* and *standard overhead cost;* and this terminology is used in this chapter. However, it should be observed that standard material, labor, and overhead costs are really budgeted material, labor, and overhead costs.

ESTABLISHING STANDARD COSTS

Great care and the combined efforts of people in accounting, engineering, personnel administration, and other management areas are required to establish standard costs. Time and motion studies are made of each labor operation in a product's production or in performing a service. From these studies, management learns the best way to perform the operation and the standard labor time required under normal conditions for performance. Exhaustive investigations are commonly made of the quantity, grade, and cost of each material required; and machines and other productive equipment are subject to detailed studies in an effort to achieve maximum efficiencies and to learn what costs should be.

However, regardless of care exercised in establishing standard costs and in revising them as conditions change, actual costs incurred in producing a given product or service commonly vary from standard costs. When this occurs, the difference in total cost is likely to be a composite of several cost differences. For example, the quantity and/ or the price of the material used may have varied from standard. Also, the labor time and/or the labor price may have varied. Likewise, overhead costs may have varied.

VARIANCES

When actual costs vary from standard costs, the differences are called *variances.* Variances may be favorable or unfavorable. A favorable variance is one in which actual cost is below standard cost, and an unfavorable variance is one in which actual cost is above standard.

When variances occur, they are isolated and studied for possible remedial action and to place responsibilities. For example, assume the standard material cost for producing 2,000 units of Product A is $800, but material costing $840 was used in producing the units. The $40 variance may have resulted from paying a price higher than standard for the material. Or, a greater quantity of material than standard may have been used. Or, there may have been some combination of these causes. The price paid for a material is a purchasing department responsibility; consequently, if the variance was caused by a price greater than standard, responsibility rests with the purchasing department. On the other hand, since the production department is usually responsible for the amount of material used, if a quantity greater than standard was used, responsibility normally rests with the production department. However, if more than a standard amount of material was used because the material was of a grade below standard, causing more than a normal waste, responsibility is back on the purchasing department for buying a substandard grade.

ISOLATING MATERIAL AND LABOR VARIANCES

As previously stated, when variances occur, they are isolated and studied for possible remedial action and to place responsibilities. For example, assume that XL Company has established the following standard costs per unit for its Product Z:

```
Material (1 lb. per unit at $1 per lb.) ............   $1.00
Direct labor (1 hr. per unit at $3 per hr.) .........    3.00
Overhead ($2 per standard direct labor hour) .....      2.00
            Total standard cost per unit ..............   $6.00
```

Material Variances

Assume further that during May, XL Company completed 3,500 units of Product Z, using 3,600 pounds of material costing $1.05 per pound, or $3,780. Under these assumptions the actual and standard material costs for the 3,500 units are:

```
Actual cost:    3,600 lbs. @ $1.05 per lb. ...........   $3,780
Standard cost: 3,500 lbs. @ $1 per lb. .............     3,500
            Material cost variance (unfavorable) .........   $  280
```

Observe that the actual material cost for these units is $280 above their standard cost. This unfavorable material cost variance may be isolated as to causes in the following manner:

```
QUANTITY VARIANCE:
    Actual units at the standard price .......  3,600 lbs. @ $1.00  =  $3,600
    Standard units at the standard price .....  3,500 lbs. @ $1.00  =   3,500
        Variance (unfavorable) ............    100 lbs. @ $1.00  =             $100
PRICE VARIANCE:
    Actual units at the actual price ..........  3,600 lbs. @ $1.05  =  $3,780
    Actual units at the standard price .......  3,600 lbs. @ $1.00  =   3,600
        Variance (unfavorable) ............  3,600 lbs. @ $0.05  =              180
        Material cost variance
            (unfavorable) ..............                                    $280
```

The analysis shows that $100 of the excess material cost resulted from using 100 more pounds than standard, and $180 resulted from a unit purchase price that was $0.05 above standard. With this information management can go to the responsible individuals for explanations.

Labor Variances

Labor cost in manufacturing a given part or in performing a service depends on a composite of the number of hours worked (quantity) and the wage rate paid (price). Therefore, when the labor cost for a task varies from standard, it too may be analyzed into a *quantity variance* and a *price variance*.

For example, the direct labor standard for the 3,500 units of Product Z is one hour per unit, or 3,500 hours at $3 per hour. If 3,400 hours costing $3.10 per hour were used in completing the units, the actual and standard labor costs for these units are:

```
Actual cost:    3,400 hrs. @ $3.10 per hr. ........  $10,540
Standard cost: 3,500 hrs. @ $3.00 per hr. ........   10,500
        Direct labor cost variance (unfavorable) .....  $    40
```

In this case, actual cost is only $40 over standard, but isolating the quantity and price variances involved reveals the following:

```
QUANTITY VARIANCE:
    Standard hours at standard price ...  3,500 hrs. @ $3.00  =  $10,500
    Actual hours at standard price .....  3,400 hrs. @ $3.00  =   10,200
        Variance (favorable) .........    100 hrs. @ $3.00  =            $300
PRICE VARIANCE:
    Actual hours at actual price ........  3,400 hrs. @ $3.10  =  $10,540
    Actual hours at standard price .....  3,400 hrs. @ $3.00  =   10,200
        Variance (unfavorable) .......  3,400 hrs. @ $0.10  =              340
        Direct labor cost variance
            (unfavorable) ..........                                    $ 40
```

The analysis shows a favorable quantity variance of $300, which resulted from using 100 fewer direct labor hours than standard for the units produced. However, this favorable variance was more than offset by a wage rate that was $0.10 above standard.

When a factory or department has workers of various skill levels, it is the responsibility of the foreman or other supervisor to assign to each task a worker or workers of no higher skill level than is required to accomplish the task. In this case, an investigation could reveal that workers of a higher skill level were used in producing the 3,500 units of Product Z. Hence, fewer labor hours were required for the work. However, because the workers were of a higher skill level, the wage rate paid them was higher than standard.

CHARGING OVERHEAD TO PRODUCTION

When standard costs are used, factory overhead is charged to production by means of a predetermined standard overhead rate. The rate may be based on the relationship between overhead and standard labor cost, standard labor hours, standard machine-hours, or some other measure of production. For example, XL Company charges its Product Z with $2 of overhead per standard direct labor hour; and since the direct labor standard for Product Z is one hour per unit, the 3,500 units manufactured in May were charged with $7,000 of overhead.

Before going on, recall that only 3,400 actual direct labor hours were used in producing these units. Then, note again that overhead is charged to the units, not on the basis of actual labor hours but on the basis of standard labor hours. Standard labor hours are used because the amount of overhead charged to these units should not be less than standard simply because less than the standard (normal) amount of labor was used in their production. In other words, overhead should not vary from normal simply because labor varied from normal.

ESTABLISHING OVERHEAD STANDARDS

A variable or flexible factory overhead budget is the starting point in establishing reasonable standards for overhead costs. A flexible budget is necessary because the actual production level may vary from the expected level; and when this happens, certain costs vary with production, but others remain fixed. This may be seen by examining XL Company's flexible budget shown in Illustration 26–4.

Observe in Illustration 26–4 that XL Company's flexible budget has been used to establish standard costs for four production levels ranging from 70% to 100% of capacity. When actual costs are known, they

Illustration 26–4

XL COMPANY
Flexible Overhead Costs Budget for Month Ended May 31, 198A

	Budget Amounts	Production Levels			
		70%	80%	90%	100%
Production in units	1 unit	3,500	4,000	4,500	5,000
Standard direct labor hours		3,500	4,000	4,500	5,000
Budgeted factory overhead:					
Fixed costs:					
Building rent....................	$1,000	$1,000	$1,000	$1,000	$1,000
Depreciation, machinery	1,200	1,200	1,200	1,200	1,200
Supervisory salaries	1,800	1,800	1,800	1,800	1,800
Totals	$4,000	$4,000	$4,000	$4,000	$4,000
Variable costs:					
Indirect labor	$0.40	$1,400	$1,600	$1,800	$2,000
Indirect materials	0.30	1,050	1,200	1,350	1,500
Power and lights	0.20	700	800	900	1,000
Maintenance	0.10	350	400	450	500
Totals	$1.00	$3,500	$4,000	$4,500	$5,000
Total factory overhead		$7,500	$8,000	$8,500	$9,000

should be compared with the standards for the level actually achieved and not with the standards at some other level. For example, if the plant actually operated at 70% capacity during May, actual costs incurred should be compared with standard costs for the 70% level. Actual costs should not be compared with costs established for the 80% or 90% levels.

In setting overhead standards, after the flexible overhead budget is prepared, management must determine the expected operating level for the plant. This can be 100% of capacity, but it seldom is. Errors in scheduling work, breakdowns, and, perhaps, the inability of the sales force to sell all the product produced are factors that commonly reduce the operating level to some point below full capacity.

After the flexible budget is set up and the expected operating level is determined, overhead costs at the expected level are related to, for example, labor hours at this level to establish the standard overhead rate. The rate thus established is then used to apply overhead to production. For example, assume XL Company decided that 80% of capacity is the expected operating level for its plant. The company then would calculate a $2 per direct labor hour overhead rate by dividing the budgeted $8,000 of overhead costs at the 80% level by the 4,000 standard direct labor hours required to produce the product manufactured at this level.

OVERHEAD VARIANCES

As previously stated, when standard costs are used, overhead is applied to production on the basis of a predetermined overhead rate. Then, at the end of a cost period the difference between overhead applied and overhead actually incurred is analyzed and variances are calculated to determine what was responsible for the difference.

Overhead variances are computed in several ways. A common way divides the difference between overhead applied and overhead incurred into (1) the *volume variance* and (2) the *controllable variance*.

Volume Variance

The *volume variance* is the difference between (1) *the amount of overhead budgeted at the actual operating level achieved during the period* and (2) *the standard amount of overhead charged to production during the period.* For example, assume that during May, XL Company actually operated at 70% of capacity. It produced 3,500 units of Product Z, which were charged with overhead at the standard rate. Under this assumption the company's volume variance for May is:

VOLUME VARIANCE:
Budgeted overhead at 70% of capacity $7,500
Standard overhead charged to production (3,500 standard
    labor hours at the $2 per hour standard rate) 7,000
               Variance (unfavorable) .... $ 500

To understand why this volume variance occurred, reexamine the flexible budget of Illustration 26–4. Observe that at the 80% level the $2 per hour overhead rate may be subdivided into $1 per hour for fixed overhead and $1 per hour for variable overhead. Furthermore, at the 80% (normal) level, the $1 for fixed overhead exactly covers the fixed overhead. However, when this $2 rate is used for the 70% level, and again subdivided, the $1 for fixed overhead will not cover all the fixed overhead because $4,000 is required for fixed overhead and 3,500 hours at $1 per hour equals only $3,500. In other words, at this 70% level the $2 per hour standard overhead rate did not absorb all the overhead incurred; it lacked $500, the amount of the volume variance. Or again, the volume variance resulted simply because the plant did not reach the expected operating level.

An unfavorable volume variance tells management that the plant did not reach its normal operating level; and when such a variance is large, management should investigate the cause or causes. Machine breakdowns, failure to schedule an even flow of work, and a lack of sales orders are common causes. The first two may be corrected in the factory, but the third requires either more orders from the sales force or a downward adjustment of the operating level considered to be normal.

Controllable Variance

The *controllable variance* is the difference between (1) *overhead actually incurred* and (2) *the overhead budgeted at the operating level achieved.* For example, assume that XL Company incurred $7,650 of overhead during May. Since its plant operated at 70% of capacity during the month, its controllable overhead variance for May is:

CONTROLLABLE VARIANCE:
Actual overhead incurred $7,650
Overhead budgeted at operating level achieved   7,500
        Variance (unfavorable) . . . . $ 150

The controllable overhead variance measures management's efficiency in adjusting controllable overhead costs (normally variable overhead) to the operating level achieved. In this case, management failed by $150 to maintain overhead costs at the amount budgeted for the 70% level.

The controllable overhead variance measures management's efficiency in adjusting overhead costs to the operating level achieved. However, an overhead variance report is a more effective means for showing just where management achieved or failed to achieve the budgeted expectations. Such a report for XL Company appears in Illustration 26–5 on the next page.

Combining the Volume and Controllable Variances

The volume and controllable variances may be combined to account for the difference between overhead actually incurred and overhead charged to production. For example, XL Company actually incurred $7,650 of overhead during May and charged $7,000 to production. Its overhead variances may be combined as follows to account for the difference:

VOLUME VARIANCE:
Overhead budgeted at operating level achieved $7,500
Standard overhead charged to production (3,500 standard
hours at $2 per hour) 7,000
  Variance (unfavorable) $500
CONTROLLABLE VARIANCE:
Actual overhead incurred $7,650
Overhead budgeted at operating level achieved 7,500
  Variance (unfavorable) 150
  Excess of overhead incurred over overhead charged to
   production $650

CONTROLLING A BUSINESS THROUGH STANDARD COSTS

Business operations are carried on by people, and control of a business is gained by controlling the actions of the people responsible for its revenues, costs, and expenses. When a budget is prepared and standard costs established, control is maintained by taking appropriate action when actual costs vary from standard or from the budget.

Reports like the ones shown in this chapter are a means of calling

Illustration 26–5

XL COMPANY
Factory Overhead Variance Report
For Month Ended May 31, 198A

VOLUME VARIANCE:
Normal production level . . . . 80% of capacity.
Production level achieved . . . . 70% of capacity.
Volume variance . . . . $ 500 (unfavorable)
CONTROLLABLE VARIANCE:

	Budget	Actual	Favorable	Unfavorable
Fixed overhead costs:				
Building rent	$1,000	$1,000		
Depreciation, machinery	1,200	1,200		
Supervisory salaries	1,800	1,800		
Total fixed costs	$4,000	$4,000		
Variable overhead costs:				
Indirect labor	$1,400	$1,525		$125
Indirect materials	1,050	1,025	$ 25	
Power and lights	700	750		50
Maintenance	350	350		
Total variable costs	$3,500	$3,650		
Total controllable variances . . .			$ 25	$175
Net controllable variance (unfavorable) .			150	
			$175	$175

management's attention to these variations, and a review of the reports is essential to the successful operation of a budget program. However, in making the review, management should practice the control technique known as *management by exception*. Under this technique, management gives its attention only to the variances in which actual costs are significantly different from standard; it ignores the cost situations in which performance is satisfactory. In other words, management concentrates its attention on the exceptional or irregular situations and pays little or no attention to the normal.

Many companies develop standard costs and apply variance analysis only when dealing with manufacturing costs. In these companies, the master budget includes selling, general, and administrative expenses, but the subsequent process of controlling these expenses is not based upon the establishment of standard costs and variance analysis. However, other companies have recognized that standard costs and variance analysis may help control selling, general, and administrative expenses just as well as manufacturing costs. Students should understand that the previous discussions of material and labor cost variances can easily be adapted to many selling, general, and administrative expenses.

STANDARD COSTS IN THE ACCOUNTS

Standard costs can be used solely in the preparation of management reports and need not be taken into the accounts. However, in most standard cost systems such costs are recorded in the accounts to facilitate both the record-keeping and the preparation of reports.

No effort will be made here to go into the record-keeping details of a standard cost system. This is reserved for a course in cost accounting. Nevertheless, when standard costs are taken into the accounts, entries like the following (the data for which are taken from the discussion of material variances on pages 901–902) may be used to enter standard costs into the Goods in Process account and to separately identify variances in variance accounts.

May	31	Goods in Process	3,500.00	
		Material Quantity Variance	100.00	
		Material Price Variance	180.00	
		Materials		3,780.00
		To charge production with 3,600 pounds of material @ $1.05 per pound.		

Variances taken into the accounts are allowed to accumulate in the variance accounts until the end of an accounting period. If at that time the variance amounts are immaterial, they are closed directly to Cost of Goods Sold. However, if the amounts are material, they may be prorated between Goods in Process, Finished Goods, and Cost of Goods Sold.

GLOSSARY

Controllable variance. The difference between overhead actually incurred and the overhead budgeted at the operating level achieved.

Fixed budget. A budget based on a single estimate of sales or production volume that gives no consideration to the possibility that the actual sales or production volume may be different from the assumed amount.

Flexible budget. A budget that provides budgeted amounts for all levels of production within the relevant range.

Flexible budget performance report. A report designed to analyze the difference between actual performance and budgeted performance, where the budgeted amounts are based on the actual sales volume or level of activity.

Performance report. A financial report that compares actual cost and/or revenue performance with budgeted amounts and designates the differences between them as favorable or unfavorable variances.

Price variance. A difference between actual and budgeted revenue or cost caused by the actual price per unit being different from the budgeted price per unit.

Quantity variance. The difference between actual cost and budgeted cost that was caused by a difference between the actual number of units used and the number of units budgeted.

Standard costs. The costs that should be incurred under normal conditions in producing a given product or part or in performing a particular service.

Static budget. A synonym for fixed budget.

Variable budget. A synonym for flexible budget.

Volume variance. The difference between the amount of overhead budgeted at the actual operating level achieved during the period and the standard amount of overhead charged to production during the period.

QUESTIONS FOR CLASS DISCUSSION

1. What is a *fixed* or *static* budget?
2. What limits the usefulness of fixed budget performance reports?
3. What is the essential difference between a fixed budget and a flexible budget?
4. What is the initial step in preparing a flexible budget?
5. Is there any sense in which a variable cost may be thought of as being constant in amount? Explain.

6. A particular type of cost may be classified as variable by one company and fixed by another company. Why might this be appropriate?

7. What is meant by contribution margin?

8. What is a flexible budget performance report designed to analyze?

9. In cost accounting, what is meant by a *variance?*

10. A cost variance often consists of a price variance and a quantity variance. What is a price variance? What is a quantity variance?

11. What is the purpose of a *standard cost?*

12. What department is usually responsible for a material price variance? What department is generally responsible for a material quantity variance?

13. What is a *predetermined standard overhead rate?*

14. In analyzing the overhead variance, explain what is meant by a *volume variance?*

15. In analyzing the overhead variance, explain what is meant by a *controllable variance?*

16. What is the relationship between standard costs, variance analysis, and *management by exception?*

CLASS EXERCISES

Exercise 26–1

A company manufactures and sells wood tables and generally operates eight hours a day, five days per week. On the basis of this general information, classify the following costs as fixed or variable. In those instances where further investigation might reverse your classification, comment on the possible reasons for treating the item in the opposite manner.

a. Varnish.
b. Nails and glue.
c. Direct labor.
d. Shipping expenses.
e. Electricity to run saws.
f. Management salaries.
g. Repair expense on saws.

h. Office supplies.
i. Fire insurance on property.
j. Depreciation on saws.
k. Sales commissions.
l. Packaging expenses.
m. Utilities (gas and water).
n. Wood.

Exercise 26–2

Jackson Company's fixed budget for the second quarter of 198A is presented below. Recast the budget as a flexible budget and show the budgeted amounts for 24,000 units and 27,000 units of production.

Sales (25,500 units)		$357,000
Cost of goods sold:		
Materials	$66,300	
Direct labor	73,950	
Production supplies	10,200	
Depreciation	7,500	
Plant manager's salary	11,000	(168,950)
Gross profit		$188,050

Selling expenses:
Sales commissions	$29,580	
Packaging expense	7,650	(37,230)

Administrative expenses:
Administrative salaries	$15,000	
Insurance expense	3,800	
Office rent expense	12,500	
Executive salaries	25,000	(56,300)
Income from operations		$ 94,520

Exercise 26–3

Fashion Furniture Company has just completed 150 units of its finest dining table using 22,800 board feet of lumber costing $29,868. The company's material standards for one unit of this table are 146 board feet of lumber at $1.25 per board foot.

Required:

Isolate the material variances incurred in manufacturing these tables.

Exercise 26–4

Fashion Furniture Company takes its standard costs into its cost records. As a result, in charging material costs to Goods in Process, it also takes any variances into its accounts.

Required:

1. Under the assumption that the materials used to manufacture the tables of Exercise 26–3 were charged to Goods in Process on March 5, give the entry to charge the materials and to take the variances into the accounts.
2. Under the further assumption that the material variances of Exercise 26–3 were the only variances of the year and were considered immaterial, give the year-end entry to close the variance accounts.

Exercise 26–5

A company has established the following standard costs for one unit of its product:

Material (1 unit @ $6 per unit)	$ 6
Direct labor (1 hr. @ $8 per hr.)	8
Factory overhead (1 hr. @ $5 per hr.)	5
Standard cost	$19

The $5 per direct labor hour overhead rate is based on a normal 80% of capacity operating level and the following monthly flexible budget information:

	Operating Levels		
	75%	80%	85%
Budgeted production in units	18,750	20,000	21,250
Budgeted overhead:			
Fixed overhead	$50,000	$50,000	$50,000
Variable overhead	46,875	50,000	53,125

During the past month, the company operated at 75% of capacity, producing 18,750 units of product with the following overhead costs:

Fixed overhead costs	$50,000	
Variable overhead costs	47,500	
Total overhead costs	$97,500	

Required:

Isolate the overhead variances into a volume variance and a controllable variance.

PROBLEMS

Problem 26–1

Bozo Company's master (fixed) budget for 198A was based on an expected production and sales volume of 13,800 units, and included the following operating items:

BOZO COMPANY
Fixed Budget
For Year Ended December 31, 198A

Sales..		$276,000
Cost of goods sold:		
Materials	$69,000	
Direct labor	41,400	
Machinery repairs (variable cost)	2,070	
Depreciation of plant	7,500	
Utilities (40% of which is a variable cost)	13,800	
Supervisory salaries	18,000	(151,770)
Gross profit		$124,230
Selling expenses:		
Packaging	$ 6,900	
Shipping	10,350	
Sales salary (an agreed-upon, annual salary)	21,000	(38,250)
General and administrative expenses:		
Insurance expense	$ 4,500	
Salaries	31,500	
Rent expense	24,000	(60,000)
Income from operations		$ 25,980

Required:

1. Prepare a flexible budget for the company and show detailed budgets for sales and production volumes of 12,600 units and 15,000 units.
2. A consultant to the company has suggested that developing business conditions in the area are reaching a crossroads, and that the impact of these events on the company could result in a sales volume of approximately 17,000 units. The president of Bozo Company is confident that this is within the relevant range of existing production capacity but is hesitant to estimate the impact of such a change on operating income. What would be the expected increase in operating income?
3. In the consultant's report, the possibility of unfavorable business events was also mentioned, in which case production and sales volume for 198A would likely fall to 12,000 units. What amount of income from operations should the president expect if these unfavorable events occur?

Refer to the discussion of Bozo Company in Problem 26–1. Bozo Company's actual statement of income from 198A operations is as follows:

BOZO COMPANY
Statement of Income from Operations
For Year Ended December 31, 198A

Sales (15,000 units)		$285,000
Cost of goods sold:		
Materials	$67,500	
Direct labor	46,500	
Machinery repairs	1,500	
Depreciation of plant	7,500	
Utilities (50% of which was a variable cost)	16,560	
Supervisory salaries	17,550	(157,110)
Gross profit		$127,890
Selling expenses:		
Packaging	$ 6,750	
Shipping	11,850	
Sales salary	21,000	(39,600)
General and administrative expenses:		
Insurance expense	$ 4,650	
Salaries	32,250	
Rent expense	24,000	(60,900)
Income from operations		$ 27,390

Required:

1. Using the flexible budget you prepared for Problem 26–1, present a flexible budget performance report for 198A.
2. Explain the sales variance.

Munday Manufacturing Company makes a single product for which it has established the following standard costs per unit:

Material (5 lbs. @ $0.70 per lb.)	$ 3.50
Direct labor (1 hr. @ $7 per hr.)	7.00
Factory overhead (1 hr. @ $4.60 per hr.)	4.60
Total standard cost	$15.10

The $4.60 per direct labor hour overhead rate is based on a normal, 90% of capacity, operating level and the following flexible budget information:

	Operating Levels		
	80%	90%	100%
Production in units	16,000	18,000	20,000
Standard direct labor hours	16,000	18,000	20,000
Fixed factory overhead	$49,680	$49,680	$49,680
Variable factory overhead	$29,440	$33,120	$36,800

During March, the company operated at 80% of capacity, producing 16,000 units of product that were charged with the following standard costs:

Material (80,000 lbs. @ $0.70 per lb.) .... $ 56,000
Direct labor (16,000 hrs. @ $7 per hr.) 112,000
Factory overhead costs (16,000 hrs. @ $4.60 per hr.) 73,600
　　　　Total standard cost $241,600

Actual costs incurred during March were:

Material (81,000 lbs.) .... $ 53,460
Direct labor (15,500 hrs.) 111,600
Fixed factory overhead costs 49,680
Variable factory overhead costs 29,400
　　　　Total actual costs $244,140

Required:

Isolate the material and labor variances into price and quantity variances and isolate the overhead variance into the volume variance and the controllable variance.

Problem 26–4

Slippery Company has established the following standard costs per unit for the product it manufactures:

Material (4 lbs. @ $3.00 per lb.) $12.00
Direct labor (3 hrs. @ $6 per hr.) 18.00
Overhead (3 hrs. @ $2.50 per hr.) 7.50
　　　　Total standard cost $37.50

The $2.50 per direct labor hour overhead rate is based on a normal, 85% of capacity, operating level and the following flexible budget information for one month's operations.

	Operating Levels		
	80%	85%	90%
Production in units.......................	2,560	2,720	2,880
Standard direct labor hours	7,680	8,160	8,640
Budgeted factory overhead:			
Fixed costs:			
Rent of factory building	$ 3,500	$ 3,500	$ 3,500
Depreciation expense, machinery	1,800	1,800	1,800
Taxes and insurance	876	876	876
Supervisory salaries	2,800	2,800	2,800
Total fixed costs...................	$ 8,976	$ 8,976	$ 8,976
Variable costs:			
Indirect materials	$ 1,920	$ 2,040	$ 2,160
Indirect labor.......................	5,760	6,120	6,480
Power..............................	768	816	864
Maintenance	2,304	2,448	2,592
Total variable costs	$10,752	$11,424	$12,096
Total factory overhead costs	$19,728	$20,400	$21,072

During May 198A, the company operated at 90% of capacity, produced 2,880 units of product, and incurred the following actual costs:

Material (11,600 lbs. @ $2.90 per lb.)		$ 33,640
Direct labor (8,590 hrs. @ $6.20 per hr.)		53,258
Overhead costs:		
Rent of factory building	$3,500	
Depreciation expense, machinery	1,800	
Taxes and insurance	876	
Supervisory salaries	2,800	
Indirect materials......................	2,080	
Indirect labor	6,370	
Power	820	
Maintenance	2,850	21,096
Total costs		$587,994

Required:

1. Isolate the material and labor variances into quantity and price variances and isolate the overhead variance into the volume variance and the controllable variance.
2. Prepare a factory overhead variance report showing the volume and controllable variances.

Problem 26–5

Blanko Company has established the following standard costs for one unit of its product:

Material (8 lbs. @ $1.30 per lb.)	$10.40
Direct labor (2 hr. @ $9 per hr.)	18.00
Overhead (2 hr. @ $3.90 per hr.)	7.80
Total standard cost	$36.20

The $3.90 per direct labor hour overhead rate is based on a normal, 80% of capacity, operating level, and at this level the company's monthly output is 16,000 units. Following are the company's budgeted overhead costs at the 80% level for one month:

BLANKO COMPANY
Budgeted Monthly Factory Overhead at 80% Level

Fixed costs:		
Depreciation expense, building	$24,000	
Depreciation expense, machinery	19,200	
Taxes and insurance	4,800	
Supervision	28,800	
Total fixed costs		$ 76,800
Variable costs:		
Indirect materials	$19,200	
Indirect labor	11,520	
Power	7,680	
Repairs and maintenance	9,600	
Total variable costs	48,000	
Total overhead costs	$124,800	

During August 198A, the company operated at 70% of capacity and incurred the following actual costs:

Material (113,100 lbs.)	$141,375
Direct labor (27,400 hrs.)	254,820
Depreciation expense, building	24,000
Depreciation expense, machinery	19,200
Taxes and insurance	4,800
Supervision	28,800
Indirect materials	17,400
Indirect labor	9,600
Power	7,080
Repairs and maintenance	8,640
Total costs	$515,715

Required:

1. Prepare a flexible overhead budget for the company showing the amount of each fixed and variable cost at the 70%, 80%, and 90% levels.
2. Isolate the material and labor variances into quantity and price variances and isolate the overhead variance into the volume variance and the controllable variance.
3. Prepare a factory overhead variance report showing the volume and controllable variances.

ALTERNATE PROBLEMS

Problem 26–1A

In the process of preparing a master budget for 198A, Slade Company assumed a sales volume of 27,000 units. The resulting budgeted income statement included the following items that comprise income from operations.

SLADE COMPANY
Fixed Budget
For Year Ended December 31, 198A

Sales		$472,500
Cost of goods sold:		
Raw materials	$108,000	
Direct labor	61,506	
Factory supplies	6,291	
Depreciation of plant	11,700	
Utilities (of which $9,000 is a fixed cost)	17,694	
Salary of plant manager	27,000	(232,191)
Gross profit		$240,309
Selling expenses:		
Packaging	$ 56,997	
Sales commissions	37,800	
Shipping	21,303	
Salary of vice president—marketing	21,000	
Promotion (variable)	23,625	(160,725)
General and administrative expenses:		
Depreciation	$ 10,500	
Consultant's fees (annual retainer)	21,750	
Administrative salaries	48,750	(81,000)
Income from operations		$ (1,416)

Required:

1. Prepare a flexible budget for the company, showing specific budget columns for sales and production volumes of 30,000 units and 33,000 units.
2. What would be the expected increase in income from opertions if sales and production volume were 31,500 units rather than 27,000 units?
3. Although the management of Slade Company believes that the master budget was a conservative estimate of sales and production volume, it is possible that the level of activity could fall to 24,000 units. What would be the effect on income from operations if this occurs?

Problem 26–2A

Refer to the discussion of Slade Company in Problem 26–1A. Slade Company's actual statement of income from 198A operations is as follows:

SLADE COMPANY
Statement of Income from Operations
For Year Ended December 31, 198A

Sales (30,000 units)		$585,000
Cost of goods sold:		
Raw materials	$117,000	
Direct labor	73,500	
Factory supplies	7,350	
Depreciation of plant	11,700	
Utilities (of which 50% is a fixed cost)	18,600	
Salary of plant manager	27,000	(255,150)
Gross profit		$329,850
Selling expenses:		
Packaging	$58,500	
Sales commissions	46,800	
Shipping	22,425	
Salary of vice president—marketing	21,000	
Promotion (variable)	27,375	(176,100)
General and administrative expenses:		
Depreciation	$10,500	
Consultant's fees	24,450	
Administrative salaries	46,875	(81,825)
Income from operations		$ 71,925

Required:

1. Using the flexible budget you prepared for Problem 26–1A, present a flexible budget performance report for 198A.
2. Explain the sales variance.

Problem 26–3A

A company has established the following standard costs for one unit of its product:

Material (3 lbs. @ $5 per lb.)	$15.00
Direct labor (1½ hrs. @ $7 per hr.)	10.50
Overhead (1½ hrs. @ $6 per hr.)	9.00
Total standard cost	$34.50

The $6 per direct labor hour overhead rate is based on a normal, 90% of capacity, operating level for the company's plant and the following flexible budget information for April 198A.

	Operating Levels		
	80%	90%	100%
Production in units	800	900	1,000
Direct labor hours	1,200	1,350	1,500
Fixed factory overhead	$4,500	$4,500	$4,500
Variable factory overhead	$3,200	$3,600	$4,000

During April, the company operated at 80% of capacity, producing 800 units of product having the following actual costs:

Material (2,350 lbs. @ $5.10 per lb.) $11,985
Direct labor (1,250 hrs. @ $6.80 per hr.) 8,500
Fixed factory overhead costs 4,500
Variable factory overhead costs 3,325

Required:

Isolate the material and labor variances into price and quantity variances and isolate the overhead variance into the volume variance and the controllable variance.

Problem 26–4A

Atlantic Company has established the following standard costs per unit for the product it manufactures:

Material (4 lbs. @ $0.75 per lb.) ..... $ 3.00
Direct labor (1 hr. @ $7 per hr.) 7.00
Overhead (1 hr. @ $5 per hr.) 5.00
Total standard cost $15.00

The $5 per direct labor hour overhead rate is based on a normal, 80% of capacity, operating level and the following flexible budget information for one month's operations.

	Operating Levels		
	75%	80%	85%
Production in units	1,500	1,600	1,700
Standard direct labor hours	1,500	1,600	1,700
Budgeted factory overhead:			
Fixed costs:			
Depreciation, building	$1,200	$1,200	$1,200
Depreciation, machinery	1,700	1,700	1,700
Taxes and insurance	300	300	300
Supervisory salaries	1,600	1,600	1,600
Total fixed costs	$4,800	$4,800	$4,800
Variable costs:			
Indirect materials................	$ 750	$ 800	$ 850
Indirect labor	1,500	1,600	1,700
Power	375	400	425
Maintenance	375	400	425
Total variable costs	$3,000	$3,200	$3,400
Total factory overhead	$7,800	$8,000	$8,200

During August 198A, the company operated at 75% of capacity, produced 1,500 units of product, and incurred the following actual costs:

Material (5,900 lbs. @ $0.78 per lb.)		$ 4,602
Direct labor (1,530 hrs. @ $6.90 per hr.)		10,557
Overhead costs:		
Depreciation expense, building	$1,200	
Depreciation expense, machinery	1,700	
Taxes and insurance	300	
Supervisory salaries	1,600	
Indirect materials.......................	735	
Indirect labor	1,560	
Power	385	
Maintenance	340	7,820
Total		$22,979

Required:

1. Isolate the material and labor variances into price and quantity variances and isolate the overhead variance into the volume variance and the controllable variance.
2. Prepare a factory overhead variance report showing the volume and controllable variances.

Problem 26–5A   Prince Company has established the following standard costs for one unit of its product:

Material (3 lbs. @ $1.25 per lb.)	$3.75
Direct labor (¼ hr. @ $6 per hr.)	1.50
Overhead (¼ hr. @ $5.20 per hr.)	1.30
Total standard cost	$6.55

The $5.20 per direct labor hour overhead rate is based on a normal, 80% of capacity, operating level, and at this level the company's monthly output is 4,000 units. Following are the company's budgeted overhead costs at the 80% level for one month:

PRINCE COMPANY
Budgeted Monthly Factory Overhead at 80% Level

Fixed costs:		
Depreciation expense, building	$1,000	
Depreciation expense, machinery	800	
Taxes and insurance	200	
Supervision	1,200	
Total fixed costs		$3,200
Variable costs:		
Indirect materials	$ 800	
Indirect labor	480	
Power	320	
Repairs and maintenance	400	
Total variable costs		2,000
Total overhead costs		$5,200

During July of the current year, the company operated at 70% of capacity and incurred the following actual costs:

Material (10,620 lbs.)	$12,744
Direct labor (850 hrs.)	5,185
Depreciation expense, building	1,000
Depreciation expense, machinery	800
Taxes and insurance	200
Supervision	1,200
Indirect materials	725
Indirect labor	400
Power	295
Repairs and maintenance	360
Total costs	$22,909

Required:

1. Prepare a flexible overhead budget for the company showing the amount of each fixed and variable cost at the 70%, 80%, and 90% levels.
2. Isolate the material and labor variances into quantity and price variances and isolate the overhead variance into the volume variance and the controllable variance.
3. Prepare a factory overhead variance report showing the volume and controllable variances.

PROVOCATIVE PROBLEMS

Provocative
Problem 26–1,
Art Company

Art Company's management plans to sell artistic, plaster statues for $15 each. Each statue should require 2 pounds of a specially processed plaster that the company expects to purchase for $2.50 per pound. The statues ought to be produced at the rate of two statues per direct labor hour, and the company should be able to hire the needed laborers for $7.50 per hour. Each statue will be packaged in a cardboard container which weighs one-half pound, and the company will seek to buy cardboard for $0.40 per pound.

If actual sales and production volume range from 16,000 to 24,000 statues, the manager would expect the company to incur administrative and sales personnel salaries of $50,000, depreciation of $10,000, utilities expenses of $9,000, and insurance expense of $6,000.

In 198A, Art Company actually produced and sold 20,000 statues at $14.50 each. It used 45,000 pounds of plaster, purchased at $2.60 per pound. Laborers were paid $7.30 per hour and worked 11,000 hours to produce the statues. Cardboard was purchased for $0.425 per pound and 9,600 pounds were used. All other expenses occurred as planned.

Although the above facts are all available to management, they have expressed considerable confusion over the matter of evaluating the operating performance of the company. They recognize that the actual operating income was different from the expected amount but are not able to sort out which items caused the change. They also expressed interest in learning the magnitude of the impact of price changes in specific items purchased by the company as well as any other factors that might be of help in evaluating the company's performance. Can you help management?

Provocative
Problem 26–2,
Special Products
Company

Jay Pauls has been an employee of Special Products Company for nine years, the last seven of which he has worked in the casting department. Eight months ago he was made foreman of the department, and since then has been able to end a long period of internal dissention, high employee turnover, and inefficient operation in the department. Under Jay's supervision, the department's production has increased, employee morale has improved, absenteeism has dropped, and for the past two months the department has regularly been beating its standard for the first time in years.

However, a few days ago Carol Hall, an employee in the department, suggested to Jay that the company install new controls on the department's furnace similar to those developed by a competitor. The controls would cost $15,000 installed and would have a 10-year life and no salvage value. They should increase production 10%, reduce maintenance costs $500 per year, and do away with the labor of one person.

Jay's answer to Carol was, "Forget it. We are doing OK now; we don't need the extra production; and besides, jobs are hard to find and if we have to let someone go, who'll it be?"

Do you think standard costs had anything to do with Jay's answer to Carol? Explain. Do you agree with Jay's answer? Should Jay be the person to make a decision such as this? How can a company be sure that suggestions such as Carol's are not lost in the chain of command?

Provocative
Problem 26–3,
Kallas Company

Kallas Company manufactures Tiffles which have a seasonal demand and which cannot be stored for long periods; consequently, the number of units manufactured varies with the season. In accounting for costs, the company charges actual costs incurred to a goods in process account maintained for the product, which it closes at the end of each quarter to Finished Goods. At the end of last year, which was an average year, the following cost report was prepared for the company manager:

KALLAS COMPANY
Quarterly Report of Costs for Tiffles
Year Ended December 31, 198A

	First quarter	Second quarter	Third quarter	Fourth quarter
Materials	$ 31,200	$ 38,900	$ 15,700	$ 7,900
Direct labor	93,400	116,000	47,000	23,600
Fixed overhead costs..............	42,000	42,000	42,000	42,000
Variable overhead costs	51,200	63,900	25,900	13,000
Total manufacturing costs	$217,800	$260,800	$130,600	$86,500
Production in units	40,000	50,000	20,000	10,000
Cost per unit	$5.445	$5.216	$6.530	$8.650

The manager has asked you to explain why unit costs for the product varied from a low of $5.216 in the second quarter to a high of $8.650 in the last quarter, and to suggest a better way to accumulate or allocate costs. The manager feels that the quarterly reports are needed for purposes of control, so attach to your explanation a schedule showing what last year's material, labor, and overhead costs per unit would have been had your suggestion or suggestions been followed for the year.

Capital Budgeting, Managerial Decisions

After studying Chapter 27, you should be able to:

Describe the impact of capital budgeting on the operations of a company.

Calculate a payback period on an investment and state the inherent limitations of this method.

Calculate a rate of return on an investment and state the assumptions on which this method is based.

Describe the information obtained by using the discounted cash flow method, the procedures involved in using this method, and the problems associated with its use.

Explain the effects of incremental costs on a decision to accept or reject additional business and on a decision whether to make or buy a given product.

State the meaning of sunk costs, out-of-pocket costs, and opportunity costs, and describe the importance of each type of cost to decisions such as to scrap or rebuild defective units or to sell a product as is or process it further.

Define or explain the words and phrases listed in the chapter Glossary.

A business decision involves choosing between two or more courses of action, and the best choice normally offers the highest return on the investment or the greatest cost savings. Business managers at times make decisions intuitively, without trying to measure systematically the advantages and disadvantages of each possible choice. Often they make intuitive decisions because they are unaware of any other way to choose; but sometimes the available information is so sketchy or unreliable that systematic measurement is useless. Also, intangible factors such as convenience, prestige, and public opinion are at times more important than the factors that can be reduced to a quantitative basis. Nevertheless, in many situations it is possible to reduce the anticipated consequences of alternative choices to a quantitative basis and measure them systematically. This chapter will examine several areas of decision making in which more or less systematic methods of analysis are available.

CAPITAL BUDGETING

Planning plant asset investments is called *capital budgeting*. The plans may involve new buildings, new machinery, or whole new projects. In all such cases, a fundamental objective of business firms is to earn a satisfactory return on the invested funds. Capital budgeting often requires some of the most crucial and difficult decisions faced by management. The decisions are difficult because they are commonly based on estimates projected well into a future that is at best uncertain. Capital budgeting decisions are crucial because (1) large sums of money are often involved; (2) funds are committed for long periods of time; and (3) once a decision is made and a project is begun, it may be difficult or impossible to reverse the effects of a poor decision.

Capital budgeting involves the preparation of cost and revenue estimates for all proposed projects, an examination of the merits of each, and a choice of those worthy of investment. It is a broad field, and the discussion of this chapter must be limited to three ways of comparing investment opportunities. They are the *payback period*, the *return on average investment*, and *discounted cash flows*.

Payback Period

Generally, an investment in a machine or other plant asset will produce a *net cash flow*, and the *payback period* for the investment is the time required to recover the investment through this net cash flow. For example, assume that Murray Company is considering several capital investments. One investment involves the purchase of a machine to be used in manufacturing a new product. The machine will cost $16,000, have an eight-year service life, and no salvage value. The company estimates that 10,000 units of the machine's product will be sold each year, and the sales will result in $1,500 of after-tax net income, calculated as follows:

Annual sales of new product..........................		$30,000
Deduct:		
Cost of materials, labor, and overhead other than		
depreciation on the new machine..................	$15,500	
Depreciation on the new machine	2,000	
Additional selling and administrative expenses	9,500	27,000
Annual before-tax income		$ 3,000
Income tax (assumed rate, 50%)		1,500
Annual after-tax net income from new product sales		$ 1,500

Through annual sales of 10,000 units of the new product, Murray Company expects to gain $30,000 of revenue and $1,500 of net income. The net income represents an inflow of assets that will be available to pay back the new machine's cost. Also, since depreciation expense does not involve a current outflow of assets or funds, the amount of the annual depreciation charge represents an additional inflow of assets that will be available to pay back the machine's cost. The $1,500 of net income plus the $2,000 depreciation charge total $3,500, and together are the *annual net cash flow* expected from the investment. Furthermore, this annual net cash flow will pay back the investment in the new machine in 4.6 years, calculated as follows:

$$\frac{\text{Cost of new machine, \$16,000}}{\text{Annual net cash flow, \$3,500}} = \text{4.6 years to recover investment}$$

The answer just given is 4.6 years. Actually, when $16,000 is divided by $3,500, the result is just a little over 4.57; but 4.6 years is close enough. Remember that the calculation is based on estimated net income and estimated depreciation; consequently, it is pointless to carry the answer to several decimal places.

In choosing investment opportunities, a short payback period is desirable because (1) the sooner an investment is recovered the sooner the funds are available for other uses and (2) a short payback period also means a short "bail-out period" if conditions should change. However, the payback period should never be the only factor considered because it ignores the length of time revenue will continue to be earned after the end of the payback period. For example, one investment may pay back its cost in three years and cease to produce revenue at that point, while a second investment may require five years to pay back its cost but will continue to produce income for another 15 years.

Rate of Return on Average Investment

The *rate of return on the average investment* in a machine is calculated by dividing the after-tax net income from the sale of the machine's product by the average investment in the machine.

In calculating the average investment, an assumption must be made as to the timing of the cost recovery from depreciation. If sales are earned evenly throughout the year, the cost recovery from depreciation may be assumed to occur at the middle of the year. Under these conditions, the average investment each year may be calculated as the average of the beginning-of-year book value and the end-of-year book value. If Murray Company's $16,000 machine is depreciated $2,000 each year, the average investment each year and the average investment over the life of the machine may be calculated as shown in Illustration 27–1.

Illustration 27–1

Year	Beginning-of-year book value	Average investment each year		
1	$16,000	$15,000		
2	14,000	13,000		
3	12,000	11,000		
4	10,000	9,000	$\dfrac{\$64,000}{8}$ =	$8,000 average investment over life of machine
5	8,000	7,000		
6	6,000	5,000		
7	5,000	3,000		
8	2,000	1,000		
Totals	$72,000	$64,000		

More simply, the average investment may be calculated as:

$$\$16,000 \div 2 = \$8,000$$

Note that the above example is simplified by the fact that the machine has no salvage value. If the machine had a salvage value, the average investment would be calculated as (Original cost + Salvage value) ÷ 2.

After average investment is determined, the rate of return on average investment is calculated. As previously stated, this involves dividing the estimated annual after-tax net income from the sale of the machine's product by average investment. Since Murray Company expects an after-tax net income of $1,500, the expected rate of return is calculated as follows:

$$\$1,500 \div \$8,000 = 18\tfrac{3}{4}\% \text{ return on average investment}$$

In some investments, the revenue from the investment is not spread evenly over each year and may be received near the end of each year. If the revenue is expected to be received at the year's end, the cost recovery from depreciation also occurs at the year's end. Thus, the average investment each year is the beginning-of-year book value. Referring back to Illustration 27–1, these assumptions result in the following calculation of average investment:

$72,000 ÷ 8 = $9,000 average investment over life of investment

Instead of adding the beginning-of-year book values and averaging over eight years, a shorter way to the same answer is to average the book values of the machine's first and last years in this manner:

$16,000 book value at beginning of (and throughout) first year
  2,000 book value at beginning of (and throughout) last year
$18,000

$18,000 ÷ 2 = $9,000 average investment over life of investment

Note that if the machine had a salvage value, the book value at the beginning of (and throughout) the last year would be the salvage value plus the depreciation expense of the last year.

Given a $9,000 average investment, the return on investment is:

$1,500 ÷ $9,000 = 16⅔% return on average investment

At this point the question naturally arises whether 16⅔% or 18¾% are good rates of return. Obviously, 18¾% appears better than 16⅔%. However, even this may not be true. A project that is expected to yield 18¾% may be much riskier than another project having a 16⅔% expected return. And, depending on other available investment alternatives, neither may be acceptable. In other words, a return is good or bad only when related to other returns and taking into consideration the differing riskiness of the alternatives. However, when average investment returns are used in comparing and deciding between capital investments, the one having the least risk, the shortest payback period, and the highest return for the longest time is usually the best.

Rate of return on average investment is easy to calculate and understand, and as a result has long been used in selecting investment opportunities. Furthermore, when the opportunities produce uniform cash flows, it offers a fair basis for selection. However, a comparison of *discounted cash flows* with amounts to be invested offers a better means of selection.

An understanding of discounted cash flows requires an understanding of the concept of present value. This concept was explained in Chapter 12, beginning on page 413. That explanation should be re-

viewed at this point by any student who does not fully understand it. The present value tables in Chapter 12, on pages 415 and 417, must be used to solve some of the problems that follow the present chapter.

Discounted Cash Flows

When a business invests in a new plant asset, it expects to secure from the investment a stream of future cash flows. Normally it will not invest unless the flows are sufficient to return the amount of the investment plus a satisfactory return on the investment. For example, assume that the cash flows from Murray Company's investment will be received at the end of each year. Will the investment in the machine return the amount of the investment plus a satisfactory return? If Murray Company considers a 10% compound annual return a satisfactory return on its capital investments, it can answer this question with the calculations of Illustration 27–2.

To secure the machine of Illustration 27–2, Murray Company must invest $16,000. However, from the sale of the machine's product it will recapture $2,000 of its investment each year in the form of depreciation; in addition, it will earn a $1,500 annual net income. In other words, the company will receive a $3,500 net cash flow from the investment each year for eight years. The first column of Illustration 27–2 indicates that the net cash flows of the first year are received one year hence, and so forth for subsequent years. This means that the net cash flows are received at the end of the year. To simplify the discussion of this chapter and the problems at the end of the chapter,

Illustration 27–2

Analysis of Proposed Investment in Machine			
Years Hence	Net Cash Flows	Present Value of $1 at 10%	Present Value of Net Cash Flows
1	$3,500	0.9091	$ 3,181.85
2	3,500	0.8265	2,892.75
3	3,500	0.7513	2,629.55
4	3,500	0.6830	2,390.50
5	3,500	0.6209	2,173.15
6	3,500	0.5645	1,975.75
7	3,500	0.5132	1,796.20
8	3,500	0.4665	1,632.75
Total present value			$18,672.50
Amount to be invested			16,000.00
Positive net present value			$ 2,672.50

the net cash flows of a company's operations are generally assumed to occur at the end of the year. More refined calculations are left for consideration in an advanced course.

The annual net cash flows, shown in the second column of Illustration 27–2, are multiplied by the amounts in the third column to determine their present values, which are shown in the last column. Observe that the total of these present values exceeds the amount of the required investment by $2,672.50. Consequently, if Murray Company considers a 10% compound return satisfactory, this machine will recover its required investment, plus a 10% compound return, and $2,672.50 in addition.

Generally, when the cash flows from an investment are discounted at a satisfactory rate and have a present value in excess of the investment, the investment is worthy of acceptance. Also, when several investment opportunities are being compared, and each requires the same investment and has the same risk, the one having the highest positive net present value is the best.

Shortening the Calculation

In Illustration 27–2, the present values of $1 at 10% for each of the eight years involved are shown. Each year's cash flow is multiplied by the present value of $1 at 10% for that year to determine its present value. Then, the present values of the eight cash flows are added to determine their total. This is one way to determine total present value. However, since in this case the cash flows are uniform, there are two shorter ways. One shorter way is to add the eight yearly present values of $1 at 10% and to multiply $3,500 by the total. Another even shorter way is based on Table 12–2 on page 417. Table 12–2 shows the present value of $1 to be received periodically for a number of periods. In the case of the Murray Company machine, $3,500 is to be received annually for eight years. Consequently, to determine the present value of these annual receipts discounted at 10%, go down the 10% column of Table 12–2 to the amount opposite eight periods. It is 5.3349. Therefore, the present value of the eight annual $3,500 receipts is $3,500 multiplied by 5.3349, or is $18,672.15. The $0.35 difference between this answer and the answer shown in Illustration 27–2 results from the fact that the numbers in Tables 12–1 and 12–2 are rounded.

Cash Flows Not Uniform

Present value analysis has its greatest usefulness when cash flows are not uniform. For example, assume a company can choose one capital investment from among Projects A, B, and C. Each requires a $12,000 investment and will produce cash flows as follows:

Years	Annual Cash Flows		
Hence	Project A	Project B	Project C
1	$ 5,000	$ 8,000	$ 1,000
2	5,000	5,000	5,000
3	5,000	2,000	9,000
	$15,000	$15,000	$15,000

Note that all three projects produce the same total cash flow. However, the flows of Project A are uniform, those of Project B are greater in the earlier years, while those of Project C are greater in the later years. Consequently, when present values of the cash flows, discounted at 10%, are compared with the required investments, the statistics of Illustration 27–3 result.

Illustration 27–3

	Years Hence	Present Values of Cash Flows Discounted at 10%		
		Project A	Project B	Project C
	1	$ 4,545.50	$ 7,272.80	$ 909.10
	2	4,132.50	4,132.50	4,132.50
	3	3,756.50	1,502.60	6,761.70
Total present values		$12,434.50	$12,907.90	$11,803.30
Required investments		12,000.00	12,000.00	12,000.00
Net present values		+$ 434.50	+$ 907.90	−$ 196.70

Note that an investment in Project A has a $434.50 positive net present value; an investment in Project B has a $907.90 positive net present value; and an investment in Project C has a $196.70 negative net present value. Therefore, if a 10% return is required, an investment in Project C should be rejected, since the investment's net present value indicates it will not earn such a return. Furthermore, as between Projects A and B, other things being equal, Project B is the better investment, since its cash flows have the higher net present value. Although the present value numbers in Illustration 27–3 show dollars and cents, present values are always approximations. Hence, it would be appropriate to round such calculations to the nearest whole dollar.

Salvage Value and Accelerated Depreciation

The $16,000 machine of the Murray Company example was assumed to have no salvage value at the end of its useful life. Often a machine is expected to have a salvage value, and in such cases the expected salvage value is treated as an additional cash flow to be received in the last year of the machine's life.

Also, in the Murray Company example, depreciation was deducted on a straight-line basis; but in actual practice, an accelerated depreciation method is commonly used for tax purposes. Accelerated depreciation results in larger depreciation deductions in the early years of an asset's life and smaller deductions in the later years. This results in smaller income tax liabilities in the early years and larger ones in later years. However, this does not change the basic nature of a present value analysis. It only results in larger cash flows in the early years and smaller ones in later years, which normally make an investment more desirable.

Selecting the Earnings Rate

The selection of a satisfactory earnings rate for capital investments is always a matter for top-management decision. Formulas have been devised to aid management. But, in many companies, the choice of a satisfactory or required rate of return is largely subjective. Management simply decides that enough investment opportunities can be found that will earn, say, a 10% compound return; and this becomes the minimum below which the company refuses to make an investment of average risk.

Whatever the required rate, it is always higher than the rate at which money can be borrowed, since the return on a capital investment must include not only interest but also an additional allowance for risks involved. Therefore, when the rate at which money can be borrowed is around 10%, a required after-tax return of 15% may be acceptable in industrial companies, with a lower rate for public utilities and a higher rate for companies in which investment opportunities are unusually good or the risks are high.

Replacing Plant Assets

In a dynamic economy, new and better machines are constantly coming on the market. As a result, the decision to replace an existing machine with a new and better machine is common. Often, the existing machine is in good condition and will produce the required product; but the new machine will do the job with a large savings in operating costs. In such a situation, management must decide whether the after-tax savings in operating costs justifies the investment.

The amount of after-tax savings from the replacement of an existing machine with a new machine is complicated by the fact that depreciation on the new machine for tax purposes is based on the book value of the old machine plus the cash given in the exchange. There can be other complications too. Consequently, a discussion of the replacement of plant assets is deferred to a more advanced course.

ACCEPTING ADDITIONAL BUSINESS

Costs obtained from a cost accounting system are average costs and also historical costs. They are useful in product pricing and in controlling operations. But, in a decision to accept an additional volume of business they are not necessarily the relevant costs. In such a decision, the relevant costs are the additional costs, commonly called the *incremental* or *differential costs.*

For example, a company operating at its normal capacity, which is 80% of full capacity, has annually produced and sold approximately 100,000 units of product with the following results:

Sales (100,000 units @ $10)		$1,000,000
Materials (100,000 units @ $3.50)	$350,000	
Labor (100,000 units @ $2.20)	220,000	
Overhead (100,000 units @ $1.10)	110,000	
Selling expenses (100,000 units @ $1.40)	140,000	
Administrative expenses (100,000 units @ $0.80)	80,000	900,000
Operating income		$ 100,000

The company's sales department reports it has an exporter who has offered to buy 10,000 units of product at $8.50 per unit. The sale to the exporter is several times larger than any previous sale made by the company; and since the units are being exported, the new business will have no effect on present business. Therefore, in order to determine whether the order should be accepted or rejected, management of the company asks that statistics be prepared to show the estimated net income or loss that would result from accepting the offer. It received the following figures based on the average costs previously given:

Sales (10,000 units @ $8.50)		$85,000
Materials (10,000 units @ $3.50)	$35,000	
Labor (10,000 units @ $2.20)	22,000	
Overhead (10,000 units @ $1.10)	11,000	
Selling expenses (10,000 units @ $1.40)	14,000	
Administrative expenses (10,000 units @ $0.80)	8,000	90,000
Operating loss		$ (5,000)

If a decision were based on these average costs, the new business would likely be rejected. However, in this situation, average costs are not relevant. The relevant costs are the added costs of accepting the new business. Consequently, before rejecting the order, the costs of the new business were examined more closely and the following additional information obtained: (1) Manufacturing 10,000 additional units of product would require materials and labor at $3.50 and $2.20 per unit just as with normal production. (2) However, the 10,000 units could be manufactured with overhead costs, in addition to those already incurred, of only $5,000 for power, packing, and handling labor. (3) Commissions and other selling expenses resulting from the sale would amount to $2,000 in addition to the selling expenses already incurred. And (4), $1,000 additional administrative expenses in the form of clerical work would be required if the order were accepted. Based on this added information, the statement of Illustration 27–4 showing the effect of the additional business on the company's normal business was prepared.

Illustration 27–4 shows that the additional business should be accepted. Present business should be charged with all present costs, and the additional business should be charged only with its incremental or differential costs. When this is done, accepting the additional business at $8.50 per unit will apparently result in $20,000 additional income before taxes.

Incremental or differential costs always apply to a particular situation at a particular time. For example, adding units to a given production volume may or may not increase depreciation expense. If the additional units require the purchase of more machines, depreciation expense is increased. Likewise, if present machines are used but the additional units shorten their life, more depreciation expense results. However, if present machines are used and their depreciation depends more on the passage of time or obsolescence rather than on use, additional depreciation expense might not result from the added units of product.

Illustration 27–4

	Present business		Additional business		Present plus the additional business	
Sales		$1,000,000		$85,000		$1,085,000
Materials	$350,000		$35,000		$385,000	
Labor	220,000		22,000		242,000	
Overhead	110,000		5,000		115,000	
Selling expenses	140,000		2,000		142,000	
Administrative expense	80,000		1,000		81,000	
Total		900,000		65,000		965,000
Operating income		$ 100,000		$20,000		$ 120,000

BUY OR MAKE

Incremental or differential costs are often a factor in a decision as to whether a given part or product should be bought or made. For example, a manufacturer has idle machines that can be used to manufacture one of the components (Part 417) of the company's product. This part is presently purchased at a $1.20 delivered cost per unit. The manufacturer estimates that to make Part 417 would cost $0.45 for materials, $0.50 for labor, and an amount of overhead. At this point a question arises as to how much overhead should be charged. If the normal overhead rate of the department in which the part would be manufactured is 100% of direct labor cost, and this amount is charged against Part 417, then the unit costs of making Part 417 would be $0.45 for materials, $0.50 for labor, and $0.50 for overhead, a total of $1.45. At this cost, the manufacturer would be better off to buy the part at $1.20 each.

However, on a short-run basis the manufacturer might be justified in ignoring the normal overhead rate and in charging Part 417 for only the additional overhead costs resulting from its manufacture. Among these additional overhead costs might be, for example, power to operate the machines that would otherwise be idle, depreciation on the machines if the part's manufacture resulted in additional depreciation, and any other overhead that would be added to that already incurred. Furthermore, if these added overhead items total less than $0.25 per unit, the manufacturer might be justified on a short-run basis in manufacturing the part. However, on a long-term basis, Part 417 should be charged a full share of all overhead.

Any amount of overhead less than $0.25 per unit results in a total cost for Part 417 that is less than the $1.20 per unit purchase price. Nevertheless, in making a final decision as to whether the part should be bought or made, the manufacturer should consider in addition to costs such things as quality, the reactions of customers and suppliers, and other intangible factors. When these additional factors are considered, small cost differences may become a minor factor.

OTHER COST CONCEPTS

Sunk costs, out-of-pocket costs, and *opportunity costs* are additional concepts that may be encountered in managerial decisions.

A sunk cost is a cost resulting from a past irrevocable decision, and is sunk in the sense that it cannot be avoided. As a result, sunk costs are irrelevant in decisions affecting the future.

An out-of-pocket cost is a cost requiring a current outlay of funds. Material costs, supplies, heat, and power are examples. Generally, out-of-pocket costs can be avoided; consequently, they are relevant in decisions affecting the future.

Costs as discussed thus far have been outlays or expenditures made to obtain some benefit, usually goods or services. However, the concept of costs can be expanded to include *sacrifices made to gain some benefit.* For example, if a job that will pay a student $1,200 for working during the summer must be rejected in order to attend summer school, the $1,200 is an opportunity cost of attending summer school.

Obviously, opportunity costs are not entered in the accounting records; but they may be relevant in a decision involving rejected opportunities. For example, decisions to scrap or rebuild defective units of product commonly involve situations which evidence both sunk costs and opportunity costs.

SCRAP OR REBUILD DEFECTIVE UNITS

Any costs incurred in manufacturing units of product that do not pass inspection are sunk costs and as such should not enter into a decision as to whether the units should be sold for scrap or be rebuilt to pass inspection. For example, a company has 10,000 defective units of product that cost $1 per unit to manufacture. The units can be sold as they are for $0.40 each, or they can be rebuilt for $0.80 per unit, after which they can be sold for their full price of $1.50 per unit. Should the company rebuild the units or should it sell them in their present form? The original manufacturing costs of $1 per unit are sunk costs and are irrelevant in the decision; so, based on the information given, the comparative returns from scrapping or rebuilding are:

	As scrap	Rebuilt
Sales of defective units	$4,000	$15,000
Less cost to rebuild		(8,000)
Net return	$4,000	$ 7,000

From the information given, it appears that rebuilding is the better decision. This is true if the rebuilding does not interfere with normal operations. However, suppose that to rebuild the defective units the company must forgo manufacturing 10,000 new units that will cost $1 per unit to manufacture and can be sold for $1.50 per unit. In this situation the comparative returns may be analyzed as follows:

	As scrap	Rebuilt
Sale of defective units	$ 4,000	$15,000
Less cost to rebuild the defective units		(8,000)
Sale of new units	15,000	
Less cost to manufacture the new units	(10,000)	
Net return	$ 9,000	$ 7,000

If the defective units are sold without rebuilding, then the new units can also be manufactured and sold, with a $9,000 return from the sale of both the new and old units, as shown in the first column of the analysis. Obviously, this is better than forgoing the manufacture of the new units and rebuilding the defective units for a $7,000 net return.

The situation described here also may be analyzed on an opportunity cost basis as follows: If to rebuild the defective units the company must forgo manufacturing the new units, then the return on the sale of the new units is an opportunity cost of rebuilding the defective units. This opportunity cost is measured at $5,000 (revenue from sale of new units, $15,000, less their manufacturing costs, $10,000 equals the $5,000 benefit that will be sacrificed if the old units are rebuilt); and an opportunity cost analysis of the situation is as follows:

	As scrap	Rebuilt
Sale of defective units	$4,000	$15,000
Less cost to rebuild the defective units		(8,000)
Less opportunity cost (return sacrificed by not manufacturing the new units)		(5,000)
Net return	$4,000	$ 2,000

Observe that it does not matter whether this or the previous analysis is made. Either way there is a $2,000 difference in favor of scrapping the defective units.

PROCESS OR SELL

Sunk costs, out-of-pocket costs, and opportunity costs are also encountered in a decision as to whether it is best to sell an intermediate product as it is or process it further and sell the product or products that result from the additional processing. For example, a company has 40,000 units of Product A that cost $0.75 per unit or a total of $30,000 to manufacture. The 40,000 units can be sold as they are for $50,000 or they can be processed further into Products X, Y, and Z at a cost of $2 per original Product A unit. The additional processing will produce the following numbers of each product, which can be sold at the unit prices indicated:

Product X	10,000 units @ $3
Product Y	22,000 units @ $5
Product Z	6,000 units @ $1
Lost through spoilage	2,000 units (no salvage value)
Total	40,000 units

The net advantage of processing the product further is $16,000, as shown in Illustration 27–5.

Illustration 27–5

Revenue from further processing:		
Product X, 10,000 units @ $3	$ 30,000	
Product Y, 22,000 units @ $5	110,000	
Product Z, 6,000 units @ $1	6,000	
Total revenue		$146,000
Less:		
Additional processing costs, 40,000 units @ $2	$ 80,000	
Opportunity cost (revenue sacrificed by not		
selling the Product A units)	50,000	
Total		130,000
Net advantage of further processing		$ 16,000

Note that the revenue available through the sale of the Product A units is an opportunity cost of further processing these units. Also notice that the $30,000 cost of manufacturing the 40,000 units of Product A does not appear in the Illustration 27–5 analysis. This cost is present regardless of which alternative is chosen; therefore, it is irrelevant to the decision. However, the $30,000 does enter into a calculation of the net income from the alternatives. For example, if the company chooses to further process the Product A units, the gross return from the sale of Products X, Y, and Z may be calculated as follows:

Revenue from the sale of Products X, Y, and Z		$146,000
Less:		
Cost to manufacture the Product A units	$30,000	
Cost to further process the Product A units	80,000	110,000
Gross return from the sale of Products X, Y, and Z		$ 36,000

DECIDING THE SALES MIX

When a company sells a combination of products, ordinarily some of the products are more profitable than others, and normally management should concentrate its sales efforts on the more profitable products. However, if production facilities or other factors are limited, an increase in the production and sale of one product may require a reduction in the production and sale of another. In such a situation, management's job is to determine the most profitable combination or sales mix for the products and concentrate on selling the products in this combination.

To determine the best sales mix for its products, management must have information as to the contribution margin of each product, the facilities required to produce and sell each product, and any limitations on these facilities. For example, assume that a company produces and sells two products, A and B. The same machines are used to produce both products, and the products have the following selling prices and variable costs per units:

	Product A	Product B
Selling price	$5.00	$7.50
Variable costs	3.50	5.50
Contribution margin	$1.50	$2.00

If the amount of production facilities required to produce each product is the same and there is an unlimited market for Product B, the company should devote all its facilities to Product B because of its larger contribution margin. However, the answer differs if the company's facilities are limited to, say, 100,000 machine-hours of production per month and one machine-hour is required to produce each unit of Product A but two machine-hours are required for each unit of Product B. Under these circumstances, if the market for Product A is unlimited, the company should devote all its production to this product because it produces $1.50 of contribution margin per machine-hour, while Product B produces only $1 per machine-hour.

Actually, when there are no market or other limitations, a company should devote all its efforts to its most profitable product. It is only when there is a market or other limitation on the sale of the most profitable product that a need for a sales mix arises. For example, if in this instance one machine-hour of production facilities are needed to produce each unit of Product A and 100,000 machine-hours are available, 100,000 units of the product can be produced. However, if only 80,000 units can be sold, the company has 20,000 machine-hours that can be devoted to the production of Product B, and 20,000 machine-hours will produce 10,000 units of Product B. Consequently, the company's most profitable sales mix under these assumptions is 80,000 units of Product A and 10,000 units of Product B.

The assumptions in this section have been kept simple. More complicated factors and combinations of factors exist. However, a discussion of these is deferred to a more advanced course.

GLOSSARY

Capital budgeting. Planning plant asset investments; involves the preparation of cost and revenue estimates for all proposed projects, an examination of the merits of each, and a choice of those worthy of investment.

Discounted cash flows. The present value of a stream of future cash flows from an investment, based on an interest rate that gives a satisfactory return on investment.

Incremental cost. An additional cost resulting from a particular course of action. Also called differential cost.

Opportunity cost. A sacrifice made to gain some benefits; that is, in choosing one course of action, the lost benefit associated with an alternative course of action.

Out-of-pocket cost. A cost requiring a current outlay of funds.

Payback period. The time required to recover the original cost of an investment through net cash flows from the investment.

Rate of return on average investment. The annual, after-tax income from the sale of an asset's product divided by the average investment in the asset.

Sunk cost. A cost incurred as a consequence of a past irrevocable decision and that, therefore, cannot be avoided; hence, irrelevant to decisions affecting the future.

QUESTIONS FOR CLASS DISCUSSION

1. What is capital budgeting? Why are capital budgeting decisions crucial to the business making the decisions?
2. A successful investment in a machine will produce a net cash flow. Of what does this consist?
3. If depreciation is an expense, explain why, when the sale of a machine's product produces a net income, the portion of the machine's cost recovered each year through the sale of its product includes both the net income from the product's sale and the year's depreciation on the machine.
4. Why is a short payback period on an investment desirable?
5. What is the average amount invested in a machine during its life if the machine cost $28,000, has an estimated five-year life during which reve-

nue is earned at the end of each year, and an estimated $3,000 salvage value? Assume straight-line depreciation.

6. Is a 15% return on the average investment in a machine a good return?

7. Why is the present value of the expectation of receiving $100 a year hence less than $100? What is the present value of the expectation of receiving $100 one year hence, discounted at 12%?

8. What is indicated when the present value of the net cash flows from an investment in a machine, discounted at 12%, exceeds the amount of the investment? What is indicated when the present value of the net cash flows, discounted at 12%, is less than the amount of the investment?

9. What are the incremental costs of accepting an additional volume of business?

10. A company manufactures and sells 250,000 units of product in this country at $5 per unit. The product costs $3 per unit to manufacture. Can you describe a situation under which the company may be willing to sell an additional 25,000 units of the product abroad at $2.75 per unit?

11. What is a sunk cost? An out-of-pocket cost? An opportunity cost? Is an opportunity cost typically recorded in the accounting records?

12. Any costs that have been incurred in manufacturing a product are sunk costs. Why are such costs irrelevant in deciding whether to sell the product in its present condition or to make it into a new product through additional processing?

CLASS EXERCISES

Exercise 27–1

Machine X cost $24,000 and has an estimated four-year life and no salvage value. Machine Y cost $30,000 and has an estimated five-year life and a $5,000 salvage value. Calculate the average investment in each machine under the assumptions that revenues and cost recovery from depreciation occur (a) uniformly throughout each year and (b) at the end of each year.

Exercise 27–2

A company is planning to purchase a machine and add a new product to its line. The machine will cost $50,000, have a four-year life, no salvage value, and will be depreciated on a straight-line basis. The company expects to sell 10,000 units of the machine's product each year. Production will occur throughout the year. However, the product is only marketable during the holiday season at the end of each year, and all sales will occur during the last 15 days of the year. Expected annual results are as follows:

Sales		$125,000
Costs:		
Materials, labor, and overhead excluding depreciation on the new machine	$65,000	
Depreciation on new machine	12,500	
Selling and administrative expenses	37,500	115,000
Operating income		$ 10,000
Income taxes		5,000
Net income		$ 5,000

Required:

Calculate *(a)* the payback period and *(b)* the return on the average investment in this machine.

Exercise 27–3

After evaluating the risk characteristics of the investment described in Exercise 27–2, the company concludes that it must earn at least a 12% compound return on the investment in the machine. Based on this decision, determine the total present value and net present value of the net cash flows from the machine the company is planning to buy.

Exercise 27–4

A company can invest in each of three projects, A, B, and C. Each project requires a $25,000 investment and will produce cash flows as follows:

Years Hence	Annual Cash Flows		
	Project A	Project B	Project C
1	$ 6,000	$10,000	$14,000
2	10,000	10,000	10,000
3	14,000	10,000	6,000
	$30,000	$30,000	$30,000

Required:

Under the assumption the company requires a 10% compound return from its investments, determine in which of the projects it should invest.

Exercise 27–5

A company has 10,000 units of Product X that cost $2 per unit to manufacture. The 10,000 units can be sold for $30,000, or they can be further processed at a cost of $14,000 into Products Y and Z. The additional processing will produce 4,000 units of Product Y that can be sold for $4 each and 6,000 units of Product Z that can be sold for $4.50 each.

Required:

Prepare an analysis to show whether the Product X units should be further processed.

PROBLEMS

Problem 27–1

A company is planning to add a new product to its line, the production of which will require new machinery costing $63,000 and having a five-year life and no salvage value. This additional information is available:

Estimated annual sales of new product $210,000

Estimated costs:
Materials 42,000
Labor 56,000
Overhead excluding depreciation on new machinery 53,200
Selling and administrative expenses 35,000
State and federal income taxes 50%

Required:

Using straight-line depreciation, calculate *(a)* the payback period on the investment in new machinery, *(b)* the rate of return on the average investment, and *(c)* the net present value of the net cash flows discounted at 14%. In calculating the rate of return and the net present value, assume that all cash flows occur at the end of each year.

Problem 27–2

A company has an opportunity to invest in either of two projects. Project A requires an investment of $45,000 for new machinery having a five-year life and a $5,000 salvage value. Project B requires an investment of $38,500 for new machinery having a seven-year life and a $3,500 salvage value. The products of the projects differ; however, each will produce for the life of the machinery an annual profit of $3,000 after subtracting straight-line depreciation and taxes of 50%.

Required:

1. Assuming the revenues are earned uniformly throughout each year, calculate the payback period and return on average investment for each project.
2. Now assume that the machines related to both projects have zero salvage values and that the expected annual profits after deducting depreciation and taxes of 50% are $2,800. Assume also that the annual cash flows from each project occur at year-end. Calculate the return on average investment and the net present value of the cash flows from each project, discounted at 10%.

Problem 27–3

Bend'n Mend Company manufactures a small tool that it sells to wholesalers at $3.20 each. The company manufactures and sells approximately 200,000 of the tools each year, and a normal year's costs for the production and sale of this number of tools are as follows:

Materials	$120,000
Direct labor	100,000
Manufacturing overhead	150,000
Selling expenses	60,000
Administrative expenses	50,000
	$480,000

A mail-order company has offered to buy 20,000 of the tools at $2.20 each to be marketed under the mail-order company's trade name. If accepted, the order is not expected to affect sales through present channels.

A study of normal costs and their relation to the new business reveals the following: *(a)* Material costs are 100% variable. *(b)* The per unit direct labor costs for the additional units will be 50% greater than normal since their production will require overtime at time and one half. *(c)* Of a normal year's manufacturing overhead costs, two thirds will remain fixed at any production level from zero to 250,000 units and one third will vary with volume. *(d)* There will be no additional selling costs if the new business is accepted. *(e)* Acceptance of the new business will increase administrative costs $3,000.

Required:

Prepare a comparative income statement that shows *(a)* in one set of columns the operating results and operating income of a normal year, *(b)* in the second set of columns the operating results and income that may be expected from the new business, and *(c)* in the third set of columns the combined results from normal and the expected new business.

Problem 27–4

La Grange Company is considering a project that requires a $120,000 investment in machinery having a six-year life and no salvage value. The project will produce $42,000 at the end of each year for six years, before deducting depreciation on the new machinery and income taxes of 50%.

For tax purposes, the company may choose between two alternative depreciation schedules, as follows:

Year	Straight-line depreciation schedule	ACRS depreciation schedule
1	$12,000	$18,000
2	24,000	26,400
3	24,000	25,200
4	24,000	25,200
5	24,000	25,200
6	12,000	–0–

Required:

1. Calculate the company's cash flow from the project for each of the six years with depreciation for tax purposes calculated according to *(a)* the straight-line depreciation schedule and *(b)* the ACRS depreciation schedule.
2. Calculate the net present value of the net cash flows discounted at 14% assuming the straight-line depreciation schedule is used.
3. Calculate the net present value of the net cash flows discounted at 14% assuming the ACRS depreciation schedule is used.
4. Explain why the ACRS depreciation method increases the net present value of this project.

Problem 27–5

Lambert Company's sales and costs for its two products last year were:

	Product X	Product Y
Unit selling price	$40	$30
Variable costs per unit	$24	$10
Fixed costs	$120,000	$140,000
Units sold	8,000	9,000

Through sales effort the company can change its sales mix. However, sales of the two products are so interrelated that a percentage increase in the sales of one product causes an equal percentage decrease in the sales of the other, and vice versa.

Required:

1. State which of its products the company should push, and why.
2. Prepare a columnar statement showing last year's sales, fixed costs, variable

costs, and income before taxes for Product X in the first pair of columns, the results for Product Y in the second set of columns, and the combined results for both products in the third set of columns.

3. Prepare a like statement for the two products under the assumption that the sales of Product X are increased 25%, with a resulting 25% decrease in the sales of Product Y.

4. Prepare a third statement under the assumption that the sales of Product X are decreased 25%, with a resulting 25% increase in the sales of Product Y.

ALTERNATE PROBLEMS

Problem 27–1A A company is considering adding a new product to its line, of which it estimates it can sell 24,000 units annually at $11.50 per unit. To manufacture the product will require new machinery having an estimated five-year life, no salvage value, and costing $72,000. The new product will have a $4.80 per unit direct material cost and a $2.40 per unit direct labor cost. Manufacturing overhead chargeable to the new product, other than for depreciation on the new machinery, will be $39,600 annually. Also, $30,000 of additional selling and administrative expenses will be incurred annually in producing and selling the product, and state and federal income taxes will take 50% of the before-taxes profit.

Required:

Using straight-line depreciation, calculate *(a)* the payback period on the investment in new machinery, *(b)* the rate of return on the average investment, and *(c)* the net present value of the net cash flows discounted at 12%. Assume that revenues are received at year-end.

Problem 27–2A A company has the opportunity to invest in either of two projects. Project X requires an investment of $28,000 for new machinery having a seven-year life and no salvage value. Project Y requires an investment of $30,000 for new machinery having a five-year life and no salvage value. Sales of the two projects will produce the following estimated annual results:

	Project X		Project Y	
Sales		$65,000		$75,000
Costs:				
Materials	$15,000		$18,000	
Labor	13,500		17,500	
Manufacturing overhead including depreciation on new machinery	19,000		22,000	
Selling and administrative expenses	12,500	60,000	12,500	70,000
Operating income		$ 5,000		$ 5,000
State and federal income taxes		2,500		2,500
Net income		$ 2,500		$ 2,500

Required:

Calculate the payback period, the return on average investment, and the net present value of the net cash flows from each project discounted at 12%. State which project you think the better investment and why. Assume that revenues are received at year-end.

Problem 27–3A

Thermodynamics Unlimited annually sells at $5 per unit 50,000 units of its product. At the 50,000-unit production level the product costs $4.50 a unit to manufacture and sell, and at this level the company has the following costs and expenses:

Fixed manufacturing overhead costs	$25,000
Fixed selling expenses	12,500
Fixed administrative expenses	15,000
Variable costs and expenses:	
Materials ($1.00 per unit)	50,000
Labor ($1.25 per unit)	62,500
Manufacturing overhead ($0.75 per unit)	37,500
Selling expenses ($0.25 per unit)	12,500
Administrative expense ($0.20 per unit)	10,000

All the units the company presently sells are sold in this country. However, recently an exporter has offered to buy 5,000 units of the product for sale abroad, but he will pay only $4.45 per unit, which is below the company's present $4.50 per unit manufacturing and selling costs.

Required:

Prepare an income statement that shows *(a)* in one set of columns the revenue, costs, expenses, and income from selling 50,000 units of the product in this country; *(b)* in a second set of columns the additional revenue, costs, expenses, and income from selling 5,000 units to the exporter; and *(c)* in a third set of columns the combined results from both sources. (Assume that acceptance of the new business will not increase any of the company's fixed costs and expenses nor change any of the variable per unit costs and expenses.)

Problem 27–4A

Tyler Company is considering a project that requires a $360,000 investment in machinery having a six-year life and no salvage value. The project will produce $42,000 at the end of each year for six years, before deducting depreciation on the new machinery and income taxes of 50%.

For tax purposes, the company may choose between two alternative depreciation schedules, as follows:

Year	Straight-line depreciation schedule	ACRS depreciation schedule
1	$36,000	$54,000
2	72,000	79,200
3	72,000	75,600
4	72,000	75,600
5	72,000	75,600
6	36,000	–0–

Required:

1. Calculate the company's cash flow from the project for each of the six years with depreciation for tax purposes calculated according to *(a)* the straight-line depreciation schedule and *(b)* the ACRS depreciation schedule.
2. Calculate the net present value of the net cash flows discounted at 12% assuming the straight-line depreciation schedule is used.
3. Calculate the net present value of the net cash flows discounted at 12% assuming the ACRS depreciation schedule is used.
4. Explain why the ACRS depreciation method increases the net present value of this project.

Problem 27–5A   Sutter Cutter Company manufactures and sells a machine called a subdivider. Last year the company made and sold 700 subdividers, with the following results:

Sales (700 units @ $90)		$63,000
Costs and expenses:		
Variable:		
Materials.............................	$13,860	
Labor	11,340	
Factory overhead	9,450	
Selling and administrative expenses	6,300	
Fixed:		
Factory overhead	9,500	
Selling and administrative expenses	6,000	56,450
Income before taxes		$ 6,550

The state highway department has asked for bids on 100 subdividers almost identical to Sutter Cutter Company's machine, the only difference being a counter not presently installed on the Sutter Cutter Company subdivider. To install the counter would require the purchase of a new machine costing $300, plus $2 per subdivider for additional material and $2.50 per subdivider for additional labor. The new machine would have no further use after the completion of the highway department contract, but it could be sold for $100. Sale of the additional units would not affect the company's fixed costs and expenses, but all variable costs and expenses, including variable selling and administrative expenses, would increase proportionately with the volume increase.

Required:

1. List with their total the unit costs of the material, labor, and so forth, that would enter into the lowest unit price the company could bid on the special order without causing a reduction in income from normal business.
2. Under the assumption the company bid $80 per unit and was awarded the contract for the 100 special units, prepare an income statement showing *(a)* in one set of columns the revenues, costs, expenses, and income before taxes from present business; *(b)* in a second set of columns the revenue, costs, expenses, and income before taxes from the new business; and *(c)*

in a third set of columns the combined results of both the old and new business.

PROVOCATIVE PROBLEMS

Silverdime Company operates metal alloy producing plants, one of which is located at Birmingham. The Birmingham plant no longer produces a satisfactory profit due to its distance from raw material sources, relatively high electric power costs, and lack of modern machinery. Consequently, construction of a new plant to replace the Birmingham plant is under consideration.

The new plant would be located close to a raw material source and near low-cost hydroelectric power; but its construction would necessitate abandonment of the Birmingham plant. The company president favors the move; but several members of the board are not convinced the Birmingham plant should be abandoned in view of the great loss that would result.

You have been asked to make recommendations concerning the proposed abandonment and construction of the new plant. Data developed during the course of your analysis include the following:

Loss from abandoning the Birmingham plant. The land, buildings, and machinery of the Birmingham plant have a $1,900,000 book value. Very little of the machinery can be moved to the new plant. Most will have to be scrapped. Therefore, if the plant is abandoned, it is estimated that only $400,000 of the remaining investment in the plant can be recovered through the sale of its land and buildings, the sale of scrap, and by moving some of its machinery to the new plant. The remaining $1,500,000 will be lost.

Investment in the new plant. The new plant will cost $6,000,000, including the book value of any machinery moved from Birmingham, and will have a 20-year life. It will also have double the 12,500-ton capacity of the Birmingham plant, and it is estimated the 25,000 tons of metal alloy produced annually can be sold without a price reduction.

Comparative production costs. A comparison of the production costs per ton at the old plant with the estimated costs at the new plant shows the following:

	Old plant	New plant
Raw material, labor, and plant costs (other than depreciation)	$300	$252
Depreciation	20	12
Total costs per ton	$320	$264

The higher per ton depreciation charge of the old plant results primarily from depreciation being allocated to fewer units of product.

Prepare a report analyzing the advantages and disadvantages of the move, including your recommendation. You may assume that the Birmingham plant can continue to operate long enough to recover the remaining investment in the plant; however, due to the plant's high costs, operation will be at the break-even point. Furthermore, a shortage of skilled personnel would not allow the company to operate both the Birmingham plant and the new plant. Present any pertinent analyses based on the data given.

Provocative
Problem 27–2,
Raytan
Company

Raytan Company has operated at substantially less than its full plant capacity for several years, producing and selling an average of 32,500 units of its product annually and receiving a per unit price of $13. Its costs at this sales level are:

Direct materials	$133,250
Direct labor	104,000
Manufacturing overhead:	
Variable	40,625
Fixed	20,000
Selling and administrative expenses:	
Variable	19,500
Fixed	40,000
Income taxes	50%

After searching for ways to utilize the plant capacity of the company more fully, management has begun to consider the possibility of processing the product beyond the present point at which it is sold. If the product is further processed, it can be sold for $15 per unit. Further processing will increase fixed manufacturing overhead by $8,250 annually, and it will increase variable manufacturing costs per unit as follows:

Materials	$0.21
Direct labor	0.19
Variable manufacturing overhead	0.15
Total	$0.55

Selling the further processed product will not affect fixed selling and administrative expenses, but it will increase variable selling and administrative expenses by 25%. Further processing is not expected to either increase or decrease the number of units sold.

Should the company further process the product? Back your opinion with a simple calculation and also a comparative income statement showing present results and the estimated results with the product further processed.

Provocative
Problem 27–3,
Allentown
Company

Allentown Company manufactures and sells a common piece of industrial machinery, selling an average of 84,000 units of the machine each year. The company generally earns an after-tax (50% rate) net income of $32 per unit sold. Allentown Company's production process involves assemblying the several components of the machine, some of which are manufactured by the company and others of which are purchased from a variety of suppliers.

One of the components that has been manufactured by the company is a pump which is also available from other suppliers. Allentown Company uses special equipment to make the pump, and the equipment has no alternative uses. The equipment has a $63,000 book value, a seven-year remaining life, and is depreciated at the rate of $9,000 per year. In addition to depreciation of the equipment, the costs to manufacture the pump are: direct materials, $4.00; direct labor, $3.20; and variable overhead, $0.80.

One of Allentown's suppliers has recently offered the company a contract to purchase pumps from the supplier at a delivered cost of $8.52 per unit. If the company decides to purchase the pumps, the special equipment used to manufacture them can be sold for cash at its book value (no profit or loss) and the cash can be invested in other projects that will pay a 14% compound after-tax return, which is the return the company demands on all its capital investments.

Should the company continue to manufacture the pump, or should it sell the special equipment and buy the pump? Back your answer with explanations and computations.

Tax Considerations in Business Decisions

28

After studying Chapter 28, you should be able to:

Explain the importance of tax planning.

Describe the steps an individual must go through to calculate his or her tax liability, and explain the difference between deductions to arrive at adjusted gross income, deductions from adjusted gross income, and tax credits.

Calculate the taxable income and net tax liability for an individual.

State the procedures used to determine the tax associated with capital gains and losses.

Describe the differences between the calculations of taxable income and tax liability for corporations and for individuals.

Explain why income tax expenses shown in financial statements may differ from taxes actually payable.

Define or explain the terms and phrases listed in the chapter Glossary.

Years ago, when income tax rates were low, management could afford to ignore or dismiss as of minor importance the tax effects of a business decision; but today, when nearly half the income of a business might be paid out in income taxes, this is no longer wise. Today, a successful management must constantly be alert to every possible tax savings, recognizing that it is often necessary to earn two "pretax dollars" in order to keep one "after-tax dollar," or that a dollar of income tax saved is commonly worth a two-dollar reduction in any other expense.

TAX PLANNING

When taxpayers plan their affairs in such a way as to incur the smallest possible tax liability, they are engaged in *tax planning*. Many business deals can be designed in more than one alternative way. For example, equipment might be purchased for cash, purchased through borrowed money, or perhaps even leased from the owner. Tax planning involves evaluating each alternative in terms of its tax consequences and selecting the one alternative that will result in the smallest tax liability.

Normally tax planning requires that a tax-saving opportunity be recognized prior to the occurrence of the transaction. Although it is sometimes possible to take advantage of a previously overlooked tax saving, the common result of an overlooked opportunity is a lost opportunity, since the Internal Revenue Service usually deems the original action in a tax situation the final action for tax purposes.

Since effective tax planning requires an extensive knowledge of both tax laws and business procedures, it is not the purpose of this chapter to make expert tax planners of elementary accounting students. Rather, the purpose is to make students aware of the merits of effective tax planning, recognizing that for complete and effective planning, the average student, business executive, or citizen should seek the advice of a certified public accountant, tax attorney, or other person qualified in tax matters.

TAX EVASION AND TAX AVOIDANCE

In any discussion of taxes, a clear distinction should be drawn between tax evasion and tax avoidance. *Tax evasion* is illegal and may result in heavy penalties, including prison sentences in some instances; but *tax avoidance* is a perfectly legal and profitable activity.

Taxes are avoided by preventing a tax liability from coming into existence. This may be accomplished by any legal means, for example, by the way in which a transaction is completed, or the manner in which a business is organized, or by a wise selection from among the options provided in the tax laws. It makes no difference how, as long as the means is legal and prevents a tax liability from arising.

In contrast, tax evasion involves the fraudulent denial and concealment of an existing tax liability. For example, taxes are evaded when taxable income, such as interest, dividends, tips, fees, or profits from the sale of stocks, bonds, and other assets, is unreported. Taxes are also evaded when items not legally deductible from income are deducted. For example, taxes are evaded when the costs of operating the family automobile are deducted as a business expense, or when charitable contributions not allowed or not made are deducted. Tax evasion is illegal and should be scrupulously avoided.

STATE AND MUNICIPAL INCOME TAXES

Most states and a number of cities levy income taxes, in most cases modeling their laws after the federal laws. However, other than noting the existence of such laws and that they increase the total tax burden and make tax planning even more important, the following discussion is limited to the federal income tax.

HISTORY AND OBJECTIVES OF THE FEDERAL INCOME TAX

Although the federal government first used an income tax during the War between the States, the history of today's federal income tax dates from the 1913 ratification of the Sixteenth Amendment, which cleared away all questions as to the constitutionality of such a tax. Since its ratification, Congress has passed more than 50 revenue acts and other laws implementing the tax, placing the responsibility for their enforcement in the hands of the Treasury Department acting through the Internal Revenue Service. Collectively, the statutes dealing with taxation that have been adopted by Congress are called the *Internal Revenue Code*.

The original purpose of the federal income tax was to raise revenue, but over the years this original goal has been expanded to include the following and other nonrevenue objectives:

1. To assist small businesses.
2. To encourage foreign trade.
3. To encourage exploration for oil and minerals.
4. To redistribute the national income.
5. To control inflation and deflation.

6. To stimulate business.
7. To attain full employment.
8. To support other social objectives.

Also, just as the objectives have expanded over the years, so have the rates and the number of people required to pay taxes. In 1913, the minimum rate was 1% and the maximum for individuals was 7%. This contrasts with today's minimum 11% rate for individuals and maximum of 50%. Likewise, the total number of tax returns filed each year has grown from a few thousand in 1913 to well over 100,000,000 in recent years.

SYNOPSIS OF THE FEDERAL INCOME TAX

The following brief synopsis of the federal income tax is given at this point because it is necessary to know something about the federal income tax in order to appreciate its effect on business decisions.

Classes of Taxpayers

Federal income tax law recognizes three classes of taxpayers: individuals, corporations, and estates and trusts. Members of each class must file returns and pay taxes on taxable income.

A business operated as a single proprietorship or partnership is not treated as a separate taxable entity under the law. Rather, single proprietors must include the income from their businesses on their individual tax returns; and although a partnership must file an information return showing its net income and the distributive shares of the partners, the partners are required to include their shares on their individual returns. In other words, the income of a single proprietorship or partnership, whether withdrawn from the business or not, is taxed as the individual income of the single proprietor or partners.

The treatment given corporations under the law is different, however. A business operated as a corporation must file a return and pay taxes on its taxable income. Also, if a corporation pays out in dividends some or all of its "after-tax income," its stockholders must report these dividends as income on their individual returns. Because of this, it is commonly claimed that corporation income is taxed twice, once to the corporation and again to its stockholders.

A discussion of the federal income tax as applied to estates and trusts is not necessary at this point and is deferred to a more advanced course.

The Individual Income Tax

The amount of federal income tax individuals must pay each year depends upon their gross income, deductions, exemptions, and tax credits. The typical calculation of the tax liability involves the sequence shown in Illustration 28–1.

To determine the federal income tax liability of an individual, the amounts of gross income, deductions, exemptions, tax credits (if any), and prepayments are listed on forms supplied by the federal government. Then, the appropriate calculations (additions, subtractions, and so forth) are performed in accordance with the instructions. The listing of the items on the forms is not precisely the same for all classes of taxpayers and does not always follow the general pattern shown in Illustration 28–1; however, the illustration does show the relation of the items and the basic mathematics required in completing the tax forms.

The items that appear on a tax return as gross income, adjusted gross income, deductions, exemptions, tax credits, and prepayments require additional description and explanation.

GROSS INCOME. Income tax law defines *gross income* as *all income from whatever source derived, unless expressly excluded from taxation by law*. Gross income therefore includes income from operating a business, gains from property sales, dividends, interest, rents, royalties, and compensation for services, such as salaries, wages, fees, commissions, bonuses, and tips. Actually, the answers to two questions are all that is required to determine whether an item should be included or excluded. The two questions are: (1) Is the item income? (2) Is it

Illustration 28–1

Gross income		$xx,xxx
Less: Deductions to arrive at adjusted gross income		(xx,xxx)
Adjusted gross income		$xx,xxx
Less: Itemized deductions	$x,xxx	
Less: Zero bracket amount (formerly called standard deduction)	(x,xxx)	
Itemized deductions in excess of zero bracket amount	$x,xxx	
Deduction for exemptions	x,xxx	(x,xxx)
Taxable income		$xx,xxx
Gross tax liability from tax rate schedule		$xx,xxx
Less: Tax credits and prepayments		(xx,xxx)
Net tax payable (or refund)		$ xxx

expressly excluded by law? If an item is income and not specifically excluded, it must be included.

Certain items are specifically excluded from gross income, for example, gifts, inheritances, scholarships, social security benefits, veterans' benefits, workmen's compensation insurance, and in most cases the proceeds of life insurance policies paid upon the death of the insured. Because these items are excluded from gross income, they are nontaxable.

Another item that is specifically excluded from gross income is interest on the obligations of the states and their subdivisions. The Supreme Court has held that a federal income tax on such items would, in effect, amount to having the power to destroy these governmental units. Thus, a federal income tax on the interest from bonds or other obligations of states or their subdivisions would violate constitutional guarantees. With a few exceptions, interest from such items is therefore nontaxable.

For many years, the law has also allowed individuals to exclude a limited amount of dividend income. The maximum exclusion is $200 for married individuals filing a joint return and $100 for all other individuals. One reason for this exclusion (among others) is to partially recognize the fact that corporation income is taxed twice, first as income earned by the corporation and second as dividends received by stockholders.

DEDUCTIONS TO ARRIVE AT ADJUSTED GROSS INCOME. These are generally deductions of a business nature. For example, all ordinary and necessary expenses of carrying on a business, trade, or profession are deductions to arrive at *adjusted gross income.* To understand this, recognize that under income tax law, gross profit from sales (sales less cost of goods sold) is gross income to a merchant, that gross legal fees earned are gross income to a lawyer, and gross rentals from a building are gross income to a landlord. Consequently, the merchant, the lawyer, and the landlord may each deduct all ordinary and necessary expenses of carrying on the business or profession, such as salaries, wages, rent, depreciation, supplies used, repairs, maintenance, insurance, taxes, interest, and so on.

Also, as with the business executive, employees may deduct from gross income certain expenses incurred in connection with their employment if paid by the employees. These include transportation and travel expenses, expenses of an outside salesperson, and moving expenses. Employees who work in more than one place during a day may deduct transportation costs incurred in moving from one place of employment to another during the day. However, as a general rule they may not deduct the cost of commuting from home to the first place of employment or from the last place of employment to home. Travel expenses include in addition to transportation expenses, the cost of meals and lodging while away from home overnight on employment-connected business. Expenses of outside salespersons are expenses incurred in soliciting orders for an employer while away from the employer's place of business. They include such things as transportation, telephone, stationery, and postage. Moving expenses are expenses incurred by employees (or self-employed individuals) in moving their place of residence upon being transferred by their employer or to take a new job. Certain minimum requirements as to the distance moved and the length of employment in the new location must be met. Commonly, an employer reimburses employees for the foregoing expenses. In such cases, employees may deduct only that portion of their expenses not reimbursed by the employer; and if the reimbursement exceeds the expenses, employees must include the excess in their gross income.

Expenses of producing rent income are another category of deductions to arrive at adjusted gross income. Examples of such deductions include depreciation, repairs, real estate taxes, and insurance expense related to the rent property.

To reduce the effect of progressive tax rates on married couples when both spouses work, Congress enacted a special deduction for two-earner married couples. This deduction is subtracted to arrive at adjusted gross income. The maximum two-earner deduction is 10% of the lesser of: *(a)* $30,000, or *(b)* the salary or wages, less employment-associated expenses, of the spouse with the lower amount of earnings. For example, assume that Bob and Janet Allen file a joint return. Bob's salary is $28,000, and Janet's is $36,000. Neither has any expenses associated with employment. Their two-earner deduction is $2,800 (10% × $28,000).

In addition to the foregoing business expenses, from a tax management point of view, a very important deduction from gross income is the long-term capital gain deduction. This permits (under certain circumstances) the deduction from gross income of 60% of the net long-term gains from capital asset sales and exchanges. More detailed discussion is given to the long-term capital gain deduction later in this chapter.

Deductions from Adjusted Gross Income

By legislative grace an individual taxpayer is permitted certain deductions from adjusted gross income. These are of two kinds: (1) the zero bracket amount or deduction of itemized personal expenses and (2) the deduction for exemptions.

The first type consists of certain personal expenses that the taxpayer is allowed to itemize and deduct, or alternatively, it consists of a *zero bracket amount*. The taxpayer chooses between these two. Regarding the zero bracket amount, all individual taxpayers are entitled to have a certain minimum amount of taxable income before owing any income taxes. This amount is known as the zero bracket amount; formerly it was referred to as the *standard deduction*. In other words, if the taxpayer reports taxable income not in excess of the zero bracket amount, the schedules of tax rates will show that zero tax is levied against this amount. The zero bracket amount is a flat amount that depends upon the taxpayer's filing status. For a single taxpayer, the zero bracket amount is $2,300; for married taxpayers filing a joint return or for a surviving spouse, it is $3,400; and for a married taxpayer filing a separate return, the zero bracket amount is $1,700.

Instead of choosing the zero bracket amount, taxpayers may itemize their allowable deductions and deduct the amount by which the itemized deductions are in excess of the zero bracket amount. Obviously, taxpayers tend to elect whichever alternative results in the largest deduction. Itemized deductions include the taxpayer's personal interest expense, state and local taxes, charitable contributions, casualty losses after reducing each loss by $100, casualty losses are deductible to the extent they exceed 10% of adjusted gross income, and a medical expense deduction. The medical expense deduction consists of that portion of prescription drugs, doctor, dental, hospital, and medical insurance expenses in excess of 5% of the taxpayer's adjusted gross income.

In addition to itemized deductions or the zero bracket amount, a taxpayer is allowed a deduction for exemptions. For each exemption, the taxpayer may deduct $1,000 from adjusted gross income, and a taxpayer is allowed one personal exemption plus one for each dependent. Additional exemptions are allowed if the taxpayer is 65 or over or is blind. If a husband and wife file a joint return, each is a taxpayer and they may combine their exemptions.

To qualify as a dependent for whom an exemption may be claimed, the person must meet these tests: (1) be closely related to the taxpayer or have been a member of the taxpayer's household for the entire year; (2) have received over half his or her support from the taxpayer during the year; (3) if married, has not and will not file a joint return with his or her spouse; and (4) had less than $1,000 of gross income during the year. An exception to the gross income test is granted if the person claimed as a dependent is a child of the taxpayer and under 19 years of age at the end of the tax year or was a full-time student in an educational institution during each of five months of the year. This exception is always of interest to college students because it commonly results in two exemptions for such students if they qualify in all other respects as a dependent. One exemption may be taken by the parent who claims the student as a dependent and the other exemption may be taken on the student's own tax return.

Observe in the discussion thus far that there are *deductions to arrive at adjusted gross income* and also *deductions from adjusted gross income*. Furthermore, it is important that each kind be subtracted at the proper point in the tax calculation because the allowable amounts of some deductions from adjusted gross income are determined by the amount of adjusted gross income.

FEDERAL INCOME TAX RATES. Federal income tax rates are progressive in nature. By this is meant that each additional segment or bracket of taxable income is subject to a higher rate than the preceding segment or bracket. This may be seen by examining Illustration 28–

Illustration 28–2

Schedule X—Single Taxpayers
For taxable years beginning after 1983.—

If taxable income is:	The tax is:
Not over $2,300	No tax.
Over $2,300 but not over $3,400	11% of the excess over $3,400.
Over $3,400 but not over $4,400	$121, plus 12% of the excess over $3,400.
Over $4,400 but not over $6,500	$241, plus 14% of the excess over $4,400.
Over $6,500 but not over $8,500	$535, plus 15% of the excess over $6,500.
Over $8,500 but not over $10,800	$835, plus 16% of the excess over $8,500.
Over $10,800 but not over $12,900	$1,203, plus 18% of the excess over $10,800.
Over $12,900 but not over $15,000	$1,581, plus 20% of the excess over $12,900.
Over $15,000 but not over $18,200	$2,001, plus 23% of the excess over $15,000.
Over $18,200 but not over $23,500	$2,737, plus 26% of the excess over $18,200.
Over $23,500 but not over $28,800	$4,115, plus 30% of the excess over $23,500.
Over $28,800 but not over $34,100	$5,705, plus 34% of the excess over $28,800.
Over $34,100 but not over $41,500	$7,057, plus 38% of the excess over $34,100.
Over $41,500 but not over $55,300	$10,319, plus 42% of the excess over $41,500.
Over $55,300 but not over $81,800	$16,115, plus 48% of the excess over $55,300.
Over $81,800	$28,835, plus 50% of the excess over $81,800.

Schedule Y—Married Filing Joint Returns and Qualifying Widows and Widowers
For taxable years beginning after 1983.—

If taxable income is:	The tax is:
Not over $3,400	No tax
Over $3,400 but not over $5,500	11% of the excess over $3,400.
Over $5,500 but not over $7,600	$231, plus 12% of the excess over $5,500.
Over $7,600 but not over $11,900	$483, plus 14% of the excess over $7,600.
Over $11,900 but not over $16,000	$1,085, plus 16% of the excess over $11,900.
Over $16,000 but not over $20,200	$1,741, plus 18% of the excess over $16,000.
Over $20,200 but not over $24,600	$2,497, plus 22% of the excess over $20,200.
Over $24,600 but not over $29,900	$3,465, plus 25% of the excess over $24,600.
Over $29,900 but not over $35,200	$4,790, plus 28% of the excess over $29,900.
Over $35,200 but not over $45,800	$6,274, plus 33% of the excess over $35,200.
Over $45,800 but not over $60,000	$9,772, plus 38% of the excess over $45,800.
Over $60,000 but not over $85,600	$15,168, plus 42% of the excess over $60,000.
Over $85,600 but not over $109,400	$25,920, plus 45% of the excess over $85,600.
Over $109,400 but not over $162,400	$36,630, plus 49% of the excess over $109,400.
Over $162,400	$62,600, plus 50% of the excess over $162,400.

2 which shows the rates for an unmarried person not qualifying as a head of household and for married persons filing a joint return or qualifying widows or widowers.

The Tax Rate Schedules shown in Illustration 28–2 are used by taxpayers who do not qualify to use simplified Tax Tables, which are discussed later in the chapter. To use the rate schedules of Illustration 28–2, a taxpayer reads down the first two columns of the appropriate schedule until arriving at the bracket of his or her taxable income. For example, if an unmarried taxpayer's taxable income is $29,000, the taxpayer reads down the proper columns to the bracket "over $28,800 but not over $34,100." The remaining columns explain that the tax on $29,000 is $5,705 plus 34% of the excess over $28,800, or is $5,705 + (34% × $200), or is $5,773.

A husband and wife have a choice. They may combine their incomes and use the rate schedule shown for married individuals (Schedule Y) or they may each file a separate return using a rate schedule (not shown) that results in a tax for each somewhat in excess of that shown in Illustration 28–2 for single taxpayers. The phrase *qualified widows and widowers* in the title of Schedule Y refers to surviving spouses who, if they are not remarried and if they have a dependent child, may continue to use Schedule Y for two tax years after the year of their spouse's death.

Also, a person who can qualify as a *head of household* may use a rate schedule (not shown) in which the rates fall between those for unmarried individuals and those for married couples filing jointly. Generally, a head of household is an unmarried or legally separated person who maintains a home in which lives his or her unmarried child or a qualifying dependent.

Regardless of the rate schedule used, it is generally recognized that our federal income tax rates are steeply progressive. Proponents claim that this is only fair, since the taxpayers most able to pay, those with higher incomes, are subject to higher rates. Opponents, on the other hand, claim the high rates stifle initiative. For example, a young unmarried executive with $41,500 of taxable income per year, upon being offered a new job carrying additional responsibilities and a $6,000 salary increase, might turn the new job down, feeling the after-tax increase in pay insufficient to compensate for the extra responsibilities. In this case, the executive could keep after federal income taxes just $3,480 or 58% of the increase.

In a situation like that described here, a decision as to whether another dollar of income is desirable or worth the effort depends on the *marginal tax rate* that applies to that dollar. The marginal tax rate is the rate that applies to the next dollar of income to be earned. For example, the highest rate that is applicable to the young executive before taking the new job is 38% on the taxable dollars between

$34,100 and $41,500 (see Illustration 28–2). However, if the new job is taken, the marginal rate on the next $13,800 of taxable income goes up to 42%.

Whether or not our progressive income tax rates stifle initiative is probably open to debate. However, there is no question that the progressive nature of the tax rates causes high-income taxpayers to search for tax-saving opportunities.

TAX CREDITS AND PREPAYMENTS. After an individual's gross income tax liability is computed from the appropriate tax rate schedule, the individual's tax credits, if any, and prepayments are deducted to determine the net tax liability. *Tax credits* represent direct, dollar for dollar, reductions in the amount of tax liability, that is, a $100 tax credit reduces the tax liability by $100. By comparison, deductions (as discussed earlier) reduce the amount of taxable income, against which is applied the appropriate tax rates to determine the gross tax liability. Thus, a tax credit of $100 is more valuable to the taxpayer than would be a tax deduction of $100. Assuming a marginal tax rate of 30%, an additional tax deduction of $100 effectively reduces the tax liability by $30 ($100 × 30%), whereas a tax credit of $100 reduces the tax liability by $100.

Examples of tax credits include the following. A retired taxpayer with retirement income may receive a "credit for the elderly." A taxpayer who has paid income taxes to a foreign government may be eligible for a "foreign tax credit." A taxpayer who has contributed to a political candidate or party may be eligible for a "political contribution credit." The latter credit is limited to one half the donation with a maximum of $50 on a separate return and $100 on a joint return.

An "investment tax credit" up to 10% of the purchase price of certain qualified property is also available to taxpayers. And taxpayers may also qualify for an "earned income credit" equal to 10% of "earned income up to $5,000," or (10% × $5,000 = $500). "Earned income" consists of wages, professional fees, and certain compensation for personal services. But, as earned income or adjusted gross income, whichever is larger, increases from $6,000 to $10,000, the amount of the earned income credit gradually declines from $500 to $0. The earned income credit, unlike the other tax credits, can generate a tax refund. Thus, it is similar to a negative income tax.

In addition to tax credits, any prepayments of tax are also deducted in order to determine the net tax liability. Most taxpayers have income taxes withheld from their salaries and wages. Other taxpayers have income that is not subject to withholding and on which they are required to estimate the tax, file an estimated tax return, and pay the estimated amount of the tax on the income in advance installments. Both the income tax withholdings and the estimated tax paid in advance are examples of tax prepayments that are deducted in determining a taxpayer's net tax liability.

Special Tax Treatment of Capital Gains and Losses

From a tax-saving point of view, one of the most important features of our federal income tax laws is the special treatment given long-term gains from *capital asset* sales and exchanges. For individuals, the usual effect of this special treatment is a tax on net long-term capital gains that is only 40% as high as the tax on an equal amount of income from some other source, commonly called ordinary income. For this reason, whenever possible, tax planners try to cause income to emerge in the form of long-term capital gains rather than as ordinary income.

The Internal Revenue Code defines a capital asset as any item of property except *(a)* inventories; *(b)* trade notes and accounts receivable; *(c)* real property and depreciable property used in a trade or business; and *(d)* copyrights, letters, and similar property in the hands of the creator of the copyrighted works or his or her donee and certain other transferees. Common examples of capital assets held by individuals and subject to sale or exchange are stocks, bonds, and a personal residence.

A gain on the sale of a capital asset occurs when the proceeds of the sale exceed the *basis* of the asset sold, and a loss occurs when the asset's basis exceeds the proceeds. The basis of a purchased asset is generally its cost less any depreciation previously allowed or allowable for tax purposes. Not all capital assets are acquired by purchase; but rules for determining the basis of an asset acquired other than by purchase are at times complicated and need not be discussed here.

For tax purposes, a distinction is made between short- and long-term *capital gains and losses.* Short-term gains and losses result when capital assets are held 12 months or less before being sold or exchanged, and long-term gains and losses result when such assets are held more than 12 months. Furthermore, under the law, net short-term gains must be reported in full and are taxed as ordinary income; but only 40% of the amount of any excess net long-term capital gains over net short-term capital losses, if any, must be included in adjusted gross income.

For example, if an individual taxpayer has $1,000 of long-term gains, no losses, and other income that places these gains in a 38% bracket, the individual is required to include only $400 of the gains in adjusted gross income and to pay only a $152 ($400 × 38% = $152) tax thereon. Consequently, the effective tax rate on the gains is 15.2% ($152 ÷ $1,000 = 15.2%), and is only 40% of what it would be if the $1,000 were ordinary income.

In the preceding paragraphs, the terms *net long-term gains* and *net short-term gains* appear. When long-term gains exceed long-term losses, a net long-term gain results. Likewise, when long-term losses exceed long-term gains, a net long-term loss occurs. Short-term gains and losses are combined in a like manner to arrive at either a net short-term gain or loss.

When an individual's net short-term capital losses exceed net long-term capital gains, the individual may deduct up to $3,000 of the excess losses ($1,500 for a married taxpayer filing a separate return) from ordinary income in the year of the loss. However, when net long-term capital losses exceed net short-term capital gains, the individual may in any one year deduct from ordinary income only one half of the excess losses up to $3,000 ($1,500 for a married taxpayer filing a separate return). A carry-over provision is available to allow deduction in subsequent years of amounts that exceeded the $3,000 or $1,500 limitations.

One last point in regard to real property and depreciable property used in a taxpayer's trade or business (see definition of capital assets in a previous paragraph). Such properties are legally not capital assets; consequently, when sold or exchanged, the excess of losses over gains is fully deductible in arriving at taxable income. However, if such properties are held over 12 months, the excess of gains over losses is eligible for capital gain treatment, except to the extent of certain amounts of depreciation taken after 1961. As to depreciation taken after 1961, there may be a share of the gain equal to a portion or all of this depreciation, depending on the nature of the property and the method of depreciation, which must be treated as ordinary income.

TAX TABLES. As previously mentioned, not all taxpayers are required to use the Tax Rate Schedules such as those shown in Illustration 28–2. Instead, most individual taxpayers use simplified Tax Tables. The Tax Tables are constructed from the Tax Rate Schedules, and they incorporate the zero bracket amount. Individuals who use the Tax Tables have to calculate their taxable income according to the formula of Illustration 28–1 and then search through the appropriate Tax Table to determine their gross income tax liability.

The Corporation Income Tax

For federal tax purposes, the taxable income of a corporation organized for profit is calculated in much the same way as the taxable income of an individual. However, there are important differences, five of which follow:

a. Instead of the $100 ($200 on a joint return) dividend exclusion of an individual, a corporation may deduct from gross income the first 85% of dividends received from stock it owns in other domestic corporations. This in effect means that only 15% of such dividends are taxed. However, if two corporations qualify as affiliated corporations, which essentially means that one owns 80% or more of the other's stock, then 100% of the dividends received by the investor corporation from the investee corporation may be deducted.

b. The capital gains of a corporation are also treated differently. Recall that the taxable income of individuals must include only 40% of their long-term capital gains in excess of short-term capital losses. Corporations must include 100% of such gains in income. However, a 28% alternative tax rate is available on all such gains accruing to a corporation.

c. A corporation may only offset capital losses against capital gains; and if in any year the offset results in a net capital loss, the loss may not be deducted from other income, but it may be carried back to the three preceding years and forward to the next five years and deducted from any capital gains of those years.

d. The zero bracket amount and the deduction for exemptions do not apply to a corporation, and a corporation does not have certain other deductions of an individual, such as that for personal medical expenses.

e. In addition, the big difference between the corporation and the individual income tax is that the corporation tax is progressive in just five steps. The corporate income tax rates are as follows:

Amount of taxable income	Tax rate
Portion from $0 to $25,000	15%
Portion from $25,000 to $50,000	18
Portion from $50,000 to $75,000	30
Portion from $75,000 to $100,000	40
Portion in excess of $100,000	46

Thus, for a corporation with $110,000 of taxable income, its tax liability is $30,350; that is, [(15% × $25,000) + (18% × $25,000) + (30% × $25,000) + (40% × $25,000) + (46% × $10,000)].

TAX EFFECTS OF BUSINESS ALTERNATIVES

Alternative decisions commonly have different tax effects. Following are several examples illustrating this.

Form of Business Organization

The difference between individual and corporation tax rates commonly affects one of the basic decisions a business executive must make, which is to select the legal form the business should take. Should it be a single proprietorship, partnership, or corporation? The following factors influence the decision:

a. As previously stated, a corporation is a taxable entity. Its income is taxed at corporation rates, and any portion distributed in dividends is taxed again as individual income to its stockholders. On the other hand, the income of a single proprietorship or partnership, whether withdrawn or left in the business, is taxed as individual income of the proprietor or partners.

b. In addition, a corporation may pay reasonable amounts in salaries to stockholders who work for the corporation, and the sum of these salaries is a tax-deductible expense in arriving at the corporation's taxable income. In a partnership or a single proprietorship on the other hand, salaries of the partners or the proprietor are nothing more than allocations of income.

In arriving at a decision as to the legal form a business should take, a business executive, with the foregoing points in mind, must estimate the tax consequences of each form and select the best. For example, assume that Ralph Jones is choosing between the single proprietorship and corporate forms, and that he estimates the business will have annual gross sales of $250,000, with cost of goods sold and operating expenses, other than his own salary as manager, of $185,000. Assume further that $45,000 per year is a fair salary for managing such a business and that Mr. Jones plans to withdraw all profits from the business. Under these assumptions, Mr. Jones will fare taxwise as shown in Illustration 28–3.

Under the assumptions of Illustration 28–3, the smaller tax and the larger after-tax income will result from using the single proprietorship form. However, this may not be true in every case. For instance, if Mr. Jones has large amounts of income from other sources, he may find he would incur less tax if the business were organized as a corporation.

Furthermore, in the example just given it is assumed that all profits are withdrawn and none are left in the business for growth. This happens. However, growth is commonly financed through the retention of earnings; and when it is, the relative desirability of the two forms may change. This is because income retained in a business organized as a corporation is not taxed as individual income to its stockholders,

Illustration 28–3

	Proprietorship		Corporation	
Operating results under each form:				
Estimated sales...............................		$250,000		$250,000
Cost of goods sold and operating expenses				
other than owner-manager's salary............	$185,000		$185,000	
Salary of owner-manager	–0–	185,000	45,000	230,000
Before-tax income		$ 65,000		$ 20,000
Corporation income tax at 15%.................		–0–		3,000
Net income		$ 65,000		$ 17,000
Owner's after-tax income under each form:				
Single proprietorship net income		$ 65,000		
Corporation salary.............................				$ 45,000
Dividends				17,000
Total individual income		$ 65,000		$ 62,000
Individual income tax (assuming a joint return with itemized deductions of $9,100 (less the zero bracket amount of $3,400) and a deduction for exemptions of $2,000 under both forms plus a $200 dividend exclusion under the corporation form)		14,142		12,926
Owner's after-tax income		$ 50,858		$ 49,074

but the income of a single proprietorship or partnership is so taxed, whether retained in the business or withdrawn.

For instance, if the business of Illustration 28–3 is organized as a single proprietorship, the tax burden of the owner remains the same whether he withdraws any of his profits or not. But, in case of the corporation, if all $17,000 of the earnings are retained in the business, the owner is required to pay individual income taxes on his $45,000 salary only. This would reduce his annual individual income tax from the $12,926 shown in Illustration 28–3 to $6,967, and would reduce the total tax burden with the corporation form to $9,967 ($3,000 + $6,967), which is $4,175 less than the tax burden under the single proprietorship form.

The foregoing is by no means all of the picture. Other tax factors may be involved. For example, a corporation may incur an extra tax if it accumulates more than $250,000 of retained earnings and such accumulations are beyond the reasonable needs of the business. Also, under present laws a corporation may elect to be taxed somewhat like a single proprietorship, thus eliminating the corporate tax. Furthermore, in a decision as to the legal form a business should take, factors other than taxes are often important, for example, lack of stockholder liability in a corporation.

Dividends and Growth

It was pointed out earlier in this chapter that it is normally to a taxpayer's advantage to have income emerge in the form of long-term capital gains rather than as ordinary income. Furthermore, earnings paid out in dividends result in ordinary income to stockholders, but earnings retained in an incorporated business commonly result in its growth and an increase in the value of its stock, which may be turned into long-term capital gains through a later sale of the stock. For this reason, it is often to the advantage of the owner of an incorporated business to forgo dividends and at a later date, through the sale of the business, to take the profits of the business in the form of long-term gains resulting from growth.

Method of Financing

When a business organized as a corporation is in need of additional financing, the owners may supply whatever funds the corporation needs by purchasing its stock. However, an overall tax advantage may often be gained if instead of purchasing stock, they supply the funds through long-term loans. Insofar as the owners are concerned, beyond the allowable dividend exclusion, it makes no difference on their individual returns whether they report interest or dividends from the funds supplied. However, whether the corporation issues stock or floats a loan usually makes a big difference on its return. Interest on borrowed funds is a tax-deductible expense, but dividends are a distribution of earnings and have no effect on the corporation's taxes. Consequently, if owners lend the corporation funds rather than buy its stock, the total tax liability (their own plus their corporation's) will be reduced. In addition, the repayment of long-term debt always is considered to be a return of capital transaction. The redemption of stock, however, may result in the proceeds being treated as dividend income to the shareholders.

In making financial arrangements such as these, owners must be careful not to overreach themselves in attempting to maximize the interest deduction of their corporation. If they do so and thereby create what is called a thin corporation, one in which the owners have supplied an unreasonably "thin" portion of capital, the Internal Revenue Service may disallow the interest deductions and require that such deductions be treated as dividends. Furthermore, repayments of "principal" may also be held to be taxable dividends.

Timing Transactions

The timing of transactions can be of major importance in tax planning. For example, securities may be held a little longer in order to make the gain on their sale subject to treatment as a long-term capital gain. Or as another example, if a company has several items of real or depreciable property to be sold and some of the sales will result in losses and others in gains, the losses should be taken in one year and the gains in another. The losses and gains should be taken this way because if the losses and gains are both incurred in the same year, they must be offset. However, if the losses are taken in one year and the gains in another, the losses may be deducted in full from other ordinary income, while the gains become eligible in their year for long-term capital gain treatment, at least to the extent they exceed depreciation taken after 1961.

Forms in which Related Transactions Are Completed

The tax consequences of related transactions are often dependent upon the forms in which they are completed. For example, the sale of one property at a profit and the immediate purchase of another like property normally results in a taxable gain on the property sold, but an exchange of these properties may result in a tax-free exchange.

A tax-free exchange occurs when like kinds of property are exchanged for each other, or when one or more persons transfer property to a corporation and immediately thereafter are in control of the corporation. Control in such cases is interpreted as meaning that after the transfer the transferring persons (or person) must own at least 80% of the corporation's voting stock plus at least 80% of the total number of shares of all other classes of stock.

At first glance it seems that it should be to anyone's advantage to take a tax-free exchange rather than to pay taxes, but this may not be so. For example, 10 years ago a corporation acquired, for $50,000, land then at the edge of the city. Today, due to booming growth, the land is well within the city and has a fair market value of $250,000. Aside from a fully depreciated fence, the land is without improvements, having been used over the years for storage of idle equipment and excess inventory. The corporation plans to move part of its operations to a suburb and has an opportunity to trade the city property for vacant suburban acreage on which it would build a factory. Should it make the trade? From a tax viewpoint, since the new land is not depreciable, the answer is probably, yes, the company should make the tax-free exchange.

However, if the suburban property rather than being vacant consisted of land having a fair market value of $25,000 with a suitable factory building thereon valued at $225,000, the corporation would probably be better off if it sold the city property, paid the tax on its gain, and purchased the suburban factory and its site. The corporation would probably be better off because the gain on the city land would be taxable as a long-term capital gain on which the tax would not exceed $56,000 (28% of [$250,000 − $50,000] = $56,000). However, by purchasing the new factory, the corporation gains the right to deduct the building's $225,000 cost. This deduction reduces its taxable income over a period as short as 15 years under the accelerated cost recovery system.

Accounting Basis and Procedures

With certain exceptions, the accounting basis and procedures used by taxpayers in keeping their records must also be used in computing taxable income. Generally, taxpayers keep their records on either a cash or an accrual basis (see page 95); but regardless of which they use, the basis and any procedures used must clearly reflect income and be consistently followed.

When inventories are a material factor in calculating income, taxpayers are required to use the accrual basis in calculating gross profit from sales. Also, plant assets cannot be expensed in the year of purchase but must be depreciated over their useful lives. However, other than for gross profit from sales and depreciation, taxpayers may use the cash basis in accounting for income and expenses. Furthermore, this is often an advantage, since under the cash basis, taxpayers can often shift expense payments and the receipt of items of revenue other than from the sale of merchandise from one accounting period to the next and thus increase or decrease taxable income.

An accrual-basis taxpayer cannot shift income from year to year by timing receipts and payments; however, somewhat of the same thing may be accomplished through a choice of accounting procedures. For example, recognition of income on a cash collection basis (see Chapter 1) commonly shifts income from one year to another. Likewise, a contractor may use the percentage-of-completion basis (Chapter 1) to shift construction income from one year to another and to level taxable income over a period of years.

Furthermore, any taxpayer may shift taxable income to future years through a choice of inventory and depreciation procedures. For example, during periods of rising prices the LIFO inventory method results in charging higher costs for goods sold against current revenues, and thus reduces taxable income and taxes. It may be argued that this only postpones taxes since in periods of declining prices the use of LIFO results in lower costs and higher taxes. However, the history of recent years has been one of rising prices; therefore, it may also be argued that LIFO will postpone taxes indefinitely.

Depreciation methods that result in higher depreciation charges in an asset's early years and lower charges in later years, such as the accelerated cost recovery system (ACRS), also postpone taxes. And while tax postponement is not as desirable as tax avoidance, postponement does gives the taxpayer interest-free use of tax dollars until these dollars must be paid to the government.

Before turning to a new topic, it should be pointed out that the opportunities for tax planning described in these pages are only illustrative of those available. The wise business executive will seek help from a tax consultant in order to take advantage of every tax-saving opportunity.

TAX CHANGES SCHEDULED TO TAKE EFFECT IN 1985

In 1981, Congress adopted several changes to the law for which it chose 1985 as the effective date. One of these changes provides for a limited form of indexing so that inflation will have less of an effect on individuals' tax liabilities. Under indexing, the tax brackets, the exemption deductions, and the zero bracket amount will be indexed annually for changes in the consumer price index (CPI). For example, if the CPI rose by 10%, the exemption deduction would increase from $1,000 to $1,100 and the zero bracket amount from $1,700, $2,300, and $3,400, to $1,870, $2,530, and $3,740, respectively. Similarly, the tax brackets for single taxpayers would be as follows: no tax on taxable income up to $2,530, 11% on taxable income of $2,531–$3,740, 12% on taxable income of $3,741–$4,840, and so on. There are no indexing provisions for corporations. As this book goes to press, some congressmen are proposing repeal of the indexing provisions.

Another provision with a 1985 effective date allows a limited exclusion for interest income. The maximum tax-free interest is 15% times the lesser of: *(a)* $3,000 ($6,000 on a joint return) or *(b)* the individual's interest received net of interest paid. Interest income does not have to be reduced, however, for interest paid on a home mortgage or for business purposes. The largest possible exclusion on a joint return is $900 (15% × $6,000).

TAXES AND THE DISTORTION OF NET INCOME

Financial statements for a business should be prepared in accordance with generally accepted accounting principles. Tax accounting, on the other hand, must be done in accordance with tax laws. As a consequence, income (before taxes) measured in accordance with generally accepted accounting principles is not always the same as income subject to state and federal income taxes. They may differ for two reasons. The first reason is that some items may be included in (or excluded from) the calculation of taxable income but be excluded from (or included in) net income according to generally accepted accounting principles. These items involve permanent differences between taxable income and net income. For example, interest received on state and municipal bonds must be included in net income on the financial statements of the company that owns the bonds. In contrast, such interest usually is not subject to tax and therefore is not included in taxable income.

The second reason why there may be a difference between taxable income and income before taxes on the financial statements involves timing differences between tax procedures and financial statement procedures. In other words, a business may select different procedures for tax purposes and for financial statement purposes where the difference between the procedures is a matter of timing. For example, unearned income such as rent collected in advance usually is taxable in the year of receipt. However, under the accrual basis of accounting such items are taken into income in the year earned regardless of when received. As another example, a business may apply straight-line depreciation over the estimated useful life of an asset for accounting purposes. At the same time, it may use the accelerated cost recovery system for tax purposes.

When a corporation uses different procedures for tax and financial statement purposes and the difference between the procedures is a matter of timing, a problem arises in measuring net income. The problem involves deciding how much income tax expense should be shown on the income statement. If the actual tax to be paid is shown as an expense, the amount of tax will appear inconsistent with the known tax rate. Consequently, the APB ruled that income taxes should be allocated so that distortions caused by timing differences between tax accounting procedures and financial accounting procedures are avoided.[1]

To appreciate the problem involved here, assume that in January 1984 a corporation purchased a fleet of light trucks for $100,000, which will produce a half million dollars of revenue in each of the succeeding five years and $80,000 of income before depreciation and taxes. Assume further that the company must pay income taxes at a 40% rate (round number assumed for easy calculation) and that it plans to use straight-line depreciation in its records but the *accelerated cost recovery system (ACRS)* for tax purposes. The fleet has a five-year life, no salvage value, and is included in the three-year class of property for tax purposes. Under ACRS, property in the three-year class is depreciated 25% in the first year, 38% in the second year, and 37% in the third year.

---

[1] APB, "Accounting for Income Taxes," *APB Opinion No. 11* (New York: AICPA, 1967). Copyright (1967) by the American Institute of CPAs.

(See Illustration 10–2 on page 361.) Depreciation calculated by each method will be as follows:[2]

Year	Straight line	ACRS
1	$ 20,000	$ 25,000
2	20,000	38,000
3	20,000	37,000
4	20,000	–0–
5	20,000	–0–
Totals	$100,000	$100,000

And since the company has elected the accelerated cost recovery system for tax purposes, it will be liable for $22,000 of income tax on the first year's income, $16,800 on the second, $17,200 on the third, $32,000 on the fourth, and $32,000 on the fifth. The calculation of these taxes is shown in Illustration 28–4.

Illustration 28–4

Annual income taxes	Year 1	Year 2	Year 3	Year 4	Year 5	Total
Income before depreciation and income taxes	$80,000	$80,000	$80,000	$80,000	$80,000	$400,000
Depreciation for tax purposes (ACRS method)	25,000	38,000	37,000	–0–	–0–	100,000
Taxable income	$55,000	$42,000	$43,000	$80,000	$80,000	$300,000
Annual income taxes (40% of taxable income)	$22,000	$16,800	$17,200	$32,000	$32,000	$120,000

Furthermore, if the company were to deduct its actual tax liability each year in arriving at income to be reported to its stockholders, it would report the amounts shown in Illustration 28–5. Observe in Illustration 28–5 the significant fluctuation in annual income after depreciation and taxes. Even though income before depreciation and income taxes is $80,000 each year and straight-line depreciation is $20,000 each year, the subtraction of the actual tax liability results in a signifi-

---

[2] This discussion, as well as the problems at the end of the chapter, has been simplified by the assumption that the company purchasing depreciable assets does not claim an investment tax credit. If a company claims an investment tax credit, the amount of cost eligible to be depreciated is reduced by one half of the credit. Thus, in the above illustration, if the corporation claimed $6,000 investment tax credit on the trucks, its ACRS deduction would be 25%, 38%, and 37% of $97,000 ($100,000 less one half of $6,000) for the first, second, and third years, respectively. To repeat, in the interest of simplicity, the remaining discussion assumes that no investment tax credit is claimed. Therefore, the above illustration shows that the entire purchase cost is depreciated.

Illustration 28–5

Income after deducting actual tax liabilities	Year 1	Year 2	Year 3	Year 4	Year 5	Total
Income before depreciation and income taxes	$80,000	$80,000	$80,000	$80,000	$80,000	$400,000
Depreciation per books (straight line)	20,000	20,000	20,000	20,000	20,000	100,000
Income before taxes	$60,000	$60,000	$60,000	$60,000	$60,000	$300,000
Income taxes (actual liability of each year)	22,000	16,800	17,200	32,000	32,000	120,000
Remaining income	$38,000	$43,200	$42,800	$28,000	$28,000	$180,000

cant fluctuation in the remaining income. This fluctuation is generally thought to be a distortion of the final income figures.

If this company should report successive annual income figures of $38,000, $43,200, $42,800, $28,000, and $28,000, some of its stockholders might be misled as to the company's earnings trend. Consequently, in cases such as this the APB ruled that income taxes should be allocated so that the distortion caused by the postponement of taxes is removed from the income statement. In essence, *APB Opinion No. 11* requires the following: When a procedure used in the accounting records and an alternative procedure used for tax purposes differ in respect to their timing of expense recognition or revenue recognition, the tax expense deducted on the income statement should not be the actual tax incurred, but the amount that would have resulted if the procedure used in the records had also been used in calculating the tax.

If the foregoing is applied in this case, the corporation will report to its stockholders in each of the five years the amounts of income shown in Illustration 28–6.

In examining Illustration 28–6, recall that the company's tax liabilities are actually $22,000 in the first year, $16,800 in the second, $17,200

Illustration 28–6

Net income that should be reported to stockholders	Year 1	Year 2	Year 3	Year 4	Year 5	Total
Income before depreciation and income taxes	$80,000	$80,000	$80,000	$80,000	$80,000	$400,000
Depreciation per books (straight line)	20,000	20,000	20,000	20,000	20,000	100,000
Income before taxes	$60,000	$60,000	$60,000	$60,000	$60,000	$300,000
Income taxes (amounts based on straight-line depreciation)	24,000	24,000	24,000	24,000	24,000	120,000
Net income	$36,000	$36,000	$36,000	$36,000	$36,000	$180,000

in the third, \$32,000 in the fourth, and \$32,000 in the fifth, a total of \$120,000. Then observe that when this \$120,000 liability is allocated evenly over the five years, the distortion of the annual net incomes due to the postponement of taxes is removed from the income statements.

ENTRIES FOR THE ALLOCATION OF TAXES

When income taxes are allocated as in Illustration 28–6, the tax liability of each year and the deferred taxes are recorded with an adjusting entry. The adjusting entries for the five years of Illustration 28–6 and the entries in general journal form for the payment of the taxes (without explanations) are as follows:*

Year 1	Income Taxes Expense	24,000.00	
	Income Taxes Payable		22,000.00
	Deferred Income Taxes		2,000.00
Year 1	Income Taxes Payable	22,000.00	
	Cash		22,000.00
Year 2	Income Taxes Expense	24,000.00	
	Income Taxes Payable		16,800.00
	Deferred Income Taxes		7,200.00
Year 2	Income Taxes Payable	16,800.00	
	Cash		16,800.00
Year 3	Income Taxes Expense	24,000.00	
	Income Taxes payable		17,200.00
	Deferred Income Taxes		6,800.00
Year 3	Income Taxes Payable	17,200.00	
	Cash		17,200.00
Year 4	Income Taxes Expense	24,000.00	
	Deferred Income Taxes	8,000.00	
	Income Taxes Payable		32,000.00
Year 4	Income Taxes Payable	32,000.00	
	Cash		32,000.00
Year 5	Income Taxes Expense	24,000.00	
	Deferred Income Taxes	8,000.00	
	Income Taxes Payable		32,000.00
Year 5	Income Taxes Payable	32,000.00	
	Cash		32,000.00

* To simplify the illustration, it is assumed here that the entire year's tax liability is paid at one time. However, as previously explained, corporations are usually required to pay estimated taxes on a quarterly basis.

In the entries, the $24,000 debited to Income Taxes Expense each year is the amount that is deducted on the income statement in reporting annual net income. Also, the amount credited to Income Taxes Payable each year is the actual tax liability of that year.

Observe in the entries that since the actual tax liability in each of the first three years is less than the amount debited to Income Taxes Expense, the difference is credited to *Deferred Income Taxes.* Then note that in the last two years, since the actual liability each year is greater than the debit to Income Taxes Expense, the difference is debited to Deferred Income Taxes. Now observe in the following illustration of the company's Deferred Income Taxes account that the debits and credits exactly balance each other out over the five-year period:

Deferred Income Taxes

Year	Explanation	Debit	Credit	Balance
1			2,000.00	2,000.00
2			7,200.00	9,200.00
3			6,800.00	16,000.00
4		8,000.00		8,000.00
5		8,000.00		–0–

At the end of years 1, 2, 3, and 4, the credit balance in the Deferred Income Taxes account is reported in the balance sheet as a separate item between long-term liabilities and stockholders' equity.

GLOSSARY

Accelerated cost recovery system (ACRS). A unique, accelerated depreciation method prescribed in the tax law for assets placed in service after 1980.

Adjusted gross income. Gross income minus ordinary and necessary expenses of carrying on a business, trade, or profession, or in the case of an employee, gross income minus expenses incurred in connection with his or her employment if paid by the employee.

Basis. In general, the cost of a purchased asset less any depreciation previously allowed or allowable for tax purposes.

Capital asset. Any item of property except (1) inventories, (2) trade notes and accounts receivable, (3) real property and depreciable property used in a trade or business, and (4) copyrights or similar property.

Capital gain or loss. The difference between the proceeds from the sale of a capital asset and the basis of the asset.

Deferred income taxes. The difference between the income tax expense in the financial statements and the income taxes payable according to tax law, resulting from financial accounting and tax accounting timing differences with respect to expense or revenue recognition.

Gross income. All income from whatever source derived, unless expressly excluded from taxation by law.

Head of household. An unmarried or legally separated person who maintains a home in which lives his or her unmarried child or a qualifying dependent.

Internal Revenue Code. Collectively, the statutes dealing with taxation that have been adopted by Congress.

Marginal tax rate. The rate that applies to the next dollar of income to be earned.

Standard deduction. The name formerly used in reference to the zero bracket amount.

Tax avoidance. A legal means of preventing a tax liability from coming into existence.

Tax credit. A direct, dollar for dollar, reduction in the amount of tax liability.

Tax evasion. The fraudulent denial and concealment of an existing liability.

Tax planning. Planning the affairs of a taxpayer in such a way as to incur the smallest possible tax liability.

Zero bracket amount. The amount of income, after subtracting all allowable deductions, that is not subject to tax; for married taxpayers filing jointly and qualifying widows and widowers, $3,400; for married taxpayers filing separately, $1,700; and for an unmarried taxpayer, $2,300.

QUESTIONS FOR CLASS DISCUSSION

1. Jackson expects to have $500 of income in a 50% bracket; consequently, which should be more desirable to him: *(a)* a transaction that will reduce his income tax by $100 or *(b)* a transaction that will reduce an expense of his business by $150?

2. Why must a taxpayer normally take advantage of a tax-saving opportunity at the time it arises?

3. Distinguish between tax avoidance and tax evasion. Which is legal and desirable?

4. What are some of the nonrevenue objectives of the federal income tax?

5. What questions must be answered in determining whether an item should be included or excluded from gross income for tax purposes?

6. Name several items that are not included in gross income for tax purposes.

7. What justification is given for permitting an individual to exclude a limited amount of dividends from domestic corporations from his or her gross income for tax purposes?

8. For tax purposes, define a capital asset.

9. What is a short-term capital gain? A long-term capital gain?

10. An individual had capital asset transactions that resulted in nothing but

long-term capital gains. What special tax treatment may be given these gains?

11. For tax purposes, what is *ordinary income?*

12. Why do tax planners try to have income emerge as a long-term capital gain?

13. It is often a wise tax decision for the owner of an incorporated business to forgo the payment of dividends from the earnings of his or her business. Why?

14. Why does the taxable income of a business commonly differ from its net income?

CLASS EXERCISES

In some of the Exercises and Problems that follow, the taxpayers would qualify to use the simplified Tax Tables (not provided in the book) rather than the Tax Rate Schedules. However, to restrict the length of the chapter and to facilitate student understanding of the underlying concepts, calculations of individual tax liability should be based on the Tax Rate Schedules shown in Illustration 28–2 on page 959.

Exercise 28–1

List the letters of the following items and write after each either the word *included* or *excluded* to tell whether the item should be included in or excluded from gross income for federal income tax purposes.

a. A computer game having a $300 fair market value that was received as a door prize.

b. Gain on the sale of a personal automobile bought and rebuilt.

c. Social security benefits.

d. Scholarship received from a state university.

e. Cash inherited from a deceased parent.

f. Dividends amounting to $100 from stock in domestic corporations received by an individual.

g. Tips received while working as a waiter.

h. Workmen's compensation insurance received as the result of an accident while working on a part-time job.

Exercise 28–2

Julie Bush earned $34,000 during 1984 as an employee of a law firm. She is unmarried and furnishes more than half the support of her brother, a college student living in a dormitory. Julie had $6,300 of federal income tax and $2,278 of FICA tax withheld from her paychecks. She received $300 interest on a savings account and $90 in dividends from a domestic corporation in which she owned stock. During the year, she paid $800 state income tax, $950 interest on the balance owed on a car she purchased, and gave her church $1,800. Show the calculation of Julie's taxable income in the manner outlined in Illustration 28–1. Then, using the rate schedule of Illustration 28–2, show the calculation of the net federal income tax payable or refund due Julie.

Exercise 28–3   In 1984, a married taxpayer who files a joint return and had no other capital gains, sold for $9,200 a number of shares of stock he had purchased for $6,200. Use the rate schedule of Illustration 28–2 and determine the amount of federal income tax the taxpayer will have to pay on the gain from this transaction under each of the following unrelated assumptions:

a. The taxpayer had $30,000 of taxable income from other sources and had held the shares four months.
b. The taxpayer had $30,000 of taxable income from other sources and had held the shares for 14 months.
c. The taxpayer had $36,000 of taxable income from other sources and had held the shares six months.
d. The taxpayer had $36,000 of taxable income from other sources and had held the shares for 12 months and one day.
e. The taxpayer had $165,000 of taxable income from other sources and had held the shares for two months.
f. The taxpayer had $165,000 of taxable income from other sources and had held the shares for 15 months.

Exercise 28–4   Don Persons, Lori Hampton, and Jim Barr are unmarried and have three income tax exemptions each. None qualify as a head of household. Last year their adjusted gross incomes were Persons, $34,000; Hampton, $39,000; and Barr, $58,000. Their itemized deductions were Persons, $8,200; Hampton, $1,300; and Barr, $9,800. Prepare calculations to show the taxable income of each person.

Exercise 28–5   Dick and Carol Day had $31,000 of adjusted gross income in 1984. They are 35 and 38 years old, respectively, and have two children, ages 9 and 14. Last year their automobile having a fair value of $5,600 was stolen and their insurance did not cover the loss. They donated $500 to the college from which they had both graduated and incurred the following expenses during the year: local property taxes, $800; interest on home mortgage, $660; hospital insurance, $1,650; and uninsured doctor and dentist bills, $840. Prepare a calculation to show their taxable income on a joint return.

Exercise 28–6   In January of 1984, a machine was purchased for $60,000. It will be used six years in research and development activities and then discarded with no salvage value. Straight-line depreciation is taken for financial statement purposes, and the accelerated cost recovery system is used for tax purposes. If the company earns $90,000 income before depreciation and taxes during 1984, and the machine is in the three-year class for tax purposes, make the journal entry to record income tax expense and liability for 1984. Assume a 40% tax rate. (Note: No investment tax credit is claimed by the company.)

PROBLEMS

Problem 28–1   Annette and Ray Groves are married and are also partners in Old World Art, a profitable business that averages $400,000 annually in sales, with a 40%

gross profit and $90,000 of operating expenses. The Groves file a joint tax return, have no dependents, but each year have $3,000 of itemized deductions and two exemptions. In the past, the Groves have withdrawn $30,000 annually from the business for personal living expenses plus sufficient additional cash to pay the income tax on their joint return.

Annette and Ray think that they can save taxes by reorganizing their business into a corporation beginning with the 1984 tax year. If the corporation is organized, it will issue 1,000 shares of no-par stock, 500 to Annette and 500 to Ray. Also, $30,000 per year is a fair salary for managing such a business, and the corporation will pay that amount to Annette.

Required:

1. Prepare a comparative income statement for the business showing its net income as a partnership and as a corporation.
2. Use the rate schedule of Illustration 28–2 and determine the amount of federal income taxes the Groves will pay for themselves on a joint return and for the business under each of the following assumptions: *(a)* the business remains a partnership; *(b)* the business is incorporated, pays Annette a $30,000 salary, but pays no dividends; and *(c)* the business is incorporated, pays Annette a $30,000 salary, and pays $20,000 in dividends, $10,000 to Annette and $10,000 to Ray. (They may exclude the first $200 of dividends.)

Problem 28–2

Tim and Joy Brown, husband and wife who file a joint return, own all the outstanding stock of Brown Corporation. The corporation has an opportunity to expand, but to do so it will need $70,000 additional capital. The Browns have the $70,000 and can either lend this amount to the corporation at 10% interest or they can invest the $70,000 in the corporation, taking its presently unissued stock in exchange for the money.

They calculate that with the additional $70,000 the corporation will earn a total of $40,000 annually after paying Tim $30,000 per year as president and manager but before interest on the loan, if made, and before income taxes. They require $45,000 for personal living expenses and their own income taxes. Consequently, if they invest the additional $70,000 in the corporation, they will pay $15,000 per year to themselves in dividends in addition to Tim's salary. But if they lend the corporation the $70,000, they will use the interest on the loan, plus $8,000 in dividends and Tim's salary, for their personal expenses.

Required:

Determine whether the loan to the corporation or an investment in its stock is to the best interest of the Browns. Assume that the decision is being made in 1984.

Problem 28–3

Nancy Hall owns all the outstanding stock of Minibond Company. The corporation is a small manufacturing company; however, over the years it has purchased and owns stocks costing $110,000 (present market value much higher) which it holds as long-term investments. The corporation has seldom paid a dividend, but it does pay Ms. Hall a $50,000 annual salary as president and manager. In 1984, the corporation earned $42,000, after its president's salary but before income taxes, consisting of $26,000 in manufacturing income and $16,000 in dividends on its long-term investments.

Ms. Hall has no dependents, but she had $11,400 of itemized deductions during 1984 plus a single $1,000 exemption deduction. She had no income other than her corporation salary and $3,000 in interest from a real estate loan.

Required:

1. Prepare a comparative statement showing for 1984 the operating income, investment income, total income, share of the dividend income deducted, taxable income, and income tax of the corporation under the *(a)* and *(b)* assumptions which follow. *(a)* The corporation owns the investment stocks and had the operating income just described. *(b)* The corporation had the operating income described; but instead of owning the investment stocks, over the years it paid dividends (none in 1984) and Ms. Hall used them to buy the stocks in her own name rather than in the corporation name.

2. Calculate the amounts of individual income tax and corporation income tax incurred by Ms. Hall and the corporation under the *(a)* assumptions, and the amounts that would have been incurred under the *(b)* assumptions. Also calculate the amount of individual income tax Ms. Hall would have incurred with the business organized as a single proprietorship and the stocks registered in Ms. Hall's name. Under this last assumption remember that the corporation's operating income plus its president's salary equal the operating income of the single proprietorship. Use the rate schedule of Illustration 28–2 in all individual income tax calculations.

Problem 28–4   Layton Corporation purchased a fleet of light trucks at a $150,000 total cost early in January 1984. It was estimated the trucks would have a five-year life, no salvage value at the end of that period, and would produce $75,000 of income before depreciation and income taxes during each of the five years. The company allocates income taxes in its reports to stockholders since it uses straight-line depreciation in its accounting records but the accelerated cost recovery system for tax purposes. In this problem, disregard the investment tax credit.

Required:

1. Prepare a schedule showing 1984, 1985, 1986, 1987, 1988, and total net income for the five years after deducting ACRS depreciation and actual income taxes. Assume a 40% tax rate.

2. Prepare a second schedule showing each year's net income and the five-year total after deducting straight-line depreciation and actual taxes.

3. Prepare a third schedule showing income to be reported to stockholders with straight-line depreciation and allocated income taxes.

4. Set up a T-account for Deferred Income Tax and show therein the entries that will result from allocating income taxes.

Problem 28–5   Mr. and Mrs. Jerry Mozena are both 43 years old and file a joint income tax return. They have two children, Cindy and Tim. Cindy is a student in high school, lives at home, and earned $930 for baby sitting jobs in 1984. Tim is 20 years old and a sophomore in college. He was a full-time student for two semesters in 1984; however, he did not go to summer school but drove a delivery truck and earned $2,600 during the summer, which was less than half what his parents paid during the year for his tuition, books, and other items of support. Mr. and Mrs. Mozena had the following cash receipts and disbursements during 1984:

CASH RECEIPTS

Mr. Mozena:

Salary as manager of Shelter Island Marina ($42,000 gross pay less $7,980 federal income taxes, $2,392 FICA taxes, and $1,400 hospital and medical insurance withheld)	$29,328
Dividends from stocks in domestic corporations	460
Interest on bonds of the city of Denver	590

Mrs. Mozena:

Rentals from a small house purchased in January 1984 (the house cost $30,000 and is depreciated on a straight-line basis under the assumption that it had 15 years of remaining life with no salvage value when purchased)	3,300
Salary from part-time position in Art Store ($12,000 gross pay less $1,250 federal income taxes and $804 FICA taxes)	9,346
Proceeds of insurance received on the death of an aunt	10,000

CASH DISBURSEMENTS

Charitable contributions	2,400
Interest on mortgage on family residence	2,930
Property taxes on family residence	1,850
Property taxes on Mrs. Mozena's rental house	690
Interest on mortgage on rental house	760
Plumbing repairs at rental house	340
Insurance (one year) on rental house	310
Uninsured doctor and dental bills	1,670
Prescription drugs	860
Advance payments of estimated federal income tax on income not subject to withholding	1,000

Also, Mr. Mozena had a $3,400 capital gain on shares of stock held 15 months and a $1,250 capital gain on shares held 7 months.

Required:

Follow the form of Illustration 28–1 and use the rate schedule of Illustration 28–2 to calculate the net federal income tax payable or refund for Mr. and Mrs. Mozena.

ALTERNATE PROBLEMS

Problem 28–1A

Judy Garber has operated The Garden Store for a number of years with the following average annual results:

THE GARDEN STORE
Income Statement for an Average Year

Sales		$300,000
Cost of goods sold	$150,000	
Operating expenses	90,000	240,000
Net income		$ 60,000

Ms. Garber is unmarried and without dependents and has been operating The Garden Store as a single proprietorship. She has been withdrawing $40,000 each year to pay her personal living expenses, including $7,300 of charitable contributions, state and local taxes, and other itemized deductions. She has no income other than from The Garden Store.

Required:

1. Assume that Ms. Garber is considering the incorporation of her business beginning with the 1984 tax year and prepare a comparative income statement for the business showing its net income as a single proprietorship and as a corporation. Assume that if she incorporates, Ms. Garber will pay $40,000 per year to herself as a salary, which is a fair amount.
2. Use the rate schedule of Illustration 28–2 and determine the amount of federal income tax Ms. Garber will have to pay for herself and for her business under each of the following assumptions: *(a)* the business is not incorporated; *(b)* the business is incorporated, pays Ms. Garber a $40,000 annual salary as manager, and also pays her $6,100 per year in dividends; and *(c)* the business is incorporated, pays Ms. Garber a $40,000 salary, but does not pay any dividends.

Problem 28–2A

Margin Corporation needs additional capital for a new investment that will cost $300,000 and will increase its earnings $60,000 annually before interest on the money used in the expansion, if borrowed, and before income taxes. The Hill family owns all the outstanding stock of Margin Corporation, and will supply the money to finance the investment, either investing an additional $300,000 in the corporation by purchasing its unissued stock or lending it $300,000 at 12% interest.

The corporation presently earns well in excess of $300,000 annually and pays $60,000 per year to the family in dividends. If the loan is made, the dividends will be reduced by an amount equal to the interest on the loan.

Required:

Prepare an analysis showing whether it would be advantageous for the family to make the loan or to purchase the corporation's stock.

Problem 28–3A

Will White, Jr., recently inherited the business of his father. The business, Makeit, Inc., is a small manufacturing corporation; however, a share of its assets, $150,000 at cost, consists of blue-chip investment stocks purchased over the years by the corporation from earnings. The father was the sole owner of the corporation at his death, and before his death he had paid himself a $30,000 annual salary for a number of years as president and manager. Over the years, the corporation seldom paid a dividend but instead had invested any earnings not needed in the business in the blue-chip stocks previously mentioned. At the father's death the market value of these stocks far exceeded their cost.

Will's mother is dead, and after Will graduated from college, the father had no dependents. The father's tax return for the year before his death (1984) showed $33,000 of gross income, consisting of his $30,000 corporation salary plus $3,000 interest from real estate loans. It also showed $5,300 of itemized deductions plus a single $1,000 exemption deduction. The corporation had earned during the year before the father's death $46,000 from its manufacturing operations plus $20,000 in dividends from its investments, a total of $66,000 after the president's salary but before income taxes.

Required:

1. Prepare a comparative statement showing for the year before the father's death the corporation's operating income, dividend income, total income, share of the dividend income deducted, taxable income, and income tax under the following *(a)* and *(b)* assumptions. *(a)* The corporation owns the investment stocks and had the operating income just described. *(b)* The corporation had the operating income described; but instead of owning the investment stocks, over the years it paid dividends (none last year), and Will White, Sr., used the dividends to buy the stocks in his own name rather than in the corporation name.

2. Calculate the amounts of individual income tax and corporation income tax incurred by Mr. White, Sr., and the corporation for the year before Mr. White's death under the foregoing *(a)* assumptions, and the amounts that would have been incurred under the *(b)* assumptions. Also calculate the amount of individual income tax Mr. White would have incurred with the business organized as a single proprietorship and the stocks registered in his own name. Under this last assumption remember that the corporation's operating income plus the salary paid its president equal the operating income of the single proprietorship. Use the rate schedule of Illustration 28–2 in the individual income tax calculations.

Problem 28–4A

Klasson Company completed the installation of a new machine in its plant at a $180,000 total cost on January 2, 1985. It was estimated that the machine would have a five-year life, no salvage value, and that it would produce $150,000 of income during each of the five years, before depreciation and income taxes. The company allocates income taxes in its reports to stockholders, since it uses straight-line depreciation in its accounting records and the accelerated cost recovery system (ACRS) for tax purposes. The machine falls in the three-year asset class for tax purposes.

Required:

1. Prepare a schedule showing 1985, 1986, 1987, 1988, 1989, and total net income for the five years after deducting depreciation and actual taxes. Assume a 40% income tax rate. (No investment tax credit is claimed by the company.)
2. Prepare a second schedule showing each year's net income and the five-year total after deducting straight-line depreciation and actual taxes.
3. Prepare a third schedule showing income to be reported to stockholders with straight-line depreciation and allocated taxes.
4. Set up a T-account for Deferred Income Taxes and show therein the entries that will result from allocating income taxes.

Problem 28–5A

John and Sara Black are both 44 years old, have three sons, and file a joint tax return. Their oldest son, Bobby, is a junior high school student and earned $870 last year working at odd jobs. The other two sons earned nothing during the year. Mr. and Mrs. Black had the following cash receipts and disbursements last year:

CASH RECEIPTS

Salary to John Black from his employer, an insurance firm, for which John is an outside salesman ($32,000 gross income less $4,100 federal income taxes withheld, $2,145 FICA taxes, and $400 for hospital insurance premiums)	$24,455
Dividends from General Motors common stock (jointly owned)	2,000
Interest from savings account owned by Sara Black........................	420
Interest from bonds issued by City of Austin, Texas	2,400
Proceeds from sale of IBM common stock which had been acquired 30 months ago at a cost of $8,000 (jointly owned)	15,000

CASH DISBURSEMENTS

Cost of John driving from home to business office and back	$ 700
Cost of John driving from business office to visit customers	670
Entertainment of customers while soliciting insurance sales	800
Telephone charges for calls made to customers	60
Contributions to church	1,500
Local property taxes	1,200
Contribution to political campaign of State Senator	120
Interest on home mortgage	1,800
Uninsured doctor and dentist bills	3,650
Donation to college from which John and Sara graduated	600
Advance payment of federal income tax	840

Required:

Follow the form of Illustration 28–1 and use the rate schedule in Illustration 28–2 to calculate for the Blacks the amount of federal income tax due or to be refunded.

PROVOCATIVE PROBLEMS

Provocative Problem 28–1, Windfall Corporation

Terry Taft and his wife own all the outstanding stock of Windfall Corporation, a company Terry organized several years ago and which is growing rapidly and needs additional capital. Cal Cook, a friend of the family, examined the following comparative income statement, which shows the corporation's net income for the past three years and which was prepared by its bookkeeper. Cal expressed a tentative willingness to invest the required capital by purchasing a portion of the corporation's unissued stock.

WINDFALL CORPORATION
Comparative Income Statement, 198A, 198B, 198C

	198A	*198B*	*198C*
Sales	$700,000	$800,000	$900,000
Costs and expenses other than depreciation and federal income taxes....................	$450,000	$480,000	$520,000
Depreciation expense	90,000	100,000	110,000
Federal income taxes	56,000	76,000	92,000
Total costs and expenses	$596,000	$656,000	$722,000
Net income	$104,000	$144,000	$178,000

However, before making a final decision, Cal Cook asked permission for his own accountant to examine the accounting records of the corporation. Permission was granted, the examination was made, and the accountant prepared the following comparative income statement covering the same period of time.

WINDFALL CORPORATION
Comparative Income Statement, 198A, 198B, and 198C

	198A	198B	198C
Sales	$700,000	$800,000	$900,000
Costs and expenses other than depreciation	$450,000	$480,000	$520,000
Depreciation expense*	90,000	100,000	110,000
Total costs and expenses	$540,000	$580,000	$630,000
Income before federal income taxes	$160,000	$220,000	$270,000
Applicable federal income taxes	64,000	88,000	108,000
Net income	$ 96,000	$132,000	$162,000

* Under the accelerated cost recovery system, the corporation deducted $110,000 of depreciation expense on its 198A tax return, $130,000 on its 198B return, and $170,000 on its 198C return.

Terry Taft was surprised at the difference in annual net incomes reported on the two statements and immediately called for an explanation from the public accountant who set up the corporation's accounting system and who prepares the annual tax returns of the corporation and the Tafts.

Explain why there is a difference between the net income figures on the two statements, and account for the difference in the net incomes. Prepare a statement that will explain the amounts shown on the corporation bookkeeper's statement. Assume a 40% federal income tax rate. (No investment tax credit was claimed by the company.)

Provocative Problem 28–2, Flat Bed, Inc.

Flat Bed, Inc., is about to invest $160,000 in a fleet of light trucks. The new trucks will be purchased in January 1985; are expected to have a five-year life and no salvage value; and you, the company's accountant, have prepared the following statement showing the expected results from the services provided by the new trucks. The statement is based on the assumption that the new trucks will be depreciated on a straight-line basis and that the company must pay out 50% of its before-tax earnings in state and federal income taxes.

FLAT BED, INC.
Expected Results from Sale of New Product

	1985	1986	1987	1988	1989	Totals
Sales	$375,000	$375,000	$375,000	$375,000	$375,000	$1,875,000
All costs other than depreciation and income taxes	250,000	250,000	250,000	250,000	250,000	1,250,000
Income before depreciation and income taxes	$125,000	$125,000	$125,000	$125,000	$125,000	$ 625,000
Depreciation expense	32,000	32,000	32,000	32,000	32,000	160,000
Income before income taxes	$ 93,000	$ 93,000	$ 93,000	$ 93,000	$ 93,000	$ 465,000
Income taxes	46,500	46,500	46,500	46,500	46,500	232,500
Net income	$ 46,500	$ 46,500	$ 46,500	$ 46,500	$ 46,500	$ 232,500

When the company president examined your statement, he said he knew that regardless of how calculated, the company could charge off no more than $160,000 of depreciation on the new trucks during their five-year life. Furthermore, he said he could see that this would result in $465,000 of earnings before taxes for the five years, $232,500 of income taxes, and $232,500 of net income, regardless of how depreciation was calculated. Nevertheless, he continued that he had been talking to a friend on the golf course a few days back and the friend had tried to explain the tax advantage of using the accelerated cost recovery system. He said he did not understand all the friend had tried to tell him; and as a result he would like for you to prepare an additional statement that calculates income after actual tax payments but based on ACRS depreciation. He said he would also like a written explanation of the tax advantage the company would gain through the use of the accelerated cost recovery system, with a dollar estimate of the amount the company would gain in this case. The president also expressed the belief that straight-line depreciation was the best method to use in financial statements. As a consequence, he wants you to explain the impact that ACRS depreciation for tax purposes will have on the income statements. Prepare the information for the president. (In making your estimate, assume the company can earn a 10% after-tax return, compounded annually, on any deferred taxes. Also, to simplify the problem, assume that the taxes must be paid the first day of January following their incurrence. The trucks are classified as three-year property under ACRS.)

APPENDIX

TEXAS INSTRUMENTS: 1982 Annual Report.

EQUIFAX INC.: Consolidating Financial Statements and Financial Review, 1982.

1982
ANNUAL
REPORT

To the Stockholders of Texas Instruments:

TI's net sales billed for 1982 were $4327 million, an increase of 3% over 1981, primarily because of volume increases in government electronics and home computers. Net income increased 33% to $144.0 million, up from $108.5 million in 1981. Earnings per share for 1982 were $6.10, compared with $4.62 in 1981.

Profit from operations as a percentage of net sales billed was 5.4% in 1982, compared with 6.0% in 1981. Substantial gains in consumer electronics, continued strength in government electronics and modest improvement in semiconductors did not fully offset sharply lower operating results in geophysical exploration, seismic equipment, and data systems, as well as softness in metallurgical materials and electrical controls. In addition, weakness in international currencies against the U.S. dollar adversely impacted margins in 1982.

Profit before tax as a percentage of net sales billed was 4.9% in 1982, compared with 4.2% in 1981. Results for 1981 included $36.6 million of pretax costs accrued in the second quarter for product phaseouts and employment reductions. Results for 1982 reflect pretax charges of $11.6 million, in connection with previously announced reductions of employment levels during the year. While these reductions were necessary in order to cut expenses, selective people additions were also made to support growth in government electronics and home computers. At year-end 1982, employment was 80,007, compared with 83,714 one year ago.

TI's effective tax rate in 1982 was 32.4%, down from 38% in 1981, primarily as a result of increased research and development tax credits.

For the fourth quarter of 1982, net sales billed were $1107 million, up 6% from the same quarter a year ago. Net income increased 16% to $42.6 million. Earnings per share were $1.80, compared with $1.56 in the fourth quarter of 1981.

TI continues to maintain a strong balance sheet. Cash and short-term investments increased during 1982 to $420 million, up from $150 million at year-end 1981, reflecting continued tight control of assets, plus cash provided from operations. These higher balances available for investment, together with reduced average borrowings, changed net interest from $30.4 million of expense in 1981 to $0.9 million of income in 1982.

Capital expenditures were $342 million in 1982, compared with $350 million in 1981. Capital spending for new semiconductor equipment and government electronics facilities increased, while cutbacks were made in expenditures for geophysical exploration. Authorizations carried over for capital expenditures in future years were approximately $288 million at year-end 1982. Depreciation for the year was $339 million, compared with $333 million in 1981.

TI's backlog of unfilled orders was $2592 million as of December 31, 1982, an increase of $247 million over year-end 1981, due primarily to contracts in government electronics and home computer demand.

TI-funded research and development expenditures increased 8% to $236 million. In addition, customer-funded R&D was $191 million for 1982, up from $154 million in 1981.

Despite increased unit volumes, semiconductor revenues for the year were essentially unchanged from 1981. Semiconductor orders, while up slightly for the full year, remained flat from the third quarter to the fourth. The market continues to be characterized by excess industry capacity, sluggish demand, and erosion of prices in both MOS and bipolar integrated circuits. Fourth quarter 1982 results, although still well below acceptable levels, were the best in seven quarters. Performance has improved steadily since the low point in the first quarter of the year, as a result of reduced overhead costs and increased shipments of higher complexity products.

Government electronics net sales billed exceeded $1 billion in 1982 for the first time. Growth came primarily from increased shipments of infrared and radar systems. Margins remained stable.

Shipments of minicomputers, terminals and peripheral products, used primarily in commercial data processing applications, declined in 1982, and orders remained flat. Operating results deteriorated with the reduced volume, the cost of carrying excess manufacturing capacity, and delays in availability of new products. With greatly improved product availability in the fourth quarter, both orders and shipments of TI's new Business System series of computers have picked up sharply. Heavy investment continues in development of new products and marketing programs.

Success of the 99/4A home computer was a major factor in the improvement of TI's consumer electronics business in 1982. Cost reductions and sharply higher second-half shipments of 99/4A home computer consoles, peripherals and software favorably impacted profitability. Our $100 rebate program, announced last August, was a key element in stimulating the exceptional growth of the home computer market. Although, in the fourth quarter, demand exceeded production capacity, we expect this market to be highly competitive in 1983.

For both electrical controls and metallurgical materials, shipments declined in 1982, reflecting poor world economic conditions, specific weaknesses in the appliance and housing markets, and lower U.S. auto production. As a result, margins declined from 1981, particularly for electrical controls. Emphasis continues on tight cost control to minimize the adverse effect of lower volumes. Most customer inventories remain at low levels.

The geophysical exploration market declined precipitously throughout 1982. The U.S. land market was particularly affected, with active industry contractor crews down nearly 40% from a year ago. Overcapacity in the seismic industry created heavy pricing pressures and reduced margins for geo-physical exploration. Shipments of seismic equipment also dropped sharply and results deteriorated. Despite this situation, geophysical exploration was a major contributor to TI profits in 1982, because of a strong first quarter. Actions to align capacity and expenses with the declining markets will continue in the face of lower operating levels expected for this business in 1983. Programs to improve productivity in data collection and processing and to develop new seismic technologies will also be maintained.

For all of its problems, 1982 has been an important year of accomplishment for TI. We have made substantial progress on an agenda of key strategic and organizational decisions, aimed at establishing a sound basis for return to satisfactory growth and earnings performance as economic recovery begins. While the outlook for sustained recovery is by no means certain, lower interest rates and reduced inflation have already created a better environment for future growth. Even if sluggish business conditions persist through much of 1983, TI will benefit from several important strengths. We have a broad range of new products in consumer, data systems, semiconductors, and industrial controls; there is a large and growing backlog in government electronics; our R&D and capital spending have stayed at high levels; our strong financial position gives us the resources and flexibility to pursue promising new opportunities; and we have planned our 1983 expenses on a conservative basis, with capacity available to respond quickly to a general economic upturn.

To all Tiers we extend our congratulations and thanks for their contributions to this strengthening of the company.

Mark Shepherd, Jr.
Chairman and Chief
Executive Officer

J. Fred Bucy
President and Chief
Operating Officer

Dallas, Texas
February 7, 1983

Consolidated Financial Statements

In millions of dollars, except per share amounts.

	For the year ended December 31		
	1982	*1981*	*1980*
Income and Retained Earnings			
Net sales billed	**$4,326.6**	$4,206.0	$4,074.7
Operating costs and expenses			
Cost of goods and services sold	**3,343.6**	3,238.7	2,922.8
General, administrative and marketing	**699.6**	674.1	636.7
Employees' retirement and profit sharing plans	**47.7**	40.3	96.5
Total	**4,090.9**	3,953.1	3,656.0
Profit from operations	**235.7**	252.9	418.7
Other income (expense) net	**10.5**	(36.6)	4.6
Interest on loans	**(33.1)**	(41.3)	(44.3)
Income before provision for income taxes	**213.1**	175.0	379.0
Provision for income taxes	**69.1**	66.5	166.8
Net income	**144.0**	108.5	212.2
Retained earnings at beginning of year	**1,070.3**	1,008.8	842.7
Cash dividends declared on common stock ($2.00 per share in 1982, 1981 and 1980)	**(47.2)**	(47.0)	(46.1)
Retained earnings at end of year	**$1,167.1**	$1,070.3	$1,008.8
Earned per common share (average outstanding during year)	**$ 6.10**	$ 4.62	$ 9.22
Changes in Financial Position			
Sources of cash			
Net income	**$ 144.0**	$ 108.5	$ 212.2
Depreciation	**338.5**	333.3	257.3
Net decrease (increase) in working capital (excluding cash and short-term investments, loans payable, dividends payable, and current portion long-term debt)	**118.1**	42.9	(93.9)
Provided from operations	**600.6**	484.7	375.6
Net change in total long-term debt	**1.8**	.9	192.7
Proceeds from sale of common stock	**.7**	32.7	41.1
Other	**30.0**	25.2	19.9
	633.1	543.5	629.3
Uses of cash			
Additions (net) to property, plant and equipment	**329.3**	341.4	542.2
Decrease (increase) in loans payable	**(16.3)**	138.0	8.9
Dividends paid on common stock	**47.2**	46.9	45.9
Purchase of common stock of the company for employee stock option and incentive plans	**2.9**	7.0	9.1
	363.1	533.3	606.1
Increase in cash and short-term investments	**$ 270.0**	$ 10.2	$ 23.2

See accompanying notes.

Texas Instruments Incorporated and Subsidiaries

	December 31 **1982**	December 31 *1981*
Balance Sheet		
Assets		
Current assets		
Cash and short-term investments	**$ 420.0**	$ 150.0
Accounts receivable, less allowance for losses of		
$72.7 in 1982 and $62.4 in 1981	**641.7**	590.6
Inventories (net of progress billings)	**360.0**	372.0
Prepaid taxes and expenses	**105.2**	84.3
Total current assets	**1,526.9**	1,196.9
Property, plant and equipment at cost	**2,083.8**	1,939.0
Less accumulated depreciation	**987.5**	833.5
Property, plant and equipment (net)	**1,096.3**	1,105.5
Other assets and deferred charges	**8.2**	8.1
Total assets	**$2,631.4**	$2,310.5
Liabilities and Stockholders' Equity		
Current liabilities		
Loans payable	**$ 48.7**	$ 32.4
Accounts payable and accrued expenses	**784.0**	614.3
Income taxes payable	**68.8**	67.0
Accrued retirement and profit sharing contributions	**44.6**	38.0
Dividends payable	**11.8**	11.8
Current portion long-term debt	**.8**	1.3
Total current liabilities	**958.7**	764.8
Deferred liabilities and credits		
Long-term debt	**214.0**	211.7
Incentive compensation payable in future years	**6.8**	9.1
Deferred credits and other liabilities	**91.1**	64.8
Total deferred liabilities and credits	**311.9**	285.6
Stockholders' equity (common shares outstanding at year-end:		
1982—23,652,416; 1981—23,580,096)	**1,360.8**	1,260.1
Total liabilities and stockholders' equity	**$2,631.4**	$2,310.5

See accompanying notes.

Notes to Financial Statements

Accounting Policies and Practices

The consolidated statements include the accounts of all subsidiaries. Intercompany balances and transactions have been eliminated. Provision has been made for income taxes on undistributed earnings of subsidiaries (principally non-U.S.) to the extent that dividend payments from such companies are expected to result in additional income tax liability. The remaining undistributed earnings have been reinvested; therefore, no provision has been made for U.S. income taxes on these earnings. Even if distributed, the related U.S. income taxes on these earnings, after giving effect to available tax credits, would not be material.

With regard to accounts recorded in currencies other than U.S. dollars, current assets (except inventories), current liabilities and long-term debt are translated at exchange rates in effect at year-end. Inventories, property, plant and equipment, depreciation thereon, and other assets are translated at historic exchange rates. Revenue and expense accounts other than depreciation for each month are translated at the appropriate month-end rate of exchange. Net unrealized gains and losses from currency translation and exchange contracts are charged or credited to income currently. The effect of net exchange gains and losses on net income has not been material.

Inventories are stated at the lower of cost, current replacement cost, or estimated realizable value. Cost is generally computed on a currently adjusted standard (which approximates current average costs) or average basis except for certain metals and metal products, which are computed on the last-in, first-out (LIFO) basis.

Substantially all depreciation is computed by either the declining balance or the sum-of-the-years-digits method. Fully depreciated assets are written off against accumulated depreciation.

Investment tax credit is taken into income over the lives of the related property. However, for tax purposes the credit is taken currently.

Cash and Short-Term Investments

Cash and short-term investments were primarily in unrestricted interest-bearing deposits, most of which were in Eurocurrency instruments.

Inventories

	Millions of Dollars	
	1982	*1981*
Raw materials and purchased parts	$216.8	$177.5
Work in process	250.0	317.1
Finished goods	105.0	102.8
Inventories before progress billings	571.8	597.4
Less progress billings	211.8	225.4
	$360.0	$372.0

Approximately 37% of the December 31, 1982, and 44% of the December 31, 1981, inventories before progress billings related to long-term contracts and programs.

Net sales billed under long-term fixed price and fixed price incentive contracts are recognized as deliveries are made, or as performance targets are achieved. Net sales billed under cost reimbursement contracts are recorded as costs are incurred and include estimated earned fees.

Inventories relating to long-term contracts and programs are stated at actual production costs, including manufacturing overhead and special tooling and engineering costs, reduced by amounts identified with net sales billed recognized on units delivered or with progress completed. Such inventories are reduced by charging any amounts in excess of estimated realizable value to cost of goods sold. The costs attributed to units delivered under long-term contracts and programs are based on the estimated average cost of all units to be produced under existing firm orders and are determined under the learning curve concept, which anticipates a predictable decrease in unit costs as tasks and production techniques become more efficient through repetition. At December 31, 1982, production costs included in inventories in excess of the estimated average cost of all units to be produced were not material.

The replacement cost of LIFO inventories exceeded the stated values by approximately $49.4 million at December 31, 1982, and $42.5 million at December 31, 1981.

Property, Plant and Equipment

		Millions of Dollars	
	Depreciable Lives	1982	1981
Land		$ 45.4	$ 40.8
Buildings and improvements	5—40 years	844.5	784.0
Machinery and equipment	3—10 years	1,193.9	1,114.2
		$2,083.8	$1,939.0

Authorizations for property, plant and equipment expenditures in future years were approximately $288 million at December 31, 1982, and $258 million at December 31, 1981.

Loans Payable

Loans payable consist of bank loans by non-U.S. subsidiaries.

	Millions of Dollars	
	1982	1981
Unused short-term lines of credit:		
U.S. (available to support commercial paper borrowings)	$167.5	$167.5
Non-U.S.	78.3	121.2

Accounts Payable and Accrued Expenses

	Millions of Dollars	
	1982	1981
Accounts payable	$269.9	$223.7
Advance payments from customers	155.8	90.0
Accrued salaries, wages and vacation pay	108.7	102.8
Other accrued expenses and liabilities	249.6	197.8
	$784.0	$614.3

Long-Term Debt

	Millions of Dollars	
	1982	1981
U.S. borrowings:		
4.80% sinking fund debentures due 1986 to 1990	$ 10.1	$ 10.1
12.70% sinking fund debentures due 1991 to 2005	200.0	200.0
Non-U.S. borrowings	3.9	1.6
	$214.0	$211.7

Stockholders' Equity

	Millions of Dollars		
	1982	1981	1980
Cumulative preferred stock, $25 par value; authorized 750,000 shares	$ —	$ —	$ —
Common stock, $1 par value:			

Shares (000s)		
1982	1981	1980

	1982	1981	1980
Authorized	30,000	30,000	30,000
Issued	23,826	23,728	23,431
	23.8	23.7	23.4
Paid-in capital	186.6	181.2	149.5
Retained earnings	1,167.1	1,070.3	1,008.8
Less treasury stock, at cost	(16.7)	(15.1)	(17.2)
	$1,360.8	$1,260.1	$1,164.5

Treasury Stock

	Shares (000s)		
	1982	1981	1980
Treasury stock held at year-end for employee stock option and incentive plans	174	148	177
Treasury stock acquired during the year for above plans	155	63	89

Paid-in Capital

	Millions of Dollars		
	1982	1981	1980
Paid-in capital at beginning of year	$181.2	$149.5	$107.8
Excess over par on stock sold to profit sharing trusts	—	30.9	37.5
Excess over par on stock issued on exercise of stock options (97,735 shares in 1982; 19,600 shares in 1981; 39,687 shares in 1980)	6.7	1.5	3.3
Common stock transactions, including tax effects, in connection with employee stock option and incentive plans	(1.3)	(.7)	.9
Paid-in capital at end of year	$186.6	$181.2	$149.5

Research and Development Expense

	Millions of Dollars		
	1982	1981	1980
Research and development expense	$236.5	$219.4	$188.5

Notes to Financial Statements

Other Income (Expense) net

	Millions of Dollars		
	1982	1981	1980
Interest income	$34.0	$ 10.9	$17.3
Other expense (net)	(23.5)	(47.5)	(12.7)
	$10.5	$(36.6)	$ 4.6

Other expense includes $11.6 million of employment reduction costs in 1982 and $36.6 million of product phaseout and employment reduction costs in 1981.

Stock Options and Reservations of Common Stock

The company has stock options outstanding to key employees under two stockholder-approved plans. The 1965 Stock Option Plan provides for options to expire not more than 10 years from date of grant. The 1974 Stock Option Plan provides for incentive stock options to expire not more than 10 years, and for options which are not incentive stock options to expire not more than 10 years and one day, from date of grant. Certain incentive stock options currently outstanding become exercisable in the second through fourth years of the option terms in percentage installments, cumulatively. Other options currently outstanding become exercisable over the last nine years of the option terms in percentage installments, cumulatively, upon attainment of specified earnings per share except that the options will be exercisable in full during the tenth year without regard to earnings per share.

The company also has options outstanding under the TI Employees Stock Option Purchase Plan approved by stockholders in 1974. The plan provides for options to be offered to all eligible employees in amounts based on a percentage of the employee's prior year's compensation. If the optionee authorizes and does not cancel payroll deductions which, with interest, will be equal to or greater than the purchase price, options granted become exercisable 13 months, and expire not more than 27 months, from date of grant.

Summary of Plans

	1965 Stock Option Plan	1974 Stock Option Plan	TI Employees Stock Option Purchase Plan
Options (shares):			
Outstanding at beginning of 1982	219,758	881,927	195,032
Granted	—	180,670	292,368*
Terminated	15,000	47,844	138,060*
Exercised	126,058	48,448	52,856
Outstanding at end of 1982	78,700	966,305	296,484
Exercisable at end of 1982	78,700	376,331	38,236
Becoming exercisable in 1983	—	208,063	258,248
Consideration received for options exercised during 1982 (millions)	$9.0	$ 3.6	$ 4.7
Aggregate purchase price of options outstanding at end of 1982 (millions)	$7.2	$76.5	$26.1

*Excludes options offered but not accepted.

There would have been no significant effect on earnings per share for the years 1980 through 1982 had the calculation included in outstanding shares from the beginning of each year those shares of common stock reserved for then outstanding options.

At year-end 1982, 78,700 shares of common stock were reserved for options granted under the 1965 Stock Option Plan, which terminated as to future grants in 1974.

At year-end 1982, 145,776 shares were available for future grants under the 1974 Stock Option Plan and 383,188 shares under the TI Employees Stock Option Purchase Plan. However, no more than a total of 1,250,000 authorized and unissued shares may be sold pursuant to the 1974 Stock Option Plan and the TI Employees Stock Option Purchase Plan combined. Through year-end 1982, 51,769 authorized and unissued shares had been sold under the two plans combined. At year-end 1982, 1,198,231 shares were reserved for options granted or to be granted under the two plans combined. The company from time to time acquires outstanding shares of its common stock for use under stock option plans.

Profit Sharing and Retirement Plans

There was no profit sharing expense in 1982, $1.1 million in 1981 and $63.8 million in 1980. Under the plans, except in France where a government-prescribed formula is used, the annual contributions are a function of consolidated after-tax return on assets, a People Effectiveness Index (defined as consolidated net sales billed divided by total payroll and payroll-related benefit costs), and the aggregate compensation of the participants. Total payroll and payroll-related benefit costs of Texas Instruments Incorporated and all subsidiaries in 1982 were $1.85 billion. The People Effectiveness Index was 2.3 in 1982. The annual contributions are subject to a ceiling of the lesser of 25% of consolidated income before profit sharing and income taxes, or an amount which, together with all previous contributions, does not exceed 15% of the cumulative compensation paid to all participating employees for all plan years. No contribution is made for any year in which the contribution would be less than 3% of the aggregate compensation of participating employees for that year. The calculated amount was less than 3% for 1982 and 1981, and therefore no contributions were provided. These plans are stock bonus plans under which each year's cash contributions are invested in TI common stock by the trustees through purchases of outstanding shares or through purchases of previously unissued shares offered from time to time by the company. The board of directors has authorized the issuance of up to 1,200,000 previously unissued shares for this purpose. During 1981, from contributions for 1980, the trustees of the plans purchased 52,624 outstanding shares of TI common stock and 277,500 previously unissued shares. During 1980, the trustees of the plans purchased 206,483 outstanding shares of TI common stock and 335,700 previously unissued shares.

Employees of the company and certain of its subsidiaries are covered by TI retirement plans. The company's policy is to fund retirement costs annually. Total expense under the plans was $47.7 million in 1982, $39.2 million in 1981 and $32.7 million in 1980. A comparison of accumulated plan benefits and plan net assets for the company's significant U.S. defined benefit plans is presented in the following table:

| | Millions of Dollars | |
	January 1, 1982	January 1, 1981
Actuarial present value of accumulated plan benefits:		
Vested	$172.9	$141.6
Non-vested	23.6	15.9
	$196.5	$157.5
Net assets available for benefits	$338.7	$303.4

The weighted average assumed rate of return used in determining the actuarial present value of accumulated plan benefits was 6%.

The benefit and net asset information above excludes the company's non-U.S. pension plans because comparable information is not available.

Incentive Compensation Plan

Under a stockholder-approved Incentive Compensation Plan, all key employees of the company are eligible to receive performance units payable, upon achievement of performance goals, in cash and/or common stock and incentive awards of cash and/or common stock, limited to the amount available from time to time in the incentive compensation reserve.

The board of directors determines the amount, if any, which is credited each year to the incentive compensation reserve, which cannot be greater than 10% of the amount by which the company's net income (as defined) for the year exceeds 6% of net capital (as defined), and cannot be greater than the amount paid out as dividends on the common stock of the company during the year.

Performance units and incentive awards may be payable in single amounts or in installments over not more than ten and five years, respectively. The obligation to pay installments terminates if the participant's employment terminates other than for retirement, disability or death, or if the participant engages in any activity harmful or prejudicial to the interest of the company. The company acquires outstanding shares of its common stock from time to time for awards under the plan.

Expense with respect to the plan was $3.0 million in 1982, $2.7 million in 1981 and $12.8 million in 1980.

Notes to Financial Statements

Rental Expense and Lease Commitments

Rental and lease expense was $112.5 million in 1982, $91.2 million in 1981, and $86.2 million in 1980. The company conducts certain operations in leased facilities and also leases a portion of its data processing and other equipment, as well as certain geophysical survey vessels.

At December 31, 1982, the company was committed under non-cancelable leases, principally for facilities, with minimum rentals in succeeding years as follows:

Non-cancelable Leases

	Millions of Dollars
1983	$ 32.9
1984	24.4
1985	15.5
1986	10.4
1987	6.4
Later years	19.3
Total	$108.9

Industry Segment and Geographic Area Operations

The company is engaged in the development, manufacture and sale of a variety of products in the electrical and electronics industry for industrial, consumer and government markets. These products consist of components (semiconductors, such as integrated circuits, and electrical and electronic control devices); digital products (such as minicomputers, data terminals, industrial controls, home computers, electronic calculators and learning aids); and government electronics (such as radar, infrared surveillance systems and missile guidance and control systems).

The company also produces metallurgical materials (primarily clad metals) for use in a variety of applications such as automotive equipment, appliances and telecommunications equipment, and provides services, primarily through the electronic collection and processing of seismic data in connection with petroleum exploration.

Industry segment and geographic area profit is not equivalent to income before provision for income taxes due to exclusion of general corporate expenses, net interest, currency gains and losses, product phaseout and employment reduction costs and other items along with elimination of unrealized profit in assets.

Identifiable assets are those associated with segment or geographic area operations, excluding cash and short-term investments in excess of operating needs, internal company receivables and tax-related timing differences. Generally, net sales billed between industry segments and between geographic areas are based on prevailing market prices or an approximation thereof.

Net Sales Billed

	Millions of Dollars		
	1982	*1981*	*1980*
Components			
Trade	$1,349	$1,460	$1,767
Intersegment	154	72	132
	1,503	1,532	1,899
Digital Products			
Trade	1,138	1,064	987
Intersegment	35	67	65
	1,173	1,131	1,052
Government Electronics			
Trade	1,059	876	738
Intersegment	25	22	33
	1,084	898	771
Metallurgical Materials			
Trade	136	146	138
Intersegment	47	54	70
	183	200	208
Services Trade	629	649	432
Eliminations	(245)	(204)	(287)
Total net sales billed	$4,327	$4,206	$4,075

Net sales billed directly to federal government agencies in the United States, made principally by the government electronics segment, aggregated $684 million for 1982, $569 million for 1981 and $476 million for 1980.

Profit

	Millions of Dollars		
	1982	*1981*	*1980*
Components	$ 34	$ 26	$ 263
Digital Products	23	26	64
Government Electronics	161	135	88
Metallurgical Materials	12	19	27
Services	81	119	63
Eliminations and corporate items	(98)	(150)	(126)
Income before provision for income taxes	$ 213	$ 175	$ 379

Industry Segment Identifiable Assets

	Millions of Dollars		
	1982	*1981*	*1980*
Components	$ 918	$ 971	$1,113
Digital Products	737	579	584
Government Electronics	315	304	331
Metallurgical Materials	85	92	92
Services	254	325	228
Eliminations and corporate items	322	39	66
Total	$2,631	$2,310	$2,414

Property, Plant & Equipment

	Millions of Dollars	
	Depreciation	Additions (net)
1982		
Components	$ 164	$ 140
Digital Products	48	44
Government Electronics	49	86
Metallurgical Materials	9	4
Services	74	48
Eliminations and corporate items	(5)	7
Total	$ 339	$ 329
1981		
Components	$ 175	$ 155
Digital Products	48	48
Government Electronics	45	45
Metallurgical Materials	11	10
Services	65	108
Eliminations and corporate items	(11)	(25)
Total	$ 333	$ 341
1980		
Components	$ 140	$ 300
Digital Products	38	73
Government Electronics	43	64
Metallurgical Materials	8	18
Services	37	105
Eliminations and corporate items	(9)	(18)
Total	$ 257	$ 542

The following geographic area data includes revenues, costs and expenses generated by and assets employed in operations located in each area.

Net Sales Billed

	Millions of Dollars		
	1982	*1981*	*1980*
United States			
Trade	$2,998	$2,866	$2,677
Interarea	233	213	237
	3,231	3,079	2,914
Europe			
Trade	678	724	870
Interarea	44	29	28
	722	753	898
East Asia			
Trade	273	263	233
Interarea	514	547	534
	787	810	767
Other Areas			
Trade	379	353	294
Interarea	69	68	72
	448	421	366
Eliminations	(861)	(857)	(870)
Total net sales billed	$4,327	$4,206	$4,075

Geographic Area Profit

	Millions of Dollars		
	1982	*1981*	*1980*
United States	$ 167	$ 136	$ 267
Europe	38	61	106
East Asia	56	69	68
Other Areas	36	37	43
Eliminations and corporate items	(84)	(128)	(105)
Income before provision for income taxes	$ 213	$ 175	$ 379

Identifiable Assets

	Millions of Dollars		
	1982	*1981*	*1980*
United States	$1,531	$1,508	$1,608
Europe	346	310	355
East Asia	308	306	281
Other Areas	153	183	142
Eliminations and corporate items	293	3	28
Total assets	$2,631	$2,310	$2,414

Notes to Financial Statements

Income Taxes

Income Before Provision for Income Taxes

Millions of Dollars

| | Geographic area profit | | Elims. & | |
	U.S.	Non-U.S.	corp. items	Total
1982	$167	$130	$ (84)	$213
1981	136	167	(128)	175
1980	267	217	(105)	379

With the exception of inter-area elimination of unrealized profit in assets which totaled $16 million in 1982, $5 million (reduction) in 1981, and $26 million in 1980, the remaining corporate items consist primarily of general corporate expenses. These expenses are applicable to both U.S. and non-U.S. operations but are generally deductible for tax purposes in the U.S.

Provision for Income Taxes

Millions of Dollars

1982	U.S.	Non-U.S.	Elims.	Total
Currently payable	$ 1	$67	$ —	$ 68
Net timing differences	1	7	(7)	1
Total	$ 2	$74	$ (7)	$ 69
1981				
Currently payable	$(24)	$77	$ —	$ 53
Net timing differences	22	(10)	2	14
Total	$ (2)	$67	$ 2	$ 67
1980				
Currently payable	$ 74	$92	$ —	$166
Net timing differences	8	5	(12)	1
Total	$ 82	$97	$(12)	$167

The effective income tax rates were 32.4% in 1982, 38.0% in 1981, and 44.0% in 1980. Investment tax credit amortization reduced the provision for income taxes by $22 million in 1982, $19 million in 1981, and $16 million in 1980. The unamortized balance is included in deferred credits and other liabilities on the balance sheet. The research and development tax credit reduced the provision for income taxes by approximately $8 million in 1982.

Net Timing Differences

| | Millions of Dollars | | |
	1982	1981	1980
Undistributed earnings of non-U.S. subsidiaries, net of effect of dividends received	$ 8	$11	$13
Elimination of unrealized intercompany profits	1	(1)	(12)
Depreciation and amortization	(34)	(10)	(9)
Other timing differences between financial statements and tax returns, net of reversals of similar items for prior years:			
Inventory valuation	32	23	12
Other	(6)	(9)	(3)
Net timing differences	$ 1	$14	$ 1

Net accumulated tax-related timing differences are classified in the balance sheet as prepaid taxes and expenses, and deferred credits and other liabilities, as appropriate.

Report of Certified Public Accountants

The Board of Directors
Texas Instruments Incorporated

We have examined the consolidated balance sheet of Texas Instruments Incorporated and subsidiaries at December 31, 1982 and 1981, and the related consolidated statements of income and retained earnings and changes in financial position for each of the three years in the period ended December 31, 1982. Our examinations were made in accordance with generally accepted auditing standards and, accordingly, included such tests of the accounting records and such other auditing procedures as we considered necessary in the circumstances.

In our opinion, the financial statements referred to above present fairly the consolidated financial position of Texas Instruments Incorporated and subsidiaries at December 31, 1982 and 1981, and the consolidated results of its operations and the changes in its consolidated financial position for each of the three years in the period ended December 31, 1982, in conformity with generally accepted accounting principles applied on a consistent basis during the period.

Arthur Young & Company

Dallas, Texas
January 29, 1983

Summary of Selected Financial Data

Year Ended December 31	1982	1981	1980	1979	1978	1977	1976	1975	1974	1973
Millions of Dollars										
Net sales billed	**$4,326.6**	$4,206.0	$4,074.7	$3,224.1	$2,549.9	$2,046.5	$1,658.6	$1,367.6	$1,572.5	$1,287.3
Operating costs and expenses	**4,090.9**	3,953.1	3,656.0	2,904.8	2,296.4	1,835.7	1,496.0	1,252.8	1,403.1	1,141.8
Profit from operations	**235.7**	252.9	418.7	319.3	253.5	210.8	162.6	114.8	169.4	145.5
Other income (expense) net	**10.5**	(36.6)	4.6	8.9	12.3	9.3	23.8	11.9	4.1	6.7
Interest on loans	**(33.1)**	(41.3)	(44.3)	(19.5)	(8.4)	(9.2)	(8.3)	(10.8)	(10.7)	(6.7)
Income before provision for income taxes	**213.1**	175.0	379.0	308.7	257.4	210.9	178.1	115.9	162.8	145.5
Provision for income taxes	**69.1**	66.5	166.8	135.8	117.1	94.3	80.7	53.8	73.2	62.3
Net income	**144.0**	108.5	212.2	172.9	140.3	116.6	97.4	62.1	89.6	83.2
Earned per common share (average outstanding during year)	**$6.10**	$4.62	$9.22	$7.58	$6.15	$5.11	$4.25	$2.71	$3.92	$3.67
Cash dividends declared per common share	**2.00**	2.00	2.00	2.00	1.76	1.41	1.08	1.00	1.00	.62
Common shares (average shares outstanding during year, in thousands)	**23,609**	23,483	23,021	22,799	22,794	22,842	22,933	22,920	22,854	22,691

December 31	1982	1981	1980	1979	1978	1977	1976	1975	1974	1973
Millions of Dollars										
Working capital	**$ 568.2**	$ 432.1	$ 327.9	$ 200.7	$ 304.3	$ 365.7	$ 364.8	$ 360.7	$ 314.3	$ 307.0
Property, plant and equipment (net)	**1,096.3**	1,105.5	1,097.4	812.5	572.7	394.1	302.9	253.7	280.4	219.9
Total assets	**2,631.4**	2,310.5	2,413.7	1,908.2	1,494.1	1,234.3	1,110.2	933.6	960.4	822.4
Long-term debt	**214.0**	211.7	211.7	17.6	19.1	29.7	38.2	47.5	72.8	67.7
Stockholders' equity	**1,360.8**	1,260.1	1,164.5	952.9	821.3	723.9	642.8	577.4	536.6	463.6
Employees	**80,007**	83,714	89,875	85,779	78,571	68,521	66,162	56,682	65,524	74,422
Stockholders of record	**28,994**	31,460	28,370	28,405	26,247	24,438	22,425	21,359	18,977	16,135

Supplemental Financial Information

Management Discussion and Analysis of Financial Condition and Results of Operations

The management discussion and analysis of the company's financial condition and results of operations consists of the Letter to the Stockholders set forth on pages 2—3 and the following additional information on financial condition, 1981 results of operations, and impact of inflation.

Financial Condition

The company's needs for cash depend on its real growth rate of net sales billed and on the rate of inflation, as well as on its profitability and asset usage. These needs are met primarily with funds provided from operations. In addition, the company maintains short-term sources of liquidity in the form of unused lines of credit.

The company's sources of long-term funding include retained earnings, the sale of common stock and long-term debt. The company may sell previously unissued shares pursuant to its stock option plans and by offerings to trustees of the company's stock bonus profit sharing plans. In 1982, proceeds from such sales of new shares were $1 million, compared with $33 million in 1981. The company's long-term debt at the end of both 1982 and 1981 consisted primarily of $200 million of 12.70% sinking fund debentures issued in 1980. The company anticipates maintaining a mix of equity and debt in its capital structure that will assure the continuation of high debt-quality ratings that provide access to worldwide capital markets.

1981 Results of Operations Compared with 1980

Net sales billed for the year 1981 were $4206.0 million, an increase of 3% over 1980. Net income was $108.5 million, down 49% from 1980. Earnings per share were $4.62, compared with $9.22 in 1980. Income before provision for taxes as a percentage of net sales billed was 4.2% in 1981, compared with 9.3% in 1980. The principal reasons for the decline were adverse results in semiconductors and distributed computing, along with the effect of weaker international currencies. Results for 1981 included the effect of $36.6 million of pretax costs accrued in the second quarter for product phaseouts and employment reductions. The employment reductions were taken as a result of weakness in world market demand for semiconductor, consumer, and, to a lesser degree, distributed computing products. In addition, the decision was made to phase out certain product activities where returns were inadequate and prospects for future returns were judged insufficient to justify continued investment. The activities included: digital watches, liquid crystal displays, magnetic bubble memories, plasma panel displays, TI Supply Company's distribution operations in the U.S., appliance electronics, and selected lines of low-margin discrete semiconductors.

The combined effect of investment tax credits and lower profits reduced the effective tax rate to 38% in 1981, down from 44% in 1980.

Semiconductor operating results in 1981 were severely affected by pricing pressures, reflecting excess capacity and weaker customer demand. Also contributing to the decline from 1980 were start-up costs associated with new products.

Demand for TI's distributed computing products weakened in 1981. High interest rates particularly affected medium-performance minicomputer systems sold through third parties. For the year, margins were well below those of 1980 because of higher marketing expenses and excess production capacity. In consumer electronics, overall results in 1981 were down from 1980 because of weakness in U.S. and European calculator markets.

The government electronics business approached the $1-billion level in 1981, paced by increased shipments of infrared systems and radar equipment. TI's geophysical exploration business grew faster than the overall market and performance improved over 1980.

In electrical controls and metallurgical materials, increased penetration of the automotive market and strong growth of copper-clad aluminum wire shipments to the cable TV market only partially offset the effects of the slump in autos and housing. Margins were down from 1980.

Backlog of unfilled orders was $2345 million as of December 31, 1981, an increase of $280 million over year-end 1980. TI-funded research and development expenditures increased 16% in 1981 to $219 million. Additional R&D funded by our customers was $154 million for the year. Capital expenditures were down from $548 million in 1980 to $350 million in 1981 due primarily to reduced spending for semiconductor capacity. Depreciation was $333 million, up from $257 million in 1980.

Impact of Inflation

For a discussion of the impact of inflation and the effects of changing prices, see "Effects of Changing Prices," following.

Effects of Changing Prices

This information measures the effects of inflation using two calculation methods, current cost and constant dollar.

Current Cost Method

This method reflects the current price of resources used rather than their historical cost. Current prices of property, plant and equipment and depreciation expense were approximated primarily using specific price indexes. Inventories and cost of goods and services sold were measured on recent production costs.

Accelerated depreciation is used for historical cost reporting to reflect ongoing technological obsolescence and offset inflationary effects. To avoid overcompensating, depreciation methods for assets not normally subject to technological obsolescence (certain buildings and improvements and long-lived equipment) have been changed to the straight-line method for purposes of this item only. Current cost depreciation expense for 1982 is $378 million. The current cost of property, plant and equipment (net) is $1.6 billion at year-end 1982.

Cost of goods and services sold on the current cost basis exceeds the historical cost amount. Most of this increase is due to the effects of increased depreciation, with minor adjustments made for average cost inventories and other items. The current cost of inventories, net of progress billings, which are unchanged, is $418 million at year-end 1982.

Constant Dollar Method

This method uses the Consumer Price Index for All Urban Consumers (CPI-U) as a measure of general inflation to express amounts in dollars of equivalent purchasing power.

Supplemental Financial Information

Constant dollar depreciation expense totals $386 million for 1982. The straight-line depreciation method has been utilized for certain assets as previously discussed.

Constant dollar cost of goods and services sold exceeds the related historical and current cost amounts because the costs are adjusted by the general inflation rate. As this rate is not representative of the company's manufacturing cost trend experience, the company does not believe this approach is a proper measure of the effects of inflation on the company.

Statements of Income for the Year 1982
Adjusted for the Effects of Inflation

Millions of Dollars, Except Per Share Amounts

	Historical Cost as Reported	Current Cost	Constant Dollar
Net sales billed	$4,327	$4,327	$4,327
Operating costs and expenses:			
Cost of goods and services sold	3,344	3,383	3,404
Other operating costs and expenses	747	751	752
Total	4,091	4,134	4,156
Profit from operations	236	193	171
Other income/interest (net)	(23)	(23)	(23)
Income before provision for income taxes	213	170	148
Provision for income taxes	69	69	69
Net income	$ 144	$ 101	$ 79
Earned per common share	$ 6.10	$ 4.28	$ 3.35
Effective tax rate	32%	41%	47%

The following five-year table shows selected inflation-oriented financial data for 1982 and certain prior periods, all stated in terms of average 1982 dollars as measured by the CPI–U.

Five-Year Table

	Average 1982 Millions of Dollars, Except Per Share Amounts and CPI–U				
	1982	1981	1980	1979	1978
Net sales billed	$4,327	$4,464	$4,774	$4,288	$3,773
Constant dollar:					
Net income	79	37	171	166	
Earned per common share	3.35	1.58	7.43	7.24	
Stockholders' equity	1,723	1,672	1,638	1,456	
Current cost:					
Net income	101	77	213	202	
Earned per common share	4.28	3.30	9.27	8.83	
Stockholders' equity	1,943	1,848	1,850	1,715	
Net increases in specific prices of inventories and property, plant and equipment	103	92	142	229	
Less increase in general price level of these items	76	181	238	217	
Excess	27	(89)	(96)	12	
Purchasing power gain on net monetary items	1	14	22	—	
Cash dividends declared per common share	2.00	2.12	2.35	2.66	2.60
Market price per common share at year-end	133.11	82.68	135.04	110.66	113.98
Consumer Price Index (1967 = 100)	289.1	272.4	246.8	217.4	195.4

Quarterly Financial Data

1982

Millions of Dollars, Except Per Share Amounts

	1st	2nd	3rd	4th
Net sales billed	$1,078.5	$1,092.9	$1,048.3	$1,107.0
Profit from operations	46.5	63.6	62.7	63.0
Income before provision for income taxes	43.9	57.7	50.1	61.4
Net income	27.7	36.9	36.9	42.6
Earned per common share	$ 1.17	$ 1.56	$ 1.57	$ 1.80

1981

Millions of Dollars, Except Per Share Amounts

	1st	2nd	3rd	4th
Net sales billed	$1,063.0	$1,055.6	$1,038.7	$1,048.7
Profit from operations	72.9	65.8	47.1	67.1
Income before provision for income taxes	59.0	18.1	40.7	57.2
Net income	34.2	10.5	27.1	36.7
Earned per common share	$ 1.47	$ .44	$ 1.15	$ 1.56

Income before provision for income taxes includes $7.2 million of net employment reduction costs in the third quarter of 1982 and $36.6 million of product phaseout and employment reduction costs in the second quarter of 1981.

Common Stock Prices and Dividends

TI common stock is listed on the New York Stock Exchange and traded principally in that market. The table below shows the high and low prices of TI common stock on the composite tape as reported by *The Commercial and Financial Chronicle* and the dividends paid per share for each quarter during the past two years.

		Quarter		
	1st	2nd	3rd	4th
Stock Prices:				
1982 High	$ 85.75	$ 93.75	$102.75	$152.50
Low	70.50	76.875	80.625	92.00
1981 High	$125.25	$126.25	$ 97.25	$ 88.125
Low	102.75	97.00	79.875	75.00
Dividends paid:				
1982	$ .50	$ .50	$ .50	$ .50
1981	.50	.50	.50	.50

Annual Meeting of Stockholders

The 1983 Annual Meeting of Stockholders of Texas Instruments Incorporated will take place on Thursday, April 21, in the North Building cafeteria at 13500 North Central Expressway, Dallas, Texas.

Board Advisory Council

The board advisory council advises the board of directors on a wide range of economic, political and social issues. Members are available on a group or individual basis, and spend between seven and 30 days a year performing such duties. Mark Shepherd, Jr. serves as chairman of the council. (See back cover.)

TI Fellow

A TI scientist or technologist who is recognized by TI management and by peers for outstanding performance in a field of specialty, as measured by patents awarded, publication of professional and technical papers and key contributions making the difference between success or failure of TI projects. (See back cover.)

New York Transfer Agent & Registrar

Morgan Guaranty Trust Company of New York, 30 West Broadway, New York, N.Y. 10015.

Dallas Transfer Agent & Registrar

RepublicBank Dallas, N.A., P.O. Box 2964, Dallas, Texas 75221.

Executive Offices

13500 North Central Expressway, (P.O. Box 225474), Dallas, Texas 75265.

SEC Form 10-K

Stockholders may obtain a copy of the company's annual report to the Securities and Exchange Commission on Form 10-K without charge (except for exhibits) by writing to: Manager of Investor Relations, P.O. Box 225474, Mail Station 413, Dallas, Texas 75265.

An Equal Opportunity Employer

EQUIFAX INC.

Consolidated Financial Statements and Financial Review, 1982

Equifax Inc.
CONSOLIDATED STATEMENTS OF INCOME

(in thousands of dollars except for per share amounts)

Year Ended December 31	1982	1981	1980
Revenue:			
Operating revenue	$434,691	$401,785	$371,108
Gain on sale of Northwest Credit Bureau	—	4,950	—
Gain on condemnation of land	—	1,046	—
Other income	2,014	1,792	1,032
Total revenue	436,705	409,573	372,140
Costs and Expenses:			
Costs of services rendered	329,177	311,662	285,548
Selling, general and administrative expenses	82,304	70,561	67,671
Loss on anticipated disposal of assets	3,152	—	—
Total costs and expenses	414,633	382,223	353,219
Income before provision for income taxes	22,072	27,350	18,921
Provision for income taxes	9,838	11,539	8,390
Net income	$ 12,234	$ 15,811	$ 10,531
Net income per share of common stock	$1.79	$2.35	$1.58
Dividends per share of common stock	$1.305	$1.200	$1.175

The accompanying notes are an integral part of these statements.

Contents

Equifax Inc.
CONSOLIDATED STATEMENTS OF SHAREHOLDERS' EQUITY

(in thousands of dollars)

Year Ended December 31	1982	1981	1980
Common Stock:			
Balance at beginning of year	$ 8,463	$ 8,383	$ 8,383
Effect of two-for-one stock split	8,417	—	
Shares issued for acquisitions	707	80	—
Balance at end of year	$17,587	$ 8,463	$ 8,383
Paid-In Capital:			
Balance at beginning of year	$ 2,275	$ 2,297	$ 2,335
Shares issued for acquisitions	1,924	(22)	—
Excess of cost over option price of shares issued under stock option plan	(210)	—	(38)
Balance at end of year	$ 3,989	$ 2,275	$ 2,297
Retained Earnings:			
Balance at beginning of year	$58,832	$51,099	$48,402
Effect of two-for-one stock split	(8,417)	—	
Net income	12,234	15,811	10,531
Cash dividends paid	(8,944)	(8,078)	(7,834)
Retained earnings of acquired company	420	—	
Balance at end of year	$54,125	$58,832	$51,099
Treasury Stock, at Cost:			
Balance at beginning of year	$ 491	$ 491	$ 615
Shares issued under stock option plan	(467)	—	(124)
Balance at end of year	$ 24	$ 491	$ 491
Accumulated Foreign Currency Translation Adjustment:			
Cumulative effect of change in accounting principles related to translation of foreign currency financial statements	$ 286	$ —	$ —
Adjustment during year	371	—	—
Balance at end of year	$ 657	$ —	$ —
Net Unrealized Loss on Long-Term Investments in Preferred Stocks:			
Balance at beginning of year	$ 2,194	$ 1,925	$ 1,422
Increase (decrease) during year	(552)	269	503
Balance at end of year	$ 1,642	$ 2,194	$ 1,925

The accompanying notes are an integral part of these statements.

Equifax Inc.
CONSOLIDATED BALANCE SHEETS

(in thousands of dollars)

December 31	1982	1981
Assets		
Current Assets:		
Cash and short-term investments	$ 3,861	$ 9,753
Accounts receivable	68,598	60,119
Other	7,823	8,112
Total current assets	80,282	77,984
Long-Term Investments in Preferred Stocks, at Market or Mandatory Redemption Price	4,069	3,517
Property and Equipment:		
Land and buildings	18,595	16,960
Furniture and equipment	41,738	41,707
Leasehold improvements	1,246	930
	61,579	59,597
Less — Accumulated depreciation	22,833	24,926
	38,746	34,671
Other Assets:		
Costs in excess of net assets of businesses acquired	13,455	11,725
Investments in tax benefits	6,547	3,224
Other	7,915	4,760
	27,917	19,709
	$151,014	$135,881

December 31	1982	1981
Liabilities and Shareholders' Equity		
Current Liabilities:		
Short-term bank notes	$ 6,500	$ 9,000
Current maturities of long-term debt	1,535	3,556
Accounts payable and accrued expenses	23,475	16,518
Income taxes	17,489	15,928
Compensated absences	7,888	7,377
Other	5,222	1,389
Total current liabilities	62,109	53,768
Long-Term Debt, Less Current Maturities	6,403	7,417
Deferred Income Taxes	9,124	7,811
Commitments and Contingencies (Notes 6, 7 and 12)		
Shareholders' Equity:		
Common stock, $2.50 par value, 7,500,000 shares authorized, 7,034,924 and 3,385,241 shares issued	17,587	8,463
Paid-in capital	3,989	2,275
Retained earnings	54,125	58,832
	75,701	69,570
Less—Treasury stock, at cost, 948 and 19,500 shares	24	491
Accumulated foreign currency translation adjustment	657	—
Net unrealized loss on long-term investments in preferred stocks	1,642	2,194
Total shareholders' equity	73,378	66,885
	$151,014	$135,881

The accompanying notes are an integral part of these balance sheets.

Equifax Inc.
CONSOLIDATED STATEMENTS OF CHANGES IN FINANCIAL POSITION

(in thousands of dollars)

Year Ended December 31	1982	1981	1980
Funds Were Provided By:			
Operations —			
Net income	**$12,234**	$15,811	$10,531
Depreciation and amortization	**7,077**	6,983	6,513
Deferred income taxes	**(1,275)**	278	883
Provided from operations	**18,036**	23,072	17,927
Increase in short-term bank notes	**—**	—	7,900
Long-term borrowings	**—**	3,407	517
Stock issued for acquisitions	**3,075**	—	—
Long-term debt issued for acquisitions	**844**	1,278	—
Credit to deferred income taxes from			
investments in tax benefits	**2,688**	1,117	—
Decrease in other assets	**1,521**	—	—
Increase in current liabilities,			
excluding debt	**9,835**	2,876	1,167
Stock options exercised	**257**	—	86
	36,256	31,750	27,597
Funds Were Used For:			
Additions to property and equipment, net	**9,188**	7,550	7,143
Cash dividends paid	**8,944**	8,078	7,834
Repayment of long-term debt	**3,880**	4,971	2,688
Decrease in short-term bank notes	**2,500**	—	—
Increase in accounts receivable	**5,284**	1,908	6,978
Purchase of tax benefits, net	**3,323**	3,224	—
Increase in other assets	**—**	682	945
Acquisitions —			
Assets acquired	**10,574**	2,499	—
Less — Cash and short-term investments			
included in assets purchased	**(1,293)**	(66)	—
Liabilities assumed	**(3,012)**	(859)	—
Costs in excess of net assets of			
businesses acquired	**2,760**	197	—
	42,148	28,184	25,588
Increase (Decrease) in Cash and			
Short-Term Investments	**$ (5,892)**	$ 3,566	$ 2,009

The accompanying notes are an integral part of these statements.

Equifax Inc.

NOTES TO CONSOLIDATED FINANCIAL STATEMENTS

1. Significant Accounting and Reporting Policies

Principles of Consolidation. The consolidated financial statements include the accounts of the Company and all wholly owned subsidiaries. All significant intercompany transactions and balances have been eliminated.

Investments in Preferred Stocks. Investments in preferred stocks are stated at the lower of cost, market or mandatory redemption price. Since the cost of these investments ($5,711,000) exceeded market at December 31, 1982, 1981 and 1980, a valuation allowance to reflect this difference has been established by a charge to shareholders' equity. There were no sales of preferred stocks during 1982, 1981 or 1980.

Depreciation, Maintenance and Property Retirements. The cost of property and equipment is depreciated over the estimated lives of such assets, primarily using the straight-line method as follows:

Classification	Predominant Rates
Buildings	2% to 10%
Furniture and equipment	5% to 20%
Leasehold improvements	Useful life, not in excess of lease term

Included in land and buildings is $1,130,000 of construction in progress. Depreciation expense is not recorded on such additions until placed in service. The Company anticipates completion of the project in late 1983 at a total cost approximating $7,300,000.

Maintenance and repairs are charged to expense as incurred. Additions and improvements are capitalized. The cost of property (other than furniture and equipment) retired or otherwise disposed of is removed from the asset account and the related accumulated depreciation is removed from that account. The resulting gain or loss is included in the consolidated statements of income. Furniture and equipment additions are recorded at cost. Furniture and equipment are removed from the asset and related accumulated depreciation accounts at the earlier of disposal, trade-in date or the end of the depreciable lives.

Costs in Excess of Net Assets of Businesses Acquired. Costs in excess of net assets of businesses purchased prior to November 1, 1970 are not amortized. For purchases of businesses subsequent to that date, such costs are amortized over forty years.

Investments in Tax Benefits. During 1982 and 1981, the Company entered into certain "Safe Harbor" lease agreements for the purchase of Federal income tax benefits with terms ranging from 5 to 20 years. The total investments have been allocated between benefits for investment tax credits and timing benefits for tax deductions. The net gains from the investments in investment tax credits are amortized into other income at a constant rate of return based on the unrecovered investments at the beginning of each accounting period. Amortization of these net gains totaled $454,000 in 1982 and $303,000 in 1981. When the cash received on tax savings exceeds the initial investments in timing benefits, the investments will be amortized into other expenses at a constant rate of return over the lease terms.

Litigation. A number of lawsuits seeking damages are brought against the Company each year as a result of reports issued by the Company. Most of the suits are eventually disposed of without cost to the Company except for legal fees involved in defending them and, in some cases, nominal settlements. The Company provides for estimated legal fees and settlements relating to pending lawsuits.

Foreign Currency Translation. Effective January 1, 1982, the Company adopted Financial Accounting Standards Board Statement No. 52, "Foreign Currency Translation". Accordingly, all balance sheet items are translated at the current rate of exchange as of the end of the accounting period and statement of income items are translated at average currency exchange rates. The resulting translation adjustment is recorded as a separate component of shareholders' equity. Prior to 1982, such adjustments were included in the statements of income. The effect of adopting the new method of accounting in 1982 was not material. Foreign currency transaction gains and losses charged to income in 1982, 1981 and 1980 were not material.

Net Income Per Share of Common Stock. Net income per share of common stock is based on the weighted average number of shares outstanding during the year (6,842,602 in 1982, 6,726,084 in 1981 and 6,666,968 in 1980).

2. Acquisitions and Dispositions

During 1982 the Company acquired the following businesses:

Month Acquired	Company	Consideration
July	Credit Bureau Marketing, Inc. (provides automated processing of credit card applications, credit promotions and related services)	180,000 common shares
October	Enercom, Inc. (provides applications software for the utility industry)	$3,570,000 cash
November	Quick Test, Inc. (marketing research)	$2,840,000 cash $844,000 note 102,942 common shares

These acquisitions have been accounted for as purchases with the exception of Credit Bureau Marketing, Inc., which was accounted for as a pooling of interests. The results of operations have been included from the date of acquisition and were not significant to the operations of the Company.

Portions of the purchase prices of Quick Test, Inc. ($2,507,000) and Enercom, Inc. ($2,470,000) have been assigned to lease agreements for opinion center locations and to computer software costs, respectively. These amounts are included in other assets and are being amortized into expense over four to five year periods from acquisition date. Costs in excess of net assets of businesses acquired in 1982 amounted to $2,760,000.

During 1984 through 1986, the Company could pay additional consideration of up to $2,000,000 for the acquisition of Quick Test, Inc., based on its profitability for specified periods through 1985. Any additional consideration paid will be recorded as costs in excess of net assets of businesses acquired.

In March, 1981, the Company realized a net gain of $727,000 (net of $319,000 in income taxes) or $.11 per share on the condemnation of land adjacent to its headquarters.

In June, 1981, the Company sold substantially all of its credit reporting operations in Oregon and Washington to Credit Northwest Corporation. This sale resulted in a net gain of $3,320,000 (net of $1,630,000 in income taxes) or $.49 per share.

3. Loss on Anticipated Disposal of Assets

In 1982, the Company provided $3,152,000 for the loss on the anticipated sale of the assets of the medical administrative services operations. This loss reduced net income by $1,714,000 or $.25 per share.

4. Debt

Short-term bank notes include amounts borrowed by the Company under its lines of credit. Short-term borrowings are payable on demand, with interest ranging from the Federal funds rate plus ¼% to the prime rate. The maximum outstanding borrowings were $11,000,000 in 1982 and $9,000,000 in 1981 and 1980. The weighted average interest rates, computed on the average month-end borrowings of $3,438,000, $3,491,000 and $4,418,000 were 14.9%, 18.3% and 14.3% in 1982, 1981 and 1980, respectively. Unused lines of credit with banks totaled $13,500,000 at December 31, 1982.

Long-term debt at December 31, 1982 and 1981 is comprised of the following:

(in thousands of dollars)	1982	1981
Mortgage note, interest at 11¼%, payable in installments to February, 1996	$1,636	$ 1,644
Industrial revenue bond, interest at 54% of prime rate plus 1%, payable in installments to September, 1988	798	964
Bank note, interest at 10½%, paid in August, 1982	—	2,000
Other notes, interest primarily from 7¾% to 9%, payable in various installments to June, 1987	5,504	6,365
	7,938	10,973
Less-Current maturities	1,535	3,556
	$6,403	$ 7,417

5. Income Taxes

The Company and certain of its subsidiaries maintain their accounts and file their income tax returns on the cash basis. The accompanying financial statements have been prepared on the accrual basis of accounting by application of memorandum entries to reflect uncollected revenues and unpaid expenses. The resulting estimated additional accrual basis income tax liability over the cash basis liability was $16,623,000 in 1982 and $15,033,000 in 1981 and is included in the current liability for income taxes.

The provisions for income taxes for 1982, 1981 and 1980 are reconciled with the Federal statutory rate as follows:

(in thousands of dollars)	1982	1981	1980
Provision computed at Federal rate	$10,153	$12,581	$8,704
State and local taxes, net of Federal tax effect	723	941	557
Investment tax credits, net of recapture (flow-through method)	(685)	(744)	(588)
Capital gains	—	(1,197)	—
Other	(353)	(42)	(283)
Provision for income taxes	$ 9,838	$11,539	$8,390

The provisions include state income taxes of $1,339,000 in 1982, $1,743,000 in 1981 and $1,032,000 in 1980, and foreign income taxes of $1,318,000 in 1982, $1,576,000 in 1981 and $1,006,000 in 1980.

Deferred income taxes are provided for timing differences in the recognition of revenues and expenses for financial reporting and income tax purposes. The components of the deferred tax provisions (benefits) are as follows:

(in thousands of dollars)	1982	1981	1980
Loss on anticipated disposal of assets	$(1,438)	$ —	$ —
Depreciation expense	831	365	105
Performance share plan expense	(665)	(172)	
Pension expense	—	58	923
Other	(3)	27	(145)
	$(1,275)	$278	$883

Income before provision for income taxes includes foreign income, primarily from Canadian subsidiaries, of $2,372,000 in 1982, $2,773,000 in 1981 and $1,673,000 in 1980. Accumulated undistributed earnings after foreign taxes for Canadian subsidiaries amounted to approximately $7,327,000 at December 31, 1982. No provision for Canadian withholding or United States Federal income taxes is made on foreign earnings because it is management's intent that dividends will be paid only under circumstances which will not generate additional net tax expense.

6. Lease Obligations

The Company and its subsidiaries conduct their branch office operations primarily from leased office space. In addition, the Company leases some equipment, mainly computers and related items. Rentals under such operating leases were $17,762,000 in 1982, $16,755,000 in 1981 and $15,252,000 in 1980. Future minimum obligations for noncancellable operating leases extending beyond one year are as follows:

Year (in thousands of dollars)	Rental
1983	$ 9,926
1984	7,984
1985	4,860
1986	3,496
1987	2,121
Thereafter	2,062
	$30,449

7. Litigation

In January, 1983 a superior court jury in Los Angeles County, California rendered a verdict awarding $5,100,000 to a man who alleged that his disability claim had been improperly denied by the insurer on the basis of a medical examination arranged by the Company. In February, 1983 the trial court let stand the award of $100,000 in compensatory damages, but ruled that the jury's award of punitive damages in the amount of $5,000,000 was excessive as a matter of law. The punitive damages were reduced to $1,000,000. The Company believes that the modified verdict of $1,100,000 is not supported by any credible evidence, and the Company will continue to vigorously contest this verdict and will appeal to a higher court. While there can be no assurance as to the eventual outcome of the appeal, in the opinion of management the final result of this matter will not have a material adverse effect on the financial condition or results of operations of the Company.

8. Common Stock

In July, 1982, the Board of Directors approved a two-for-one common stock split, in the form of a stock dividend, effective in September, 1982. The weighted average number of shares outstanding, per share data, common share references (except shares issued and outstanding in 1981 in the accompanying balance sheets) and the related notes have been restated to give effect to this split.

During 1981, the shareholders approved a performance share plan for certain key officers who may be awarded up to 200,000 shares of the Company's common stock at the end of three-year measurement periods, based upon the growth in earnings per share during those periods. At December 31, 1982, 130,000 shares had been designated for future distribution for the measurement periods commencing January 1, 1981 and 1982. The total expense under this plan was approximately $1,358,000 in 1982 and $350,000 in 1981.

In 1969, the Company established a qualified stock option plan whereby up to 200,000 shares of common stock could be sold to officers and certain key employees. The plan provided that no options could be granted after January 28, 1979. Thus for the purpose of granting additional options, the plan is now terminated. Such termination does not, without the consent of an employee to whom an option has been granted, alter or impair any rights or obligations under any option which has been granted under the plan. Stock options were granted at fair market value at date of grant. Additional information concerning stock option shares is as follows:

	1982	1981	1980
Outstanding at beginning of year	43,500	60,500	94,500
Options:			
Granted	—	—	—
Expired	—	(13,000)	(21,000)
Forfeited	(500)	(4,000)	(3,000)
Exercised	(19,552)	—	(10,000)
Outstanding at end of year	23,448	43,500	60,500

Options outstanding at December 31, 1982 have an exercise price of $13.13 per share or $308,000 in the aggregate and expire in January, 1983. No accounting recognition is given to stock options until they are exercised.

In January, 1983, the Board of Directors increased, subject to shareholder approval, the Company's authorized common stock to 25,000,000 shares.

9. Employee Benefits

The Company and its subsidiaries have noncontributory qualified retirement plans covering most salaried employees, including certain employees in foreign countries. The total pension expense under these plans was approximately $7,924,000 in 1982, $7,707,000 in 1981 and $7,381,000 in 1980, including amortization of unfunded prior service costs over various periods up to forty years. The Company's policy is to fund pension plan costs accrued. The comparison of accumulated plan benefits and plan net assets as of January 1, 1982 and 1981, the two most recent actuarial valuation dates for the domestic plan, is as follows:

(in thousands of dollars)	1982	1981
Actuarial present value of accumulated plan benefits:		
Vested	**$72,428**	$57,612
Nonvested	**4,662**	2,340
	$77,090	$59,952
Net assets available for benefits	**$85,404**	$75,659

The increase in 1982 in accumulated plan benefits was primarily the result of certain changes to the plan provisions. The expected rates of investment return used in determining the actuarial present value of accumulated plan benefits were 8%.

The Company's foreign pension plan is not required to report to certain governmental agencies pursuant to the Employee Retirement Income Security Act of 1974 and does not otherwise determine the actuarial value of accumulated benefits or net assets available for benefits as calculated and disclosed above. For this plan, the net assets of the plan exceeded the actuarially computed present value of vested benefits as of the date of its latest valuation, January 1, 1982.

In 1982, the Equifax Inc. Employee Stock Ownership Plan was established retroactive to January 1, 1981. The Plan provides for annual contributions by the Company at the discretion of the Board of Directors for the benefit of eligible employees in the form of cash or common stock of the Company. The Company made cash contributions of $277,000 to the Plan in 1982.

10. Quarterly Financial Data (unaudited)

Summarized quarterly financial data (in thousands of dollars except for per share amounts) is as follows:

Quarter	Total Revenue	Income Before Taxes	Net Income Amount	Net Income Per Share
1982				
First	$103,524	$ 4,615	$2,510	$ .37
Second	109,784	6,903	3,618	.54
Third	108,848	6,883	3,643	.53
Fourth	114,549	3,671	2,463	.35
1981				
First	$ 98,576	$ 6,884	$3,769	$ .56
Second	107,716	10,674	6,279	.93
Third	100,242	5,127	2,656	.40
Fourth	103,039	4,665	3,107	.46
1980				
First	$ 89,850	$ 5,094	$2,721	$ .41
Second	92,550	4,220	2,341	.35
Third	92,519	4,442	2,501	.37
Fourth	97,221	5,165	2,968	.45

Significant amounts included in the above data and the related increase (decrease) in net income per share are as follows:

Quarter	Description	Effect on Net Income Per Share
Fourth-1982	Loss on anticipated disposal of assets	$(.25)
Fourth-1982	Gain on investments in tax benefits	.05
First-1981	Gain on condemnation of land	.11
Second-1981	Gain on sale of Northwest Credit Bureau	.49
Fourth-1981	Gain on investments in tax benefits	.05
Fourth-1981	Gain on foreign currency translations	.04

11. Industry Segment Information

The 1980 through 1982 information contained on pages 30 and 31 is presented in conformity with the requirements of Statement of Financial Accounting Standards No. 14, "Financial Reporting for Segments of a Business Enterprise", and is an integral part of the consolidated financial statements.

12. Subsequent Event

In February, 1983, the Company acquired Credit Northwest Corporation, Olympia Credit Bureau, Inc. and the Credit Bureau of Lewis County, Inc., firms with credit bureau and collection operations in Oregon, Washington and Alaska, for an aggregate purchase price of approximately $13,350,000. These acquisitions will be accounted for as purchases in 1983.

AUDITORS' REPORT

To the Shareholders of Equifax Inc.:

We have examined the consolidated balance sheets of Equifax Inc. (a Georgia corporation) and subsidiaries as of December 31, 1982 and 1981, and the related statements of income, shareholders' equity and changes in financial position for each of the three years in the period ended December 31, 1982. Our examinations were made in accordance with generally accepted auditing standards and, accordingly, included such tests of the accounting records and such other auditing procedures as we considered necessary in the circumstances.

In our opinion, the financial statements referred to above present fairly the financial position of Equifax Inc. and subsidiaries as of December 31, 1982 and 1981, and the results of their operations and the changes in their financial position for each of the three years in the period ended December 31, 1982, all in conformity with generally accepted accounting principles applied on a consistent basis.

ARTHUR ANDERSEN & CO.

Atlanta, Georgia,
February 25, 1983.

MANAGEMENT'S REPORT

The consolidated financial statements presented in this report, which were prepared by the Company, are based on generally accepted accounting principles applied on a consistent basis and are considered by management to reflect the financial position of the Company at December 31, 1982 and 1981, and the results of operations and changes in financial position for each of the three years in the period ended December 31, 1982.

The integrity and objectivity of data in these financial statements, including estimates and judgments relating to matters not concluded by year-end, are the responsibility of management. The Company and its subsidiaries maintain accounting systems and related controls, including a detailed budget and reporting system, to provide reasonable assurance that financial records are reliable for preparing the consolidated financial statements and for maintaining accountability for assets. The system of controls also provides reasonable assurance that assets are safeguarded against loss from unauthorized use or disposition, and that transactions are executed in accordance with management's authorization. Periodic reviews of the system and controls are performed by the internal auditors.

The system of controls includes the careful selection of people, a division of responsibility consistent with cost effectiveness and the application of formal policies and procedures that are consistent with good standards of accounting and administrative practices.

H. A. PHILLIPS, JR.
Vice President & Treasurer

Equifax Inc.
SUMMARY OF SELECTED FINANCIAL DATA

(in thousands of dollars except for per share amounts)	1982	1981	1980	1979	1978
Operating revenue	$434,691	$401,785	$371,108	$339,629	$307,202
Costs and expenses	410,015	380,205	351,193	320,378	289,356
Loss on anticipated disposal of assets	3,152	—	—	—	—
Operating income	21,524	21,580	19,915	19,251	17,846
Nonoperating income	2,014	7,788	1,032	827	714
Interest expense	1,466	2,018	2,026	1,468	687
Income before provision for income taxes	22,072	27,350	18,921	18,610	17,873
Provision for income taxes	9,838	11,539	8,390	8,271	8,357
Net income	12,234	15,811	10,531	10,339	9,516
Dividends paid	8,944	8,078	7,834	7,315	7,217
Net income per share	1.79	2.35	1.58	1.56	1.44
Dividends:					
Per share	1.305	1.200	1.175	1.100	1.100
Percent of net income	73%	51%	74%	71%	76%
Average number of shares outstanding	6,842,602	6,726,084	6,666,968	6,649,106	6,603,670
As a percent of operating revenue:					
Operating income	5.0%	5.4%	5.4%	5.7%	5.8%
Net income	2.8%	3.9%	2.8%	3.0%	3.1%
Assets at December 31	$151,014	$135,881	$123,515	$113,456	$ 99,675
Long-term debt at December 31	6,403	7,417	8,319	10,246	4,903

Management's Discussion and Analysis of Financial Condition and Results of Operations
This discussion and analysis is to be read in conjunction with the Consolidated Financial Statements and related notes and the Segment Information presented on pages 30 through 31. Special attention should be given to note 6 on page 31 describing the reclassification of prior year segment information to conform with the 1982 presentation.

Results of Operations
In 1982 operating revenue increased 8.2 percent despite the national recession, with all segments of the Company's business showing a year-to-year increase in operating revenue. Net income declined; however, after adjusting for the capital gains in 1981 and the anticipated capital loss in 1982, net income increased 18.6 percent. In 1981 operating revenue increased 8.3 percent and net income, after adjusting for the capital gains, increased 11.7 percent.

Operating Revenue. Risk management services, the largest segment of the Company's business, increased revenues 5.1 percent in 1982 after an 8.0 percent increase in 1981. In both years the distributed data processing for property and casualty insurers realized unit gains while property and casualty underwriting reports realized unit declines. Life and health underwriting reports experienced unit declines in both 1982 and 1981; however, product mix changes contributed to a revenue increase of 9 percent in 1982. The home energy audit business continued its growth and contributed to the revenue increase in this segment by approximately $4,100,000 in 1982 and $3,400,000 in 1981. Price adjustments in the risk management services segment averaged 9 percent in 1982 and 10 percent in 1981.

The financial control services segment increased revenue by approximately 20.5 percent in 1982. The United States and Canadian credit reporting revenue experienced unit gains, especially in the fourth quarter of 1982. The acquisition of Credit Bureau Marketing contributed $6,600,000 to this segment's revenue increase. The modest revenue increase in 1981 was the net result of a 9.5 percent increase in United States and Canadian credit bureau operations offset by a planned elimination of unprofitable lines of service in the medical administrative services business. Price increases in this segment averaged 4 percent in 1982 and 6 percent in 1981.

Printing segment revenue increased 5.2 percent in 1982. The 1982 growth was below that experienced during the past several years, primarily because of the recession, with volume growth below expectations at all three plants. The revenue growth in 1981 was due to growth on existing business and the acquisition of Hutton-Roach Lithographers which contributed $2,139,000 to 1981 printing revenues.

Other general business services revenue increased 39.7 percent in 1982. The majority of this increase came from the Company's marketing research subsidiary, Elrick and Lavidge. Two recent acquisitions, Quick Test and Enercom, are included in this segment. Enercom contributed $853,000 to the 1982 revenue increase. Quick Test was acquired late in the year and had a minimal impact in 1982. The 1981 revenue decline reflects the sale of the health systems division at the end of 1980. The marketing research revenue increased 7.1 percent from 1980 to 1981.

Operating Income. 1982 operating income was essentially unchanged from 1981; however, the 1982 results contain a $3,152,000 loss on the anticipated disposal of the medical administrative services assets. Before this loss, operating income increased 14.3 percent in 1982 after an 8.4 percent increase in 1981.

Risk management services increased operating income by 8.9 percent in 1982 and 10.6 percent in 1981. The improved margin in both years was the result of cost containment and a very strong performance by the distributed data processing for property and casualty insurers business.

The financial control segment's operating income increased 11 percent in 1982. The operating income figures include the $3,152,000 loss on the anticipated disposal of assets of the medical administrative services business. Credit reporting operating income in the United States and Canada was up sharply as revenue levels were well above the break-even point and directly improved profitability. Medical administrative services continued to show a loss; however, there was substantial improvement from the $1,600,000 loss experienced in 1981. The increase in this segment's 1981 operating income reflects a recovery from 1980, which was depressed due to Federal credit restrictions.

Printing experienced poor operating income performance, losing $143,000 in 1982. The primary reason for the loss was lower than expected revenue at all three printing plants, causing them to operate at or below break-even levels. The printing segment also experienced higher than normal bad debt write-offs in 1982. The decrease in operating income in 1981 was influenced by two primary factors. First, the Hutton-Roach acquisition experienced start-up costs which resulted in no contribution to income. Secondly, the move into a larger plant in Houston disrupted production and required significant one-time moving expenses.

The increased 1982 operating income from the other general business services segment resulted from the improved performance of the marketing research business. Quick Test was acquired late in 1982 and had a minimal impact on operating income. Enercom was acquired in October, 1982, and contributed approximately $269,000 to this segment's profit increase. The improved operating profit in 1981 was primarily the result of the sale, at the end of 1980, of the health systems division.

The Company is not subject to the requirements of Statement of Financial Accounting Standards No. 33 (Financial Reporting and Changing Prices). Most components of the Company's costs increase with the general rate of inflation; however, were the Company to restate income using either replacement cost or cost adjusted for changes in the general purchasing power of the dollar, higher depreciation and cost of goods sold (printing segment) expense would result.

Nonoperating Income, Interest Expense and General Corporate Expense. Nonoperating income in 1981 included $5,996,000 in capital gains from the land and Northwest credit bureau sales. After adjustment for these gains, the increases from 1980 are the result of higher levels of dividend and temporary investment income and gains from the investments in tax benefits.

The decline in interest expense was the result of a lower average interest cost on the short-term debt and lower levels of long-term debt. Interest expense remained constant between 1980 and 1981 as lower 1981 borrowing levels were offset by higher interest rates.

The increased general corporate expense since 1980 is the result of inflation, compensated absence accruals and the performance share plan. Performance share plan expense totaled $350,000 in 1981 and $1,358,000 in 1982.

Financial Condition

The Company's overall financial position remained strong during 1982. Normal capital investment and working capital needs were financed with internally generated funds and both short- and long-term debt were substantially reduced. The acquisitions were financed with cash, Company stock and a note to the sellers of the businesses. In 1983 the Company will require additional external borrowing to finance the expansion of the home office building, the Credit Northwest acquisition and capital investment requirements. Initially these requirements will be financed with short-term borrowings from normal credit facilities. The short-term debt will be converted to longer term arrangements as conditions warrant. The proceeds from the anticipated sale of the medical administrative services business will be used to reduce the required external borrowing.

The Company's primary source of capital has traditionally been from internal sources. Acquisitions and capital expenditures over the past three years have required external financing in the form of bank borrowings and in some instances stock and notes issued for acquisitions. External financing will be required in 1983 as described above. Additional external financing beyond 1983 may be necessary as the Company continues to position itself in growth markets. The Company feels it has adequate borrowing capacity through unused lines of credit with banks and additional long-term debt capacity to meet its future capital requirements.

Equifax Inc.
INDUSTRY SEGMENT INFORMATION

(in thousands of dollars)	1982 Amount	1982 % of Total	1981 Amount	1981 % of Total	1980 Amount	1980 % of Total
Operating revenue:						
Risk Management Services	$321,694	74%	$306,196	76%	$283,641	77%
Financial Control Services	73,000	17	60,583	15	56,717	15
Printing	27,136	6	25,797	7	21,456	6
Other General Business Services	12,861	3	9,209	2	9,294	2
	$434,691	100%	$401,785	100%	$371,108	100%
Intersegment sales (Printing)	$ 5,478	100%	$ 4,966	100%	$ 5,142	100%
Income before provision for income taxes:						
Risk Management Services	$ 24,420	77%	$ 22,426	75%	$ 20,278	76%
Financial Control Services	6,615	20	5,962	20	4,916	18
Printing	(143)	—	1,534	5	1,847	7
Other General Business Services	886	3	167	—	(229)	(1)
Operating income	31,778	100%	30,089	100%	26,812	100%
Non-operating income	2,014		7,788		1,032	
Interest expense	(1,466)		(2,018)		(2,026)	
General corporate expense	(10,254)		(8,509)		(6,897)	
	$ 22,072		$ 27,350		$ 18,921	
Identifiable assets at December 31:						
Risk Management Services	$ 63,908	42%	$ 61,997	46%	$ 59,884	48%
Financial Control Services	32,975	22	30,294	22	32,997	27
Printing	23,407	16	25,796	19	16,954	14
Other General Business Services	13,939	9	3,875	3	3,622	3
	134,229	89	121,962	90	113,457	92
Corporate assets	16,785	11	13,919	10	10,058	8
	$151,014	100%	$135,881	100%	$123,515	100%

Description of Segments

Risk Management Services. Informational services which include underwriting and claim reports; adjusting, loss control and health screening services; employment evaluation services; administrative self-insurer services; rapid data transmission services; energy audit services; mortgage loan reports and mortgage servicing aids; and business analysis and inventory finance and control services. (NOTE: Mortgage loan reports and mortgage servicing aids and business analysis and inventory finance and control services are financial in orientation and are provided primarily to credit grantors. For these reasons, these services are grouped and described with other financial control services elsewhere in this Annual Report. Additionally, energy audit services are described with other general business services elsewhere in this Annual Report. Except for revenue amounts, it is not practicable to segregate other financial information relating to these services because they are generally investigative in nature and utilize common production facilities with risk management services. Consequently, all financial data for these services are included in the risk management services segment for this presentation.)

Financial Control Services. Informational and administrative services which include consumer and commercial credit reports; credit promotions and collections; automated credit application processing; and medical administrative services.

Other General Business Services. Includes marketing research, applications software for the utility industry and epidemiological services (business sold in 1980).

Notes to Industry Segment Information

Additional information required by Statement of Financial Accounting Standards No. 14, dealing with financial reporting for segments of a business enterprise, is as follows:

(1) Operating revenue by industry is sales to unaffiliated customers only.
(2) Operating income is operating revenue less operating expenses. In computing operating income, none of the following items have been added or deducted: interest expense, gains, other income and income taxes.
(3) Identifiable assets by industry segment are those assets that are used in the Company's operations in each industry. Corporate assets are primarily cash and short-term investments, long-term investments in preferred stocks, property and equipment and investments in tax benefits.

(4) Depreciation and amortization by industry segment for 1982, 1981 and 1980 are as follows:

(in thousands of dollars)	1982	1981	1980
Risk Management Services	$2,564	$2,557	$2,394
Financial Control Services	2,398	2,923	2,806
Printing	1,202	863	741
Other General Business Services	441	197	132
	$6,605	$6,540	$6,073

(5) Capital expenditures by industry segment (includes property and equipment acquired in acquisitions accounted for as purchases) for 1982, 1981 and 1980 are as follows:

(in thousands of dollars)	1982	1981	1980
Risk Management Services	$3,009	$2,769	$2,222
Financial Control Services	1,816	491	3,720
Printing	2,449	6,052	902
Other General Business Services	1,062	517	135
	$8,336	$9,829	$6,979

(6) In 1982 medical administrative services and mortgage loan reporting, formerly included in other general business and financial control services, were merged into financial control and risk management services. The 1981 and 1980 segment information has been reclassified to conform with the 1982 presentation.
(7) Income before provision for income taxes for 1982 for financial control services includes a $3,152,000 loss on the anticipated disposal of the assets of medical administrative services.

Index

This book has been set VideoComp, 10 and 9 point Gael, leaded 2 points. Part numbers and titles and chapter numbers are 24 point Avant Garde Extra Light, and chapter titles are 18 point Avant Garde Extra Light. The size of the type page is 33 by 47½ picas.